P9-CSE-663

Warman's
English & Continental
POTTERY &
PORCELAIN

4TH EDITION • SUSAN AND AL BAGDADE

Identification and Price Guide

Published by

kp books

An imprint of F+W Publications, Inc.

700 East State Street • Iola, WI 54990-0001
715-445-2214 • 888-457-2873

Our toll-free number to place an order or obtain
a free catalog is (800) 258-0929.

Library of Congress Catalog Number: 2004093876

ISBN: 0-87349-505-5

Designed by: Wendy Wendt
Edited by: Dan Brownell

Printed in the United States

CONTENTS

PREFACE TO THE FOURTH EDITION

In order to keep this book "fresh" and meeting collectors' interests, several changes have been made. Several new categories were added, including Wade, Royal Wilton, Oyster Plates, and Cornishware. Strong interest in art pottery, especially British art pottery, has resulted in the inclusion of Bretby, Pilkington, and Ruskin, which are the "darlings" of art pottery collectors. Recent publications have shed new light on these subjects and, as a result, have piqued collectors' interest.

Another category that is making its debut is Picasso ceramics. Here again, it has begun to find its way into the top auction houses and upper end antiques shows. A major auction of Picasso ceramics took place near the end of this year.

Several categories have been moved into more appropriate categories, as too little material has reached the public to warrant a stand-alone category. Frankenthal, Furstenberg, Ludwigsburg, and Nymphenburg have been added to Minor German Factories; Gardner has joined the Russia category; and St. Cloud and Chantilly have been moved to France where they belong. Cottage Ware has been taken from the English category and now has a category of its own. The same is true for Feather Edge ceramics, which had been scattered among several categories.

We believe that the fourth edition will continue to be the "bible" of the ceramics field.

This year saw the passing of my wife and co-author Susan, and as a result, this book is dedicated to her memory. She truly loved the world of antiques and especially the people. She was a breath of fresh air and will surely be missed!

Susan and Al Bagdade,
Northbrook, Illinois

ACKNOWLEDGMENTS

This book would not have been possible without the cooperation of hundreds of antiques dealers who allowed us to gather information and photograph their wares at antique shows and in their homes and shops. We also owe a debt of gratitude to all the auction houses who gave us complimentary subscriptions to their catalogs for all pottery and porcelain auctions. Thank you!

HOW TO USE THIS BOOK

ORGANIZATION OF THE PRICE GUIDE

Listings: More than two hundred categories and subcategories dealing with English and Continental pottery and porcelain are listed alphabetically in this price guide. Most categories refer to a single manufactory. A general category by country includes smaller firms that are not dealt with individually.

Every effort had been made to make the price listings descriptive enough that specific objects can be identified by the reader. Emphasis has been placed on examples being sold in the marketplace today. Some harder-to-find objects were included to provide a full range in each category.

History: Every category has a capsule history that details the founding of the company, its principal owners, the nature of its wares, the patterns used, and general information on the specific company. Notes about marks are included in the history, collecting hints, or a marks section.

References: Reference books are listed whenever possible to encourage the collector to learn more about the category. Books are listed only if there is a substantial section on the category being considered. Included in the listing are the author, title, publisher (if published by a small firm or individual, we have indicated "privately printed"), and date of publication or most recent edition.

Some of the books listed may be out of print and no longer available from the publisher; these will usually be available in public libraries or through inter-library loan. Readers may also find antiques book dealers at antiques shows, flea markets, and advertised in trade papers and journals. Search services are another source for out-of-print books. Many dealers provide mail-order services. Also, the Internet is an excellent source for locating hard-to-find books.

Periodicals: In addition to publications of collectors' clubs, numerous general-interest newspapers and magazines devote considerable attention to pottery and porcelain. A sampling includes the following:

Antique Monthly, P.O. Drawer 2, Tuscaloosa, AL 35402

Antique Review, P.O. Box 538, Worthington, OH 43085

Antique Showcase, Amis Gibbs Publications, Ltd., Canfield, Ontario, Canada NOA1CO

Antique Trader Weekly, P.O. Box 1050, Dubuque, IA 52004

Antique Week, P.O. Box 90, Knightstown, IN 46148

Antiques and Collecting, 1006 S. Michigan Avenue, Chicago, IL 60605

Antiques and The Arts Weekly, 5 Church Hill Road, Newtown, CT 06740

Antiques (The Magazine Antiques), 551 Fifth Avenue, New York, NY 10017

China and Glass Quarterly, David & Linda Arman, P.O. Box 39, Portsmouth, RI 02871

Collector News, Box 156, Grundy Center, IA 50638

The Daze, P.O. Box 57, Otisville, MI 48463

Maine Antique Digest, P.O. Box 645, Waldboro, ME 04572

New York-Pennsylvania Collector, Drawer C, Fishers, NY 14453

Porcelain Collector's Companion, Dorothy Kamm, P.O. Box 7460, Port St. Lucie, FL 34985

Southern Antiques & Southeast Trader, P.O. Box 1550, Lake City, FL 32055

West Coast Peddler, P.O. Box 5134, Whittier, CA 90607

Museums: Museums are listed if significant collections in the category are on display. Many museums have large collections of pottery and/or porcelains, but did not provide a listing for inclusion in this book.

Collectors' Clubs: All collectors' clubs have been verified to be active. Addresses are listed for membership information. Some clubs have regional and local chapters. English clubs listed welcome American members.

Reproduction Alert: Where reproduction alerts are listed for a particular category, the collector should be extremely careful when purchasing examples. Some reproductions are unmarked; the newness of their appearance is often the best clue as a reproduction. We recommend strongly that collectors subscribe to *Antique & Collectors Reproduction News*, P.O. Box 12130, Des Moines, IA 50312-9403, to receive current information on reproductions. Antiques newspapers also provide news of reproductions when they appear in the marketplace.

Collecting Hints: This section calls attention to specific hints if they are applicable to a category. Clues are also given for spotting reproductions when known.

Additional Listings: When more than one category is covered by a specific listing, other listings are added to help the reader find additional information.

Marks: When pottery and porcelain ware are marked, we have included representative marks for that manufactory. However, to see the full range of marks used by a firm, one must consult one of the marks books listed in the bibliography.

Photographs: We have used representative photographs for each category. However, to see a full range of examples, one must consult one of the specialized books listed for that category.

DERIVATION OF PRICES USED

The majority of the prices listed in this book was derived from "on-site" inspection, which required a good deal of shoe leather and gas, but provided a realistic feel for what ceramics are selling for in the marketplace. The prices reflect what the collector should pay for an item., i.e., the retail price.

Antiques shops and markets, flea markets, antiques shows, and antiques malls from all sections of the country were a major source for prices. The explosion of antiques malls, as well as mega-malls in the last few years, has placed a large number of antiques under one roof; this allows for comparison shopping. Prices were also obtained from the smaller-sized antiques shows, as well as major international expositions and other shows in varying ranges.

Auction houses located in the United States, London, and the Continent were a source for upper-level ceramics, but were also useful for middle- and lower-range material in some instances. Specialized auctions have increased in number and have provided pricing material for collectors with specific interests. Those pieces derived from auction houses are noted with an (A) preceding the price in the listings and represent the actual hammer price along with the buyer's premium where applicable.

Antiques newspapers, antiques magazines, and antiques journals were a rich source of information. Antiques dealers' price lists, both generalized and specialized, were used extensively in deriving prices for numerous categories.

Since the second edition of this price guide, the Internet has become a major marketplace for buying and selling ceramics. Many dealers maintain Web sites with constantly changing inventories, and these sites were used for comparative pricing. Numbers of these sites located worldwide should expand significantly over the next few years and, as a result, a larger number of collectors will visit these sites to shop for their collections. It also allows for comparison shopping in the comfort of the home. Auction houses have also found the Web and are using it to supplement their printed catalogs. Now a collector can build or add to a collection without ever leaving home.

When conflicting prices occurred for similar pieces, an additional source was sought, which included consulting ceramics specialists to confirm or reject a specific item's value.

It is unlikely that the collector will be able to match exactly a specific piece with listings in this price guide. Each category represents a range of examples and prices from each manufactory. It should act as a *guide* to the collector, rather than an absolute determination of what a collector would have to pay for a specific piece.

CONDITION OF WARES

Condition plays an important role in determining the value of ceramics. Prices for porcelain and pottery from the early periods (16th to 18th century, and rare pieces) are less affected by condition than the more recent ceramic examples. One would be less concerned about missing fingers on a figure by the Meissen modeler Kaendler than by the same damage found on a 19th or 20th century Dresden "lace" figure. Availability is the key word.

Middle- and lower-priced pieces that are damaged should not be completely overlooked, though. In some cases, they may act as "filler" pieces for a collection until better examples become available. However, these damaged pieces should reflect lower prices than fine examples. The price should be directly proportional to the extent of the damage. As an example, tin-glazed earthenware often shows wear along the rim. Glaze flakes in this area are to be expected. However, glaze flakes affecting the central design are less acceptable, even if they are smaller in diameter.

Outright chips also should be reflected by a lower price. Under-the-rim chips are more tolerable than those on the surface or at the margin. Major defects such as breaks, cracks, fades in the design, pieces missing (knobs, handles, covers, etc.) or heavy cuts in the glaze greatly diminish the value of a piece. Remember that an age crack is still a crack and should be treated as such. It is wiser to spend extra dollars to purchase the best examples available.

Repaired examples should be evaluated critically because casual examination of a piece may not show the location or extent of a repair. A reglued handle detracts considerably from the value of a piece. A professionally restored handle may be more acceptable to the collector.

Changes in the glaze, brilliance, or texture, or slight variations in decorative colors are often signs of a repair. By examining the inside of a hollow figure, a repaired fracture may be quite visible because inside cosmetics were often overlooked during exterior restorations. It behooves the buyer to examine a piece carefully under a strong light or black light before purchasing the piece, as repaired merchandise is difficult to return when discovered at a later time.

THE CARE AND FEEDING OF CERAMICS

Ceramics by nature are fragile and should be treated with the utmost care. Dirt and dust are natural enemies to all ceramics and should be removed whenever encountered. The natural impulse is to plunge the dirty object into a sinkful of hot, sudsy water and give it a good "once-over." This, however, is the wrong procedure to follow. Care was used in selecting the piece; care should also be used in the cleaning process.

Visual examination of the piece is the first step. Check for obvious repairs, hairline cracks, and crazing, as these factors require additional care when cleaning the piece. It is important to know what the piece is made of, as this also controls the method of cleaning. Unglazed ceramics are washed differently than glazed pieces.

Set aside a work area that is uncluttered and near running water. A textured towel makes a good work surface and adds support for the piece. Remove loose dirt and dust with a soft brush such as an artist's brush. Never use a stiff brush because this can disturb surface decorations. Proceed slowly and carefully, especially around projections and handles. A good portion of the grime can be removed in this manner. In addition, pieces with hairlines will less likely soak up dirt when the washing process starts.

A solution of mild soap in lukewarm water with ammonia (1 ounce of ammonia to 10 ounces of water) is an ideal working solution. Enough soap should be added to create suds. Cotton swabs or balls dipped into the solution and applied gently to the surface will loosen and remove years of grime. Stains such as grease and unknown stains should be approached cautiously.

On vertical pieces such as figures, begin at the top and work toward the base. Constantly change the wash water, as it tends to become dirty with use. Continually rinse away the soapy solution using clean water and cotton swabs. Never use abrasive materials such as scouring pads or harsh detergents. Unglazed ceramics like earthenware and bisque should be wiped with moist, soft swabs.

Though the dishwasher is a handy device for commercial dishware, it is not a friend to early ceramics. Hot water and strong detergents can dissolve water-soluble glue joints and remove surface decorations. Pieces with metal bases should not be immersed in water. This is especially true for ormolu.

Never use bleach. This material is harmful to certain types of decoration. In addition, bleach can cause a stain to spread rather dramatically. Dry pieces with equal care using cotton swabs or linen towels. A hair dryer can be a handy tool for getting into hard-to-reach areas. If stains are persistent, are of unknown origin, or if a glue joint separates, call a professional restorer.

Once the pieces are clean, storage is the next consideration. Certain precautions apply. All pieces must be dried thoroughly before storing. When stacking plates, always keep the same sizes and shapes together. Tissue or felt should separate each plate. Cups should be hung from plastic-coated hooks or stored individually. Never stack cups or bowls, as this tends to damage surface decorations.

Plate hangers serve a purpose, but should be used with discretion. Always use the proper size. A hanger that is too large will not provide sufficient support. A hanger that is too small will place excessive pressure on a piece. Wrap wire projections in plastic tubing to help protect the rim glaze.

For additional hints on the care of ceramics, consult one of the following books: Frieda Kay Fall, *Art Objects: Their Care and Preservation*, Museum Publications, 1967; Albert Jackson & David Day, *The Antiques Care & Repair Handbook*, Alfred A. Knopf, 1984; Judith Larney, *Restoring Ceramics*, Watson-Guptil Publications, 1975; Judith Miller, *Care & Repair of Everday Treasures: A Step-by-Step Guide to Cleaning & Restoring Your Antiques & Collectibles*, Putnam Pub Group, 1997; Mette Tang Simpson, Ed. & Michael Huntley, Ed., *Sotheby's Caring for Antiques: A Guide to Handling, Cleaning, Display and Restoration*, Antique Collectors' Club, Ltd., 1996; V.P. Wright, *Pamper Your Possessions*, Barre Publishers, 1972.

STATE OF THE MARKET

With the explosion of trade on the Internet, it becomes a little more difficult evaluating the status of the ceramics market. Collectors are searching the world for items from the comfort of their homes, and dealers are buying and selling through this electronic marketplace. No longer is it possible to sit and chat with dealers to find out whatís selling and what's not. However, the "old" methods of legwork still work.

What has emerged is that the ceramics market is still somewhat "soft." Much of this can be tied to the sluggish economy, but when rare upper level pieces reach the public, they are quickly snatched up for very solid prices. In addition, those with available cash are finding many bargains.

The Skinner auction of upscale Wedgwood from the Lloyd Bleier collection illustrates a few of these points. A handsome green jasper rectangular plaque with exceptional cameos sold for a remarkable price of $25,850, more than doubling the pre-auction estimate. Also, Fairyland luster continues to be a collector's favorite. A large pillar vase fetched $11,163 at the same auction and large, unusually decorated pieces of Fairyland continue to show strength. Other lusters such as Dragon, Butterfly, and Hummingbird are still somewhat sluggish, however.

The large number of copper luster reproductions hitting the market in the past few years has driven collectors from this material. This appears to be changing as the reproductions are winnowed out and the fine pieces are again gaining strength. This also holds for other lusters that languished but appear to be back in good graces—especially silver luster, which is scarce to begin with.

Mid-range antiques are holding their own. Fine examples of well-printed, crisp transfer ware and rare scenes are selling briskly, but ordinary single color pieces are languishing. English majolica is selling better than its European counterparts. Excellent examples of Minton, George Jones, and Holdcroft are climbing in price as well as interest. Rare pieces such as garden seats and figural teapots top the list along with oyster plates. Again reproductions are also beginning to surface; therefore, this segment will bear watching for future trends. Mustache cups, as well as Austrian, Dresden, and Bohemian porcelain are quite soft.

Robust sales were recorded for unusual Schlegelmilch porcelains. The Woody auction of R.S. Prussia showed that unusual pieces reflect collector interest. A simple bone-shaped box with a simple floral design sold for $375, but the same box with a design called "Midst Snow & Ice," showing scenes from Byrd's Expedition, found an appreciative collector for $9,300. Also, a large two-handled vase decorated with a lion theme crossed the block at more than $13,000, and a large cobalt decorated centerpiece bowl raised eyebrows at $11,000.

Well-printed, dark blue examples of American Historic Staffordshire show signs of strength, especially unusual shapes and scenes. The same cannot be said for their English cousins, which are often overlooked by collectors. Staffordshire figures, long a sign of health for products from this region, are also on the "mushy" side, with exceptions including examples by Obadiah Sherratt.

Low-end ceramics such as Rudolstadt, Hutschenreuther, Angelica Kauffmann, and others of this caliber of material, remain gathering dust. Of course, artist-signed pieces and unusual shapes counter this trend.

Once again, the "hot" categories fall under the general heading of Art Deco, but more specifically, British art pottery. Ruskin, Pilkington, Poole, Charlotte Rhead, Martin Brothers, and Clarice Cliff continue to catch the collector's attention. Whether it's the experimental glazes found on Ruskin and Pilkington, or the bright paints of Cliff, clean, well executed pieces are drawing top prices. In addition, European and English studio potters are showing strength. Studio lines of Rosenthal, Royal Copenhagen, Rorstrand, and lesser known artists are on the rise.

Along the same lines of artist-inspired pieces are those from the Ditmar-Urbach studios. While most Czechoslovakian ceramics are rather mundane and overlooked by ceramic enthusiasts, the brightly painted pieces of Mrazek Peasant and the figural pitchers are on the rise.

The International Ceramics Fair held each year in New York City is always a bellwether for top-of-the-line pieces. Finely executed Meissen, Lowestroft, Worcester, and Caughley are among the best sellers. Rare spatter and mocha patterns also continue to show signs of strength.

The chintz market, which skyrocketed a few years ago, has come back to earth. Part of this is due to the re-issuing of many of the earlier patterns by Royal Winton. This grouping may regain its feet in the near future.

Finally, the economy appears to be on the upswing. How long it will take to affect the ceramics market is a guess, but the next year or so may give us a more realistic picture of how healthy this market will be. We will be watching!

ABBREVIATIONS

c	circa		lg	large
C	century		lt	light
circ	circular		med	medium
cov	cover		mk	mark
d	diameter		MOP	mother of pearl
dbl	double		mtd	mounted
dk	dark		mts	mounts
dtd	dated		#	numbered
emb	embossed		no.	pattern number
ext	exterior		oct	octagonal
ftd	footed		pr	pair
ground	background		prs	pairs
h	height		PUG	print under glaze
H-H	handle to handle		rect	rectangular
hex	hexagonal		sgd	signed
horiz	horizontal		sm	small
HP	hand painted		SP	silver plated
imp	impressed		sq	square
int	interior		unmkd	unmarked
irid	iridescent		vert	vertical
irreg	irregular		w	width
l	length			

EDGE, MALKIN & CO.

c. 1871

ABC AND MAXIM WARE

Staffordshire, England and Continental
19th Century

History: Nineteenth century English ABC plates from Staffordshire are not considered great works of art, but are quite collectible. They were made in soft paste by many potteries, most of whom did not mark the plates with a factory mark.

ABC plates were designed to teach a child letters and numbers. In addition, knowledge of important people, places, or things also was transmitted via these plates at mealtimes.

ABC plates were made in forty-four different sizes, ranging from 4" to the large size of approximately 9". Usually the alphabet was on the rim of the plate, either applied (transferred) or embossed (raised). The center of the plate usually had a scene of people, domestic or wild animals, birds, sports, occupations, places, months, military, Indians, or some other type of design transferred onto it.

When the picture was transferred to the plate and fired, the basic color was added as well. When additional colors were used, the plate had to be fired one or more additional times depending on the number of colors.

ABC plates also were made in Braille for the blind child. These are quite rare today.

Some English ABC plates were marked with the diamond British Registry mark from 1812-1883, while some marks were transferred, stamped, or pressed onto the soft paste.

English Staffordshire soft paste alphabet mugs are difficult to find in perfect condition. Mugs were cylindrical with a thick wall. Usually two or three consecutive letters appeared with transfer illustrations. Some mugs had a capital and lower case letter with an illustration. Others had just one letter that was used to begin a short verse. Very few mugs were marked. Subjects included animals, children, birds, rhymes, and stories, or just letters of the alphabet with an illustration.

Benjamin Franklin's *Poor Richard's Almanac* was the source for many of the maxims and moral lessons used on maxim ware. Biblical passages and nursery rhymes also were used on these plates to present a message to the child.

Plates are most frequently encountered. Teapots, cups, bowls, and porringers also carried lessons for the young. Most of the maxims were illustrated with transfer printed pictures that helped make the lesson more palatable. Some were hand painted, but most were multicolored transfers. The same maxim or rhyme frequently was illustrated by various manufacturers, each using a slightly different drawing.

Manufacture of ABC plates and cups began about 1890 in Germany, much later than in England. The examples were made in hard paste and were thinner and whiter than the Staffordshire pieces. Decals were used in place of transfers on the German wares. The alphabet was usually embossed and sometimes trimmed with gilt. Subjects included chickens, cats, animals, and people.

References: Mildred & Joseph P. Chalala, *A Collector's Guide to Plates, Mugs & Things*, Pridemark Press, 1980; Irene & Ralph Lindsay, *ABC Plates & Mugs*, Collector Books, 1997. David & Irving Shipkowitz; *The ABC's of ABC Ware*, Schiffer Books, 2002.

Collectors' Clubs: ABC Collector's Circle, Joan M. George, 67 Stevens Avenue, Old Bridge, NJ 08857, $25 per year for quarterly newsletter.

Collecting Hints: Interest in ABC plates has increased dramatically in the past five to ten years. Make certain the transfers are in good to very good condition. Avoid pieces that are seriously cracked or crazed.

*Mug, 3" h, red and black letters, "U" for umpire, "V" for volume, Black transfers w/yellow and green accents, int red line, **$235.00***

Feeding Dish
6 1/2" d, multicolor decal of 4 children w/musical instruments, green printed alphabet on ext, Bavaria, ... **50.00**
7 1/2" d, multicolored decal of Jack and Jill and verse in center, printed alphabet border,

"Schumann, Bavaria" mk, ... **68.00**
Milk Jug, 3" h, blue transfer of alphabet on front, gold accented rim and handle, ... **25.00**

*Plate, 7 1/4" d, black transfer w/ochre, red, & green accents, black lined rim, raised alphabet border, **$325.00***

Mug
2 1/2" h
Black printed children playing w/sailboats and "Lost Time Is Never Found Again...," **425.00**
Brown printed panel of seaside scene w/beached boat on front, printed alphabet, Brownhill, ... **425.00**
Yellow overlay of letter "K" and black transfer of woman helping man with cane and dog w/yellow and red overlay, yellow overlay of letter "L" and Lord sitting w/four children, red and yellow overlay, rim chips, (A), ... **110.00**
2 5/8" h, "Franklin's Maxim-Now I Have a Sheep and Cow," black printed gentleman w/cow and sheep, red, brown, and green tints, ... **375.00**
2 3/4" h
Letter "O" and owl and orange, red transfer, ... **250.00**
Rooster and goat, printed alphabet, blue/green transfer, ... **175.00**
2 7/8" h, brown printed and tinted panels of girl at fence and cottage or two cows grazing, mother and child, brown printed alphabet, ... **410.00**

Plate

6 3/4" d

Multicolored decal of 2 children riding in donkey cart, windmill in bkd, raised alphabet border, ... **95.00**

Organ grinder and children, brown transfer w/red, blue, and green accents, raised alphabet border, ... **45.00**

"Rugby," blue transfer, raised alphabet border, ... **265.00**

Plate, 6 7/8" d, magenta, brown, and green transfer, raised alphabet border, **$145.00**

6 7/8" d, children spilled from wicker wagon pulled by dog and rabbit, brown transfer, raised alphabet border, ... **50.00**

7" d

Diamond center, brown English hunt scene, brown transfer w/polychrome accents, raised alphabet border, ... **275.00**

"Franklin's Proverbs-Three Removes Are As Bad As A Fire. Rolling Stone Gathers No Moss," woman in carriage pulled by 2 horses, multicolored, raised alphabet border, red lined rim, ... **225.00**

"Hey Diddle Diddle," cow jumping over moon, black transfer w/polychrome accents, printed alphabet border, ... **215.00**

Multicolored decal of 3 Victorian children and flowers in center, raised alphabet border, ... **90.00**

"The Lord's Prayer" and "For Thine is the Kingdom...," brown transfer w/maroon accents, raised alphabet border, ... **255.00**

"The Walk," black print of walking horse and rider, color tints, raised alphabet border, red lined rim, ... **66.00**

"The Young Sargeant," black transfer w/red, blue, green, and yellow accents, raised alphabet border, "imp Elsmore & Son" mk, rim chips, ... **120.00**

Plate, 7 1/8" d, brown transfer, blue accents, British reg. mark, **$195.00**

7 1/8" d

Multicolored scene of boys stealing hat from sleeping man, raised alphabet border, Elsmore, ... **195.00**

"Stag And Fawn," black transfer w/red, brown, and green accents, raised alphabet border, "Elsmore & Son England" mk, ... **80.00**

"Wild Animals The Lion," brown lion w/green foliage in center sq, brown printed alphabet border, ... **230.00**

7 1/4" d

"Baked Taters All Hot," couple selling potatoes, black transfer w/blue, green, red, and orange overpaint, raised alphabet border, ... **115.00**

"Crusoe Finding The Foot Prints," brown transfer w/blue, green, yellow, and dk brown accents, brown printed alphabet border, "B. P. Co. Tunstall England" mk, ... **110.00**

"Fox Hunt" design, blue transfer, raised alphabet border, ... **285.00**

"Franklin's Maxim-Handle your tools without mittens," young

men in center, black transfer, border of red, blue and green accented relief molded flowers, (A), ... **132.00**

"Going To Market," black transfer w/red, yellow, and blue accents, raised alphabet border, ... **125.00**

Horse head and fan in center, printed alphabet border, blue transfer, "W. Adams & Co." mk, ... **350.00**

"Steeplechase" in diamond, blue transfer, raised alphabet border, ... **247.00**

"Titmouse-Bird Series," printed alphabet on other half, ... **325.00**

"Wild Animals-The Lion," center sq w/brown lion, green foliage, brown printed alphabet, "Brownhills Pottery & Co." mk, ... **120.00**

7 3/8" d

Clock and calendar design w/alphabet, brown transfer, ... **450.00**

"Nations Of The World- Japanese," brown printed oriental couple w/blue, yellow, and red accents, brown printed alphabet, ... **385.00**

7 1/2" d

"Crusoe Rescues Friday," brown transfer w/colors, printed alphabet border, ... **350.00**

Farm animals in barn in center w/"Fs for the fowls, and farm where they dwell, Gs for the girlie who feeds them so well," blue transfer, raised alphabet border, rope rim, ... **80.00**

Franklin's Maxim

"A Dead Bee maketh No Honey," black transfer w/green, yellow, and blue accents, molded lily of the valley on border, blue lined rim, "J. & G. Meakin" mk, ... **155.00**

"Forage and Want...," black transfer w/green, red, and yellow accents, raised alphabet border, rope rim, ... **325.00**

Punch and Judy, blue-green transfer, raised alphabet border, ... **195.00**

7 3/4" d

Monkey shaving in mirror, pink transfer, raised alphabet border, ... **275.00**

"Queen Victoria," black transfer, raised alphabet border, ... **750.00**

Two girls in garden, printed alphabet border, brown transfer, ... **65.00**

8" d

"Franklin's Proverbs," center scene of farmer plowing, black transfer w/green and yellow accents, "He that by the plough would thrive himself must either hold or dive" around center, raised alphabet border w/3 petal flowers from pink lined rim, ... **150.00**

"The Guardian," dog protecting sleeping child, black transfer w/blue and green accents, raised alphabet border, green lined rim, ... **250.00**

Young child artist in center, brown transfer w/yellow, green, blue, and red accents, printed alphabet border, ... **75.00**

8 1/4" d

Brown printed sq w/"Wild Animals The Stag," brown stag, green bkd, cream body, brown printed alphabet, ... **100.00**

Decal of brown cat and yellow kitten in center, black printed alphabet border, England, ... **45.00**

Green transfer of bust of dog wearing glasses and fan, printed alphabet border, ... **115.00**

Polychrome scene of man sliding down hill, raised alphabet border, ... **195.00**

Tinted and brown printed "Birds of England-Wandering Pie," brown printed alphabet separated by blue diagonal, rim chip, ... **135.00**

Train emerging from tunnel, brown transfer, raised alphabet border, ... **395.00**

9 1/2" d, "Playing at Lovers," little boy courting girl, black transfer w/polychromes, raised alphabet border, ... **395.00**

Soup Plate, 8" d, Franklin's Proverbs, multicolored transfer of farm scene in center and "He that by the plough

would thrive himself must either hold or thrive," raised alphabet border w/raised flowerheads, pink lined rim, ...**150.00**

ADAMS

Burslem, Staffordshire, England 1770 to Present

The Adams family established themselves in Burslem. The first potter was William Adams, but this name was used repeatedly throughout the Adams' history. Eventually there were Adams potteries in seven different locations. Most of the potteries, if they marked their works, simply used the name "Adams."

William Adams Brick House, Burslem and Cobridge 1770-c1820

He produced blue-printed wares with chinoiserie patterns early in the 1780s. They were probably not marked. Two of his potteries were lent to other potters among whom were James and Ralph Clews in 1817.

William Adams Greengates, Tunstall, c1779-1805 (1809)

Blue-printed wares were made. They were the first pottery in Tunstall to do so. William died in 1805, but the works were continued by trustees. Benjamin, his son, took over in 1809.

William Adams Stoke-on-Trent 1804-1819

Large quantities of blue and white transfer wares were made both for the home market and for export to America. In 1810, William, his son, joined the partnership, and three other sons joined soon after. The company was then called "William Adams & Sons."

Benjamin Adams Greengates, Tunstall 1809-1820

Benjamin used the impressed mark "B. Adams." He continued making blue-printed wares.

William Adams & Sons Stoke-on-Trent 1819 to Present

William Adams died in 1829; William, his eldest son, took over. In 1834, the Greenfield pottery was added to the firm. The Stoke factory was closed in 1863. The Greengates pottery was added to the group in 1858. William Adams joined the Wedgwood Group in 1966.

Adam's Rose 1820s-1830s

This pattern was named for its maker William Adams & Sons of Stoke-on-Trent. It consisted of a border of large red roses with green leaf sprigs on a white ground.

G. Jones & Son, England, produced a variation known as "Late Adam's Rose." The colors were not as brilliant. The background was a "dirty" white.

References: A.W. Coysh, *Blue-Printed Earthenware 1800-1850*, David & Charles, 1972. David Furness, J. Wagner, Judith Wagner, *Adams Ceramics: Staffordshire Potters & Pots*, 1779-1998, Schiffer Books, 1999.

Berry Bowl, 5 3/8" d, "Rural Scenery" pattern, girl feeding sheep, ducks, and turkey in center, checkerboard border w/lozenges of florals, red transfer, scalloped rim, ... **40.00**

Biscuit Barrel, 6 1/4" h, multicolored Dickens scenes on sides, overhead woven handle, repair, ... **35.00**

Bone Dish, 9" l, "Cattle Scenery" pattern, blue transfer, ... **90.00**

Bowl

7 1/2" l, diamond shape, Titian Ware, HP red and orange fruit and green foliage in center, border of fruit and flowers, ... **35.00**

7 3/4" d, "In God is Our Trust The Farmers Arms," grey-black transfer w/colors, ... **15.00**

10" d, Mariner's compass on side, sailing ship on reverse, black transfers w/colors, roses and green foliage band on inner rim, ... **150.00**

Coffeepot, 9" h, Calyx Ware, "Metz" pattern, figural flower knob, ... **85.00**

Creamer, 4 1/2" h, basket of flowers design, dk blue transfer, "imp ADAMS" mk, (A), ... **125.00**

Cup and Saucer

Black outlined center band of cobalt centered orange flowerheads, cobalt and purple foliage, wide yellow border band, set of 4, ... **25.00**

Cup and Saucer, "The Seasons of Blossoms" on cup, "A Mountain Home" on saucer, black transfers w/color accents, "B. Altman & Co. NYC" mk, $10.00

Calyx Ware
"Chinese Garden" pattern,
.... **10.00**
"Ming Toi" pattern, ... **15.00**
"English Scenic" pattern, red
transfer, set of 10, ... **225.00**
Ironstone
"DuBarry" pattern, brown
transfer, set of 6, ... **32.00**
"Tokio" pattern, blue transfers,
.... **35.00**

Cup and Saucer, Handleless,
"Seasons" pattern, brown transfers,
.... **95.00**

Dish, Cov, 11 1/4" l x 8 3/8" w, oval,
Titian Ware, "Lakewood" pattern,
band of red flowerheads and green
foliage, ... **125.00**

Fruit Bowl, 6" d, Calyx Ware,
"Singapore Bird" pattern, blue-
green, ... **10.00**

Gravy Boat
7" l, "Adam's Rose" pattern, blue,
green, and red, unmkd,
.... **50.00**
7 1/2" l, "Tokio" pattern, blue transfer,
.... **48.00**
8 1/2" l x 4" h, ironstone, "Sharon"
pattern, brown transfer,
.... **10.00**

Jug, 3 3/4" h, dk blue printed chinoiserie
vignettes, net ground, ridged strap
handle w/foliate terminal,
.... **115.00**

Mustard Pot, 3 1/2" h, stoneware, white
body w/relief of classic figures,
brown glazed neck and spout,

hinged SP cov, early 19th C, (A),
.... **120.00**
Pitcher
3" h, Calyx Ware, sm pink roses,
green foliage, dk red band of
chevrons on rim, pale blue
ground, ... **22.00**

Pitcher, 7 1/2" h, "Standing Rock Picturesque, Wisconsin Dells" and "The Narrows, Wisconsin Dells" on reverse, multicolored transfers, $75.00

4" h, Titian Ware, raised orange,
green, purple, blue, and yellow
flowers on sides, black outlined
yellow band on collar, black lined
handle, ... **10.00**

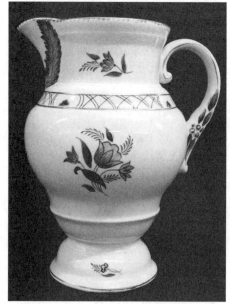

Pitcher, 9 1/2" h, "Calyx Ware", gilt outlined purple flowers, rust trim, purple feather on spout, cream ground, $75.00

5 1/4" h, Calyx Ware, "Regent"
pattern, lt blue ground, ... **10.00**

7" h, ironstone, paneled, "Victoriana"
pattern, sprig of leaves on sides,
dot and diamond border, blue
and white, molded vert fluted
base, ... **40.00**

Plate, 7 1/2" d, pearlware, "Tendril" pattern, blue and white, gilt rim, c1810, pr, $575.00

Plate
6 1/8" d, "Chinese Bird" pattern, blue
transfer, ... **6.00**
7" d
"Adam's Rose" pattern, red, blue,
and green, ... **35.00**
"Tokio" pattern, blue transfer,
.... **35.00**
7 1/2" d, "Adam's Rose" pattern,
green and red, "imp ADAMS"
mk, c1830, ... **100.00**
8" d
"Adam's Rose" pattern, green
and red, ... **125.00**
Titian Ware, lg red and white
clover in center, panels of
blue dot flowers on border,
.... **15.00**
8 1/2" d
"Adam's Rose" pattern, green
and red, ... **135.00**
Ironstone, "Habana" pattern,
central Spanish courtyard
scene, 5 medallions of
Spanish nobles on border
separated by sm
flowerheads, red-pink
transfer, "Ironstone Habana
W. Adams" mk, ... **95.00**
8 7/8" d, oct, Titian Ware, gaudy red
flowerhead and blue and yellow
florals, wide black border,
.... **8.00**
9" d, Titian Ware, HP lg garden
flowers and foliage, raised white

acorn design border, brown lined rim, ... **25.00**

9 3/8" d, oct, "Cries of London-Sweet China Oranges," **115.00**

9 1/2" d

"Adam's Rose" pattern, green and red, ... **150.00**

"Cries of London-Knives, Scissors and Razors to Grind," **20.00**

9 3/4" sq, "Chelsea Sprays" pattern, blue sprays, ... **5.00**

10" d

"Cries of London-New Mackerel, New Mackerel," **25.00**

"David Copperfield-Mr Micawber Delivers Some Valedictory Remarks," **28.00**

Ironstone, "Ming Jade" pattern, pale green ground, fluted border, ... **20.00**

10 1/4" d

"Cupid and Roses," dk blue transfer, ... **750.00**

"Faneuil Hall, Cradle of Liberty, 1742," flower border, red transfer, scalloped rim, "Wm Adams & Co., England, eagle" mk, (A), ... **130.00**

Pastoral scene of cattle in field, leaf and flower border, scalloped rim, dk blue transfer, "imp Adams Warrented Staffordshire" mk, (A), ... **275.00**

10 1/2" d

"Adam's Rose" pattern, green and red, ... **195.00**

"Chinese Ching" pattern, cobalt, red, orange, and tan oriental garden scene, ... **50.00**

"Cries of London-Fresh Gathered Peas Young Wastings," **35.00**

"Winter in the Country-The Old Grist Mill," black transfer w/pink and yellow floral border, ... **28.00**

10 7/8" d, "Lorraine" pattern, med blue transfer, "imp B. Adams" mk, ... **310.00**

Platter

11 1/2" l x 9" w, Titian Ware, "Blossomtime" pattern, molded basketweave border, ... **20.00**

11 3/4" l x 9" w, rect w/cut corners, Calyx Ware, "Cambodia" pattern, blue, yellow, green, and pink center flower spray, border sprigs, pale green ground, gold rim, ... **25.00**

14 1/4" l x 10 1/2" w, ironstone, "Cattle Scenery" pattern, blue transfer, ... **70.00**

16 1/2" l x 11" w, oct, Calyx Ware, "Singapore Bird" pattern, pale blue ground, ... **150.00**

Sandwich Plate, 9 3/4" H-H x 8 3/4" w, rect, Titian Ware, HP lg yellow and sm blue flowers, green foliage, ... **16.00**

Sauce Tureen, Cov, 8" H-H, w/undertray and ladle, "Cattle Scenery" pattern, med blue transfers, ... **325.00**

Serving Bowl, 9 1/2" l, oval, ironstone, "Sharon" pattern, ... **15.00**

Soup Plate

9" d, ironstone, "Shanshai" pattern, med blue transfer, ... **15.00**

10 1/2" d, "Adam's Rose" pattern, green and red, ... **195.00**

Sugar Bowl, Cov

5 3/4" h, Calyx Ware, "Mandalay" pattern, ... **26.00**

7 1/2" h, paneled steeple shape, blue "Berlin Groups" pattern, "W. Adams & Sons" mk, ... **235.00**

Teapot

4 7/8" h, Calyx Ware, "Carolynn" pattern, flower knob, ... **38.00**

8" h, ironstone, paneled, "Veruschka" pattern, ... **165.00**

Toddy Plate, 5 7/8" d, "Temple Warriors" pattern, red transfer in center, black border transfer, mkd, ... **185.00**

Vase

6" h, "Oliver Twist-Oliver Asking For More," multicolored transfer, ... **100.00**

8 3/4" h, oct, trumpet shape, "Cattle Scenery" pattern, blue transfer, c1910, ... **200.00**

Vegetable Bowl

9 1/2" d, oct, ironstone, "Vermont" pattern, border band of red, blue, and gold florals, ivory ground, ... **15.00**

9 3/4" l, "Lancaster" pattern, ... **30.00**

10 1/8" l x 7 1/4" w, "Adam's Rose" pattern, red, green, and blue, ... **150.00**

Waste Bowl, 6 1/4" d, ftd, "Adam's Rose" pattern, red and green, (A), ... **44.00**

AFTER 1892

AFTER 1892

AMPHORA

Turn-Teplitz, Bohemia
1892 to Present

History: Hans and Carl Riessner, Rudolf Kessel, and Edward Stellmacher started the Amphora Porzellan Fabrik in 1892 for the manufacture of earthenware and porcelain. This pottery was established at Turn-Teplitz, Bohemia (now the Czech Republic). It produced mostly porcelain figures and Art Nouveau styled vases that were widely exported. Many of the wares were hand decorated. They marked their wares with a variety of stamps, some incorporating the name and location of the pottery with a shield or a crown.

Edward Stellmacher left Amphora to start his own company from 1905-1912. The factory was then named "Riessner & Kessel Amphora Werke" until Kessel left in 1910. When Carl Riessner died in 1911, it left Hans Riessner as the sole proprietor. World War I and the Depression affected the company as it decreased in size, and finally it faded out during World War II.

They used the Art Nouveau style on their original forms and decorations. Molded animals were applied to the vases in the form of leopards, panthers, frogs, salamanders, lions, various birds, alligators, monkeys, bats, mice, and elephants. Vases depicting sea life were some of their best works. Paul Dachsel and Alfred Stellmacher were excellent designers for Amphora. Portrait vases were also made. A tremendous variety of glazes was utilized.

After World War I, there were fewer designs and less glaze experimentation. Stoneware pieces were made with hard enamel designs using Egyptian or Art Deco motifs. Before WWI, Bohemia was part of the Austro-Hungarian empire so that the name "Austria" may have been used as part of the mark. After World War II, the name "Czechoslovakia" may be part of the mark.

The Amphora Pottery Works was only one of a number of firms that was located in Teplitz, an active pottery center at the turn of the century.

References: Richard L. Scott, Lenka Pankova, & Dr. Jan Mergl, *House of Amphora*, Self Published, 2003.

Museum: Antiken Museum, Basel, Switzerland.

Basket

8" h x 6" w, corset shape, enameled orange, blue, or red flowerheads on border, lt green stylized foliage, dk blue fencing, tan textured ground, enamel dots on base, "Amphora Made in Czecho-Slovakia" mk, ... **70.00**

9 1/2" h x 11 1/4" w, standing figural cherub w/bunches of pink roses next to woven basket w/brown, rope border, lt green center handles, "Amphora Made in Czechoslovakia" mk, ... **295.00**

Candleholder, 6" l x 3 1/2" h, figural kneeling tan camel, red fringed blue blanket on back, brown harness, ... **265.00**

Ewer, 6" h x 7" w, applied molded white orchid and leaves, lt yellow-green body, Ernst Wahliss, ... **395.00**

Figure

14 1/2" h x 20" l, brown accented bull, green sculptured base, ... **895.00**

16" h, period woman in irid gold gown, holding 2 grey baskets at sides, repairs, ... **700.00**

17" h, nymph leaning on tree stump, rock base, green and gilt shades, matte finish, Ernst Wahliss, ... **2,500.00**

Marriage Jug, 7" h, dbl spout w/center overhead handle, brown, tan, and orange enameled bust of prince in medallion, dk blue matte ground w/orange stars, green fleur-de-lys, and blue and orange dots, ... **175.00**

Pitcher, 8 3/4" h, bulbous base, tapered neck, everted rim, 2 handles and spout, tube lined black outlined blue flowerhead and diamonds on base, textured tan ground, textured purple neck w/herringbones and blue and gold ovals on rim, "Amphora Made in Czechoslovakia" mk, ... **65.00**

Planter

2 3/4" h x 2 3/4" d, enameled brown sailboat, green sail, blue waves, dk blue enameled stars separated by vert swirls, matte brown ground, green "jewels" on collar, brown "jewels" on base, ... **140.00**

4 1/4" h, sq shape, cuenca design of pink and cream tulips w/lt green whiplash leaves, med green ground, irreg rim, hairline, (A), ... **200.00**

Vase

3 1/4" h, spherical shape, faux verdigris and bronze leaf

designs w/polychrome "jewels," unmkd, (A), ... **115.00**

4 1/2" h, trumpet shape, relief matte herringbone pattern, blue, yellow, maroon, and white enameled stones on base, dk blue enamel handles and rim, "Amphora Czechoslovakia" mk, ... **55.00**

5 1/2" h, squat shape, blue ground w/strings of blue beads, lt blue bubbles on rim, gold figural dragonfly handles, ... **1,100.00**

6" h, yellow-green bisque body w/tan mottling, incised and enameled dk green, lt blue, rose, and white Art Deco butterfly on front and reverse, 2 sm ear handles, "Amphora Made in Czechoslovakia" mk, ... **55.00**

6 3/4" h

Cylinder shape w/wide collar, 4 gold handles on base, bust of woman wearing bonnet in raised gilt circle, bird in gilt circle on reverse, raised gilt ribbon on neck, cobalt ground, "Amphora Austria, red Turn Teplitz" mk, ... **250.00**

Gourd shape, 2 sm handles on base, emb fruits and flowers on base and rim, matte green glaze, "stamped AMPHORA 10-40" mk, (A), ... **115.00**

8" h, gourd shape, relief of pink cyclamen blossoms, whiplash stems, heart shaped leaves, and handles on collar, hammered blue lustered ground, ... **1,900.00**

8 1/2" h

Applied brown pinecones, vines, and leaves, taupe basketweave ground, gilt accents, cream int, "imp Amphora, Austria, castle" mk, ... **600.00**

Enameled black crows w/orange breasts, white, red, and blue feathered wings, tan crackle base, white and red enameled cottages, "blue Amphora Made in Czechoslovakia" mk, ... **180.00**

9 1/2" d, squat shape, 2 red and black handles, applied green flowerheads, black stems,

mauve ground, black rim, "R.ST.K. Amphora" mk, ... **350.00**

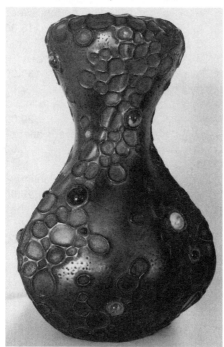

Vase, 9" h, jeweled, gold to dk red to green luster ground, "Amphora Austria" mk, $1,295.00

10" h

Bulbous base, tapered neck, brown textured ground, 4 horiz rows of enamel "jewels," "Amphora, Made in Austria" mk, ... **100.00**

Gourd shape w/pinched waist, applied dk blue grape clusters, moss green leaves, rose colored accents, tan ground, ... **1,500.00**

Tapered shape, raised enameled red, blue, white, or orange flowerheads, dk brown stems, leaf outlines, matte tan ground, sm cobalt handles, "imp crown AMPHORA AUSTRIA" mks, ... **300.00**

11 1/2" h, dbl gourd shape w/short, straight neck, sculpted stylized leaves under tan, gold, and brown matte glaze, (A), ... **863.00**

12" h, swollen shape, 2 handles shoulder to rim, Art Nouveau style pink and white flowers and buds, curved green stems and leaves, chocolate brown ground w/burgundy highlights, Julius Dresser, ... **750.00**

13" h, tapered shape, emb ivory Arctic scene of polar bear and terns on umber matte ground, rising sun border, (A), ... **650.00**

14" h, squat base, long tapered neck, applied bouquet of red or cream flowerheads, green buds and stems, tan washed basketweave ground, burnished gold rim, irid int, ... **475.00**

14 1/4" h, tan matte straight body w/raised white enamel dots and spread foot, swollen cobalt enamel collar below rim w/4 tube openings and handles, blue, yellow, and green enamel stylized leaf and geometric designs on body and collar w/gold accents, repairs, (A), ... **690.00**

15" h, squat ball base, long flared neck, applied red flowers, gold buds, green stems, textured gold-green ground, gold accents, "imp crowned AMPHORA" mk, ... **1,295.00**

Vase, 16" h, multicolored parrot, gray-green ground, "Amphora, Austria, and crown" mark, $650.00

17" h, spread base, tapered body, applied blackberries, green and copper leaves, streaked matte brown ground, "imp crowned AMPHORA" mk, ... **525.00**

ANGELICA KAUFFMANN

Switzerland
1741-1807

History: Marie Angelique Catherine Kauffmann (1741-1807), a Swiss artist, worked primarily in a neo-classical style. Many artists copied her original paintings and used them on hand decorated porcelains during the 19th century.

Cake Plate, 10" H-H, decal of classical lovers seated in garden w/cherub watching, white border, open handles, gold wavy rim, ... **60.00**

Charger

11 1/2" d, multicolored scene of classic seated woman w/attendants, dancing woman w/cherub and tambourine player, sgd, "Victoria Carlsbad Austria" mk, ... **85.00**

Cake plate, 10" H-H, multicolored decal in center, shaded blue-green border w/gold stenciling, sgd, "Victoria Austria" mk, $85.00

12" d, multicolored classic garden scene of warrior seated on rock, dancing nymphs, and lyre player, undulating rim, sgd "Kauffmann," **225.00**

Creamer and Sugar Bowl, Cov, 5" h, gilt oval w/multicolored classic scenes, green center bands, green bases, scattered pink roses w/gilt accents, sgd "Kauffmann," pr, ... **35.00**

Cup and Saucer, multicolored decal of 2 classic women and cherub in center of cup, hanging red and green wreaths, gilt stenciled accents, ... **23.00**

Dresser Set, 2 bottles, 7" h, 2 candlesticks, 5 1/2" h, 2 cov dishes, 4" w, pin tray, 4 1/4" w, tray, 19" l, multicolored classic transfers, gold trim. $275.00

Ewer

10" h, classic Renaissance form, center multicolored scene of classic ladies and child, shadowed leaves on reverse, cream and green ground, maroon top and base, gold handle and trim, sgd "Angelica Kauffmann," **345.00**

11" h, gold arrowhead outlined oval of multicolored scene of classic women in garden, dk green ground w/gold overlay, sgd "Angelica Kauffmann," **95.00**

Patch Box, 1 3/4" d, hinged, multicolored scene of 4 classic ladies in garden scene, white body, ... **55.00**

Plaque, 14" d, multicolored scene of classic people in garden, gold rim, pierced for hanging, sgd "Kauffmann," blue "Victoria Austria" mk, ... **125.00**

Plate

6 1/4" d, Multicolored

Dancing classic women, nude reclining male in bkd, gold arched wreath on border, Hutschenreuther, ... **30.00**

Scene of 3 classic women in garden in gold zigzag inner border, burgundy ground w/3 lobed cream and gold drape, Victoria Austria, ... **65.00**

7 1/2" d, multicolored scene of classic woman w/three attendants and putto in garden, blue sky, shaded tan ground, sgd "Kauffmann," "Victoria Austria" mk, ... **50.00**

8" d, multicolored transfer of "Cupid Bound by the Graces" in center, lg purple and white roses on border, gold indented rim, "E.S.

Germany Prov. Saxe" mk,
.... **95.00**

8 1/2" d, "Bacchanalian,"
multicolored transfer of 3 classic
women holding grapes and vines
in meadow, gold border w/dk
red, green, and white
embellishments, sgd
"Kauffmann," blue beehive mk,
.... **100.00**

9 1/2" d, Multicolored Scene
Center w/2 classical women
playing w/infant, inner gold
band of geometric drops,
cobalt border w/gold fluted
overlaid rim, Royal Austria,
.... **15.00**

Plate, 9" d, multicolored center, maroon border, sgd "Kauffmann," $125.00

Three classic ladies attending a
seated woman, inner white
border, cobalt outer border
w/molded designs, sgd
"Kauffmann," unmkd,
.... **75.00**

Powder Box, 3 1/4" d, multicolored
transfer of 3 classic women in
garden, kneeling male companion,
gold rim, blue body, sgd "Angelica
Kauffmann," **25.00**

Urn, Cov, vasiform body, ovoid lid,
green ground w/central painted
scene of 3 graces in gold dentil
surround, sq base w/similar scene,
gold tracery and urn knob, gilt scroll
handles, "Victoria Altrohlau
Bohemia," mk, early 20th C, (A),
.... **400.00**

Vase

5" h, flattened ball shape, long neck,
long rect handles to neck, center
medallion of classic woman,
child, and handmaidens, teal
and rose ground, gilt accents,

sgd "Kauffmann," "blue beehive,
Austria" mk, ... **50.00**

7" h, waisted shape, 2 handles, HP
multicolored circ scene of classic
ladies w/cherubs in garden,
cobalt body, sgd "Kauffmann,"
.... **75.00**

12" h, cylinder shape, flared ft, cup
rim, multicolored oval of classic
figures in garden or 2 classic
women w/wreath and infant,
green ground w/vert yellow
separations and gold overlay,
reverse w/gold cartouche and
gold star on white ground, yellow
ft and rim w/gold overlay, white
sq handles from shoulder to
neck, purple luster shoulder and
base, sgd "Kauffmann," pr,
.... **800.00**

AUSTRIA

16th Century to Present

History: Salzburg was the center of
peasant pottery or pottery stove making
during the 16th and 17th centuries. These
wares were similar to those being made in
Germany at the same time. Sometimes
they were colored with tin enamels.
Factories in Wels, Enns, and Steyr also
made this type of pottery ware.

Peasant pottery, known as "Habaner
ware" or Hafner ware, was decorated in an
unsophisticated style with flowers, animals, and figures. These faience wares
were made in Salzberg and Wels during
the late 17th century. Most were used
locally.

The only porcelain being produced in
the early 18th century was made by a
Vienna factory founded by Claudius I Du
Paquier in 1718 with assistance from Meissen workers. This was the second factory
in Europe to make hard paste porcelain.
The factory was sold to the Austrian State
in 1744.

Many of the later Austrian porcelain
factories such as Schlaggenwald,
Klosterle, Prague, Dallwitz, Pirkenhammer,
and Elbogen were classified with Bohemia
porcelain because of their location.

A number of porcelain factories originated in the 19th and 20th centuries to

make utilitarian and decorative porcelains.
These included Brux, Frauenthal, Turn,
Augarten, Wienerberger, Spitz, and Neumann.

In 1897 the Vienna Secession Movement provided a stimulus to Austrian
ceramics. A group of young painters,
sculptors, and architects desired to overthrow conservatism in the arts and design
to revolutionize taste. Moser and Peche
were designers of tableware and decorative porcelains associated with this movement.

In 1903 Moser and Peche founded the
Wiener Werkstatte, an association of artisans, along with porcelain maker Joseph
Bock. They made innovative designs in
both shape and pattern.

Michael Powolny and Berthold Loffler
founded the Wiener Keramik Studio in
1905, which produced advanced tablewares and figure designs in earthenware
and porcelains. Products included black
and white majolica, generally decorated
with Cubist inspired geometrical patterns
from designs by J. Hoffmann, D. Peche,
and Powolny. Figures were modeled by Loffler and Powolny. Art Nouveau and Art
Deco designs were utilized. The products
of the Wiener Keramik Studio became the
foundation for the international Modern
Movement that developed after World War
I.

References: George Ware, *German and
Austrian Porcelain*, Lothar Woeller Press,
1951.

Museums: Osterreisches Museum fur
Angewandtekunst,Vienna, Austria; Vienna
Kunsthistoriches Museum,Vienna, Austria.

Cigar Holder, 9 1/2" l, black jacket, brown pants, yellow scarf, brown barrel, green & gold bucket, "Austria" mk, (A), $250.00

Bonbon Dish, 7" l x 5 1/2" w, gold leaf
and flower bands on MOP ground,
wide gold wavy band, "M.Z. Austria"
mk, ... **50.00**

Bowl

9 1/2" d

Ftd, lobed, white roses, foliage,
shaded brown to pale blue
ground, relief molded
geometric shaped rim, rose

ext, "green M.Z. Austria, eagle" mk, ... **25.00**

Lg dk red roses, blue-green leaves, green to red-brown to cream shaded ground, gold scalloped border and rim, ... **45.00**

9 3/4" d, transfer of purple gowned maiden holding lyre, shaded green border w/gold stenciling, ... **85.00**

Charger

11 1/2" d, sq center cartouche of reclining classic lady and putto in meadow, border of pink roses and green foliage, Victoria, Austria, ... **225.00**

13 1/2" d, HP scene of lady making daisy chain, beckoning to Cupid, titled "Komm zu mir," sgd "Ullman," early 20th C, (A), ... **940.00**

Cheese Dish, Cov, 7 1/2" l x 6" w x 7" h, slant top, sm red roses, molded designs, worn gold trim, ... **135.00**

Chocolate Service, pot, 9 1/4" h, creamer, 3" h, cov sugar bowl, 3 7/8" h, cracker jar, 5 1/2" h, 5 cups, 5 saucers, gold outlined and veined cobalt flowerheads and leaves, red accents and dots, half loop borders, gold rims, ... **550.00**

Cologne Bottle, 5 1/2" h, squat shaped base, pink roses and green leaves on blue and cream shaded ground, gold ball stopper, Vienna, ... **135.00**

Cracker Jar, 5 1/2" h x 6 3/4" H-H, ribbed, bulbous shape, pink roses, green leaves in black outlined rects w/pink and blue ground, satin cream body, gold piecrust rim, handles, and knob, "M.Z. Austria" mk, ... **35.00**

Dish, 13 1/2" H-H, oval, 4 molded squares on border w/decals of pink roses and green foliage, "Victoria Austria" mk, ... **15.00**

Ewer

8" h, purple and grey blossoms and leaves, gold bicycle chain handle, ... **85.00**

14" h, lg red and yellow tulips, sm yellow and purple flowers, gold accented molded swirls, matte

cream ground, 4 sm feet, gold outlined fancy handle, "red crowned RH Made in Austria" mk, ... **75.00**

14 1/2" h, red-purple spider chrysanthemums, yellow-green foliage, tan ground, gold rococo handle, ... **90.00**

Figure

5 1/2" h, bust of Austrian child, flowered yellow cap, gold scarf, off-shoulder blue and orange dress, gold accented waisted base, ... **475.00**

7" h, young boy w/basket on brown stump, green trousers, blue striped tie, Augarten, ... **100.00**

Fruit Bowl, 10" w, 8 panels, blue bird in center and alternating panels, 4 pierced panels, "Victoria Austria" mk, ... **125.00**

Hair Receiver, 2 3/4" h x 4 1/2" d, decals of sm pink flowers, green foliage, gold outlined raised arches on base, crenellated opening, ... **110.00**

Meat Platter, 16 1/4" H-H, oval, scattered sprigs of rose red flowers, green leaves, fluted border, molded beaded rim, ... **15.00**

Milk Pitcher, 4" h, white horiz bands w/red stripe in center bordered by black stripes alternating w/lt blue vert bands, orange luster rim and spout, c1930, ... **25.00**

Nappy, 6 1/2" d, 2 lavender and grey birds on branch, black accents, green rim, "M.Z. Austria" mk, ... **20.00**

Pin Tray, 6 1/2" l, oblong, band of HP pink roses, green foliage on inner border, burnished gold rim, "M.Z. Austria" mk, ... **35.00**

Planter

8" l x 7" w, canoe shape, sm purple shaded violets, green leaves, brown to purple shaded ground, aqua int, c1925, ... **150.00**

12" l x 8" h, squat shape, decals of garden flowers and sprigs, 2 vert handles at each end shaded red to cream and relief molded swirls, shell motif on border, 4 sm aqua shaded feet, "Royal Floretta Austria" mk, ... **100.00**

Plate

8 1/4" d, multicolored center scene of classic ladies, green border

w/gilt accents, "Emerald Victoria Austria" mk, ... **12.00**

9" d, multicolored decal of 3 classic women dancing under flowering tree, dk green border w/molded rays and gold trim, ... **40.00**

9 1/4" d, multicolored center scene of 2 maidens in meadow, gold stenciled inner border, dk green border w/8 ovals of roses separated by dk pink triangles, ... **75.00**

Plate, 10 1/2" d, multicolored portrait, auburn hair, raised gold flower and trellis border, green rim, sgd "F. Tenner," A-$747.00

Rose Bowl

4 1/2" h, HP violets and foliage, gold outlined wavy rim, gold feet, ... **125.00**

5" h, HP red or white roses, green foliage, gold netting on ground, gold outlined wavy rim, gold feet, ... **150.00**

Sardine Box, 5 1/4" l x 4 1/2" w x 3" h, fan-shaped ribbed ground, scattered red roses and foliage, figural grey-black fish handle, "Victoria Austria" mk, ... **195.00**

Serving Bowl, 17 1/2" l x 12 1/2" w, oval, scattered purple violets, molded and lobed border, gold outlined molded handles, beaded rim, "Basset Austria" mk, ... **80.00**

Sugar Bowl, Cov, 4 1/4" h x 5 3/4" H-H, bulbous, lobed shape, pink and green grapes, vines, and leaves, pierced handles, gold trim, scalloped ft and rim, pink roses on cov, "M.Z. Made in Austria" mk, ... **20.00**

Talc Shaker, 4 1/2" h, HP blue forget-me-nots on lt blue upper section

shaded to cream base, gold top, ... **95.00**

Tankard

12 1/2" h, HP multicolored scene of seated Victorian woman quilting by seaside, "M.Z. Austria" mk, ... **150.00**

14 3/4" h, pink and white apple blossoms, green leaves, brown, pink, and green ground, sgd "Gallios," "Hapsburg, Austria" mk, ... **385.00**

Tea Caddy, 4 3/4" h, flat sides w/arched shoulder, HP orange, yellow, blue, green, and violet tulips and rose on sides, sprigs on sides and cov, gilt rims, ... **60.00**

Teapot, 7" h, multicolored scene of "Falstaff" and woman in gilt cartouche on front, burgundy body, gilt bird spout, bird form handle, and bird knob, ... **100.00**

Tea Set, pot, 8 1/4" h, cov sugar bowl, 5 1/2" h, creamer, 3 1/2" h, pink roses on brown branch w/green leaves, ivory ground, gold Greek key handles, gold spread base w/sm feet, gold spout, gold wreath knobs, "MZ Austria" mks, ... **300.00**

Vase

5" h, amphora shape, cup throat, gilt sq handles from neck to body, gilt tooled oval cartouche of classic ladies and cherub in garden, burgundy red ground w/gold geometrics, white spread ft w/gold curlicues, "blue beehive and Austria" mk, ... **35.00**

5 1/2" h, bag shape, short, flared neck, multicolored English garden scene, "red G.B. & C. Made in Austria" mks, pr, ... **385.00**

8" h, goblet shape, Art Nouveau style, raised hanging gilt drops w/red faux "jewels," matte shaded brown, green, and rust ground, 2 sm gilt handles on shoulder, "stamped AUSTRIA" mk, pr, (A), ... **85.00**

8 1/2" h, Secession, 2 buttressed handles, emb medallion, matte green glaze, (A), ... **260.00**

9" h

Inverted heart shape, trailing red roses and bouquet, green

foliage on sides, gold aesthetic collar and handles, rect ft, ... **60.00**

Straight sided base, flared neck w/piecrust rim, bouquet of multicolored garden flowers, molded beading on neck, fancy scroll handles w/gold trim, matte cream ground, "red RH Made in Austria" mk, ... **25.00**

9 1/2" h

Bulbous w/straight neck, 2 tone brown texture on lower section, raised fish on dk brown ground on neck, c1930, ... **95.00**

Three blue streaked joined cylinders w/gilt horiz ribs, gilt molded handles on each cylinder and raised gilt geometrics, sgd "Gudrin Baudisch," (A), ... **2,530.00**

9 3/4" h, bottle shape, Art Nouveau style, painted iris, swirling green foliage, pea green ground, ... **950.00**

11" h, cylinder shape, HP multicolored peacock w/long tail in pink and white apple blossoms and brown branch, shaded gold top to pink and blue ground, "MZ Austria" mk, ... **80.00**

11 1/2" h, hourglass shape w/2 handles, emb yellow berries and green leaves on mottled yellow and brown matte ground, "JBD Austria" mk, (A), ... **172.00**

12" h

Cylinder shape w/slightly flared ft and molded and gilt ruffled rim, lady wearing diaphanous gown holding blowing olive green scarf overhead, leafless tree and ocean on reverse, blue streaked ground, gold curled handles, c1860, ... **475.00**

Tapered cylinder shape, aqua body, band of pink or red roses between gold bands on collar, ... **215.00**

12 1/8" h, cylinder shape, short collar, painted pastel blue, yellow, and pink Geishas w/umbrellas, hanging vines, gold ground, c1910, ... **395.00**

BAVARIA

Bayreuth, Bavaria
c1713-1852

History: By the 18th century, many factories were established in the Bavarian region. Bauscher at Weiden produced utility wares, some of which featured cobalt blue ornamentation. J.N. Muller at Schonwald supplied painted and unpainted utility wares. Other factories operating in Bavaria included Schuman; Thomas; and Zeh, Scherzer and Company.

J.G. Knoller founded the Bayreuth factory in Bavaria and produced faience and brown glazed wares with silver, gilt, and engraved decorations. The finest work was done from 1728 until 1745. Bayreuth brown glazed wares were a lightly fired reddish earthenware covered with a manganese brown or red glaze. Yellow glazed wares were lighter in body and were covered with a buff or pale yellow glaze. About 1745 Frankel and Schrock took over and started to make porcelain. J.G. Pfeiffer acquired the firm, later selling it in 1767.

After 1728, the pottery and porcelain pieces were marked frequently. The mark consisted of the initials of the place and the owner, along with the painter's mark.

Museum: Sevres Museum, Sevres, France.

Tirschenreuth
1838 to Present

The Tirschenreuth Porcelain Factory was established in 1838 and made tablewares, utilitarian and decorative porcelains, figures, and coffee and tea sets. In 1927 the company was acquired by the Porcelain Factory Lorenz Hutschenreuther in Selb.

Additional Listing: Hutschenreuther.

Bowl

6" d, 10 sides, red and green grapes in center, vert pierced sides, purple rim, ... **10.00**

8 1/2" d, HP yellow daffodils, long green leaves, green and gold ribbon border, c1903, ... **85.00**

9" d

Decal of white roses, green foliage, gold rim, mkd, ... **20.00**

Multicolored sprig of garden flowers on int, molded border w/orange and grey shading and scattered sprigs, ... **20.00**

11" d, multicolored decal of yellow, red, or pink roses, int border of molded curls w/orange splashes, shaped rim, "J.S.V. Bavaria" mk, ... **85.00**

Cake Plate

9 7/8" H-H, red and pink roses on green shaded border, gilt rim, "Sevres Bavaria" mk, ... **35.00**

12" H-H, 3 lg red poppies joined by gold band on border, whiplash stems to center, gold rim and open handles, ... **385.00**

Candy Dish, 8" l, pink and red rose w/green foliage in center, band of pink and yellow roses w/green foliage, vert pierced sides, gilt rim, ... **10.00**

Celery Tray, 12 1/2" l x 5" w, pink roses w/thorny stems, moss green shaded ground, "Z.S. & C. Bavaria" mk, ... **25.00**

Chocolate Set

Pot, 9 1/2" h, 6 cups and saucers, HP lg white camellias, shaded lt blue to pink ground, "crowned rampant lion Bavaria" mks, ... **285.00**

Pot, 9 3/4" h, creamer, 3 1/2" h, cov sugar bowl, 3" h, HP lg white and red roses, garden flowers, gold rococo handles, rims, and knobs, mkd, ... **350.00**

Chop Plate

12 1/2" d, lg pink or red roses, green foliage, sm yellow flowers in bkd, dk red to yellow shaded ground, gold rim, ... **110.00**

13" d, multicolored bouquet in center, olive green border panels outlined in raised gold w/gold dots, ... **10.00**

Condensed Milk Container, 5 3/4" h, stenciled red grapes, brown branch, green leaves, matte gold rims, handles, and knob, "Jaeger Bavaria" mk, ... **155.00**

Creamer, 2 3/4" h, multicolored clown seated on lg blue ball, airbrushed

grey ground and border, "gold BAVARIA" mk, ... **35.00**

Cup and Saucer

Cream and pink dogwoods, gold swirl overlays, cream to grey shaded ground, gold edged rim, base, and handle, ... **15.00**

Decal of pink roses on black ground in gold and lt blue cartouches, orange luster splashes, ... **15.00**

Multicolored crocuses, relief molded scrolling on saucer rim, white ground, Johann Seltmann, ... **15.00**

Dessert Plate, 7 1/2" d, oct, white or pink roses on border, band of gold semicircles on rim, "Z.S. & Co. Bavaria" mks, set of 6, ... **130.00**

Dish, 7 1/2" d, 3 scattered bouquets of multicolored florals, scroll molded border w/shading, ... **10.00**

Plate, 10" d, multicolored floral bouquet and scattered florals, gold swags, "H. & C. Selb, Bavaria Heinrich & Co." mk, **$48.00**

Dresser Tray, 11 1/2" H-H x 8" w, rect, multicolored decal of 2 period women on patio w/fencing, pale orange border, molded handles at ends, ... **215.00**

Service Plate, 11" d, multicolored bouquet in center, gold inner border, green border w/cream band and multicolored florals and vases, **$35.00**

Jardiniere, 4" h x 8" d, HP pink roses, green foliage, shaded blue-green ground, burnished gold wavy rim, base, and feet, ... **300.00**

Pancake Dish, Cov, 9 3/4" d, HP blue and purple bellflowers, green stem leaves on cov, crown knob, matte gold rim, artist sgd, ... **225.00**

Plate

7 3/8" d, multicolored clover and daisies in center, gilt swags and molding on border, indented rim, "Z.S. & Co. Bavaria" mk, ... **8.00**

9 3/4" d

Blue, dk red, and gold relief of Neuschwanstein castle, molded rococo border, Johann Seltmann, ... **50.00**

Printed and HP lg white rose, red and white petaled flower, green foliage, green to brown shaded ground, ... **50.00**

Plate, 10" d, gilt rim, pierced rocaille gilt and polychrome floral cavetto, green ground with orange, yellow, purple, and magenta flowers and alternating panels of multicolored courting scenes, "Schumann Bavaria" mark, **$190.00**

10" d

HP lg yellow roses and foliage on brown shaded ground on border, gold rim, "Sevres Bavaria" mk, ... **95.00**

Red lobster in center, brown and white clams, oysters, and shells on border, ... **15.00**

Shaker, 4 1/2" h, HP violets, pale violet ground, metal top, "BAVARIA" mk, ... **95.00**

Sugar Bowl, Cov, 4" h x 6" H-H, pink roses from yellow hanging border swags, "Z.S. & Co." mk, ... **8.00**

Spittoon, 5 1/2" h, 7 3/4" d, lg orange and purple flowers, gold outlined leaves, molded swirled body, blue-green shaded ground, "J.S. Bavaria" mark, $90.00

Teapot

5" h, "Ming" pattern, oriental branch of florals, green transfer, gold lined handle, spout, and ft, gold flame knob, ... **25.00**

9 1/2" h, HP white and magenta roses, green foliage, shaded green to cream ground, gold handle and loop knob, "Sevres Bavaria" mk, ... **160.00**

Tray

8 1/2" l x 5" w, oval, "Mignon" pattern, lg red-centered yellow roses on border w/gold geometric overlay, shaded green ground, open handles, scalloped rim, "Z.S. Bavaria" mk, ... **20.00**

10 1/4" l x 7 3/4" w, rect w/indented sides, multicolored decal of fruit and stems in center, gold rim, "Empire Z.S. & Co. Bavaria" mk, ... **35.00**

Vase, 6" h, tapered shape, HP band of purple violets in center between wide gold bands, white ground, gold everted rim, ... **150.00**

1751-96

BELGIUM-GENERAL

1751-1891

History: Belgium's principal pottery and porcelain manufacturing center was Tournai. When Francois J. Peterinck came from Lille to Tournai in 1751, he took over a faience factory belonging to Carpentier. Empress Maria-Theresa gave him a grant to make porcelains. The early decorations were done in underglaze blue. Oriental patterns, mostly derived from Chantilly, and some Meissen-style decorations were used.

In 1763, Duvivier joined the factory as chief painter and added Sevres-style decorations, adopting the Louis XVI style in 1780. The principal background colors were bleu de roi and yellow. Figures and groups also were made in biscuit and glazed porcelain.

When Peterinck died in 1799, the factory experienced difficulties. Peterinck's descendants continued production until 1815, when the firm went bankrupt. Henri de Bellingnies reopened the factory in 1817 and managed it until 1850. Porcelains with a blue ground, similar to earlier styles, were made. The Boch brothers of Luxembourg purchased the factory in 1850. They made creamwares until 1891.

Francois Peterinck's son Charles established a second factory for stoneware production at Tournai that operated from 1800 to 1855.

Another smaller porcelain center in Belgium was in Brussels and its suburbs. Several factories operated on a small scale, mostly as decorating workshops utilizing the Paris style of decoration.

Museums: Chateau Mariemont, Brussels, Belgium; Musee du Cinquantenaire, Brussels, Belgium.

Barber Bowl, 13 1/2" l x 9 1/2" w, gilt sprigs, gilt feather rim, white ground, ... **385.00**

Cache Pot, 7" h, 4 molded dragonflies on border, green drip over tan, gloss brown base, 2 sm handles, ... **45.00**

Coffee Can and Saucer, multicolored crest flanked by Belgian flags, cobalt borders w/gilt overlay and hanging fleur-de-lys designs, Dresden-style red, purple, and green sprigs on reverse, c1830-50 .... **300.00**

Figure, 9 1/4" h, tin glazed, putti as "Summer" w/flowered wreath in hair, "Winter" holding brown brazier, foot resting on brown cup, purple headpiece, domed sq bases enriched w/green, Brussels, c1760, pr, (A), ... **3,585.00**

Floor Vase, 16 1/2" h, Arts and Crafts style, celadon and ochre drip over Prussian blue ground, ... **500.00**

Jardiniere and Pedestal, 51" h, brown centered sunflowers, green foliage, maroon ground, Nimy les Mons, c1910, ... **3,600.00**

Jar, Cov, 6 1/4" h, blue and white, Tournai, $325.00

Pitcher, 7 1/2" h, art pottery, matte dk brown drip over tan and dk green streaked body, turquoise int, "raised BELGIUM" mk, ... **50.00**

Plate

8" d, underglazed blue "Saxon Flowers" pattern, 4 pie-shaped panels, flowerhead in center hub, raised molded scales on outer rim, Tournai, ... **275.00**

Plate, 8 1/8" d, black transfer, $65.00

8 3/4" d, lg naively painted red rooster, green foliage in center, red single stroke border, "Made in Belgium" mk, ... **75.00**

9" d, spirally molded, basketweave border, underglaze blue bouquet in center, blue floral sprigs on border, Tournai, ... **100.00**

9 1/4" d, blue transfer of Napoleon Marching on Madrid-"Bataille du

Some Sierro 30 Novembre 1808," crowned N on border, ... **45.00**

Platter, 16" l x 11" w, oval, pink cyclamen flowers on long stems, green pad leaves, "Manufacture Imperiale & Royale 17898-NIMY Belgium" mk, ... **40.00**

Soup Plate, 10 3/4" d, HP single stroke red tulips, green foliage in center, blue pentagon-shaped striped border w/blue stylized flowerheads, green foliage and red drops, ... **125.00**

Vase

4 1/8" h, squat base, flared neck, Art Nouveau style matte red, white, blue, and orange swirls and geometrics, black ground, mkd, ... **128.00**

6" h, bottle shape covered in brown shades, molded red-brown reclining male figure around body and neck, "imp Emile Muller" mk, (A), ... **1,610.00**

6 1/2" h, bowl shape, orange to yellow drip over lt tan-grey ground, "Ceramique de Bruxelles" mk, ... **10.00**

6 3/4" h, bulbous, horiz ribbing, roping around rim and down sides, mottled green glaze, ... **175.00**

7" h, 5 sides, gloss green glaze on rim, matte cream body w/black and tan specks, ... **95.00**

Waste Bowl, 5 3/4" d, dk blue transfers of lg flowerheads on int and ext, ... **20.00**

Beswick Ware.
MADE IN
ENGLAND
1936

BESWICK

Staffordshire, England
Early 1890s to Present

History: James Wright Beswick and John, his son, acquired the Gold Street Works in Longton, Stoke-on-Trent, in 1896. They made utilitarian and ornamental wares, but are best known for their series of figures of horses and domestic pets. All of their animals are created with utmost accuracy

and attention to details. In 1918, the Beswicks added the Warwick China Works in Longton.

After James Beswick died in 1920, John took over the firm. In 1934, John was succeeded by John Ewart Beswick, his only son. John Ewart worked along with Gilbert Ingham Beswick. They expanded the firm and increased their reputation for excellent equestrian figures. The firm was called John Beswick Ltd. from 1936.

The firm continued to expand by acquiring the site of Williamson & Son's factory in 1945 and Thomas Lawrence's site in 1957. They were converted to a public company in 1957.

Since neither Ewart or Gilbert had a successor to take over, they sold the firm to Royal Doulton Tableware Ltd. in 1969. Their reputation for figures of animals continues to the present day.

Beswick's best known models of horses are part of the "Connoisseur Series." Though the "Connoisseur Series" was developed in the early 1970s, it incorporated figures that had been made many years before. Cats, dogs, farm animals, birds, wildlife, and figures identified with children's literature such as *Winnie the Pooh*, *Alice in Wonderland*, and the works of Beatrix Potter have been modeled by Beswick.

The Beswick name is stamped on most pieces, but the earliest examples are unmarked. Every item made since 1933 is assigned a model number.

References: Diana & John Callow, *The Charlton Standard Catalogue of Beswick Animals, 2nd Edition*, Charlton Press, 1996; Diana & John Callow, *The Charlton Standard Catalogue of Beswick Pottery*, Charlton Press, 1997; Jean Dale, *Royal Doulton Beswick Jugs, Third Edition*, Charlton Press, 1995; Jean Dale, *Royal Doulton Beswick Storybook Figurines, Third Edition*, Charlton Press, 1996; Harvey May, *The Beswick Collector's Handbook*, Kevin Francis Publishing Ltd. 1986; Harvey May, *The Beswick Price Guide, 3rd Edition*, Francis Joseph Publications, 1995; Doug Pinchin, *Beatrix Potter & Bunnykins Price Guide*, Francis Joseph Publications, 1995.

Collecting Hints: It is usually best to start a collection by selecting a specific theme or subject.

Basket, 10 1/8" h, overhead handle, relief molded tan, green, and violet Hawaiian palm tree, gilt accents, sky blue ground, hairline, ... **85.00**

Butter Dish, 5" h x 7 1/2" l, figural brown log cabin, grey stone chimney, green grass base, mkd, ... **50.00**

Candlestick

2 1/4" h x 4 1/4" w, matte mottled yellow ground, "Beswick England" mk, pr, ... **45.00**

*Teapot, 7" h, "Sam Weller," green cap, yellow collar, brown shirt, **$395.00***

9" h, matte black glaze, "Beswick England" mk, ... **15.00**

Celery Dish, 11 7/8" l x 5 1/2" w, cream figural celery stalk on green basketweave ground, beaded rim, "Beswick England Made in England" mk, ... **15.00**

Charger, 15 1/2" d, stylized red, blue, and yellow exotic bird and flowers in center, green foliage w/red and yellow flowers, pierced for hanging, ... **300.00**

Cheese Dome

3 1/2" h x 7" l, "Sundial," brown and white stepped brick cov, pink flowering tree on sides, green base, sundial knob, ... **65.00**

4" h x 7" l x 6" w, green basketweave w/molded leaf, figural red strawberry knob, "Beswick M.1. England" mk, ... **25.00**

Coffee Set, paneled, pot and stand, 9" h, cov sugar bowl, 7" H-H x 5" h, creamer, 5" h, cake plate, 12" l, "Flowerkist" pattern, pastel florals, ... **225.00**

Dish

10" l x 7" w, free form, molded red centered yellow flowerheads, green leaves on edge, med green shaded body, ... **25.00**

10 1/2" l x 7 1/2" w, rect, molded orange fruit, dk green leaves, green leaf molded ground, "BESWICK ENGLAND" mk, ... **40.00**

Figure

2 1/2" h

Beatrix Potter, "The Old Woman Who Lived in a Shoe," brown

shades, lt blue shoe,
.... **15.00**
Standing bulldog, brown and
white, ... **35.00**
2 3/4" h, "Diggory Diggory Delvet,"
BP3c, ... **38.00**
3" h, Beatrix Potter
"Miss Moppet," 1st variation, BP2
gold oval mk, ... **60.00**
"Mr. Jeremy Fisher," **90.00**

*Figure, 3 1/4" h, Ribby and Patty Pan,
multicolored, Royal Albert mark, $35.00*

3 1/4" h, Beatrix Potter
"Appley Dapply," BP3b mk,
.... **45.00**
"Mrs. Tittlemouse," **50.00**
3 1/2" h
Beatrix Potter
"Hunc Munc Sweeping," mauve
peasant dress, BP 3a mk,
.... **30.00**
"Old Mr. Brown," brown feathers,
white body w/black accents,
.... **35.00**
"Timmy Tiptoes," grey squirrel,
pink jacket, BP 3b mk,
.... **38.00**
"Tommy Brock," brown BP 3b
mk, ... **50.00**
Brown owl w/white breast, black
eyes, green perch, "Beswick
England" mk, ... **15.00**
3 3/4" h, Beatrix Potter
"Duchess Holding Flowers,"
BP3h, (A), ... **2,115.00**
"Cottontail," BP3c mk, ... **35.00**
"Ginger," BP3b mk, ... **280.00**
"Poorly Peter Rabbit," red
blanket, ... **20.00**

"Squirrel Nutkin," gold BP2 mk,
.... **110.00**
"Timmy Tiptoes," BP2 mk,
.... **155.00**
4" h
Beatrix Potter
"Benjamin Bunny," gold BP2 mk,
.... **300.00**
"Mrs. Flopsy Bunny," brown mk,
late version, ... **50.00**
"Pigling Bland," pink, blue tie
and vest, red basket, "Beatrix
Potter's Pigling Bland-F.
Warne & Co. Ltd., Beswick,
England" mk, ... **20.00**
"Pig Wig," brown BP1 mk,
.... **300.00**
Brown-black, white, and yellow
Evening Grosbeck perched
on brown branch, tan trunk,
#2190, ... **70.00**
4 3/8" h, Beatrix Potter, "Mrs. Flopsy
Bunny," **15.00**
4 1/2" h, owl, split tail, brown, white
breast and face, yellow and
black eyes, ... **35.00**
4 3/4" h, Foxy Whiskered Gentleman,
gold mk, ... **160.00**
5 1/4" h
Seated deer, lustered blue glaze,
.... **20.00**
Standing pony, brown shades,
#1197, ... **30.00**
5 1/2" h
Girl riding brown and white pony,
grey jacket, black hat,
.... **260.00**
Golden Retriever, golden brown
glaze, ... **26.00**
"Romany Rhinestone," Brindle
dog, ... **200.00**
Standing Corci dog, dk brown
back, tan face and legs,
.... **72.00**
6" h, "Fantail Pigeon," white glaze,
yellow beak, green and purple
base, #NR1614, ... **675.00**
6 1/4" x 8" l, standing Siamese
cat, tan w/dk brown tail,
head, and paws, ... **40.00**
7 1/4" h
Standing giraffe, brown and
white, #853, ... **125.00**
Swimming angelfish, silver and
green-brown, red tipped fins,
#1047, ... **395.00**
9 1/2" l, mallard duck, brown
feathers, green head and tail
feathers, white base, ... **180.00**

Jug
2 3/4" h, figural "Tony Weller," mkd,
.... **25.00**
6" h, drip type shaded rose, green,
and grey ground, twisted handle,
.... **65.00**
9" h, "Palm Tree" pattern, white,
.... **70.00**

*Jug, 11 1/2" h, magenta, turquoise, mustard
yellow, and brown, cream ground, c1930s,
$595.00*

Pitcher
8" h, "Romeo and Juliet,"
multicolored, "Farewell" on
reverse, ... **185.00**
9" h, emb enameled green and
brown palm tree and lt brown
trunk on sides, gilt accents, gloss
burgundy ground, figural
bamboo handle, cream and gilt
int, ... **100.00**
Plaque
7 1/4" w
Brown figural horsehead w/dk
brown bridle through white
horseshoe, ... **60.00**
Bust of young boy, red-brown
hair, #612, ... **215.00**
8 1/2" l, 10 1/2" w, flying duck, green
head, brown wings, white breast,
#596-1, #596-2, pr, ... **95.00**
Sandwich Tray, 11 1/4" l x 5 3/4" w,
brown bird on green bramble
branch, ... **40.00**
Teapot
5" h, "Sairy Gamp," multicolored,
.... **110.00**
6" h, "Peggotty," multicolored,
.... **65.00**

6 5/8" h, modeled black and white seated panda, bamboo form handle, ... **525.00**

Toast Rack, 6 1/2" l, 5 bars, "Green fingers" pattern, girl in tan skirt, blue blouse, hoeing blue, yellow, lavender, and green flowers on ends, cream ground, "Beswick England" mk, ... **10.00**

Vase

7 1/2" h, Art Deco style, water pitcher shape, rect w/flat sides, incised curl, round ends, green to orange to purple shaded ground, ... **65.00**

8" h, molded green apples, brown leaves around shoulder, ... **160.00**

10" h

Flared shape w/reverse flared base, relief molded w/sea shells, coal, and sea creatures, pastel colors, ... **110.00**

Spread disk foot, relief of satyr and nymph on sides, leaf molded handles, green, ... **25.00**

12" h, ovoid, Art Deco style, tan and brown squares on mottled aqua ground, horiz ribbing on top, hairline, ... **85.00**

Wall Mask, 11 1/2" h, profile of brown haired woman w/curls on end, red pearls, yellow or blue flowers behind, ... **675.00**

Whisky Miniature, 4 1/2" h, figural eagle, brown shades, "BENEAGLES SCOTCH WHISKY," **25.00**

20 TH CENTURY

BING AND GRONDAHL

Copenhagen, Denmark
1853 to Present

History: The Bing and Grondahl Porcelain Factory was established in Copenhagen in 1853 when Frederich Grondahl left the Royal Copenhagen Porcelain Manufactory due to an artistic disagreement and joined with M.H. and J.H. Bing. The Bing brothers provided the business expertise, while Grondahl was the artistic force.

About one and one-half years after the company started, Grondahl died. The

Bings hired top designers and decorators to continue fabricating utilitarian and art wares. In 1886 the firm first used underglaze painting. Previously, the firm manufactured pieces with "biscuit" or overglaze porcelain decorations.

In 1895 the first Christmas plate was issued. A seven inch blue and white plate utilizing the underglaze technique is made every year, with the molds being destroyed after Christmas to prevent later restrikes. From 1910 to 1935, Easter plaques also were issued.

Several great artists were employed by the company such as J.F. Willusmen, Effie Hegermann-Lindercrone, Fanny Garde, Haus Tegner, Kai Nielsen, and Jean Gauguin. In 1914, stoneware was made for the first time. Soft paste porcelain began in 1925. In 1949 a new factory was built for producing dinnerwares.

Every piece of Bing and Grondahl work is signed with either the artist's name or initial. While today's collectors know Bing and Grondahl primarily for its figurals and annual Christmas plates, the company still produces a porcelain line.

Reference: Pat Owen, *The Story of Bing & Grondahl Christmas Plates*, Viking Import House, Inc. 1962. Caroline & Nick Pope, *Bing and Grondahl Figurines, Schiffer Publications*, 2003.

Museums: The Bradford Museum, Niles, IL; Metropolitan Museum, New York, NY.

Bowl, 5 5/8" d, celadon green ground w/incised dragonflies and lizards, matte black ft, "B & G towers" mk, #1209/9/384, ... **150.00**

Bud Vase

5 1/4" h, slightly tapered shape, lily of the valley and foliage, shaded green ground, mkd, ... **35.00**

6 1/2" h, HP dogwood blossoms and branches, "3 tower, B & G" mk, ... **30.00**

Cabinet Vase, 4 3/4" h, wide shoulder tapered to narrow base, short collar, white Calla lily w/brown accents, med blue ground, c1915, ... **195.00**

Compote, 5 7/8" h x 10" d, bouquet of garden flowers in center, blue, pink, and blue and purple flowers on stem, gold rims, ... **200.00**

Cup and Saucer

Scattered multicolored floral sprigs, relief molded and gilt swirls, mkd, ... **20.00**

"Seagull" pattern, blue shades, ... **48.00**

Dish

8" w, white center, tan coiled figural rope border w/blue-grey figural anchor on end, #2377, ... **125.00**

10" w, leaf shape w/end handle, blue and white seagull pattern, ... **125.00**

Figure

4" h, seated Great Dane dog, grey, brown, and green shading, #2189HC, ... **80.00**

4 1/2" h, seated lt and dk brown pan holding grey grapes, sgd "Lkai Nielsen," 3 royal towers mk, ... **275.00**

5" h x 3 1/2" w, kneeling little girl, blue sweater, white skirt, petting white cat in tan woven basket, ... **165.00**

6 1/4" h x 8" l, swimming carp, blue-grey glaze, ... **125.00**

Figure, 8 1/2" h, dk blue scarf, lt blue jacket, white apron, green dress, #2233, $475.00

6 3/4" h, little girl holding kitten in apron, rose and blue, #1779, ... **95.00**

7 1/2" h x 8 1/2" l, kneeling blue and white milkmaid milking blue-grey spotted cow, cat at side, sgd "Axil Locher," #2017 ES, ... **395.00**

8 1/2" h, brother and little sister dancing, grey-blue and white, ... **295.00**

9 1/2" h

"Hans Christian Anderson" seated in brown suit, talking to young girl in blue-grey dress, #2037, ... **300.00**

Seated woman playing guitar, white gown, tan guitar w/grey neck, #1684, ... **500.00**

10" h, standing lg goose, white body, grey and pink accents, #1593, ... **395.00**

Match Holder, 6 1/2" h x 5" w, seated little girl, mauve shawl, blue dress, resting against white brick chimney match holder, #1655, ... **200.00**

Nut Dish, 8" w, lobed, white dogwood blossom, green leaves in center blue shaded ground, #42A, ... **40.00**

Vase, 7 1/8" h, "JULEN 1918" on base, blue shades, A-*$100.00*

Plate

6" d, blue and white seagull design, molded basketweave border, set of 4, ... **40.00**

7 1/4" d, bouquet of 3 garden flowers and foliage in center, sprigs on border, gold rim, ... **16.00**

Soup Plate, 9 5/8" d, blue slender stems and flowers, molded woven border, ... **95.00**

Teapot, 3 1/4" h, dk blue stylized flowers in basket, swirls, starburst on cov, white ground, mkd, ... **35.00**

Tray, 7" l x 6 1/2" w, Art Nouveau style figural seaweed, blue tones, brown stem, #1112, ... **190.00**

Vase

4 3/4" h, swollen shape, short neck, white calla lily, med blue ground, 92/198, ... **195.00**

4 7/8" h, swollen shape, short neck, ring rim, relief of flowers under overall cream glaze, "3 towers, Kjobenhavn Denmark" mk, ... **240.00**

Vase, 6 1/4" h, red, green, and brown matte copper type glaze, (A), *$300.00*

7 1/4" h, bulbous shape, short collar, blue, grey, and white windmill scene, pale blue ground, ... **75.00**

BISQUE

English/Continental 1750 to Present

History: Bisque, or biscuit china, is white, marble-like, unglazed hard porcelain or earthenware that has been fired only once. The composition of the body and the firing temperature are most important to achieve the matte, porous surface of the figure. Since there is no glaze or decoration, the surface has to be completely free of imperfections. Razor-sharp modeling of details is made possible by the absence of glaze.

Bisque figures first were produced around 1751 at Vincennes and Sevres in France. They became very fashionable. Many French porcelain factories during the latter part of the 18th century added them to their product lines. Bisque figures also were made at Meissen in Germany.

Beginning in 1773, Derby was the principal manufacturer of bisque figures in England. Bisque figures in soft paste porcelain have a great smoothness to the touch and a warm soft tone.

About 1850 German factories produced bisque dolls. Delicacy of coloring and realism of features could be achieved with this material. In the late 1850s, France also started producing bisque dolls. Both French and German factories manufactured bisque dolls in the image of children rather than ladies during the 1880s. They were called "bebes", even though they depicted girls from about eight to twelve years old.

Most bisque examples are unmarked.

Museums: Bayerisches National Museum, Munich, Germany; Victoria & Albert Museum, London, England.

Figure, 11 1/4" h, 11" h, boy w/yellow hat, gilt trimmed grey jacket, tan boots, lt grey pants, girl w/grey hat, gilt trimmed lt grey dress, yellow basket, dk tan shoes, yellow bases, unmkd, pr, *$250.00*

Candelabra, 8 1/2" h, 2 arm, 2 socket, coral and white rococo stems, male or female period couple on base, blue and white w/gold accents, pr, ... **275.00**

Figure

1 3/4" h, child kneeling and praying, blond hair, white gown, ... **35.00**

4" h x 5" l, little girl sitting on transom of tan boat, orchid dress w/white collar, brown sun hat w/flowers, Germany, ... **30.00**

4 1/2" h, seated Dutch boy next to white basket, lt blue peaked hat, red jacket, olive brown pants, Hertwig, c1910, ... **145.00**

5" h

Child wearing pink and white outfit, seated atop grey elephant on blue, pink, and gold blanket, ... **85.00**

Standing Dutch girl holding grey jug, leaning on grey fence, white cap, red jacket, lt blue scarf, Germany, ... **55.00**

6" h, young period man in red collared yellow jacket, grey trousers, young girl in red apron, purple skirt, under blue lined purple umbrella, circ base, unmkd, ... **135.00**

6 1/4" h, standing brown haired nude woman, tan rock base w/blue and green vert folds and swirls, gold accents, Germany, ... **130.00**

6 1/2" h, bust of Bismarck, black soft hat and suit, marble waisted base, Ernst Bohne & Sons, c1900, ... **140.00**

7" h x 7 7/8" l, period couple seated on semicircular couch w/ring handle ends, white, Sevres, ... **1,140.00**

7 1/2" h, cherub emerging from purple flowerhead in center, reaching for maiden standing at end in pink-purple gown, base of gown swirls to opposite side joined by purple ribbon at end, ... **200.00**

8 1/4" h, white seated cat on rect base, "imp Sevres Manufacture Nationale France" mk, c1900, ... **1,500.00**

8 7/8" h, bust of Napoleon, waisted circ socle, France, ... **145.00**

10" h, Scottish girl, red, white, and blue plaid dress, pink, maroon, and yellow scarf, blue hat w/feather, pink pantaloons, gold trim, circ base, France, ... **225.00**

12 3/4" h, figures of Louis XVI in armour and Benjamin Franklin at table holding document inscribed "INDEPENDENCE DE L'AMREIQUE and LIBERTIE DES MERS," c1780-85, Niderville, (A), ... **108,000.00**

13 1/4" h, period man or woman, yellow accented clothes w/gilt trim, man holding yellow roses, stone base, c1900, pr, ... **650.00**

*Figure, 7 3/4" h, blond hair, lt blue or pink clothes, green and brown base, "blue R in diamond" mark, Germany, **$295.00***

15" h, period woman in flowing gown, holding open book in hand, raised rock base, uncolored, France, c1890, ... **345.00**

16 1/2" h, Madonna and Child, Mary wearing gold crown, yellow robe, yellow-lined blue skirt, c1890, ... **300.00**

18" h, woman in 1920s full blue bathing suit w/raised vert blue dots, gold trim, in diving pose, supported by rock, ... **375.00**

48" h, nude female seated on draped tree trunk w/leg crossed, doves on base, overall white, repair to foot, ... **2,695.00**

Planter

7" h x 7" l, Art Nouveau style, opened flowerhead body, curved panels w/hanging purple grapes alternating w/flower panels, 4 green swirl feet, 2 green upright handles, applied figure of winged Cupid on rim, med blue int, repairs, ... **765.00**

14" h, white, urn set on center pedestal, 3 female figures of musicians at side, circ base, France, ... **700.00**

Tobacco Jar, 5" h, head of Arab boy wearing cream turban scarf w/orange and green stripes, gold earrings, ... **175.00**

Vase, 9 1/4" h, dbl, standing woman in blue-green gold accents blouse, pink skirt w/gold trim, standing between blue and tan relief molded leaf and swirl trunks, ... **195.00**

AFTER 1882

BLUE ONION

German
c1730 to Present
English/Continental
1800s to Present

History: The Blue Onion or bulb pattern was started in Meissen, Germany, about 1728 and was based on a Chinese aster pattern from the late Ming Dynasty. After Horoldt perfected the underglaze blue paint technique in 1739, the onion pattern took on its more familiar form. This pattern really had nothing to do with onions. The flower in the center has been described as a chrysanthemum, peony, or aster. The bulbs or fruits on the border were not onions either, but resembled pomegranates and peaches. In later years, they resembled onions more closely.

More than sixty European and oriental manufacturers copied the onion pattern and called it by a variety of names. In German, the pattern is called "Zwiebelmuster."

The pattern underwent various changes and was produced in tremendous numbers. It was less expensive to make and could be painted by less experienced workers.

The Royal Prussian Manufactory in Berlin was one of the most serious competitors utilizing the onion pattern from the 18th to the 20th century. They utilized the scepter mark.

Popularity increased in the second half of the 19th century, and the onion pattern appeared on other items such as pots, boxes, tablecloths, and napkins.

Most of the onion pattern pieces available today were made after 1865. Some examples have a gilt edge, or the fruits and plants are heightened with gold or red contours.

Some of the European manufacturers produced blue onion stoneware in addition to their porcelain examples. Since the pattern was not copyrighted, it could be used by any factory. To protect the actual Meissen examples, the factory utilized the crossed swords mark in the lowest part of the bamboo cane about 1888. Pieces without this mark date before 1888.

Carl Teichert's factory combined with Melzer's as the Meissen Stove and Fireclay Factory and copied the Meissen onion pattern exactly. They hand painted their copies. In 1882 they registered a trademark with the name "Meissen" that caused much confusion. Other factories were established that used similar marks to add to the confusion. There were disputes with Meissen over the marks. Another popular producer of the onion pattern was L. Hutschenreuther, who printed the pattern rather than hand painting it, since they produced it in quantity for everyday use.

The Meissen Stove and Porcelain Factory acquired a factory in Eichwald, Bohemia, which later became B. Block's factory. He continued to produce the onion pattern.

Additional changes in the factory and borders put the Block factory in Czechoslovakia after 1918, but Block still utilized marks that caused confusion. With World War II, more changes occurred and the factory came under German jurisdiction.

After World War II, the factory returned to Czechoslovakia and, with other factories, became Duchsovsky Porcelain. This Dubi branch continued to make the onion pattern.

After 1900, Meissen added "MEISSEN" to its mark impressed into the piece before firing and then glazed over it. "Made in Germany" was printed in blue under the glaze for export pieces.

Other factories in Germany and abroad also copied the onion pattern in both porcelain and stoneware. Examples are available from English, French, Japanese, Austrian, and Czechoslovakian manufactories.

Plate, 8 1/2" d, pierced border, "blue Meissen in oval," "imp Meissen" mks, $85.00

Bell, 4 1/2" h, "blue X'd swords" mk, ... **250.00**

Bowl
9" d, "Staffordshire Kensington England" mk, ... **20.00**
10" d, "B. Bloch" mk, ... **250.00**

Butter Dish, Cov, 7" d, attached underplate, rose knob, "blue X'd swords" mk, ... **295.00**

Cake Plate, 10 1/2" H-H, molded, open handles, unmkd, ... **25.00**

Charger
12" d, indented rim, "blue X'd swords" mk, early 20th C, ... **650.00**
13 3/4" d, unmkd, ... **350.00**

Cheese Dish, 9 1/4" d, "blue X'd swords Germany" mark, A-$75.00

Chocolate Pot, 8" h, flower knob, "blue X'd swords" mk, c1920, ... **195.00**

Chop Plate, 14" d, ... **350.00**

Compote, 11" d x 9 3/4" h, reticulated border, Germany, ... **950.00**

Creamer, 3" h, Cov Sugar Bowl, 3" h, rosebud knob, "blue X'd swords, Germany" mks, c1921-24, .. **225.00**

Cream Jug, 5" h, ear handle, "blue X'd swords" mk, ... **175.00**

Cutting Board, 8" l x 5 1/2" w, pierced for hanging, "blue X'd swords" mk, ... **295.00**

Dish, 8" l x 7 1/2" w, arced indented sides, c1850, ... **250.00**

Dish, Cov, 11" d, Schoenau, ... **450.00**

Gravy Boat
9" l, w/attached underplate, .. **250.00**
10" l, lg loop handle, scalloped rim, ... **100.00**

Invalid Feeder, 6 1/2" l, gold accents, ... **200.00**

Knife Rest, 3 3/4" l, bowtie shape, "blue X'd swords" mk, ... **30.00**

Meat Platter, 16" l x 12" w, oval, wavy rim, ... **295.00**

Plate
6" d, Open weave border w/3 cartouches, "crowned SAXE" mk, ... **42.00**
7 1/4" d, Staffordshire, ... **45.00**
7 1/2" d, unmkd, ... **65.00**
8" d
Reticulated border, "blue X'd swords" mk, ... **225.00**
Scalloped rim, "blue X'd swords" mk, ... **32.00**
9 1/8" d, pierced quarter panels on border alternating w/ovals of florals, "blue Meissen, imp Meissen" mks, ... **20.00**
9 1/2" d, Cauldon, ... **10.00**
9 5/8" d, lobed rim, "crown Morkische Steingut Fabrik Vordamm in shield" mk, ... **35.00**
9 3/4" d, "Meissen in oval" mk, ... **40.00**
10" d
Reticulated border w/alternating cartouches of sprigs, scalloped rim, Hutschenreuther, ... **30.00**
Staffordshire, ... **25.00**

Platter
12" l, oval, scalloped rim, ... **80.00**
13 1/4" l, oval, "blue X'd swords" mk, ... **450.00**
13 1/2" l, oval, "imp Cauldon" mk, ... **50.00**
14" l x 10" w, oval, Villeroy & Boch, ... **140.00**
14 1/4" l x 10 3/4" w, oval, Brown, Westhead, Moore & Co., ... **160.00**
19" l x 13" w, oval, wavy rim, "imp and blue Meissen" mks, ... **225.00**

Serving Bowl, 9" sq, reticulated sides, "blue X'd swords" mk, pr, ... **1,025.00**

Serving Dish, 11 3/8" l, dbl molded shells, overhead ring handle, "blue X'd swords" mk, ... **100.00**

Serving Plate, 11" H-H, "blue X'd swords" mk, ... **70.00**

Soup Bowl, 9 1/2" d, "Meissen England" mk, ... **95.00**

Soup Plate
8" d, Johnson Brothers, ... **14.00**
9" d, "blue X'd swords" mk, c1860, ... **150.00**
9 1/2" d, Germany, ... **95.00**

Soup Tureen, Cov
11" H-H, Meissen, c1820, ... **1,100.00**
14" H-H, flower knob, ... **1,050.00**

Tea Service, pot, 8 1/4" h, cream jug, 4" h, cov sugar bowl, 4 cups and saucers, tray, 14 1/2" l x 12" w, figural rose knobs, "blue X'd swords" mks, ... **3,250.00**

Tea Trivet, 7" d, Franz Mehlem, ... **15.00**

Tid Bit Dish, 12" d, painted silver center handle, ... **20.00**

Tid Bit Stand, 14" h, 3 tier, reticulated panels on borders, swirl molded base, club-shaped open handle at top, "oval MEISSEN, imp MEISSEN, blue X'd swords" mks, ... **350.00**

Vegetable Bowl, 9 3/8" l, "Onion Staffordshire England Rd No. 57681" mk, ... **50.00**

KERAMIS
MADE IN BELGIUM
c1900

BOCH FRERES KERAMIS

La Louviere, Belgium
1841 to Present

History: The Boch Freres factory at La Louviere, called Keramis, was founded in 1841 by Victor and Eugene Boch and Baron J.G. Nothomb. Previously, the Boch brothers were associated with the Villeroy and Boch concern.

The designs of Alfred William Finch, an English artist, and Marcel Goupy, a French artist, were produced at the Keramis factory. Finch signed vases, dishes, jugs, and candlesticks featuring a rough, red earthenware body covered with slip and glazed in ochre, blue, bottle green, or fawn along with incised linear decoration and dots of light-colored glaze in the Art Nouveau style.

Marcel Goupy made earthenware services decorated in ochre and blue for the Keramis factory. His pieces usually were signed.

Tiles were made from the 1880s at a branch factory in France. The Keramis factory also produced earthenware and stoneware similar to Staffordshire wares. Imitations of Delft china were produced along with Rouen and Sevres copies.

Museum: Museum voor Sierkunst, Ghent, Belgium.

Bud Vase, 10" h, squat base, long foot, yellow glaze on neck, blue drip on base, "Boch Freres Belgium" mk, ... **150.00**

Pitcher, 8" h, yellow and lt green vert streaks, gloss green ground, lt green int, "Boch Freres Belgium" mk, ... **150.00**

Plate

9 1/2" d, "Grand Bouquet" pattern, dk blue flowerheads and vines in center, bouquets on border, ... **20.00**

9 3/4" d, "Les Sports," multicolored transfer of comical scene of man fishing, another watching, French saying below, sgd "L.E.C.," "Fabrication Belge, Made in Belgium, Boch-F. & S. Lalouviere" mk, ... **10.00**

Tray, 9 1/4" d, ftd, blue outlined enameled white flowers, lt turquoise ground, gold vert handles, mkd, ... **85.00**

Vase

6 1/2" h, bulbous body, short, straight neck, semi-matte tan and white spoked flower-circles, tan outlined lt and dk blue leaves, black ground, blue and white horiz striped neck, "blue Boch Freres Keramis" mk, ... **250.00**

7" h

Art Deco, gloss lt blue ovoid body, white stepped geometric handles on shoulder, mkd, ... **75.00**

Teardrop shape, short neck, ftd, enameled black outlined red circles, black outlined yellow leaves on neck, 2 vert panels of yellow leaves and red circles, white crackle ground, Catteau, ... **400.00**

9" d, ball shape, rose-red stylized flowerheads, sm yellow centered blue flowers, brown saw-toothed leaves, gloss white ground, 2 gold ribbon handles, "BOCH LA

LOUVIERE MADE IN BELGIUM" mk, ... **225.00**

Vase, 9" h, orange, brown, and tobacco glaze, artist sgd, (A), **$250.00**

9 1/4" h, ball shape, red shields, blue feather designs, vert green feather leaf designs, red clovers, white ground, black collar, "Keramis Made in Belgium" mk, ... **950.00**

9 1/2" h, bulbous shape, flared rim, red centered yellow flowers, green leaves, blue dotted yellow lobes, black ground, matte finish, "Keramis Made in Belgium" mks, pr, ... **900.00**

Vase, 10 1/2" h, red centered dk blue circles on turquoise vert bands, white crackle ground, dk blue rim, "Ch. Catteau, Made in Belgium" mk, **$495.00**

10 3/8" h, bag shape, wide flared rim, enameled red-brown and black stylized flowerheads, white crackle ground, red-brown neck w/black stripe, Charles Catteau, c1925, ... **600.00**

12 1/2" h, swollen shape, vert enameled blue, green, and orange stylized hanging florals, white ground, "Boch La Louviere Made in Belgium" mk, ... **450.00**

13" h, dbl gourd shape, Art Deco, enameled white and pink flowers, stylized blue and tan leaves and stems, black ground w/gold and blue dots, textured brown banded rim, "BFK" mk, ... **595.00**

13 3/8" h, ovoid, short collar, enameled cobalt, med blue, orange, white, or yellow nasturtium florals and leaves, lt to med blue shaded crackle ground, cobalt int, Charles Catteau, ... **825.00**

*Vase, 13 1/2" h, eggshell birds, blue and turquoise striped ground, yellow line borders, "Made in Belgium, Bausch Firienze LaLouviere, Catteau" mark, A-***$1,035.00**

13 1/2" h, tapered cylinder shape, wide shoulder, short flared neck w/cobalt rim, vert triangles of cobalt, yellow, turquoise and green enameled geometrics and stylized flowerheads, white crackle ground, ... **750.00**

13 3/4" h, tapered form, flared rim, 4 handles of applied off-white descending rings from peg, off-white circ base, sky blue body, ... **225.00**

18 1/2" h, slightly tapered shape, sm neck, yellow roses, dk blue arbor, lt blue ground, gold stars, pr, ... **1,995.00**

MODERN MARK

BOHEMIA-GENERAL

Germany
Late 1700s to Present

History: Franz Anton Haberditzel pioneered the Bohemian porcelain industry. In 1789, along with twenty-five partners, he established a factory in his native Rabensgrun near Schlaggenwald. Johann Gottlieb Sonntag of Rudolstadt was the technical director. When Haberditzel died in 1792, Sonntag carried on. The company disbanded in 1793 due to the unsatisfactory nature of the porcelain.

The first successful porcelain factory in Bohemia was started by Johann George Paulus and Georg Johann Reumann at Schlaggenwald. Production initially was limited to earthenware because their patent to produce porcelain was refused in 1793 as a means of protecting the porcelain production in Vienna. Louise Greiner acquired the firm in 1800, enticed workers to move from Meissen in 1808, and received a regional patent in 1812. After 1876 the firm became Haas and Czizek.

Johann Nikolas Weber established a porcelain factory at Klosterle in 1794. This firm was rented by Christian Noone in 1799 to distribute Volkstedt porcelain. In 1820 Count Thun assumed management of the factory. Karl Venier, as director, improved the quality of the porcelain and produced examples that were richly gilded. Important sets, such as the "Empire" set (1851) and the "Thun" service (1856), and fine figures were made during his tenure.

Christian Noone set up a new factory near Carlsbad. After Noone died in 1813, Anton Hladik took over. There was a succession of owners. The factory eventually was sold to Johann Schuldes.

Johann Wenzel, Karl Kunerle, Josef Longe, and Josef Hubel started a factory in Prague in 1795. At first stoneware was made. Later the plant became the largest porcelain factory in Bohemia. In 1800, the firm was called Hubel and Company. It was sold to J.E. Hubel in 1810, who took in his son in 1820. Many figures were made during the 1840s for the wealthy bourgeois of Prague.

Friedrich Hocke established the Pirkenhammer factory in 1803 near Carlsbad. He sold out to Johann Fischer and Christof Reichenbach in 1811. By 1830, this was a fine Bohemian porcelain factory. All kinds of subjects were used on their porcelains: views, flowers, mythological, antique, and allegorical themes. Lithophane bedside lamps, dessert dishes, vases, and figures were made.

Christian Fischer became managing director in 1831. Fischer bought out Reichenbach in 1846. From that date until 1853, Reichenbach was the sole proprietor. In 1853 Ludwig von Mieg, Reichenbach's son-in-law, entered the business. The name was changed to Fischer and Mieg from 1857 to 1918 and was used after both Fischer and Mieg died. After 1875 the wares became less important artistically and more practical. In 1918, the firm operated at Branch Pirkenhammer by Opiag. The name eventually was changed to Epiag and existed until 1945.

By the mid-19th century, there were thirty new porcelain factories in Bohemia. Forty-three factories existed by the end of the century.

References: E. Poche, *Bohemian Porcelain*, Artia, 1954. Dr. James D. Henderson, *Bohemian Decorated Porcelain*, Schiffer Publications, 1999.

Museums: Industrial Art Museum, Prague, Czechoslovakia; Museum of Bohemian Porcelain in the State Castle Klosterle, Czechoslovakia.

Pitcher, 8 1/4" h, flying crane on blue ground, gilt outlined cobalt flowerheads, gilt stems, matte yellow ground, pink, brown, and green shaded handle, "crowned RH shield" mk, $195.00

Beaker, 3 3/4" h, Boston, Faneuil Hall, Bunker Hill, and Old State House, multicolored transfer and polychrome enameled highlights, ... **95.00**

Ewer, 13" h, gilt edged pink, yellow and red flowers, brown leaves, ivory ground, gold trim, brown handle, Pirkenhammer, $275.00

Bowl

9" d, HP flower sprigs on int, gold outlined cutout and pierced flower designed sides and rim, Bawo & Dotter, c1890, ... **25.00**

9 1/2" d, transfer and tinted pink, blue, and purple flying bird in woodland setting, green stenciled inner border, shaded green border w/raised gold accented designs, Fischer & Mieg, ... **125.00**

Bud Vase

5 3/4" h, 2 handles, molded vert loops on base, HP gilt edged lt and dk pink peonies, green and brown leaves, blue foliage, "Porzellon Fabrik Viktor Schmidt & Co." mk, ... **18.00**

8 1/2" h, muted yellow, orange, brown, and green flowers, tan ground, Fischer & Mieg, ... **45.00**

Coffeepot, 9 3/4" h, blue printed scene of bird stealing flowers from vase, stylized garden and rockery, flat lid, button knob, ... **640.00**

Cup and Saucer, relief of gold and black flowers w/3 applied black flowers, horiz gilt handle, border bands of gilt squares w/center dots, Pirkenhammer, ... **195.00**

Dish, 8" sq, indented sides, dk red flower sprig in center, dbl inner border of dk red geometrics over floral sprigs, Pirkenhammer, ... **20.00**

Egg Cup, 3" h, w/attached underplate, swirl molded body, painted flowers and insects, gold lined rim and base, Fischer & Mieg, ... **30.00**

Figure

9 1/4" h, Art Deco woman in lt blue 1920s suit, dk blue banded hat, clutching brown purse, white Scottie dog on base, Pirkenhammer, ... **240.00**

13 1/2" h, "EUROPA," draped nude woman riding bull, rect tilted base, white glaze, Pirkenhammer, ... **400.00**

Hostess Set, 8 1/2" l, iron-red, cobalt, and orange Imari pattern of chrysanthemums and lined swirls, gilt accents and outlined cobalt pagoda on int of cup, scalloped rims, gilt rims and handle, Fischer & Mieg, ... **150.00**

Jardiniere, 5 3/8" h x 9" l, boat shape, HP pink dogwood blossoms, green leaves on sides, gold scrolling rim, pierced fan type shells on rim and ends, oval base w/4 curled feet, Robert Hanke, ... **335.00**

Jardiniere and Pedestal, 43 1/2" h, earthenware, ovoid bowl, baluster form pedestal w/ovoid foot, green, taupe, and brown glazed relief molded shell motifs, acanthus leaves, and C-scrolls, Dressler, (A), ... **940.00**

Plate

8 3/4" d, HP flying birds, butterflies, and insects around flowers and plants, gilt rim, Fischer & Mieg, set of 12, ... **325.00**

Plate, 8 3/4" d, polychrome center, magenta and blue floral border, set of 6, 3 women, 3 men, $2,800.00

9" d

Border of ivory and pink flowers in oval cartouches, gold beaded inner and outer rims, set of 11, ... **395.00**

Gold bird flying above gold flowering branches, gold rim, Pirkenhammer, ... **30.00**

9 1/2" d, HP enameled spray of flowers onto pink shaded border w/raised gilt swirls, Fischer & Mieg, Pirkenhammer, set of 10, ... **650.00**

Scent Bottle, 7 1/2" h, gilt oval w/HP scene of castle on front, palace and mountain on reverse, gilt leaves on sides, gilt banding, chip, ... **450.00**

Sweetmeat Stand, 16 1/2" h, 3 graduated tier, wide pink borders w/gold scrolling, scalloped rims, pink and gold center stem and loop handle, "Hegewood Bohemia" mk, ... **375.00**

Tobacco Jar

5 1/2" h

Figural bust of Slav, black circ cap, flesh face, grey mustache and hair, brown bow tie, "imp B.B." mk, ... **350.00**

HP lg red roses, sm garden flowers, green and brown leaves, figural lily-of-the-valley knob, c1890, ... **425.00**

7 1/2" h, figural brown robed monk wearing white apron next to brown barrel, Bernard Bloch, ... **795.00**

Vase

9 3/4" h, bulbous body, trumpet neck, curved handles, lg yellow roses, green leaves, shaded green, lt violet, and amber ground, molded diamonds on neck, stiff leaves on rim, c1900-18, ... **155.00**

10 1/4" h, bottle shape w/long straight neck, raised gold cherry blossoms and branches, pink ground, gold dragon handles, Robert Hanke, ... **165.00**

14" h, earthenware, Egyptian Revival, baluster shape, blue, brown, terra cotta, white, and gold enameled incised chevrons, lines, beading, stylized flowerheads, Egyptian pictographs and hieroglyphs, black ground, molded bird head handles on rim, molded Egyptian

maiden heads on rim, "W.S. & S." mk, c1870-80, ... **3,800.00**

1760 - 76

BOW

East End of London, England c1741-1776

History: The Bow factory, one of the earliest English porcelain factories, was located from c1741-1776 in what is now the East End of London. Mostly utilitarian wares that imitated the imported Chinese porcelains were made; underglaze-blue designs also were made. Bow's porcelains were the soft paste variety, incorporating a high percentage of bone ash in the paste mixture.

In the 1760s and 1770s, numerous decorative figures and animal models were made. The back usually had a square hole to hold a metal candle holder. Bow figures were press molded and thick walled.

Bow pieces of the 1760s are not marked with a true factory mark. They usually have the painter's mark or a reference number painted under the base. Later pieces often have an anchor and dagger mark painted in red enamel.

Bow porcelains found a willing audience in American buyers. Many pieces were exported. American clay also was utilized to manufacture some of the wares.

References: Elizabeth Adams & David Redstone, *Bow Porcelain*, Faber & Faber, 1981; Anton Gabszewicz & Geoffrey Freeman, *Bow Porcelain*, Lund Humphries, 1982; Egan Mew, *Old Bow China*, Dodd, Mead & Co. 1909; H.Tait, *British Museum Catalogue of the 1959 Bow Exhibition*, Faber & Faber.

Museums: British Museum, London, England; Victoria & Albert Museum, London, England; Fine Arts Museums, San Francisco, CA.

Dish, 9 1/2" l, blue and white, c1755, $2,800.00

Basket, 5 1/8" d, diamond pierced sides, blue painted int w/scattered flowers and loose bouquets, florets at intersections on ext, (A), ... **825.00**

Chocolate Cup, Cov, relief molded banded pinecone pattern, blue painted cell pattern borders, loop handles and knob, c1770, (A), ... **440.00**

Coffee Cup, polychrome enameled Chinese style figures in landscape on ext, iron-red line over semicircles on int rim, c1760, ... **800.00**

Dish

8 1/4" d, oct, molded prunus border, white glaze, c1755, ... **885.00**

8 1/2" l x 7" w, soft paste, emb blue grape, vine, and leaf motif, c1760, ... **1,700.00**

9" l x 7 1/2" w, oval, painted multicolored scattered garden flowers, lobed purple lined rim, c1755, ... **1,100.00**

Figure

2 5/8" h, cat seated on haunches, puce accented fur, yellow eyes, puce accented scroll base, c1758, (A), ... **3,825.00**

Figure, 6 3/4" h, "Neptune," rust sash with yellow floral int, purple shaded plumed bird, $1,900.00

3 1/4" h, standing classical female wearing, yellow-lined, blue dotted mauve loose drape, standing before tree stump, shaped oval base w/applied flowers, c1755, chips, (A), ... **880.00**

4" h, emblematic of "America" as Negress in feathered headdress, yellow sash, w/crocodile, or "Asia" in yellow gown w/blue lined puce flowered sash, holding red flowered urn,

damage, c1760, pr, (A), ... **750.00**

4 1/2" h, seated Harlequin in puce scale jacket w/pink or yellow sleeve, holding horn, seated Columbine in blue bodice, gilt edged white blouse, red trimmed yellow skirt, playing hurdy-gurdy, round base, c1755-65, pr, (A), ... **2,870.00**

4 1/2" l, recumbent lion w/paw on branch, white glaze, opposite pair, c1750, pr, (A), ... **2,625.00**

7" h, "New Dancer," young bow, wide brimmed feathered hat, puce coat flowered trousers, floral rock base, c1760, ... **850.00**

8 1/8" h, modeled gallant and companion in flowered pink, green, and gilt hunting dress flanking stylized spouting fountainhead, orange, pink, blue, and yellow flowered bocage bkd, 4 scroll feet, "red anchor, dagger" mks, c1765, (A), ... **1,195.00**

8 3/4" d, iron-red and cobalt "Two Quails" pattern, shaped rim, ... **1,200.00**

9" h, "New Dancers," classic male or female in multicolored flowered costumes, flower and leaf borage, puce, gilt, and turquoise scroll molded base, c1768, pr, (A), ... **1,435.00**

10" h, "Air," female w/billowing puce and lt blue cape, brown eagle at side, puce scroll molded base, c1765, restored, ... **2,700.00**

10 1/2" h, standing woman, red vest, flowered pink dress, green sash, holding basket of flowers, green bocage, turquoise scroll base, ... **775.00**

Jug, 3" h, "sparrow beak," HP polychrome florals, red drape band on rim, c1765, ... **700.00**

Plate

8 7/8" d, painted famille rose style scattered flower sprays, iron red inner border, molded prunus on border, c1755, (A), ... **1,050.00**

9" d, painted bouquet of polychrome flowers in center, molded scroll border enclosing sm flower sprays and insects, green leaf spray on reverse, c1765, (A), ... **480.00**

Platter

12 3/8" l, oct, Kakiemon enamel colors and style "Quail" pattern, (A), ... **825.00**

20" l x 16" w, oct, soft paste, blue and white oriental fisherman in boat in center, border parcels of fisherman or florals, powder blue ground, c1765, ... **4,850.00**

Sweetmeat Dish, 5 3/4" w x 3 1/4" h, white w/blue trim, c1750, $2,650.00

Sauceboat, 7 1/4" l, lobed body, pagoda scene, foliate sprays and sprigs, cell diaper border, underglazed blue on white, c1760, ... **650.00**

Sweetmeat Dish, 6 3/4" h, 3 molded scallop shells painted in famille rose enamels w/flowering prunus and rockwork, shaded puce ext, molded multicolored rockwork base w/shells, coral, and green algae, grey conch shell knob, c1755, ... **10,000.00**

Teabowl and Saucer, molded prunus blossoms, overall white glaze, hairlines, c1755, (A), ... **425.00**

Teapot

4" h, barrel form, blue printed w/2 milkmaids holding buckets on heads, Robert Hancock, "blue and imp anchor" mks, ... **2,450.00**

4 7/8" h, globular form, molded floral sprays, overall white glaze, hairline and chip, (A), ... **1,800.00**

6 1/4" h, globular form, blue painted bird perched on oriental flowers, trellis border, c1765, cracks, (A), ... **450.00**

Tureen, 4 3/8" l, modeled as drake or hen, green-headed drake w/purple and green accents, brown-headed hen w/green and black accents, c1755, pr, (A), ... **59,750.00**

c. 1884

BRETBY

Woodville, Derbyshire
1882-1996

History: Founded as Henry Tooth & Company in conjunction with William Ault for the production of art pottery at the Woodville location. Tooth was influence by the designer Christopher Dresser during his early years. He honed his skills at the T.G. Green & Company factory and developed a series of innovative glazes while working at Linthorpe Pottery.

When Linthorpe closed, Tooth and Ault purchased the molds and offered a line of "reasonably" price artistic pieces based on slip casting techniques. These were the heart of Tooth & Company. These included ashtrays to floor vases and jardinieres with matching pedestals. The experimental glazes and surface treatments set Bretby products apart from their competitors. Examples included "Ligna Ware," which produced a hammered copper effect, and "Lustre Ware," which was introduced in 1911. Old molds were often recycled using different glazes resulting in new products. Ault left Bretby to form his own company.

Fred Parker purchased Bretby from the Tooth family in 1933. In 1938, Neville Chamberlain presented Adolph Hitler with a Bretby jug modeled in the form of King Edward VIII.

References: Michael David Ash, *Bretby Art Pottery, A Collectors Guide.*

Bookend, 6" h, sq stepped base, vert sq, mottled green glaze, pr, ... **100.00**

Bowl
6" w, wavy shaped rim, running brown, blue, and tan glazes, ... **95.00**
9" w, squat w/inverted rim, overall yellow glaze, "imp half sunburst, BRETBY ENGLAND" mks, ... **25.00**

Bud Vase, 6 7/8" h, squat, flattened base, long, slender neck, green frog skin on orange ground, ... **65.00**

Dish
10" l x 7" w, green textured base, trompe l'oille Huntley and Palmer crackers, c1880, ... **525.00**
10 3/4" d, figural flowerhead, blue center w/brown ground and molded tendrils, green overlapped petals on border, ... **35.00**

Ewer, 12" h, Art Nouveau style, hammered copper type ground,

pewter colored curled handle and strapping, ... **125.00**
Figure, 7" h, seated cat, matte black glaze, green glass eyes, "imp BRETBY ENGLAND" mk, chips, ... **50.00**
Flower Bowl, 7" d, pink ground w/dk pink marbling, "imp BRETBY MADE IN ENGLAND" mk, hairline, ... **40.00**
Flower Frog, 7 1/4" h, Bowl, 10" d, figural green, yellow, blue, and purple parrot w/glass eyes, perched on pierced rock, blue bowl, ... **350.00**

Jardiniere
4" h x 6" d, lobed, med grey glaze, mkd, ... **15.00**
7" h x 8 1/2" d, 3 black stylized butterflies on sides, bright green ground, mkd, ... **125.00**
12" h x 14" d, Art Nouveau, green relief of swirling foliage on lt green ground, pinched flared rim, ... **250.00**

Jardiniere and Pedestal, 43 1/2" h, red-brown drip over molded vert flowerheads and stems, dk brown body, yellow int, ... **1,325.00**
Jug, 6 1/2" h, dk orange ground, ribbed base, ... **45.00**
Planter
5" d, 2 sm arrowhead handles, pea green glaze w/black stripe on shoulder, ... **75.00**
8 5/8" d x 6 1/4" h, molded florals and seed heads, maroon base shaded to green border, wavy rim, ... **50.00**
15 3/4" d, relief of yellow flowers, green foliage on red basketweave ground in leaf cartouche, red body, 2 ear handles, c1880, ... **640.00**
Plaque
6" l x 4" w, rect, multicolored scene of Dutch couple at sea port, blue self frame, ... **78.00**
13" d, brown and blue relief of 2 oriental women in tea room, blue relief border w/oriental geometrics, ... **50.00**
Tulip Vase, 5 1/2" h, 4 spouts, "flown" green, blue, brown, orange, and cream glazes, ... **160.00**
Vase
2 1/2" h, dish shape, rolled inverted rim, mint green, ... **10.00**
5" h, wide shoulder, tapered body, spread ft, short neck, black and maroon flambe, ... **65.00**
7 1/4" h, tapered shape, wide base to narrow shoulder, textured tan

body w/raised multicolored period man and boy w/"Oliver & The Beadle," dk brown neck and base, ... **55.00**

Vase, 5" h, blue, green, ivory, and red drip glaze, rim repair, (A), $210.00

7 1/2" h, gourd shape w/sm everted rim, green and brown streaked glaze, imp mk, ... **450.00**
8" h, waisted shape w/short rim, Art Nouveau style, relief of green and yellow flowerheads on shoulder, blue, yellow, and brown swirling stems, pale yellow ground, imp mk, ... **90.00**
8 1/2" h, cylinder shape w/slightly flared collar and base, 2 matte black panels w/polychrome birds on branches and flowers, lg gloss brown loop handles to collar and bands extending to gloss brown base, ... **50.00**

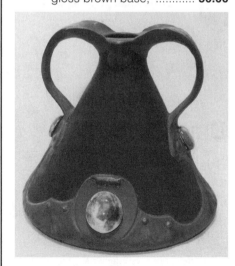

Vase, 9" h, applied blue "jewels," copper glaze on handle and base, dk brown matte ground, (A), $375.00

Warman's English & Continental Pottery & Porcelain, 4th Edition ——— 31

9" h, Arts and Crafts
Bottle shape, tapered neck,
metallic orange glaze,
.... **60.00**
Squat base, tapered neck,
everted rim, 2 handles from
body to rim, gloss dk green
glaze, imp mk, ... **100.00**
10" h, ball base, cylinder neck, tan
ground w/relief or oriental women
playing instruments, lotus
blossom and lizard on base,
gloss dk brown accents, 2 figural
bamboo handles, imp mk,
.... **25.00**
10 1/4" h, relief of orientals at window
and w/tea service, matte cobalt,
ivory, and rose, 2 side handles,
molded base, ... **215.00**
11 1/2" h, figural tan and white crane
eating bamboo, standing next to
lg green bamboo flower holder,
mkd, ... **125.00**
11 7/8" h, tapered form, 3 pierced
handles from body to neck, pink
lotus, green foliage, tan to brown
ground, pr, ... **1,045.00**
15" h, tapered shape, 2 loop
handles, spread foot, Ligna
Ware, applied butterfly and bee
on side, grasshopper on reverse,
black textured metallic type
body, ... **595.00**
18 1/2" h, tapered form, straight
neck, brown streaks over hunter
green glaze, "imp Bretby
England 228" mk, (A),
.... **465.00**

3
1770-81

BRISTOL

Bristol, England
c1749-1752, soft paste
c1770-1781, hard paste

History: Soft paste porcelain called
"Lund's Bristol" was made in Bristol,
c1749-52. Pieces show a strong Chinese
influence. There usually was no factory
mark. Hence, it is easily confused with
early Worcester porcelains. In 1752 the
Worcester Porcelain Company, under Dr.

John Wall, purchased the Bristol soft paste
factory and relocated it at Warmstry House
in Worcester.

In 1770 a second porcelain factory at
Bristol was established by William Cookworthy. This venture made hard paste porcelain, rather than soft paste. Richard
Champion continued the factory between
1774 and 1778. A group of Staffordshire
potters bought Champion's patent for hard
paste porcelain and formed the New Hall
Company, closing the Bristol factory in
1781.

Bristol porcelains of the 1770-78
period are rare. Tea services, dessert services, and dinner wares were made with
simple floral patterns. Some gilding was
used. Figures and vases were decorated
with florals too. The factory is best known
for its oval biscuit floral encrusted plaques.

Much Bristol porcelain was unmarked.
Sometimes a cross in blue was accompa-
nied by a painter's or gilder's mark. Copies
of Dresden crossed swords were used on
some Bristol pieces.

References: F.S. Mackenna,
*Cookworthy's Plymouth & Bristol
Porcelains*, F. Lewis, 1947; F. Severne,
Champion's Bristol Porcelain, F. Lewis,
1947; Dr. B. Watney, *English Blue & White
Porcelain of the 18th Century*, Rev. Ed.
Faber & Faber, 1973.

Museum: Gardiner Museum of Ceramic
Art, Toronto, Canada.

Collecting Hints: Fake Bristol porcelains
often bearing the cross mark with a date
are in the marketplace.

*Plate, 9 1/8" d, tin glazed, red, blue, green,
yellow, and manganese, $375.00*

Bowl, 10 5/8" w, blue painted Chinese
pavilions, river, and landscape on
ext, blue flower sprays on int, c1780,
repairs, ... **150.00**

Charger
13 1/2" d, tin glazed, multicolored
oriental lake scene in center,
bianco-sopra-bianco border,
c1760, ... **1,500.00**
14" d, tin glazed, blue and yellow
painted standing Queen Anne
holding orb, "A" and "R" flanking
head, blue sponged trees at
sides, blue and yellow ground in
blue and yellow surround, blue
dash rim, c1710, (A),
.... **10,755.00**
13 3/4" d, tin glazed, painted bird
perched on flowering branch
watching insects, branches
w/buds and leaves, blue and
white, 18th C, rim chip,
.... **975.00**
Dish, 14 1/4" d, tin glazed, blue painted
peacock in center in flowering
shrubs, blue painted birds in
flowering branches on border,
repaired chip, c1710, (A),
.... **2,700.00**
Jug, 9" h, and Basin, 12 3/8" d,
pearlware, jug w/bocage of yellow,
ochre and blue-grey flowers in green
foliage, border bocage on inner lip,
sepia border on rim of mouth, base,
and strap handle, basin w/bocage
around dbl banded ochre scalloped
shell border and green flowerhead in
center, c1800, ... **2,300.00**

*Plate, 9 1/4" d, med blue design, lt blue ground,
c1760-80, $300.00*

Plate, 9" d, tin glazed, dk blue design of
fisherman on dock, boat in
foreground, village in bkd, pale blue
ground, bianco-sopra-bianco
flowerheads on border, rim chip,
.... **325.00**

Salt, 5 1/4" w, figural shell w/3 claw-and-ball feet, painted loose spray of flowers and sprigs, Cocksworthy, c1775, ... **5,000.00**

Soup Plate, 8 1/2" d, tin glazed, blue scene of oriental man swinging two balls from curtain, buildings in bkd, c1740, ... **700.00**

Teabowl and Saucer, ogee fluted form, green floral swags, gilt embellishments, ... **135.00**

Tulip Vase, 6 3/4" h, 3 stems, HP red, blue, and yellow flowers and green leaves on sides, dk red lines, dashes, and rims, c1830, ... **455.00**

BRITISH ROYALTY COMMEMORATIVES

Staffordshire, England
1600s to Present

History: British commemorative china dates from the 1600s, although the early pieces were rather crude in form and design. When transfer printing was developed about 1780, the likeness of the king or queen was much improved.

With coronations or jubilee celebrations of England's royalty, a great number of souvenir wares appeared on the market to commemorate the occasion. This practice started in earnest with the coronation of Queen Victoria and has been in use ever since.

Most of these wares were manufactured in the Staffordshire district of England. Many small potters, finding a ready market for these souvenir products, produced them well in advance of any upcoming celebration. At times this was premature. The number of pieces prepared for the coronation of Edward VIII is an excellent example. With his abdication of the throne, the coronation ware quickly became abdication ware. Since large quantities were produced and sold previously, wares for this event that never happened are not scarce.

It was not long before the major houses such as Minton, Royal Doulton, Aynsley, and Wedgwood began producing commemorative wares. Plates, jugs, pitchers, and tea sets were the popular pieces.

Transfers and decals that often featured busts of the king or queen and the consort graced most pieces. Other royal symbols used on the pieces included crowns, dragons, royal coats of arms, national flowers, swords, sceptres, dates, messages, and initials.

Some items were issued in limited quantities and are very desirable, but much of the materials prepared for coronation and jubilee celebrations were mass produced and are readily available.

From 1887-1937, the Golden Jubilee period through the coronation of George VI, are the most popular periods for collecting royal commemoratives. Queen Victoria's commemoratives are the single most popular theme for collectors due to her popularity and longevity. For her Diamond Jubilee there were great quantities of memorabilia made because she was the longest reigning monarch in English history.

References: M.H. Davey & D.J. Mannion, *Fifty Years of Royal Commemorative China 1887-1937*, Dayman Publications, 1988; Douglas H. Flynn & Alan H. Bolton, *British Royalty Commemoratives*, Schiffer Publishing Ltd. 1994; Lincoln Hallinan, *British Commemoratives*, Antique Collectors' Club, 1995; Josephine Jackson, *Fired for Royalty*, Heaton Moor, 1977; Peter Johnson, *Royal Memorabilia*, Dunestyle Publishing Ltd.1988; John May, *Victoria Remembered, A Royal History 1817-1861*, London, 1983; John & Jennifer May, *Commemorative Pottery 1780-1900*, Heinemann, 1972; David Rogers, *Coronation Souvenirs & Commemoratives*, Latimer New Dimensions Ltd. 1975; Sussex Commemorative Ware Centre, *200 Commemoratives*, Metra Print Enterprises, 1979; Geoffrey Warren, *Royal Souvenirs*, Orbis, 1977; Anthony B. Zeder, *British Royal Commemoratives With Prices*, Wallace-Homestead, 1986.

Collectors' Clubs: Commemorative Collectors Society, 25 Farndale Close, Long Eaton, United Kingdom, NG 10 3PA, $25.00 per year, *Journal of the Commemorative Collectors Society*; Royalty Collectors Association of North America, 30 E. 60th Street, Suite 803, New York, NY 10022. $15.00 per year, annual newsletter.

Museums: Brighton Museum, Brighton, England; London Museum, Kensington Palace, London, England; Victoria & Albert Museum, London, England.

Collecting Hints: Some collectors specialize in just one monarch, while others include several different ones. Another approach is to collect only pieces for special occasions, such as coronations, jubilees, marriages, investitures, births, or memorials. Others specialize in one specific form such as mugs, teapots, spoons, etc.

Newsletter: *The Commemorative Collector*, Douglas H. Flynn, P.O. Box 294, Lititz, PA 17543-0294, quarterly, $18.00 per year.

Edward VII

Beaker, 4" h, Coronation, swirl molded, multicolored decal of royal crest, red roses on int, ... **40.00**

Cup and Saucer, Coronation, multicolored busts of Edward and Alexandra in ovals, fluted saucer w/busts and crest, ... **150.00**

Beaker, 3 1/2" h, Coronation, multicolored transfer, reverse w/multicolored transfer of St. George on horse, "ER, 1937," inner band of green leaves, brown berries, Royal Doulton, $60.00

Egg Cup, 3" h, black transfer of "H.M. Queen Alexandra," pink luster base, ... **18.00**

Figure, 8 1/4" h, Coronation, parian, bust of Edward, socle base, "imp R. & L." mk, ... **275.00**

Jug

5" h, flat sides, Wedding, multicolored busts of Edward and Alexandra and "In Commemoration of the Wedding March 10th," three feathers in shield on reverse, ... **75.00**

6" h

Coronation, color portraits of Edward and Alexandra in gold ovals, red crown and flowers on front, brown branch handle, ... **145.00**

Wedding, relief designs of royal crests, crowns, and orbs, lt brown, "Albion Cobridge" mk, ... **300.00**

6 1/4" h, Coronation, sepia portraits of Edward and Alexandra in red

crowned ovals, Edward on throne w/lion below, ... **175.00**

Mug, 3 7/8" h, Coronation, "King George V Queen Mary 1911," and "Crowned June 22nd," "County Borough of Brighton Thomas Stanford Mayor" on reverse, blue transfers, $100.00

Mug, 3" h, Memorial, multicolored bust of Edward and "Edward VII Peace Maker," "1841-1910" on reverse, ... **175.00**

Pitcher, 6 1/4" h, Coronation, multicolored busts of Edward and Alexandra in wreath ovals, flags, and crests, "CORONATION, KING EDWARD VII QUEEN ALEXANDRA" in ribbon, reverse w/crown and flags and "TO COMMEMORATE THE CORONATION OF EDWARD VII KING & EMPEROR," molded rim, ... **32.00**

Plate

7 1/2" d, Memorial, multicolored bust of Edward in uniform in black wreath in center, "Peace Maker," "Born Nov. 9th 1841, Died May 6th 1910," feathered border, gilt rim, ... **150.00**

Plate, 6 3/4" d, Coronation, multicolored transfer, unmkd, $55.00

9 1/4" d, Coronation, profile bust of Edward in center, Mayor and Mayoress of Worcester below, "Coronation, Celebration, Worcester 1902" on border, brown transfer, ... **120.00**

9 3/4" d, Proclamation, busts of Edward and Alexandra surrounded by colored flags and "Long Live The King Edward Proclaimed King Jan 24 1901," bust of Victoria and "Britannia Mourns Her Immortal Queen," molded swirl border, gold shaped rim, ... **475.00**

Vase, 11" h, Coronation, polychrome medallion bust of Edward on front, Alexandra on reverse, raised blue and rose flowerheads on white centerband, tan inscribed bands, cobalt base and flared neck, Doulton Lambeth, (A), ... **345.00**

Edward VIII

Beaker, 4" h, Coronation, multicolored bust of Edward in oval w/crests of England, Ireland, Scotland, and Wales, Royal Doulton, ... **95.00**

Bowl, 4 5/8" d, Coronation, sepia bust of king flanked by multicolored flags and crown, "Et Mon Dieu Droit" below, banner w/ "Coronation of H.M. King Edward VIII 12th May 1937," molded woven shell border, ... **70.00**

Figure, 5 1/4" h, bust of Edward, ivory, ... **120.00**

Loving Cup

3 1/4" h x 5 1/4" H-H, Coronation, multicolored decal of Royal Crest on front, "purple HM King Edward VIII at Westminster Abbey on May 12th 1937" under handle, gold figural lion handles, Paragon, ... **95.00**

6 1/4" h, Coronation, tan relief profile of Edward in green wreath w/multicolored flags and "Crowned Edward VIII 12 May 1937," reverse w/relief of blue "ER" in green wreath, green wreath rim, red and green flowers on handles, brown ground, Paragon, ... **85.00**

Mug,

4 1/2" h, Coronation

Bust of Edward on red ground in gold garter, reverse w/crown and "ER," "CORONATION OF KING EDWARD VIII MAY 1937" on rim, Copeland-Spode, ... **85.00**

Raised profile of Edward in wreath on side, "ER" in

wreath on reverse, mottled green, musical base, ... **245.00**

Plate, 5" d, Coronation, sepia bust of Edward in gold wreath, "CORONATION," and "H.M. EDWARD VIII" above and below, flanked by multicolored flags, crowned "ER and wreath on opposite border, ... **20.00**

Tea Set, Coronation, pot, 4 1/2" h x 7 1/2" w, creamer, 2 1/2" h, cov sugar bowl, 4 1/4" h, white cameo of crowned profile bust of Edward in wreath, royal crest on sugar bowl, "ER" in wreath on creamer, bands of interlocking circles, dk blue jasper ground, "imp WEDGWOOD MADE IN ENGLAND" mks, ... **1,750.00**

Elizabeth

Box, Cov

4 1/4" h, white cameo of bust of Elizabeth in wreath on front, Philip on reverse, stiff leaves on cov, blue jasper ground, Wedgwood, ... **145.00**

5 1/2" l x 5" w, Coronation, raised blue bust of Elizabeth in wreath and crown, white ground, "Dartmouth Pottery Devon" mk, ... **65.00**

Cup and Saucer, Coronation

Crowned photo bust of Elizabeth in uniform, flanked by multicolored flags, lion and unicorn, "CORONATION" in banner, Windsor China, ... **55.00**

Sepia bust of Elizabeth in multicolored Royal crest, "Coronation, June 2nd 1953" below, gold rim, crowned "ER" on saucer, Clarice Cliff, ... **70.00**

Cup Plate, 4 1/2" d, Coronation, emb gold crowned "ER" in center, yellow border between gold lines, Wedgwood, ... **10.00**

Jug, 9 1/4" h, Silver Jubilee, relief molded scene of Coronation at Westminster abbey around middle, lt blue top and base, figural crown handle, Burleigh Ware, ... **165.00**

Loving Cup, 3 1/2" h, Coronation, bone china, multicolored Royal Crest w/"Queen Elizabeth II Coronation Souvenir" below, relief molded thistle, daffodil, clover, and rose on reverse, multicolored molded flowerheads on handles, "C. & E." mk, ... **40.00**

Mug, Coronation

3" h, bone china, blue, red, green, and yellow decal of crest, "ER" and "The Queen," horseshoe and flowers on reverse, "Long Life & Happiness To Her Majesty" on int rim, gold trim, Hammersley, ... **95.00**

5 1/2" h, terra cotta ground, raised designs of crests, "Elizabeth II Regina Coronation June 2nd 1953" on base, lion handle, white wash, Prinknash Pottery, ... **35.00**

Pin Tray, Coronation

2" w x 3" h, Multicolored bust of Elizabeth in green wreath w/red crown, indented gilt rims, Royal Crown Derby, ... **50.00**

3" sq, sq w/cut corners, indented sides, black photo bust of queen in multicolored royal crest, gold rim, Coalport, ... **25.00**

Plate

8 1/4" sq, oct, Coronation, multicolored decal of Elizabeth in oval w/crown and flags, "black ELIZABETH II CROWNED JUNE 2, 1953," relief molded border, gold rim, Royal Winton, ... **33.00**

8 3/8" d, Coronation, bust of Elizabeth II in center, flags, leaves, and acorns on border, red transfer, "John Maddock & Son Ltd England" mk, ... **25.00**

8 1/2" sq, rounded corners, Coronation, black bust of queen, flanked by multicolored flags and "Coronation of HM Queen Elizabeth II" under, crossed flags on border, molded gold edged rim, Alfred Meakin, ... **24.00**

9 1/2" d, Silver Jubilee, multicolored crest in center, "Queen Elizabeth" and "Silver Jubilee 1952-1977" on border, Wood & Sons, ... **10.00**

10 1/2" d, Coronation, sepia bust of Elizabeth, mint green border, molded rim, ... **55.00**

George IV

Jug, 6" h, lobed, Memorial, black printed quarter portrait of king, reverse w/"To The Memory of His Late Majesty King George The IV Born Aug. 12 1762 Ascended The Throne Jan. 29 1820 Publicly Proclaimed 31 Departed the Life June 26 1830 Age 68 Years," "Goodwin, Bridgewood & Harris" mk, ... **1,250.00**

Plaque

3" d, Coronation, puce printed "GOD Save The KING" below crown, "GR IV, Crowned 10th July 1821," green and yellow relief molded acorns and leaves on border between blue lines, pierced for hanging, (A), ... **1,125.00**

7 1/4" l x 6 1/4" w, relief of half bust of George, blue, yellow, and black, in yellow swag w/"George IIII," molded black rect frame, pierced for hanging, c1815-20, ... **5,750.00**

Plate, 8 1/2" d, Pratt-type, molded bust of George in center, blue uniform w/yellow sash, ochre and blue ozier molded border panels w/crowns over roses and thistles, (A), ... **930.00**

Soup Plate, 8 1/4" d, pearlware, relief molded bust of Queen Caroline, pink luster cap w/green plume, green gown, multicolored molded crowns, roses, and thistles, and Prince of Wales on border, ... **1,000.00**

George V

Beaker

3" h, Silver Jubilee, brown overlapping profiles of George and Mary flanked by multicolored flags, gold-brown border band w/"Silver Jubilee George V and Queen Mary," unmkd, ... **18.00**

3 1/2" h, Coronation, "Coronation June 22nd 1911" over multicolored busts of George and Mary, flanked by crown, flags, banner w/"Long Live," reverse w/"County Borough of Eastbourne" and crest, Shelley, ... **90.00**

Cream Jug, 3 1/8" h, multicolored transfer of bust of George in uniform, ... **8.00**

Cup and Saucer

Multicolored bust of George on front of cup, Mary on reverse, both on saucer in ovals w/flags, ... **45.00**

Silver Jubilee, bust of George in oval on side of cup, Mary on reverse, saucer w/ busts and flags and crest, ... **45.00**

Figure, 3 1/4" h, parian bust of George or Mary, black painted stepped base, c1915, pr, ... **150.00**

Jug, 5" h, Silver Jubilee, raised profile of George on side, tan ground, raised silver horiz bands and handle, Mason, ... **85.00**

Mug

2 7/8" h, Coronation, multicolored frontal busts of George and Mary separated by Union Jack shield, topped by X'd scepters and crown, "Coronation, June 22nd 1911," and ribbon w/"George V & Mary Long Live," reverse w/lion holding tablet w/"Coronation 1911," Shelley, ... **160.00**

3" h

Coronation

Bust of George V and "Rulers of an Empire on Which the Sun Never Sets" and "Send Them Victorious, Happy and Glorious Long to Reign Over Us," gold trim, ... **135.00**

Multicolored busts of George and Mary flanked by flowers, foliage, and crown, blue banner beneath w/"June 22nd 1911," "God Save The King..." on reverse, Royal Winton, ... **35.00**

Multicolored royal crest on front, ... **75.00**

3 1/8" h, Silver Jubilee, named sepia busts of George and Mary flanked by multicolored flags, crest and "1910-1935," "Silver Jubilee" below, reverse w/multicolored decal of crest, red lined rim, "Green & Co. Ltd" mk, ... **85.00**

3 1/2" h

Coronation, green toned crowned busts of George and Mary, ribbon below w/"Coronation 1911," Royal Doulton, ... **100.00**

Silver Jubilee, grey battleship on blue sea, blue sky, "H.M.S. Queen Elizabeth Flagship Mediterranean Fleet 1933-1935," reverse w/gold oval and overlapping busts of George and Mary, flanked by multicolored flags, gold banner on rim w/George V and Mary, Silver Jubilee," cream ground, Minton, ... **45.00**

Pin tray, 9" l, white ground w/multicolored bust of "H.M. QUEEN MARY," piecrust border, artist sgd,

"Schmidt & Co. Czechoslovakia" mk, ... **60.00**

Plate

4" d, Silver Jubilee, multicolored busts of George and Mary in ovals w/flags and crown, "1910-1925 Jubilee," "Accession May 6 1910 Long May They Reign." green rim, "New Chelsea Pottery" mk, ... **48.00**

8" d, Coronation, multicolored portrait of George in blue uniform in center, "Coronation 1911," gilt rim, Royal Doulton, ... **55.00**

9" d

Coronation, multicolored busts of George and Mary in wreaths crowned w/crest, wreath of flowers on inner border, relief molded flower border, scalloped rim, ... **27.00**

Silver Jubilee, sepia busts of George and Mary and multicolored flags, crest on border, blue lined rim, ... **25.00**

10" d, Coronation, busts of George and Mary in ovals in center flanked by flags, crown and "Coronation" above, warships, Empire shields, and regalia on border, blue transfer, ... **165.00**

Teapot, 5 1/2" h x 9" w, Silver Jubilee, multicolored portraits of George and Mary in rectangles, yellow sun rays behind, red trim, ... **165.00**

Tile, 6" sq, Coronation, black busts of king and queen flanked by colored flags, crown, and florals, "George V" and "Mary," "A Souvenir of the Coronation" in pink ribbon below, turquoise majolica border w/red flowerheads and green foliage, ... **360.00**

Toothpick, 2" h, 2 handles, multicolored decal of bust of Queen Mary, ... **150.00**

George VI

Beaker, Coronation

3 1/2" h, busts of George and Elizabeth in gilt ovals w/multicolored flags and red crown, ... **18.00**

4 1/4" h, multicolored royal crest of front, crest of London on reverse w/"LONDON COUNTY COUNCIL" in banner, "GEORGE & QUEEN ELIZABETH" on border, "MAY 1937" on base, ... **40.00**

Cookie Jar, 7 1/2" h, paneled, Coronation, black portrait of George in military uniform in green wreath, multicolored flags at side, Queen Elizabeth on reverse, Maling, ... **165.00**

Cup and Saucer, Canadian Trip, black busts of George and Elizabeth, flanked by multicolored flags, "Long May They Reign" in ribbon, yellow borders, "Coclough China" mk, ... **45.00**

Loving Cup, 6" H-H, George and Queen first visit to Canada, 1939, ... **95.00**

Mug, Coronation

2 5/8" h, figural bust of George, cobalt, gold, and white officer's cap, navy coat, brown handle, Royal Winton, ... **140.00**

3" h, black frontal busts of Elizabeth, George, and children on blue ground, black wreaths, Wedgwood, ... **69.00**

3 1/2" h, overlapping busts of George and Elizabeth in blue garter, green thistle on sides, names on rim, Minton, ... **22.00**

Plate, 7 1/2" sq, Coronation, sepia portrait of George VI, multicolored flags, gold lined rim, "L. & Sons Ltd Henley, Made in England" mark, $60.00

Plate

9 3/4" l x 8 3/4" w, Royal Visit to Canada 1937, lt yellow ground w/sepia busts of king and queen in multicolored wreaths flanked by flags, "To Commemorate The Visit...," below, relief molded roses and florals on border, gold beaded rim, Royal Winton, ... **78.00**

10" d, 12 sides, Coronation, sepia busts of George VI and Elizabeth flanked by British flags and "Long May They Reign" below,

red and blue striped inner and outer borders, "John Maddock & Sons, Ltd Made in England" mk, ... **50.00**

10 1/2" d, Coronation, multicolored royal crest w/lion and unicorn in center, "King George VI and Queen Elizabeth" on rim, Paragon, ... **220.00**

Scuttle Mug, 4" h, Coronation, sepia portraits of George and Elizabeth in gold ovals, multicolored flags and crown and "Coronation 1937," red and blue striped rim, ... **85.00**

Tankard, 3 1/2" h, tapered, Coronation, busts of George and Elizabeth in gilt ovals w/multicolored flags and red crown, ... **18.00**

Victoria

Beaker, 6" h, Diamond Jubilee, stoneware, relief bust of queen, blue printed flowers, blue spattered rim and foot, ... **385.00**

Bowl, 5 1/4" d, Coronation, black transfer bust of Victoria and Windsor Castle, "crown over VICTORIA" on int of bowl, ... **650.00**

Butter Dish, Cov, 6 1/8" l, rect, Golden Jubilee, bust of Victoria, "Wales, Scotland, Ireland, and England" on lid, red transfers, MOP finish, ... **185.00**

Figure, 16 1/2" h, Golden Jubilee, white dress w/florals, blue diag sash, "gilt Queen of England & Empress of India. Crowned June 20th 1837. Year of Jubilee 1887" on base, (A), ... **280.00**

Jug

4" h, stoneware, Diamond Jubilee, relief medallions of busts of young and old Victoria and 1837, 1897, roses, shamrocks, and thistle, dk brown rim, tan body, Doulton Lambeth, ... **125.00**

5 1/4" h, waisted shape, white cameos of full length portraits of Victoria on front, Albert on reverse, blue ground, scroll molded white handle and spout, hairline, ... **650.00**

6 1/4" h, Marriage of Princess Royal, black printed scene "Princess Royal and the Prince of Prussia," lustered cartouche of Prussian Royal Palace on reverse, blue tinted ground w/luster accents, ... **650.00**

7" h

Paneled, relief bust of Victoria and Prince Albert, blue glaze, ... **455.00**

Squat shape, Coronation, green transfer bust of queen w/thistle and shamrocks, "Victoria Regina Crowned June 28 1838" on base, green diapered border, fancy branch handle, ... **850.00**

Marriage, yellow band w/white panel of puce printed bust of Victoria and Albert, copper luster body, handle, and spout, chips, ... **650.00**

8" h, ovoid, Coronation, relief molded standing queen and "Queen Victoria," relief molded roses, thistle, and shamrocks, scalloped rim, overall blue glaze, ... **725.00**

Mug

3 1/8" h, Golden Jubilee, gold crown and banners w/"Queen Victoria" and "1837 Jubilee Year 1887," raised gold band on shoulder and rim, ... **100.00**

3 1/4" h

Diamond Jubilee, black transfer of bust of Victoria, banners of "Leicester Commemoration, Diamond Jubilee, Queen Victoria," and "1837-1897" on front, black transfer of bust of "J. Herbert Marshall Mayor of Leicester" on side, Mayoress on reverse, Brownfields, ... **59.00**

Golden Jubilee, black transfers of bust of queen, royal crest, and crest of City of Peterborough, and "21st June 1887," unmkd, ... **85.00**

Pitcher, 7 1/2" h, ovoid, Coronation, blue printed bust of queen under spout and black "John Howarth 1838," thistles, shamrocks, figural lion handle, ... **1,650.00**

Plaque

6 3/4" d, MEMORIAL, multicolored half bust of Victoria, "In Memorium Queen Victoria," "Born May 24th 1809, Ascended The Throne 1837, Entered Into Rest Jan 22, 1901," and "The Wrought Her People Lasting

Live," gilt rim, Grimwades, ... **125.00**

11" d, Diamond Jubilee, brown transfers w/colors of queen in center, circ scenes of 4 castles, "Victoria Diamond Jubilee 1897" at top, "Empress of India" and "Queen of England" at sides, "Crowned 1837" on bottom, molded border, pierced for hanging, ... **290.00**

Plate

5" d, Marriage, green painted royal couple on horseback, Windsor castle in bkd, "Her Most Gracious Majesty Queen Victoria and Prince Albert" below, molded horse border w/red, green, and yellow dashes, ... **650.00**

5 7/8" d, oct, Marriage, black printed and polychromed crown and wreath and "Victoria and Albert Married Feb 10 1840," molded floral head border, red rope rim, ... **625.00**

6 1/2" d, Coronation, blue printed bust of queen and "Victoria Regina Crowned 28th of June 1838 Born 24th of May 1819, Proclaimed 20th June 1837," multicolored enameled flowers and pink luster border, cracked, ... **1,250.00**

9" d, Diamond Jubilee

Gold hanging banner w/"Accession 1837 Diamond Jubilee 1897," gold V.R., border w/relief bust of Victoria and thistles and flowers, gold outlined shaped rim, Copeland Spode, pr, ... **150.00**

Sepia busts of young and old queen in laurel wreaths on painted crowned blue and red shield, banner w/"LONGEST AND NOBLEST REIGN 1837-1897," HP roses, thistles, and shamrocks and relief designs on border, ... **250.00**

9 1/2" w, oct, Golden Jubilee, black transfer of "Victoria Queen & Empress," "Jubilee year 1887," busts of Queen Victoria and Prince of Wales, maps of British Empire w/yellow accents, crests

of Canada, Australia, Cape Colony, and India, English protector in center w/polychrome accents, gold rim, ... **115.00**

Teapot, 4 1/2" h x 7" w, Diamond Jubilee, multicolored busts of young and old queen in swirl cartouches and "God Save The Queen," banner w/"Sixty Years Glorious Run," "1837 - 1897," and "H.M. Queen Victoria," molded beaded and swirl body, gold rims, ... **75.00**

Tea Tile

6" w, oct, Diamond Jubilee, multicolored transfer of bust of Victoria over Windsor castle, "VICTORIA OUR QUEEN" in circle and banner w/"1837-1897, Long May She Reign," yellow rim, unmkd, ... **35.00**

6 1/4" d, Golden Jubilee, black printed bust of Victoria crowned w/veil, flower border, "Royal Jubilee" on reverse, ... **185.00**

William IV
Jug

4 5/8" h, ovoid, Coronation, black printed quarter bust of William and Adelaide, "WILLIAM IV AND QUEEN ADELAIDE CROWND SEPT 8 1831," border of roses, thistles, and shamrocks, rim chips, ... **950.00**

5 3/4" h, Coronation, red transfers of William crowned at Westminster Abbey, "William & Adelaide Crowned Sept 8, 1831" on sides, ... **975.00**

6 1/4" d, purple transfer of bust of William and "William the Fourth, King of Britain" overhead, leaf molded border, c1832, ... **210.00**

6 1/2" h, Coronation, blue printed bust of William in scrolling cartouche on side, Queen Adelaide on reverse, floral throat, Minton, ... **875.00**

7" h, purple printed half portrait of William and "OUR BELOVED KING WILLIAM 4TH" and bust of queen and "OUR AMIABLE QUEEN ADELAIDE," garter star under spout, molded scroll handle, restored, ... **1,000.00**

Mug, 3" h, white relief bust of William and Adelaide on blue ground, white beaded rim, fancy handle, hairline, ... **650.00**

Plate, 7" d, oct, black transfer of William and "William The Fourth, King of Great Britain," relief molded daisy border, rim chip, ... **625.00**

c.1930s

BURLEIGH WARE JUGS

Middleport Pottery, Burslem, England 1931-1950s

History: This firm was started as Hulme and Booth in 1851 and became Burgess and Leigh in 1877. Their new factory was built at Middleport in 1889. The company remained in the hands of these two families until the death of R.S. Burgess, when it passed to the Leigh family, who are still the owners. Burgess and Leigh became a Limited Company in 1919. They are still located in Middleport.

From 1926 to 1931, Charlotte Rhead worked at Burgess and Leigh, where she trained a team of tube liners. She then moved on to A.G. Richardson.

Burleigh Ware was an important aspect of English Art Deco ceramics. During the 1930s, they produced the geometric, embossed, and hand painted yellow earthenware "flower jugs" that became very popular and were eagerly collected. Ernest Bailey, as an apprentice modeler in 1931, made the Squirrel, Parrot, Dragon, Kingfisher, Flamingo, Harvest (a rabbit in a corn stalk), Highwayman, and Pied Piper jugs. The elaborately molded figural handle formed the main subject of the jug, while the body had appropriate decoration to coordinate with the handle.

Another designer of many jugs was Charles Wilkes, who added Butterfly, Budgerigar, Village Blacksmith, and Stocks in 1938. Later, Coronation, Tally-ho (a hunting scene), and Sally in the Alley were made.

A series of larger sports-people jugs also were made including the golfer, cricketer, and the tennis player, but less of these were made. Jugs were made in a variety of sizes and often in several colorings.

The usual mark is a beehive with leaves around it and "Burleigh Ware Made in England."

References: Judy Spours, *Art Deco Tableware*, Rizzoli International Publications, 1988; Howard and Pat Watson, *Collecting Art Deco Ceramics,*

2nd Edition, Wallace-Homestead, 1997.

Collecting Hints: Burleigh Ware jugs are sought by collectors of Art Deco ceramics, as well as by collectors who are just interested in the jugs for their subject matter or design.

Jug, 8" h, "Kingfisher," blue and green bird, yellow ground, rose handle, black dash rim, mkd, $395.00

4" h, Art Deco "Zenith" pattern, bluebells and brown tree trunks on green grass patch, yellow ground, bluebells and green leaves on handle, brown dash rim, ... **75.00**

5 1/4" h, "Pixie," running pixie in green sack hat, yellow ground w/relief molded leaf designs, green branch handle, ... **60.00**

6" h, Tony Weller, multicolored, ... **40.00**

7" h
Brown squirrel handle, yellow ground w/brown tree trunk, green and brown acorns, brown dash rim, shaded lt green base, ... **250.00**
Overall molded yellow grape body, green molded leaves on base and spout, brown branch handle, ... **350.00**
"Rabbit in the Haystack" pattern, red flowerheads, brown dash rim, red int, ... **225.00**

7 1/4" h, Charles Dickens character, black hair and beard, seated on stack of books, holding feather pen, lapel of blue coat, brown base, ... **50.00**

7 1/2" h, Pied Piper, castle on mint green ground, multicolored

figural handle of Pied Piper, ... **200.00**

7 3/4" h
Art Deco, relief of blue-grey or orange leaves on stem from neck through lg curved handle to base, green outlined margins, ... **125.00**
Dragon, green, orange, yellow, and red figural dragon handle, yellow ribbed body, black dash rim, ... **275.00**

8" h
Brown branch around middle w/green pine needles, mottled brown ground, faceted band around base and collar, brown dashes on rim, salmon int, ... **38.00**
Pied Piper, tan castles, brown rocks on yellow ground, green int, brown dash rim, figural Pied Piper handle, repaired hairline, ... **215.00**
Yellow ground w/orange accents, black dash rim, green, blue, red, and black figural parrot handle, ... **145.00**

8 1/2" h, "Village Blacksmith," polychrome blacksmith at forge, branch handle, ... **165.00**

8 5/8" h, "Galleon" design, Art Deco shape, cream and brown sailing galleon on lilac ground, orange swimming fish, green spout, handle, and wave type base, ... **300.00**

9 1/2" h, pale green ground w/relief of flying flamingo, relief molded and HP polychrome reeds and plants, reed handle, ... **95.00**

9 3/4" h
"Sally in Our Alley" pattern, lantern handle, white glaze, ... **135.00**
"Wolf and Stork," brown wolf, yellow horiz ribbed body, green figural stork handle, green dash rim, (A), ... **425.00**

10" h
Art Deco style yellow-brown leaping gazelle on yellow zigzag ground, black and green vert zigzag stripes, sq base, ... **400.00**

*Pitcher, 9 1/2" h, pink dress, yellow vest, green coat, black pantaloons, brown brick, green window, brown lantern handle, "Sally in our Alley" on base, c1940, **$279.00***

Ironstone, "Meal Time" pattern, relief of 3 dogs and woman eating, molded brick wall, white glaze, shaded dk blue top and base, figural hound handle, ... **65.00**

Relief molded wolf, sheaf of corn on reverse, figural crane handle, matte lt green glaze, ... **125.00**

11" h, "Bulrushes" pattern, grey-white relief of bulrushes, flowing blue base, border, and handle, ... **130.00**

c1760 - EARLY 20TH C

CAPODIMONTE

Near Naples, Italy
1743-1759
Buen Retiro,
near Madrid, Spain
1760-1812

History: Capodimonte was a royal palace in Naples where a porcelain factory was established in 1743. Charles III, the Bourbon King, and his Queen, who had brought quantities of porcelain from Meissen, were the founders. The factory produced primarily soft paste porcelain in a milky white color for the court.

Guiseppe Gricci was the chief modeler. His specialties included religious subjects (madonnas, pietas, and holy water

stoups), snuff boxes, and mythological figures. Gricci was in charge when the factory created an entire room for the king that featured porcelain panels in high relief decorated in chinoiserie and which can be viewed today at the Museo di Capodimonte in Naples. Pieces usually were marked with the armorial fleur-de-lys of the Bourbon family.

When Charles inherited the throne of Spain and became king in 1759, he moved the factory and workers to Madrid with him. Gricci, now signing his works Jose Gricci, also made the transition. The new factory, located on the palace grounds, was called Buen Retiro. They continued to make soft paste porcelains similar to those made at Capodimonte, including elaborate tablewares, centerpieces, flowers, and figures. Sometimes the factory used the Bourbon fleur-de-lys mark. An attempt to make hard paste porcelains was made shortly before the factory closed.

When Ferdinand IV governed Italy in 1771, he revived the royal factory. Styles were influenced by a classical revival, inspired by the unearthed treasures at Pompeii. Best known are the pieces decorated with mythological reliefs.

After 1807 the factory declined and closed several years later. In 1821 the molds and models were sold to the Ginori factory at Doccia.

Museums: Metropolitan Museum of Art, New York, NY; Museo di Capodimonte, Naples, Italy; Woodmere Art Museum, Philadelphia, PA.

Reproduction Alert: Many factories in Hungary, Germany, France, and Italy copied Capodimonte examples. Many of the pieces on the market today are of recent vintage. Many reproductions are made with the red mark underglaze.

*Box, 8 1/2" l, multicolored, "Italy" mk, **$95.00***

Box

3 7/8" l x 3" w x 2" h, relief of angels on cov, band of relief molded mythological figures on sides, beaded rims, "blue crowned N" mk, ... **145.00**

4" w, clover shape, relief of cherubs at pursuits on cov, ... **290.00**

4 1/2" l x 3 1/2" w, relief of gladiator in chariot w/horse on cov, relief of cherubs on sides, white, metal mts, ... **475.00**

Cup and Saucer, relief of frolicking cherubs, "crown N" mk, ... **195.00**

*Plate, 9 1/4" d, gold, red, & blue crest of Pope Pius IX in center, multicolored border, gilt rim, "blue crowned N" mk, c1870, **$385.00***

Cup and Saucer, Demitasse, relief of mythical figures, pedestal and oil lamp, twisted gold and red feather handle, "blue crowned N" mk, ... **175.00**

Dessert Plate, 6" d, 4 different polychrome armorials in center, molded polychrome and gilt classical figures on border, "blue crowned N" mks, set of 4, ... **425.00**

*Ewer, 16 1/2" h, polychrome, "gold crown over blue dash" mark, **A-$375.00***

Figure, 14" h, period gentleman, tan top hat, brown jacket, woman in black flowered dress, bonnet, circ base, "crowned N" mk, c1900, ... **600.00**

Inkstand, 8" l x 7" w, inkwell w/multicolored cherubs, multicolored transfer of floral bouquet on tray w/gilt cell border, "crowned N" mk, c1900, ... **550.00**

Jewel Casket, 8 1/4" l x 5" w, oval, polychrome mythological scene on cov, mythological heads, florals, and goats on body, bronze mts, ... **950.00**

Napkin Ring, 1 1/2" d, polychromed relief of frolicking cherubs, .. **100.00**

Planter on Stand, 44 3/4" h, cylindrical, continuous polychrome band of nude nymphs in fluted border, pedestal w/fluting, standard w/vert relief bands of cavorting putti w/continuous scene of classic figures, reeded stepped ft, gilt details, early 20th C, (A), ... **345.00**

Plaque, 9 1/2" l x 6 1/2" w, rect, polychromed relief of goddess, soldiers, animals, and cherubs, ... **650.00**

Platter, 21 3/4" l, oval, molded scene of swans and water birds in pond, border of flowering vines, gilt scalloped rim, (A), ... **295.00**

Urn
8 1/4" h, gilt w/white and pink feathered rim and base, putti on shoulder, relief of polychrome mythological figures around center, sq handles, "gilt crowned N" mks, pr, (A), ... **440.00**

Urn, 10" h, polychrome neo-classical figural scene, gilt rim, gilt garland band, relief molded horned satyr masks and garlands, faux marble and acanthus pedestal, plinth base, pr, A-$850.00

14 1/2" h, multicolored relief of mythological scene around center, sq base w/relief of gold accented scrolling, collar w/gold accented relief molded foliage, gold accented curled handles, "crowned N" mk, ... **255.00**

Vase
12" h, goblet shape, multicolored cherubs, flowers, and interwoven curls and swirls, "Italy" mk, ... **390.00**

13 1/4" h, campana urn shape, relief of Roman mythological putti, satyrs, and goats, festooned ivy wreath, 2 horiz gilt handles, swirl fluted pedestal on sq base w/gilt scrolling, "blue crowned N" mk, mid-19th C, ... **795.00**

c1883

CARLSBAD-GENERAL

Bohemia, now Czechoslovakia 1848 to Present

History: Carlsbad and the vicinity surrounding it was the center of the Bohemian porcelain industry. Many factories used the name Carlsbad in their marks even though they were not located in the city itself. The factories manufactured household and decorative porcelains and gift items.

Opiag, Austrian Porcelain Industry AG, changed its name to Epiag after Bohemia was removed from the Austrian Empire at the end of World War I to become part of the newly created state of Czechoslovakia. Epiag was nationalized after World War II.

Cracker Jar, 9" h, multicolored transfer, gold trim, $65.00

Plate, 11 1/4" d, pink edged yellow flowerhead, mauve flowers, green and brown foliage, mint green ground, gold outlined pierced leaf border w/grape clusters, gold rim, "imp CARLSBAD AUSTRIA" mk, $89.00

Biscuit Jar, 7" h, bunches of blue forget-me-nots, green leaves, beige ground, brass collar, cov, and overhead handle, Royal Carlsbad, ... **125.00**

Bud Vase, 9" h, ball base, trumpet neck, HP purple violets, green foliage, ivory ground, gold accents, ... **25.00**

Cabinet Cup and Saucer, multicolored panels of period couples on cup and saucer borders, maroon body w/gold flower overlay, 4 gold feet, lg gold scroll handle, ... **75.00**

Cake Plate
9 3/4" H-H, multicolored decal of classic scene of woman playing tambourine, assistants, and cherub, blue shaded swirl molded border w/gold dusted rim, open handles, ... **20.00**

11" d, multicolored garden flowers, gold rim, molded in body handles, ... **125.00**

Canned Milk Holder, 4" h, painted multicolored flowers on dk blue marbled ground, gold handles and knob, ... **130.00**

Charger
11" d, multicolored print of 3 classic women grooming fourth, child at side, blue border, yellow, red and gold geometric rim, ... **25.00**

11 1/2" d, decal of young girl in red dress, holding handkerchief, lt to dk green shaded ground, gold stenciled border, ... **95.00**

12" d, center multicolored transfer of 2 classic ladies and cherubs, teal border w/5 cartouches of cherubs and gold overlay,

pierced for hanging, "Victoria Carlsbad Austria" mk,
.... **125.00**

Chocolate Service, pot, 10" h, tray, 16 1/2" H-H, 6 cups and saucers, multicolored transfer of classical scenes in gold cartouches, cobalt ground w/gold floral stenciling, cream borders w/gold stenciling, molded rococo handles, hairline on pot, ... **995.00**

Cup and Saucer, sprigs of yellow-centered blue petaled flowers, sm pink flowers, green leaves, brown stems, gold dust borders, "W. & Co. Carlsbad Austria" mk, ... **15.00**

Dish

6 1/2" l, HP pink floral spray, cream to pink shaded ground, gold trim, Carl Knoll, ... **25.00**

15 3/4" l x 9 1/2" w, sm scattered florals, vert ribbed border, gilt trim, mkd, ... **50.00**

Ewer, 12" h, period woman in pink gown w/puffed sleeves, blue sash, green foliage bkd, gold rococo handle, ... **80.00**

Hair Receiver, 4" d, transfer of purple florals, emb basketweave on lid, scrolling design on sides,
.... **48.00**

Dresser Set, tray, 11 1/2" l, 7 3/8" w, ring tree, cov box, candlesticks, 7 3/4" h, pink, yellow, and red flowers, green leaves, white ground, "Victoria Carlsbad" marks, $275.00

Pitcher, 9" h, vert fluting, bunches of pink accented sm blue flowers, green foliage, fancy gold handle, gold accented spout and rim,
.... **75.00**

Plaque, 13" d, multicolored classic scene of women in garden w/temple columns, irreg gilt lined rim,
.... **150.00**

Plate

7" d, pair of thrushes in pines, dk red rim, ... **18.00**

8 1/4" d, border of pansies, indented aqua rim, "Victoria Carlsbad" mk,
.... **18.00**

8 1/2" d

Decal of 3 classical maidens and cherubs in gold outlined quatrefoil, matte green pierced border w/gold accented relief molding,
.... **200.00**

Multicolored bust of nobleman in gold outlined cartouche, sea green border w/molded designs, gold molded rim, artist sgd, ... **125.00**

9 3/8" d, center w/loose mass of violets, border of hanging swags of violets alternating w/green leaf from gilt band, "red AUSTRIA CARLSBAD" mk, ... **20.00**

Rose Bowl, 4 3/4" h x 5" d, yellow flowers, brown foliage, gold accents, scalloped rim, "crowned Carlsbad" mk, ... **85.00**

Salt Dish, 3" sq, green transfer printed floral border, "G.B.M. CARLSBAD" mk, set of 11, ... **110.00**

Teapot, 8 3/4" d, decal of lg pink floral spray on front, sprig on reverse, lime green shaded borders, gold rim, stem knob, ... **65.00**

Tea Set, pot, 5" h, cream jug, 5 1/2" h, cov sugar bowl, 5" h, pink ground w/gold and white raised band on shoulders, gold trim, figural gold and white eagle handles, dragon spout on teapot, figural gold and white eagle knobs, "Elbogen, Carlsbad" mks, ... **80.00**

Vase

5 1/2" h, swollen base, long straight neck, lg white water lilies, green foliage and meandering stems, shaded lt blue ground, "Carlsbad Made in Austria" mk, ... **30.00**

7" H-H, free form, irid glaze, gilt trim and handles, pink int, "Carlsbad Made in Austria" mk, ... **200.00**

9 1/4" h, bottle shape, HP red centered white rose, brown foliage, cream ground, molded gold stems on neck, "crowned Carlsbad" mk, c1900, ... **40.00**

13" h, white standing female in gown holding flowers, leaning on beige to rust drip trunk, c1920, hairlines, ... **950.00**

14" h, organic form, pale magenta veined stylized opening flower bud, green stem handle around neck, green leaf pad base, restored, ... **798.00**

CARLTON WARE

Stoke-on-Trent, Staffordshire, England c1890-1992

History: Staffordshire porcelain and earthenware were produced at the Carlton Works, Stoke-on-Trent, from about 1890 by a firm that traded as Wiltshaw and Robinson. Carlton Ware became the factory's trade name in 1894.

In the early 1920s, luster wares were made in twelve colors and were one of the main lines of the factory between the two world wars. Vases, bowls, ginger jars, wall plaques, dishes, and potpourri holders in classic shapes were decorated with a variety of patterns including Egyptian, Byzantine, Persian, Chinese, Japanese, and Art Deco styles. Motifs included angel fish, birds of paradise, waterlilies, butterflies, bluebirds, sunbursts, shooting stars, and lightning flashes.

Due to the complex nature of the luster process, luster pieces comprised the luxury end of Carlton Ware's production. Luster pieces often had mother-of-pearl interiors. Background colors could be marbled, mottled, bubbled, or splashed. Enameled paint and gilding enriched the surface of the pieces.

In the mid-1920s, novelty earthenware was introduced, including the cruets that were characteristic of this firm. Jampots were made in the shape of fruit, and small figurines were made, along with napkin rings. Advertising and promotional items were made as well as china commemoratives and crested wares.

Following the takeover of Birks, Rawlins & Company in 1920, china production was expanded to teawares in floral patterns such as "Delphinium," "Springime," and "Sunshine" that utilized hand painting and transfer printing.

Embossed salad ware was made in green and red from the 1920s until 1976, when regulations about lead paint eliminated the red color that was utilized for the tomatoes and lobster claws. A tremendous variety of shapes was made in this embossed ware.

In 1929 Carlton Ware introduced oven-to-table utilitarian wares with banding in three colors.

The most collectible Carlton Ware lines are the floral embossed pieces based on

leaf and flower shapes. "Oak Tree" from 1934 in blue and cream was made for plaques, vases, jugs, candleholders, bookends, match holders, and cruets. "Garden Ware" from 1935 was made in similar objects and also matte glazed. "Handcraft" was a less expensive version of the luxury luster examples.

Highly glazed lines included "Buttercup," "Waterlily," "Apple Blossom," "Wild Rose," "Foxglove," "Primula," and "Poppy."

After World War II, Carlton Ware had major improvements and expansions. Designs became more sophisticated in two-tone colors with more exotic flowers motifs. In 1967 Arthur Wood & Sons took over the factory and expanded the export trade. Fruits replaced flowers as a popular theme.

With the 1980s recession, Carlton Ware finally stopped production in 1992.

Until about 1927, most products were identified with a circular printed mark with W & R/STOKE ON TRENT enclosing a swallow and topped by a crown. "Made in England" was added in the early 1900s. Later a variety of script marks was used.

References: Francis Salmon & others, *Collecting Carlton Ware*, Francis Joseph Publications, 1994; Judy Spours, *Art Deco Tableware*, Rizzoli, 1988. David Serpell, *Collecting Carlton Ware*, Krause Publications, 1999.

Collectors' Club: Carlton Ware Collectors International, Helen and Keith Martin, P.O. Box 161, Seven Oaks, Kent TN15 6GA England, Membership: $55.00, four magazines per year, *The Carlton Times*. Carlton Ware Collectors Club, Leley Crowther at Fraces Joseph, 5 Southbrook Mews, London SE 12 8 LG.

Collecting Hints: Collectors have given their own names to many patterns where the names are not known. Most patterns can be identified by pattern number, but some patterns were made in several background colors, so the same numbers are repeated.

Biscuit Barrel, SP rim, cov, and overhead handle
  6" h, "Peony" pattern, multicolored oriental flower scene, bluebird mk, ... **285.00**
  6 5/8" h, "Fantasia" ware, multicolored scenes from "Flower Fairy," **70.00**

Bowl
  7 1/4" d, pedestal base, lg purple, yellow, red, and blue hollyhocks, green leaves, lustered, mottled orange ground, ... **345.00**
  8" w, lobed triangle shape, red, orange, or purple anemones, green foliage, ... **45.00**

9" d, Rouge Royal, green, yellow, and orange enameled grasses, insects, and spider web on int, red luster ground, wavy gold rim, ... **350.00**
10 1/4" d, molded conc rings, mauve ground w/blue sponging, ... **25.00**
12 1/4" l, oval, pedestal base, green and black weeping tree w/orange blossoms on cream ground, lustered orange mottled handles and foot, scalloped rim, ... **295.00**

Bud Vase, 6" h, swollen base, long narrow neck, flared rim, multicolored Egyptian designs, gilt accents, mkd, ... **265.00**

Charger, 13" d, "Mephisto," HP red devil w/black shadow on red brick road, yellow, red, and blue stylized flames, black clouds, Lorna Bailey, ... **120.00**

Chocolate Cup, 4 1/4" h, Australian Ware, "Flowers and Basket" pattern, mauve and red flowers, green relief woven ground, yellow relief molded woven handle, ... **30.00**

Cup and Saucer, Demitasse, gold stems, gold outlined dk blue leaves, white enameled berries, mottled blue ground, gold rims, handle, and int, ... **38.00**

Dish
  7" l x 6 1/2" w, lime green molded water lily head, ... **28.00**
  7 1/4" l, leaf shape, cream w/red and white flowerhead, green leaves, brown branch handle, ... **15.00**
  8" l x 5 1/2" w, oak leaf shape, relief of dk brown branch w/yellow and rust brown acorns on blue-grey radiating ground, ... **15.00**
  11" l x 9" w x 4" h, pedestal base, Australian Ware, leaf molded yellow ground w/relief of purple foxglove and foliage, ... **35.00**

Egg Cup, 2 1/2" h, "Walking Ware," figural egg, green figural shoes, ... **20.00**

Egg Dish, 13 1/2" d, Australian Ware, red lobster in center, white coral textured ground, ... **55.00**

Flower Holder, 10" d, "Harebell," purple, yellow, and pink flowers, blue ground, ... **395.00**

Ginger Jar, 7 3/4" h, "Rouge Royale," enameled white and multicolored flowers, shaded green leaves, burgundy luster ground, "Carlton Ware Made in England Trademark" mark, $595.00

Ginger Jar, 7 1/2" h, enameled orange, lt and dk green, and red swimming oriental bird under trees w/hanging willow leaves, Rouge Royal ground, ... **245.00**

Gravy Boat, 7" l, w/underplate, Australian Ware, red convolvulus, green foliage on sides, lt green ground, ... **15.00**

Honey Jar, Cov, 4 1/2" h, Australian Ware, "Foxglove" pattern, tan leaf ground, ... **90.00**

Jam Dish, 3 1/2" w, Australian Ware, figural buttercup blossom, orange w/green stamen and stem handle, ... **30.00**

Jar, Cov
  9" h
    "Handcraft," pink and white flowers, grey and black branches, blue mottled ground, gold Foo dog knob, ... **350.00**
    Orange, green, aqua, lavender, and yellow enamel and gold oriental man and woman w/fans near house, birds in sky, lacy gold bands on base w/blue flowers, dk blue ground, domed cov, ... **425.00**
  14 1/2" h, paneled, multicolored enameled oriental scenes of pagodas, bridges, and trees, gilt accents, teal green ground, gilt Foo dog knob, pr, ... **1,695.00**

Jug
  2" h, Australian Ware, brown gum nuts, green textured ground, ... **25.00**

6" h, "Silk Sand," lt green glaze, gold trim and handle, ... **30.00**

6 1/8" h, musical, "Doing The Lambeth Walk," figural rose head handle, ... **445.00**

Lamp Base, 8" h, orange, green, maroon, and gold flying Chinese bird, dk blue luster ground, MOP int, ... **495.00**

Mug

3 1/2" h, bust of 2 men, whiskey bottle, and "We are given our relations, thank God we can choose our friends," saying on reverse, green lined rim, ... **35.00**

Pitcher, 7 1/4" h, Rouge Royal, green, orange, and yellow enamels, gold accents, gold handle, "Carlton Rouge Royal" mk, $240.00

5 1/4" h, hanging Pilgrim, black suit, brown tree, whiskey bottle in green wreath on side and "In loving memory," and "There are several reasons for drinking...," blue base and rim, figural red devil handle, repaired chip, ... **65.00**

Pitcher

6" h, "Vert Royal" glaze, eggshell int, gold handle, ... **45.00**

6 3/4" h, "Rouge Royal," lg enameled green, orange, and white flying bird, gold accents, gold rect handle, MOP int, ... **475.00**

Plate, 11 1/4" d, Australian Ware, lg red hydrangea, green stem and leaves, molded border, cream ground, shaped indented rim, ... **85.00**

Preserve Jar, Australian Ware

3" h, lt green lobed body, HP relief of cherries on cov, green stem knob, ... **30.00**

4 1/8" h, relief molded red foxglove, green shading, ... **50.00**

Serving Dish, 11 1/4" d, 5 section, yellow textured center shaded to orange rim, ... **35.00**

Teapot

6" h, "Aeroplane," figural white biplane, brown pilot wearing goggles, ... **160.00**

8" h, black and white standing figural cat, brown and white mouse knob, ... **60.00**

9 1/2" h, lighthouse shape, yellow w/dk brown band of paisley curls on base, dk brown knob, ... **20.00**

Tennis Set, 8 1/2" w, triangle shaped saucer, printed yellow buttercups, yellow lined edge on one side of saucer, ... **12.00**

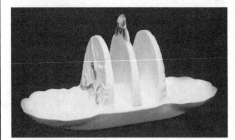

Toast Rack, 4" h x 7 3/4" l, Australian Ware, yellow body w/yellow overlapping leaves on bars, lt pink flowers on end, sm red flower on top, $85.00

Toast Rack, 2" h x 4 1/2" l, 3 bar, Art Deco style, orange and black edges, orange or black end handles, cream ground, ... **60.00**

Vase

4 1/8" h, Australian Ware, overlapped swirl shape, mint green, gold trim, ... **30.00**

4 1/2" h, blue lustered squat base and trumpet neck, 2 gilt dbl loop handles, pearl luster int, .. **30.00**

7 1/2" h

Swollen shape, short collar, "Devil's Copse" pattern, enameled and gilt florals on cobalt luster ground, shape #456, (A), ... **495.00**

Tapered form w/horiz ribbed base, "Bleu Celeste" glaze, MOP int, ... **250.00**

11" h, swollen base, spread ft, long trumpet neck, multicolored enamel and gilt oriental man paddling boat w/ladies, temple on shore and bridge, dk blue ground, MOP int, ... **345.00**

Vase, Cov

7 3/8" h, swollen shape, gold outlined multicolored luster oriental home, woman, and man, luster blue ground, gold outlined pagoda cov w/gold knob, ... **245.00**

9 3/8" h, ovoid, flared base, "Rosetta" pattern, enameled lt blue, orange, and blue flowers, black stems, mustard yellow ground, gold accents, (A), ... **1,145.00**

1775-90   c 1775-1790

CAUGHLEY

Royal Salopian Porcelain Manufactory Shropshire, England c1775-1799

History: Thomas Turner, who received his training at the Worcester porcelain factory, converted an existing pottery at Caughley in Shropshire in 1772 to make possible the manufacture of porcelain products. He developed a uniformly smooth, transparent glaze that lent itself well to the transfer printed decorations. Basic Caughley porcelain had a white soapstone body.

Blue and white ware with printed transfer decorations in a Chinese design was the chief item of manufacture. The "willow pattern," c1780, and the "Broseley dragon" were two of the most characteristic and popular Caughley patterns. Sometimes the Caughley blue and white china was painted in underglaze blue as well as transfer printed. The china often was enriched with bands of gilding.

Turner established a London warehouse called the "Salopian China Warehouse" in 1780 for the sale of Caughley chinaware. Tablewares, tea and coffee services, and other utilitarian items were the chief Caughley products. Few decorative pieces were made.

In 1870 Turner brought back several French china decorators, leading to a greater variety in decoration. Turner sent some of his porcelain pieces to be gilded and enameled at the Chamberlain factory at Worcester. By 1796 hard paste porcelain was introduced.

The factory was taken over by John Rose of nearby Coalport in 1799 and continued to offer whiteware for decoration at London and Coalport until its closing in 1814.

References: G.A. Godden, *Caughley & Worcester Porcelains, 1775-1800*, Herbert Jenkins, 1969.

Museums: Clive House Museum, Strewbury, England; Metropolitan Museum of Art, New York, NY; Victoria & Albert Museum, London, England.

Teabowl and Saucer, blue printed "Pagoda" pattern, gilt trim, "blue S" mk, $385.00

Asparagus Holder, 3" l, blue printed "Fisherman" pattern, "blue S" mk, c1785, pr, ... **545.00**

Basket, 9 1/2" l x 7 3/4" w x 3 3/4" h, reticulated, 2 handles, blue printed "Pine Cone" pattern, c1780, ... **3,920.00**

Berry Bowl, 11" l, kidney shape, underglazed blue and gilded flowers, leaves, and festoons, palmate border, "blue S" mk, ... **750.00**

Bottle, 10" h, blue printed "Fisherman" pattern, "blue S" mk, (A), .. **1,765.00**

Butter Boat
2 3/4" w, leaf shape, 3 pad feet, blue printed oriental scene of man, house, and mountains, blue cell border, "blue S" mk, ... **220.00**
4" l x 2 1/2" h, underglazed blue oriental temple and trees, blue lined rim, "blue S" mk, .. **300.00**

Coffee Cup
"Fence and House" pattern, blue, "blue S" mk, c1785, ... **315.00**
"Fenced Garden" pattern, blue, c1785, ... **320.00**
"Tower" pattern, blue, gilt foot and handle, ... **345.00**

Coffee Cup and Saucer, blue printed "Temple" pattern, gilt rims, "S" mk, ... **235.00**

Coffeepot, 9" h, baluster shape, blue printed "Three Flower" pattern, scrolling ring knob, c1776, (A), ... **795.00**

Cream Jug, 3 3/4" h, blue printed "Fence" pattern, "blue S" mk, c1780, ... **185.00**

Cup, "Mansfield" pattern, underglazed blue print, c1770, ... **300.00**

Cup and Saucer, meandering gilt buds and vine, cobalt border band w/gilt

ovals and lines, "blue S" mk, ... **160.00**

Creamer, 4" h, overglazed gold design, black florals, c1810. $125.00

Dessert Dish, Shell Shape
6 1/2" l x 5 1/2" w, blue printed "Fisherman" pattern, cell border, c1770, ... **655.00**
8 1/8" l x 7 3/4" w, blue printed "Full Nankin" pattern, "S" mk, c1785, ... **220.00**

Egg Strainer, 3 3/4" w, bowl w/blue painted flowers and radiating triangular piercing, shell molded handle, "blue S" mk, ... **570.00**

Jug, 5" h, blue, rust, and black transfer of fishing before castle, Salopian, $295.00

Jug, 9" h, molded cabbage leaf body, underglazed blue flower sprays, mask head spout, C-scroll handle, "blue C" mk, c1785, ... **1,050.00**

Mug
4 1/2" h, blue printed "Parrot Pecking Fruit" pattern, ... **450.00**
5 1/4" h, cold gilt and brown armorial crest of William, Earl of Essex, initialed badge and lion crest on sides, c1790, ... **2,370.00**
5 1/2" h, blue printed "La Promenade Chinoise" and "La Peche" patterns, C shaped handle, "blue C" mk, c1780, ... **1,065.00**

Pickle Dish, 4 3/4" w, leaf shape, blue printed "Fisherman" pattern, c1785, ... **135.00**

Plate
8" d, pearlware, blue printed carnation and sprigs in center, molded panels of basketweaving, blue lobed rim, "blue S" mk, ... **190.00**
8 1/4" d
Blue carnation in center, paneled and lobed basketweave border, "blue S" mk, chips, ... **150.00**
Blue printed "Temple" pattern, half chrysanthemums, florals, and cell designs on border, indented rim, "blue S" mk, ... **275.00**
8 3/4" d, oct, blue printed "Full Nankin" pattern, Fitzhugh-type border, ... **725.00**
9 1/4" d, blue printed bouquet and insects in center, half circles inner border, blue feathered edge, "blue S" mk, ... **200.00**

Platter, 22" l x 17 1/2" w, oct, "Full Nanking" pattern, blue transfer, ... **2,400.00**

Sweetmeat Dish, 6 1/4" d, blue printed, A- $495.00

Sauceboat
6 1/2" l, blue printed "Doughnut Tree" pattern, ... **650.00**
6 3/4" l, lobed, blue printed oriental landscape scene, med blue transfer, ... **550.00**

Spoon Tray, 6 1/4" l x 3 1/4" w, blue printed "Pagoda" pattern, gilt lined wavy rim, c1785, ... **175.00**

Tankard, 4" h, underglazed blue sliced fruit and flowers on sides and handle, solid blue crescent mk, hairline, ... **165.00**

Teabowl, fluted, blue pagoda design, blue inner sprig, blue swirl inner band, ... **40.00**

Teabowl and Saucer
Blue printed "Pagoda" pattern, gilt rims, "S" mk, ... **250.00**
Flute, blue and gilt "Dresden Sprig" pattern, c1785, ... **50.00**
Fluted, gilt sprigs and rims, .. **75.00**

Tea Caddy
3 1/2" h, blue printed "Three Flower" pattern, "blue C" on base, rim chips, ... **285.00**
4 1/2" h, barrel shape, blue printed bouquet of garden flowers, "blue S" mk, ... **550.00**

Teapot, 5 1/2" h, blue printed "Fisherman" pattern, cell and foliate borders, "blue S" mk, (A), ... **560.00**

Teapot Stand, 6" l x 5" w, oval, blue painted oriental tower design, scalloped edge, ... **375.00**

Waste Bowl, 6" d, half fluted, ftd, blue printed pagoda and lg tree on ext, blue cell int border, ... **220.00**

Wine Taster, 2 1/8" w, blue printed "Fisherman" pattern, leaf handle, c1780, ... **485.00**

CAULDON ENGLAND
1905-20

CAULDON

Shelton, Hanley, England
1905-1962

History: This Staffordshire pottery, a direct descendant of the Ridgway potteries, operated from 1905 to 1920 at Cauldon Place, Shelton, Hanley. After John Ridgway dissolved his partnership with William, his brother, in 1830, he operated the Cauldon Place Works. A wide variety of china and earthenware was made, including utilitarian and decorative pieces.

Ridgway sold to T.C. Brown-Westhead, Moore & Company in 1855. Brown-Westhead, Moore & Co. (1862-1904) became Cauldon Ltd. in 1905. From 1920 to 1962, the firm operated as Cauldon Potteries, Ltd., at which time it became known as Cauldon Bristol Potteries, Ltd. It was eventually acquired by Pountney & Co. Ltd. of Boston in 1962.

Bowl, 6" d, overall lg red, yellow, and white peonies, blue-green stems and leaves, c1886, set of 4, ... **105.00**

Candlestick, 6" h, cobalt ground w/gilt oriental pagoda designs, gold handle, gold lined pinched rim, "Cauldon England" mk, ... **60.00**

Coffeepot, 7 3/4" h, "Pershore" pattern, ... **50.00**

Creamer, 4" h
Blue chrysanthemums and foliage, thumb rest on handle, ... **30.00**
Two dragons, floral reserves, diaper border and base, blue transfer, gilt accents, ... **145.00**

Cup and Saucer
Band of blue dragons and oriental foliage, gilt lined rim, "dragon, Cauldon England" mk,
.... **15.00**
"Barberry" pattern, Royal Cauldon,
.... **30.00**
Vert gold stripes, "CAULDON ENGLAND" mk, c1910,
.... **30.00**

Jug
4" h, blue and white dragons, floral reserves, diaper borders top and base, ... **125.00**
7" h, Art Deco style, "Arabian" pattern, gold outlined med blue, white, cream, orange, and blue-black circles and geometrics, blue collar and handle,
.... **100.00**

Pin Tray, 6" l x 4" w, rect w/indented sides, Roman chariot and horses before temple, fleur-de-lys and scale border, rope rim, blue transfer, "Cauldon, England" mk, ... **40.00**

Pitcher, 4" h, "The Triumphal Car" pattern, horse drawn chariot and driver before ancient temple, med blue transfer, "Cauldon England" mk,
.... **35.00**

Plate
8 1/8" d, blue starburst in center flanked by curlicues and swirls, blue zigzag border, gold rim, "CAULDON LTD ENGLAND" mk,
.... **20.00**
8 7/8" d, "Corinthian Flute" pattern, cobalt transfer, "J.R. CORINTHIAN FLUTE CAULDON ENGLAND" mk, ... **30.00**
9" d
Berries and leaves in center, basketweave molded border, lobed rim, cobalt transfer,
.... **10.00**
Multicolored design of "Eastern Bluebird" in center, emb

border, lobed rim, "Royal Cauldon" mk, ... **10.00**
9 1/4" d, apple green border w/3 gilt scroll and flowerhead reserves of multicolored flowers, rim band of gilt arrowhead leaves and berries, "Cauldon England" mk, set of 5, ... **350.00**
9 1/2" d, multicolored butterflies in center, relief molded textured border, "Butterflies of the World" series, ... **10.00**
10" d
Multicolored turkey walking in field, floral border, beaded lobed rim, blue transfer, "blue CAULDON ENGLAND" and "imp CAULDON" mks, c1900, (A), ... **302.00**
"Victoria" pattern, mauve, blue, green, and yellow floral and diaper border, "Royal Cauldon" mk, ... **10.00**
10 1/4" d
Greek columns, red tinged roses and cobalt leaves in center, blue Moresque type border w/cell design and hanging red roses or yellow daffodils, gilt rim, ... **10.00**
HP yellow outlined orchid colored lilies, green leaves in center, border band of lilies, buds, and foliage, "imp Cauldon" mk, ... **25.00**

Plate, 10 1/2" d, multicolored, "Cauldon England" mk, **$89.00**

10 1/2" d, multicolored transfer of red-coated hunter and horse falling over broken fence, "Cauldon, England" mk,
.... **195.00**

Plate, 10 1/2" d, banded and stamped parcil gilt and cobalt border, "green Cauldon China England" mark, set of 12, (A) **$715.00**

Platter, 15" l x 10 1/2" w, "Blue May" pattern, blue transfer, ... **22.00**

Platter, 17" l x 12 1/2" w, "Teutonic" pattern, blue transfer, "Cauldon England" mk, **$365.00**

Sandwich Plate, 10 1/2" H-H, border transfer of blue foliage, florals, and fruit, gold accented molded open handles, shaped gold lined rim, ... **15.00**

Soup Plate, 9" d, "Dragon" pattern on rim, blue transfer, ... **20.00**

Teapot, 6" h, Roman scenery of temple, charioteers, fan and geometrics on borders, blue transfers, hairlines, ... **135.00**

Turkey Set, platter, 21 1/4" l x 18" w, 8 plates, 10" d, center multicolored transfers of turkey in field, border of meandering vines, leaves, and flying game birds, band of sm flowerheads on shaped rims, ... **595.00**

Urn, 13 1/4" h, underglazed blue chintz type florals w/overglazed iron-red, yellow, and purple accents, 2 arched handles, c1910, ... **375.00**

Vegetable Bowl, Cov, 12" H-H, oval, multicolored transfer border bands of florals and foliage, brown outlined

handle and floral terminals, "Cauldon England" mk, hairlines, ... **75.00**

Vegetable Bowl, Cov, 10 1/2" H-H, pink and yellow flowers, lt blue ground, gold outlined handles and knob, "Royal Cauldon" mk, **$110.00**

Bursley-Ware Charlotte Rhead England

c. 1920s

CHARLOTTE RHEAD

Tunstall, England
1912-1960

History: Charlotte Rhead came from a family of designers connected to English potteries since the 18th century. She was trained with her sister Dolly by her father, Frederick, and her brothers. Charlotte joined her father at Wood and Sons in 1912 and remained there until 1926. Her works were not signed while she worked at Wood. Popular patterns from that period were "Seed Poppy" and "Pomona." Charlotte also worked for a Woods subsidiary—Ellgreave Pottery—and created "Lottie Rhead Ware" there.

Tube lining became Charlotte Rhead's signature while she worked at Burgess and Leigh from 1926 until 1931. She trained workers at this firm to execute her designs with tube lining techniques. Charlotte designed tablewares and sandwich sets at Burgess and Leigh, using designs such as "Paisley" pattern for tablewares and the Richmond shape for sandwich sets.

Charlotte made many successful patterns for Burgess and Leigh, such as "Florentine," "Sylvan," "Garland," and "Laurel Band." All her works from this time were signed "L. Rhead" along with the Burleigh Ware backstamp. Charlotte often wrote the "C" of her signature as an "L" with a long underline since she preferred to be known as Lottie. The number in the mark refers to the pattern. Fruits and flowers were the central motifs of her patterns. She also experimented with luster during this time.

The pattern "Carnival" was done in bright colors to compete with patterns from Clarice Cliff, Susie Cooper, and inexpensive Czechoslovakian imports entering England at this time.

In 1931 Charlotte Rhead moved on to A.G. Richardson (Crown Ducal) and remained there for more than a decade. There, her artistic and technical influences were seen in their ceramics. Although she designed a range of tablewares and utilitarian pieces, she is well known for her art ware and tube-lined designs for lamp bases, vases, bowls, and wall chargers called Rhodian ware.

Charlotte experimented with various glazes and lusters. Some patterns had a mottled effect such as "Persian Rose" and "Granada." In 1936, her snow glaze was used on "Foxglove" and "Wisteria." "Stitch" and "Patch" were produced by trainees from Rhead designs and were never marked with the Rhead signature. Other patterns included "Byzantine," "Persian Rose," and "Golden Leaves." Most other patterns have the Richardson trademark "Crown Ducal" with a tube-lined "C. Rhead."

During World War II, there was a large drop in pottery production, and in 1942 Charlotte was unemployed. She then worked for Harry Wood with a new range of tube-lined wares for H.J. Wood Ltd. Most of these examples were made for export during and immediately after the war. Although Charlotte died in 1947, her designs continued to be made until 1960.

References: John Barlett, *English Decorative Ceramics 1875-1939*, Kevin Frances Publishing, 1989; Bernard Bumpus, *Charlotte Rhead: Potter & Designer*, Kevin Frances Publishing, 1987; Susan Scott, *Charlotte Rhead Ceramics*, Antique Trader Weekly, August 31, 1994; Judy Spours, *Art Deco Tableware*, Rizzoli International Publications, 1988. Bernard Bumpus, *Collecting Rhead Pottery, Charlotte, Frederick, Frederick Hurten*, Francis Joseph Publications, 1999.

Bowl, 11 1/2" H-H x 6 1/2" h, orange, dk brown, and green flowers, tan leaves, orange and green dashes, cream ground, tan handles, orange lined int, sgd "Rhead," "Crown Ducal Made in England" mk, **$590.00**

Basket, 2 3/4" h x 6" l x 4 1/2" w, Bursley Ware, orange centered blue flowerheads, blue-green leaves, yellow ground, gilt accents, blue-green mottled ext and overhead handle, mkd, ... **175.00**

Bon Bon Basket, 6" h x 6 1/2" w, "Tulip" pattern, blue trimmed yellow tulips, green overhead handle, ... **475.00**

Bowl

9" d, HP and tube-lined brown and tan oblongs w/cream curls on int, lt blue inner border band, mkd, ... **150.00**

10" d

"Padua" pattern, black, cream, orange, and red overlapping huts, #3637, ... **1,900.00**

Tube lined pink, red, and grey flowers on ext, int banding, gilt wavy rim, pattern #6778, Crown Ducal mk, ... **265.00**

Box, 5" l x 4 1/4" w, blue bellflower, curled tendrils and leaves on cov, dash border, hairpin and dot band on base, ... **225.00**

Candlestick, 2 1/4" h, boldly painted lt and dk leaves, red buds, orange ground, mkd, pr, ... **395.00**

Charger

12" d, brown spider web in center, border of orange and tan stylized flowerheads, brown leaves w/blue-green accents, gold rim, pierced for hanging, "Bursley Ware Charlotte Rhead, England" mk, ... **155.00**

12 3/4" d, tube-lined yellow centered orange, red, or blue flowerheads, green foliage, lt grey matte ground, ... **775.00**

14 1/4" d, lavender center, blue and lavender squeeze bag irises and foliage, white and grey speckled ground, lavender dot rim, (A), ... **410.00**

17 1/2" d, lg red and white flowerheads, black outlined spear leaves, mottled purple-red ground, red dash rim, mkd, ... **525.00**

Dish, 3" w, heart shape, 2 oranges on branch w/blue and green leaves, sm pale purple flowers, ... **145.00**

Ewer, 13 1/2" h, "Rustic Trellis" pattern, brown, orange, and yellow, "Bursley Ware Charlotte Rhead, England" mk, ... **700.00**

Flower Bowl, 6 1/4" d x 2 1/2" h, flattened shape, boldly painted purple and blue Art Deco style flowerheads, purple and blue circles, blue-green leaves, #TL38, ... **230.00**

Ginger Jar, 10" h, tube-lined tan, green, and red stylized flowers, green

foliage, mottled tan ground, mottled green borders top and base, blue stripes, blue half flowerheads on cov, base chip, ... **190.00**

Jar, Cov, 6 1/4" h, Bursley Ware, yellow and pink leaves, iridized leaves and trim, beige ground, ... **300.00**

Jug, 8" h, enameled orange flower and buds, green foliage on side, yellow-cream ground, ribbed orange neck, "Charlotte Rhead, Crown Ducal, Gainsborough England" mk, ... **95.00**

Jug, Bursley Ware

5 1/4" h, lg blue shaded orchid and foliage, Green key design on base, blue handle, ... **200.00**

6 1/2" h, tube-lined orange, green, and blue stylized fruit and leaves, white and blue band on throat, green handle, ... **105.00**

Pitcher, 7 1/2" h, "Arabesque," cream base w/dk brown squares, green, red, and blue flowerheads on collar, brown handle, mkd, ... **295.00**

Teapot, 4" h, "ARRAS" pattern, Bursley Ware, red, brown, and tan flower and streak designs, mkd, ... **260.00**

Urn, 9" h, tube-lined orange flowerheads, hanging blue or orange leaves, brown diagonals on collar, tan ground, ... **270.00**

Vase

5 1/2" h

Narrow base, flared body, spread ft, wavy rim, lg yellow and pink flowers, iridized leaves and trim, beige ground, ... **185.00**

Slightly bulbous shape, med blue stylized stenciled leaves and flowerheads, gold veining and dots, tan ground, "Bursley Ware Charlotte Rhead" mk, ... **135.00**

5 3/4" h, horiz lobing, tube lined apple green and dk grey interlocking loops, apple green stripes, orange stripes w/drops, cream ground, graduated apple green triple loop handles, ... **235.00**

6 1/2" h, slightly swollen shape, "Aztec" pattern, red, black, and cream stacked geometric designs, matte tan base, #2800, ... **375.00**

7 1/2" h, tapered shape, short, flared rim, "Arabesque," pink, lavender, and blue flowers, grey ground,

blue and yellow chevrons on shoulder, "Woods Arabesque Charlotte Rhead" mk, ... **210.00**

7 3/4" h, swollen shape, "Lotus Leaves" pattern, tan and brown w/lt blue accents, matte finish, ... **440.00**

8 3/4" h, slightly swollen shape, flared rim, yellow and orange stylized flowerheads, brown leaves, gold mottled ground, blue trim, ... **275.00**

12" h, ball base, long, trumpet neck, molded blue and yellow exotic birds on brown branches, blue or brown finger leaves, tan body, "Charlotte Rhead, Crown Ducal" mk, ... **110.00**

 c1752-1769

 1769-84

CHELSEA

London, England
c1745-1769

History: As early as 1745, soft paste porcelains were being manufactured in London at Chelsea, one of the most famous English porcelain factories. Nicholas Sprimont, originally a silversmith, was manager of the factory for most of its history. Chelsea porcelains were the most richly decorated of English 18th century ceramics. Pieces were ornate and made for the higher class market.

Various periods of Chelsea porcelain are classified according to the anchor-like mark. But before these were used, there was an incised triangle mark, c1745, and a painted mark of a trident piercing a crown.

From 1749 to 1752, a "raised-anchor" mark was used. This mark was relief molded on a small applied oval pad. Porcelains of this period have the tin-added glaze and mostly are decorated with oriental motifs or simple, floral designs.

The "red-anchor" period (1752-56) has the anchor painted directly on the porcelain. Small light colored "moons" can be seen on these porcelains when held up to the light.

Animal fables and botanical studies were characteristic of this period, along with florals and oriental motifs.

The Chelsea "gold-anchor" period dates between c1786 and 1769. Porcelains of this era were richly decorated and ornately gilded. The glazes tend to be thickly applied.

The anchor period dates are only approximations. More than half of all Chelsea porcelains had no mark at all.

William Duesbury of the Derby factory purchased the Chelsea factory in 1770. The wares of the 1770-1784 period are called "Chelsea-Derby." Because of the interaction of these two factories and the interchange of molds, clay, and workmen, it is difficult to distinguish between the Chelsea and Derby porcelains of this period. Further complications resulted when Duesbury used the Chelsea gold anchor mark on some Derby pieces. A "D" and anchor mark also was used, as was a crowned anchor mark. By 1784 the last of the Chelsea works was demolished and the molds and workers transferred to Derby.

References: John C. Austin, *Chelsea Porcelain at Williamsburg*, Colonial Williamsburg Foundation, 1977; John Bedford, *Chelsea & Derby China*, Walker & Co.1967; Yvonne Hackenbroch, *Chelsea and other English Porcelains, Pottery and Enamel in the Irwin Untermeyer Collection*, Harvard University Press, 1957; William King, *Chelsea Porcelain*, Benn Brothers, 1922; F. Severne Mackenna, *Chelsea Porcelain, The Triangle & Raised Anchor Wares*, F. Lewis, 1948; F. Severne Mackenna, *Chelsea Porcelain, The Red Anchor Wares*, F. Lewis, 1951; F. Severne Mackenna, *Chelsea Porcelain, The Gold Anchor Period*, F. Lewis, 1952. Elizabeth Adams, *Chelsea Porcelain*, David and Charles, 1999. Margaret Legge, *Flowers and Fables: A Survey of Chelsea Porcelain, 1745-69*, National Gallery of Victoria.

Museums: Colonial Williamsburg Foundation, Williamsburg, VA; Fine Arts Museums, San Francisco, CA; Fitzwilliam Museum, Cambridge, England; Gardiner Museum of Ceramic Art, Toronto, Canada; Henry E. Huntington Library & Art Gallery, San Marino, CA, (gold anchor); Museum of Fine Arts, Boston, MA.; Seattle Art Museum, Seattle, WA; Victoria & Albert Museum, London, England; Wadsworth Atheneum, Hartford, CT; Walters Art Gallery, Baltimore, MD.

Reproduction Alert: Samson made copies of Chelsea pieces, but these were generally marked as copies. Many forgeries and imitations are seen every year bearing red or gold anchors.

Basket

7 1/2" d, painted purple plums in center int, applied green leaves on pierced border, puce rim, "brown anchor" mk, c1760, ... **1,875.00**

11 1/4" H-H, oval, HP multicolored scattered floral sprigs in center, pierced border w/molded red or yellow flowerheads on ext intercises, green handles

wrapped w/red ribbon and flowerhead terminals, "red anchor" mk, ... **800.00**

Beaker

2 1/2" h, painting hanging floral swag, gilt dentil rim, Chelsea-Derby, c1775, chip, pr,
.... **1,035.00**

3" h, fluted, relief molded and polychrome accented "Tea Leaf" pattern, scattered flowerheads on int, brown lined scalloped rim, c1745-49, (A), ... **4,200.00**

Bowl, 9 1/2" d, painted peach, cherries, orange, lemon, and plums, stems, and foliage, scattered insects, iron-red shaped rim, c1760, "brown anchor" mk, (A), ... **1,075.00**

Candlestick, 6 5/8" h, asymmetrical scrolling shape w/flowers, applied flowers and leaves, green, puce, and gilt accents, "gold anchor" mk, c1760, firing crack, pr, (A),
.... **3,700.00**

Dessert Dish, 7 1/2" sq, gilt central classical urn and flowers, entwined gilt husk swags and scattered insects on border, green enameled scattered garden flowers on reverse, Chelsea-Derby, "gold anchor" mk,
.... **1,095.00**

Dish

7" l, dbl leaf molded, center painted w/fruit, foliage, and insects, brown lined rim, "red anchor" mk, c1758, ... **2,500.00**

Dish, 9 1/4" l, multicolored bouquet in center, puce veining, shaded yellow to green border, "red anchor" mk, **$1,400.00**

9" l, figural cabbage leaf, purple veins, painted flower spray in center, green and yellow shaded border, "red anchor" mk, c1755,
.... **450.00**

10" l, Silver Shape Burgundy, brown, blue-green, and yellow exotic birds w/green and red brown

foliage in center, green and gilt accented molded handles, swirl molded border, chocolate lined indented rim, brown anchor mk period, c1758, ... **2,500.00**

Painted iris or wild tulip, trailing iron-red leaves on reverse, molded green streaked borders, pink and gilt shell handles, "gold anchor" mks, c1760, pr, (A), ... **956.00**

10 7/8" l x 8 1/4" w, painted loose bouquet and scattered flowers in cartouches, fruit, vegetables, and flowers in center panel, claret ground w/gilt trellis work borders, turquoise and gilt feather molded border, c1760,
.... **6,500.00**

13" l, oval, 4 rococo shaped cartouches of multicolored birds, claret ground w/gold trellis work, shaped rim, c1769, gold anchor period, ... **6,500.00**

16 1/2" d, sprigs of blue, red, and yellow flowers and tulips overlapping border, shaped brown line rim, red anchor period, ... **12,000**

16 1/2" w, botanic group of yellow, brown, mauve, and blue garden flowers, molded mauve trimmed border w/shaped rim, red anchor period, c1755, ... **15,000**

Ecuelle, Cov and Stand, 7 5/8" w, painted scattered bouquets, brown line rims, branch handles, cherry knob, "red anchor" mks, c1758, (A),
.... **1,912.00**

Figure, 8 3/4" h, purple jacket, yellow dress, iron red, black, and green trim, gilt scrolled base, "gold anchor" mark, **$1,100.00**

Figure, 8 1/4" h, white, gold trim, restored, unmkd, $900.00

Figure, 2 1/4" h x 2 1/8" l, standing grey shaded billy goat, applied flowerheads on gilt lined oval base, "gold anchor" mk, ... **495.00**

Plate

7 1/2" sq, classic urn w/flowers and insects in center, entwined green husk swag border, green sprigs on reverse, gilt dentil rim, Chelsea-Derby, ... **1,100.00**

8 3/8" d, lg painted exotic bird on rock ledge, green foliage in center, 2 sm exotic birds and foliage on border, brown branch and green foliage molded rim, "brown or gold anchor" mks, pr, (A), ... **4,540.00**

8 1/2" d

Multicolored fruit and butterflies, turquoise shaped rim, "red anchor" mk, c1755, ... **2,200.00**

Overall botanical of red flowers, green foliage, shaped rim, "brown anchor" mk, c1758, ... **870.00**

Painted specimen honeysuckle and rose, brown lined shaped rim, "brown anchor" mk, c1759, (A), ... **300.00**

8 5/8" d, oct, HP orchid specimen in center, 3 insects, 2 sprigs on border, brown lined lobed rim, c1760, (A), ... **10,930.00**

8 3/4" d, 3 gilt edged cornucopia cartouches w/HP flying exotic birds, claret ground w/gilt ribbon tied swags and scattered sprigs, "gold anchor" mk, c1768, (A), ... **4,780.00**

9" d

Meissen style painted bouquet in center, relief molded florals on border w/4 panels of painted sprigs, "red anchor" mk, ... **975.00**

Scattered floral sprigs in center, rococo molded gilt border w/multicolored exotic birds in foliage, c1760, ... **980.00**

Silver shape, HP Meissen style floral bouquet and scattered sprigs, indented chocolate lined rim, "red anchor" mk, c1755, ... **250.00**

9 1/2" d, basket molded center w/painted bouquet of flowers, pierced woven basketweave border w/green applied leaves, "red anchor" mk, c1756, restorations, ... **2,395.00**

10" d, iron-red and cobalt "Brocade" pattern, c1755, ... **2,100.00**

Sauceboat, 7 1/2" l, leaf shape, painted loose sprays of flowers and sprigs on sides, 4 leaf molded feet, green branch handle w/strawberries from green leaf terminals, brown lined rim, "red anchor" mk, c1765, (A), ... **795.00**

Teabowl and Saucer, fluted, Kakiemon enamel painted butterflies, prunus, and bamboo, scalloped rims, restorations, c1750-52, (A), ... **1,285.00**

Tray, 10 1/2" l, magenta, red, yellow, and grey bird, lt blue and gold border, "brown anchor" mark, $1,500.00

Vase, 7 1/4" h, flattened baluster form, painted lg exotic birds on ground and in branches, reverse w/birds perched on leafy branches, puce, turquoise, and gilt dbl rococo handles, gilt lined rim, "gold anchor" mk, pr, (A), ... **1,425.00**

CHILDREN'S WARE

English/German
Late 17th C to Present

History: Initially, miniature English china dinnerware sets were made primarily to furnish miniature decorative rooms, but by the late 19th century, the emphasis had shifted. Most of these dinnerware and tea sets now were made as children's playthings. They served a dual purpose—first as playthings and second as a means of teaching social graces to children of wealthy families.

Children's dinnerware sets were made in two basic sizes. One size was used by children to entertain their friends. A smaller size was used when playing with dolls. Various designs were used on these sets, including historical scenes, moral and educational phrases, botanical lessons, and art works of famous illustrators.

Children's feeding dishes, often divided into sections, were made during the late 19th and early 20th century, and were used for children's meals. Many have a unit to hold hot water to keep the food warm during the meal. These dishes were designed with colorful animals, nursery rhymes, and children's activities to make mealtime fun for the child.

German children's dishes also were designed with rhymes, animals, children, and florals. Paints, decals, and lusters were used in abundance on these dishes. Among the leading German manufacturers was the R.S. Prussia factory of Schlegelmilch.

References: Maureen Batkin, *Gifts for Good Children Vol. 2*, Richard Dennis, 1996; Doris Anderson Lechler, *Children's Glass Dishes, China, & Furniture*, Collector Books, 1983; *Volume 2*, 1986; Doris Anderson Lechler, *English Toy China*, Antique Publications, 1990; Lorraine May Punchard, *Child's Play*, published by the author, 1982; Lorraine Punchard, *Playtime Pottery and Porcelain from Europe and Asia*, Schiffer Publishing Ltd. l996; Noel Riley, *Gifts for Good Children, Vol. 1*, Richard Dennis, 1991; Margaret & Kenn Whitmyer, *Children's Dishes, Collector Books*, 1984. Lorraine Punchard, *200 Years of Playtime Pottery & Porcelain 2003 Values*, Schiffer Publications, 2003.

Collectors' Club: Toy Dish Collectors' Club, Shelley Smith, Box 159, Bethlehem, CT 06751, Membership: $25.00, Quarterly newsletter. Treasures For Little Children, *Tiny Times Quarterly*, Lorraine Punchard, 8201 Pleasant Ave, Bloomington, MO.

Museums: Museum of Childhood, Douglasville, PA.

Chocolate Service, pot, 6 3/4" h, 6 cups, 6 plates, 5" d, multicolored transfers, gold trim, "red GERMANY" mks, $190.00

Mug

2 1/2" h

"Wooden Bowls and Spoons," black transfer of salesman, houses in bkd w/housewives, polychrome accents, red stripe on int, (A), ... **145.00**

2 5/8" h

"A Present For A Good Boy," children at play, green transfer, ... **195.00**

Two strolling cats in woods, brown transfer w/color accents, crazing, ... **20.00**

2 3/4" h

"A BROTHER'S GIFT" in wreath, "JOSIAH" on reverse, green transfers, ... **275.00**

Black transfers of "YOUNG COTTAGERS," mother and 2 children before cottage, reverse w/"On Time" verse, ... **100.00**

Boys playing ball and "Cricket," green transfer, leaf designs on handle terminals, ... **250.00**

Children playing lawn bowling, blue transfer w/yellow and green accents, strap handle w/trefoil terminals, hairlines, ... **145.00**

Cottage design, "Have a little drink," Torquay, ... **55.00**

"FRENCH AND ENGLISH," black transfer w/polychrome accents of children playing tug of war, ... **425.00**

Occupational-"The HP Gatherer," black transfer w/green, red, and yellow accents, . **195.00**

Ribbon cartouche w/"If You Would Have Business Done, Go If Not Send," black transfer, ... **225.00**

2 7/8" h, "FOOTBALL" design, black transfer w/green, red, blue, and yellow overlay, c1850, (A), ... **385.00**

3" h

Christening, gold "Emma" on front, ... **135.00**

Cowboy design on front, horse on reverse, orange and yellow inner rim stripes, Susie Cooper, ... **125.00**

Little girls, geese, and doll, brown transfer w/pink, blue, green, and yellow enamel accents, ... **295.00**

Multicolored Decal

Children grooming sheep, "OG Germany" mk, ... **50.00**

Humpty Dumpty on wall, "raised Made in England" mk, ... **10.00**

Plate

4 7/8" d

Black transfer of "Eagle" in center w/rabbit in talons, emb rose, thistle, and shamrock orange luster border, (A), ... **253.00**

Rabbit in leaves in center, blue transfer, raised Roman and Arabic numbers on border, c1840, ... **300.00**

5" d

Black printed rural scene of couple milking cow, molded rim, c1830, Swansea, ... **95.00**

"INDIAN ANTELOPE," teal green transfer, ... **125.00**

5 3/8" d, woman and 3 children standing under umbrellas, purple transfer, raised daisy heads on border, purple lined rim, ... **75.00**

6" d

Black transfer of "Diverting History of John Gilpin," comical man riding running horse through town, molded clover border, ... **130.00**

Multicolored decal of "The House That Jack Built" in center, rooster, rabbit, and cat on border, gold rim, Germany, ... **40.00**

Plate, 6 3/4" d, multicolored scene on grey-black transfer, emb flowerhead border, copper luster rim, $125.00

Overall pink luster w/heart shaped center w/multicolored

decal of children playing tea party, ... **28.00**

6 3/8" d, bird in flowering branch, black transfer w/red, yellow, and green accents, relief molded floral border, unmkd, ... **90.00**

6 1/2" d

Multicolored Decal

Roosevelt bears playing various sports, "B. & S. Austria" mk, ... **100.00**

Three mice dressed in clothes and "Three Blind Mice-See How They Run," pink inner line and rim, Swinnertons, ... **65.00**

Oct, "The FAVOURITE," black transfer w/red, blue, green, and yellow tints, cat seated on stool, little girl at side, molded daisy border, blue lined rim, ... **150.00**

Purple transfer of boy and begging dog, relief molded flower and leaf border, purple lined rim, ... **75.00**

"Syntax Sketching the Lake," brown transfer w/blue, green, orange, and yellow clobbering, molded rosehead border, ... **525.00**

7" d, "Pixie-I TOOK SOME FAIRIES IN MY PLANE, SOME WANTED...," Mabel Lucie Attwell, Shelley, ... **200.00**

7" w, oct

"Father Mathew-May God Bless You...," black transfer w/blue, green, and red accents, 2 blue beaded stripes on half loop and curlicue molded border, ... **120.00**

Multicolored transfer of Robinson Crusoe and Friday, relief molded border, serrated rim, ... **110.00**

7 1/2" d, multicolored decal of "Little Boy Blue," Wileman Shelley, ... **90.00**

7 5/8" d, "Gathering Flowers," 2 children picking flowers, brown transfer, raised enameled flowers in border segments, ... **125.00**

8" d, blue printed Scottish Highland dancers, relief molded daisy border, "Moore & Co." mk, ... **50.00**

Platter 4 1/2" l x 3 1/2" w, Toy "Chinese Bells" pattern, mulberry transfer, ... **195.00**

Pearlware, red-purple printed seated mother w/child in lap holding baby's bonnet overhead, blue lined rim, ... **85.00**

Soup Plate, 3 1/4" d, creamware, Wedgwood, set of 6, ... **180.00**

Teapot, 4 1/2" h, pastoral scene w/cows and pillars, flower band on lid, red transfers, "DAVENPORT" mk, ... **185.00**

Tea Service

Five Piece, pot, 5 3/4" h, cream jug, 2 3/4" h, cov sugar bowl, 3 3/4" h, 2 cups and saucers, vert fluting, black printed oval of children playing w/balloons or kites, red, yellow, and blue accents, ... **200.00**

Seven piece

Pot, 5 1/2" h, creamer, 3" w, sugar bowl, 4" d, 4 cups and saucers, "Humphrey's Clock" pattern, blue transfers, ... **595.00**

Pot, 6" h, creamer, 2 3/4" h, sugar bowl, 2" h, 2 cups and saucers, decal of dbl red roses, original box, Germany, ... **75.00**

Pot, 6 1/2" h, creamers, 3 1/2" h, cov sugar bowl, 4 1/2" h, 4 cups and saucers, wide green center bands around center and covs, Germany, ... **250.00**

Pot, 8 1/2" h, creamer, 2 1/4" h, cov sugar bowl, 2 1/4" h, 4 cups and saucers, yellow ext, white int on cups w/multicolored bouquet of flowers, Czechoslovakia, ... **175.00**

Nine piece, pot, 4 1/2" h, creamer, 3 1/8" h, cov sugar bowl, 4" h x 4 3/4" H-H, 2 cups, 4 plates, 5" d, "Girl With Goat" pattern, red transfers, chips and stains, unmkd, (A), ... **385.00**

Twelve piece, pot, 4 1/2" h x 6 1/2" w, creamer, 3" w, sugar bowl, 3 1/4" d, 4 cups and saucers, serving plate, 5 3/4" sq, 4 plates, 5 1/2" d, "blue Spode's Towers" pattern, ... **1,995.00**

Tete-a-Tete, pot, 2 3/4" h, creamer, 1 1/4" h, cov sugar bowl, 1 3/4" h, 2 cups and saucers, tray, 6" l x 3 1/2" w, gold ribbed waves on bases and rims, gold handles, Germany, c1910, ... **185.00**

CHINTZ CHINA

Stoke-on-Trent, Staffordshire, England
1880s-Present

History: The earliest chintz wares date back to the 1800s when transfer printing was popular. Today's collectors seek chintz china that was made from the 1930s to the 1960s.

Royal Winton
Stoke-on-Trent, England
1886-Present

History: The Grimwade brothers firm was founded in 1885 by Leonard, Edward, and Sidney Grimwade at Winton Pottery in Stoke-on-Trent. They immediately started adding additional companies and built a new pottery. In 1900 they changed the name to Grimwades, Ltd. By 1913 they were one of the largest pottery firms in the area.

Royal Winton was the pre-eminent producer of chintz china since it made more than sixty patterns from the late 1920s to the 1960s. The early chintz china patterns were tightly grouped small floral patterns reminiscent of chintz fabrics.

"Marguerite" was Royal Winton's first pattern made in 1928. The chintz pattern was applied by the lithographic process. Many patterns were similar to each other. The pattern name was often incorporated into the back-stamp, while the name impressed in the body of the piece was a shape name.

In 1931 "Delphinium" was added, 1932 saw "Summertime," and by 1936 there were "Queen Anne," "Cranstone," "Sweet Pea," and "Hazel." Shapes included Ascot, Norman, Countess, Athena, and Rose Violet. Nearly all the chintz pieces that came in a tremendous variety of sizes and shapes were marked. Chintz china was earthenware, not expensive china.

Cake plates, trays, salt and pepper sets, teapots, vases, honey pots, sugar bowls, creamers, cruet sets, nut dishes, divided sweet-meat dishes, plates, cups and saucers, and platters were made in the delightful and colorful chintz patterns.

Pattern names were mostly taken from English garden flowers, girls' names, or places. Some chintz patterns were used by several firms with different names. Fac-tories were always looking to create new shapes as well as patterns.

Highly sought out Royal Winton examples include breakfast sets, condiments, teapots, and unusual sizes and shapes in the popular patterns. Black background patterns such as "Hazel," "Majestic," "Balmoral," and "Florence" are very desirable.

During World War II and until 1952, the British government restricted potteries from making products with a design; they could only make undecorated ware. Some decorated ware was made for export only.

In 1964 the pottery was taken over by Howard Pottery Company of Shelton, but the Royal Winton name was retained. From that time on, there was a succession of owners, but the Royal Winton name continued.

Crown Ducal
Tunstall, England
1915-1974

History: A.G. Richardson developed its first chintz motifs in earthenware in 1918 under the Crown Ducal name after it bought Gordon Pottery. Its designs fell between the early Victorian and later tightly patterned, all-over florals.

In 1922 the company introduced tennis or hostess sets (trays with cups) followed by console sets—10" candlesticks with a matching bowl—in 1923. Next in line was a 12" lily bowl with a black matte interior.

Numerous Crown Ducal chintz patterns were made, including "Florida" in 1925, "Primrose" in 1936, "Peony" in 1937, "Pansy" in 1938, and "Priscilla" in 1940.

A.G. Richardson was acquired by Enoch Wedgwood Ltd. of Tunstall in 1974, and this firm was taken over by the Wedgwood Group in 1980 and renamed Unicorn Pottery.

James Kent
Longton, England
1897-Present

History: James Kent took over the Old Foley Pottery at Longton in 1897 and renamed it James Kent, Ltd. Popular patterns were "DuBarry" and "Hydrangea." This firm was bought by M.R. Hadida Fine Bone China Ltd. in the 1980s.

Elijah Cotton Ltd.
(Lord Nelson)
Hanley, England
1889-1981

History: This firm operated at Nelson Pottery in Hanley starting in 1889. "Black Beauty" and "Green Tulip" were its most popular chintz patterns. The chintz patterns at this firm were never applied to handles or spouts because this required special skills.

W.R. Midwinter, Ltd.
Burslem, England
1910-Present

History: "Springtime," "Lorna Doone," and "Brama" were the most popular chintz patterns at W.R. Midwinter. In 1968 this firm merged with J & G Meakin Ltd. and was taken over by the Wedgwood Group in 1970.

Shelley Potteries, Ltd.
Longton, England
1872-1966

History: This firm began in 1872 as Wileman & Company and became Shelley Potteries, Ltd. in 1925. In 1966 they were taken over by Allied English Potteries and acquired by Doulton & Company in 1971. These companies formed Royal Doulton Tableware Ltd.

The company made chintz patterns on earthenware bodies before World War II, but after the war they only made bone china chintz. Black ground patterns were the most popular.

Additional English potteries that made chintz ware included Barker Brothers, Ltd.; Brexton, Empire Porcelain Co. Ltd.; Ford & Sons; Myott Son & Co.; Wade & Co.; and Wood & Sons, Ltd.

References: Linda Eberle & Susan Scott, *The Charlton Standard Catalogue of Chintz, 3rd Edition*, Charlton Press, 1996; *2nd Edition*, Charlton Press, 1997; Bonnie Heller, Joy Humphrey, & Felicity Finburgh, *Chintz By Design*, Chintz International, 1997; Muriel Miller, *The Chintz Collectors Handbook*, Krause Publications, 1998; Muriel Miller, *Collecting Royal Winton Chintz*, Frances Joseph Publications, 1996; Jo Anne Welsh, *Chintz Ceramics*, Schiffer Publishing Ltd. 2000.

Collectors' Clubs: The Chintz Collectors' Club, P.O. Box 50888, Pasadena, CA 91115, $40.00, Quarterly newsletter; Chintz Connection, P.O. Box 222, Riverdale, MD 20738, $25.00, Quarterly newsletter; Royal Winton International Collectors' Club, Ken Glibbery, Dancer's End, Northall, Bedfordshire, LU6 2EU England, $50.00, Bi-monthly newsletter. Chintz World International, P.O. Box 50888, Pasadena, CA 91115, $58.00, Website www.chintznet.com.

Newsletter: *The Crazed Collector*, ed. by Char Jorgenson & Debbie Rusconi, P.O. Box 2635, Dublin, CA 94568.

Reproduction Alert: Chintz patterns have been copied in Germany, Czechoslovakia, and Japan. Examples marked "Erphila" come from Germany and Czechoslovakia. Japanese chintz called Mano and Halton wares copied Royal Winton patterns.

Royal Winton is reproducing the "Julia" pattern in a stacking teapot in a limited edition of 1,000, and the "Florence" pattern in an 11" octagonal footed vase in a limited edition of 2,000.

Collecting Hints: Be sure to check that sets are always complete and that the patterns match—not just similar patterns. Check to make sure finials have not been reglued, and check for chips on spouts of tea and coffeepots. Check to see if the lithographs have been applied properly, and the patterns match. Some pieces in the same pattern vary in color over the years they were made. Since this is earthenware and not bone china, check the crazing in the glaze.

Collectors seek out either a particular pattern in a number of shapes, or they pick a particular shape such as a stacking teapot and collect as many patterns as possible. Patterns and shapes affect the price of chintz pieces. Different examples are more or less desirable in different parts of the country. Some of the most desirable examples include wall clocks, musical boxes, wall pockets, breakfast sets, and small, unusual pieces such as a stand with eggcups and tiny salt and pepper sets.

Biscuit Jar, 6 1/2" h, "Hazel" pattern, Royal Winton, ... **1,500.00**
Bonbon Dish, 6 1/2" H-H, "Windsor" pattern, "Erphila Czechoslovakia" mk, ... **75.00**
Bowl
  3 1/2" d, "Sweet Pea" pattern, Royal Winton, ... **25.00**
  4 1/8" d, "Ascot" pattern, Crown Ducal, ... **65.00**
Bud Vase
  3 1/4" h, "Sunshine" pattern, Royal Winton, ... **285.00**
  5" h, "Hazel" pattern, Royal Winton, ... **288.00**
  5 1/4" h, "Kinver" pattern, Royal Winton, ... **395.00**
Butter Dish, Cov, 3" h x 6 1/2" l, "Floral Garden" pattern, Royal Winton, ... **230.00**
Butter Pat, 3" d, "Current" pattern, ... **28.00**
Cake Plate, 12 1/4" sq, "Sweet Pea" pattern, Royal Winton, ... **340.00**

Cheese Keeper, 6 1/2" l x 5 1/2" w x 4 7/8" h, "Anemone" pattern, Royal Winton, $280.00

Cake Plate, Chrome Center Handle
  7 1/2" d, "Anemone" pattern, Royal Winton, ... **110.00**

  9" d, "Regency" pattern, ... **95.00**
Candy Dish, 6 3/4" H-H, x 5" w, "Hydrangia" pattern, James Kent, ... **140.00**
Cheese Dish, Cov, 7 1/4" l, "Rosalynde" pattern, James Kent, ... **295.00**

Chop Plate, 11" d, "Rosalynde" pattern, James Kent, ... **175.00**
Coffeepot
  7 1/4" h, "Melody" pattern, Shelley, ... **475.00**
  7 3/4" h
    "Old Cottage Chintz" `pattern, Perth shape, Royal Winton, ... **800.00**
    "Summertime" pattern, Albans shape, Royal Winton, ... **1,200.00**
  8" h
    "Hazel" pattern, Perth shape, Royal Winton, ... **1,160.00**
    "Rose Chintz" pattern, Johnson Brothers, ... **80.00**
    "Summertime" pattern, Perth shape, Royal Winton, ... **1,200.00**

Coffee Service, pot, 8 1/2" h, creamer, sugar bowl, 8 cups and saucers, "Melody" pattern, Shelley, $995.00

Compote
  6 1/2" d x 2 1/4" h, "Sweat Pea" pattern, Royal Winton, ... **45.00**
  7 1/8" l x 5 3/4" w x 2 1/2" h, "Queen Anne" pattern, Royal Winton, ... **60.00**
Condiment Set, creamer, 3" h, sugar bowl, 4" h, tray, 8" l x 5" w, "Bedale" pattern, Royal Winton, ... **100.00**
Cup and Saucer
  "Fleur" pattern, Poole, ... **25.00**
  "Kew" pattern, Royal Winton, ... **90.00**
  "Melody" pattern, Shelley, ... **48.00**
  "Morning Glory" pattern, Brexton Pottery, ... **40.00**
  "Pekin" pattern, Royal Winton, ... **55.00**

"Rock Garden" pattern, Shelley, ... **135.00**
"Rosalynde" pattern, James Kent, ... **60.00**
"Rosina" pattern, ... **50.00**

Dessert Set, cake plate, 9 1/2" d, creamer, 3 3/4" h, sugar bowl, 3" h, 4 dessert plates, 6 1/2" d, 6 cups and saucers, "Elizabeth" pattern, "Royal Stafford Bone China" mks, ... **495.00**

Dish
4 3/4" H-H, tab handles, "Old Cottage" pattern, Royal Winton, ... **80.00**
6 7/8" l, "DuBarry" pattern, James Kent, ... **58.00**

Egg Cup, 2 1/2" h, "Evesham" pattern, Royal Winton, ... **200.00**

Egg Set, tray, 6" l x 5 3/4" w, overhead metal handle, 4 egg cups, 1 1/2" h, "Queen Anne" pattern, Midwinter, ... **320.00**

Hot Water Pot
6" h, "Cotswold" pattern, Albans shape, Royal Winton, ... **795.00**
7" h, "Welbeck" pattern, Royal Winton, ... **1,275.00**

Jug
3" h, "DuBarry" pattern, James Kent, **85.00**
4 1/2" h, "Sommerset" pattern, Royal Winton, ... **135.00**

Pin Dish, 4 1/2" l x 3 1/2" w, "English Rose" pattern, Royal Winton, ... **80.00**

Pitcher, 6 1/4" h, "Marina" pattern, Lord Nelson, ... **200.00**

Plate
6 1/2" d
"Morning Glory" pattern, Brexton Pottery, ... **50.00**
"Rose Chintz" pattern, Johnson Brothers, ... **5.00**
6 5/8" d, "Marion" pattern, Royal Winton, ... **30.00**
6 3/4" d, "Joyce-Lynn" pattern, Royal Winton, ... **75.00**
8" d, "Ascot" pattern, Crown Ducal, ... **60.00**
8" sq
"Rosale" pattern, Empire, ... **20.00**
"Welbeck" pattern, Royal Winton, ... **75.00**
9" sq, "Summertime" pattern, Royal Winton, ... **50.00**

Platter, 12" l x 10" w, oval, "Old Cottage Chintz" pattern, Royal Winton, ... **450.00**

Posey Ring, 7 1/4" d, "Melody" pattern, Shelley, ... **529.00**
Sandwich Set, tray, 10 1/4" l x 6" w, 4 plates, 5 1/4" sq, "English Rose" pattern, Royal Winton, ... **850.00**
Sandwich Tray, 12 1/2" l, "Rose Chintz" pattern, Johnson Brothers, ... **45.00**
Serving Dish, 9 1/2" l, dbl, "Rapture" pattern, James Kent, ... **35.00**

Stacked Teapot, 5 1/2" h, "Chelsea Chintz" pattern, multicolored florals, black ground, "Royal Winton Grimwades Made in England" mark, **$900.00**

Stacking Teapot
2 1/2" h, "Balmoral" pattern, Royal Winton, ... **1,800.00**
5 1/2" h, "Morning Glory" pattern, Royal Winton, ... **895.00**
5 3/4" h, "Summertime" pattern, Royal Winton, ... **2,000.00**
6" h, "Royal Brocade" pattern, Lord Nelson, ... **950.00**
6 1/2" h, "Briar Rose" pattern, Royal Winton, ... **475.00**

Sugar Shaker, 6" h, "Julia" pattern, Royal Winton, ... **950.00**

Teapot
4 1/2" h x 8" w, "Welbeck" pattern, "Ajax" shape, Royal Winton, ... **1,800.00**
5" h, "Primula" pattern, Crown Ducal, ... **260.00**
5 1/2" h
"Old Cottage Chintz" pattern, Elite shape, Royal Winton, ... **550.00**
"Summertime" pattern
Albans shape, ... **1,000.00**
Elite shape, ... **1,200.00**
"Sweat Pea" pattern, Royal Winton, ... **420.00**
6" h,
"Rose Bouquet" pattern, Arthur Wood, ... **85.00**
"Summertime" pattern, Ascot shape, ... **1,000.00**
6 1/2" h, "Dorset" pattern, Albans shape, Royal Winton, ... **500.00**

8" h, "Royal Brocade" pattern, Lord Nelson, ... **465.00**
Tea Set, pot, 7" h, cream jug, 3" h, sugar bowl, 2 3/4" h, "Welbeck" pattern, Royal Winton, ... **245.00**

Tennis Set, 9 1/4" l, "Summertime" pattern, "Royal Winton Grimwades Made in England" mark, **$125.00**

Tennis Set
7 3/4" l, "Old Cottage" pattern, Royal Winton, ... **225.00**
9" l x 6 1/4" w, "Summertime" pattern, Royal Winton, ... **200.00**

Tidbit Stand, 13 1/2" h, 3 tier, 6 1/2", 7", 10" d, "Rose Chintz" pattern, goldtone center bar and ring handle, Johnson Brothers, ... **50.00**

Toast Rack, 7" l
"Eleanor" pattern, Royal Winton, ... **295.00**
"Julia" pattern, Royal Winton, ... **750.00**
"Marguerite" pattern, Royal Winton, ... **298.00**

Trio
Plate, 6" d, cup, saucer "Queen Anne" pattern, Royal Winton, ... **115.00**
Plate, 7" d, cup, saucer, "Pekin" pattern, Royal Winton, ... **110.00**
Tureen, 12" H-H x 8" h, "Rose Chintz" pattern, Johnson Brothers, ... **150.00**

Vase
5 1/4" h, "Marina" pattern, Lord Nelson, ... **245.00**
9" h, "Julia" pattern, Royal Winton, ... **140.00**

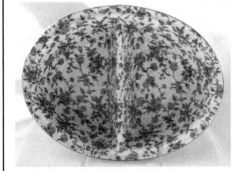

Vegetable Bowl, Divided, 9 3/4" l, "Old Cottage" pattern, Royal Winton, **$385.00**

Vegetable Bowl, 9 3/4" l x 7 5/8" w, "Rosebud" pattern, Spode-Copeland, ... **145.00**

Vegetable Bowl, Cov, 10 1/4" H-H, "Rose Chintz" pattern, Johnson Brothers, ... **100.00**

Wall Pocket, 8 1/2" l, "Rosebud" pattern, Royal Winton, ... **900.00**

c 1836 -1900

CHOISY-LE-ROI

Seine, France
1804 to Present

History: This French factory produced porcelain and white earthenware at Choisy-le-Roi in Seine, France, from 1804. First, table services and toilet sets that featured French views or classical scenes printed in red or black were made here. Later, relief decorative motifs were added.

The factory began making earthenware about 1830. Black transfer prints were used with occasional touches of color. After 1860 more relief work was used, and some pieces were glazed with brilliant colors. Majolica wares were made with careful glazing and naturalistic colors. Other works included tiles and trompe l'oeil pieces in the form of ducks, pigs, and plates of asparagus or oysters.

Beginning in 1836, the factory traded as Hautin and Boulanger. Marks incorporated Choisy, or Ch le Roy, or HB & Cie. The factory still remains in operation.

Bowl, 6" d, ftd, stenciled blue irises, green stems and grasses, "Terre de Fer Choisy le Roi" mk, ... **25.00**

Coffee Can and Saucer, canary yellow ground, black lined rims, "P. & H. CHOISY 22" mks, ... **95.00**

Dish, 9 7/8" w, shell molded w/rolled handle, multicolored bird on branch w/flowers and leaves, mkd, ... **50.00**

Figure, 21 1/4" h, bare breasted classic woman in blue gown, holding attacking leopard by rose and foliate chain collar, stepped oval base, c1880, ... **12,800.00**

Match Holder, 21 1/4" h, standing figure of rooster, brown-tan back feathers, red-brown and blue-grey breast, blue-grey tail, standing next to rect box w/green ivy, brown-green textured base, "imp Louis Carrier Belleuse," **8,250.00**

Mug, 3 5/8" h, grey rabbits, dk red fruit, ivory ground, rabbit handle, mkd, **$565.00**

Pitcher, 7" h, relief of dk brown bird on med brown branches, red blossoms, green foliage, white bark ground, red int, mkd, ... **265.00**

Plate

6" d, 3 molded pink, purple, or yellow pansies on border, ... **230.00**

7" d, painted dk red, green, and yellow rooster against green foliage, border of dk red painted scrolls, ... **145.00**

Plate, 7 3/4" d, multicolored transfer in center, green leaf and berry rim, "Choisy-Le-Roi HB Tere de Fere" mks, pr, (A), **$60.00**

7 3/8" d, green relief of woman and child holding animal in center, burgundy red inner border, green relief molded border of dog, chicken, and pig, "HB & Co. Choisy Le Roi" mk, ... **185.00**

8" d, "Vue due Village de Marmaren en Turgovie Sur le Lae Inferier de Constance," leaf and flowerhead border, black transfers, canary yellow ground, "imp P. & H. CHOISY" mk, ... **185.00**

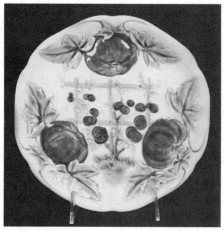

Plate, 8 3/4" d, red tomatoes, green leaves, yellow-green trellis, **$215.00**

8 1/2" d, tin glazed, lg red strawberries, lg green and sm blue leaves, ... **250.00**

Plate, 8 1/2" d, olive green glaze, "imp H.B. & Cie Choisy Le Roi" marks, **$45.00**

9" d

Multicolored transfer of French satirical scene in center and "L'indescrete No.1," relief molded flower and vine design on border, green lined rim, "H. & B. Choisy" mk, ... **40.00**

Relief of 4 brown and cream rabbits, green grass, cream ground, "HB & Cie Choisy Le Roi" mk, ... **255.00**

Relief of 6 grey-brown and cream rabbits, green foliage, cream ground, lobed rim, ... **225.00**

Relief of swimming white swan, blue water, green and brown bulrushes, "Hautin & Boulanger, Choisy-Le-Roi" mk, ... **100.00**

Platter

13 1/8" l x 10" w, maple leaf in center, branch and leaves on border,

blue transfer, blue lined rim, ... **15.00**

15 1/2" h x 12 1/4" w, oval, painted song birds on branch and butterflies, "HB Choisy-Le-Roi" mk, ... **295.00**

Soup Plate, 10 1/2" d, brown center transfer of "Le Movin," French country scene, slate blue border of foliage, indented rim, ... **15.00**

Teapot, 9 1/2" h, oriental style, paneled, moss green and gold molded geometrics, "Hippolyte Boulenger" mk, ... **200.00**

Vase, 11" h, tapered form w/cylinder neck, painted cornflowers on gloss brown ground, ... **850.00**

Wall Pocket, 11 3/4" h, figural purple pansie or white pansie, brown tinged green stem and leaves, pr, ... **2,195.00**

Clarice Cliff
WILKINSON LTD
ENGLAND
c1930

CLARICE CLIFF

Burslem, England
1925-1963

History: Clarice Cliff, 1899-1972, began her training at Stoke-on-Trent at age 13 when she joined the staff at A.J. Wilkinson, Ltd. Royal Staffordshire Pottery at Burslem. The company acquired the adjoining Newport factory along with a huge supply of undecorated bowls and vases that were assigned to Clarice Cliff to decorate. She utilized vivid colors and eccentric Art Deco designs with chunky, angular shapes that contrasted sharply with the flowing lines of the earlier Art Nouveau period. Cliff became art director of A.J. Wilkinson, Ltd. in 1930.

Cliff's earthenwares were gay, colorful, and all hand painted. Circles, squares, colored bands, diamonds, conical shapes, and simple landscapes were incorporated in the designs. Pattern names included "Applique," "Bizarre," "Fantasque," "Gay Day," "Latonia," "Lodore," "Ravel," and the most popular "Crocus." These patterns were all mass produced and achieved tremendous popularity in both England and America.

Shapes also had special names such as Athens, Biarritz, Chelsea, Conical, Daffodil, Iris, Lotus, Lynton, Stamford, and Trieste. A customer could order the shape desired and have it decorated with a pattern of choice. Many novelty pieces such as flower holders, vases, inkwells, candle-

sticks, cruet sets, bookends, umbrella stands, and even a ceramic telephone cover all were made in Clarice Cliff designs.

Clarice Cliff used several different printed marks, each of which incorporated a facsimile of her signature and usually the name of the pattern.

In 1965, Midwinter bought Wilkinson. Midwinter merged with J & G Meakin in 1968, and in 1970 Meakin was absorbed by the Wedgwood Group.

References: Richard Green & Des Jones, *The Rich Designs of Clarice Cliff*, Rich Designs, 1995; Leonard Griffin, *Taking Tea with Clarice Cliff: A Celebration of her Art Deco Teaware*, Pavilion Books, 1996; Leonard Griffin & L & S Meisel, *Clarice Cliff: The Bizarre Affair*, Adams, 1988; Howard Watson, *Collecting Clarice Cliff*, Kevin Francis, 1988; Pat and Howard Watson, *Clarice Cliff Price Guide, 1st Edition*, Kevin Francis Publications, 1995; Peter Wentworth-Shields & Kay Johnson, *Clarice Cliff*, L'Odeon, 1976. Helen C. Cunningham, *Clarice Cliff & Her Contemporaries; Susie Cooper, Keith Murray, Charlotte Rhead and the Carlton Ware Designers*, Schiffer Publications, 1999.

Collectors' Club: Clarice Cliff Collectors Club, Leonard R. Griffin, Fantasque House, Tennis Drive, The Park, Nottingham NG7 1AE Great Britain. Membership: £55, *Review*, three times a year, *Newsletter*, six times a year.

Museum: Brighton Museum, Brighton, England.

Reproduction Alert: 1993 Wedgwood reproductions in limited editions of 500 patterns were Sliced Circle, May Avenue, Orange Roof Cottage, Trees and Houses, Carpet and Lighting which were issued as sugar dredges priced at $125 each.

Fakes are also appearing on the market.

In 1985 Midwinter produced a series of "limited edition" reproductions marked with a 1985 backstamp.

1997 Clarice Cliff reproductions included two Stamford shape teapots each with a different design on either side—Summerhouse with Tennis, and Red Roofs with Apples, based on the originals from the book *Taking Tea with Clarice Cliff*. They have a full commemorative backstamp and are in a strictly limited edition.

Two of Clarice Cliff's figurines from the "Age of Jazz" from 1930—the piano player and banjo player, and the couple dancing—are being reproduced by Pastimes of England. The reproductions are cast as one piece instead of with blocks as the old ones were done.

Collecting Hints: Unmarked pieces of Clarice Cliff china are rare. The large number of back stamps that were used leads to confusion in dating examples.

"Bizarre"(1928-1937) and "Fantasque"(1929-1934) are the most actively sought patterns. "Crocus," the most popular pattern she ever created, was created in 1928.

There is a big demand for regular tableware items such as tea sets, vases, and fruit bowls, but decorative wares such as wall plaques and her lotus jugs are also big sellers.

Biscuit Barrel
6 1/8" h, "Crocus" pattern, wicker handle, Bizzare Ware, ... **525.00**
6 5/8" h, "Secrets" pattern, brown, yellow, green, and red house and rolling hills, SP rim, cov, and overhead handle, Bizarre Ware, (A), ... **530.00**

Bone Dish, 6 1/2" l, "Tonquin" pattern, black transfer, ... **9.00**

Bowl
5 1/2" d, "Blue Crocus" pattern, ... **395.00**
8" d, "Patchwork Leaves" pattern, SP rim, ... **1,200.00**
8 1/2" d, "Night and Day" pattern, blue, mauve, purple, yellow, and red geometric designs, "Bizarre By Clarice Cliff" mk, ... **3,000.00**
8 5/8" d, low profile, inverted rim, "Gibraltar" pattern, "Fantastique Bizarre Clarice Cliff" mk, ... **1,350.00**
8 3/4" l x 6 3/4" w x 5" h, figural waterlily, lt yellow flower, purple/blue base, ... **160.00**
10" d, "Sunshine" pattern, ... **180.00**

Cake Plate, 8 1/2" w, "Rhodanthe" pattern, ... **165.00**

Candle Holders, 1 1/2" h x 3 1/2" d, "Celtic Harvest" pattern. Bizarre Ware, pr, ... **150.00**

Charger, 17 3/4" d, "Applique Blue Lagoon" pattern, blue, yellow, brick-red, green, and black, Bizarre, (A), ... **19,390.00**

Coffee Cup and Saucer, "Mondrian" pattern, ... **1,345.00**

Coffeepot
7 3/8" h, "Caprice" pattern, tapered conical shape w/horiz ribbing, ... **435.00**
8" h, "Rodanthe" pattern, Bonjour shape, ... **1,250.00**

Creamer and Sugar Bowl, 2 7/8" h, "Rhodanthe" pattern, "Clarice Cliff," "WILKINSON ENGLAND" mks, ... **310.00**

Creamer, 3 1/2" h, "Tonquin" pattern, blue transfer, ... **22.00**

Cream Jug, 3" h, Sugar Bowl, 3 3/4" d x 2 1/2" h, "Duvivier" pattern, ... **60.00**

Cup and Saucer
"Melon" pattern, Fantasque, **500.00**
"Old Bristol" pattern, swirled body, ... **20.00**
"Sunshine" pattern, Fantasque, ... **400.00**

Cup and Saucer, Demitasse
"Gayday" pattern, ... **165.00**
"Tonquin" pattern, blue transfers, ... **22.00**

Dish, 9 5/8" w, oct, "Japan" pattern, orange, yellow, green, purple, blue, and black oriental teahouse scene, Bizarre, (A), ... **565.00**

Fern Pot, 2 3/4" h, "Gayday" pattern, "GAYDAY HAND PAINTED Bizarre By Clarice Cliff" mk, ... **150.00**

Honey Pot, 3 1/2" h, "Autumn Crocus" pattern, ... **620.00**

Jam Pot, 3" h, "Autumn Crocus" pattern, "Handpainted Bizarre By Clarice Cliff Newport Pottery England, Made in England" mk, ... **425.00**

Jug
4 3/4" h, "Autumn-Blue Balloons" pattern, Bon Jour shape, Cafe-Au-Lait, ... **500.00**
9" h, "Coral Firs" pattern, c1930s, ... **1,850.00**
10" h, blue, orange, and black "Pine Grove" pattern, yellow banded handle, burnt orange int rim, Lotus shape, ... **1,200.00**
11 1/2" h, "Sliced Circle" pattern, Lotus shape, strap handle, ... **9,400.00**
12 1/2" h, "Anemone" pattern, Lotus shape, ... **700.00**

Pitcher
5 1/8" h, "Crocus" pattern, green bands on rim and base, "Clarice Cliff Newport Pottery England" mk, ... **225.00**
7 1/4" h, orange-red fish, pink shells, brown coral, green ground, yellow branch handle, Bizarre Ware, ... **495.00**

Plate
6 1/4" d, "Tree and House" pattern, orange border, ... **650.00**
6 3/8" d, "Spring Crocus" pattern, ... **45.00**
6 1/2" l x 5 1/2" w, rect, "Aurea" pattern, Biarritz, ... **245.00**
7" d
"Delecia" pattern, Coronet shape, ... **460.00**
"Star" pattern, blue inner pinwheel star on black outlined orange and brown star design, tan border, ... **600.00**
"Tennis" pattern, "Bizarre by Clarice Cliff" mk, ... **825.00**
"Tralee" pattern, ... **745.00**
8 1/2" d, "Sunkissed" pattern, HP fruit and slices, set of 6, ... **60.00**
9" d, "House and Bridge" pattern, ... **1,950.00**
10" d
"Charlotte" pattern, basket overflowing w/flowers, blue transfer, "Royal Staffordshire Clarice Cliff" mk, ... **25.00**
Oct, "Tartan" pattern, Bizarre Ware, ... **425.00**
"Pine Grove" pattern, ... **600.00**
"Rural Scenes" pattern, men cutting trees, brown transfer w/colors, ... **25.00**
"Tonquin" pattern, mulberry transfer, "Royal Staffordshire Clarice Cliff Made in England" mk, set of 8, ... **110.00**

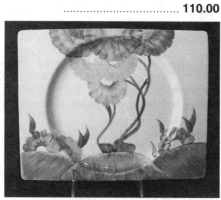

Plate, 10 1/2" l, "Biarritz," green, rose, and yellow flowers, brown branches, cream ground, "The Biarritz Clarice Cliff" mark, $595.00

10 1/2" d, "Blue Crocus" pattern, ... **40.00**

Preserve Dish, 4 3/4" d, w/spoon, raised purple flowers, green leaves, yellow ground, mkd, ... **110.00**

Sauceboat
5 1/4" l, "Tonquin" pattern, green transfer, ... **20.00**
7" l, w/underplate and fishtail ladle, applied blue, orange, and green carp, ... **280.00**

Sugar Bowl, 4 1/4" w, paneled, "Bobbins" pattern, red and orange w/blue-green leaves, tan ground, mkd, ... **300.00**

Sugar Sifter
3" h, conical, "Blue Crocus" design, ... **170.00**

5" h, Bonjour Shape
"Rodanthe" pattern, c1930, ... **750.00**
"Windbells" pattern, "Fantastique Bizarre," **1,550.00**
5 1/2" h
"Autumn Crocus" pattern, ... **600.00**
"Brookfields" pattern, base chip, (A), ... **670.00**
"Fruit Burst" designs, "Clarice Cliff Bizarre Fantastique" mk, ... **1,125.00**
"Marguerite" pattern, ... **735.00**
"My Garden" pattern, brown ground, ... **475.00**
"Summer Crocus" pattern, "Hand Painted Bizarre By Clarice Cliff" mk, ... **455.00**

Teapot, 4 7/8" h, "Farmhouse" pattern, Stamford shape, $3,950.00

Teapot
4 3/4" h, "Gayday" pattern, Stamford shape, ... **1,150.00**
5" h x 9" w, globe shape, "Crocus" pattern, c1928, ... **850.00**
5 1/4" "Cubist" pattern, orange, yellow, blue, green, and black, Athens shape, (A), ... **885.00**
5 3/4" h, "Pink Pearls" pattern, Stamford shape, ... **1,475.00**
6" h, green "Cowslip" pattern, Bonjour shape, "Bizarre by Clarice Cliff" mk, ... **1,150.00**
6 1/4" h, "My Garden" pattern, ... **500.00**
7" h, "Teepee" pattern, (A), ... **633.00**

Toast Rack, 5" l, 3 bar, "Blue Chintz" pattern, "Clarice Cliff Bizarre, Fantastique, Newport Pottery" mks, ... **480.00**

Tray, 11 3/4" l, rect w/cut corners, "Delecia" pattern, red, green, blue, and orchid streaks, ... **155.00**

Trio, cup, saucer, plate, 6" d, "Orange Secrets" pattern, ... **1,375.00**

Vase

4 3/4" h, squat base, straight neck w/horiz ribbing, "Goldstone" pattern, "Goldstone Hand Painted Bizarre By Clarice Cliff" mk, ... **220.00**

4 7/8" h, "Rhodanthe" pattern, Bonjour shape, ... **300.00**

5 1/2" h, "My Garden" pattern, orange ground, "Bizarre by Clarice Cliff" mk, ... **550.00**

6" h, trumpet shape
"Red Gardenia" pattern, **835.00**
"Umbrellas" pattern, "Fantastique Clarice Cliff" mk, ... **750.00**

Vase, 7 3/4" h, raised yellow flowers, blue leaves, dk brown and green branches and stems, mint green int, "Newport Pottery 990 Clarice Cliff" mark, $325.00

7" h
Standing cornucopia, celadon glaze, modeled multicolored flowers on handle and base, ... **280.00**
Trumpet shape, "My Garden" pattern, mushroom ground, multicolored flowers on base, ... **265.00**

8" h
"Persian" pattern, red and tan shades, ... **450.00**
"Raffia" pattern, orange, brown, and green, ... **450.00**
Red, yellow, blue, and green "Fruit" pattern on purple diagonal hatched ground,

---

shape #358, "Hand Painted, Fantastique, Clarice Cliff" mk, **1,285.00**

Vase, 8 1/4" h, "Autumn" pattern, shape #362, $3,000.00

8 1/8" h, trumpet shape, "Latona Cartoon Flowers" pattern, c1930s, ... **2,200.00**
9" h, single handle, "My Garden" pattern, mushroom ground, ... **265.00**
9 1/2" h
Squat shape, horiz ribbing, "Etna" pattern, HP mountainous scene, ... **8,225.00**
"Sunrise" pattern, Isis shape, ... **4,500.00**
14 1/8" h, "Inspiration Bouquet" pattern, green and dk blue leaf designs on streaked med blue ground, "Mei Ping" shape, (A), ... **795.00**
19" h, trumpet shape, "Secrets" pattern, green and yellow hillsides, brown roofed houses, stylized tree over lake, (A), ... **1,870.00**

Wall Pocket, 7" h, mask of woman's face, Inspiration Blue w/red, blue, and green flowers in hair, red lips, ... **425.00**

c1818-1834

CLEWS

Cobridge Works, Staffordshire, England 1818-1834

History: James and Ralph Clews were Staffordshire potters who operated the Cobridge Works from 1818 to 1834. They were known for the fine quality of their blue transfer-printed earthenwares, mostly made for the American market. American views used on their wares were taken from contemporary prints. In addition, designs were taken from books—e.g. the Clews series of *Dr. Syntax* and *Don Quixote*. Plates also were made from the comic pictures drawn by Sir David Wilkie. The company's English views consisted chiefly of castles, abbeys, and cathedrals.

Reference: N. Hudson Moore, *The Old China Book*, Charles E. Tuttle Co., Second printing, 1980.

Museums: Cincinnati Art Museum, Cincinnati, OH; Metropolitan Museum of Art, New York, NY.

Collecting Hints: The two most famous patterns by Clews are "Landing of Lafayette" and the "States." The "Landing of Lafayette" pattern contains an extremely large number of accessory pieces.

Cup and Saucer, Handleless

Basket and vase floral design, med blue transfer, "imp CLEWS WARRANTED STAFFORDSHIRE" mk, chips, (A), ... **220.00**
Blue, green, and gold gaudy floral design, "Clews Warranted Staffordshire" mk, (A), ... **248.00**
"Jessamine" pattern, classic building and deer, flower and floral border, mauve borders, "R. & J. Clews" mk, ... **95.00**
Soft paste, bold blue, tan, and green floral and foliate pattern, wide blue border stripes, "imp CLEWS" mk, rim chip, ... **275.00**
Two setter dogs hunting, leaf borders, dk blue transfers, mkd, ... **425.00**
Vase and flowers design, dk blue transfers, foot chip, imp mk, ... **245.00**

Dish, 6 1/2" d, children and dog design, dk blue transfer, "Clews" mk, (A), ... **206.00**

Plate

6 3/4" d, "Doctor Syntax and a Blue Stocking Beauty," dk blue transfer, hairline, ... **175.00**
7 1/2" d, "Playing at Droughts," The Wilkie Series, med blue transfer, ... **350.00**

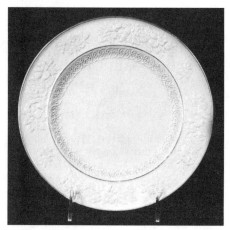

Plate, 8 5/8" d, drabware, gold inner and outer rims, "imp CLEWS" mk, c1825-30, **$150.00**

8 3/4" d, "Doctor Syntax Reading His Tour," dk blue transfer, "imp CLEWS" mk, ... **280.00**

9 3/4" d, "Italian Scenery," man and donkey before columns, floral and leaf border, med blue transfer, ... **260.00**

10" d

"Coronation" pattern, vase w/flowers and birds in center, vine border, med blue transfer, "Coronation Clews" mk, (A), ... **195.00**

"Death of a Bear-Indian Sporting Series," med blue transfer, c1810, ... **695.00**

Plate, 10 1/2" d, oriental scene, dk blue transfer, "imp CLEWS" mk, (A), **$100.00**

"Don Quixote-Knighthood Conferred On Don Quixote," med blue transfer, ... **425.00**

"Doctor Syntax Painting A Portrait," med blue transfer, ... **650.00**

"Escape of the Mouse-Wilkies Series," med blue transfer, ... **425.00**

Plate, 6 5/8" d, "Christmas Eve," med blue transfer, "imp CLEWS" mark, **$225.00**

"The Valentine," Wilkie Series, dk blue transfer, ... **625.00**

Vase of flowers seated on table, leaf border, med blue transfer, "imp James & Ralph Clews" mk, ... **350.00**

Platter

15 1/4" l x 11 1/4" w, oct, "Coronation" pattern, bouquet in vase on table, leaf border, med blue transfer, c1820, ... **1,400.00**

19" l x 14" w, "Dr. Syntax Amused With Pat in the Pond," med blue transfer, ... **2,500.00**

Soup Bowl, 7 5/8" d, "The Meeting of Sancho and Dapple," flower and bird border, dk blue transfer, unmkd, (A), ... **193.00**

Sugar Box, Cov, 5 1/4" h x 5 1/2" w, black basalt, "Bellflower and Acanthus" relief molded pattern, "imp CLEWS" mk, ... **495.00**

Teapot, 8" h, reserves of Neptune on seashell on sides, shells on border, dk blue transfers, unmkd, repairs to lid and spout, (A), ... **385.00**

Toddy Plate

4 1/2" d, "Devon Ivy Bridge" design, flowerhead border, dk blue transfer, imp mk, (A), ... **55.00**

4 5/8" d, "Puss 'n Boots" in center, dk red transfer, molded leaf border, beaded rim, imp mk, ... **150.00**

Toy Plate, 2 1/2" d, creamware, iron-red wide and narrow rim stripes, tan ground, "imp CLEWS WARRANTED STAFFORDSHIRE" mk, c1820, ... **55.00**

Tray, 9 3/4" l x 5 1/2" w, "Dr. Syntax Making a Discovery," med blue, ... **595.00**

Vegetable Bowl, 9 1/4" l x 7" w, "Dr. Syntax Copying The Wit Of The Window," dk blue transfer, "imp CLEWS WARRANTED STAFFORDSHIRE" mk, ... **725.00**

COALPORT

Severn Gorge, Shropshire, England c1796 to Present

History: After John Rose completed his apprenticeship at Caughley, he established a pottery at Coalport in Shropshire in 1796. Rose expanded his original factory with the purchase of Caughley in 1799. His original soft paste formula eventually was superseded by bone china ware.

By 1822 molds, models, and some key personnel were acquired from the South Wales porcelain manufacturers at Swansea and Nantgarw and incorporated into the Coalport factory. In 1820 John Rose won a Society of Arts medal for his lead-free glaze.

The most characteristic type of Coalport porcelains are the distinctive rococo style flower-encrusted decorative pieces called "Coalbrookdale." "Indian Tree," first made in 1801, and "Hong Kong," made c1805 are two tableware patterns that are still popular to this day.

John Rose died in 1841. Production at Coalport continued under Thomas Rose, his son, W.F. Rose, his nephew, and William Pugh. The influence of Sevres was reflected in the style and decoration of table and ornamental wares made during the mid-19th century.

In 1885 the Bruff family took over. The Coalport firm was sold to Cauldon Potteries Ltd. in Staffordshire in 1923 and moved to the Staffordshire area in 1926 along with many of the workers.

By 1936 both Coalport and Cauldon became part of Crescent potteries at Stoke-on-Trent. In 1958 Coalport was acquired by Brain of Foley China and preserved its separate identity. Many traditional patterns and lines were revived. In 1967 Coalport became part of the Wedgwood group. The Coalport name continues a line of modern china products.

References: G. Godden, *Coalport and Coalbrookdale Porcelains*, Praeger,

1970; Compton MacKenzie, *The House of Coalport, 1750-1950*, Collins, 1951; Michael Messenger, *Coalport 1795-1926*, Antique Collectors' Club, 1995. Alf Willis, *Coalport Collectibles*, Charlton Press, 2000; Tom Power, Gaye-Blake Roberts, *Coalport Figurines*, 2nd Edition, Charlton Press, 1999.

Museums: Cincinnati Museum of Art, Cincinnati, OH; Coalport China Works Museum, Ironbridge Gorge Museum Trust, Shropshire, England; Victoria & Albert Museum, London, England.

Basket, 9" l
6 3/4" h, orange swirled ground w/gilt accents, applied multicolored flowers on body, rim, and handle, Coalbrookdale, c1840, ... **2,500.00**
9" h, HP garden flowers on int, applied flowerheads on rim, blue ext w/gilt swirls and applied flowerheads, overhead handle w/applied flowerheads, Coalbrookdale, ... **1,145.00**

Box, 6" w, heart shape, gilt scrolled cartouche of blue and Italianate and gondola scene, gilt ground w/overall turquoise jeweling, ... **2,300.00**

Cabinet Cup and Saucer, quatrefoil shape, overall gilding w/graduated turquoise jewels, gilt int, c1900, ... **695.00**

Chestnut Basket, 9 1/2" l x 4" h, reticulated body w/flowerheads at intersections, c1800, ... **1,875.00**

Cream Jug, 3 3/4" h, "Batwing" pattern, floral bouquets in hanging swags on sides, gilt wing borders, green cell pattern on front and back w/gilt foliage above, gilt ribbed rim, c1890, ... **100.00**

Cup and Saucer
Burgundy ground w/gilt swags and ovals on borders, silver mtd cup, dtd 1925, ... **185.00**
"Dragon in Compartments" pattern, multicolored, ... **135.00**
Iron red, black, and gilt band of buzzsaw type stylized leaves, c1815, ... **65.00**
"Ming Rose" pattern, ... **20.00**
Swirl molded, gold outlined raised leaves on borders, gold and white bead wrapped handle, gold int, ... **195.00**

Cup and Saucer, Demitasse, fluted, yellow ground w/gilt fleur-de-lys designs, turquoise jewels and gold beads on gold band, c1900, ... **245.00**

Dessert Service, Part, oval compote, ftd and branch handles, 13 1/4" w, 2 cov sauce tureens w/stands, 8 1/2" l, 4 lozenge shaped dishes, 11 1/8" l, 4 shell shaped dishes, 7 5/8" w, 4 dishes, 8 3/8" sq, 24 dessert plates, 7 1/2" sq, border of iron-red flowers w/diamond shaped petals and green foliage on trailing gilt vines, c1820, (A), ... **11,350.00**

Gravy Boat, 5 1/2" l, w/underplate, bone china, "Ming Rose" pattern, ... **45.00**

Meat Platter, 14" l x 11" w, "Hong Kong" pattern, cobalt, iron-red, and salmon oriental flowers, ... **395.00**

Mug, 3 1/2" h
Overall HP multicolored garden flowers w/gilding, c1830, ... **1,025.00**
Overlapping playing cards on green ground, gilt rim and base, c1840, ... **575.00**

Plate
7 1/2" d, "Rossellini" pattern, ... **10.00**
8 1/2" d
Chinoiserie "Tree of Life" pattern, cobalt, iron-red, green, and gilt, c1810, ... **485.00**
Multicolored chinoiserie bird in center w/lg tree, packets of flowers and chrysanthemums on border, c1800, ... **730.00**
8 7/8" d, HP multicolored birds both perched and flying, gilt border of flowerhead cartouches and scrolling acanthus leaves, c1815, pr, ... **1,500.00**

Plate, 10"d, cobalt, iron-red, orange, and gilt, c1840, **$85.00**

9" d
HP sm bouquet of garden flowers in center, hanging gilt curls on inner rim, sage green border w/3 gilt outlined

panels of HP floral sprigs, gilt rim, pr, ... **110.00**
"Money Tree" pattern, cobalt, iron-red, and green oriental tree and bridge in center, compartments on border, c1820, ... **495.00**

Plate, 9"d, blue and gilt, "green crown, Coalport England Leadless Glaze" mark, set of 16, A- **$770.00**

9 1/4" d, HP red poppy, blue cornflower, green foliage, c1880, ... **80.00**
10" d, "Japan" pattern of fan shaped panels, orange-red, cobalt, green, and gilt, c1820, ... **600.00**
10 3/4" d, HP fruit and foliage, gilt gadrooned rim, sgd "F.R. Ball," **120.00**

Porringer, Cov, 5 1/2" H-H, band of gilt anthemion, gilt rims, ... **190.00**

Sauce Tureen, Cov, 7 1/2" l x 6 3/4" h, w/undertray, Chinese shape, enameled pink, turquoise, yellow, green, and iron-red "Tobacco Leaf" pattern, gilt accents, scroll knob, c1805, ... **950.00**

Soup Plate, 10" d, "Finger and Thumb" pattern, cobalt, iron-red, and green, c1820, ... **600.00**

Sugar Bowl, Cov, 5 1/2" h, band of iron-red, gilt and gilt edged cobalt chrysanthemums and leaves on salmon cell ground in gilt and cobalt arches, gilt knob and base line, c1815, ... **600.00**

Urn, 6 3/8" h, lg orange florals, orange, green and gilt foliage, sq handles, c1800, ... **1,900.00**

Urn, Cov, 20 3/4" h, HP w/classical females leaning on vase holding leafy garlands, russet ground, reverse painted w/trophies in oval panel, acanthus scroll handles w/Bacchus mask terminals, circ foot on sq base, gilt accents, (A), ... **4,500.00**

Vase

5 5/8" h, sq baluster shape, pink ground w/gold molded snail, gilt rim and base, c1890, ... **135.00**

10 1/4" h, moon flask shape, 2 sm handles on shoulder, Islamic style lt blue enamel raised shaped cartouches w/gilt star ground, ... **2,500.00**

Waste Bowl, 6 1/4" d, overlapping this red circles w/blue and black enamel dots and sm swags, border of band of gilt ovals and stars, ... **185.00**

COPELAND-SPODE

London and Stoke-on-Trent, England 1833 to Present (see Spode for early history)

History: William Copeland died in 1826, and Josiah Spode II died in 1827. In 1833 William Taylor Copeland bought the Spode share in the London showroom and warehouse as well as the Spode Factory. Copeland took Thomas Garrett, a London colleague, as a partner and the firm was known as Copeland & Garrett from 1833 to 1847.

About 1842 Copeland's statuary porcelain body was developed and achieved success. Statuary porcelain, a major new art product, was sponsored by the new Art Unions. Many competitors adopted it, renaming it "Parian." Copeland statuettes, portrait busts, and other objects dominated the market until 1914. Production was halted after that date.

The name Spode was subordinated to that of Copeland after 1847, but the high standards of quality in all its products both in design and execution were maintained. The Spode Factory has held Royal Warrants from 1806 to the present time. The

Spode Factory survived many difficult times, constantly striving to maintain its reputation as the producers of fine ceramic wares.

In 1966 the Copeland family sold the firm to the Carborundum Company Ltd. who injected much needed capital to help the firm compete with the other English pottery and porcelain companies. In 1970 the bicentenary year of the firm's establishment, the name of the company was changed back to Spode to honor the founder. In 1976 Spode joined with the Worcester Royal Porcelain Company to form Royal Worcester Spode.

Up to 1833 the name "Spode" referred to the period during which the two Josiahs controlled the company. From 1833 onwards "Spode" referred to the Spode Factory irrespective of ownership. From about 1842 to 1880 the name Spode seldom appeared on its products. Keep in mind that all Copeland & Garrett and Copeland wares were Spode factory productions.

Copeland & Garrett 1833-1847

Copeland c1847-1970

Spode 1970-Present

References: see Spode.

Museums: see Spode.

Bon Bon Dish, 8" H-H x 4" w, "Spode's Byron" pattern, green and brown transfer of country landscape, "Copeland Spode England" mk, ... **65.00**

Bone Dish, 8 1/2" w, printed and accented "Chelsea" pattern, dtd 1910, ... **18.00**

Bowl

9 1/4" d, lg bunches of purple grapes, brown twisted vines, lg green leaves on int, c1890, Copeland-Spode, c1890, ... **195.00**

9 1/2" d, "Italian" pattern, blue transfer, "Copeland Spode's Italian England" mk, ... **75.00**

Bread Tray, 11" l x 3" w, "Spode's Italian" pattern, blue transfer, "blue Copeland Spode's Italian England" and "imp COPELAND" mks, ... **160.00**

Butter Pat

3" d, "Spode's Camilla" pattern, red transfer, ... **35.00**

3 1/4" d, "Spode's Tower" pattern, red transfer, ... **15.00**

Cabinet Plate, 9" d, HP multicolored center scene of "Lake of Como," turquoise border w/molded ovals joined by gilt chain links, c1870, ... **135.00**

Centerpiece, 9" h x 9" d, 3 figural cherubs w/gold sashes holding gilt edged shell formed pink int shell bowl, gilt accented base, ... **600.00**

Charger, 12 1/2" d, "Seasons" pattern, blue transfer, dtd 1907, Spode-Copeland, ... **20.00**

Coffee Can and Saucer, fluted, cobalt, iron red, yellow, and gilt Imari pattern on upper portion, gilt line above white lower section, ... **100.00**

Condiment Dish, 5 3/4" l x 5 1/4" w, "Spode's Italian" pattern, blue transfer, c1910, ... **250.00**

Cup and Saucer

"Berlin" shape, molded florals, white w/gilt rims, Copeland and Garrett, ... **50.00**

"Cabbage Leaf" pattern, "Copeland Late Spode New Stone" mk, c1900, ... **225.00**

"Chelsea Garden" pattern, pink, blue, and green florals, paneled borders and sides, scalloped rims, gilt trim, ... **14.00**

"Mayflower" pattern, blue transfers w/colors, "Copeland Spode England Spode's Mayflower" mk, ... **25.00**

"Spode's Blue Tower" pattern, ... **18.00**

Cup and Saucer, Demitasse, HP multicolored parrot, insects in center of saucer, cobalt borders w/gilt cell overlay and gilt ovals of HP flowers, ... **120.00**

Dish, Cov, 4 5/8" d, pink shells, red coral knob, "blue COPELAND" mk, $275.00

Dish

7 3/4" H-H, abbey in center, oak leaf and acorn border, 2 open gold accented handles, "blue COPELAND" mk, ... **55.00**

10 1/4" l x 8 1/2" w, leaf form, blue accented molded strawberry

handle, blue printed oriental scene of fisherman w/bridge, molded floral designs on margins, Copeland-Spode, ... **30.00**

11 1/2" l x 7 1/2" w, cut corners, indented sides, multicolored "Chinese Pheasant" pattern, "Copeland Late Spode" mk, ... **85.00**

Fish Platter, 23" l x 11" w, "Spode's Tower" pattern, blue transfer, ... **200.00**

Meat Platter

13" l 10" w, "Byron" pattern, blue printed w/yellow, red, and green accents, Copeland Spode, ... **30.00**

16 3/4" l x 13" w, w/drain, blue printed "Statice" pattern, star crack, Copeland Spode, ... **465.00**

Mug, 3 1/8" h, painted grey dog w/blue collar, seated on pink cushion, gilt banded rim and foot, c1880, Copeland-Spode, ... **500.00**

Pitcher, 4 5/8" h, white cameos of continuous hunt scene, white geometrics, matte dk tan ground, c1850, **$285.00**

Pitcher

6 1/2" h, Agateware, blue, grey, black, and white swirls, Copeland and Garrett, ... **315.00**

7" h, "Shakespeare-Ferdinand, Ariel, Audrey, and Touchstone," flower border, blue transfers, "W.T.Copeland & Son" mk, ... **55.00**

Plate

6 1/2" d

"Constable" pattern, lg bouquet of red rose and foxglove, blue delphinium, yellow daisies,

green foliage in center, scalloped border, Copeland-Spode, ... **9.00**

Pitcher, 6" h, grey-white cameos, med blue ground, c1875, **$175.00**

"Spode's Tower" pattern, blue transfer, ... **20.00**

7 1/4" d

Cobalt and brick red Imari pattern, "Copeland & Garrett Spode's New Stone" mk, c1840, ... **15.00**

"Tobacco Leaf" pattern, gilt outlined lg blue leaf, sm iron-red flowerheads, blue stems, peach accents, "blue Copeland Late Spode" mk, ... **58.00**

Plate, 7 1/2" d, "Italian" pattern, blue transfer, "Copeland Spode's Italian England and imp Copeland and crown" marks, **$65.00**

7 3/4" d, "The Ruins" pattern, oak leaf and acorn border, brown transfer, ivory ground, ... **10.00**

8" d, spiral fluted, "Fairy Dell" pattern, Copeland Spode, ... **10.00**

8 7/8" d, painted botanical specimens, green border, gilt dentil scalloped rim, dtd 1852, set of 7, (A), ... **285.00**

9" d

"Cairo" pattern, brown transfer, ... **35.00**

HP "Newark Castle," or "Auld Brig O Doon" in center, med green border w/raised gilt shells and feather designs, white and gilt rope rim, "W.T. Copeland & Sons, Ltd" mks, pr, ... **245.00**

Red poppy, green foliage in center, relief molded daisy heads on border, green lined indented rim, "Copeland-Spode" mk, ... **25.00**

9 1/4" d, "Grasshopper" pattern, med blue transfer, "imp Spode New Stone" mk, ... **65.00**

10" d

"Bologna-Byron Views," lady and 2 men walking in classical gardens, view of bay, acanthus and scroll border, med blue transfer, "Copeland & Garrett Late Spode" mk, ... **95.00**

Camel and couple in scroll w/flying birds in center, geometric and snowflake border design, indented rim, brown transfer, "W.T. Copeland & Sons" mk, ... **35.00**

10 1/2" d

"Camilla" pattern, lt blue transfer, ... **58.00**

"Chinese Rose" pattern, ... **12.00**

"Buttercup" pattern, "Chelsea Wicker" shape, yellow buttercups in center w/sm blue flowers and green and brown foliage, brown inner border, molded basketweave border w/florals, scalloped rim, "Copeland Spode England Buttercup" mk, ... **15.00**

"Marina" pattern, lg bouquet of loose flowers in center, scattered floral border, scalloped rim, brown transfer, ... **35.00**

10 3/4" d

"Geranium" pattern, black transfer, crimped rim,

"Copeland Late Spode Geranium" mk, ... **35.00**

Turkey walking in field, multicolored transfer, red flowerhead on blue ground on border, lobed rim, "blue COPELAND LATE SPODE ENGLAND" and "imp COPELAND SPODE" mks, c1887-94, set of 4, (A), ... **412.00**

11" d, "Carolyn" pattern, multicolored scattered floral sprigs, ... **15.00**

Platter

9 1/2" l x 6 1/4" w, rect w/cut corners, "Spode's Peacock" pattern, multicolored, ... **60.00**

15" d, "Spode's Tower" pattern, blue transfer, molded rope rim, ... **100.00**

15" l, "Cowslip" pattern, mauve blue, yellow, and red transfer, molded diaper border, "Copeland Spode England Spode's Cowslip" mk, ... **55.00**

15 1/2" d, "Fairy Dell" pattern, mustard yellow, fuchsia, violet, lime green, dk blue, and maroon flora and fauna, ivory ground, fluted border, Copeland Spode, ... **65.00**

Serving Dish, 8" w, 3 section, 3 molded cabbage leaves joined at center ring handle, white glaze, ... **50.00**

Soup Bowl

6 1/4" H-H, w/underplate, 7 1/8" d, "Camilla" pattern, pink-red transfers, "Spode's Camilla Copeland ENGLAND" mk, ... **25.00**

7 1/2" d, "Buttercup" pattern, yellow floral, molded wicker border, piecrust rim, Copeland-Spode, ... **16.00**

Sugar Bowl, Cov, 3 7/8" h, vert ribbing, "Madeira" pattern, basketweave relief band, Copeland Late Spode, ... **10.00**

Teapot

5 1/2" h x 10" w, blue "Italian" pattern, ... **225.00**

6" h, med blue center band w/white cameos of hunting scene and dogs, cov w/white stiff leaves on blue ground, dtd 1898, .. **110.00**

6 1/4" h, Cadogan style, applied flower sprigs and berries, manganese brown glaze, "imp COPELAND & GARRETT" mk, ... **175.00**

6 3/4" h, paneled, HP red and tan flying birds in brown bamboo w/green leaves, bamboo handle, pewter cov, "Copeland & Sons" mk, ... **425.00**

Toast Rack, 6 1/2" l, 5 bars, "Spode's Italian" pattern, blue transfer, c1902, ... **150.00**

Tray, 6 3/4" H-H, "Polka Dot" pattern, multicolored fruit and flowers in center, blue polka dot ground blue lined rims, blue dash tab handles, ... **25.00**

Trio, cup, saucer, plate, 6 1/4" d, "Chinese Rose" pattern, "Copeland-Spode England" mk, ... **30.00**

Urn, 24 1/2" h, amphora shape, cobalt ground, applied gilt C-scroll handles, gilt accented rococo base, gilt accents on shoulder an interior rim, Copeland and Garrett, c1833-47, pr, ... **6,850.00**

Vase, 12 1/4" h, ovoid shape, socle foot, sq gilt base, turquoise ground, named painted scene of "Geneva" in rect gilt frame, reverse w/panel of flowering plants, wall, and urn, or named painted scene of "Tophana" in rect gilt frame, reverse w/rivers, dome and balcony, flowers at side on reveres, gilt swirls on foot, gilt winged female handles, Copeland-Garrett, pr, ... **12,500.00**

Vegetable Bowl, Cov

9" sq, "Spode's Peacock" pattern, multicolored, c1920s, ... **85.00**

11" H-H, "Billingsly Rose" pattern, ... **175.00**

c. 1930

c. 1930

CORNISH WARE

**T.G. Green
Church Gresley Potteries
Burton on Tent,
South Derbyshire
1860-Present**

History: Developed in the 1920s and 1930s to counter a slowdown in business following the war, Green turned ordinary white ware into stylish kitchenware by adding wide blue stripes. Canisters, storage jars, and some tableware were introduced, many of which carry black names such as "Cocoa, Milk, and Soda," to name a few. The use of yellow stripes was introduced as an alternative color scheme.

Some experimental colors, including red, brown, lilac, orange, and black, never made their way to the kitchen. From 1968 to 1980, Judith Onions restyled many of the pieces by introducing new colors and shapes. Mason Cash & Company continues to manufacture Cornish Ware today.

References: Paul Atterbury, *Cornish Ware & Domestic Pottery By T.G. Green*, Richard Dennis Publications, 2001.

Collecting Hints: Collectors seek early examples, so dating by backmark is important. Storage containers such as "Apricots" and "Borax," are highly prized.

Butter Dish, Cov, 6" d x 4" h, black "BUTTER" on center white stripe, alternating yellow and white horiz stripes, ... **60.00**

Canister, 5 1/2" h, black "COFFEE," blue and white horiz stripes, ... **90.00**

Coffeepot, 7 1/2" h, cylinder shape, yellow and white horiz bands, "T.G. Green" mk, ... **155.00**

Cereal Bowl, 6 1/2" d, blue and white horiz banding, green mk, ... **60.00**

Cream Pitcher, blue and white horiz banding, "T.G. Green" mk

2 7/8" h, ... **45.00**

3 1/2" h, ... **35.00**

Cup and Saucer, blue and white horiz banding, ... **25.00**

Egg Cup, 3 1/4" h, dbl, blue and white horiz banding, ... **30.00**

Milk Jug, 3" h

Blue and white horiz banding, "T.G. Green Cornish Kitchen Ware" mk, ... **20.00**

Yellow and white horiz banding, ... **50.00**

Mixing Bowl

6" d, blue and white horiz bands, ... **55.00**

8" d, blue and white horiz bands, "T.G. Green" mk, ... **30.00**

9 3/4" d, blue and white horiz bands, "T.G. Green" mk, ... **25.00**

Mug, 4 3/8" h, blue and white horiz bands, "T.G. Green & Co." mk, ... **55.00**

Mustard Pot, Cov, 2 1/2" h, "Blue Domino" pattern, ... **45.00**

Pitcher, 5" h, gold and white horiz bands, "T.G. Green Co Ltd Cornish Kitchen Ware Made in England" mk, ... **20.00**

Plate

9" d, yellow and white border bands, ... **25.00**

10" d, blue and white border bands, ... **15.00**

Pudding Bowl, 4" h x 6" d, blue and white horiz bands, green mk, ... **50.00**

Rolling Pin, 18" H-H, blue and white bands, blue wood handles, "T.G. Green Co." mk, ... **120.00**

Salt Pig, 5" w, black "SALT" on white band, blue and white horiz bands, green mk, ... **295.00**

Salt Shaker, 4 3/4" h, black "SALT" on white band, blue and white horiz bands, ... **40.00**

Shaker, 5" h, black "FLOUR" on white center band blue and white horiz bands, "T.G. Green & Co." mk, ... **60.00**

Storage Caddy, 5 1/2" h, black "COCOA" on white band, blue and white horiz bands, ... **500.00**

Storage Jar, 3 5/8" h, "black BAKING POWDER," blue and white horiz bands, $125.00

Storage Jar

3 1/2" h

Black "Bl. CARB. SODA" on white center band, blue and white horiz bands, ... **120.00**

Black "CREAM OF TARTAR" on white center band, blue and white horiz bands, ... **100.00**

5" h

Black "CANDIED PEEL" on white center band, blue and white horiz bands, "T.G. Green" mk, ... **120.00**

Black "COCOA" on white center band, blue and white horiz bands, "T.G. Green" mk, ... **150.00**

Yellow and white horiz stripes, "T.G. Green & Co." mk, ... **25.00**

5 1/2" h

Black "CORNFLOUR" on center white band, blue and white horiz bands, ... **200.00**

Black "PEAS" on center white band, blue and white horiz bands, ... **195.00**

Black "RICE" on center white band, blue and white horiz bands, black mk, ... **195.00**

Black "SOAP FLAKES" on center white band, blue and white horiz bands, ... **600.00**

6 1/4" h, black "RICE" on white center band, blue and white horiz bands, ... **45.00**

6 1/2" h

Black "PEARL BARLEY" on white center band, blue and white horiz bands, ... **225.00**

Black "STONED DATES" on white center band, blue and white horiz bands, ... **65.00**

Yellow and white horiz bands, black mk, ... **25.00**

Sugar Bowl, 4 1/2" d, white domino pattern on med blue ground, "T.G. Green Co." mk, ... **10.00**

Sugar Shaker, 4 1/2" h, screw lid, black "SUGAR" on white band, blue bands top and base, "T.G. Green Co." mk, ... **50.00**

PRICE BROS

MADE IN ENGLAND

c. 1934-61*

COTTAGE WARE

England and Germany 1920s-1990s

History: Household items were shaped like cottages, pubs, historic buildings, and "crime cottages," which were the scenes of famous crimes. Cookie jars, teapots, jugs, toast racks, and multiple pieces of tableware were molded and painted in bright colors, often including "climbing vines" and foliage.

Price Brothers was the major manufacturer of this charming ware, although Shelley and Royal Winton were also major players.

References: Eileen Rose Busby, *Cottage Ware*, Schiffer Publications, J. Donnelly, *The Charlton Standard Catalogue of Cottageware*, The Charlton Press, 2000.

Bank, 5" h x 4 1/2" w, brown thatched roof, dk brown window frames and door, slot in roof for coins, Price Kensington, ... **30.00**

Biscuit Barrel

5 3/4" h, shades of tan and brown, replaced woven overhead handle, "Arthur Wood Made in England" mk, ... **50.00**

7 1/2" h, brown thatched roof, dk brown window, woven overhead handle, Price Kensington, ... **25.00**

Box, Cov, 4" h, lt and dk brown, red and green vines, Price Brothers, ... **30.00**

Butter Dish, Cov

6" w x 4" h, lt brown roof, blue windows, tan cobblestone base, chimney knob, ... **15.00**

6 1/2" l x 5 1/2" h, lt and dk brown, white body, Price Kensington, ... **25.00**

Cottage Ware, Butter Dish, 4 3/4" h, 6 3/4" l, HP brown and yellow, "Keele St. Pottery Company" mark, $100.00

Cheese Dish, Cov

4" h x 6" sq, "Trellis Rose" pattern, climbing rose vine on cov, brown trellis base, Royal Winton, ... **1,100.00**

5" h x 8" w, cottage, tan thatched roof w/red chimney pots, lt brown house w/red and green molded foliage, green base, "Olde England, Royal Winton" mk, ... **85.00**

5 1/2" h x 5 1/2" w, 2 story manor house, med brown body w/molded cross timbers, green trailing foliage from roof to base,

dbl chimney knob, Arthur Wood, ... **65.00**

6 1/4" h x 6 1/4" w, brown thatched roof w/dk brown chimney, cream stone cottage w/dk brown doors and framed windows, green textured ground, Beswick, ... **60.00**

6 3/8" l x 5 1/4" w, med blue thatched roof, dk brown windows and door, dbl chimney knob, Burlington, ... **40.00**

7" l, country house, lt brown thatched roof w/2 chimney pots, cream house, dk brown window frames w/blue windows, green base, Carlton, ... **45.00**

Coffee Cup and Saucer, med brown ground, dk brown arched windows, green border on saucer, Price brothers, ... **15.00**

Condiment Set

4" h, w/tray, 6" l, salt, pepper, and cov jar, figural cottages, Price Kensington, ... **35.00**

4 1/2" h, "Trellis Rose" pattern, shakers w/brown arbor and vines topped by green foliage and red roses, stepped base w/multicolored florals, Royal Winton, ... **600.00**

Cream Jug

2 1/2" h

Oct, lt and dk brown, white body, Price Kensington, ... **13.00**

Sq, brown vines w/orange-red and yellow leaves, green handle, brown int, ... **30.00**

2 3/4" h, sq, brown thatched roof w/light green foliage, brown body w/dk brown windows and door, Keele Street, ... **10.00**

3 1/4" h, sq, tan brick ground, dk brown windows, brown thatched roof, Burlington, ... **10.00**

Cup and Saucer

Lt yellow ground, Keele Street, ... **45.00**

Tan ground, dk brown windows, Burlington, ... **15.00**

Dish

5" d, relief molded cottage, brown brick road in front, blue sky, dk brown rim, Price Kensington, ... **15.00**

8 1/2" sq, "Ye Olde Inne" pattern, relief molded, Royal Winton, c1935, ... **435.00**

Egg Set, 4 cups, 2" h, tray, 6" sq, lt and dk brown, white windows, Price Kensington, ... **20.00**

Honey Pot, Cov, 4" h, w/spoon, brown thatched roof, tan body w/dk brown windows, dk red and green trim, Price Kensington, ... **30.00**

Hot Water Pot, Cov, 9 1/2" h, 3 story brown house w/dk brown windows, "green Kensington Made in England Cottageware" mk, ... **30.00**

Jam Jar, 5" h, circ form, brown thatched roof, white stone body, violet door, Babbacombe Devon, ... **25.00**

Jar, 6 1/2" h, turret shape, brown roof w/red flowers, dk brown window and door frames, Price Kensington, ... **20.00**

Jug

3" h, tan and brown, Price Kensington, ... **10.00**

5 1/2" h, circ timbered house, overall green glaze, Price Brothers, ... **15.00**

8 1/2" h, Pixie Ware, red pixie seated next to stone building wall, green foliage w/purple fruit at top, mushrooms on base, Royal Winton, ... **680.00**

Jug, Cov, 4 3/4" h, red roof, green foliage, tan water wheel on side, ... **110.00**

Mug, 3 1/2" h, tapered, brown body and handle, dk brown window frames, green foliage, Price Brothers, ... **10.00**

Pitcher

4 3/4" h, corset shape, med brown upper section, dk brown window frames, Price Kensington, ... **15.00**

7 1/4" h, relief molded cottage, trees, and shrubs, tan ground, molded red flowerhead on handle, "Price Bros. Made in England Cottage Ware Reg. No. 845007" mk, ... **50.00**

8" h

Circ 4 story house, dk brown window frames, green foliage on sides, Price Kensington, ... **35.00**

Sq, peaked roof, med brown, dk brown window frames, green foliage on base, molded hunter on horse w/hounds at side, Price Kensington, ... **60.00**

Planter, 10" l x 6" w x 3 1/2" h, rect, "Ye Olde Inne" pattern, brown timbered inn, hanging swan sign, brown and green relief molded tree, rose path, Royal Winton, ... **2,400.00**

Preserve Jar, 4 1/2" h

Brown thatched roof, dk brown timbers, red door, chimney knob, Babbacombe Devon, ... **20.00**

Circ shape, orange-brown tiled roof, dbl green swirl knob, white imp diamond pattern on body, mint green base, Shorter, ... **15.00**

Sauceboat, 3 3/4" h x 7" l, w/underplate, med brown w/green foliage, white gables, dk brown window frames, Price Kennsington, ... **30.00**

Storage Jar, 8 1/2" h, circ brown brick house, dk brown window frames, green foliage, Price Kensington, ... **35.00**

Sugar Shaker, 5" h, old mill, red-brown roof, green foliage on tan building, brown water wheel, Royal Winton, ... **625.00**

Teapot

4 1/2" h x 4 1/2" l, lt and dk brown, white body, twig handle and spout, Price Kensington, ... **15.00**

5" h, circ, HP Cotswold style of brown washed grey stone body, lt brown thatched roof, green door, Sylvac, ... **68.00**

6" h

Brown thatched roof, dk brown brick chimney knob, tan brick body, green foliage on base, blue windows, green door, Sylvac, ... **25.00**

Devon Cottage, red-brown thatched roof, dbl chimney, dk brown beams, blue windows, green grass base, "John Shaw Burlington Ware Staffordshire England" mk, ... **53.00**

Figural florist shop, brown thatched roof, blue window, dk brown door, foliage and flowers, "FLORIST" in blue oval, ... **10.00**

"Ye Olde Swan Inn," 2 story figural inn, red roof w/green accents, dk brown vert timbers over yellow upper walls, tan lower walls w/sign and swan at corners, Royal Winton, ... **65.00**

Teapot, 6 1/2" h x 9 1/2" l, brown roof, yellow body, red and green foliage, "Paramount Pottery Co. England Ltd" mk, $45.00

6 1/2" h
Ann Hathaway's Cottage, tan body, rose florals, green foliage handle and spout, Royal Winton, ... **1,475.00**
Brown thatched roof, dk brown window frames, green foliage, Price Brothers, ... **75.00**

Tea Set
Pot, 6" h, creamer, 3 1/2" d, cov sugar bowl, circ bodies, tan thatched roofs, green doors, brown brick, Sylvac, ... **225.00**
Pot, 7" h, creamer, 3" h, cov sugar bowl, 4" h, cov jam jar, 4 1/4" h, brown and tan thatched roofs, cream stone bodies, lt brown window frames, Keele Street Pottery, ... **50.00**
Toast Rack, 4" h x 5 1/2" l, 5 bar, brown body and chimney handle, dk brown window frames, Price Kennsington, ... **25.00**

COW CREAMERS

Staffordshire, England Second half of 18th C to mid-19th C Delft, Holland c1755

History: Cow creamers are cow-shaped cream jugs. They feature an oval hole opening in the top of the back of the cow for filling the creamer. The spout is the mouth, with the curved tail serving as a handle. Most filling holes had lids, but today they are often missing.

Some cow creamers have a seated milkmaid alongside the creamer. The earliest earthenware cow creamers were made in Staffordshire during the second half of the 18th century.

English cow creamers were made in Whieldon ware, creamware, Prattware, and many other ceramic types. Large size versions often were called cow milk jugs. Cow creamers in tin-glazed ware, c1755, were made at Delft, Holland.

Museum: City Museum and Art Gallery, Stoke-on-Trent, Hanley, England.

Covered
5" h
5 1/2" l, orange-brown spotting, molded green grass base, ... **350.00**
7" l
Lg orange-brown spots, white body, oval base, ... **395.00**
Overall brown glaze, stepped oval base, c1850, ... **40.00**

---

7 1/4" l, brown, yellow, and orange sponging, blue lined moss green base, ... **1,850.00**

Cov., 5" h, 6 1/2" l, green, rust, and chartreuse florals, gold horns, iron-red and mustard stiped base, unmkd, A-$207.00

Jackfield, gloss black glaze w/gold spots, ... **300.00**
Willow pattern, blue, c1840, ... **1,095.00**
5 1/4" h x 6 3/4" l, black spotted body on white ground, brown muzzle, black interlocking half circles on sides of rect base, England, c1940, ... **250.00**
5 1/2" h
6 1/2" l, standing goat, mottled blue and white, brown tipped tail and hooves, green rect base w/canted corners, c1800, repairs, replaced cov, ... **6,500.00**
Ochre and brown sponging, seated milkmaid in translucent green dress, ... **570.00**
Spattered bands of black and dk orange, black haired milkmaid in dk green dress, dk green base, ... **1,200.00**
5 3/4" h, iron-red spots, pink luster splotches, green rocky base, Swansea, repairs, ... **600.00**
6" h
Brown and black sponged circles, white ground, green textured base, ... **1,650.00**
Pink luster and brown spotting, raised green oval base, restored tail, Swansea, ... **625.00**
6" l, brown-red shaded spots and dashes, white ground, rect base w/vert fluting, ... **2,250.00**
6 1/2" l, lg blue and purple luster splashes, green wash base, Swansea, (A), ... **300.00**
7" l
Heavy manganese sponging, seated milkmaid in orange dress, green shaded base, c1800, ... **1,850.00**

Med brown body, dk brown legs, white face w/brown spotting, green textured base, Swansea, replaced cov, ... **1,000.00**
7 1/2" l, blue printed oriental scenes on sides, brown muzzle, white body, molded green oval base, repaired horn, ... **200.00**
8" l, pink sponged body, black horns, seated milkmaid in green blouse, pink sponged skirt, green shape base, (A), ... **500.00**

Open
3" h x 6 1/2" l, cow lying down, black glaze, ... **120.00**

Open, 3 3/8" h, 7 1/2" l, rust glaze, unmkd, A-$35.00

3 3/8" h x 7" l, reclining, "Victorian Chintz" pattern, Burleigh, ... **50.00**
3 1/2" h
5 1/2" l, blue windmill on side, flowers on reverse, blue outlined eyes and hooves, white ground, ... **10.00**
5 3/4" l, lg brown shaded spots, bell on neck, Goebel, blue full bee and V, ... **60.00**
7" l, reclining, black to grey shading, ... **45.00**

Open, 4" h, 7 1/4" l, blue shades, unmkd, A-$45.00

4" h
7" l, overall white glaze, ... **10.00**
7 1/4" l, tin glazed, "Chantilly" style painted garden flowers, brown horns and hooves, blue striped tail, ... **295.00**
4 1/4" h x 6 1/4" l, overall orange-brown color, black hooves, eyes, and tail, ... **42.00**

4 1/2" h

7" l, reclining cow, "Calico" pattern, blue overall sheet design, Burleigh, ... **20.00**

7 1/4" l, brown airbrushed top, white underbody Germany, c1930s, ... **115.00**

Seated cow, blue flowers on sides, blue collar and bell, white ground, unmkd, ... **20.00**

Cov, 5" h x 6 1/2" l, black spotting, white ground, orange udder, gold lustered horns, green base, (A), $125.00

4 3/4" h

4 1/2" w, cow seated on haunches, amber-brown glaze, black tail handle, ... **25.00**

7" l, standing cow, black, grey, and white shading, salmon pink ears, nose, and horns, France, ... **200.00**

7 3/8" l, gloss brown shaded ground, Germany, horn chip, ... **18.00**

7 1/2" l, standing bull, black top, white underside, "GERMANY" mk, ... **115.00**

5" h x 7 1/2" l, Delft style blue windmill and sailboat on side, sailboat on reverse, figural udder, ... **65.00**

5" l, reclining, white w/multicolored crest of "Cowes," unmkd, ... **28.00**

5 1/8" h, 6 1/4" l, orange-brown splashes, grey horns, green oval base, ... **75.00**

5 1/4" h

7" l, standing cow, head raised, tan upper section, white underbody, c1930, ... **185.00**

Comical, standing wearing yellow dress, white collar, orange dots on cuffs, lt blue scarf, pink underskirt, repaired horn, ... **95.00**

5 1/2" h x 9 1/2" l walking cow, dk brown back and head, white legs, underbody, and tail, Czechoslovakia, ... **125.00**

5 3/4" h, seated cow, Delft style blue and white design of windmills on sides, flowers on chest, blue horns, ... **15.00**

6" h

6" l, black spotting on white ground, black tail handle, unmkd, ... **50.00**

8" l, black spotted white cow, standing milkmaid w/hole in hat, blue shaded flowered dress, brown accented oval green base, restored horns and ears, ... **260.00**

10" l, brown shading, ... **425.00**

6 1/2" l, blue Willow pattern, unmkd, ... **18.00**

7" l, reclining, white body w/brown shading, "GT Yarmouth" mk, ... **26.00**

CREAMWARE

English/Continental c1740 to Present

History: Creamware (cream-colored earthenware) provided a fine form and thin body in addition to a clean and brilliant glaze. Creamware made no pretense to imitate porcelain in color, form, or decoration. Yet, it found a ready acceptance in the marketplace.

Creamware was made from the beginning of the 18th C. The materials were identical to those used to make salt glaze. The principal difference was that creamware was fired at a lower temperature and glazed with lead.

In 1740 Enoch Booth of Tunstall in Staffordshire developed a fluid glaze that provided a brilliant, transparent cream color. Thomas Whieldon and Josiah Wedgwood both used this glaze. By 1760 enameled decoration was being added to the creamware glaze. Derbyshire, Liverpool, Yorkshire, and Swansea also produced creamware products.

Creamware was improved in 1768 by introducing china clay and china stone from Cornwall into the body and glaze. This resulted in creamware that was paler in color, as well as lighter and more brilliant in the glaze.

Since there was much interchange and copying of ideas among a number of potteries, similarities in both the body and glaze were found. Hence, it is quite difficult to assign early creamware to a particular factory because most creamware was unmarked prior to that manufactured by Wedgwood.

Creamware was the main product in England between 1760 and 1820 and had supplanted the manufacture of white salt glaze by c1780. Creamware's prominence during these years provided the death blow to tin-glazed earthenware in England and on the Continent. From c1760, English creamware was exported to nearly every European country.

Many Staffordshire potters left England and established factories in France, thus threatening the faience factories and undercutting the sale of porcelains. The European factories turned to manufacturing creamware in self defense.

Reference: Donald Towner, *Creamware*, Faber & Faber, 1978.

Museums: Castle Museum, Norwich, England; Cincinnati Art Museum, Cincinnati, OH; City Museum & Art Gallery, Hanley, Stoke-on-Trent, England; Victoria & Albert Museum, London, England.

Basket Stand, 7 1/2" d, molded basketweave body w/knot in center, open loop border, ... **150.00**

Cheese Cradle, 11 1/2" l x 5 1/2" h, quarter moon shape, oval pedestal base, c1820, hairline, ... **565.00**

Coffeepot, 10" h

Blue painted flowers, stems, and leaves, blue accented molded mask under spout, c1780, restored, ... **1,475.00**

Dbl strap handle, pewter hinge, figural convolvulus knob, ... **1,600.00**

Dish, 10" l x 8" w, molded basketweave body, green outlined oval and diamond in center, green outlined reticulated border, Neale, c1760, ... **950.00**

Feeding Pot, Cov, 4 3/4" h, perforated spout tip, overall white glaze, restored chip, ... **800.00**

Figure, 12 7/8" h, standing brown spotted yellow giraffe before brown tree trunk, rect base w/black marbleized top and red marbleized sides, early 19th C, (A), ... **1,795.00**

Fruit Bowl, 12 1/2" l, oval, scalloped and pierced sides, molded swags, c1790, ... **2,000.00**

Jug, 10 3/4" h, black printed "James Whiffin Thorp Market 1794" in cartouche under spout, oval panel w/Apollo as Sun God in chariot, surrounded by signs of zodiac, reverse w/Venus as Moon Goddess, border of love and trophies, restored, (A), ... **710.00**

Mug

4 1/4" h, bat printed w/classical scenes in gilt reserves, star crack, (A), ... **250.00**

6 5/8" h, tinted black printed man, woman, and dog, sailing ship in

bkd w/"Jack on a cruise," and "Avast there, back you main topsail." **1,900.00**

Pepper Pot, 3 1/2" h, monument shape w/sq base, white glaze, pr, .. **245.00**

Pitcher, 7 1/2" h, paneled base, molded figural Toby top, gold trim, late 19th C, ... **145.00**

Plaque, 6" h, oval, molded relief of bust of Duke of Cumberland, brown hair, green sash, ochre rimmed shirt, green foliage border, ... **2,175.00**

Plate, 7 3/4" d, molded "husk" pattern, c1780, **$360.00**

Plate

8 1/4" d, dk blue stylized meandering flowerheads, stems, and leaves, molded inner borders, reticulated rim w/blue line, "imp Vienna" mks, set of 6, ... **175.00**

Continental, Plate, 8" d, dk brown transfer, "imp Gien" mark, **$125.00**

8 1/2" d

Lg blue stem w/2 carnations and bud, blue banded vert lined rim, ... **100.00**

Molded basketweave center, reticulated loop border, ... **52.00**

9 3/8" d, red and green famille rose style design in center, inner band of red and green buds and leaves, red streaks and cells on border, c1780, ... **95.00**

England, Plate, 8" d, "incised beehive" mark, A- **$35.00**

9 3/4" d, silver shape, press molded, indented wavy rim, c1780, ... **110.00**

10" d, black transfer of 3 masted sailing ship, black lined rim, rim chips, Shorthose and Heath, c1815, ... **120.00**

Platter, 16" d, silver shape, press molded shaped rim, pale yellow glaze, c1780, ... **300.00**

Porringer, 4 3/4" d, applied handle, sponged mang ground w/ochre and green spotting, c1770, hairline, ... **1,250.00**

Sauceboat, 5 3/4" l, molded figural dolphin, head spout, tail forms handle, brown and green accents, c1780, ... **1,500.00**

Serving Dish, 8" w, 3 molded scallop shells form body, figural bird on branch center handle, ivory glaze, England, c1780, (A), ... **1,875.00**

Soup Plate, 9 1/4" d, molded basketweave, dot, and diaper border, scalloped rim, overall brown translucent glaze, Staffordshire, c1760, (A), ... **325.00**

Sugar Shaker, 4 1/4" h, ovoid, pierced diamond pattern on neck, c1800, ... **395.00**

Tankard

5 3/4" h, black printed "A West View of the Iron Bridge at Sunderland," hairlines, (A), ... **350.00**

6" h, "Mr John Bowker of Bowker Bank 1777" in maroon and pink wreath, hairline, ... **550.00**

Teabowl and Saucer, lg red cabbage rose w/green foliage, scattered sprigs, molded beaded inner rim on saucer, chips, ... **185.00**

Teapot

4 1/4" h, modeled as pineapple, underglazed yellow and green enamels, flower knob, Staffordshire, chips, c1765, (A), ... **7,050.00**

4 3/8" h, bullet shape, leaf molded spout, strap handle, relief molded accent fruit and vegetables in basket accented w/green, yellow, grey, and brown, basket molding on cov, flower knob, William Greatbatch, repairs, c1770, (A), ... **700.00**

5 1/2" h, globular, lead glazed melon design of alternating green and yellow vert striping, leaf molded spout, dbl scrolled handle, applied leaves and florets, Staffordshire, c1770, glaze missing, (A), ... **8,225.00**

Tureen, Cov, 8 1/4" l, w/attached undertray, molded palm frond handles, flowerhead knob, England, ... **1,250.00**

CREIL
LM& Cie
MONTEREAU
1841-1895

CREIL

Seine-et-Marne and Oise, France 1784-1895

History: About 1784 the Englishman Bagnad, in association with M. de St. Cricq-Cazeaux, established a factory for manufacturing English-style earthenware. These two founders united with Montereau during the early 19th century, forming a firm that continued until 1895.

The Creil factory was the first French pottery to use transfer printing on earthenware. Transfer views of Paris, French chateaux, portraits of important people, English country houses, fables of La Fontaine, and paintings of religious or allegorical subjects in monochrome graced white or cream colored ware. Porcelain never was made.

Marks were either stamped in the paste or stenciled. They included Creil et Montereau or LM & C.

Lavabo, fountain, 21" h, basin, 14" w, blue printed classic scenes on reclining woman and cherubs in molded swirl cartouches, blue streaked molded cov, c1885, hairlines and restorations, ... **1,400.00**

Plate

7 3/4" w, oct, "HISTOIRE ROMAINE, ENTREE DE CLEOPATRE A TARSE AN DE ROME 7" or "CONDEMNATION DE MANIUS, AN DE ROME 37," grapevine border, black transfer, pr, ... **295.00**

8" d

"Le Fou Qui Vend Le Sagesse Fables," multicolored jester slapping gentleman, brown tree branches in bkd, "CM" mk, ... **45.00**

Man or woman hunters, holding rifles in center of dominos, border of ribbons and hunting horn, ... **80.00**

"The Cannons," border w/instruments and lions in wreath designs, black transfers, white ground, ... **175.00**

8 1/8" d, "Le Tour Du Monde En 80 Jours," border of palm fronds, lion heads, and birds, blue-black transfer, "Creil et Montereau L.M." mk, ... **100.00**

8 1/4" d

"Halte de Chasse," fallen hunter, black transfer, yellow ground, ... **300.00**

"La Lion de Martin," lion tamer feeding lion in center, floral and geometric border, brown transfer, "imp CREIL" mk, ... **55.00**

Plate, 8 1/2" d, black transfer, cream ground, "imp Creil" mark, $375.00

Man in water reaching for gentleman in top hat on shore w/trees, French saying below, classic leaf border band, black transfers, rim chip, ... **45.00**

8 1/2" d, center black transfer of sign for March For Women, man w/woman being led by rope around neck and gentleman w/French saying, multicolored border of flowers and panels and French military pieces, ... **195.00**

8 5/8" d, black transfer bust of "Louis XVII," "Roi de France et de Navarre," border of lilies, imp mk, ... **450.00**

9 1/4" d, "Place Vendome a Paris," oak leaf and acorn border, black transfers, yellow ground, unmkd, ... **110.00**

Plate, 9 1/2" d, dk red and green grasshopper, blue bird, green leaves, streaked blue rim, "Creil et Montereau" mk, $725.00

9 1/2" d, faience, pink, rose, and green transfer printed and color accented botanical specimen, butterfly, and insect, dk blue feathered rim, "Leboef & Miller" mk, late 19th C, ... **70.00**

9 3/4" d, "Eglise de la Sorbonne a Paris" in center, leaf border band, black transfers, white ground, ... **175.00**

Vase, 22 1/2" h, hex paneled, bulbous middle, flared neck and rim, hex ft, 2 gilt notched C-form handles, painted pseudo Arabic writing in panels, red, black, green, teal blue, and iron-red oriental house, flowerheads, and bridges on reverse, alternating panels of flowerheads on white or dk blue w/gilt designs, center dk red band on neck w/white and green

flowerhead, mkd, c1850, pr, ... **12,000.00**

CROWN AND ROYAL CROWN DERBY

Osmaston Road, Derby, England 1876 to Present

History: Edward Phillips, formerly of the Royal Worcester Company, established the Royal Crown Derby Porcelain Company on Osmaston Road in Derby in 1877. This new company had no connection with the original Derby works. By 1878 the new factory was producing earthenwares called "crown ware" in addition to porcelains.

The new Derby porcelain was richly decorated in the old "Japan" patterns featuring reds and blues along with rich gilding very much in the manner of the earlier Derby porcelains. Additionally, the new Derby company produced ornamental forms including figures and highly decorated vases and services.

The beginning of the Royal Crown Derby period began in 1890 when the company was appointed manufacturers of porcelain to Queen Victoria, and "Royal Crown Derby" was added to the trademark.

Desire Leroy was the most distinguished artist employed by Royal Crown Derby. He trained at the Sevres factory, went to Minton in 1878, came to Royal Crown Derby in 1890, and stayed until his death in 1908. His most successful contribution was the use of white enamels painted over rich dark blue ground in the style of Limoges enamels. He exhibited a great versatility of design and remarkable use of colors. His lavish designs usually featured birds in landscapes, fruits, flowers, and occasional figures. He also added gilt embellishments.

In 1904, toy shapes were produced that attracted the attention of miniature collectors. Figures were made in the late 1920s and early 1930s. During the postwar period, Arnold Mikelson modeled lifelike birds and animals.

In 1935, the Royal Crown Derby company purchased the small King Street works which had been established by some former Derby workers in 1848. This provided a link with the original Derby factory founded by William Duesbury in the mid-18th century.

References: F. Brayshaw Gilhespy, *Crown Derby Porcelain*, F. Lewis Ltd. 1951; F. Brayshaw Gilhespy & Dorothy M. Budd, *Royal Crown Derby China*, Charles Skilton Ltd. 1964; John Twitchett & Betty Bailey, *Royal Crown Derby*, Barrie & Jenkins, Ltd. 1976.

Museums: Cincinnati Art Museum, Cincinnati, OH; Gardiner Museum of Ceramic Art, Toronto, Canada; Royal Crown Derby Museum, Osmaston Road, Derby; Derby Museums & Art Gallery, The Strand, Derby; Victoria & Albert Museum, London, England.

Collecting Hints: Royal Crown Derby continues production to the present day as part of Royal Doulton Tablewares Ltd. From 1882 onwards, all Crown Derby can be dated. A year cypher appears under the trademark, the key for which can be found in Geoffrey A. Godden's *Victorian Porcelain*, Herbert Jenkins, 1961.

Bowl, 9" d, oct, panels of iron-red, cobalt, and gilt Imari designs, Crown Derby, ... **1,125.00**

Box, Cov, 4 1/2" sq, Imari style cobalt, iron-red, peach, and gilt stylized flowerheads and diamonds in compartments on cobalt ground w/gilt accents, Royal Crown Derby, ... **170.00**

Coffee Cup and Saucer, Imari pattern #1128, arched panels of flowerheads, cobalt, iron-red, and gilt, Royal Crown Derby, set of 6, ... **665.00**

Cup and Saucer
Iron-red, cobalt, and gilt Imari pattern #8310, dtd 1920, Royal Crown Derby, ... **80.00**
"London" shape, iron-red and cobalt bouquet in center of saucer, sprigs on border and cup, Crown Derby, ... **150.00**

Dinner and Dessert Service, Part, 2 soup tureens, 11 3/4" h, 4 sauce tureens and stands, 8 1/4" l, oval platter, 18 1/4" l, 3 oval platters, 14 1/2" l, 2 oval platters, 12 1/2" l, 4 cov rect dishes w/loop handles, 10 1/4" w, 4 lozenge shaped dishes, 9 3/4" l, 4 kidney shaped dishes, 9 3/4" w, dish, 9 3/4" sq, 54 dinner plates, 9 3/4" d, 18 soup plates, 9 3/4" d, 32 dessert plates, 8 1/8" d, "Formal Lotus Tree" pattern, iron-red, cobalt, green, and gilt, "iron-red crowned X'd batons and D" mks, Royal Crown Derby, c1815, (A), ... **41,825.00**

Dish, 9 1/2" w, hex shape, Imari pattern #6285, flat bowl of oriental flowers on table, cobalt, iron-red, and gilt, dtd

1911, Royal Crown Derby, pr, ... **630.00**

Figures, 7 1/8" - 7 1/2" h, "Earth, Water, and Air," lt blue, dk blue, yellow, pink, and red, gold accented bases, "iron red crown, X'd batons and D" marks, set of 3, A-$320.00

Flower Holder, 4 3/4" h, figural lilac nautilus shell, relief molded white coral and shells, Royal Crown Derby, c1880, ... **250.00**

Goblet, 4 1/2" h, iron-red, cobalt, and gilt Imari pattern of flowers, gilt diamond, flowing flowers in compartments, Royal Crown Derby, ... **180.00**

Jug
6 1/4" h, "Stanley," raised gold flowerheads and swirled stems, cream ground, gold accented grid paneled neck, Royal Crown Derby, ... **110.00**
10 1/2" h, figural white owl w/gilt outlined oak leaves on base and around rim, Royal Crown Derby, (A), ... **188.00**

Meat Platter, 17" l x 13 1/2" w, border of cobalt outlined brick red cartouches w/white stylized flowerhead and basket, cobalt curlicues between, Crown Derby, ... **100.00**

Muffin Dish, Cov
8" d, "Wilmot" pattern, iron-red brocade style flowerheads and butterflies, cobalt band on base, gilt accents, Royal Crown Derby, ... **175.00**
8 3/4" d, Imari pattern #2712, cobalt and iron-red scattered loose oriental flowers, border of Moorish style pockets of cell designs, Royal Crown Derby, ... **100.00**

Plate
7" d, 5 petaled stylized cobalt, iron-red, and gilt flowerhead in center, alternating border panels of red flowerhead or white and blue scale on cobalt ground, gilt accents, lobed rim, pattern

#1128, Royal Crown Derby, ... **180.00**
8" d
"Peacock" pattern, 3 stylized peacocks, blue transfer, dtd 1892, Royal Crown Derby, ... **20.00**
Two hunters on horseback and fencing in center, wavy fluted gilt and jeweled border, Royal Crown Derby, ... **145.00**
9" d, "Mikado" pattern, oriental man w/staff, another on bridge, tiered house on border, lg hanging, arched trees, blue transfer, Royal Crown Derby, ... **20.00**

Tea Plate, 6 1/4" d, bone china, "Blue Mikado" pattern, blue transfer, Royal Crown Derby, ... **35.00**

Teapot, 5 3/4" h, "Olde Avesbury" pattern, painted Chelsea style bird on each side, Royal Crown Derby, ... **195.00**

Vase
4 1/4" h, straight sides w/curved top and base, sm ft, tapered collar, HP multicolored hanging florals and compass rose, c1877, Crown Derby, ... **115.00**

Vase, 7 1/2" h, gold outlined orange, iron-red, or blue flowers, shaded cream to gold ground, cobalt neck and shoulder w/gold designs, Royal Crown Derby, **$695.00**

*Vase, 6" h, magenta and orange florets, gold outlined leaves, pink ground, cobalt trimmed neck, gold handles, Crown Derby, **$850.00***

7 1/4" h
Ball shape, Japanese style red, cream, blue, or mauve peonies and chrysanthemums, raised gilt accents gilt ground w/raised gilt and enameled flowerheads and leaves, short cobalt neck w/gilt comb design, Royal Crown Derby, ... **1,250.00**
Slightly swollen shape w/flared neck, raised gold leaves, flowers, and butterfly on yellow ground, Royal Crown Derby, ... **450.00**
9" h, tapered shape, lg shoulder, short, straight neck, raised and tooled gilt floral bouquet on front and reverse, teal blue ground, vert gilt lines on neck, gilt crisscross fencing on base, Crown Derby, ... **900.00**
11 1/2" h, bulbous shape, short neck, lg blue iris w/gilt accents on ivory ground, scattered gilt stems, cobalt neck w/gilt flowerheads, Royal Crown Derby, c1883, ... **595.00**
15 1/8" h, ovoid w/trumpet neck, molded and gilded spread ft, gilded neo-classical handles, painted lg spray of English garden flowers on front and reverse in raised gold scrollwork borders reserved on cobalt

ground, Royal Crown derby, dtd 1920, (A), ... **7,400.00**
Vase, Cov
5 3/4" h x 6" H-H, campana form, conical cov, gilt scroll handles, painted panels of flowers in gilt beaded trellis cartouches w/turquoise enameled jewels, rims and ft w/gilt foliage, spire knob w/turquoise enamel jewels, dtd 1900, Royal Crown Derby, (A), ... **11,350.00**
15" h, globular, raised gilt foliate decoration on cobalt ground, 2 gilt horiz handles on shoulder, gilt flowerhead knob, Royal Crown Derby, c1894, (A), ... **2,585.00**

CROWN DEVON

Stoke-on-Trent, England
1870 to 1982

History: S. Fielding and Co. Ltd. established a pottery at Stoke-on-Trent, England in 1870. This Staffordshire factory produced a wide variety of products including majolica wares, terra cotta wares, and earthenwares for domestic use.

Abraham Fielding acquired the pottery soon after it began. Its "majolica argenta" was a white body and glaze introduced in the early 1880s. The wares were decorated with high temperature colors and designs in relief.

After majolica fell out of fashion, it was replaced by vellum—a range of pale, biscuit colored ware with gilding and hand painted floral or topographical patterns that was made until World War I. A huge variety of patterns was made in cream and ivory grounds. "Royal Devon" was the most popular pattern made in vellum. Other "Royal" patterns included "Essex," "Sussex," "York," "Scotia," and "Suffolk."

From 1913 luster wares were sold under the trade name Crown Devon, including works done in the Art Deco style. In the early 1920s the lusterware was made for the higher end market, while embossed salad ware, tableware, and novelty items were made for the lower end market. Crown Devon Art Deco patterns included "Aztec," "Espanol," "Moresque," "Mattajade," "Mattajung," "Fairy Castle," and "Rustic Lustrine."

Ivrine figurines were made from 1919 for more than a decade. In addition to animals and birds, there were figurines of Gainsborough Girl, War Officer, Italian woman and man, Grecian lady and numerous others. In the late 1920s and 30s, Kathleen Parsons made Art Deco figures of Spring, Gina, Caroline, Ballerina, Old Kate, Flapper Girl, Bathing Girl, and Windy Day, and others.

In 1932 son Arthur Ross Fielding took over and added a range of musical pottery, including the John Peel Series, Widdicombe Fair, Auld Lang Syne, Daisy Bell, and Ilkla Moor Baht. Tankards, jugs, cigarette boxes, and salad bowls were designed which, when lifted, played popular tunes. He also made Art Deco colors and shapes with vivid patterns of stylized fruit and flowers, many of which had dark backgrounds.

After World War II, Reginald Fielding took over, and modern shapes and sharp contemporary color contrasts were used. Crown Devon also made souvenir and commemorative wares, as well as Christmas plates and Cries of London plates.

A fire in 1951 was the beginning of the end for Crown Devon. After 1967, Fieldings were no longer involved in the operations. The factory closed in 1982, a victim of the recession.

Marks used were an impressed "FIELDING" and "SF & CO" printed with the title of the pattern.

References: Ray Barker, *The Crown Devon Collectors Handbook, First Edition,* Francis-Joseph Books, 1997; Susan Hill, *Crown Devon,* Jazz Publications, 1993; Irene & Gordon Hopwood, *The Shorter Connection,* Richard Dennis, 1992.

Collecting Hints: The 1920s and 30s pieces are sought by collectors. There is a lot of interest in luster pieces, as well as mattajade and mattasung.

Bone Dish, 6 7/8" l, overall floral design, blue transfer, ... **8.00**
Box, Cov
4" sq, "Garden Path" pattern, pale yellow molded stone ground, green streaked rims, ... **115.00**
4 7/8" sq, 4 3/8" h, cream honeycomb ground w/relief of bees and floral feet, black, yellow, and blue figural knob, ... **210.00**
Bud Vase, 6 7/8" h, multicolored "Country Cousins" design on base, ... **10.00**
Candle Holder, 5 1/2" h, 2 nozzle, Art Deco style, black outlined red, orange, and yellow vert stripes on nozzles, yellow supports, sgd "Dorothy Ann," **15.00**
Cup and Saucer
"Chelsea" pattern, brown transfers, ... **10.00**

"Harlequin" pattern, white fruit on black ground, turquoise int of cup, "Crown Devon Fielding Harlequin" mk, ... **10.00**

Dish

5 1/4" w, triangle shape w/wavy gilt rim, multicolored decal of "Blacksmith Shop Gretna Green," **15.00**

11" H-H, sm blue, red, or white enameled flowers w/gilt, dk red and gilt accented ground, beaded rim, ... **35.00**

11" l, oval, sm orange or blue flowerheads, green foliage on border, pink ground, gold lobed rim, "Crown Devon Made in England" mk, ... **25.00**

Dresser Set, tray, 11 3/4" l, 2 jars, 4 1/4" d, "Fife" pattern, red and yellow roses, red and yellow flowerheads, green swags and curlicues, .. **20.00**

Figure

5" h x 6" l, "Churchill Bulldog," standing ivory dog w/brown patches, navy hat, black bow tie, smoking cigar, ... **725.00**

7" h x 4 1/2" w, Art Deco woman's face, red hat w/black rim, black eyes, red lips, ... **15.00**

Fruit Bowl, 10" l x 8 1/2" w, "My Garden" pattern, ... **45.00**

Ginger Jar, 5" h, ovoid shape, red, brown, green, and gilt oriental figures on bridge w/pagoda, dk blue ground, ... **100.00**

Gravy Boat, 6" l, w/undertray, 6 1/2" l, HP red tomatoes, green leaf molded ground, gold trim, ... **30.00**

Hatpin Holder, 4 1/2" h, "Wye" pattern, multicolored hanging florals, gold rim, ... **30.00**

Jug

3 1/2" h, "Glenwood" pattern, ... **35.00**

4" h

"Chelsea Pensioner," multicolored, ... **55.00**

Lg painted green and yellow flowerheads, brown stems and wavy lines, ... **20.00**

4 3/4" h, musical, "Killarny," couple in horse-drawn cart, branch handle, ... **175.00**

5 1/4" h, Art Deco shape, "Tiger Trees" pattern, orange and green balloon trees, artist sgd, ... **35.00**

5" h, gilt and enamel dragon on side, gilt symbols on neck, rouge luster ground, ... **125.00**

5 1/2" h

Enameled red grapes, gilt leaves and tendrils, maroon ground, MOP int, gilt handle, ... **45.00**

Horiz ribbing, dk red body, blue-grey wax drip, red drip rim, ... **20.00**

6 1/8" h, musical, "John Peel," mauve coat, blue scarf, yellow vest, holding riding crop, reverse w/fox head and crop, brown figural hound handle, ... **190.00**

7 1/8" h, musical, HP molded figures seated by hearth, cream ground, printed "Auld Lang Syn" on reverse, ... **400.00**

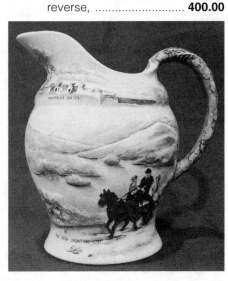

Jug, 8" h, musical, multicolored relief horse and cart scene, "The Irish Jaunting Car" and "Muckross Gates" at top, "Kilarney" verse on side, $185.00

7 7/8" h, musical, "Sarie Marais," young girl in green dress in landscape, brown figural lion handle, (A), ... **1,235.00**

8 1/2" h, musical, "Daisy Bell," couple on bicycle, red daisy and green stem figural handle, ... **260.00**

8 3/4" h, horiz ribbing, HP enameled orange, lt blue, mauve, and yellow flowerheads, blue luster ground, yellow luster int, gold lined rim and handle, ... **40.00**

9" h, Art Deco style pink, black, white, and yellow panels and zigzag designs, ... **55.00**

Jug, 8 5/8" h, musical, multicolored relief of carriage scene, "Bermuda," poem on reverse, $175.00

Pitcher 8" h

Stylized brown, orange, or red overlapped flowerheads, green single stroke foliage, cream ground, brown lined circ base, dbl handle, ... **45.00**

"Wye" pattern, red, yellow, or blue flowers, hanging chains, peach blush to white ground, molded swirls on border, ... **60.00**

Planter, 10 1/2" l, canoe shape, Arts and Crafts style muted florals on side on pale green ground, ... **175.00**

Plate

8" d, "Morning Glory" pattern on border, ... **8.00**

8 7/8" w, oct, Art Deco, painted trees, butterflies, and flowering shrubs, gold rock border, orange-red luster ground, ... **120.00**

10" d, multicolored center scene of Windsor Castle w/swans, lt green scrolling border, gilt rim, ... **160.00**

11" d, "Cries of London-Do You Want Any Matches," multicolored decal in center, molded geometrics on border, ... **50.00**

Scent Bottle, 3 1/2" h, "Devon Violet" pattern, ... **10.00**

Teapot, 5 1/4" h x 9 3/4" w, Art Deco style "Stockholm" pattern, leaping deer, red lined rims, ... **78.00**

Tea Service, teapot and stand, 5 1/2" h, hot water pot, 7 1/2" h, milk jug, 3" h, sugar bowl, 3 1/2" h, "Georgian Pearline," pink luster w/gold trim, ... **45.00**

Toby Jug, 8 1/2" h, "The Chelsea Pensioner," seated gentleman, red coat, holding black boots, ... **120.00**

Vase

4 1/4" h, squat shape, flared neck, horiz 1/2 circle handles, horiz ribbing in center, blue luster glaze w/mauve splashes, ... **72.00**

4 1/2" h, jar shape, "Pegasus," white horse and trees, red glazed ground, ... **35.00**

5" h, bulbous, spread foot, figural ram head handles, streaked orange-tan ground, ... **15.00**

5 1/2" h, bulbous w/ear handles, fan fluted base, Art Deco style brown tree w/green leaves and colored florals, ... **50.00**

6" h, bag shape, enameled "Fairy Castle," flowers, burgundy ground, gilt rim, ... **175.00**

7" h, tapered w/lg curled handles on rim, enameled sm lt or dk blue, yellow, or purple flowers, blue luster crackled ground, gold rim, ... **250.00**

7 3/4" h, trophy shape, spread ft, enameled orange, blue, white, or yellow oriental flowers, vert bamboo designs, med green ground, 4 gold ram's head handles, lt yellow int, ... **395.00**

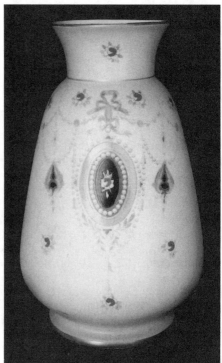

Vase, 8 5/8" h, red and green trim, gold accents, shaded matte tan ground, **$120.00**

8" h

Cylinder shape w/overlapping horiz sections, 3 sm horiz handles on side, 2 on reverse, stylized earthtone turquoise, orange, and tan flowerheads, brown rolling ground on base, ... **75.00**

Molded overlapping leaves and scrolls, white glaze, ... **28.00**

Ovoid, ruffled rim w/2 sm handles, flared base, enameled purple, green, orange, yellow, and gold garden scene w/butterflies, cobalt luster ground, ... **110.00**

Urn shape, ribbed base, 2sm curved handles, brown deer jumping near green trees, cream ground, dk red int, ... **75.00**

9" h

Bulbous base, flared neck, 2 loop handles, Art Deco style blue and green leaves on shaded pink ground, ... **45.00**

Vase, 9" h, orange tipped yellow flowers, sm blue flowers, green leaves, dk blue base, gold trim, matte yellow ground, 1930s, **$295.00**

Bulbous body, flared neck, classic design of hanging yellow baskets w/red roses, yellow sconces hanging from swags and chains w/red

roses, gold rim, "DEVON WARE SF & CO. STOKE ON TRENT ENGLAND ETNA RDNO 578617 CROWN DEVON" mk, ... **25.00**

11" h, transfer printed flying geese over cattails on front, flying goose on reverse, black ground, ... **95.00**

Wall Plaque

5 7/8" h x 5 7/8" w, figural head of Dalmatian dog, black spots on white ground, mkd, ... **125.00**

10" h, figural Tyrolean lad, hand shading eyes, green hat w/orange feather, orange jacket, lt brown knapsack, lt blue short pants, ... **150.00**

C. TIELSCH-GERMANY

Silesia, Germany, now Walbrzych, Poland 1845-1945

History: Beginning in 1845, the C. Tielsch and Company factory located at Altwasser made household, hotel, and decorative porcelain, along with coffee and tea sets. The C.M. Hutschenreuther Company in Hohenberg acquired most of the stock of Tielsch in 1918 and merged the factory with its own. Hutschenreuther continued using the C. Tielsch name until after World War II.

Dresser Tray, multicolored florals in center, lt blue ground, shaded green corners, "green C.T. Germany" mk, **$26.00**

Bowl

12 1/2" d, pink and yellow flowers around int border, cut out cream and gilt leaves on border, ... **190.00**

13" l, bouquet of multicolored flowers in center, raised gold border, scalloped rim, ... **40.00**

Cake Plate, 10" H-H

Decal of country village scene w/peddlers and dog and cart, gold tracery, "C.T. eagle" mk, ... **10.00**

Pink flowers, butterflies, gold trim, pink outlined molded open handles, pink lined rim, "C.T." mk, ... **20.00**

Celery dish, 12" l x 6" w, yellow, lilac, and pink sprigs of asters and chrysanthemums, molded florals garlands on borders and ends, floral rim band, ... **120.00**

Charger

12" d, transfer of florals in center, gold outlined molded reticulated leaf border, gold rim, "eagle, C.T. Germany" mk, ... **95.00**

13 1/2" d, bunches of purple violets and molded curl and swirl designs on border, gold indented rim, "green eagle C.T." mk, ... **95.00**

Cream Jug, 5 1/8" h, melon ribbed body w/scattered multicolored florals, wreath of florals on neck, gold rim, ivory ground, "green C.T. eagle" mk, ... **10.00**

Cup and Saucer, sm blue forget-me-nots, green foliage, brown stems, red to cream shaded ground, brushed gold rims and handle, "green eagle, C.T. Altwasser" mk, ... **40.00**

Dessert Bowl, 4 1/4" d, border band of sm pink roses, lt blue flowers, green leaves, black stylized branching, inner gold leaf band border, "C. Tielsch Altwasser, Silesia, Germany" mk, set of 4, ... **135.00**

Dish, 10 5/8" w, multicolored garden flowers in center, gold accented shell molded border, heavy gold swirl border, ... **225.00**

Divided Dish, 14 1/2" w x 9" w, scattered florals, brown molded border, center handle, ... **75.00**

Plate

7" d, border of hanging chains of pink roses entwined w/chain of green leaves, "C.T. Altwasser, Silesia" mk, ... **20.00**

8" d, lg yellow or mauve roses and sm bunches, green foliage on border, ... **10.00**

Serving Dish

12" d, multicolored bouquet of garden flowers in center, molded white leaves w/gold trim on border, gold rim, "C.Tielsch" mk, ... **105.00**

14" H-H, decal of bouquet of garden flowers in center, gold molded fancy border and handles, ... **295.00**

Tea Tile, 7" d, decal of pink floral bouquet, emb skirt w/gilt florals, beaded rim, ... **25.00**

Vase, 8 5/8" h, tapered form, narrow at base to wide shoulder, reverse tapered collar, 2 gilt outlined white rect handles, cream and blue hanging webs and flower sprays from gilt bands, cream-pink ground w/sm flowers, gilt collar w/pink flowers, "C.T. Altwasser Silesia, eagle" mk, ... **225.00**

Made in
Czechoslovakia
c 1920

CZECHOSLOVAKIA-GENERAL

1918 to Present

History: In 1918 the Czechs and Slovaks became free of Austro-Hungary domination and were granted their own country, Czechoslovakia. Portions of the regions of Bavaria, Bohemia, Moravia, and Austrian Silesia made up the new country. Bohemia, now the metropolitan area of Czechoslovakia, was the chief ceramic producing area in the Austro-Hungarian empire in the 19th century.

A variety of china wares was made by the many Czechoslovakian factories, among which are Amphora in Egyptian and Art Deco styles, and Erphila Art Pottery. Decorative items such as flower holders and wall pockets in the form of birds were produced. Creamers, salt and peppers, and napkin rings were made in interesting shapes. Kitchen or cereal sets and complete dinner sets, with pattern names such as "Iris," "Royette," "Royal Bohemia," "Ivory Rose," kept factory production high.

The Karlsbad Porcelain Factory "Concordia" Brothers Lew & Co. operated from c1919 until 1937. From 1939 until 1945, the factory was operated by Winterling & Co. It was nationalized in 1945 and merged with the former Count Thun's Porcelain nationalized factory in Klosterle.

Several other factories such as Meierhofen, Alp, and Altrohlau merged with Epiag in Karlsbad about 1939. This merged firm was nationalized in 1945.

Between 1871 and 1940, B. Bloch & Company made table, household, and decorative porcelain and earthenware, some in the onion pattern. After 1920 the name was changed to the Eichwald Porcelain and Stove Factory Bloch & Co., then to the Eichwald Porcelain Stove and Tile factory from 1940 until 1945.

Works of Ditmar Urbach feature boldly painted designs and are highly prized by collectors. An endless variety of patterns were produced.

Most items are stamped "Made in Czechoslovakia" with an ink stamp.

References: Dale & Diane Barta & Helen Rose, *Czechoslovakian Glass and Collectibles, Book II*, Collector Books, 1997; Ruth A. Forsythe, *Made in Czechoslovakia*, Richardson Printing Corp.1982; Ruth A. Forsythe, *Made in Czechoslovakia, Book 2*, Antique Publications, 1996. Sharon Bowers, Sue Closser, Kathy Ellis, *Czechoslovakian Pottery: Czeching Out America*, The Glass Press, 1999.

Collectors' Club: Czechoslovakian Collectors Guild International, P.O. Box 901395, Kansas City, MO 64190. Newsletter. Czechoslovakian Collectors Association, Cheryl Goyda, Box 137, Hopeland, PA, 17533, *Journal of Czechoslovakian Decorative Arts*-Biannual.

Ash Receiver, 7 7/8" h x 5 1/2" w, figural swimming white swan, airbrushed brown wingtips, yellow beak, "Ditman Urbach," **40.00**

Basket

4 3/4" h x 5 1/2" w, lg magenta and white blossoms on green ground, overhead handle, "green CZECHOSLOVAKIA" mk, ... **45.00**

5" h, yellow centered lg red or blue flowerheads, black leaves, stems, and vert lines, ivory ground, ... **30.00**

5 1/4" h x 4" d, mint green molded base, brown molded border and overhead handle, "Made in Czecho Slovakia" mk, ... **10.00**

Biscuit Barrel, 5 1/2" h, continuous black silhouette of dancing family, white ground, woven overhead handle, "Erphila Art Pottery Czechoslovakia" mk, ... **135.00**

Bookend, 4 3/8" h x 4 1/2" l, airbrushed blue figural penguin on white base, "Made in Czechoslovakia" mks, pr, ... **185.00**

Figure

7" h, rose parrot, steel-grey spread wings, perched on tan branch, "Made in Czechoslovakia" mk, ... **28.00**

7 3/4" h x 10" w, walking horse w/flowing mane, rock base, white glaze, ... **20.00**

8" h

Art Deco bust of woman, glazed yellow hair w/orange curls, unglazed brown face w/red lips, sq turquoise base, ... **110.00**

Dancing peasant couple, woman in red vest, flowered dress over red trimmed brown skirt, man holding hat overhead, brown jacket, black trousers, circ base, ... **185.00**

Fruit Bowl, 8 1/2" d, spray of tulips and garden flowers in int, pierced sides w/red or blue flowerheads, gold paneled rim, ... **20.00**

Hatpin Holder, 4 1/2" h, black lined yellow band, black and white block pattern on neck, white body, black stripe on base,....................... **100.00**

Jam Pot, 5" h, figural orange, overall orange luster glaze, stem knob, black "Made in Czechoslovakia" mk, ... **30.00**

Jewel Casket, 3 1/2" h x 4" l, gold outlined raised swirls, decals of sm red roses on side and cov, ... **150.00**

Jug, 4 1/2" h, blue, brown, and green paisley style floral design, orange and yellow bands, brown wavy rim, Erphila,.................................. **18.00**

Pickle Tray, 13" l, green int, white ext, "Made in Czecho" mk, ... **20.00**

Pitcher

3 1/2" h, yellow luster glazed ext, white int, Erphila, ... **20.00**

3 7/8" h, figural 18th C Englishman, black hat, red coat, white bow tie, pink-white curls, "Made in Czechoslovakia" mk, ... **25.00**

4 1/2" h, Figural

Parrot, red, lt blue, and tan, ... **28.00**

Strawberry, black stem w/green leaf terminals, "Czecho-Slovakia" mk, ... **40.00**

5" h

Multicolored decal of 2 classic ladies on side, molded rim and handle, "red CZECHO-SLOVAKIA" mk, ... **15.00**

Overall red-orange glaze, ... **25.00**

Paneled, multicolored decal of desert scene of men on camels on cream bkd, orange body, green lined rim, "red Made in Czecho-Slovakia" mk, ... **110.00**

6" h

Art Deco, horiz ribbing, white and blue floral spots, brown ground, "MADE IN CZECHO-SLOVAKIA" mk, ... **25.00**

Bust of period man, red hat, white collared green coat, blue tie, yellow handle, ... **25.00**

Decal of hunter on horseback, shaded orange ground, green rim, mkd, ... **25.00**

Figural toucan, red and black, tan body, "Erphila Czechoslovakia" mk, ... **125.00**

Green and brown tree trunk body, green, black, tan, and red figural woodpecker handle, "red Made in Czecho Slovakia" mk, ... **60.00**

6 1/4" h, blue and red circ discs, green airbrushed top and base, figural cat handle, ... **25.00**

7" h

Brown stone type ground, black outlined orange center band, mkd, ... **65.00**

Vert rows of red, green, yellow, and blue raised dots, MOP ground, red lined rim and red lined piecrust base, ... **10.00**

7 1/2" h, decal of 2 women in pastoral scene on side, shaded brown body, cornucopia spout, and stepped handle, 4 sm feet, "Made in Czecho-Slovakia" mk, ... **75.00**

8" h

Alternating mottled turquoise bands and mottled dk pink bands, fancy curved handle, ... **175.00**

Orange top, blue base, center band of lavender and white peaks and valleys, black handle, "Ditmar Urbach Made in Czech." mk, ... **155.00**

Relief molded pears, grapes, peaches, and plums, yellow ground, red border and sq handle,....................... **20.00**

8 1/4" h, multicolored decal of pastoral scene of man, woman, and sheep, green starburst webbing, brown to cream shaded ground, fancy handle, ... **25.00**

*Planter, 9 1/2" H-H, lg orange flowers, green leaves, white ground, orange rim, base, and handles, **$95.00***

Planter

4" h x 4" d, raised blue, red, and purple flowers, green leaves and stems, white pebble ground, ... **25.00**

4 1/8" h, sq, HP orange petaled stylized flowers in black circles, blue dot centers, white ground, blue and yellow striped border, ... **96.00**

5" h x 5" sq, black outlined white streaked 5 petaled blue flower, black netting, white enamel dots, caramel ground, "CZECHOSLOVAKIA HAND PAINTED" mk, ... **65.00**

6" h, figural white stork standing in green grasses, brown rock base, ... **37.00**

7 1/2" w, figural duck, orange and black accents, yellow body, ... **650.00**

8" l x 7" w x 4 1/2" h, bean shape, painted magnolia flowers, buds, and foliage around middle on rose to aqua shaded ground, yellow int, wavy rim,......... **165.00**

Plaque

7" h x 7" w, Art Deco bust of woman and child, woman w/pink face, orange lips and hair, blue scarf, black headwrap, brown haired child; pierced for hanging, sgd "Strobach," **65.00**

8 1/4" h x 6" w, profile of Art Deco woman's bust, lt brown curly hair, white collar, mkd, ... **60.00**

Plate

7 1/2" d, man and woman sowing seeds in center, yellow and red lower half, red top, Victoria Czechoslovakia, ... **38.00**

Vase, 7 3/4" h, black outlined blue flowers, yellow-gold ground with white enamel dots, "Czechoslovakia Hand Painted" mark, $375.00

Vase

12" h, swollen body, flared neck and ft, black outlined oval w/stylized red, blue, and yellow flowerheads, white body w/black leaves and stems, orange neck and ft, ... **375.00**

14" h, triple gourd shape, HP overlapping black outlined tan leaves, sm lt blue centered black flowerheads, mottled blue ground, 4 small tube openings on waist, 2 arched handles, mkd, ... **300.00**

Vegetable Bowl, 9 1/4" l x 6 1/4" w, decal of scattered pink roses, gilt lined rim, "TK CZECHOSLOVAKIA" mk, ... **15.00**

Wall Plaque, 4 3/8" h x 3 5/8" w, profile bust of Cleopatra, straight black hair, orange head band w/blue stone, "Made in Czechoslovakia, acorn in triangle" mk, ... **290.00**

Wall Pocket

5" h x 4 1/2" w, figural red, yellow, and blue-green finch perched on brown tree trunk, (A), ... **45.00**

5 1/2" h, red figural parrot w/black beak, brown branch w/3 openings, "red CZECHOSLOVAKIA" mk, ... **10.00**

5 3/4" h, red and blue bird perched on brown birdhouse on green tree branch, mkd, ... **20.00**

Water Pitcher, 5" h, ball shape, red glaze, ... **10.00**

DAVENPORT STONE CHINA
1805-20

DAVENPORT
LONG PORT
STAFFORDSHIRE
1870-1886

DAVENPORT

Longport, Staffordshire, England 1794-1887

History: John Davenport and family established their factory in 1794. Earthenware, ironstone, porcelains, caneware, black basalt, and glass were made. Few of the early examples were marked. Porcelains were not manufactured until 1805 to 1810. The earliest Davenport porcelains were marked with the word "Longport" in red script.

About 1825, Davenport teawares and dessert services came under the influence of the rococo revival. The shapes of pieces resembled the Coalport forms of this period. Landscape decorations were used frequently.

Porcelain painted plaques were decorated both at the factory and by independent artists about 1860 to 1880. Earthenware table services for use on ships became a specialty product. Colorful Japan patterns were produced in the Derby manner in the 1870s to 1880s. These were a specialty of the Davenport factory. The firm ceased operation in 1887.

References: T.A. Lockett, and Geoffrey A. Godden, *China, Earthenware & Glass, 1794-1884*, Random Century, 1990.

Museums: British Museum, London, England; Cincinnati Art Museum, Cincinnati, OH; Hanley Museum, Stoke-on-Trent, England; Liverpool Museum, Liverpool, England; Victoria & Albert Museum, London, England.

Baker, 9 1/4" d, blue printed design of stucco house, lg trees at sides, gentlemen, branch and leaf inner border, wavy rim, "imp anchor" mk, ... **110.00**

Bowl, 6 5/8" d, multicolored transfer on int, wide lt blue band w/relief of white grape leaves and tendrils on ext border, gold rim, c1820, $195.00

Bough Pot, 5 1/4" h, demilune form, gilt curved ring handles, roses and garden flowers in shaped and shaded orbs on white ground, gilt and apricot vert stripes on base, "imp anchor" mks, c1807-12, pr, (A), ... **1,015.00**

Coffee Can and Saucer, fluted, printed and HP blue ribbon and hanging red roses and leaves, scattered bluebells and pink carnations, gilt rims, ... **125.00**

Comport, 11 1/4" d x 2 1/2" h, Stone China, blue, orange, yellow, green, and pink oriental style bird above foliage and tree branch, ... **75.00**

Cup and Saucer

Molded vert fluting, painted bouquets of roses joined by claret and gilt ribbon, gilt dentil rim on int of cup, c1860, ... **45.00**

Scattered sm red berries and green leaves, shaped red rims, ... **20.00**

Dessert Service, 2 ftd dishes, 11" l, 7 3/4" w, 9 plates, 9 1/2" d, green border with gilt florals and molded shells, "Davenport and anchor" marks, A-$287.00

Dessert Dish, 9 5/8" l x 7 1/2" w, indented sides, ironstone, "Flying Bird" pattern, c1815-25, ... **775.00**

Dessert Service, 12 plates, 9 1/4" d, 2 oval dishes, ftd, 11" l, 2 rect dishes, ftd, 11" l, 2 shell dishes, ftd, 9 1/2" l, orange ground panels overlaid w/gilt florals and scrollwork, central gilt design of leaves and dbl roundel, open work borders, "puce crown and DAVONPORT LONGPORT STAFFORDSHIRE, gold #865" mks, c1845-55, ... **9,500.00**

Dish, 8 1/8" H-H, "Ceres" pattern, dk red morning glories, tan wheat, flowing blue accents, open handles, imp mk, ... **100.00**

Jelly Mold, 5" l x 4" w, creamware, "imp DAVENPORT" mk, ... **70.00**

Jug, 5 1/2" h, ironstone, paneled, "Jardiniere" pattern, blue, orange, green, peach, and gold, red and green serpent handle, c1805-20, ... **450.00**

Pitcher, 12" h, relief of purple tinged Calla Lily on shoulder w/red, brown, and green leaves, stem handle, gilt rim and accents, dtd 1877, ... **100.00**

Meat Platter, 17 3/4" l x 13 3/4" w, well and tree, "The Villagers" pattern, med blue transfer,.............. **1,200.00**

Pitcher, 8 3/8" h, ironstone, paneled, waisted baluster form, blue and iron-red chinoiserie designs, snake handle w/luster accents, ... **250.00**

Plate

8 1/4" d, 10 sides, central gilt geometric design, orange border w/white ground pockets of gilt stems and leaves and gilt overlay, gilt molded rim, .. **32.00**

Plate, 8 1/8" d, Imari, iron-red, orange, and green, flower designs, gilt outlined cobalt leaves, "red DAVENPORT, anchor" mk, $165.00

9" d

"Davenport III" pattern, oriental man at riverbank, border of birds and flowers, purple transfer, ... **125.00**

HP botanical in center, matte pale green inner border, pale pink outer border w/gilt rim and embellishments, c1870, ... **70.00**

9 1/2" d

Pearlware, med blue print country scene of man and dog approaching cottage, floral border, ... **60.00**

Sq sea scene, oval scene of child fishing, fans, florals, and geometrics, brown transfer, ... **25.00**

10" d, pearlware, "Knighthood Conferred on Don Quixote," flowerhead border, dk blue transfer, ... **350.00**

10 1/2" d, "Florentine Fountain" pattern, med blue transfer, c1840s, ... **175.00**

10 5/8" d, blue printed scene of river crossing w/boatmen, trees, and monastery in bkd, scroll and flower border, scalloped rim, "blue DAVENPORT, imp DAVENPORT, anchor" mks, c1820-40,......................... **100.00**

Platter

16 1/2" l x 13" w, "Rustic Scenery Series," soldier holding flag at river edge near boat, lg building and fortress in bkd, flowerhead border, med blue transfer, "imp DAVENPORT" mk, ... **390.00**

18" l x 15" w, view of castle and village, flowing river, purple transfer, "imp anchor Davenport" mk, ... **675.00**

Sauceboat, 8 1/2" l, w/attached underplate, lobed, blue printed mountainous scenic panorama, dtd 1844, ... **395.00**

Sauce Tureen, 7 1/4" h x 7 1/2" l x 4 1/2" w, w/undertray, 8 1/2" l x 6 1/2" w, and ladle, 6" l, "Davenport II" pattern, brown transfers, rose bud knob w/applied stem and leaves, "brown DAVENPORT and anchor" mk, c1820-60, (A), ... **1,100.00**

Soup Plate, 10 1/4" d, lg floral bouquet in center, lg and sm flowerheads on border, lobed rim, lt blue transfer, "imp anchor DAVENPORT" mk, ... **60.00**

Tea Caddy, 4 3/4" h, iron-red, cobalt, and gilt Imari pattern of diamonds and swirls in compartments, SP lid and bail handle, "crowned Davenport Longport Staffordshire" mk, ... **150.00**

Tureen, Cov, 7 3/4" l, leaf-molded boat shape, HP flowers on sides and cov, chocolate brown wavy rims, curled handles, green grape bunch knob, "imp DAVENPORT, anchor" mk, (A), ... **1,125.00**

Wine Cooler, 9 3/4" h, caneware, relief molded grapes, tendrils, and foliage, applied satyr mask handles, tan, "imp anchor and DAVENPORT" mk, ... **3,700.00**

MODERN MARK

DELFT, DUTCH AND ENGLISH

**Holland
c1613 to Present
Bristol, Lambeth,
and Liverpool, England
1690-1790
Dutch**

History: Tin enamel ware was first manufactured in Delft about 1613 as a result of Italian potters immigrating to Holland and bringing the techniques with them. Prior to this, the Dutch relied heavily on the Dutch East India Company's importing Chinese porcelains to fulfill their china need.

When the imported supply was reduced because of disruption of the trade routes, the local Dutch pottery industry thrived. Idle breweries were refitted as potteries. By the mid-1600s, more than thirty pottery manufacturers were operating out of the defunct breweries, making imitations of Chinese and Japanese porcelains in blue and white tin-glazed wares. A transparent lead glaze was added as a "flashing," or overglaze, to make the tin-enamel copies closely resemble Chinese porcelain.

Two types of blue and white wares were made. The first type featured blue and white motifs in the monochrome Chinese style. The blue and white motifs of the second type included Dutch subjects such as landscapes, windmills, sailing ships, portraits, Bible stories, views of towns, and other "series" plates. The prime period of production for both types of blue and white wares was 1640 to 1740. Other towns in Holland also produced blue and white in addition to Delft. Few pieces are found with identifying maker's marks.

After 1700 more polychrome wares were produced in tones of copper green, iron red, and yellow. Japanese Imari wares were the source of inspiration for the polychrome wares. In addition to plates, tiles, vases, and other dishes, Delft potters also specialized in novelties such as shoes, cow milk jugs, violins, and small figures, especially of animals.

The decline of Dutch Delft was accelerated by the introduction of Wedgwood's creamware in the second half of the 18th century. In addition, the works of Meissen and Sevres surpassed the tin-glazed wares from Delft. By the beginning of the 19th century, the number of pottery manufacturers in Delft was reduced to three.

Today only one of the original producers of Delftwares remains in operation. De Porceleyne Fles began producing pottery in 1653. This firm was saved from bankruptcy in 1870 by Joost Thooft. To make the company competitive, Thooft made some changes in the manufacturing process, among which was importing white baking clay from England. Each piece is marked with the logo of De Porceleyne Fles, Joost Thooft's initials, and the initials of the decorator.

English

History: Tin enamel pottery came to England from Antwerp in the Netherlands in the 16th century. At first the tin-glazed earthenware was called "galley-ware." The name changed to Delftware in the mid-18th century because of its similarity to Dutch Delft products. English Delft production was centered in Bristol, Lambeth, and Liverpool after strong beginnings in London in the mid-17th century.

At Lambeth, apothecary wares, barber basins, and puzzle jugs were among the most popular forms produced. In Bristol, the glaze had a more bluish tone. Plates, bowls, and flower holders with a naive treatment predominated. Liverpool Delft, with its harder body, resembled Chinese porcelains more closely than those made elsewhere. By 1790 tin-enamel glaze wares fell into decline in England due to the rise of Wedgwood's creamware.

References: John C. Austin, *British Delft at Williamsburg*, Decorative Arts Services, 1994; John Bedford, *Delftware*, Walker & Co. 1966; Frank Britton, *London Delftware*, Jonathan Horne, 1987; Carolene Henriette De Jonge, *Delft Ceramics*, Praeger, 1970; H.P. Fourest, *Delftware*, Rizzoli, 1980; F.H. Garner & Michael Archer, *English Delftware*, Faber & Faber, 1972; Ivor Hume, *Early English Delftware from London and Virginia*, The Colonial Williamsburg Foundation, 1977; Diana Imber, *Collecting European Delft and Faience*, Praeger, 1968; Anthony Ray, *English Delftware Pottery in the Robert Hall Warren Collection*, Boston Book & Art Shop, 1968. Peter Francis, *Irish Delftware, An Illustrated History*, Jonathon Horne, 2001. Louis Lipski & Michael Archer, *Dated English Delftware*, Philip Wilson, 1984. Amanda E. Lange, *Delftware At Historic Deerfield, 1600-1800*, University of Virginia Press, 2001.

Museums: Ashmolean Museum, Oxford, England; Fitzwilliam Museum, Cambridge, England; Gemeente Museum, Arnhem, Holland; Gardiner Museum of Ceramic Art, Toronto, Canada; Henry Ford Museum, Dearborn, MI; Hius Lambert van Meerten Museum, Delft, Holland; Musees Royaux d'art et d'Historie, Brussels, Belgium; Prinsenhof Museum, Delft, Holland; Rijksmuseum, Amsterdam, Holland; Royal

Factory "De Porceleyne Fles" Collection, Delft, Holland; Sheffield City Museum, Sheffield, England; The Colonial Williamsburg Foundation, Williamsburg, VA; Victoria & Albert Museum, London, England; William Rockhill Nelson Gallery of Art, Kansas City, MO.

Reproduction Alert: The old Dutch wares have been copied as souvenirs and are quite popular with the foreign traveler. Be careful not to confuse these modern pieces with the older examples. There are many reproductions on the market, particularly from 1960 to the present day. Both new and old marks are generally in blue under the glaze. Many new pieces have made-up marks that are not used on older pieces.

Many 16" Delft platters were invented for interior decorators and antique reproduction wholesalers and have been made for over thirty years. Examples with the marks Delfts are less than thirty to forty years old. New pieces are transfer decorated and not hand painted with visible brush strokes.

Dutch

Bowl, 14" d, lg bowl of ferns in center, inner band of circlets, flowerheads and sprigs on border, blue and white, blue lined scalloped rim, "De Metalen Pot," c1750, rim chip, ... **430.00**

Box, 7 1/2" l, modeled dk purple Concord grapes, stem extending to green leaf stand, "blue APK" mk, c1750, (A), ... **4,185.00**

Charger
  12" d, blue and white, 2 horses under tree in center, half circles and curlicues on border, ... **1,600.00**
  13 1/4" d, blue, iron-red, green, yellow, and manganese fountain w/feather tree, fencing, and florals, 17th C, chips, (A), ... **1,808.00**
  13 1/2" d, orange and blue bust of Prince William of Orange, "P-W-O-3" overhead, gadrooned and lobed border w/orange and blue meandering flowering and fruiting branches, hairlines, ... **1,875.00**
  14 1/4" d, blue and white, florals from vase on mat, lg island w/rocks, lg chrysanthemum head, cell and scroll inner and outer rim, c1750, ... **1,750.00**
  16" d, blue and white, blue painted oriental warrior w/bow and arrow on horseback in center, border of compartments w/oriental figure alternating w/geometrics, ... **2,700.00**

Comport, 6" h x 8 3/4" d, HP red, blue, and green stylized flowerheads and half flowerheads, red dash spokes, band of yellow centered red flowerheads on scalloped border, ... **250.00**

Dish, 9 1/8" d, cobalt, manganese, yellow, and green, 18th C, **$450.00**

Dish
  10" d, Chinese garden landscape, foliage border, blue and white, ... **170.00**
  13 1/2" d, blue painted oriental figures below gazebo, border w/panels of seated figures and scrolls, "blue claw" mk, 18th C, (A), ... **390.00**

Figure
  4 1/4" h x 5" l, standing cow, HP blue, green, red, and purple flowers, iron-red scrolling on rect base, ... **385.00**
  4 7/8" h x 6 3/8" l, standing cow w/manganese splotches and garlands, head turned, flanked by standing man w/one hand in pocket of yellow trousers, other holding staff, blue sponged base, 18th C, ... **750.00**
  4 1/2" w, 2 modeled red to yellow shaded cherries on green stems, lg green leaves, green base, ... **1,250.00**
  7" h, seated blue sponged cat on dk blue and white pillow w/tassels, "AP" mk, (A), ... **525.00**
  9 3/8" h, prancing horse, fringed saddle blanket under saddle, canted rect base w/molded vining, overall white glaze, mid-18th C, pr, (A), ... **2,870.00**

Fruit Bowl, 11 1/2" d, multilobed, white glaze, ... **445.00**

Garniture, 6" h, 3 piece, 2 oct vases w/bust of man or woman below flowerhead and "PVO," baluster vase w/urn of flowers, polychrome, repairs, (A), ... **300.00**

Jar, Cov

14" h, baluster shape, blue painted Dutch village scene on mirror cartouche on body and cov, cell pattern ground, stiff leaves on border and base, pr, ... **1,495.00**

24 1/2" h, oct, inverted baluster shape, blue painted oriental figures in various pursuits in landscape below band of flowerheads scrolls and band of leaves, Foo dog knob, c1900, (A), ... **675.00**

Plate

8 1/2" d, blue and yellow stylized tulip, buds, and foliage in center, yellow and blue feather type foliage and dots on border, blue claw mk, ... **275.00**

Plate, 9" d, dk blue designs, pale blue tinted ground, c1780, $300.00

9" d, HP

Chinese style design of red center star, orange, red, green, and blue stylized flowerheads, part flowerheads, foliage, and fencing, c1740, rim chips, ... **300.00**

Chinoiserie design of man under weeping willow tree, blue painted, ... **265.00**

Manganese chinoiserie fenced garden, bamboo shoots and rock in foreground, green leaves, stylized manganese floral border, ... **750.00**

Plate, 9" d, polychrome decoration, "blue AK" mark, late 18th C, $235.00

9 1/8" d, blue and white vase and feathers design, yellow lined rim, porcelain claw mk, ... **350.00**

9 3/8" d, lg blue flower design from stylized vase, lg ovals and sprigs on border, blue and white, rim chips, 18th C, ... **150.00**

Shaving Bowl, 10" w, blue, green, and dk red band of beads in center, blue, yellow, green, and red swirls, and feathers on border, c1800, chips on rim, ... **675.00**

Teapot, 5 1/2" h, convex w/flat sides, HP red, blue, and green vase of flowers on sides in red band of "x's," red, blue, and green quatrefoil leaf designs on body, reed molded lid w/quatrefoil leaves, ear handle, c1720, ... **1,775.00**

Tobacco Jar, 10 3/4" h, oviform, blue painted "No. 3 St. Vinsent" in floral cartouche, flanked by pillars and American Indians smoking pipes, contemporary cov, 18th C, (A), ... **1,900.00**

Tureen, Cov

7 5/8" h, sq, HP blue florals, birds, and butterflies, diapering on corner pillars, figural fish knob, Porcelyne Fles, hairlines, ... **450.00**

7" l x 6" w, figural melon, green and yellow striped cov, branch knob, 3 applied green leaves and blue or red flowerheads, yellow stand w/grey and black striping, c1710, pr, ... **45,000.00**

Vase

7 5/8" h, corset shape, lg blue flowers, trailing foliage, leaves, and bud, 18th C, ... **670.00**

8 1/4" h, beaker shape, blue and white oriental lady in landscape in molded scroll border, c1770, ... **255.00**

Vase, 9" h, dk blue designs, white ground, "blue claw" mark, mid-18th C, pr, $1,280.00

9 3/4" h, baluster shape, brown slip ground, simulated lacquer design, yellow painted oriental scene of man seated at tea table, standing woman holding fan, trees, foliage and flying birds, green key design on collar, "De Twee Scheepjes" mk, c1680, chips and scratches, (A), ... **2,870.00**

13 3/8" h, bulbous body, trumpet neck, flared rim, panels of blue painted florals and foliage, vert banding, ... **225.00**

14 1/4" h, garlic form, blue painted oriental scholars and foliage on body, faceted neck w/florals and fretwork, stiff leaves on base, ... **565.00**

English

Bottle, 10 1/4" h, bulbous, blue painted Chinese style garden w/bird on fence, lg trailing flowers, stylized flowers around neck, mid-18th C, (A), ... **1,875.00**

Bowl, 12 1/2" d, silver, dbl lobed shape, black outlined cherub w/sword and shield accented w/brown, and ochre in center, alternating ochre and blue stylized ferns and loops around center, blue pendent tassels from rim, London, c1700, rim chips, ... **3,600.00**

Plate

11" d, blue chinoiserie scene of fisherman, village, and boat in lake on powder blue ground, bianco supa bianco floral border, c1765, ... **1,000.00**

Posset Pot, Cov, 8 1/4" h, blue ovals w/diapering in center and borders, scrolling vines, blue dash spout and handles, London, repaired chip, ... **7,350.00**

Pot, 4 1/2" h, cobalt and dk red flowers and foliage, cobalt and dk red alternating vert stiff leaves on foot, blue dash handles, London, c1720, ... **2,800.00**

Punch Bowl, 10" d, painted blue flowerheads and foliage on ext, leaf sprigs on int, c1760, ... **2,600.00**

Puzzle Jug, 7 1/4" h, blue and white, "Here Gentlemen come try your skill, I'll hold A wager if you will, That you don't Drink this Liquor all, Without you spill or let some fall," elongated neck w/heart and oval piercing, 3 spouts on rim, mid-18th C, repairs, (A), ... **1,400.00**

DENMARK-GENERAL

1759 to Present

History: Louis Fournier, a Frenchman, made soft paste porcelain in Denmark from 1759 to 1765. These wares had a yellow tone with a dull glaze and were decorated with flowers and cupids in the French style. The principal products were tablewares.

Franz Muller made the first hard paste porcelain in Denmark in 1773. From 1779 until his death, Muller managed the Royal Porcelain Manufactory in Copenhagen. Furstenberg and Meissen models were copied. Anton Carl Luplau, master modeler, came from Furstenberg to work in Denmark. His strawflower pattern in underglaze blue achieved tremendous popularity.

Neo-classical decorations were used on the majority of Copenhagen porcelains. In about 1815, Gustav Hetsch served as managing director of the Royal Porcelain Manufactory. During the 1830s, many state services were designed for the royal residences. Denmark's national sculptor Berthel Thorwaldsen made numerous sculptures and reliefs during the 1840s. Copies of his works were made in biscuit

porcelain, and these statuettes sold extensively. Christian Hetsch continued his father's neo-classical style at the Royal Porcelain Manufactory, but enhanced the pieces with colorful decorations, relief, and gilt.

Financial problems occurred after 1850. By 1868 the factory was Royal in name only, as it was privately owned. In 1882 the firm regained some prominence when it merged with the Faience Alumina factory, which had been established in Copenhagen in 1863. Philip Schou served as manager.

Arnold Krog became artistic director in 1885. He reinstituted the original straw-flower ornamentation and designed new tableware shapes. Krog's revival of underglaze blue decoration utilizing the straw-flower and other patterns started a prosperous period for Copenhagen. Animal sculptures were introduced by Carl Liisberg in 1888.

The Bing and Grondahl factory was the second factory established in Copenhagen. Starting in 1852, the sculptor Hermann Bissen produced biscuit statuettes and reliefs based on the same models as the Royal Porcelain Manufactory. Harold Bing became managing director in 1885. He appointed Pietro Krohn as artistic director in 1886. Krohn's greatest design was the "Heron Service," in which the heron appeared on each piece.

References: Caroline & Nick Pope, *Dahl-Jensen Porcelain Figures 1897-1985*, Schiffer Publications, 2003. Robin Hecht, *Scandinavian Art Pottery, Denmark & Sweden*, Schiffer Publications, 2000.

Museum: Royal Porcelain Factory, Copenhagen, Denmark.

Bowl, 3" d x 3 1/2" h, ftd, hand thrown, incised conc rings, green glaze, ... **200.00**

Ewer, 7 1/4" h, vert bands of white inverted hearts, red glazed ground, "Zeuthen Denmark" mk, ... **65.00**

Figure

4 3/4" h, stylized angel, dk red hair, white gown w/green stars and dashes and dk red and yellow flowerheads and streaks, white halo, ... **12.00**

5 1/4" h, kneeling brown faun holding white water jug, Dahl Jensen, ... **450.00**

6" h, seated Danish girl holding doll in lap, tans and rose shades, Dahl Jensen, #1295, ... **318.00**

Pitcher, 6 1/2" h, lt leaf form w/blue and brown mixed surface shades, Herman Kahler, c1910, ... **75.00**

Sugar Bowl, Cov

3 1/2" h, single handle, matte blue ground, green vert streaks and

red dots, "DYBDAHL DENMARK" mk, ... **10.00**

*Figure, 9" h, "Girl From Amager," dk brown skirt, blue scarf, flowered belt, tan skirt, "DJ Copenhagen" mark, **$675.00***

7" h

9" l, standing Airedale dog, dk brown accents on med brown body, Dahl Jensen, ... **475.00**

14 1/2" l, brown spotted dog tugging blue pants from boy in white shirt, oval base, Dahl Jensen, ... **925.00**

8" h, little girl in blue dress hugging grey spotted fox terrier, Dahl Jensen, ... **775.00**

Vase

4 3/4" h, "Lilje" design, Art Deco bust of woman, vases of florals, and geometrics, black on white ground, Bjorn Winnblad, ... **70.00**

6 1/2" h x 8" w, orange ball w/dk brown swirl band around center w/dk brown vert stripes and 4 handles to dk brown rim, ... **950.00**

9 1/2" h, bulbous shape w/wide collar, HP dk blue swirling vert leaves, dk sm red flowerheads, cream ground, gloss finish, imp mk, ... **145.00**

15" h, bulbous shape, flared neck and rim, HP dk red dot flowerheads, olive green and black curled stems, black rim, white ground, Herman Kahler, ... **400.00**

Vase, 8 1/4" h, orange, yellow, blue, or red fruit, black outlined blue and green leaves top and base, matte tan ground, artist sgd, c1920,
$195.00

DERBY

1820-40

1782-1825

Derby, England
1755 to Present

History: William Duesbury I opened the Derby works at the Nottingham Road factory in 1755. Tablewares and ornamental wares were produced. Chinoiserie designs, exotic bird paintings, and blue and white patterns were the favorite design motifs. Derby had no factory mark before Duesbury purchased the Chelsea factory.

In 1769 Duesbury acquired the Chelsea factory and transferred some of the extremely skilled craftsmen from Chelsea to Derby. The production of the first biscuit or unglazed porcelain and figure groups began in 1770. Originally developed at the Sevres factory about 1752, biscuit figures were to make Derby famous.

In 1784, Duesbury closed the Chelsea works, moving the remainder of the craftsmen to Derby. Duesbury died in 1786, and William Duesbury II, his son, assumed control.

Between 1786 and 1797, under the guidance of Duesbury II, the Derby factory became a major British pottery. Great advances were made in body, glaze, potting, and decoration. A tremendous variety of lavishly decorated objects was made. Added to the popular floral patterns were landscapes, maritime subjects, and hunting scenes. Duesbury's group of painters and craftsmen were among the finest in England during the 18th century.

In 1795 Duesbury took Kean as his partner. Duesbury died in 1791. Kean continued to produce landscape and marine subjects, but the quality of the body and the glaze deteriorated. Robert Bloor leased the factory in 1811 and then took over completely. The shapes tended to be larger, utilizing flamboyant gilded decoration as a reflection of the current tastes. The Japan, or Imari patterns, with their rich colorings and lavish use of gold, typified the period. Imari patterns that started about 1770 are still being produced. Many figures were also modeled during the Bloor period. Bloor experienced a long illness, during which the factory declined. He died in 1846. In 1848 the factory was sold.

The Nottingham Road factory closed. Several of the potters and painters began manufacturing china at King Street, trading as Sampson Hancock until the eventual merger with Royal Crown Derby in 1935. Utilitarian wares were made with an emphasis on the popular Japan and Imari designs. This small factory is the link to the claim of continuous china production in Derby.

References: F.A. Barrett & A.L. Thorpe, *Derby Porcelain 1750-1848*, Faber & Faber, 1971; Gilbert Bradley, *Derby Porcelain 1750-1798*, Seven Hills Books, 1992; F.B. Gilhespy, *Derby Porcelain*, Spring Books, 1961; Dennis Rice, *Derby Porcelain—The Golden Years, 1750-1770*, Hippocrane Books, 1983; John Twitchett, *Derby Porcelain, The Illustrated Dictionary*, Antique Collectors' Club, Ltd. 1997.

Collectors' Club: Derby Porcelain International Society, Membership Secretary, The Old Barracks, Sandon Road, Grantham, Lincolnshire NG31 9AS England, £25 Membership, quarterly newsletter, journal, occasional essays.

Museums: see Crown & Royal Crown Derby.

Asparagus Server, 3" w, blue painted pagoda beside estuary, c1778, (A), ... **270.00**

Basket, 11" l, oval, underglazed blue printed oriental scene of pagoda, lake, lg willow tree, and man fishing in center, reticulated sides w/blue painted flowerheads at intercises on int, relief molded flowerheads on ext, dk blue rope twist handles, rope ft, 18th C, pr, ... **4,875.00**

Bowl, 11" l x 4 1/2" h, circ base, vert gilt outlined handles, scattered multicolored and gilt sm floral sprigs and leaves, molded lion mask corners, ... **450.00**

Cabinet Plate, 9" d, HP named "View of Leicestershire," cobalt border w/gilt shell motifs, 5 gilt stripes on scalloped rim, c1825, ... **85.00**

Candlestick, 7 1/8" h, 2 speckled white doves perched blue flowered green arched bocage, brown streaked fox reaching for birds, white candle stem, gilt accented scroll molded base, c1770, pr, (A), ... **720.00**

Centerpiece, 5" h x 6 1/2" w, 3 molded scallop shells, blue ring base w/encrusted cockle, periwinkles, and corals, blue encrusted coral between shells, blue conch shell knob, blue painted floral sprigs and insects in wells, inner border of band of blue whelk shells, patch marks, Duesbury, c1765, ... **4,800.00**

Cup and Saucer

Gilt outlined dk blue acanthus leaf designs, gilt lines, c1810, mkd, ... **80.00**

HP iron red flowerhead, cobalt leaves, gilt accents, ... **50.00**

Imari pattern, gilt outlined cobalt and iron-red oriental florals and foliage, cobalt rims w/gilt zigzags, ... **50.00**

Dessert Dish, 9" d, HP sm bouquets of summer flowers in center, fluted gilt border w/stiff leaf and floral motifs, "iron-red crowned D and X'd batons" mk, (A), ... **135.00**

Dish

8 1/8" w, figural peony, yellow centered, puce edged overlapping petals, applied green stalk handle, puce veining, applied buds, c1760, (A), ... **1,060.00**

11" l

8" w, 2 lg orange and red or purple and yellow tulip, gilt trim, open work indented borders w/gilt painted flowers on mottled blue ground at corners, c1810-20, ... **4,000.00**

8 1/2" w, oval, sm red flower spray, green foliage in center, wide

fluted border w/sm sprigs, red lined rim, Bloor Derby, ... **250.00**

13 1/2" l x 9 1/2" w, fluted lozenge shape, painted specimen fruits and insects, puce and teal blue accented molded scallop shells at points, gilt line rim, unmkd, c1765, ... **3,800.00**

Figure

4" h, seated red-brown fox, tapered rect green base, c1770, ... **2,870.00**

5 1/2", 6" l, running boar or boar seated on haunches, puce-brown dry edged painted accents, black hooves, mound base w/applied flowers, Duesbury & Co., c1755, pr, (A), ... **20,315.00**

5 3/4" h, period gentleman wearing med blue coat w/gold buttons, red crisscrossed and flowered yellow vest, black hat under arm, holding cane, rect base, c1820, restorations, ... **1,020.00**

6 1/2" h, "Mansion House Dwarf," card-decorated tall peaked yellow hat w/dk red slash, flowered jacket w/slashed sleeves, red and gold striped breeches, holding staff, green washed base w/flower clumps, (A), ... **600.00**

7 1/4" h, "Minerva," black hair, blue flowered orange-red gown, yellow sash on shoulder, bird on outstretched hand, brown eagle on scroll molded base, c1800, ... **1,350.00**

9 1/2" h, male or female w/feathered turban, seated on tree trunk, holding basket in lap, flowers in hand, hound or sheep on scroll molded base, white glaze, c1760-70, chips, pr, ... **7,500.00**

9 7/8" h, "Ranelagh Dancers," male in tricorn hat, purple cloak, floral jacket and breeches, hand on hip, other hand extended holding flower, female w/plumes in hair, pink bodice, floral skirt, scroll molded bases, pr, c1765, (A), ... **975.00**

10 7/8" h, "Britannia," plumed helmet, floral dress, gilt breast plate, yellow and purple cloak, holding shield w/English and Irish flags, lions and trophies at feet, scroll molded base, c1765, (A), ... **450.00**

18 1/2" h, "Jupiter and Eagle," standing figure holding bundle of arrows, eagle at feet, yellow cloak w/red outlined circles and sm flowers, blue-green drape on shoulder, gilt accented scroll molded base, c1760, ... **15,000.00**

Jug, 6 1/4" h, painted panels of flying birds in landscapes front and reverse in burnished gilt bands reserved on blue ground w/gilt foliate scrolls and flowers, "iron-red crowned X'd batons, D" mk, Bloor-Derby, c1813-20, (A), ... **1,795.00**

Monteith, 10 1/4" H-H x 5" h, ovular w/rounded crenellated rim, applied shell form handles, painted hanging red berries from brown stems and lg green leaves, scattered multicolored butterflies and moths, gilt outlined rim, base, and handles, "puce crowned X'd batons, dot and D" mk, c1785, pr,......................... **19,500.00**

Mug

3 3/4" h, figural Bacchus head, flesh face w/grey beard, relief molded red grapes and green leaf wreath on head, gilt rim and outlined handle, "puce crowned X'd batons" mk, repaired chip, ... **350.00**

5 1/8" h, painted named panel of "In Westmoreland," scattered gilt floral, border of gilt feathers and shells between gilt lines on collar, Bloor Derby, ... **1,400.00**

Plate

8 3/8" d, spiral fluted, floral sprigs in mazarine and gilt diamond cartouche of dentil, scale, and flowerhead designs, scattered multicolored floral sprigs, mazarine and gilt wavy rim, c1765, pr,...................... **1,250.00**

8 1/2" d, pearlware, green outlined relief of overlapping leaves, c1820, ... **65.00**

8 5/8" d, branch of Purple Ragwood, gilt border of stylized lily of the valley, "blue Purple Ragwood, crown, X'd batons and D" mks, c1810,........................... **1,250.00**

9 7/8" d, HP cobalt and iron-red oriental flowers in center, border of hanging cobalt packets w/iron-red circles, cobalt border w/molded beading, gilt accents, gadrooned rim, Bloor-Derby, c1830, ... **75.00**

Platter, 13" l, scattered purple, red, yellow, or green florals and sprigs, dk blue border band w/gold grape leaves and vines, "blue crowned D" mk, (A), **$225.00**

10 1/4" d, iron-red oriental flowers, dk blue leaves, border of iron-red flowers, blue leaves, gilt stems, c1825, ... **30.00**

Potpourri Jar, 7 3/4" h, applied multicolored flowerheads and bows on cov, applied flowerheads and enameled floral bouquet on body, gold rim, stress cracks and chips, pr, ... **3,450.00**

Soup Plate, 9 3/4" d

HP garden bouquet in center, 4 individual flowers on border, gold rim, "red X'd batons, D" mk, ... **690.00**

"Kings" pattern, cobalt, iron-red, and gilt floral and oriental scrolling and berry border, c1820, ... **500.00**

Sugar Box, Cov, 4" h, painted cherries, green branches, and leaves, scattered fruit and insects, white ground, rose knob, Duesbury, c1780, ... **1,700.00**

Teapot

5 1/2" h, globular, blue printed runny blue Worcester-style carnations, roses, asters, and insects, blue open crescent mk, c1770, ... **3,000.00**

6 5/8" h, campana shape, panel painted w/basket of flowers, cobalt ground w/gilt foliate motifs and swans, snake handles, c1820, pr, (A), ... **180.00**

7" h, molded fluted body, blue line on shoulder w/gilt floral band and gilt dentil band, gilt dashes on spout, gilt ring knob, "red crowned X'd batons D" mk, ... **200.00**

Vase

3 1/2" h, baluster base, elongated trumpet neck, gilt oval w/HP red roofed barn, trees, and mountains on front, white ground

w/gilt swirls, "red crowned X'd batons, D" mk, ... **300.00**

4 5/8" h, tapered form, oval gilt cartouche w/garden flowers of passion flowers, roses, carnations, and stocks, reverse w/fruit lying on ground under tree, white body w/yellow border and gilt band accents, turned yellow and cobalt ft, cobalt and gilt scrolling handles, "blue crowned X'd batons and D" mk, c1790, pr, (A), ... **1,900.00**

13" h, krater shape, painted flowers around flared neck, lower body, foot, sq base, and handles w/gilt foliate scrolls and anthemion, "iron-red crown, X'd batons, D" mks, c1820, pr, (A), ... **7,170.00**

14" h, teardrop shape w/sm flared rim, ftd, gold handles, HP cattle at waterhole, blue sky, forest on reverse, sgd "Bradshaw," pr, ... **265.00**

*Vegetable Dish, Cov, 11" sq, "King's" pattern, gold and iron-red florals, cobalt trim, **$600.00***

20" h, campana shape, tapered waisted sq base, gilt vert handles at waist terminating in Etruscan masks, painted Derbyshire hunting scene w/dogs in forest, gilt anthemion and scrolling on lower section, base, and inner rim, "red crowned X'd batons, dot and D" mk, Duesbury & Kean, c1815, ... **24,000.00**

1880-1902

ROYAL DOULTON ENGLAND c1902-1929

DOULTON BURSLEM ENGLAND 1882-1902

DOULTON BURSLEM 1882-1902

DOULTON AND ROYAL DOULTON

DOULTON OF LAMBETH

Lambeth, near London 1815-1956

History: In Lambeth, near London, John Doulton founded the Doulton Lambeth pottery in 1815. Utilitarian salt glazed stonewares were the mainstay. When John Watts joined the firm, it became known as Doulton and Watts (1820-1853). Stoneware barrels, bottles, spirit flasks, and jugs were produced in vast quantities.

Henry Doulton, John's second son, joined the firm in 1835. His inventiveness led to the application of steam to drive the potter's wheel, placing Lambeth Pottery ten years ahead of the other potteries. Architectural terracotta and garden ornaments were added to the catalog. Production of stoneware drainpipes, conduits, and other sanitary wares also began.

The Lambeth School of Art, under John Sparkes' direction, became associated with the Doulton wares. Through Sparkes, George Tinsworth began working with Doulton in 1866. Hannah and Arthur Barlow, students at the school, joined Doulton in 1871. They made pots with incised decorations worked directly into uncoated clay. During the next twenty years, the number of artists and designers grew; 250 artists were at work by 1885. The monogram, initials, or signature of the artist appeared on the piece; often the assistants' initials appeared too. In 1887 Queen Victoria knighted Henry Doulton for his achievements in the advancement of ceramic art.

Sir Henry died in 1897; Henry Louis Doulton succeeded his father. In 1899 the family company became Doulton & Co. Ltd. During the 20th century, reductions took place in the production of artist-signed pieces from Doulton Lambeth. By 1925 only 24 artists were employed. Leslie Harradine did excellent stoneware figures of Dickens' characters. He also modeled spirit flasks of contemporary politicians.

During the 1920s and 1930s, collectors' pieces in simple shapes, subtle colors, and uncluttered decorations were made. A large range of commemorative wares also was produced. Agnete Hoy, working at Lambeth from 1951 to 1956, achieved fame for her cat figures. She used salt glaze techniques and developed a new transparent glaze. In 1956 production ceased at the Doulton Lambeth pottery.

DOULTON OF BURSLEM

Staffordshire, England 1877 to Present

History: In 1877 Henry Doulton acquired the Nile Street pottery located in Burslem, Staffordshire, from Pinder, Bourne & Co. The name was changed to Doulton & Co. in 1882. Beginning in 1884, porcelains of the highest quality were manufactured. Simple, inexpensive earthenware tablewares also were made. A large group of artists under the direction of John Slater assembled at the Burslem factory.

Doulton's china was exhibited at the Chicago Columbian Exposition in 1893. Charles Noke, who joined the company in 1889 and became one of the most important workers at Burslem, exhibited his vases. Many Noke figures portrayed contemporary people as historical personages. His early achievements included Holbein, Rembrandt, and Barbotine wares plus a popular range of flasks, jugs, and other shapes in subdued colors. Rouge Flambe was perhaps the most important ware introduced by Noke. He became art director in 1914. Noke also used many oriental style dragons in high relief.

Other notable artists included Percy Curock, Daniel Dewsbury, Edward Raby, and George White. They used many experimental glazes including Chang ware, Chinese Jade, and Sung. Doulton artists often used nature as their theme. Flowers and animals, especially farm animals such as cows and goats, were used. Many landscapes were also hand painted.

At the Burslem factory, a tremendous amount of tableware was produced. In addition to the earthenwares, fine bone china ornamented in gold and frequently exhibiting elaborate designs also was manufactured. In 1901 King Edward VII granted the Royal Warrant of appointment to Doulton. From that point on, they used the word "ROYAL" to describe their products.

Royal Doulton Figures

Nearly all of Royal Doulton figures are made at the Burslem factory. Three basic ingredients—china clay, Cornish stone, and calcined bone ash—are blended together with water to make a fine body able to withstand the high-temperature firings needed to produce a superfine, yet strong translucent ceramic body. Figurine subjects include child studies, street sellers, and historical, literary, or legendary characters in large and miniatures sizes.

In 1913 Royal Doulton began marking each new figurine design with an "HN" number. Harry Nixon was the artist in charge of painting the figures. The "HN" numbers refer to him. "HN" numbers were chronological until 1949, after which blocks of numbers were assigned to each modeler. Over two thousand different figures have been produced. New designs are added each year, and older designs are discontinued. Approximately two hundred designs are currently in production.

Character And Toby Jugs

Character jugs depict the head and shoulders, whereas Toby Jugs feature the entire figure, either standing or seated. Noke revived the old Staffordshire Toby tradition in the 20th century by modeling characters based on songs, literature, legends, and history. The first jugs were produced by Noke in 1934. Large jugs measure 5 1/4" to 7 1/2", small jugs 3 1/4" to 4", miniatures 2 1/4" to 2 1/2", and tinies 1 1/4" tall or less. The shape and design of the jug handle aids in establishing the age of a jug. For a brief period, all seated Tobies were discontinued. Production of the seated Tobies began again in 1973.

Series Ware

Series Ware, created by Charles Noke, used a large number of standard blank shapes decorated with a selection of popular characters, events, and illustrators. A series ranged from two to three to as high as twenty scenes.

A variety of printing techniques was used on Series Ware. Transfer printing from engraved plates and lithography supplemented with hand coloring was one technique. The block printing and silk screening techniques produced denser, more colorful images. A photographic process captured famous views and characters.

Series Ware production was interrupted by World War II. However, a revival of decorative plate production led to the Collectors International plates during the 1970s, featuring plates for special holidays such as Valentine's Day and Christmas, and designs by international artists.

Today Doulton and Company is the largest manufacturer of ceramic products in the U.K. Minton, Royal Crown Derby, Ridgway, Royal Albert, Royal Adderley, Colclough, Paragon, John Beswick, and Webb Corbett are all part of the company.

References: Jean Dale, *The Charlton Standard Catalogue of Royal Doulton Beswick Figurines, 5th Edition*, The Charlton Press, 1996; Richard Dennis, *Doulton Character Jugs*, Malvem Press, 1976; Michael Doulton, *Discovering Royal Doulton*, Swan Hill, 1994; Desmond Eyles & Richard Dennis, *Royal Doulton Figures Produced at Burslem, Staffordshire 1892-1994*, Richard Dennis Publications, 1994; Desmond Eyles, *The Doulton Burslem Wares*, Royal Doulton & Barrie Jenkins, 1980; Desmond Eyles, *The Doulton Lambeth Wares*, Hutchinson, 1975; Louise Irvine, *Royal Doulton Bunnykins Collectors Book*, Richard Dennis, 1993; Louise Irvine, *Royal Doulton Limited Edition Loving Cups &*

Jugs; Louise Irvine, *Royal Doulton Series Ware, Vol. 1 & 2, Vol. 3 & 4*, Richard Dennis, 1980, 1984; Ralph & Terry Kovel, Kovels' *The Illustrated Price Guide to Royal Doulton, Crown, 1980*; Katherine Morrison McClinton, *Royal Doulton Figurines & Character Jugs*, Wallace-Homestead, 1978; Kevin Pearson, *The Doulton Figure Collectors Handbook*, Kevin Francis Publishing Ltd. 1988; Doug Pinchin, *The Beatrix Potter & Bunnykins Price Guide*, Francis Joseph Publications, 1995; Doug Pinchin, *The Doulton Figure Collectors Handbook, 4th Edition*, Francis Joseph Publications, 1996; Francis Salmon, Ed. *The Character Jug Collectors Handbook, Sixth Edition*, Francis Joseph Publications, 1995. Jean Dale, *Royal Doulton Animals*, The Charlton Press, 2000. Jean Dale & Louise Irvine, *Royal Doulton Bunnykins*, The Charlton Press, 3rd Edition, 2003.

Gallery: Sir Henry Doulton Gallery, Doulton Fine China, Nile Street Pottery, Burslem, England.

Collectors' Club: Mid-America Doulton Collectors, P.O. Box 483, McHenry, IL 60060. Annual membership: $20.00 per year, Newsletter: 6 per year; Royal Doulton International Collectors Club, 701 Cottontail Lane, Somerset, NJ. 08873, annual membership: $50.00 per year, Quarterly magazine. Doulton & Beswick Collectors Club, Lesley Crowther At Francis Joseph, 5 South brook Mews, London SE 12 8LG.

Newsletter: *Character Jug Report*, Box 5000, Caledon, Ontario, LONIC0, Canada; *Collecting Doulton*, P.O. Box 310, Surrey TW9 1 FS, UK. Bi-monthly magazine; *Doulton Divvy*, Quarterly magazine, Betty J. Weir, P.O. Box 2434, Joliet, IL 60434.

Burslem

Biscuit Barrel, 5 1/2" h, fluted body, 4 panels w/multicolored transfers of flowers, HP accents, brown borders, gilt accents, SP cov and overhead handle, ... **160.00**

Cabinet Plate, 9" d, gilt outlined red flowers, red-brown, brown, and blue autumn leaves and branches, ivory ground, swirl molded border, shaped rim w/tan feathers on dk brown band, ... **155.00**

Chamber Pot, 11 1/2" d, blue printed floral design w/gold splashes, ... **255.00**

Dresser Jar, 6 1/8" d, blue printed botanical designs, gold dusted rims, ... **175.00**

Ewer
9 1/2" h, lg cobalt blue irises w/leaves and stems, tan ground, gold accents, ... **595.00**

10 1/2" h, renaissance shape, painted pink fuchsia flowers, lg bronze waterlily leaves, painted bronze handle, ... **395.00**

Figure, Daffy-Down-Dilly, HN 1712, (A), **$425.00**

Figure, Gossips, red and cream, HN 2035, **$495.00**

Jar, 7" h, lg flowing blue pomegranates, gold accents, ... **200.00**

Jardiniere, 11 1/2" h, "Babes in Woods," blue and white, c1891, **$2,950.00**

Jardiniere, 5" h x 5" w, "Morrisian" pattern, blue printed maidens dancing in garden, stiff leaf base, ... **450.00**

Pin Dish, 4 3/4" w, shell form, HP foxglove flowers, ... **95.00**

Pitcher, 5 1/2" h, gilt centered blue and white meandering flowers and stems, stiff leaves on collar, ... **260.00**

Plate

7 1/4" d, lg blue flowerheads, gold overlay of leaves and rims, set of 12, ... **450.00**

9" d, HP Monarch butterfly feeding on gilt outlined white and lt blue flowers, lt brown foliage, cream ground, gilt lobed rim, c1875, ... **355.00**

9 1/4" d

Bone china, multicolored scene of boat, bridge, and steepled buildings, scalloped and fluted border w/gold tendrils, ... **150.00**

HP pink edged white irises, green and brown foliage and stems, gold shaded lobed border w/fluting, sgd "Dewsberry," **175.00**

9 7/8" d, "Madras" pattern, oriental temples in center w/figures by water, border of oriental flowers and buildings, blue-grey transfer, "Doulton Burslem England" mk, ... **15.00**

10" d, 12 sides, "Nankin" pattern, multicolored floral, geometric, and swirl border, ... **15.00**

Platter, 13 1/8" l x 10 5/8" w, "Madras" pattern, dk blue transfer, "Doulton Burslem" mk, (A), ... **135.00**

Pitcher, 8 1/2" h, blue and white, **$450.00**

Pitcher

5" h, transfer of blueberries, lime green leaves, yellow centered blue flowerheads, brown shaded stems, gold accents, pewter lid w/ceramic thumblift, dtd 1888, ... **130.00**

Pitcher, 9" h, incised black design, tan to brown ground, cobalt flowerheads and int, Hannah Barlow, imp mks, **$1,450.00**

11" h, red flowers, leaves, and stalks on body, red collar w/white curlicues, ... **150.00**

Sauceboat, Cov, 4 1/2" h x 8" H-H, w/undertray, scattered floral sprigs, gold rims and handles, fluted borders, gold acanthus knob, "brown DOULTON BURSLEM ENGLAND" mk, ... **20.00**

Teapot, 4 1/2" h, "Empire" pattern, blue sprigs, dk blue handle, spout, flowerhead knob, ... **300.00**

Urn, 9 1/2" h, HP pink and white dogwood blossoms, green foliage, bluebell flowers on reverse, shaded lt green to cream ground, pink spread base w/gilt leaf designs, 2 gilt curved handles from shoulder to rim, artist sgd, ... **200.00**

Vase

6 1/2" h

Bulbous, short collar, HP gold tube lined pink peonies on

cream ground, raised gilt tooled floral base, ... **395.00**

Teardrop shape, flared neck, multicolored garden flowers on cream ground, gilt accents, fancy gilt scrolled handles w/painted flowers, ... **275.00**

7" h, wide shoulder, papered body, flared base, HP white flowers, red hanging buds, gold-green foliage, cream ground, red and brown circ base, brown rim, yellow int, ... **430.00**

Vase, 16" h, raised tan buds, med blue swirls, dk blue ground, Eliza Simmance, c1891, **$1,950.00**

8" h, long, slightly swollen shape, everted rim, arched bracket feet, white enameled centered gilt flowerheads, raised gilt scrolls and trailing branches, gilt filigree tracery, cobalt ground, ... **300.00**

Lambeth

Biscuit Barrel, 10 1/4" h, black outlined incised horse design on tan ground between bands of molded bamboo, bluebells on base, SP rim, cov, and overhead handle, Hannah Barlow, (A), ... **880.00**

Cache Pot, 3 5/8" h, piecrust rim, brown stoneware, turquoise and white enamel stylized flowerheads, gilt accents, cobalt int, ... **50.00**

Ewer, 7 1/4" h, "Carrara" ware, spiral bands of foliage and turquoise beads on matte cream ground, ... **1,600.00**

Jardiniere, 8" h x 9" d, Silicon Ware, white center band of curlicues w/borders of blue bands of fleur-de-lys, star bursts on base, brown stone body, ... **350.00**

Jardiniere and Pedestal, 39" h, Art Nouveau style, jardiniere w/gold ground, dk red and white slip trailed stylized peonies, brown and green whiplash stems, white enamel dots on ground, brown collar w/green stiff leaves, mottled blue base, repeat design on pedestal, waisted circ foot w/mottled blue borders and olive green swirls, c1890, (A), ... **10,158.00**

Jug

5 1/4" h, stoneware, "Harvest," tan base, dk brown top, applied white scenes of men drinking, hunter w/horn, and trees, c1895, ... **165.00**

5 1/2" h, stoneware, tan base, brown top, raised white flowerheads joined by stems and leaves, band of white 4 leaf clovers on neck, "Doulton Lambeth" mk, ... **250.00**

7" h, raised enameled bands of white flowerheads, med blue leaves, dk blue swags, white and lt blue band on neck, matte brown body, "Doulton Silicon Lambeth England" mk, ... **95.00**

Mug

5" h, beaker shape, relief of blue flowers, olive green leaves and stems, dk blue mottled ground, brown int and handle, ... **225.00**

6 1/4" h, dk brown border, tan glazed body w/applied figures hunting deer, peasant family and hog eating, 3 applied ribbed handles, "imp DOULTON LAMBETH" mk, (A), ... **60.00**

Pitcher, 8" h, stoneware, applied snowflakes on upper dk brown section, textured tan lower section w/applied cream flowers, "imp Doulton Lambeth England" mk, c1890, ... **200.00**

Plate, 9" d, "Norfolk" pattern, blue and white Dutch scene, ... **40.00**

Tea Kettle, 8 1/4" h, white and blue enameled stylized flowerhead, brown curled petals, meandering enameled green foliage, white enamel accented tan textured ground, brown simulated bundled wood spout and overhead handle w/white enamel wraps, Frank Butler, (A), ... **1,145.00**

Vase, 7 3/4" h, tan shades, blue trim, "Doulton Lambeth" mark, **$450.00**

Vase

4" h, bulbous body, slightly flared base, HP enameled blue and white leaf shaped designs on textured gold scroll ground, cobalt rim and int, "imp DOULTON LAMBETH SLATER'S PATENT" mk, ... **45.00**

5" h, bulbous middle, incised design of ewes grazing around middle, blue glazed spread base w/cobalt streaks, short collar w/incised blue jewels, sgd "Hannah Barlow," **775.00**

5 1/4" h, squat shape, everted rim, faience, painted polychrome enameled apple blossoms, dk

blue ground, brown lined rim, dtd 1877, ... **1,650.00**

6 1/2" h, Silicon Ware, applied pale blue flowerheads, white curlicues, blue stiff leaves on collar and base, orange-brown ground, c1880, ... **1,250.00**

8" h, ball body, long straight neck, dk pink crystalline pattern, ... **750.00**

9" h, bulbous, rounded shoulder, short, flared rim, pink-white flowerheads, mottled green and blue ground, ... **225.00**

9 1/4" h, incised "New Forest Ponies" around middle, incised stiff leaf design on base, sgd "Hannah Barlow," Silicon Ware, ... **2,250.00**

12" h, stoneware, tube lined green centered red and cream or maroon flowerheads, olive leaves, tan neck, mottled blue body, ... **595.00**

Royal Doulton

Animal Figure

Cairn Terrier, HN 2589, ... **100.00**

Crouching tiger, 14" l, flambe, #809, ... **995.00**

Dalmatian, "Ch. Goworth Victor," HN 1113, ... **225.00**

Dog lying on back, brown and white, RN 1098, ... **135.00**

Dolphin, "The Leap," flambe, #2949, (A), ... **1,235.00**

English Setter, black and white, HN 1050, ... **175.00**

Greyhound, HN 1066, (A), ... **495.00**

Irish Setter, red-brown, HN 1055, ... **175.00**

Owl, flambe, #2449, (A), ... **320.00**

Penguin With Chick, K-20, ... **280.00**

Persian Cat, blue-grey, HN 2539, ... **250.00**

Peruvian Penguin, flambe, 585, (A), ... **440.00**

Siamese Cat, DA130, ... **50.00**

Thrush Chicks, green base, HN 2552, ... **450.00**

Brambly Hedge

3 1/4" h, Mrs. Apple, BP3b brown mk, ... **25.00**

Bunnykins

Bank, 9 1/4" h, 2nd version, ... **210.00**

Bowl

6" d, "Baking," **15.00**

6 1/2" d, "Family in the Garden," **25.00**

Figure, 4" h, Bunnykins, Master Potter Bunnykins, **$150.00**

Feeding Dish, 6 1/2" d,
    "Wheelbarrow Race," **35.00**
Figure
    2 1/2" h, Jogging Bunnykins,
        DB22, BK2, ... **98.00**
    3 1/2" h, Daisie Springtime, DB7,
        BK1, ... **225.00**

Figure, 4 1/2" h, Bunnykins, Father, Mother, and Victoria Bunnykins, **$40.00**

4" h
Be Prepared, DB56, BK5,
    .... **55.00**
Grandpa's Story Bunnykins,
    .... **435.00**
Playtime, ... **55.00**
4 1/4" h, Friar Tuck, DB243,
    .... **35.00**
4 1/2" h, Paperboy Bunnykins,
    .... **150.00**

Plate
    6 1/2" d, "Apple Picking," SF25,
    .... **45.00**
8" d
    "Baking," **15.00**
    "Dancing in the Moonlight,"
    .... **55.00**
    "Topping The Fruit Cart,"
    .... **20.00**

Figure, Betsy, HN 2111, **$295.00**

Figure
    Abdullah, HN 2104, ... **400.00**
    A Child of Williamsburg, HN 2154,
    .... **175.00**
    Afternoon Tea, HN 1747, ... **425.00**
    A Gentleman From Williamsburg, HN
        2227, ... **230.00**
    An Old King, HN 2134, ... **595.00**
    A Stitch in Time, HN 2252, ... **250.00**
    Autumn Breezes, HN 1934,
    .... **275.00**

Babie, HN 1679, ... **110.00**
Ballad Seller, HN 2266, ... **335.00**
Balloon Clown, HN 2894, ... **245.00**
Biddy Penny Farthing, HN 1843,
    .... **165.00**
Bluebeard, HN 2105, ... **495.00**
Carolyn, HN 2112, ... **425.00**
Coralie, HN 2307, ... **150.00**
Country Lass, HN 1991, ... **180.00**
Curley Knob, HN 1627, ... **425.00**
Daffy Down Dilly, HN 1712, .. **455.00**
Day Dreams, HN 1731, ... **215.00**
Dimity, HN 2169, ... **400.00**
Elegance, HN 2264, ... **255.00**
Elfreda, HN 2078, ... **975.00**
Enchantment, HN 2178, ... **250.00**
Flower Seller's Children, HN 1342,
    .... **695.00**
Gay Morning, HN 2135, ... **250.00**
Giselle, HN 2140, ... **550.00**
Good King Wensceslas, HN 2118,
    .... **175.00**
Grace, HN 2318, ... **235.00**
Grizel, HN 1625, (A), ... **960.00**
Her Ladyship, HN 1977, ... **300.00**
Hostess of Williamsburgh, HN 2209,
    .... **220.00**
In Grandma's Days, HN 362,
    .... **3,000.00**
Janet, HN 1537MC, ... **150.00**
Jovial Monk, HN 2144, ... **135.00**
Karen, HN 1994, ... **400.00**
Lambing Time, HN 1890, ... **145.00**
LaSylphide, HN 2138, ... **550.00**
Laurianne, HN 2719, ... **225.00**
Lorna, HN 2311, (A), ... **110.00**
Lunchtime, HN 2485, ... **135.00**
Mendicant, HN 1365, ... **325.00**

Figure, Midsummer Noon, HN 2033, **$495.00**

Michelle, HN 2234, ... **140.00**
Midinette, HN 2090, 2nd edition,
    .... **200.00**
Milkmaid, HN 2057, ... **245.00**
Miss Muffet, HN 1936, ... **150.00**

Noella, HN 2179, ... **600.00**
Old Meg, HN 2494, ... **150.00**
Olga, HN 2463, ... **225.00**
Pamela, HN 1469, dtd 1932, potted
   mk, ... **950.00**
Parson's Daughter, HN 564,
.... **395.00**
Paula, HN 2906, ... **210.00**
Polly Peachum, HN 550, ... **495.00**
Pope John Paul II, HN 2888,
.... **310.00**
Queen Victoria, HN 3125A, (A),
.... **530.00**
Sir Walter Raleigh, HN 2015,
.... **475.00**
Solitude, HN 2810, ... **325.00**
Spring Flowers, HN 1807, ... **375.00**
Sunday Best, HN 2698, ... **265.00**
Swimmer, pink and purple, HN 1326,
   (A), ... **4,350.00**
Tea Time, HN 2355, ... **175.00**
Thanksgiving, RN 2446, ... **225.00**
The Balloon Man, HN 1954, **225.00**
The Ballerina, purple dress, HN
   2116, ... **425.00**
The Begger, HN 2175, ... **375.00**
The Captain, HN 2260, ... **200.00**
The Cobbler, HN 1706, ... **400.00**
The Curtsey, lavender, HN 57B, (A),
.... **1,585.00**
The Doctor, HN 2858, ... **275.00**
The Gossips, HN 2025, ... **495.00**
The Judge, HN 2443, ... **265.00**
The Potter, HN 1493, ... **350.00**
The Skater, HN 2117, ... **450.00**
The Wayfarer, HN 2363, ... **125.00**
Tinker Bell, HN 1677, ... **95.00**
Victoria, HN 2471, ... **139.00**
Viking, HN 2375, matte, ... **225.00**

Jugs

Anne Boleyn, Lg, D6644, ... **125.00**
Anne of Cleaves, 2nd version, Lg,
   D6653, ... **150.00**
Apothecary, Sm, D6574, ... **75.00**
Arriet, Tiny, D6256, ... **225.00**
Arry, Tiny, D6255, ... **235.00**
Auld Mac
   Lg, D5823, ... **70.00**
   Tiny, D6257, ... **325.00**
Beefeater
   Lg, D6206, ... **135.00**
   Miniature, D6251, G.R. on
     handle, ... **85.00**
Bonnie Prince Charlie, Lg, D6858,
.... **180.00**
Captain Henry Morgan, Lg, D6467,
.... **95.00**
Cardinal, Tiny, D6258, ... **280.00**
Catherine of Aragon, Lg, D6643,
.... **100.00**

Catherine Parr, Lg, D6664, ... **220.00**
Charles Dickens, Style B, Lg, D6939,
.... **330.00**
David Copperfield, Tiny, D6680,
.... **95.00**
Dick Turpin,
   Lg, old version, D5485,
   .... **125.00**
   Mini, D6542, ... **25.00**
   Sm, D6535, ... **75.00**
Dick Whittingham, Lg, D6375,
.... **395.00**
Falstaff
   Lg, D6287, ... **150.00**
   Sm, D6385, ... **85.00**
Fat Boy, Tiny, D6142, ... **135.00**
Fortune Teller, D6503, Sm, ... **280.00**
Gondolier, Lg, D6589, ... **625.00**
John Barleycorn, Sm, D5735,
.... **68.00**
John Peel
   Miniature, D6130, ... **70.00**
   Sm, D5731, ... **85.00**
King Charles I, 3 handles, Lg,
   D6917, ... **385.00**
Lawyer, Mini, D6524, ... **55.00**
Little Nell, Tiny, D6681, ... **95.00**
Mephistopheles, Sm, wo/verse,
   D5758, (A), ... **670.00**

Jug, Robin Hood, large, D-6527, **$125.00**

Mine Host, Lg, D6468, ... **170.00**
Mr. Bumble, Tiny, D6686, ... **100.00**
Mr. Micawber, D6143, ... **130.00**
Mrs. Bardell, Tiny, D6687, ... **95.00**
Old Charley
   Miniature, D6046, ... **65.00**
   Tiny, D6144, ... **50.00**
Old King Cole
   Lg, D6036, ... **225.00**
   Musical, D6041, (A), ... **1,765.00**
Old Salt, Mini, D6557, (A),
.... **695.00**
Oliver Twist, Tiny, D6677, ... **95.00**

Paddy
   Mini, D6042, ... **50.00**
   Tiny, D6145, ... **50.00**
Parson Brown, Sm, D5529, ... **70.00**
Pearly Boy, Lg, Variation 3, brown
   hat, coat, and buttons,
.... **2,800.00**
Pied Piper, Lg, D6403, ... **85.00**
Poacher, Mini, D6515, ... **45.00**
Robin Hood, Sm, D6252, ... **100.00**
Sairy Gamp, Tiny, D6146, ... **50.00**
Sam Weller, Tiny, D6147, ... **100.00**
Santa Claus
   Lg, doll handle, D6668,
   .... **250.00**
   Tiny
     Candy cane handle, D6980,
     .... **60.00**
     Parcels handle, D7020, ... **68.00**
Scrooge, Tiny, D5731, ... **55.00**
Simple Simon, Lg, D6374, ... **580.00**
Sir Francis Drake, old version, Lg,
   D6805, ... **125.00**
The Pendle Witch, Lg, D6826,
.... **250.00**
Town Crier
   Lg, D6530, ... **185.00**
   Sm, D6537, ... **55.00**
Ugly Duchess, SM D6603, ... **350.00**
Vicar of Bray, Lg, D5615, ... **150.00**
   Lg, D6496, ... **170.00**
   Mini, D5526, ... **145.00**

Miscellaneous

Butter Dish, Cov, 8 7/8" d, 4 3/8" h,
   w/drain, oct, "Mandarin" pattern,
   bands of multicolored oriental
   figures and butterflies, dtd 1893,
   .... **175.00**
Coffeepot, 8 1/4" h, "Tosca" pattern,
   ivory ground, ... **75.00**
Creamer, 2 3/4" h, "Castles and
   Churches Series-Bodiam
   Castle," D4504, ... **70.00**
Creamer, 4" h and Sugar Bowl, 2 1/2"
   h, "Rialto" pattern, ... **100.00**
Cup and Saucer
   "Crocus" pattern, ... **70.00**
   "Old Leeds Sprays" pattern,
   .... **50.00**
   "Poppy" pattern, ... **250.00**
Fruit Service, master bowl, 9 1/2" d,
   oct, 6 bowls, 6 1/2" d, oct,
   "Norfork" pattern, blue and white
   windmill and country scenes,
   .... **105.00**
Ginger Jar, 10 3/4" h, globular shape
   w/domed cov, black, green, blue,
   and orange enameled exotic bird
   and stylized flowerheads, yellow
   ground, dtd 1925, (A),
   .... **1,315.00**

Tobacco Jar, 5 1/2" h, matte brown bark body, cobalt base, rim, and cov, ... **120.00**

Toby Jugs
Cliff Cornell
  Lg
    Blue suit, ... **250.00**
    Dk Brown suit, ... **330.00**
    Tan Suit, ... **660.00**
    Sm, blue suit, ... **385.00**
Falstaff, Lg, D6062, ... **75.00**
Fat Boy, Sm, D6264, ... **220.00**
Old Charlie
    Lg, D6030, ... **330.00**
    Sm, D6069, ... **210.00**
The Squire, Med, D6319, ... **425.00**

Trio
"Clamis" pattern, ... **75.00**
"Magma" pattern, ... **110.00**
"Rialto" pattern, ... **90.00**

Vase
5 3/4" h, slightly swollen shape, everted rim, applied ribbon-tied brown washed hanging swags and vines, blue-green hammered ground, ... **45.00**
6" h, classic form, 2 high handles, Sung, red and black mottled coloring, ... **900.00**
7" h
    Lobed tulip form, flambe Sung, c1930, ... **780.00**
    Shield shape, flared neck, black outlined green circle flowers and blue spade shaped leaves, black stems, purple to blue mottled ground, ... **293.00**
8" h
    Bottle shape, flambe veining, red shading over oxblood base, ... **260.00**
    Elongated ovoid shape, Japanese style tube lined wheat and lt green wheat pattern on upper section, blue mottled ground, ... **500.00**
9" h, bottle shape, relief of band of blue and grey geometrics on tan ground on neck, overall mottled blue ground, "Royal Doulton England" mk, ... **95.00**
10 3/4" h, bulbous, straight neck, flared rim, magenta, purple, green, and brown incised fruit and flowers, blended grey and white upper section, med blue lower section, Maude Bowden, (A), ... **385.00**

16" h, squat ball body, stick stem, enameled turquoise, white, and gold flowerheads on beige textured ground w/gold splashes, gloss cobalt neck w/lt blue stiff leaves, beige flared rim, ... **125.00**
16 3/4" h, Titanian Ware, bulbous shape, flared rim, HP multicolored deer, mountains, and forest, gold emb rim, sgd "A. Eaton," **2,025.00**

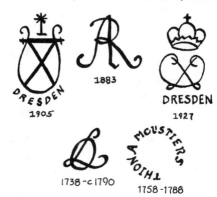

DRESDEN

Germany
1694 to Present

History: Two men, working for Augustus II Elector of Saxony, rediscovered the technique to make hard paste porcelain of the oriental type. Count Tschimhaus, who began his research in 1694, was joined by Johann Bottger, an alchemist, in 1701. At first they produced a red stoneware. By 1709 Bottger was producing white porcelain. Tschimhaus did not live to enjoy their success, having died in 1708. The king established the Royal Saxon Porcelain Factory in Dresden in 1710 and then moved it to Meissen one year later.

During the 18th century, Americans and English used the name "Dresden china" for the porcelain ware produced at Meissen. This has led to much confusion. Dresden, the capital of Saxony, was better known in 18th century Europe than the city of Meissen, fifteen miles away. In addition, Meissen products were sold in Dresden. Hence, Dresden became a generic term for all porcelains manufactured and decorated in the city of Dresden and its surrounding environs, including Meissen.

In the mid-19th century, about thirty factories were operating in the city of Dresden, producing and decorating porcelains in the style of Meissen wares. Marks were adopted that were similar to the crossed swords of the original Meissen factory. Many simply faked the Meissen mark.

Helena Wolfson and her successors imitated AR Meissen porcelain between

1843 and approximately 1949. Her firm had a large staff of painters trained to imitate the 18th century porcelain. Wolfson also purchased "white" china blanks from the Meissen factory and had them decorated by her own staff of painters and gilders. After much litigation, Wolfson was forced to abandon the AR mark. About 1880 the firm adopted a mark using the word "Dresden" with the letter "D" surmounted by a crown.

Meyers and Son was the greatest rival of Wolfson in the production of imitation Meissen porcelains. They used the crossed swords with an "M" to mark their examples. Franziska Hirsch, another copyist, used a mark similar to that of Samson, the French potter, on her Meissen and Vienna imitations made between 1894 and 1930.

The porcelain factory of Carl Thieme of Potschappel produced rococo imitations of Meissen pieces from 1872 until 1972, often marketing them as Meissen 18th century figures. They also produced household, table, and decorative porcelains, knick knacks, souvenirs, and gift articles, all decorated in the Meissen and Vienna styles.

A "Dresden style" came into being when four decorators, Richard Klemm, Donath and Co., Oswald Lorenz, and Adolph Hamann, all registered the same mark in 1883. The mark was a crown with "Dresden" underneath in blue. Later this group altered their marks. Eight other decorators then used the "Dresden" and the crown mark.

Donath and Co. produced porcelain in the Meissen and Vienna styles from 1872 until 1916. The company merged with Richard Klemm's decorating workshop for three years. In 1918 the firm became the Dresden Art Department of C.M. Hutschenreuther, continuing in that relationship until 1945. Adolph Hamann, another member of the "Dresden style" group, operated a porcelain decorating workshop from 1866 until 1949. It was acquired by Heinrich Gerstmann in 1933 and continued with its earlier name.

Franz Junkersdorf, A. Lamm, Henfel and Co., Anton Richter, Max Robra, Wilhelm Koch, and others had decorating workshops from the last quarter of the 19th century and extending into the 20th century. All of these firms imitated Meissen porcelains.

Dresden "lace" figures were introduced by Meissen in 1770. Real lace was dipped into liquid porcelain, then cut and applied to figures. The lace threads were burned off during the firing process. It is often found with applied flowers. The large groups were called "Crinoline" groups. Such companies as Donath & Company, Richard Klemm, Adolph Hamann, and Oswald Lorenz popularized these figures.

References: Susan & Jim Harran, *Dresden Porcelain Studios*, Collector Books, 2002.

Museums: Bayerishes National Museum, Munich, Germany; Kunstgewebemuseum, Berlin, Germany; Museum fur Kunst and Gewerbe, Hamburg, Germany; Staatliche Porzellansammlung, Dresden, Germany.

Additional Listings: see Hutschenreuther.

Baker, 8 1/4" l x 6 1/8" w, lg bouquet of garden flowers in center, vert fluted border w/gold rim and sprigs on ext, Helena Wolfson, ... **125.00**

Basket, 5 1/2" sq, dk red rose, green foliage in center, open weave body, molded wave rim, "blue crowned Dresden" mk, ... **65.00**

Bowl

4 1/2" l x 2 3/4" w, vert fluted body, HP multicolored garden flowers, gold curls on base, gold outlined ruffed rim, ... **25.00**

6" d, lg red rose and foliage in center, woven lattice sides, gilt accented rope rim, "blue crowned Dresden" mk, ... **18.00**

8 1/2" d, ftd, applied pink, orange, blue, and lavender flowerheads, applied green leaves, reticulated body, gold overlay, "Dresden Germany" mk, ... **40.00**

Cabinet Cup and Saucer

Cup w/6 panels of multicolored Watteau courting scenes separated by gold vert lines and wide gold band on int, 9 scenes on saucer w/gold accents, ... **95.00**

Cup w/painted continuous panel of period woman and 4 cherubs eating grapes, lt yellow ground w/bands of raised gilt beading and fleur-de-lys, Ambrosius Lamm, ... **600.00**

Cabinet Plate, 7 7/8" d, 4 gilt lacework edged quatrefoil cartouches of iron-red scenes of travelers reserved on cream ground w/gilt lacework border, Adolph Hamann, ... **85.00**

Centerpiece, 35" h, bowl w/border of applied multicolored flowers and cut leaf and flower design on body, HP flowers on int, supported by center shaft w/3 figures of gold clad women and applied flowers and salmon outlined seashells, base w/figures of 3 gold clad kneeling women holding shells, molded swirls w/painted flowers and scroll feet and hanging shells on margins, ... **795.00**

Chocolate Cup and Saucer, Cov, alternating panels of HP classical scenes and black panels w/flowers separated by gilt scroll and line

borders, gilt loop knob set on pink lapped ribbon, zig-zag handle, ... **150.00**

Chocolate Pot, 9 1/2" h, rect HP panel of 2 women, child on wash day under spout, green side panels w/pastel flower inserts and gold scroll work, handle, and spout, ... **1,210.00**

Cup and Saucer, panels of HP scenes of period couples alternating w/burgundy panels and flowers separated by gold bands, gold accents, Helena Wolfson, ... **100.00**

Cup and Saucer, Demitasse

HP multicolored floral sprays, gold swags, gold int dentil rim, Richard Klemm, ... **50.00**

Sm scattered purple violets, green foliage, gilt trim, ... **75.00**

Figure, 5" h

Period boy wearing pink jacket, blue and pink striped trousers, feeding greens to 2 ducks on gilt scroll base, ... **220.00**

Seated female dancer, lilac ruffled layered lace dress, red bodice, brown hair, ... **135.00**

Nodder, 11 1/2" h, multicolored floral designs, white kimono, grey hair, yellow trim, Carl Thieme, c1901, (A), **$500.00**

Jardiniere, 3 7/8" l, w/stand, flared rect shape, black scenes of hunter shooting deer on side, reverse w/hunters and horn, flowers on ends, gilt trim, Carl Thieme, ... **250.00**

Plaque, 5 1/2" h x 3 1/2" w, rect, titled "Vestalin," seated figure in white classic gown, holding oil lamp, late 19th C, (A), ... **2,585.00**

Plate

6" d, center panel of garden flowers, yellow reticulated border w/3 oval panels of garden flowers, wavy shaped rim, ... **32.00**

7 1/2" d, 4 fan shaped panels, 2 HP scenes of courting couples on white ground, 2 panels of flowers on yellow ground, panels separated by gold swirls, border of gold swirls and shells, Richard Klemm, ... **45.00**

*Plate, 7 1/4" d, magenta and blue flower border, orange and raised gilt in center, A-***$50.00**

9 1/4" d, HP cantaloupe, blueberries, and nuts in center, lt blue to dk brown shaded ground, ... **65.00**

9 1/2" d, painted scene of courting couples and floral sprays on yellow ground, separated by scrolling gilt bands, Richard Klemm, pr, (A), ... **235.00**

Plate, 10" d, named HP portrait of "Duchess d' Angouleme," red-brown feathers in hair, white drape, med blue gown, cobalt border w/gilt accents and enamel dots, gilt rim, "blue DRESDEN" mk, (A), **$650.00**

Ramekin, 3 1/2" d, w/underplate, 5" d, fluted body, flared ruffled borders, HP sprays of garden flowers w/gilt trim, "Dresden, Crown over H" mk, ... **35.00**

Serving Bowl, 13" H-H x 9" w, HP red roses, lg garden flowers, gilt rope twist handles and wavy rim, gilt leaves on ext, Ambrosius Lamm, ... **900.00**

Tea Set, pot, 9" h, creamer, 6 1/4" h, cov sugar bowl, 6 1/4" h, tray, 8" l x 7" w, rect, gilt and white Empire style designs of leaves and hanging drapery, griffin handles, Helena Wolfson, ... **1,500.00**

Urn, Cov

12 1/2" h, HP red, pink, and lavender rose bouquets, garden florals, gold leaf designs on borders, gold pointed knob, "blue crowned D" mk, ... **470.00**

30" h, HP scene of period courting couple in garden on front in flowered and applied flower cartouche, applied flowers on body w/gilt accents, figural female bust handles, encrusted flower circ base, gilt accented curled feet, multiple applied flower knob, ... **2,600.00**

Vase

9" h, shield shape w/circ socle and base, pierced flared collar, 2 gold accented curl handles w/mask terminals, gilt edged cartouche of period people in garden reverse w/loose spray of garden flowers, Carl Thieme, repaired handle, ... **120.00**

10" h, lower section w/scattered purple and red roses, dk blue flowers, green foliage, reticulated shoulder and neck w/gold outlined molded curlicues, sm painted flowerheads between reticulations, "blue crown Dresden" mk, ... **40.00**

12 1/2" h, ball base, long, slender neck, yellow panels w/multicolored flowers, white panels w/flowers, white panels w/multicolored scenes of period couple, gold filigree designs separating panels, ... **275.00**

1749-55

ENGLAND-GENERAL

Porcelain
1700 to Present

History: Before the 1740s, porcelains available in England were of Chinese or

Japanese origin and were imported by the British East India Company. Many early English pottery manufacturers tried to duplicate Oriental porcelains and the Continental porcelains of Meissen and Sevres, but achieved only limited success.

The earliest English porcelains date to about 1745 and were made at the Chelsea factory. This porcelain was the soft paste type. By the mid-18th century, production of soft paste porcelain was well established at Bow and Chelsea. Other factories, including Bristol, Longton Hall, Derby, Worcester, Liverpool, and Lowestoft soon followed. The English factories were private enterprises, not subsidized by royal families or princely households, as were those on the Continent.

Soft paste was fragile. Hot liquids could crack it. Sometimes it collapsed or lost its shape in the kiln. Efforts were mounted to find a material that was more stable in the kiln and durable. The Bow factory tried adding ash of calcined bones. Bristol and Worcester incorporated a soapstone paste to their mix to strengthen their porcelains.

Many credit William Cookworthy of Plymouth with the rediscovery of the Chinese method of hard paste porcelain manufacture in England about 1768. He made hard paste type porcelain at Plymouth for only two years, 1768-70. In 1771, he moved to Bristol.

Pieces from the Plymouth pottery have an oriental influence. Some under-the-glaze blue designs are enhanced with over-the-glaze enamels. Figurines and animal and bird groups also were made. The second Josiah Spode of Stoke developed bone china by adding bone ash to the ingredients of hard paste porcelain. This "bone" china led to the development of cream colored earthenware. Based on the hard paste rediscovery and Spode's bone china, England became a major supplier to the worldwide market.

Pottery

17th Century to Present

History: Early pottery wares in England included stoneware, Delftware, slipware, and salt glaze ware. Potters such as Thomas Toft, John Dwight, and the Elers were among the principal manufacturers.

During the early 17th century, Staffordshire became the center of the pottery industry due to an abundant supply of coal, availability of clays and adequate transportation to the marketplace. Astbury, Whieldon, and the Woods experimented with all forms of earthenwares from figure groups with colored glazes to numerous types of vessels and dishes. Earthenware production dominated the first half of the 18th century.

As the newly perfected cream-colored earthenwares introduced by Josiah Wedgwood in the 1760s came to the forefront, Staffordshire salt glazed wares started to go out of fashion. Numerous Staffordshire

makers such as the Turners, Elijah Mayer, Palmer and Neale, Wilson of Hanley, Leeds, William Adams of Tunstall, and Josiah Spode of Stoke copied Wedgwood's cream-colored earthenwares. They also imitated Wedgwood's black basalt, jasper, and cane-colored stoneware. Spode introduced the manufacture of blue-printed earthenwares.

During the 1800s, lusterwares became popular with the Staffordshire potters. New techniques in the early 19th century included overglaze transfer printing and ironstone china. Underglaze blue printing was developed in the first half of the 19th century.

Figures, depicting all sorts of people and animals, were made during the 1800s by John Walton, Ralph Salt, and Obadiah Sherratt. During the reign of Queen Victoria, earthenware cottage mantelpiece figures were decorated in enamels and some gilding. Underglaze blue was the most important color used. Sampson Smith was the principal manufacturer. Pot lids were another 19th century product with decorations in polychrome underglaze.

Other pottery firms making utilitarian and decorative wares during the 19th century included H.& R. Daniels, Miles Mason, W. Ridgway & Co., Cauldon Place Works, John Davenport, Job Meigh, Lakin & Poole, Mintons, and Doulton of Lambeth.

Since the late 1800s, the studio potter had become important in England. This movement was a reaction against the emphasis on mass-produced pieces. The studio potter usually threw his own wares, with the glazing and decorating done either by himself or under his supervision. The first of the studio potters was William de Morgan and the Martin Brothers. Bernard Leach of the St. Ives Pottery made stoneware influenced by early Chinese and Japanese wares. The studio potters used many traditional methods of manufacture such as tin glaze, salt glaze, slipware, agate ware, and sgraffito work.

Patent Office Registration Marks: From 1842 until 1883, many manufacturers' wares were marked with the "diamond mark," which was an indication that the design or form of the piece was registered with the British Patent Office and protected against piracy for three years. The mark could be applied by either printing, impressing, or applying a molded piece of clay. Pottery and porcelains were in Class IV. In the diamond, the numbers or letters in each corner were keyed. A ceramic marks book is necessary to decipher the mark and discover the date the design was registered with the Patent office. After 1884, the diamond mark was replaced by a registry number.

References: Cyril G.E. Bunt, *British Potters & Pottery Today*, F. Lewis Publishers, 1956; J.P. Cushion, *English China Collecting for Amateurs*, Frederick Muller, 1967; B. Watney, *English Blue & White Porcelain, Rev. Ed.* Faber & Faber, 1973.

Museums: British Museum, London, England; City Museum & Art Gallery, Stoke-on-Trent, England; Cranbrook Academy of Art Museum, Bloomfield Hills, MI; Gardiner Museum of Ceramic Art, Toronto, Canada; Norwich Castle Museum, Norwich, England; Victoria & Albert Museum, London, England.

Additional Listings: Adams, Beswick, Bisque, Bow, Bristol, Carlton Ware, Caughley, Cauldon, Chelsea, Clews, Coalport, Copeland-Spode, Creamware, Crown & Royal Crown Derby, Davenport, Delft, De Morgan, Derby, Doulton, Flow Blue, Ironstone, Jackfield, Leeds, Liverpool, Longton Hall, Lowestoff, Lusterware, Majolica, Martin Brothers, Mason, Meakin, Meigh, Minton, Mocha Ware, Moorcroft, Nantgarw, New Hall, Pot Lids, Pratt, Ridgway, Rockingham, Royal Worcester, Salt Glaze, Slipware, Spode, Staffordshire, Stoneware, Swansea, Wedgwood, Whieldon Ware, Willow Ware, Enoch Wood, Ralph Wood, Worcester.

Candlestick, 7 1/4" h, modeled hen turkey standing next to tree stump w/applied grapes and leaves, mound w/applied flowerheads and leaves, overall white glaze, c1750, missing sconce, chip, ... **6,850.00**

Coffee Cup, "Root and Peony" pattern, polychrome enamels, c1757, rim chips, ... **345.00**

Cup and Saucer, 2 fighting dragons, oriental foliage, green transfers, ... **25.00**

Dessert Dish, 9 1/4" d, painted center w/flower bouquet, painted insects and sprigs, border molded w/red puce, and green accented berries and leaves, pr, ... **6,600.00**

Dish, 9" w, figural leaf shape, floral sprig in center, molded green outlined leaves on rim, green branch handle, puce rim, c1758, restored chips, pr, ... **3,500.00**

Dish, 9 7/8" l, fluted oval, painted titled scene of Stork w/chicks or Spoonbill on shore, pr, (A), ... **300.00**

Figure, 17 3/8" l, pig seated on haunches, "Cabbage Rose" pattern, painted red roses, foliage, green shamrocks, Wemyss, (A), ... **6,170.00**

Garniture, vase, 5" h, HP landscape in cartouche on front, maroon ground w/band of white beading above and below, 2 vases, 4 1/2" h, HP continuous landscape, maroon upper and lower borders w/white beading above and below design, ... **1,400.00**

Jardiniere and Stand, 4 7/8" h, bucket shape, sepia painted oval landscape scenes reserved on upper and lower gilt bands joined vert by gilt stripes and iron-red and turquoise floral garlands, gilt applied ring handles, Pinxton, c1798-1800, (A), ... **5,650.00**

Jug
6" h, alternating bands of relief of green or red daisy flowerheads, c1835, Wales, ... **500.00**
6 3/8" h, pear shape, sparrow beak spout, strap handle, painted iron-red, green, black, and yellow full flower spray w/old English roses, lilies, and tulips, scattered sprigs and sm sprigs of cherries, inscribed "MR 1764," salt glaze finish, Cockpit Hill, (A), ... **1,095.00**

Liquor Dispenser, 12 3/4" h, pottery, gold rect cartouches w/gold "S. WHISKY, RUM, GIN, I. WHISKY, BRANDY," wooden spigot, set of 5, ... **2,850.00**

Milk Jug, 3 5/8" h, oval silver shape, painted band of moths and ladybirds on gilt scrolling foliage between gilt band lines, angular handle, Pinxton, c1800-10, (A), ... **1,100.00**

Mixing Bowl, 9" d, molded flowerheads in circles on yellow ext, white int, ... **25.00**

Pitcher, 9" h, paneled, oct base, mottled yellow and brown glaze, (A), ... **100.00**

Plaque, Rect
8" h x 6" w, painted view of Lion Rock, Dovedale, Derbyshire, sgd "W.E.J. Dean," c1920, (A), ... **920.00**
17 1/2" l x 11 1/2" w, painted view of sacking of city, soldiers, men, and women before city ramparts, artist sgd, late 19th C, (A), ... **440.00**

Plate
7 1/2" d, HP enamel Meissen style sprays and sprigs, molded radiating paneled border, scalloped rim, c1750-60, pr, ... **900.00**
8" d, HP red cherries, green foliage, green lined rim, "yellow WEMYS" mk, ... **120.00**

8 1/2" d, red and dk blue Willow type pattern, band of red and dk blue fan designs on rim, "Ferrybridge Pottery Yorkshire" mk, ... **25.00**
9" d, lg red centered yellow roses, green foliage in center, cobalt border, gold dentil rim, ... **125.00**
9 1/4" d, "Strawberry Leaf" pattern, rose, purple, iron-red, green, yellow, and blue bouquet, sprays, and sprigs in center, molded rim w/iron-red strawberries, green stems, puce veined green leaves, c1755, firing cracks, ... **520.00**
9 3/8" d, chinoiserie design of deer in woods w/gilt bamboo and enamel flowerheads and butterflies overhead, scalloped rim, c1770, pr, ... **3,500.00**
9 1/2" d, multicolored floral bouquet and sprigs in center, green molded leaves on border, c1755, ... **1,390.00**
9 3/4" d, painted bouquets and scattered sprigs, strawberry fruit and leaf molded border, c1775, pr, (A), ... **2,870.00**

Potpourri, Cov, 17 3/4" h, painted panel of exotic birds, reverse w/flowers, blue splashed ground, cov and ft, pierced and molded w/oak leaves and acorns, branch handles and knob, mid-19th C, (A), ... **900.00**

Spill Vase, 5 1/2" h, flared, HP lg bouquet of garden flowers, cobalt collar w/gilt flowers and leaves, gilt base, white beaded base and collar, gilt lined rim, c1820, pr, ... **1,600.00**

Sweetmeat Dish, 6" l, modeled as scallop shell w/coral, limpets, and shells on base, white glaze, c1755, pr, (A), ... **3,585.00**

Teapot, 8" h x 11 1/2" w, blue striping, white ground, Castleford, c1800, $1,100.00

Teapot and Stand, 9 1/2" h, "Meashan Ware," "A Present To A Friend," multicolored enameled flowers, brown ground, c1870, $695.00

Tea Service, Part, pot and stand, 6 5/8" w, cream jug, 5 7/8" w, cov sugar bowl, 7 1/8" H-H, waste bowl, 6 1/8" d, dish, 8 1/8" d, 11 tea cups, 12 coffee cups, 12 saucers, wide orange band on body and covs w/gilt trailing vines and foliage, c1805, (A), ... **3,825.00**

Vase

4 1/2" h, triangle base, inverted triangle top, ftd, 2 sm handles, red and yellow speckles, blue-green ground, Dover, ... **20.00**

11" h, cylinder shape, tan and brown horiz bands of geometrics, grooved top and base, "Denby Made in England" mk, ... **45.00**

FAIRINGS AND TRINKET BOXES

Locket, Elbogen, Germany Possneck, East Germany
c1840 - 1900s

Staffordshire, England

History: Fairings, common during the Victorian era, were small porcelain groups of gaily colored human and animal china figures designed to catch the eye with their humor and sentimentality. One figural, captioned "The last in bed to put out the light," showed a man and woman bumping heads as they jumped into bed while a lighted candle stands on a table nearby. "Five o'clock tea" featured humanized cats at a tea party. Fairings were made to be given away as prizes or purchased at English fairs.

Fairing themes included courtship and marriage scenes, events in the lives of the people, war, politics and the law, children at work and play, and animals behaving like people. Most fairings had inscriptions written in English. Often these were naive or intended to be risqué.

Colors mainly were shades of pink and blue with the inscriptions in black or gold. Early examples were usually 3 1/2" to 4 1/2" high with plain, undecorated bases. Gilt was used sparingly. After 1890 the colors became more garish.

Fairings were made of white heavy paste. Most had numbers incised or impressed beneath their bases, though the earliest and best examples had no numbers.

Although fairings were associated with English fairs, they were actually made by German makers Springer and Oppenheimer of Locket, Elbogen, Germany, which is now part of the Czech Republic, and Conta and Boehme of Possneck, Germany.

Trinket boxes usually had a utilitarian purpose. They were designed to hold pins, rings, watches, or other trinkets after being taken home from the fairs. Early boxes usually were not marked, but by the late 1860s they had incised or scratched numbers.

The marks on boxes made by Conta and Boehme and Springer and Company were similar. Conta and Boehme had an arm holding a sword in an enclosed shield, while Springer had a bent elbow in a shield crest with a crown. Conta and Boehme porcelain boxes had identifying numbers on the base or underside of the cover. Most of the boxes were exported to England and America.

Box styles included bureaus or dressers, figurals, baskets, furniture, and others. Some had fairing-type subjects in a variety of sizes. Many boxes had mirror frames. Boxes could also be a combination of bisque and glazed finishes. Conta and Boehme made more than four hundred different designs for boxes. Fairing boxes were captioned on the front base or side in English. When fairs became less popular, boxes were sold in gift shops and other stores.

Some boxes were also match boxes with a striker on the underside of the cover. Otherwise, the design is the same as a trinket box. Beginning in the 20th century, production and interest declined and nearly ceased during World War I. The factory finally closed in 1931.

Small English Staffordshire porcelain trinket boxes were sold at fairs and seaside resorts. They ranged in size from about 3" to 5" in length and usually were several inches tall. The lids were decorative and featured subjects similar to the fairings from Germany. Many had animals or children on them. Most were white and had gilt trim.

References: Margaret Anderson, *Victorian Fairings & Their Values*, Lyle Publications, 1975; W.S. Bristowe, *Victorian China Fairings*, A & C Black, 1964; Nancy Neely, *Victorian Fairing Boxes*, Antique Trader Weekly, March 9, 1994; Janice and Richard Vogel, *Victorian Trinket Boxes*, PoBneck Publishing Co. 1996. Janice & Richard Vogel, *Conta & Boehme Porcelain, Identification & Value*, Privately Printed, 2001.

Museums: Strong Museum, Rochester, NY

Reproduction Alert: An increasing number of fairings are being reproduced in England and sold as original Conta and Boehme pieces. These examples have captions printed in black caps and have numbers on the solid bottom from the 1800 series. They also have a crude copy of the mark. Reproductions are also coming from Germany and Japan.

Collecting Hints: Boxes in mint condition with the original gold and paint command the highest prices. Make sure the top and bottom match each other.

Fairings

2 3/4" h x 4 1/4" w, "What Peace, When The Old Girl Sleeps," woman in blue shawl, dk red coat, sleeping on sofa, another in brown robe sleeping in chair, ... **675.00**

3 1/2" h, 3 1/2" l, "Who is coming?" man in lt blue jacket, pink striped pants, woman in gold dotted white gown, blond hair, gold trimmed base, c1850, $295.00

3" h x 3 5/8" l

Couple climbing into bed, white w/polychrome accents, unmkd, base, ... **350.00**

Woman in bed, standing nurse feeding baby, blue blanket, yellow pillow, ... **365.00**

"Before Marriage," man in purple coat, kneeling before seated woman in pink jacket, lt purple skirt, gold trim, ... **255.00**

"Tug of War," seated child holding red sock overhead away from leaping brown and white dog, gold accented fence in bkd, ... **300.00**

3 1/4" h

3 5/8" l, "Come Pussy Come," man and woman in nightclothes climbing into bed, cat on back board, multicolored accents w/gold trim, "red MADE IN GERMANY" mk, ... **225.00**

5" l, "In Chancery," 2 men pulling at ends of brown spotted cow, seated woman milking, polychrome, Conte & Boehme, c1870, ... **1,125.00**

3 1/2" h x 3 3/4" l, "Returning at One O' Clock in the Morning" on base, white ground w/puce, gold, and black accents, (A), **$30.00**

3 1/2" h

"Checkmate," man kissing woman, seated near chest table, another woman looking away, polychromes, ... **550.00**

"Return From The Ball," mother in red flowered white gown carrying child up blue carpeted stairs, ... **585.00**

"Slack," seated worker in orange jacket, brown striped trousers, another in brown trousers leaning on broom, ... **165.00**

"Some Contributions To Punch," characters from *Punch Magazine*, polychrome, Conte & Boehme, c1870, ... **675.00**

"The Welch Tea Party," 3 women seated at table, tall black hats w/white stripe, red dresses, red checked or striped aprons, ... **130.00**

"Three O'Clock Tea," 3 brown and white kittens seated before cups and kettle, cats on base, ... **370.00**

"Twelve Months After Marriage," figure of husband and wife in bed, ... **100.00**

"Wedding Night," man and woman before fireplace w/clock, polychrome accents, ... **100.00**

2 3/4" h x 3" w, green top, overall white glaze, **$135.00**

3 5/8" h x 4" l, "Will We Sleep First or How-," man and woman in bed, red and blue blankets, gold trim, ... **100.00**

3 3/4" h

3 1/4" w, "If You Please Sir," man seated at table drinking, hand on standing woman's posterior, dk red apron, c1870, chips, ... **600.00**

3 1/2" w, "Arriving Home at 3 O'Clock in the Morning," woman spanking man lying across bed, ... **55.00**

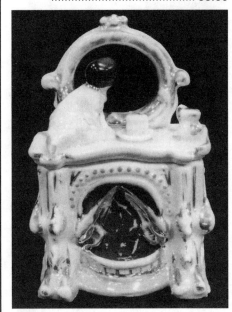

4 3/8" h, blue hearth, white ground, orange luster base, gold trim, **$125.00**

4" h x 3 1/2" w

"The Orphans," brown, brown and white, grey and white pugs in

chair, wearing collars w/bells, ... **400.00**

"Modesty," man in green and orchid checkered trousers in bathroom, pushing door against woman in orchid gown, ... **90.00**

4 1/2" h x 3" w, "Paddling His Own Canoe," figural child seated in bowl w/gold oars and shield on cov, bureau base w/molded gilt fruit bowl, red dots on base, Conta & Boehme, ... **125.00**

5" h

"A Privileged Pet," seated little girl wearing red ribboned yellow hat, green stockings w/brown and white dog nipping, gold trimmed 3 panel screen in bkd, brown table at side, c1890, ... **95.00**

Father in pink nightcap and gown feeding child in lap wearing blue gown, "The Pitfalls of Matrimony" on base, ... **180.00**

4" h, 3 1/2" l, green and blue coverlet, red and blue clothes, brown posted bed, "Shall We Sleep First Or How" on base, **$225.00**

Trinket Boxes

Baby Princess Elizabeth in Cradle, 2 3/4" h x 4 3/4" l, black helmet shaped cradle w/white eagle emblem, white cushion w/turquoise stripes, child wearing purple and gold trimmed white dress, brown hair, red shoes, green foliate base, c1860, ... **300.00**

Brown and White Fox Jumping over Tan Fence, grey and white goose in mouth, ... **180.00**

Bureau

2 1/8" h, 2 red and blue trimmed birds on surface before worn gold accented mirror, gold accented base, "imp shield

Conta & Boehme" mk, c1850, ... **50.00**

2 3/8" h, wash set w/pitcher and bowl on top, mirror frame, worn gold accents, ... **50.00**

3 7/8" h, pocket watch and mirror on top, white w/gold trim, ... **65.00**

4" h x 3 1/4" w
Molded figure on blue ground on front, gold accented clock, jars, and mirror frame, orange border, ... **95.00**

Red beaked dove w/blue ribbon and envelope around neck, molded floral base, blue vert stripes, c1880, ... **93.00**

4 1/2" h x 3" w
Figural monkey beating drum before mirror frame, gold accents, ... **375.00**

Blond haired figural boy in blue-green outfit, seated on bureau top reading red outlined book, gold accented mirror frame and base, "imp Conta and Boehme" mk, ... **90.00**

Gold and orange dashes on base, 3 figural pups on top w/mirror frame, ... **75.00**

5 1/2" h, oval mirror, 2 vases and clock on top, molded flowerheads on borders, gold accents, chips, ... **175.00**

Casket
3" l x 2 1/2" h, figural crown, scepter, and orb on cov, white w/red, blue, and gold accents, ... **40.00**

4 1/2" h, gold accented fan on base, brown accented figural dog and puppy on stool on cov, arbor arch in bkd, unmkd, ... **145.00**

Child in Highchair, 2 3/4" h, brown chair, brown-gold hair, blue striped white gown, holding bowl, ... **115.00**

Clown, 3 1/2" h x 3" w, green striped trousers, blowing horn, seated on red trimmed drum, applied band of flowerheads on cov, molded vines and beading on white base, ... **125.00**

Dishes on Table, 3" l x 3 1/2" h, white glaze, Germany, ... **125.00**

"Ernst und Marie," polychrome couple seated on tree trunk w/bocage bkd, Conta & Boehme, ... **200.00**

Fireplace
4 1/4" h x 3" w
Gold outlined blue hearth w/orange enamel dots, child

wearing orange shoes lying on mantle, looking in gold mirror frame, ... **90.00**

Orange dots on base, figural child w/hoop before mirror frame on cov, ... **250.00**

4 1/2" h x 3" w, orange dots around hearth opening, figural child w/trumpet seated on red and gold drum, mirror frame, ... **285.00**

Hand Holding Crowned Box, 3 1/2" h, blue drape on box, dk red loops on cov, Conta & Boehme, ... **35.00**

Hand and Tub, 2 1/2" h x 3 1/2" w, figural hand and applied flowerheads on cov, deer head in beaded frame on front of vert ribbed tub, 4 claw feet, red flowerheads on border, ... **40.00**

Hunter, brown ground w/raised white wild boar and deer, antlers at corners, white figural hound knob, ... **115.00**

Man and Horse, 3 1/2" h x 2 1/2" w, tricorn hat, knee breeches, overall white glaze, ... **110.00**

Pug, 2 1/2" h, standing tan dog on cov, oval box w/blue oblong on side, gold trim, Staffordshire, ... **220.00**

Queen Seated on Throne, 6" h, blue top w/pink sash, lt blue gown w/gold trim, Conta & Boehme, ... **285.00**

Reclining Black Spotted Dog, 3" h x 2 1/2" l, blue blanket w/trumpet at side, scroll molded and fluted base, ... **38.00**

Seated Girl Holding Group of Rabbits in Arms, 3 3/4" h x 3 1/4" w, white glaze, ... **50.00**

Swan on Cov, 2 3/4" h x 3" l, black face, brown bill, white body and base, ... **195.00**

FEATHER EDGE CERAMICS

Staffordshire, Leeds, France, Delft
1790-1880s

History: One of the simplest forms of decoration on creamware and pearlware tableware was created by adding color to the rim or border. Molded or plain rims received blue or green streaking as a decorative technique. The molding took the form of shells or streaks. Not only were rims treated in this fashion, feathering was used as a decoration on center sections such as pepper pots and coffeepots.

Feathering was also used in conjunction with center designs. These can be

found on Leeds-type wares, as well as Dutch Delft and tin-glazed French Faience, most notably at Strasbourg.

References: Lisa A. McAllister, *Collector's Guide To Feather Edge Ware: Identification & Value*, Collector Books, 2000.

Bowl
12" d, beaded blue feather edge, (A), ... **150.00**

Charger
9 1/2" d, Leeds, blue, yellow, and gold peacock w/black spots, on green and brown branch, green feather edge, (A), ... **1,700.00**

14 1/4" d, blue and yellow brown polychrome flowers, green foliage, white ground, blue scalloped feather edge, rim chip, (A), ... **825.00**

14 3/8" d, painted dbl handled yellow urn and brown swags holding cobalt, brown, and yellow flowers, green foliage, brown inner line border, blue scalloped feather edge, (A), ... **1,870.00**

Cup and Saucer, green feather rims, France, pr, ... **160.00**

Pepper Pot, 4 1/4" h, blue stylized starburst on cap, blue feathered edge, $265.00

Cup Plate
4 1/4" d, green, gold, blue, and brown Leeds type Dahlia in center, dk green molded feather

and fishscale edge, (A),
.... **1,210.00**
4 3/8" d, brown eagle, blue and gold
American shield, green branch,
scalloped blue feather edge, (A),
.... **1,980.00**

Egg Cup, 2 3/4" h, blue ruffled rim, blue
lined body and base, Leeds, c1810-
20, hairlines, ... **160.00**

Fish Drain, 18 1/2" l, blue feather edge,
c1800, ... **495.00**

Gravy Boat
6 1/4" l, lobed, blue feather edge,
hairline, (A), ... **150.00**
7" l, pearlware, blue feather edge,
blue dash handle, ... **125.00**

Pepper Pot, 4 1/2" h, 2 tooled bands
w/blue feathering, base repaired,
(A), ... **85.00**

Plate
7" d, oct, pearlware, brown American
eagle w/red and blue shield
breast, holding arrows and green
balls, molded green feather
edge, ... **700.00**
7 1/8" d, blue, yellow, and ochre
peafowl on branch, green
sponged leaves, green feather
edge scalloped rim, Leeds,
.... **475.00**
8 3/8" d, pearlware, cobalt pagoda,
fence, and trees, blue diaper
border, blue wavy feather edge,
c1780-1800, ... **130.00**
8 3/4" d
Blue feather edge, (A), ... **25.00**
Gaudy yellow, green, gold, and
dk brown floral design in
center, molded green feather
edge w/leaves and fish
scales, (A), ... **880.00**
9 3/8" d, blue feather edge,
.... **30.00**

*Plate, 9 1/2" d, creamware, blue Leeds style design, blue feather edge, **$225.00***

9 1/2" d
Blue feather edge, (A), ... **35.00**
Oct, green feather edge, pr, (A),
.... **230.00**
Pearlware, underglaze blue
painted oriental figure
holding open umbrella in
front of pagoda, garden, and
fencing, inner border band of
ovals, blue feather edge,
c1780, ... **130.00**
9 3/4" d
Leeds type, blue pagoda,
mountains, and landscape,
blue feather edge, ripple rim,
chips, (A), ... **195.00**
Molded blue feather edge, **65.00**
10" d
Blue feather scalloped edge
w/ribbing, (A), ... **55.00**
Creamware, HP blue house,
tiered tree, lake and island,
blue feather edge, c1810,
.... **375.00**
Pearlware, oriental temple,
mountains and trees,
interlaced inner border, blue
and white, blue feather edge,
.... **200.00**

Platter
9 3/8" l, oval, basketweave body,
reticulated border, blue feather
edge, ... **250.00**
12" l x 15 3/4" w, oct, blue feather
edge, (A), ... **110.00**
13 1/2" l x 10 3/8" w, oct, blue feather
edge, "Stone Ware P.W. & Co."
mk, ... **50.00**
15 1/4" l, blue feather edge, . **175.00**
16" l x 12 1/2" w, oval, pearlware, lg
blue sprig and sm sprigs in
center, blue feather edge, late
19th C, ... **950.00**
16 1/8" l x 13" w, oct, creamware,
green feather edge, unmkd,
.... **375.00**
17" l x 13 5/8" w, rect, dk blue feather
edge, "imp Stubbs Longport"
mk, ... **225.00**

Soup Plate
7 3/4" d, pearlware, blue feather
edge, ... **65.00**
10" d, blue feather edge, (A),
.... **40.00**

Toddy Plate, 4 1/2" d, dk blue shell
molded rim, lt blue overall ground,
.... **100.00**

Tray
9 1/4" l x 6 3/4" w, blue feather edge,
(A), ... **65.00**

17 3/4" l x 13 3/4" w, blue feather
edge, (A), ... **100.00**

Tureen, Cov
7 1/2" l x 5 1/2" h, blue feather edge,
(A), ... **185.00**
12 1/2" l x 7 3/4" h, blue feather
edge, (A), ... **200.00**

Vegetable Bowl, 7 1/2" l, rect w/canted
corners, blue feather edge, (A),
.... **95.00**

M F
1880

FISCHER

Herend, Hungary
c1839 to Present

History: Moritz Fischer established a
porcelain manufactory at Herend,
Hungary, about 1839. His factory was
noted for the high quality of its
reproductions of Chinese porcelains and
18th century European porcelains from
Meissen, Vienna, Capodimonte, and
Sevres. Reticulated vases, ewers, and
chimney ornaments also were made in
very bright enamel colors, almost
majolica-like in appearance. Oriental
patterns such as famille rose, famille verte,
and Imari decorations were imitated by
Herend craftsmen. They employed no
independent designers, only craftsmen.
Every piece was hand painted.

When the Imperial Vienna factory
closed in 1864, Fischer received the right
to use the patterns and models selected
by Emperor Franz Joseph for continued
use. These old Vienna molds and patterns
were marked with a beehive. Many wares
were exported to the United States.

Fischer was raised to the nobility and
used the name Farkashazi in 1865. Fischer
was succeeded by his sons. The factory
failed in 1874 and then underwent a series
of changes in ownership.

New prosperity was achieved under
Jeno Farkashazi, the grandson of Moritz.
The factory was taken over by the state in
1948. The factory continues to produce
hard paste porcelain dinnerware, vases,
and figures similar to those of Meissen and
Sevres.

Herend porcelain is still produced
today. Although figures are very popular,
Herend is most known for its tablewares.
Patterns are never discontinued, so it is
always possible to order replacements.

Museum: Victoria & Albert Museum,
London, England.

Cache Pot, 8" h, painted red centered
blue stylized flowerheads, mauve
stylized leaves and stems, mauve
zigzag border, applied gilt

flowerheads on border, "Fischer Budapest" mk, ... **350.00**

Carafe, 11 3/4" h, Middle Eastern shape, Persian style paisley motif in colors, "FISCHER J. BUDAPEST" mk, ... **625.00**

Cup and Saucer, cup w/2 white panels and HP courting couples, 2 yellow panels w/blue stylized flowerheads separated by vert gilt columns of curlicues, saucer w/2 white panels of courting couples, 2 pink panels w/flowers, separated by gilt curlicue lines, gilt curlicue rims, ... **495.00**

Ewer
12" h, HP lg oriental flowers on body, gold base, gold fluted flared rim, gold fancy branch handle, ... **500.00**
18 3/4" h, Moorish style, ext reticulated w/cartouches enamel decorated w/Asian type branches and insects, part reticulated rim, dragon handle, quatrefoil trumpet foot, "J. Fischer Budapest" mk, (A), ... **700.00**

Ewer, Cov, 18" h, Turkish motif, dbl walled gold and white shields on sides, applied gold accented white flowerheads on neck, tooled gold flowerhead and leaf bands, "blue Fischer Budapest" mk, ... **850.00**

Planter, 13 1/2" l x 10" h, figural pagoda boat w/figural dragon figurehead, cobalt ground w/gold accents, multiple tiny feet, mkd, ... **750.00**

Puzzle Jug, 8 1/2" h, multicolored Persian motif w/butterfly, "imp FISCHER J. BUDAPEST" mk, ... **350.00**

Vase, 8 1/4" h, brown-red and gold accents, dk red ground, **$1,250.00**

Vase
9 1/2" h, ewer shape, enameled blue-centered red flowers, dk

blue tulips, lt and dk green foliage, gold textured ground, lg arched handles w/flowers, "blue Fischer Budapest" mk, ... **275.00**

Vase, 12 7/8" h, med blue leaves, gold reticulation, pale blue ground, **$375.00**

12 1/2" h, Aesthetic, ovoid body, cylinder neck, 2 figure "8" handles, blue and maroon printed and painted flowers, gilt accents, "J. Fischer Budapest" mk, late 19th C, (A), ... **350.00**
12 3/4" h, Aladdin lamp shape, spread ft, 2 fancy loop handles, multicolored cherub scene on front, reverse w/vase and garden flowers, multicolored scattered flowers and trellis, "Fischer Budapest Hungary" mk, ... **495.00**

FLOW BLUE

Staffordshire, England
Early Victorian 1835-1850s
Mid Victorian 1860s-1870s
Late Victorian 1880s, 1890s, and the early 1900s

History: "Flow" or "Flowing" Blue was developed for commercial consumption in the 1820s by Josiah Wedgwood. Other well-known makers included W.T. Copeland, Samuel Alcock, and William Davenport. Flow Blue was being marketed in many countries including France, Germany, Holland, and the U.S. The peak production period was from the mid-1800s to the early 1900s.

The Flow Blue process occurred when a transfer printed design, originally in cobalt oxide, received volatizing agents such as lime of chloride or ammonia, causing the pattern to "bleed" during the glaze firing stage. The cobalt, when first applied, was brown in color and changed to a deep blue during the firing. The degree of flowing varied considerably, with some designs barely discernable, while others showed a slight hazing of the pattern.

The earliest patterns were Oriental in style and named in most cases by the manufacturer. These names often are found incorporated with the maker's mark. Scenics and florals were popular during the Victorian period. Some Art Nouveau designs were produced. Most designs were applied by transfers. In some cases, hand painted designs were done.

Though some of the designs were registered, it was not unusual to find the same name used by two different companies for two entirely different designs. Manufacturers also had a habit of changing design names. Over 1,500 patterns were manufactured during the peak years of Flow Blue production.

Early Flow Blue was characterized by a dense coloration. Later pieces had a softer look to them. By the mid-Victorian era, colors, as well as gold embellishments, were added to enhance the designs.

Many early examples were made of stoneware, but porcelain and semi-porcelain also served as bodies for the Flow Blue patterns. By the later half of the 19th century, semi-porcelain was the material of choice. The designs of this period usually were sharper and cleaner. The body design was more elaborate.

Back stamps usually provided the pattern name and initials or name of the maker. Often the location of the factory was included. Transfer marks outnumber all other types. Marks with a pattern name date after 1810.

References: Sylvia Dugger Blake, *Flow Blue*, Wallace-Homestead, 1971; Robert Copeland, *Spode's Willow Pattern and*

Other Designs After the Chinese, Rizzoli, 1980; Mary Gaston, *The Collector's Encyclopedia of Flow Blue China*, Collector Books, 1983, values updated 1996; Mary Gaston, *Collector's Encyclopedia of Flow Blue, 2nd Series*, Collector Books, 1994, values updated 2000; Veneita Mason, *Popular Patterns of Flow Blue China with Prices*, Wallace-Homestead, 1982; Jeffrey B. Snyder, *A Pocket Guide to Flow Blue, Revised & Expanded*, Schiffer Publishing, Ltd. 2000; Jeffrey B. Snyder, *Flow Blue, A Collectors Guide to Pattern, History & Values*, Schiffer Publishing, Ltd. 2003; Jeffrey B. Snyder, *Historic Flow Blue*, Schiffer Publishing, Ltd. 1994; Petra Williams, *Flow Blue China, An Aid to Identifications*, Fountain House East, 1971; Petra Williams, *Flow Blue China 11*, Fountain House East, 1973; Petra Williams, *Blue Flow China & Mulberry Ware, Rev. Ed.* Fountain House East, 1981; William & Van Baskirk, *Late Victorian Flow Blue & Other Ceramic Ware, A Selected History of Potteries & Shapes*, Schiffer Publications, 2002.

Collectors' Clubs: Flow Blue International Collectors' Club, Inc. P.O. Box 205, Rockford, IL 61105. $30 annual dues, Bi-monthly newsletter, *Blueberry Notes*.

Museums: Margaret Woodbury Strong Museum, Rochester, NY.

Reproduction Alert: New Flow Blue has been manufactured by Blakeney Pottery Limited in Stoke-on-Trent since 1968. Objects are termed "Victorian Reproductions" and are made with large blue roses in many forms. Evidence shows that some of these items have been sold as old.

A reproduction barber bowl is marked "Made in China" with a paper label. Pitcher and bowl sets are also being reproduced. Some pieces have an enormous backstamp with "Victoria Ware" and "Ironstone."

Reproductions of Touraine pattern have surfaced from China. They have an underglazed Stanley Pottery Co. mark. Reproductions do not carry "England" in the mark as the originals did. Plates measuring 8", 9", and 10" have been reproduced, as have 8", 11" and 17" platters, bone dishes, vegetable dishes, teapots, and cups and saucers.

Collecting Hints: The center for collecting Flow Blue is the United States. Even though the vast majority of Flow Blue was made in England, the English do not attach much antique value to Flow Blue because it was mass produced, transfer decorated, and inexpensive. Since most was exported to the U.S. during the 19th century, it is not prevalent in the English market.

Miniatures and children's dishes are scarce in Flow Blue because few examples were made. Art and decorative items are harder to find than ordinary table and utilitarian wares.

Abbey Pattern
Bowl, 4 3/4" d, "Jones & Co." mk, ... **145.00**
Pitcher, Cov, 7 3/4" h, "G. Jones & Co." mk, ... **110.00**
Plate, 10" d, Petrus Regout, ... **85.00**
Punch Bowl, 9" d, George Jones, ... **525.00**

Agra Pattern
Bowl, 8" d, Winkle, ... **135.00**

Albany Pattern
Gravy Boat, 9" l x 4" h, "W.H. Grindley" mk, ... **229.00**

Alhambra Pattern
Plate, 8" d, ... **25.00**
Sauce Tureen, 6" l, w/undertray, ... **215.00**

Althea Pattern
Condiment Dish, 9 1/2" l x 5" w, Villeroy & Boch, ... **225.00**
Plate, 9 1/2" d, Villeroy & Boch, ... **195.00**
Soup Plate, 9 3/4" d, Villeroy & Boch, ... **195.00**
Vegetable Bowl, Cov, 11 3/4" l, Villeroy & Boch, ... **595.00**

Amoy Pattern
Berry Bowl, 5 1/8" d, "blue AMOY, imp DAVENPORT anchor" mks, (A), ... **88.00**
Butter Dish, Cov, 4" h, paneled cov, ... **795.00**
Milk Pitcher, 5 1/2" h, Davenport, ... **495.00**
Plate, 9 1/8" d, Davenport, ... **195.00**
Platter
    13 3/8" l x 10" w, Davenport, ... **395.00**
    18" l x 14" w, oct, ... **895.00**
Sugar Bowl, Cov, 6 1/2" h x 8 1/4" l, "blue AMOY, imp DAVENPORT anchor" mks, (A), ... **605.00**

Andorra Pattern
Butter Pat, 3" d, Johnson Brothers, ... **58.00**

Arabesque Pattern
Plate, 10" d, "T.J. & J. Mayer Longport" mk, ... **165.00**

Argyle Pattern
Butter Dish, Cov, 8" w, "W.H. Grindley" mk, ... **400.00**
Gravy Boat, 7 1/2" l, ... **225.00**
Plate, 8 7/8" d, "W.H. Grindley" mk, ... **55.00**
Platter, 15 1/4" l x 10 3/4" w, "W.H. Grindley" mk, ... **275.00**
Soup Plate
    8 3/4" d, Ford & Sons, ... **40.00**
    9 1/2" d, Ford & Sons, ... **35.00**
Vegetable Bowl, Cov, 11" H-H, "W.H. Grindley" mk, ... **350.00**

Ashburton Pattern
Platter, 18" l x 14 1/2" w, ... **250.00**

Astral Pattern
Ladle, 7 3/8" l, Grindley, ... **100.00**

Atlanta Pattern
Plate, 10 1/2" d, Wedgwood, .. **22.00**

Beaufort Pattern
Gravy Boat, 8 1/2" l, "W.H. Grindley" mk, ... **185.00**

Beauty Roses Pattern
Plate
    7" d, ... **18.00**
    8" d, "W.H. Grindley" mk, ... **20.00**
    9 1/2" d, Grindley, ... **25.00**

Bejapore Pattern
Platter, 13 1/2" l x 10 1/4" w, "blue IRONSTONE, BEJAPORE, G. PHILLIPS LONGPORT" mks, (A), ... **330.00**

Belmont Pattern
Platter, 11" l x 8" w, "J.H. Weatherby & Sons" mk, ... **185.00**
Vegetable Bowl, Cov, 12" l x 9" w, gilt accents, "Weatherby & Sons" mk, ... **78.00**

Bentick Pattern
Soup Plate, 8 7/8" d, Cauldon, ... **85.00**

Vegetable Bowl, Cov, 13" H-H, "Brampton" pattern, "F. & Sons Ltd Burslem" mk, c1900, $595.00

Brooklyn Pattern
Vegetable Bowl, Cov, 12" l x 6 1/2" w, c1910, ... **200.00**

Blue Danube Pattern
Plate, 10" d, ... **160.00**
Platter, 15 7/8" l, ... **500.00**
Vegetable Bowl, 7 1/2" l, ... **600.00**

Brush Stroke Pattern
Children's Tea Service, Part, teapot, 5 1/4" h, creamer, 3 1/4" h, cov sugar bowl, 4 3/4" h x 4" w, 4 plates, 5 1/2" d, cup, repaired, 2 cup plates, Dahlia pattern, c1870-80, (A), ... **660.00**
Cup and Saucer, (A), ... **55.00**
Plate
    6 3/8" d, Aster and Grape Shot pattern, set of 4, (A), ... **77.00**

10 3/8" d, "Fairy Villas" pattern, Adams, $75.00

Fairy Villas Pattern
Teapot, 6" h, Adams, ... **650.00**
Vegetable Bowl, 9" d, Adams,
.... **135.00**
Fason Pattern
Cake Stand, 9" d x 3 3/4" h, Villeroy
and Boch, ... **595.00**
Festoon Pattern
Cup and Saucer, "W. Adams
England" mk, ... **20.00**
Florida Pattern
Bowl, 7 1/2" d, Johnson Brothers,
.... **110.00**
Butter Pat, 3" d, set of 3, ... **125.00**
Cup and Saucer, Johnson Brothers,
.... **35.00**
Plate
7" d, ... **80.00**
9" d, Johnson Brothers,
.... **85.00**
Vegetable Bowl, 10 1/2" l, Johnson
Brothers, ... **250.00**
Formosa Pattern
Coffeepot, 13 1/4" h, ironstone,
paneled, ... **4,950.00**
Plate, 9 3/8" d, (A), ... **195.00**
Platter, 13 1/4" l x 10 1/4" w, "blue
lion, circle, FORMOSA, T.J. & J
MAYER" mks, (A), ... **330.00**
Gainsborough Pattern
Vegetable, Cov, 11 1/4" H-H,
Ridgway, ... **350.00**
Geisha Pattern
Creamer, 4" h, Ford, ... **175.00**
Cup and Saucer, c1893, ... **145.00**
Gem Pattern
Plate, 8 1/2" d, ironstone,
Hammersley, (A), ... **121.00**
Geneva Pattern
Platter, 16" l, ... **185.00**
Gironde Pattern
Cake Plate, 10 1/2" d, ... **250.00**
Gravy Boat, 8" l, w/undertray, 8 3/4" l
x 4 3/4" w, "W.H. Grindley" mk,
.... **275.00**

Platter
13" l x 8 3/4" w, oval, "W.H.
Grindley" mk, ... **95.00**
15" l, oval, "W.H. Grindley" mk,
.... **55.00**
19" l x 12" w, oval, "W.H.
Grindley" mk, ... **140.00**
Vegetable Bowl
9" d, ... **135.00**
11" l x 7 3/4" w, ... **120.00**
Grace Pattern
Bone Dish, 7" l, "W.H. Grindley" mk,
gilt accents, ... **110.00**
Grenada Pattern
Bone Dish, 6" l, "Henry Alcock &
Co." mk, ... **65.00**
Platter, 15" l x 10 1/4" w, Alcock,
.... **60.00**
Grosella Pattern
Cup and Saucer, Handleless, (A),
.... **55.00**
Haddon Pattern
Platter, 10 1/4" l, oval, ... **52.00**
Soup Bowl, 9" d, ... **55.00**
Hindustan Pattern
Platter, 18" l x 14" w, oct, ... **750.00**
Holland Pattern
Charger, 12 1/4" d, Johnson
Brothers, ... **180.00**
Pitcher, 7 1/4" h, Johnson Brothers,
.... **315.00**
Plate, 10" d, ... **70.00**
Sauceboat, 7 1/2" l, ... **135.00**
Vegetable Bowl, Cov, 9 3/4" H-H,
Johnson Brothers, ... **135.00**
Hong Kong Pattern
Plate, 9 1/4" d, ... **145.00**
Idris Pattern
Cup and Saucer, c1910, ... **110.00**
Indian Jar Pattern
Gravy Boat, 9" l, Furnival, ... **395.00**
Plate, 7" d, Furnival, ... **112.00**
Soup Plate, 9" d, Furnival, ... **250.00**
Iris Pattern
Butter Dish, Cov, 7 1/2" d, ... **255.00**
Plate, 8" d, ... **15.00**
Ivy Pattern
Platter, 18 1/4" l x 15 1/4" w,
"Cockson & Chetwynd" mk,
.... **750.00**
Kelvin Pattern
Plate, 9" d, "Alfred Meakin," ... **75.00**
Kenworth Pattern
Berry Bowl, 5" d, "Johnson Brothers"
mk, ... **35.00**
Knox Pattern
Platter, 10 1/2" l, oval, "N.W.P." mk,
.... **125.00**

Kyber Pattern
Plate
7 1/4" d, Meier, ... **150.00**
9"d, "Wm. Adams" mk,
.... **110.00**
10" d, "W. Adams & Co." mk,
.... **140.00**
Platter
10" l x 7 1/4" w, "W. Adams & Co."
mk, ... **150.00**
17" l x 13" w, Adams, ... **1,395.00**
Lahore Pattern
Plate
9 1/2" d, 14 sides, "T. Phillips &
Son" mk, ... **165.00**
10 1/2" d, "T. Phillips & Son" mk,
.... **100.00**
Waste Bowl, 7" d, ... **295.00**
Larch Pattern
Sauceboat, 8" l x 6 1/2" h,
w/undertray, 8 1/4" l x 6" w,
"Hancock & Sons" mks, .. **145.00**
Lonsdale Pattern
Platter
11 1/2" l, oval, Ridgways,
.... **245.00**
15" l x 12 1/2" w, rect, "Samuel
Ford & Co. Lincoln Pottery"
mk, ... **300.00**
Lorne Pattern
Gravy Boat, 8 1/2" l, beaded and
emb rim, ... **185.00**
Plate, 10" d, ... **125.00**
Platter
11" l x 8" w, ... **160.00**
16" l x 11" w, "W.H. Grindley" mk,
.... **335.00**
Louvre Pattern
Plate, 7" d, J. & G. Meakin, ... **35.00**
Lugano Pattern
Plate, 9" d, ... **90.00**
Lyndhurst Pattern
Plate, 5 1/2" d, "W.H. Grindley" mk,
.... **65.00**
Madras Pattern
Plate
7 1/2" d, Royal Doulton, ... **45.00**
8 1/4" d, ... **95.00**
Sauce Tureen, Cov, 8 1/2" H-H,
w/undertray, 8 3/4" l, ... **495.00**
Mandarin Pattern
Platter, 11 1/4" l x 8 1/4" w, oval,
Poultney, ... **85.00**
Vegetable Bowl, Cov, 11 1/4" l x 9" w
x 6" h, ... **400.00**
Manhattan Pattern
Soup Plate, 9" d, Adcock, ... **195.00**
Manilla Pattern
Bowl, 10" d, "P.W. & Co." mk,
.... **185.00**

Plate
7 3/4" d, "P.W. & Co." mk,
.... **150.00**
9" d, (A), ... **50.00**
9 1/2" d, "P.W. & Co." mk, (A),
.... **70.00**
10 3/8" d, "P.W. & Co." mk,
.... **130.00**
10 3/4" d, "P.W. & Co." mk,
.... **110.00**
Platter, 15 3/4" l x 12" w, "MANILLA
PW & CO, IRONSTONE" mk, (A),
.... **990.00**

Marechel Niel Pattern
Bowl, 4 7/8" d, ... **30.00**
Platter, 14 1/2" l x 10" w, oval, "W.H.
Grindley" mk, ... **250.00**

Marguerite Pattern
Bone Dish, 6 1/8" l, "W.H. Grindley"
mk, ... **20.00**
Charger, 13 1/2" d, c1895, ... **395.00**

Maria Pattern
Plate, 8" d, "W.H. Grindley" mk,
.... **145.00**

Matlock Pattern
Vegetable Bowl, Cov, 11 1/2" l,
c1890, ... **175.00**

Melbourne Pattern
Gravy Boat, 8" l, ... **275.00**
Plate, 6" d, ... **55.00**
Platter, 14" l x 9 5/8" w, "W.H.
Grindley" mk, ... **245.00**
Soup Tureen, 14" l, w/undertray,
"W.H. Grindley" mk, ... **1,195.00**
Vegetable Bowl, 10" l x 7 1/2" w,
"W.H. Grindley" mk, ... **150.00**

Melrose Pattern
Dish, 7 3/4" H-H, "imp COPELAND"
mk, ... **55.00**

Milton Pattern
Platter, 16 1/2" l x 12 1/2" w, oval
Wood & Son, ... **180.00**

Monarch Pattern
Plate, 7" d, "Myott & Sons" mk,
.... **20.00**

Mongolia Pattern
Butter Dish, 7 1/4" d, w/drain,
.... **320.00**
Plate
7" d, Johnson Brothers, ... **45.00**
8" d, Johnson Brothers, ... **60.00**
8 3/4" d, Johnson Brothers, set of
8, (A), ... **400.00**

Moyune Pattern
Soup Bowl, 7 3/4" d, Ridgway,
.... **55.00**

Nankin Pattern
Cup and Saucer, ... **125.00**
Plate
8" d, Doulton, ... **30.00**
9 1/4" d, ... **95.00**

Ning Po Pattern
Pitcher, 8" h, oct, R. Hall, c 1845 (A),
.... **935.00**

Non Pariel Pattern
Cup and Saucer, Burgess & Leigh,
.... **125.00**
Meat Platter, 13 3/8" l, Burgess &
Leigh, ... **295.00**
Plate
8 3/4" d, Burgess & Leigh,
.... **55.00**
9 3/4" d, Burgess & Leigh,
.... **70.00**
Platter
11" l x 9" w, "Burgess & Leigh
Middleport Pottery" mk,
.... **200.00**
12" l
9 1/2" w, Adams, ... **350.00**
10" w, Burgess and Leigh,
.... **170.00**
Tureen, Cov, 9" H-H x 6" h, w/ladle,
gilt accented flower knob,
Burgess & Leigh, ... **450.00**

Normandy Pattern
Bowl, 6" d, Johnson Brothers,
.... **20.00**
Gravy Boat, 7 1/4" l, "Johnson
Brothers" mk, ... **275.00**
Plate, 9" d, Johnson Brothers,
.... **110.00**
Platter
9 3/4" l x 7 1/2" w, "Johnson
Brothers" mk, ... **185.00**
10 1/2" l x 8" w, "Johnson
Brothers" mk, ... **195.00**
12 1/2" l x 9 1/4" w, "Johnson
Brothers" mk, ... **250.00**
Potato Bowl, 9 1/2" d, "Johnson
Brothers" mk, ... **195.00**
Vegetable Bowl
9" l x 7" w, "Johnson Brothers"
mk, ... **150.00**
9 3/4" l x 7 1/2" w, "Johnson
Brothers" mk, ... **185.00**

Oregon Pattern
Plate
7 1/2" d, "T. J. & J. Mayer
Longport" mk, ... **125.00**
8 3/4" d, "T. J. & J. Mayer
Longport" mk, c1843,
.... **190.00**
9 1/2" d, ... **155.00**
Platter, 17 3/4" l x 14" w, rect w/cut
corners, T. J. & J. Mayer, (A),
.... **770.00**
Sugar Bowl, Cov, 8" h x 6 1/2" H-H,
"OREGON CHINESE
PORCELAIN T.J. & J MAYER
LONGPORT" mk, repair to rim,
(A), ... **247.00**

Oriental Pattern
Plate
7 1/2" d, Ridgways, ... **40.00**
8 1/2" d, "N.W.P." mk, ... **110.00**
9" d, ... **60.00**
9 3/4" d, ... **75.00**
11" d, ... **125.00**
Platter, 13" l x 11" w, Ridgways,
c1891, ... **275.00**
Serving Bowl, 8 1/2" d, Ridgways,
.... **185.00**
Soup Plate, 10 1/2" d, c1850,
.... **35.00**

Ormande Pattern
Plate, 6 3/4" d, Alfred Meakin,
.... **65.00**

Osbourne Pattern
Soup Plate, 10 1/8" d, ... **110.00**
Soup Tureen, Cov, 13 1/2" l,
Ridgway, ... **595.00**
Vegetable Bowl, Cov, 8 1/2" H-H x 5
1/4" w, "T. Rathbone & Co." mk,
.... **275.00**

Oxford Pattern
Pitcher, 4 1/4" h, ... **200.00**

Pagoda Pattern
Cup and Saucer, ... **58.00**
Vegetable Bowl, Cov, 11" l x 7 1/2" w,
"J. & G. Meakin" mk, ... **350.00**

Pekin Pattern
Dessert Tray, 11" l x 8 1/4" w,
scalloped rim, ... **395.00**
Soup Tureen, 12" H-H, ... **375.00**

Pelew Pattern
Cup Plate, 5" d, Challinor, ... **40.00**

Plate, 8 3/4" d, ironstone, "Pelew" pattern, Challinor, **$200.00**

Plate
8" d, "E. Challinor" mk, c1842,
.... **200.00**
8 1/2" d, ... **200.00**
9 3/4" d, "E. Challinor" mk,
c1842, ... **250.00**

Teabowl and Saucer, Challinor,
.... **150.00**

Penang Pattern

Platter, 19 1/2" l x 14 1/2" w, Wm
Ridgway, ... **1,695.00**

Persian Pattern

Plate, 9" d, Johnson Brothers, c1902,
.... **55.00**

Tureen, Cov, 12" H-H x 7 1/2" h,
.... **495.00**

Portman Pattern

Gravy Boat, 9" l, w/undertray, "W.H.
Grindley" mk, ... **295.00**

Sugar Bowl, Cov, 8" H-H, ... **295.00**

Vegetable Bowl, Cov, 13" l, oval,
"W.H. Grindley" mk, ... **395.00**

Queen Pattern

Platter, 11 3/4" l x 11" w, rect w/cut
corners, "T. Rathbone &
Company" mk, ... **110.00**

Raleigh Pattern

Bowl, 5" d, Burgess & Leigh, . **15.00**

Regal Pattern

Casserole, Cov, 11" l, Leighton
Pottery, ... **165.00**

Soup Bowl, 9" d, "J. G. Meakin,"
.... **145.00**

Rhone Pattern

Platter, 15" l x 11" w, unmkd, (A),
.... **247.00**

Richmond Pattern

Platter, 16 3/8" l, ... **600.00**

Rose Pattern

Plate, 7" d, W.H. Grindley, ... **15.00**

Roseville Pattern

Plate, 9" d, Maddock, c1880,
.... **125.00**

Soup Plate, 9" d, Maddock,
.... **95.00**

Salem Pattern

Cup and Saucer, Handleless,
.... **325.00**

Pitcher, 8 1/4" h, ... **1,195.00**

Scinde Pattern

Cup and Saucer, Handleless, "imp
ORIENTAL STONE, blue
SCINDE" mks, (A), ... **100.00**

Fruit Comport, 4" h x 13" l x 10" w,
reticulated, "J. & G. Alcock" mk,
.... **3,250.00**

Plate

7 1/4" d, "J. & G. Alcock" mk,
.... **150.00**

9 1/2" d, Alcock, ... **165.00**

10 1/2" d, Alcock, c1840,
.... **250.00**

Soup Bowl, 9 1/2" d, "blue SCINDE"
mk, (A), ... **137.00**

Vegetable Bowl, 9 1/4" l x 7" w,
Alcock, ... **395.00**

Vegetable Bowl, Cov, 12 1/2" l x 10"
w x 7 1/2" h, paneled, "imp J. &
G. Alcock" mk, (A), ... **550.00**

Waste Bowl, 5 1/4" d, 16 panels,
.... **400.00**

Shanghai Pattern

Cup and Saucer, ... **145.00**

Plate

6" d, W.H. Grindley, (A), ... **28.00**

7" d, "W.H. Grindley," **60.00**

8 1/2" d, "Adams & Sons" mk,
.... **40.00**

9 3/4" d, Adams, ... **45.00**

10" d, ... **49.00**

Platter, 14" l x 10" w, oval, "W.H.
Grindley" mk, ... **400.00**

Soup Bowl, 8" d, "W.H. Grindley" mk,
.... **95.00**

Vegetable Bowl, 10" l, oval, "W.H.
Grindley" mk, ... **165.00**

Shapoo Pattern

Cup Plate, 4 1/8" d, "imp STONE
CHINA" mk, (A), ... **68.00**

Plate, 9 1/2" d, "T. & R. Boote" mk,
c1842, ... **250.00**

Platter, 18" l x 13 1/2" w, scalloped
corners, "SHAPOO T. & R." mk,
(A), ... **550.00**

Sobraon Pattern

Tray, 7 1/2" l x 6 1/4" w, ... **145.00**

*Plate, 7 1/4" d, "Spinach" pattern, "Maastricht"
mark, A-$15.00*

St. Louis Pattern

Platter, 16" l x 12" w, Johnson
Brothers, ... **95.00**

Sydney Pattern

Plate, 9 1/4" d, "Sydney, New Wharf
Pottery England" mk, ... **65.00**

The Hofburg Pattern

Plate, 8 3/4" d, "W.H. Grindley" mk,
.... **7.00**

The Temple Pattern

Coffeepot, 8 1/2" h, paneled,
repaired finial, (A), ... **770.00**

Pitcher, 6 1/4" h, paneled, (A),
.... **413.00**

Plate

8 3/4" d, "blue THE TEMPLE,
PEARL STONE WARE, PW &
CO" mks, (A), ... **70.00**

9" d, "PW & CO" mk, (A),
.... **110.00**

9 3/4" d, "blue THE TEMPLE,
PEARL STONE WARE, PW &
CO" mks, (A), ... **110.00**

Teabowl and Saucer, "P.W. & Co."
mk, ... **325.00**

Togo Pattern

Plate

8" d, "Colonial Pottery" mk,
.... **30.00**

10" d, ... **130.00**

Tonquin Pattern

Coffeepot, 13 1/2" h, paneled,
repaired chip, (A), ... **6,750.00**

Cup Plate, 4" d, Joseph Hewath,
c1850, (A), ... **110.00**

Platter

13 1/2" l x 10 1/4" w, rect w/cut
corners, "TONQUIN
IRONSTONE W. ADAMS &
SONS" mk, (A), ... **247.00**

15" l x 12" w, rect w/cut corners,
.... **500.00**

Relish Dish, 8 3/4" l x 4 3/4" w, (A),
.... **137.00**

Vegetable Bowl, Cov, 9" d, Adams,
.... **850.00**

Touraine Pattern

Bone Dish, 6" l, "Touraine Semi
Porcelain Henry Alcock & Co.
England" mk, pr, ... **135.00**

Butter Pat, 3" d, ... **60.00**

Creamer, 5" h, Alcock, ... **495.00**

Egg Cup, 3 1/4" h, Alcock, ... **550.00**

Plate

8 1/2" d, Stanley, ... **55.00**

9" d, gold rim, Henry Alcock,
.... **70.00**

Troy Pattern

Plate, 7 1/4" d, "TROY IMPROVED
STONE CHINA" mk, (A), ... **60.00**

Turin Pattern

Plate, 7" d, Johnson Brothers,
.... **20.00**

Vermont Pattern

Bone Dish, 6 1/2" l, Burgess & Leigh,
.... **72.00**

Butter Pat, 3" d, ... **50.00**

Celery Dish, 8" l x 5" w, ... **95.00**

Plate

8" d, "SEMI PORCELAIN
ENGLAND BURGESS &
LEIGH BURSLEM" mk, (A),
.... **12.00**

9" d, "SEMI PORCELAIN ENGLAND BURGESS & LEIGH BURSLEM" mk, (A), ... **30.00**

Soup Bowl; 9" d, "SEMI PORCELAIN ENGLAND BURGESS & LEIGH BUSLEM" mk, (A), ... **22.00**

Verona Pattern

Platter, 17" l x 13" w, rect, "Ford & Sons" mk, ... **540.00**

Vinranka Pattern

Vegetable Bowl, 10 1/4" l, ... **85.00**

Violette Pattern

Plate, 8 1/4" d, Keller and Guerin, c1890, ... **25.00**

Wagon Wheel Pattern

Cup and Saucer, ... **110.00**

Waldorf Pattern

Creamer, 2 3/4" h, New Wharf Pottery, ... **495.00**

Cup and Saucer, "N.W.P." mk, ... **130.00**

Plate

8 1/2" d, "N.W.P." mk, ... **110.00**

9" d, "N.W.P." mk, ... **150.00**

Platter, 10 1/4" l x 7 3/4" w, ... **195.00**

Serving Bowl, 9 5/8" d, "N.W.P." mk, ... **185.00**

Soup Bowl, 9" d, ... **150.00**

Vegetable Bowl, 9" d, "N.W.P." mk, ... **250.00**

Walmer Pattern

Platter, 17 1/2" l x 14" w, oct, ... **1,000.00**

Watteau Pattern

Cup and Saucer, ... **20.00**

Milk Pitcher, 6 1/4" h, Doulton Burslem, ... **395.00**

Pitcher, 5 1/4" h, "N.W.P." mk, ... **350.00**

Plate

8 1/2" d, Doulton, ... **80.00**

10" d, "NWP Co. Eng." mks, set of 8, ... **925.00**

10 1/4" d, Doulton, ... **40.00**

Sauceboat, 7 1/2" l, ... **75.00**

Soup Plate, 10 1/4" d, Doulton, ... **95.00**

Waverly Pattern

Platter, 14" l, "W.H. Grindley" mk, ... **275.00**

Wellbeck Pattern

Vegetable Bowl, Cov, 11" l, Samson Hancock & Sons, ... **275.00**

Whampoa Pattern

Cheese Stand, 10 3/4" d x 2 1/2" h, Mellor Venables, ... **285.00**

Plate, 7 1/2" d, ironstone, ... **50.00**

Yeddo Pattern

Bowl, 10 1/4" d, Ashworth, ... **175.00**

Cake Stand, 2 1/2" h x 12" d, ... **750.00**

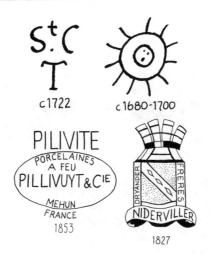

FRANCE-GENERAL

Rouen
1673-1696

Louis Poterat, a faience maker, was granted a patent to make the earliest French soft paste porcelain at Rouen in 1673. The decorations were dark blue in the style of faience ware with lambrequins and gadroons. Relief work appeared on the body of pieces such as salt cellars, mustard pots, and vases. Poterat died in 1696.

Lille
1711-1817

Barthelemy Dorenz and Pierre Pelissier established a soft paste porcelain factory in Lille in 1711. Pieces were decorated with Chinese designs. Leperre Ducot began manufacturing hard paste porcelains in 1784. The French Dauphin became a patron of the factory in 1786. The dolphin was chosen as the factory's mark.

St. Cloud
Seine-et-Oise, France
c1690-1773

In about 1675, Pierre Chicanneau established a factory for the production of faience and soft paste porcelain at St. Cloud. Shortly after Chicanneau's death in 1678, Berthe, his widow, assumed control of the works.

St. Cloud porcelain was thickly potted, with a yellowish color to the body. The glaze was very glassy, with a somewhat orange peel texture to the surface. The pieces were decorated in strong polychromes or in the simple blue motifs similar to the faience examples from Rouen, especially in the use of the baroque diapering pattern. Many forms featured plain white and relief patterns. Fishscale-type embellishments were used as the method of decoration.

The variety of wares produced was quite large, exhibiting applied decoration. Accessory pieces, e.g. knife and cane handles, and novelty pieces, some of which were silver mounted, were made. Many of the designs incorporated elements from silverware such as reeding or gadrooning.

Family squabbles plagued the St. Cloud pottery. In 1722 Berthe Coudray died. Henri-Charles Trou II, backed by the sponsorship of the Duc d'Orleans, took control. The St. Cloud factory ended its operations about 1773.

Strasbourg
1721-1781

Charles Hannong, who started a porcelain factory in Strasbourg in 1721, manufactured clay pipes and stoves that were decorated in relief and glazed. For a short time, he was a partner with Johann Wachenfeld, who came from Meissen. Together they made faience and porcelain wares. In 1724 a second factory was established in Haguenau.

Hannong transferred the factories to his sons, Paul Antoine and Balthasar, in 1732. Between 1745 and 1750, hard paste porcelains were produced that were decorated in red and pale gold. Adam Lowenfinck arrived from Hochst in 1750 and became co-director of the porcelain factory. He brought the rococo style and introduced flower painting to Strasbourg.

By 1753 Paul Hannong assumed control of both factories. When Louis XV of France ordered him to dismantle his porcelain factory and demolish his kilns, Paul Hannong went to Frankenthal. As a result, early Strasbourg ware and Frankenthal ware resembled each other.

By 1766 Joseph-Adam, Hannong's son, tried to re-establish a hard paste porcelain factory in Strasbourg. Opposition by the authorities forced its closure in 1781.

Sceaux
1748-1795

Under the patronage of Duchess de Marne, the architect de Bay established a porcelain factory that was managed by Jacques Chapelle. The firm's soft paste porcelains were decorated with exotic birds, flowers, and cupids in the fashion of the Louis XVI period. The factory closed in 1795.

Niderviller
1754-1827

Baron Beyerle established a faience factory in 1754. Porcelains were produced by 1765. When opposition arose from the Sevres potters in 1770, Beyerle took Count de Custine into partnership because of his influence at the French Court. On Custine's death, the factory was sold to Claude-Francois Lanfrey and continued until 1827. Tea sets, tablewares, and services were made and decorated in the manner of Sevres.

Paris Area

The majority of French hard paste porcelains available in today's market was made at numerous small factories in the Paris area. Production of porcelain began in the early 18th century.

References: W.B. Honey, *French Porcelain of the 18th Century*, 1950; George Savage, *Seventeenth & Eighteenth Century French Porcelain*, Hamlyn Publishing Co. Ltd, 1969.

Museums: Frick Collection, New York, NY; Louvre, Paris, France; Musee des Arts Decoratifs, Paris, France; Musee des Beaux-Arts et de la Ceramique, Rouen, France; Musee National de Sevres, Sevres, France; Victoria & Albert Museum, London, England; Wadsworth Atheneum, Hartford, CT.

Additional Listings: Choisy-le-Roi, Creil, Faience, Limoges, Malicorne, Old Paris and Paris, Quimper, and Sevres.

Basket

10 1/2" h x 10 1/2" d, flared reticulated white basket w/gilt serrated rim, supported by 2 kneeling bisque females, sw base w/blue frieze and gilt floral pattern, ... **3,450.00**

10 7/8" H-H, oval HP loose bouquets of roses and cornflowers on int, puce lined pierced sides w/painted floral sprigs, scalloped rim, rope tied branch handles, blue lined rim, "blue hunting horn" mk, c1750, pr, (A), ... **11,350.00**

Beaker and Saucer, paneled, Kakiemon palette of 2 quails in prunus, chocolate brown rims, "red hunting horn" mk, ... **3,450.00**

Bowl, 7 1/2" d, yellowware, center band of orange centered white petaled flowers alternating w/green leaves, brown ground, white band on rim, Alsace, c1900, ... **15.00**

Bud Vase, 6 3/4" h, bulbous base, tapered neck, yellow, green, and blue crystalline glaze, Pierrefonds, (A), ... **315.00**

Cabinet Cup and Saucer

HP garden flowers in rect reserve, gilt over cobalt ground w/anthemion and leafy vine bands, gilt handle w/lion head terminal, gilt int, ... **1,850.00**

Sevres style, painted period couple playing w/dog in gilt tooled surround, cobalt ground, saucer w/painted floral center, cobalt border w/floral cartouches, late 19th C, (A), ... **800.00**

Cabinet Plate, 9 1/2" d, Sevres style painted center of Watteau lovers in garden setting, bleu celeste border w/4 ovoid reserves of painted garden flowers in gilt surrounds, late 19th C, (A), ... **175.00**

Cake Plate, 11" H-H, blue-grey transfer, "Windmill, Nord, Orchies, Moulin des Loups & Humage France" mark, $75.00

Cache Pot

6 3/4" h, Sevres style, painted scene of Dionysus and goddess in chariot drawn by lions and putti, fruits and flowers on reverse both in gilt rococo scroll, mesh, and rose surrounds, cerulean blue ground, late 19th C, (A), . **940.00**

7 1/2" h, HP garden bouquet ands scattered sprigs between raised gilt lines, maroon border band, molded ring handles, c1840, pr, ... **650.00**

8 1/4" h, HP bouquet of garden flowers on white ground in gilt surround, dk red ground, gilt edged ear handles, artist sgd, ... **500.00**

Cider Jug, 13" h, dk red unglazed clay, ... **50.00**

Chocolate Cup, Cov and Saucer,

trembleuse saucer, multicolored panel of oriental figures w/enamel accents in gilt cartouche on cup, cobalt ground w/gilt diapering, scrolling, and flowerheads, saucer w/2 panels of roosters and flowers, cobalt ground and gilt diapering, scrolls, and flowerheads, gilt flowerhead knob, ... **600.00**

Chocolate Pot, 8 1/2" h, rococo style swirl, fluted, and emb loop sides, emb foliate scroll and gilt diaper spout, "S"-scroll handle, HP enameled purple, blue, yellow, and red floral bouquets, green foliage, gilt feather knob, ... **385.00**

Compote, 4 1/2" h x 5" d, fluted hex bowl, gold roses in bowl and base, ivory ground, ... **55.00**

Crock, Cov, 13 1/2" H-H, yellowware, red-brown glazed int, Alsace, ... **100.00**

Cup and Saucer

Overall relief molded pinecones, white glaze, St. Cloud, c1740, ... **2,250.00**

Trembleuse, gadrooned body and saucer border, blue lappets and hanging lambrequins, St. Cloud, c1720, (A), ... **1,675.00**

Dish, 7 3/4" l, lozenge shape, painted center hunt scenes in tooled gilt surround, turquoise border w/triple gilt lined rim, mid-19th C, pr, (A), ... **835.00**

Figure, 13 3/4" h, brown haired man, turquoise jacket, mauve pantaloons, gilt trim, blond haired woman, white gown w/gilt trim, lt blue and pink flowers, orchid overgown, med blue and gilt bases, "blue D & T, anchor" marks, c1880, pr, $2,800.00

Figure

3 1/8" h x 4 1/2" l, wild boar seated on haunches, white body w/blue florals on back, spots on body and legs, and solid spout, ... **195.00**

6 3/8" h, little boy w/blue sash over shoulder, holding basket of roses on tree stump, little girl sucking thumb, reclining on corn stalks, gilt hair band, puce striped cloth on thigh, puce scroll molded base, chips, Niderville, c1760, chips, (A), ... **720.00**

10" h, bust of woman, lt blue eyes, "bee sting" mouth, gold ribbon in hair, gold garland wrap on base, c1900, ... **225.00**

Urn, Cov, 30" h, Sevres style, classic courting scene on front, woodland and pastoral scene on reverse in raised gilt scrolled cartouches, cobalt ground w/gilt accents, dore bronze mts and female mask handles, ... **8,500.00**

Vase

4 1/2" h, swollen middle, Art Deco style metallic lustered glazed yellow shells, turquoise banding on shoulder, blue drip over lustered burgundy body, Montieres, ... **825.00**

5 1/4" h, bottle shape, multi toned brown matte glaze on base and rim, blue gloss glaze on upper section, Louis Louriox, (A), ... **288.00**

5 1/2" h, figural hand holding vase, enameled flowers and beading, ... **105.00**

6 1/2" h, ball base, short, flared rim, grey body w/green drip on shoulder, pr, ... **90.00**

6 3/4" h, teardrop shape, flared neck, painted scenes of children dancing in gilt surround and scrollwork, reverse w/lake scenes, turquoise ground, pr, (A), ... **1,435.00**

16 5/8" h, flared beaker shape, painted blue, red, yellow, and green enamel oriental figures in fan shaped panels between bands of flower panels, borders painted w/bands of stylized chrysanthemums, gilt accents, 19th C, ... **400.00**

22 1/2" h, amphora shape, lt sky blue ground w/gold ribbon-tied quivers, torches, arrows, and flowers, gold molded satyr handles, raised gold stiff leaves on base, spread circ ft, "FRANCE" mk, ... **675.00**

Veilleuse, 9" h, HP courting scene on front of burner, gold overall ground, figural animal spout, flame knob, c1840, ... **2,950.00**

1738-c1790

1758-1788

FRENCH FAIENCE

Nevers
c1632-1800

Rouen
1647-c1800

Moustiers
1670-1800

Marseilles
1677-c1800

Strasburg
1721-1780

History: Faience, a porous pottery, was lightly fired earthenware that was painted and then covered with an opaque stanniferous glaze. Tiny particles of tin oxide suspended in the glaze provided the characteristic white, opaque nature of the pottery.

Italian potters migrated to France in the 1600s, first to Nevers, and later to Rouen, Moustiers, Marseilles, and other pottery centers. In **Nevers** the potters transformed the Italian majolica tradition into something distinctively French. The Nevers potters developed a Chinese style employing oriental subjects and the Chinese blue and white color scheme. They also added a richly intertwining border pattern of leaves and flowers. Nevers was the leader during the 17th century.

In the third-quarter of the 17th century, four main schools—Rouen, Moustiers, Marseilles, and Strasburg—developed. **Rouen** faience was characterized by "decor rayonnant," a richly intricate pattern of stylized leaves and florals that adorned the outer border, cascading in swags around a central flower burst that was adapted from the delicate lace and iron work of the mid-18th century rococo patterns. Polychrome chinoiserie styles also were introduced.

Moustiers derived its early system of decoration from Nevers. The pioneer was Pierre Clerissy (1679-1739). The Chinese influence is in evidence in pattern design, form, and the blue and white palette. The use of "grotesques," fantastic human or animal figures in scenes of wild vegetation, added excitement to the pieces.

In 1677 Joseph Clerissy came from Nevers to **Marseilles**. The Marseilles potters used border patterns that were heavier than at Moustiers. Landscape panels, acanthus leaves, or birds with foliage followed the Nevers style.

Strasburg faience was influenced by the rococo motifs from Rouen. In 1748-1749, a group of artists who had worked at Meissen arrived in Strasburg from Hochst. They applied enamel painting techniques, giving the wares a more German than French appearance.

Before the French Revolution, faience factories were thriving. After the revolution and the treaty of commerce between England and France, English potters flooded the market with their industrial pottery that was cheaper to make, lighter in weight, easier to transport, and less liable to chip or crack under heat. This pottery appealed to both wholesale dealers and the public. The French factories experienced great difficulties competing. Many factories closed. By 1850 the French pottery industry was practically extinct.

References: Diana Imber, *Collecting European Delft and Faience*, Frederick A. Praeger, 1968; Arthur Lane, *French Faience*, Faber and Faber, 1970; Millicent S. Mali, *French Faience*, United Printing, 1986; Francois Piton, *C'est du Desvres*, 2001.

Museums: Musee Ceramique, Rouen, France; Musee des Arts Decoratifs, Paris, France; Victoria and Albert Museum, London, England.

Reproduction Alert: Collectors of French faience should be very wary of imitations being made in large quantities in modern day Paris. Genuine French faience is rare and only is offered for sale when a famous collection is dispersed.

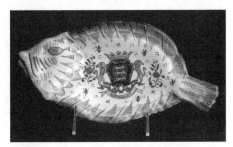

Fish Plate, 10 3/4" l, blue outlined "Normandie" crest w/yellow lions on red ground, red dashes on yellow ground border, blue dash rim, **$165.00**

Asparagus Dish, 12 1/2" l x 4" h, multicolored florals, gold and blue rim on cradle, multicolored scattered florals, gold and blue zigzag rim on base, Desvres, ... **750.00**

Bottle, 16" h, painted winged cherubs riding dolphins, wavy blue ground, figural ram head handles, stiff leaf stopper, Nevers, ... **3,200.00**

Bowl

9" d, HP stylized yellow centered blue petaled flowers, sm ochre flowers, green foliage on int, ochre and green sprigs on border, shaped rim, ... **140.00**

9" w, sq shape, HP red, blue, and yellow flower spray in center, floral garland border banding, scalloped rim, Nevers, early 19th C, ... **595.00**

12" d, HP blue rose and red flower spray, pitted cream ground, 19th C, ... **695.00**

Box, Cov

3" h x 7" w, painted green grotesques and geometric swirls, white ground, bronze mts, pink int, Moustiers, ... **400.00**

3 1/2" h x 5" l, oval, polychrome scene of country men seated on white fence w/green ribbon wrap, raised handles ends, dog knob, ... **400.00**

Candlestick

5 1/2" h, lg yellow and orange fleur-de lys on shaft, crest of France on base, blue loop and red dot rim and ft, scattered ermine tails, "CA" mk, (A), ... **220.00**

6" h, figural curved dragon w/blue accents, blue dash handle, Desvres, ... **155.00**

Chamberstick, 7 1/4" w, red, green, blue, orange Rouen style, figural fleur-de-lys base w/crest of Cherbourg, painted floral handle, ... **100.00**

Cup and Saucer

Lobed, red and yellow fleur-de-lys, 4 blue dots, lg blue and green and sm black ermine tails, blue chain linked rims, ... **50.00**

Painted flying bird, red and white blossoms, black outlined green leaves, olive green handle and rims, yellow ground, ... **85.00**

Dish

9 1/4" sq, lg floral bouquet in center, scattered sprigs, shaded pink shaped rim, Gien, ... **120.00**

11" d, center band of blue stylized leaves, border of red, orange, green, and blue curlicues and geometrics between blue lines, 18th C, chips, ... **220.00**

Egg Cup, 3" h, w/attached underplate, alternating yellow-gold fleur-de-lys and blue ermine tails, border bands of blue half circles and red dots, "CA" mk, ... **250.00**

Flower Frog, 5 3/4" l, figural turtle, crest on back, black ermine tails, gold fleur-de-lys, blue outlined holes, border of blue half circles and red dots, (A), ... **150.00**

Inkwell, 3" h x 3 1/21" w, hex, HP black lined alternating yellow and dk red stripes on base, band of red flowerheads, green leaves, black ground on border, green lined rims,

sm sprigs on top surface and cov, "Aladin France" mk, chips, ... **50.00**

Inkwells, 5 1/2" l, 4 blue dots, yellow beaks, blue outlined wings, green tails, multicolored floral sprigs, "blue CM" mks, pr, $170.00

Jardiniere

13" H-H, painted multicolored parrot, tulip, insects, and crest of Brittany on sides, green and yellow molded wave on rim, blue accented shell handles, Desvres, c1890, ... **875.00**

17" l x 8" w x 7" h, 4 curved feet, blue, red, and yellow geometrics, blue figural fans above rims, George Martel, ... **225.00**

Jardiniere and Pedestal, 21" w x 41" h, painted baskets of flowers in gold, red, and blue molded swirls and curls, fancy curved handles, shell feet, int painted florals, pedestal w/same designs, scroll molded red, gold, and blue bottom, Desvres, ... **4,000.00**

Jug, 5" h, painted male peasant leaning on shovel, trees and meadow, dk blue rim, yellow handle w/dk blue dots, ... **395.00**

Knife Rest, 4" l, figural dog, white ground, black outlined blue and yellow flowerheads, Desvres, ... **125.00**

Mug, 2 1/2" h, red and yellow fleur-de-lys on side, reverse w/red-brown hedgehog on green ground, blue wavy rim w/red dots, red dashes on handle, "AMBOISE" on base, "CA" mk, ... **110.00**

Pitcher

5 3/4" h, lying yellow dog w/bone on red ground in black scrolling cartouche, scattered black fleur-de-lys, blue loop and red dot rim, grey crackle ground, blue dash handle, "CA" mk, ... **400.00**

6" h, HP

Lg dk blue iris, sm red flowers, green leaves on meandering stems, yellow ground, green and blue dash handle, unmkd, c1890, ... **300.00**

Simple red or blue flowers, green leaves, yellow ground, hairline, ... **300.00**

Plate, 9" d, magenta and yellow robe, blue pants, green umbrella, mauve rim, Luneville, c1850, $225.00

Plate

7 5/8" d, yellow rooster, red comb, brown tail in center, blue dentil rim, grey ground, St. Clement, ... **40.00**

9" d

Center sprig of puce painted dbl carnation, green foliage, scattered sprigs on border, shaped rim, c1760, pr, ... **1,500.00**

HP stylized single stroke yellow centered red daisy, sm blue flowers, green leaves in red and yellow 2 handled flowerpot on green base, red streaked rim, ... **75.00**

Lg HP stylized yellow-centered blue sunflower flanked by green foliage and red and yellow stylized flowers, yellow and blue border stripes, St. Clements, pr, ... **395.00**

Painted scene of Mt. St. Michel in center, lattice pierced border, blue, green, yellow, and blue molded curlicues on rim, Desvres, ... **95.00**

Strutting black rooster, blue tail, red comb, walking on lt brown patch, blue lined rim, "Faiencerie du Midi A B & CK" mk, ... **35.00**

9 1/4" w, HP bouquet and side sprigs in center, mauve shaded border, sq rim w/lobes and pointed peaks, "Gien" mk, ... **115.00**

9 1/2" d, green enameled flower sprigs from center to border, green shaped rim, Veuve Perrin, c1760, ... **975.00**

9 3/4" d, painted French couple, man holding sword, border of yellow centered blue petaled flowerheads and green edged pyramids, lobed rim, Joseph Olerys Moustier, ... **165.00**

9 7/8" d, black outlined running pink pig on green and black ground in center, green and black scattered stylized florals on border, orange outlined indented rim, unmkd, ... **70.00**

10" d, Rouen pattern, blue stylized basket and single stroke flowers, border band of blue squiggles and blobs, black back, Nevers, unmkd, (A), ... **275.00**

Quintal, 9 3/4" h, heart shape w/indentations, flat sides, 5 paneled tubes, 2 handles, rect base, painted red rose, green foliage on sides, sm yellow flowers, brown stems, green leaves on tubes, red dots on handle and base, red streaked rims, Paul Hannong, Strasbourg, ... **245.00**

Soup Tureen, 12" H-H x 8" h, w/undertray, painted orange-yellow, green, and blue exotic birds, florals, and butterfly, orange-yellow lined rim, figural orange-yellow pear knob, sculpted orange-yellow trimmed border on undertray, Moustier, ... **480.00**

Trinket Box, 4 3/4" l x 2 1/4" w, red, blue, and yellow cornucopia and lg flowers on sides, white ground, Gien, ... **55.00**

Vase, 6 1/4" h, quilted body, painted blue, yellow, or orange flowers, stepped base, "FF" mk, c1880, ... **120.00**

1846 - 1904

GALLE

Nancy, France
1874-1904

History: Emile Galle, a leading designer and manufacturer of art glass, first made faience in Nancy, France, in 1874. Later he experimented with both stoneware and porcelain. Galle's decorations included heraldic motifs and scenes that resembled Delft ware. A series of souvenir dishes was made to commemorate the Franco-Prussian War.

Glazes used were flowing and opaque in nature. Sometimes several colors were mixed together. Most of the forms were simple in design.

Victor Prouve, an artist friend of Galle, provided designs for figures of bulldogs and cats. The most popular figures were painted yellow with blue hearts and circles, black and white with pale indigo blue, or beige with pink and green decorations of naturalistic flowers. Green glass eyes were used. Prouve's designs were used for candlesticks of heraldic lions and grotesque and fantastic ducks, fox, owls, swans, and parakeets. Plant designs of dandelions, chrysanthemums, and orchids were used in Art Nouveau style decorations that duplicated Galle's work on glass.

All of Galle's ceramics were marked with the impressed initials E.G. Em. Galle Faiencerie de Nancy, or some version of his signature.

Museums: Bowes Museum, Barnard Castle, Durham, England; Musee des Arts et Metiers, Paris, France.

Collecting Hints: Galle faience now is prevalent in the American antiques market. Cat, parrot, and dog figures are seen in various colors and sizes. Sets of plates, three sectioned dishes, tureens, wall vases, and inkwells are eagerly sought. Large candlesticks with figures of lions are among the most expensive pieces.

Dish, 16" l, dk red scattered florals on int, red outlined arched reticulated sides w/raised medallions, buttressed corners and feet, ... **1,100.00**

Ewer
8" h, emb blue, black, and brown beetle, terra cotta tree and flowers, overall blue, gold, and brown sponged ground, rect handle, mkd, ... **850.00**

9" h, long neck, painted pansies on mottled yellow, blue, white, cobalt, and brown ground, (A), ... **900.00**

Figure, 9 1/4" l, pottery, lady's shoe, grey-black streaked body, med blue ruffled rim, applied lg red roses and foliage on toe, mkd, ... **200.00**

Inkstand, 8 1/4" h x 11 1/2" l, molded blue ribbon on backplate, painted ovals of cherubs, painted scattered butterflies and sprigs, open loop design on front, center drawer, covs missing, "Galle Nancy" mk, ... **550.00**

Inkwell, 3 3/4" h x 7" sq, tin glazed, blue painted Cross of Lorraine and thistle on sides, blue feathered edges, blue flowerhead cov, "E. Galle Nancy, E./Lorraine cross, G" mks, ... **1,000.00**

Jardiniere
9" h x 9 3/4" w, painted garden bouquet on side, molded vert fluted border w/mauve streaking, mauve rim, and ear handles, "Galle Nancy" mk, c1890, ... **1,795.00**

9 1/2" h x 23" l, tin glazed, blue and white, interwoven pierced body, swirl feet and side crest w/fleur-de-lys, blue feather int rim, 2 curled overlapped handles, ... **3,250.00**

Plaque, 13" d, HP tan, brown, and cream bust of young court gentleman after Holbein painting, dk brown ground, pierced for hanging, "black E. Galle Nancy" mk, ... **5,700.00**

Plate, 8 3/4" d, brown, red, green, and cream glazes, "E.G. E. Galle Nancy Edward VI H. Holbein" mark, A-**$350.00**

Plate, 8 1/2" d, HP blue weed leaves and butterfly, pierced lattice border, c1890, ... **195.00**

Vase, 4 1/2" h, blue, red, and green flowers and swags, white ground, "Galle France" mark, A-**$165.00**

Vase

5" h, squat shape, slender neck, 2
lug handles on shoulder, Islamic
style design of raised gilt
dragonfly on side, flower on
reverse, yellow ground
w/burgundy splashes, "EFG
Depose E. Galle Nancy" mk,
.... **250.00**

12" h, bulbous base, straight neck,
applied bisque bust of jester
w/split hat and beard, red
lustered ground, "imp EG" mk,
.... **7,500.00**

20" h, squat base, long trumpet
neck, earthenware, seated boy
or girl peasant on brown base
w/applied snails and reptiles, lt
blue neck, "E.G." mks, pr,
.... **2,250.00**

GAME PLATES AND SETS

English/Continental
c1870-1915

History: Game plates and sets, usually
including a large platter, serving plates,
and a sauce or gravy boat, were popular
between 1870 and 1915, both in England
and on the Continent. They are specially
decorated plates used to serve game and
fish. Subjects utilized by the makers
included all types of game birds, quail,
snipe, pheasants, mallards, etc. and fish.

Among the principal French manufac-
turers were Haviland and firms in Limoges.
Makers in England included Crescent and
Sons, Mason, Royal Doulton, Wedgwood,
and Royal Worcester. Factories in Bavaria,
Villeroy and Boch in Germany, and Royal
Vienna in Austria also made game plates
and sets.

Reproduction Alert: Game plates were
imported to the United States by
reproduction wholesalers and giftware
distributors during the 1970s and 80s. The
new pieces are full-color transfers that
were also used on urns, vases, and
compotes in addition to plates. These
carry Germany and Austrian backstamps
as well as facsimile signatures. Beware of
gold trim that is too shiny.

Fish Platter, 23" l x 12" w, oval, blue
printed swimming pike, sm fish in
sea grasses, shells and fish on
border, Wedgwood, ... **1,250.00**

Fish Sets
Platter
15 3/4" l x 11" w, oval, 5 plates,
11" d, multicolored decal of

swimming fish in center, sm
fish on borders, indented
rims, Germany, ... **395.00**

*Fish Set, platter, 23 1/2" H-H, 12 plates, 7 3/8"
sq., multicolored fish in center, different fish on
each plate, gold rim, "CFH/GDM" marks, A-
$375.00*

19 1/2" l x 9 1/4" w, 12 plates, 9"
d, fish swimming in seaweed
and plants, border band of
seaweed, blue and white,
"imp CAULDON" mks,
.... **750.00**

20 1/2" H-H, 12 plates, 8 3/8" d,
multicolored decals of
swimming fish in aquatic
plants, beaded borders, gold
scalloped rims, Victoria
Austria, ... **1,000.00**

22 1/2" l
8 plates, 9 3/4" d, cov tureen, 10
1/2" l, HP swimming fish in
water scenes, floral sprig
border, molded rim w/gilt
beaded edges, "Z.S.
Bavaria" mks, ... **800.00**

*Charger, 12" d, blue, brown, and white bird,
winter scene, shaded mustard yellow, green,
and tan bkd, off-white and blue sky, "Germany"
mk, c1920s, $135.00*

12 plates, 8 3/4" d, sauce boat
w/underplate, multicolored
swimming game fish in
seaweed w/gilt accents,
shaded salmon borders, gold
indentations on rims, "M R
Limoges" mks, ... **1,295.00**

24" l
12 plates
9" d, swimming multicolored fish
on borders, gold lobed rims,
T.V. Limoges, ... **1,500.00**

9 1/2" d, 2 swimming pike off
shore in center, gold serrated
rims, Limoges, ... **1,795.00**

24 3/4" l x 10 1/4" w, oval, 10
plates, 9 1/4" d, sauce boat, 8
1/4" l, HP multicolored
individual fish swimming in
water plants, gold trim, artist
sgd, "L.S & S. Limoges,
Lewis Straus & Sons" mks,
.... **1,495.00**

25 1/4" l x 8 1/2" w, 6 plates, 8
1/4" l x 7 1/2" w, HP swimming
fish in vegetation, pink
flowers on borders, gilt lined
rims, Limoges, c1900,
.... **990.00**

26 1/2" l x 11" w, oval, 10 plates,
10" d, sauceboat 10 1/2" l,
w/underplate, prs of
multicolored game fish
swimming in seaweed,
quilted borders, "Gien France
Loire" mks, chips, ... **385.00**

*Plate, 9" d, multicolored bird in forest setting, lt
blue and mauve bkd, molded matte gold border,
"MR France" mark, set of 6 different birds,
$390.00*

Game Plates

Bowl, 9 3/8" d, center decal of stag
in woods, gold hanging swags
on inner border, shaded pea

green luster rim w/molded shell designs, "Germany" mk, .. **30.00**

Plate, 9 3/4" d, brown and green fish, seaweed and red dots, molded shell border, gold outlined rim, Bing and Grondahl, set of 11, A-$144.00

Charger

10 3/4" d, multicolored transfer of male and female peasant walking in leaf strewn field, dk blue rim w/gold beading, "S.T. Bavaria, blue beehive" mks, ... **100.00**

11 1/2" d

Two HP grouse in woodland setting, gold rococo border, sgd "G. Rosser," "LRL" mk, c1920, ... **150.00**

Two multicolored pheasants in Fall forest setting, bright blue border w/gold stenciled scrolling, gold flowerhead rim, Royal Vienna, ... **165.00**

12" d, multicolored decal of grouse in meadow, border of pink rose hanging swags, lt blue scalloped rim, "C.T. Altwasser" mk, ... **90.00**

12 1/2" d, multicolored sandpiper in field in center, border of blooming pink or pink tinged white roses, gold outlined shaped rim, Austria, ... **75.00**

13" d, multicolored woodcock in meadow, raised gold scalloped border, Royal Munich, ... **90.00**

Plaque

9 3/4" d, HP swimming cod, green water plants, green to pink shaded ground, irreg gold rim, sgd "ROH," pierced for hanging, "LDBC Limoges Flambeau" dbl mks,

.... **125.00**

10" d, HP sandpipers in marsh w/cattails, gold rococo border, Limoges, ... **155.00**

10 1/4" d, HP walking quail in meadow, rococo molded border, Limoges, ... **225.00**

11" d, 2 HP nesting ducks in brown reeds, gold molded rim, artist sgd, Coronet Limoges, ... **410.00**

12 1/4" d, HP partridge in forest w/white flowers at side, gold rococo border, pierced for hanging, sgd "Baumy," "B & H Limoges" mk, ... **795.00**

12 1/2" d, HP flying brown and white flying quail, shaded green ground, gold rococo border, Limoges, ... **365.00**

12 3/4" d, multicolored transfer of grouse in meadow, brown border band w/ovals of game birds, molded beaded and gold accented lobed rim, pierced for hanging,

.... **125.00**

13" d, HP game birds feeding in snow covered ground, forest in bkd, gold rococo border, artist sgd, ... **450.00**

15 1/2" d, HP w/2 grouse seated in meadow and purple flowers, 2 flying grouse, gold rococo border, sgd "Dubois," "L.R. & L. Limoges France" mk, ... **700.00**

Plate

8 1/2" d

HP duck standing in marsh, gold ribbon border, Minton,

.... **125.00**

Three walking grouse in marsh, border band of leaves, "L.S.& S. Carlsbad" mk, ... **20.00**

Walking, teal, dk orange, and brown duck, border panel of daisies, shaded lt blue to lt green ground, molded fan designs on rim, gold scalloped rim, Limoges,

.... **80.00**

9" d

HP

Capercaille in meadow, shaded pink to blue sky, green border w/molded rim, Burgess & Leigh, ... **25.00**

Eider Duck, gilt shaded piecrust border, sgd "J. Birbeck," Royal Doulton, c1902,

.... **250.00**

Quail in meadow, molded leaf border, gold dusted rim, sgd "Roche N," Limoges,

.... **125.00**

Pheasant in flight, HP copper shaded foliage border, gilt scalloped rim, Royal Doulton,

.... **50.00**

Tin glazed, walking yellow, blue, red, and brown pheasant, green ground, indent rim, France, ... **95.00**

Walking pheasant in woods, border band of florals and foliage, blue transfer, Cauldon, ... **35.00**

9 1/4" d, flying "Red Grouse" over field, lake in bkd, gilt geometric and floral inner band, gilded geometric border, Minton, ... **325.00**

9 1/2" d

HP peacock at edge of pond, unilateral red rococo border, gold molded rim, sgd "C. Saquel," Limoges, ... **695.00**

HP scene of 2 quail in meadow, flying quail above, gilt rococo border, sgd "Muville," Limoges, ... **150.00**

Multicolored Transfer

Pheasant in field, shaded green border w/moldings, scalloped rim, "Petrus Regout Maasstricht, Made in Holland" mk, ... **10.00**

Three pheasants in field, white border w/molding, shaped rim, Germany, ... **35.00**

9 3/4" d, multicolored walking quail in meadow, pale blue border, gold rim, Bavaria,

.... **50.00**

10" d

Brown transfer of grouse in field in center, dbl zigzag and dot design border, Wedgwood, c1879, ... **135.00**

HP

Multicolored grouse standing in field, shaded blue to pink bkd, shaped and molded rim, artist sgd, Limoges,

.... **100.00**

Swimming fish, waterlilies, salmon pink shaded ground, gold rococo border, artist sgd, "LOBC torch Limoges" dbl mks, ... **175.00**

Two deer in forest setting, gold rococo border, sgd "Rey," Limoges, ... **425.00**

Two wild ducks in marsh, emb relief design border, green shaded ground, gilt rim, artist sgd, Coronet Limoges, ... **100.00**

11 1/2" d, brown transfer of running rabbit in winter setting, med blue border w/gold accents and rim, Bavaria, ... **395.00**

Platter, 18" l x 11 3/4" w, 3 painted partridges in meadow by lake in gilt scroll cartouche at top, pink ground, gold shell rim, Limoges, ... **395.00**

Game Sets

Platter

16 1/2" l x 12" w, 6 plates, 8 3/8" d, lg flying pheasant, grouse, duck, etc in center, lobed border w/multicolored fruit, flowers, and foliage, gold accented relief molded swirls, Carlsbad, ... **975.00**

18" l x 12 1/2" w, 6 plates, 9 1/4" d, sauce bowl, 6" d, HP dbl game birds in centers and foliage, cobalt rococo borders w/gold lacework, shaped rims, artist sgd, "L.S. & S. Limoges" mks, ... **4,000.00**

18 1/2" l

6 plates, 9 1/2" d, multicolored game birds in center, fluted borders, molded blue and gilt rims, artist sgd, "J.P. Limoges" mks, ... **950.00**

8 plates, 9 1/2" d, HP multicolored flying game birds, lg pink roses and foliage on border, gold scrolling borders, sgd "Daruy," Limoges, . **1,795.00**

J & R. Riley

1802-1828

GAUDY DUTCH

Staffordshire, England
c1810-1830

History: Staffordshire pottery with a Gaudy Dutch motif was made for the American trade and experienced wide popularity from c1810 to 1830. White earthenwares, mostly plates and tearwares, were made by a number of Staffordshire potters, among whom were Riley and Wood. Painted patterns included Butterfly, Grape, King's Rose, Oyster, Single Rose, Strawflower, Urn, and War Bonnet. Dominant colors were cobalt blue, bright yellow, green, red, and pink.

References: Eleanor J. Fox and Edward G. Fox, *Gaudy Dutch*, privately printed, 1970; Sam Laidacker, *Anglo-American China Part 1*, Keystone Specialties, 1954; Earl F. Robacker, *Pennsylvania Dutch Stuff*, University of Pennsylvania Press, 1944; John A. Shuman, III, *The Collector's Encyclopedia of Gaudy Dutch & Welsh*, Collector Books, 1998 values.

Collectors' Club: Gaudy Collector's Society, P.O. Box 274, Gates Mills, OH 44040.

Museums: Henry Ford Museum, Dearborn, MI; Philadelphia Museum of Art, Philadelphia, PA; Reading Art Museum, Reading, PA.

Reproduction Alert: Cup plates, bearing the impressed mark "CYBRIS," have been reproduced and are collectible in their own right. The Henry Ford Museum has issued pieces in the Single Rose pattern, although they are of porcelain and not soft paste.

Bowl, 6" d, "Grape" pattern, ... **1,450.00**

Cup and Saucer, Handleless

"Carnation" pattern, ... **1,000.00**

"Dbl Rose" pattern, blue overpainted band on saucer, (A), ... **231.00**

"Grape" pattern, (A), ... **413.00**

"Oyster" pattern, ... **475.00**

"Single Rose" pattern, ... **900.00**

Cup Plate

3 1/2" d

"Grape" pattern, (A), ... **990.00**

"Warbonnet" pattern, (A), ... **1,375.00**

3 5/8" d, "Double Rose" pattern, ... **1,320.00**

3 3/4" d, "Urn" pattern, (A), ... **2,200.00**

4" d, "Rose" pattern, (A), ... **990.00**

Plate

6"d

"Grape" pattern, ... **1,350.00**

"Warbonnet" pattern, ... **1,350.00**

6 1/4" d, "Oyster Variant" pattern, ... **450.00**

7" d, "Single Rose" pattern, ... **1,850.00**

7 1/8" d, "Grape" pattern, (A), ... **440.00**

7 1/4" d, "Carnation" pattern, (A), ... **330.00**

8 1/4" d

"Grape" pattern, cobalt, green, orange, and yellow, (A), ... **440.00**

Pitcher, 8 3/4" h, "Carnation" pattern, blue and iron-red, green handle, A-$258.00

"Single Rose" pattern, (A), ... 413.00

Plate, 8 1/4" d, "Sunflower" pattern, $875.00

"Strawberries" pattern, pink border, ... 395.00

Plate, 9 5/8" d, "Warbonnet" pattern, c1800, $1,600.00

10" d, "Dove" pattern, ... **5,800.00**

10 1/8" d, pearlware, "Double Rose"
pattern, ... **255.00**
Sugar Bowl, Cov, 5 1/4" h x 7 3/4" l,
"Grape Variant" pattern, orange,
yellow, green, and blue, wishbone
handles, (A), ... **923.00**

*Tea Set, pot, 6 1/4" h, creamer, sugar bowl,
"Carnation" pattern, repairs, $2,100.00*

Teapot, 6" h, squat shape, "Leaf"
pattern, restorations, (A), ... **880.00**
Toddy Plate, 5 1/8" d, "Warbonnet"
pattern, cobalt, green, orange, and
yellow, (A), ... **195.00**
Waste Bowl, 6 1/4" d, "Dove" pattern,
orange, cobalt, yellow, and green,
hairlines, (A), ... **360.00**

GAUDY IRONSTONE

Staffordshire, England
1850-1865

History: Gaudy Ironstone was produced
in the Staffordshire district between 1850
and 1865. Edward Walley's "wagon wheel"
was a popular Gaudy Ironstone design
similar to the design of Gaudy Welsh.
Walley, who worked at Villa Pottery in
Cobridge, utilized bright colors and floral
designs to give a country or folk character
to his pieces.

While some of the examples used the
same colorations as Gaudy Welsh, other
pieces used varying shades of red, pink,
and orange with light blue and black
accents. Some designs utilized copper
luster, while others did not. The flow blue
technique also was used on some Gaudy
Ironstone pieces.

Collectors' Club: Gaudy Collector's
Society, P.O. Box 274, Gates Mills, OH
44040

Bowl
5" d, "Seeing Eye" pattern, .. **280.00**
13 1/2" d, 12 sided, "Morning Glory"
pattern, red, yellow, green,
flowing blue, and copper luster,
(A), ... **825.00**
Charger, 13" d, blue, red, and green
polychrome flowers in center, black
transfer of rabbits and frogs on
border, crazing, (A), ... **1,100.00**

Creamer, 3 1/4" h
"Chicken Feet" pattern, cobalt, iron-
red, and copper luster, (A),
.... **77.00**
"Wagon Wheel" pattern, cobalt, iron-
red, and copper luster, (A),
.... **137.00**
Cup and Saucer
"Morning Glory" pattern, ... **300.00**
"Pinwheel" pattern, cobalt, iron-red,
and copper luster, (A), ... **50.00**
Cup and Saucer, Handleless
"Blackberry" pattern, iron-red,
cobalt, yellow, and copper luster,
(A), ... **143.00**
"Feather" pattern, cobalt, iron-red,
green, and copper luster, (A),
.... **165.00**
Red roses, green foliage, purple cut
sponge flowers, "John Meir &
Son England" mk, set of 6, (A),
.... **220.00**
"Urn" pattern, cobalt, green, pink,
and copper luster, ... **175.00**
Jug, 7 1/2" h, relief molded "Resting
Child" design, flowing blue w/copper
luster swirls, ... **295.00**
Milk Pitcher, 7 3/4" h, "Seeing Eye"
pattern, cobalt, iron-red, green, and
copper luster, (A), ... **1,320.00**
Mixing Bowl, 9" d, pink, yellow, green,
and blue tulips, "stamped Hand
Painted Germany Wittenberg," (A),
.... **75.00**
Mug, 3" h, "Chicken Feet" pattern,
cobalt, iron-red, and copper luster,
(A), ... **110.00**
Pitcher
4" h, "Chicken Feet" pattern, cobalt,
iron-red, and copper luster,
.... **195.00**
6" h, "Dahlia" pattern, cobalt
brushstroke flowerheads
w/copper luster overlay, red
berries, ... **295.00**
7 1/2" h, red strawberries, green
stems and leaves w/copper
luster accents, emb diamond
ground, ... **120.00**
Plate
6 3/4" d, "Wagon Wheel" pattern,
cobalt, iron-red, and copper
luster, set of 4, (A), ... **110.00**
7 1/2" d, "Wagon Wheel" pattern,
cobalt, iron-red, and copper
luster, (A), ... **88.00**
8" d
Flowing blue coral and emb leaf
design on border, copper
luster rim, ... **40.00**

*Plate, 8" d, "Blinking Eye" pattern, iron-red,
cobalt, green, and copper luster, c1840,
$325.00*

Twelve sides, flow blue and
copper luster bittersweet,
"imp Real Ironstone" mk, (A),
.... **83.00**

*Plate, 7 5/8" d, "Urn" pattern, iron-red, cobalt,
green, and copper luster, $245.00*

8 1/4" d
Ten sides, "Primrose" pattern,
cobalt, iron-red, green, and
copper luster, ... **350.00**
Twelve sides, flowing blue
morning glory flowers,
copper luster overlay and
rim, ... **135.00**
"Wagon Wheel" pattern, cobalt,
iron-red, and copper luster,
.... **150.00**
8 1/2" d
"Blackberry" pattern, iron-red,
cobalt, yellow, and copper
luster, (A), ... **132.00**
Flow blue "Urn" pattern w/pink
and red flowers, copper
luster, (A), ... **110.00**
Paneled, "Feather" pattern,
cobalt, iron-red, green, and
copper luster, (A), ... **198.00**

Plate, 8 5/8" d, iron-red flowers, gold outlined cobalt leaves, sm green flowerheads, copper luster rim, c1845, **$275.00**

Ten sides, "Seeing Eye" pattern, flowing cobalt, dk red, green, and luster, ... **125.00**

8 3/4" d
Ten sides, "Seeing Eye" pattern, flowing blue, rust-red, and grey, copper luster rim, ... **85.00**

Twelve sides, "Morning Glory & Strawberries" pattern, cobalt, iron-red, green, and luster, ... **350.00**

9" d, "Morning Glory" pattern, cobalt and copper luster, c1860, ... **175.00**

9 1/2" d, paneled
"Feather" pattern, iron-red, cobalt, and green flowers and stems, cobalt and copper luster feather-type designs, (A), ... **187.00**

"Seaweed" pattern, (A), **110.00**

Platter, 11" l x 8 1/2" w, oct, "Pinwheel" pattern, cobalt, iron-red, and luster, ... **215.00**

Soup Plate
8" d, cobalt, iron red, pink, green, and luster scattered chrysanthemums, peonies, and joined stems, unmkd, ... **65.00**

10 1/4" d, paneled, "Pinwheel" pattern, iron-red, cobalt, and copper luster, (A), ... **308.00**

Tureen, Cov, 10 1/2" l x 9 1/2" w x 7" h, red roses, green and cobalt foliage, "Heal & Son, London" mk, (A), ... **200.00**

Waste Bowl
5" d, "Seeing Eye" pattern, iron-red, cobalt, green, copper luster accents, ... **280.00**

5 1/2" d, "Fern" pattern, iron-red, cobalt, green, and copper luster, (A), ... **121.00**

6 1/2" d, "Pinwheel" pattern, iron-red, cobalt, and copper luster, (A), ... **176.00**

GAUDY WELSH

England, Wales
1820-1860

History: Gaudy Welsh, manufactured between 1820 and 1860, was produced for the working class people in England and Wales. It traced its decorative motifs to Japanese Imari. Gaudy Welsh was identified by its colors of underglaze cobalt blue (often in panels), rust (burnt orange), and copper luster on a white ground, plus its decoration, which most often was floral, although trees, birds, or geometric forms were sometimes used. The body can be earthenware, creamware, ironstone, or bone china.

Swansea and Llanelly were the two areas in Wales where the Gaudy Welsh motif began. At least four firms in Newcastle and two Sunderland firms copied the design to their wares. However, it was the Staffordshire potteries at Stoke-on-Trent that produced the greatest amount of Gaudy Welsh.

Grape leaves, panels, cartouches, fences, and flower petals appeared repeatedly in Gaudy Welsh designs and reflected the Oriental influence. Many patterns had names indicative of the design, e.g. "Tulip," "Sunflower," "Grape," and "Oyster," while other names were more fanciful and bore little resemblance to the decorative motif. True Gaudy Welsh had the cobalt portion of the design under the glaze and the additional enamel colors including the lusters over the glaze. In addition to the bold colorations of cobalt, orange, and luster decorations, pieces can be found with shades of green and yellow highlights added. As many as 300 designs have been identified.

Tea cups and saucers were made more than any other forms. Most Gaudy Welsh designs were painted on the inside of the cups. Tea sets, jugs, bowls, and miniatures were produced in smaller quantities.

Much of the Gaudy Welsh was unmarked. Design and techniques allowed some pieces to be traced to specific companies.

References: John A. Shuman, III, *The Collector's Encyclopedia of Gaudy Dutch & Welsh*, Collector Books, 1998 values; Howard Y. Williams, *Gaudy Welsh China*, Wallace-Homestead 1978.

Collectors' Club: Gaudy Collector's Society, P.O. Box 274, Gates Mills, OH 44040

Museums: Royal Institution of South Wales, Swansea, Wales; St. Fagen's Welsh Folk Museum, near Cardiff, Wales; Welsh National Museum, Cardiff, Wales.

Reproduction Alert: Gaudy Welsh has been reproduced during this century by several Staffordshire potteries. The most prolific was Charles Allerton & Sons (1859-1942), who specialized in jugs in the "oyster" pattern. The orange-red pigment, often streaked and uneven, is the sign of a reproduction.

Bowl
6" d
"Oyster" pattern, ... **175.00**
"Tibet" pattern, ... **300.00**
6 1/2" d, ftd, "Columbine" pattern, ... **95.00**
8 1/2" d, "Grape" pattern, variant, chips, ... **200.00**

Cake Plate
7 3/4" d, "Sunflower" pattern, **195.00**
10" H-H, "Tulip" pattern, ... **145.00**

Center Bowl
9" d, ftd, "Oyster" pattern, ... **590.00**
10" d, ftd, "Grape" pattern, ... **245.00**

Creamer, 3 7/8" h, "Buckle" pattern, (A), ... **45.00**

Compote, 5" h, 9" d, "Grape" pattern, blue, green, lavender, and iron-red, A-**$287.00**

Cup and Saucer
"Angels Trumpet" pattern, ... **195.00**
"Basket" pattern, (A), ... **165.00**
"Bath" pattern, ... **260.00**
"Buckle" pattern, ... **90.00**
"Columbine" pattern, ... **75.00**
"Drape" pattern, ... **195.00**
"Feather" pattern, ... **145.00**
"Floret" pattern, ... **110.00**
"Garland" pattern, ... **70.00**
"Grape Variant" pattern, (A), ... **98.00**
"Lotus" pattern, ... **75.00**
"Oyster" pattern, ... **75.00**
"Pyrethrum" pattern, ... **140.00**
"Rocking Urn" pattern, ... **100.00**
"Sunflower" pattern, ... **190.00**

"Tricorn" pattern, (A), ... **35.00**
"Urn" pattern, ... **125.00**
"Venus" pattern, ... **195.00**
Dessert Service, 6 tea plates, 6" d, 6 cups and saucers, cake plate, 9" l x 8 3/4" w, "Oyster" pattern, ... **975.00**
Dish, 9 1/4" l x 8 3/4" w, "Grosmont" pattern, ... **245.00**
Fruit Bowl, 5 1/2" h x 9 1/2" d, ftd, "Amherst Japan" pattern, repaired chip, (A), ... **200.00**
Jug
3" h, "Pansy" pattern, repairs, ... **85.00**
4" h, hex shape, "Rose Haulwen" pattern, ... **75.00**
4 1/2" h
"Oyster" pattern, ... **75.00**
"Grape III" pattern, (A), ... **65.00**
Paneled, "Gwent" pattern, ... **300.00**
"Rainbow" pattern, ... **200.00**
5" h
"Cambrian" pattern, ... **375.00**
"Sunflower" pattern, snake handle, "ALLERTONS EST.1831, MADE IN ENGLAND" mk, (A), ... **55.00**
"Teahouse" pattern, restored hairline, ... **470.00**
5 1/2" h, paneled, "Grape" pattern, ... **60.00**
6" h
"Drape" pattern, ... **275.00**
"Sunflower" pattern, snake handle, "ALLERTONS EST. 1831" mk, (A), ... **100.00**
6 1/4" h
"Capel Curig" pattern, ... **525.00**
"Cardiff" pattern, ... **350.00**
6 3/4" h, "Celyn" pattern, figural swan handle, ... **475.00**
7 1/4" h, "Llanelly Poppy" pattern, ... **350.00**
7 1/2" h
"Aberdare" pattern, ... **460.00**
"Grape" pattern, ... **400.00**
Milk Jug, 8" h, "Oyster" pattern, . **82.00**
Mug
2 1/4" h, "Tulip" pattern, c1860, ... **200.00**
2 1/2" h, "Grape Variant" pattern, (A), ... **70.00**
2 3/4" h, "Drape" pattern, ... **190.00**
3" h
"Asian" pattern, ... **195.00**
"Forget-Me-Not" pattern, **450.00**
"Oyster" pattern, ... **195.00**
"Pansy and Gate" pattern, ... **375.00**

3 1/2" h, "Chinoiserie" pattern, ... **115.00**
3 3/4" h, "Grape Variant" pattern, (A), ... **193.00**
4" h, "Oyster" pattern, Allerton, (A), ... **110.00**
Pitcher
4" h, "Oyster" pattern, ... **36.00**
4 3/4" h, "Tulip" pattern, ... **95.00**
5" h, "Oyster" pattern, ... **100.00**
5 1/2" h, paneled, "Cambrian Rose" pattern, (A), ... **200.00**
6 1/8" h, "Grape" pattern, vine molded handle and spout, (A), ... **225.00**
6 1/2" h, "Cardiff" pattern, c1840, ... **350.00**
7 1/2" h, "Bell Flower and Vase" pattern, rim chip, (A), ... **110.00**
Plate
5" d
"Oyster" pattern, "Allerton's England" mk, ... **40.00**
"Tulip" pattern, ... **15.00**
6 1/4" d, "Oyster" pattern, ... **85.00**
6 1/8" d, "Tulip" pattern, ... **20.00**
7" d, "Tricorn" pattern, ... **100.00**
7 1/2" d, pattern #634, ... **50.00**
7 3/4" d, "Oyster" pattern, ... **95.00**
8" d, "Sea Waves" pattern, Middleborough Earthenware company, ... **95.00**
8 1/8" d, paneled, "Pinwheel" pattern, (A), ... **85.00**
8 1/2" d
"Grape" pattern, ... **175.00**
"Urn" pattern, (A), ... **55.00**
9" d
"Flower Basket II" pattern, ... **175.00**
"Lotus" pattern, ... **195.00**
"Oyster" pattern, ... **35.00**
9" sq, "Columbine" pattern, ... **40.00**

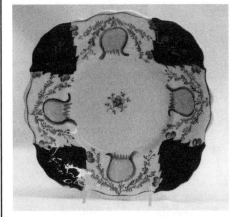

*Plate, 9 1/4" d, "Tulip" pattern, 1860, **$125.00***

9 1/2" d
"Pinwheel" pattern, ... **275.00**
Twelve sided, "Dutch Rose" pattern, stains, (A), ... **100.00**

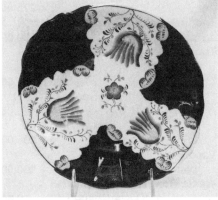

*Plate, 9 1/2" d, "Tulip" pattern, blue, yellow, and iron-red, **$45.00***

10" d, "Flower Basket II" pattern, ... **110.00**
10" l x 9" w, "Coral" pattern, scalloped rim, ... **170.00**
Punch Bowl, 10" d, "Grape" pattern, rim chip, ... **140.00**
Soup Plate, 10 1/4" d, "Oyster" pattern, (A), ... **85.00**
Spill Vase, 3 1/4" h, "Asian" pattern, ... **550.00**
Sugar Bowl, Cov
7" h, "Tulip" pattern, ... **325.00**
7 1/2" h, "Venus" pattern, ... **250.00**
Teapot
3 1/2" h, miniature, "Oyster" pattern, ... **200.00**

*Teapot, 8 1/2" h x 11" w, "Rocking Urn" pattern, c1885, **$390.00***

7" h, "Tulip" pattern, ear handle, ... **500.00**
7 1/2" h
"Buckle" pattern, ... **650.00**
"Chinoiserie" pattern, c1850, ... **675.00**
"Glowing Pagoda" pattern, ... **425.00**

"Warbonnet" pattern, base
crack, ... **340.00**
8" h, "Columbine" pattern, molded
feet, handle, spout, and knob,
(A), ... **275.00**
Toddy Plate, 5 1/2" d, "Oyster" pattern,
.... **30.00**
Tray, Molded Handles
9" H-H, "Buckle" pattern, hairlines,
(A), ... **45.00**
9 1/8" H-H, "Drape" pattern, stains,
(A), ... **70.00**
9 1/4" H-H, "Tulip Variant" pattern,
(A), ... **138.00**
Vase, 4 1/2" h, urn shape, "Grape"
pattern, ... **160.00**
Waste Bowl
5 1/4" d, "Oyster" pattern, ... **50.00**
6 3/8" d, "Drape" pattern, ... **68.00**
6 1/2" d, "Grape" pattern, pink luster
rim, ... **195.00**

GERMAN FACTORIES-MINOR

History: Many small, but highly important factories were established in the German provinces during the last half of the 18th century. Some were started by princes, but the majority were private commercial enterprises.

Ansbach
Hesse
1758-1860

Under the patronage of Hohenzollern Margrave Alexander of Brandenburg, and with the help of workers from Meissen, this porcelain factory was established in 1758 in connection with an old faience works. In 1762 the firm moved to a hunting castle at Bruckberg. Fine pieces were made during the rococo period, c1775. The factory was sold to private interests in 1807 and continued to make a variety of wares until 1860.

Wares imitated those made at Berlin, Meissen, and Nymphenburg. Exotic groups and figures, white and painted decorative and utilitarian wares, especially coffeepots, souvenir plates, monogrammed cups and saucers, and silhouette medallions were made. The principal mark in the c1760 to 1785 period was an "A" of varying sizes and shapes.

Bayreuth
Bavaria, Germany
1899-1920

Siegmund Paul Meyer's factory produced utilitarian and hotel porcelains. The firm changed its name to First Bayreuth Porcelain Factory in 1920, continuing to make ovenproof pots and coffee machines.

Frankenthal
Palatinate, Germany
1755-1799

History: Paul Hannong established the Frankenthal hard paste porcelain factory in 1755 with the consent and patronage of the Prince Elector Karl Theodor of Palatinate. Previously Hannong worked at Strasbourg, France, 65 miles south of Palatinate.

Dinner services and accessory pieces were marketed along with biscuit and decorated figures, some of which were excellent artistically. The rococo style dominated and was similar to that appearing on Vincennes-Sevres pieces. Frankenthal decorators used a full range of colors along with the Vienna style of raised gilt work. Classical and natural themes proved the most popular.

Despite high quality pieces, the company suffered from financial difficulties. In 1762 Karl Theodor purchased the factory and personally supervised its operation. Modelers Luck and Melchior fashioned figural pieces of note. Nevertheless, the company failed in 1799. Nymphenburg acquired the Frankenthal molds to reproduce the old forms. The Nymphenburg factory used the blue lion mark and "CT" with a crown on their pieces made from Frankenthal molds.

Frankenthal's forty-four years of production were the shortest production period experienced by a major German porcelain manufacturer. However, Frankenthal's high quality and variety of products produced during this brief period were enough to rank it among the greatest of the German factories.

Fulda
Hesse
1765-1790

This factory was established for the Prince-Bishop of Fulda in 1765. The predominant decorative style was from the late rococo period. The products resembled those manufactured at Frankenthal. The main subjects of the figures were shepherds, children, ladies, cavaliers, and comedians positioned on rococo trellises. The factory mark in underglaze blue was a double "F" with or without a crown. A few pieces were marked with a cross.

Fursternberg
Brunswick, Germany
1747-1859 Royal-State
1859 to Present-Private

History: The Furstenberg factory was founded in 1747 in the castle of Karl I, Duke of Brunswick, primarily to satisfy his vanity. Six years passed before porcelain was produced in 1753. The technique came from artists who left Hochst. Raw materials for the paste and glaze had to be imported from a great distance. By 1770 the porcelain paste closely approximated that made at Meissen.

Many figures were modeled, but the amount of production was not great. The figures imitated figural molds and decorations produced at Meissen and Berlin. English styles from Bow, Wedgwood, and Chelsea, and Sevres from France also were copied. After 1760, Frankenthal vases became famous. China services and various utilitarian and decorative wares were competitive with those produced by other 18th century factories.

The period of 1770 to 1790 was the golden age at the Furstenberg factory. Materials improved considerably, additional enamel colors were utilized, and gilding was employed in the border patterns. After 1775, neo-classical influences appeared.

During the French occupation, Brunswick was part of the Kingdom of Westphalia ruled by Napoleon's brother, Jerome Bonaparte. The factory became the Royal Porcelain Manufactory from 1807 to 1813. After Napoleon's defeat, Brunswick regained its independence. In 1813 the former name was restored. The factory continued to produce tablewares, decorative porcelains, figures, and coffee and tea sets.

In 1859 Furstenberg was leased by the Brunswick government. Private ownership took over again in 1876. The company was reorganized as a joint stock company and named Furstenberg Porcelain Factory AG. Today, the factory still manufactures a great variety of vases, tablewares, and other porcelains.

Gotha
1757-1782

Wilhemn von Rotberg established this factory in 1757. His cream-colored paste had a translucent glaze. Products included coffee sets, tea sets, and decorative porcelain figures. At first, the rococo style was predominant. Later, the Louis XVI and neo-classical styles were used. Underglaze blue marks were first an "R" and then "R-g" and "G." The factory survived until 1782.

Kassel
Hesse
1766-1788

Friedrich II founded the factory. It made attractive tablewares with underglaze blue decoration and some simple figures. The mark was a lion or "HC" in underglaze blue.

Figure, 7" h, 6 3/4" w, peach-pink blouse, lt purple sleeves, green flowered overdress, gilt trim, dtd 1762, **$1,650.00**

Kloster Veilsdorf
1760 to Present

The factory was established in 1760 under the patronage of Friedrich Wilhelm Eugen. Tablewares and decorative porcelains, coffee sets, tea sets, and figures were made. The typical decorations were large freely painted purple, red, and yellow flowers evolving from thread-like stems. The underglaze blue monogram "CV" was used, occasionally supplemented with a coat of arms. After 1799, the mark became a three-leaf clover.

Limbach
1772 to Present

Gotthelf Greiner established this factory in 1772. Porcelains were decorated primarily in blue and purple tones. Figures were rustic subjects and small-town people. The marks "LB" or crossed "Ls" were applied on the glaze in red, purple, or black. About 1787 an underglaze blue cloverleaf mark was used. Later, cloverleaf marks were purple, black, or red.

Greiner and his five sons acquired other factories such as Grossbreitenbach in 1782 and Kloster Veilsdorf in 1791. From 1797 to1850, G. Greiner's Sons made utilitarian and decorative porcelains and figures.

Ludwigsburg
Wurttemberg, Germany
1758-1824

History: Karl Eugen, Duke of Wurttemberg, founded a hard paste porcelain manufactory in 1758 at Ludwigsburg, twelve miles north of Stuttgart. A faience factory was established two years later. Joseph Jacob Ringler directed the porcelain factory from 1759 to 1799. Initially, copies of Meissen wares were made.

The peak period of production was between 1758 and 1776. Utilitarian wares decorated with birds and ornamental wares, e.g., candlesticks, were produced. Riedel, the major designer and modeler during this period, crafted mythological and classical figures. Berger, another sculptor, made small figural groups comprised of peasants, work, and ballet groups. These figures did not match the quality of the figurines from Meissen, Nymphenburg, or Frankenthal. Initially, the Ludwigsburg shapes and decoration were in the rococo style. The factory changed its forms and designs as tastes changed. Rococo gave way to neo-classical, followed by Empire styles. Ludwigsburg porcelain started to decline after 1770. The enterprise never really was profitable or highly successful. Duke Karl Eugen died in 1793. Production deteriorated even more after his death. The factory struggled on for thirty more years before it closed in 1824. During the 19th century, the Ludwigsburg molds were sold to Edward Kick, at Amberg in Bavaria. Kick reissued a number of the pieces.

Nymphenberg
Near Munich, Bavaria, Germany
1747 to Present

History: The Nymphenburg Porcelain Factory, located in Neudeck ob den Au, near Munich, was founded in 1747 by the Bavarian Elector. As production increased, the factory was moved to the grounds of Nymphenburg Palace in Munich.

As with many German porcelain firms, Meissen pieces strongly influenced the types of wares produced at Nymphenburg. By 1765, under the guidance of the Elector, Nymphenburg became the most renown hard paste factory in Europe. Shortly thereafter, a series of wars and economic reversals created a decline in the popularity of the porcelain. By 1770 the Nymphenburg factory was hard pressed for markets in which to sell its products.

During the early years at Nymphenburg, production was devoted to table services, accessory pieces, and household wares that were painted in a rococo style featuring birds, fruits, flowers, and the popular pastoral scenes. However, it was the modeling of Franz Bustelli, the Swiss craftsman who worked at Nymphenburg from 1754 to 1763, that contributed the most to the success of the company. Bustelli's figures were modeled in a light, graceful rococo style that found a ready market with the gentry.

The Nymphenburg pottery was transferred to the control of the Elector of Palatinate who also owned the Frankenthal factory, a competitor of Nymphenburg. With more emphasis placed on the Frankenthal pottery, Nymphenburg experienced a period of neglect and subsequent decline. When the Frankenthal Factory closed in 1799, many of the workers and artisans were moved to Nymphenburg to revitalize the ailing concern.

Melchior, who achieved fame at Hochst and Frankenthal, was chief modeler at Nymphenburg between 1797 and 1822. He produced many biscuit portraits and busts.

When Melchior died in 1822, Friedrich Gartner was appointed artistic director. He preferred to produce vases in a variety of decorative motifs. Gartner showed little interest in producing tableware. As a result, the factory declined economically. Royal commissions for Ludwig I (1825-1848) did result in the manufacture of several outstanding state services.

When Eugen Neureuther assumed control as director in 1848, the factory's finances were poor. Ludwig I abdicated in favor of Maximilian II, his son. Maximilian II had almost no interest in the pottery factory. Steps were taken to try to alleviate the problem. For example, popular wares such as paperweights, toothbrush racks, and cigar holders were made to attract working capital, and tablewares regained favor. But the factory still lost money. In desperation, the factory switched to industrial porcelains.

In 1862 the Royal Manufactory was leased to a private concern. The new managers produced art porcelain and reissued some of the earlier rococo figures. The pottery again became profitable.

Albert Keller from Sevres and Louis Levallois, a student from Sevres, developed an Art Nouveau line for Nymphenburg based on the underglazed painting of figures. When Theodor Karner, a sculptor, came to Nymphenburg, he introduced a number of successful animal sculptures that were modeled after the animals and birds in Bavaria and the Munich Zoo. Animal motifs also were used on modern tablewares. Other tablewares were produced in the Art Nouveau style that encompassed linear decorations, stylized designs, and angular handles.

The popularity of the neo-classical, Empire, and Biedermeier movements that swept across Europe during the late 19th century achieved the same success at Nymphenburg. In 1887, the Baum family from Bohemia gained control of the company. They still guide its fortunes today. Recently the company reproduced a number of pure white figures from its old models. The company still has not regained the position of prominence it enjoyed in the past.

Thuringian Factories
From 1757

Nine hard paste porcelain factories were established in theThuringian region. The three main ones were Gotha, Kloster Veilsdorf, and Volkstedt-Rudolstat. (see Volkstedt-Rudolstat)

Wallendorf
1764-1833

Johann W. Hammann established this factory in 1764. The first products had rococo style decoration. Later dinner services were made in formal styles. Pastoral and street scenes in monotones of purple, brown, black, and grey tones featured figures of rural characters. The factory's mark was an underglaze blue "W." In 1833 the factory was sold to Hutschenreuther, Kampfe, and Heubach.

Reference: George W. Ware, *German & Austrian Porcelain*, Crown, Inc. 1963; Alfred Ziffer, *Nymphenburg Porcelain, The Bauml Collection*, Arnold Sche, 1997. George W. Ware, *German and Austrian Porcelain*, Crown Publishers, Inc. 1963.

Museums: Bayeriches National Museum, Munich, Germany; Gardiner Museum of Ceramic Art, Toronto, Canada; Museum fur Kunst und Gewerbe, Hamburg, Germany; Schloss Museum, Berlin, Germany; Victoria & Albert Museum, London, England; Cincinnati Art Museum, Cincinnati, OH.

Ansbach

Figure, 7 1/2" h, monk, brown-grey habit, yellow sheaf of corn on back, hiding young girl, white cap, red heeled turquoise shoes, shaped gilt scroll molded pad base w/applied foliage and flowers, c1770, chips, (A), ... **3,050.00**

Mug, 5" h, painted vignette of boat in harbor, classical ruins, above scrolling leaves and scattered sprigs, gilt dentil rim, dbl scroll leaf molded handle, c1770, (A), ... **485.00**

Bayreuth

Ewer, 13" h, lead glazed, lg blue floral spray and bird, white ground, chips, ... **2,325.00**

Brunswick

Figure, 3 1/2" h, faience, ochre and manganese cat seated on haunches, manganese splashed rect mound base, C1760, (A), ... **880.00**

Erfurt

Tureen, 6 1/4" w, right and left opposing figural reclining pug, yellow-green coat, manganese muzzle, red tongue, blue outlined eyes, chips and crack, c1760, pr, (A), ... **12,545.00**

Coffee and Tea Service, coffeepot, 8 1/4" h, teapot, 5 3/4" h, missing cov, cov sugar bowl, 5 3/4" h, waste bowl, 5 1/8" d, tea caddy, 4 5/8" h, 10 coffee cans, 10 saucers, painted green and brown oak leaf and acorn borders and sprays, white ground, "painted F" mks, c1890-1908, repairs, $350.00

Frankenthal

Basket, 8 1/2" H-H, int painted w/loose spray of flowers, bowl pierced w/trellis pattern, "blue crowned CT" mk, c1765, (A), ... **440.00**

Cream Jug, 4" h, mauve and purple flowers, green leaves, brown lined rim and outlined feet, "blue crowned CT" mark, $975.00

Charger, 15 1/2" d, 2 enameled bunches of garden flowers in center, molded paneled basketweave border w/flower sprigs, ... **1,000.00**

Figure

5 1/2" h, "Lemon Seller," white jacket, yellow bows, puce breeches, yellow bow garters, standing before brown tree trunk, lemon in outstretched hand, dish of lemons in other, green base w/added grass, gilt scrolled bottom, "blue crowned CT," c1780, ... **2,200.00**

6" h, young man, black tricorn, green coat and britches, standing by garden tub, mound base molded w/puce and white scrolls, "blue rampant lion" mk, c1765, (A), ... **620.00**

6 7/8" h, "Falconer," black hat, yellow lined blue edged white jacket, white shirt, red breeches, holding red and blue bird on arm, standing bare foot on cloud molded base, "blue crowned interlaced Cs" mk, c1770, cracks and repairs, (A), ... **1,075.00**

7" h, "Winter," ice-blue painted January w/natural colored face, face mask on reverse, holding medallion of nymph pouring water, another of December blowing flames in brazier, ermine lined cloaks and hats w/yellow and brown enameled accents, gilt scroll molded bases, "blue crowned CT" mks, c1762-66, pr, (A), ... **10,160.00**

Plate

9" d, painted vignettes of birds in branches in pierced and molded trellis pattern border, "blue crowned CT" mk, c1765, (A), ... **495.00**

9 1/2" d, HP puce and yellow sprig in center, molded border panels of florals w/painted sprigs, "blue rampant lion" mk, ... **1,200.00**

Furstenberg

Figure, 4 1/8" h, standing Chinese woman, black peaked hat, puce coat w/scrolling designs, yellow sash, holding parrot on branch in hand, puce scroll molded base, "blue F" mk, c1775, restored hat, (A), ... **2,330.00**

Fruit Bowl, 12" d, burgundy, mauve, and green-yellow fruit and apples in center, dry burnished gold crosshatched diapering and scrolling on border, "crowned F Furstenberg" mk, ... **50.00**

Letter Holder, 9" l x 6" h, 3 slots, HP Dresden style flowers, gilt accented scroll molded rims, ... **1,200.00**

Pin Tray, 3 7/8" d, black printed "Rathaus Zu Rendsburg," mkd, ... **15.00**

Pitcher, 3 1/4" h, hanging green leaf swags on shoulder, "blue crowned F Furstenberg Germany" mk, ... **25.00**

Charger, 14" d, polychrome enameled designs, c1780, $5,500.00

Plate, 9 1/2" d, sprig of red dogwood, blue bachelor button, and sm yellow flowers, yellow and green foliage, shaded blue border, c1920, ... **15.00**

Vase
9 1/2" h, swollen slender shape, long flared neck, pink, blue, and green floral designs, wide gold rim band, ... **135.00**
16" h, trumpet shape, spread ft, center tan band w/gilt curlicues and blue panel w/gilt florals, blue ft w/gilt lines and geometrics, ... **200.00**

Hanau
Salt, 5" h, ftd, blue painted overall floral design, c1720, ... **2,700.00**

Kunersberg
Jug, 15" h, faience, painted mang oval w/"FGR," suspended from blue bow, over yellow, green, and mang flower spray, hinged pewter lid, (A), ... **315.00**

Ludwigsburg
Cup and Saucer, painted loose bouquets and scattered sprays, ozier molded borders, brown lined rims, "blue crowned interlaced Cs" mks, (A), ... **510.00**

Cup and Saucer, **Handleless**, painted peasants gathering and tending vegetables, simple landscape, puce rims, "blue crowned CC" mks, (A), ... **310.00**

Dessert Service, Part, 3 bowls, 9 3/4" d, 6 bowls, 7 5/8" d, painted puce loose bouquet in center w/scattered sprigs, border of alternating molded panels of scrolling foliage or plain w/puce sprigs, gilt shaped rim, "blue crowned interlaced Ls" mks, c1775, (A), ... **1,795.00**

Figure, 7" h, purple dress with green leaves, yellow bodice, "blue interlocking Cs" mark, spoon missing, $475.00

Figure
4 3/8" h, huntress, green cap, green trimmed white dress, gilded buttons, game bag on shoulder, holding game bird and rifle, scroll molded mound base, c1765, "blue interlaced Cs" mk, restorations, ... **550.00**
5" h, "Hurdy-Gurdy Player," female w/black choker and gilt pendant, red bodice, white blouse, yellow-lined pink apron, yellow-centered blue flowered skirt, gilt buckled black shoes, hurdy-gurdy under arm, gilt scroll molded mound base, "black interlaced Cs" mk, c1765, chips, (A), ... **1,615.00**
5 3/4" h, street vender, woman in white cap, yellow bodice, white blouse, blue edged white apron, puce skirt, holding dead

chicken, basket and apron of vegetables, red shoes, circ mound base w/gilt C-scrolls, "blue interlaced Ls" mk, c1765, chips, (A), ... **3,050.00**
13 1/4" h, Venus and Adonis, embracing semi-nude figures, female in draped green lined pink robe w/purple flowers, rockwork base w/applied green moss, blue and green scaled dolphin in green seaweed, "blue interlaced Cs" mk, c1765, (A), ... **8,775.00**

Nymphenburg
Figure
5" h, Shetland pony, black shred mane and tail, blue edged red saddle, rect gilt base w/red line, "imp and green printed shield" mks, late 19th C, (A), ... **1,195.00**

Figure, 4" h, blue shield, white ground, pr, $225.00

6" h, seated little boy playing flute to seated little girl, or little boy kissing little girl, freeform base, white glaze, "imp shield" mks, pr, chips, ... **200.00**
7 3/4" h, seated dachshund, brown shades, ... **385.00**

Figure, 4 3/4" h, 6 1/4" l, white glaze, imp mark, A-$150.00

8 1/4" h, standing oriental man wearing gilt lined green cap, flowered red jacket, green floral trimmed white gown, lg brown book under arm, gilt edged base, ... **275.00**

Figure, 5 3/4" h, 5 1/4" l, green leaf hat, lt yellow gown with lilac trim on rt figure, iron-red trimmed pants, blue flowered top, grey hair on lt figure, gilt trimmed base, "imp shield" mark, $500.00

10" l x 5 1/2" h, reclining shepherd dog, white glaze, sgd "Theodor Karner," **125.00**

14" h, standing white lion holding blue and white shield, Bavarian figures on base, Ernst Andrea Rauch, ... **1,400.00**

Salt, 3 1/2" l, bombe shape, painted German flowers, 4 gilt and blue accented scroll feet, "imp shield" mk, c1765, (A), ... **560.00**

Chocolate Service, pot, 7" h, milk jug, 2 cups and saucers, tray, 13 1/4" l, painted hunt scenes, green ground, Nymphenburg, (A), $270.00

Teapot, 4 1/4" h, squat shape, swirled body, HP garden flowers on sides, gilt accents, branch handle, gold rose knob, ... **250.00**

Wallendorf

Teabowl and Saucer, blue onion type pattern, c1780, firing crack, ... **85.00**

1907   1914   1895

GERMANY-GENERAL

Pottery

15th Century to Present

History: Some of the earliest forms of German decorative pottery were made by the Hafner or stove-makers. The stove tiles of the 15th century were covered with a green lead glaze. Later 16th century stoves contained tiles of yellow, brown, and white clays or with tin-glaze over red clay bodies. Hafner wares also included large vessels or jugs made in Nuremberg.

In 1712 Marx and Hemman first made tin-glazed earthenwares. They continued in a series of partnerships until 1840. Most of the wares were decorated in blue with baroque style scrolls, foliage, or strapwork. Subjects encompassed landscapes, heraldic shields, and biblical or mythological scenes.

Hamburg faience came in the period of the second quarter of the 17th century. Pear-shaped jugs decorated with a coat-of-arms in a blue motif were best known.

The most prolific center of German faience was at Hanau, near Frankfort-am-Main, from 1661 until 1806. The wares imitated Delftware. Many Chinese forms were copied. At first only blue decoration was used. By the early 18th century, wares were decorated with landscapes and biblical scenes in a variety of colors. Naturalistic flowers in enamel colors dominated the mid-18th century wares.

Ansbach, Bayreuth, Cassel, Erfurt, Frankfurt-am-Main, Proskau, and Schrezheim were other areas where faience factories were established.

Porcelain

16th Century to Present

History: In Germany there were many small principalities that competed with each other in establishing porcelain factories. Each developed an individual style. There was no royal monopoly in Germany as there was in France because there was no unified Germany.

In addition to the major German factories of Berlin, Frankenthal, Furstenberg, Hochst, Ludwigsburg, and Meissen, at least twenty minor manufactories were established in the German provinces during the last half of the 18th century. Some of these include Ansbach, Fulda, Gera,

Gotha, Grossbreitenbach, Gutenbrunn, Ilmenau, Kassel, Kelsterbach, Kloster Veilsdorf, Limbach, Ottweiler, Rauenstein, Volkstedt, and Wallendorf.

Though some of these factories were established by princes, most were formulated as private commercial enterprises to make wares that could be sold competitively. For the most part, these wares copied works of the major German factories, such as Frankenthal and Meissen, etc. The majority of the minor factories were able to continue operation despite changes in ownership, economic disruptions, and competition from larger firms, especially those established in the 19th and 20th centuries that were close to the source of raw materials.

Independent painters developed soon after the establishment of the Meissen factory about 1720. Porcelains painted by these independent decorators in their homes or studios were known as Hausmalerei. The painters were designated as Hausmaler. Hausmalers were experienced painters of faience and other ceramics. The large porcelain factories feared their competition. Hausmalers obtained Meissen and Vienna blanks and painted them as they wished. Ignaz Bottengruber of Breslau was the best known of the independent decorators. Hausmalers were active for about forty years during the mid-18th century.

A smaller group of factories was in operation during the last half of the 18th century. These included Baden-Baden, Blankenhain, Eisenberg, Ellwangen, Hanau, Hoxter, Schney, and Tettau. Only Tettau still operates today.

Germany was in the forefront of the hard paste porcelain industry. Many new factories, making high quality utilitarian and decorative porcelains, were established during the 19th and 20th centuries. Most of these 19th and 20th century factories, approximately two hundred of them, were concentrated near the source of porcelain's raw materials, i.e. the central and eastern regions of Germany (mainly North Bavaria, Thuringia, Saxony, and Silesia). Among the dominant factories are Sitzendorf, Rosenthal, Schumann, Hutschenreuther, and Heinrich. Factories located at Altwasser, Passau, Plaue, Potschappel, Rudolstadt, and Selb concentrated on the production of utilitarian and decorative porcelains.

Reference: William B. Honey, *German Porcelain*, Faber & Faber, 1947.

Museums: Arts & Crafts Museum, Prague, Czechoslovakia; Bayerishes National Museum, Munich, Germany; Kunstgewerbemuseum, Berlin, Germany; Metropolitan Museum of Art, New York, NY; Museum fur Kunst und Gewerbe, Hamburg, Germany.

Additional Listings: Bavaria, Bohemia, Carlsbad, C.T. Germany, Dresden, Frankenthal, Furstenberg, Heubach, Hochst, Hutschenreuther, KPM,

Ludwigsburg, Minor German Factories, Meissen, Nymphenburg, Rosenthal, Royal Bayreuth, Royal Dux, Rudolstadt, Schlegelmilch, Sitzendorf, and Volkstedt.

Ashtray, 2 3/4" h, green figural frog smoking gold pipe seated on gold edged white figural leaf base, ... **75.00**

Basket, 2" h x 3" l, Elfinware, molded green moss ground w/applied white and pink rose and purple violets on side, applied band of sm blue flowers on rim, "red GERMANY" mk, ... **30.00**

Bell, 5 1/2" h, figural period lady, blond hair w/black hat, pink gown w/yellow ribbons and jacket, ... **85.00**

Berry Set, master bowl, 10" d, 4 bowls, 5" d, HP pink and white roses, green foliage, shaded steel grey ground w/shadow leaves on borders, ... **185.00**

Biscuit Barrel, Cov, 7" h, Delft-style blue and white sailboats in harbor scene, sm blue flowers on cov, ... **325.00**

Bookend, 6" h x 4 1/4" l, seated figural Dutch boy or girl, boy wearing brown hat and trousers, blue scarf, girl w/blue jumper, white apron, red cap, "Erphila Germany" mks, pr, ... **20.00**

Bowl, 9 1/4" d, red and yellow roses, green leaves, shaded green border with gold stenciling, **$68.00**

Bowl
7 1/4" d, center multicolored medallion of period couple in meadow in gilt frame and band of HP pink roses on int, 4 part pierced shapes around sides over HP gilt relief molded shell and scrolling on ext, drops of red-pink roses and green leaves from inner border, Von Schierholz, ... **125.00**

8" l x 6 1/2" w, red roses, creamy yellow and blue shaded ground, gold curled handles, crimped rim, and feet, MOP int, ... **145.00**
10" d, purple and white orchid in center, molded border panels w/green luster finish, raised circles on lobed rim, ... **35.00**
11" d, blooming white or dk red hydrangeas, brown and green foliage, dk red shaded border, rim molded w/gold shell designs, ... **95.00**

Cake Plate, 9 1/2" H-H, transfer of red and purple grape bunches, green foliage, green and purple luster border trim, ... **32.00**

Candlestick, 9 1/2" h, molded curlicues and leaves, white glaze, "blue KPM scepter" Krister Porcelain Manufacturer mk, c1885, pr, .. **85.00**

Canister Set
Three canisters, 6" h x 4" sq, gold "Tea, Farina, and Oatmeal," green bellflowers, ribbons, and flowers, HP purple violets, "G.M.T. & Bros. Germany" mks, set of 3, ... **145.00**
Six canisters, 8 1/2" h, "Coffee, Tea, Barley, Rice, Sugar, and Farina," 6 canisters, 4 1/2" h, "Pepper, Allspice, Ginger, Cinnamon, Cloves, and Nutmeg," 2 bottles, 9" h, "Oil and Vinegar," hanging box, 6 1/2" h, blue Dutch scenes of windmills, black lettering, ... **800.00**

Centerpiece, 18" l x 13" w x 8 1/2" h, oval center bowl supported by 4 multicolored putti, applied flowers on scroll molded base, Von Schierholz, ... **2,500.00**

Chocolate Set, pot, 10 1/4" h, 6 cups and saucers, yellow roses, brown to yellow shaded ground, **$250.00**

Chocolate Pot, 9 1/2" h, oval decal of basket of pink roses on side, green luster finish, "Made in Germany" mk, ... **65.00**

Creamer
3 1/2" h, spotted orange luster ground, black rim and handle, ... **25.00**
3 3/4" h, brown and green figural tree trunk, orange, yellow, and green figural woodpecker handle, ... **55.00**

Cup and Saucer, Multicolored
Bucket shape, continuous landscape, blue band w/horiz gilt beaded band above, short gilt acanthus scroll handle, 3 gilt paw feet, beaded and gilt saucer, (A), ... **1,035.00**
Dutch scene, "G. Zell S. Germany" mk, ... **25.00**
Sparrow, branches, holly and holly berries, mkd, ... **65.00**

Figure, 12 1/2", 11 3/4" h, polychrome florals on white gowns, gold medallion w/white cameo portrait, applied flowers on gilt scroll base, pr, (A), **$400.00**

Figure
4 1/2" h, little girl wearing mint green hat, white dress w/sm red and blue flowers, holding Teddy bear wearing red bow, seated on blue tasseled yellow sled, Hertwig, ... **175.00**
6" h, brown haired little boy in yellow coat, pink trousers, little girl in white cap, aqua apron, pink skirt, both hunched under grey umbrella, molded rock base, ... **90.00**
8" h x 7" l, young boy mounted on horse drinking from bucket, sm boy at side feeding chickens on base, blanc-de-chine, ... **750.00**
13" h
Seated nude boy wearing small hat, holding apple, blanket in

lap, sq base, white glaze, Karl Ens, ... **1,200.00**

Standing winged putto w/bird on finger, torch in other hand, floral sash, applied multicolored flowerheads on base, ... **1,200.00**

Flower Frog, 6 3/4" h, figural dancing nude holding drape, pierced paneled base, white glaze, ... **15.00**

Fruit Bowl, 12 3/4" l x 9" w, lavender flowers, green leaves, gold outlined reticulated border, ... **85.00**

Hair Receiver, 3 1/2" d, lg white or purple-red flowerheads, cream to lt green-tan shaded ground, ... **95.00**

Humidor, 9" h, brown, green trim, yellow doors, red roof, **$200.00**

Half Doll, 5 1/2" h, period woman, blond hair, white trimmed blue gown, holding pink and white fan, ... **125.00**

Herring Box, 2" l x 1 1/4" w, relief of lt blue herring on cov and dk blue "Heringe," c1900, ... **175.00**

Mug, 4" h, figural Bacchus head, molded purple grape and green leaf crown, black beard, orchid handle and rim, gilt accents, ... **190.00**

Plate

7 1/2" d, caneware, relief of windswept trees in center, molded interlocking loop border, tan, ... **150.00**

Lemonade Set, pitcher, 7" h, 8 tumblers, 4 7/8" h, multicolored decals, green rims, pale yellow ground, hairlines, "Zell Germany" mks, **$100.00**

8" d, "Mignon the Monk" drinking beer in center, maroon border w/gold floral and geometric overlay, shaped rim, "Zeh, Scherzer, & Co." mk, ... **220.00**

Powder Jar, 2 1/4" d x 1" h, multicolored decal of bird in foliage on cov, ... **45.00**

Relish Tray, 9 3/4" H-H x 4 1/2" w, HP sm red fruit, green foliage on border, pale blue to cream shaded ground, matte gold open handles, artist sgd, "KPM Germany" mk, Krister, ... **25.00**

Serving Dish, 11 3/4" l, sm pink flowers, green leaves in center, shaded pink border, gold rim and handle, "blue scepter Germany" mk, Krister, (A), **$30.00**

Syrup Jug, Cov, 5" h, w/underplate, 6" d, pink, white, and green bouquet on sides, green shaded ground w/shadow leaves, "GERMANY" mk, ... **40.00**

Tazza, 12 3/8" h, reticulated basket, brown tree trunk pedestal w/figure of boy on ladder w/apples, magenta pants, white shirt, figural girl standing on gilt trimmed base, pink skirt, white apron, orange top, girl seated on base wearing blue dress, pink, magenta, and yellow applied

flowers and green leaves, Von Schierholz, ... **565.00**

Teapot, 6" h, caramel luster, black spout, handle, and knob button, ... **60.00**

Tea Set, pot, 6" h, creamer, 5 3/4" h, cov sugar bowl, 4" h, green luster borders, gold rims, "Made in Germany" mks, ... **50.00**

Tray, 10" H-H, green pears, white blossoms, brown to green shaded ground, "3 Crowns Germany" mk, ... **45.00**

Vase, 8 3/4" h, dk green ground, gold trim, gold handles, Ludwig Wessel, "Imperial Bonn Germany" mark, **$150.00**

Vase, 5" h, Art Deco, paneled trumpet flowerhead shape w/2 figural ladies seated on haunches on base, white glaze, ... **20.00**

Vegetable Bowl, 9" l x 8" w, rect, band of blue interlocking florals on border, blue floral sprigs on ext, "Meissen, star in oval" mk, ... **150.00**

Wall Pocket, 5" w x 4 1/2" h, house in country scene, brown shades, ... **30.00**

GINORI

Doccia, near Florence, Italy
1737 to Present

History: In 1737 the Ginori family established a factory to manufacture porcelain and earthenware at a villa in Doccia, a few miles from Florence. Marquis Carlo Ginori, the founder, operated the factory until 1757. Carlo Ginori's management was known as the "first period."

Stencil decorated dark blue plates, teapots, coffeepots, and cups were the earliest wares. Ginori produced many examples of snuff boxes, extremely popular in the 18th century, in a variety of shapes and decorations. Sculptures and large reliefs depicting mythological or religious subjects also were made.

In 1757 Lorenzo, his son, took over. This is the "second period." Lorenzo introduced an imitation Sevres blue ground, and strong use of colors. He continued making figurals in the rococo style.

Anton Maria Fanciullacci served as director from 1791 to 1805, the "third period," changing the designs to reflect the Empire style. In 1792 the manufacture of creamware helped subsidize the production of porcelain.

Doccia was the only Italian pottery that survived and prospered during the 19th century. It remained in the control of the Ginori family. Around 1821 the Doccia factory acquired Capodimonte molds from the Naples factory and continued production. Ginori used the Old Naples mark on these examples.

Lorenzo Ginori II took charge in 1848. The firm started to make lithophanes, majolica, and egg-shell porcelains. A large number of pieces were decorated with urban scenes enclosed within a shield-shaped reserve on a white ground in the classical style. The crowned "N" mark was used on some of the wares. Industrial ceramics for the electrical industry also were manufactured on a large scale.

In 1896 the firm incorporated with Societa Ceramica Richard in Milan to become Societa Ceramica Richard-Ginori. The Art Nouveau style was introduced. In addition to modern forms and decorations, some traditional motifs such as cockerels, narrative reliefs, and tulip motifs continued to be used.

Early Ginori porcelains were frequently not marked. During the third period, the "F" or "PF" incised marks appeared. In the 19th century, "G," "Ginori," or a "N" crowned and impressed was used. The present mark is "Richard-Ginori" with a crown.

References: Arthur Lane, *Italian Porcelain*, Faber & Faber, 1954; Francesco Stazzi, *Italian Porcelain*, G.P. Putman's Sons, 1964.

Museums: Doccia Museum at Sesto Fiorentino, Florence, Italy; Fitzwilliam Museum, Cambridge, England; Metropolitan Museum of Art, New York, NY; Victoria & Albert Museum, London, England.

Box, 4 3/4" h x 5" l x 4 1/2" w, lobed, rect panels of landscapes, gilt border trim and leaf banding, gilt rose and leaf knob, ... **400.00**

Coffeepot, 11" h, HP hanging purple plums, green foliage, gold border and handle, ... **125.00**

Cream and Sugar Set, creamer, 5" h, cov sugar bowl, 4" h, blackberries, green and lt purple leaves, pale violet flowers, cream ground, gold handle, rims, and knob, "red crowned Ginori Italy Handpainted" mks, c1910, ... **110.00**

Cup and Saucer, overall green glaze, gold rims, ... **12.00**

Ewer, 10" h, applied lg red or orange rose, sm blue flowers, green foliage, rope twist handle w/applied flowerhead, ... **165.00**

Figure
10 1/2" h, parian, standing maiden w/shawl and gown, holding basket under arm, "blue crowned N" mk, ... **135.00**
15" h, standing nude pinching nipples, brown hair w/blue band, circ base, "blue crowned N" mk, ... **695.00**

Dish
4 3/4" sq, oct, multicolored transfer of floral stem, gold luster rim, "Richard Ginori Italy" mk, ... **30.00**
10 5/8" l, oval, silver shape, painted scattered flowers, iron-red and cobalt shell molded ends, dk blue scroll molded rim, (A), ... **1,135.00**

Figure, 8 1/2" h x 13" l, polychrome elderly couple seated at yellow and floral clothed dinner table, female plucking goose, man eating w/spoon, brown sleeping dog at feet, gold scroll molded base, artist sgd, ... **975.00**

Plate
8 3/4" d, HP green and red raspberries, dk red, green, and yellow leaves, gold beaded rim, artist sgd, ... **50.00**
9" d, Firenzeware, HP lg pink and ivory roses, green foliage, gold trim on shaded rose ground, wavy gold rim, artist sgd, . **35.00**
9 1/4" d, HP mauve to pink clover, green leaves, shaded brown to apple green ground, gold rim, artist sgd, ... **40.00**

Platter, 14 1/4" l, oval, silver shape, painted "Tulipano" pattern of multicolored tulips in center, shaped border w/sm flower sprays and molded rim, c1775, (A), ... **540.00**

Serving Dish, 8 1/4" sq, black transfer of boy carrying sack over shoulder, inner gilt band of leaves, gilt and blue lined indented rim, "Richard Ginori Made in Italy" mk, ... **125.00**

Soup Bowl, 7 7/8" d, gold center, brown band, gold rim, "Richard Ginori Italy" mark, set of 12, $240.00

Sugar Sifter, 6" h, black bat printed classic rural scenes in black and gilt frame, gilt loop and dot border, rose knob, ... **95.00**

Tankard, 10 1/4" h, HP red poinsettia, shaded green ground, gold dbl handle w/mask terminal and rim, artist sgd, ... **645.00**

Tea Caddy, 4 1/2" h, sloped shoulder, "Paradise" pattern, HP red-headed bird w/yellow and lt blue feathers, perched on branch, scattered flowerheads, gilt lines on cov, "Richard Ginori Italy" mk, ... **40.00**

Teapot
4 5/8" h, "King Collection," blueberry and butterfly motif, molding on body and cov, gilt dentil rim on cov, ... **400.00**
6 1/2" h, wreath of green ivy and brown stem on shoulder, scattered green ivy leaves, "crowned Richard Ginori Italy" mk, ... **35.00**
7 1/2" h, painted green clover, raised gold ribbons and bows around body, cov, and handle, ... **275.00**

Tray, 8" l x 6 1/4" w, oval, 2 brown and orange roosters in clouds, lg tree and sprigs, shaped rim, "crowned Richard Ginori Italy" mk, ... **40.00**

Trio, cup, saucer, plate, 7 5/8" d, "Italian Fruit" pattern, ... **45.00**

Vase
8 1/4" h, flattened shape, oval opening, 2 flattened serpent

handles on shoulder, faceted body, clear glaze over white earthenware body, c1927, ... **650.00**

10" h, amphora shape w/2 wide handles, yellow and gold stylized flowers, leaves, and stems on alternating cobalt or white horiz bands, "blue crowned Ginori" mks, pr, ... **850.00**

18" h, ball body, long trumpet neck, flared rim and ft, polychrome tin glazed classic motifs of winged grotesques, "blue crowned Ginori" mk, ... **365.00**

GOEBEL

Rodental, Bavaria, Germany
1871 to Present

History: In 1871 Franz and William Goebel, father and son, applied for a permit to manufacture porcelain in the village of Oeslau near the city of Coburg. When Duke Ernst II of Saxe-Coburg intervened, the permit finally was granted in 1879. The firm, F.D. & W. Goebel Porcelain Works, began manufacturing dinner services, milk pitchers, beer steins, and egg cups.

When Franz died in 1909, William expanded the porcelain dinnerware and figurine business into an export-oriented concern. Max-Louis, William's son, took over in 1912 when William died. Max-Louis introduced many new porcelain figurine designs and added a ceramic figurine line as well. Frieda, wife of Max-Louis, Franz, son of Frieda and Max-Louis, and Dr. Eugene Stocke, Frieda's brother, assumed control when Max-Louis died in 1929.

Franz Goebel first saw Sister Maria Innocentia Hummel's sketches in 1934. In March 1935 the first "M.I. Hummel" figure was made. These were an immediate success, especially in America.

During World War II the Goebel works concentrated on the manufacture of dinnerware for the domestic market. A few figurines were made. When the United States Military Government of Germany lifted the wartime embargo and gave permission for production and exportation of "M.I. Hummel" figurines and other objects in 1946, a rapid recovery was accomplished by this firm.

When Franz died in 1969, the management of the company transferred to Wilhelm, his son, and Ulrich Stocke, Eugene's son. They continued expansion of the company and acquisition of other factories.

Today the Goebel factories manufacture high quality porcelain dinnerware for the home and export markets. In addition to the popular Hummel series, they manufacture figurine series that include Disney characters, birds, animals, and Friar Tuck monks. A collectors' plate series also is made. A wide variety of Friar Tuck and Cardinal Tuck versions have been made including salt and pepper shakers, cookie jars or biscuit barrels, banks, and cruets.

Marks: There are six trademarks by Goebel. They are called "Trademark 1," "Trademark 2," etc. and also referred to as "crown," "bee," "stylized bee," "3-line," "Goebel bee" and "Goebel." Trademark 1, the crown trademark, is the oldest; Goebel, or Trademark 6, is the current mark.

Trademark information is generally stamped on the bottom of the piece. Mold numbers, and often the year the item was sculpted, are incised on the bottom. Mold numbers are an accurate method of identifying pieces.

References: Eric Ehrmann, *Hummel*, Portfolio Press Corp. 1976; John F. Hotchkiss, *Hummel Art 11*, Wallace Homestead, 1981; Thomas E. Hudgeons, III, Ed., *The Official Price Guide to Hummel Figurines and Plates*, House of Collectibles, 1980; Carl F. Luckey, *Hummel Figurines and Plates, 5th Edition*, Books Americana, 1984; Robert L. Miller, *M.I. Hummel: The Golden Anniversary Album*, Portfolio Press, 1984; Wolfgang Schwatlo, *W. Goebel Porzellan, Part I: Figurines*, Sammlerverlag Schwatlo GmbH, 1996; Lorie A. Wuttke, *Fired Up Over Friar Tuck*, *Antique Trader Weekly*, December 17, 1997; Rocky Rockholt, *Goebel Figurines & Prints by Charlot Byj*, Schiffer Publications, 2001

Collectors' Clubs: Friar Tuck Collectors' Club, P.O. Box 262, Owego, NY 13827, Membership: $18.00, quarterly newsletter; Goebel Networkers, P.O. Box 396, Lemoyne, PA 17043, $15.00 per year, quarterly newsletter.

Museum: Goebel Museum, Tarrytown, NY.

Bank

3" h x 5" l, figural white pig w/green shamrocks, ... **15.00**

4 1/4" h, figural cottage, orange roof, white house w/brown timbers, ... **10.00**

5 3/4" h, seated long haired dachshund, orange-brown w/grey muzzle, black nose, "Goebel W. Germany" mk, ... **50.00**

8 1/2" h, Co-Boy, "Pete the Pirate," **295.00**

Candleholder, 3 1/2" h, figural angel playing guitar, red tinged wings, green streaked robe, ... **15.00**

Cookie Jar, 9 3/4" h, Friar Tuck, brown robe, ... **285.00**

*Cream and Sugar Set, creamer, 4" h, sugar bowl, 4 3/4" h, tray, 7" l, Friar Tuck, brown robes, flesh faces, brown lined rim on tray, "blue V and full bee" mark, **$125.00***

Creamer

4" h, Friar Tuck, full bee, TMK-2 mk, ... **10.00**

4 1/2" h, figural elephant seated on haunches, lt blue, TMK-1 mk, ... **112.00**

5" h, figural seated cat, turquoise eyes, ... **58.00**

Cruet Stand, 3 3/4" h x 5" w, figural golfer, red cap, lt blue trousers, holding brown golf club, crossed golf clubs on base, green platform, "V bee" mk, ... **375.00**

Cup and Saucer, HP Art Decor woman's face on ext of cup, yellow borders, ... **190.00**

Decanter, 10 1/2" h, Friar Tuck, full bee, TMK-2 mk, ... **58.00**

Egg Cup, 2" h, cardinal, red robe, "V-sm bee, W. Germany" mk, E95/4, ... **125.00**

Figure

2 3/4" h, cardinal, red robe, ... **235.00**

3 1/2" h, angel wearing white fringed blue robe, holding lantern, "ROB412," **35.00**

3 3/4" h, orange glazed terrier, head turned toward tail, full bee mk, ... **80.00**

4" h

4 1/2" w, "Off-Key," Charlotte Byj, ... **50.00**

"Butch," paw extended, black and white, "bee in V, W. Goebel, Western Germany" mk, ... **285.00**

4 1/4" h, "Plenty of Nothing," Charlotte Byj, "BYJ27," **45.00**

4 1/2" h
"E-e-eek," Charlotte, Byj, 3 line mk, ... **100.00**
Standing schoolgirl, orange-red dress w/horseshoe designs, brown shoes, ... **15.00**
4 1/2" l, 2 white mice seated on yellow and green ear of corn, ... **30.00**

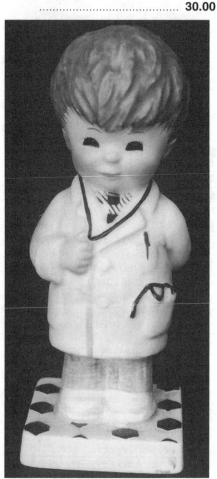

Figure, 5 1/4" h, "Red Top M.D.," Charlotte Byj, **$125.00**

5" h, nativity, Joseph, Mary, and baby Jesus, multicolored, "HX-152-68," **50.00**
5 1/2" h
Little girl seated on rock reading book, red jacket, green trousers w/red bottoms, blue bird on hat brim, Nasha, c1935, ... **140.00**
"Sleepyhead," blue outfit, Charlotte Byj, ... **110.00**
"The Stolen Kiss," red haired boy kissing blond girl, "Charlotte Byj 18," **65.00**
6" h
Austrian girl, polychrome, ... **100.00**

Standing blond cherub and white lamb wearing gold bell, blue V and full bee mk, ... **50.00**
6 1/2" h, St. Joseph, standing figure, blue robe, brown belted sash, holding lantern, ... **40.00**
8" h, goblin stirring pot, tall blue hat, white beard, yellow jacket, blue heart on pot, 3 line TMK-4 mk, ... **185.00**
8 1/2" h
"Afternoon Tea," brown haired period woman, yellow gown, holding purse, ... **100.00**
Parrot perched on branch, green body w/red slashes, orange-yellow face w/blue accents, bee in V mk, ... **175.00**
9 1/2" h
"Ball Ballet," Olympic female athlete holding ball in outstretched hand, extended rt arm, circ base, ... **600.00**
Pierrot holding pantaloon sides, yellow outfit w/geometric designs, black outlined white ruffled collar, peaked hat on base, "imp and blue crowned GW" mks, ... **550.00**
9 3/4" h, rearing stallion, white glaze, "blue V bee, W. Goebel, W. Germany" mk, ... **125.00**
Flower Frog, 10" h, Art Deco young girl wearing stepped ballet skirt, stepped circ base, white glaze, ... **150.00**
Game Tureen, 6 1/2" h x 8" l, yellow-brown body, white tusked brown boar's head knob, stamped "Goebel W. Germany" mk, ... **75.00**
Honey Pot, 4 1/2" h, figural black and yellow bee, ... **350.00**
Juice Reamer, 6 1/2" d, figural harlequin face, mint green rim and hat, red hearts on cheeks, c1920, ... **80.00**
Jug
2 1/4" h, Friar Tuck, ... **30.00**
5 1/2" h, Friar Tuck, ... **35.00**
Lamp, 6" h, figural Art Deco woman's bust, orange cap, yellow pierced head band, green shaded eyes, c1920, ... **275.00**
Mug
5" h, figural bar keeper, red hat, green vest, brown trousers, holding stein, ... **75.00**
5 1/4" h, Friar Tuck, brown robe, full bee mk, ... **80.00**
Music Box, 7" h, "Skater's Waltz" pattern, Charlotte Byj, ... **350.00**

Mustard Pot, 3 3/4" h, figural Cardinal, ... **180.00**
Perfume Lamp, 5 1/2" h, seated Scottie dog, ... **250.00**
Pitcher
6 1/2" h, Friar Tuck, ... **375.00**
7 1/2" h, figural clown, black hat, orange collar, lg blue buttons, ... **135.00**
Plaque, 9 1/4" h, Art Deco style bust of brown haired woman, orange-red hat w/purple ribbon, tan dress w/sm red and yellow flowers, blue-green scarf, Nasha, c1935, ... **175.00**
Shakers
2" l, figural walking elephants, grey, "V and bee" mk, pr, ... **25.00**
2 1/2" h
Figural boy wearing green cap, lt blue jacket, brown lederhosen, figural girl wearing green hat, yellow and black vest, red skirt, small bee and V, pr, ... **15.00**
Munich monk holding red heart or blue-grey stein, yellow centered black robe, "full bee and V," pr, ... **40.00**
Storage Jar, 5" h, Friar Tuck, ... **21.00**
Sugar Bowl, 4 1/2" h, Friar Tuck, full bee, TMK-2 mk, ... **25.00**
Teapot, 7 1/2" h, 4 teacups, white ground w/tan and lt brown edging, white grapes, tan vines, lt coral, yellow, and blue flowers on white center band, ... **250.00**
Wall Mask, 7 1/2" h, bust of brown, curly haired woman, blue eye shadow, red tinged flower on shoulder, ... **465.00**

Goldscheider 1845 - 1897

GOLDSCHEIDER PORZELLAN 1927

GOLDSCHEIDER

Vienna, Austria
1885 to Present

History: Friedrich Goldscheider founded the Goldscheider Porcelain and Majolica Factory in 1885. Goldscheider's family owned a factory in Pilsen, Czechoslovakia, along with decorating shops in Vienna and Carlsbad. Decorative earthenwares and porcelains, faience, terra cotta, and figures were made.

Regina Goldscheider and Alois Goldscheider, her brother-in-law, ran the firm from 1897 until 1918. They made figures along with sculptured vases in the Art Nouveau style. Regina's sons, Walter and Marcel, took control in 1920 and adopted styles prevailing in Vienna during the 1920s.

The factories experienced several name changes both before and after World War I and II. Following Hitler's invasion of Austria, the family left and settled in Trenton, New Jersey, in the early 1940s. They established a factory in Trenton and made art objects and tablewares.

After World War II, Marcel Goldscheider established a pottery in Staffordshire, England, to manufacture bone china figures and earthenware. The company's mark was a stamp of Marcel's signature.

Figure

8" h, young girl wearing checked orange dress and hat, holding umbrella, looking down at black and white dog on base, "Goldscheider, Made in Austria" mk, ... **375.00**

11 1/2" h, Art Deco style, standing lady w/black bra top, holding edges of black gown w/blue shaded peacock eyes, circ stepped base, "Goldscheider, Wien, Made in Austria Lorenzl," mks, ... **1,850.00**

12" h
  Art Deco
  Nude lady, flesh colored, rotating spread arms, circ base, Lorenzl, ... **3,000.00**
  Woman holding lg floppy hat on head, grey lace layered dress, domed circ base, Lorenzl, ... **950.00**
  Blond lady in sweeping green dress w/black stripes, holding brown hat, sgd "Dakon," Austria, ... **1,750.00**

13" h
  Art Deco lady, purple shorts and bow scarf, pink shirt, hands in pocket, sgd "Dakon," "Goldscheider Austria" mk, ... **3,000.00**
  Dancer holding edges of green gown w/magenta floral accents, Austria, ... **1,300.00**
  Period woman holding basket of fruit under arm, offering bunch of grapes, red, blue, and green flowered gown, mauve underdress, "Goldscheider Wien 3862" mk, ... **1,000.00**

14" h
  Lady wearing yellow dress, hand on hip, reaching for basket on ground, floppy hat, Austria, ... **1,350.00**
  Young girl w/bonnet, white gown, lt blue shoes, 4 white and lt yellow chicks on base, "Persuir" on brown textured base, imp mk, early 20th C, chips, ... **750.00**

15 3/8" h, kneeling nude woman, hands on head, HP terra cotta, mkd, ... **475.00**

Figure, 16" h, white glaze, sgd "K. Lorenzl," $3,250.00

16" h
  Lady wearing red gown, lg floppy hat, white borzoi w/brown spots, Austria, ... **3,500.00**
  Standing and reclining Russian Wolfhounds, white w/black markings, "green Goldscheider Made in Austria" mk, ... **595.00**

18 1/2" h, bust of country girl, white lace cap w/blue trim, blue drape gown, white bodice, waisted socle base, "Friedrich Goldscheider Wien" mk, ... **925.00**

19" h, "Bat Girl," arms extended holding blue wings of dress, black hair, pink florals, "Lorenzl Austria" mk, ... **4,750.00**

Figure, 19" h x 12 1/2" w, lt brown bodice and cap w/blue and turquoise "jewels," raised "Carlotta" on brown base, sgd "Dupre, Goldscheider," c1880, $4,000.00

Mask

9 1/4" h, woman's face, brown shaded skin, brown tinged green leaves around head w/blue molded grapes for hair and at throat, "Goldscheider Wien Made in Austria" mk, ... **325.00**

11 1/4" h x 9" w, Art Deco style woman's face, white ground, brown curly hair, holding black half mask in hand, "red Goldscheider Wien Made in Austria" mk, ... **1,950.00**

Vase

16 3/4" h, flattened profile, relief of seated Art Nouveau woman holding branch, hammered brass colored glaze, mkd, ... **1,500.00**

22" h, terra cotta, 2 modeled children climbing simulated tree trunk, brown streaked glaze, tapered base, ... **1,765.00**

W. H. GOSS
c1862

GOSS AND CRESTED WARE

Stoke-On-Trent, England
1858-1930

History: William Henry Goss founded the Goss China Company in 1858 at Stoke-on-

Trent. Goss began producing a fine grade parian that was used for figural groups, busts of famous people both past and present, pierced baskets, and a variety of other items. Terra cotta tobacco jars and wine vases decorated with transfers also were produced. Goss developed a method of embedding colored glass into the parian body to make "jewelled" vases, patenting the technique in 1872. Fine tea services appeared in his catalog by 1880.

In 1883 Adolphus, William's son, joined the firm. William's aggressiveness helped launch the company into new and profitable fields. It was William who introduced crested china.

Victorian England had increased leisure time and great accessibility to the seacoast and resort areas. These vacation sites were perfect for the introduction of inexpensive souvenir items. Adolphus, much to the chagrin of William, produced and marketed the now famous white glazed souvenir pieces complete with enameled decorations and coats of arms of various towns and resorts. The technique was simple. A paper transfer was applied to the glazed body, and the colors were hand painted in the design. These heraldic souvenirs were an instant success. Shops were established in the resort areas to sell Goss crested china. Other factories quickly imitated the Goss crested ware.

In 1893 Goss China began producing miniature full color buildings, duplicating every detail of the original buildings from which they were modeled. Expansion was necessary to meet the demands for the Goss products. Victor and Huntley, Adolphus' sons, became partners in 1900. Goss china even published its own journal, *Goss Records*, to promote its products.

The company suffered during the Great Depression. Its assets were sold to Cauldon Potteries in 1929. Cauldon began manufacturing figurines of young girls similar to the Royal Doulton figurines. Coalport China Co. purchased the rights to Goss in 1945; Ridgway and Adderly took control in 1954. The company currently is part of the Royal Doulton organization.

Other manufacturers of crested ware in England were Arcadian, Carlton China, Grafton China, Savoy China, Shelley, and Willow Art. In Germany, Gemma also made crested wares.

References: Sandy Andrews, *Crested China*, Milestone Publications, 1980; Sandy Andrews & Nicholas Pine, *1985 Price Guide to Crested China*, Milestone Publications, 1985; John Galpin, *Goss China*, 1972, published by author; Nicholas Pine, *Goss China: Arms, Decorations & Their Values, Rev. Ed.* Milestone Publications, 1982; Nicholas Pine, *The Concise Encyclopedia & Price Guide To Goss China*, Milestone Publications, 1989; Lynda Pine, *A Collectors Guide To Goss & Crested Wares*, Miller Books, 2001.

Collectors' Clubs: Goss Collectors Club, The Secretary, 4 Khasiaberry, Walnut Tree, Milton Keynes, MK7 7DP, England. Membership:£18, monthly newsletter; The Crested Circle, 42 Douglas Road, Tolworth Surbiton, Surely KT6 7SA, England. Membership:£7. Bimonthly magazine and *Crested Circle* annual magazine. This circle covers the products of W.H. Goss, Arcadian, Carlton, Grafton, Shelley, and Savoy factories and commemoratives from the different factories.

Collecting Hints: Early Goss pieces tend to be heavier and less perfectly rounded than later pieces, gilding tends to come off easily if rubbed, and a heavy mold line is often apparent. By 1890 to 1900, the molding technique was improved and resulted in a thinner, more precise mold. Gilding also was of better quality and did not rub off easily. Greater color and more precision was used in the application of the coats of arms transfers.

Atwick Roman Vase, 2 1/4" h, crest of "Queen Anne Boleyn," "W.H. Goss" mk, ... **16.00**

Avebury Celtic Urn, 4 1/8" h, crest of "Devizes," Goss mk, ... **110.00**

Ball Cream Jug, 2" h, blue forget-me-nots forming "T" under spout, "W.H. Goss" mk, ... **50.00**

Bali Vase, 1 7/8" h, crest of "Aberdeen," "Wm. Holmes & Co." mk, ... **8.00**

Beachy Head Lighthouse, 4 3/8" h, multicolored crest, Sussex China, ... **30.00**

Beaker
1 1/2" h, 3 sm feet, crest of Germany, Goss mk, ... **8.00**
1 7/8" h, 3 sm feet, crest of "Exeter," Grafton, ... **9.00**
4 1/2" h, "Of creamie clay the potter fashioned me, That I with creamie milk might filled be, With milk to make fayre ladyes face more fayre, And give strong man more strength to doo and dare," "black W.H. Goss gosshawk" mk, ... **40.00**

Bobby's Helmet, 2 1/2" h, crest of "Dover," Swan Company, ... **58.00**

Bouloge Milk Pail, 2 7/8" h, crest of "Willton," Goss, ... **65.00**

Box of Matches, 2 7/8" l, crest of Littlehampton, Shelley, ... **70.00**

British Submarine, 4 7/8" l, crest of "Exeter," Carlton, ... **190.00**

Bud Vase, 3 1/2" h, crest of "Hastings," MOP finish, "Carlton China" mk, ... **5.00**

Burn's Chair, 3 1/2" h, crest of "Barry," Shelley, ... **15.00**

Cardinal Beaufort's Candlestick, 6" h, crest of "Harrismith O.R.C.," Goss, ... **220.00**

Cauldron, 2 3/8" h, crest of "Hobart," "Willow Art Longton" mk, ... **15.00**

Celtic Urn, 2 1/8" h, "Deedham" crest and "Arms Of Henry Navarre King of France," multicolored, "Model of Celtic Urn Found at Gerrans Cornwall," Goss, ... **30.00**

Chair, 3 1/2" h, "MODEL OF BURNS CHAIR" on front, crest of "West Australia," "Leadbeater Art China Longton" mk, ... **10.00**

Charger, 14" d, parian, relief of arms of Canterbury Cathedral, "Manners Makyth Men," yellow, red, and blue-green accents, W.H. Goss, .. **700.00**

Cheese Dish, 2 1/4" w, crest of "Clacton-on-Sea," Gemma, ... **23.00**

Chester Vase, 2 1/2" h, crest of "Harrow," "W.H. Goss" mk, ... **18.00**

Christchurch Ancient Bowl, 2 3/8" d, crest of "City of Wells," Goss, . **24.00**

Cinerary Urn, 2 1/2" h, crest of "Guildford," multicolored, Shelley, ... **18.00**

Coffee Can, 2 1/4" h, Welsh hat, crown w/3 feathers, oak bough and sickle, ... **65.00**

Colchester Vase, 1 3/4" h, crest of "Hastings," "Model of the Famous Colchester Vase in the Museum," "W.H. Goss" mk, ... **8.00**

Cream Jug
2" h, crest of "Goring On Thames," "W.H. Goss" mk, ... **10.00**
2 1/4" h, "Shakespeare's Arms," "W.H. Goss" mk, ... **16.00**
2 1/2" h, crest of "Birmingham," Foley, ... **20.00**
5" h, lobed, crest of "Nova Scotia," Old Foley, ... **75.00**

Cup and Saucer
"Blackpool" crest, multicolored, Willow mk, ... **19.00**
"Dalbeatie" crest on cup and saucer, multicolored, Goss, ... **25.00**
"Edinburgh" crest, multicolored, ... **8.00**
"Northampton" crest, multicolored, Goss, ... **10.00**
"Norwich" crest, multicolored, Shelley, ... **80.00**
"St. Ives" crest, multicolored, Goss, ... **25.00**
"St. Mawgen" crest, multicolored, ... **25.00**

Dish, 5 1/2" l x 4" w, crest of "Bristol England," gold accents, Shelley, ... **35.00**

Plate

7" d

Black printed "Llanwyrtyd Bridge," gold rim, "W.H. Goss" mk, ... **30.00**

Crest of "Bath," pierced rim, unmkd, ... **7.00**

Portland Vase, 1 3/4" h, crest of "London County Council," "W.H. Goss, Model of the Portland Vase in the British Museum" mks, ... **15.00**

Pot

2 1/2" h, crest of "Hastings," "Maxim China" mk, ... **8.00**

Crest of "Ramsey Isle of Man," Arcadian, ... **12.00**

Poy Holder, 2 3/8" h, 5 tube, crest of "Bournemouth," **8.00**

Puff Box, 3 1/4" d, crest of "Scarborough," **25.00**

Raleigh Ancient Crock, 1 1/8" h, crest of "Earl of Leicester," **28.00**

Reading Jug, 3 1/4" h, crest of "Leicestershire," "Goss and Model of 15th Cent Jug Dug in Munster St. Reading" on base, ... **10.00**

Red Cross Van, 3 3/8" l, crest of "Birmingham," Clays, England, ... **68.00**

Queen Victoria Slipper, 4" l, crest of "Sidmouth," blue trim, "Model exact size of first shoes worn by Queen Victoria-H.M. The late Queen (Who died Jan 22nd 1901) Made at Sidmouth in 1819," "black W.H. Goss" mk, ... **35.00**

Roman Bowl, 2" h, crest of "Honiton," unmkd, ... **10.00**

Roman Ewer, 2 3/4" h, crest of "Douglas," "Goss and Roman Ewer From Original in Hospitium Found at York" on base, ... **7.00**

Roman Pot, 2" h, crest of "Shoreham," "Model of Roma Pot Found At Ifold Vill Goss" mk, ... **10.00**

Roman Vase, 1 1/2" h, crest of "Floreat Etona," "W.H. Goss, Model of Roman Vase in Lewes Castle" mks, ... **10.00**

Roman Vase Found Near Canterbury, 2 3/4" h, crest of "West Bromich," Arcadian, ... **12.00**

Sack Vase, 1 3/4" h, crest of "Tunbridge Wells," "W.H. Goss" mk, ... **25.00**

Sandwich Plate, 6" d, crest of "Seal Of The Corporation Of Dredgers Of Whisable 1793," "W.H. Goss" mk, ... **15.00**

Scarboro Kettle, 2 3/4" h, crest of "Arms of Newton Abbot," "W.H. Goss, Gosshawk" mk, ... **18.00**

Sevres Vase, 3 3/4" h, crest of "Strathpeffer Spa," gold trim, "Model of a Sevres Vase, Shelley" mk, $75.00

Shoe, 4" l, crest of "Scarborough," unmkd, ... **6.00**

Silchester Vase

2" h

Crest of "City of Peterborough," "W.H. Goss" mk, ... **8.00**

Crest of "Swansea," "Model of Vase From Silchester in Reading Museum, W.H. Goss" mk, ... **18.00**

2 1/8" h, crest of "Teignmouth," Arcadian, ... **12.00**

Sofa, 3 1/8" l, crest of "Town of Alcester," Florentine, ... **23.00**

Spanish Jug, 2 1/4" h, crest of "Weymouth and Melcombe Regis," "W.H. Goss" mk, ... **14.00**

St. Ives Ancient Church Font, 3 1/2" h, crests of "St. Buryan," and "Lamorna," glazed, Goss, ... **55.00**

St. Paul's Cathedral, 5 1/2" h, crest of "City of London," Grafton, ... **60.00**

Stockton Ancient Salt Pot, 2 7/8" h, crest of "South-on-Sea," Goss, **28.00**

Sugar Bowl, 2" h, crest of "Whitley Bay," gold outlined crimped rim, "black Willow Art China Longton," **15.00**

Tankard, 2 1/2" h, crest of "Broadstairs," "Willow Art China" mk, ... **50.00**

Teapot

2" h x 3 1/2" w, crest of "Liverpool," **45.00**

5" h x 9 1/4" w, crest of "Hamilton Ontario, Canada," Fairy Shape, Shelley-Wildman, ... **130.00**

Tea Set, pot, 4 3/8" h, cream jug, 2 5/8" h, sugar bowl w/underplate, 1 3/8" h, crests of "Eastbourne," unmkd, ... **45.00**

Teapot, 5 1/8" h, Bagware, "Buckinghamshire" and "Arms of Wycombe" crests, turquoise handle, "Published By Symond's Brothers High Wycombe" and Goss marks, $195.00

Toothpick Holder, 1 1/2" h, crest of "Buxton," unmkd, ... **10.00**

Trench Mortar Gun, 3" l, crest of "Crowborough," Arcadian, ... **38.00**

Tulip Vase, 3 Tubes

2 1/2" h, crest of "Torquay," Carlton, ... **15.00**

3" h, crest of "City of Bristol," "Dolphin Bazaar Bristol" mk, ... **8.00**

Tyge, 2" h, crest of "City of London, " "GEMMA" mk, ... **35.00**

Urn, 3 1/2" h, crest of "Bath," Grafton China, ... **18.00**

Vase

1 3/4" h, crest of "Southam, Near Leamington in Warwickshire," Arcadian, ... **15.00**

2" h

Crest of "City of Bristol," unmkd, ... **10.00**

Crest of "Paisley," "W.H. Goss" mk, ... **9.00**

Crest of "Southampton," Aracadian, ... **2.00**

2 3/8" h

Crest of "Cwmllynfell," gilt rim, Balmoral China, ... **8.00**

Crest of "Paignton in Devon," "Model of Sacred Vase From Temple in Tibet" on base, Shelley, ... **10.00**

2 1/2" h, crest of "Arms of Lymington," Carlton, ... **30.00**

2 3/4" h, 2 vert handles, crest of "Dublin," gold trim, ... **8.00**

3" h

Sq handles, crest of "Bournemouth," **12.00**

Two loop handles, crest of "Southend on Sea," "Willow Art China Longton" mk, ... **8.00**

3 1/8" h, figural hand holding tulip, crest of "Blackpool," gold trim, "Willow Art China Longton" mk, ... **5.00**

4 3/8" h, crest of "Dover," Goss, ... **10.00**

Walmer Vase, 2 3/4" h, crest of "Herne Bay," "Model of Roman Vase Found at Walmer Lodge, W.H. Goss" mk, ... **12.00**

Water Can, 3" h, crest of "Blackpool," **10.00**

Water Pitcher

3 1/8" h, crest of "Gillingham," **20.00**

6 1/4" h, crest of "Arms of Wales," gold trim, unmkd, ... **125.00**

Welsh Hat, 2 7/8" d, crest of "Towyn," Goss, ... **38.00**

Welsh Leek, 3 1/2" h, crest of "Tenby," Goss, ... **68.00**

Whelk Shell, 3 3/4" l, crest of "Saffron Walden," Florentine, ... **25.00**

Worcester Jug, 2 1/2" h, crest of "Ealing," **30.00**

Zeppelin Bomb, 2 1/2" h, "Model of German Bomb Dropped on Bury St. Edmonds From a Zeppelin, April 1915," crest of "Swanage," Goss, ... **45.00**

MADE IN

Zuid Holland

c 1897

GOUDA

Gouda, Holland
17th Century to Present

History: Gouda and the surrounding areas of Holland have been producing Dutch pottery wares since the 17th century. Originally Delft-type tin glazed earthenwares were manufactured along with the clay smokers' pipes.

When the production of the clay pipes declined, the pottery makers started producing art pottery wares with brightly colored decorations. These designs were influenced by the Art Nouveau and Art Deco movements. Stylized florals, birds, and geometrics were the favorite motifs, all executed in bold, clear colors. Some Gouda pieces have a "cloisonne" appearance.

Other pottery workshops in the Gouda region included Arnhem, Plazuid, Regina, Schoonhoven, and Zenith. Utilitarian tartan wares, vases, miniatures, and large outdoor garden ornaments also were included in the product line.

References: Gene Ritvo, *The World of Gouda Pottery*, Font & Center Publishers, 1998.

Reproduction Alert: With the recent renewal of interest in Art Nouveau and Art Deco examples, reproductions of earlier Gouda pieces now are on the market. These are difficult to distinguish from the originals.

Bottle, 10" h, figural, Dutch boy, black cap, red striped shirt, hands in black trousers w/yellow buttons, yellow wooden shoes or Dutch girl in white cap, flowered blouse, black jacket, flowered waist, black apron over red and blue striped skirt, holding "BOLS" bottle, c1930s, "Zenith" mks, pr, (A), ... **300.00**

Bowl, 14" d, "Feller" pattern, lg brown abstract shields, yellow sunray design, turquoise, cobalt, and tan abstracts, matte glaze, "Feller Plaz, Holland" mk, ... **300.00**

Bud Vase, 4" h, flattened base, long, narrow neck, stylized purple, blue, black, and green puffy geometrics, black and dk red ground, gloss glaze, pr, (A), ... **460.00**

Candlestick, 16 3/8" h, tapered trumpet base, lg drip pan, exaggerated handle, mottled matte green w/blue bands, green leaves, blue tulips, "blue Damascus, house, Holland" mks, pr, (A), ... **660.00**

Card Tray, 10" l, rect, gloss design of red windmill on green shore next to lt blue lake on int, abstract green and brown border designs, "Made in Zuid Holland PW" mk, (A), ... **248.00**

Chamberstick, 5 1/2" d, Art Nouveau style dk blue outlined rust, orange, green, and yellow geometrics, black bkd, matte finish, dk blue handle, "BEEK PLAZUID, AK GOUDA HOLLAND, house" mk, ... **70.00**

Charger

11" d, multicolored bird on branch, multicolored matte finish, "Bejo GL" mk, c1920, ... **450.00**

20" d, lavender, red, navy blue, gold and white slip swirling paisley and floral designs, Henri Breetvelt, PZH Gouda, (A), ... **2,310.00**

Coffeepot, 8 1/2" h, Turkish style, dk orange, mustard yellow, dk blue and green geometrics, gunmetal grey ground, matte finish, (A), ... **500.00**

Figure, 3 3/4" h, stylized lamb, irid streaked brown, blue base, .. **165.00**

Floor Vase, 24" h, amphora shape, gloss glazed purple, magenta and blue wild tulips, green and brown stylized leaves, hunter green handles, dk blue circ base, "Zuid Holland" mk, (A), ... **2,200.00**

Vase, 9 1/4" h, gold outlined lt blue, rust, cobalt, and yellow geometrics, rust, cobalt, and turquoise striped base, matte finish, "Grotius house" mk, $265.00

Gravy Boat, 8" w, w/attached undertray, scattered floral bouquets of red, blue, yellow, and green florals, cream ground, "N.V. KONINK PLATEEL BAKRERY ZUID-HOLLAND GOUDA A PLAZUID" mk, ... **20.00**

Jar, Cov, 15 1/2" h, "Maryke" pattern, lg lavender or gold florals, med blue-green spattered dots, ivory ground, black wave type design on base, matte finish, "Maryke, Koninkylk, Royal Holland" mk, (A), ... **550.00**

Jardiniere

6" d x 4 3/4" h, center band of multicolored petaled flowerheads on orange and gold swirled ground between blue teardrop bands, black top and base, matte finish, "GOUDA ZUMER" mk, 1921, ... **185.00**

11 1/4" d x 10 1/2" h, stylized purple pansy, green swirl stems, black outlined cream, brown, and green swirls, med green leaf collar, gloss finish, house, Zuid Holland, ... **995.00**

Pipe Rack, 12" w, shield shape, lavender, purple, magenta, yellow, and green pansy and foliage, turquoise and plum purple ground, gloss finish, "Ivora Gouda Holland" mk, repaired chip, (A), ... **245.00**

CFH
GDM
FRANCE
c1891

H & C°
L
c1885

HAVILAND

Limoges, France
1842 to Present

History: David and Daniel Haviland, two brothers, had a china import business in New York. When traveling to France in search of china, David decided to remain in Limoges, the leading center for the manufacture of pottery. By 1842 David and his family were firmly established in Limoges. David supervised the purchasing, designing, and decorating of stock for export from several Limoges companies. In 1865 he acquired a factory in Limoges to produce porcelains directly. Instead of sending whiteware to Paris to be decorated, David established studios at his own factory. He hired and trained local decorators.

In 1852 Robert Barclay Haviland sent his son, Charles Field Haviland, to learn the business from Uncle David. Charles Field married into the Alluaud family, who owned the Casseaux works. When Charles Field took over, the mark used on the whiteware was "CFH."

Charles Edward and Theodore, sons of David Haviland, entered the firm in 1864. By 1878 the Haviland factory was the largest in the Limousin District. When David died in 1879, the firm passed into the hands of his two sons. A difference of opinion in 1891 led to the liquidation of the old firm. Charles Edward produced china under the "Haviland et Cie" name. After Charles died in 1922, his firm lost significance and went out of business in 1931. Theodore started his own factory, "La Porcelaine Theodore Haviland," which produced china until 1952.

In 1875 Charles and Theodore Haviland founded a faience studio in Paris that was headed by Bracquemond, the famous engraver. This Auteuil Studio gathered the greatest artists and decorators of the period. By the end of the 19th century, the entire French china production was influenced by this studio's output.

William David, son of Theodore, took over in 1919. William David's three sons, Theodore II, Harold, and Frederick, eventually became involved. Members of the Haviland family, all direct descendants from the founder David Haviland, always have directed the French firm in Limoges. Each has chosen to retain U.S. citizenship.

Marks: Until 1870 only one back mark was used for the "H & Co." or the Haviland & Co. After that time, two back marks were used—one for the factory where a piece was made and the other for the factory in which the piece was decorated. Department stores, hotels, railroads, and restaurants that placed special orders received individual marks.

All the whiteware marks were under the glaze. The decoration back marks were over the glaze. Various colorings used in the back marks designated different periods in Haviland factory production. Pattern names often appeared on many older sets between the whiteware and decorating marks.

References: Jean d'Albis & Celeste Romanet, *La Porcelain de Limoges*, Editions Sous le Vent, 1980; Mary Frank Gaston, *Haviland Collectibles & Objects of Art*, Collector Books, 1984; Mary Frank Gaston, *The Collector's Encyclopedia of Limoges Porcelain*, Collector Books, 1980; G.T. Jacobson, *Haviland China: Volume One & Volume Two*, Wallace-Homestead, 1979; Arlene Schleiger, *Two Hundred Patterns of Haviland China, Books I-V*, published privately, Omaha; Nora Travis, *Haviland China, The Age of Elegance, Revised 2nd Edition*, Schiffer Books, 1998; Harriet Young, *Grandmother's Haviland*, Wallace-Homestead, 1970; Nora Travis, *Evolution of Haviland China Design*, Schiffer Publishing, 2000.

Collectors' Club: Haviland Collectors Internationale Foundation, Dept. AT 96, P.O. Box 802462, Santa Clarita, CA 91380-2462, Membership: $30.00, Quarterly newsletter, Annual convention.

Collecting Hints: The term "blank" refers to the whiteware piece before any pattern decoration has been applied. A blank can be a simple, all-white finished glazed piece. Blanks can be smooth or have embossed edges and designs in the whiteware itself. Decorations and gold trims were applied later.

One must know both the blank number and the pattern number to make an exact match of a Haviland piece. The width and placings of the gold trims also exhibited tremendous variety and must be checked carefully.

Haviland matching services use Arlene Schleiger's reference books to identify patterns. Xerox a plate on both sides and indicate colors of the patterns when sending a sample to a matching service.

Monsieur Jean d'Albis, Haviland & Company historian, believes that more than 20,000 patterns were created and produced by artists of the company. Many old patterns have been discontinued, but Haviland Limoges porcelain dinnerware still is being made and sold in department and specialty stores.

In addition to the popular floral pattern tablewares, collectors of Haviland also should be alert for the art objects and richly decorated tableware and the unique non-tableware items that the company also manufactured.

Vase, 4" w, painted and applied yellow-brown floral design, med blue enamel dots, brown ground, Ernest Chaplet, (A), **$20.00**

Cabinet Plate, 9" d, HP center of Psyche gazing into reflecting pool, lt lavender border w/raised gilt shell forms, sgd "A.A. Elliott," "H. & Co." mk, ... **295.00**

Cake Plate
9 1/2" sq, enameled purple and green thistle, yellow forsythia, gold rim and molded handles, "C.F.H." mk, ... **125.00**
13" d, overall pink and yellow roses, shaded creamy yellow, blue, pink, and green bkd, tab handles, ... **95.00**

Center Bowl, 9 1/2" d x 5" h, pedestal base, sea green, blue, and gold interwoven geometrics, brown border, "HAVILAND FRANCE" mk, ... **250.00**

Coffeepot, 7 1/2" h, band of multicolored cornflowers, ring handle and knob, "Haviland France" mk, ... **300.00**

Compote, 5" h x 9 3/4" d, "Moss Rose" pattern, orange lined rim, "green H. & Co.," "red Haviland & Co. Limoges" mks, ... **295.00**

Creamer, 4" h, Cov Sugar Bowl, 5" h, pink and green dogwood blossoms, apron feet, gold handles and knob, "green Haviland France, red Haviland & Co. Limoges" mks, ... **125.00**

Cup and Saucer
Band of purple and gold clover, gold ribbon handle, "Haviland & Co." mk, ... **40.00**
Lobed, pink, green, blue, and violet floral sprays on int and ext, gilt handle w/molded leaf design, gilt rim, "green Haviland France," "red Haviland & Co. Limoges" mks, ... **85.00**
"Mozart-Chantoung" pattern, Charles Field Haviland, ... **45.00**

Decanter, 8 1/2" h, "Chantilly" pattern, ... **75.00**

Dresser Tray, 12 1/4" w, 3 lobed, HP dk red spider chrysanthemums, green foliage, Charles Field Haviland, ... **50.00**

Figure, 9" h, bisque, white bust of "Jenny Lind," circ socle, sq base, "imp HAVILAND" on side, ... **550.00**

Gravy Boat, 8 3/4" l, w/undertray, pink and burgundy wild roses, green shaded leaves, "GDA" mk, ... **15.00**

Jardiniere, 4 1/2" h x 11" w, lg red strawberries, green foliage, molded gold accented rim and elaborate curled leaf handles, pink int, "Haviland Limoges" mk, ... **495.00**

Lemonade Pitcher, 7 3/4" h, "Tarascon" pattern, sm lavender violets, gold trim and accented ribbon handle, "Haviland France, Haviland & Co. Limoges" mks, ... **250.00**

Pedestal Basket, 7 1/2" h x 9" d, pierced loops and arches on basket, pedestal base, white glaze, gold bands and stripes, "CFH" mk, hairline, ... **45.00**

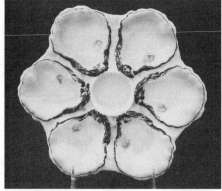

Oyster Plate, 8 3/4" d, purple shells, white ground, "Haviland & Company Made For Burley and Tyrrell Chicago" marks, set of 12, A-$345.00

Plate

6" d, border band of sm white dogwood blossoms, green leaves, long red tendrils, scalloped rim, "green Haviland France" mks, set of 8, ... **120.00**

6 1/2" w, "Ranson" blank, gold outlined rim, "Haviland France" mk, set of 4, ... **30.00**

6 3/4" sq, folded corners, polychrome costumed Japanese woman in center, Japanese characters on border, "H & Co./L" mk, set of 4, ... **600.00**

7 1/2" d, HP dk pink and white columbine, blue cornflowers on border, "GDM/CFH" mk, set of 3, ... **180.00**

8" sq, napkin fold corners, HP pr of grey and black birds on red flowering brown branch, gold rim, "H. & Co. L" mk, ... **25.00**

8 1/2" d
HP purple and yellow crocus, lt blue shaded ground, "Haviland & Co." mk, .. **75.00**

Lg orange poppy in center, white radiating leaves and stems on black center ground extending to orange poppies on bold border, artist sgd, "Haviland France" mk, ... **195.00**

9 1/2" d, cloisonne style enameled flowers on gold ground in center medallion and border, "CFH/GDM" mk, (A), ... **1,000.00**

10 1/2" d, "Madeleine" pattern, ... **25.00**

Sherbet, 3" h, white and brown flowers on red-brown, shaded brown ground, "Haviland France" mk, ... **45.00**

Soup Tureen, 11" H-H, grey and pink flowers, gold rims, gold accented knob, "C.F.H., CH FIELD HAVILAND LIMOGES" mks, ... **130.00**

Sugar Bowl, Cov, 3 1/2" h, "Montmery" pattern, sm blue forget-me-nots on gold branches, flame knob, "Haviland & Co." mk, ... **50.00**

Tankard,12" h, lobed and tapered, cascading pink roses, green foliage, gold lobed rim and base, gold accented handle, pattern #29L, "Haviland & Co." mk, chip on base, ... **340.00**

Teapot

6" h x 9 1/4" l, sm hanging dk pink roses, gilt hanging swags on rims, gilt accents, "Haviland France," "Haviland Co. France" mks, ... **75.00**

7 3/4" h, "Floradora" pattern, "red Haviland Limoges, green Floradora Haviland France" mks, ... **120.00**

Tea Service, pot, 8 1/2" h, creamer, 6" h, cov sugar bowl, 7 1/2" h, 3 plates, 7 1/2" d, 4 berry bowls, 4 3/4" d, 4 cups and saucers, pink-centered yellow flowers, grey leaves, "C.F.H." mks, ... **200.00**

Tureen, Cov

9 3/4" H-H, bands of pink and turquoise flowers on rims, gold accented curled handles and knob, "CFH/GDM" mk, ... **50.00**

10 1/2" h x 14" H-H, "Moss Rose" pattern, gold trim, rim chip, ... **400.00**

Vase, 5 1/2" h, 2 ovals w/lady in red gown, lg black hat, tan, rose, brown, baskets and garlands of flowers, white ground, "Charles Field Haviland and GDA" mks, ... **265.00**

Vegetable Bowl, Cov, 11" H-H, "Sylvia" pattern, "Haviland & Co." mk, ... **90.00**

c 1882   c1909

HEUBACH

Thuringia, Germany
1840s to Present

History: Christoph and Philip Heubach founded the Heubach factory to manufacture decorative and household porcelains, figures, doll heads, and dolls. Their doll heads, animal figures, and piano babies were their most famous products. There was no connection between this factory and the Ernst Heubach factory in Koppelsdorf.

After World War II, the company was nationalized and experienced several name changes. The present company name is VEB United Decorative Porcelainworks Lichte.

Bud Vase, 5 3/4" h, squat, flattened body, transfer of Pre-Raphaelite woman holding hem of green trimmed white gown on green splashed bkd, white body, ... **75.00**

Figure

3 1/2" h, seated Dutch girl w/hands on knees, orange skirt, white blouse w/green scarf, white cap, ... **95.00**

3 3/4" h, bisque, blond child in ruffled white blouse, seated in grey and brown shoe, child's feet sticking out through hole in shoe, mkd, ... **100.00**

4 3/4" h, seated German short haired pointer, white w/brown splotches and ears, pink nose, "GH rising sun" mk, ... **255.00**

5" h, seated Pierrot, black hair and ruffled collar, ... **185.00**

6" h, bisque, seated Dutch boy, orange jacket, yellow trousers,

black and white scarf, grey hat
and shoes, unmkd, ... **195.00**

Figure, 5" h, blue shades, "imp sunburst" marks, pr, $395.00

6 1/2" h, bisque, "A Dark Secret,"
standing little black girl in pink
dress, little black boy in red hat,
white shirt, tan trousers,
whispering in her ear, ... **200.00**
7" h, 2 little blond boys playing in lg
white shirt, intaglio eyes,
sunburst mk, ... **795.00**
7 1/4" h, bisque, Dutch boy and girl
standing back to back, red,
black, and grey outfits, .. **495.00**
7 1/2" h, seated Dutch boy in red
jacket, grey trousers, seated
Dutch girl wearing white cap,
olive green shawl, red skirt, imp
sunburst mks, pr, ... **650.00**

Figure, 11 7/8" h, bisque, "Blind Man Buff," pink shirt, pastel green dress, gold accents, blond hair, green kerchief over eyes, green ribbon band in hair, $1,300.00

12 1/2" h, bisque, Pierrot, red and
green flowered white costume,
gold accents, lg blue puffy
buttons, red cap, rising sun mk,
.... **310.00**
Perfume Lamp, 7" h, paneled, tapered
top and base w/wide middle, art
deco purple and red stylized flying
birds and border striping, "HEU
BACH" mk, ... **125.00**
Vase
7" h x 6" l, figural walking elephant
w/tasseled saddle, young girl at
side holding water jug, grey,
black, and white shading, red
lips and cheeks on girl,
.... **395.00**

Vase, 6" h, white, green, yellow, and blue enameled bird, black waves, matte red-orange ground, white int, printed mark, $95.00

10 1/2" h, molded pink cherub
holding figural pelican on side,
bkd of multicolored dogwood
blossoms, ... **595.00**

1756-76   1767-79

Hochst

Hesse, Germany
1746-1796

History: Though in existence for only a
short time, the porcelain factory at Hochst
produced a high quality product. Johann
Goltz and Johann Clarus, his son-in-law,
founded the porcelain factory together

with Adam Friedrich von Lowenfinck, a
decorator, who came from Meissen. The
group did not work well together and soon
split up. By 1750 Johann Benchgraff from
Vienna joined Glotz and Clarus to produce
porcelains.

After Benchgraff left in 1753, Goltz had
financial difficulties. The Prince-Elector,
Friedrich Carl von Ostern, from Mainz, took
over. Johann and Ferdinand Maass were
appointed managers of the factory, now
known as the Prince-Electoral Privileged
Porcelain Factory, from 1756 to 1776.
Tablewares, decorative porcelains, coffee
and tea sets, and figures were made. Oriental, rococo, and neo-classical decorative themes were used. Piercing and
fretwork were common design elements.

Hochst porcelain was probably best
known for the figurals that were modeled
under the supervision of Johann Melchior.
These painted and biscuit figures showed
a high degree of artistic ability. Religious
and pastoral groups, figures of children,
and mythological characters were modeled with special attention to detail. Pinks
and light rose tones were most prominently
used by Melchior on his figures of children.

The new Prince-Elector, Breidbach-
Burresheim, converted the company into a
joint stock company in 1776. The factory
was renamed the Prince-Electoral Fay-
ence Manufactory. With the departure of
Melchior to the Frankenthal factory in
1779, a gradual decline in quality
occurred, although attempts at modeling
continued. The factory ceased operations
in 1796.

Reference: George Ware, *German &
Austrian Porcelain*, Crown, Inc.1963.

Museums: Dixon Gallery, Memphis, TN;
Metropolitan Museum of Art, New York, NY;
Museum fur Kunsthandwerk, Frankfurt,
Germany; Schlossmuseum, Berlin,
Germany; Seattle Art Museum, Seattle,
WA.

Reproduction Alert: Following the closing
of the Hochst factory, many of the molds
were sold to the Muller factory in 1840 at
Damm near Aschaffenburg. Muller
produced many of the more popular items,
including the figures. The Hochst mark
was used, but these new copies lacked
the subtle coloration of the earlier Hochst
originals.

The Fasold & Stauch Company of
Bock-Wallendorf, and the firm Dressel,
Kister & Co. of Volkstedt employed a mark
that is often confused with Hochst. The
quality of their products differs significantly
from the high quality of the Hochst material.

Cup and Saucer, "Camaieu Rose"
painted scene of seated man
holding pipe on cup, seated man
under tree holding stein on saucer,
gilt rims, ... **350.00**
Cup and Saucer, **Handleless**, painted
period couple in landscape

w/mountains, puce scalloped borders, "red wheel" mk, c1750-60, (A), ... **310.00**

Dish, 9 3/4" d, painted floral bouquet and scattered flowers in center, molded pink, gold, or blue scrolling on puce rococo molded border, blue wheel mk, ... **3,500.00**

Figure

4 3/4" h, young girl offering pear, holding basket, mauve flowered skirt, blue striped shawl, green circ base, ... **215.00**

5 1/4" h, seated nun in red sprigged yellow lined cowl, gilt edged puce striped tunic, reading from brown book, oval mound base, "iron-red wheel, incised IHC" mks, c1750, restorations, (A), ... **750.00**

Figure, 7 1/2" h, 12" l, brown and black highlights, green accents, "blue wheel" mark, **$3,500.00**

7 1/4" h, "The Grape Thief," young man in yellow brimmed hat, pink breeches, seated on brown stone wall, offering bowl of grapes to kneeling girl in flowered dress, young man reaching into another bowl of grapes, green mound brown rock base, "blue wheel" mk, c1765, restorations, (A), ... **10,760.00**

14" h, 3 pairs of figures around central mound w/vase atop sq pedestal on grass base, young girl holding apron picking flowers, barefoot child at side, tub w/grapes in bkd, group w/man holding bunch of grapes, arm extended to woman gardening holding rake, group w/vender having container on back, child at side w/hurdy gurdy, multicolored, chips, ... **9,500.00**

Plaque, 3 5/8" h, HP scene of 3 people by sea w/sailboat, pale orchid border, self stand, ... **590.00**

Teapot, 6" h, bulbous shape, faience, painted and applied puce flowers, green foliage, figural female handle, green and yellow bird head spout, puce flowerhead knob, c1760, ... **3,750.00**

1755 - 1773

1897

HOLLAND-GENERAL

Porcelain
1757-1819

Porcelain by Dutch manufacturers was not as well known as the country's Delftware. Dutch porcelain factories at Weesp, Oude Loosdrecht, Amstel, and The Hague produced some wares, although production was limited and frequently imitated styles from other areas.

Hard paste porcelain was made at the **Weesp** factory near Amsterdam beginning in 1757. The factory was sold to Count Diepenbroick in 1762. The factory used French and German styles for inspiration, e.g. white porcelains decorated with flowers and other motifs in relief. Perforated baskets were made, along with rococo relief-decorated wares featuring landscapes in cartouches or adorned with birds or flowers. The factory did not prosper and was sold in 1771. The mark used by Weesp was a copy of the Meissen crossed swords in underglaze blue with the addition of three dots between the points of the blades on either side.

De Moll bought the factory, and the company moved to **Oud Loosdrecht** between Utrecht and Amsterdam. The wares exhibited more Dutch characteristics. Landscapes were especially popular. The mark used at Loosdrecht was "M.O.L." either incised or in underglaze blue, black, or colored enamels.

The company moved again in 1784 to **Ouder-Amstel** and was taken over by Frederick Daeuber. The wares now imitated the Empire style wares from Sevres.

In 1800 the factory belonged to the firm George Dommer and Co. It was moved to **Nieuwer-Amstel** in 1809 and was closed in 1819. Sometimes the "M.O.L." mark was used with the word Amstel. Other wares were marked "Amstel" in black.

Lynker, a German, established a porcelain factory in 1775 at **The Hague**. It produced hard paste porcelain similar to

Meissen. The pieces were decorated with landscapes, seascapes, and birds. The factory also decorated china from other sources. It closed in 1786. The Hague mark was the stork from the city arms in blue underglaze. When other blanks from other firms were decorated, the mark was painted on the glaze.

Pottery

The earliest pottery in Holland was made before 1609, long before Holland became an independent nation state. Tin-glazed wares of the early 16th century made in Antwerp, Haarlem, Rotterdam, and Amsterdam were similar to Italian wares known as majolica. Mid-16th century dishes made in Antwerp utilized the "blue-dash" around the edges that was later a design element found on 17th century English wares. Drug jars and spouted drug pots painted in high temperature blue tones similar to Italian wares were quite popular in the Netherlands.

With the founding of the Dutch East India Company in 1609, trade flourished with both China and Japan. As the Dutch potters became familiar with Far Eastern porcelains, they imitated the oriental designs on the earthenware. By the early 17th century, Delftware had developed.

When English salt-glazed stonewares and cream-colored earthenwares were imported from England in large quantities about the 1760s, Dutch potteries experienced a decline. Customers preferred the English goods over the tin-glazed wares made in Holland.

Museums: Gemeente Museum, The Hague, Holland; Municipal Museum, Amsterdam, Holland.

Additional Listings: Delft, Gouda, Maastricht, and Rozenburg.

Bowl, Cov, 4 1/2" h x 5 1/2" d, w/undertray, molded overlapped green lettuce leaves, ... **26.00**

Bud Vase

7 3/8" h, band on HP blue stiff leaves and yellow dots on lower body, banded neck, ... **500.00**

12" h, "Elrakka" pattern, red, white, and blue geometrics on tan bands top and base, blue ground, Arnhem, ... **300.00**

Figure

4 3/4" h, 2 monks wearing brown cowled habits, holding rod, ... **320.00**

8 3/4" h, seated potter forming pot, dk brown glaze, c1920, ... **195.00**

Plaque, 12" d, multicolored harbor scene w/Dutch man, woman, and child on dock, sailboats in water, pierced for hanging, ... **20.00**

Platter, 11 1/2" l, oval, multicolored landscape and cottage scene, gold inner and outer rims, c1820, ... **260.00**

Tray, 11" l x 5 1/4" w, rect w/cut corners, lg yellow centered red or blue flowerheads, foliage in center, red curlicue inner border, blue and yellow foliage border, Makkum Pottery, pr, ... **175.00**

Vase, 5 1/2" h, dk and lt grey over black, Mobach, $100.00

Vase

7" h, ovoid, flared rim, stylized white swimming swans, gloss brown ground, mkd, ... **40.00**

8 1/4" h, tapered shape w/sloping shoulder, mottled lt blue and tan ground, teardrop reticulated shoulder, gold rim, "Made in Holland" mk, ... **50.00**

8 3/4" h, squat bottle shape, organic floral and foliate motif in jewel tones on brown ground, high gloss glaze, (A), ... **400.00**

11" h, hand thrown cylinder shape w/3 imp horiz depressions, textured matte brown ground w/yellow and black highlights, "Utrecht, Holland" mk, (A), ... **110.00**

15" h, tapered form, high luster multicolored glaze, St. Lukes, c1909-20, ... **510.00**

1743 - 1826

HUNGARY-GENERAL

Holitsch
1743-1827

History: The Holitsch pottery factory was established in 1743 by Francis of Lorraine, consort of the Empress Maria Theresa. Decorative motifs followed the popular Strasbourg style. Tureens were made in the form of birds. Most of the painting favored a Hungarian peasant pottery style. When the firm started to produce English style earthenwares in 1786, they used workers from the Vienna factory. It continued in operation with state support until 1827.

The early faience wares were marked with the "HF" monogram for "Holitscher Fabrik." Later creamwares bear the full name "HOLICS" or "HOLITSCH."

References: Tivadar Artner, *Modern Hungarian Ceramics*, Art Foundation Publishing House, 1974; Gyorgy Domanovszky, *Hungarian Pottery*, Corvina Press, 1968.

Additional Listings: Fischer and Zsolnay.

Bowl, 9 1/2" sq, multicolored, gold lined rim, Herend, c1930s, $450.00

Bowl, 3 3/8" h x 6 1/4" d, flared hex shape w/spread ft, "Chinese Bouquet" pattern, Herend, ... **140.00**

Breakfast Service, teapot, 5" h, coffeepot, 6 1/2" h, cov milk jug, 6 3/4" h, cov muffineer, 7 3/4" d, milk jug, 3 1/2" h, creamer, 2 5/8" h, egg cup, 3 3/4" h, dbl salt, 5 3/4" w, 3 shakers, 2 1/4" h, 6 coffee cups and saucers, 2 teacups and saucers, 4 cereal bowls, 6 1/2" d, 8 plates, 10

1/4" d, 6 plates, 9" d, 6 plates, 8 1/8" d, 3 plates, 6 1/2" d, iron-red and gilt flowers and butterflies, peach border w/molded basketweave ground, shaped rims, "blue Herend shield" mks, 20th C, (A), ... **4,183.00**

Coffeepot, 8 1/4" h, pear shape, domed cov, blue "Nanking" pattern, gold accents, flower knob, Herend, ... **210.00**

Cream Jug, 2 1/2" h, blue "Nanking" pattern, basketweave border, Herend, ... **50.00**

Dessert Service, master plate, 11" d, 4 plates, 6 1/2" d, painted center w/tulip and garden flowers, border panels of flower sprigs alternating w/molded basketweave designs, Herend, ... **185.00**

Dish, 6 1/2" l x 6" w, lobed, open handle, HP floral sprigs, gold accented swirls and shell designs, Herend, ... **125.00**

Plate, 9 1/4" d, raised swans, brown cranes, green and gray water plants, multicolored floral border, gilt rim, Herend, "gold crest and cross" mark, $450.00

Figure

6 7/8" h, Art Deco stylized bust of woman, brown braided hair, turquoise lined mauve wrap, sgd "H. Rahmer," c1910, ... **400.00**

9" h, brown haired white nude female scarf dancer, "Herend Hungary" mk, ... **580.00**

15" h x 10 3/4" l, peasant man riding grey donkey, brown feathered hat, black jacket and boots, holding pipe, rect base, Herend, c1940, ... **850.00**

Fruit Bowl, 9" d, HP bunches of garden flowers, gilt outlined overlapping open loop border, Herend, ... **360.00**

Salad Dish, 8" l, kidney shape, "Fruit and Flowers" pattern, Herend, ... **100.00**

Soup Plate, 9 1/2" d, "Blue Garden" pattern, Herend, ... **55.00**

Teapot, 8 1/4" h, dome shape, HP blue "Nanking" pattern, gold rims, figural flower knob, c1920, ... **210.00**

Tea Service, Demitasse, pot, 6 1/2" h, creamer, 3 1/2" h, cov sugar bowl, 3 1/2" h, 6 cups and saucers, HP gilt trimmed green flowers and foliage, osier molded borders, yellow roses knobs, fancy handles, Herand, ... **695.00**

Vase

4" h, inverted bell shape, 3 sm gold feet, gold lined base, "Rothschild" pattern, painted birds, branches, plants, and butterfly, gilt rim, Herend, ... **75.00**

5 1/2" h, swollen bulbous shape w/short collar, lg red tulip, sm yellow centered purple or blue flowers, green foliage on side, scattered flowers on reverse, gold trimmed base, Herend, ... **32.00**

HUTSCHENREUTHER

Hohenberg, Bavaria, Germany
1814 to Present

History: Carl Magnus Hutschenreuther established a German porcelain factory—Hutschenreuther A.G.—at Hohenberg, Bavaria, in 1814. When Carl Magnus died in 1845, he was succeeded by Johanna, his widow, and Christian and Lorenz, his sons. Lorenz was not satisfied simply to carry on the family business. He was bought out by his partners and established his own porcelain factory in Selb. The Lorenz Hutschenreuther and Carl Magnus Hutschenreuther porcelain factories co-existed as two totally independent businesses. When Lorenz Hutschenreuther died in 1856, Viktor and Eugen, his sons, took over his company.

The Lorenz family enlarged their firm through acquisitions and the creation of new factories during the first part of the 20th century. In 1906 they acquired the porcelain factory Jaeger, Werner & Co. in Selb. In 1917 Lorenz Hutschenreuther bought the Paul Muller Porcelain Factory in Selb. In 1927 they purchased the Tirschenreuth Porcelain Factory and Baus-

cher Brothers Porcelain Factory in Weiden. The following year they added the Konigszelt Porcelain Factory.

Both branches of the Hutschenreuthers were noted for the high quality of their tablewares and figures. In 1969 all branches of the Magnus and Lorenz firm were united under the group name Hutschenreuther AG.

A merger with Porzellanfabrik Kahla AG of Schoenwald in 1972 brought the Arzberg and Schonwald brands of porcelain along with two earthenware factories into the Hutschenreuther group of enterprises. The company is still in business today producing limited edition plates, figures, dinnerware, and other china. Distribution companies have been established in France, the United States, Canada, Scandinavia, Belgium, and Italy.

Bowl, 9 1/2" d, HP green and lt purple grapes, white blossoms, green to red shaded ground, gold accented molded rim, c1900, ... **95.00**

Bowl, Cov, 8" H-H, border bands of sm pink and white flowers, gold handles and open knob, ... **85.00**

Box, Cov, 3 3/4" h x 3 1/2" w, swirl molded, HP scattered magenta flowers, gilt outlined flowerhead knob w/leaf terminals, ... **125.00**

Cabinet Cup and Saucer, ext of cup w/band of pink roses and gilt, int gilt border and saucer w/cobalt cartouches of pink roses, ... **250.00**

Charger, 12 1/2" d, pink and yellow painted orchid, green foliage, cobalt ground, artist sgd, ... **60.00**

Celery Tray, 9 1/4" H-H, small bunch of pink roses, shaded green border, matte gold handles, "Hutschenreuther Favorite" mk, ... **45.00**

Coffeepot, 7 3/4" h, "Silvia" mold, lightly lobed body, band of HP pink roses and foliage around base, lobed base, rococo handle, gold rims and accents, ... **150.00**

Cup and Saucer

Blue, green, pink, red, and yellow flower sprigs, raised gold scrolling trim, ... **68.00**

Blue, pink, green, red, and yellow florals in gilt molded mirror cartouches, gilt trim, **68.00;** trim, HP orange star and half leaf design, gilt netted ground, ... **45.00**

"Maple Leaf" pattern, gold rims, ... **15.00**

Cup and Saucer, Demitasse, multicolored pheasant on branch

w/pink flowers, gold rims, cup base, and handle, ... **44.00**

Figure, 18" h, Emperor Penguin and Chick, grey-black body, orange-yellow to white shaded breast, black accents, sgd "Gunther R. Donger," $950.00

Figure

3 1/4" h x 3" l, circus elephant on circ stand, overall white glaze, gold rim, c1920, ... **95.00**

8 1/2" h, white glazed kneeling nude woman holding 3 yellow chicks, ... **495.00**

8 3/4" h, seated nude girl holding bowl of multicolored flowers to grey deer behind, ... **570.00**

Gravy Boat, 11 1/4" l, Platter, 17" l, multicolored florals, white ground, burnished gold borders, "CM Hutschenreuther and blue scepter" marks, gravy boats, pr, A-$920.00

Pitcher, 5" h, figural crow, black w/yellow beak, ... **100.00**

Plaque, 5 3/4" h x 4" w, rect, brunette lady in classic robe, marguerites in hair, artist sgd, giltwood frame, (A), ... **1,410.00**

Plate

6 7/8" d, orange and green peaches, green foliage, orange to green shaded ground, lobed rim, mkd, ... **15.00**

7 1/2" d, white daisy pattern around border, gold rim, set of 12, ... **125.00**

7 3/4" d, painted lilies, irises, peonies, and daffodils, artist sgd, ... **70.00**

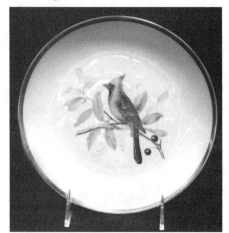

Plate, 8" d, multicolored bird, gold rim, "Cardinal From the Drawings of Audubon," "CM Hutschenreuther Selb" mks, set of 5, (A), **$60.00**

Platter, 15" l x 10" w, pink rose and buds w/lt green and pink leaves on border, ... **30.00**

Service Plate, 10 1/2" d, center scene of courting couple in meadow in blue 5 pointed star cartouche, blue border w/5 mirror cartouches of classic scenes, gilt accents on border, set of 12, ... **2,400.00**

Serving Dish, 13" l x 9" w, oval, "Dresden" pattern, molded border design, white glaze, ... **30.00**

Tureen, Cov, 14" H-H, border band of green and pink geometrics, gold accented handles and knob, artist sgd, ... **155.00**

Urn, Cov, 24" h, 3 section, HP continuous rural scene, gilt hanging drape, 3 leaf band, and beading on base, gilt flame knob, 2 gilt fancy handles, ... **9,800.00**

Vase

7 1/2" h, inverted pear shape, stylized gilt foliage designs on royal blue ground, gilt open work collar, c1913, ... **150.00**

8" h, rect flattened form, HP pink and yellow irises, long green leaves, yellow marsh marigold, sgd "Leonard," **30.00**

Vegetable Bowl, 10 1/4" l, oval, scattered multicolored floral sprigs, ... **25.00**

INDIAN TREE

English
Mid-1800s to Present

History: Indian Tree is a popular dinnerware pattern that was made by English potters such as Burgess & Leigh, Coalport, John Maddock & Sons, S. Hancock & Sons, and Soho Pottery from the middle of the 1800s until the present. The main theme is an Oriental landscape with a gnarled brown branch of a pink blossomed tree. The remainder of the landscape features exotic flowers and foliage in green, pink, blue, and orange on a white ground.

Berry Bowl, 5 1/4" w, 10 sides w/indentations, Coalport, ... **6.00**

Bone Dish, 9 3/8" w, brown, Copeland Spode, ... **40.00**

Bowl

5 1/4" d, "C.M. Hutschenreuther" mk, ... **7.00**

6" d, "COALPORT" mk, wavy border, ... **16.00**

6 5/8" d, Myott, ... **7.00**

9" l x 6 3/4" w, oval, "Johnson Brothers" mk, ... **10.00**

Bowl, Cov, 9 1/2" d, "Johnson Brothers" mk, ... **65.00**

Breakfast Cup and Saucer, Cauldon, ... **30.00**

Cake Plate

8 1/2" H-H, tab handles, Coalport, ... **200.00**

10" H-H, Grafton China, ... **30.00**

11 1/2" H-H, ... **75.00**

Cereal Bowl, 6 1/2" d, ... **12.00**

Chop Plate, 12" d, "Johnson Brothers" mk, ... **35.00**

Coffee Can and Saucer, Aynsley, ... **30.00**

Coffeepot, 8" h, Johnson Brothers, ... **45.00**

Creamer, 4 1/2" h, Coalport, ... **15.00**

Cream Soup

5 1/2" H-H, Myott, ... **15.00**

7 1/4" H-H, "Johnson Brothers" mk, ... **25.00**

Cup and Saucer, Johnson Brothers, ... **7.00**

Cup and Saucer, Demitasse, Coalport, ... **275.00**

Cup and Saucer, Handleless, "Anchor China England" mk, ... **8.00**

Dessert Bowl, 5 3/4" d, paneled, Coalport, set of 10, ... **120.00**

Dessert Set, platter, 12 1/4" d, 6 dessert plates, 8" d, 6 dessert bowls, 5 1/8" d, 6 cups and saucers, Johnson Brothers, ... **50.00**

Dish, 9" w, lobed, applied mauve streaked shell handle, ... **7.00**

Fruit Bowl, 5 1/8" d, Johnson Brothers, ... **4.00**

Gravy Boat

7 1/2" l, Enoch Wood, ... **9.00**

8" l, "Soho Pottery Cobridge England" mk, ... **10.00**

Jug

2" h, Coalport, ... **68.00**

2 1/2" h, Wood, ... **32.00**

Meat Platter, Well and Tree

18 3/4" l x 15" w, Copeland, .. **435.00**

20" l x 15 1/2" w, "imp SPODE STONE CHINA" mk, ... **2,250.00**

Mug, 3 1/4" h, Coalport, ... **75.00**

Plate, 10" d, "John Maddock & Son" mk, **$10.00**

Plate

6 1/4" d, molded fluted border, Myott, ... **6.00**

6 1/2" d, Johnson Brothers, ... **5.00**

6 3/4" d, ... **5.00**

7" d, England, ... **8.00**

7 1/2" d

Fan shaped molded border, Myott, ... **4.00**

"Wedgwood & Son" mk, .. **12.00**
7 3/4" sq, Johnson Brothers, ... **4.00**
8" d
  Straight rim, Johnson Brothers,
  .... **6.00**
  Wavy rim, "COALPORT" mk,
  .... **20.00**
9" sq, cut corners, Colclough, . **8.00**
9 1/2" d, "Till & Sons" mk, ... **8.00**
9 3/4" d, Coalport, ... **10.00**
10" d
  Copeland, ... **15.00**
  Fluted border, Myott,........... **5.00**
"J. & G. Meakin" mk, ... **20.00**
10 1/4" d, "Bridgewood England"
  mk, ... **15.00**

Platter
12" l, oval, "John Maddock & Sons-
  Vitrous" mk, ... **20.00**
12 1/2" l x 9 1/2" w, oval, "Johnson
  Brothers" mk, ... **10.00**
12 3/4" l x 9 3/4" w, oval, Spode,
  .... **35.00**
13" l x 10" w, oval, "W.T. Copeland &
  Sons, Stoke on Trent" mk,
  .... **120.00**
14" l x 11" w, oval, Johnson Brothers,
  .... **10.00**
14 1/2" l x 13" w, oval, Myott,
  .... **15.00**
15" l x 10 1/2" w, oval, "John
  Maddock & Sons" mk, ... **25.00**
19" l x 11" w, Copeland, ... **375.00**
Relish Tray, 8 1/2" l, Johnson Brothers,
  .... **25.00**

Sauceboat, 8" d, attached underplate, Myott,
$65.00

Serving Bowl
9 1/4" l x 4" w, oval, Johnson
  Brothers, ... **15.00**
10 1/4" l x 9 1/2" w, Johnson
  Brothers, ... **20.00**
Serving Plate, 8 3/4" d, unmkd, (A),
  .... **20.00**
Serving Tray, 15" d, Coalport, ... **230.00**

Soup Bowl, 5 1/2" d, Johnson Brothers,
  .... **5.00**
Soup Plate
8" d, Johnson Brothers, ... **7.00**
8 1/2" d, Crown Ducal, ... **8.00**
9 1/2" d, Spode, ... **195.00**
Soup Tureen
8" l, England, unmkd, ... **195.00**
10 1/2" H-H, Copeland, ... **795.00**
14 1/4" H-H, Johnson Brothers,
  .... **110.00**
Sugar Bowl, Cov, 3 1/2" h, Wood,
  .... **42.00**
Sweet Dish, 7" d, oct, "Royal Albert"
  mk,................................. **55.00**
Teapot, 5" h x 7" w, ribbed, gold trim,
  Sadler, ... **10.00**
Tea Set, pot, 9" h, creamer, 4 1/2" h, cov
  sugar bowl, 5" h, Greek key rims, "J.
  & G. Meakin" mks, c1930, ... **150.00**
Tray, 15" d, Coalport, ... **230.00**
Vase
4 1/2" h, HP pattern, "H.J. Wood
  Staffordshire" mk, ... **15.00**
11" h, tapered shape, Sampson
  Hancock, ... **265.00**
Vegetable Bowl, 9" l x 6 7/8" w, oval,
  "Johnson Brothers" mk, ... **35.00**

Vegetable Bowl, 10" l, "green Coalport" mark,
$110.00

Vegetable Bowl, Cov, 12 1/2" H-H, ftd,
  gold trim, "imp COPELAND" mark,
  .... **85.00**

IRISH BELLEEK

County Fermanagh, Ireland
1857 to Present

History: Pottery production using native clay deposits began in 1857 in Belleek in County Fermanagh, Ireland. Although David McBurney and Robert Armstrong, the founders, started with earthenwares, they soon produced Belleek parian china, a fine porcelain. William Bromley brought some workers from the Goss factory at Stoke-on-Trent when he moved to Belleek about 1860.

Native marine motifs, such as seashells, corals, marine plants and animals, seahorses, and dolphins were the subjects of early Belleek pieces. The Irish shamrocks also were a favorite subject. Many of these motifs continue in production. From its beginning, the factory produced both utilitarian and decorative wares.

Belleek porcelain is extremely thin and light with a creamy ivory surface and iridescent luster. Probably its most distinctive quality is its delicate cream or pastel tone with a pearl-like luster. All pieces are hand crafted.

William Henshall's introduction of basketwork and flowers in 1865 gave Belleek porcelains a world wide audience. Each basket was woven out of fine rods of clay, not cast; each leaf and flower was made by hand. These intricate and highly decorative pieces are most sought after by collectors. Belleek baskets were dated according to whether they were made with three strands or four strands. Also, the pieces were identified with strips of Belleek parian with various impressed wording to indicate the date.

The company's first gold medal was won at the 1865 Dublin International Exposition. Irish Belleek parian china still is hand crafted, just as it was more than a hundred years ago. Each piece is made by one craftsman from start to finish; no assembly line methods are used.

References: Richard K. Degenhardt, *Belleek: The Complete Collectors' Guide & Illustrated Reference, 2nd Edition*, Wallace-Homestead, 1993; Marion Langham, *Belleek Irish Porcelain*, Quiller Press, Ltd. 1994; Walter Rigdon, *Illustrated Collectors' Handbook*, Wilkins Creative Printing, 1978.

Marks: Belleek pieces are marked with the Belleek backstamp consisting of an Irish Wolfhound, a Harp, a Round Tower, and Sprigs of Shamrock. This first mark was used from 1863 to 1890. The marks were either printed or impressed into the china. Early marks were usually black, but could also be red, blue, green, or brown.

With the second mark, 1891 to 1926, "Co. Fermanagh, Ireland" was added along with a ribbon. The third mark was used from 1926 to 1946 and included a round scroll with three Gaelic words—

"Deanta in Eirinn"—and celtic design with circle. The fourth mark in green, from 1946 to 1955, was the same as the third. The fifth mark in green, from 1955 to 1965, was the same as the fourth, but with the addition of the letter "R" in circle. The sixth mark in green, from 1965 to 1980, was the same trademark reduced in size, ribbon shortened, and "Co. Fermanagh" deleted, leaving only "Ireland." The seventh mark, from 1993 to the present, is similar to the second but in navy blue. The current change reflects the 130th anniversary of Belleek.

Museums: National Museum, Dublin, Ireland; Ulster Museum, Belfast, Ireland; Victoria & Albert Museum, London, England; Visitor's Center, The Belleek Pottery, Belleek, Co. Fermanagh, N. Ireland; Irish American Heritage, 4626 N. Knox Ave, Chicago, IL.

Collectors' Club: The Belleek Collectors' International Society, 9893 Georgetown Pike, Suite 525, Great Falls, VA 22066, phone 800-Belleek, Membership: $35.00, Society journal newsletter.

Collecting Hints: Specialty shops and department stores usually carry contemporary Belleek wares. These are good sources for comparing the new examples with the older ones. In the modern pieces, the paste has a creamy white appearance and the high, brilliant glaze has a yellowish color tone. Modern pieces usually have more color used in the design than their older counterparts. Every genuine Belleek piece carries the company crest. Christmas collector plates were started in 1970. Reed and Barton is now the exclusive distributor of Belleek products in the United States.

Basket, 9" d, 4 strand, applied pink, yellow, or blue flowers, turquoise handles, ivory ground, pad mk, (A), **$190.00**

Basket, 5 1/8" w, heart shape, 4 strand basketweave base, single strand woven sides, applied pastel flowerheads on rim, "BELLEEK FERMANAGH IRELAND" pad mks, ... **260.00**

Basket, Cov, 9 5/8" d, 3 strand wicker work, recessed rim w/basket work loops and dbl rose twig handles, applied sm flowers, cov w/applied rose, carnation, sunflower, and shamrock, bird finial, "BELLEEK CO FERMANAGH" pad mk, c1863-91, restorations, (A), ... **1,125.00**

Biscuit Barrel, Cov, 6" h
   Diamond pattern, 2nd black mk, ... **825.00**
   Shamrock pattern, 1st green mk, ... **210.00**

Bowl
   4" H-H, "Ivy" pattern, rope twist handle, 3rd black mk, ... **120.00**
   5" w, heart shape, 3rd black mk, ... **120.00**
   8 1/2" h, green tinged figural nautilus shell on coral stand, 2nd black mk, ... **4,950.00**

Bread Plate, 11" H-H, "Limpet" pattern, 3rd black mk, ... **180.00**

Butter Dish, 6 1/2" l x 5 1/4" w, figural cottage, branch handle from end to roof peak, 3rd green mk, ... **200.00**

Cake Plate, 9 1/2" H-H, 4 strand, twig handles, pearl glaze, "BELLEEK CO FERMANAGH IRELAND" pad mk, ... **1,185.00**

Candelabra, 13 3/4" h, modeled nude child seated on rocks w/coral stems, 3 bowls supported on coral stems, removable sconces, beaded stepped circ base, 1st black mk, (A), ... **2,550.00**

Celery Vase, 12" h, pink w/gilt accents, 1st black mk, pr, ... **16,850.00**

Cream Jug, 2 1/2" h
   "Lily" pattern, 2nd green mk, ... **78.00**
   "Tridacna" pattern, 1st black mk, ... **120.00**

Cream Jug, 3 1/4" h, Sugar Bowl, 3" d x 2 3/4" h, "Shamrock" pattern, 3rd black mk, ... **75.00**

Cup and Saucer
   "Harp and Shamrock" pattern, 3rd black mk, ... **90.00**
   HP gilded ivy leave on meandering brown stems, 2nd black mk, ... **485.00**
   "Neptune" pattern, 2nd black mk, ... **110.00**
   "Limpet" pattern, 3rd black mk, ... **85.00**
   "Mask" pattern, 3rd black mk, ... **215.00**
   "Shamrock" pattern, 2nd black mk, ... **95.00**

Shell shape, shaded pink ground, 3 shell feet, 2nd black mk, ... **125.00**

Dish
   5 1/8" w, heart shape, fluted, 2nd black mk, ... **30.00**
   5 1/2" w, oak leaf shape, 3rd black mk, ... **125.00**
   8 1/4" w, crescent shape, HP fuchsia bouquet, 2nd black mk, ... **1,350.00**

Flower Holder, 3 1/4" h x 5" l, figural half horse and trumpet, yellow luster trim, 3rd black mk, ... **400.00**

Jar, Cov, 7" h, "Shamrock" pattern, gold mk, **$225.00**

Jardiniere
   7" h, "Thorn," scalloped form, applied meandering florals on shoulder over molded peony, 2nd black mk, (A), ... **1,050.00**
   7 5/8" h, encrusted w/rose and other flowers, barbed rim, 2nd black mk, (A), ... **750.00**
   11 7/8" h, paneled, shoulders w/applied meandering florals and 2 birds perched on branches, molded stiff leaf scrolled feet, c1891-1926, (A), ... **630.00**

Jug
   3 1/2" h, "Ivy" pattern, rope twist handle, 3rd black mk, ... **120.00**
   5 3/4" h, "Thorn," pink and gold, 1st black mk, ... **1,160.00**
   7 1/2" h, "Florence," tan, 1st black mk, ... **1,175.00**

Marmalade Jar, Cov, 4 1/2" h, "Shamrock" pattern, 3rd black mk, ... **225.00**

Mirror, 10 5/8" h, oval, encrusted w/flowerheads between beaded rims, c1863-90, (A), ... **480.00**

Pitcher
3" h, "Lotus" pattern, 1st green mk, ... **139.00**
5" h, "Maskware" pattern, 3rd black mk, ... **125.00**
5 1/2" h, "Ribbon" pattern, 2nd green mk, ... **90.00**

Plate
6 3/4" d, "Shamrock" pattern, basketweave border, 3rd black mk, ... **35.00**
8 1/4" d
"Limpet" pattern, Cobb tint, 3rd black mk, ... **65.00**
"Shamrock" pattern, 1st green mk, ... **20.00**

Pot, Cov, 3" h x 3 3/8" d, "Shamrock" pattern, basket weave ground, 3rd black mk, ... **90.00**

Salt Dish
3" l
2" w, 4 joined pectin shells, "Shamrock" pattern, 3rd black mk, ... **40.00**
2 1/8" w, shell molded, coral accents, yellow luster glaze, 2nd black mk, ... **70.00**
3 1/2" l x 2 1/8" w, pink tinged diamond shape w/molded fluting, pink shaded spoon w/coral handle and scallop shell bowl, 1st black mk, pr, ... **765.00**

Spill Vase
5" l x 3 3/4" h, sm pink tulip blossom and bud on green and brown branch, 1st black mk, ... **1,320.00**
9" h, "Lizard," 1st black mk, pr, ... **5,500.00**

Teakettle, 7" h, w/underplate, "Grasses" pattern, bird spout, 1st black mk, ... **2,135.00**

Teapot, 5 1/2" h, "Limpet" pattern, cob luster handle, 2nd green mk, ... **295.00**

Tea Service, teapot, 4" h, cream jug, 3 3/4" h, sugar bowl, 2" h, milk pitcher, 4" h, 6 plates, 6 1/2" d, 4 plates, 7" d, 8 plates, 8" d, 2 cake plates, 9" H-H, 6 cups, 7 saucers, "Shamrock" pattern, basketweave ground, 3rd black mk, (A), ... **400.00**

Tennis Set, saucer-tray, 7 1/2" l x 5" w, "Tridacna," green tinged rims, pink tint, 2nd black mk, ... **365.00**

Vase
2" h x 4" d, ball shape, "Shamrock" pattern, gilt rim, 2nd black mk, ... **48.00**
3 1/2" h
"Gothic," lt green wreaths, 2nd black mk, ... **855.00**

Swirl shell molded, applied flowerheads, 2nd black mk, ... **450.00**
3 3/4" h, "Typha" design, 2nd green mk, ... **50.00**
4 1/8" h, swirl molded body, applied lg rose and leaves and Irish shamrocks, 2nd black mk, ... **350.00**
5 1/4" h, "Thistle" pattern, 2nd black mk, ... **395.00**
5 3/8" h, pink shaded vert cornucopia set on grey rock base, 2nd black mk, ... **165.00**
5 7/8" h, "Feather" pattern, #D155, 3rd green mk, ... **55.00**
8 1/2" h, figural "Owl," 1st green mk, ... **145.00**
12 1/2" h, "Rose Isle," 2nd black mk, ... **1,125.00**

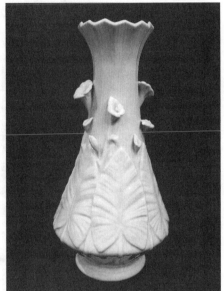

Vase, 13 1/2" h, "Nile" pattern, 3rd black marks, **$575.00**

13" h, "Nile," lilies and broad leaves, 1st black mk, ... **2,650.00**

IRONSTONE, PATTERNED AND WHITE

Staffordshire, England
Early 1840s-1891

History: White ironstone in Gothic shapes was first produced from Staffordshire in the early 1840s. Gothic shapes already had been used by Staffordshire potters for cobalt and mulberry transfer wares. Roses, lilies, and human profiles comprised the finials or the trim under the handles.

The firm of James Edwards of Burslem made a tremendous variety of designs in white ironstone. T.J. & J. Mayer designed "Prize Puritan" and "Prize Bloom." "Adam's Scallop," "Line Trim," and "Scalloped Decagons" by J. Wedgwood and Davenport all used scallops in the pottery design. "Fluted Pearl" by J. Wedgwood and "Fig" by J. Wedgwood and Davenport are among the most collectible patterns.

William Adams, John Alcock, E. Challinor & Co., Davenport, C. Meigh & Son, and J. Wedgwood were some of the firms making white ironstone in the 1840s and 50s. Thomas and Richard Boote's "Octagon Shape" in 1851 was the forerunner of the famous "Sydenham Shape" from 1853. Many potters then copied these popular shapes.

"President" by James Edwards and "Columbia," made by six different companies, were registered in 1855. The potters of "Columbia" used the same borders on the plates and platters, but used varied finials and foliage decorations. "Dallas," "Mississippi," and "Baltic Shapes" also were registered in that year. Many other shapes appeared from the Staffordshire Potteries during the 1850s.

Many white ironstone patterns used corn, oats, and wheat in their designs such as "Corn & Oats" manufactured by J. Wedgwood and Davenport from 1863; "Wheat & Blackberry" by J. & G. Meakin from 1865; "Prairie Shape" from 1862; and "Ceres" by Elsmore and Forster from 1859.

During the 1860s, gardens and woods inspired the designers of white ironstone. Patterns such as "Sharon Arch," "Hanging Arch," "Winding Vine," and "White Oak and Acorn" are just a few that were developed. Flowers also influenced the Staffordshire potters during the 1860s in such patterns as "Morning Glory" by Elsmore & Forster, "Moss Rose" by J. & G. Meakin, "Bordered Fuchsia" by A. Shaw, and "The Hyacinth" by J. Wedgwood.

Ribbed patterns also were popular as in Meakin's "Ribbed Raspberry with Bloom" and Pankhurst's "Ribbed Chain" during the 1860s. A classical revival was seen in "Athens Shape" by Podmore Walker & Co. and "Athenia" by J.T. Close.

Rectangular shapes became popular during the 1870s and 1880s. After 1891 ironstone diminished as the demands for porcelains increased.

References: Dawn Stoltzfus & Jeffrey B. Snyder, *White Ironstone*, Schiffer Publishing, Ltd. 1997; Jean Wetherbee, *A Look at White Ironstone*, Wallace-Homestead, 1980; Jean Wetherbee, *A Second Look at White Ironstone*, Wallace-Homestead, 1984; Jean Wetherbee, *White Ironstone: A Collectors' Guide*, Antique Trader Books, 1996; J. Godden, *Godden's Guide to Ironstone: Stone & Granite Wares*, Antique Collector's Club, 1999; Ernie & Bev Dieringer, *Ironstone China 1840-1890, Plate Identification Guide*, Schiffer Publication, 2001.

Collectors' Club: White Ironstone China Association, Inc. Diane Dorman, P.O. Box 855, Fairport, NY 14450-0855, www.ironstonechina.org, Membership: $25.00, Quarterly newsletter *White Ironstone Notes*.

Patterned
Bowl
7 1/2" d, ftd, "Amherst Japan" pattern, orange, blue, green, and gold, unmkd, ... **100.00**
8 1/4" d, red, green, yellow, and dk blue stylized floral on int border, red lined rim, (A), ... **195.00**
Butter Dish, Cov, 5" h x 8 1/2" d, cobalt, iron-red, and gilt "Amherst Japan" pattern, (A), ... **192.00**
Center Bowl, 5 1/2" h x 12 1/2" H-H, ftd, Imari style cobalt and iron-red florals, bands of cobalt crisscross design alternating w/ovals of florals, tan rim, ... **100.00**

Dish, 11" l x 7 1/2" w, cobalt, yellow, turquoise, iron-red and gilt, c1800, $595.00

Dish, 10 1/4" H-H x 9 1/4" w, Imari palette of chinoiserie village scene and lake w/boats, cobalt border w/gilt accents and ovals of mons and geometrics, blue molded scrolling handles, scalloped rim, "crowned Ironstone Stone China" mk, ... **250.00**

Drain, 14 1/2" l x 11" w, "Seasons" pattern, blue transfer, "T. Goodwin" mk, ... **250.00**
Ice Pail, Cov, 12" h, w/liner, painted gold and iron-red peonies and chrysanthemums, gilt outlined and veined cobalt foliage, gilt and cobalt figural beast handles, gilt acorn knob, c1800, pr, (A), ... **2,870.00**
Jug, 5 3/4" h, paneled, Imari pattern, underglazed cobalt, overglazed iron-red oriental flower design, green snake handle w/iron-red, green, and luster head, unmkd, ... **245.00**
Mug, 3" h, black printed chinoiserie design of pagoda, bridge, and fence w/peacock, polychrome enamel accents, Ashworth, ... **45.00**
Pitcher, 7" h, scattered floral sprigs and foliage, brown transfers, molded fan designs on sides and rim, thumb rest on handle, "Alpine Dalehall Pottery Co. England" mk, ... **25.00**

Pitcher, 7 3/4" h, purple transfer, hunting scene of hunters and horses, England, $100.00

Plate
8 3/8" d
"Bandana & Vase" pattern, stylized black and white vase in center, mottled Chinese red border w/black and white dragon dogs, "Imp Ashworth" mk, ... **120.00**
"Trophies" pattern, dk green, pink, orange, dk blue, and gilt, Ashworth, ... **250.00**
8 1/2" d, turquoise vase w/flowers in center, turquoise border w/dragons, red rim, Ashworth, ... **125.00**
9" d, "Prunus Bush" pattern, cobalt, orange, green, and peach,

flowing waves on border, lustered rim, c1835, ... **65.00**
9 1/2" d, ten sides, multicolored seashells and butterflies, purple squiggle ground, ... **275.00**
10" d, red roses, bluebell flowers, green foliage, (A), ... **40.00**
10 1/4" d
"Indian Flower" pattern, mauve transfer w/iron-red, yellow, blue, and green, ... **30.00**
"Table and Flower Pot" pattern, blue and pink lg vase w/red peonies, green foliage on table, cobalt border w/mons, half flowerheads, and curlicues, "imp ASHWORTH REAL IRONSTONE CHINA" and "black PELLATT & WOOD 25 BAKER ST. PORTMAN SQUARE LONDON" mks, (A), ... **250.00**

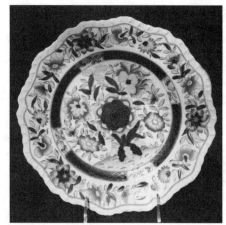

Plate, 10 1/2" d, cobalt, orange, iron-red, and gilt, unmkd, c1820, $285.00

10 1/2" d, cobalt, burnt orange, green, and rose "Japan Vase" pattern, leaf and rose border, set of 8, ... **680.00**
Platter
10 7/8" l x 8 1/2" w, oval, iron-red, cobalt, and gilt Imari pattern of vase w/lg cobalt plumes on rect table, scattered flowerheads and stems, Ashworth, ... **595.00**
15" l x 11" w, rect, gilt outlined cobalt lily of the valley, gilt stems and sponged border, ... **100.00**
17" l x 13" w, oct, iron-red, blue, green, and yellow oriental floral pattern, c1820, ... **775.00**
22" l x 18 1/2" w, semi-rect, "Tree of Life" pattern, polychrome, ... **500.00**

White

Plate

9 3/4" d

"Hyacinth" pattern, Burgess, ... **10.00**

"Lily of the Valley" pattern, "H. Burgess" mk, ... **35.00**

Raised "Wheat" pattern, Wilkinson, ... **10.00**

10" d, "Hebe" shape, Alcock, ... **30.00**

Platter

11" l x 8" w, "Sydenham" shape, "T. & R. Boote" mk, ... **50.00**

11 3/4" l, "Wheat" pattern, Ceres shape, Elsmore and Forster, ... **95.00**

12" l x 9 1/4" w, "Berlin Swirl" pattern, rim chips, ... **70.00**

13 3/4" l x 10 3/4" w, "Wheat" pattern, "Ceres" shape, Elsmore & Forster, ... **150.00**

14 1/2" l, "Ceres" shape, "W.E. Corn" mk, ... **110.00**

14 3/8" l x 10 3/4" w, oval, Anthony Shaw, ... **50.00**

16 1/4" l

11 5/8" w, "Sydenham" shape, "T. & R. Boote Sydenham Shape" mk, (A), ... **35.00**

12 3/4" w, "1851 Octagon" shape, "T. & R. Boote" mk, ... **100.00**

17" l x 12" w, "Victor" shape, "F. Jones" mk, ... **125.00**

17 5/8" l x 13 7/8" w, "Gothic" shape, J. Heath, ... **115.00**

18" l x 14" w, "Scalloped Decagon" shape, Wedgwood, ... **100.00**

18 3/4" l, "Wheat" pattern, Ceres shape, Elsmore and Forster, ... **125.00**

Relish Tray, 9 3/4" H-H, Johnson Brothers, ... **20.00**

*Tureen, 8 1/4" h, 13" H-H, "Ribbed Chain" shape, "J.W. Pankhurst Stone China Hanley, Royal Arms" mark, **$225.00***

*Tureen, 11 3/4" H-H, 8" h, "J.F. Ironstone China, Royal Arms" mark, **$225.00***

Sauce Tureen

8" h x 5 7/8" d, "Sydenham" shape, "T. & R. Boote Sydenham Shape" mk, (A), ... **88.00**

8" H-H, w/undertray and ladle, "Pankhurst Stone China England" mk, ... **85.00**

8 1/4" H-H, "Virginia" shape, Brougham and Mayer, (A), ... **80.00**

8 3/4" H-H, w/undertray, "Wheat and Hops" pattern, (A), ... **100.00**

Soap Dish, 3 3/4" h x 5 1/2" l x 4 1/4" w, rect, "Ironstone China G. Wooliscroft" mk, drain missing, (A), ... **110.00**

Soup Plate

7 1/2" d, "Gothic" shape, 12 sided, Alcock, ... **20.00**

8" d, "Wheat" pattern, "Wilkinson, Ltd" mk, set of 4, ... **30.00**

9" d, Alfred Meakin, ... **12.00**

9 3/4" d

"Chinese" shape, "T. & R. Boote" mk, ... **25.00**

"Columbia" shape, ... **30.00**

10" d, Alfred Meakin, ... **15.00**

10 1/8" d, "Budded Vine" design, "Meakin & Co." mk, ... **45.00**

10 5/8" d, "Hebe" pattern, "imp John Alcock, Cobridge" mk, ... **32.00**

Soup Tureen

9" w x 9 1/2" h, "Berry Cluster" shape, Jacob Furnival, (A), ... **80.00**

10 3/4" w x 6 1/2" h, "Union" shape, Davenport, ... **225.00**

11 1/2" h x 12 3/4" H-H, "Curved Gothic" shape, "T.J. & J. Mayer's Improved Ironstone China" mk, (A), ... **110.00**

12" H-H, "Ceres" shape, "Elsmore and Forster" mk, ... **250.00**

13" h, w/underplate and ladle, "President Shape," John Edwards, ... **950.00**

Sugar Bowl, Cov

7" h, "Bow and Tassel" pattern, "Burgess & Goddard" mk, ... **140.00**

8" h, "Sydenham" shape, T. & R. Boote, ... **110.00**

Syrup Pitcher, 6" h, "Lily of the Valley" pattern, pewter lid, "James Edwards & Sons" mk, ... **335.00**

*Teapot, 10" h, "Pear" pattern, Anthony Shaw, **$125.00***

Teapot

6 1/2" h, "Athena" pattern, "Johnson Bros.-Made in England" mk, ... **30.00**

7" h, "Empress Shape," Adams, ... **70.00**

9 1/2" h

"Atlantic Shape," "T. & R. Boote" mk, ... **525.00**

"President Shape," emb fuchsia and forget-me-nots, Meir, ... **325.00**

9 3/4" h, "Ribbed Oak" pattern, "W. & E. Corn" mk, c1878, ... **150.00**

Vegetable Bowl

9 3/4" l x 7 3/8" w, "W.& E. Corn England" mk, ... **42.00**

10" sq, vert ribbing, Alfred Meakin, ... **135.00**

Vegetable Bowl, Cov

7" h, 13" H-H, "Prairie" shape, "Clementson Brothers Royal Patent Stoneware" mk, ... **100.00**

8 1/4" d, "Sydenham" shape, "T.& R. Boote Sydenham Shape" mk, (A), ... **230.00**

11 1/8" l, "Vintage" shape, (A), ... **55.00**

12" H-H
8" h,
"Gothic" shape, George
Woodscroft, ... **160.00**
"Fuschia" pattern, "J. & G.
Meakin" mk, ... **125.00**
12 1/2" l x 8" w x 6 3/4" h, "Forget-
Me-Not" pattern, "E. & C.
Challinor," mk, (A), ... **55.00**
Water Pitcher, 12" h, England, ... **75.00**

ITALIA
1901

ITALY-GENERAL

Venice
1727-1812

Hard paste porcelain was made by
Francesco and Guiseppe **Vezzi** in Venice
between 1720 and 1727 with workers
brought from Meissen. The products
resembled the early Meissen and Vienna
wares. Tea wares were the most popular
form. The oldest pieces had black and
gold coloring. Later Venetian red was
used. Porcelains were marked with various
forms of the word Venice: VENEZIA, VEN,
or Va, in either gold, underglaze blue, or
red.

After the Vezzi factory closed, a new
factory was established by Friedrich
Hewelke in 1758. His china was marked
with the letter "V." The factory failed in
1763 during the Seven Years War.

A more successful factory to manufacture hard paste porcelain was established
by Geminiano **Cozzi** in 1764 and ran until
1812. Both utilitarian and ornamental
wares were made and exported throughout Europe. Cozzi's wares featured pouring spouts on coffeepots molded with leaf
decorations. Figures from the Italian Com-
edy were made along with colored and
white tea sets, services, and vases. Pieces
were marked with an anchor in red, blue,
or gold.

Le Nove
1750 to Late 19th Century

Pasquale Antonibon established a
porcelain factory in Le Nove in 1750. He
took Francisco Parolini as a partner in
1781. The painter Giovanni Marconi was
the factory's most prolific decorator. He
signed several Meissen type examples of
harbor scenes and rural romances. The
factory was leased to Baroni in 1802,
reverted to the Antonibon family in 1825,
and continued to produce until the late
19th century. Its principal production was
tableware. Special pieces included fish-
shaped tureens. The Sevres influence was

strong. The mark used was a comet or a
star in red, blue, or gold.

Naples
1771-1807

King Ferdinand IV, son of Charles IV,
established the Royal Naples Factory in
Naples in 1771 to manufacture porcelain
and fill the gap left by the transfer of
Capodimonte to Buen Retiro in Spain in
1759. Neo-classical wares were made
along with the rococo styles formerly used
by the Capodimonte workers. Domenico
Venuti was director from 1779 until 1807.
Filipo Tagliolini modeled figures of people
from Naples in the fashions of the day. The
factory was taken over by the French in
1807 and then closed in 1834.

The marks used were "FRF" under a
crown until 1787 and then a crowned "N"
impressed or painted in underglaze blue.

Vinovo
1776-1840

Gian Brodel from Turin and Marchese
Birago of Vische, assisted by Peter
Hannong, established a hard paste
porcelain factory in Vinovo in 1776. It went
bankrupt after a few years. Dr. Victor
Gioanotti, and Tamietti, a modeler,
reopened the factory in 1780. They made
mythological figures in colored and white
porcelain, services with rococo
decorations, vases with rural landscapes,
groups and statuettes in the Capodimonte
style, and busts of famous people in
biscuit ware. The factory remained in
operation until 1815 when Gioanotti died.

Giovanni Lamello, after working there
as a sculptor from 1798, bought the factory in 1815. The factory marks imitated
those of Sevres and the Meissen swords.
The marks were either impressed or
painted in underglaze blue or in red, grey,
or black on the glaze.

Maiolica or Faience
1400 to Present

The earliest maiolica was produced by
potteries located near Florence at Orvieto,
Faenza, Siena, and Arezzo, and used
manganese-purple and copper-green
decoration on pieces made for everyday
use. These wares were inspired by earlier
Spanish examples. Early in the 15th
century, a cobalt blue was introduced from
the Middle East. In about 1450, new colors
of yellow, turquoise, and orange appeared.

The rise of Faenza coincided with the
brilliant colors used in the istoriato, or pic-
toral, style of Urbino. The entire surface of
the piece was covered with historical,
classical, mythological, or Biblical scenes.
Subjects included heraldic lions, birds,
portraits, and foliage designs. Large drug
jars (albarelli) with strap handles were
made. Grotesques and arabesques were
introduced in the 16th century. Faenza
wares were at their finest from about 1480
until 1520.

Pictorals in the istoriato style were
done at Castel Durante and Urbino. Venetian maiolica exhibited an Oriental influence due to trade with the East. Large
globular jars were a favorite shape.

Savona in Liguria made maiolica in the
17th and 18th centuries. A wide variety of
wares was made including tea wares and
figures. Castelli near Naples, made maiolica in the 17th and 18th centuries, reviving
the istoriato style.

During the 17th and 18th centuries,
many factories produced maiolica wares.
Eventually they turned to the production of
lead-glazed earthenwares in the English
style. Manufacturing of tin-enamel wares
still continues in Italy. Some of the production is directed toward making souvenirs
for tourists.

Cantagalli
1878-1901

Cantagalli, an Italian potter, opened his
faience factory in Florence in 1878 and
used the crowing cock as its mark. The
firm traded as Figli di Giuseppe Cantagalli.
This factory manufactured imitations of
early Italian maiolica, similar to pieces
from Urbino, Faenza, Gubbio, Deruta, and
at the Della Robbia workshop. The factory
also imitated tin-glazed earthenwares in
the Isnik and Persian styles. Art Nouveau
style is found in vases decorated with
elongated plant motifs. Vases and dishes
designed by William De Morgan were
manufactured. Among its original products
were decorative tablewares.

References: A. Lane, *Italian Porcelain*,
Faber & Faber, 1954; B. Rackham, *Italian
Maiolica, 2nd Ed.*, Faber & Faber, 1963;
John Scott-Taggart, *Italian Majolica*,
Hamlyn Publishing Group, Ltd. 1972.

Museums: Bargello Museum, Florence,
Italy; Birmingham Museum of Art,
Birmingham, AL; British Museum, London,
England; Gardiner Museum of Ceramic
Art, Toronto, Canada; Musee National de
Ceramique, Sevres, France; Museo Civico,
Turin, Italy; National Museum of Wales,
Cardiff, Wales; Seattle Art Museum,
Seattle, WA; Victoria & Albert Museum,
London, England; Wadsworth Atheneum,
Hartford, CT.

Additional Listings: Capodimonte,
Deruta, and Ginori.

Albarello
6 1/2" h, waisted shape, lead glazed,
painted green and ochre
scrolling leaves on blue ground,
blue crosshatched base, 17th C,
Sicily, cracks, pr, (A),
.... **1,675.00**
6 3/4" h, black "PING.ANSER." in
center band, blue and yellow
birds and foliage, chips,
.... **2,250.00**

Beaker and Trembleuse Stand, 3 1/4" h, overall blue painted lambreguin bands, Savona, 18th C, (A), ... **450.00**

Bowl

10 1/4" d, HP yellow, pink, blue, and green geometrics, lines, spokes, and curves, ... **25.00**

10 1/2" d, orange, blue, green, and dk red stylized dragon, yellow-centered green flowerheads, 3 brown rope twist handles, Deruta, ... **60.00**

16" d, band of lg yellow lemons, blue-green leaves, border of blue dashes, "Montelupo Italy" mk, ... **125.00**

Cache Pot, 5 3/4" h x 6 1/2" d, Della Robbia, relief of 10 child figures around sides w/pink and green florals on blue ground, orange-brown rim and base, "Della Robbia XVI Century Made in Italy" mks, ... **45.00**

Cake Plate, 11" d, chipped pedestal, blue and white design of Order of St. Augustine, "flaming heart" pierced by swords, c1700, ... **750.00**

Center Bowl, 10" h x 15" d, cobalt ground w/painted soldier and satyrs on int, yellow and green grapevines and leaves on ext, 3 serpent handles, Deruta, late 19th C, repairs, ... **1,600.00**

Charger, 11 1/4" d, tin glazed, multicolored scene of royal Italian gentleman and guard in wooded landscape, brown lustered rim, "Benozzo Pazzoli Palozzo Riccardi Firenze, blue rooster" mks, 19th C, (A), $1,200.00

Charger

14 1/4" d, majolica, painted center scene of "Ascension" in lt blue inner frame line, border of dk blue foliage, c1680, ... **4,200.00**

17" d, faience, yellow, blue, and green, center medallion of 2 cherubs holding shield, border of grotesques, fowl, and animals, hairlines, ... **1,200.00**

17 1/2" d, HP half portrait of Italian lady holding hand mirror, multicolored arabesques, stylized flowers and buds on border, Deruta, ... **1,950.00**

Coffeepot, 9 1/2" h, classic woman wearing blue-green crisscross design gown, blue-green or yellow flowers, burgundy red ground, Deruta, ... **225.00**

Cup and Saucer, tin glaze, yellow centered red or blue flowerheads, green foliage, brown line rims, "rooster, Italy" mk, ... **25.00**

Dish

8 5/8" d, Istoriato, painted scene of nude female reclining under blue and orange canopy, Cupid w/bow at rt, yellow lined rim, Venice, c1560, chips, star crack, (A), ... **5,020.00**

13 5/8" d, lead glazed, green, ochre, blue, and yellow painted musketeer holding sword in outstretched hand, border of yellow dashes below conc blue and green lines, yellow rim, 18th C, (A), ... **425.00**

Drug Jar, 7" h, center banner w/black "Anari," blue and ochre scrolling foliage and shield designs, blue acanthus designs on base and collar, Deruta, hairlines, ... **125.00**

Egg Dish, 10" l x 8 1/2" w, oval, yellow, pink-red, and green rooster in center, 12 green dash lined oval wells, mkd, ... **20.00**

Figure, 5 3/4" h, standing zebra, relief of black stripes, red eyes, Raymor, "Italy" mk, ... **30.00**

Garden Seat, 17" h x 24" l, figural standing grey elephant, tan saddle, yellow blanket, dk red girth strap, repaint, ... **650.00**

Inkwell, 5 7/8" h, tin glazed earthenware, relief of swags of fruit from ribbons in stem w/yellow molded rope on base of stem, green leaves on cov, green and multicolored fruit, flowers, and foliage on base border, "rooster" mk, chips, ... **80.00**

Jar, 11 1/8" h, painted bust of Venetian woman w/pearl earrings in yellow ground roundel w/red streaks, reverse w/bearded man wearing

beret and ruffled collar, iron-red, blue, white, and green scrolled body w/trailing flowers and sgraffito tendrils, c1560, (A), ... **14,340.00**

Jug

3" h, yellow crawling leopard, yellow scattered leaves, blue buds, dbl red striped rim, blue dash handle, Deruta, ... **25.00**

6 1/4" h, tin glazed, center ochre medallion w/dk blue "BEVI CARA," vert ochre stripes separating blue curlicues, blue and ochre dashes and dots, white ground, c1820, ... **200.00**

7 1/2" h, ovoid, tin glazed, blue, yellow, ochre, and dk purple grotesques and scroll work, serpent handle, c1640, ... **525.00**

Master Salt, 7 1/2" h, tin glazed, figural woman seated before open basin on scroll work base, yellow hat, yellow-trimmed blue coat, green, yellow, and blue base and stand, mid-18th C, chips, ... **4,500.00**

Milk Jug, 3 7/8" h, painted loose sprays of flowers and scattered sprigs, bearded mask spout, branch handle w/fruiting vines, c1780, (A), ... **490.00**

Pilgrim Flask, Cov, 14" h, Istoriato, painted mythological scene of Apollo and Daphne w/cupid in clouds on shoulder, reverse w/Apollo reaching for Daphne who changes to a tree, pierced oval ft, screw cov, gold horned long eared lion's mask handles, Urbino, c1550, (A), ... **80,665.00**

Pitcher, 4 1/2" h, tin glazed, HP violet morning glories, leaves, and stems, white ground, violet dash handle, ... **25.00**

Pitcher, Cov, 6 1/8" h, tin glazed, blue-green and purple dragon on front, white ground, blue-green bands and cov, Deruta, ... **20.00**

Planter, 6 3/8" h, lg dk red stylized flowerheads, open loops on border, dk brown rim, Deruta, ... **30.00**

Plaque, 13" l x 9 1/2" w, rect, lead glazed, painted blue, green, and ochre scene of Virgin w/arms outstretched, 3 kneeling figures, "P.G.R." below lt green border, 18th C, (A), ... **1,050.00**

Plate

7 3/4" d, silver shape, painted figure in pink and yellow clothes, plumed hat leaning on stick,

flying insect, flanked by trees, brown lined shaped rim, Milan, c1760, (A), ... **4,660.00**

8" d, center painted w/pink, blue, or orange-yellow flowers and foliage, border w/flowerhead on alternating panels separated by honeycombs, overall brown bark ground, shaped, rim, ... **12.00**

9 1/8" d, tin glazed, HP blue, yellow-ochre, and green stylized bouquet in center, border of ochre-brown, blue, and green flowers and curls, c1700, rim chips, ... **510.00**

9 1/2" d, Kakiemon style prunus from tree trunk w/yellow tiger, c1765, ... **2,325.00**

9 3/4" d, shaded green molded artichoke design, center well, set of 6, ... **250.00**

10" d, multicolored painted overall peacock feather design, mkd, ... **95.00**

10" sq, HP crowing yellow rooster, red comb, blue-green tail, green and brown ground, "Italy" mk, ... **20.00**

10 1/4" d, HP orange, yellow, and brown rooster in center, blue geometric border, ... **15.00**

Platter, 9 3/4" l x 7 1/4" w, tin glazed, painted yellow and green fox in center, shaped border and rim w/scattered sprigs, ... **245.00**

Urn, 4 3/4" h, black painted garden scene w/figures, orange-brown rim, gold trim, c1880, **$385.00**

Serving Dish, 9" w, 3 molded shell sections, mottled grey in center, mottled grey and turquoise border, dk red flowerhead center handle, ... **35.00**

Tray, 10" H-H x 5 3/8" w, "Raffaellesco" pattern, 2 orange-yellow dragons in center, yellow border, red dash tab handles, scalloped rim, ... **26.00**

Urn, 8" h, tin glazed, white and yellow heart designs on blue ground, white stiff leaves on neck and base, 2 fancy handles, Deruta, ... **45.00**

Vase

6" h, ball shape w/short neck, faience, 4 heart shaped quadrants of gold-ochre and white swirls, curls, and leaves on blue ground, ... **65.00**

9 1/2" h, lg ear handles, upper section w/painted gold stylized scrolling foliage on blue ground between bands of foliage and dot designs, lower section w/spiral gadroons and conc bands on circ spreading ft w/radiating flowers and stiff leaves, c1530, hairlines and restored handle, (A), ... **7,175.00**

10" h, flared and lobed, lg yellow and orange flower, green foliage, lt brown mottled ground, brown streaked rim, artist sgd, ... **150.00**

24" h, baluster shape, HP scene of horse mtd king, reverse w/Italian lake scene, serpent handles, ... **1,500.00**

Water Pitcher

7 1/2" h, terra cotta body, HP blue and red stylized flowerheads and stems, off-white ground, c1800, chips and glaze skips, ... **75.00**

12" h, 2 pink "old" roses, green foliage in wavy blue line and ermine tails, red dot border on side panels, single rose panel under spout, gold separate panels w/red scrolling designs, blue lined rim, red dash fancy handle, Deruta, ... **250.00**

Wet Drug Jar, 9 1/4" h, blue scrolling medallion w/birds and "A.Q.A. di LINO," blue notched line designs, white ground, strap handle, ... **375.00**

Wet Drug Jar, 8 1/2" h, majolica, blue and olive green designs, yellow stripe and spout, grey ground, late 17th C, repair to spout, A-$550.00

JACKFIELD

Staffordshire and Shropshire, England
Second half of 18th century

History: Jackfield was a generic term used for black-glazed earthenware made during the second half of the 18th century. The red clay body was covered with a blackish glossy slip that was ornamented with scrollwork and relief flowers, oil gilding, and unfired painting. Jackfield was named after the Shropshire Pottery Center.

From c1750 to 1775 the Jackfield factory was managed by Maurice Thursfield. John Rose of Coalport assumed control of the firm about 1780. Staffordshire potters such as Astbury and Whieldon also produced Jackfield wares.

References: R.G. Cooper, *English Slipware Dishes, 1650-1850*, Tiranti, 1968; *The Jackfield Decorative Tile Industry*, pamphlet, published by Ironbridge Gorge Museum Trust, England, 1978.

Museum: British Museum, London, England.

Cow Creamer, Cov, 5 1/2" h

7" l, gold spots on body and face, gold horns **200.00**

7 1/2" l, gold trim around horns, oval stepped base, ... **195.00**

Creamer

3 1/4" h, stippled and rose bands, figural eagle handle, (A), ... **50.00**

3 3/4" h

Baluster form, 3 sm feet, molded flowers on front, (A), ... **66.00**

Redware body, molded fruit on flowers on upper half, vert molding on lower half,
.... **55.00**

Figure

7" h, seated cat, gold star on neck, gilt accented face, gilt outlined oval base, ... **260.00**

12" h, seated spaniel, c1865, pr, ... **850.00**

Jug

7 3/4" h, printed and enameled oriental figures, gilt accents, Dudson, c1890, ... **325.00**

8 1/2" h, paneled, oil gilt designs of foliage and dots, molded beaded rim, dbl loop handle,
.... **65.00**

Match Holder, 3 1/2" h, engine turned horiz ribbing on center section, raised beaded rim, ... **30.00**

Milk Pitcher

3 3/4" h, black glazed body w/green ground and lg gold edged and veined leaf form, scattered white enameled dots, ... **10.00**

Pitcher, 5 5/8" h, HP polychrome bird on front, violet barn on reverse, gold trim, c1780, $375.00

4" h, gold leaf and stem overlay, gloss black ground, ... **10.00**

8" h, aesthetic, HP enameled blue-green and gold palm trees, diagonal and geometric gold and enamel designs, gloss black ground, ... **225.00**

Mug, 3 3/8" h, blue sprigged classic figure offering crown, reverse w/sprigged blue flowers, gloss black ground, c1810, ... **75.00**

Teapot

2 3/4" h x 6 1/2" l, bachelor's size, horiz ribbing, Staffordshire, ... **110.00**

4" h x 4 3/8" w, relief molded wicker type body, molded leaf rim, floral spout and handle, chips, (A), ... **75.00**

Teapot, 9" h, unmkd, c1760-80, $1,250.00

4 3/4" h

Engine-turned design, c1820, ... **200.00**

Molded and gilt oriental florals, branch handle and spout, 3 paw feet, bird knob, ... **180.00**

5" h, globular shape, chips, ... **75.00**

6 3/4" h, molded thistles and roses, ram's horn mask on handle, (A), ... **60.00**

9" h, enameled yellow-centered white daisies, lt brown and green leaves, repair to lid, ... **40.00**

Tobacco Jar, 4" h, center band of enameled green leaves, white grape bunches, band of white enamel beading on cov, int chip, ... **25.00**

Vase, 8 1/2" h, pilgrim bottle shape, enameled flowers and butterflies, black glazed ground, gilt dolphin handles, Dudson, pr, ... **495.00**

JASPER WARE

Staffordshire, England
Continental
1774 to Present

History: About 1774 Josiah Wedgwood perfected a hard, unglazed stoneware whose body was capable of being stained throughout its substance with metallic oxides. Shades of blue, lavender, sage, olive green, lilac, yellow, and black could be used. With jasper dip, the color was applied only on the surface.

Many firms, in addition to Wedgwood, produced jasper wares. Adams made jasper from the early 1800s into the 20th century. Adams blue jasper was distinguished from that of Wedgwood because it had a faint violet shade. Initially Adams modeled many of the designs for his jasper ware. In 1785 he employed Joseph Mongenot from Switzerland as a modeler. Together they designed the bas-reliefs and border decorations that were applied in white jasper to the colored bodies of vases, urns, tea and coffeepots, plaques, medallions, and candelabra drums. Most of the Adams jasper is marked.

Another producer of jasper ware was Spode. Other Staffordshire manufacturers produced marked jasper ware. Unfortunately, many examples do not include a maker's mark. Several Continental potters, e.g. Heubach, also manufactured jasper ware.

Museums: British Museum, London, England; Memorial Hall Museum, Philadelphia, PA; Museum of Fine Arts, Boston, MA; Victoria & Albert Museum, London, England.

Biscuit Barrel

5" h, white cameos of classic figures separated by trees and columns, border band of grape leaves and tendrils between lines, dk blue jasper ground, SP rim, cov, bail handle, unmkd, ... **135.00**

5 1/2" h, ovoid shape, white classic cameos, dk blue ground, SP rim, cov, and overhead handle, "imp Wm. Adams" mk, ... **425.00**

7" h, white cameos of classic figures, Cherub on pedestal, trees and shrubs, stiff leaves and acorns on cov, med blue jasper ground, acorn knob, unmkd, ... **70.00**

Bowl, 9 1/2" d, white cameos of chariots and horses w/drivers, dk blue jasper ground, silver rim, Brownshill, ... **460.00**

Box, Cov, 4 3/8" d, white cameo of bust of Art Nouveau woman holding vase of flowers on cov, green jasper ground, ... **250.00**

Additional Listing: Wedgwood jasper ware pieces are found in the Wedgwood listing.

Cheese Keeper

5 1/4" d, 2 1/2" h, circ, white cameos of rural scenes of horses jumping fences and dogs, dk blue jasper ground, EPNS lid, Adams, ... **400.00**

8 1/2" h x 11" d, white cameos of classic figures, dog, and trees, band of leaves on base and cov rim, star shaped snowflake design on cov, med blue ground, Adams, ... **425.00**

Cheese Dome, 8" h x 8 3/4" d, white cameos, med blue ground, unmkd, $650.00

9" h x 12" d, white cameos of ferns, fronds, grasses, and calla lilies, petals around air holes, brown jasper ground, band of white of stiff leaves around base rim, unmkd, ... **495.00**

Clock Case, 6" h, white cameos of seated classic lady holding winged cherub, 2 children and dog seated beneath arched trees, molded scroll borders, green jasper ground, ... **165.00**

Creamer

2 1/4" h x 3 1/2" w, white cameos of classic women and children and trees, leaf band on handle, cobalt jasper ground, Adams, chip, ... **50.00**

3" h

Raised cameo figure of queen on sides, flowers, and figures, raised grapes and leaves around top, green base, Germany, ... **55.00**

White cameo of seated angel, playing mandolin, bird on knee, green cameos of foliage under rim and spout, violet jasper ground, .. **20.00**

4" h, white cameos of man, woman, dog, deer, and bird around sides, lt blue jasper ground, Dudson, England, ... **35.00**

Creamer and Sugar Bowl, creamer, 3 1/4" h, sugar bowl, 2" h x 3 1/2" d, white cameos of classic figures, dk blue jasper ground, white gloss ints, "imp ADAMS TUNSTALL ENGLAND" mks, ... **30.00**

Flask, Cov, 7" h, w/handle, sq white cameo cartouche of minstrel and lady, Cupid on neck, green jasper ground, ... **95.00**

Hair Receiver, 5" w, heart shape, white cameos of woman, winged cherub, and birds, blue jasper ground, ... **295.00**

Jam Pot, 4" h, white cameos of classic figures on med blue jasper ground, SP cov and spoon, Wm. Adams, ... **35.00**

Milk Pitcher, 5 1/2" h, white cameos of classic women musicians and dancing cherubs, hanging wreaths from border, green jasper ground, Germany, ... **25.00**

Pitcher

4 1/4" h, white Kewpies playing, white floral border, med blue ground, "Rose O'Neill, Kewpie" mk, ... **245.00**

4 1/2" h, white cameo of cherub drinking from jug held by kneeling woman, winged shell design on base, band of curlicues on border, molded shell on straight handle, med blue jasper ground, unmkd, ... **25.00**

4 3/4" h

White cameo band of dancing classic women, hanging swags on shoulder, blue jasper ground, tan rim, spout, base, and handle, Copeland, ... **185.00**

White cameos of classic figures of women, children, and dog, band of grape leaves and tendrils on rim, dk blue ground, ... **225.00**

6" h, white cameos of muses w/white cameo vert dividers, band of sprigs on border, sage green ground, Dudson, ... **45.00**

7 1/2" h

Applied lt tan vert fern fronds, med blue jasper ground, applied white rope twist handle, ... **110.00**

White cameos of classic figures between cameo arches, white cameo starburst border, med blue jasper ground, "Adams & Bromley" mk, ... **295.00**

8" h, white cameos of classic figures w/columns, Cupids, and warriors, herringbone handle w/mask terminal, dk blue jasper ground, Dudson, ... **65.00**

10" h, white cameos of swags hanging from lion's heads, border of grapes, leaves, and tendrils, med blue jasper ground, Dudson, ... **135.00**

Planter, 8" h, white cameos of hunt scene on base, white cameo drape on border, med blue jasper ground, Adams, c1890, ... **745.00**

Plaque

5 1/2" d, white cameos of child and cat reaching for piano, doll on ground, fancy rim, green jasper ground, ... **85.00**

5 3/4" l x 5" w, oval, white cameos of Indian on horseback w/bow and arrow chasing buffalo, green jasper ground, shaped rim, ... **135.00**

6" d, white cameo of frontal view of American Indian woman, flowerhead border, dk green ground, ... **195.00**

6" l x 4 1/2" w, oval, white cameos of Cupid fanning reclining lady, pink cameo flowerheads and scroll border, dk blue jasper ground, c1900, ... **60.00**

6 1/4" l x 4 1/2" w, pink relief of bust of Art Nouveau woman, pink scrolling and border, blue-grey jasper ground, pierced for hanging, unmkd, ... **80.00**

6 1/2" h x 5 1/2" w, rect, white cameos of "The Melon Eaters" on green jasper ground, Goebel, c1914, pr, ... **495.00**

7 1/2" d, white cameo bust of Beethoven, med blue jasper ground, unmkd, ... **160.00**

8 1/2" h x 5 1/2" w, white cameos of period male kissing hand of maiden, scrolling border w/flowerhead top and base, sage green ground, unmkd, ... **35.00**

8 3/4" h x 6" w, white cameos of period courting couple, rococo border, pink ground, "blue X'd swords" mk, Germany, ... **20.00**

Spill, 4 1/2" h, cylinder shape, white cameos of classic figures w/instruments, kissing doves, and trees, hanging swag on shoulder, med blue jasper ground, SP rim, "imp ADAMS" mk, ... **420.00**

Tankard, 8" h, w/circ stand, white cameos of dancing women, med blue ground, band of white leaves on rim, ... **255.00**

Teapot, 4 1/2" h, white cameos of classic figures and trees, band of leaves at spout connection, dk blue jasper ground, Adams, chip, ... **55.00**

Tea Set, pot, 5 1/4" h, creamer, 5 1/2" w, cov sugar bowl, 6 3/4 H-H, band of white cameos of classic figures and trees, bands of leaves on borders, white cameo starburst on cov, med blue jasper ground, Copeland-Spode, ... **490.00**

Tobacco Jar, 6" h, white cameos, dk blue ground, SP collar, cov, and handle, "imp ADAMS" mk, $175.00

Tobacco Jar, 5" h, white cameos of dancing classic maidens holding ribbons, band of chevrons on base, geometrics on cov, med blue jasper ground, "imp Adams EST 1657 Tunstall England" mk, ... **125.00**

Vase
  6" h, trumpet shape, flared rim, band of white cameos of flowerheads on base, vert stiff leaves, band of flowers and curlicues on neck, dk green ground, ... **185.00**
  6 3/4" h, corset shape, white cameos of classic figures and trees around base, interlocking curls and loops on neck, dk blue ground, Adams, ... **275.00**
  7 1/2" h, triangle shape, white cameos of classic woman dropping flowers into urn, cameo wreaths of cherubs on other sides, green jasper ground, unmkd, ... **265.00**
  7 3/4" h, paneled straight shape, white cameo of bust of Art nouveau woman in relief of beaded heart, relief molded ribbons, sage green jasper ground, ... **25.00**
Waste Bowl, 3 1/8" d, white cameos of dancing Grecian females, dk blue jasper ground, Dudson, ... **25.00**

Urn, 6" h, dk brown classical scene of putti in landscape, beaded border, yellow jasper ground, unmkd, A-$75.00

JOHNSON BROTHERS

Staffordshire, England
1883 to Present

History: Henry, Robert, Alfred, and Fred, the four Johnson brothers, founded a pottery in 1883 in Staffordshire, England. Although begun on a small scale, it soon expanded. Its principal success was derived from earthenware tablewares that were quite successful in both England and the United States.

By 1914 the Johnson Brothers had five factories scattered throughout Hanley, Tunstall, and Burslem. Some popular patterns included "Granite," made for the overseas market, as well as "Green & Golden Dawn," and "Rose." Johnson Brothers' wares originally were white ironstone, but they were replaced by a ware known for its uncommon lightness and finish.

Johnson Brothers became part of the Wedgwood Group in 1968.

Reference: Mary J. Finegan, *Johnson Brothers Dinnerware: Pattern Directory and Price Guide*, Marfine Antiques, 2000.

Berry Bowl, 5" d, "Dorchester" pattern, multicolored, ... **3.00**

Bowl
  5 1/4" d, "Century of Progress-Art Institute of Chicago-1833-1933," red transfer, vert red dash rim, ... **35.00**
  6 1/2" d, "Tally-Hoe-Stirrup Cup" pattern, multicolored, ... **25.00**
  7" w, oct, "Devonshire" pattern, brown transfer w/colors, ... **14.00**
  8 1/4" d, "Nordic" pattern, blue transfer, ... **12.00**
  8 3/8" d, "The Friendly Village-Autumn Mist," brown transfer w/colors, ... **20.00**
  9" l, oval, "Sheraton" pattern, multicolored, ... **20.00**
Butter Pat, 4" d, "Haddon Hall" pattern, blue transfer, ... **10.00**
Casserole, Cov, 10 1/2" d, "Strawberry Fair" pattern, red transfers, ... **215.00**
Cereal Bowl, 6 1/8" d, "Coaching Scenes" pattern, blue transfer, **12.00**
Coffeepot, 8 1/2" h, "Old Britain Castles-Blarney Castle and Dunstanburg Castle," blue transfer, ... **90.00**
Cookie Jar, 9 1/4" h, "The Friendly Village," figural tan house, red shutters and roof, ... **20.00**
Creamer
  3 1/2" h, "Winchester" pattern, red floral transfer w/green and blue accents, ... **15.00**
  3 3/4" h, "Strawberry Fair" pattern, ... **40.00**
  4 3/4" l, "Winchester" pattern, pink, green, yellow-gold, and blue transfer, rope rim, ... **50.00**
Creamer and Sugar Bowl, 3 1/8" h, "Fruit Sampler" pattern, pr, ... **20.00**
Creamer, 4 3/4" h, Sugar Bowl, Cov, 5 1/2" h, "Rose Bouquet" pattern, ... **30.00**

Cup and Saucer
  "Azalea Garden" pattern, pink, blue, and brown, ... **10.00**
  "Chippendale" pattern, red transfers, ... **32.00**
  "Indies Blue" pattern, ... **10.00**
  "Olde English Countryside," brown transfer w/colors, ... **10.00**
  "The Friendly Village-The Ice House" pattern, ... **5.00**
  "Tulip Time," blue transfer, ... **25.00**
  "Winchester" pattern, multicolored, ... **20.00**
Dish, 11" l x 9" w, scalloped rim, "The Friendly Village" pattern, ... **30.00**
Fruit Bowl, 5" d, "Old Britain Castles-Alnwich Castle in 1792," red transfer, ... **6.00**

Dish, 11" l x 7 1/2" w, cobalt, yellow, turquoise, iron red and gilt, c1800, $595.00

Ginger Jar, Cov, 6 1/2" h, "Old Britain Castles-Karlick Castle 1792," red transfers, ... **325.00**

Gravy Boat
8" l
  3 3/4" h, "Sheraton" pattern,
  .... **35.00**
  W/undertray, 8 1/2" l, mottled cobalt upper band, gold garland of hanging swags, ivory base, ... **20.00**
8 1/4" l, "Poppy" pattern, yellow, dk blue, and brown, ... **35.00**

Milk Jug, 4 1/2" h, "The Friendly Village" pattern, multicolored transfer, ... **70.00**

Pickle Dish, 8" l, "Devonshire" pattern, brown transfer w/colors, ... **50.00**

Plate
6 1/4" d, "Olde English Countryside" pattern, brown transfer, ... **4.00**
6 1/2" d
  "Azalea Garden" pattern, pink, blue, and brown, ... **3.00**
  "The Old Mill" pattern, brown transfer, maroon and blue accents, ... **7.00**
8" d, "Dorchester" pattern, multicolored, ... **8.00**
10" d
  "Apple Blossom" pattern, brown transfer w/colors, molded rim, ... **10.00**
  "Azalea Garden" pattern, pink, blue, and brown, ... **12.00**
  "Chippendale" pattern, red transfer, ... **20.00**
  "Olde English Countryside" pattern, brown transfer, ... **7.00**
  "Strawberry Fair" pattern, ... **35.00**
  "The Friendly Village-The Schoolhouse" pattern, ... **15.00**

Platter
9 1/4" l, oval, "Historic America-Erie Canal" pattern, red transfer, ... **35.00**
11 1/2" l x 8 7/8" w, "Winchester" pattern, pink, green, yellow-gold, and blue transfer, rope rim, ... **30.00**
12" l
  9 1/4" w, "Blue Tulip Time" pattern, ... **15.00**
  9 1/2" w
  "Garden Bouquet" pattern, pink, purple, blue and green flowers, green foliage, molded fluted rim, ... **15.00**

Tureen, 17 1/4" H-H, 9 3/4" h, "Harvest Time" pattern, polychrome transfer, $250.00

  "Old English Countryside," brown transfer w/color accents, ... **40.00**
12 1/4" d, "Henley" pattern, blue/grey transfer, gold trim, ... **25.00**
12 1/4" l x 9 1/2" w, oval, "Castle on the Lake" pattern, brown transfer w/polychrome accents, ... **39.00**
13 3/4" l x 11" w, oval, "Devonshire" pattern, brown print, ... **65.00**
14" l
  "English Bouquet" pattern, ... **99.00**
  "Rosedale" pattern, blue/black transfer, ... **15.00**
  White, molded piecrust border, ... **20.00**
14 1/2" l x 11" w, oval
  "Constance" pattern, purple transfer, ... **30.00**
  "Pareek" pattern, ... **39.00**
16" l, oval
  Gold floral outlined rim and molded handles, white ground, mkd, ... **20.00**
  "Pomona" pattern, ... **200.00**
  White, molded acanthus leaf border, ... **75.00**
18" l x 13" w, "Holland" pattern, ... **99.00**

20" l, "The Friendly Village" pattern, brown transfer w/colors, ... **225.00**
25" l, oval, lobed, "Fish" series, multicolored swimming fish, ... **125.00**

Ramekin, 3 7/8" d, "Summer Chintz" pattern, ... **7.00**

Sandwich Tray, 12 3/4" l x 7 3/8" l, "Old Britain Castles-Dudley Castle in 1792," blue transfer, ... **25.00**

Serving Bowl
8 1/4" d, "Winchester" pattern, pink, green, yellow-gold, and blue transfer, rope rim, ... **40.00**
9 1/4" w x 10" l, "Old Britain Castles-Bolover Castle," blue transfer, ... **18.00**

Serving Plate, 12" w, "Olde English Countryside" pattern, brown transfer w/colors, ... **15.00**

Soup Bowl, 7 1/2" d, "Dorchester" pattern, multicolored, ... **7.00**

Soup Plate, 8" d, "Old British Castles-Chatsworth in 1792," blue transfer, ... **15.00**

Soup Tureen, Cov
11 1/2" H-H, w/underplate, white ground w/gold outlined molded borders and flower knob, ... **25.00**
17" l , "The Friendly Village," pattern, brown transfers w/colors, ... **350.00**

Sugar Bowl
2 7/8" h x 6 1/4" H-H, "Strawberry Fair" pattern, ... **38.00**
6 3/4" H-H, "Carnation" pattern, gold trim, ... **13.00**
7" H-H, "Eastbourne" pattern, multicolored, ... **10.00**

Teapot
4 1/2" h x 10" w, "American Heritage-Mt. Vernon" pattern, blue transfers, ... **145.00**
5 1/2" h, 4 sm feet, "Old Britain Castles-Farnham Castle-1792," red transfer, ... **235.00**
6" h, "The Friendly Village" pattern, ... **50.00**
6 1/4" h
  "Dorchester" pattern, ... **200.00**
  "Pink Rose Chintz" pattern, ... **80.00**
9" h, "Tulip Time" pattern, blue transfers, ... **95.00**

Turkey Platter, 20 1/2" l x 16 1/4" w, oct, "BARNYARD KING" pattern, brown transfer, ... **165.00**

Turkey Service, platter, 20" l x 14" w, 8 plates, 10 1/2" d, "Wild Turkeys" pattern, multicolored flying turkeys, brown fruit and floral borders, ... **1,475.00**

Vegetable Bowl, 9 3/4" l, "Old Britain Castles—Arundel Castle in 1792" pattern, red transfer, **$40.00**

Vegetable Bowl

9" l x 7" w, "Olde English Countryside" pattern, red transfer, ... **15.00**

9 1/8" l 6 7/8" w, "Castle on the Lake" pattern, multicolored, ... **45.00**

9 1/2" l, "Devonshire" pattern, brown transfer w/colors, ... **45.00**

Vegetable Bowl, Cov

10" H-H, "Athena" pattern, white glaze, ... **30.00**

11 1/2" H-H, "Worcester" pattern, ... **125.00**

KG Luneville 1788 - 19TH CENTURY C.M Golfe·Juan· (A·M) 1845-1917

KELLER AND GUERIN

Luneville, France
1778 to Present

History: Keller and Guerin bought the old faience factory of Jacques Chambrette from Gabriel, his son, and Charles Loyal, his son-in-law, in 1778. The factory made blue decorated faience similar to that of Nevers, and rose and green faience that imitated old Strasbourg motifs.

Schneider was the most celebrated of the potters who worked at Keller and Guerin. The company commissioned designs from sculptors Ernest Bussiere and E. Lachenal, among others. Biscuit porcelain figures, especially of large animals, were a specialty.

The company switched from faience to English-style earthenware at the end of the 19th century. Majolica and transfer-printed wares entered the product line. The company still is in operation.

Creamer and Cov Sugar Bowl, 3" h, dk brown drip glaze, ball knob w/molded leaf terminal, ... **40.00**

Jam Pot, 3" h, w/underplate, tin glazed, meandering dk red cabbage rose, stems, and buds, streaked dk red tab handles, figural lemon knob, red lined rim, ... **95.00**

Milk Jug, 5" h, "Elysee" pattern, mauve and black flowers, med brown streaked ground, ... **10.00**

Pitcher, 8" h, lg red poppies, green foliage, shaded green ground, serrated rim, "K. & G. Luneville France" mk, ... **75.00**

Planter, 14" l, 8" w, 6" h, brown and black stylized foliage, white ground, "Keller & Guerin, Monterey" mark, A-$110.00

Planter, 7 1/2" h x 11" d, Art Nouveau style cream irises, green stems, blue shadow flowerheads w/whiplash stems, lt blue ground, dk blue shoulder w/gold lines, ormolu feet, collar, and handles, "K. & G. Luneville" mk, ... **595.00**

Plate

8" d

"La Boxe," black and tinted comical scene of boxer and another lying flat, "La Defaite," "K. & G. Luneville France" mk, ... **20.00**

"Timor" pattern, 2 oriental figures in center, multicolored, iron-red rim, ... **48.00**

"Violette" pattern, flowing blue violets in center and border, "K. & G. Luneville" mk, ... **85.00**

8 1/2" d

HP bouquet of red tulip, red chrysanthemums, purple flowers, green leaves in center, red outlined vert reticulated rim, mkd, ... **15.00**

HP hanging red cherries, brown stems, green leaves, shaded green to cream ground, artist sgd, ... **50.00**

HP yellow, green, or red hanging grape bunches, blue-green foliage, rose-burgundy shaded ground, "K & G Luneville France" mk, ... **18.00**

9" d, molded purple tipped green asparagus stalks, green and turquoise swirled foliage, pink shaded sauce well at end, c1885, ... **235.00**

9 3/4" d, Art Nouveau style, brown, tan, and yellow clothed couple kissing, lg pink flowers, twisting green stems, green lined rim, "K. & G. Luneville, France" mk, ... **20.00**

10" d, 2 lg pink and red roses and buds at side, shaded green ground, ... **75.00**

Platter, 20 1/2" l x 14 1/2" w, blue printed Tom, hen, and chick turkeys, molded panel border, gold rim, ... **40.00**

Soup Plate, 9 1/2" d, "Veronique" pattern, mauve flowers, chocolate brown leaves and rim trim, honey brown glaze, piecrust rim, ... **10.00**

Tea Set, pot, 7 1/2" h, creamer, 4" h, cov sugar bowl, 3 1/2" h, tin glazed, red Strasbourg tulip on sides, pink rims, fruit knobs, "K. & G. Luneville France" mks, ... **225.00**

Vase, 8" h, slightly swollen body and collar, white Art Nouveau style swamp flowers, green stems and pads, olive green ground, "KG Luneville France" mk, ... **130.00**

KPM 1844-1947 *KPM 1835-44* *1870-PRESENT*

KING'S PORCELAIN MANUFACTORY (KPM)

Berlin, Germany
1763 to Present

History: The King's Porcelain Manufactory (KPM) was purchased and controlled by Frederick the Great. He ran the factory according to his own ideas and was responsible for its successes and failures, even though he employed Johann Grieninger as director.

The early porcelains were characterized by a dense, clear glaze over a fine white body. Many of the more talented German painters were employed by Frederick, resulting in products that competed with the highly successful Meissen factory.

The 18th century at KPM was characterized by technically superior figures in the glazed and biscuit state that showed a critical attention to details. However, the mainstay of the company was a line of popular, fine tablewares and ornamental pieces. Large quantities of tablewares were decorated with detailed florals and period and pastoral paintings. These early pieces showed a discriminating use of gilding, often used to highlight rather than to decorate. The later periods saw an increase in the use of gilding to the point of excessiveness. After the death of Frederick the Great in 1786, the factory continued to produce dinner services and other utilitarian and decorative porcelains.

The King's Porcelain Manufactory also was known for the fine miniature plaques in porcelain that featured copies of popular paintings of the period. KPM, along with other major European houses, kept up with the times and changing styles, adopting the rococo, neo-classical, and Empire styles as each became fashionable. KPM was among the first to produce lithophanes. During the 19th century, the emphasis shifted to simple, clean designs.

From its beginnings, KPM was under the control of the Prussian monarchy. With the abdication of William II, the last of the kings, in 1918, KPM became the property of the Prussian state. It was renamed the States Porcelain Manufactory Berlin. Severe damage from bombings during World War II resulted in the factory being moved to Selb, where it leased the porcelain factory of Paul Muller.

After WW II, the factory in Berlin was reconstructed. Since the two factories were in separate occupation zones, both branches remained legally separated until 1949. When the Federal Republic of Germany was established in 1949, the factory in Berlin became the property of the City of Berlin (West Property). The branch in Selb returned to Berlin in 1957. Products from Selb have an "S" beneath the scepter.

References: Winfred Baer, *Berlin Porcelain*, Smithsonian Institution Press, 1980; George W. Ware, *German and Austrian Porcelain*, Crown, Inc. 1963.

Reproduction Alert: This mark is one of the most frequently copied and reproduced marks on china and porcelain. Imitations and modern reproductions have little or no hand painting; they are transfer printed. Other factories used similar marks to KPM. A mark without the scepter is not authentic. KPM must appear in combination with scepter, orb, or eagle on authentic marks.

Bowl, 8 3/8" w, oct and flared, blue and gilt flowers in gilt filigree sq in center, side panels of painted scenes of shore scenes and harbors, alternating dk red panels of garden flowers or narrow white panels w/flowers, gilt filigree rim, blue scepter mk, ... **300.00**

Cabinet Cup and Saucer, gilt oval w/multicolored bust of military man, gilt rims and star burst on saucer, gilt edged scroll handle w/white beading, "blue scepter, iron red eagle, orb, and KPM" mks, c1800, ... **825.00**

Coffee Set, pot, 11 1/2" h, cream jug, cov sugar bowl, multicolored armorials, gilt accents, 19th C, A-$605.00

Compote, Cov, 12 1/2" h, HP scene of family pleading w/tax man and family leaving home on body, cov w/painted scene of men eating, another w/men drinking, border bands of sm red flowers and green foliage, gilt rims, figural knob of standing cherub holding wine glass and carafe, blue scepter mk, ... **2,950.00**

Cup and Saucer, HP

Floral bouquets, raised gold panels and scrolling, c1830, "iron-red orb and KPM, blue scepter" mks, ... **470.00**

Grey, yellow, and orange tulip, sm blue flowers, green foliage, orange rims, "blue scepter, KPM" mks, ... **325.00**

Dish, 15" l x 11 1/8" w, oval, HP tulip and flower sprigs, indented lobed rim, c1775, ... **220.00**

Lithophane, 7 1/4" h x 5 7/8" w, rect. portrait of Saint Peter, imp scepter, KPM, ... **400.00**

Plaque

9" h x 6 5/8" w, oval, HP half portrait of lady, green gown, holding flute, "imp KPM scepter" mk, ... **1,795.00**

9 1/4" l x 6 1/8" h, rect, nude brunette relining on leopard skin, next to pool, "imp KPM, scepter" mks, (A), ... **4,995.00**

9 1/2" h x 6 1/2" w, rect, HP classic lady, sheer white gown, peach waist drape, butterfly on hand, pastoral bkd, "imp KPM scepter" mk, ... **3,250.00**

9 3/4" h

5 3/4" w, HP standing classic maiden wearing pink gown, brown sandals, standing in hallway, holding tray of flowers, "imp scepter, KPM" mks, ... **12,000.00**

7 1/2" w, rect, "Whispering Secrets," HP peasant girl whispering to another holding shielded candle, artist sgd, "KPM, scepter" mks, ... **1,175.00**

12 1/2" h x 10" w, bust of classic Italian lady, "La Fiammetta V. Lefebvre Cop V.F. Wagner Wein," "imp KPM, scepter" mks, ... **17,500.00**

12 3/4" h x 6 1/2" w, "The Muse of Music," young girl holding instrument next to tree, gold and white satin gown, "imp scepter, KPM" mks, ... **13,500.00**

Plate, 8 1/2" d, HP fruit, white ground, raised gold border and rim, "blue scepter, iron-red KPM, orb" mks, set of 5, (A), $350.00

Plate

9 1/2" d, painted white, yellow, or red lilies, or white, pink, or blue convolvulus, apricot border w/gilt scrolling foliage, "brown eagle, KPM, blue scepter" mks, pr, (A), ... **5,740.00**

9 5/8" d, painted scene of "Winter" as child in animal skin seated at brazier before reclining goat, skates in foreground, lt apricot border w/gilt diamond flowerheads in diamond band,

tooled gilt inner border, "blue scepter" mk, c1830, (A), ... **1,075.00**

Platter

15 1/2" l x 12" w, oval, painted garden bouquet and sprigs in center, swirl molded border, gilt drape rim, "blue scepter" mk, ... **1,500.00**

19 1/4" l x 14 3/4" w, oval, floral bouquet in center and scattered sprigs, scalloped border, gilt rim, "blue scepter" mk, ... **2,100.00**

Pot Au Creme, 4 5/8" h, blanc-de-chine, trembleuse saucer, 2 handles, asparagus knob, blue scepter mk, ... **125.00**

Tea and Coffee Service, Part, teapot, 5 1/2" h, coffeepot, 9 1/2" h, pitcher, 5 1/2" h, creamer, 3 3/4" h, cov sugar bowl, 4 1/2" h, waste bowl, 6 1/2" d, 17 cups, 18 saucers, 6 plates, 7" d, tray, 12" H-H, textured weave ground, HP sprigs of garden flowers, gilt rims, "blue scepter, red orb, KPM" mks, c1830, ... **4,500.00**

Tea Caddy, 5 1/4" h, multicolored florals, gilt trim, "blue scepter" mk, late 19th C, $225.00

Tea Caddy, 4 1/2" h, flat sides, arched shoulder, HP painted bouquets on sides, puce and green butterfly on corner, figural rose knob, gilt line on cov, "blue scepter" mk, ... **435.00**

Teacup and Saucer, painted polychrome exotic birds and butterflies, gilt scrolling rims, gilt leaf end handle, blue scepter mk, c1840, ... **625.00**

Teapot, 4 1/2" h, multicolored turkeys in frame on front, chickens on reverse, salmon colored ground, set in lid, gilt ear handle and spout, 3 gilt paw feet, late 19th C, (A), ... **645.00**

Vase, 3 3/4" h, squat shape, blanc de chine, intaglio medallion of classical semi-nude woman on side, blue scepter mk, ... **125.00**

KING'S ROSE AND QUEEN'S ROSE

Staffordshire, England
c1820-1830

History: The King's Rose pattern, decorated on a soft paste body, was related closely to Gaudy Dutch in form as well as in the colors used in decoration. A large orange or red cabbage rose with green, yellow, and pink leaves surrounding it as accents formed the center of the design. Many plates also featured relief motifs.

The Queen's Rose pattern had a pink rose as the center with the accent colors in more delicate tones.

Coffeepot, 11 1/2" h, dome top, King's Rose variant, lg red rose, yellow chrysanthemum, blue cornflower, pink banded rims, restored, (A), ... **880.00**

Cup and Saucer, yellow centered pink rose, green dash foliage, pink lustered leaves, stems, and rims, ... **150.00**

Cup and Saucer, Handleless

King's Rose, lg iron-red rose, pink border w/diamond designs, unmkd, ... **245.00**

Queen's Rose, pink rose, green leaves, borders of pink lozenges, ... **175.00**

Jug, 5 5/8" h, King's Rose, iron-red rose, blue and yellow flowers, green leaves, (A), ... **220.00**

Plate

5 7/8" d, Queen's Rose, pink rose, red, green, and yellow foliage, basketweave border, (A), ... **85.00**

6" d, pearlware, King's Rose, magenta flower, green leaves, emb border, ... **80.00**

6 1/2" d

King's Rose, lg red rose, yellow centered blue petaled flowers, green foliage, dk red

dbl lined border, Wood, ... **150.00**

Pearlware, Queen's Rose, lg pink rose, green leaves, sm flowers in center, 2 pink luster bands on border w/raised waffle pattern between, ... **60.00**

Plate, 7 1/2" d, Queen's Rose, pink flower, red and green border, pink luster rim, $385.00

7 1/2" d, pearlware, Queen's Rose, lg pink rose, green leaves, sm flowers in center, raised pink-purple luster border of seashells and green leaves, c1820, ... **50.00**

7 3/4" d, King's Rose

Lg iron-red rose, yellow centered red dashed flowerheads, green foliage, red flowerheads on border, ... **165.00**

Lg red rose, yellow centered blue petaled flowers, green foliage, dk red dbl lined border, ... **200.00**

Plate, 8 1/4" d, lg mauve flower, yellow and green leaves, border with iron-red and mauve flowerheads, green leaves, iron-red lines, c1840, $150.00

8" d, pearlware, King's Rose, magenta flower, green leaves, emb border, ... **185.00**

8 1/4" d, King's Rose, lg iron-red rose in center w/yellow centered red dashed flowerheads, green leaves, pink lozenges on border, ... **495.00**

8 1/2" d, creamware, King's Rose, iron-red rose, yellow-centered red dash petaled flowers, green foliage, sm red roses and circular lines on border, ... **230.00**

9 1/8" d, King's rose, lg iron red flower, yellow centered flowers w/blue petals, green foliage, Adams, c1830, ... **350.00**

10" d, pink Queen's Rose and leaves in center, vert molded and scalloped rim, (A), ... **165.00**

Teapot, 5 3/4" h, Queen's Rose, lg pink rose, green leaves on sides, pink lozenges on borders, ... **425.00**

LEEDS

Yorkshire, England
c1757-1878

History: The original Leeds factory was located in Yorkshire and was founded by John and Joshua Green about 1757. Among its products were saltglaze, basalt, and stoneware, plus a very fine pearlware using a bluish glaze similar to that of Wedgwood. Figures, transferwares, lusters, and mottled wares, similar to Whieldon's, also were produced.

Probably the most recognized Leeds product was yellow-glazed creamware, first produced about 1760. This creamware was characterized by its soft yellow-cream color and the extensive use of perforations and open work, especially evident in the border treatments.

All types of utilitarian and decorative items were made in creamware from the simplest plate to elaborate, multi-sectioned fruit coolers and figural groups. The basic body often was augmented with painted and printed designs. Floral and fruit finials were a Leeds trademark.

The Green brothers had several different partners in their enterprises; shortly after forming the company, it traded as Humble, Greens & Co. Financial difficulties beset the Yorkshire pottery. After several additional owners and attempts at resurrection, the company failed and closed its doors in 1878.

Only a small amount of Leeds wares bore factory marks.

References: Heather Lawrence, *Yorkshire Pots and Potteries*, David & Charles, 1947; Donald Towner, *The Leeds Pottery*, Cory, Adams & MacCay, 1963.

Museums: City Art Gallery, Leeds, England; Everson Museum of Art, Syracuse, NY; Fitzwilliam Museum, Cambridge, England; Museum of Fine Arts, Boston, MA, Victoria & Albert Museum, London, England.

Basket, 10" H-H, flared, pierced sides, ... **80.00**

Bowl, 10 3/4" d x 4 3/4" h, ftd, blue, yellow, green, and brown finely painted vert lobes, band of brown vining on int, hairlines and restorations, (A), ... **660.00**

Centerpiece, 18 1/4" h, creamware, 3 tiers of molded shells supported by figural dolphins, female figure at top holding cornucopia, triangular perforated base, ... **11,000.00**

Coffeepot

10" h, creamware, blue painted flowers, buds, and stems, blue accented molded Indian mask under spout, restored chip, ... **1,575.00**

11" h, dbl bulbous form, lg blue flowerheads, leaves, blue center band w/dk blue half circles, repaired lid, rim, and spout, (A), ... **880.00**

Creamer, 2 3/4" h, Cov Sugar Bowl, 2 1/2" h, miniature, lg blue stylized flowerheads w/green and brown buds and stems, tooled handle on creamer, (A), ... **330.00**

Cream Jug, 3 3/4" h, lg blue, tan, and green floral and leaf decoration, blue lined rim, (A), ... **265.00**

Cup and Saucer, Handless

Band of yellow and black netting w/rect panels of red and blue fans, (A), ... **190.00**

Blue, yellow, green, and goldenrod floral design, (A), ... **220.00**

Brown rim stripes blue, green, golden yellow, and yellow floral swags, chips, (A), ... **138.00**

Miniature

Grid design of green w/orange dots and blue circles, hairline, (A), ... **220.00**

Pearlware, gold flower w/green and brown leaves, (A), ... **275.00**

Yellow band w/brown tulips, (A), ... **65.00**

Yellow, blue, and green floral in center of saucer, band of florals on border and cup, hairline, (A), ... **275.00**

Yellow centered lg blue flowerheads, green and tan leaves and buds, (A), ... **220.00**

Figure, 17" h x 14" l, pearlware, standing stallion, marbled cream coat, white halter w/blue leather joints, rect base w/canted corners, green sponging and raised dk pink leaf molded border, c1820-30, ... **32,000.00**

Fruit Bowl, 10" d, molded basketweave base, reticulated border, unmkd, ... **495.00**

Jug, 9 1/2" h, vert ribbing on lower body and foot, flowered terminals for handles, c1780, ... **1,890.00**

Mug, 6" h, band of stylized yellow, green, orange, and blue flowers and foliage around middle between brown lines, hairlines, (A), ... **522.00**

Plate

6" d, creamware, molded fluted inner border, pierced flowerhead lattice border, "Leeds Pottery" mk, c1780, rim chips, ... **320.00**

7" d, yellow, blue, and gold peafowl w/green leaves, (A), ... **495.00**

8" d, red rosebuds, green leaves, forget-me-nots, panels of red cross hatching on border, c1800, ... **425.00**

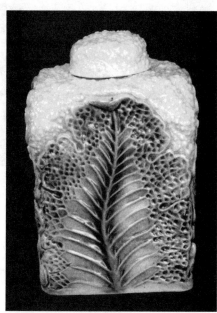

Tea Caddy, 5" h, cauliflower form, green leaves, cream ground, "imp LEEDS POTTERY" mk, c1790, $1,200.00

8 3/4" d, creamware, press molded rosette in center, garland and open work border, shaped rim, c1790, ... **90.00**

Platter

10 1/4" l, purple intertwined "FB" in center, green leaf inner border, basketweave border w/brown dashes, open loop rim, c1790, ... **365.00**

11 1/8" l x 10" w, oval, molded fan design w/blue diamond and oval line in center, border of molded basketweave, applied blue outlined open oval loop rim, ... **485.00**

Teabowl and Saucer, creamware, HP iron-red flowers, molded beaded rims, c1785, ... **510.00**

Teapot

3 1/4" h, green and brown leaves, blue and orange flowers, (A), ... **300.00**

4" h, blue bordered yellow bands, green, orange, blue, and brown sprigs, (A), ... **400.00**

4 1/8" h, yellow band w/orange and blue buds, hairlines, (A), ... **415.00**

4 1/4" h, yellow band w/brown tulips, (A), ... **100.00**

Tea Caddy, 6 3/4" h, black transfers, pink-purple luster trim, c1820, **$650.00**

4 3/4" h x 7 1/2" w, pearlware, globular, underglazed blue, iron-red, and gilt overall oriental scene of pagodas, curved spout, acanthus leaf molded base, twisted strap handle w/4 floral

and foliate terminals, flower knob, ... **2,500.00**

6 1/2" h, blue and yellow figure "8" flowers, green leaves, brown stripes, (A), ... **248.00**

Toddy Plate, 6 3/8" d, yellow and green pineapple in center, blue and tan leaf vine border, chips, and hairline, (A), ... **825.00**

Waste Bowl

4 1/4" d, blue band w/green, gold, black, and mustard hanging leaves, (A), ... **110.00**

6" d, green and gold leaves w/blue accents, hairlines, (A), ... **115.00**

Vase, 8" h, sq gadrooned base, pr, A-**$900.00**

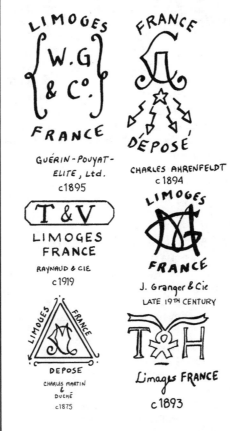

LIMOGES
W.G & Co.
FRANCE
GUÉRIN-POUYAT-ELITE, Ltd.
c1895

FRANCE
A
DÉPOSÉ
CHARLES AHRENFELDT
c1894

T&V
LIMOGES
FRANCE
RAYNAUD & CIE
c1919

LIMOGES
FRANCE
J. Granger & Cie
LATE 19TH CENTURY

LIMOGES FRANCE
A
DEPOSE
CHARLES MARTIN & DUCHÉ
c1875

T&H
Limoges FRANCE
c1893

LIMOGES

Limousine region of France
c1770 to Present

History: The region was the center for porcelain production due to the abundance of natural resources, wood for kilns, and rivers for transportation. Limoges' first hard paste porcelain dated from about 1770 and was attributed to the company of Massie, Grellet, and Fourneira. Permission was granted to make porcelain by the Council of the Court. The company came under the patronage of Comte d'Artois, brother-in-law of King Louis XVI, in 1777. Since the company was financed and supported by the court, the products were marked with the initials "C.D."

Due to financial and technical problems, the company was sold to the King in 1784. He used the factory as a branch of Sevres. Whitewares were made at Limoges and sent to Sevres for decoration.

Grellet served as manager from 1784 until 1788. J. Francoise Alluaud followed as manager and remained until 1794. About that time, the factory was sold to Joubert, Cacate, and Joly, three of the workers.

At the end of the French Revolution, c1796, the progress of porcelain making continued at Limoges with the addition of many new factories. Alluaud, Baignol, and Monnerie were among those establishing their own factories during the 1790s.

Additional factories developed between 1800 and 1830, among which were two factories begun in 1825 at Saint-Leonard, the Recollet factory, which remained in production until 1963, and the Pont de Noblat factory, still in production. These factories responded to the growing demands of a large export market for Limoges porcelains, with America as the largest customer. The mid- to late-19th century was the golden age for Limoges porcelain.

David Haviland also established himself in Limoges during the 1850s. Many of the other factories imitated his techniques. Limoges porcelain is usually more bold than Haviland.

With the tremendous amount of porcelain produced, the market could not absorb all the wares. After World War I and the economic crises of the 1920s and 1930s, many older companies were forced out of business. There was some revitalization after World War II. Today Limoges still is the center of hard paste porcelain production in France.

A wide range of objects was made with vivid decoration of florals, fruit, figural, and scenic themes that were embellished with gold. Decorative pieces included vases, large plaques, trays, tankards, mugs, bowls, plates, paintings, and jardinieres.

Smaller accessory pieces such as dresser sets, trinket boxes, cache pots, candleholders, baskets, and inkwells added variety. In addition, a whole range of dinnerware sets, compotes, fish and game services, and coffee, tea, and chocolate sets bore the Limoges mark.

Early Limoges porcelain whiteware blanks were sent to Paris for decoration over the glaze. Decoration under the glaze did not begin in Limoges until the late 1800s. Transfer decoration was used mostly on tablewares. Hand painting usually appeared on accessory art pieces and decorative porcelain pieces. Mixed decoration, in which the transfer outline was filled in or trimmed with hand painting, was used primarily on tablewares. The decoration was found on both over- and under-the-glaze styles.

Floral decor was most prominent on Limoges porcelain. Fruit themes of berries, cherries, and grapes were next. Oyster, fish, and game sets had birds and marine life subjects. Figurals of either allegorical subjects or portraits also were used, but in a more limited context.

Most of the Limoges colors were deep and vivid. The lavish gold embellishments had a rich patina.

References: Mary Frank Gaston, *The Collector's Encyclopedia of Limoges Porcelain*, Collector Books, 1980; *3rd edition*, 2000, Values updated, 2000; Keith & Thomas Waterbrooke-Clyde, *Distinctive Limoges Porcelain: Objects d'Art, Boxes, & Dinnerware*, Schiffer Publications, 2001; Debbie DuBay, *Living With Limoges*, Schiffer Publications, 2001; Keith & Thomas Waterbrooke-Clyde, *The Decorative Art of Limoges Porcelain & Boxes*, Schiffer Publications, 1999; Debbie DuBay, *Antique Limoges*, Schiffer Publications, 2002; Faye Strumpf, *Limoges Boxes*, Krause Publications, 2000; Keith & Thomas Waterbrooke-Clyde, *Atelier Le Tallec: Hand Painted Limoges Porcelain For Connoisseurs, Royalty, & Tiffany & Company*, Schiffer Publications, 2002.

Museums: Limoges Museum, Limoges, France; Musee National Adrien Dubouche, Limoges, France; Sevres Museum, Sevres, France.

Additional Listing: Haviland

Collecting Hints: Limoges porcelains are still in production. Marks aid the collector in determining the age of a piece of Limoges.

The quality of the craftsmanship and decoration on the older pieces was superior to the new examples. Less gold decoration is used on newer pieces.

The newer marks usually are found over the glaze. Many pieces have factory whiteware marks in addition to marks to indicate whether the piece was decorated at the factory or at another decorating studio.

Beverage Set, tankard, 14 1/2" h, 4 mugs, 6" h, HP purple and green grapes, berries, red strawberries, flowers, and foliage, molded curlicues, shaded brown to pale green ground, gold rims, artist sgd, "W.G. & Co. Limoges France" mks, ... **1,895.00**

Biscuit Jar, 7" h, lobed body w/molded shell top, gold stylized flowers, turquoise and blue accents, gilt flower knob, ... **350.00**

Bowl, 11" d, white water lilies, red and white buds on sinuous stems, shaded yellow to green ground, gilt rococo border, ... **315.00**

Bud Vase
4 1/2" h, squat shape, painted black and white swimming ducks, teal ground, flat, gold rim, "J.P.L. France" mk, ... **295.00**
8" h, lg open green centered rust poppy, green leaf design, reverse w/pink/lavender or rust poppies, bud, green shaded leaves, cream to green shaded ground, gold handles from shoulder to gold rim, sgd "Teret," "J.P.L. Limoges" mk, ... **175.00**

Butter Dish, Cov, 7" d x 4 3/4" h, w/drain, scattered pink flowers, sm sprigs, gold accents, dbl mks, **89.00**

Cache Pot, 8 1/4" h, cylinder shape, yellow and coral red flowers, multicolored shaded ground, 2 ring handles, 4 green ball feet, William Guerin, ... **475.00**

Cake Plate, 11" H-H, yellow or purple ring of pansies and foliage on border, gold rim and open handles, "T. & V. Limoges" dbl mks, ... **185.00**

Candlestick
3 1/2" h, blue lined base w/molded conc circles and blue dots on surface, nozzle w/flowing blue rim, "W.G. Limoges" mk, ... **38.00**
5 1/2" h, HP yellow roses on base, aqua ground, gold int of stem, pr, ... **165.00**

Charger
11 1/2" d, HP multicolored scene of boy fishing near boat, lake, and woods, molded rococo border, c1900, ... **295.00**
13 1/4" d, HP multicolored bird perched on branch facing lg red and pink roses, sm yellow centered white flowers, green and lt blue foliage, cream to

green-blue shaded ground, gilt indented rim, "Limoges B & C France" mk, ... **485.00**
14 1/2" d, HP hollyhocks, lt blue ground, gold scalloped rim, "T. & V. Limoges" mk, c1907, .. **550.00**

Chocolate Cup and Saucer, green grapes, gilt tendrils, gilt borders and handle, sgd "Duva," **68.00**

Chocolate Cup and Saucer, Cov, bands and bunches of pink flowers on heavy gilt ground, white base, 2 ornate gilt handles, gilt flame knob, trembleuse saucer, ... **295.00**

Chocolate Pot, 10 3/4" h, lg pink roses, cream ground, gold rims, swirl knob, gold outlined sculpted handle, "green J.P.L." mk, ... **475.00**

Chocolate Service, pot, 9" h, 6 cups and saucers, shaped tray, 14 1/2" H-H x 12 1/4" w, scattered purple pansies, gilt twig handles and rims, c1904, ... **895.00**

Chop Plate, 12 3/4" d, 3 lg lavender and yellow pansies on border, gold border, sgd "Duval," **265.00**

Cider Pitcher, 6 1/2" h,
HP pear and strawberries, shaded green ground, gold trim, "W.G. & Co." dbl mks, ... **320.00**
Lg HP pink tinged white and dk pink roses, tan ground, sgd "Sena," **325.00**

Coffee and Tea Set, coffeepot, 11" h, teapot, 10" h, creamer, 6 3/4" h, cov sugar bowl, pedestal bases, flame knobs, fancy handles, overall white glaze, Giraud, c1900, ... **325.00**

Compote, 6 1/2" sq x 4 1/2" h, scattered multicolored and gilt flying insects, "Ebeling & Reuss Co. Limoges France" mk, ... **85.00**

Cracker Jar, 4 1/2" h x 6" d, clusters of gold leaves on front, back, and lid, gold handles and rims, ivory ground, ... **380.00**

Cup and Saucer
Band of cherry blossoms, green foliage on white honeycomb ground, gold tracery on cup base and saucer int, "T.& V. Limoges" mk, ... **75.00**
Raised gold shamrocks and hanging Celtic designs on dk blue ground, gold handle, ... **30.00**

Dresser Set
Match holder, 3" h, cov box, 5 1/4" l x 3 3/4" w, cov powder jar, 4 1/2" d, hair receiver, 3 piece, 4 1/2" d, candlestick, 8 3/4" h, hatpin holder, 4 1/2" h, pin tray, 5 1/2" l x

4 1/2" w, tray, 9 1/2" l x 7 1/2" w, tray, 12 1/2" l x 9 3/4" w, gold stenciled band of flowers, gold rims and knobs, "PL Limoges France" mks, c1915, ... **395.00**
Pin dish, 4" l x 3 1/4" w, hair receiver, 4" d x 2 1/2" h, ring tree, 2" h, tray, 12 1/2" l x 8" w, HP lg pink and white roses, blue-green leaves, sky blue to cream shaded ground, gold rims and accents, "J.P.L." mks, ... **545.00**

Dresser Tray, 12 3/4" l x 9 3/4" w, freeform, blue printed forget-me-nots, gold rim, Charles Ahrenfeldt, ... **110.00**

Humidor, 5 3/4" h, HP grey bat flying by moon, shaded blue ground, brown and tan figural pipe knob, artist sgd, "T. & V. Limoges" mk, ... **400.00**

Ice Cream Set
Master bowl, 16 3/4" l x 10 1/4" w, 12 plates, 7 1/8" d, HP dk pink roses and green foliage in center, border of similar roses on shaded pale green ground, gilt rococo rims w/gilt molded handles, George Borgfeldt dbl mks, ... **1,400.00**
Platter, 14 1/2" l, oval, 6 dishes, 7 1/2" d, white flower pattern, green tendrils, green and brown foliage, pale green ground, gold trim, Jean Pouyet, ... **440.00**

Jardiniere
9" h x 9 1/2" w, HP peach peonies, raised gold designs, scalloped rim, 3 open scrolled gold feet, ... **1,750.00**
9 3/4" h x 7 1/2" w, HP continuous scene of 2 classic women seated in forest by river, 4 sm gold feet, molded gold ring handles, artist sgd, "Limoges W.G. & Co." mk, ... **500.00**

Oyster Plate, 9 1/8" d, multicolored floral transfers, lt blue fan molded border, "Limoges, France" mark, **$165.00**

Pickle Dish, 6 3/8" l x 4 1/2" w, fleur-de-lys shape, gilt and black period couple in center, gilt inner border and lined rim, "A. Giraud & Brousseau Limoges" mk, ... **45.00**

Picture Frame, 9 3/4" h x 6 1/4" h, multicolored transfers of cherubs, floral garlands, and swags, gold rococo border, c1920, ... **185.00**

Plaque
11 1/2" d
HP purple or irises, long green and tan leaves, wide gilt rococo border, artist sgd, ... **335.00**
Multicolored scene of kneeling Prince w/slipper and maiden on wall, gold rococo border, pierced for hanging, unmkd, ... **245.00**
12 3/4" d, HP shepherd w/flock of sheep in forest, gold rococo border, pierced for hanging, sgd "Baumy," **1,795.00**
15 1/2" d, HP grapes and red pomegranates, gilt rococo border, pierced for hanging, sgd "DuBois," "LR & L Limoges" mk, ... **1,295.00**
15 3/4" d, HP yellow, white, or red roses and buds, green foliage, brown to cream shaded ground, "T & V Limoges France" mk, ... **895.00**

Plate
8 1/4" d, gold outlined pink and maroon flowers in center, cream center ground shaded to coral pink border, gold outlined irreg border, "J.P. Limoges" mk, ... **55.00**
8 7/8" d, HP purple grapes, green and blue foliage, shaded dk red to cream ground, ... **100.00**
9 1/2" d, HP
Pink roses, buds, and foliage, dk green molded and scalloped border, "T. & V. Limoges" mk, ... **35.00**
Three groups of violets in gold filigree, pale blue border, gold rim, "T. & V. Limoges" mk, c1900, ... **125.00**
White daisies and foliage in center, molded gold outlined neo-rococo border w/seafoam green accents, "green Limoge France" mk, ... **95.00**

12 1/2" d, HP scene of shepherd and flock in meadow, gold rococo border, pierced for hanging, sgd "Baumy," "Blakeman & Henderson Limoges France" mk, ... **395.00**

Powder Box, 8 1/2" d x 4" h, HP pink, burgundy, or yellow roses, gold beading, lt green borders w/gold accented relief molded swirls, "Bawo & Dotter, Elite/L France" mks, ... **695.00**

Punch Bowl, 16" d x 9 1/4" h, red or purple bunches of green grapes, green foliage int and ext, green shaded ground, gold rim, "T & V Limoges, D. & Co." mks, ... **4,000.00**

Sugar Scuttle, 5 1/4" l, gold vine on lt green ground, gold trimmed curled handle, ... **35.00**

Syrup Pitcher, cov, 5 1/4" h, sm pink and blue hanging flower chains, upper section w/urn of flowers on lt blue ground, lt blue cov, burnished gold handle and knob, "A.K.D. France" mk, ... **95.00**

Tankard
5" h, HP portrait of monk eating, artist sgd, c1891, ... **250.00**
15" h, HP red and green bunches of grapes, shaded tan and green leaves, tendrils, shaded cream to green ground, lg gold figural dragon handle, sgd "Pankhurst," "J.P.L. France" mk, ... **1,650.00**
16" h, HP grapes, tendrils, and foliage, "T & V. Limoges" mk, ... **995.00**

Tea Set, pot, 4 1/2" h, cov sugar bowl, 6 1/4" H-H, creamer, 2 1/2" h, tray, 12" H-H, Art Nouveau style HP thick gold thistle, leaves, and clover, cream ground, gold borders and knobs, artist sgd, late 19th C, ... **395.00**

Tray, 12 /4" H-H, pink, red, blue, and green, gold trim, "J.P.L. & J. Poyet Limoges" marks, **$35.00**

Tray

11 1/2" l x 9" H-H, side handles, HP yellow roses, blue-grey leaves, heavy gold rim and open side handles, artist sgd, "B. & C. Limoges" mk, c1900, ... **95.00**

16" l x 12 1/2" w, cartouche shape, HP Arab riding camel in desert, gilt band border, "W. Guerin" mk, c1900, ... **745.00**

16 1/2" l x 10 3/4" w, oval, HP Irish Setter walking in field, relief molded floral and swirl border, shaped wavy rim, artist sgd, "Elite/L France" mk, ... **895.00**

18 7/8" H-H, oval, HP village scene w/church and creek, sgd "Luca," "Vignaud Limoges" mk, ... **1,500.00**

Tureen, Cov, 12 1/2" H-H, "Marguerite" pattern, leaf and berry handles, white glaze, T. & V., ... **110.00**

Urn, 12" h, shield shape w/spread ft, HP dancing nude woman, raised gilt diamonds and bands on base, pierced gilt diamond rim, gilt wing handles, artist sgd, ... **225.00**

Vase, 16" h, 3 orange, blue, turquoise, and gold peacocks, white, orange, and gold butterflies on gold border band, blue-black ground, (A), $225.00

Vase

5" h, ball shape, short, flared neck, painted red or yellow trailing roses, green foliage, white ground, "D. & C. Limoges" mk, ... **285.00**

6" h, horseshoe shape, painted blue birds, orange and black butterflies, raised gold branches, red or white screens, med blue ground, gold loop handles, 4 spread gold feet, ... **175.00**

9 1/4" h, pillow style, HP lg pink roses, green foliage, lt blue marbled ground, gold dragon handles, ... **550.00**

13" h, swollen middle, tapered base and neck, HP dk red roses on front, yellow roses on reverse, gold rim, "T V Limoges" mk, ... **1,395.00**

LIVERPOOL

City and port of Liverpool, England
c1754-1840

History: During the 18th century, a group of potteries in Liverpool were producing mostly tin-glazed Delft type wares and some porcelains. Utilitarian wares usually were made without distinguishing factory marks. Among the Liverpool potteries were the following:

Richard Chaffers & Co.
c1754-65

Made soapstone-type porcelain. Chaffers' blue-and-white and enameled pieces featured Oriental designs.

Samuel Gilbody
c1754-61

Took over his father's earthenware pottery and switched production to enameled porcelains.

William Ball
c1755-69

Used a soapstone body with a glossy glaze that gave a wet appearance to his Chinese designs in underglaze blue.

William Reid & Co.
c1755-61

Also used underglaze blue Oriental motifs on an almost opaque body.

Philip Christian & Co.
c1765-76

Took over Chaffers' factory and made soapstone-type porcelains, mostly with underglaze blue designs.

Pennington & Part
c1770-99

Produced lesser quality wares decorated with underglaze blue prints. Their enameled pieces exhibited simple decorations.

Thomas Wolfe & Co.
c1795-1800

Made hard paste porcelains.

Herculaneum-Liverpool factory at Liverpool
c1796-1840

Established by Samuel Worthington. Most of the workers were brought from the Staffordshire Potteries. At first only earthenwares and stonewares were made.

"Herculaneum Pottery" was the name of the factory. Some pieces were marked with an impressed "Herculaneum." About 1800 porcelains were introduced. Some Empire-style vases were manufactured, but the principal production focused on teawares. Extremely large jugs were a specialty.

References: Dr. Knowles Boney, *Liverpool Porcelain of the 18th Century and Its Makers*, B.T. Batsford, 1957; H. Boswell Lancaster, *Liverpool and Her Potters*, W.B. James & Co. 1936; Robert McCauley, *Liverpool Transfer Designs on Anglo-American Pottery*, Southworth-Anthoensen Press, 1942; Alan Smith, *The Illustrated Guide to Liverpool Herculaneum Pottery 1796-1840*, Barrie & Jenkins, 1970; B. Watney, *English Blue and White Porcelain of the 18th Century*, Faber & Faber, 1936; Bernard M. Watney, *Liverpool Porcelain of the Eighteenth Century*, Antique Collectors' Club, Ltd. 1997.

Museums: City of Liverpool Museum, Liverpool, England; Henry Ford Museum, Dearborn, MI; Potsdam Public Museum, Potsdam, NY.

Reproduction Alert: Modern imitations of old marine-decorated Liverpool jugs 8 1/2" to 11" high decorated in black transfer on one side with "The Shipwright's Arms," reverse with ship flying the American flag in colors on a green sea entitled "Ship Caroline," and under the spout with the name "James Leech" in a wreath. These have been showing up at various auctions. Some have artificially produced age cracks and glaze crackle.

Beaker, 2 3/8" h, oct w/circ ft, blue painted "Jumping Boy" pattern, seated lady holding bouquet watching boy jumping w/arms outstretched, paneled diaper inner border, Chaffers, c1758, (A), ... **2,645.00**

Bowl, 6" d, underglaze blue and overglaze iron-red oriental buildings, hanging trees, and flowers, blue and iron-red crisscross inner rim, gilt accents, Chaffers, c1760, ... **350.00**

Canister, 4 3/8" h, tea party on front, fishing scene on reverse, black transfers, pewter cov, Sadler & Green, c1770, $380.00

Coffee Can, polychrome floral sprays, Chaffers, ... **560.00**

Coffeepot, Baluster Shape
9" h, famille rose enamel painted scene of seated Chinese lady talking to standing figure, same on reverse, loop border on rim and cov, strap handle, mushroom knob, Chaffers, c1760-65, (A), ... **1,550.00**
9 3/4" h, "Pilgrim Shell" blue transfer, Seth Pennington, repairs, ... **1,200.00**

Cream Jug, 3 1/2" h, HP, blue oriental scene of 2 figures and tree, blue lined rim, sparrow beak, Pennington, c1780, ... **870.00**

Cup and Saucer, black transfers of Cadmus, American eagle perched on shore, Fulton's Steamboat passing West Point, pink luster line on cup and saucer, hairline, ... **375.00**

Jug
4 1/4" h, "Enterprise and Boxer," and "United States and Macedonian"

sailing ships, black transfers, pink luster trim, ... **1,850.00**

Jug, 8 1/2" h, black transfers w/colors, restored back, $3,250.00

6" h, overall Masonic emblems and signs, black transfers, black stripes on rim, ... **850.00**
7" h, stoneware, sprigged design of Nelson, trophies, and battle scenes, grey, Herculaneum, c1805, ... **1,095.00**
7 1/4" h, ship w/flags on side, reverse w/Jefferson's Poem, black transfers, hairlines, ... **6,500.00**

Jug, 11 1/4" h, creamware, black transfers, sailing ship on reverse on reverse, "Great American Eagle" under spout, $6,800.00

8 1/4" h, ship building scene and poem about shipbuilding, reverse w/ship and American flag, seal of United States under spout, black transfers, hairlines, ... **1,800.00**
8 1/2" h, black transfers of farmer carrying rake, wife at side,

haystack and farm in bkd, reverse w/classic temple ruins, river and boat, ... **495.00**
9" h, seated "Hibernia" on side, sailing ship on reverse, "Ye Sons of Hibernia Rejoice in the Freedom of Your Extensive Commerse" on outside, black transfers, c1790, ... **1,300.00**

Pickle Dish, 7 3/4" l, leaf shape w/blue accents and molded inner leaf, 3 sm feet, c1765, ... **545.00**

Pitcher, 5" h, Commodore Bainbridge on front, Commodore Lawrence on reverse, black transfers and trim, restored, $650.00

Pitcher
7" h, men and women seated and drinking, reverse w/man playing flute to woman and "Wine Cannot Cure The Pain I Endure For My Chloe," black transfers, c1800, ... **795.00**
8 1/2" h, black printed American sailing ship and "Success to Trade," reverse w/couple and verse "Abbas and Abra," staining and damage, (A), ... **330.00**
9 1/4" h, black transfer w/green, yellow, red, and blue accents of "Brig Adventure of Salem," reverse w/black transfer of East Coast of United States, George Washington and Lady Liberty, American eagle and "James Barr" under spout, (A), ... **4,675.00**
10" h, black transfers of "Peace, Plenty, and Independence" on side, Washington monument w/names of 13 states on reverse, Masonic emblem over Washington and "First in War, First in Peace..." eagle and "E Pluribus Unum" under spout, ... **2,600.00**

11" h, American ship under sail, reverse w/Washington memorial and "Ascending into Glory," Liberty holding American shield and eagle at foot in circ border under spout, black transfers, repairs and overpainting, c1800, ... **4,200.00**

Plate

9 1/8" d, Delft-style, painted lg blue peony design and scattered flowers, narrow trellis pattern on border, (A), ... **175.00**

9 1/2" d, pearlware, "Bamboo" pattern, iron-red, lt blue, and cobalt, c1820, ... **325.00**

10" d, "Lancaster" pattern, med blue transfer of 2 ladies, child, and farmer on river bank, Lancaster city in bkd, St. Mary's Church, Cherub Medallion border, "imp Herculaneum" mk, c1822, ... **195.00**

Punch Bowl, 5 1/2" h x 12 3/4" d, en grisaille, painted stylized flowerhead in circle on int w/scattered sprigs, inner and outer border w/lined half circles, ext w/scattered sprigs, ... **3,250.00**

Tankard, 7 1/2" h, blue printed chinoiserie scenes of gardens, flowers, rockwork, and fence, cell border, John Pennington, c1775, ... **2,000.00**

Teabowl and Saucer

Blue, pink, green, red, and yellow painted chinoiserie scene of pagodas on rocky islands, dbl lined rim, flower spray on bowl int, Chaffers, c1757-58, (A), ... **710.00**

Blue scallop shell and flowerhead design, bud and dot border, rim chips, ... **300.00**

Teapot, 5 1/4" h, globular, famille rose palette of flowering peony from rockwork, trailing vine on cov, Richard Chaffers, c1765, chips, (A), ... **970.00**

Vase, 3 1/2" h, baluster shape, blue painted willow tree w/peony and bamboo, Christian, c1770, crack, (A), ... **790.00**

Waste Bowl, 6 3/8" d, "Old Bill" pattern, polychrome enameled Chinese style characters on ext, iron-red line over band of half circles over band on dots on int border, Phillip Christian, c1770, ... **1,300.00**

LLADRÓ

HAND MADE IN SPAIN
1951

LLADRO

Almacera, Spain
1951 to Present

History: The Lladro brothers, Juan, Jose, and Vicente, started their small studio in 1951 in Almacera, Spain. They built their own kiln and began making small flowers for decorative lamps. All three brothers shaped the porcelains. Only Juan and Jose decorated them; Vicente supervised the firing.

As their business expanded, they formed Lladro Porcelanas in 1958 and produced their first porcelain figurine of a ballet dancer. Their distinctive style emphasizes the elongated look in porcelain sculpture. The figurines were hand painted in a variety of pastel colors.

Salvador Furio was one of the most senior and prolific sculptors at Lladro. His "Clown with Concertina" was the first figurine he designed for Lladro. Furio has become the Lladro sculptor specializing in particular thematic subjects such as historic characters, figures of literature, and personalities in public life.

Today the Lladro complex is located in Valencia, Spain, and is known as "Porcelain City."

In the late 1960s, a new line entitled Nao by Lladro was added to respond to different aspects of the marketplace. The logo features a sailing ship in tandem with the company name. The three brothers are involved in Nao, as they are in Lladro, but there are two separate manufacturing facilities.

There are some shared design themes, but there are differences in the detail work and palette of colors applied. Some sculptural lines are similar.

Nao retired in 1992.

Reference: Dr. Glenn S. Johnson, *The Official Lladro Collection Reference Guide, First Edition*, Clear Communications, 1996; Peggy Whiteneck, *Collecting Lladro, Identification & Price Guide*, Krause Publications, 2001.

Museums: Lladro Museum, Los Angeles, CA; Lladro Museum, New York, NY.

Collectors' Club: Lladro Society, 1 Lladro Drive, Moonachie, NJ 07074, Membership: $45.00, Quarterly magazine *Expressions*; e-mail:society@Lzladro.com Lladro Collectors Society, 43 W. 57th St, New York City, 10019-3498.

Newsletter: *Lladro Antique News*, Lladro Mail Center, Dept. 909, 41 Jackson Street, Worcester, MA 01608

3" h, Dog and Butterfly, #4917G, ... **750.00**

3 1/8" h, Hedgehog, #2037, ... **450.00**

4 1/2" h, Angel Praying, #4538, ... **90.00**

5" h

Bird on Cactus, #1303, ... **735.00**

Boy With Cymbals, #4613, ... **200.00**

Donkey in Love, #4524, ... **450.00**

5 1/2" h

Eskimo Boy With Pet, #5238, ... **110.00**

Joy in a Basket, #5595, ... **575.00**

5 7/8" h, Tern, #1051, ... **425.00**

6" h, Skye Terrier, #4643, ... **700.00**

6 1/4" h

Bird Watcher, #4730, ... **250.00**

Little Eagle Owl, #2020, ... **150.00**

6 1/2" h

Little Bo Peep, #1312, ... **400.00**

Spring Is Here, #5223, ... **125.00**

7" h

Decorative Peacock, #4766.3, ... **730.00**

Girl With Doll, #1083, ... **280.00**

Girl With Pig, #1011, ... **100.00**

Shepherdess With Dove, #4660, ... **350.00**

7 1/2" h, Full Moon, #1438, ... **685.00**

7 3/4" h

German Shepherd With Pup, #4731, ... **900.00**

Girl Clown With Dice, #1176, ... **300.00**

8" h, White Cockerel, #4588, ... **250.00**

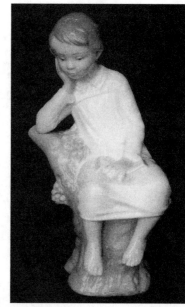

Figure, 8 1/4" h, "Thinker, Little Boy," #4876, **$195.00**

8 1/4" h
- Bar Mitzvah Day, #6004, ... **285.00**
- Coquette, #5599, ... **125.00**
- Girl Gathering Flowers, #1172, ... **295.00**
- German Shepherd With Pup, #4731, ... **1,050.00**
- Papillon Dog, #4857, ... **600.00**

8 1/2" h
- Boy From Madrid, #4898, ... **100.00**
- Fisher Boy, #4809, ... **155.00**
- Girl With Bonnet, #1147, ... **300.00**
- Girl With Candle, matte, #4868, ... **100.00**
- Group of Musicians, #4617, ... **475.00**

8 3/4" h, Garden Song, #7618, ... **245.00**

*Figure, 9 1/2" h, #1255, **$695.00***

9 1/2" h
- Curious Angel, #4960, ... **125.00**
- Seesaw, #1255, ... **695.00**

9 3/4" h
- Little Gardener, #4726, ... **375.00**
- New Shepherd, #4577, ... **300.00**
- Partridge, #1290, ... **2,000.00**

9 7/8" h
- Floral Jug, #1115, ... **375.00**
- White Cockeral, #4588, ... **525.00**

10 1/4" h
- Peddler, #4859, ... **490.00**
- The Flower Peddler, #5029, ... **1,375.00**

10 1/2" h
- Boy With Goat, #4506, ... **295.00**
- Bride and Groom, #1247, ... **225.00**
- Girl with Basket, #1034, ... **225.00**
- Hindu Goddess, #1215, ... **1,100.00**
- Pan With Pipes, #1007, ... **625.00**
- Sultanita, #1173, ... **550.00**
- You and Me, #4830, ... **800.00**

11" h
- Glorious Spring, #5284, ... **500.00**
- Mardi Gras, #4580, ... **1,300.00**

11 1/2" h
- Chrysanthemum, #4990, ... **350.00**
- Countryman, #4664, ... **400.00**
- Hebrew Student, #4684, ... **350.00**

11 3/4" h
- Lady At Dressing Table, #1242, ... **3,000.00**
- Young Sultan, #1174, ... **550.00**

11 7/8" h, Don Quixote Vase, .. **1,470.00**

12 1/4" h
- Boys Playing With Goat, #1129, ... **2,000.00**
- Columbus Bookend, #4627, . **800.00**
- Country Man, #4664, ... **525.00**
- Florist, #1243, ... **6,285.00**
- Pelusa, #1125, ... **1,925.00**

12 1/2" h, Quiet Afternoon, #5843, ... **1,100.00**

13" h
- At The Circus, #5052, ... **1,200.00**
- Maja Head, #4668, ... **785.00**
- Monk, #2060, ... **295.00**
- Mother and Child, #4575, ... **300.00**
- The Race, #1249, ... **2,450.00**

13 1/4" h
- Golfing Couple, #1453, ... **390.00**
- Hansom Carriage, #1225, . **6,500.00**

13 3/4" h
- Boys Playing With Goat, colored, #1129, ... **2,225.00**
- Gres Nuns, #2075, pr, ... **215.00**
- Here Comes The Bride, #1445, ... **990.00**
- Marketing Day, #4502, ... **345.00**
- Old Man, #4622, ... **725.00**
- Opal Blue Lamp, #4776, ... **420.00**
- The Grandfather, #4654, ... **800.00**
- You And Me, #4830, ... **1,050.00**
- Woman with Girl and Donkey, #4666, ... **1,000.00**

14" h
- Old Man With Violin, #4622G, ... **1,650.00**
- Shepherd Sleeping, #1004, ... **1,600.00**
- Violinist, #4887, ... **700.00**

14 1/4" h, Song Lessen, #4973, ... **1,850.00**

14 1/2" h, Don Quixote, #1030, . **700.00**

15" h, Artist, #4732, ... **890.00**

15 3/4" h
- Genteel, #5014, ... **1,900.00**
- King Gaspar, #1018, ... **1,895.00**

16 1/2" h
- Anemones Bunch, #1184, . **2,100.00**
- Lady With Shawl, #4914, ... **675.00**

16 7/8" h, Dentist, #4762, ... **600.00**

17" h, Herald, #1078, ... **1,125.00**

17 1/4" h
- A Tribute To Peace, #2150, ... **795.00**

- The Flirt, #4564, ... **900.00**

17 3/8" h, Rescue, #3504, ... **4,200.00**

17 3/4" h, Horse's Group, #1021, ... **2,590.00**

18" h
- Hunters, #1048, ... **1,650.00**
- Torero, #2004, ... **1,365.00**

18 1/2" h
- Girl to the Fountain, #2023, .. **250.00**
- Star Fruit Bowl-3 Levels, #4739, ... **2,000.00**

18 7/8" h, Bird Vase, #1619, ... **3,570.00**

19" h
- Vase, Green Peonies, #4753, **650.00**
- With Rose, #3517, ... **675.00**

19 1/4" h, Girl With Umbrella, #4805, ... **235.00**

20 1/2" h, #2121, ... **1,150.00**

21" h, Hunting, #1308, ... **7,350.00**

22" h, Herons, #1319, ... **1,850.00**

23 5/8" h, Allegory To Peace, #1202, ... **8,925.00**

LONGWY
20ᵀᴴ CENTURY

LONGWY

Lorraine, France
1798 to Present

History: A French faience factory, known for its enameled pottery that resembled cloisonne, was established in 1798 at Lorraine. Utilitarian wares were made in addition to the enameled pieces.

About 1875 Emaux de Longwy introduced wares that were decorated with Persian-inspired motifs. His designs were first outlined with black printed manganese resist and filled in with brightly colored glazes, especially the turquoise color for which the pieces are most famous. The company achieved its greatest fame for pieces with Art Deco motifs featuring bold colors and geometric designs.

Marks used on Longwy examples incorporate "LONGWY," either impressed or painted under the glaze.

Ashtray, 3 1/2" h, rose and dk red enamel flowerheads, green stems, med blue ground, dk blue rim w/tan scrolling and cigarette rest, turquoise int, ... **65.00**

Basket, 6 1/4" h, pink and red enameled flowerheads, turquoise ext and rope twist handle, int w/painted lg red flowerheads, green leaves, white crackle ground, mkd, ... **375.00**

Box
5" w, triangle shape w/cut corners, yellow lobed cartouche of red

and yellow enamel flowers, green leaves on white crackle ground, lavender curl and geometric body, white crackle rims, ... **150.00**

Box, 6" d, dk blue, brown, yellow, and orange center in cobalt circle, aqua crackle ground, Primavera, $580.00

6 " sq, oct, enameled white parrot w/black trim, perched on black branches and foliage, lt and med brown hills on cov, med blue ground, yellow and yellow and red beaded designs on sides, ... **860.00**

Bud Vase, 3 7/8" h, lg red tipped white lily w/green base, red berries, brown stems, lt blue ground, ... **75.00**

Charger
14 1/4" d, 3 pink, yellow, and black enameled storks standing in marsh in center cartouche, enameled pink, yellow, and red flowerheads and stems on blue ground, pierced for hanging, "Decor Ala Main E. Maux Longwy" mk, ... **795.00**

15" d
Art Deco, enameled, two running tan antelopes, dk brown, tan, and red foliage, cream crackle border, red rim, ... **775.00**
Med blue ground w/black printed gazelle in forest in circ center, border of dbl circles and spots, "Atelier Primavera Longwy France" mk, ... **560.00**
Two blue, red, and green sparrows on bramble branches, red berries, green, tan, and red tinged leaves, cream ground, ... **650.00**

Clock, 13 1/4" l x 7 3/4" h, Art Deco style, enameled multicolored birds, flowers on turquoise ground, cream brick imp side panels w/blue vert stripes, dk blue base, ... **1,950.00**

Creamer, 2 3/8" h, lg enameled pink flowerheads, sm dk blue and rose flowers, green leaves, turquoise ground, dk blue rim and handle, white int, ... **55.00**

Cup and Saucer, enameled red centered pink blossoms, brown branches, green leaves, turquoise ground, blue-black rims and handle, ... **80.00**

Dejeuner Set, coffeepot, 6" h, cream jug, 4" h, cov sugar bowl, 3" h, side plate, 5" d, oct tray, 14" x 11" w, enameled orange stylized flowerheads, green leaves, cream crackle ground, brown rims and vert stripes, ... **1,350.00**

Fruit Compote, 11 7/8" d x 6 5/8" h, orange and dk orange geometric swirls and lines on cream crackle glaze int, cream crackle ext w/dk orange vert stripes to oct base, black lined rim and ft, ... **400.00**

Pin Tray, 4 1/2" l, pink centered white enameled flowerheads, brown stems and branches, green leaves, med blue ground, ... **40.00**

Pitcher, 10" h, enameled turquoise vert ovals w/sm white and red flowerheads and red wavy lines, vert stems w/red and white flowerheads and turquoise foliage, red and turquoise wavy base, cream crackle ground, turquoise rope handle, mkd, ... **400.00**

Plate, 7 1/2" d, "Poissons et Pecheurs," black transfer in center, blue-green transfer border, "LONGWY PECHEURS" mk, $85.00

Plate
8" d, yellow centered two tone red flowerheads, yellow centered

blue flowerheads, two tone green foliage, brown branches, sm red and yellow flowerheads, turquoise ground, mkd, .. **165.00**
8 3/4" d, pink and red enameled flowers and buds, green and dk blue curved stems, med blue ground, ... **195.00**
9" d, 2 enameled cranes w/cream feathers, dk red, yellow, and blue-green feathers, tan bamboo, blue and green leaves, tan ground, blue water, lt blue crackle bkd, black lined rim, ... **495.00**
9 1/4" d, enameled rose, blue, and brown bird perched on red flowered brown branch and green leaves, cream crackled ground, brown indented rim, ... **65.00**
10" d, enameled red roofed cream house at water's edge framed in cobalt swirls, chartreuse, blue, yellow, dk red and pink florals on med blue ground, scalloped cobalt rim, "Emaux de Longwy France" mk, ... **415.00**

Porringer, 9 3/4" H-H, enameled blue and purple flower medallion on int, white crackle ground, dk blue border w/lt blue beaded rim, sm enamel yellow and lt blue flowers on tab handles, white crackle ext, ... **125.00**

Serving Dish, 12" w, 3 section, enameled brown-red centered white dogwood blossoms, red tinged white flowers, brown stems, med blue ground, black loop center handle, c1920, ... **680.00**

Teapot, 5" h, pink, mauve, and yellow enamel flowers, med blue ground, cobalt handle, knob, and spout rim, ... **775.00**

Tete-a-Tete, pot, creamer, cov sugar bowl, 2 cups and saucers, tray, 13" l, 12" w, pink and cream enameled blossoms, brown branches, turquoise ground, dk blue handles, med blue and brown knobs, marsh bird in cartouche on tray, $795.00

Tea Tile, 6" sq, 2 multicolored birds perched on brown branches, red and purple flowers, blue and green foliage, grey crackle ground, turquoise border w/red, yellow, and green florals and foliage, "raised LONGWY" mk, ... **195.00**

Tray, 15 3/4" H-H x 7 1/4" w, multicolored pheasant in branches w/yellow flowerheads, green leaves in center, blue multistrand woven ribbon border w/red flowerheads and green leaf swirls, ... **350.00**

Vase

3" h, slightly swollen shape, short collar, lg black outlined red tinged yellow flowerheads, med blue lower section, lt blue upper section, med blue collar, c1900, ... **110.00**

8" h, bulbous base, flared neck, enameled pink and red florals, green leaves, brown meandering branches, turquoise ground, black lined rim and foot, ... **795.00**

9" h, tapered cylinder shape, black outlined orange geometrics on base and border, orange rim, white crackle ground, "LONGWY Made in France, Vase 3011" mk, ... **115.00**

11" h, tapered shape, Art Deco style, dk red enameled monkeys, cobalt leaves, white tree trunks, cream crackle ground, .. **200.00**

*135
7 913
✕ ☽
c1775-1790*

LOWESTOFT

Bell Lane, Lowestoft, England
c1757-1799

History: Soft paste porcelains were made in Lowestoft beginning about 1757 and ending in 1799. The principal production was utilitarian wares for the local community. Until 1770 all the designs used blue and white Oriental motifs. Sales were direct from the factory.

Later, formal floral patterns were introduced. During the 1770s, blue-printed designs, copied from Worcester and Caughley, were produced. Lowestoft's enameled wares of the 1780s resembled the Chinese Export figure- and flower-painted wares imported by the English East India Company. Rarer examples of

Lowestoft have naturalistic flower painting and English views.

No Lowestoft factory marks were used.

References: G. A. Godden, *The Illustrated Guide to Lowestoft Porcelain*, Herbert Jenkins, 1969; W.W.R. Spelman, *Lowestoft China*, Jarrold & Sons, 1905.

Museums: Castle Museum, Norwich, England, Christ-church Mansion, Ipswich, England; Fitzwilliam Museum, Cambridge England; Lowestoft Museum, Lowestoft, England; Museum of Fine Arts, Boston, MA; Victoria & Albert Museum, London, England.

Coffee Cup, pink and red enameled flower sprays, c1785, ... **275.00**

Creamboat, 2 1/4" h, molded serpentine flutes, painted bouquet of flowers, flowerheads on reverse, gilt scalloped raised rim, angled loop handle, c1770, ... **3,250.00**

Cream Jug, Sparrow Beak

3 3/8" h, blue painted oriental garden scene w/fencing, hairlines, (A), ... **330.00**

3 3/4" h, blue painted house above stone bridge and river, blue banded int rim, scroll handle, c1770, ... **1,125.00**

Cup and Saucer, underglazed blue scattered florals, inner rim band of sprigs on cup and saucer border, handle w/thumb rest, open blue crescent mk, ... **200.00**

Pickle Dish, 4 1/4" l, blue and white, c1775, $395.00

Plate, 8 3/4" d, blue painted oriental fisherman on bridge, lattice border w/reserves of flower panels and willows, c1765, (A), ... **4,200.00**

Sauceboat, 6 1/4" l, pleated form, curved, peaked rim, blue painted w/3 floral panels in floral molding, floral spray on int, c1775, crack, (A), ... **420.00**

Sugar Bowl, 3 3/4" d, "Redgrave" pattern, underglaze blue and overglazed enamels, hairline, ... **155.00**

Trio, "Redgrave" pattern, iron-red, cobalt, puce, green, and gold, c1770, $695.00

Teabowl and Saucer

Blue painted oriental house and bridge scene, blue border band of geometrics, c1770, rim chip, ... **250.00**

Gilt outlined cobalt and iron-red oriental marsh birds and stylized trees, ... **550.00**

Iron-red and cobalt pagodas, gilt accents, ... **575.00**

"Mandarin" pattern, multicolored orientals at tea service w/table, cup, and pot, ... **525.00**

Tankard, 4 1/2" h, blue printed oriental pagoda and trees, blue cell rim, scroll handle w/thumb rest, hairline on base, ... **385.00**

Waste Bowl, 9 1/2" d, "Curtis" pattern, iron-red, puce, green, and lavender, c1782, $295.00

LUSTER

English
19th Century to Present

History: The exact beginning of luster decoration on British pottery cannot be

dated accurately. The first pieces dated from the first quarter of the 19th century; the luster process still is used today.

Luster decoration was achieved by applying thin metallic films to earthenware or china bodies. Gold luster comes from gold oxide, copper luster from copper oxide, silver luster from platinum, and pink or purple luster from "purple of cassius."

All-over lustering imitated metallic wares made in gold, silver, or copper. Luster decorations also were used on rims, details, and decorative highlights.

The "resist" process involved keeping parts of the object white through temporarily resisting them with wax or paper cutouts so that when the luster solution was applied to the object, it would not affect the resisted portions. Reserved panels could be left plain, painted, or transfer printed. Stenciling also was used. Overglaze enamels could be added to the lustered ground.

Sunderland or "splash luster," a mottled type of pink luster used on a white body, was very popular. The splash effect came from spraying an oil on the wet luster that had just been applied to the white ware. The oil expanded in the kiln to form bubbles and splashes. Manufacturers who used this technique were Southwick, Dixon & Austin, and Ball's. A large portion of Sunderland luster was produced at Newcastle-upon-Tyne.

Jugs, mugs, tea, and tablewares were among the most popular luster forms. An enormous variety of jugs was made, some featuring mottled pink with verses and others silver or other colors. Inscriptions on luster ware varied greatly. Events, landmarks in history, and popular sentiments were commemorated. Plaques had either mottos or verses, sailing ships, or landscapes within painted frames.

Staffordshire and other potteries that made a wide variety of luster ware types included Spode, Wedgwood, Lakin & Poole, Ralph & Enoch Wood, Davenport, New Hall, and Minton.

References: John Bedford, *Old English Lustre Ware*, Walker & Co. 1965; W. Bosanko, *Collecting Old Lustre Ware*, George H. Doran Co. 1916; Jeanette R. Hodgon, *Collecting Old English Lustre*, Southworth-Anthoensen Press, 1937; W.D. John & W. Baker, *Old English Lustre Pottery*, Ceramic Book Co. 1951; J.T. Shaw, *The Potteries of Sunderland & District*, Sunderland Library, 1961; Michael Gibson, *19th C Lustreware*, Antique Collectors' Club, 1999

Museums: Art Institute of Chicago, Chicago, IL; Cincinnati Museum of Art, Cincinnati, OH; City Museum & Art Gallery, Stoke-on-Trent, Hanley, England; Cleveland Museum of Art, Cleveland, OH; Laing Art Gallery & Museum, Newcastle, England; Potsdam Public Museum, Potsdam, NY; Sunderland Museum, Sunderland, England.

Reproduction Alert: Portmeiron Potteries Ltd., a Stoke-on-Trent firm, produces jugs that are reproductions of older luster types in museums and private collections. These new pieces have the maker's mark and are not intended to confuse the collector. Sometimes the mark is removed, and these reproductions are offered as old pieces.

Copper

Beaker, 2 7/8" h, cream center band of raised polychrome accented flowers, molded beaded rim, luster body, ... **55.00**

Bowl, 5" d, tan center band w/stylized leaves, luster body, unmkd, .. **100.00**

Cache Pot, 5" h, lt brown center band w/enameled relief molded green, yellow, blue, and white birds and flowers, applied ring handles w/dragon masks, copper luster body, ... **210.00**

Creamer, 3" h, dk red enamel center band w/copper luster resist foliage, copper luster body w/beaded rim, MOP int, unmkd, ... **25.00**

Cup and Saucer, blue center band w/copper luster floral sprays, copper luster bodies, c1840, ... **65.00**

Figure, 12 1/2" h, rearing stallion over hedge, overall copper luster, Staffordshire, c1917, pr, ... **600.00**

Goblet, 4 3/8" h, purple and blue florals, green leaves, copper luster body, $75.00

Goblet

4 1/4" h, HP stylized cabbage rose, green/yellow leaves, luster body, ... **125.00**

4 1/2" h
Enameled pink stylized flowerheads, green and yellow leaves, white birds, molded beaded rim, horiz ribbing on lower body, ... **75.00**
Pink luster splashes, copper luster ground, ... **165.00**

Pepper Pot, 4 1/8" h, lt rust band w/pink luster foliage and blue berries, (A), ... **165.00**

Mug

2 1/2" h, waisted shape, wide blue-green center band, pink luster int rim, luster body, ... **25.00**

2 3/4" h, blue-grey center band, yellow stripes molded beaded rim, luster body, ... **100.00**

3 1/8" h, tan center band w/copper luster stems and leaves, luster body, ... **110.00**

3 1/2" h, wide blue center band w/HP enamel red, yellow, and orange flowers, green foliage, molded beaded rim, copper luster body and handle, ... **145.00**

Pepper Pot, 3 1/2" h, blue center band w/copper luster stylized flowerheads and leaves, luster body, ... **85.00**

Pickle Dish, 5 1/4" w, leaf shape, copper luster stylized flowerheads and stems, copper luster rim, ... **250.00**

Pitcher, 4 3/8" h, yellow and red enameled fruit, green leaves, copper luster body, $65.00

Pitcher

2 1/2" h, center tan sandy textured band, copper luster body, ... **150.00**

2 3/4" h, white textured bottom, luster top, pink luster int, ... **25.00**

4 1/8" h, white stylized flower and dots on sides, luster body, white int, Price Kensington, ... **15.00**

Pitcher, 4" h, cartouches of 2 birds on branch, rust, black, and dk yellow, silver luster body, unmkd, (A), $100.00

4 5/8" h, HP enameled red, green, and blue florals, diamond molded base and top, copper luster body, fancy handle, ... **325.00**

4 3/4" h, enameled polychrome flowers in basket on body, sprigs on neck, mask spout, serpent handle, luster ground, ... **295.00**

5 1/2" h, enameled pink or yellow flowerheads, green foliage on sides, scroll handle, luster body, ... **30.00**

7" h

Blue base band w/red, lt blue, and yellow enameled fruit from yellow vase, green foliage, molded mask spout and beaded rim, luster body, ... **70.00**

Pitcher, 6 3/4" h, relief of brown spotted dogs, red fruit in trees, green foliage, pink luster rim and base, $450.00

Peach stripes w/copper luster leaf band on shoulder and berry and squiggles on lower band, luster body w/molded beading on center and rim, fancy handle, ... **75.00**

White, pink, green, and yellow enameled stylized flowers and foliage, molded diamond design on lower body, fancy handle, luster body, unmkd, ... **225.00**

8" h

Pink and yellow enameled flowers, green spear foliage, copper luster body, white int, Wales, ... **25.00**

Relief of dancing couple on sides, blue scrolling design on rim, ... **125.00**

Salt

2" h x 3 1/8" d, ftd, blue enamel center band w/orange and pink circles, luster body, ... **30.00**

2 1/4" h, ftd, center band of pink luster house and trees on white band, luster body and ft, ... **42.00**

Sugar Caster, 4 7/8" h, center med blue band w/raised red rose and copper luster leaves, ... **65.00**

Vase, 4" h, cream center band w/raised red or blue morning glories, green foliage, copper luster body, ... **70.00**

Pink

Bowl, 5 1/4" d, "The Mother's Grave," pink transfer, pink luster inner rim, ... **20.00**

Creamer

3 1/2" h, black transfer of mourners at tomb and "TO THE MEMORY OF PRINCESS CHARLOTTE," beaded pink luster band, pink luster rim, ... **550.00**

4" h, HP stylized half red petaled flowerheads w/yellow margins, hanging green wreath w/flower buds, pink luster rim, ... **250.00**

Cup and Saucer, pink luster chinoiserie scene and banding, A-$55.00

Cup and Saucer

Pink luster body resisted w/iron-red centered white grapes and iron-red veined white leaves, ... **65.00**

Purple bat printed design of sheep in pasture, pink luster stylized flowerheads on borders, ... **155.00**

Three cartouches of red flowerhead, sm blue flowerheads, green foliage, pink ground w/pink luster leaves, stems, and rims, ... **145.00**

Cup and Saucer, Handleless, black transfers of woman and 2 children playing paddle ball, pink luster rims, Staffordshire, ... **110.00**

Jug, 5" h, relief molded hunting dogs and foliage picked out w/green enamel and pink luster, molded rope rim, Staffordshire, c1820, ... **270.00**

Master Salt, 2" h x 3" d, pink luster house flanked by trees, pink luster rim, ... **70.00**

Pitcher

2 3/4" h, pink luster cottage and stylized birds, band of stylized leaves on border, "Old Castle England" mk, ... **40.00**

4" h, relief of Indian, pink luster cloud design, ... **40.00**

6" h, pink lustered bordered center pink band w/pink luster wavy line, pink luster rim, HP dk red tulips, and leaves, green foliage, pink luster stems, ... **75.00**

Plate, 9 1/8" d, dk red flowerheads on pink border, pink luster leaves and rim, c1840, $75.00

Plate

5 1/4" d, pink luster cottage and fence in center, dbl row of raised daisy heads on border, pink luster rim, ... **60.00**

6 3/8" d, pink luster "House" pattern, emb floral border, pink luster lined rim, c1810-30, ... **65.00**

6 3/4" d, pink luster stylized building and trees in center, geometric molded border, pink luster lined rim, ... **20.00**

8" d, lg red stylized flower in center, green leaves and stem, pink luster leaves and sm flowerheads on border, pink luster rim, ... **135.00**

9" d, pink transfer of couple walking in farmland, blue and green accents, band of pink luster flowerheads on border, shaped rim, unmkd, c1840, ... **95.00**

Teabowl and Saucer

Bands of small pink luster fleur-de-lys, pink luster rims, ... **135.00**

Black transfer of period couple in garden setting, pink luster lined rims, ... **40.00**

Teapot, 5 3/4" h x 9 1/2" w, blue center band w/stylized copper luster leaves, $650.00

Teapot

5 1/2" h x 9" w, pearlware, center band of orange, pink, blue, and green flowerheads and ferns, pink luster lines, dashes, and rims, ... **150.00**

7 1/2" h

Black transfers of woman holding tennis racquet and child on sides, black transfers of Rachel and Rebecca on cov, pink luster borders and accents on spout and ft, c1830, ... **125.00**

Pink luster cottage pattern on body and domed cov, luster dashes on open knob, leaf molded spout, swag base w/4 feet, ... **150.00**

Tea Service, pot, 7" h, creamer, 3 3/4" h, cov sugar bowl, 5" h, 6 plates, 6 3/4" d, 6 cups and saucers, pink luster

house design w/pink florals and rims, c1880, ... **245.00**

Silver

Bulb Pot, 6 1/2" l x 9" w, semicircular shape, silver luster and orange shield design on front, silver luster and orange leaf and branch designs on sides, 4 emb vert columns w/silver luster and orange accents, orange outlined emb semicircular border band, c1820, ... **190.00**

Cream Pitcher

3 1/2" h x 5 1/2" w, raised dot outlined bowtie design on sides, vert fluted base, overall silver luster, unmkd, ... **95.00**

4 1/2" h, inverted helmet shape, center band of silver luster stylized leaves and Chinese red branching, silver luster banding on rim, lip, and handle, ... **75.00**

5" h, molded vert loops on lower section, ear handle, overall silver luster, ... **85.00**

Figure, 13" h, bust of Princess Charlotte, shaped plinth, overall luster, repaired chip, ... **2,500.00**

Jug

4" h, "Farmer's Arms," black transfer w/polychrome accents, "The Husbandman Diligence..." in floral cartouche and other sayings, silver luster bands on neck, ... **190.00**

4 1/4" d, grey bat printed scene of children on side, reverse w/"Faith" in silver luster wreaths, silver luster rim, c1810, ... **90.00**

4 1/2" h, silver resist white daisies, sm flowers on curved stems, grapes and tendrils on collar, ... **120.00**

5" h

Circ cartouche of Masonic symbols and pink ribbon, 6 pointed star on reverse, starburst under spout and handle, silver resist ground w/leaf and stylized flowerhead designs, c1890, ... **295.00**

Molded ribbing and beading w/painted reserve of starbursts, border of molded roses, silver luster ground, c1810, ... **375.00**

Silver resist exotic bird in field of leaves, reverse w/chrysanthemum flowerhead, band of ovals on collar, ... **495.00**

5 1/4" h

Silver resist fishscale design on body, band of silver resist and white flowerheads on collar, c1820, ... **750.00**

Vert fluted base, band of beading around middle, overall silver luster, "imp Gibsons England" mk, **50.00**

5 1/2" h, silver resist vert white curled fern fronds, collar w/interwoven ovals, c1880, ... **725.00**

5 3/4" h, silver resist overall sprig pattern, leaf design on collar, c1810, ... **675.00**

6" h

Pineapple diamond base, silver luster body, early 19th C, ... **250.00**

Silhouettes of birds, flowers, and leaves against silver luster ground, border bands of silver luster vert hearts, star crack on base, ... **750.00**

6 1/4" h, pineapple diamond body, burnt orange and silver luster flowers and leaves, leaf design on collar, spout repair, (A), ... **110.00**

6 3/4" h, soft paste, transfer and HP "Odd Fellows" and "God is our Guide," reverse w/rearing horseman, silver luster band of foliage on collar, and rim, (A), ... **400.00**

Loving Cup, 5 3/8" h, gadrooned lower body, spurred handle terminals, pedestal stem and base, copper luster int, c1830, ... **85.00**

Mug, 3 3/8" h, blue transfer printed scene of huntsman and dogs in landscape in silver resist ground, England, (A), ... **295.00**

Mug, Miniature, 2" h, wide silver resist stripe of foliage and zigzag design on upper half, unmkd, (A), ... **28.00**

Pitcher, 4 1/4" h, silver resist florals, leaves, and geometric loops, $265.00

Pitcher

5 1/2" h, silver resist ground w/lt blue transfers of bird hunters in woods, polychrome accents, hairline, (A), ... **185.00**

7 5/8" h, black transfers of hunters, horses, and dogs on sides, lt tan ground, silver luster collar and rim, (A), ... **440.00**

Sugar Bowl, Cov, 4 1/8" h x 7" H-H, ribbed middle band, curled handles, flanged cov, overall silver luster, (A), ... **77.00**

Teapot

6" h

9 1/2" w, sprigged white cameos on classic figures w/horses and chariot on brown ground, silver luster base, spout, handle, collar, and cov, "Gibson's Made in England" mk, ... **80.00**

Pitcher, 5 1/8" h, HP red tipped white blossoms, green and yellow leaves, green stems, red and white buds, Wales, c1820-40, $250.00

10" l, silver shape, vert fluting on base, wishbone handle, ... **95.00**

7" h, squat shape, 4 sm feet, overall luster, ... **90.00**

10 1/4" h, urn shape, narrow pedestal, soft paste, band of silver luster florals and red leaves, cov hairline, (A), ... **80.00**

Tea Set, pot, 10 1/2" h, creamer, 4 1/2" h, cov sugar bowl, 5 1/2" h, neo-classical style, overall silver luster, Hutschenreuther, repairs, ... **165.00**

Toby Jug, 5" h, overall silver luster, early 19th C, ... **325.00**

Water Pitcher, 7 3/4" h, ball shape, applied handle, overall silver luster, (A), ... **55.00**

Sunderland

Bowl

7" d, int w/busts of Victoria and Napoleon III, multicolored flags, lion and unicorn and pink splashing, ext w/black transfers of French and English sailors and "the Sailor's Tear," pink splashed sides, ... **950.00**

7 3/4" d, ftd, black transfer of Garibaldi on int, "Ensigns Of State That Feed Our Pride" and "Ancient Order of Foresters" on ext, pink bubble luster trim, ... **495.00**

9 1/4" d, ftd, black transfers on ext of "Ancient Order of Foresters," "Forget Me Not" poem and print of ship, int w/print of "Mariner's Arms," "the Sailors Tear" poem and "Sailors Fairwell," bowl center w/"West View of the Cast Iron Bridge Over the River Wear Built By R. Burdon, Esq." "Span 236 Feet, Height 100 Feet-Begun 24 Sept. 1793 Open 9 Augt. 1796," pink bubble luster between, ... **3,000.00**

12" d, black transfer of ship and "SHIP CAROLINE" on int w/pink bubble luster border, ext w/black transfers of 2 sailors poems in ovals, pink bubble luster on body, Grey's Pottery, ... **300.00**

Cup and Saucer, overall bubble burst pink luster design, ... **115.00**

Jar, Cov, 5" h, 5 3/4" H-H, black transfer of clipper ship w/brown coloring in green and brown wreath of leaves and branches, reverse w/black printed "From Rocks & Sands And every ill May God preserve The Sailor still" and clipper ship in wreath, applied green handles, pink bubble luster splashes on body and cov, c1820, (A), ... **600.00**

Jug, 4 1/2" h, black transfer of Iron Bridge, verse on reverse, splashed pink lustered body, $175.00

Jug

7" h, black transfer

Bust of Garibaldi on side, pink luster clouds, pink luster lined rim, ... **650.00**

Mariner's Compass on side, reverse w/"Thou Noble Bark of Brightest Fame," ... **950.00**

7 1/4" h, 3 oval HP orange, red, and green medallions w/black transfer of sailing ship under spout, religious verse on side, Captain's verse on reverse, pink splash luster on collar, (A), ... **550.00**

7 7/8" h, black transfer of "The Ancient Order of Foresters" crest on side, Alexander Pope poem on reverse, pink bubble luster frames and rim, rim chip, ... **400.00**

8" h, dk red transfer of 2 sailors, ship, verse and "Mariner's Arms," red, green, yellow, and blue enamel accents, pink splash luster ground, (A), ... **770.00**

Jug, 5 3/4" h, black Masonic transfer, verse on reverse, pink luster clouds and rim bands, $450.00

Mug

2 5/8" h, overall pink bubble design, ... **175.00**

4" h

Black transfer of sailor and girl w/sailing ship in bkd, hunting verse on reverse, pink bubble luster ground, figural frog on int, ... **250.00**

"MARY ELLEN, 1854," sailing ship, iron bridge, black transfers, pink luster and bubble luster arches and borders, applied handle w/tendril terminals, ... **650.00**

Sailing ship "Barque" on side, sailors w/capstan and "Heave Oh Cheerly..." on reverse in splashed pink luster reserves, black transfers w/colors, ... **225.00**

4 1/2" h, black transfer of "Cast Iron Bridge of the River Weir...Began 24 Sept. 1793 Open 9 Aug. 1796" in pink bubble luster cartouches on front, pink bubble luster rim and base, figural frog on int, star crack, ... **545.00**

4 3/4" h, black print of clipper ship w/brown overlay in brown and green wreath of leaves and branches, reverse w/black printed "From hence in the deep May divisions be tof'd And Prudence What folly has loft" in black printed design of sm circles and green and brown wheat, floral, and bows, overall pink bubble splash, c1820, (A), ... **495.00**

Mug, Cov, 5 1/4" h, overall pink bubble luster, button knob, hairline, (A), ... **70.00**

Pepper Pot, 4 1/2" h, overall bubble luster, wear to rim and holes, **125.00**

Pitcher, 2 1/4" h, overall bubble burst pattern, gilt rim and handle, "Grey's Pottery" mk, ... **20.00**

Plaque, 9 1/4" l x 8 1/4" w, black transfer, pink bubble luster self frame, copper luster rim, pierced for hanging, $600.00

Plaque

5 1/4" d, "black PREPARE TO MEET THY GOD," angel above w/yellow accents, green streaks, pink bubble luster rim, ... **525.00**

8" d, "black PREPARE TO MEET THY GOD," pink luster border w/white bubble bursts, copper luster rim, ... **450.00**

8 1/2" d, "black MATE SOUND THE PUMP MORNING NOON & NIGHT in wreath," pink bubble

luster border, copper luster rim, c1820-40, ... **3,900.00**

8 1/2" l, Rect

7 1/4" w, "black THOU GOD SEEIST ME," pink luster stylized flowers in corner, self framed pink bubble luster border, copper luster rim, pierced for hanging, ... **650.00**

7 3/4" w, "black Job.8.20, Behold. God will not cast away a perfect man, neither will he help the evil-doers" in red, yellow, and green floral wreath, pink bubble luster self frame, c1830, ... **235.00**

8 3/4" l

7 1/2" w, rect, "black THOU GOD SEEST ME in wreath," self framed pink bubble luster border, pierced for hanging, ... **550.00**

7 3/4" h, rect, "black Behold God will not cast away a perfect man, neither will he keep the evil-doers," self framed pink bubble luster border, pierced for hanging, ... **550.00**

8 1/2" h, center romantic landscape scene, black transfer, pink bubble luster and copper luster accented self frame, "Dixon & Phillips & Co." mk, (A), ... **275.00**

9" l x 8" w, rect

Black transfer

Iron bridge scene w/yellow and brown overlay and pink luster swirls, black printed "A West View of the Iron Bridge over the Wear under the Patronage of R. Burton Esq. M.P.," pink bubble luster frame border, copper luster rim, pierced for hanging, (A), ... **440.00**

"THOU GOD SEEST ME" in red, green, and yellow floral wreath, orange luster frame, pierced for hanging, c1860, ... **125.00**

Sailing ship, black transfer w/colors, pink bubble luster self frame, pierced for hanging, ... **650.00**

9 1/4" l x 8 1/4" h, "black FROM MAN DIETH AND WASTETH AWAY YE MAN GIVETH UP THE GHOST," multicolored floral wreath, pink lustered corners, pink bubble

luster self frame, purple luster rim, ... **575.00**

9 1/2" l x 8 1/2" w, rect, black transfer of sailing ship w/yellow, brown, and blue overlay, black printed "May Peace & Plenty On our Nation Smile and Trade with Commerce Bless the British Isle," pink bubble luster frame border w/copper luster rim, pierced for hanging, (A), ... **440.00**

9 3/4" l x 8 1/2" w, rect, black transfer of Mariner's Compass, flanked by man and woman w/orange color added, pink luster dashes top and bottom, self framed pink bubble luster frame, copper luster rim, pierced for hanging, ... **695.00**

Plate

7 3/8" d, overall pink bubble luster, c1800-20, ... **45.00**

10" d, bust of Pike and "Be Always Ready To Die For Your Country," black transfer in center, yellow inner border, pink bubble luster border, ... **165.00**

Salt, 2 1/8" h x 3" d, overall bubble luster, ... **52.00**

Soup Plate, 8" d, polychrome transfer of sailing ship w/"Success to the Tars of old England," pink bubble luster border, ... **950.00**

Tankard, 5" h, multicolored center band of family in glenn, red and green flowerheads and "Where I So Tall To Reach The Pole..," pink bubble luster bands w/black stripes top and base, ... **1,200.00**

c1836-1878

Petrus Regout & C°
MAASTRICHT

c1878

MAASTRICHT

Maastricht, Holland
1836 to Present

History: Petrus Regout founded a glass and crystal works in 1834 in Maastricht, Holland. In 1836 he expanded his operation to include the De Sphinx Pottery that had a work force recruited from England. It was Regout's desire to introduce the manufacture of ironstone, a ware that had greatly reduced the market for Delftware.

From 1836 to 1870, Petrus Regout manufactured dinnerware in the style of English ironstone decorated with transfer printed patterns with scenic or romantic themes. Pattern names were back stamped in English for wares exported to English and American markets. Patterns included "Amazone," "Mythology," "Pleasure Party," "Ruth & Boaz," "Wild Rose," and "Willow." Until about 1870, Regout's decorations had been printed only in one color, either blue, black, violet, or red. If a second color was desired, the piece was first decorated with a printed black transfer and the second color then hand applied. In 1870 lithographic decalcomania made possible multicolor printing on china. Brightly colored dinnerware became the rage until the end of the century.

When Regout died in 1878, his sons reorganized the company. They adopted the Sphinx trademark. During the 20th century, tastes became more conservative. Today the firm is called "N.V. Konmklijke Sphinx." Since 1974, it has been part of the British conglomerate Reed International.

Pieces usually had a printed back stamp. Most dinnerware was marked with a pattern name. The company also made blanks for others to decorate. The phrase "Royal Sphinx" was authorized in 1959 and used on decorative tiles.

Other potteries in Maastricht during the 1840s and 1850s included N.A. Bosch; W.N. Clermont and Ch. Chainaye; and G. Lambert & Co., which merged with Sphinx in 1958.

References: John P. Reid, "The Sphinx of Maastricht," *The Antique Trader Weekly*, December 20, 1984.

Collecting Hints: Early Regout pottery always had a heavily crazed glaze. After the 1870s, the glaze was free of crazing. The tan luster did not wear well. The quality of the printing varied with the different transfers.

Bowl, 7 5/8" d, "Pajong" pattern, black transfer, lt orange accents, "Petrous Regout Co. Maastricht Pajong" mk, **$60.00**

Bowl, 6" d, 3 11/4" h, "Abbey" pattern, green transfer, orange accents, **$35.00**

Bowl
5 5/8" d, "Canton" pattern, black transfer w/polychrome accents, "Petrus Regout, Maastricht" mk, ... **15.00**
6" d, "Honc" pattern, green transfer w/colors and tan luster, ... **25.00**
7 3/8" d, "Timor" pattern, 2 oriental figures in center in colors, "Petrus Regout Maastricht" mk, ... **95.00**
8 1/4" d, "Slamat" pattern, multicolored, "Petrus Regout Maastricht Made in Holland" mk, ... **75.00**
8 3/4" d, "Fishing" pattern, couple fishing in classical setting, floral border, red transfer, "Petrus Regout Maastricht" mk, ... **35.00**
11 1/4" d
"Hong" pattern, black transfer w/color accents, ... **65.00**
"Vlinder" pattern, polychrome and transfer printed butterflies and flowering branches, geometric and spearhead border, iron-red rim, tan luster accents, Petrus Regout, ... **145.00**
Candleholder, 4" h, dk blue transfer of butterfly and flowers, lt blue ground, "Royal sphinx Maastricht Made in Holland" mk, ... **20.00**
Charger, 13" d, dk red quarter moon and star in center, dk red border w/white quarter moons and stars, "The Maestricht Ceramique Societe, Made in Holland" mk, ... **20.00**
Creamer, 4" h x 5 3/8" l, "Cambridge" pattern, blue transfer, "Petrus Regout Maastricht" mk, ... **20.00**
Cup and Saucer
"Honc" pattern, green transfer w/tan luster and orange rims, "Petrus Regout & Co. Maastricht Holland, sphinx" mk, ... **20.00**

"Tea Drinker" pattern, red transfers, "Socite Maastricht" mk, ... **40.00**
Cup and Saucer, **Demitasse**, "Border" pattern, band of florals and geometrics w/interwoven fencing, red transfers, sphinx mk, ... **8.00**
Cup and Saucer, **Handleless**, "Pajong" pattern, black oriental transfers w/orange luster overglaze, "sphinx, P. REGOUT MAASTRICHT PAJONG, Made in Holland" mk, ... **20.00**
Ginger Jar, 10 1/8" h, "Delft" pattern, blue and white, "sphinx, Maastricht" mk, ... **45.00**
Plate
7 1/4" d, "Amazone" pattern, purple transfer, Petrus Regout, ... **10.00**
7 3/8" d, stylized Dutch country scene, tan and brown shades, Societe Ceramique, ... **10.00**
8 1/4" d
Red, blue, yellow, and green butterfly and foliage in center, butterflies and insects on border, Greek key rim, "P. Regout Maastricht" mk, ... **65.00**
"Timor" pattern, tan transfer w/orange, black, and green accents, orange rim, "P. Regout Maastricht Timor" mk, ... **30.00**
9" d, lt purple inner border, outer border of red and blue stamped sq flowerheads, scattered yellow flowerheads, red lines, ... **5.00**
9 1/8" d, "Castillo" pattern, blue transfer, "Petrus Regout Maastricht, Holland" mk, ... **25.00**
9 1/4" d, "Hollandia" pattern, windmill scene, med blue transfer, pierced for hanging, ... **45.00**
9 1/2" d, "Tecla" pattern, lg oriental style flowers, buds, and leaves, oval cartouches on border of flowerheads between sm flowerhead pattern, red transfer, "Petrus Regout Maastricht TECLA" mk, ... **25.00**
9 5/8" d, "Amazone" pattern, red transfer, "Petrus Regout Maastricht, Holland" mk, ... **13.00**
Soup Plate, 8 1/4" d, "Bima" pattern, oriental flying animals in center, packets of drawing and painting

instruments on border, red transfer, "Petrus Regout Maastricht BIMA" mk, ... **30.00**

Tureen, Cov, 8" h, overall blue printed calico type pattern, white piecrust rim, ear handles, mkd, ... **110.00**

Tray, 11" H-H x 7 1/2" w, sm multicolored flowerheads on border and handles, ... **10.00**

Vase, 14 1/2" h, amphora shape, painted eagle perched on brown rocks, tan and aqua bkd, 2 handles, "Societe Ceramique Maestricht Made in Holland" mk, c1930, ... **170.00**

Vegetable Bowl, 13" l x 9 1/2" w, "Timor" pattern, "Petrus Regout Maastricht" mk, ... **15.00**

Waste Bowl, 5 1/2" d, "Pomeia" pattern, black transfer of bottle on int and ext and leaves and scrolls, blue, green, and iron-red accents, "Petrus Regout Maastricht POMEIA" mk, ... **25.00**

1874~1924
GEORGE JONES

1890 - 1939

MAJOLICA

English and Continental
1850 to Present

History: During a visit to Rouen in 1849, Herbert Minton saw flower pots with a green glaze. When he returned to England, Minton instructed Leon Arnoux, his firm's art director, to copy these wares. Arnoux introduced English Majolica, an opaque tin-glazed earthenware, in 1850. The name Majolica originally came from the Spanish island of Majorca. Its popularity in England remained strong through the second half of the 19th century.

Minton's early majolica wares closely imitated Palissy ware, a pottery made by Bernard Palissy at Saintes, France, between 1542 and 1562 and later in a workshop on the grounds of the Palais des Tuileries in Paris.

Palissy ware was characterized by relief figures and ornaments that were covered with colored glazes—mainly yellow, blue, and grey, highlighted with brown and manganese. Palissy was known for naturalistic designs of leaves, lizards, snakes, insects, shells, and other natural objects in high relief on plates and dishes. He also made vases, ewers, and basins. The reverse of his wares was covered with a mottled glaze in brown, blue, and manganese. Palissy developed the applique technique, which consisted of making plaster casts resembling the natural objects separate from the main body and applying these later.

Early Minton majolica wares were modeled by the French sculptors Emile Jeannest, Albert Carrier-Belluse, and Hugues Protat. Protat made the models from which the wares were cast. Leading artists from the Victorian period who decorated the wares included Thomas Allen, Thomas Kirkby, and Edouard Rischgitz.

Early majolica wares by Minton also attempted to emulate Italian majolica, basic earthenware that was coated with an opaque white glaze or covering slip. English majolica were earthenwares decorated with deep semi-transparent lead glazes. Typical Victorian majolica examples included large garden ornaments such as seats and jardinières, plus many types of plates and dishes for utilitarian and decorative use.

Daniel Sutherland and Sons of Longton established a pottery in 1863 to manufacture the majolica wares. A tremendous variety of articles was made. Other manufacturers included Brown/Westhead; W. Brownfield and Company of Cobridge; Holdcraft; George Jones and Sons; Moore and Company; and Wedgwood. George Jones, who was employed by Minton until he established his own Trent Pottery in Stoke in 1861, made lidded vases, ornamental bowls, candelabras, and wall plaques, along with more ordinary everyday majolica wares.

Wedgwood's majolica took the form of molded leaves and vegetables that were decorated with a translucent green glaze. Other Wedgwood majolica wares were covered with colored glazes on a white body that was molded with high quality relief ornamentation. Vases, umbrella stands, wall brackets, candlesticks, compotes, plates, and a variety of dishes were made.

Majolica wares were made on the Continent by Sarreguimines in France, by Villeroy and Boch and Zell in Germany, and by companies in Austria, Bavaria, and Italy. Nineteenth century majolica was different from the earlier Italian majolica wares.

References: Victoria Bergesen, *Majolica: British, Continental and American Wares, 1851-1915*, Barrie & Jenkins, 1989; Leslie Bockol, *Victorian Majolica*, Schiffer Publishing, Ltd. 1996; Helen Cunningham, *Majolica Figures*, Schiffer Publishing, Ltd. 1997; Nicholas M. Dawes, *Majolica*, Crown Publishers, Inc. 1990; Marilyn G. Karmasn with Joan B. Stacke, *Majolica: A Complete History and Illustrated Survey*, Harry B. Abrams, 1989; Marshall P. Katz & Robert Lehr, *Palissy Ware: Nineteenth Century French Ceramists from Avisseau to Renoleau*, Athlone Press, 1996; Mariann Katz-Marks, *Collectors' Encyclopedia of Majolica*, Collector Books, 2000; D. Michael Murray, *European Majolica*, Schiffer Books, 1997; Julia E. Poole, *Italian Majolica*, Cambridge University Press, 1997; Mike Schneider, *Majolica, 3rd Edition*, Schiffer Publishing, Ltd. 1999; Jeffrey B. Snyder & Leslie J. Bockol, *Majolica: American, British, & European Wares*, Schiffer Publishing, Ltd. 2001; Alan-Caiger Smith, *Tin-Glaze Pottery in Europe & the Islamic World*, Faber & Faber, 1973; Jeffrey B. Snyder, *Marvelous Majolica: An Easy Reference & Price Guide*, Schiffer Publications, 2001; Robert Cluet, *George Jones Ceramics, 1861-1951*, Schiffer Publications, 2002.

Collectors' Club: Majolica International Society, David Stone treasurer, 4144 E. Admiral Place, Tulsa, OK, 74115, www.majolicasociety.com, Membership: $35.00, Quarterly newsletter, *Majolica Matters.*

Museums: British Museum, London, England; Cooper Hewitt Museum, NY; Henry Ford Museum, Dearborn, MI; Cleveland Museum of Art, Cleveland, OH; City Museum and Art Gallery, Stoke-on-Trent, England; Metropolitan Museum of Art, New York, NY; Minton Museum, Stoke-on-Trent, England; J. Paul Getty Museum, Los Angeles, CA; Strong Museum, Rochester, NY; Victoria & Albert Museum, London, England; Wadsworth Atheneum, Hartford, CT; Wallace Collection, London, England; Wedgwood Museum, Barlaston, England.

Reproduction Alert: Original majolica always was thick walled, with smooth interior walls showing no sign of the pattern. Most new majolica is much lighter in weight than Victorian counterparts. Check the glazes because new ones are not as rich or deeply colored. Some marks have also been reproduced.

Reproductions coming from China are now close copies of some of the original Victorian majolica. The Chinese examples have hollow handles, unglazed bottoms, dull, rough surface glazes, and poorly molded details. The dark background colors are predominately yellow-brown or gold-brown. Patterns on the outside of vases and pitchers can also be seen and felt on the inside of these pieces. Many Chinese examples have a matte finish, while original pieces utilize bright colors and shiny glazes. Old examples have solid handles that were made separately and applied to the body of the piece, so there are no firing holes. With the hollow handles, these pieces were cast as a single piece, so there is a firing hole by the handle.

Some reproductions from China can carry dangerous amounts of lead and should not be used to serve food.

To complicate matters, some reproductions are better made and have shiny, smooth glazes and bright colors, but they are generally heavier than the originals they are copied from.

The desirable "Monkey" teapot has been reproduced in 1993. Also "Chinaman," and "Tortoise" have been reproduced.

English

Bowl

2 1/2" h x 3 7/8" w, figural brown bamboo and rope ext, turquoise int, "imp MINTON" mk, ... **475.00**

9" d, relief of yellow and red fruit in center, brown basketweave ground, ... **225.00**

Bowl, Cov, 7" h, pierced green and ochre scrolls and leaves, brown branch twist handles, cream flower knob, Wedgwood, c1860-80, (A), ... **900.00**

Celery Tray, 16" l x 5" w, dk green leaf in center, molded brown border, ... **75.00**

Comport, 6 3/4" h, 3 green twisted dolphins support green leaf dish, lt green and pink dolphin heads on purple vert lined triangular base, Wedgwood, dtd 1873, (A), ... **630.00**

Creamboat, 9" h, figural cream nautilus shell w/blue end and brown streaks, grey figural dolphins on green gadrooned oval base, dtd 1862, pr, (A), ... **3,825.00**

Creamer, 3 1/2" h, overlapping pink edged scallop shells, brown branch handle, brown coral base, c1880, ... **325.00**

Crocus Pot and Stand, 10 1/2" l, figural hedgehog, brown, green, and ochre glaze, Wedgwood, (A), ... **975.00**

Cup and Saucer

Lavender and yellow molded shells, turquoise int, c1880s, ... **495.00**

Red daffodil and buds on brown branches around middle, green leaves, white pebble ground, lt blue int, c1880s, ... **325.00**

Tan, white, and lt blue Japanese fans, pink half chrysanthemum blossoms, cobalt pebble ground, tan rim, brown branch handle, British reg mk, ... **100.00**

Dish

9" l, lg green centered mauve flowerhead, swirled tan leaves, brown molded border, Shorter, ... **20.00**

11" l, oval, molded yellow and red tinged green leaves in center, green and grey berries, brown molded ground and dbl

overhead handle, Wedgwood, c1875, (A), ... **510.00**

Figure

8" h x 9 1/2" w, standing brown elephant, red fringed turquoise and blue saddle blanket, dk brown based cream, dk blue, and turquoise sedan chair, yellow harness, "Hadley" mk, Royal Worcester, ... **1,500.00**

12" h, parrot, yellow comb, green body, perched on grey-brown tree branch, "MINTON ENGLAND" mk, c1900, ... **600.00**

Flower Holder, 16" h, seated Arab in white cloak holding hookah, brown recumbent camel w/white, black, green, and brown saddle, grey-black stone flower holder in bkd, brown stone base, Brown, Westhead, and Moore, c1870, (A), ... **3,750.00**

Game Pie Dish, 9" l, tan hanging game, green foliage and fruiting vines, brown ground, figural brown crouching rabbit knob, Wedgwood, (A), ... **825.00**

Game Tureen, 14 3/8" l, w/liner, oval, relief molded brown rabbits in green grasses, ivy, and oaks on turquoise ground, brown branch rim and entwined handles, relief of partridge and chicks in grasses on cov, George Jones, c1860, repairs, (A), ... **17,625.00**

Garden Seat

18 1/2" h, crouching brown and white monkey, holding yellow and green coconut, cobalt pillow w/green edge, yellow tassels on head, oct faux rattan base, MINTON, dtd 1873, (A), ... **16,730.00**

19" h, seated blackamoor boy, brown lion skin on shoulders, yellow-gold lined green jacket, purple striped yellow-brown sash, red boots, supporting red tasseled green quilted cushion on shoulders, seated on green quilted red tasseled base, Minton, c1867, chips and restorations, (A), ... **17,250.00**

Jam Pot, Cov, 4 1/2" h, lg yellow rayed sun w/pink flower and flying pink, brown and yellow flying bird on turquoise disk, brown textured ground, brown branch handles and knob, ... **150.00**

Jardiniere, 10 3/4" h x 10 1/2" d, blackberry brambles, red centered white blossoms, pink edged green leaves, brown stems on dk brown bark ground, lt brown entwined stems on rim, twig feet, turquoise int, Wedgwood, dtd 1868, hairline, ... **1,295.00**

Jug, 9 1/4" h, green vine leaves molded on cobalt ground, brown branch handle, Minton, (A), ... **975.00**

Jug, Cov, 13" h, "Tower," polychrome medieval merrymakers, figural jester knob, Minton, dtd 1877, (A), ... **780.00**

Pitcher

5" h, yellow centered brown flower, green leaves on sides, white bamboo ground w/molded raindrops, ... **145.00**

6" h, figural monk, tan and green drip robe, blue collar and hat, c1880, restored rim chip, ... **395.00**

6 3/4" h, 4 panels, relief of white storks, brown bullrushes, blue ground, brown handle and rim, ... **300.00**

Pitcher, 8" h, white and yellow irises, green foliage, lavender ground, sm red and white flowers on base, yellow rim, yellow entwined brown branch handle, lavender int, George Jones, $6,900.00

8" h, green ivy meandering on lt yellow brick ground, brown branch handle, c1870, ... **485.00**

8 1/2" h, brown, tan, pink, and green bamboo pattern on beige textured ground, Brownhill Pottery, ... **170.00**

9" h, figural ear of yellow and gold corn, green leaves, mauve int, ... **475.00**

10" h, figural
Grey nautilus shell, pink coral handle, green leaf terminals, ... **695.00**
Yellow corn cob, green leaves and handle, c1880, .. **500.00**
10 1/2" h, figural gurgling fish, grey body, brown fins, green foliage on circ base, c1880, ... **425.00**

Plate
8" d, white and pink molded conch shell and coral, turquoise netted ground, Fielding, ... **600.00**
8 1/4" d, 2 green budgies perched on dk brown branches w/green foliage, med brown patches on border w/triangle designs, pale blue ground, dk brown lined rim, British reg mk, ... **275.00**
8 1/2" d, relief of half bust of Spanish lady wearing shawl in center, basketweave inner border, molded geometric swirls on border, overall dk green glaze, Wedgwood, ... **165.00**
8 3/4" d
Green melon w/orange slice, red raspberries, purple plums, brown foliage, cream w/brown dashes and rim, Wedgwood, ... **695.00**
Three brown carp fish w/pink facial accents, brown sea plants and lined rim, "imp WEDGWOOD" mk, c1870, ... **360.00**
9" d
Brown tipped green oak leaf on cream and rose lined ground, tan rim, mottled reverse, George Jones, ... **250.00**
Red winged, white breasted, crowned bird on branch, brown pebbled border w/butterflies and leaves, tan bamboo rim, English reg mk, dtd 1875, ... **185.00**
Three black fan panels, 3 panels w/multicolored bird on branch in each, Wedgwood, ... **195.00**
9 1/4" d, sm yellow centered red or blue flowerheads, red tipped green spiked foliage, pink basketweave ground, brown bamboo rim, ... **165.00**
9 1/2" d, green center, overlapped radiating orange tinged yellow petals, Burslem, ... **15.00**
Platter, 13" l, figural radiating yellow corn in center, green leaves on border, ... **895.00**

Sardine Box, 8 1/2" w x 7 3/4" l, grey, white and red crossed fish on cov, green seaweed, turquoise ground, brown rims, George Jones, ... **2,875.00**
Spill Vase, 7 1/2" h, kneeling cherub w/purple drape, brown and grey woven basket on back, turquoise, green, and brown circ base w/beading, Wedgwood, c1872, (A), ... **630.00**
Spooner, 5" h, white dogwood blossoms, brown branches, lt blue bark ground, Holdcroft, hairline, ... **275.00**
Strawberry Server, 10 1/2" l x 10 1/4" w, green leaf shape w/molded strawberry leaves and white blossoms, 2 lg white blossom holders, brown center stem handle, ... **195.00**

Teapot
5 1/2" h, ball shape, pink body w/green branch and orange flowers, green and brown overhead branch handle, "imp MINTON" mk, dtd 1873, ... **800.00**
5 5/8" h x 10 1/2" l, figural fish swallowing fish, grey, green, pink, and yellow, c1872, ... **1,595.00**
9" h, Gothic style, lt brown circ panels on sides w/white flowerheads, green foliage on lt blue ground, cobalt borders w/white dot flowerheads, dk brown panels, 4 sm feet, lilac int, repaired chip, ... **2,035.00**
11 1/2" l, figural crowing cockerel, white body, red comb, green and brown base, George Jones, c1875, (A), ... **4,541.00**

Tray, 12" d, brown and yellow butterfly, yellow wheat with green leaves, turquoise ground, brown border, George Jones, **$2,175.00**

Tray, 12" H-H x 9" w, yellow centered blue or red daisies, yellow wheat, blue pebbled ground, brown rope rim, blue ribbon handles, Fielding, ... **695.00**
Umbrella Stand, 40" h, standing white stork, snake in beak, standing in green bullrushes, frog underfoot, Minton, dtd 1916, (A), ... **9,000.00**

Vase, 6 1/8" h, white doves, cobalt jar w/mauve and green accents, turquoise int, "imp MINTON" mk, **$3,800.00**

Vase
6 3/4" h, cobalt bombe body w/red, green, and ochre geometrics, 3 tan lion paw feet w/tan lion mask terminals and green shells, green, tan, and dk brown striped triform base, lilac int, ... **345.00**
9 3/8" h, modeled as elongated bird's nest, brown twigs entwined around green bullrushes, brown figural bird perched on side facing pad base w/insect, lily leaves, and flowers, George Jones, c1874, (A), ... **7,755.00**
10 3/4" h, brown squirrel climbing grey and white tree trunk, green leaves w/yellow-brown fruit, Minton, dtd 1877, (A), ... **7,500.00**
27 3/4" h, "Queen's Vase" form w/purple gadrooned trumpet neck, molded green grape leaves, tan tendrils, purple grapes, brown ground, purple gadrooned base, brown rect branch handles w/pink tied ribbons framing brown cat's

heads, turquoise int, c1880, Minton, (A), ... **11,353.00**

Asparagus Plate, 9 1/8" d, purple asparagus strips, red border flowers, green trim, cream ground, $95.00

Continental

Asparagus Dish, 9 1/4" d, molded yellow shaded grey asparagus stalks, dk red and green stylized flowers and leaves on border, "St. Clement" mk, set of 6, ... **270.00**

Bank, 4 3/4" h, figural white cat's head, rose collar, St. Clement, ... **495.00**

Basket, 11 1/4" h, emb pinecone clusters on green and white woven ground, Austria, (A), ... **200.00**

Bowl, 7 1/4" sq, white lily of the valley, red flower buds, green leaves in center, turquoise rayed and basketweave ground, "Made in Germany" mk, ... **20.00**

Cake Stand, 3" h x 9 3/8" d, yellow water lilies, green whiplash stem and leaves, turquoise textured ground, Germany, ... **150.00**

Charger, 16 1/8" d, red-yellow pomegranates, green leaves and stems, yellow and brown butterfly in center, yellow-gold inner border, dk brown border molded w/tulips and leaves in alternating compartments, shaped rim, Austria, ... **180.00**

Creamer, 4 1/8" h, stylized owl face, brown, green, yellow, and pink, unmkd, ... **135.00**

Cup, 2 1/2" h x 3 1/2" H-H, Art Nouveau modeled woman's face w/flowing hair, shaded green to pink, pink int, France, ... **185.00**

Cup and Saucer
Brown and olive brown acorns, leaves, and oak leaves, turquoise int, France, ... **70.00**

Relief of blue-green leaves and stems, brown bark ground, turquoise int, France, ... **85.00**

Dish
12" d, Palissy ware, molded red beatles and green lizards on brown mottled ground, c1890, ... **1,550.00**
12 1/2" w, oval, 2 molded red and green apples in center, green tinged overlapped brown molded leaf ground, Sarreguemines, ... **77.00**

Jardiniere
5 3/4" h x 9" d, yellow centered white blossoms, vert blue-green leaves, textured brown bark ground, France, ... **725.00**
6" h x 11" d, red and yellow irises on turquoise ground, cobalt base w/dk red and green leaves, France, ... **320.00**
8" h x 13 1/4" l,
Oval shape, cream ground w/brown outlined panels of blue and red flowers, green and brown foliage, brown base and rim, aqua int, France, ... **495.00**
Molded pink thistles, vert green stems and leaves at corners, green drip rim, white ground, France, ... **195.00**

Pitcher
6 1/2" h, emb gold-brown bird on green branch on sides, mottled green, gold, pink, and green ground, ... **175.00**
8" h, figural yellow and green ear of corn, France, c1890, ... **750.00**
8 1/2" h, green bamboo leaves and stems, relief molded brown shaded bamboo ground, turquoise int, Sarreguemines, ... **160.00**
8" h, standing cat playing banjo, red jacket, blue bow tie, France, ... **430.00**
11" h, figural standing black, grey, and white penguin w/yellow breast, white ice block support and handle, Orchies, France, ... **450.00**
13" h, figural standing rooster, green wing feathers, red and yellow breast, yellow head, red comb, Saint Clement, ... **100.00**

Planter, 8 5/8" h x 7 7/8" sq, turquoise picket fencing, 2 brown horiz bands top and base, red tinged green

leaves from raised brown stems, brown stem feet and side handles, pink int, France, ... **480.00**

Planter, 18 3/4" H-H x 8" h, blue-green berries, red tinged yellow-brown leaves, dk brown leaves on base, dk brown branch handles, maroon int, "Frie Onnaing Made in France" mk, $1,150.00

Plaque
10" d, 2 white herons in blue water w/marsh grass, rose-red peonies on brown shore, pierced for hanging, Italy, ... **125.00**
12" d
Palissy style, raised red and yellow pears, green leaves, pink blossoms, shaded green ground, Longchamp, ... **780.00**
Two red poppies, 2 green leaves, brown ground w/leaf and stem designs, Sarreguemines, ... **65.00**
12 3/8" d, relief of red cherries, green leaves, blue and brown shaded ground, pierced for hanging, France, ... **235.00**

Plate
5 1/2" d, HP classic youth erupting from urn, curlicues and hanging swags and drapes, indented rim, yellow, blue, and gold, Italy, ... **45.00**
6" d, blue angel and cherub on tan streaked ground in center, cobalt border w/4 white ram heads, scattered fruit, tan wavy rim, "imp W.S. & S." mk, ... **175.00**
6 1/2" d, green maple leaf w/red margins, cream ground, "G.S. Zell Germany" mk, ... **10.00**
6 5/8" d, blue centered 12 petaled green flower in center, white lily of the valley on brown border, Villeroy and Boch, ... **75.00**
7 1/4" d, yellow waterlily blossoms, dk green leaves, whiplash stems, turquoise ground, "Schramberger" mk, ... **90.00**
7 3/8" d
Brown relief of 2 rabbits w/rifles hunting in center, turquoise

border w/relief of cattails and leaves, Villeroy & Boch, ... **130.00**

Two red headed yellow and brown birds perched on branches w/green and red leaves, purple grapes, turquoise ground and curlicue molded border, brown rim, France, ... **125.00**

7 1/2" d

Blue-green center w/molded rose red grapes, green leaves, brown tendrils, brown molded inner border, brown wrapped and green molded rim, med blue reverse, Germany, ... **80.00**

Sm salmon pink flowers in center, brown rayed lines, border band of med blue curlicues and leaves, scalloped rim, ... **60.00**

7 3/4" d, lg green chestnut leaf in center, sm red flowers on tan pebbled ground, green interwoven loop border, St. Clements, ... **165.00**

8" d

Figural blossom, yellow and green center, red-brown stamens, pink shaded lobed border, France, ... **380.00**

Two blue and white birds perched on brown branches, lg green leaves, hanging red berries, med blue ground, relief band of curls on rim, ... **80.00**

8 1/4" d

Two grey and white birds perched on branches, green leaves, red berries, lt blue ground, indented rim, France, ... **60.00**

Yellow figure of Joan of Arc holding banner, grey castle in bkd, in center, turquoise, yellow, and green ribbons on border w/French sayings, ... **125.00**

9" d

Relief of 2 black birds eating purple berries, dk green shaded leaves, green ground w/molded curlicue rim, unmkd, ... **50.00**

9 3/4" d, molded green asparagus stalk, blue curlicues on border, shaped rim, c1880, ... **125.00**

10" d, 2 pink roses, brown, green and blue leaves on white rayed ground, 4 border panels w/pink scalloped shells, molded blue rim, France, ... **90.00**

Platter, 13" H-H, dk red hibiscus, dk green leaves, med green basketweave ground, rope twist rim and handles, Germany, ... **50.00**

Serving Bowl, 12" H-H, lg white-centered red iris, green leaves, tan molded basketweave ground, rope handles, Germany, ... **210.00**

Teapot, 8 1/4" h, figural dachshund seated on haunches begging, tan and dk brown, paw forms spout, Germany, ... **295.00**

Tobacco Jar, 7 1/4" h, dk red jacket, grey-green suit, brown pipe, unmkd, **$895.00**

Tobacco Jar, 6 1/2" h x 9 1/4" l, figural mill and waterwheel, tan thatched roof, grey chimney and house, green tree trunk match holder, brown and green base, France, ... **250.00**

Urn, 13 1/2" h, relief of reclining nude woman and cherub in garden, grey ground w/trees, gargoyle head handles, brown top and base, green rim w/molded white oblongs, ... **4,250.00**

Vase

11" h, pink and blue tree trunk body w/drip and pink roses, green leaves, wide green loop handles from rim to body, sm figural boy holding roses, brown jacket, pink trousers, wide brimmed hat, c1911, ... **125.00**

15" h, 2 figural overlapping birds w/heads turned upward, brown-

red heads, blue-green feathered bodies, France, c1890, ... **1,150.00**

22 1/2" h, ovoid w/wavy rim, lg yellow irises, long green and brown stems and leaves, cream to brown shaded ground, pink int, Austria, ... **2,200.00**

Wall Pocket, 8 1/2" h, green ivy, tan flowerheads, brown cicada, purple grapes and vines, med brown board bkd, France, ... **450.00**

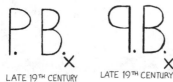

MALICORNE

West of Paris, France
Last Quarter 19th Century to 1952

History: Pouplard established his Malicorne factory in the Sarthe region west of Paris during the last quarter of the 19th century. He was making fine quality reproductions of the typical Quimper patterns, especially those of the Porquier Beau factory.

To add to the confusion, Pouplard used the "P" from his own name and the "B" from his wife's name Beatrix to form a "PB" mark of his own. Though the design differed from the "PB" mark of Porquier-Beau because the letters were separated and followed by a small "x," Porquier-Beau still brought suit against Pouplard. When the suit was settled in 1897, Malicorne was ordered to cease production and forced to destroy all of his remaining pottery molds. He continued to sign pieces with the PBx mark, only he no longer used the Breton designs. He ceased doing business in 1952.

In 1924, Emile Tessier, a colleague of Pouplard, opened his own workshop producing latticework baskets. The company became the largest factory in Malicorne, but economic crisis resulted in it closing in 1984.

References: Sandra V. Bondhus, *Quimper Pottery: A French Folk Art Faience*, privately published, 1981, *Rev. Ed.* 1995; Millicent S. Mali, *French Faience*, United Printing, 1986; Stephane Deschang, *Les Faiences de Malicorne*, 2001.

Museum: Sevres Museum, Sevres, France; Tessier Museum, Malicorne; Municipal Museum, Malicorne.

Bank, 3 1/2" h x 4 1/4" l, figural house, male peasant w/walking stick on roof, scattered red and blue flowerheads, yellow-green foliage, unmkd, (A), ... **205.00**

Bowl, 9 1/4" sq, tan scarf, green blouse, red apron, blue dress, yellow flowerheads with green and iron-red accents, $245.00

Charger

13" d, frontal view of male peasant wearing red-lined purple jacket, green vest, blue trousers, holding riding crop, border band of red, yellow, and green nuts and fruit, crackle glaze, indented rim, unmkd, ... **395.00**

13 1/2" d, center scene of male peasant seated at grinding wheel next to barn door, 3 children watching, crest of Brittany on border w/blue-green acanthus border design, orange shaped rim, "PBx" mk, (A), ... **775.00**

Cider Jug,
5" h, male peasant under spout, vert red, green, and yellow flowers and dot flowerheads, wavy blue lined rim w/red dots, blue stylized foliage on overhead and side handle, "PBx" mk, ... **175.00**

Egg Server,
11" l x 8" w, central panel of seated peasant woman knitting, 6 blue dash outlined egg cups w/scattered florals, black ermine tails between, blue dashed indented border, "Pbx" mk, (A), ... **990.00**

Holy Water Font,
7" h, kneeling female peasant before wayside cross, blue acanthus top, blue molded rococo sides, crest of Brittany on bowl, "PBx" mk, (A), ... **525.00**

Jug

5 1/4" h, 2 tone blue fleur-de-lys on sides, blue banded shoulder, rim, and base, blue dash handle, white ground, unmkd, ... **100.00**

5 1/2" h, male peasant holding flower and umbrella, scattered blue and

---

yellow sprigs, yellow and blue striped collar, black "PBx" mk, ... **75.00**

Pitcher, 6 3/8" h, green blouse, red apron, blue skirt, red, blue, or green florals, 4 blue dot designs, blue lined rim and base, single stroke floral handle, "Pbx" mk, $295.00

Pitcher,
10 1/2" h, flat sides, wide, flared rim, 2 male peasants holding basket of vegetables or walking stick, reverse w/yellow wildflowers, buds, green leaves, and tendrils, blue and yellow acanthus front and back sides, blue sponged handle, crest of Brittany on throat, blue lined rim, "PBx" mk, (A), ... **650.00**

Plate, 9 1/2" d, purple shawl, green blouse, yellow apron, blue dress, red, blue, yellow, and green trim, unmkd, $275.00

Plate, 9 3/4" d

Frontal view of male peasant wearing blue jacket, pink pantaloons, or female with yellow blouse, blue dress, pink apron holding flowers, blue and yellow banded borders, pr, ... **145.00**

Walking male peasant w/umbrella under arm, red, blue, and green vert flowers, border of scattered ajonc florals, indented rim, ... **160.00**

Porringer,
7 1/4" H-H, female peasant, red, yellow, and green florals, yellow and blue striped rim, blue and red striped tab handles, mkd, ... **150.00**

Serving Dish,
8 1/2" w, 3 leaf shaped sections w/brown knot center handle, male in one, female in second, pink and blue floral spray in third, blue and orange lined rims, "Pbx" mk, ... **230.00**

Snuff Bottle,
3" h, figural bagpipe, Breton lady on front, flower spray on reverse, red ribbon around opening, (A), ... **210.00**

Tray,
12" l x 7 3/4" w, frontal view of female peasant holding basket of eggs, male peasant leaning on walking stick, scalloped ribbon rim design w/yellow dots, blue sponged rope twist handles, (A), ... **525.00**

Vase

6" h, cylinder shape, male peasant holding leafy branch or frontal view of female peasant, blue and yellow Ruenesque scrolling upper border, geometric band of blue and red diamonds and dots, and stars on flared base, "PBx" mks, pr, (A), ... **325.00**

6 1/4" h, figural fleur-de-lys, seated male peasant playing bagpipe, geometric red green lattice on yellow round on sides, blue striped and gold branches of fleur-de-lys, shield of Brittany on ft, unmkd, (A), ... **375.00**

8 1/4" l, flat back, curved front and sides, pierced top, Rouen designs, multicolored cornucopia spilling flowers, birds, and butterflies on front, red and blue flowerhead stem openings on top, blue dbl loop borders, late 19th C, "PBx" mk, ... **150.00**

Wall Pocket

6 1/4" w, figural envelope, kneeling male peasant w/baskets of

---

cherries on flap, red and yellow floral sprays on folds, pierced for hanging, "PBx" mk, (A),
.... **350.00**

6 1/2" h, fan shape, male or female peasant, floral sprigs on molded backplate, dk red outlined wavy rims, unmkd, pr, ... **175.00**

c1895

MARTIN BROTHERS

Fulham, England
1873-1877

London and Southall, England
1877-1914

History: Robert, Walter, Edwin, and Charles Martin, the first of the English "studio potters," were four brothers who produced salt glaze stoneware called "Martinware." The Martin tradition evolved around ornately engraved, incised, or carved designs on salt glazed ware. Glazes usually were mottled with colors including, grey, brown, blue, and yellow in muted tones.

Robert initially worked for the Fulham Pottery of C.J.C. Barley. He and his three brothers established their own workshop in 1873 at Pomona House in Fulham. They fired their wares in the kiln at Fulham Pottery. When that kiln was no longer available, they leased a kiln at Shepherd's Bush.

Robert, known as Wallace, was the sculptor and director of the Martin team. He received his training at the Lambeth School of Art. He was an experienced stone carver and modeler of figures. Wallace modeled grotesques, now eagerly sought by collectors, for over thirty years. Grotesque birds were called "Walley-birds" after their maker.

Walter was in charge of throwing the large vases, mixing the clays, and the firing process. Edwin decorated the vases and other objects with naturalistic forms of decoration. Often he used incised or relief designs of fish, florals, and birds. Charles handled the business aspects of the concern.

In 1877 the brothers founded a pottery in Southall and built their own kiln. They opened a shop in London the next year. The Southall Pottery declined in 1910 with the death of Charles Martin. When Walter died in 1912, production ceased.

All pieces of Martinware were signed with their name, the place of production, and numerals and letters signifying the month and year. The information was incised into the soft clay before firing.

Between 1873 and 1883 the pottery was incised "R.W. Martin" followed by "Fulham" if fired at the Fulham Pottery, "London" if fired at Shepherd's Bush, and "Southall" if made at their own works. From 1879 when the shop was operating, the words "and London" were added to "Southall." From 1883 the full mark was "R.W. Martin & Bros. London & Southall."

References: C.B. Beard, *Catalogue of the Martinware in the Collection of F. I. Nettleford*, privately published, 1936; Malcolm Haslam, *The Martin Brothers Potters*, Wittenborn Art Books, 1978; Hugh Wakefield, *Victorian Porcelain*, Herbert Jenkins, 1962.

Museum: Victoria & Albert Museum, London, England.

Bowl, 2 3/4" l, rect, 4 sm feet, painted and incised tan and brown crawling snail, lt blue textured ground, (A),
.... **1,150.00**

Bud Vase, 10 1/2" h, tapered gourd shape, 4 vert buttresses, incised indigo wavy horiz lines on matte white ground, "Martinware Southall 13-37" mk, ... **1,200.00**

Jug
7 1/4" h, dbl face designs, brown shades, ... **4,700.00**
9" h, incised slip brown vert florals and foliage, mottled brown ground, cobalt leaf handle terminals, "Martin Brothers London and Southall" mk,
.... **470.00**

Urn, 7 1/2" h, brown and tan, "R.W. Martin Bros. London & Southhall" mark, ***$1,950.00***

Posy Holder, 2 balls joined by swirling leaves and pierced lotus blossoms,

shell and coral base, whiplash handles, white glaze, c1870,
.... **470.00**
Urn, 8 3/4" h, carved blue-centered yellow flowers, green leaves, brown and ivory ground, 2 loop handles from body to neck, "R.W. Martin/London & Southall" mk, (A),
.... **800.00**

Vase
1 3/4" h, molded swirl body w/blue and white swirls, "Martin Bros. London" mk, ... **330.00**
2 3/4" h, ball shape w/short neck, flared rim, painted and incised dk brown birds and grasses, tan and brown mottled ground, mkd, (A), ... **575.00**
5 1/8" h, sq, bulbous base, flared neck, blue, green, and tan frog skin finish, "incised Martin Ware Southall" mk, (A), ... **615.00**

Vase, 9" h, 4 panels, carved green, blue, rust, and ivory sea creature, restored lip, (A),
$1,725.00

7" h, tapered shape w/long, straight neck, blue and tan birds on brown and pale green leafy branches, gloss brown spread base and neck, "incised R.W. Martin" mk, ... **1,950.00**
8" h, bulbous shape, brown streaked flared ft and neck, stoneware,

carved cream grotesque face, overlapping tan fans w/blue-green margins, "incised Martin Bros., London & Southall" mk, (A), ... **1,035.00**
9" h
Bag shape w/long tapered neck, painted winged insects on branches and thistles, ivory ground, ... **2,250.00**
Ball shape w/flared rim, incised blue flowers, leaves, chestnut brown ground, ... **2,475.00**
9 3/8" h, organic form, indented sides, matte brown ground w/overall white squiggles, mkd, ... **1,300.00**

c1845

c1829-1845

FENTON STONE WORKS

_No 306_

c1825

MASON

Lane Delph, Staffordshire, England
c1804-1848

History: Although ironstone is the most familiar product associated with Mason's name, Miles Mason actually began his business career as an importer of china wares, specializing in matching pieces for incomplete sets. After studying the manufacturing methods at Worcester and Derby, Mason joined Thomas Wolfe in Liverpool in 1780 to manufacture Chinese-style porcelain tablewares.

After the dissolution of the Wolfe-Mason partnership in 1804, Mason started a second concern at Lane Delph in Fenton, Staffordshire. The Fenton factory was devoted to the manufacture of quality blue and white transferware. Within a short time, the factory was relocated at Minerva Works and expanded to incorporate the Bagnell factory. The new factory was known as the Fenton Stone Works.

Charles and George, Miles' sons, eventually became the managers. In 1813 they patented the ironstone formula and manufacturing technique. They were not the first to produce this hard and durable

earthenware, but they certainly were the most successful. Mason's Patent Ironstone China became dominant in the market. Ironstone, designed to meet the middle class needs for utilitarian, durable china tablewares, was produced at Fenton from 1813 to 1848.

The first designs were Oriental in nature. The most common method of applying the design was by transfer. Areas were highlighted with touches of enamel. Hand painting and gilding of the ironstone blanks was not uncommon, especially in floral and scenic patterns. Every conceivable form was fashioned in ironstone, from common tableware to fireplace mantles.

Economic difficulties beset the works in 1848. Charles was forced to sell the family business to Francis Morley. Morley, in partnership with Ashworth from 1849 to1862, acquired the Mason designs and molds. Ashworth reissues of Mason's original shapes and decorative patterns were hard to distinguish from those produced at the Fenton works.

For over one hundred years, Ashworth and Brothers, Ltd. have been selling vast quantities of their Mason's type ware with the traditional Oriental-styled patterns. In 1968 the firm took the new name "Mason's Ironstone China, Ltd," and the old mark was reinstituted.

References: Geoffrey A. Godden, _Godden's Guide to Mason's China & Ironstone Wares_, Antique Collectors Club, Ltd. 1980; Geoffrey A. Godden, _The Illustrated Guide to Mason's Patent Ironstone China,_ Barrie & Jenkins, 1971; Reginald Haggar & Elizabeth Adams, _Mason Porcelain and Ironstone 1796-1853_, Faber & Faber, 1977; R.G. Haggar, _The Masons of Lane Delph_, Lund Humphries, 1952.

Collectors' Club: Mason's Ironstone Collectors' Club, Susan Hirshman, 2011 East Main Street, Medford, OR, 97520, Membership: $25.00, Six newsletters per year.

Museums: City Museum & Art Gallery, Hanley, Stoke-on-Trent, England; Potsdam Public Museum, Potsdam, NY.; Victoria & Albert Museum, London, England.

Reproduction Alert: Mason's has reissued 19th century transfer patterns such as the "Quail pattern" on old shapes such as two-handled soups, mugs, teapots, and creamers in brown and blue with similar backstamps. However, "Made in England" appears in the cushion part of the mark and this was not done on pre-1900 examples.

Mason's reproductions are also being made in China with the crown mark. Some have paper labels identifying their China origin, but these are easily removed.

Collecting Hints: Don't overlook the Ashworth reissue pieces. They qualify as true antiques.

Ashtray, 3 1/2" sq, ironstone, "Mandarin" pattern, cobalt, rust, and

gold florals, "Mason's Patent Ironstone England Mandarin" mk
.... **15.00**
Bullion Cup and Underdish, 7" H-H, "Regency" pattern.................. **20.00**
Bowl
5" d, oct, "Vista" pattern, blue transfer............................. **240.00**
8" d, "Mandalay" pattern, cobalt, brick red and gilt, cream ground
.... **65.00**
8 1/2" d, ironstone, "Applique" pattern, green, red, and gold oriental flowers.................... **80.00**
10" d, ftd, ironstone, "Ascot" pattern, red transfer, wavy rim, "crowned Mason's, Patent Ironstone in banner" mk, ... **85.00**
Bud Vase, 6 1/2" h, paneled, ironstone, oriental house, bridge, and trees, dk blue transfer **50.00**
Candleholder, 5 1/2" h, ironstone, "Mandalay Red" pattern, ... **25.00**
Chamber Pot, 6" h x 10 1/2" d, blue, iron-red, yellow, or mauve shaded peonies and buds, blue and yellow perched birds, gold trimmed cobalt handle, lt blue inner border w/florals and geometrics, "blue crowned MASON'S, PATENT IRONSTONE CHINA in banner" mk, ... **225.00**
Charger, 15 1/2" d, "Vista" pattern, red transfer, "red MASON'S crown, PATENT IRONSTONE CHINA, drapery, VISTA ENGLAND" mk,
.... **90.00**
Compote, 9" d x 3 3/4" h, "Vista" pattern, med blue transfer, ... **220.00**
Cooler, 10" h, hex shape, spread ft, iron-red and cobalt "Japan" pattern, green and luster animal mask handles, ... **2,775.00**
Cream Jug
4 1/2" h, paneled, "Ivory" design, gilt outlined rim and snake handle, "MASON'S over crown, PATENT IRONSTONE in banner, IVORY, MADE IN ENGLAND" mk,
.... **20.00**
5 1/2" h, center band of orange flowers, gilt leaves between gilt bands, Miles Mason, ... **295.00**
Cup and Saucer
"Black Chinese" pattern, "crown MASON'S PATENT IRONSTONE CHINA ENGLAND BLACK CHINESE" mk, ... **90.00**

Plate

10" d, "Chinese Mountain" pattern, blue transfer, c1835, ... **65.00**

10 1/2" d, ironstone
Black ground, green, salmon, and white floral sprigs in center and on border, early 20th C, ... **50.00**
"Manchu" pattern, ... **8.00**
"Vista" pattern, red transfer **10.00**

Platter

10" l x 7 3/4" w, ironstone, "Chinese Scroll" pattern, orientals crossing a bridge, dk red and dk green border, "crowned Mason's, Patent Ironstone China in scroll" mk, ... **595.00**

11 3/8" l x 9" w, oval, ironstone, "Watteau" pattern, brown transfer, ... **25.00**

16" l x 12" w, oct, ironstone, "Grasshopper" pattern, "Mason's crown over Patent Ironstone China in banner" mk, ... **785.00**

17" l x 13 1/4" w, ironstone, "Asiatic Pheasant" pattern, blue transfer **1,550.00**

17 1/4" l x 13 1/2" w, oct, cobalt, dk orange, green, and gilt oriental design of vase on table w/shrubs and peonies, border of flowers and tree branches, "imp PATENT IRONSTONE CHINA" mk, c1813-25, (A), ... **715.00**

18" l x 14" w, red "Vista" pattern, "Mason's, crown, Patent Ironstone China in banner, Vista England" mk, ... **125.00**

Potpourri Jar, 5 1/4" h, 6 3/4" d, cobalt, orange, and gilt Imari pattern, "imp Ironstone China Patent" mark, pr, A-$632.00

Relish Dish, 8" l, oval, "Amberley Oak" pattern, multicolored decal of people under arched oaks w/castle in bkd, relief molded border, ... **15.00**

Potpourri Jar, 11 3/4" h x 13" H-H, "Schoolhouse" pattern, iron-red, cobalt, peach, and gold, gold handles, imp mk $3,750.00

Serving Bowl, 9 1/2" H-H, ironstone, "Regency" pattern, red, blue, green, and orange Chinese peony designs, molded handles, "Mason's Patent Ironstone China Regency England" mk, ... **35.00**

Soup Plate

7 7/8" d, blue "Dragon" pattern, "MASON'S crowned PATENT IRONSTONE CHINE in drape" mk, ... **70.00**

9 1/2" d, Ironstone
"Japan" pattern, cobalt, lt blue, and iron-red oriental florals and fencing, ... **150.00**
"The School House" pattern, iron-red, cobalt, salmon, and gilt, "MASON'S PATENT IRONSTONE CHINA" mk, c1820, ... **170.00**

10 1/2" d, ironstone, "Blue Pheasants" pattern, med blue transfer, c1920, ... **75.00**

10 3/4" d, lt blue, dk orange, green, lt yellow, and mauve "Flying Bird" pattern, scalloped rim, "blue MASON'S, crown, PATENT IRONSTONE CHINA in drapery" mk, (A), ... **50.00**

Tea Caddy, 6 1/2" h, hex shape, ironstone, lt blue, yellow, and red, "Plantation Colonial" pattern, .. **65.00**

Teapot, 6 1/4" h, "Vista" pattern, mulberry transfer, metal lid, "Mason's over crown, Patent Ironstone China in ribbon, England" mk, ... **35.00**

Toast Rack, 5" l, 4 bar, "Vista" pattern, red transfer, ... **650.00**

Tray, 10" H-H, sq shape, "American Marine" pattern, mulberry transfer, ... **125.00**

Tureen, Cov, 14" l x 10" h
"Mandalay" pattern, cobalt and brick red, ... **435.00**

"Vista" pattern, red transfer, "red MASON'S, crown, PATENT IRONSTONE CHINA, banner VISTA ENGLAND" mk, ... **165.00**

Vase, 9 3/8" h, spread ft and collar, "Japan" pattern, lg red flowerheads, cobalt, gilt and tan bridge over lt blue water, gilt loop handles w/mask terminals, unmkd, (A), ... **440.00**

Vase, Cov, 15 1/4" h, oct, ironstone, "Woodland" pattern, blue transfers, . **625.00**

Vegetable Bowl, 10" l x 8" w, "Fruit Basket" pattern, multicolored, pink rim, ... **120.00**

Vegetable Tureen, Cov

9" H-H, "Regency" pattern, multicolored, ... **95.00**

10" l x 9" w, "Woodland" pattern, med blue transfer, c1910, ... **210.00**

11" H-H, "Vista" pattern, pink transfer, "MASON, crown, PATENT IRONSTONE VISTA ENGLAND" mk, ... **150.00**

Warming Dish, Cov, 9" w, "Regency" pattern, multicolored, original stopper, "blue MASON's, crown, PATENT IRONSTONE CHINA, banner, Regency, ENGLAND, C4475," mk, ... **165.00**

c.M
Golfe·Jurn·
(A·M)
1845-1917

MASSIER

Golfe-Juan, France
1881-1917

History: Clement Massier, who started work in 1881 in Golfe-Juan, France, was an artist and potter who produced earthenware with metallic luster decoration. He used plant motifs and other nature themes on shapes that were Art Nouveau in style.

Massier's wares usually are marked with an incised "Massier" or have his initial or the location of the pottery.

Museums: Musee d'Art Moderne de la Ville de Paris, Paris, France; Musee d'Orsay, Paris, France; Musee Municipal de Ceramique et d'Art Moderne, Vallauris, France.

Bud Vase

4 1/2" h, squat shape, green drip over green ground, "incised CLEMENT MASSIER GOLFE JUAN AM" mk, ... **175.00**

13 1/4" h, gourd base, long swollen neck, "sang-de-boeuf" glaze, "C. MASSIER GOLFE-JUAN" mk, ... **900.00**

Cache Pot, 11 1/2" l x 6" w x 6 1/2" h, figural pink flower petals, green foliage, white int, Delphin Massier, ... **940.00**

Jardiniere and Pedestal, 61 1/4" h, Moorish style globular bowl w/3 upright scalloped pistol handles molded w/entwined lattice and knotwork, similar molded circ base, pedestal formed w/4 columns ending in stylized shells, quatrefoil foot, mottled blue ground, Clement Massier, c1880, (A), ... **7,170.00**

Planter

4 1/2" h x 3" sq, 3 figural birds on rim, lustered blue, green, and brown feathers and heads, green grass blades on base, "Massier Vallauris" mk, ... **50.00**

8" h x 8" l x 7 1/2" w, 4 figural multicolored birds perched on rect log body, 4 sm log feet, Jerome Massier, c1880, ... **2,775.00**

Serving Dish, 13 1/4" d, figural flowerhead, red to white shaded petals, green center, brown twig overhead handle, Delphin Massier, ... **1,750.00**

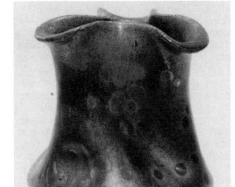

Vase, 3 1/2" h, metallic floral glaze, Jerome Massier, rim and hairline repair, (A), $425.00

Vase

4" h, baluster form, painted red fleur-de-lys on purple and green

lustered ground, restored rim, Clement Massier, (A), ... **285.00**

4 1/2" h, tapered shape w/flared rim, metallic blue, purple, magenta, green, and gold, streaking, unmkd, ... **300.00**

5 1/2" h, swollen shape, red and white splotched glaze w/charcoal highlights, imp mk, (A), ... **173.00**

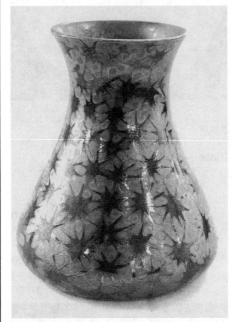

Vase, 6" h, starburst design, irid purple, red, gold, and blue, "Clement Massier, Golfe Juan A.M." mark, A-$502.00

6 3/4" h, squat form w/3 molded serpents at lip, irid metallic green glaze w/incised designs, mkd, (A), ... **1,150.00**

7" h, vert undulations, painted green frogs seated by water, yellow moon, blue textured ground, white int, Delphin Massier, c1900, ... **2,500.00**

9 1/2" h

Sq tapered shape to round base, applied gold clovers, painted waves, coffee brown ground, Clement Massier, ... **525.00**

Tapered shape, green-gold metallic glaze leaves and flowers on red and blue ground, Clement Massier, ... **855.00**

11" h, bulbous body, long straight neck, turquoise flambe glaze over green ground, Clement Massier, restored rim, (A), ... **115.00**

Vase, 15" h, daisies and leaves, irid gold, blue, and red, "D.M. Vallauris A.M." mark, repairs, A-$605.00

16 3/8" h, amphora shape w/2 handles, stylized trees on lustered ground, Clement Massier, ... **2,175.00**

MEAKIN

Hanley, England

Alfred Meakin
1873 to Present

History: Alfred Meakin was a Staffordshire potter who made a wide range of earthenware and ironstone china at his Royal Albert Works in Tunstall starting in 1873. Beginning in 1877 the firm traded as Alfred Meakin Ltd., a name it still uses today.

The earthenware was marked with a crown and "ALFRED MEAKIN/ENGLAND."

J. & G. Meakin
1845 to Present

History: James Meakin established a pottery in Longton in 1845 and transferred it to Hanley in 1848. When he retired in 1852, James and George, his sons, succeeded him. The firm traded as J. & G. Meakin.

The Meakins built the Eagle Works in 1859 and enlarged it in 1868. Later there were branches of the factory at Cobridge and Burslem. Both earthenware and graniteware were produced. The wares were decorated in the style of French porcelain and made for export to the American market. Meakin also produced romantic Staffordshire and flow blue decorated pieces.

J. & G. Meakin joined the Wedgwood Group in 1970.

Reference: Bernard Hollowood, *The Story of J. and G. Meakin*, Bemrose Publicity Co. Ltd. 1951.

Berry Bowl
    5 3/8" d, ironstone, "Windsong" pattern, yellow flowers, J. & G. Meakin, ... **5.00**
    5 1/2" d, oct, "Wicker" pattern, brown wicker transfer on border, ... **6.00**
Bowl, 8 1/4" d, multicolored "Kasmir" pattern, fluted border, J. & G. Meakin, ... **10.00**
Chamber Pot, Cov, 11 1/2" d, blue-black transfers of rambling garden flowers and foliage, white ground, Alfred Meakin, ... **245.00**
Coffeepot, 8 1/2" h, sprays of violets, sponged gold trim, J. & G. Meakin, ... **35.00**
Creamer, 2 3/4" h, Sugar Bowl, 5" d, "Centenary" pattern, red transfers, J. & G. Meakin, ... **20.00**
Cup and Saucer
    "Chatsworth" pattern, blue transfer, fluted saucer, J. & G. Meakin, ... **8.00**
    "Coaching Days" pattern, med blue transfers, Alfred Meakin, ... **15.00**
Dish, 6" H-H, "Sunshine" pattern, brown, orange, yellow, and green flowers and leaves, tab handles, ... **10.00**
Gravy Boat, 8 1/4" l, "Castillian" pattern, black and white striped band w/red florals and gold trim, "J. & G. Meakin" mk, ... **20.00**

Jug, 4 3/8" h, "Colonial Garden" pattern, green transfer, "J. & G. Meakin" mk, ... **8.00**
Milk Pitcher, 7" h, "Tintern" pattern, red transfer, Alfred Meakin, ... **28.00**

Platter, 12 1/2" l, "Gleneagle" pattern, cobalt, orange, mauve, green, and gold, Alfred Meakin, **$62.00**

Plate
    5 3/4" d, "Rose Duet" pattern, lg yellow and pink rose, green leaves, "J. & G. Meakin" mk, ... **8.00**
    8 1/2" d, brown transfer of cows in pasture, relief of flowerheads on border, Alfred Meakin, ... **22.00**
    10 1/2" d, "Fair Winds" pattern, blue transfer, Alfred Meakin, ... **10.00**

*Sugar Bowl, 7" h, ironstone, "Moss Rose" pattern, pink flowers, blue and green leaves, gold trim, Alfred Meakin, A-***$28.00**

Teapot, 7" h
    Paneled, "Blue Vanity Fair" pattern, "J. & G. Meakin England" mk, ... **15.00**
    "Scandia" pattern, blue and white, ... **35.00**
Tureen, Cov, 11 3/4" H-H x 6 1/2" h, molded vert ribbing forming sections, relief molded grapes and leaves on cov, branch knob, overall white glaze, Henry Meakin, ... **50.00**

Vegetable Bowl, Cov, 10 1/8" H-H, "Fleur-De-Lis" pattern, blue printed, white ground, "J. & G. Meakin" mk, c1891, **$330.00**

MEIGH

Staffordshire, England
c1305-1834 Job Meigh
1835-1901 Charles Meigh

History: Job Meigh operated the Old Hall Pottery at Hanley in the Staffordshire District beginning around 1805 and ending in 1834. Charles, his son, joined the firm. Charles operated the pottery under his own name between 1835 and 1849. The factory produced earthenwares and stonewares.

Charles Meigh was famous for his firm's white stoneware jugs with relief decorations. The decorations were part of the mold from which the pieces were cast. During the 1840s, jugs with Gothic details were made. The "Minister" jug of 1842 was the most famous. Classical jugs featuring designs of sporting events and drinking scenes were produced during the 1840s and 50s.

For two years, 1850 to 1851, the firm operated as Charles Meigh, Son & Parkhurst. For the next eleven years, 1851 to 1861, the company was known as Charles Meigh & Sons.

Museum: Potsdam Public Museum, Potsdam, NY.

Cake plate, 9" d, green printed oriental scene of 2 bridges, chrysanthemums, flower border, scalloped rim w/gold accented molded designs, Hicks & Meigh Stone China, ... **135.00**
Dinner Service, Part, soup tureen and stand, 13 5/8" w, meat platter, well

and tree, 21" l, platter, 19 1/8" l, oct, 2 cov vegetable bowls, 9 1/2" sq, vegetable bowl, 12 3/4" l, cov sauce tureen and stand, 7 1/4" l, 13 soup plates, 9 1/2" d, 10 rimmed bowls, 8 1/4" d, 15 plates, 9 3/4" d, blue printed and gilt accented chinoiserie scenes of flowering trees, plants, and exotic bird, leaf tip cavettos, flower spray border, twisted grape vine handles, grape bunch knobs, orange luster lined rims, Hicks, Meigh, and Johnson, c1822-35, (A),...... **7,770.00**

Garniture, 3 piece, vase, 9 1/4" h, 2 vases, 8" h, HP garden flowers on gunmetal bluish ground, gold handles and sq bases,
.... **9,500.00**

Mug, 5" h, relief molded "Bacchanalian Dance" pattern, white, ... **85.00**

Plate

8 1/4" d, ironstone, "Lotus" pattern, pink, orange, green, cobalt, and gilt, Hicks & Meigh, ... **325.00**

9" d, ironstone, "Ceylon" pattern, cobalt, pink and green shades, "Ceylon C.M." and "imp Stone China" mk, c1835-49, ... **120.00**

9 1/4" d, "Orleans" pattern, red transfer w/green, blue, and yellow accents, ... **25.00**

9 1/2" d

Apple, peach, pineapple, grapes, and basket in center, vine and berry foliage, blue rim, "imp Charles Meigh Opaque China" mk, ... **12.00**

Ironstone, "Grosvenor" pattern, center red rose and garden spray, 5 quatrefoils w/florals on grey-green border w/scrolling, red lined rim, "Charles Meigh & Son" mk,
.... **25.00**

9 3/4" d, 2 lg exotic birds in center w/florals, border of cartouches and flowerheads, med blue transfer, Hicks, Meigh, and Johnson, c1825, ... **95.00**

10" d, "Amherst Japan" pattern, cobalt vase w/iron-red chrysanthemums and fencing,
.... **100.00**

10 1/4" d, ironstone, "Belisarious" pattern, bush in center, dk blue, orange, pink, yellow, and green, heavy floral design on cobalt border, Hicks, Meigh & Johnson,
.... **250.00**

10 1/2" d, Imari pattern, blue, iron-red, and gold oriental vase on table w/lg flowerheads and

bouquet, wavy rim, flowers and stems on ext border, "Hicks, Meigh, & Johnson" mk, ... **80.00**

Platter, 15" l, 11 3/4" w, ironstone, cobalt, red, and gold Imari pattern, "Royal Arms and Stone China" mark, A-**$110.00**

Platter

11 1/2" H-H, "California" pattern, iron-red, cobalt, and green florals, relief molded open handles and terminals, "C.M.S. & P. California" mk, ... **245.00**

12 3/4" l x 9 1/2" w, oct, ironstone, dk orange, cobalt, lt blue, and gilt floral and leaf design in center w/dk orange and lt blue latticed inner border, floral and leaf border, canton/comb back, "STONE CHINA and royal arms" mk, c1804-22, (A), ... **275.00**

16 1/2" l x 13 1/2" w, cobalt, iron-red, and yellow-gold "Amherst Japan" pattern, "Amherst Japan No. 62 Stone China in scroll" mk,
.... **185.00**

Soup Bowl, 9" d, oriental scene of 2 bridges and flowers, med blue transfer, wavy blue lined gadrooned rim, Hicks & Meigh, c1820,
.... **155.00**

Soup Plate, 9 7/8" d, ironstone, "Flying Bird" pattern, dk blue, orange, yellow, and green, sprigs on dk blue border, Hicks, Meigh & Johnson,
.... **195.00**

MEISSEN

Saxony, Germany
1710 to Present

History: The history of Meissen porcelain design falls into distinct periods that were determined by the director of the company and the kings who appointed and controlled them. Located in the Saxon district of Germany, the Meissen factory, or Royal Saxon Porcelain Manufactory, was founded in 1710 by Frederich August I and first directed by Johann Boettger. It was Boettger who developed the first truly white porcelain in Europe. His white porcelain was exceptionally plastic and could be molded into a variety of applied decorations. Silver shapes were most popular.

After 1720 Meissen porcelain was decorated with fine enamel painting, even surpassing some of the Chinese porcelains. During this period, most of the Meissen tablewares were of relatively simple form, which provided ample backgrounds for the beautiful painted decorations. The original crossed swords factory mark was adopted in 1723.

When Johann Horoldt was manager during the last ten years of the reign of Augustus the Strong (1694-1733), the porcelain was a brilliant pure white. Horoldt did pseudo-Chinese scenes in scrollwork of red, gold, and luster, plus other adaptations of Chinese, Japanese, and other Oriental wares and motifs. Johann Kirchner (1727-1733) made life-size figures of animals and birds for Augustus the Strong's Japanese Palace.

When Joachim Kaendler, a modeler, came to Meissen in 1731, he began producing figures, especially the Crinoline figures and groups. About 1738 Kaendler created numerous miniature figures used for lavish banquet decorations for the court of Dresden. He designed the world famous swan set for Count von Bruhl. Kaendler also introduced tablewares with low relief borders in the style of silver.

The rococo influence occurred after 1740. The famous onion pattern appeared about that time. The factory was severely damaged during the Seven Years' War (1756-1763) and was occupied by the victorious Prussians.

Following a major reorganization, the master modeler Michel Victor Acier came to Meissen in 1764 and became the dominating influence. He moved the factory into the neo-classical period with emphasis on mythological figures. Pictorial decoration was copied from Sevres. Under the directorship of Marcolini (1774-1813), the style shifted to that of Louis XVI. The Marcolini Period ended with the cessation of the Napoleonic Wars in 1814.

The factory experienced a decline in production under the management of Von Oppel from 1814 to 1833. The wares during this phase often imitated other successful European concerns.

The period from 1833 to 1870 is called the "Kuhn Period," after a director of the factory. The company's fortunes improved,

both technically and economically. A revival of production of the great pieces from one hundred years earlier was carried out. Many figures were copied in the rococo style, which was the popular taste of the times. Sales of the china wares continued to increase.

A system of grading was introduced in 1869. Meissen used four grading marks. First-choice painted porcelain had no incisions. Second grade had 2 slashes. Third grade had 3, and fourth, or least desirable, received 4 slashes. This system is in effect today.

The "New Period" at Meissen started in 1870 when Kuhn died and Raithel became director. Exports of china to America increased during this time. Utilitarian wares in blue underglaze grew in popularity. Improvements continued to be made in the china production process.

From 1895 to 1901 the factory was managed by Brunnemann. A conflict developed between the supporters of old and new ideas of china manufactory. Between 1901 and 1910 there was increasing success artistically and financially, culminating with the two hundredth anniversary Jubilee year of 1910. Many reforms were carried out. New buildings were constructed for furnaces and studios. A new drawing school was established at the factory.

Following World War II, the factory was reorganized. Today it operates as the State's Porcelain Manufactory. New models are made as close as possible to the old shapes. Ornamentation also tends to follow the old models. In addition, some new forms are made. The Meissen factory also manufactures various commemorative wares for coronations, Christmas plaques, and Easter plaques.

References: Dr. K. Berling, Editor, *Meissen China, An Illustrated History*, Dover, 1972; Yvonne Hackenbroch, *Meissen & Other Continental Porcelain Faience & Enamel in the Irwin Untermeyer Collection*, Harvard University Press, 1956; W.B. Honey, *Dresden China: An Introduction to the Study of Meissen Porcelain*, Dresden House, 1946; Ingelore Menzhausen, *Early Meissen Porcelain in Dresden*, Thames & Hudson, 1990; Robert E. Rontgen, *The Book of Meissen, Revised Edition*, Schiffer Publishing Co; Otto Walcha, *Meissen Porcelain*, G.P. Putman's Sons, 1981; Samuel Wittwer, *A Royal Menagerie: Meissen Porcelain Animals*; Lawrence Mitchell, *The Meissen Collector's Handbook*, Antique Collectors Club, 2002, Yvonne Adams, *Meissen Figures, 1730-1775, The Kaendler Period*, Schiffer Publications, 2002.

Museums: Art Institute of Chicago, Chicago, IL; Cincinnati Art Museum, Cincinnati, OH; Cummer Gallery of Art, Jacksonville, FL; Dixon Gallery, Memphis, TN; Dresden Museum of Art & History, Dresden, Germany; Gardiner Museum of Ceramic Art, Toronto, Canada; Meissen Porcelain Museum, Meissen, Germany; Metropolitan Museum of Art, New York, NY; National Museum of American History, Smithsonian Institution, Washington, D.C.; Robertson Center for the Arts and Sciences, Binghamton, NY; Schlossmuseum, Berlin, Germany; Stadtmuseum, Cologne, Germany; Wadsworth Atheneum, Hartford, CT; Woodmere Art Museum, Philadelphia, PA; Zwinger Museum, Dresden, Germany.

Collecting Hints: Collectors must distinguish between the productions from the greatest period—1710-1756—and later works. During the 19th century, Meissen reproduced some of its 18th century molds in addition to making new ones.

Numerous Dresden factories also reproduced Meissen wares and figures, some copying the original marks. One should be aware of the Dresden decorating shop of Helena Wolfsohn, who used the Augustus Rex (AR) monogram, which was not used by Meissen after 1730, but was applied by Wolfsohn to reproductions of much later works. About 1833 the Royal Porcelain Manufactory in Meissen obtained a court decision against Wolfsohn ordering her to cease and desist using the AR mark.

Helena Wolfsohn operated the decorating shop, but probably did not produce her own porcelain. However, most of her AR pieces have the AR mark underglaze. Since this mark was applied before glazing and final firing, Helena Wolfsohn must have ordered the white porcelain blanks with the AR mark from some porcelain factory. The manufacturer is not known. Wolfsohn sold many thousands of pieces with the "AR" mark.

The Meissen factory itself used the "AR" mark in 1873 as a trademark and still uses it on special pieces. Therefore, every "AR" marked piece must be studied very carefully.

Basket, 16 3/4" H-H, painted multicolored bouquet in center, flared diamond cut reticulated sides, green twist handles w/flowerhead terminals, gilt lobed rim, (A), ... **1,100.00**

Beaker
2 3/4" h, painted ribbon tied bouquet of puce and blue flowers, trailing branches, brown line rim, "blue X'd swords, 24" mks, c1740, pr, (A), ... **3,100.00**
5 1/4" h, gilt quatrefoil cartouche of red painted period group in garden on front, florals on reverse, yellow ground, gilt webbing on int rim, ... **3,500.00**

Bowl, 7" d, Kakiemon palette and style alternating coiled phoenix and prunus sprays, "blue X'd swords" mk, (A), ... **4,065.00**
Cabinet Plate, 10" d, painted court musicians in pastoral setting in center in raised gilt foliate cartouche, pink inner border, pierced latticed border w/alternating panels of lt blue forget-me-nots, "blue X'd swords, imp 6 and 49" mks, late 19th C, (A), ... **1,912.00**
Cache Pot, 10" H-H, oval, overall encrusted multicolored flowers and foliage, brown branch handles extending to branch feet, c1870, ... **5,500.00**
Candlestick, 10 1/4" h, fluted column, modeled green hanging wreath and wreath around base, band of flowers on ft, blue and gold horiz stripes, c1790, pr, ... **3,500.00**
Chocolate Pot, 6 3/4" h, reeded, puce and gilt sprays of Indian flowers, gilt metal mts, turned wood handle, c1745, "blue X'd swords" mk, (A), ... **880.00**

Coffee Can and Saucer
Lg blue bow suspending brown basket w/multicolored flowers, ochre rims and sq handle, "blue star and X'd swords" mk, Marcolini, c1800, ... **715.00**
Multicolored continuous harbor scene on cup, same in center of saucer w/dbl iron-red inner border lines, gilt lined rims, scrolled lyre handle, "blue X'd swords" mk, c1740, ... **3,500.00**

Coffeepot
7" h, baluster shape, painted harbor scenes in gilt quatrefoil cartouches front and reverse, powder purple ground, gilt mask spout, gilt trimmed wishbone handle, "blue X'd swords" mk, (A), ... **2,870.00**
8" h, Turkish style, globular form w/slender, cylindrical neck, foliage molded dbl scroll handle and spout, beast head spout, Kakiemon painted w/branches of flowering prunus, peony, pomegranates, corn husks, and scattered flowerheads, pine cone knob, gilt accents, "blue X'd swords" mk, c1730, (A), ... **7,920.00**

Hot Milk Jug, 6" h, pear shape, painted river landscapes reserved in black quatrefoil cartouches on sides and cov, yellow ground w/Indian flowers, shell molded beak spout w/Kakiemon flowers and gilt, wishbone handle w/thumbrest, "blue X'd swords" mk, c1735, (A), ... **2,400.00**

Nodder, 8 5/8" h, seated scholar in black robe holding marble covered book, nodding head and jaw, (A), ... **17,310.00**

Plaque, 12 3/4" h x 10 1/2" w, rect, oval painted scene of lt haired girl, seated on rock in pastoral setting, brown and white dog at feet, flute at side, "blue X'd swords" mk, late 19th C, (A), ... **9,560.00**

Plate

8" d, HP multicolored exotic birds in center, butterflies on border, gilt netted rim, "blue X'd swords, slash" mks, 19th C, ... **150.00**

8 1/2" d, Kakiemon palette, painted flying bird next to flowering chrysanthemum from green and turquoise rocks, scattered sprays, red dbl line int border, 3 trailing flower branches on border, "blue X'd swords" mk, c1735, (A), ... **2,690.00**

8 3/4" d, painted polychrome butterfly on flowering branch, scattered sprigs, brown lined petal shaped rim, "blue X'd swords" mk, c1730-35, ... **2,200.00**

9 1/4" d, Kakiemon painted birds flying and perched on pine, prunus, and bamboo from pierced rockwork, scattered florals on shaped border, brown lined rim, "blue X'd swords" mk, c1740, (A), ... **5,485.00**

9 3/8" d, HP scattered garden flower sprigs, molded basketweave border, c1750, ... **130.00**

Platter, 13 1/2" l, 9 3/4" w, lg mauve and yellow flowers, yellow, blue, and red pansies and garden flowers, multicolored insects, gilt lined rim, "blue X'd swords" mark, $550.00

Platter

15 3/4" l x 11 1/4" w, oval, gilt edged spoked panels w/8 alternating burgundy or white ground and HP pink, yellow, or green flowers or period couples in garden setting, dk red center hub w/painted flowers, gilt scroll and feather border, "blue X'd swords" mk, ... **2,900.00**

16" l x 11 1/2" w, HP multicolored game birds in forest in center, birds on border w/gilt panels and shaped rim, "blue X'd swords" mk, ... **600.00**

19" l x 14 1/4" w, oval, sm purple and black flowers, blue feather leaves, scalloped gilt rim, "blue X'd swords" mk, (A), ... **275.00**

Potpourri Vase, 13" h, painted vignette of period couple in wooded landscape in fruit and flower encrusted surround, mint green reed handles, beaded socle w/applied figures of putti, reticulated cov w/applied flower bouquet, "blue X'd swords" mk, late 19th C, pr, (A), ... **3,100.00**

Rose Bowl, 5 1/2" h x 6" w, "Schneeballen," applied lg yellow or pink roses and brown meandering stems and feet, white snowball ground, ... **975.00**

Salt, 3 7/8" w, shell form, painted figures in landscape in quatrefoil cartouches w/pendant gilt diapered tassels at each end, center painted w/sm blue or lg red flowers, foliage, and insect, gilt scale and scroll border, gilt lined rim, 3 C-scroll feet, "blue X'd swords" mk, c1735, (A), ... **4,085.00**

Soup Plate, 8 7/8" d, silver shape, polychrome enameled exotic bird, blue branch from brown rock, border of multicolored sprigs, lobed rim, "blue X'd swords, star" mk, ... **250.00**

Sugar Caster, 7" h, baluster shape, painted w/loose bouquets and scattered sprigs, "Sugar" on base, pierced ogee shaped dome, "blue X'd swords, dot" mk, c1765, (A), ... **795.00**

Sugar Box, Cov

3 1/2" h x 4 7/8" l, bombe shape, painted scenes of merchants and sailors in harbor setting in gilt and brown lines quatrefoil cartouches reserved on powdered purple ground, gold knob, "blue X'd swords" mk, c1735-40, (A), ... **3,585.00**

4" h x 4 1/2" d, painted tulip, roses, pansies, and cornflowers, sm sprigs, brown lined rims, mid-18th C, ... **1,275.00**

Tankard, 3 5/8" h, purple painted scene of schoolmaster instructing group in wooded landscape w/church and cottages, blue kite mk, c1745, (A), ... **2,870.00**

Teabowl and Saucer

Ext of bowl w/painted Kakiemon flowering shrubs in 2 purple lined quatrefoil cartouches, pea green ground w/scattered shrubs, int w/flower spray, saucer painted w/flying exotic bird and insects, flowering shrubs and rocks on pea green ground, gilt banded footrim, brown lined rims, "blue X'd swords, imp" mks, c1735, (A), ... **2,150.00**

HP harbor scenes in gilt cartouches, after Herold, ... **3,500.00**

Iron-red tied ribbon entwined w/sm yellow, red, or blue flowers, green entwined foliage, and iron-red and blue quiver and arrows on cup, brown bow on saucer, gilt lined rim, Marcolini, blue X'd swords, star, press numbers, c1780, set of 8, (A), ... **1,370.00**

Tea Caddy

4 1/4" h, rect, painted scenes of merchants and harbor in brown lined oblong quatrefoil cartouches front and reverse, lavender ground, Indian blooms on shoulder, gilt lined rims, 2 vignettes of landscapes on cov, gilt flame knob, "blue X'd swords" mk, c1740, ... **2,630.00**

5 1/2" h, sq shape w/sloping shoulders, painted scenes of workers on estuaries in shaped gilt quatrefoil cartouches edged w/gilt, iron-red and puce scrolls and puce sgraffito panels at sides, scattered Kakiemon flowerheads and sprays, vert gilt lines on corners, Laub und Bandelwork on shoulder, cylinder cov painted w/flowers and 4 faceted gilt knobs, green lined rim on cov, "blue X'd swords, gilders" mks, c1735, (A), ... **13,145.00**

Teacup and Saucer, purple floral sprig on int of cup, purple painted cherubs in clouds on ext and saucer, gilt rims, "blue X'd swords and dot" mk, ... **1,200.00**

Teapot

3 1/4" h, globular, molded prunus on body, dragon spout, wishbone handle, overall white glaze, "blue X'd swords" mk, c1730, (A), ... **1,435.00**

3 5/8" h, bullet shape, yellow ground, painted harbor scenes in black quatrefoil cartouches on sides, gilt lined borders, iron-red, puce and gilt accented wishbone handle and bird head spout, cov w/painted cartouches, strawberry knob, "blue X'd swords" mk, c1740, (A), ... **4,185.00**

3 3/4" h x 7" w, silver shape, painted fruit, flowers, and mushrooms, gilt accented bird spout, clip shaped handle, flower form knob, "blue X'd swords" mk, ... **1,980.00**

Trivet, 5 7/8" d, little girl holding fan, little boy w/sword spearing bee, period clothes, gilt rim and 3 bun feet, "blue X'd swords, J102" mk, ... **750.00**

Vase, 4 7/8" h, baluster form, painted w/2 birds in Indian style flowers from rockwork, flared neck painted iron-red and gilt half flowerheads on purple diaper ground, gilt lined ft, "blue X'd swords" mk, c1730, (A), ... **20,110.00**

Vase, Cov, 9 1/2" h, ovoid shape, incised, painted, and gilt trailing chrysanthemums on orange ground, green frog knob, "blue X'd swords" mk, (A), ... **1,765.00**

MINTON

Stoke-on-Trent, Hanley, England
1793 to Present

History: Thomas Minton established his pottery in Stoke-on-Trent. During the early years, he concentrated on blue transfer-printed earthenware, cream-colored earthenware, and plain bone china. By 1810 production expanded to include stoneware, Egyptian black and printed and painted bone china. A tremendous number of shapes, styles, and decorations with printed, enameled, or gilded designs was manufactured. Many 19th century Minton patterns resembled those of Spode, Miles Mason, New Hall and Pinxton, the company's principal rivals. Most pieces were unmarked.

Between 1816 and 1824, production at the Minton factory was concentrated on earthenwares and cream-colored wares. Bone china production resumed in 1824. A large selection of figures and ornamental wares augmented the traditional tableware line.

Much of Minton's success could be attributed to the decorations applied by the staff of painters. French porcelain artists and ex-Derby decorators were employed by Minton. By the late 1830s, Minton had achieved a quality of modeling and decoration on bone china that was unequaled in Europe.

In 1836 Herbert took complete charge when his father died. Herbert Minton, Thomas' son, gradually changed the factory from a small scale producer into one of the greatest Victorian potteries in Europe. By 1858 Minton employed over 1,500 people utilizing new technologies and decorative styles. Encaustic floor tiles and Parian porcelain were developed under Herbert's jurisdiction.

Leon Arnoux became art director at Minton in 1849. He encouraged many French artists to move to Stoke-on-Trent and introduced a revival of the Renaissance styles. Arnoux also developed a series of colored glazes for a "majolica" line.

Colin Minton Campbell took control in 1858. The acid gold process was developed, allowing rich gold decorations in bas relief. Louis Marc Solon came to Minton from Sevres in 1870 and brought with him the technique of pate-sur-pate decoration. Pate-sur-pate became a major contribution by Minton to the 19th century English ceramics heritage. After Campbell's death in 1885, Minton continued to be the leading English pottery manufacturer of the 19th century.

In 1968 Minton became a member of the Royal Doulton Tableware Group. Minton china still is being produced today. The company retains its reputation for high quality hand-painted and gilded tablewares.

References: Paul Atterbury & Maureen Batkin, *The Dictionary of Minton, Rev. Ed.* Antique Collectors' Club, Ltd. 1999; G.A. Godden, *Minton Pottery & Porcelain of the First Period. 1793-1850,* Herbert Jenkins, Ltd. 1968; G.A. Godden, *Victorian Porcelain,* Herbert Jenkins, 1961; Joan Jones, *Minton: The First Two Hundred Years of Design and Production,* Antique Collectors' Club, Ltd. 1993; Joan Jones, *Minton,* Shire Album; Gillian Neale, *Miller's Blue & White Pottery,* Antiques Collectors Club, 2000.

Museum: Minton Museum, London Road, Stoke-on-Trent, England.

Asparagus Dish, 10" l x 7" w, center stand, molded asparagus stalks on side, white glaze, "imp MINTON" mk, ... **55.00**

Bowl

6 1/8" d, HP chinoiserie designs of Chinese boy building house of cards or Chinese boy bowling, stylized trees and foliage between, gilt rim, ... **1,500.00**

9 1/2" d

Fluted, "Genevese" pattern, Swiss lakeside cottage scene, blue transfer, "MINTON, globe, GENEVESE" mk, ... **38.00**

Japanese style gilt and platinum continuous scene of cranes, fencing, and bamboo trees on pink ground, dtd 1881,

10 1/2" d, ftd, "Amherst Japan" pattern, ... **150.00**

Candlestick, 5" h, hemisphere base, squeezebag design of blue grape clusters on blue and chartreuse ground, (A), ... **235.00**

Chamber Pot, 9" d x 5" h, HP red and gilt meandering flowers and leaves, red rim, imp mk, ... **50.00**

Charger

11 7/8" d, painted scene of Artemis-nude female, leaning against tree, snaring putti in net, blue drape on hip, sgd "MLS 72," dtd 1871, "Minton & Co." mk, (A), ... **5,735.00**

15" d, Secessionist, white water lilies, green pads, dk to light green water, splashed purple ground, (A), ... **1,500.00**

Comport, 9" w, oct, HP enameled baby chick and insect, dk brown ground, gold chain rim, ... **295.00**

Creamer, 4 1/4" h, "Amherst Japan" pattern, cobalt, iron-red, and gold,

French shape w/3 paw feet, ... **150.00**

Cream Soup, 4 1/2" H-H, w/underplate, 6 3/4" d, "Kashmir" pattern, ... **40.00**

Cup and Saucer

"Amherst Japan" pattern, #824, c1825, ... **175.00**

Japanese style painted gold birds on branches, cobalt ground, gold rims and handle, dtd 1882, ... **245.00**

Orange and rust meandering branches, gold rims, c1890, ... **75.00**

Dessert Plate, 9 1/8" d, painted specimen flowers on each, cavetto or inner border w/beaded gilt scrollwork, turquoise border, gilt shaped rim, dtd 1863, set of 12, (A), ... **2,390.00**

Dinner Service, Part, soup tureen, 12" w, 2 vegetable dishes, ftd, 11 7/8" H-H, 2 cov sauce tureens and stands, 9" w, 21 plates, 10 1/8" d, puce and green rose sprigs between puce and green twisted ribbon bands, gilt accented handles w/wheat leaf terminals, pattern #2043, c1845, (A), ... **2,870.00**

Dish, 8 3/4" l x 7 1/2" w, shell form, multicolored chinoiserie pattern of 2 men and child catching ball, gilt rim, c1810, pr, ... **3,000.00**

Egg Cup, 3 1/2" h, w/attached underplate, HP iron-red, mauve, and blue loose flowers, gilt accents, dtd 1882, ... **30.00**

Figure

6" h, 8" l, seated or lying panther, bright yellow glaze, c1891-1910, pr, ... **35.00**

13" h, seated "Young Warrior," unglazed olive body, glazed white toga, mask at feet, sgd "John Bell," c1848, chip, ... **1,125.00**

Food Mold, 6" l, oval, molded fruit, white glaze, mkd, ... **65.00**

Jar, Cov, 3" h, cylinder shape, HP sm individual garden flowers, white ground, gilt rims, ... **295.00**

Jug, 7 1/2" h, lobed, alternating blue feather or vert floral sprigging, ... **160.00**

Luncheon Service, Part, teapot, 6 7/8" w, cup and saucer, trapezoidal 2 handled tray, painted hunting and musical trophies in floral garlands suspended from turquoise and gilt

line and dot ribbons, (A), ... **1,435.00**

Jug, 6" h, "Chinese Temple" pattern, black transfer w/red, green, blue, and yellow accents, **$235.00**

Meat Platter, 18 1/4" l x 14 1/4" w, oct, "Bewick Stag" pattern, med blue transfer, ... **2,750.00**

Plate

7 3/4" d, "Amherst Japan" pattern, cobalt, red, pink, and gilt, ... **55.00**

8" d

Border ovals of orange, dk orange, ochre, and green HP gargoyles, Italianate foliage, apples in cornucopia on black transfer, ... **30.00**

Cobalt and red oriental flowers in basket design, floral border, ... **25.00**

9" d

Enameled oriental center medallion of rose shaded peonies, brown prunus from brown box planters w/dk blue feet, green foliage on sky blue ground, gold cavetto of curl designs, cream border, burnt orange and gold chevrons on blue rim, dtd 1874, (A), ... **690.00**

"Green Cockatrice" pattern #4863, red exotic bird in gold curlicue cavetto, green border w/cartouches of flowers, ... **60.00**

Yellow enameled daisies, green foliage, brown butterfly in center, pink rim w/sm molded gold ribbons, c1870, ... **135.00**

9 3/8" d, HP yellow and black butterfly, lady bug on red grasses, green stems, turquoise border w/raised and printed gilt inner border and rim, "imp MINTON" mk, dtd 1873, ... **120.00**

9 1/2" d

Lobed shape, HP named "Lineluden College" in center, inner gilt border, red border w/crisscross band and beaded rim, dtd 1850, ... **50.00**

Two painted butterflies, tall brown, green, and purple grasses, and wheat shafts, pale blue ground, border of band of gilt dots below gilt band w/raised gilt dots, gilt rim, c1862-71, ... **145.00**

10" d, transfer of red lotus in center w/blue stylized leaves, border of red lotus and buds, and blue leaves, ... **45.00**

10 1/4" d

Secessionist, white stylized flowerheads w/hanging stamens, blue-green whiplash stem, splashed bright purple ground, (A), ... **1,060.00**

Wide border w/Moorish-style teal blue, cobalt, gold and orange palmettes, int gold rim, retail mks, set of 12, (A), ... **1,585.00**

10 1/2" d, "Brocade" pattern, multicolored floral sprig in center, pink border w/gilt floral design, set of 12, ... **1,200.00**

Platter

15" l x 11 1/2" w, "Grasmere" pattern, ... **40.00**

17" l x 13 3/4" w, oval, "Jaffa" pattern, lg mons in center, blue and green Japanese flowers sprays, molded basketweave border, piecrust rim, ... **60.00**

18" l x 14" w, bone china, painted and relief molded cranes and bamboo on border, rim w/painted and molded bamboo, ... **170.00**

20 1/2" l x 17" w, "Clematis" pattern, shaped rim, "imp STONE CHINA" and Minton mks, dtd 1850, ... **1,500.00**

Pot, 14" h, blue neo-classical pot w/white garland on border supported by 3 white figural doves, tricorn base, ... **85.00**

Pot, Cov, 6 1/2" h x 11" H-H, HP named "Lydford Cascade," waterfall, and rockwork on front, HP floral painting on reverse, applied and molded flowerheads, buds, and stems, gilt accents, orange flowerhead knob, green branch handles, chips, ... **4,000.00**

Preserve Jar, Cov, 4" h, "Haddon Hall" pattern, multicolored florals, .. **50.00**

Punch Bowl, 10" d, lg iron-red flowerheads and green and gilt trim, green and gilt striped ftd base, c1805, ... **3,275.00**

Serving Dish, Cov, 12" l x 8" w x 4" h, rect, well and tree, "Green Cockatrice" pattern, ... **125.00**

Soap Dish, 8" H-H, w/drain, scattered sm pink roses, inner green band of leaves, lime green rim, c1915, ... **150.00**

Soup Plate, 10 1/4" d, "Basket Japan" pattern, blue transfer, set of 8, ... **950.00**

Teapot, 5 1/2" h, molded swirl body, "Haddon Hall" pattern, ... **175.00**

Urn, Cov, 28" h, blue and tan scene of Roman chariot and horses, pink ground, blue petal margins, on cov and ft, gilt handles, crocus shaped knob, c1870, ... **3,800.00**

Wine Cooler, 10 1/4" h, relief molded "Bacchus" pattern, grey, c1875, pr, $5,250.00

Vase

6 1/2" h, flattened circ shape, spread ft, HP landscapes on front and reverse, pink banded side w/gilt accents, c1830, pr, ... **1,100.00**

Vase, 7 1/2" h, pale red squeeze bag stylized iris design, blue flambe ground, green base, unmkd, (A), $325.00

10" h, dbl gourd bottle shape, turquoise ground, figural green, gold and blue scarab beetle on middle, cloisonne style gilt outline green, iron-red, and dk blue strapwork and scrolls, gilt rim w/red enamel dots and green, cream, red, and cobalt pendants, Christopher Dresser, dtd 1874, pr, (A), ... **19,120.00**

Vase, 11 1/2" h, Secessionist, tube-lined turquoise peacock, olive green ground, dk green handles, blue base, $2,200.00

17 1/4" h, moon flask shape, rect base, 2 sm handles, HP multicolored birds and foliage scenes on shaded tan ground, dk brown top and base, pr, ... **1,800.00**

MOCHA WARE

Staffordshire, England
1760-1939

History: Inexpensive utilitarian wares with tree-like, feather, moss, and worm designs, known as "Mocha" wares were made during the 19th century. The name came from the mocha stone or moss agate that the design resembled.

William Adams made the first examples at his Cobridge factory in 1799. Since these wares were mainly used in public houses, jugs, tankards, coffeepots, porringers, and butter dishes were the principal shapes that were manufactured.

Basically, the decorative portion of a piece consisted of a broad band of colored slip, usually blue, grey, or coffee-colored in tone, upon which was the design itself. To achieve the "tree" design, mocha ware potters utilized a mixture called "tea" that was put into the slip while still damp, thus causing the color to spread out into tree-like fronds that contrasted with the white earthenware beneath. On some examples, black rings were added.

Mocha ware exhibited a large variety of patterns. Arboration was made with an acidic solution, forming patterns such as Tree, Shrub, Fern, Seaweed, and Landscape. Cat's Eye and Worm patterns evolved from the use of a three-chambered slip bottle. Marbled and splotched pieces were made by using a blow pipe.

When the background was green, brown, cream, or orange, the designs usually were brown or black. Ale mugs, chamber pots, jugs, pitchers, and shrimp and nut measures are the forms most frequently found with mocha decoration.

It is rare to find a piece with a maker's mark. Among the known manufacturers of Mocha ware are Edge and Malkin in Burslem between 1871 and 1890 and T.G. Green & Co. in Derbyshire from 1864 to 1939. Additional mocha ware makers included Adams of Tunstall, Cork and Edge of Burslem, Broadhurst of Fenton, Tams of Longton, Macintyre of Cobridge, Pinder and Bourne of Burslem, Green of Church Gresley, and Maling of New Castle-on-Tyne.

Museum: City Museum and Art Gallery, Stoke-on-Trent, England.

Reproduction Alert: An American firm, East Knoll Pottery in Torrington, Connecticut, is producing mocha on yellow ware bodies. Pitchers, bowls, batter bowls, and colanders are hand thrown with applied strap handles. These pieces are plainly marked.

Bowl

4" d, ftd, yellowware, white striped wide brown band w/black seaweed, hairlines, (A), ... **358.00**

5" d x 3 1/4" h, ftd, blue, white, and black agate over brown ground, white slip int, c1830-50, ... **230.00**

6 1/4" d, lt sea green center band w/black tree designs, 2 black bands at top, single at base, (A), ... **385.00**

6 3/8" d, white, dk and lt brown balloon design, burnt orange ground, dk brown rim, hairline, (A), ... **7,040.00**

7 1/4" d, pearlware, blue and brown bands and earthworm designs, restorations, c1820, (A), ... **259.00**

8 1/4" d, flared, brown, opaque white, and blue earthworm pattern on wide blue band, (A), ... **523.00**

10 1/4" d, white, rust, and brown earthworm designs on lt blue bands separated by black stripes, tooled green rim, hairline, (A), ... **3,850.00**

Butter Tub, 4 3/4" h x 7" w, angular handles, yellowware, alternating bands of yellow, white slip, and painted cobalt, ... **260.00**

Canister, 4 1/2" h, cafe au lait bands w/dk brown stripes and seaweed designs, conical lid, (A), ... **2,090.00**

Creamer, 4 1/2" h, white, tan, and dk brown cat's eye design, grey bands, brown and tooled stripes, molded leaf handle, (A), ... **990.00**

Jug

6 1/2" h, brown, opaque white, and blue earthworm on grey band above narrow blue band flanked by 4 brown stripes above and below, (A), ... **578.00**

7" h

Creamware, rust, green, and black banding w/tree designs, (A), ... **3,737.00**

Two bands of copper green over rouletting on base and neck, lg sky blue band w/black seaweed designs, dk amber center band w/multiple rows of grey, blue, and black cat's eye designs, chips, ... **6,575.00**

Mug, 5 1/8" h, tan center band w/black trees or seaweed, wide blue border band w/dk brown-black stripes, white molded crest, early 19th C, hairline, $175.00

Mug

2 5/8" h, sage green bands, blue stripes, applied handle w/molded leaves, (A), ... **245.00**

3 1/2" h, tooled black and white scalloped lines on middle, tan border stripes w/tooled green bands, molded leaf handle, (A), ... **1,540.00**

4 7/8" h, tan, brown, white and gold marbleized ground, dk brown rim and base, molded leaf handle, hairline, (A), ... **2,420.00**

5" h, brown band w/black tree design in middle and blue band above, 2 brown stripes at top and base, brown transfer w/trees and "PINT," crown, letter "C" and "R," and "490 S," c1850, (A), ... **385.00**

Mustard Pot, 3 3/4" h

Blue band w/tooled blue band, black stripes and brown, black, white, and blue earthworm pattern, leaf molded handle, (A), ... **1,320.00**

White w/brown tooled lines, (A), ... **1,210.00**

Wide brown band w/black stripes and seaweed design, molded leaf handle, (A), ... **275.00**

Pepper Pot

4" h

Black checkered middle, green tooled band, lt brown stripes, (A), ... **1,320.00**

Tooled green band on shoulder w/burnt umber stripes, taupe top and wide white band w/white, umber, and black feather designs, (A), ... **2,750.00**

4 1/2" h

Dk brown, tan, and lt blue cat's eye designs, tan and dk brown stripes, (A), ... **2,750.00**

Lt blue and black stripes, chips, (A), ... **110.00**

4 3/4" h, grey stripes, black band, lt blue, orange, and white wavy line in center, cobalt feathered top, hairline, (A), ... **1,155.00**

5 1/8" h, pearlware, black and brown bands, c1800, restoration to foot, (A), ... **1,380.00**

Pitcher

5 5/8" h, brown, tan, and white feathered marbling, tooled green rim, (A), ... **3,190.00**

7 1/8" h, black, white, and slate blue dbl earthworm design on tan banded neck, earthworm w/tricolor balls on lower body on tan band, separated by slate blue stripes, molded leaf handle, (A), ... **4,125.00**

7 1/4" h, brown stripes on top, base, and middle, scattered blue and white cat's eyes, ivory ground, stains, (A), ... **500.00**

7 5/8" h, yellowware, white slip center band w/blue trees, white slip bands on shoulder, ... **1,650.00**

9" h, ovoid, alternating horiz bands of dk blue, black, and brown, applied ear handle, (A), ... **1,100.00**

Sugar Bowl, Cov, 5" h, incised green herringbone pattern on border, black seaweed on yellow-tan ground, damage to knob, (A), ... **2,450.00**

Tumbler, 2 1/2" h, gold, white, brown, and black feathered marbling, tooled green rim, (A), ... **3,520.00**

Waste Bowl, 6 1/2" d, white, dk brown, and lt blue earthworm designs on brown band w/dk brown stripes, hairlines, (A), ... **330.00**

c1919

MOORCROFT

Burslem, Staffordshire
1897 to Present

History: William Moorcroft was first employed as a potter by James Macintyre & Co. Ltd. of Burslem in 1897. Moorcroft believed in ornamentation that enhanced rather than disguised the shape of the ware. Most pots had to be hand thrown. He created his designs on the pot itself, rather than on paper, achieving an extraordinary marriage of shape and design.

Moorcroft's early works included vases, bowls, and biscuit jars that were decorated in blue, red, and gold plant forms called "Aurelian" ware.

Moorcroft also made "Florian" ware in a wide variety of shapes and types of decorations. "Florian" ware featured poppies, violets, or cornflowers applied in relief or portrayed in slip trail outlines or tube lining techniques. It was marketed under various trade names such as "Claremont," a toadstool design; "Hazledene," a landscape with trees; "Honesty;" "Pansy;" "Pomegrante;" and "Flamminian" luster wares. The principal markets were in London, New York, Paris, and San Francisco. The signature "W. Moorcroft" appeared on each piece along with the standard Macintyre printed mark.

In 1913 Moorcroft built his own small factory, the Washington Works, at Burslem, employing potters and decorators with whom he worked at James Macintyre & Co. A line of "Powder Blue" speckled tableware was designed in 1913 and continued in production for almost fifty years.

"Persian" was introduced in 1914 and was followed by "Late Florian" with orchid designs, narcissus, damson plums, and cornflowers. In 1921 Moorcroft experimented with trees in blues and greens on a powder blue ground called "Moonlit Blue." This was followed by "Eventide" and "Dawn."

Moorcroft continued the floral styles, but now used simpler and bolder designs. Dark colored exotic flowers adorned many pieces. Landscapes were done in the trailed outline technique. Monochrome luster glazes were produced until the 1920s, followed by flambe glazes in the decade that followed. The flambe or transmutation glazes provided the most interest for Moorcroft.

W. Moorcroft was appointed potter to Queen Mary in 1928. The impressed phrase "Potter to H.M. The Queen" was added to his mark. During the 1930s, fruits, fish, birds, and boats joined the traditional decorative motifs. Matte glazes

found favor. When Moorcroft died in 1945, Walter, his eldest son, continued the Moorcroft company.

At first, Walter used his father's designs. In the 1950s, he developed a more personal style with exotic designs and more dramatic use of color, especially with the eccentric Caribbean and marine life designs. He continued the flambe experiments and increased the range of flambe colors until 1973.

Walter was in charge for more than forty years. Changes during that time included the use of electric kilns, and casting replaced throwing. They still utilized William's styles and basic methods. During the 1970s, Walter designed the magnolia range.

In 1984 Walter's brother John became managing director, and the Moorcroft family sold a controlling interest to the three Roper brothers. This relationship lasted only two years, and the Dennis and Edwards families took over. Walter retired in 1987, and Sally Tuffin became Moorcroft designer along with Phillip Richardson.

Since 1994, Rachel Bishop has been Moorcroft's designer. Today, Moorcroft is selling more of its wares all over the world than it did in its heyday in the mid-1920s.

Marks: Various types of marks include the Moorcroft signature or initials, printed or impressed factory marks, retailers' marks, design registration numbers, and pattern or shape marks. Some paper labels with printed factory marks also were used starting in the 1920s. Rectangular ones were used first. After the awarding of the Royal Warrant in 1928, circular paper labels were used until 1978, when the Royal Warrant expired.

References: Paul Atterbury, *Moorcroft: A Guide to Moorcroft Pottery 1897-1993, Rev. Ed.* Richard Dennis and Hugh Edwards, 1990; A. W. Coysh, *British Art Pottery, 1870-1940*, Charles E. Tuttle, 1976; Richard Dennis, *William & Walter Moorcroft, l897-1973*, an exhibition catalog, 1973; Francis Salmon, *Collecting Moorcroft Pottery*, Francis Joseph Publications, 1994; Susan Scott, *Moorcroft, Antique Trader Weekly*, March 29, l995; Walter Moorcroft, *Memories of Life & Living*, Richard Dennis, 1999.

Museums: Everson Museum of Art, Syracuse, NY; Moorcroft Museum, Stoke-on-Trent, England; Victoria & Albert Museum, London, England.

Collectors' Club: Moorcroft Collectors Club, W. Moorcroft Plc., Sandbach Road, Burslem Stoke-on-Trent, Staffordshire, ST 62 Dq England, www.moorcroft.com, Membership: $30.00, 3 newsletters per year. Collectors' Club pieces issued yearly.

Bonbonniere, Cov, 7" h, "Rose Garland" pattern, gold lined handles and knob, "MacIntyre, green signature" mks, ... **1,725.00**

Bowl
5 1/2" d, "Fresia" pattern, moss green ground, "imp Moorcroft" mk, ... **150.00**
7" d, "Eventide" pattern, ... **1,450.00**
8 1/2" d, "Anemone" pattern, cobalt ground, "Moorcroft, Made in England" mk, ... **675.00**
9 1/2" H-H, "Pomegranate" pattern, cobalt ground, "blue W Moorcroft" mk, ... **625.00**

Box, Cov, 6 1/2" h, sq, "Flamminian," green glaze, for "Liberty & Co," chip, (A), ... **540.00**

Candlestick, 6" h, "Moonlit Blue" pattern, "blue W.M." mk, c1925, pr, ... **3,375.00**

Coffeepot, 5 1/2" h, powder blue, "imp W Moorcroft," "MADE IN ENGLAND, POTTER TO MARY THE QUEEN" mks, ... **65.00**

Cup and Saucer, "Leaf and Berry" pattern, green ground, ... **445.00**

Dish, 4 3/8" d, "Claremont" pattern, red capped yellow mushrooms, sm blue mushroom, med blue rim, (A), ... **530.00**

Ginger Jar, 6 1/8" h, "Magnolia" pattern, dk blue ground, "green WM" mk, ... **545.00**

Inkwell, 2 3/8" h x 3 1/8" sq, "Mushroom" pattern, lt blue ground, "WM, W Moorcroft" mks, ... **1,230.00**

Jug
6" h, MacIntyre, blue "Poppy" pattern, pewter lid, c1905, ... **1,420.00**
6 1/4" h, "Fresia" pattern, shaded cream to blue-green ground, hairline, (A), ... **390.00**

Nut Bowl, 3" d, red and green floral on int, shaded green to dk blue ext, mkd, ... **100.00**

Pipe Stand, 5 1/4" h, "Orchids" pattern, cobalt ground, "blue WM" mk, ... **1,400.00**

Pitcher, 5 7/8" h, "Butterfly" pattern, green leaves, shaded blue rim, "WM MOORCROFT MADE IN ENGLAND" mks, ... **650.00**

Plate, 8 1/4" d, Florian, "Daffodil" pattern, "green W.M. des," "Florian" mks, c1900, ... **1,125.00**

Urn, 3" h, Orchid design, yellow and red flowers w/purple accents, cobalt ground, ... **210.00**

Vase
1 3/4" h, ball shape, flared foot, rolled rim, dk blue and purple iris on cream-yellow cartouche, med green ground, ... **460.00**

Vase, 12" h, "Florian Ware," red, yellow, and lt green tube lined iris pattern, dk green ground, (A), $5,500.00

12" h

Corset shape, "Knightswood" pattern, multicolored stained glass effect, olive green ground, ... **1,150.00**

Ovoid, red "Tudor Rose" pattern, yellow-tan ground w/black circles and stripes, ... **2,150.00**

Squat shape, flared rim, red and orange "Pomegranates," purple hanging grapes, green and yellow streaked ground, "green signature," (A), ... **7,475.00**

16" h, tapered form, orange and red "Leaf and Berries" pattern, "imp MOORCROFT, blue William Moorcroft" mks, ... **5,500.00**

17" h, ovoid, "Pansy" pattern, cobalt ground, "MADE IN ENGLAND MOOCROFT, script" mks, ... **1,600.00**

19 7/8" h, bottle shape, "Flamminian," orange-red spades on disc, orange-red ground, (A), ... **1,500.00**

MULBERRY WARE

Staffordshire, England
1835-1855

History: Mulberry ware was made by many of the same Staffordshire potters who produced Flow Blue. In fact, many patterns with identical design and name are found on both types of wares. The bulk of the Mulberry ware production occurred during the early Victorian period, 1835 to 1855.

The mulberry color was achieved by a chemical reaction combining red, brown, grey, and purple dyes. Mulberry referred to the color of berries from the English black mulberry trees. Some mulberry patterns on earthenware or ironstone were "flown," producing a soft, hazy effect. Most were presented with a sharp, clear design.

Mulberry ware was a response to the public's need for something new and different. Its popularity did not last. Few pieces were made after 1855.

References: Petra Williams, *Flow Blue China & Mulberry Ware, Similarity and Value Guide, Rev. Ed.* Fountain House East, 1981.

Collecting Hints: Previously, mulberry prices always had been priced higher than Flow Blue examples. However, in the past few years, there has been a reversal. Mulberry ware now sells for about one-third less than the prevailing price for a comparable Flow Blue piece.

Abbey Pattern
Cup Plate, 4 1/8" d, ... **80.00**

Avon Pattern
Cup Plate, 3 3/4" d, ... **80.00**

Blantyre Pattern
Platter, 21 1/2" l x 17" w, Charles Meigh, ... **450.00**

Bochara Pattern
Plate
8 1/2" d, "J.E." mk, ... **95.00**
9 1/8" d, ... **45.00**
10 1/2" d, "J.E." mk, ... **125.00**
Platter, 15" l oct, ... **350.00**
Relish Dish, 9" l x 5" w, "J. Edwards" mk, ... **195.00**

Bryonia Pattern
Soup Bowl, 9" d, Sarreguemines, ... **32.00**

Buda Pattern
Plate, 9 1/2" d, ... **85.00**

Calcutta Pattern
Plate, 9 3/4" d, E. Challinor, ... **70.00**

Corea Pattern
Cup Plate, 4" d, ... **80.00**
Plate, 7" d, "J. Clementson" mk, ... **35.00**

Corean Pattern
Plate
8 1/2" d, ... **56.00**
9" d, "P.W. & co." mk, ... **30.00**
9 3/4" d, "P.W. & Co." mk, ... **65.00**
10" d, ... **50.00**
Platter, 13 3/4" l x 10 1/4" w, oct, "P.W. & Co." mk, ... **200.00**
Posset Cup, 3" h, unmkd, (A), ... **110.00**
Sauce Tureen, 7 1/2" h x 7" w, ftd, w/undertray, 8 1/2" H-H, "COREAN, PW & CO." mks, (A), ... **495.00**

Cyprus Pattern
Cup Plate, 4 1/8" d, Davenport, ... **80.00**
Plate
9 1/4" d, ... **45.00**
10" d, ... **125.00**
Platter, 16" l x 12" w, oct, Davenport, chips, ... **230.00**

Foliage Pattern
Platter, 15 1/2" l oct, ... **275.00**

Fruit Basket Pattern
Soup Plate, 10 1/2" d, ... **110.00**

Genoa Pattern
Cup and Saucer, ... **38.00**
Plate, 9 3/8" d, Davenport, ... **35.00**

Gothic Pattern
Platter, 22 1/2" l x 17 1/2" w, oct, unmkd, ... **400.00**

Hadden Pattern
Plate, 9 1/2" d, ... **125.00**

Jeddo Pattern
Jug, 9 1/2" h, oct, "Wm Adams & Sons Ironstone" mk, (A), ... **145.00**
Plate
7 1/2" d, "W. Adams & Sons" mk, ... **85.00**
9 1/4" d, 14 panels, "W. Adams & Sons" mk, ... **130.00**
Sugar Bowl, Cov, 7 3/4" h, "Wm. Adams" mk, ... **100.00**

Kyber Pattern
Plate, 9" d, J. Meir, ... **75.00**

Loretta pattern
Plate, 8" d, ... **65.00**
Vegetable Bowl, 9 1/2" l, ... **125.00**

Lozere Pattern
Teapot, 11" h, paneled, ... **250.00**

Marble Pattern
Pitcher, 5 5/8" h, John Wedgwood, ... **100.00**

Platter, 17 1/2" l x 14" w, R.
Wedgewood, ... **495.00**
Teapot, 9 1/2" h, Gothic Shape,
.... **350.00**

Medina Pattern
Plate, 9 3/4" d, 10 sides, ... **25.00**

Milan Pattern
Plate, 7 1/4" d, 12 sides, ... **185.00**

Moss Rose Pattern
Plate
9" d, c1840, ... **110.00**
10 1/4" d, Furnival, ... **80.00**

Ning Po Pattern
Bowl, 6" d, Hall, ... **45.00**

Non Pariel Pattern
Pitcher, 7 1/2" h, "T. & J. Mayer" mk,
.... **595.00**

Panama Pattern
Pitcher, 7 1/2" h, "T.& J. Mayer" mk,
.... **595.00**
Plate, 9 5/8" d, 12 sides, "E. Challinor
& Co." mk, ... **65.00**

Platter, 13 5/8" l, "Orpheus" pattern, Davenport,
$370.00

Pelew Pattern
Cup and Saucer, Handless, .. **50.00**
Cup Plate, 4" d, ... **80.00**
Plate
7 3/4" d, E. Challinor, ... **40.00**
10" d, Challinor, ... **100.00**
Vegetable Bowl, Cov, 10 5/8" d, oct,
.... **300.00**

Panama Pattern
Plate, 7" d, 12 s "imp IMPROVED
STONE CHINA" mk, (A), .. **53.00**

Percy Pattern
Plate, 9" d, ... **70.00**

Peruvian Pattern
Plate
7 5/8" d, ... **60.00**
10 1/2" d, (A), ... **50.00**

Rhone Scenery Pattern
Plate
9 1/4" d, "T.J. & J. Mayer" mk,
c1845, ... **95.00**
9 3/4" d, "T.J. & J. Mayer" mk,
.... **95.00**

Rose Pattern
Plate, 8 1/2" d, Challinor, ... **50.00**

Platter, 13 3/4" l x 10 3/4" w, oval, E.
Challinor, ... **150.00**

Simla Pattern
Bowl, 12" d, 12 panels, "Bagshaw &
Meir" mk, ... **150.00**

Singan Pattern
Creamer, 5 3/4" h, c1850, ... **235.00**

Sydenham Pattern
Platter, 17 3/4" l x 14" w, oct, "J.
Clementson" mk, ... **450.00**

Teapot, 10" h, "Corea" pattern, c1834-1859,
$745.00

Temple Pattern
Cup and Saucer, Handless, "P.W. &
Co." mk, ... **75.00**
Plate, 10 1/2" d, "P.W. & Co." mk,
.... **50.00**
Teapot, 9 1/4" h, paneled, ... **200.00**

Tivoli Pattern
Vegetable Bow, Cov, 8 3/4" h x 11" H-
H, oct, Charles Meigh, (A),
.... **385.00**

Venus Pattern
Plate, 8 3/4" d, "P.W. & Co." mk,
.... **50.00**

Vincennes Pattern
Plate, 10" d, ... **40.00**
Teabowl and Saucer, Alcock,
.... **65.00**

Washington Vase Pattern
Cream Jug, 5 1/4" h, oct, (A),
.... **88.00**
Cup and Saucer, Handleless,
.... **55.00**
Cup Plate, 4 1/4" d, ... **100.00**
Plate
7 3/4" d, 12 sides, "P.W. & Co."
mk, ... **48.00**
8" d, "WASHINGTON VASE,
PEARL STONE WARE, PW &
CO." mks, (A), ... **48.00**
9" d, ... **42.00**

10 3/8" d, ... **110.00**
Platter, 15 3/4" x 12 1/4" w, rect, "P.W.
& Co." mk, (A), ... **220.00**
Sugar Box, Cov, 8 1/4" h, oct, emb
lion head handles, (A), ... **275.00**
Teapot, 9 1/2" h, oct, unmkd, (A),
.... **467.00**

Whampoa Pattern
Pitcher, 9" h, paneled, ... **400.00**

 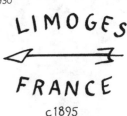

MUSTACHE CUPS

English, Continental
1830 to Present

History: The mustache cup was a
Victorian innovation that owed its origin to
Harvey Adams, a Stoke-on-Trent potter
who introduced the design in 1830. It was
a drinking cup used for sipping or coffee,
featuring a raised lip guard attached from
rim to rim of the cup to keep the mustache
and beard from touching the liquid. The
guard had one semicircular opening.
Originally called "Napoleons and
Saucers," after the small beards popular at
the time, mustache cups reached the peak
of their popularity in the 1890s, when
wearing a mustache was the rage.

Mustache cups were first sold singly.
Some had matching saucers, but most
stood alone. As their popularity increased,
they were included in dinnerware sets. Gift
sets that included a cup with a mustache
rim for the gentleman and an identical rim-
less cup for madam were common. Right-
and left-handed cups were produced.
Left-handed examples are scarce.
Although originating in England, the manufacture of mustache cups quickly spread
to other areas including France, Germany,
and Austria.

Many different media were used for
the body, including earthenware, porcelain, and bone china. Free-hand painting
by artists, along with transfer printing and
other decorative techniques were used.
Heavy raised and burnished decorations
and rich gilding proved popular. These are

the most frequently encountered pieces today. Some mustache cups employed several techniques to catch the fancy of the buyer.

Many of the major houses produced mustache cups and marked their products accordingly. Crown Derby, Wedgwood, Meissen, and Limoges all provided cups for the mustached gentleman. However, many of the examples found in today's market are unmarked.

The size of mustache cups ranges from demitasse to quart. The eight-ounce size is most commonly found.

References: Dorothy Hammond, *Mustache Cups*, Wallace-Homestead, 1972; Thelma Schull, *Victorian Antiques*, Tuttle, 1963; Glenn Erardi & Pauline Peck, *Mustache Cups, Timeless Victorian Treasures*, Schiffer Publications, 2001.

Reproduction Alert: Reproduced matching left-handed and right-handed mustache cups have found their way to antique shops. Since matched sets are very rare, collectors should be careful to make sure the matched set is old, not a reproduction.

Collecting Hints: Sayings and mottos are fairly common but do not add significantly to the value of the piece. Advanced collectors seek out Majolica, Imari, Rose Medallion, Sunderland, Luster, and Belleek cups.

Note: All listings are for right-handed cups unless indicated otherwise.

Cup, 3 1/4" h, orange zigzag ribbon, yellow centered red flowers, green leaves, red rose handle, gold accents and mustache bar, unmkd, $45.00

Cup

Applied sm yellow, lg white flowers, cobalt leaves, gold trimmed handle and rim, "red Made in Germany" mk, ... **60.00**

Crusted gold "PRESENT" on front, raised sm red flowerheads, Germany, ... **28.00**

Decal of garden flowers, gold border w/drape, gold outlined handle, ... **20.00**

Decal of pink and red flowers, green foliage, blue to white shaded ground, unmkd, ... **12.00**

Gold centered and edged applied red flowerhead, gold buds, gold outlined and veined relief molded leaves, blue shaded border, vert fluted base w/yellow lustering, ... **65.00**

"Gold Forget Me Not" in banner, HP red or blue flowerheads, green leaves, shadow leaf ground, ... **10.00**

HP

Brown cabin in snow scene, unmkd, ... **60.00**

Lily of the valley, lavender, and pink flower bouquet, molded curls on rim and base, gold rim, c1900, ... **65.00**

Red centered green or white flowers, raised green beading, buds, and border swirls, Germany, ... **20.00**

Yellow centered red blossoms, hanging bluebell, green and brown foliage, molded lt blue fishscale base, gold accents and rim, "C. Telsch" mk, ... **18.00**

Left Handed, decal of carnations and foliage molded swirls top and base, gold rim, sculpted handle, unmkd, ... **10.00**

Lg pink, white and blue flowerhead, brown and green cattails, and foliage, "periwinkle" blue ground, gold accents, ... **35.00**

Mauve, orange, and purple flowers, raised gold designs, "green CT eagle" mark, A-$25.00

Multicolored bouquet of flowers, molded swirl border, gold dust rim, gold handle, pale green base w/sm feet, c1900, ... **40.00**

Pink ground w/gold accented raised white diamonds, band of raised gold flowerheads on throat, 4 sm curled feet, ... **55.00**

Raised gilt trimmed pine trees, lt blue sky and tan ground, 2

sheep, farmer and fencing on reverse, ... **30.00**

Raised gilt accented "PRESENT" on front, applied blue forget-me-nots on base, gilt accents, Germany, ... **25.00**

Raised gold fruit, flowers, and foliage, white ground w/raised swirls, ... **25.00**

Red strawberries, white blossoms, green foliage, orange luster border, Altenburg, Germany, ... **20.00**

Squat form, lg pink roses, green foliage on white center band, lt blue base and border, gold outlined fancy loop handle, Germany, ... **25.00**

White ironstone, molded diamond pattern on base, ... **35.00**

Cup and Saucer

Blue bands w/trailing red foxglove, "gold Forget Me Not" on front, Germany, ... **75.00**

Bucket shaped cup, multicolored scene of "Sister Dora Monument" in oval on cup, pink ground, pink band on border of saucer, Germany, ... **75.00**

"Eddystone Lighthouse," black transfers, gold trim, ... **75.00**

Eight flutes, multicolored decal of classic scene w/cup on cup, pea green borders w/gold stenciled overlay, ... **50.00**

Fluted, scalloped rim

Flowing green body, white daisy style flowers and foliage in raised gold ovals, ... **50.00**

"Gold A Present" in white banner w/gold and white flowers, pink body, white fan fluted saucer w/pink rim, Germany, ... **45.00**

Gold foliage on cup, gold handle, and rim, sm red roses, green and gold foliage on saucer, ... **65.00**

"Gold Think of Me," in raised white and gold stylized flower chain, pink ground, saucer w/radiating fluting, pink shaded ground, gold trim, unmkd, ... **25.00**

Ironstone, blue printed roses and foliage, blue streaked rims, ... **30.00**

Hanging blue forget-me-nots from rim, shaded pink ground, gold molded borders, ... **30.00**

HP lt yellow luster ground, emb red, blue, and green flowers and

foliage, emb swirls on saucer, Germany, ... **50.00**

Maroon, blue, green, and gold wide swirls on pink ground, ... **75.00**

Multicolored decal of garden flowers, molded beaded swirls, gold lined rims and bar, fancy handle, "C.T. Germany" mk, ... **50.00**

Multicolored scene of period couple in grass in raised gilt scrolling cartouche, pink border and saucer w/raised designs, Germany, ... **145.00**

Pale green ground w/raised PRESENT, applied blue forget-me-nots and base of cup, "Made in Germany" mk, ... **45.00**

Paneled cup, fluted saucer, pale yellow and white apple blossoms, brown toned leaves and stems, "Gutherz Carlsbad" mk, ... **75.00**

Purple flowers, yellow paneled wavy borders w/gold crisscrossing and flowers, gilt fancy handle, ... **15.00**

Scattered sprigs of garden flowers, gold lined rims and bar, ... **30.00**

Swirled, paneled body, gold banded borders w/sm flowerheads and hanging drape, gold outlined mustache bar, ... **60.00**

Tan-violet printed scrolling and geometric borders w/orange-red, blue, yellow and green enamel accented flowers between, ... **50.00**

Tridacna pattern, Irish Belleek, 2nd black mk, ... **225.00**

Willow design, blue, unmkd, c1900, hairline, ... **220.00**

1812-35

NEW HALL

Staffordshire Potteries, England
c1731-1735

History: A group of partners purchased Champion's patent to make translucent porcelains. In 1781 they established the New Hall China Manufactory at Hanley in

Staffordshire to make hard paste porcelains based on the patent. Tea and dessert sets, along with blue and white wares showing Chinese influences, were characteristic products at New Hall. Gold was used in both simple and elaborate designs. Many early pieces only had elegant gilt borders.

Fidelle Duvivier, who had been employed at Worcester and Derby, worked at New Hall from 1781 to 1790. He did figure and landscape compositions and flower subjects on presentation jugs. Early New Hall teapots were globular in form. Pieces made during the hard-paste period were not marked. Pattern numbers were used instead.

About 1812-1814, bone china that was lighter and whiter was introduced at New Hall. The pieces were marked "New Hall" in a double-lined circle along with a pattern number. Work declined after about 1820. The factory was put up for auction in 1831. Various firms using the original site continued the name until 1836.

References: David Holgate, *New Hall & Its Imitators, Rev. Ed.* Faber & Faber, 1988; G.E. Stringer, *New Hall Porcelain*, Art Trade Press, 1949.

Museums: City Museum & Art Gallery, Stoke-on-Trent, Hanley, England; Victoria & Albert Museum, London, England.

Bowl

5" d, painted red rose, yellow buds, green leaves, unmkd, ... **50.00**

7 1/4" d, black bat printed scene of English castle and countryside on int, c1820, ... **195.00**

Center Bowl, 11" d, painted floral sprig on int, red int border w/white rects, painted multicolored floral sprays on ext, black and red geometric rim, ... **3,500.00**

Coffee Can and Saucer, multicolored bat print landscape scene in gilt cartouche, thatched cottage on saucer, ... **115.00**

Coffee Cup, 2 1/2" h, underglazed blue hanging swags and pendants, gilt accents, c1782, ... **125.00**

Coffee Cup and Saucer, London shape, band of puce and red flowers and lg pad type green leaves, ... **70.00**

Cream Jug

5 1/2" l, scattered iron-red and blue summer flower sprigs w/green leaves, puce lined rim, ... **175.00**

5 3/4" l, green grapes, gilt tendrils, gilt outlined white leaves, cobalt ground, gilt lined rim and handle, c1805, ... **480.00**

Cream Jug, 4 1/2" h, puce cartouches of iron-red, puce, and green flowers, magenta lined rim, **$245.00**

Cup and Saucer

"Boy in the Window" pattern, multicolored, ... **125.00**

Painted oriental women and musicians and pagoda, red, yellow, blue, and green, red stiff leaf interior cup border, blue and red panels on saucer border, c1780, ... **125.00**

Tan border bands, scattered gilt sprigs, "elf ear" handle, ... **75.00**

"Tobacco Leaf" pattern, c1820, ... **325.00**

Dish

7 1/2" l x 6" w, rect, 3 adult oriental men and child in court in center, floral border, multicolored, c1810, ... **275.00**

8 1/4" d

"Boy in the Window" pattern, c1820, ... **565.00**

Puce and green floral sprigs and flowing ribbons, c1790, ... **175.00**

8 1/4" w, dk blue border band w/gilt outlined 3 lobed leaves, gilt banding, ... **45.00**

Jug, 4 1/4" h, silver shape, HP black rose and sprigs on sides, black lined border, #461, ... **145.00**

Pitcher, 5 1/4" h, helmet shape, painted flowers from brown basket on sides, wavy dk red dentil line on throat, ... **135.00**

Plate

8 1/4" d, "Boy in the Window" pattern, multicolored, c1820, ... **565.00**

8 5/8" d, blue oriental flowerheads on dk blue stems, green leaf forms, pink roses, cobalt, and gilt border, c1820, ... **675.00**

Sugar Box, Cov, 7 1/2" H-H x 5" h, 2 vert loop handles, gilt outlined dk blue leaves, gilt and blue acorns, gilt tendrils and knob, c1805, ... **100.00**

Teabowl and Saucer
  Black bat printed fruit design, sm gilt flower on int of bowl, gilt lined rims, ... **125.00**

Teabowl and Saucer, orange urn, pink, red, and green flowers and foliage, iron-red diaper borders, (A), $95.00

  Painted multicolored scene of oriental child, 2 adults, cherry tree, and insects, ... **150.00**
  Multicolored overall pseudo "Tobacco Leaf" and sprigs pattern, blue gilt flower on int of bowl, blue gilt and acanthus scroll borders, c1810, ... **650.00**

Teapot, 8 1/4" h, with stand, "Boy in the Window" pattern, orange, blue, green, and white cartouches, $1,200.00

Teapot
  5" h, boat shape, center band of multicolored enameled sprigs, iron-red and magenta borders, c1800, ... **950.00**
  6" h, "Boy in the Window" pattern, ... **975.00**

---

  7 1/2" h, "Boy Chasing Butterfly" pattern, multicolored enamels, "red N421" mk, c1810, ... **525.00**
Teapot Stand, 6 7/8" l x 5 5/8" w, polychrome "Boy in the Window" pattern, ... **150.00**

SILESIA

Clairon
LATE 1800s

OLD IVORY

Silesia, Germany
Late 1800s

History: Old Ivory dinnerware was made during the late 1800s in the pottery factories in Silesia, Germany. The Ohme Porcelain Works (1882-1928) produced the majority of the dinnerware. It derived its name from the background color of the china.

  Marked pieces usually had a pattern number stamped on the bottom. The mark also may include a crown and "Silesia."

References: Alma Hillman, David Goldschmitt & Adam Szynkiewicz, *Collector's Guide to Old Ivory China*, Collector Books, 1998.

Collectors' Club: Old Ivory Porcelain Society, Jo Ann Hamlin, Route 3, Box 18B, Spring Valley, MN 55975. Membership: $25.00, *Elegance of Old Ivory*, 3 times a year newsletter.

Berry Set, master bowl, 9 1/2" d, 6 bowls, 5 1/2" d
  #XXVIII pattern, (A), ... **85.00**
  #75 pattern, Silesia Ohme, ... **325.00**
Bowl
  9 1/4" d, #122 pattern, Clairon, (A), ... **325.00**
  9 1/2" d, #82 pattern, Ohme, (A), ... **38.00**
Bun Tray, 12 1/2" l, #122 pattern, (A), ... **220.00**
Butter Pat, 3" d, Etalle, Clairon, set of 8, ... **175.00**

Cake Plate, Open Handles
  10" d, #XI pattern, Clairon, (A), ... **75.00**
  11" d,
    #XI Clairon, (A), ... **110.00**
    #XII pattern, Clairon, (A), ... **165.00**
    #16 pattern, Clairon, (A), ... **55.00**

Cake Plate, 10" H-H, #XXII pattern, A-$155.00

Cereal Bowl, 6 1/2" d, #XII pattern, Clairon, set of 6, ... **200.00**
Charger, 13" d
  #11 pattern, Clairon, (A), ... **200.00**
  #XXI, Clairon, (A), ... **650.00**
  #82 pattern, Clairon, (A), ... **600.00**
Chocolate Cup and Saucer, #137 pattern, Rivoli, (A), ... **247.00**
Coffee Cup and Saucer, Clairon
  #X pattern, (A), ... **44.00**
  #22 pattern, (A), ... **330.00**
  #73 pattern, (A), ... **350.00**
Condensed Milk Container, 6 1/2" h, lg brown tinged pink and white rose, gold trim, "Old Ivory Germany" mk, ... **350.00**

Cracker Jar, 7 3/4" h, 8 3/4" l, #84 pattern, A-$310.00

Creamer and Sugar Bowl, creamer, 4" h, sugar bowl, 5 3/4" h, #84 pattern, A-$410.00

Coupe Plate
7 3/4" d, Silesia, #82 pattern,
.... **69.00**

9 1/2" d, #X pattern, Clairon, (A),
.... **110.00**

Cup and Saucer, Silesia, #84 pattern,
.... **80.00**

Cup and Saucer, Demitasse
#XV pattern, Clairon, (A), ... **165.00**
#XXVIII pattern, Empire, Clairon (A),
.... **200.00**
#73 pattern, Clairon, (A), ... **135.00**

Dresser Tray, 11 1/2" l, #XV pattern,
Clairon, (A), ... **80.00**

Nappy, 6 1/2" d, #16 pattern, ... **125.00**

Pickle Dish, 8" l, #75 pattern, Empire,
(A),
.... **88.00**

Plate
6" d, Silesia
#16 pattern, ... **50.00**
#84 pattern, ... **55.00**
6 1/4" d
Clairon
#XI pattern, (A), ... **10.00**
#XXII pattern, (A), ... **28.00**
Silesia
#11 pattern, ... **45.00**
#16 pattern, ... **55.00**

Plate, 6 1/2" d, #16 pattern, $75.00

6 1/2" d, #69 Florette, (A), ... **35.00**
7" d, #XXVIII, (A), ... **11.00**
7 1/2" d, Silesia
#16 pattern, ... **50.00**
#XL pattern, (A), ... **125.00**
#84 pattern, ... **50.00**
7 3/4" d
Silesia, #16 pattern, ... **85.00**
#118, Empire, (A), ... **35.00**
8" d, Silesia, #11 pattern, ... **69.00**
8 1/4" d
#XXXIII, Empire, (A), ... **50.00**
#73 pattern, Clairon, (A),
.... **90.00**

8 3/8" d
#XXII pattern, Clairon, (A),
.... **165.00**
#75 pattern, Empire, (A), .. **68.00**
8 1/2" d, #82 pattern, Ohme, (A),
.... **38.00**
8 3/4" d, Silesia, #71 pattern, **100.00**
9" d, #84 pattern, ... **295.00**

Platter, 11 1/2" l, #84 pattern, ... **200.00**

Soup Bowl, 7 3/4" d, #16 pattern,
Clairon, (A), ... **85.00**

Sugar Bowl, Cov, 6" H-H, #VIII pattern,
.... **18.00**

Tea Cup and Saucer, #X pattern,
Clairon, (A), ... **22.00**

NAST
a
PARIS
1782 - MID 19TH CENTURY

J.P
1830-62

H. DECK
c1859

OLD PARIS AND PARIS

Paris, France
18th and 19th Centuries

Old Paris

History: Old Paris referred to porcelains made in the 18th and 19th centuries by various French factories located in and around Paris. Shapes were usually classical in design, decorations were elegant, and gilding was popular. Although some examples were marked, many were not.

Paris

History: Most of the early porcelain factories of France were located in and around Paris. Without marks, it was difficult to differentiate between the various factories because their shapes and designs were similar. Strewn flower sprigs, especially the cornflower, and lots of gilding were favorite decorative motifs.

Fabrique du Conte d'Artois was founded by Pierre-Antoine Hannong in 1773. Hannong's polychrome flower painting was similar in style to that of Sevres. Coal was used to fire the ovens because the woods around Paris had been depleted by earlier porcelain manufactures. In 1787, Hannong was granted the rights to make figures in biscuit, to paint in color, and to use gilding. Production ended about 1828.

Hannong used the letter "H" as his mark.

Fabrique de la Courtille was founded by Jean-Baptiste Locre de Roissy, a potter from Leipzig, in 1773. He imitated German porcelains, including those of Meissen. Large vases were a specialty. The factory was taken over by Pouyat of Limoges about 1800. No exact date is known for its closing.

The factory mark was a pair of crossed torches that closely resembled the Meissen crossed swords.

Fabrique de la rue de Reuilly was established by Jean Joseph Lassia of Strasbourg about 1775. He used an "L" mark. Production ceased in 1784. **Henri-Florentin Chanou** had a factory nearby from 1779 to 1785. His mark was a "CH."

Fabrique de Clignancourt was founded by Pierre Deruelle in 1771. Porcelains rivaling Sevres were made. The decorative motifs included polychrome flower sprays and landscapes along with gilding. Some figures also were made.

The first mark was a windmill, a tribute to the windmills of Montmartre located nearby. A later mark was "LSX," a monogram for Louis XVIII.

Fabrique de la Reine was organized by Andre-Marie Leboeuf about 1778 under the protection of Marie-Antoinette. Products were called "porcelaine de la Reine."

The decorations included small sprigs of cornflowers, daisies, and roses, bird paintings, and some gilding. The factory was sold by Guy in 1797.

Fabrique Duc d'Angouleme was established by Dihl in 1780. Guerhard became his partner in 1786. The firm's main pattern was called "Angouleme Sprig," featuring strewn cornflowers. The pattern was copied by many other factories. Biscuit figures were made. Dihl introduced the painting of portraits on porcelain. The favored decorative motif was designs in the Empire style. The factory was transferred to Fabrique rue du Temple in 1796.

Marks included "GA," "Dihl," "Guerhard and Dihl," or "Rue de Bondy."

Fabrique de la Popincourt, founded by Lemaire, was bought by Johann Nast in 1782. He moved it to Popincourt in 1784. Biscuit porcelains, biscuit clock cases, and Wedgwood imitations were made. The factory's marks were "Nast a Paris" or "N."

Fabrique du Duc d'Orleans was started by Louis de Villers and Augustin de Montarcy in 1784. Its mark was a monogram "MJ." In 1786 the factory changed hands. The mark became "LP." A single rose decoration appears on some pieces.

The factory of the "Prince de Galles," or the "Prince of Wales" factory, was established in 1789 by the Englishman Christopher Potter. He was the first in Paris to use the transfer printing method. The factory changed hands several times. The first mark was "Potter Paris," then "EB" for

E. Blancheron, the manager in 1792, and finally "PB."

Fabrique de Petit rue Saint Gilles was started by Francois-Maurice Honore in partnership with Dagoty about 1785. They made vases in the style of Wedgwood. The names "Honore and Dagoty" were used in the marks.

Fabrique du Jacob Petit was established by Jacob Petit Fontainebleau in 1834. Much of Petit's porcelain was inspired by 18th century French and German examples. His animal tureens and figurals all looked to the past for inspirations; he used English shapes for his tea services. Many pieces contained relief ornamentation in the form of flowers, jewels, and fruit. The factory closed in 1866.

Reference: George Savage, *Seventeenth & Eighteenth Century French Porcelain*, Spring Books, 1969.

Museums: Musee National Adrien-Dubouche, Limoges, France; Musee National de Ceramique, Sevres, France; Munson-Williams-Proctor Institute, Utica, NY; Victoria & Albert Museum, London, England.

Cologne Bottle, 8" h, multicolored figures, fruit on reverse, peach ground, cobalt side bands, gilt accents, unmkd, pr, (A), $800.00

Basket, 8 1/8" h x 9 5/8" h, pedestal base, oct shape, arched pierced sides, gilt horiz bands and trim, wear to gilt, ... **350.00**

Breakfast Set, teapot, 11" h, chocolate pot, 9" h, creamer, 7" h, sugar bowl, 5" h, 6 cups and saucers, side plate, 5" d, band of gilt ferns, tendrils, and leaves on borders, gilt overlapping ovals on body, wide gilt bands, gilt accented mask spouts, c1825, ... **4,500.00**

Cabaret Set, teapot, 5" h, cream jug, 5 1/4" h, cov sugar basin, tray, 11" sq, cup and saucer, paneled, lt orange ground w/gold and red neo-gothic tracery inset w/faux cabochon emeralds in center, Paris, c1830, ... **12,500.00**

Cabinet Plate, 9 1/4" d, HP scene of "The Chateau de Pierrefond," cobalt border w/applied gilt swags and drops, c1870, ... **595.00**

Coffee Cup and Saucer, cup w/4 gilt lined teardrops w/HP wildflowers in each, coral ground between, 3 teardrops on saucer, acorn and leaf handle, ... **45.00**

Coffee Service, Part, pot, hot water pot, creamer, cov sugar bowl, 7 cups and saucers, multicolored landscape scenes, gilt accents, A-$467.00

Dessert Service, comport, 9" d x 4 1/2" h, 3 comports, 9" d x 2 3/8" h, HP floral bouquet in center, med blue banded borders and stands, ... **260.00**

Jardiniere, 7 1/2" h x 10" l x 6 1/2" w, painted center band of reclining woman w/looking glass and putti, putto w/florals on reverse, molded gilt beaded inner border, med blue base band w/gilt antheniom, 4 gilt feet, 2 gilt and blue scroll handles, Old Paris, ... **995.00**

Plate

8 1/2" d, multicolored HP scene of early harbor scene in center, underglazed blue and fancy gilt border, c1825, ... **820.00**

9" d, center multicolored scene of "Muse in Clouds," muse painting on canvas w/cherubs, gilt interwoven wreath int border, gilt hanging lambrequins on border, ... **500.00**

9 1/4" d, center painted scene of "The Chateau de Pierrefond," cobalt border w/gilt swags and leaves, wavy rim, Paris, .. **595.00**

9 3/8" d, center painted w/nude couple, holding shield, armor at feet, female holding white cloth on thighs, dk brown ground in gilt circ cartouche, border of gilt male heads, sun masks, scrolls, and anthemion between gilt bands, c1810, (A), ... **670.00**

9 7/8" d, HP lg bouquet of garden flowers in center, gilt keyed inner

border, pea green border w/3 gilt trimmed oval cartouches of HP flower sprigs, gilt lobed rim, Le Feuillet Studio, c1825, set of 12, ... **24,000.00**

Solitaire Set, teapot, 4 1/8" h, cream jug, 4 1/2" h, cov sugar bowl, 4 5/8" h, cup and saucer, shaped sq tray, 9 3/4" w, painted still life of flowers and vegetables on ledge in circ and oval gilt roundels, reserved on gold ground, borders of HP flower garlands, Potter & Blancheron, c1790, (A), ... **3,825.00**

Soup Tureen, 13 1/4" h, w/undertray, rect shape w/tapered canted corners, wide lt yellow band w/lg bouquet of polychrome flowers, "Rose Wreath" band on border on cov and undertray, gilt scroll handles, gilt shell knob, Paris, ... **14,000.00**

Spill Vase, 5 1/2" h, HP political allegorical animal figures, wide gilt bands, 3 sm feet on gilt lined circ base, c1840, pr, ... **3,200.00**

Teapot, 8 3/8" h, pear shape w/gooseneck spout, loop handle, leaf and pear knob, emb spout and handle, gilt banded rims and outlines, c1870, ... **175.00**

Tobacco Jar, 6" h, "black Tabac" on front, brown and green topped palm trees, blue, purple, and red grasses, brown branch knob, Old Paris, ... **295.00**

Urn, 7 5/8" h, multicolored florals, gold banding, c1820-30, $375.00

Urn, 9 1/2" h, HP front panel of orientals fishing from balcony, reverse w/HP trailing bouquet of flowers on tan ground, gilt rim, gilt accented horiz handles, circ ft, and sq base, ... **900.00**

Vase

10 1/2" h, urn shape, HP multicolored panel of landscape view of farmland and figures, reverse w/painted flower garland on purple ground, gilt body, figural swan handles, socle and sq base, c1825, pr, ... **4,500.00**

11 1/2" h, oviform, platinum ground w/painted exotic flying and perched birds on resist plants and branches, burnished gilt fixed ring handles and rims, Paris, c1878, pr, (A), ... **8,965.00**

12 3/4" h, urn shape, multicolored bust of cavalier or lady in gilt tooled cartouche, gilt molded scroll and hanging loop handles, gilt geometric cross on reverse, gilt wavy rim, c1850, pr, ... **650.00**

Vase, 13" h, multicolored allegorical scenes on front, gilt trophy on reverse, maroon ground, gilt body, pierced handles and sq base, pr, $950.00

14" h, swollen shape, narrow gilt base and flat ft, HP birds perched on branch w/lg pink and

sm blue flowers below, platinum ground, pierced gilt collar, Paris, ... **7,500.00**

17 1/8" h, campana form on gilt circ socles on stepped sq base, HP garden bouquet in gilt foliage cartouche, dk blue ground, gilt mask handles, band of red and blue oval faux cabochons, gilt sawtooth rim, base w/painted garden bunch in gilt foliate quatrefoil, dk blue ground, c1835, pr, ... **15,000.00**

18" h, tapered shape w/flared neck and rim, band of lg HP roses on burgundy ground, base swagged w/needlework designs, white neck w/gilt hanging swags, c1860, pr, ... **9,000.00**

Veilleuse, 9 1/2" h, gilt outlined ovals of multicolored garden flowers, pink ground, gilt tipped knob, c1850, ... **495.00**

MINTON

c. 1862

OYSTER PLATES

1860-1910

History: Serving oysters reached its highpoint during the Victorian era when specialized dishes were introduced. Large quantities were shipped to officers at the front in the American Civil War. Deep welled bowls—with scallops for holding ice and oysters in the half shells—were forerunners of later models. A second type of plate was designed to hold oysters on the half shell without ice. These carried less well-defined wells for the shells. A third type featured shallow wells for oysters out of the shell. Each of the wells was shaped like an oyster shell. Wells ranged in number from one to six, with two wells being the most rare. Large plates often held one to three dozen oysters. Minton potted a three-tiered example that held twenty-seven oysters.

Many of the plates carried a center well for sauces or large center or side wells for lemon wedges. The plates were made in France, England, Austria, and Germany by such companies as Haviland, Minton, Copeland, and Utzcheider of Sarreguemines. Haviland examples usually used soft, pastel colors, while Limoges examples often embellished the plates with gold.

Decorations often incorporated ocean scenes with the extensive use of coral, seaweed, and shells.

References: Jeffrey B. Snyder, *Collecting Oyster Plates With Price Guide*, Schiffer Publications, 2002. Vivian & Jim Karsnitz, *Oyster Plates*, Schiffer Publications.

Collectors' Club: Oyster Plate & Collectibles Society, Andrea Sullivan Treasurer/Secretary, P.O. Box 632 Brigantine, NJ, 08203.

Collecting Hints: Majolica and HP examples, as well as unusual shapes, are highly prized by collectors.

Reproduction Alert: Reproductions of Haviland examples are appearing on the scene. Majolica fish-head oyster plates are being reproduced.

7" d, majolica, 6 molded shells, 5 pink edged, violet, and gold shell wells, one white shell well, green seaweed and coral ground, Wedgwood, ... **900.00**

7 1/2" d, 5 well, gold outlined mottled pink ground wells, dk pink border w/gold accents, France, late 19th C, ... **370.00**

8" d, 5 wells, gold starfish in center, sea green wells w/gold scalloped edging, Limoges, ... **220.00**

8" w, oct, scalloped shell, 5 molded oyster shells, yellow and pink tinged, med blue ground, gold rim, c1880, ... **100.00**

8 1/4" d, 5 wells, center lemon well, magenta and yellow florals, sm blue flowers and green leaves, white ground, "Haviland & Co. Limoges; H. & Co. L" mks, $38.00

8 1/4" d

5 Wells

Brushed gold oyster shaped wells, scallop shell sauce well in center, fluted and dot molded border w/sm red centered blue flowers, green leaves, Germany, ... **135.00**

Center sauce well, HP Delft style blue painted Dutch scenes in each well, blue edged wells, Weimar Germany, c1900-20, ... **535.00**

6 Wells

Band of roses on outer border, gold outlined shells, center sauce well, gilt dentil rim, Haviland, ... **200.00**

Oct, gold outlined oyster shaped shells, border of blue dots w/gold vert chains, med blue rim, France, ... **275.00**

8 3/8" d, 4 gold to bronzed edged oyster shaped wells, HP mussels in each shell, lg scallop shell lemon holder and 2 sm condiment wells, swirl molded ground w/fishscale designs and purple painted sea grass, Germany, ... **225.00**

8 1/2" d

Blue dashed outlined wells, 2 wells w/bust of male or female Breton peasant, 4 wells w/red single stroke half flowerhead, band of red centered blue circlets, center sauce well w/green circlets, ivory ground, blue lined rim, "HenRiot Quimper" mk, ... **395.00**

Five raised gilt swirl outlined blue wells w/gold floral sprig, center sauce well, lt blue ground, Limoges, ... **265.00**

8 5/8" d, majolica, 6 pink edged black shell molded wells, teal blue center lemon well, teal blue molded ground between wells, Longchamps, ... **695.00**

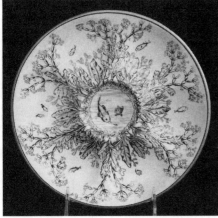

8 3/4" d, 6 wells, center sauce well, brown transfer, gold rim, "George Jones" mk, $495.00

8 3/4" d

Five raised oyster shaped shells, relief molded seaweed and shell bits, overall white glaze, "green H & Co." mk, ... **300.00**

Five swirled wells, center sauce well, pink ground w/spattered gold border, "CFH GDM" mk, ... **300.00**

8 7/8" d, 6 shell wells, center sauce well, transfers of floral sprigs in each well and border, gold lined rim, Carlsbad, Austria, ... **150.00**

9" d

Center sauce well, 6 oval wells, lg side cracker well, "Bombay" pattern, blue oriental flower designs in each well, white ground, Minton, ... **975.00**

Five molded swirl shells, Center well, transfer of sm blue and yellow flowing flowers and foliage, gold rim, "C.F.H." mk, c1880, ... **85.00**

Raised pink coral in center, pink rim, Brownfield, c1883, ... **400.00**

Lg molded shell form w/5 swirled wells, raised pink coral in center, pink rim, Brownfield, ... **400.00**

Majolica, green center well w/band of white shells, 6 green wells w/molded cowry shells between, lt blue reverse, "imp MINTON" mk, set of 8, ... **3,100.00**

Six oyster shaped wells, cream w/multicolored local florals, red, green, and black striped center sauce well, cream ground w/green and brown sponged rim, "HenRiot Quimper" mk, ... **100.00**

Six pink and blue shells, lg shell for lemons, center well surrounded by pink flowerheads, green shells between wells, Minton, ... **100.00**

Six molded med brown scallop shells, dk brown center sauce well, dk brown ground, Sarreguemines, ... **50.00**

Six molded wells, white glaze, gold edged center well, gold lined rim, Limoges, ... **110.00**

Six wells w/center sauce well, molded coral separating wells, overall white glaze, "green H. & Co./L" mk, ... **45.00**

Six white molded shells, pink center sauce well, lt blue ground, ... **70.00**

Yellow lemon center well, 6 dk red to brown oyster shell shaped wells, dk green spatter ground, Vallauris, ... **60.00**

9" w, crescent shape, 5 pink oyster shaped wells, turquoise ribbed ground w/molded grey clam shells, 2 sm yellow shells, Germany, ... **175.00**

9 1/4" d

Art Deco style, brown edged yellow hex center well, 6 elongated hex pink edged oyster wells, green stylized water plants between wells, blue rim, ... **275.00**

Center well, 6 side wells, white ground w/floral sprigs in each well, "K. & G. Luneville" mk, ... **95.00**

Six lt green and pink wells and fan shaped lemon well, pink flowerheads on lt yellow ground around center sauce well, med green ground between wells, Minton, ... **100.00**

Six gold outlined pink shaded oyster shaped wells, salmon pink center well, turquoise ground between, Bohemia, ... **100.00**

Six side wells, center sauce well, side kidney shaped lemon well, Aesthetic style "blue Bombay" pattern, Minton, ... **595.00**

Seven well, 6 oyster, side lemon well, center sauce holder, blue printed "Bombay" pattern in each well, Japanese fans and carp, Minton, ... **595.00**

9 3/8" d, 6 wells, molded starfish in center, spiral shells on border, mustard yellow glaze, Vallauris, ... **35.00**

9 1/2" d, 6 wells

Center Sauce Well

Brown edged scallop shells w/blue int lines, green

seaweed border, brown
bamboo rim, France,
.... **255.00**
Rose to ivory shaded shell wells,
sea green ground,
Rudolstadt, ... **145.00**
Scattered red roses, yellow
daisies, green leaves, white
ground, "KG LUNEVILLE
FRANCE DEMI
PORCELAINE" mk, ... **55.00**
Molded browned edged white
scallop shells, center sauce
well, green basketweave
ground, Longchamp,
.... **120.00**
Molded half shells, center sauce
well, molded relief of
seaweed between wells,
overall brown glaze,
Sarreguemines, ... **50.00**
9 7/8" sq, 5 molded shell wells,
center sauce well, gilt and blue
enameled flowers, fish, and birds
on border, scalloped rim, Austria,
(A), ... **170.00**
10" d, Majolica
Six fish head molded wells,
center sauce well, green
shades w/brown accents,
unmkd, ... **195.00**
Three molded shell lemon wells
in center, 6 molded scallop
shells on border, blue shaded
edges, blue coral between,
sm button feet, Vielillard,
.... **375.00**
Three turquoise, 3 purple shell
wells, purple center sauce
well, brown ground w/green
seaweed, unmkd, ... **495.00**
Yellow lemon center well, 6 dk
green-black shaded shell
molded wells, France,
.... **490.00**
10" l x 9" w, 5 pink edged oyster
shaped wells, center sauce well,
dbl lemon well on side, black
pearlized ground, gold trim,
Germany, ... **100.00**
10" w, half moon shape, 5 pink shell
shaped wells, green coral, brown
ground, Holdcroft, ... **1,300.00**
12 1/2" d, 3 lg, 2 sm blue outlined
and blue netted shells, 6 side
wells w/blue and yellow flowers,
separated by blue lines,
Portugal, ... **150.00**

Server
13 1/8" d, 2 center and 10 side
molded white scallop shell wells,
green basketweave ground,
brown striped rope rims,
Longchamp, ... **170.00**
14" l, majolica, center dk gold
starfish w/cream sauce well, 12
cream oyster wells w/green
border, Sarreguemines,
.... **600.00**
17 3/4" l x 11 7/8" w, 16 red wells, 2
lemon wells, blue-green textured
ground, 6 plates, 8 7/8" d, 6 red
wells, lemon well, blue-green
textured ground, Vallauris,
.... **175.00**
Server and Plates, server, 15 1/2" l x 13"
w, 12 plates, 9 1/2" d, server w/12
white shell shaped wells and center
well, blue-green ground, red center
starfish w/arms between wells,
plates w/6 wells, Sarreguemines,
.... **1,445.00**

1862

PARIAN

English/Continental
Early 1840s to 20th Century

History: Parian had a slightly translucent,
natural creamy white body fired to a matte
finish. It was introduced in the early 1840s
and remained popular during the entire
Victorian era. Parian's strong resemblance
to marble appealed to the Victorians
because it suggested elegance,
opulence, and wealth.

The best parian examples were characterized by the delicacy of the ware's texture. Its excellent molding versatility made
it suitable for figures, utilitarian wares, and
even floral jewelry pieces.

Copeland is one of the many firms that
have made parian china from the 1840s to
the present. Pieces often were marked
with an impressed "Copeland." After 1862
Minton impressed its parian with the name
of the company and occasionally added
the impressed year mark.

Parian also was manufactured by Bel-
leeck in Ireland, and by Coalport, Goss,
Robinson and Leadbeater, Wedgwood,
and Royal Worcester in England. Gustavs-
burg and Rorstrand in Sweden carried

parian wares as part of their line. Most
leading firms marked their parian wares.
Smaller firms were less likely to do so.

References: Paul Atterbury, Editor, *The
Parian Phenomenon*, Shepton
Beauchamp, 1989; G.A. Godden,
Victorian Porcelain, Herbert Jenkins,
1961; C.& D. Shinn, *The Illustrated Guide
to Victorian Parian China*, Barrie &
Jenkins, 1971.

Museum: Victoria & Albert Museum,
London, England.

Cheese Dish, Cov, 8" d, overall relief
molded flowers and leaves, flower
knob, ... **295.00**
Comport, 16" h x 11 1/2" d, pierced
bowl set on leaves, supported by 3
cherubs holding grapes, pedestal
base w/scroll feet, unmkd, ... **550.00**
Creamer, 3 1/2" h, relief molded
Cherubs at play, white glazed, "T. J.
& J. Mayer Longport" mk,
.... **125.00**
Drinking scene, man in vineyard on
reverse, white, ... **75.00**

*Figure, 9 1/2" h, Queen Alexandra, Robinson
and Leadbeater, $375.00*

Figure
6 1/4" h, seated young boy reading
book, c1850, ... **250.00**
7 1/2" h, "The Defeat" design, child
seated at work table w/bowl,
c1850, ... **250.00**

Amphora

Vase, 12 3/4" h, Ernst Wahliss, ...**18,000.00**

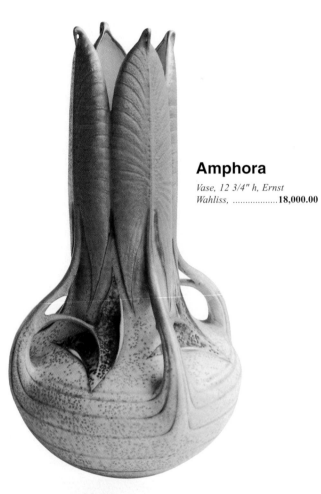

Bing and Grondahl

Jar, Cov, 9 5/8" h, ...**14,000.00**

Bing and Grondahl

Vase, 16" h, artist sgd, ...**21,000.00**

193

Boch Freres

Vase, 10 1/4" h, "Boch Freres Made in Belgium"
*mk, ...***3,500.00**

Bow

*Mug, 3 1/2" h, sprigged design, c1750, ...***1,295.00**

Bow

Sweetmeat Dish, 7 1/4" h x 10" w, c1760, ... **2,650.00**

Bretby

*Vase, 9" h, 3 handles, (A), ...***100.00**

Clarice Cliff

*Jardiniere, 7" h, (A), ...***500.00**

Clews

*Plate, 8" d, "imp CLEWS" mk, ...***245.00**

Denmark

*Vase, 16" h, Hermann August
Kahler, "imp DENMARK" mk,
c1900, ...***4,500.00**

Derby

*Cooler, 12" h, removable insert, c1790, ...***2,850.00**

195

Derby

Sauceboat, 7 1/8" l x 5 1/8" h, cos lettuce, c1758-62, pr, ...**2,600.00**

Doulton Lambeth

Jardiniere, 9" w, "imp DOULTON LAMBETH SLATER'S PATENT" mk, (A), ...**150.00**

Royal Doulton

Vase, 13" h, sgd "Noke," Royal Doulton, ...**28,000.00**

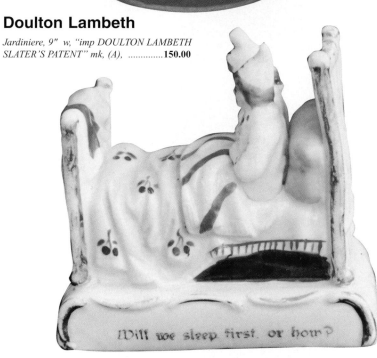

Fairing

Fairing, 3 5/8" h, ...**175.00**

Flow Blue

Platter, 12" l x 8 1/2" w, "Melbourne"
*pattern, ...***285.00**

France

*Asparagus Plate, 10" d, Longchamps, ...***195.00**

France

*Bowl, 8 3/4" d, sgd "Andrew Methey", ...***8,500.00**

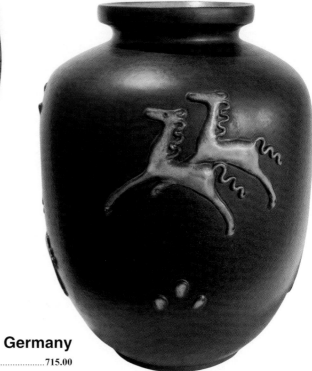

Germany

*Vase, 14" h, (A), ...***715.00**

Ironstone - Pattern

*Soup Tureen, 12" h x 14 1/4" H-H, w/undertray, 15 1/2" l, and ladle, c1880, ...***1,650.00**

Haviland

Vase, 15 1/2" h, sgd "Ernst Chaplet,"
*rosary mk, ...***45,000.00**

Luster

*Teapot, 9 1/2" l x 5 1/4" h, ...***225.00**

Lowestoft

*Pickle Dish, 5 1/4" w, c1757, ...***5,000.00**

Luster

Plaque, 9" l x 8 1/4" w, c1815-30, ...**425.00**

Majolica

Plaque, 9 1/2" d, Palissy, ...**1,400.00**

Majolica

Planter, 14 1/4" l, France,
.................................**5,500.00**

Majolica

Centerpiece, 14 1/4" l x 10" h, "imp COPELAND" mk,
....**4,100.00**

Meigh

*Plate, 9 3/4" d, "Stone China" mk, ...***165.00**

Malicorne

*Planter, 13" l x 4 1/8" h, ...***450.00**

Martin Brothers

*Vessel, 9 1/4" h, (A), ...***19,800.00**

Massier

Wall Pocket, 14" l x 10" w, Clement Massier,
*...***23,000.00**

Minton

Plate, 9 1/4" d, ...**110.00**

Minton

Plate, 10 1/2" d, "Bombay" pattern, c1840, ...**225.00**

Moorcroft

Vase, 12 1/2" h, (A), ...**6,600.00**

Old Paris and Paris

Plate, 8 1/4" d, named view on reverse, c1820,
....**450.00**

Relief Molded Jug

7 1/2" h, "Silenus" pattern, ...**400.00**

Quimper

Platter, 17 1/2" H-H x 10 1/2" w, Porquier Beau, ...**2,200.00**

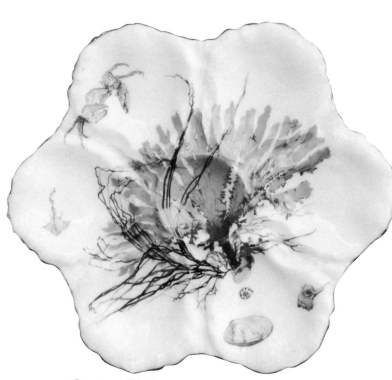

Oyster Plate

9" d, "H. & Co., Haviland & Co." mks, ...**450.00**

Relief Molded Jug

10 1/4" h, "Family" pattern, pewter lid,
"T. J. & J. Mayer" mk, ...**375.00**

Royal Copenhagen

Dish, 16" w, dtd 17-2-28,
....**28,000.00**

Royal Bonn

Vase, 12 1/2" h, (A), ...**605.00**

Ridgway

*Jugs, 7" , 7 3/4" , 9 3/4" h, "imp
anchor" mks,* **1,200.00**

Royal Copenhagen

Vase, 11 1/4" h, ...**5,500.00**

Royal Copenhagen

Vase, 9 3/4" h, sgd "Salto," **18,000.00**

Royal Worcester

Plate, 9" d, purple mk, ...**125.00**

Rozenberg

Vase, 5" h, (A), ...**1,760.00**

Ruskin

Vase, 4" h, (A), ...**1,100.00**

Sarreguemines

Jug, 7 1/2" h, "Puck," "imp SARREGUEMINES" mk,
....**395.00**

Sevres

Vase, 6" h, sgd "Taxtile Doat," (A), ... **1,320.00**

Sevres

Vase, 7 3/4" h, imp mk, (A),
....**440.00**

Slipware

Pitcher, 5" h, Jaspe, ...**110.00**

Spode

*Cup and Saucer, Handleless, "Tobacco Leaf" pattern, "blue SPODE Stone China" mk, ...***165.00**

Staffordshire - General

Hen on Nest, 6 3/4" h x 7 1/4" w, bisque,
*...***375.00**

Staffordshire - Romantic

Plate, 9 3/8" d, "Washington" pattern,
*"Washington E.W. & S." mk, ...***125.00**

Staffordshire - Romantic

Vegetable Bowl, Cov, 7 1/4" h x 12 3/8" l x 8 3/4" w,
*"Canova" pattern, ...***695.00**

Swansea

Pitcher, 9 3/4" h, c1815,
....**750.00**

Teplitz

*Vase, 9 3/4" h, pr, (A), ..***800.00**

Toby Jug

*9" h, ...***495.00**

Wedgwood - Basalt

*Basalt-Urn, Cov, 13 1/8" h, "imp
WEDGWOOD" mk, c1880,*
....**5,650.00**

Wedgwood - Jasper

Jasper-Potpourri, 15 1/2" h, "imp WEDGWOOD" mk, c1810, ...**5,000.00**

Wedgwood - Luster

Luster, Jardiniere, 9 3/8" d, "Fairyland Luster-Candlemass," **25,000.00**

Worcester

Teapot, 6 1/4" h, Dr. Wall period, "blue crescent" mk, c1770, ...**1,150.00**

Worcester

Serving Dish, 12 3/4" l x 9 1/2" w, blue scale, "chop" mk, c1770, pr, ...**6,325.00**

Zsolnay

Vase, 10" h, Henry Darilek, (A), ...**6,600.00**

7 1/2" w, 2 recumbent King Charles spaniels resting atop each other, shaped rect base w/gilt braid and tassels, Copeland, c1855, (A), ... **670.00**

8" h, bust of Oliver Wendell Holmes, sq base, Robinson & Leadbeater, chips, ... **85.00**

8 1/2" h, bust of Lord Burton, Hewett & Leadbeater, "inscribed A. Willis Sculptor Feb 26th 1909," white, ... **165.00**

9" h

Bust of angel sleeping in enfolded wings, draped pedestal, "imp COPELAND" mk, ... **800.00**

Bust of Count D'Orsay, "W.T. Copeland, Spode Works Stoke Staffordshire Potteries" mk, dtd 1852, ... **125.00**

9 1/2" h

Bust of Clytie, circ base, c1860, ... **150.00**

Bust of Shakespeare, ... **95.00**

Little standing girl crying, broken bowl on oct base, ... **125.00**

9 3/4" h, Hermes seated on rocks, winged sandals, c1850-60, base chip, ... **345.00**

10" h, lion seated on haunches, oval base, c1870, (A), ... **300.00**

Figure, 10 1/4" h, unmkd, **$400.00**

10 1/2" h, bust of Sir Isaac Pitman, Robinson Leadbeater, white, ... **395.00**

11 1/4" h, "Dorothea," woman seated on rocks, shoes and satchel at feet on base, unmkd, England, (A), ... **265.00**

11 1/2" h

Bust of Apollo, circ socle, ... **370.00**

Standing boy grooming dog, c1850, ... **300.00**

12" h x 12" w,

"Paul and Virginia," Copeland, restruck fingers, ... **1,085.00**

Shepherd holding hat and staff, reclining goat on base, unmkd, ... **160.00**

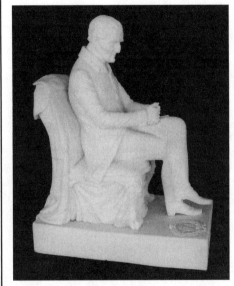

Figure, 12" h, "Duke of Wellington," Samuel Alcock, c1850, **$750.00**

12 1/4" h, mother kneeling by infant in cradle, "incised A. Carrier-Belleuse," Minton, c1872, (A), ... **1,765.00**

13" h

"Autumn," draped classic woman holding wheat sheaves in arm, circ base, chips, ... **200.00**

"Dorothea," seated woman w/armor, Minton, c1868, (A), ... **265.00**

13 1/2" h, girl wearing chain mail, and sword; and barefoot girl, shoes and sack nearby, each seated on rock, John Bell, Minton, pr, (A), ... **495.00**

14" h x 12" w, nude woman seated on crouching lion, cherub,

serpent, lambs, and grapes on oval base, repairs, ... **1,125.00**

14 1/2" h

Bust of Prince of Wales, "inscribed Albert Edward" and "Art Union of London 1864," Brown-Westhead, Moore & Co., white, chip, ... **950.00**

Semi-nude nymph emerging from foliage, holding inverted amphora jar, circ base w/"R & B," Robinson & Leadbeater, c1890, ... **725.00**

15" h

Bust of "Alexandra," waisted circ socle, raised title, Copeland, c1868, (A), ... **440.00**

Standing woman holding child on shoulder, bulrushes in opposite hand, circ base, unmkd, ... **125.00**

15 1/4" h, "Evangeline and Benedict," unmkd, ... **875.00**

15 1/2" h

"Bell's Miranda," girl seated on rock, flowing hair, conch shell at feet, "imp Minton" mk, (A), ... **440.00**

Nude boy carrying lamb on shoulder, "imp GERMANY" mk, ... **600.00**

"Young England's Sister," young girl holding book and pencil, Copeland, c1879, base chips, (A), ... **235.00**

15 3/4" h, "The Bather," classic semi-nude woman seated on rocks w/flowers, placing foot in water, ... **770.00**

17" h, "The Three Graces," draped and nude women embracing, oval stepped base, ... **275.00**

17 3/4" h, "Abyssinian Slave," standing semi-nude woman, beads on neck, hands clasped on thigh, "incised Abyssinian Slave sc Sept 1868" on base, Minton, (A), ... **1,410.00**

19" h, standing Queen Victoria, mourning clothes, holding Bible, ... **795.00**

19 1/4" h, wood nymph, seated nude w/deer and fawn, "inscribed C.B. Birch," England, c1865, (A), ... **1,525.00**

19 1/2" h, "Sunshine," standing female shading eyes, holding

flowers in apron, titled tree stump base, Copeland, c1858, (A), ... **747.00**

20 1/4" h, "Niobe and Daughter," mother shielding child w/gown, England, c1870, rim chips, (A), ... **1,000.00**

20 3/4" h
Bust of "Daphne," waisted circ socle, England, (A), ... **2,470.00**
"Temperance," standing figure pouring water into wine ewer at feet, Minton, c1874, (A), ... **825.00**

22" h, "Reaper and the Flowers," winged female holding baby in arms, Copeland, missing finger, (A), ... **1,175.00**

25" h, "Chastity," standing robed woman w/flowers under arm, raised circ plinth, "imp J. Durnam SC pub Sep 1 1865," chips, (A), ... **1,295.00**

27 1/2" h, "Rape of the Sabines," standing nude bearded man grasping female in arms, old man kneeling on rock base, England, ... **6,000.00**

43 1/4" h, flower seller, woman holding apron full of flowers, flowers overhead, tree stump on circ base, England, chips, (A), ... **7,345.00**

Jug
4 1/2" h, vert fluted body and neck, Minton, ... **50.00**
7 1/2" h, raised blue Grecian figures, trees, and columns, raised head on handle, white ground, unmkd, ... **165.00**

Pitcher
6" h, red-orange Greek key around collar, vert fluted body, orange-red Vitruvian scroll base, ... **325.00**

Vase
5" h, relief modeled woman's face front and reverse w/flowing hair, beaded necklace, molded leaf top, white, ... **60.00**
5 1/4" h, bowl shape, flared base, relief of dancing classic women playing instruments, unmkd, ... **75.00**
7" h, cylinder shape, white relief of birds in foliage, open floral rim, blue ground, c1850, ... **250.00**

PATE-SUR-PATE (PASTE ON PASTE)

Austria, England, France, and Germany
c1860 to 1900s

History: During the early 1860s, several Sevres potteries attempted to copy the Chinese technique of pate-sur-pate. Pate-sur-pate designs exhibit a cameo-like decorative motif achieved by using tinted parian as the background and adding layers of white parian slip that then were carved into the design before the firing. When fired, the layers of white parian slip becomes semi-translucent and vitrified. The dark ground shows through the thinner parts.

Marc Louis Solon, who trained at Sevres, brought the Victorian pate-sur-pate process to England in 1870 when he began employment at Minton. At first he depicted tall, thin classical female figures in diaphanous drapery. Later, he expanded his repertoire to include children and cupids. Each creation was unique and signed.

Solon enjoyed a great reputation for his pate-sur-pate pieces. Since the painstaking pate-sur-pate technique was exceptionally slow and the market demand was great, Solon trained a series of apprentices while at Minton, the most talented of which were A. Birks and L. Birks. Solon worked at Minton until 1904. After retirement, he worked free-lance until he died in 1913.

Not all pate-sur-pate examples were made at Minton. Royal Worcester, Grainger-Worcester, the Crescent Potteries of George Jones, and several other firms manufactured pate-sur-pate pieces. F. Schenk produced many examples for Crescent Pottery at Stoke. These pieces were inferior and repetitive when compared to those made at Minton and Worcester.

Meissen, Berlin, and Vienna on the Continent were known for the production of pate-sur-pate. Pieces from these factories lacked the finesse of Solon's works and tended to be heavy and Germanic in style.

References: Paul Atterbury & Maureen Batkin, *Dictionary of Minton*, Antique Collectors' Club Ltd. 1996; Bernard Bumpers, *Pate-Sur-Pate*, Barrie & Jenkins, 1992; G.A. Godden, *Victorian Porcelain*, Herbert Jenkins, 1961.

Museums: National Collection of Fine Arts, Smithsonian Institution, Washington DC; Victoria & Albert Museum, London, England.

Collecting Hints: Collectors should be aware that some George Jones wares are being sold as Minton products in today's marketplace.

Box, Cov
3 1/4" d, cov design of white slip design of winged cherub dropping flower petals on mauve ground, raised gilt band w/mauve enamel dots, aqua blue lozenges w/gilt swirl margins, body w/purple-brown band, aqua trim, gilt loops and rims, "blue X'd swords" mk, ... **2,000.00**
4" d, white slip design of satyr and dancers, blue ground, Limoges, ... **575.00**
4 3/8" l x 3 7/8" w, white slip design of 2 cherubs w/lute in gilt leaf surround on cov, cobalt ground, sgd "Tharaud," Limoges, ... **300.00**
5" d
Slip painted seated nude woman, standing winged cherub, trees at sides, band of ivy around body, blue ground, Limoges, ... **350.00**
White slip painted scene of 2 cherubs in clouds holding ring on blue ground on cov, white body, Camille Tharaud Limoges, ... **100.00**

Charger
13 3/4" d, white slip design of Bacchante nymph pouring wine from vessel to kneeling Pan in gilt surround on celadon green ground, cream border w/Art Nouveau style gilt stylized and enameled forget-me-nots and roses, "blue scepter, iron-red orb" mks, c1895, (A), ... **5,380.00**

Coffee Can and Saucer
band of white slip decorated flowers and foliage, green ground, gilt rims, Locke & Co., (A), ... **195.00**

Panel
4 7/8" w, fan shape, white slip painted nymphs and putti at fountain, grey ground, Minton, pr, (A), ... **475.00**

Pilgrim Bottle, Flattened, Circ Firm
6" h, white slip decorated scene of 3 putti playing w/bird in florals, carved gilt edged slip decorated lt blue daisy and buds, green foliage on sides, olive green ground, gilt rim and feet, Minton, c1880, (A), ... **7,170.00**
10" h, peacock blue ground w/water as putti in ribbon tied gilt berried pate-sur-pate surround, reverse w/fishing trophy or Earth as putti w/grapes in same surround,

gardening trophy on reverse, gilt handles, Minton, c1875, pr, (A), ... **14,340.00**

Plaque

4 1/4" h x 2 3/4" w, oval, white slip of nymph in thin gown holding grapes overhead or grapes in gown, dk green ground, artist sgd, pr, ... **1,000.00**

6 7/8" h x 5 3/4" w, rect, white slip lightly clad nymph holding anthemion leaf fans in each hand, putti in flight, salmon ground, sgd "L.A. Birks," England, c1900, (A), ... **2,630.00**

7" l x 5" w, rect, white slip decorated design of Cossack riding horse, cobalt ground, Limoges, ... **495.00**

7 1/2" h x 5 3/4" w, rect, white slip decoration of woman w/spear and putti, pale blue ground, France, (A), ... **530.00**

8 1/2" l x 6 1/8" w, rect, white slip scene of recumbent nymph on terrace serenaded by 2 putti, blue ground, giltwood frame, Limoges, (A), ... **5,019.00**

9 1/2" h x 6 3/4" w, rect, "Water" and "Air," white slip decorated nymph holding basket of fish before putto, or nymph in forest w/putto shooting bow and arrow, grey ground, sgd "Auguste Riffaterre," Limoges, c1890, pr, (A), ... **4,780.00**

10 5/8" h, oval, white cameo of classical female playing harp, blue ground, Limoges, (A), ... **295.00**

11 3/4" l x 7 3/4" w, rect, white slip scene of shepherd and shepherdess resting w/sheep in landscape, lt coral ground, artist sgd, Sevres, c1865, (A), ... **880.00**

14 1/4" h x 10 1/4" w, rect, white slip decorated Dawn flanked by putto blowing horn and another holding nest of chicks, or dusk flanked by sleeping putto and other holding torch, olive green ground w/gilt stars, sgd "L. Solon," Minton, pr, (A), ... **31,070.00**

Plate

9 1/2" d, gilt scrolled central roundel, border of white slip decorated dolphins and seashells on sky

blue ground, geometric reticulated border, sgd "T. Mason," Minton, set of 5, (A), ... **6,485.00**

11" d, white slip design of 2 nymphs beside rock pool, tree at side, dk green ground, gold rim, Frederick Schenk, George Jones, c1880, (A), ... **1,575.00**

Vase, 8 1/2" h, white cameo on lilac ground, pink and blue enameled flowers, green leaves, med blue ground, gilt trim, "Made in Germany" mark, **$850.00**

Vase

4" h, teardrop shape, 2 loop handles, narrow flared neck, white slip design of seated woman w/arm extended on pink panel front and reverse, cobalt ground w/gold leaves, Heubach, c1912, ... **90.00**

6 3/8" h, globular shape w/flat sides, white slip design of woman and child fishing in gilt border, holly leaf band on neck, green-brown ground, gold ring handles, England, (A), ... **880.00**

7 1/4" h, slip painted Greek woman kneeling, releasing 2 doves, blue ground, gilt banding, Limoges, ... **400.00**

8 1/2" h, oviform, white slip painted standing nymph and 2 putti, ribbon tied laurel swag, dk brown ground, gilt scale shoulder, sgd "Birks," Minton, c1900, (A), ... **4,780.00**

10 1/2" h, ovoid, white cameos of cherubs w/smoke trails, mint green ground, white "Man in the Moon" face handle w/flowing beard trailing to body, ... **400.00**

Vase, 11 1/2" h, white slip decorated Cupid on front, bird on branch w/acorns and oak leaves, celadon ground, gilt bronze putto mask and leaf handles, sq base, pr, **$3,800.00**

12 1/4" h, shield shape, circ socle, sq plinth, white slip decorated flying putti in clouds, dk teal blue ground, gilt anthemion on neck and socle, gilt floral molded vert ring handles, Louis Solon, Minton, c1895, pr, (A), ... **8,050.00**

PEARLWARE

English
c1780-c1865

History: Pearlware, a variation of white creamware body, had a slightly bluish tint due to the addition of a small quantity of cobalt to the glaze. Pearlware was closer in general appearance and whiteness to porcelain than creamware. Wedgwood first made pearlware about 1779.

Pearlware was made mostly in tablewares. Among the leading Staffordshire manufacturers were Herculaneum, Phillips Longport, Davenport, Clews, T. Mayer, Enoch Wood, Rogers, and Stubbs. Potteries at Leeds and Swansea also produced pearlware.

Polychrome floral decorations on pearlware became popular about 1800 and continued for approximately twenty years. These designs, usually in yellow, green, orange, or on silver luster resist, were most commonly found on pitchers and jugs. Mocha decoration also was used on pearlware bodies.

Vast quantities of pearlware were shipped to the United States between 1790 and 1830. Some firms, such as Enoch Wood, produced pearlware specifically for the American market. Shell-edge plates were decorated with the American eagle and shield in polychrome; other plates depicted prints of American ships with polychrome flags. Later blue transfer prints of American landmarks were applied to pitchers, plates, and chamber pots.

Museum: Victoria & Albert Museum, London, England.

Bowl, 6 1/2" d, Salopian style yellow, green, and blue transfer printed rural scene of milk maid milking cow, cottage and church in bkd, repairs, ... **575.00**

Coffeepot, 10 1/2" h, high dome shape, blue printed "Fallow Deer" pattern, repairs to lid and body, c1820, ... **445.00**

Cup and Saucer
Blue printed scene of oriental man seated under arches, trees, and table, flowerhead border on int of cup and saucer, c1810, ... **75.00**
Underglazed brown transfer w/yellow, aqua, orange, and green scene of figures on bridge w/umbrella and oriental buildings, floral border, ochre rims, c1815, ... **185.00**

Cup Plate, 3 1/2" d, "Girl Musician" pattern, med blue transfer, Riley, ... **150.00**

Dish
8 1/4" d, 3 classical figures in floral wreath surround, border band of florals, rose red underglaze transfer w/yellow, green, blue, brown, and orange accents, ... **130.00**
10 1/8" l, oval, pierced diamond and heart border, molded hanging swags, white, c1785, ... **630.00**

Figure
2 1/4" h x 3 1/2" l, reclining lamb, brown legs, ears, and tail, lt green base, (A), ... **165.00**
3 1/4" h x 2 7/8" l, seated dog, brown and gold spots, (A), ... **511.00**

Figure, 8 3/4", 9 1/4" h, Minerva and Poseidon, yellow and white clothes, turquoise dolphin, green lined base, pr, A-$380.00

6" h x 8" l, standing horse, pink and purple luster spots, green rect base, c1800, ... **5,500.00**
7" h, boy wearing red coat, yellow knickers, carrying nest of birds, green stump base, (A), ... **275.00**

Figure, 8 1/4" h, orange, green, and yellow, (A), **$125.00**

Invalid Feeder, 6 1/4" l, overall blue veining design, c1820, ... **170.00**

Jug
5 3/4" h, named bust of George Washington under spout, black transfer, blue stripes and hanging swags on neck, blue stripe on foot, Herculaneum, ...**15,000.00**
6 3/4" h, "A Token of Gratitude and Respect," reverse w/"Daniel and Mary Cotton," flower spray under spout, c1820, ... **185.00**
6 5/8" h, relief molded "Royal Sufferers" on side, "Duke of York" on reverse, molded acanthus leaves, oak leaves, and ribbons, pink, green, brown, and black, crazing, (A), ... **495.00**
11 1/4" l, black sponged cow nursing her black sponged calf, canted rect base sponged green w/pink dots and blue fret designs, c1800, (A), ... **7,768.00**
17 3/4" h, bust of Shakespeare, red lined green cape, gold tassels on yellow vest, brown-black beard and hair, marbled socle base, early 19th C, (A), ... **1,950.00**

Mug
4 7/8" h, black transfer of "Farmer's Arms" design, winter scene, and poem, molded frog on int, band of black leaves on int rim, ... **350.00**
5" h, black printed w/polychrome accented scene of Duke of York on horseback, "His Royal highness FREDERICK DUKE OF YORK" on rim, c1794, hairline crack, (A), ... **1,200.00**

Mustard Jar, Cov, 2 7/8" h, blue streaked center band, blue lined base, blue streaked cov, ... **140.00**

Pickle Dish, 5 1/4" l x 5" w, leaf form, blue painted veins and sawtooth rim, "imp Rogers" mk, c1820, pr, ...**275.00**

Plate
6 1/2" d, classic scene of boy and goat under statue, bordered by trees, bridges, and cottages, med blue transfer, indented rim, c1820, ... **50.00**
6 3/4" d, dk brown stylized Chinese house, weeping willows, and fencing in center, orange inner border line, dk brown feathered scalloped rim, England, c1780, ... **300.00**

7 1/2" d, chinoiserie scene of pagoda, man in boat on lake, lg rocks, and tree, inner border of geometrics, border of hanging florals, blue and white, molded rope rim, unmkd, c1840, ... **40.00**

7 3/4" d, 2 deer before hunting lodge in center, houses and deer on border, black transfer w/brown, tan, and green accents, c1820, ... **420.00**

8 1/2" d, oct, scattered floral sprigs in center, hanging swags from corners, blue and white, blue lined rim, ... **200.00**

9 1/2" d

Blue transfer of classic buildings w/2 people and ox on road, floral and entwined tree border, geometric rim, c1820, ... **35.00**

"Chrysanthemum" pattern, 4 cobalt and white flowerheads, iron-red and green florals, Herculaneum, c1810, ... **530.00**

9 3/4" d, "Rural Scenery-Reaper" pattern, med blue transfer, "Bathwell & Goodwill" mk, ... **250.00**

10" d, castle tower, stone bridge and cattle, floral, leaf, and grape, border, blue transfer, ... **90.00**

Pitcher, 7" h, brown transfer w/green, blue, and yellow accents, $1,150.00

Platter

11 3/4" l x 9 1/4" w, "Village Church" pattern, flowerhead border, med blue transfer, combed back, c1825, ... **450.00**

17 3/4" l x 13" w, combed back, family walking w/dogs, and pony,

near stone bridge, castle ruins in bkd, med blue transfer, ... **595.00**

19 1/4" l x 14 3/8" w, Italian scene of Rome, St. Peters, castle Sant Angelo, bridge and boaters, med blue transfer, ... **650.00**

Punch Bowl, 9 1/2" d, blue stylized flower sprig on int, blue zigzag int border, ext w/blue vert herringbone bands alternating w/blue zigzag on red ground between blue horiz lines, repaired chip, ... **950.00**

Salt, 3 3/4" h, oval, ftd, fluted, blue underglaze hanging swags of leaves and rim, c1800, ... **330.00**

Sauceboat, 7 1/4" l, fluted, blue painted floral sprigs on sides, blue streaked rim, c1790, ... **350.00**

Sugar Bowl, Cov

5 1/2" h, black printed Adam Buck style classic figures on sides, drape on borders, flower knob, ... **425.00**

6" h, paneled, dk brown stripes w/blue and gold swags and green accents, swan knob, (A), ... **385.00**

Teabowl and Saucer, bold painted blue flowers and stems, ... **40.00**

Tea Caddy, Barrel Shape

3 3/4" h, blue bird and bird's nest, white ground, c1750, ... **475.00**

4 1/8" h, black printed classical scenes of musicians and scholars on sides, neo-classical designs on shoulder, ... **385.00**

Teapot, 6 3/4" h x 8 3/4" w, blue oriental figures, green streaking, c1790, repairs, $1,400.00

Teapot

3 1/2" h

Band of brown agate decoration, molded vert bamboo on base, flowerhead knob, ear handle, ... **2,100.00**

Rural scene on side, hatch and geometric borders, blue transfers, c1800, ... **175.00**

4 1/2" h, center band of mustard, blue, and brown foliage, brown border lines, ... **695.00**

6" h x 9" w, paneled, underglazed blue painted Chinese pavilions or panels of trees, molded designs, green drip on shoulder, 6 sm feet, figural widow knob, hairline on base, ... **560.00**

7" h, bulbous, lg brown-red cabbage rose, green and yellow leaves on sides, repaired cov, (A), ... **100.00**

Tray, 7 5/8" l x 6 1/4" w, oval, molded woven center w/cobalt geometric design, open vert looped border w/stitched rim, cobalt accents, c1790, ... **145.00**

Tulipiere, 6 3/4" h, fan shape, 5 tubes, HP chains of sm enamel flowers, blue feather edge, chips and hairline, (A), ... **495.00**

PIANO BABIES

England and Germany
19th Century

History: Piano babies, primarily in bisque, ranged in size from two to twelve inches long. They were popular additions to Victorian parlors, usually found on the top of a piano.

Piano babies were produced in a variety of poses from crawling, sitting, or lying on their stomach, to lying on their backs playing with their toes. Some babies were dressed; some were nude.

The most popular manufacturer was Heubach Brothers of Germany. Other identified makers include Hertwig and Company and Royal Doulton.

3" h, bisque, seated baby, hand on ground, blue and yellow ball in lap, blond hair, white nighty, ... **90.00**

3 3/4" l, bisque, reclining brown haired baby, white gown, hand at mouth, ... **75.00**

4" h, bisque, seated, red trimmed gown, holding bottle, ... **175.00**

4" l x 2 3/4" h, bisque, crawling baby, both feet raised, lt brown hair, white nighty, ... **395.00**

4 1/4" h, bisque, seated w/head tilted, blond hair, red cheeks, white gown, ... **85.00**

4 1/2" l, bisque

Crawling

2 1/2" h, lt blue nighty, dk blue trim, ... **160.00**

*8 1/2" h, bisque, lt yellow-green gown w/pink shoulder and blue ribbon, blond-brown hair, holding fruit, **$345.00***

3" h

Blond hair, white gown, blue ribbon, ... **165.00**

Seated blond girl, white nighty, raised left hand, ... **85.00**

4 3/4" h, bisque, seated baby, arms raised, pale blue nightie, ... **125.00**

6 1/4" h, bisque, seated child, arm raised, holding flower, white nighty, ... **350.00**

6 1/2" h x 7 1/2" l, bisque, seated baby holding toe, white gown w/green trim, repaired chip, ... **175.00**

6 1/2" l, bisque, brown haired baby in gold beaded blue gown lying on pillow, brown eared white dog holding pacifier in mouth, ... **195.00**

6 3/8" h, bisque, seated baby, white hat w/pink ribbon bow, pale blue dress w/pink sleeves and gold beaded margins, Hertwig, ... **195.00**

7 3/8" l, bisque, lying on back, holding big toe, white gown w/blue ribbon, wearing white cap w/blue ribbon, Heubach, ... **395.00**

7 1/2" h, bisque, seated holding foot, brown hair, pink cheeks, white gown w/green trimmed neck, repairs, ... **175.00**

7 1/4" l, bisque, blond baby crawling on stomach, lt blue nightie w/red ribbon on collar, ... **225.00**

*8" h, bisque, yellow gown, blue ruffles, blond hair, pink shoes, lime-green socks, **$295.00***

8" h, Bisque

Seated little boy w/ankles crossed, lg floppy hat, HP lilacs on blue gown w/beaded cuffs and collar, white kitten in lap, ... **120.00**

Seated girl pulling pink sock off, lg white pink and white bonnet, pink polka dot white dress, Heubach, ... **725.00**

8" l, bisque, crawling on stomach, one leg in air, blond hair, baby gown w/blue ribbon on back, Heubach, ... **650.00**

*10" h, lt brown hair, pink underdress, lime green nighty, gold trim, **$525.00***

9" h, Bisque

Little girl seated w/one brown shoe, pink hat, dress w/lt blue collar and bow, ... **95.00**

Seated w/legs crossed at ankles, arms raised, blue intaglio eyes, molded white gown w/pink trim, repairs, .. **650.00**

12" h, bisque, seated little girl w/bonnet, pointing to mouth, mauve dress w/ruffles, seated little boy, hat w/ball, lt green jacket, ankles crossed, c1880, pr, ... **3,950.00**

14" h, bisque, seated little girl holding cup, brown curly hair, spotted pink dress w/blue ribbons on shoulders, c1880, ... **2,950.00**

PICASSO

Spain
1881-1973

Pablo Picasso created a series of ceramic pieces that were released in limited edition numbers. Plates, plaques, and decorative jugs are highly prized by collectors and are finding their way to the major auction houses. Prices are often in the four to five figure range. Many of the designs reflect work that appeared in other media, but some designs are native to pottery.

References: Patrick O'Brian, *Pablo Ruiz Picasso, Picasso: A Biography*, W.W. Norton Co., 1994; *Picasso: A Dialogue With Ceramics: Ceramics From The Marina Picasso Collection*, Mass Market Produced.

*Bowl, 6" d, black-brown stylized bird design, mkd, (A), **$325.00***

Charger

14 1/4" d

Black flower pot w/flowers, red/orange apple, ... **350.00**

White earthenware w/engraved brown bull, blue clouds and ground, yellow matador, tan ground, sgd, ... **375.00**

16 1/2" d, "Face With Palm Leaves-Bright Mask" on reverse, green circles around black eyes, green mouth, brown-black vert stripes on border w/alternating dots, ... **5,800.00**

17" d, incised "Clock Face" design, cream, ... **3,000.00**

Jug, 12 1/2" h, "Face," green striped nose, green eyes, black lips and pupil, brown splashed accents, ... **3,800.00**

Pitcher, 7 1/2" w, stylized fish, orange-brown ground, black fins, center handle, ... **2,500.00**

Plaque

7" d, "Madoura Plein Feu," black figures, white ground, ... **950.00**

7 1/2" h x 7 3/4" w, 2 white slip stylized dancing figures, dk brown ground, "EMPRINTE DE PICASSO" mk, ... **1,000.00**

Plate

7 1/2" d, ivory slip of silhouette of female bust, matte black ground, ... **1,050.00**

8" d, "Picador," black oxide picador on horse, black dash rim, white ground, "Edition Picasso Madoura Plein Feu" mk, ... **2,500.00**

9 7/8" d, "Little Faces" design, white earthenware, engobe and enamel red-pink, blue, and brown, "Edition Picasso Madoura" mk, ... **3,900.00**

10" d

Black stick figures w/gulls at shore, green accents, hook for hanging, ... **2,000.00**

"Toro," black-brown tube lined bull's head, ... **1,650.00**

10" sq, black-brown "Vase Au Bouquet," **1,525.00**

12" d, black "Head With Mask," white enamel eyes, black mask, ... **8,000.00**

Vase, 122" h, "Wood-Owl," engobe design, black patina, ... **7,500.00**

c. 1914

PILKINGTON TILE AND POTTERY COMPANY

Church Gresley
Clifton Junction
1892-1957

History: The Pilkington family found red clay deposits at their colliery in Clifton Junction. Chemist William Burton, working at Wedgwood, determined that the deposits were of high caliber and thus the Pilkington Tile Company was founded. The original factory was located at Church Gresley, but twelve months later it was moved to its permanent home at Clifton Junction. William left Wedgwood and, with his brother Joseph, took over the management of the fledgling company. Initially, production of artistic tiles using a glaze called Sunstone was the chief source of income. Though the glaze worked well on tiles, it was a splendid glaze for hollow ware.

Employing craftsmen and chemists to develop a range of experimental glazes became Pilkington's bread and butter. Edward Radford was recognized as a master pottery thrower producing an amazing range of shapes and sizes. Two lines were associated with Pilkington. The Lancastrian line used simple glazes and shapes to produce special effects. Orange peel, egg shell, and fruit skin are the most recognizable. A line of lusters based on metallic oxides produced a different form of Lancastrian ware. Pilkington pottery was expensive because of the high cost of these unusual glazes. Lancastrian was named for Lancaster County, where the factory was located. In 1913, the company received a royal warrant, and the pottery became known as Royal Lancastrian.

Following World War I, the company revitalized its sales with the introduction of Lapis glaze. But this was reversed during the recession, and slumping sales resulted in the closing of the company in 1938. It reopened following World War II but never regained its prominence, and many of its products related to the 1950s style. The company closed its doors again, and in 1972 reopened for a short time.

Collectors Club: Pilkington Lancastrian Pottery Society: Wendy Stock, Sullom Side, Barnacre, Garstang, Preston, Lancs. PR3 IGH

Bowl

4 1/2" d, ftd, pinched tab handles, lustered gold ground w/shamrock and vert geometric designs, ... **575.00**

5 1/2" d, rolled rim, lumpy ground, green/gold luster finish, ... **60.00**

Comport, 11 5/8" H-H, Royal Lancastrian, spread foot, cobalt kingfisher glaze w/mottled green glaze, mkd, ... **125.00**

Dish, 7" H-H, purple flowers, green and yellow leaves on shaded orange to blue ground, burnished gold trim and pierced handles, ... **15.00**

Plate, 8" d, curdled white glazed center, shaded pink border, mkd, ... **45.00**

Vase, 6" h, blue-green drip, **$475.00**

Vase

2 7/8" h, bulbous, squat shape, flared rim, red snakeskin glaze, ... **60.00**

3 1/4" h, architectural, 4 buttress handles, gloss turquoise glaze, ... **145.00**

4" h, squat shape, flared neck and rim, mottled green glaze, "imp Pilkington England 2521" mk, ... **50.00**

4 3/8" h, swollen shape, slightly flared base, short neck, dk green stylized hanging leaf designs, orange vermilion luster glaze, sgd "W.S. Mycock," **95.00**

4 1/2" h, squat shape, flared rim, Arts and Crafts relief and incised design of stylized flowers and plants, mottled olive and apple green w/turquoise tones, mkd, ... **75.00**

5 1/2" h

Dbl gourd shape, matte gold-burnt orange glaze, .. **320.00**

Swollen body, short, straight neck, pale blue to pinkish-grey glaze, ... **120.00**

5 3/4" h, dbl gourd shape, gloss cobalt glaze, c1910, ... **295.00**

6 5/8" h, squat body, slender, tapering neck, aventurine glaze, ... **745.00**

7" h, squat shape, short, flared neck, molded vert leaves, gold stone drip glaze, (A), ... **633.00**

9 3/8" h, tapered body, spread ft, molded off designs flared shoulder, green eggshell glaze, c1910, ... **445.00**

9 1/2" h, ovoid, vert bands of med blue oval jewels, lt to dk blue shaded ground, imp mk, ... **245.00**

9 3/4" h, squat base, slightly flared neck, lt green leaf design, ... **329.00**

10 3/8" h, swollen shoulder tapered to narrow base, short neck, ochre glaze, ... **445.00**

10 5/8" h, bottle shape w/sm everted rim, gloss cobalt glaze, .. **595.00**

H.&S
Nº 4

1822-1830

PITCHER AND BOWL SETS

English/Continental
19th and Early 20th Centuries

History: Pitcher and bowl sets or washstand china were popular during the 19th and early 20th centuries. A typical set consisted of a pitcher (ewer) and basin, soap dish, sponge dish, toothbrush tray, and slop pail. Additional specialized pieces, e.g. hair receivers and comb box also were available. Wash sets allowed an individual to complete the washing up procedure in the privacy of the bedroom. The availability of piped water put an end to the Victorian and Edwardian jug and basin sets.

The list of manufacturers of washstand china was large. Principal English manu-facturers included Minton, Wedgwood, George Jones, Doulton, Clarice Cliff, and Ridgway. Many Continental companies also made washstand china.

Collecting Hints: Not every set has the same number of pieces. Many sets featured only the pitcher and bowl.

Two Piece

Pitcher, 2" h, bowl, 2 3/4" d, Imari pattern, bold iron-red, cobalt, and green colors w/gilt trim, Derby, c1830, ... **1,275.00**

Pitcher, 4 1/4" h, bowl, 4 1/2" d, Gaudy Welsh, "Grape Variant" pattern, cobalt, orange, green, and luster, scalloped rims, (A), ... **220.00**

Pitcher, 5" h, bowl, 6 1/2" d, chased front and back w/birds reserved in gilt shaped grass and floral cartouches, mottled dk blue ground, gilt dentil rims, gilt copper mounts, "blue interlaced Ls, A" mk, Vincennes, dtd 1753, (A), ... **14,340.00**

Pitcher, 7" h, bowl, 11 1/2" d, scattered floral sprigs, molded gold hanging leaves and horiz striping, on borders, shaped gold rims, Old Paris, ... **750.00**

Pitcher, 8" h, bowl, 9" d, Cottage Ware, 4-story tower pitcher w/brown thatched roof, yellow-green foliage, dk brown window frames, Price Kensington, ... **80.00**

Pitcher, 9" h, bowl, 12" d, "Lafayette at Franklin's Tomb," dk blue transfers, Enoch Wood, (A), ... **3,200.00**

Two piece, pitcher, 9" h, bowl, 10" d, orange flowerheads, orange-brown, tan, and green leaves, black stems, tan shaded ground, Charlotte Rhead, Crown Ducal, c1905, **$500.00**

Pitcher, 9 1/2" h, bowl, 13 1/4" d, pink, yellow, blue, and green gaudy flowers and foliage, emb floral designs and rope rim, repaired chip, "imp Wood" mk, ... **155.00**

Two piece, pitcher, 9 1/2" h, bowl, 15 1/4" d, "Wamba" pattern, blue, yellow, and green Art Nouveau style florals, white ground, Wedgwood, A-**$200.00**

Pitcher 10" h
Bowl, 15 1/4" d, blue, green, and red Asian flowers, Royal Doulton, ... **375.00**
Bowl, 16" d, faceted pitcher and bowl w/panels of stylized yellow roses, linear borders in rose, green, and blue, ivory ground, Royal Doulton, (A), ... **575.00**

Pitcher, 10 1/4" h, bowl, 13 1/4" d, gaudy red, blue, and yellow stylized roses, green fern-type foliage, red rims, "imp Wood" mks, repairs, (A), ... **1,265.00**

Pitcher, 10 1/2" h, bowl, 12" d, "Abbey Ruins" pattern, lt blue transfers, "T. Mayer Longport" mks, ... **975.00**

Pitcher, 11" h
Bowl, 13 1/4" d, "Persian" pattern, med blue transfer, "J. Heath" mks, hairline, ... **675.00**
Bowl, 14" d, HP purple, pink, and white spider chrysanthemums, grey-green foliage, lt tan ground, ... **395.00**
Bowl, 15" d, printed blue and white sheet chintz pattern, Royal Crownford, ... **795.00**
Bowl, 15 1/2" d, "Ormande" pattern, flowing blue, "Alfred Meakin" mk, ... **2,500.00**
Bowl, 16" d, "Togo" pattern, flowing blue, "F. Winkle & Co." mk, ... **925.00**

Pitcher, 11 1/2" h
Bowl, 13 1/4" d, white ironstone, "Maltese" shape, "WE.& E. Corn" mks, ... **450.00**

Bowl, 13 1/2" d, flow blue "Carlton" pattern, Alcock, repair to bowl, ... **2,195.00**

Pitcher, 11 3/4" h, bowl, 14" d, pink transfers of Warwick castle and English country houses, repairs, ... **595.00**

Pitcher, 12" h
Bowl, 13 1/2" d, white ironstone, "Fuschia" shape, "J. & G. Meakin" mks, ... **425.00**

Bowl, 17" d "Lily" pattern, blue transfers, Johnson Brothers, ... **1,500.00**

"Loire De Dijon" pattern, blue floral transfers w/gold accents, Doulton Burslem, ... **1,400.00**

Pitcher 12 1/2" h
Bowl, 13 1/2" d, white ironstone, "Sydenham" shape, Boote, ... **495.00**

Bowl, 15" d, flowing blue dragon and phoenix, red flowers, green leaves, yellow ground, Minton, ... **895.00**

Bowl, 15 1/2" d, ironstone, "Black Chinese" pattern, lg multicolored oriental flowers on black ground, Ashworth, (A), ... **385.00**

Bowl, 16 1/2" d, transfer print of rose red flowers, blue-green and blue foliage, blue geometric and swag borders, "Keeling & Co. Losol Ware" mk, ... **150.00**

Pitcher, 13" h
Bowl, 14" d, red, green, blue, black, and yellow rainbow spatter, (A), ... **25,875.00**

Bowl, 16" d, HP scene of period girl on swing from tree near water on pitcher, ruffled rim, HP girl feeding ducks on bowl w/mauve ground, Limoges, ... **1,100.00**

Pitcher 13 1/4" h, bowl, 18" d, "Glenwood" pattern, blue transfers, "Crown Pottery" mk, ... **1,100.00**

Pitcher, 13 1/2" h
Bowl, 15" d, "Pekin" pattern, multicolored oriental style vase on table w/peacock feather and florals, wide blue border bands w/gold accents, gold handle w/spread leaf terminals, Furnivals, ... **200.00**

Bowl, 16 1/4" d, "Aubrey" pattern, flowing blue, c1902, ... **1,500.00**

Bowl, 16 1/2" d, "Buttercup" pattern, blue transfers, molded bodies, gilt rims, Doulton, ... **625.00**

Pitcher, 15" h, bowl, 19" d, "Queen" pattern, blue transfers, gilt accents, unmkd, ... **200.00**

Four Piece
Pitcher, 12 1/4" h, bowl, 16 3/4" l x 13 3/4" w, rect, toothbrush holder, 5 1/8" h, soap dish w/drain, 9" d, Art Nouveau style lg white flowers, brown to white shaded ground, molded swirls, "DOULTON BURSLEM, ENGLAND" mks, (A), ... **275.00**

Pitcher, 13 1/2" h, bowl, 16 3/8" d, cov soap Dish, 5 1/2" d, shaving dish w/drain, 7 5/8" d, flowing blue and gilt "Rosslyn" pattern, Adderly, ... **1,200.00**

Five piece, pitcher, 11" h, bowl, 15 1/4" d, soap dish w/drain, 5 3/4" d, 2 chamber pots, 9 1/4" d, pink and white florals, green leaves, blue top and bottom rims and handles, white ground, "Newhall Hanley Staff. England" mks, $350.00

Five Piece, pitcher, 11 1/4" h, bowl, 16" d, cov slop basin, cov, 9 3/4" h, cov soap dish, 7 1/4" d, tumbler, 5" h, "Queen's Ware," black printed Liverpool bird design, Wedgwood, c1924, ... **700.00**

Six Piece
Pitcher, 11 3/4" h, bowl, 16" d, hot water pitcher, 6 3/4" h, mug, 3 1/2" h, cov chamber pot, 9 3/4" d, toothbrush holder, 5 1/2" h, "Huron" pattern, scattered florals, blue transfers, molded bodies, "Colonial Pottery" mks, ... **1,400.00**

Pitcher, 12 1/2" h, rect bowl, 18" l x 14 1/2" w, mug, 4" h, hot water pitcher, 7 1/2" h, cov soap dish

w/drain, crazing, 5 1/2" d, cov slop jar, 8 1/2" h, transfer of blue roses and carnations, green-brown foliage, gold outlined molded scrolling and handles, molded beading, Wilkinson, ... **785.00**

Seven Piece, pitcher, 11 1/4" h, bowl, 14 1/4" d, hot water pitcher, 7" h, toothbrush holder, 5" h, shaving mug, 3 3/4" h, cov waste bucket w/bail handle, 13" h, cov soap dish w/liner, blue sponging, white ground, blue banded trim, chips and hairline, (A), ... **1,540.00**

Eight Piece, pitcher, 10 1/2" h, bowl, 17 1/2" d, shaving mug, 3 1/2" h, cov chamber pot, 10 1/2" d x 7 1/2" h, toothbrush holder, 5 5/8" h, pitcher, 7" h, cov soap dish, 5" w, w/drain, cov waste jar, 13 1/2" h x 13 1/2" d, flowing blue "Gordon" pattern, Grindley, chips, ... **4,100.00**

PORTRAIT WARE

English/Continental
Mid-19th C to 1900

History: Plates, vases, and other pieces with portraits and busts on them were popular during the mid-19th century. Male subjects included important historical figures, such as Napoleon, Louis XVI, and James Garfield. However, most portraits featured beautiful women, ranging from the French Empress Josephine to unknown Victorian ladies.

Many English and Continental firms made portrait ware. Makers included Royal Vienna, Limoges, Schumann, and MZ Austria. Most examples were hand painted and often bore an artist's signature. Transfer prints supplemented the hand painted pieces.

Reproduction Alert: Portrait plates were imported to the United States by reproduction wholesalers and giftware distributors during the 1970s and 80s. These utilized full color transfers that also appeared on urns, vases, and compotes as well as plates. Many carried German and Austrian backstamps as well as facsimile signatures. Beware of gold trim that is too shiny.

Berry Set, master bowl, 9 1/2" d, 4 bowls, 5 3/4" d, shoulder portrait of black-haired woman wearing red-orange gown, blue scarf, orange sprayed borders, stenciled gold leaves and fruit between indents on rims, "Victoria Austria" mks, ... **75.00**

Bowl, 12" H-H, oval, bust of brown haired Victorian woman w/bun, green off the shoulder gown, maroon to dk blue shaded ground, molded shells on border w/gilt accents, "Victoria Austria" mk, ... **75.00**

Cabinet Cup and Saucer, raised gilt curlicue cartouche of half portrait lt brown-haired girl, pink rose in hair, pink gown w/gold clasp, lt blue ground, burgundy luster body w/raised gold curlicues and swirls, gilt fancy curled handle, Rosenthal, ... **225.00**

Cake Plate, 10 1/2" H-H, multicolored decal of Queen Louise in center, black hair, blue scarf and gown, pink and blue border w/molding, Franz Mehlem, ... **35.00**

Charger

11 3/4" d, bust of woman w/flowing brown hair, maroon gown, emerald green border, outer border w/gilt filigree, Germany, ... **90.00**

13 1/2" d, HP half portrait of woman wearing blue feathered hat, brown curls on shoulder, white dress, tan shaded ground, artist sgd, ... **150.00**

Cup and Saucer, Handleless, cup w/bust of brunette woman, lt blue gown on shoulder, dk red roses on blue-green base w/raised gold designs, hanging gold swags on rims, "Imperial Crown Made in Germany" mk, c1900, ... **95.00**

Dresser Jar, Cov, 4 1/2" d, cov w/named bust of "Cleopatra" in gilt roundel, maroon ground w/gilt scrollwork, sgd "Wagner," Germany, late 19th C, (A), ... **1,290.00**

Ewer, 19 1/2" h, profile bust of dk brown haired woman wearing red and white flowered cap, lt blue gown, in rect flower enclosed cartouche, relief of leaves on tan to cream shaded matte ground, sgd "Wagner," "RH Austria" mk, ... **2,750.00**

Mug, 3 1/2" h

Bust of woman w/brown floppy hat, blue feathers, pink gown w/white collar, blue and white clouds behind, tan shaded base, "red GERMANY" mk, ... **95.00**

HP bust of aristocratic 18th C woman, brown curly hair, rose on breast, gold stenciled swags of festooning flowers and vines from rim, orange to green

shaded ground, "Made in Germany" mk, ... **55.00**

Pitcher, 5" h, multicolored portrait, gold trim, shaded brown ground, "red Austria" mk, $32.00

Pilgrim Bottle, 16" h, bust of German girl, white lace cap, gold heart shaped locket on neck, blue gown, simulated champleve reverse, gold and cobalt rect base and drape handles, ... **2,500.00**

Plate, 8 1/2" d, "Amorosa," brown hair, mauve and blue gown, burgundy luster border, raised gilt accents, "Z.S. & Co. Bavaria, gold crown and shield" marks, $125.00

Plate

7 1/2" d, half portrait of woman w/flowing brown curly hair, brown to blue shaded ground, "J.P.L. Limoges" mk, ... **125.00**

8 1/2" d

Frontal bust of woman w/dk brown hair, gold loop earrings, brown dress, 6 emb cobalt and gilt flowerheads on border, cobalt rim w/gold band of leaves, Rosenthal, ... **50.00**

HP bust of period woman, brown hair w/long curls to shoulder, white gown on shoulders, gilt inner border, turquoise border, lobed rim, artist sgd, ... **200.00**

Plate, 8 3/8" d, lt blue dress, rust florals in black hair, gold inner and outer rim, "C.T. Germany" mk, $65.00

8 7/8" d, bust of young woman wearing blue Victorian gown, white lace bonnet, cross and pearls on neck, dtd 1882, Haviland, ... **150.00**

9" d, HP young woman, white cap, white gown w/blue sleeves, rose on breast, brown shaded ground, med blue border, molded gold rococo rim, artist sgd, Pirkenhammer, ... **200.00**

9 1/2" d

Half portrait of woman w/black hair and bun on top, lt blue gown, brown shaded ground w/gold overlay of hanging swags on border, gold Greek key rim design, Bavaria, ... **250.00**

Sevres style, multicolored transfer w/accents of named half portrait of "Mademoiselle de la Valliere," inner gilt border of hanging drops, lobed outer border w/gilt Greek key and drops designs, c1880, sgd "Debrie," **275.00**

10" d, HP half bust of woman playing harp, white headpiece, purple dress, cobalt border, gilt rim, Rosenthal, ... **245.00**

10 1/4" d, HP 1/2 bust of noble lady, lg plumed jeweled hat, blue collared gown w/ribbons, gold

inner border, cobalt border, sgd "W. Breidel," "Haviland France" mk, ... **650.00**

10 1/2" d, bust of period woman, black floppy w/brown feather, lt brown shoulder-length curls, blue grown, maroon border w/gold overlay, "Bayreuth Bavaria" mk, ... **75.00**

Tray, 18" d, transfer printed bust of red haired Art Nouveau woman wearing emerald circlet, gilt rim, Limoges, (A), ... **825.00**

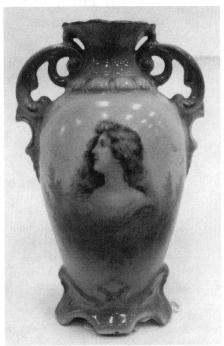

Vase, 6 1/4" h, brown hair, lt blue gown, blue bkd, olive green and brown shaded lower section, "Austria" mark, **$70.00**

Vase

10 1/8" h, tapered cylinder shape, everted rim, bust of curly haired brunette woman wearing red flowers in hair, pearl earrings, blue gown on shoulders, shaded cream to brown ground, "green C.T. Germany" mk, ... **100.00**

10 1/4" h, Ovoid

Short gilt handles, central etched gilt roundel w/maroon and turquoise jewels, of lady plucking rose stem, brown hair, blue gown w/red sash, looking back over shoulder, gilt leaf sprig border on maroon ground, turquoise jeweled short neck, titled "Unter Rosen," sgd "Wagner," Germany, (A), ... **2,115.00**

Vase, 9" h, brown hair, purple sash, multicolored bkd, gold rim, Royal Bayreuth, **$250.00**

Slender neck, gilt upright peaked handle, opalescent pink ground centering gilt surround w/maiden wearing wreath in hair, pale peach gown, titled "Sommer," sgd "Muller," Royal Vienna, late 19th C, (A), ... **1,295.00**

10 1/2" h, reverse triangle shape, trumpet neck and base, painted nude brunette woman w/arms behind head in front of spider web, gilt tracery on maroon body, shoulder w/leaftip metal band, lt yellow neck, lt yellow central band of gilt scrolls and trefoils, titled "Spinne," sgd "Wagner," late 19th C, (A), ... **1,295.00**

12" h, swollen tapered shape, raised gilt cartouche w/HP bust of brown haired woman, pink head scarf, green dress, body of white flowerheads on shaded purple ground, cobalt neck and fancy gilt accented handles, sgd "Bohme," Royal Bonn, ... **1,500.00**

15 3/4" h, ovoid w/scrolled gilt handles, trumpet foot and parcel gilt acanthus topped sq base, painted central roundel

w/brunette in red dress calling out, hand to mouth, titled "Echo," reverse w/gilt enamel cornucopia, lt yellow, green, purple, and pink shaded body, Austria, (A), ... **3,290.00**

PORTUGAL-GENERAL

Ilhavo, Portugal
1824 to Present

History: Jose Ferreira Pinto Basto established a factory to make porcelain at Vista Alegre in 1824. Soft paste porcelains and earthenwares, based on English models, were made until 1832. Anselmo Ferreira, a modeler from Lisbon, and Joseph Scorder from Germany helped develop the factory. In the early 1830s, the ingredients to manufacture hard paste porcelains were found in the region.

Vista Alegre's golden period began in 1835 when Victor Chartier-Rousseau, a French artist, arrived. He remained until his death in 1852. During his tenure, an improved hard paste porcelain became the standard product. Sevres forms replaced the earlier English influenced pieces. Classical, Gothic, and Rococo Revival influences can be found among Vista Alegre's products. Gustave Fortier served as artistic director from 1851 to 1856 and from 1861 to 1869. French influences continued. The factory prospered.

During the late Victorian period, when the Portuguese Joaquim de Oliverra (1870-1881) was head painter, the factory experienced financial difficulties. The problems continued under head painters da Roche Freire (1881-1889) and Jose de Magalhaes (1889-1921). De Magalhaes was responsible for ornamental plates with high relief decorations that featured vibrant themes and Art Nouveau characteristics.

In 1924 the factory was reorganized. An emphasis was placed on the production of classical patterns. Some contemporary designs were introduced.

The factory still is controlled by the descendants of the original owner, Jose Basto. The "VA" mark in blue has been maintained. A laurel wreath and crown symbolizing the royal patent of 1826 were added, but later abandoned.

Artichoke Plate, 10" d, 2/3 well of molded overlapping artichoke leaves, 1/3 basketweave well, center sauce well, white glaze, "Secla-Made in Portugal" mk, ... **15.00**

Bowl, 10 3/4" sq, cut corners, polychrome on black ground, yellow and green striped border, "Portugal" mark, $90.00

Bowl

6 1/2" d, HP lg blue rose and foliage on int, dbl reticulated sides, blue dash ext, blue lined rim, .. **10.00**

7" d, molded overlapping cabbage leaves, white glaze, ... **10.00**

12" d, lg red centered yellow flowers, blue-green leaves on int, blue-green rim, ... **350.00**

Coffee Set, pot, 9 1/2" h, creamer, cov sugar bowl, blue design, white ground, "Mottahedah, Visa Alegre VA" marks, $160.00

Candy Dish, 7 1/2" d, HP hanging floral swags, lobed border w/blue dots in diamonds, blue lined rim, ... **25.00**

Coffee Can and Saucer, green ground w/brown drip, "Made in Portugal" mk, ... **15.00**

Cup and Saucer, red apple, bright green leaves, olive green ground, shaded brown int, ... **5.00**

Dish, 9 1/2" d, Palissy style, lg brown beatles, green and brown salamanders, green textured ground, gloss brown reverse, pierced for hanging, ... **1,000.00**

Figure, 6" h, seated black and white Dalmatian pup, mkd, ... **25.00**

Flower Pot, 3" h, HP carnations and sprigs, pie crust rim w/painted hanging blue and yellow curls and dots, ... **15.00**

Charger, 13" d, tin glazed, brown script, blue dots and combs, yellow ground, 18th C, $950.00

Hen On Nest, 4 1/2" h x 5" l, red, yellow, and brown figural seated hen, brown molded basketweave base, ... **10.00**

Jam Pot, 4 1/2" h x 6 1/2" w, figural red strawberry, green leaf base, chips, ... **50.00**

Mixing Bowl, 8" d, stepped, cobalt ext, white int, "Made in Portugal" mk, ... **15.00**

Pitcher

4" h, HP burnt orange and mustard yellow flowers, green shaded leaves, white ground, yellow lined rim, spout, and handle, ... **10.00**

4 1/2" h, lg red flower w/yellow leaves on sides, lt blue ground, dk blue rim, spout, and handle, ... **8.00**

10" h, figural seated pig waiter, yellow coat, olive green apron, white chef's hat, holding bottle and glass, ... **30.00**

Pitcher, Cov, 11 1/2" h, relief molded hanging game on forest green ground, tan figural hound handle, white figural rabbit on forest green cov, white int, "MADE IN PORTUGAL" mk, ... **200.00**

Plate

4" d, HP yellow-brown, red, green, and blue wren on brown stylized ground, red and yellow flowers, green leaves, brown stems, red lined rim, mkd, ... **15.00**

6 1/4" d, painted boats in water under lg tree, kidney and triangle pierced border and flowerheads, green lined undulating rim, ... **25.00**

8" d, HP multicolored scene of lake, bridge, and house in center, 4 border panels of brown or white lattice alternating w/molded green and red cornucopia and painted flower sprays, mkd, ... **15.00**

9 1/4" d, relief of sheep and leaves in sq in center surrounded by intertwining loops, border of relief of leaves, overall med green glaze, mkd, ... **15.00**

Platter

10" l x 7 1/2" w, oval, HP orange, mauve, or blue flowerheads, green foliage in center, red and orange inner bar border, orange and yellow leaves, blue dash flowerheads on border, ... **25.00**

16" l x 12 1/4" w, oct, tin glazed, med blue painted allegorical animal in center, border of med blue painted stylized trees, flowerheads and leaves flanking center animal, white ground, "VL" mk, ... **110.00**

22 1/4" l x 14 1/4" w, oct, blue painted w/3 circle edged hexagons containing deer, flying birds, and foliage, border of scroll designs, artist sgd, ... **200.00**

Potpourri, 3" l x 3" d, figural drum, raised gold ropes, supports, and rims, gold band of leaves on int border, ... **15.00**

Serving Bowl, 10" l, diamond shape, HP red stylized flowerhead and foliage in center, blue lined open lattice sides, blue lobed rim, blue lined ext, ... **10.00**

Sugar Bowl, Cov, 5" h, w/underplate, beige transfers of country house, river and stone bridge, gold trim and ring handles, feather knob, "V.A. Portugal" mk, ... **45.00**

Teapot

6 1/4" h, relief molded leaves, green overall ground, molded red berries and knob, rope twist handle, "Made in Portugal" mk, ... **20.00**

7" h x 6" d, incised dragonfly design on med green ground, ... **40.00**

Tulipiere, 8" h, 5 tube, fan shaped, raised dot design, wavy rims, sq base, overall white glaze, ... **10.00**

Tureen, Cov, 8" h x 10" d, w/ladle, figural green cabbage leaves, ... **70.00**

Vase, 6" h, lobed, melon shape, painted red flower, single stroke single blue foliage, pale blue ground, dk blue painted curls on collar, ... **28.00**

F&R·PRATT·&·Cº

FENTON

c 1850

POT LIDS AND RELATED WARES

Staffordshire, England

c1840-1900

History: Pot lids were defined as under-the-glaze, chromatic transfer-printed Staffordshire pot covers. The pots were containers designed to hold foodstuffs, delicacies, and cosmetics, such as potted meats, relishes, fish paste, sauces, rouge, lip salve, hair pomades for women, and bear grease for men. First sold about 1840, they reached their popularity in the Victorian era. They were priced according to size. There were five basic sizes ranging from the smallest (under 1 3/4" diameter) to the largest (5 1/2" to 8 1/2" diameter).

The finest pot lids were made between 1850 and 1870. Production continued to the end of the 19th century. Although at least eight firms made pot lids, Pratt & Company was the major manufacturer.

In 1836 George Baxter patented his process to make an oil color printing from a number of plates and blocks. Ten years later the process was applied to ceramics. Pratt's 1847 "Grace Before Meals" was the first full chromatic transfer printed under the glaze on a pot lid. T.J. & J. Mayer followed suit in 1851. Chromatic transfer printing first involved painting a watercolor. Next a key plate was engraved. Prints from the key plate were then transferred to three other plates that held the three prime colors.

Pratt's master artist-engraver was Jesse Austin. His key plate color was brown. From 1852 to 1869 Austin engraved plates that portrayed portraits of royalty and famous people on pot lids. Between 1864 and 1873, eleven different views of London were made on pot lids. In addition to his own original watercolors, Austin also reproduced in miniature forms the paintings of famous artists.

Early Pratt lids frequently were flat topped. Shapes varied. The glaze had a bluish tint, especially before 1870. In the 1870s the glaze was more grey-blue in tone. The glaze also featured fine crazing. Forty-seven pot lids had the line and dot border design. Large Pratt pot lids made before 1863 show three stilt marks on the underside. Pratt's chief competitor from 1856 to 1862 was Cauldon Place Pottery.

References: A. Ball, *The Price Guide to Pot-Lids & Other Underglaze Multi-Colored Prints on Ware, 2nd Ed.* Antique Collectors' Club Ltd. 1980; H.G. Clarke, *The Pictorial Pot Lid Book*, Courier Press, 1960; Ronald Dale, *The Price Guide to Black & White Pot Lids*, Antique Collectors' Club, 1978; Cyril Williams-Wood, *Staffordshire Pot Lids & Their Potters*, Faber & Faber, 1972.

Museums: County Museum, Truro, England; Fitzwilliam Museum, Cambridge, England. (Collection seen by appointment only.)

Collecting Hints: Full color lids are the most popular among collectors. Most prized are pot lids with broad gold bands that were either produced for display at trade exhibits or showrooms, or as souvenirs for families and friends of the master potter.

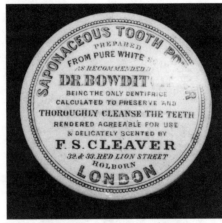

Lid and Jar, 3 5/8" d, black print, **$95.00**

LIDS AND JARS

1 1/2" d, MORRIS'S EYE OINTMENT, black printing on white, ... **125.00**

1 1/2" h

2 5/8" sq, "White Roast Paste-Teeth," black transfer, ... **145.00**

2 3/4" d, "Cracroft's Areca Nut Tooth Paste," black transfer, ... **110.00**

2 1/2" d

"Rose Cold Cream Wilson & Son Chemists Harrgate," black transfer, ... **125.00**

2 3/4" d

"Cullwicks Celebrated Skin Ointment," black transfer, ... **150.00**

"Superior Cold Cream E. Anstee Turner Chemist," black transfer, hairline, ... **120.00**

3" d, "Cherry Tooth Paste," black transfer, ... **110.00**

3 1/4" d, "ALMOND SHAVING CREAM," green print, ... **225.00**

1 5/8" h x 3" d, "Oriental Tooth Paste," "Jewsburg & Broun," black transfer, ... **110.00**

2" h

3 1/2" d, "Corona Anchovy Paste," black transfer, ... **125.00**

3 3/4" d, "S. Maw Son & Sons London, Ambrosial Shaving Cream Perfumed with Almonds," black print, ... **175.00**

4" d, "Fishing in Rockpools," multicolored transfer, ... **120.00**

4 1/4" d, "A Pair," multicolored transfer, ... **195.00**

2 1/4" h x 2 1/2" d, lg dog guarding baby in wicker cradle, multicolored transfer, (A), ... **120.00**

2 3/8" h

4 3/8" d, "The Room in Which Shakespeare Was Born 1564..." **295.00**

4 1/2" d, multicolored transfer of "Shakespeare's House Stratford on Avon," "Henley's Silk & Shave Soap" on base, rim chips, ... **100.00**

2 1/4" h x 4 1/8" d, "Thames Embankment," multicolored transfer, ... **120.00**

2 1/2" h x 2 3/4" d, "FORTNUM & MASON LMTD CAVIAR," sturgeon on side of jar, black transfers, ... **45.00**

2 7/8" d, "Cold Cream-Boots," "Cash Chemists," black transfer, ... **95.00**

3" d

"Black KLENZIT DENTAL PLATE SOAP," **175.00**

Children playing w/boat in tub, multicolored transfer, chip, ... **85.00**

3 1/8" h x 4 3/8" d, multicolored bust of Sir Walter Raleigh, "A.G. Hackney" mk, ... **60.00**

3 1/2" d, "green ALMOND SHAVING CREAM," **225.00**

3 1/2" h, "Pegwell Bay, Kent," multicolored transfer, ... **200.00**

4 1/8" d, "A Letter From The Diggings," multicolored transfer, chip on base rim, ... **100.00**

4 1/4" d, Skaters, multicolored transfer, ... **135.00**

4 3/4" d, "The Farriers," multicolored transfer, ... **130.00**

5 1/2" l x 3" w, oblong, multicolored transfer of horsemen, classic ruins, and trees, sgd "Wouwerman," chips on base rim, ... **125.00**

LIDS

1 3/4" d, black EYE OINTMENT, ... **95.00**

2 5/8" d, "WOODS ARECA NUT TOOTHPASTE..PLYMOUTH," black transfer, (A), ... **55.00**

3" d

"Alas Poor Bruin," multicolored, ... **150.00**

Fallen skater, multicolored transfer, ... **75.00**

Goats and Goat Herders, multicolored transfer, ... **95.00**

3 1/8" l x 2" w, rect, multicolored transfer of "A Sea Shore Study," **150.00**

3 3/8" d, "BURGESS ANCHOVY PASTE," black and white, ... **25.00**

3 1/2" d

"JAMES ATKINSONS BEARS GREASE," black transfer, . **46.00**

"SAPONACEOUS TOOTH POWDER," black transfer, chips, ... **20.00**

4" d

"Albert Memorial," multicolored transfer, ... **140.00**

"A Pair," multicolored transfer of old man and woman playing cards, rim chip, ... **154.00**

"A Race of Derby Day," multicolored transfer, ... **350.00**

Black "FORTNUM & MASON CHICKEN & HAM," **110.00**

"Chapel Royal," multicolored transfer, c1864, ... **225.00**

"Cries of London-Primroses-Yellow Primroses," **55.00**

"Dr. Johnson," multicolored transfer, ... **150.00**

Fallen grey horse, multicolored transfer, ... **145.00**

Fishing, multicolored transfer, ... **65.00**

"Hawling in the Trawl," multicolored transfer, ... **165.00**

"Hide and Seek," multicolored transfer, rim chips, ... **45.00**

"Holborn Viaduct," multicolored transfer, "F. & R. Pratt" mk, ... **325.00**

"Landing the Catch," multicolored transfer, ... **150.00**

"Low Life," seated dog, multicolored transfer, ... **150.00**

Old English village scene, multicolored transfer, ... **110.00**

"Preparing For The Ride," multicolored transfer, ... **145.00**

"Seven Ages of Man," multicolored transfer, c1870, chips under rim, ... **195.00**

"Shakespeare's House," multicolored transfer, ... **180.00**

Shells and coral, multicolored transfer, ... **90.00**

"The First Appeal," multicolored transfer, ... **125.00**

"The High Mettled Racer," multicolored transfer, ... **55.00**

"The New Blackfriar's Bridge," multicolored transfer, ... **295.00**

"The Poultry Woman," multicolored transfer, ... **140.00**

Three fishing boats, multicolored transfer, ... **125.00**

"Uncle Toby," multicolored transfer, ... **175.00**

"Wolf and the Lamb," multicolored transfer, ... **195.00**

4 1/8" d

"Il Pense Voso," seated man in stocks, multicolored transfer, ... **100.00**

Pot Lid, 4" d, "Albert Memorial," multicolored, $140.00

4 1/4" d

"Feeding the Chickens," multicolored transfer, ... **275.00**

Fox w/rocks and grass, multicolored transfer, ... **225.00**

"Snow Drift," multicolored transfer of wolf and sheep, ... **125.00**

"The Enthusiast," multicolored transfer of man w/gout in chair holding fishing rod, ... **195.00**

"The Village Wedding," multicolored transfer, scratches, ... **70.00**

Woman in period clothes skating w/2 gentlemen, ... **135.00**

4 1/2" d

Horse racing, multicolored transfer, ... **80.00**

"The Children of Flora," multicolored transfer of children pulling cart w/little girl, ... **275.00**

"Meeting of Garibaldi and Victor Emmanuel," multicolored transfer, c1850, ... **320.00**

4 3/4" d, "Country Quarters," multicolored stable scene of animals, ... **275.00**

5" d

"Funeral of the Late Duke of Wellington," "T.J. & J. Mayer" mk, ... **600.00**

"Stag Hunting," multicolored transfer, ... **170.00**

"The Breakfast Party," multicolored transfer, ... **295.00**

"The Grand International Building of 1851," **250.00**

5 1/2" d, "Trinity Hall, Oxford/Cambridge," multicolored transfer, ... **38.00**

Pot Lid, 5 3/4" l, Dutch battle scene, multicolored, $80.00

MISCELLANEOUS

Bread Plate, 12 3/8" d, multicolored transfer of Jesus in wheat field, orange-red inner border, relief molded green, yellow, and gilt accented corn on border, ... **225.00**

Compote

9 1/4" d x 1 3/4" h, multicolored transfer of "Forum in Rome," dk pink border, tan geometric rims, ... **125.00**

11 1/8" H-H x 2 1/2" h, "The Mountain Stream," multicolored transfer, gold outlined molded handles, ... **110.00**

13 1/2" H-H, "The Blind Fiddler" design, multicolored transfer, malachite border, gilt accented scroll handles, ... **390.00**

Creamer and Cov Sugar Bowl, creamer, 2 3/4" h, sugar 4" h, creamer w/front panel of ruins and river scene, reverse w/cattle crossing bridge, sugar w/cattle and church ruins on front, horses pulling boat on reverse, white ground, white beaded band and gold-brown bands of geometrics on borders and cov, gold outlined leaf designs on handles, "F. & R. Pratt" mks, hairline, ... **250.00**

Jar
4" h, fox hunt scene w/horse jumping fence, huntsman, black and gold transfer, pale blue ground, Pratt, ... **50.00**

4 1/2" h, multicolored underglazed transfer of harbor and village scene, Pratt, ... **135.00**

Loving Cup, 4" h, multicolored transfer of huntsmen on horseback starting hunt, reverse w/woman washing clothes in river, cattle in water, tomato red ground, gold rim, 2 gold outlined handles, gold-tan geometric int border, hairlines, ... **75.00**

Mug, 5 1/2" h, dbl handled, multicolored transfer of "The Rustic Laundrywoman" on front, "A Rural Scene" on reverse, green ground, (A), ... **60.00**

Pitcher, 4" h, multicolored transfer of "Blind Man's Bluff" in gold oval on side, reverse w/multicolored Dutch winter scene in gold oval, green ground, ... **100.00**

Plate, 8 1/2" d, "Philadelphia Public Buildings 1876," multicolored transfer, med blue border w/gold-brown rim, F. & R. Pratt, **$250.00**

Plate
4 1/8" d, "Preparing For The Ride," multicolored transfer, wide green border, gold rim, ... **110.00**

7 1/4" d, "The Trooper," multicolored transfer, tan geometric rim, ... **55.00**

7 1/2" d
Deer in forest, multicolored transfer, turquoise border, tan geometric rim, ... **100.00**

"Shakespeare's House," multicolored transfer, orchid border, tan geometric rim, ... **50.00**

8 1/4" d
"Lend a Bite," peasant couple and dog, multicolored transfer, white border, gold geometric rim, Pratt, ... **200.00**

"Scottish Hunting Party," multicolored transfer, aqua int border, tan oak leaf border, "F. & R. Pratt" mk, ... **240.00**

8 1/2" d, multicolored transfer Black water carrier, 2 children seated on ground, maroon border, gold-brown rim w/geometric designs, "PRATT FENTON" mk, ... **95.00**

Cows in front of cottage, turquoise border, brown/gold geometric rim, Pratt, ... **125.00**

Scene of man and woman dismounting from horses before stone building, blue-green border, brown bow border, Pratt, ... **125.00**

9" d, "The Ruined Temple," multicolored transfer, lustered tan border w/gold-brown geometric design rim, Pratt, ... **95.00**

9 3/8" d, "The Bully," multicolored transfer, gold acorn border w/scrolling, Pratt, ... **450.00**

Plate, 9 1/4" d, multicolored transfer, dk pink inner border, mustard yellow rim, gilt accents, "F. & R. Pratt Fenton" mark, **$125.00**

Teapot Stand, 6 1/4" d, "THE QUEEN! GOD BLESS HER!" multicolored transfer of 2 little boys and dog, white border, Pratt, ... **75.00**

Vase, 6 1/2" h, flat sides, spread ft, short neck, "Thames Embankment" on

front, "Trafalgar Square" on reverse, multicolored transfers, malachite ground, (A), ... **50.00**

PRATT WARE

Staffordshire, Shropshire, and other English pottery centers
c1785-1840

Scotland
1750-1840

History: Pratt ware was relief decorated, high-temperature fired, under-the-glaze, cream-colored earthenware and pearlware that was made between 1785 and 1840. William Pratt headed a family of potters who worked at Lane Delph and Fenton. William was the first of six generations of Prattses to make Pratt ware. Felix, John, and Richard, William's sons, managed the pottery after their father's death in 1799.

Jugs with relief-molded designs of sporting and bucolic scenes, or commemorative subjects featuring naval or military heroes or royal figures were the most popular forms. Tea caddies, plaques, flasks, teapots, dishes, mugs, cow creamers, busts, and other forms also were produced.

The body usually was white or a pale cream color. The glaze consisted of lead oxide tinged with blue. The wares were decorated with relief designs pressed from intaglio molds. Colors used for the decorations included yellow, orange, ochre, green, cobalt blue, brown, black, and mulberry. The under-the-glaze color technique that protected the colors under a transparent glaze retained the brilliance of the pieces.

The majority of Pratt's jugs were unmarked. Other potters that imitated the wares from Pratt's factory included Wedgwood, Leeds, E. Bourne, T. Hawley, and R.M. Astbury. Under-the-glaze colored figures of animal groups, Toby jugs, tall-case clocks, money boxes, and watch stands appeared. Classical scenes were featured in relief decoration under the glaze on jugs. A number of relief decorations on Pratt ware duplicated the intaglio patterns found on jasper ware.

The Scottish East Coast Potteries made Pratt ware style jugs and other forms from the mid-1700s until 1840. Some pieces contained motifs with a distinctive Scottish flavor.

Reference: John & Griselda Lewis, *Pratt Ware 1780-1840*, Antique Collectors' Club Ltd. 1984.

Museums: City Museum & Art Gallery, Stoke-on-Trent, England; Fitzwilliam Museum, Cambridge, England; Potsdam Public Museum, Potsdam, NY; Royal Pavilion Art Gallery & Museum, Brighton,

England; Royal Scottish Museum, Edinburgh, Scotland; Victoria & Albert Museum, London, England, William Rockhill Nelson Gallery of Art, Kansas City, MO.

Bowl, 9 1/2" d, blue centered ochre flowers, green foliage in center, bands of alternating blue and ochre flowers, green foliage, brown bands, ... **3,500.00**

Creamer
4 5/8" h, green and ochre edged oval of blue, ochre, and green peacocks on sides, relief of green and ochre feathers on base, vining around rim, ... **1,350.00**
4 7/8" h, molded scenes of children in hearts, stiff leaves on base, blue dk yellow, and green, (A), ... **275.00**

Figure
4" h, standing lamb, black, green, and puce splashes, c1800, ... **335.00**
5 3/4" h
Bust of man w/head turned, black hair, blue sponged chest, ochre sponged shoulders, green flared pedestal base, ... **1,800.00**

Figure, 9 3/4" h, blue jacket, yellow vest, red, blue, and black spotting, c1800, **$15,500.00**

Seated monkey, brown w/yellow collar and strap, green base, ... **3,750.00**
6" h x 6 1/2" l, standing orange and black spotted cows, black tails, lady gardener in blue and orange dress, orange apron, calf on base, or male gardener in blue coat, red-brown trousers, dog on base, blue, black, and

orange-brown sponged base, repairs, pr, ... **9,000.00**
12 3/4" l, standing lion, orange-brown coat, dk brown mane, paw on dk brown ball, rect green base, c1800, ... **10,000.00**
Flask, 4 1/4" w, overlapping blue, brown, and tan molded shells, c1800, ... **990.00**

Jug, 6 1/4" h, blue jackets, blue and ochre drape, green mounds, **$985.00**

Jug
4 7/8" h, "Mischievous Sport," and "Sportive Innocence" in heart shaped cartouches on sides, molded stylized wheat sheaves on rim, acanthus molded base, green, brown, ochre, and blue, ... **535.00**
5" h, "Pointer," relief molded brown and dk orange hunting dogs, green molded foliage, blue and orange dash border, c1810, unmkd, ... **150.00**
5 3/4" h, pearlware, relief of archery lesson, reverse w/couple and hunting horn hanging from branch, ochre, brown, and green, c1820, chip on spout, ... **325.00**
6" h, "Lord Wellington," relief of bust of Wellington w/dk brown hat, ochre and brown feather, yellow collared ochre coat, blue drape, General Hill on reverse, c1810, ... **360.00**
12 1/4" h, figure of seated Bacchus, black hair, brown sash, figural brown animal handle, green figural dolphin on head forms spout, purple and green grapes, "Wine" on base, c1800, ... **2,030.00**
Pipe, 8 1/2" l, molded dog head whistle

in center, spattered ochre, green/blue, black, and puce, ... **395.00**

Plaque
7 1/2" h, oval, relief of black-haired Vulcan at forge, brown loincloth, med blue ground, ochre rim, pierced for hanging, (A), ... **900.00**
8 1/8" h, oval, relief molded figures of Paris, Aphrodite, and Eros under tree w/"Apple of Discord," green, brown, and blue, cobalt laurel leaf inner frame, turquoise scrolling acanthus leaf outer frame, restored, ... **300.00**
13 1/2" h x 9 3/4" w, relief of Crucifixion, red-brown cross, dk brown haired angel w/ochre wings above, blue drape at sides, ochre, dk red-brown, and blue beaded rim, pierced for hanging, ... **1,750.00**
Tea Caddy, 4 3/4" h, relief of 2 men dressed in brown or blue spotted oriental robes, reverse w/2 gentlemen in brown or cobalt jackets, flowers on end panels w/black crisscross vert side margins, c1790, ... **1,500.00**
Teapot, 4" h, globular, brown swags w/black drops on body, black outlined brown band on shoulder and cov, c1800, ... **2,285.00**
Watch holder, 10" h, 2 figures flanking tall case clock, blue, ochre, and green flowers on clock and trim on figures, rect base, c1790, ... **1,750.00**
Whistle, 3 3/4" l, figure of reclining lion, brown and ochre patches, ... **1,095.00**

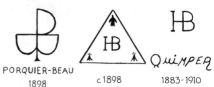

QUIMPER

Quimper, Brittany, France
1600s to Present

History: Quimper faience derived its name from the town in Brittany, in the northwest corner of France, where the potteries were located. Three of the major 17th and 18th century centers of French faience—Nevers, Rouen, and Moustiers—strongly influenced the early Quimper potters.

Jean Baptiste Bousquet settled in Quimper in 1685 and started producing functional faience wares using Moustiers-inspired patterns. Pierre, his son, took over in 1708. In 1731 Pierre included Pierre Bellevaux, his son-in-law, in the business. He introduced the Chinese-inspired blue and white color scheme, the Oriental subject matter, an intertwining border pattern of leaves and flowers, and the use of the rooster as a central theme.

From Rouen, Pierre Clement Caussy brought to Quimper many important features such as "decor rayonnant," an intricate pattern of stylized leaves and florals on the outer border, and lacy designs that resembled wrought iron trellises. By 1739 Pierre Clement Caussy had joined with Bousquet. He became the manager of the faiencerie and expanded the works.

Francois Eloury opened a rival factory in 1776, and in 1778 Guillaume Dumaine opened a second rival factory. Thus, three rival faience factories were operating in Quimper, producing similar wares by 1780.

Through marriage, Antoine de la Hubaudiere became the manager of the Caussy factory in 1782. The factory's name became the Grande Maison.

After the beginning of the 19th century, the essential Breton characteristics began to appear on the pottery—the use of primary colors, concentric banding in blue and yellow for border trims, and single-stroke brushing to create a flower or leaf. Toward the end of the 19th century, scenes of everyday Breton peasants became popular decorative motifs. Artists such as Rene Quillivic joined Grande Maison in 1920 and produced figures.

Concurrently, the Eloury factory passed to Charles Porquier and later to Adolphe Porquier. In 1872, Alfred Beau, a master artist, joined the firm and produced Breton scenes and figures.

In 1884 Jules Henriot took over the Dumaine factory. He added the Porquier factory to his holdings in 1904. Mathurin Meheut joined the Henriot factory in 1925 and introduced patterns influenced by the Art Deco and Art Nouveau stylistic trends. Other noted artists at Henriot were Sevellec, Maillard, and Nicot. During the 1920s, the HB concern introduced the Odetta line that utilized a stoneware body and decorations of the Art Deco period.

The Henriot factory merged with the Grande Maison HB in 1968, each retaining its individual characteristics and marks. Production ceased in the early 1980s. An American couple purchased the plant and renewed the production of Quimper.

Quimper pottery was made in a tremendous number of shapes and forms, among which are utilitarian pieces, all types of figures and decorative articles, and in fact, just about everything imaginable.

Marks: The "HR" and "HR Quimper" marks were found on Henriot pieces prior to 1922. The "HenRiot Quimper" mark was used after 1922. The "HB" mark covered a long span of time. The addition of numbers or dots and dashes referred to inventory numbers and were found on later pieces. Most marks were in blue or black. Consignment pieces for department stores such as Macy's and Carson Pirie Scott carried the store mark along with the factory mark. These consignment pieces are somewhat less desirable in the eyes of the collector.

References: Sandra V. Bondhus, *Quimper Pottery: A French Folk Art Faience*, published privately, 1981; *Rev. Ed.* 1995; Millicent S. Mali, *French Faience*, United Printing, 1986; Millicent Mali, *Quimper Faience*, Airon, Inc. 1979; Anne Marie O'Neill, *Quimper Pottery*, Schiffer Publishing, 2000; Marjatta Taburet, *La Faience de Quimper*, Editions Sous le Vent, 1979 (French Text); Adela Meadows, *Quimper Pottery: A guide to Origins, Styles, & Values*, Schiffer Publications, Barbara Walker & Dave Williamson, *Quest For Quimper*, Schiffer Publications, 2001.

Museums: Musee de Faiences de Quimper, Quimper, France; Musee Departemental Breton, Quimper, France; Victoria & Albert Museum, London, England; Villa Viscaya, Miami, FL.

Reproduction Alert: A line of pottery called "museum quality" has appeared on the market. These pieces featured a brownish wash over a crazed glaze surface. The marks were generally in brown as opposed to the blue or black factory marks of the earlier period. Originally these reproductions had paper labels, but the labels were removed easily. The reproductions sometimes are sold as old pieces.

The Blue Ridge Pottery and several Japanese firms have produced wares with peasant designs similar to those of Quimper. These are easily recognizable.

Peasant pottery similar in style and feel to Quimper has been produced by the Malicorne factory, near Paris. These pieces carry a Malicorne "PBx" mark. Examples have appeared on the market with the "x" removed and sold as genuine Quimper.

Modern Quimper pottery still is made and marketed in major department stores such as Neiman-Marcus and Marshall Fields; in china specialty shops; in Quimper factory shops in Paris; in the city of Quimper in France; in Alexandria, Virginia; and in Stonington, Connecticut.

An American couple now owns the Quimper factory. Many of the older patterns are being reproduced for an eager market. New pieces of Quimper are much lighter in weight than the older examples.

Imitation Quimper-style plates are being produced in Romania. These feature croisille decor. Also barber bowls signed "quimper" with a small "q" are popping up.

Collecting Hints: Most Quimper available to the collector comes from the late 1800s to the mid-1920s. Because so much was made, the collector should focus on pieces that are in very good or better condition. Missing covers to sugar bowls, teapots, inkwells, etc., greatly reduce the value of these pieces and should be avoided. Small flakes in the glaze are inherent in the nature of the pottery, and, for the most part, do not detract from their desirability.

Pieces from the Odetta period (c1920) are less desirable because of the emphasis on Art Deco designs rather than the country motif associated with the more traditional Quimper pottery.

Newsletter: *Le Monde de Quimper*, Quimper Faience, Inc., 141 Water Street, Stonington, CT 06378. Subscription: $10 for three years; USA Quimper Club, Inc., Attn Lucy Williams, 2519 Kansas Ave., Suite #108, Santa Monica, CA 90404; Quimper Club International, Attn. Diane Robertson, 5316 Seascape Lane, Plano, TX 75093, e-mail join@quimperclub.org, website, www.quimperclub.org.

Bell, 4 1/2" h, figural female peasant, cobalt skirt, lt blue apron and cap, brown hair, "HenRiot Quimper" mk, ... **150.00**

Biberon, 5" h, band of red, blue, and green single stroke florals, conc blue and yellow banding, 19th C, (A), ... **275.00**

Bookend, 5" h x 6 3/4" w, figural fisherman leaning against brown stone wall, dk blue cap, red jacket, blue trousers w/dk blue knee patches, "HenRiot Quimper 161 J.E. Sevellec" mks, pr, ... **400.00**

Bowl, 10 1/2" d, blue fleur-de-lys in center, white ground, "HenRiot Quimper" mk, ... **50.00**

Bulb Pot, 4" h x 4 1/2" d, female peasant seated on rock holding flowers, typical floral sprays, blue half circle and dot border w/orange and blue stripe, green sponged ruffled rim, "HenRiot Quimper France 117" mk, ... **120.00**

Butter Pat, 3" d, female peasant, blue blouse, red skirt, blue and yellow striped border, "HB Quimper France" mk, ... **35.00**

Gravy Boat, 3 1/2" h x 8 3/4" l, male or female peasant on sides, red, green, and yellow-centered blue dot florals on sides and int, yellow molded seashells on border and base, blue streaked rim, blue serpent handle, "HR Quimper France" mk, ... **425.00**

Holy Water Font, 6 1/2" h, raised stylized figure of Mary holding infant Jesus, red and blue dotted robe, red and orange vert striped font, blue and olive green backplate border, unmkd, (A), ... **300.00**

Ice Cream Dish, 4" d, black lined wide brown band on dish, figural female peasant handle, black blouse, orange vest, blue skirt, yellow apron, ... **95.00**

Inkstand, 7" l, rec w/backplate, 2 wells, walking male peasant on top w/red, green, and blue scattered florals, band of red, green, and blue foliage on base, blue dash borders, molded orange shell on backplate, "HR Quimper" mk, c1900, ... **450.00**

Inkwell, 3 1/4" w, heart shape, male and female peasant on front, floral garland w/bluets and 4 red dot designs, 3 blue outlined openings and knob, 3 sm feet, "HR Quimper" mk, ... **250.00**

Jardiniere, 8" l x 4 1/2" h, cradle shape, orange outlined cartouche w/seated Breton male blowing horn, female holding flowers, next to lake, reverse w/lg red flowerhead and trailing red, green, and yellow centered blue flowers, lg red starburst flowers on ends, blue zigzag and dot borders, 4 sm feet, gold knobs, "HenRiot Quimper France" mk, ... **395.00**

Knife Rest

3 1/2" l, triangle shape, male peasant, blue coat, red pantaloons, blue, red, and green vert florals on sides, blue dash margins, blue sponged rims, "HenRiot Quimper France 492" mk, ... **45.00**

4 1/2" l, figural male peasant lying on back, black hat, green shirt, blue vest, brown shoes, Maillard, "HenRiot Quimper" mk, .. **200.00**

Mug, 3 3/4" h, male or female peasant, green vert leaves w/blue and yellow florals, yellow and blue striped border, blue sponged handle,

"HenRiot Quimper France" mk, pr, ... **95.00**

Pitcher, 6 1/2" h, figural bust of female with orange and white coif, tan hair, "HB Quimper" mk, ... **125.00**

Plate, 9 1/4" d, blue jacket, red pants, blue, green, and red single-stroke border, "HB" mk, **$300.00**

Platter

10 1/2" l x 7 1/2" w, rect w/cut corners, male and female peasants w/vert foliage in center, border band of red, green, and blue single stroke florals, black ermine tails in corners, blue outlined rim, "HenRiot Quimper" mk, ... **225.00**

11" l x 8 1/2" w, oval, center bird, torch, quiver, and cornucopia in center, hanging lambrequin border, indented rim, green, blue, red, and yellow, "HB" mk, ... **550.00**

24" l, oval, male peasant leaning on staff, female standing next to lg brown barrel of corn, fencing and tress in bkd, rim band of blue semicircles, "HB" mk, ... **2,250.00**

Porringer, 4" H-H, male peasant, blue jacket, red pantaloons, red, green, and blue, vert florals, yellow and blue striped border, blue sponged handles, "HenRiot Quimper" mk, ... **35.00**

Plate

5 1/2" d, male peasant, green shirt, blue trousers, vert red, green, and blue single stroke flowers, yellow and blue striped border bands, scalloped rim, "HenRiot Quimper France" mk, ... **65.00**

7" d, female peasant, orange blouse, blue skirt, red, green, and blue,

vert florals, wide blue sponged border, "HenRiot Quimper France 82" mk, ... **40.00**

8" d

Blue and red single stroke pinwheel in center, blue and manganese striped border, grey clay, black bk, c1850, (A), ... **140.00**

Plate, 9" d, blue jacket, red pantaloons, yellow stockings, red, yellow, blue, and green florals, blue dot and red dash border on yellow ground, blue striped rim, "blue HB" mark, **$300.00**

Frontal view of female peasant w/basket on head, blue and red crisscross border panels alternating w/red and yellow stylized flowerheads, "HenRiot Quimper France" mk, ... **125.00**

8 1/8" d, lg blue outlined 6 petal flower w/red or yellow slashes, green grass stripes, blue spokes, blue and yellow border bands, "HenRiot Quimper France" mk, ... **75.00**

Plate, 9" d, yellow blouse, blue skirt, green apron, red, green, and blue vert florals, red and blue dash border, yellow and blue striped rim, "black HB" mark, **$300.00**

9 1/4" d, "Breton Broderie," enameled orange, white, and green stitched designs on med blue ground, "HB Quimper" mk, ... **110.00**

Plate, 9 3/8" d, blue jacket, black pantaloons, yellow stockings, red, yellow, blue, and green florals, blue 4 dot design, "HR" mark, $285.00

9 5/8" d, female peasant holding basket, green blouse, purple apron, gold edged blue skirt, red, green, and blue florals and 4 blue dot designs on border, indented rim, "HB" mk, ... **275.00**

10" d
Frontal view of standing male and female peasant before yellow-tan rock, cobalt acanthus (decor riche) design on yellow border and crest of Brittany, red outlined lobed rim, "HR Quimper" on front, ... **895.00**

Lg spray of white double daisies, 3 green buds, arched leaves and stem, insect on border, yellow outlined indented rim, Porquier Beau, (A), ... **1,300.00**

Male peasant blowing horn, blue top, orange pantaloons, green vert leaves w/yellow-centered blue dot flowers, border band of green leaves w/yellow-centered blue dot flowers, blue outlined indented rim, "HenRiot Quimper France 81" mk, ... **125.00**

Two tone blue fleur-de-lys in center, 2 tone blue striped rim, "HenRiot Quimper France" mk, ... **75.00**

Platter, 20 1/2" l, multicolored peasant wedding scene with musicians, gold outlined dk blue acanthus border on lt blue border ground, crest of Brittany at top, lobed rim, "HenRiot Quimper 154" mk, ... **1,850.00**

Quintal, 6 1/2" h, frontal of view blond haired male peasant, holding walking stick, reverse w/lg floral spray and red daisy, single stroke bluet branches, sprigs, and 4 blue dot designs, "HenRiot Quimper France" mk, ... **175.00**

Ramekin, 3 3/4" d, male or female peasant on int, med blue ext and handle, blue and yellow striped int border, "HenRiot Quimper" mk, pr, ... **100.00**

Sauce Boat, 10 7/8" l, w/undertray, lobed body, female peasant on side and scattered typical florals, blue lined rims, blue dash handle, "HB Quimper" mk, ... **240.00**

Serving Dish, 9 1/2" l x 9 1/4" w, 4 sections, male or female peasant in 2 sections, lg yellow centered red or blue single stroked flowerheads, blue sponged dividers, blue and yellow rim, "HenRiot Quimper France" mk, ... **150.00**

Snuff Bottle
2 1/2" h, figural clam shell, female peasant w/red and blue vert floral sprays and 4 blue dot designs on each side, blue dashes on edge, "HR Quimper" on front, (A), ... **600.00**

3 1/4" h, doughnut shape, red and green geometrics on front, "Souvenir de Bretagne" on reverse, cobalt banded edge and spout, (A), ... **400.00**

Soup Plate, 8 1/4" d, female peasant, green blouse, blue skirt, red apron, red, blue, and green vert florals, yellow and blue striped border, "HenRiot Quimper France" mk, ... **40.00**

Spoon Rest, 4 1/2" l, oval, peasant woman in center, red, green, and blue vert foliage, molded blue shell at end, blue striped rim, "HB" mk, c1895, ... **195.00**

Teapot
6" h, lobed, blue shaded fleur-de-lys and ermine tails, blue striped handle and spout, blue chain rims, flower knob, "HB Quimper" mk, ... **575.00**

Teapot, 8 1/2" h, blue blouse, red skirt, yellow apron, red, blue, and green florals, gold outlined blue striped handle, yellow ground, "HB Quimper" mark, $195.00

7 1/2" h, hex shape, painted blue open basket w/lg yellow centered red or blue flowerheads, scattered single stroke foliage, yellow banded and blue dash handle, 4 blue dot and blue dash spout, "HenRiot Quimper France 73" mk, ... **225.00**

Tea Tile, 8" w, oct, bust of female peasant, orange ribbon in white coif, blue dress, purple apron, border band of red, blue, and green single stroke flowers and foliage, green rim, "HB Quimper" mk, ... **175.00**

Tete a Tete, female peasant on cup, male on dish, orange and blue clothing, red and green vert florals, blue rims and dashes on cup, "HenRiot Quimper France" mk, ... **200.00**

Tulipiere, 7" h, female peasant holding distaff, male w/horn on front in yellow band and blue chain, reverse w/sprays of bluets and red buds, scattered 4 blue dot designs, flared base w/yellow band and blue chain, 4 tubes w/blue chains, "HR" mk, (A), ... **375.00**

Tureen, Cov
7 1/2" d x 7 1/4" h, base w/band of single stroke, red, blue, and green florals, male peasant holding pipe on cov, vert red and green single stroke foliage and 4 blue dots, blue dash scroll handles, yellow striped rim, blue striped ft, "HenRiot Quimper" mk, ... **275.00**

8 3/4" d x 8 1/2" h, Modern Movement, Breton Broderie, base w/panel of brown, cream, and dk blue bust of male or female peasant, cobalt bands w/raised ochre leaf band intersecting panels cov and base, cobalt vert handles w/ochre leaves, cobalt flowerhead knob, "HB Quimper" mk, ... **225.00**

Vase
4 1/2" h, egg shape w/zigzag border, walking Breton male holding pipe, vert green and red single stroke flowers and yellow centered blue dot flowers, blue streaked rim, blue scroll feet, "HR Quimper" mk, ... **100.00**

5" h, overlapped curved cone shape w/male peasant and typical florals mtd on blue lined rect base, blue shell designs on int of cone, "Souvenir de Bretagne" on base, "HB" mk, ... **325.00**

8" h, paneled front and back, curved sides, frontal view of male peasant, reverse panel w/red and green foliage, yellow centered blue dot flowers, orange and blue framed panels, black ermine tails, blue 4 dot designs on sides, blue dash, orange outlined dbl wishbone handles, "HenRiot Quimper France 74" mk, ... **295.00**

8 5/8" h, bag shape, female peasant holding distaff, single stroke vert foliage, reverse w/lg red single stroke flower, blue single stroke flowers, and green foliage, orange and blue zigzag raised collar, 2 orange wishbone handles w/blue dashes, "HenRiot Quimper France 72" mk, c1925, ... **145.00**

Wall Pocket
10 1/2" h, figural slipper, male peasant flanked by red and green foliage and yellow centered blue dot flowers, border of blue swags and dots, orange and blue striped rim, red, blue, and green croisille back plate, red starburst hanging hole, "HenRiot Quimper France" mk, ... **345.00**

11" h, dbl cone shape, frontal view of blond Breton man w/arms crossed or female peasant

holding distaff on each, vert single stroke blue and green florals and yellow centered red dot florals, raised blue striped band on base, overlapping blue scales on backplates, applied blue dash loop on back, "HenRiot Quimper France 96" mk, ... **300.00**

RELIEF MOLDED JUGS

England
1820-1900

History: At numerous English potteries during the 1820s, a new type of jug was molded in one process with no additional decorations.. The Staffordshire Potteries were the center of this activity, but some relief-molded jugs were made elsewhere.

The earliest jugs had hunting scenes, but by the mid-1800s, there was a wide range of designs, including historical and commemorative subjects, classical figures, naturalistic patterns, Biblical stories, religious architecture, scenes from literature and wildlife, and others. The best jugs were made during the 1840s and 50s. After that time, cheaper mass-produced jugs resulted in a lesser quality product with mostly floral or geometric patterns.

Jugs were an essential part of everyday life in the Victorian era and were used for ale, water, cider, milk, wine, and toddy. Some were made with lids of Britannia metal, some had relief-molded pottery lids, and some had strainers in the spout to feed invalids. There was a range of sizes, and some were made in sets. Jugs were produced in huge numbers, and the variety in shape, style, quality, size, decoration, and subject matter was vast.

To produce the master model for a relief-molded jug, the modeler carved the original design, often in a block of alabaster. Casts were then made from the master to form reversed master molds. Further casts produced cases. Final castings resulted in the working molds. Approximately 25 jugs could be made from a master, and then a new mold was necessary.

At first, jugs were buff colored, then pastel blues and green were used. White became the standard color. Jugs also were made in beige, grey, and brown. Some makers used enamel colors for highlighting certain aspects of the designs. After c1845 colored grounds increased in popularity.

Many relief molded jugs were marked with either impressed, printed, molded, or applied marks. Applied marks were the most common on relief-molded jugs. They were formed separately and then attached to the body using slip. Applied marks were

used mostly in the 1830s and 40s, while molded marks were used in the second half of the century. Printed marks were used in the 40s and 50s. Some marks included publication dates, which indicated when a design was first introduced. These were either applied or impressed. The diamond shape registration mark was used from 1842 until 1883. This mark designated when a design was registered, not necessarily when it was made. Registration marks provided protection for makers against copying by other makers. After the Patents, Designs and Trade Marks Act of 1883, marks were either "Rd." or "Rd. No."

There were numerous makers of relief-molded jugs. William Ridgway and Company's most famous jug, Tam O'Shanter, was based on scenes from a Robert Burns poem. He worked with James Leonard Abington from 1831 to 1860, mostly at the Church Works in Hanley. At least twenty-six different designs in a wide range of subjects were made during this thirty-year period.

Another prolific maker of jugs was Herbert Minton, who used model numbers on relief-molded jugs to identify the designs. Charles Meigh's first relief-molded jug was made in 1835. His famous Apostle jug was produced in huge quantities. This jug set the standard for others who made these jugs. William Taylor Copeland's first jug was "The Vintage Jug" made in 1844. After 1849 all his jugs were registered. Another important maker was William Brownfield who made a wide range of designs, mostly in naturalistic motifs to appeal to mid-Victorian tastes.

Additional makers included Ashworth, Doulton, Mason, Worcester, Wedgwood, Samuel Alcock and Company, and Mayer.

References: R.K. Henrywood, *Relief-Moulded Jugs 1820-1900, Rev. Ed.* Antique Collectors' Club Ltd. 1996; Kathy Hughes, *A Collector's Guide to Nineteenth-Century Jugs, Vol.1 & Vol.2*, Routledge, Kegan & Paul, 1985.

Museums: City Museum & Art Gallery, Hanley, Stoke-on-Trent, England; Potsdam Public Museum, Potsdam, NY; Victoria & Albert Museum, London, England; Wadsworth Atheneum, Hartford, CT.

4" h, Parian, white relief
Lily of the Valley flowers, "W.T. Copeland" mk, ... **170.00**
Two men seated on carpet under palm trees, mosque, lavender ground, unmkd, ... **125.00**
4 1/2" h
Apple blossoms, lt blue stoneware, unmkd, c1860, ... **40.00**
"Thespian," white relief molded theatrical figurals in arches, buff stippled ground w/white relief molded leaves on base, stepped handle, ... **170.00**

5" h, ivy leaf design, white, Minton, c1845, ... **350.00**

5 1/2" h, parian, white relief of birds eating grapes and leaves, blue stippled ground, white branch handle, Minton, ... **95.00**

5 7/8" h, parian, panels of grape vines and leaves on blue ground, mask spout, ... **175.00**

6" h
"Animal Hunting" pattern, stag hunted by hounds, wild boar and hounds on reverse, hound handle, band of leaves and vines on collar, tan, Phillips and Bagster, ... **185.00**
"Garibaldi" pattern, white cameos, blue parian ground, c1860, ... **250.00**
"John Gilpin" pattern, horse head handle, blue parian, Wm. Ridgway, ... **225.00**
White exotic birds in trees and grasses, dk brown ground, pewter lid, "imp Dudson" mk, ... **160.00**

6 1/4" h
Cherubs playing tug of war, fuchsia blossoms, lt blue stoneware, "J. & T. Locket" mk, ... **150.00**
Portland Vase, band of white classic figures on lavender ground, Alcock, ... **275.00**
Snake and dog design, sleeping child w/dog watching, stylized snake handle, grey-green stoneware, Pankhurst, c1853, ... **170.00**

6 1/2" h
"Julius Caesar and Boadicea" pattern, grey stoneware, Meigh, ... **320.00**
"Lily" pattern, celadon stippled ground, c1860, ... **135.00**
"Linenfold" pattern, white stoneware, William Ridgway, ... **60.00**
"Medieval Wedding" pattern, med blue stoneware, Ridgway and Abington, ... **140.00**
"Night & Morning" pattern, grey, Dudson, c1860, ... **200.00**
"Resting Putti" pattern, putti flanked by flowers and foliage. Lt blue, Dudson, c1850, ... **100.00**
"Severn" pattern, gilt and burgundy accent, William Brownfield, ... **175.00**
"Silenus" pattern, grey stoneware, Minton, c1830, ... **250.00**
"Willie" pattern, grey, Ridgway, c1851, ... **225.00**

6 3/4" h, "Uncle Tom's Cabin" design, grey, c1850, ... **435.00**

7" h
"Assyrian" pattern, grey stoneware, ... **350.00**
"John Barleycorn" pattern, grey, "imp Ridgeway and Abington" mk, ... **135.00**
Molded corn and leaves, white glaze, unmkd, ... **60.00**
"Wisdom and Providence" pattern, white stoneware, Alcock, ... **165.00**

7 1/4" h
"Camel" pattern, pewter lid, c1850, ... **295.00**
"Eglington" pattern, lt blue salt glaze, Wm Ridgway, ... **275.00**
"Volunteer Rifle Corps" pattern, blue stoneware, c1835, ... **165.00**

7 1/2" h
"Albion" pattern, blue, Brownfield, c1863, ... **295.00**
"Amphitrite" pattern, white stoneware, Charles Meigh, chips, ... **350.00**
"Cashmere" pattern, white on brown ground, Brownfield, ... **225.00**
"Elephant and Camels" pattern, relief of 2 elephants pulling cart, reverse w/2 camels pulling cart, palm trees, grapevine and leaf border, beige ext, lt blue int, 6 sm feet, grapevine handle, unmkd, (A), ... **220.00**
Hanging hops and leaves, branch handle, ruffled rim, rose stoneware, ... **255.00**
"Naomi and Her Daughter-in-Laws," lilac relief, white body, ... **135.00**
"Paul and Virginia" pattern, grey stoneware, unmkd, c1860, ... **195.00**
"Peace and Plenty" pattern, grey-green stippled ground, Cork and Edge, ... **185.00**
"Ranger" pattern, grey-green stoneware, metal lid, "E. Walley" mk, ... **125.00**

7 3/4" h
"Bacchanalian Revels," white, Charles Meigh, ... **475.00**
"Falstaff" pattern, grey, salt glaze, Mason, ... **450.00**
"Slavery" pattern, white, salt glaze, metal cov, Ridgway & Abington, ... **950.00**

8" h
Parian, white relief of "Music" and "Dancing," tree branches and

leaves above, blue pebbled ground, white twisted branch handle, pewter lid, maker unknown, ... **165.00**

7 3/4" h, "International," Science, Art, Music, and Commerce, white relief, med blue ground, William Brownfield, A-$70.00

"Portland Jug" pattern, white cameos, lavender ground, parian, bearded face on handle, Samuel Alcock, crack in handle, ... **150.00**
"Prince Consort" pattern, grey, restored knob, ... **450.00**

8 1/4" h
"Sleeping Beauty" pattern, stippled blue ground, Dudson, c1860, ... **110.00**
"Stag and Hounds" pattern, brown, c1840, ... **395.00**
"Westminster" pattern, grey, pewter lid, Brownfield, ... **195.00**
"York Minster" pattern, tan stoneware, Meigh, ... **135.00**

8 1/2" h, trellis and vine design, grey, c1860, ... **250.00**

8 3/4" h
"Bundles" pattern, brown glaze, Ridgway, c1840, ... **195.00**
"Four Seasons" pattern, tan, Charles Meigh, ... **395.00**

8 7/8" h
"Dancing Amorini" pattern, grey, 1845, ... **495.00**
"Monkey" pattern, bearded mask spout, tan stoneware, metal lid, ... **285.00**

9" h
"Amphitrite" pattern, white design on blue ground branch handle,

parian, Charles Meigh, dtd 1853, ... **295.00**

"Apostle" pattern, white, Charles Meigh, ... **450.00**

"Arabic" pattern, celadon ground, Alcock, c1847, ... **295.00**

"Bacchanalian Dance" pattern, grey stoneware, Meigh, c1840, ... **150.00**

Dragonfly and fruit, stiff leaves, vine handle, grey, unmkd, ... **100.00**

"Wheatsheaf" pattern, blue pebble ground, Dudson, ... **150.00**

9 1/4" h

"Hecate," relief of 2 women reading tea leaves, natural color, (A), ... **135.00**

"Idle Apprentice" pattern, tan glaze, c1840, ... **175.00**

White relief of pansies and leaves, blue enameled ground, hinged metal lid, ... **195.00**

9 1/2" h

"Apostle's" pattern, grey, Charles Meigh, 1842, ... **395.00**

Boy and eagle's nest, white parian, Keys and Mountford, chip under spout, ... **375.00**

Chinese figures in vert panels, blue glazed stoneware, "S. Hughes & Co. Staffordshire" mk, ... **175.00**

"Holy Family" pattern, tan glaze, c1845, ... **250.00**

"Pan" pattern, grey, c1830, ... **395.00**

Prince Albert Memorial, grey-white, hairline, ... **575.00**

Tam O'Shanter, Souter Johnny, and cronies, grey, William Ridgway, ... **125.00**

10 1/4" h, "Gypsy" pattern, tan, Jones & Walley, **$325.00**

10" h

"Aesthetic" design, lt green stoneware, pewter lid, "imp DUDSON" mk, ... **1,320.00**

Molded Psyche and Eros, vert wheat shaft and trees, twist handle, grey, unmkd, ... **175.00**

10 1/2" h

"Apostles," grey-white, ... **600.00**

"Falstaff," grey stoneware, c1835, ... **155.00**

10 3/4" h, "Gleaners" pattern, white, salt glaze, Walley, ... **750.00**

11" h

"Rossi" pattern, grey, "T. J. & J. Mayer" mk, 1845, ... **550.00**

White molded grapevine and birds eating grapes, stippled green ground, dtd 1849, Minton, ... **335.00**

12" h, tan glaze, **$595.00**

12 1/2" h, "Paul & Virginia" pattern, white relief, blue ground, parian, "T. J. & J. Mayer" mk, c1851, ... **595.00**

15" h, "Garibaldi" design, tan, c1860, ... **295.00**

c1818-1834

RIDGWAYS ENGLAND 2 ROYAL SEMI-PORCELAIN

c1905

JOHN RIDGWAY - c 1841-1855

RIDGWAY

Shelton, Staffordshire, England
c1808-1855

History: Job Ridgway trained at the Swansea and Leeds potteries. In 1808 he took John and William, his two sons, into partnership at his Cauldon Place Works at Shelton. At first, the company only made pottery. Later, porcelains were added to supplement the earthenware line.

The early porcelain pieces usually were unmarked. A few pieces done before Job Ridgway's death in 1813 are impressed "Ridgway & Sons." After 1813 the two brothers separated. John retained the Cauldon Place factory and made porcelains. William produced earthenwares at the Bell Works.

John Ridgway specialized in the production of fine porcelain tablewares, mostly tea and dessert services. He was appointed potter to Queen Victoria. Very few ornamental pieces were made. Most pieces remained unmarked. Hence, his wares often were attributed to other factories by scholars and collectors.

William Ridgway expanded the scope of his operation until he eventually owned six factories at Hanley and Shelton. Their principal production was utilitarian earthenwares, with a tinted bluish-mauve body. The earthenware products that were made between 1830 and 1845 had no mark, only a painted pattern number.

After 1856 there was a series of different partnerships with varying names. By 1962 the porcelain division of Cauldon was carried on by Coalport China Ltd.

The Ridgways used a distinctive system of pattern numbering, which is explained in G. Godden's *British Porcelain.*

Reference: G.A. Godden, *The Illustrated Guide to Ridgway Porcelains*, Barrie & Jenkins, 1972.

Museums: Cincinnati Art Museum, Cincinnati, OH; Potsdam Public Museum, Potsdam, NY.

Bowl, 8 1/2" d, "Coaching Days and Coaching Ways-The Journey's End," black transfer w/white accents, caramel ground, ... **75.00**

Compote

8" h x 8" d, gilt snowflake on white ground in center, green borders and ground w/gilt accented molded curlicues and swirls, ... **1,275.00**

10" H-H, blue printed "Helical" pattern, reticulated border, foliate scroll handles, ... **395.00**

Cream Jug, 4" h, overall relief design of daisies, glazed white ground, Wm. Ridgway, ... **95.00**

Cup and Saucer, Handleless, black bat printed scene of woman resting against tree, ... **150.00**

Dessert Dish, 9 1/2" l x 9" w, center painted w/landscape and tall tree, med green border w/3 gilt painted and molded cartouches of garden sprigs, gilt molded and painted fancy rim, ... **250.00**

Dessert Service, Part, 9 plates, 9 1/4" d, 2 service plates, 10 1/2" H-H, 2 rect service plates, 11 1/2" H-H, 2 oval service plates, 12" H-H, center designs of variations of multicolored basket of garden flowers, tan border w/gilt molded accents and gilt florals in urns, gilt molded rims, c1835, ... **7,500.00**

Dish, 14" H-H, diamond shape w/molded scrollwork and flower designs on handles, "Flosculous" pattern, masses of oriental style brown flowers, leaves, and sprays, c1840, ... **45.00**

Fruit Cooler, 13 1/2" h, w/liner, circ body w/painted floral sprays under blue band w/gilt lattice decoration, gilt ring handles, 3 gilt dolphin feet on trefoil base, domed cov w/flower finial, repaired hairline, c1830, pr, ... **15,000.00**

Milk Jug, 3 1/4" h, "Coaching Days & Coaching Ways," black designs of "Fresh Team" and "A Winter Days Amusement," caramel w/silver trim, ... **20.00**

Pitcher
4 1/4" h, "Coaching Days and Ways," black transfers of Henry VIII and abbot, caramel ground, silver luster rim and handle, ... **60.00**
6 1/2" h, painted pink and white flowerheads, green leaves along middle, molded interwoven rope on neck, scrolling on rim and spout, gilt trim, green ground, "Published By Wm. Ridgway & Co. Hanley, October 1, 1835" mk, ... **125.00**

Plate
8 3/4" d, "Japan Flowers" pattern, flowing blue, rose, and yellow flowers and butterflies, rope twist gilt rim, "J.W. Ridgway" mk, ... **90.00**

*Plate, 9" d, tan, green, and brown, castle scene, tan border w/gilt and white trim, unmkd, **$195.00***

9" d
"Devonshire" pattern, orange/rust rooster, fish, and bird scenes in overlapping panels on brown transfer ground, ... **95.00**
HP rose spray in center, wide med blue border w/3 burgundy edged oval cartouches holding painted sprigs, burgundy shaped rim, c1840, ... **22.00**
9 1/8" d, "Marmora" pattern, blue transfer, "W.R. & Co." mk, ... **85.00**
9 1/4" d, central landscape w/castle ruins, molded med blue border w/yellow flowerheads, gilt accented molded rim, ... **130.00**
9 3/4" d, "Windsor" pattern, red transfer, ... **8.00**
10" d
"Mr. Pickwick And The Rival Editors" in center, flower border, dk blue transfer, indented rim, ... **125.00**
"Water Lily" pattern, blue transfer, "J. Ridgway" mk, ... **50.00**
10" H-H, green oriental style plants and florals in center, scattered green foliage border, molded handles, c1830, ... **35.00**
10 1/4" d, "Asiatic Palaces" pattern, med blue transfer, ... **50.00**

Platter
16 1/2" l x 13 1/2" w, "Marmera" pattern, med blue transfer, ... **350.00**
18" l x 14 1/2" w, "Indus" pattern, brown transfer, dtd 1877, ... **375.00**

Serving Dish, Cov, 11" l, ftd, "Oriental" pattern, blue transfers, c1900, ... **100.00**

Soup Plate, 9" d, "Oriental" pattern, cartouches of flowers or oriental scenes on border, lt blue transfer, gold lobed rim, "William Ridgway" mk, ... **10.00**

Sugar Bowl, Cov
5" h x 7 1/2" H-H, drabware, relief molded flowerheads and bands of leaves, branch handles, flowerhead knob, William Ridgway, c1820, ... **495.00**
5 1/4" h x 7 1/2" H-H, "Asiatic Temple" pattern, blue transfers, chip, ... **175.00**
6" h x 7 1/2" H-H, English manor house on side, sponged type borders, teal blue transfers, ... **185.00**

Syrup Pitcher, 4 1/2" h, "Indus" pattern, brown transfer w/red accented cranes, leaves, and flowers, pewter lid, ... **425.00**

Tankard, 10 1/2" h, "Coaching Days and Coaching Ways-A Christmas Visitor and Waiting For The Coach," black transfers, caramel ground, silver trim, ... **110.00**

Teabowl and Saucer, "Berlin Vase" pattern, blue transfers, ... **50.00**

*Teapot, 6 3/4" h, ironstone, "Blenham" pattern, iron red, blue, and gold florals, white ground, "Ridgway Ironstone England Blenham" mark, **$85.00***

Teapot, 5 1/2" h, sq shape, "Iran" pattern, iron-red, cobalt, and gilt, gilt accented serpent handle, "bow and quiver" mk, ... **60.00**

Rockingham Works Bramld
c 1826-1830

ROCKINGHAM

Swinton, South Yorkshire, England
Pottery 1745-1842
Porcelain 1826-1842

History: The Rockingham factory was located on the estate of Earl Fitzwilliam, Marquis of Rockingham, near Swinton in Yorkshire. The first pottery was manufactured in 1745. The factory continued production under various owners, who concentrated on brown and yellow wares; blue-and-white dinner, tea, and coffee services; and white earthenwares. In 1806 John and William Brameld took over the business and used the name "Brameld Co." They made pottery from 1806 to 1842.

Brown ware was the best known variety of Rockingham pottery. Its common forms included teapots, coffeepots, jugs, and cadogans (a pot from which liquid will not spill). The thickly applied glaze was intense and vivid purple-brown when fired. The interior of pieces often was left white. Sometimes the brown exterior was decorated with gilding, enamel colors, or classical figures in relief. During the 19th century, many companies copied the "Rockingham" glaze of a rich brown stained with manganese and iron.

The Bramelds introduced porcelain production in 1826. Rockingham bone china porcelain had a glaze somewhat prone to fine crazing. During the next sixteen years, until 1842, many ornamental wares and some utilitarian wares were made. Rockingham tea and coffee services in both simple and ornate decoration remained a mainstay of production. Finally the company also manufactured animal groups featuring dogs, cats, squirrels, rabbits, hares, deer, or sheep. Vases, ewers, baskets, scent bottles, candlesticks, desk pieces, trays, and pieces for the dressing table constituted the principal ornamental forms.

The red griffin mark was used from 1826 to 1830 and the puce griffin mark from 1831 to 1842.

References: Alwyn Cox & Angela Cox, *Rockingham Pottery & Porcelain 1745-1842*, Faber & Faber, 1983; Arthur A. Eaglestone & Terence A. Lockett, *The Rockingham Pottery, Rev. Ed.* David & Charles, 1973; D.G. Rice, *Ornamental Rockingham Porcelain*, Adam, 1965; D.G. Rice, *Rockingham Pottery and Porcelain*, Barrie & Jenkins, 1971; Alwyn & Angela Cox, *Rockingham 1745-1842*, Antique Collectors Club, 2002.

Museums: City Museum, Weston Park, Sheffield, England; Clifton Park Museum, Rotherham, England; Rotherham Museum, Rotherham; Victoria & Albert Museum, London, England; Yorkshire Museum, York, England.

Reproduction Alert: Rockingham brown glaze was copied extensively throughout the 19th century by many factories.

Sauce Tureen, Cov, 8 1/8" h, w/attached underplate, bands of HP multicolored flowers, pale yellow border bands, gilt rims, handles, and knob, c1840, **$245.00**

Basket, 4" h x 4 1/2" d, pink flowers w/gilt accents on green center band, tan open rope weave overhead handle, ... **125.00**

Breakfast Trio, cup, saucer, plate, 7 1/2" d, pink borders w/white molded swags, gilt rims, "griffin, Rockingham Works Brameld, Manufactured to the King" mk, ... **150.00**

Bud Vase, 4" h, applied polychrome flowers and stems on body and neck, painted flowers on base and neck, "Rockingham Works, griffin" mk, ... **200.00**

Cup and Saucer, "Grey" feather and gilt grapes and vines designs, 3 spur handle, "puce Rockingham Works Brameld Manufactured to the King" mk, ... **120.00**

Dessert Service, compote, 15 1/2" H-H, 6 1/2" h, 2 cake plates, 10 1/4" l, 8 plates, 8 1/4" d, dbl open plate, 11 3/4" l, pink, orange, yellow, and purple florals, white ground, cobalt and gilt cartouche, almond brown border, almond brown, cobalt, white, and gilt pedestal bases, **$2,400.00**

Dessert Plate, 10 1/4" d, center painted w/rose and foliage, green border molded w/gilt accents and 4 cartouches of florals, gadroon shell and acanthus leaf rim, ... **600.00**

Dessert Stand, 9" d x 2 3/4" h, lg finely painted red flower and foliage in center, peach border w/band of white flowers, green foliage, molded gilt and grim rim, peach and gilt banded ft, hairline, pr, ... **315.00**

Plate

7" d, 12 sided, HP gilt wide and narrow center circles, gilt swirling foliage and vine designs on border, set of 10, ... **100.00**

7 1/2" d, overall molded veined leaf design, leaf edge, overall green glaze, "imp BRAMELD 4" mk, ... **100.00**

8 3/4" d, central painted classical landscape scene, green and gold molded scrollwork border, ... **100.00**

9" d, HP center landscape vignette, green border w/gold and white curls and lobed rim, "puce griffin" mk, (A), ... **225.00**

10 1/4" d, oct, woodman returning to thatched cottage, dog, and child, stitch design on border, med blue transfer, "imp Brameld Works Rockingham" mk, ... **130.00**

Sugar Bowl, Cov, 7 1/2" h, white panels w/HP red flowers, green foliage, gilt swirls on upper section, lower panels of gilt swirls, cobalt center band, gilt accented dbl handles, gilt and white crown knob, c1830, ... **950.00**

c1878

c1884

RORSTRAND

Near Stockholm, Sweden
1726 to Present

History: Rorstrand, established in 1726 near Stockholm, was the oldest porcelain factory in Sweden. Although formed for the production of tin-glazed earthenware, porcelain was the ultimate aim of the founder. A succession of German managers directed the production during the early years. The company made little impact on the ceramic world.

When Anders Fahlstrom became manager in 1740, the company began to flourish. Elias Ingman assumed control in 1753. The company immediately undertook to imitate the successful Sevres and Meissen wares. The company continued to prosper. Rorstrand absorbed the rival Marieberg factory in 1782.

Bengt Jeijer became manager in 1798. In the early 1800s, the fortunes of Rorstrand were altered by two major events: the introduction and popularity of Wedgwood's creamware, and the ban on the exportation of English clay. Rorstrand tottered on the brink of bankruptcy. Eventually the clay ban was relaxed. Workers from Stoke-on-Trent were imported. Rorstrand's products now had a finer clay body and strong English influence.

In the mid-1870s, a limited company was formed. Production flourished due to the infusion of the fresh ideas of talented Scandinavian artists employed at the factory. Between 1895 and 1914, Rorstrand's art director and designer was Alf Wallander. He produced a wide range of tablewares and decorative pieces in the Art Nouveau style, using delicate, sculptural modeling of figures and flowers, often in deep relief. Tonal qualities included delicate greens, pinks, and violets on a greyish off-white background. Wallander also used pale flower decorations contrasted with black grounds.

Following World War II, the entire factory was moved to the port city of Gothenburg, its present location.

The company has used the mark of three crowns of Marieberg with "ROR-STRAND" since 1884.

Reference: Bengt Nystrom, *Rorstrand Porcelain: Art Nouveau Masterpieces*, Abbeville Press, 1995.

Ashtray, 8" d, box match holder on curled end, matte brown glaze, mkd, ... **80.00**

Bowl, 4 1/4" d, tapered shape, white ground w/overall imp crowns, gold ft band, "Rorstrand Sweden G.N." mk, ... **65.00**

Bud Vase, 5 1/4" h, bag shaped base, slender neck, dk turquoise crackled glaze, ... **195.00**

Charger, 14" d, HP multicolored bust of Princess Neapolit in center, blue border w/yellow-gold swirls and feather designs, repaired rim chip, ... **245.00**

Ewer, 8 3/8" h, matte cream ground w/pale vert stripes, Gunnar Nylund, "R, 3 crowns Sweden" mk, ... **160.00**

Figure, 8 1/4" h, knelling gnome carrying horn on bk, tan wash w/blue accents, ... **100.00**

Jug, 7" h, mottled brown glaze, Gunnar Nylund, ... **60.00**

Soup Plate, 9" d, romantic center scene of Middle Eastern spired temple, trees, and water, cell border, swirl rim, purple transfer, "imp RORSTRAND" mk, ... **50.00**

Vase

2 1/2" h, flared shape, flared ft, HP garden flowers, white ground, "RORSTRAND SWEDEN" mk, ... **70.00**

3 1/2" h, squat shape w/pink tinged ivory modeled overlapped petals, short green neck w/everted dentil molded rim, (A), ... **690.00**

4" h, beaker shape, dk red circ in dk yellow arch, black vert runny streaks, blue band base, grey stone ground, ... **25.00**

Vase, 6" h, lilac spotting, pale green dragonfly, green ground, *$1,200.00*

5 3/4" h, squat shape, 4 sides, short neck, red and yellow flowerheads, green leaves, cobalt ground, chips, mkd, ... **50.00**

Vase, 7 1/2" h, blue and multi-toned purple matte glaze, Gunnar Nylund, (A), *$375.00*

Vase, 8" h, mauve pansies, green stems, cream ground, *$1,200.00*

Vase, 9" h, rust textured glaze, incised mks, (A), **$357.00**

9 1/2" h, ovoid, short collar, spread ft, enameled green centered yellow stylized daisies, pink and blue leaves and stems, off-white ground, "Rorstrand Sweden" mk, c1910, ... **45.00**

10" h, squat base, long, straight neck, 10" h, blended dk brown drip over tan body, green int, ... **145.00**

Vase, 11 3/8" h, incised design, polychrome hunter and 2 maidens, grey ground, **$425.00**

11" h, swollen, tapered shape, flared rim, painted yellow daisies, bluebells, and dk red stems, ... **100.00**

ROSENTHAL

Selb, Bavaria, Germany
1879 to Present

History: The Rosenthal factory was located in Selb, Bavaria. Philip Rosenthal started initially by purchasing whiteware from Selb's other potter, Lorenz Heutschenreuther, decorating it, and selling it from house to house. Rosenthal established his own factory in 1879.

Rosenthal's factory flourished, providing quality figure and tableware that was decorated tastefully. Simplicity of designs and high quality workmanship made Rosenthal a household word.

Several additional factories were constructed. Production rose steadily. Designers of dinnerwares included Theodor Karner, Karl Himmelstoss, Ferdinand Liebermann, Philip Rosenthal, and Walter Gropius. "Darmstadt," "Donatello," and "Isolde" originally were produced in plain white between 1904 and 1910. Later heart-shaped motifs in the Art Nouveau manner were added to "Darmstadt." "Donatello" was decorated with underglaze pate-sur-pate, painted cherries, or a geometric pattern.

Figures made during the 1920s and 1930s were shaped and decorated in the Art Deco style. Many were signed by the artists. Following World War II, most of Rosenthal's assets were destroyed or outmoded. Sources for raw materials, mainly from the Eastern Block countries, were terminated.

Philip Rosenthal II assumed control, formed Rosenthal Porzellan AG, and began the restoration of the works. Many of the older designs, except for "Maria Weiss," "Moss Rose," "Sans Souci," and "Pompadour" were abandoned in favor of fresh ideas originated by designers familiar with the modern tastes, among whom were Tapio Wirkkala from Finland, Jean Cocteau from France, and Bela Bechem from Germany.

The U.S. market was the major goal. Raymond Loewy was hired to design medium-priced dinnerware for the American market. Under Philip's supervision, Rosenthal regained its prestigious position and flourishes today.

References: Dieter Struss, *Rosenthal*, Schiffer Publishing, Ltd. 1997; Ann Kerr, *Rosenthal, Excellence For All Times: Dinnerware, Accessories, Cutlery, Glass*, Schiffer Publications.

Collectors Club: Rosenthal Collectors Club, www.rosenthal.de/

Candlestick, 6 1/4" h, white w/gold trim and base, pr, **$595.00**

Bowl, 10 7/8" w, oct on ftd oct base, green band of leaves and berries on border, ... **395.00**

Candy Dish, 7 1/2" l x 6 3/4" w, scattered violets in center, lt green ground, gold outlined wavy rim, gold circ handle on end, ... **45.00**

Creamer and Cov Sugar Bowl, creamer, 4 1/8" h, sugar bowl, 5" h, molded, twisted shape w/alternating lt blue or yellow panels and HP sprigs of blue cornflowers, gold trimmed handles, ... **120.00**

Cup and Saucer, Demitasse
Band of purple pansies on gold borders, cobalt ground, gold int and handle, ... **100.00**
"Delft" pattern, blue and white Dutch windmill scenes, "Versailles" shape, ... **85.00**
Quatrefoil shape, HP pink, blue, and purple carnations and forget-me-nots in molded gilt panels, relief molded designs on ground, ... **40.00**

Dessert Set, 12 plates, 7 7/8" d, "Chippendale" shape, 3 groups of red or yellow roses and orchid on border, cream ground, ... **180.00**

Ferner, 8 1/2" d, blue "Delft" pattern, "Sanssouci" shape, early 20th C, ... **395.00**

Figure
3 1/8" h, standing terrier dog, white w/brown mask, "ROSENTHAL GERMANY KUNSTABTEILING

SELB HANDGEMAKT V" mk, ... **150.00**

7" h

"Drinking Maiden," kneeling brown haired, flesh colored nude woman drinking from hand, white rect base, c1920s, ... **325.00**

Walking blackamoor, white suit, white cap w/gilt accents and blue feather, gilt accented vest, carrying multicolored tray of fruit, "Rosenthal Bahnhof Selb Bavaria Pastell China" mk, ... **220.00**

Plaque, 12 3/8" h x 8 1/2" w, rect, HP scene of racing sailboats, wood frame, sgd "Fritz Neumann," **2,500.00**

Plate

8" d, multicolored bouquet of garden flowers in center, border of gold outlined ovals w/garden flowers alternating w/gold outlined reticulated circles, ... **68.00**

10" d, HP grapes, shaded lavender, blue, and cream ground, gold scalloped rim, ... **165.00**

12 1/2" d, lg red, yellow, and grey flowerheads, grey stems, molded swirls on border, ivory ground, gold shaped rim, ... **40.00**

Tankard, 13" h, purple and green grapes, shaded purple borders, gold rim, mkd, ... **675.00**

Teapot, 10 1/2" h, diamond shape, multicolored quilt design on top section, brown pebble textured lower section and pyramid cov, ... **170.00**

Trio, cup, saucer, plate, 7 3/4" d, "Maria" pattern, ... **55.00**

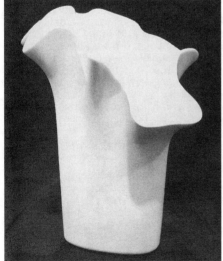

Vase, 10" h, white glaze, Studio line, **$185.00**

Vase

6" h, ball base, trumpet neck, HP pink flowers, green foliage, gold outlined relief molded leaves, cream ground, mkd, ... **50.00**

6 1/2" h, tapered shape, everted rim, soft white florals, blue vellum ground, ... **185.00**

Vase, 9" l, porcelain, textured brown crystalline glaze, (A), **$220.00**

9" w, white porcelain, organic teardrop shape w/bands of molded beading on neck, Tapio Wirhala, (A), ... **374.00**

10" h, ovoid, 2 sm purple and gold handles on shoulder, multicolored transfer of farm maiden and cows in meadow, reverse w/sm transfer of farm girl holding basket, ... **150.00**

10 3/8" h, swollen middle, trumpet neck and rim, raised white cameos of flying and standing herons in marsh, matte rust ground, pr, ... **550.00**

Vegetable Bowl, 12 3/4" l x 8" w, oct, "Maria Floral" pattern, ... **115.00**

Vegetable Bowl, Cov

5 1/4" h x 10 1/2" H-H, "Bountiful" pattern, "Winfred" shape, gold trim, ... **60.00**

12" H-H, lobed, purple grapes, brown-green leaves and tendrils, lt blue shaded ground, gold ribbon handles and knob, artist sgd, "Versailles" shape, c1920, ... **245.00**

O & EG
ROYAL
AUSTRIA
1899 - 1918

History: In 1899 Oscar Gutherz joined with Edgar Gutherz, the former manager of the New York and Rudolstadt Pottery, to manufacture household, table, and decorative porcelains, mainly for export to the United States. The mark used was "O. & E.G." and "Royal Austria" until 1918.

The Austrian Porcelain Industry combine acquired the factory, named it Opiag, Branch Altrohlau, and operated it from 1918 until 1920. Between 1920 and 1945, the factory was called Epaig, Branch Altrohlau. It produced household and decorative porcelains, gift articles, and souvenir items. After World War II, the company was nationalized.

Bowl, 5 1/2" d, HP pink rose sprays w/green leaves on int and ext, shaped rim, "O. & E.G. Royal Austria" mk, ... **35.00**

Cookie Plate, 11" H-H, tan center and ground, border band of green parakeets on alternating yellow or pink vert bands, ... **75.00**

Dish, 6" w, "Rose Pompador" pattern, HP lg dk red or pink tinged white roses and foliage, sm white baby's breath, wide indented gold border w/raised beaded band, "Rose Pompador," "O. & E.G. Royal Austria" mks, ... **20.00**

Gravy Boat, 8 1/2" w, w/underplate, scattered multicolored garden flowers and sprigs, "green O. & E.G. Royal Austria" mk, ... **35.00**

Hatpin Holder, 4 1/4" h, corset shape, HP pink and white dogwood blossoms and buds, lt green ground, gilt top, "O. & E.G. Austria" mk, ... **155.00**

Nut Bowl, 6" d, HP brown acorns, vines, and leaves on ext, green luster int, 4 gold feet, scalloped rim, ... **20.00**

Plate

6 3/8" d, HP pink, reed, yellow, or purple pansies around border, wide burnished gold rim, "green O. & E.G. Royal Austria" mk, ... **15.00**

6 5/8" d, hanging red cherries, blue and green foliage, shaded cream to maroon beaded border, shaped rim, "green O. & E.G. Royal Austria" mk, ... **30.00**

Plate, 9" d, HP pink and lt green, gold rim, "O. & E.G. Royal Austria" mark, **$35.00**

8 3/4" d
> HP lg red centered white roses, green leaves, gold indented shaped rim w/beading, "O. & E.G. Royal Austria" mk, ... **30.00**
> HP white and red roses, buds, and foliage in center, blue border w/gold overlay and band of gold hanging ivy leaves, artist sgd, ... **50.00**

8 7/8" d, HP
> Lg pink and red roses and buds, green foliage on border, scalloped rim, "green O. & E.G. Royal Austria" mk, ... **15.00**
> Three black sandbirds on brown ground, green grass bkd w/trees, blue water in distance, indented rim, "O. & E.G. Royal Austria" mk, ... **20.00**

Plate 9 5/8" d, red and white roses, green foliage, pale green to ivory ground, gold rim, artist sgd, "Hand Painted Gloire d Dijon, O. & E.G. wreath" mks, **$60.00**

9" d, HP
> Grapes and leaves on shaded green border, artist sgd, "green O. & E.G. Royal Austria" mk, ... **15.00**
> Two lg pink roses, green leaves, brown to cream shaded ground, gilt accents, artist sgd, "green O. & E.G. Royal Austria" mk, ... **125.00**
> 10 1/4" d, "Rose Pompador" pattern, HP lg dk red and pink roses, foliage, at side, green to white shaded ground, gold rim, artist sgd, "green O. & E.G. Royal Austria" mk, ... **85.00**

Salt, 1 1/2" d, bag shape, mint green, gold rim, ... **38.00**

Shaker, 3" h, yellow flowerheads, green foliage, shaded brown to ivory ground, "green O. & E.G. Austria" mk, pr, ... **20.00**

Vase, 6 1/2" h, multicolored scene of classic maidens and cherub in oval gilt cartouche, dk red, pink, and green body divided by gold beading, dbl gold handles, gold accented spread foot, ... **75.00**

Vegetable Bowl, Cov
> 10" H-H x 5" h, bunches of sm blue flowers, gilt rims, handles, and knob, ... **65.00**
> 12" H-H x 5 5/8" h, bunches of purple violets, green leaves, gold trim, molded indented rims, "green O. & E.G. Royal Austria" mk, ...**40.00**

c1903

ROYAL BAYREUTH

Tettau, Bavaria
1794 to Present

History: Wilheim Greiner and Johann Schmidt established a porcelain factory at Tettau in 1794. They also maintained an association with the Volkstedt and Kloster Veilsdorf factories in Thuringia. The factory survived numerous wars, financial difficulties, and many changes in ownership until a great fire in 1897 destroyed most of the molds and early records. A more modern factory was built and operated until World War I.

The company operated under the name Porcelain Factory Tettau from 1902 until 1957. In 1957 the company adopted the name Royally Privileged Porcelain Factory Tettau GMBH, which it still uses today.

Animal and floral forms along with other unusual figural shapes were made at Tettau between 1885 and World War I. Designs included fruits, vegetables, lobsters, tomatoes, and people. Shapes ranged from ashtrays to vegetable dishes. Individuals often bought them as souvenir and novelty items because of their inexpensive cost. Much of the production was exported.

Today the firm produces dinnerware and limited edition collectibles. The name, "Royal Bayreuth" is used in the United States to identify the company's products.

Rose Tapestry

Rose tapestry, similar in texture to needlepoint tapestry and called "matte finish" china, was made in the late 19th century. Rose tapestry had a rough effect that felt like woven cloth. It was made by wrapping the article in coarse cloth and then firing. The cloth was consumed in the firing, and the tapestry effect remained.

Decoration was added over the glaze. It varied from floral to scenic to portrait. The floral motifs included "rose tapestry," the most popular and prevalent design. The roses shaded from a pale pink to deeper red colors.

Occasionally, pale yellow or white roses were combined with the pink or red roses. Rose tapestry also can be found in an apricot and deep orange-gold shade. The rarest rose tapestry was "sterling silver." The roses were deep grey to a pale silver-grey shaded into white.

The background of rose tapestry was off-white or had a greyish or greenish tinge. Pale green leaves and small faintly tinted flowers completed the decoration.

Floral, scenic, and portrait tapestries were made in plates, pitchers, cups and saucers, vases, pin boxes, trays, bells, and many other shapes.

Sunbonnet Babies

Molly and Mae, the Sunbonnet Babies, were created by Bertha L. Corbett, an American artist, in the early 1900s. Corbett had no confidence in her ability to draw faces, so she hid them under the large bonnets. The Sunbonnet Babies were drawn to develop good character traits and teach children their daily chores, e.g. washing, ironing, sweeping dusting, mending, baking, fishing, and going to church.

Variations identified as Beach Babies and Snow Babies also were made.

References: Mary J. McCaslin, *Royal Bayreuth: A Collector's Guide*, Antique Publications, 1996; Mary J. McCaslin, *Royal Bayreuth, Book 2*, Glass Press/Antique Publications, 2000, Joan & Marvin Raines, *A Guide to Royal Bayreuth Figurals*, privately printed, 1973; Joan & Marvin Raines, *A Guide to Royal*

Bayreuth Figurals, Book 2, privately printed, 1977; Virginia & George Salley, Royal Bayreuth China, privately printed, 1969.

Collectors' Clubs: Royal Bayreuth Collectors Club, Inc., Mary McCaslin, 6887 Black Oak Court, Avon IN, 46123, Membership: $30.00, Quarterly newsletter, e-mail maryjack@indyrr.com; Royal Bayreuth International Collectors' Society, P.O. Box 325, Orrvile, OH 44667, Bi-monthly newsletter.

BABIES
Bell

3" h, Sunbonnet Babies-Fishing, ... **450.00**
3 1/4" h, Sand Babies, ... **480.00**

Creamer and Sugar Bowl, multicolored Ring Around the Rosie and girl pulling dog, blue marks, **$335.00**

Creamer

2 3/4" h, Dutch girl and dog, brown and blue banded ground w/white center, gold handle, ... **65.99**
3 1/2" h, Sunbonnet Babies-sweeping and dusting, .. **365.00**
3 3/4" h, Snow Babies-Sledding, ... **275.00**

Cup and Saucer, Demitasse

Sand Babies running, ... **125.00**
Sunbonnet Babies washing, ironing, and mending, blue mk, ... **225.00**

Milk Pitcher, 7 1/2" h, Sunbonnet Babies washing, blue mk, **$1,395.00**

Feeding Dish, 7 1/2" d, Snow Babies sledding, multicolored decal, Royal Bayreuth blue mk, ... **300.00**
Jug, 3 1/2" h, Snow Babies sledding, blue mk, ... **100.00**
Milk Pitcher, 5 1/2" h, Sunbonnet Babies fishing, ... **300.00**
Pitcher, 5" h, Sunbonnet Babies sewing and mending, blue mk, ... **500.00**
Plate, 7 1/2" d, Sunbonnet babies washing and ironing, blue mk, ... **75.00**
Toothpick, 2 1/4" h, 3 handles, Little Boy Blue, ... **365.00**
Tray, 9 1/2" l x 7" w, Snow Babies, blue mk, ... **545.00**
Vase, 4 1/4" h, Sand Babies, ... **250.00**

Ashtray, 7 1/8" l x 6 1/8" w, orange ground, blue mk, **$300.00**

FIGURAL
Ashtray, 6" d, figural elk, tan, ... **295.00**
Bowl, 5" w, figural rose, yellow, pink, white, and green, ... **650.00**
Bowl, Cov, 3 3/4" h, tomato, red body, green stem, blue mk, ... **125.00**
Candlestick, 4" h, Basset Hound, ... **495.00**
Condiment, 4 1/4" h, red lobster, green handle, ... **145.00**
Creamer

Coachman, ... **175.00**
Cow, black w/red ears and nose, ... **245.00**
Dachshund, ... **200.00**
Devil, matte black ext, red int, blue mk, ... **1,200.00**
Devil and Cards, 3 3/4" h, ... **300.00**
Dog Head, ... **265.00**
Elk, ... **95.00**
Frog, brown, black and white eyes, ... **345.00**
Lemon, green leaf spout, ... **300.00**

Lion, brown, unmkd, ... **165.00**
Lobster, blue mk, ... **185.00**
Milkmaid holding jug, green dress, blue mk, ... **440.00**
Mouse, ... **2,600.00**
Pansy, green stem handle, blue mk, ... **425.00**
Pear, ... **575.00**
Pelican, ... **275.00**
Pig, grey, pink snout, blue mk, ... **500.00**
Robin, ... **175.00**
Rooster, red comb, blue mk, ... **550.00**
Rose Bud, red and green, ... **225.00**
Spikey Shell, ... **245.00**
Strawberry, ... **125.00**
Sunflower, brown centered yellow petaled flower, green stem handle, blue mk, ... **225.00**
Watermelon, dk green stripes, ... **495.00**
Cup and Saucer, red strawberry, green leaf saucer, ... **195.00**
Cup and Saucer, Demitasse, poppy, red w/green foot and leaf saucer, ... **195.00**
Match Holder, 5" h, clown, red suit, white collar, ... **495.00**
Milk Pitcher, 5 1/2" h, figural lamplighter, blue mk, ... **425.00**
Mustard Pot

3 1/4" h, tomato, red w/green stems, blue mk, ... **50.00**
3 1/2" h, grapes, yellow, ... **250.00**
4 1/2" h, lobster, red, ... **200.00**
Nappy, 6 1/2" l, green lettuce leaf, blue mk, ... **75.00**
Pitcher

4" h, figural red lobster and green lettuce leaf, ... **195.00**
4 1/8" h, Devil and Cards, ... **400.00**
7 1/4" h, Devil and Cards, blue mk, ... **950.00**
Plate

7 1/2" d, red figural lobster on green ground, unmkd, ... **75.00**
8 1/2" d
Figural corn, 3 yellow ears, green ground, blue mk, ... **650.00**
Figural red strawberries, white blossoms, green leaves, ... **125.00**
Shakers

2 1/2" h, red tomatoes, unmkd, pr, ... **50.00**
3 1/2" h, purple grapes, green leaf bases, green mk, pr, ... **148.00**
Sugar Bowl, Cov, 3 1/2" h x 5 1/2" d, red tomato, green leaf base w/curled stem handle, ... **95.00**

Teapot, 3" h, red tomato, green stem handle, spout, and knob, ... **185.00**

Toothpick Holder, 3 1/2" h, bell ringer, ... **425.00**

Wall Pocket, 9" h, green, yellow, and red-brown figural bunch of grapes, ... **575.00**

*Water Pitcher, 7" h, blue-green feathers, cream breast, yellow beak, **$1,850.00***

Water Pitcher

6" h

    Apple, yellow and red, green stem handle, blue mk, ... **795.00**

    Tomato, ... **395.00**

6 1/2" h, red clown, nicks on collar, ... **700.00**

7 1/4" h

    Devil and Cards, ... **750.00**

    Santa Claus, pack handle, ... **4,800.00**

GENERAL

Bowl, 10 1/2" d, painted grapes and leaves in center, molded grape and leaf border, blue mk, ... **450.00**

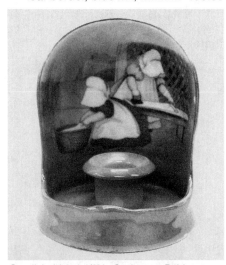

*Candleholder, 4 1/2" h, Sunbonnet Babies washing and ironing, blue mark, A-**$575.00***

Candlestick

4" h, Dutch girl, blue mk, ... **70.00**

4 1/4" h, black Corinthian design, blue mks, pr, ... **38.00**

4 1/2" h, Little Bo Peep, blue mk, ... **195.00**

5 1/4" h, farm scene in band on neck, yellow body, blue mk, ... **165.00**

*Creamer, 3 3/4" h, water buffalo, black, red trim and int, blue mark, **$145.00***

Creamer, 3 1/2" h x 4 1/4" w, Corinthian design, black, blue mk, ... **125.00**

Dresser Jar, 3" h x 4" d, pastel pink or blue flowers around rim, blue mk, ... **165.00**

Hatpin Holder

4 1/2" h, sailing boat, seagulls overhead, blue mk, ... **200.00**

5" h, multicolored swimming swans, med blue ground, ... **170.00**

Humidor, 8" h, transfer printed orange and yellow roses, blue mk, ... **450.00**

Mug, 2 3/4" h,

    Jack and the Beanstalk, blue mk, ... **195.00**

    Little Bo Peep, blue mk, ... **50.00**

Nappy, 4 1/8" w, Breton girl carrying basket, ... **100.00**

Pin Dish, 7" w, leaf shape, Little Bo Peep, blue mk, ... **195.00**

*Pitcher, 4" h, Corinthian Ware matte black ext, gilt trim on rim, lt orange to dk orange shaded int, **$150.00***

Pitcher

3 1/8" h, Dutch boy and girl standing on dock, intertwined dbl handle, ... **175.00**

3 1/4" h, multicolored cavalier design, gold trimmed handle, unmkd, ... **65.00**

3 3/4" h, black Corinthian design, orange int, ... **135.00**

3 7/8" h, multicolored sailing ship scene, blue mk, ... **245.00**

4 1/2" h, cylinder shape, black Corinthian pattern, ... **125.00**

5" h, Corinthian design, black, ... **175.00**

6 1/4" h, multicolored hunt scene chasing moose on upper section, orange-red base, ... **100.00**

7" h, "Two Musicians" pattern, ... **175.00**

7 5/8" h, red Corinthian, green int, ... **350.00**

7 3/4" h, stagecoach scene, green band, blue mk, ... **75.00**

Plate

7 5/8" d, "Little Bo Peep," blue mk, ... **175.00**

9" d, little girl and dog on leash, ... **175.00**

9 1/2" d, multicolored chambermaid on steps holding lighted candle, shaded brown ground, pierced for hanging, blue mk, ... **340.00**

Toothpick, 2 1/2" h, ball shape, ftd, multicolored cattle in pastoral bkd, unmkd, ... **55.00**

*Tray, 10" l, 7 3/8" w, man in blue jacket, purple pants, woman in orange gown, blue mark, **$485.00***

Tray, 11" l x 8" w, multicolored scene of Arab on horseback in desert, ... **250.00**

Vase

3" h

    Dbl spout, center handle, musicians decal, brown shaded ground, unmkd, ... **55.00**

Ftd, 2 sm stub handles, multicolored Dutch girl holding basket on shore, silver rim, mkd, ... **85.00**

Little Jack Horner, blue mk, ... **195.00**

3 1/4" h

Two horiz handles on shoulder, "The Fox Hunt" design, shaded green to tan ground, blue mk, ... **65.00**

Wide base, tapered top, 3 handles on base, multicolored Arabs w/camels in desert, mkd, ... **60.00**

3 1/2" h, 4 handles, multicolored decal of hunt scene, yellow to brown shaded ground, unmkd, ... **55.00**

3 3/4" h, trumpet shape, ruffled rim, multicolored Arab on horseback w/palm trees and desert, unmkd, ... **65.00**

4 1/4" h, ovoid, Corinthian, black, blue mk, ... **100.00**

5 1/2" h, Ring Around Rosie, blue mk, ... **368.00**

8 1/2" h, bulbous shape, wide shoulder, short, flared neck and rim, lg curved gilt handles, multicolored cavalier scene, shaded brown, pink, and tan ground, emb mk, ... **165.00**

TAPESTRY

Basket

4 1/2" h, 3 color roses, ... **450.00**

5 1/2" h, overhead pierced handle, pink roses, blue mk, ... **550.00**

Bell, 3 1/4" h, cavalier design, .. **325.00**

Box, Cov, 5 3/4" w, clam shell shape, pink roses, green mk, ... **475.00**

Bud Vase, 5" h, pink roses, blue mk, ... **325.00**

Cake Plate, 10 1/2" H-H, 3 color roses, blue mk, ... **465.00**

Creamer, 3 1/2" h, pink roses, ... **175.00**

Dish, 9 1/2" d, 2 cavaliers drinking or playing lute, gold accented raised rim, blue mk, ... **500.00**

Hatpin Holder, 4 1/4" h, pink roses, ... **475.00**

Nappy, 5" l x 4 1/2" w, clover shape, pink roses, blue mark, ... **295.00**

Pin Box, Cov, 3" d, multicolored period courting scene on cov, ... **350.00**

Pin Dish, 5" l x 4" w, 3 color roses, ... **250.00**

Pitcher, 5" h, cottage and mill scene, ... **425.00**

Plaque, 11 1/4" d, multicolored, gold accents, pierced for hanging, "Gobelin Ware," blue mk, **$895.00**

Plaque, 9 1/2" d

Hunting scene of man shooting gun, dog at side, gold rococo border, ... **450.00**

Pink and yellow roses, gold rococo border, pierced for hanging, ... **240.00**

Plate, 10 1/2" d, 3 color roses, blue mk, ... **465.00**

Rose Bowl, 3" h, pink roses, blue mk, ... **140.00**

Pitcher, 4 1/4" h, mill scene, ... **435.00**

Toothpick, 2 1/2" h, pink roses, ... **425.00**

Tray, 11" l x 8" w, rect, 3 color roses, ... **585.00**

Vase

2 1/2" h, fan shape, 3 color roses, 2 sm gold handles on base, ... **295.00**

4 1/4" h, barrel shape, 3 color roses, blue mk, ... **465.00**

5" h

Barrel shape, multicolored scene of ladies bathing in river w/castle in bkd, ... **500.00**

Flared shape, cottage and windmill scene, ... **335.00**

ROYAL BONN

Bonn, Germany
1836-1931

History: Franz Anton Mehlem founded a factory in the Rhineland in 1836 to produce household, decorative, technical, and sanitary earthenware and porcelain. Between 1887 and 1903, the factory reproduced Hochst figures in both porcelain and earthenware using the original molds from the defunct Prince-Electoral Mayence Manufactory in Hochst. Villeroy and Boch from Mettlach bought the factory in 1921 and closed it in 1931.

Royal was added to the mark in 1890. After that, products were marketed under the name, "Royal Bonn."

Berry Set, compote, 9" d x 3" h, 4 plates, 8 1/2" d, various multicolored German village scenes, beaded rims w/blue to pink shaded rayed scallops, ... **150.00**

Bud Vase, 5 1/2" h, squat shape, lg dk red roses, green foliage, cream center ground shaded to brown, ... **65.00**

Center Bowl, 14 1/2" l x 6 1/2" w x 10" h, HP enamel scene of house on lake, flanked by pink roses and daisies, reverse w/blue and purple cornflowers, tan circle and dot ground, ormolu winged griffin handles, ormolu rim, ormolu gargoyle feet, mkd, ... **850.00**

Charger, 11 3/4" d, lg yellow roses, green foliage in center, brown shaded relief molded border and rim w/rays, ... **110.00**

Clock Case, 11" h x 12" w, sm house w/yellow and purple flowers, green leaves, gilt accents, border molded w/puce accented curlicues, swirls, and figural lion heads, Gilbert clock, dtd 1881, ... **850.00**

Ewer, 14 1/2" h, blue forget-me-nots, gold foliage, gold rim and handle, ... **650.00**

Floor Vase, 22 1/4" h, slip decorated matte black, purple, and pink vert chains of thistle and acanthus, blue-green to brown-pink shaded ground, ... **2,200.00**

Jug, 6 1/4" h, HP lg purple and yellow flowerheads, brown stems and branches, tan body, gilt handle, ... **50.00**

Letter Holder, 3 compartment, painted flying cherub w/letter on front panel, gilt floral sprays on sides and

backplates, gilt rococo borders, "red Royal Bonn Germany" mk, chip on base, ... **200.00**

Planter, 7" h, blue printed, branch of flowers and curl leaves in mirror cartouche, overall leaf and flower design, dk orange rim and base, mkd, ... **160.00**

Plate, 11 1/2" d, yellow roses and buds in center, green border w/molding and vert molded designs, gold trim, ... **15.00**

Umbrella Stand, 22" h, vert ribs, blue poppies, mauve and green accents, mauve and gold lustered ground, sgd "J. Miller," **1,550.00**

Urn, Cov, gilt scroll cartouche of period woman and child on portico, dk blue ground w/HP gilt flowerheads and foliage, gilt vert handles and flower knob, ... **885.00**

Vase

6" h, squat shape, Art Nouveau style blue iris, black and green leaves, teal ground, "Royal Bonn Germany Ruysolael" mk, restored rim lines, (A), ... **288.00**

6 1/4" h, swollen shoulder, tapered body, spread ft and rim, HP Dutch woman carrying basket of eggs, reverse w/fence and meadow, pale blue sky, gold rim, mkd, ... **75.00**

6 3/4" h, tapered form, sm flared neck, lt yellow shaded to white roses, shaded brown to green to tan ground, gold rim, ... **275.00**

7" h, squat base, stepped neck and rim, HP yellow, lt and dk brown pansies, brown shaded ground, mkd, ... **195.00**

Vase, 7 3/4" h, magenta and yellow dahlias, blue, green, and yellow ground, gilt trim, molded leaf design on neck and base, $395.00

7 1/2" h

Ball shape, lg enameled gold irises, brown shaded ground, ... **125.00**

Bulbous shape, ftd, 2 curved handles, pie crust rim, HP red and white poppies, buds, and green foliage, ground shaded green base to blue top, molded streaks on shoulder, ... **200.00**

7 3/4" h, tapered shape wide base, narrow neck, flared rim, lg burgundy irises, green foliage, burgundy shaded ground, gold trim, ... **75.00**

8" h, tapered form, straight collar, Art Deco design, stylized white tree, white outlined black diamond leaves, white dot rim, bright red ground, mkd, ... **295.00**

9 1/2" h, bag shape body w/flared neck, HP white, purple, or red flowers, yellow shaded ground, maroon and gold neck w/branch and leaf designs, gold rococo handles, artist sgd, ... **180.00**

10" h

Tapered cylinder shape, "Tokio" pattern, blue transfer, mkd, ... **100.00**

Vase, 11 1/4" h, yellow roses, blue to lt green ground, raised gold overlay, shaded yellow neck, shaded green base, $59.00.

Waisted shape, rolled base, ruffled rim, lg red poppies, yellow-centered white daisies, shaded lt to med green ground, molded flowerheads on base, gold dust on int rim, ... **295.00**

10 1/4" h, wide shoulder tapering to narrow base, short neck, flared rim, 2 sm horiz handles, lg pink and white flowers, lt olive green to dk olive green shaded ground, molded design on neck, ... **195.00**

10 1/2" h, teardrop base, bamboo type neck, painted birds on branches, gold sun and rays, c1910, ... **350.00**

10 3/4" h, bulbous shape, tapered base, sm flared neck, dk pink center band w/gilt lilies, top and base w/stylized cream sunflowers and leaves on earthtone ground, gold beaded borders, ... **275.00**

11 1/4" h, HP polychrome full figure of woman wearing yellow accented white gown, purple sash, holding branches in arm on gold textured ground cartouche, green body w/raised gilt flowers and stems, c1880, ... **750.00**

Vase, 12 1/4" h, blue birds, tulips, florals in colors, magenta and pink vert band, cream ground, gilt foliate design, A-$150.00

12" h, bulbous body, swollen neck, piecrust rim, sq ftd base, 2 gold twisted handles, HP white camellias, shaded maroon to pale blue ground, gold trim, ... **250.00**

13" h, bulbous base, straight neck, yellow centered pale red flowerheads, brown and orange-brown leaves, dk brown branches, cream ground, gold rim, ... **100.00**

*Vase, 15" h, brown hair, country road scene on reverse, raised purple flowers, gold outlined leaves, mint green handles, "Royal Bonn Germany" mk, **$2,000.00***

15" h, ovoid shape w/flared rim, overall gilt outlined purple, white, and blue pansies, lt pink shaded ground, 2 horiz handles, pr, ... **1,650.00**

c1923

ROYAL COPENHAGEN

Copenhagen, Denmark
c1760 to Present

History: During the 1760s, the Danish royal family was interested in discovering the Chinese secret for white hard-paste porcelain. Louis Fournier, a French ceramist, came to Denmark to conduct experiments in hopes of uncovering the porcelain formula.

In 1772 Franz Muller, a Danish pharmacist and chemist, produced the first genuine hard-paste porcelain. Muller, with the Queen's support, founded the Danish Porcelain Factory in Copenhagen in 1775. By 1779 financial difficulties forced Muller to relinquish his hold to the Danish crown. The Dowager Queen Julianne Marie was the chief patron. Under her influences, the Copenhagen trademark of three wavy lines was established. Each wave represented a waterway from Kattegat to the Baltic.

Royal Copenhagen's Flora Danica, decorated with the native plants of Denmark, was a famous 18th century service begun in 1790. A total of 1,802 pieces was painted. The dinnerware was intended originally as a gift for Catherine the Great of Russia, but she died six years before its completion. All botanical illustrations were done free hand; all perforations and edges were cut by hand. The service still remains in the possession of the Danish crown. Flora Danica is still being produced today. Each piece is done entirely by hand by an individual artist who signs his work.

Royal Copenhagen's most famous pattern, Blue Fluted, was created in 1780. It is of Chinese origin and has three edge forms, smooth edge, closed lace edge, and perforated lace edge. It was copied by many other factories.

Although the quality of the porcelain kept improving during the early 19th century, and there was strong popular approval for the company's figures, vases, and accessory pieces in all pottery and porcelain compositions, the factory was not a financial asset for the crown. A. Falch, a private owner, purchased the factory in 1867. A condition of purchase was his right to continue to use the term "Royal" in the monogram. Philip Schou purchased the works from Falch in 1882 and moved to the present location at Smalzgade. Arnold Krog, who was appointed Art Director in 1885, was responsible for revitalizing Royal Copenhagen. The under-the-glaze painting technique was perfected under his control. Muller's early creations were reproduced as the "Julienne Marie Porcelain" line.

Dinner services, under-the-glaze painted figures, and vases were among the principal forms being made at Royal Copenhagen when Dalgas took over in 1902. The first Christmas plate was made in 1908. As at the Bing and Grondahl factory, the molds were destroyed each year after the holiday season to prevent restrikes in hopes of preserving the value of each plate for the collectors. During Dalgas' tenure, there also were experiments with stonewares and the renaissance of the overglaze painting techniques.

Royal Copenhagen grades its products. Pieces that fail inspection, but are worthy of sale are marked under the base by a scratch made by a grinding wheel canceling the 3 wavy lines.

References: Robert J. Heritage, *Royal Copenhagen Porcelain Animals & Figurines*, Schiffer Publishing, Ltd. 1997; Pat Owen, *The Story of Royal Copenhagen Christmas Plates*, Viking Import House, Inc. 1961; H.V.F. Winstone, *Royal Copenhagen*, Stacy International, 1984; Nick & Caroline Pope, *A Comprehensive Guide to Royal Copenhagen*, Schiffer Publications, 2001.

Museums: The Bradford Museum, Niles, IL; Rosenborg Castle, Copenhagen, Denmark.

Collecting Hints: Royal Copenhagen dinnerware sets are eagerly sought by collectors because of their high quality. The blue and white limited edition plates remain popular with collectors.

*Bowl, 10 3/8" d, mulitcolored center scene, maroon and gilt banded int, gilt ext, "Royal Copenhagen 3 blue waves" mark, **$385.00***

Bowl, 13" l x 9 1/2" w, "Flora Danica" pattern, flower names on base, ... **3,900.00**

Bowl, Cov, 11" l x 7" w, blue fluted "Half Lace" pattern, #672, ... **240.00**

*Bowl, 11 3/4" l, 5" h, blue and white, Full Lace, A-**$250.00***

Bud Vase, 4" h, lg relief molded brown and white flower petals, sgd "SALTO," **210.00**

Candelabrum, 19 1/2" h, 3 arm and center nozzle, rococo style, green and gold molded swirls and leaves, figural cherub wearing blue dotted white robe, figural cat on base, 3 gilt outlined rococo scroll feet, mkd, ... **900.00**

Candlestick, 9" h, relief molded masks and drape on sides, blue trim, pr, ... **550.00**

Centerpiece, 11 1/2" l x 5 3/8" h, Art Nouveau style, 3 Himalayan quails, 2 dragonflies, Arnold Krug, chip, ... **2,300.00**

Charger, 13" d, lg blue poppy and foliage in center, blue sprigs on molded border, repeat on reverse, 3 wave mk, ... **250.00**

Coffee and Tea Set, coffeepot, 10 1/2" h, teapot, 7" h, creamer, 4 1/2" h, cov sugar bowl, 4" h, HP red roses w/green foliage, cream ground, gold rims and knobs, c1920, ... **750.00**

Coffeepot, 11 1/2" h, blue fluted "Full Lace" pattern, flower knob, #1202, ... **450.00**

Coffee Service, pot, 10" h, cream jug, 4" h, cov sugar bowl, 5" h, 5 cake plates, 5 1/2" d, 4 cups and saucers, leaf shaped dish, 9" l, dish, 3" d, tray, 9" l, blue fluted "Plain" pattern, ... **475.00**

Compote, 9" w, 4 3/4" h, Flora Danica, "Potenilla Apaca L," or "Thymus Chamedrys FR," pr, A- $920.00

Compote, 7" d x 2 3/8" h, blue fluted "Full Lace" pattern, ... **325.00**

Cup and Saucer
Blue fluted
"Half Lace" pattern, ... **45.00**
"Plain" pattern, ... **70.00**
Flora Danica, "Oscycoccus Palustris Rupr," **700.00**

Cup and Saucer, Demitasse, blue fluted, "Full Lace" pattern, set of 6, ... **350.00**

Dinner Service, 18 plates, 8 5/8" d, 15 bowls, 4 3/4" d, 2 serving bowls, 10 1/4" d, 2 oval platters, 19" l, 2 platters, 13" d, 2 oblong dishes, 9 1/4" l, bowl, 8 3/8" d, platter, 14 3/4" l, 18 butter pats, 30 cups, 36 saucers, cov pot au creme w/underplate, "Brown Iris" pattern, (A), ... **600.00**

Dinner Service, Part, teapot, 6 3/4" h, platter, 12" l, platter, 14 1/2" l, 2 soup bowls, 7 1/2" d, 2 plates, 9 3/4" d, plate, 7 1/2" d, oval vegetable bowl, 9 1/2" l, 2 cups and saucers, blue flute "Plain" pattern, ... **995.00**

Dish, 10" l, oval, blue fluted "Full Lace" pattern, pr, ... **235.00**

Figure
4" h x 5 1/2" l
Standing elephant, matte dk and med brown spotting, black, tan, and grey accents, Knud Kyhn, ... **95.00**
Little boy in blue peaked hat and jacket, white scarf, seated on brown barrel, holding spoon, #3647, ... **95.00**
5 1/2" h
Opium Smoker, sepia and gold, white gown, #2342, ... **400.00**
Seated "Fawn With Syrinx," blue-grey and white, #1736, ... **375.00**
6 1/2" h x 6 1/2" l, boy w/calf, blue coat, brown and white calf, #772, ... **375.00**
7" h
Boy astride goat, holding dead chicken in hand, grey, white, green, and blue, #1228, (A), ... **155.00**
"Little Mermaid," #4431, ... **550.00**
Seated boy on rocks, mending nets, tools on belt, #905, ... **135.00**
7 1/2" h x 6" w, "Hans Clodhopper," blue and red striped coat, tan trousers, red cap, riding goat, carrying dead rooster, #1228, chip, ... **400.00**
8" h, "Harvest Group," woman in long blue dress, white apron, man in white shirt, blue trousers, leaning on woman, both w/garden hoes, ... **275.00**
12 3/4" h, Art Deco style terra cotta bust of Princess Eugene, blue and white head scarf, sq base, sgd "Johannes Kedegaard," **1,600.00**

18 1/2" h, "Wave and Rock," lovers kissing on rock, #1132, ... **4,995.00**

Plate
6 5/8" d, blue fluted "Half Lace" pattern, ... **25.00**
7 1/8" d, blue fluted "Half Lace" pattern, molded basketweave ground, reticulated border, #1/1135, ... **155.00**

Plate, 8 1/4" d, Flora Danica-"Sorbus Aucuparial," $400.00

8 1/2" d, blue fluted "Half Lace" pattern, #572, set of 6, ... **190.00**
9" d, blue flute, "Half Lace" pattern, 2nd quality, ... **45.00**
9 1/2" d, "Full Lace" pattern, reticulated border, ... **145.00**
9 7/8" d, lg sprig of HP flowers in center, sprigs on spirally molded basketweave border, wavy gilt dentil rim, ... **35.00**
10 1/4" d, "Flora Danica-Rosa Rubiginosa.L," **575.00**

Platter, 16 1/4" l x 12 1/2" w, blue fluted, "Plain Lace" pattern, ... **225.00**

Salad Bowl, 9 1/2" d, "Flora Danica-Tormentilla Reptans L," gilt rim, ... **1,595.00**

Serving Bowl, 10" d, "Flora Danica-Angalallus Arvensis L," **260.00**

Serving Dish, 14" l x 11 1/2" w, blue fluted "Half Lace" pattern, #533, ... **175.00**

Soup Plate, 10" d, blue fluted "Half Lace" pattern, #565, set of 6, ... **395.00**

Sugar Bowl, Cov, 4 1/2" h, blue fluted "Half Lace" pattern, toadstool knob, 2nds mk, ... **130.00**

Teapot, 6 1/2" h, blue fluted, "Half Lace" pattern, ... **190.00**

Tray, 9 1/2" l x 6 1/2" w, indented sides, blue fluted "Full Lace" pattern, ... **210.00**

Umbrella Stand, 24 1/2" h, blue and white seagull and ocean, artist sgd, #18-4-1927, ... **3,200.00**

Urn, Cov, 11 3/4" h, baluster shape, HP blue morning glories and foliage on sides, circ foot, sq base w/blue egg design, figural cherub holding mirror on cov, late 19th C, ... **400.00**

Vase, 9 1/2" h, green and brown gloss glaze, Johannes Hedegaard, (A), **$475.00**

Vase

3 1/4" h, squat shape, short neck, lt and dk green crystalline matte glaze, imp mk, (A), ... **650.00**

3 1/2" h, baluster form, blue butterfly over Hawthorn flowers, lt blue to white ground, ... **30.00**

4" h, ovoid, short neck, 2 painted dandelions w/thistles on front, dandelion w/o thistles on reverse, lt to med blue shaded ground, ... **40.00**

6" h

Bulb base, flared neck, blue stylized flowerheads, leaves and birds on base, blue stripes on neck, c1918, ... **95.00**

Pillow shape, blue, pink, and green stylized flowers, lavender leaves, white ground, turquoise ends, blue lined rim, ... **165.00**

Vase, 7" h, brown, blue, and tan design, "Royal Copenhagen Denmark, 870/3455" mark, A- **$110.00**

6 1/4" h, ftd, vert flutes, imp diamond border, white glaze, ... **50.00**

6 1/2" h, ball shape, short neck, HP yellow-centered blue flowers, red veined green leaves, dk blue ground on top, white ground base, orange geometric designs on collar, ... **225.00**

11" h, slightly swollen center, short neck, purple edged white flowers, dk purple foliage, white to blue shaded ground, ... **350.00**

12 3/4" h, tapered form, hourglass neck, painted white daffodil, green and brown leaves, lt blue to cream ground, #2640, 3 wavy line mk, ... **325.00**

13 1/4" h, cylinder shape w/everted rim, HP landscape of rolling hills, farm houses, and path, artist sgd, ... **600.00**

14" h, bulbous form, flared neck, painted sailing fishing boat on waves, blue to white shaded ground, #2869-4044, c1930, ... **1,100.00**

15" h, tapered form, flared neck, white apple blossoms, dk green leaves, grey grasses on base, blue to cream shaded ground, artist sgd, ... **650.00**

19" h, bulbous shape, everted rim, Iceland Falcon in mountains, blue, grey, and white shades, ... **1,500.00**

ROYAL DUX

Dux, Bohemia (now Duchow, Czech Republic)
1860 to Present

History: In 1860 E. Eichler established the Duxer Porcelain Manufactory in Dux, Bohemia. The factory was noted for its portrait busts and lavishly decorated vases. Much of the production was exported to America. After the turn of the century, the Art Nouveau style was used for large porcelain figures and vases.

Shortly after the conclusion of World War II, the factory was nationalized. The newly formed company produced household, decorative, and table porcelains, plus coffee and tea sets. In the 1990s, the company returned to private ownership.

New figures are produced in many of the same subjects, colors and styles of the original pre-World War II pieces. The keys to dating are the impressed marks in the pink triangles and whether the pieces are marked "Czechoslovakia" or "Czech Republic." The pink triangle mark was applied to the base using a piece of solid pink clay. Prior to WWI, the pink triangle mark was left in the bisque state. After the war, the triangle was often glaze-on-glaze, and after 1950, glazed triangles can be more uniformly found on glazed pieces.

Reproduction Alert: Examples are being made reproducing the pink triangle, but the reproductions have painted pink marks instead of solid pink triangles on the genuine pieces. A forged blue-printed triangle mark also has been found and this usually is quite faded. Facsimile signatures are another sign of a fake piece.

Centerpiece

6 1/2" h x 9 1/2" w, Art Nouveau style, figural young girl in pink wrap,

seated on brown washed rocks, fountain into jug below, lg basin bowl w/sm feet, ... **990.00**

12" h x 10 1/2" d, standing semi-nude black-haired woman wearing green split skirt, pierced stepped base flower frog, oct bowl w/lapped borders, ... **795.00**

13" h, 2 figural standing classical females, green gowns, pink sashes, next to lg cream shell, pink triangle mk, ... **1,800.00**

Comport, 8" h x 12" d, 4 figural cherubs holding lt rose, gold, and green bowl, shaped green edged base, pink triangle mk, ... **690.00**

Dish, 12" w, oblong, modeled as duck pond w/figural boy in pink shirt, green trousers at end, 2 ducks at opposite end, pink triangle mk, ... **355.00**

Ferner, 13 1/2" l, molded pink irises, lt green stems, full figured female on front w/red gown, seated on yellow straw bundle, branch handles, pink triangle mk, ... **1,400.00**

Figure, 14 3/4" h, olive green sash w/gold trim, dk pink gown, lt brown sandals, holding melons, "pink Royal Dux Bohemia E triangle" mk, $895.00

Figure

5 7/8" h, standing penguin, black w/white and grey accents, pink triangle mk, ... **90.00**

7 3/4" h, standing period woman, holding bouquet at side, lt blue flowered gown w/yellow overskirt, gold accents, pink triangle mk, c1939, ... **200.00**

8" h x10 1/2" w
Little boy in green-brown suit, pink scarf, seated on edge of handled bowl, washed colors, pink triangle mk, ... **550.00**

Two hunting dogs, standing orange-brown and seated dk brown dogs on oval base, ... **325.00**

Figure, 11 1/2" h, grey, tan, and green, raised pink triangle mark, $350.00

Seated brown-haired nude woman w/black and white butterfly on knee, pink triangle and "Royal Dux Bohemia D acorn in triangle" mk, ... **160.00**

Standing female period courtesan, arm raised w/hand held flat, maroon jacket w/yellow bow, rose skirt, puffy white trimmed lt yellow overskirt, "printed triangle E Royal Dux" mk, ... **300.00**

8 1/4" h, Art Deco, young girl wearing tan pantaloons, shaded blue and white dress, tan bonnet, holding edge of dress and bonnet against wind, ... **325.00**

8 1/2" h, 9 1/4" h, period couple dancing, pale blue wigs, white costumes w/cobalt and gold trim, mkd, pr, ... **490.00**

8 1/2" l, standing ram, brown washed cream body, oval brown base, pink triangle mk, c1920, ... **445.00**

9 1/2" h x 9" w, Art Nouveau woman seated in green-gold gown w/pink belt, seated on shell filling urn from water from cream rocks, pink triangle mk, ... **255.00**

13" h, Art Deco woman w/head back, arms outstretched upward, gold waistband w/dk red-gold hanging drape, gold sling pumps, stepped base, "pink triangle, imp Royal Dux Bohemia, Made in Czechoslovakia" mks, ... **310.00**

13 1/2" h, maiden in yellow flowered red dress and cap, holding lt blue milk jug, 2 white cats on black rect base, pink triangle mk, ... **145.00**

13 1/2", 14" h, classic standing hunter carrying geese, female carrying basket of fish, olive green, beige, and gold matte finish, pink triangle mks, pr, ... **800.00**

14 1/2" h, brown haired running nude woman, white wolfhound at side, tan tree trunk, ... **140.00**

18" h, "EURYDICE" on base, iron-red gown, holding lt blue scarf w/applied flowers overhead and on back, pink triangle mk, ... **1,450.00**

19" h, standing woman in dk red dress, olive green apron, arm resting on man in olive shirt, red trousers, seated on rocks, child wearing olive outfit reaching for man, sickle on circ base, pink triangle E mk, ... **3,250.00**

19" h, 20" h, male water carrier in pink gown, olive sash, female w/basket on head, jug at feet, pink gown, olive top, molded bases, pink triangle mks, pr, ... **675.00**

19" l, English pike, grey-black body, pink accented fins, cream and pink seaweed support, pink triangle mk, ... **300.00**

22" h, classic figures of woman in olive gown holding flowers, man in dk red cloak smelling flowers,

rock base, matte finish,
.... **2,450.00**

35" h, Art Nouveau woman, olive-brown gown, holding pink scarf arching overhead, lg pink flowerheads on side and base, pink triangle mk, ... **2,995.00**

Planter

7 1/2" h x 7 3/4" w, Art Deco, 4 overhead arms, grey mottled ground w/raised red berries, red and yellow center lt blue flowerheads, black stems, triangle and acorn mk, ... **75.00**

10" l x 4 3/4" h, oval, Art Nouveau, relief of pink waterlilies, gold foliage, tan-cream ground, stem handles, matte finish, "Bohemia, E pink triangle" mk, ... **275.00**

21" h, Art Nouveau style, standing nude wearing gold sash gown, leaning on gold open conch shell, gold washed base w/molded red flowers,
.... **2,275.00**

Vase, 19 1/4" h, tan, green, and cream shades, gold handles, matte finish, $4,500.00

Vase

5 1/2" h, center white band w/blue flowers, gold scalloped margins, dk blue band above and below, gold outlined loops on white base, 2 lg fancy gold handles,
.... **110.00**

10" h, Art Deco, 4 overhead strap handles, green and red arches, tan and yellow mottled ground,
.... **180.00**

10 1/4" h, urn shape, painted lilac flowers, gold leaves, cream

ground, 2 gold handles on shoulder, matte finish, ... **150.00**

12" h, amphora shape w/vert rect handles, applied red tinted bronze colored flowerhead and hanging cherries, matte gold ground, mkd, ... **395.00**

15" h, figural classic youth in olive-gold sash w/Greek key border seated on tall brown washed rock, feeding water cup to seated female in pink gown, brown sandals, gold trim,
.... **1,100.00**

17" h, modeled female in copper-green wrap clinging to brown stained cream tree trunk, pink tinged applied flower and red tinged base, another slightly different, pink triangle "E" mks, c1906, pr, ... **2,500.00**

18" h, modeled female figure reaching for fruit on ext of flared center trunk vase, oval red-tan glaze, pink triangle mk,
.... **1,750.00**

21" h, Art Nouveau, corset shape w/sq base and flared neck, applied matte gold hanging leaves, ivory ground, swirled reticulated top, base w/wishbone protrusions at corners, 2 whiplash handles, ... **1,200.00**

24" h, Art Nouveau, bisque, natural color, applied classic women on sides, molded floral and leaf patterns and handles, sq base, gilt accents, pink triangle mks, pr, ... **4,250.00**

1749 - 1864

ROYAL VIENNA

Vienna, Austria
1864 to Present

History: After the Imperial Porcelain Factory closed in 1864, some of the artists and workers established their own small shops. They produced the same forms and followed the same decorative motifs they used at the Imperial Porcelain Factory. The quality of the pieces varied from shop to shop. Some were over decorated; some cheaply done. Many of the pieces imitating the earlier Vienna porcelains were marked with the beehive mark.

The Vienna Porcelain Factory Augarten, that was established in 1922, considered itself the successor to the Imperial and Royal Porcelain Manufactory of Vienna, which closed in 1864. This factory still makes decorative porcelain and figures.

A company started by Josef de Cente in 1793 as a tile and stove factory made copies of the porcelain and figures from the Imperial Vienna factory after it closed in 1864. De Cente bought many of the original molds and used them. His reproductions always were marked with "de Cente," mostly impressed in the base. In 1902 the Alexandria Porcelain works in Turn-Teplitz bought the molds from the de Cente factory.

Basket, 10" w, triangle shape, painted center w/Leda and the Swan scene w/putto spying, pink and green reticulated border w/gilt accents and rim, "blue beehive" mk, late 19th C, (A), ... **480.00**

Box, 3 3/4" l x 3" w, classic scene of 3 women and cherub on cov, dore bronze mts, ... **2,750.00**

Cabinet Cup and Saucer

Gilt beaded rect cartouche of HP multicolored classic women in garden setting, pink ground w/raised gilt scrolling and dots, 3 gilt outlined white panels on saucer border, ... **125.00**

HP scene

Classic woman playing lute, cherub holding music in raised gilt scrolled cartouche, green ground w/raised gilt scrolling, webbing and center dots, gilt rims, gilt dbl scroll handle, gilt int, "blue beehive" and "Austria" mk,
.... **150.00**

Sq shape, HP classic scenes of maidens in gilt beaded vert cartouches on front and reverse, cobalt borders w/gilt chrysanthemum heads, gilt int of cup, blue beehive mk,
.... **225.00**

Woman and parrots in front panel, gold int and fancy curled handle, saucer w/alternating maroon panels w/raised gilt trophies and gold classic scenes on white panels, star in center on pale blue ground, gilt dot rim, "Mein Liebling, blue beehive" on base, ... **2,250.00**

*Charger, 13" d, center portraits of "Pierre le Grande" and "Catherine II" on pink and foliate ground, claret red and gilt border with blue reserves, inscribed on reverse, A-**$3,520.00***

Charger

19 1/4" d, HP scene of Christopher Columbus and crew at Port of Talos, gilt C-scrolls on dk red border, sgd "A. Huston," "Columbus Landet im Hafen Von Talos-1492-93," and blue beehive mks, c1890,
.... **14,500.00**

19 3/4" d, HP center scene of colonial women and children at picnic table outdoors, cobalt border w/raised gold geometrics and swirls, artist sgd, "blue beehive" mk, ... **2,500.00**

Figure

3 1/4" h, blackamoor, white turban w/gilt accents, red vest, blue striped white baggy pants, red shoes, holding blue butterfly, circ base, "blue beehive" mk,
.... **700.00**

7 1/2" h x 6" w, 2 classical ladies in flowered gowns, seated on rocky shelf, one holding bird in outstretched hand, polychrome, oval base w/gilt oval designs and short peg feet, "blue beehive" mk, ... **750.00**

16" h x 17" l, "Europa" riding bull, cherub seated on rock base, overall white glaze, ... **3,520.00**

Plaque, 5 3/4" h x 4" w, rect, multicolored transfer of "Cupid's Temptation," enamel accents,
.... **150.00**

Plate

7 1/4" d, multicolored painting of courting scene in gilt scrolling cartouche in center, cobalt border w/gilt curlicues and scrolling, "blue beehive" mk, c1890, ... **60.00**

8 1/4" d, multicolored titled "Amor and Psyche" in center, cobalt border w/gold leaves and beads, scalloped rim, "blue beehive" mk, ... **195.00**

8 7/8" d, HP center scene of "Renaldo and Armida" or seated woman holding branch beside child, cobalt border w/3 gilt edged oval cartouches of cherubs playing, gilt clover, crisscross and white enamel fields between, "blue beehive" mks, pr, ... **1,450.00**

*Plate, 9" d, HP brown hair, purple ribbon, pale blue-green gown, pink rose in bodice, cobalt border w/raised gold designs, shaped gold rim, (A), **$350.00***

9 1/2" d, HP center scene
Cherub seated on cloud offering crown to gentlemen, lt blue lozenge border w/gilt accents, beehive mk,
.... **750.00**

Classical maiden being crowned by two women in garden, cherub observing, gilt geometric border and rim, "blue beehive" mk, ... **375.00**

Three royal children and dogs titled "Die Kinder Kohl's v. Englound," border w/vignettes of swans, raised beading and gilt enameling, c1880-90, ... **900.00**

Multicolored center scene of "Lisette" holding candle, gilt scrolling and paneled border on cobalt, ... **1,100.00**

9 5/8" d, Multicolored
Center scene of 3 graces dancing and cherub playing harp, maroon border w/raised gold swirls, feather designs, and geometrics, oval inserts, "blue beehive" mk, ... **450.00**

Three classic figures, cherub in garden, cobalt border w/aqua accented gold shell forms, "blue beehive" mk,
.... **375.00**

10" d, classic woman seated in garden holding tambourine, classic standing at side, raised gold stemmed flowers, dk red border w/band of ivy leaves, lobed rim w/Greek key design, "blue beehive" mk, ... **175.00**

Platter, 15 1/4" l x 12" w, oval, HP bunch of garden flowers in center, floral sprigs on border, "blue beehive" mk,
.... **1,400.00**

*Urn, Cov, 25" h, cobalt ground, gilt filigree, continuous multicolored center band, multicolored ovals on plinth, gilt handles, "blue shield" mk, **$3,800.00***

Urn

7 1/2" h, HP classical scene of lute player in boat w/attendants on front, Neptune and attendants on reverse on gilt ground w/raised dots, cobalt collar and circ socle w/gilt swags and swirls, sq cobalt base w/gilt accents, gilt

vert handles, "blue beehive" mk,
.... **1,250.00**

17 1/2" h, HP panel of Roman
senators and orators on front,
Roman soldiers and slave on
reverse, beaded gilt rect frames,
maroon ground w/gilt feathers
and scrolls, circ ft on sq base
w/cartouches of trophies, gilt
rococo handles, "blue beehive"
mk, ... **2,750.00**

Urn, Cov, 12 1/4" h, HP center band of
classical philosophers and warriors
on gold ground w/tooled designs,
cobalt body w/gold filigree, gold
knob, "blue beehive, green Austria"
mk, (A), ... **660.00**

Vase

8 1/4" h, continuous painted classic
scene of woman and cherubs
around middle, pink neck w/vert
fluting, gold bands and handles,
"blue beehive" mk, ... **230.00**

11 3/4" h, triangle shaped body,
trumpet neck and foot, painted
scene of 3 alpine hikers on front,
courting couple at mountain on
reverse, cobalt ground, beaded
band at waist over gilt flutes on
underbody, gilt dolphin handles,
titled "Angenehme Begleitung,"
and "I Mag Di Leiden," late 19th
C, (A), ... **765.00**

13 1/8" h, bottle shape, upright gilt
scroll handles, painted figure of
maiden kneeling and praying in
gilt raised scrollwork and trellis
surround, dk red luster ground,
elongated neck w/gilt Greek key
and vine patterns w/white
enamel accents, "blue beehive"
mk, late 19th C, (A),
.... **2,868.00**

13 7/8" h, ovoid w/trumpet neck and
foot, centered band of classical
figures on gold ground in
beaded and scroll borders,
cobalt ground w/gilt tracery, late
19th C, (A), ... **1,295.00**

Vase, Cov, 12 1/4" h, ovoid w/gilt loop
handles, painted scene of dancing
lady in flower-trimmed dress in
landscape, celeste blue ground
w/gold tracery, domed cov
w/mushroom knob, titled "Tanzendes
Madchen," sgd "Wagner," early 20th
C, (A), ... **1,645.00**

GRIMWADES
ROYAL
WINTON
IVORY
ENGLAND

c. 1930+

STOKE POTTERY

GRIMWADES

c1900

ROYAL WINTON GRIMWADES

Stoke-on-Trent, Staffordshire
1885-Present

History: Founded by the Grimwade
brothers at Stoke in Staffordshire in 1885,
the company initially produced simple
utilitarian wares. In 1887, the firm moved to
larger quarters at the Winton Hotel in Stoke
and in 1890, they moved to even larger
quarters as the exporting of their goods
brought increased success to the
company.

A major move occurred in 1900 as
Grimwades purchased Winton Pottery
Company, Ltd. and Stoke Pottery. The
combined group became Grimwades Ltd,
and, about the same time, a London showroom was opened called Winton House.
Leonard Grimwades introduced a line of
art pottery utilizing innovative designs and
glazes expanding the company's inventory.

Expansion occurred again in 1906-07
with the acquisition of Rubian Art Pottery,
Upper Hanley Pottery, Atlas China of
Stoke, and Heron Cross Pottery of Fenton.
The acquisitions significantly increased
the catalog of products.

Another important change occurred in
1908 as Grimwades purchased a portion
of Chrome Transfers & Potters Supply
Company, thereby gaining control of transfers and colors necessary for the company
to compete. An innovative transfer process
was developed and addition of gold and
colors to the prints often disguised imperfections. A large selection of "Sanitary
Ware" was also introduced in this year.

The coronation of George V in 1911
saw Grimwades deliver a large number of
commemorative pieces at a low cost, as
well as introduce the company to a wider
audience. When George and Mary visited
the factory, the Grimwades saw an oppor-
tunity to add "Royal" to the Winton name.

By the outbreak of World War I, the
company employed about 1,000 employ-
ees. Following the war, Grimwades introduced long, gas-fired furnaces capable of
producing large quantities of ceramics.
Showrooms called Victorian and Excelsior

were opened at Winton House for the introduction of new lines and for clearance
products.

In the 1930s, the popular chintz patterns were introduced and with the coronation of Edward VIII and George VI, large
quantities of Royal Winton's wares hit the
market. Rosebud and cottage wares are
additional patterns prized by collectors.

The death of the last heir in 1964
resulted in the company transferring to
Howard Pottery Company, Ltd. as well as
future companies to the present.

References: Eileen Rose Busby, *Royal
Winton Porcelain, Ceramics Fit For A
King*, The Glass Press, Inc., 1998; Muriel
Miller, *Royal Winton Collector's
Handbook From 1925: Cottageware, Art
Deco, Lustreware, Pastels, Etc.*, Francis
Joseph Publications, 1999.

Collectors' Clubs: Royal Winton Chintz
Collectors Club, Normacot Road, Longton,
Stoke-On-Trent, Staffordshire, ST3 1PA,
www.royalwinton.co.uk

Collecting Hints: Many of the chintz
patterns were re-issued in the 1990s.

Biscuit Barrel, 7 1/2" h, figural brown
beehive w/molded multicolored
flowers, overhead woven handle,
.... **1,500.00**

Bowl, 5 1/2" w, squat form, rolled rim,
"Byzanta Ware," lustered lilac ext,
amber int, ... **20.00**

Butter Dish, 3 1/4" sq, "Garden State"
pattern, ... **10.00**

Butter Dish, Cov, 6 1/2" l x 4 1/2" w,
yellow and purple crocus and green
leaves at corners, gold outlined
knob and rim, ... **30.00**

Cheese Dish, Cov

5 3/4" h, figural hen on nest, yellow
and brown body, red comb,
green nest plate, ... **1,450.00**

6 1/2" l, "Red Roofs" pattern, gold
outlined rims and knob,
.... **50.00**

Comport, 6 1/2" l x 5 1/2" w x 2 3/4" h,
"Tiger Lily" pattern, molded red-pink
flowers on ends w/green foliage,
cream ground, ... **40.00**

Creamer

3 1/4" h, "Tiger Lily" pattern, green,
.... **85.00**

3 3/8" h, red rosebud and foliage on
handle, mint green ground, gold
lined rim, ... **25.00**

3 3/4" h, Sugar Bowl, 3" sq x 3" h, "Ye
Olde Inne" pattern, ... **95.00**

Cup and Saucer

"Golden Age" pattern, ... **10.00**

"Red Roof" pattern, shaded pink
borders, ... **30.00**

Cup and Saucer, Demitasse, "Red Spatter" pattern, gold rims, ... **30.00**

Dish
  5 1/2" l, maroon to gold luster ground, gilt rim, ... **15.00**
  5 7/8" l x 4 7/8" w, figural maple leaf, rose shaded to grey ground, ... **5.00**

Gravy Boat, 5 1/2" l, "Fuschia" pattern, med blue ground, ... **30.00**

Jug
  5" h, "Green Tiger Lily" pattern, ... **275.00**
  7 1/2" h, Art Deco style blue flowerheads, red petaled flowers, yellow-beige ground, brown-gold shaded top and base, blue irid int, "Royal Winton Grimwades Made in England" mk, ... **125.00**

Money Box, 5" h x 5 1/2" sq, brown molded beehive, w/green knob, blue insects and purple flowers, ... **1,650.00**

Pitcher, 10" h, Art Deco style, yellow to green shaded luster glaze, c1920, ... **150.00**

Plate, 5 1/2" sq, relief of ears of corn and stalks, rope rim, white, ... **10.00**

Preserve Pot
  1 1/4" h x 4" l, figural reclining grey-black Pekingese, red ribbon collar, ... **320.00**
  4" h, "Lotus" pattern, pale blue ground w/yellow accents, flower knob, c1930s, ... **385.00**

Sauceboat, 2 1/4" h x 5" w, w/undertray, "Beehive" pattern, ... **450.00**

Stacking Teapot, 6" h, "Rouge" w/gilt rims, and handles, ... **495.00**

Sugar Sifter, 5" h, figural green tree top, painted brown trunk, flowers on base, ... **265.00**

Teapot, 8 1/2" l x 6 1/2" h, red rose w/green leaves on handle and knob, ivory ground, **$550.00**

Teapot
  3 1/2" h, lt green ground, red figural rose on handle and knob, gold lined rims, ... **65.00**

  4 1/2" h, figural petunia, pink body, green stem handle and knob, ... **100.00**
5" h
  "Gera" pattern, white dogwood on green basketweave ground, flower knob, ... **1,100.00**
  "Hibiscus" pattern, figural red flower on handle, ... **160.00**
  6" h, brown painted tree trunks framing lake scene w/blue-grey buildings in bkd, flowers in foreground, yellow leaf canopy on top, brown handle, ... **325.00**
  6 1/2" h x 9 1/4" w, figural polychrome rooster, circ green base, ... **65.00**
  8" h x 10" w, "Golden Age" pattern, overall gold, ... **45.00**

Tea Set, pot, 6 1/2" h x 9 1/2" w, creamer, 4 1/4" h, sugar bowl, 3 3/4" h, "Chanticleer" pattern, figural rooster, white, ... **150.00**

Toast Rack
  5" l, 3 section, sm blue iris, yellow daisies, green leaves on ends, ... **25.00**
  8" l, 5 prong, "Regina," relief molded yellow and pink flower at each end w/shaded green to red ends, ... **38.00**

Trinket Box, 5 1/2" l x 4" w, multicolored floral pattern on cov, gold lined rim, pink base w/4 gold feet, ... **20.00**

Trio, raised pink petunia on handle, pink ground, gilt rims, ... **40.00**

Vase
  4 1/2" h, swollen shape, "Pekin" pattern, pink, cream, and gold oriental temple design on black ground, ... **45.00**
  5" h, shouldered form, lg carved pink rose w/apricot accents, green shaded branch and leaves, lt blue-green ground, white int, ... **16.00**

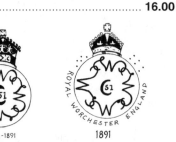

c1876–1891   1891

ROYAL WORCESTER

Worcester, England
1862 to Present

History: (see Worcester for early history) In 1862 Worcester Royal Porcelain Company Ltd. was formed by Kerr and Binns. Limoges-style enameled porcelains, figures, and many dessert services were manufactured. Vases and other ornamental pieces were painted with figure subjects. Among the factory's popular wares was ivory porcelain, a glazed parian ware.

During the 1870s, magnificent porcelains in the Japanese style were produced. Many were modeled by James Hadley, one of the finest ceramic modelers. Hadley left Royal Worcester in 1875 to freelance, but almost all his work was bought by Worcester.

In 1889 Thomas Grainger's factory was bought by the Worcester Royal Porcelain Company. Grainger had started his own factory in 1801 at St. Martin's Gate. After having several different partners, George, his son, eventually took over.

George Owens made wonderful reticulated pieces for Royal Worcester in the 1890s. The piercing was done when the piece was still in the greenware stage before biscuit firing. Pieces were exceptionally delicate and fragile.

James Hadley started his own factory in 1896 to produce ornamental art pottery. It was located near Royal Worcester's main factory. Hadley modeled figures that were decorative as well as fictional in the form of baskets, dessert centerpieces, and candlesticks. In addition to his Kate Greenaway children, he modeled a series of figures entitled "Countries of the World." By 1905 the Hadley firm was absorbed by the Royal Worcester Company. Binns retired in 1897, and Dyson Perrins took over.

Royal Worcester continued to make ordinary bone china patterns in the 20th century. Colored floral borders or blue and white transfer prints in the "Willow Pattern," "Royal Lily," and "Broseley Dragon" were most popular. Ornamental wares with a parian body were part of the product line. The ewer form was very popular at Worcester, as were shell vases.

During the 1920s and 1930s, the company maintained its fine quality wares in a depressed world market with some degree of success. Around 1924 luster wares were introduced, inspired by Wedgwood's dragon and fairyland lusters. In 1928 an electrical decorating tunnel kiln was installed, causing a great improvement in firing decorated wares and raising the standards of china production.

World War II restrictions forced china manufacturers to cut back on their production. Rich ornamental and decorated wares came to an end.

Worcester carried on production of some wares, especially the Doughty Birds for the United States market as part of the war effort involved with lend-lease. Dorothy Doughty's bird figures, and even the foliage on which they were modeled, were absolutely correct in size and color. From the 1930s until 1960, thirty different bird sculptures were made.

Other figures also were produced during the war years, including dogs by Doris Linder, Gwendoline Parnell's "London Cries," Miss Pinder-Davis's "Watteau" figures, and Eva Soper's series of small birds and children in wartime Britain. Freda Doughty modeled a series of children from foreign lands and nursery rhymes in the 1940s. She did an Alice in Wonderland series in 1957.

After World War II, things began to return to normal. A great number of young painters apprenticed to Royal Worcester. In 1948 Doris Linder modeled the first limited edition equestrian model featuring Queen Elizabeth II on Tommy. It has become the most sought after of Worcester's equestrian models.

In 1950 the biscuit kilns were replaced by gas-fired tunnel kilns, which produced even finer quality ware. The founding of the Dyson Perrins Museum at Worcester in 1951 marked the bicentenary of the Worcester Porcelain Company.

During the 1960s, Doris Lindner's equestrian models achieved great success. In addition to limited edition figures, Worcester produced tea, dinner, and oven-to-table wares using both old traditional patterns and new ones. Demands for Royal Worcester porcelain continuously increased. A new factory opened in 1970. Much of the current porcelain decoration is still done by hand. Hard porcelain ornamental wares are part of the product line. Royal Worcester commemorative pieces included mugs, jugs, and trays.

In 1976 the company was restructured and renamed Royal Worcester Spode Ltd.

Marks: Almost every piece of Worcester porcelain was marked. The principal mark on Royal Worcester was a circle containing intertwined Ws with a crescent and the number 51. The 51 represented the original date of the first Worcester pottery. There was also a crown above the circle. From 1891 to 1915, the words "Royal Worcester England" were added around the circle. The mark could be impressed or incised instead of printed. The color could be green or purple.

References: John Edwards, *The Charlton Price Guide to Royal Worcester Figurines, Models by Freda Doughty*, 2nd Edition, The Charlton Press, 2000, Geoffrey A. Godden, *Victorian Porcelain*, Herbert Jenkins, 1961; Stanley W. Fisher, *Worcester Porcelain*, Ward Lock & Co. Ltd. 1968; Susan & Jim Harran, *Royal Period Pieces Deserving of Worcester Name*, Antique Week, October 6, 1997; Henry Sandon, *Royal Worcester Porcelain*, Barrie & Jenkins, 1973.

Museums: Dyson Perrins Museum, Worcester, England; Roberson Center for the Arts and Sciences, Binghamton, N.Y.

Reproduction Alert: Both Austria and Rudolstadt made copies of Royal Worcester wares.

Bowl, 9" d, overall blue dragon pattern w/oriental stylized clouds, molded scrolling sides and handles w/gilt trim, ... **150.00**

Candle Snuffer
3 5/8" h, Mandarin man, yellow robe, red collar, green beaded necklace and cuffs, holding fan in hand, black hat, purple mk, dtd 1922, (A), ... **390.00**
3 3/4" h, kneeling monk, matte chestnut brown habit natural face and beard, purple mk, dtd 1893, (A), ... **2,230.00**

Chocolate Pot, 7" h, wide yellow center band, flanked by conc bands of florals, gilt accented relief areas, figural bamboo handle and spout, ... **200.00**

Coffee Can and Saucer, blue oriental dragons on int and ext, gilt rims, dtd 1922, ... **55.00**

Cup and Saucer, Miniature, HP pheasant in meadow setting, dtd 1926, ... **465.00**

Dinner Service, Part, 11 plates, 9 1/4" d, 8 salad plates, 9 bread and butter plates, 12 cups, 10 saucers, 4 teacups, 3 saucers, 4 oval platters, 3 cov serving bowls, gravy boat, 8 1/2" l, blue and white, dtd 1883, A-$920.00

Dish
10" d, "Evesham" pattern, painted peaches and leaves, vert crimped sides, ... **15.00**
10 7/8" l, oval, HP plums and grapes, sm leaves, brown ground, gilt lined lobed rim, sgd "R. Sebright," puce mk, dtd 1936, (A), ... **835.00**

Ewer, 6 3/4" h, HP flowers, gilt rope around neck, gilt curved handle, dtd 1889, ... **400.00**

Figure
3 1/2" h, "Candle Snuffer," **65.00**

4 1/4" h, "Little Boy Blue," **550.00**
5" h, "Peace," **245.00**
6" h, "Stephon" or "Phyllis," boy piper or girl w/tambourine leaning against tree trunk, gold clothes, matte ivory skin, pale enamel accents on base, dtd 1951, pr, (A), ... **700.00**
6 3/4" h, "The Parakeet," yellow suit, ... **250.00**
9 3/4" h, standing figure of Bacchante, holding tambourine, ivory stained body w/washed green and orange glazes, gilt accents, c1892, (A), ... **380.00**
10" h
"Ascot Lady," **225.00**
"Garden Party," **230.00**
15" h, "The Bather Surprised," partially draped female standing by tree trunk, gilded and bronzed cream coloring, c1924, (A), ... **880.00**
20" h, Grecian Water Carrier, woman w/pot on head, amphora at side, ivory w/brown and purple accents, purple mk, ... **1,765.00**

Jardiniere, 10" h x 18" H-H, peach and lt yellow molded vert leaves on body, mint green leaf molded handles, gilt trim, purple mk, ... **2,175.00**

Jug, 6 3/8" h, gold outlined tan leaves and flowerheads, satin ivory ground, gold handle, purple mk, dtd 1897, $165.00

Jug
4 1/4" h, flat back, HP red tinged white roses, yellow and green foliage, gold handle, ft, and rim, dtd 1926, ... **300.00**
5 7/8" h, tan basketweave ground w/applied gold lizard, gold

bamboo handle, dtd 1917, ... **225.00**

8 1/4" h, HP red centered yellow daffodils and green foliage on side, reverse w/purple flowers on stems, brown and green leaves on neck, gold trim, rim, and outlined branch handle, ivory ground, c1889, ... **875.00**

8 1/2" h, overall white glaze, scallop shell rim, coral handle, c1890, (A), ... **120.00**

10 1/4" h, bottle shape, enameled leaves, flowers, and berries, yellow ground, bronzed and gilt dragon handle, c1880, (A), ... **560.00**

Planter, 3 3/8" h x 3 5/8" d, HP pink and red roses, buds, and vines, gilded top and bottom rims, sgd "M. Hunt," purple mk, c1906, ... **450.00**

Plaque, 4 3/8" d, painted highland cattle on mountainside, misty sunlight and clouds, sgd "John Stinton," dtd 1914, (A), ... **3,700.00**

Plate

6 3/4" d, border of blackberries, apples, and pears, gilt rim, set of 10, ... **140.00**

8" d, blue disc in center, HP fruit on shaded ground, sgd "Ayrton," **230.00**

Potpourri Bowl, 6 1/2" d, pierced curved leaf design, white glaze, gilt accents, c1890, ... **360.00**

Potpourri Vase, Cov, 12" h, painted w/4 cattle by river, bridge in bkd, painted landscape on reverse, gilt divided white enameled panels on shoulder and cov, gilt accents, 2 horiz gilt handles on shoulder, J. Stinton, dtd 1926, (A), ... **7,800.00**

Sauce Tureen, 9" H-H, w/undertray, blue center bands w/geometrics, cream border bands, 4 sm gilt accented cream feet, figural elephant handles, fancy knob, dtd 1878, ... **595.00**

Spill Vase, 6" h, cylinder shape, raised gold and brown bamboo designs, cream ground, purple mk, ... **225.00**

Stand, 7" h, molded ribbed nautilus shell, supported on coral branch, figural shells on base, overall white glaze, ... **125.00**

Teapot, 8" h, HP red flowers, green and red leaves, ivory ground, blue or red flowers on cov, gilt spout and overhead handle, purple mk, ... **255.00**

Toothpick, 2 3/4" h, ivory stepped body w/raised burnished gold 4 petal flowerhead, burnished gold textured base, ... **75.00**

Vase, 9" h, 12" H-H, gold outlined mauve and pink flowerheads, matte cream ground, gilt accents and handles, $450.00

Vase

3 1/2" h, cylinder shape on 3 gold hands to feet supports, HP panel of garden flowers in gilt edged cartouche, turquoise ground w/gilt accents, gilt beaded upper and lower borders, gilt triangular base, sgd "Chair," c1900, (A), ... **780.00**

4 1/8" h, ovoid shape, ivory ground dbl wall, cut honeycomb cells on outer wall w/gold dots, 3 quatrelobed windows showing gold drawn country scenes, row of enamel ivory dots on gold band on shoulder, purple mk, dtd 1930, ... **825.00**

4 1/4" h, swollen middle, flared base and neck, "Sabrina Ware," lt blue Koi fish and seaweed, dk blue ground, dtd 1909, pr, ... **350.00**

4 1/2" h x 8" l, Japanese style curved cream bamboo body, blue-green bamboo overhead handle terminating in blue-green leaf, dtd 1903, ... **525.00**

5 3/4" h, ovoid, flared gilt rim, HP highland cattle in meadow, gilt and white enameled teardrop support on white bead-lined circ gilt base, c1936, puce mks, (A), ... **1,425.00**

6 1/2" h, trumpet shape, multicolored highland cattle, green and gilt scroll molded ft, gilt molded leaves on rim, purple mk, ... **1,250.00**

7 1/2" h, ovoid, ivory wicker ground, red and gilt relief foliage, 4 twig feet, restored rim, c1882, (A), ... **500.00**

8" h, bulbous base w/long slim neck, flared rim, overall HP yellow and red roses, green foliage, Hadley Ware, dtd 1905, ... **700.00**

9" h, bulbous, straight neck w/gold bands, HP red and yellow roses and foliage on ivory ground, 3 gold winding serpent handles, ... **500.00**

10 1/4" h, ovoid w/flared rim and base, lustered lt orange, green, and blue-grey landscape w/vert orange flames, c1926, (A), ... **500.00**

16" h, bulbous middle, tapered base, everted neck, Japanesque style incised turquoise ground w/stylized leaves and blossoms, raised cell design in compartments on base, pierced neck w/leaves, bronzed and gilded bamboo-form handles, c1865, repairs to handles, pr, (A), ... **4,700.00**

c1885

ROZENBURG

The Hague, Holland
1884-1914

History: W. van Gudenberg established an earthenware and porcelain factory at The Hague in 1885.

Rozenburg was best known for a line of exceptionally thin earthenware that was made during the late 19th and early 20th century in the Art Nouveau style. The delicate, translucent body had over-the-glaze decorations of flowers, foliage, and birds derived from the design of Japanese batik-printed fabrics from the Dutch East Indies, now Indonesia. Mauve, yellow ochre, orange, and shades of green were some of the vivid enamel colors used on the white ground. The decoration on later examples was stiffer and had less delicate colors. Shapes featured elongated handles and spouts contrasted with the curved and flat surfaces of the body.

S. Juriaan Kok was director of the company from 1895 to 1913. He was responsible for a series of extraordinary Art Nouveau shapes. J. Schellink was employed as a painter who decorated his works with stylized flowers in brick-red, black, purple, green, and yellow on a bottle-green ground. He also used sea horses and spiked leaves in his motifs. Schellink painted in a series of tense, nervous spots and lines with subtle color combinations. The eggshell-thin porcelain that Schellink used was unique to Rozenburg. M.N. Engelen, the firm's chemist, developed it. Production stopped with the beginning of World War I.

Pieces were marked "Rozenburg/den Haag," a crown, and a stork that was copied from the mark of the 18th century porcelain factory at The Hague.

Bottle, 11" h, w/stopper, brown lettering for liquor, sailing ship, windmills, and farmhouse on neck, chip on base, ... **195.00**

Pitcher, 12" h, orange-yellow chrysanthemums, blue stylized leaves, chocolate-brown ground, c1896, $2,950.00

Inkwell, 3" h, hex shape, HP rooster on panel, brown and yellow meandering plants, leaves, and stems, dk yellow grounds, ... **375.00**

Vase, 10" h, eggshell, multicolored parrots, yellow and orange florals, green vines, white ground, $7,500.00

Vase, 12" h, dk red, pink, and brown flowerheads, green leaves, lt brown ground, dk blue base, "stork and Rozenburg" mark, c1895, $4,200.00

Vase, 8 1/2" h, swollen shoulder, tapered collar, HP Art Nouveau stylized blue and yellow streaks and curls, white ground, repaired rim chip, ... **275.00**

c1924   c1918

RUDOLSTADT

Thuringia, Germany
1720 to Present

History: Macheleid, with the patronage of Johann Friedrich von Schwartzburg-Rudolstadt, established the Rudolstadt factory about 1720. During the factory's peak period, 1767-1797, the firm was leased to Noone. The arrangement lasted until 1800. Rococo-style tableware and large vases were made. After 1800 the firm was sold to the Greiners. A series of partnerships followed.

Ernst Bohne Sons made decorative porcelain, coffee and tea sets, and figures between 1854 and 1920. Many products were similar to R.S. Prussia pieces. After 1920 the factory became a branch of Heubach Brothers.

Lewis Straus and Sons in New York were co-owners of the New York-Rudolstadt Pottery between 1882 and 1918. This firm received the right to use the Royal Rudolstadt designation. The firm produced household, table, and decorative porcelains and served as importers for the U.S. market.

The Rudolstadt-Volkstedt Porcelain Factory was nationalized in 1960.

Biscuit Jar
5 1/2" h, 8" H-H, decals of garden flowers on satin cream ground, gold wishbone handles, rim, and knob, Beyer and Bock, ... **295.00**
7" h, swirl molded body, blue flowers, yellow foliage, gold ribbon knob, ... **149.00**

Bowl
6" d, flowerhead shape w/molded petals, red centered white flowers, gold leaves, gold outlined rim, gold tracery on ext, 3 sm gold feet, "Prussia crowned shield B Royal Rudolstadt" mk, ... **125.00**
9 3/4" d, lg pink roses, meandering green thorny stems, lt blue to brown shaded ground, ... **25.00**

Bud Vase, 4" h, HP red and yellow flowers, red foliage, gold trim, molded chevrons on neck, peach satin finish, "blue crowned RW shield Rudolstadt" mk, ... **85.00**

Cake Plate
10 1/4" H-H, HP blackberries, red tinged green leaves and branches, white ground, silver rim, open handles, Beyer & Boch, ... **165.00**
12" H-H, shaded white to red old roses, raised accents, green foliage, shaded brown to cream ground, gold rim, open handles, "crowned shield B" mk, ... **310.00**

Candlestick, 11 1/2" h, 3 figural elephant heads on base w/entwined trunks supporting nozzle on leaf base, browns and tans, "Rudolstadt Germany, L. Straus & Sons Thuringia Germany" mks, pr, ... **900.00**

Candy Dish, 2 1/2" h x 4" d, painted gilt edged red and white flowers on brown branches, gilt edged relief molded drip collar, ruffled rim, ivory ground, ... **145.00**

Chocolate Service, pot, 10" h, 6 cups and saucers, bunches of blue forget-me-nots on front and back hanging from blue border gold trim, cream shaded ground, artist sgd, ... **335.00**

Cup and Saucer

Band of black silhouettes of animals of "Flossie Fisher's Funnies," pink bands, c1915, ... **165.00**

HP purple and magenta iris on sides w/green leaves, beige ground, gold rim and handles, artist sgd, ... **85.00**

Kewpie, Rose O'Neill, ... **195.00**

Rose, holly, and berry pattern, mkd, ... **25.00**

Dish, 5 1/4" l x 5" w, shell molded, purple and dk red flowers and stems in center, molded curved shell handle, orange shaded rim, "RW in diamond, Rudolstadt" mk, ... **45.00**

Ewer, 11" h, stepped ball shape, gold leaves and stems on cream ground, fancy handle wrapped at neck, "RW diamond" mk, ... **220.00**

Figure

3" h, jumping brown deer supported by stump, oval base, ... **120.00**

5 3/4" h, seated blown and white spaniel on cushion, ... **195.00**

8" h, street musician, man seated on brown bench holding gold French horn, brown, floppy hat, purple trousers, brown cane on grassy base, ... **450.00**

Loving Cup, 6" h, multicolored decal of bust of Victorian woman, med blue ground w/dk blue and white flowerheads, sm dk blue sprigs on reverse, 3 blue bamboo handles, "RW shield" mk, ... **125.00**

Pitcher

6" h, corset shape, HP florals, molded swirls on body, molded center band w/beading, gilt handle and rim, "Germany, R W in diamond, Rudolstadt" mk, ... **85.00**

Plate, 8 1/4" d, yellow or pink roses, green foliage, gold banding w/rose designs, **$35.00**

10" h, swirl molded, serpentine handle, pink florals spray, cream ground, ruffled rim and spout, ... **295.00**

12" h, ewer shape, molded vert ribbing, scattered dk blue flowerheads, gold trimmed handle, ... **400.00**

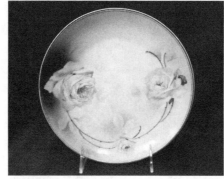

Plate, 8 1/4" d, transfer of pink and white roses with HP accents, brown, blue, and green shaded ground w/shadow leaves, gold rim, Beyer and Boch, **$28.00**

Plate

7 3/4" d, Kewpies playing in green field, gold rim, ... **235.00**

8 1/2" d, HP red-pink roses, green foliage, shaded ground, gold rim, mkd, ... **65.00**

Relish Dish, 9 1/2" l x 5" w, pink-purple orchids on border w/long green leaves, shaded orange to cream ground, artist sgd, ... **70.00**

Tea Caddy, 6 1/2" h, fluted body, HP lg purple pansies, shaded green and brown leaves, gold tracery, white ground, gold ring knob, c1900, ... **225.00**

Vase

3 1/2" h, bulbous w/spread ft and ruffled collar, lg tan-gold rose applied to sides, relief of tan-gold leaves, tan shaded spots, "raised RW diamond" mk, ... **150.00**

4" h, figural brown spattered baby chick next to white egg w/heart shaped opening, brown and green base w/chick heads along border, "Germany RW Rudolstadt" mk, ... **12.00**

6 1/2" h, bulbous shape, Art Nouveau style, relief of vert flowers on base, 4 strap handles on shoulder to neck, overall gold glaze, ... **265.00**

7 1/4" h, ball shape, lg gold outlined purple and magenta pansies and foliage, gold accents, gold

branch handles, 4 gold feet, "blue crowned RW in diamond" mk, ... **45.00**

8" h

Flattened flask shape, 2 sm handles on shoulder, 4 sm feet, multicolored branches of sm flower buds on tan ground, satin finish, "RW Rudolstadt" mk, ... **175.00**

Urn shape w/scalloped gold handles, pink and blue birds on brown and orange-brown foliage, ivory ground, "blue crowned diamond RW" mk, ... **140.00**

8 1/4" h, ball body, flared neck, HP pink flowers, gold detailing on body, reticulated shoulder, gold notched handles, painted flowers on flared top, ... **320.00**

9 1/4" h, teardrop base, straight neck, 2 gilt fancy handles, multicolored scattered florals on satin ivory ground, ... **25.00**

9 3/4" h, figural American Indian head, black and white feathered headdress, green and gold lined black coat, ... **165.00**

16" h, amphora shape, painted Roman chariot and drivers on cream ground, blue and gilt twist handles on shoulder, Greek key rim, raised gold dots, painted blue and red foliage on base, "crowned RW diamond" mk, ... **650.00**

RUSKIN
MADE IN ENGLAND

c. 1920

RUSKIN POTTERY

Smethwick, Birmingham, West Midlands
1898-1933

Founded as the Birmingham Tile and Pottery Works by Edward Taylor and his son William, the pottery derived its name from the philosopher John Ruskin, who influenced the Arts and Crafts movement. As with many fledgling art pottery companies, Birmingham introduced a line of tiles.

Many of the inspirations for Ruskin pottery and its associated glazes came from the Far East. Lead-free glazes were introduced, and these were ahead of the times. One of the recognizable glazes is called

"Souffle." It appeared as a frothy surface, usually in a single color. Lusters were introduced about 1905 and were often used overlaying other colors. William Taylor was a pioneer in high-fired glazes using metallic oxides. Colors included sang de boeuf, crushed strawberry, peach bloom, and snake green.

The 1920s saw a change in form, relying on Art Deco shapes to carry the glazes. Crystalline and matte glazes were introduced. These were less expensive to produce than the high-fired oxides.

The company closed in 1933, and many of the Ruskin secrets were lost.

References: Paul Atterbury and John Henson, *Ruskin Pottery—The Pottery of Edward Richard Taylor and William Howson Taylor, 1898-1935*, Baxendale Press, The Antique Collectors Club, ISBN 0 9520933 08, Lucille Grant, *The Albert E. Wade Collection and Ruskin Pottery, Antique and Collecting Magazine*, October, 2002, 1006 S. Michigan Avenue, Chicago, IL 60605.

Bud Vase
3" h, mottled green glaze w/dk black green islands, "RUSKIN ENGLAND" mk, ... **55.00**
4" h x 5" d, squat shape, shaded turquoise to purple lustered ground, stylized red flowers on shoulder, c1906, ... **550.00**

Bowl
4 1/2" h, high fired, blue, red, and white streaked glaze, SP cov, (A), ... **615.00**
5" d, cream and lt blue crystalline glaze, mkd, ... **70.00**
6" d, ftd, mottled lt sea green glaze w/dk area, "imp RUSKIN ENGLAND" mk, dtd 1924, ... **50.00**
10" d, mottled yellow, green, and blue int, blue streaks over yellow ext, "RUSKIN ENGLAND" mk, ... **250.00**

Coffee Can and Saucer, blue luster glaze, ... **95.00**
Jar, Cov, 7 1/4" h, fruiting vines on shoulder, med blue glaze, ... **1,195.00**
Lamp Base, 8 1/2" h, architectural form, hex w/vert buttresses, blue base shaded to orange middle to white top, ... **465.00**

Vase
3" h, flared trumpet shape, orange luster glaze, c1921, ... **50.00**
3 3/8" h, cylinder shape, spread elephant ft, green "souffle" glaze, ... **720.00**

5 3/4" h, cylinder form w/flared rim and ft, curdled cream and gold glaze, dtd 1916, ... **150.00**
6" h, tapered bowl shape, ftd, orange lustered glaze w/oilspots, "RUSKIN ENGLAND" mk, ... **125.00**
6 1/2" h, bulbous shape, green, blue, orange-brown, and ivory drip glaze, mkd, (A), ... **460.00**
7 1/2" h, ball base, trumpet neck, flared rim, blue luster oil spot glaze, "1924 Ruskin England" mk, ... **225.00**
7 7/8" h, slightly swollen shape, high fired sang-de-beouf red and white glaze, (A), ... **1,235.00**
8 1/4" h, corset shape, gloss blue glaze, ... **745.00**
9" h, amphora shape w/3 handles, copper red ground w/dk blue streak on top, lt blue streaks on base, "imp RUSKIN" mk, ... **400.00**
9 1/2" h, cylinder shape, flared rim, streaked orange luster glaze, ... **290.00**
9 7/8" h
Shoulder form, short collar, turquoise luster glaze, (A), ... **295.00**
Trumpet shape, shaded dk to med blue ext, mottled lt blue int, (A), ... **495.00**
10 7/8" h, bulbous body, spread base and foot, everted rim, orange luster glaze w/streaks, dtd 1920, ... **350.00**

ГАРДНЕРZ

EARLY 19TH CENTURY

КорНИЛОВЫХЪ

Korniloff's factory
c1835

Завода
S.Т.КУЗНЕЦОВА
Вз.Rин 5
c1835

ВРАТЬЕВЪ

Baterin's factory
1812-1820

RUSSIA-GENERAL

Early 1800s to Present

Gardner
Verbiki, near Moscow, Russia
1766-1891

History: Francis Gardner founded his factory in 1766. He brought experienced European potters and decorators to Russia. Utilitarian wares, artistic objects, and articles for sale at fairs comprised the production.

Floral motifs and pastoral scenes were favored. Many dinner sets were made on commission. The Gardner family controlled the factory until 1891, when it was acquired by the Kuznetsov family.

The initial "G" or name "Gardner" was used as the mark.

St. Petersburg, now Leningrad, Russia
1744 to Present

History: The Kuznetsov family established a factory to manufacture porcelain and faience at Novocharitonowka in 1810. Their sons, trading as the Brothers Kuznetsov, managed the factory until the 1870s. They also operated other factories around Russia.

These factories produced powder boxes, vases, and toilet sets in blue and pink porcelain that was often enameled and gilded. Figures in biscuit porcelain were painted with regional costumes and other decorative motifs. Products from these Russian factories were exported to other European countries, the Far East, and India.

In 1891 the firm acquired the Francis Gardner factory near Moscow. Marks usually incorporated "Ms. Kuznetsov" along with the place of manufacture.

Native Russian porcelains developed during the 1800s because of the high duty on imported porcelains. The Kornilow Brothers established a factory to manufacture utilitarian wares in St. Petersburg in 1835.

The Yusupov Factory near Moscow operated from 1814 to 1831. White porcelain blanks for decoration were purchased from Sevres, Limoges, and Popov. Articles made at this factory were used as gifts for the members of the Tsar's family or for the friends and relatives of the Yusopovs.

The Popov Factory, established in 1806 at Gorbunovo, made dinner services, tea sets, and porcelain figures for an urban middle-class clientele. Popov's figures of Russian craftsmen, peasants, and tradesmen, are eagerly sought by collectors. The factory closed in 1872.

Initially, the Imperial St. Petersburg porcelain factory enjoyed only limited success. Catherine the Great was associated with the factory by 1762. Her imperial patronage helped ensure success.

Most of the wares were basically French in form, but often were painted with Russian views. When Jean-Dominique Rachette became head of the modeling workshop in 1779, he increased the sculpture output by making porcelain statues, groups in bisque, and portrait busts.

Enormous dinner services were made for the Tsar's palace and the nobility of the court, e.g. the "Arabesque Service" of 973 pieces in 1784 and the "Cabinet Service" of 800 pieces. The War of 1812 disrupted production at the factory somewhat. Portraits of heroes and military motifs appeared on the porcelains during and immediately following the war.

Reorganization took place in 1901. The Art Nouveau style was utilized. About 1907 soft paste porcelains were developed. A series of figures entitled "Peoples of Russia" was designed by P. Kamensky and issued beginning in 1907. The factory's work continued after World War I and during the Civil War. The revolution inspired designs for porcelains reflecting industrialization of the country.

The factory was renamed Lomonosov Factory in 1925 in honor of M. Lomonosov, the Russian scientist. Production continues today.

Marks changed many times. Until 1917 the cypher of the reigning monarch was used.

References: R. Hare, *The Art & Artists of Russia*, Methuen & Co.1965; L. Nikiforova, Compiler, *Russian Porcelain in the Hermitage Collection*, Aurora Art Publishers, 1973; Marvin Ross, *Russian Porcelains*, University of Oklahoma Press, 1968; Ian Wardropper et. al., *Soviet Porcelain*, The Art Institute of Chicago, 1992; Tamara Kudriavtseva, *The Imperial Russian Porcelain Factory in St. Petersburg, 1760-1850*, 2001.

Museums: Hermitage, Leningrad, Russia; Russian Museum, Leningrad, Russia; Hillwood Museum & Gardens, Washington, D.C.

Bowl, Cov, 4" d, famille rose colors and designs, gilt accents, Gardner, ... **475.00**

Butter Dish, Cov, 6 1/2" w, figural reclining ram, black and white, gold trimmed horns, Kuznetsov, repairs, ... **650.00**

Coffee Can and Saucer, HP pink roses, green foliage, gold ground w/white stripes, Batenin Porcelain Factory, ... **800.00**

Cream Pitcher, 3 1/4" h, fancy handle, overall white glaze, Kuznetsov, ... **25.00**

Cup and Saucer
Band of HP octagons w/eagles, chickens, squirrels, owls, and fish around middle, dk red stars,

gilt accents, figural animal handle, Kornilov brothers, c1910, ... **40.00**
Cobalt and white crisscross design, gilt accents, c1920, ... **125.00**
HP bands of ochre and blue scroll and geometric designs, green line rims, Kornilov, ... **125.00**
Maroon ground w/gilt and white flowerheads and stems, lg half leaf from rim, gilt lined rims, ... **25.00**

Coffee and Tea Service For One, coffeepot, 7 1/2" h, teapot, 6" h, creamer, 4" h, cov sugar bowl, 4" h, cup and saucer, tray, 13 5/8" d, cobalt ground w/white ribbons and gilt accents, Imperial St. Petersburg Factory, c1796, (A), $3,750.00

Cup and Saucer, Demitasse, HP flowers and hand gilded cross hatching, swirls, and leaves, wide gilt band on int of cup, twisted branch handle, Gardner, c1850, ... **295.00**

Dish
9 7/8" H-H, oval, molded dbl-headed eagle in center, enameled forest, animals and buildings on inner border, white intertwined loops on border, gilt rim, Kornilov, ... **1,250.00**
12 1/2" d, center gilt and dk blue medallion and hanging gilt flowerheads, lt blue and pink banded border w/gilt dots, loops, and hanging designs, green accents, Imperial St. Petersburg, chips, ... **375.00**

Figure
5 1/8" l x 5 1/8" h, seated ballerina, arm extended over head, long brown braided hair, blue gown w/red lacing and accents, ... **550.00**
6" h, boy blowing horn, black tall hat, brown coat, white shirt w/sash, blue stripe trousers, rococo base, c1830, Popov, (A), ... **1,090.00**

Figure, 9" h, white blouse, cream jerkin, multicolored floral wreath, iron-red underlayer, black boots, $1,200.00

6 1/2" h, bisque, seated brown haired woman in pink cap, white peasant blouse, tan flowered skirt, infant in lap, bowl at side, brown bench base, Gardner, mid-19th C, (A), ... **860.00**
7 1/2" h
Dancing girl, hand on hip another holding kerchief, gold banded mauve hat, flowered white blouse, gilt trimmed blue dress, brown and green base, Kornilov, c1850, (A), ... **545.00**

Figure, 9 1/2" h, grey-brown jacket, blue kerchief, pink skirt, white bag with blue dots, green ground, $1,400.00

Period lady seated before gold edged white spinet piano, white cap, brown hair, gold edged green jacket, orchid scarf, and bustle, red and blue flowered lt yellow gown, flowered base, Popov, 19th C, (A), ... **1,840.00**

8 1/2" h, neo-classical grouping of seated Muse and Eros holding bust of Tsarina Catherine II on pedestal, maroon and blue rect base w/gilt accents, Imperial Russian Works, c1825, ... **4,850.00**

Jam Dish, 4" d, HP red cherries and green leaves in center, pea green and gilt indented rim, Kuznetsov, set of 6, ... **70.00**

Mug, 3 3/4" h, earthenware, blue hanging medallion w/yellow and red crest of St. George slaying the dragon, blue toothed border, blue Russian works on sides, Kuznetsov, ... **75.00**

Platter, 17" l, dk red eagle, gray and black birds, blue zigzag, dk red and brown border trim, Kornilov Brothers, A-$700.00

Plate

8" d, polychrome transfer of family camping before fire, horses, shoes on long poles, border of hanging banners of Cyrillic sayings and drapery, Siemens and Halske, ... **380.00**

9" d, HP pear, plum, and pomegranate, green foliage, molded gilt fancy rim, Kornilov Brothers, late 19th C, ... **95.00**

9 3/8" d, HP multicolored flowers and gilt leaves on brown inner ground, green outer border w/gilt leaves and sm painted flowerheads, undulating rim, c1825, ... **950.00**

9 1/2" d
Cloisonne style central design of stylized flowers and scrolls

on green ground, alternating panels of blue or gold ground w/cloisonne style flowers and scrolls, Kornilov Brothers, pr, (A), ... **2,000.00**

Painted red-orange trumpet flower, sm purple or blue flowers, molded basketweave border w/floral sprigs, gilt rim, Imperial Porcelain Factory, ... **275.00**

9 3/4" d, HP red, blue, and gilt crest of crown over scrolling "A," painted med blue border w/gilt accented relief molded scrolling leaf swirls and rim, c1822, ... **500.00**

9 7/8" d, creamware, pink-purple enamel single flower and foliage in center, pink-purple enamel hanging husk swags on border, early 19th C, set of 12, (A), ... **1,175.00**

Soup Bowl, 9 3/4" d, royal crest of Alexander II on border, gold lined rim, Imperial St. Petersburg, set of 5, ... **1,500.00**

Teapot, 8" w, ball shape, white reserve of folk style painted flowers, claret ground, white handle and knob, Kuznetzov, c1890, ... **175.00**

Toothpick Holder, 5 5/8" h, figural crouching lion, gilded initials on stem, white body w/gilt trim, beaded rims, sq base w/gilt banding, ... **110.00**

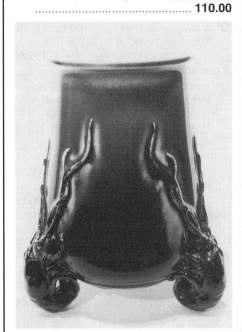

Vase, 8 1/2" h, dk red body, 3 blue and green figural lobster feet, Imperial Porcelain Factory, c1888-94, repairs, pr, A-$1,440.00

Vase, 12" h, blue, pink, and lavender leaves and flowers, brown branches, Imperial St. Petersburg, A-$3,960.00

Vase, 7 7/8" h, tapered form w/corset neck, painted gold and polychrome cornucopia, fountain, scrolling designs, and geometrics on cobalt ground, ... **2,900.00**

SALT GLAZED STONEWARE

Staffordshire, England
1671 through the 19th C

Rhineland, Germany
1500s to Present

History: Stoneware was pottery that was fired at such high oven temperature that the body vitrified and became impervious to liquids. A salt glaze was achieved by throwing salt into the high temperature oven causing the salt to volatilize. The sodium in the salt combined with the alumina and silica in the clay to form a thin vitreous coating on the surface of the stoneware. The glaze layer also was impervious and had minute pitting.

English

In the late 17th century, potters in north Staffordshire around Stoke-on-Trent began experimenting in hopes of producing a purely English style of salt glazed stoneware. John Dwight was credited with discovering the technique. In 1671 Dwight was granted a patent for the manufacturing of salt glazed stoneware.

Six villages comprised "The Potteries" in Staffordshire. The greatest concentration of potters was in Burslem. Their salt glazed stoneware pieces were thin, lightweight, and made to compete with porcelain. A brown salt glaze stoneware was developed in the second half of the 18th century and was used for beer jugs, tankards, flasks, and industrial wares.

With the advent of mold making and slip casting, more complicated shapes could be made. A wide range of utilitarian and decorative articles was produced. Few pieces contained factory marks.

The Burslem families of Wedgwood and Wood manufactured salt glaze stoneware beginning in the late 17th century. They trained a succession of master potters.

Enameled stoneware was introduced in the Staffordshire potteries about 1750. Enameled wares required a second firing—at a considerably lower temperature than the salt glaze oven—to "fix" the color to the pot. European and oriental porcelain decorative motifs were enameled on salt glaze pieces. Transfer printing also was done on white salt glazed stoneware.

The first salt glazed figures were animals. These were not marked and rarely dated. Most salt glazed figures were made by pressing slabs of moist clay into a two piece mold and then uniting the halves using a slip.

Groups of figures required combining press-molding with hand modeling. A wide variety of salt glaze bird and animal figures was made between 1725 and 1755. Usually the figures were ornamental, but cow creamers and beer baiting jugs were useful exceptions.

German

Salt glazed wares were being manufactured in Germany by the early 16th century to fill the demand for drinking vessels for taverns. These brown salt glaze wares were also exported to England for more than two hundred years.

References: J.F. Blacker, *The ABC of English Salt-Glaze Stoneware from Dwight to Doulton*, Stanley Paul & Co. 1922; Arnold R. Mountford, *The Illustrated Guide to Staffordshire Salt-Glazed Stoneware*, Barrie & Jenkins, 1971; Louis T. Stanley, *Collecting Staffordshire Pottery*, Doubleday & Co. 1963.

Museums-English: American Antiquarian Society, Worcester, MA; City Museum, Stoke-on-Trent, England; British Museum, London, England; Colonial Williamsburg, Williamsburg, VA; Fitzwilliam Museum, Cambridge, England; Museum of Art, Rhode Island School of Design, Providence, RI; Victoria & Albert Museum, London, England; William Rockhill Nelson Gallery of Art, Kansas City, MO.

Museums-German: Kunstgewerbemuseum, Cologne, Germany; Metropolitan Museum of Art, New York, NY; Rheinisches Landesmuseum, Bonn, Germany; Colonial Williamsburg Foundation, Henry Weidon Collection.

Bank, 5 1/2" h, molded brown hex cottage, Staffordshire, ... **150.00**

Basket, 11 3/4" d, press molded, center of stepped pyramids in rope inner border, cartouches w/diapering on border, scrolling cartouches w/diamond reticulation on outer border, white, Staffordshire, ... **650.00**

Basket and Stand, basket, 10" H-H, stand, 10 5/8" w, press-molded, basket w/bracket branch handles, ext reserved on basketweave ground w/6 molded teardrop cartouches of vines and berries and pierced trellis, silver shape oval stand w/molded berries into basin, white, Staffordshire, c1760, (A), ... **2,630.00**

Biscuit Barrel, 6 1/2" h, cylinder shape, relief of cobalt accented wind faces, gargoyles, and geometrics, grey ground, SP collar, lid, and handle, unmkd, c1900, ... **160.00**

Bottle
9 3/4" h, bulbous base, slightly flared long neck, white, ... **1,610.00**
11" h, lt brown base, dk brown neck, imp slab seal w/"G & JT Beller York," **75.00**

Butter Tub, 3 3/4" h, oval, white, basketweave molded body and cov Staffordshire, (A), ... **1,000.00**

Charger, 16" d, press molded border of lozenges w/molded diaper pattern, cream, Staffordshire, ... **1,595.00**

Coffeepot, 9 3/4" h, pear shape w/dragon head spout, 3 paw feet w/lion mask knees, black drawn and lt blue, pink, green, and yellow gallant and companion next to pond on side, reverse w/flute player in landscape, domed cov painted w/house in landscape, acorn knob, Staffordshire, c1765, (A), ... **2,630.00**

Cornucopia, 8 1/4" h, molded bearded mask, leaf and swag top, white, c1745, cracks, ... **1,190.00**

Cream Jug, 3 1/4" h, white, oct panels of reliefs of grotesques, birds, and animals, Staffordshire, c1745, (A), ... **700.00**

Crock, 6" h, cobalt leaf swirls on front, cobalt line on shoulder and base, cobalt striped horiz handles, France, ... **55.00**

*Creamer, 4 3/4" h, blue striping, white ground, Castleford, c1820, **$750.00***

Custard Cup, Cov, 2 3/4" h, white, press-molded as artichoke, Staffordshire, c1760, restored chips, (A), ... **470.00**

Dish
9 1/4" d, white, press molded dot, star, and diaper body w/scrolled foliate cartouches and diamond piercing, Staffordshire, mid-18th C, (A), ... **1,060.00**
12" d, lobed border w/press molded swirls and pierced diamonds, white, ... **795.00**

Figure
2 7/8" h, standing monk, brown agate, salt glazed finish, Staffordshire, mid-18th C, (A), ... **3,240.00**
4" h, seated cat, marbled white and brown clay splashed w/cobalt, Staffordshire, c1745, (A), ... **1,410.00**

Jug
5 1/8" h, famille rose style polychrome enameled oriental figures, strap handle, repairs, c1760, ... **1,120.00**
5 3/8" h, sprigged design of hunters, dogs, deer and windmills, dk brown top shaded to cream base, arched handle, ... **135.00**

Jug, Cov, 8 3/4" h, tan figural bear covered in chipped clay, snout pierced w/3 ring chain, brown accents, c1760, (A), ... **2,700.00**

Milk Jug, 7 1/4" h, beak spout, strap handle, seated gallant playing cello in park, rose, lt blue, med blue and green painting, black ext rim w/foliate scrolls on green band, diapering on int border,

Staffordshire, c1765, (A), ... **2,635.00**

Pickle Tray, 4 1/2" l, triangular, white, press-molded, relief scroll foliage and shell corners, Staffordshire, c1745, (A), ... **295.00**

Pitcher, 7 1/2" h, enamel painted relief of hanging game from blue ribbon in oval cartouche, enamel flowers and leaves on body, brown geometrics on neck, Brownhills Pottery Company, ... **225.00**

Plate, 8 1/4" d, drabware, c1840, pr, A-$450.00

Plate, 8" d, press molded waffled center, diamond pierced border w/press molded chevrons, shaped rim, white, c1750, ... **295.00**

Platter, 13" l, octafoil shape, press-molded, center molded w/graduated pleats in squares, wide border molded w/cartouches reserved on basketweave ground and diapering, pierced border sections in foliate scrolls, white, c1780, (A), ... **960.00**

Platter, 16" l x 12 1/2" w, press molded ovals in panels, off-white ground, $950.00

Punch Bowl, 7 3/4" d, scratch blue design of flowers and scrolling foliage, grey, Staffordshire, c1770, (A), ... **1,390.00**

Sauceboat

6 1/2" l, panels of weaving and diapering separated by rococo swirls, lg ribbon handle, white, ... **415.00**

6 5/8" l, molded beads, vert bars, and medallions, loop handle, c1760, crack, ... **1,575.00**

Spoon Boat, 5 7/8" l, white, press-molded scrolled form, scrolled foliate relief, Staffordshire, c1745, ... **880.00**

Strawberry Basket, 11 1/4" H-H, w/stand, press molded swirls and perforations in center, press molded cell pattern in molded lobed border panels, 3 peg feet, white, c1770, firecrack, ... **2,550.00**

Tobacco Jar, 6" h, 5 1/4" l, 3 3/4" w, brown ground, "R.H. BRIDDON" mark, A-$605.00

Teapot

3 3/4" h, globular form, band of relief of foliage and shells, blue sponged accents, 3 lion mask and paw feet, salt glaze finish, Staffordshire, c1740, repairs, (A), ... **2,700.00**

4 1/4" h x 7 1/2" w, multicolored named bust of Frederick the Great in lobed cartouche, Prussian eagle in cartouche on reverse, overall black ermine tails and dot ground, crabstock handle, salt glaze, c1760, ... **1,900.00**

5 3/8" h, modeled house form, molded Royal Arms, molded dolphin spout held by hand, scrolled handle, shingled roof cov, white, Staffordshire, c1740, repaired cov, (A), ... **310.00**

5 1/2" h, white, diamond shape, paneled sides molded w/shell centers and key band borders,

serpent spout and handle, Foo lion knob, Staffordshire, c1750, (A), ... **2,350.00**

5 3/4" h, white, relief molded tavern scene on side, hunt scene on reverse, serpent handle and spout, Staffordshire, c1750, repairs, (A), ... **1,175.00**

Vase, 8 3/4" h, bottle shape, relief molded prunus and birds, grey-cream, ... **975.00**

1845

SAMSON

Paris, France
1845-1964

History: Samson made reproductions and copies of porcelains from famous manufacturers in hard-paste porcelains. Some of the items they copied were originally only made in soft paste.

Edme Samson bought the Tinet factory in Paris. Until 1873 he decorated porcelains produced by other factories. Pieces he decorated had over-the-glaze marks, often duplicating the mark of the original factory.

Emile, his son, was the first in the family to make reproductions of decorative porcelains and figurals of the famous factories in England and the Continent. He started in 1873. The reproductions also contained a copy of the original mark under the glaze. Sometimes a small Samson mark was added over the glaze.

The Samsons owned over 20,000 originals of Meissen, Sevres, Chelsea, Capodimonte, Chinese, and Japanese porcelains. They made molds from these originals to produce their copies. Frankenthal, Ludwigsburg, Furstenburg, Vienna, Derby, Bow, Worcester, Chantilly, Tournay, Vincennes, Mennecy, and Copenhagen pieces also were copied, as were the tin-glazed earthenwares of Rouen, Sinceny, and Marseilles.

The company was operated by the Samson family until 1964 when C.G. Richarchere took over.

From about 1845 to 1905, the original marks were imitated on the pieces they copied. The company registered some trademarks after 1900 and used them under glaze after about 1905.

Reproduction Alert: Overglaze marks are removed easily. There is evidence that a large number of Samson marks have been removed so the pieces would appear to be from the original manufacturers.

Basket, Cov, 7" H-H, 6" h, pedestal base, panels of famille vert birds, flowers, sprigs, and leaves, alternating white and red lattice panels, applied handles and fan knob, ... **130.00**

Box, 3 1/2" h x 5" w, serpentine shape, HP garden flowers in gold accented molded swirls, int w/painted sprigs, metal mts, ... **280.00**

Cabinet Cup and Saucer, scattered gilt flower sprigs, band of crosshatched curls on saucer, gilt scroll handle, ... **175.00**

Cup and Saucer, Chinese style armorial crest w/greyhounds on front, blue banner w/motif, enameled purple and red flowers, gold on red chains on middle and border of cup and saucer border, ... **50.00**

Figure

4" h, red parrot, green comb, perched on white trunk w/applied green leaves, gold anchor mk, pr, ... **135.00**

4 1/4" h, Meissen style beggar boy, purple and gilt cap, purple lined green jacket, flowered vest, gilt accented circ base, "blue X'd swords" mk, ... **400.00**

5 1/2" h, standing Mercury, yellow classic gown, brown hair, gilt scroll molded base, gold anchor mk, ... **50.00**

Meissen Style

7 1/4" h, courting period couple, man in gilt lined blue coat, flowered vest, yellow breeches, woman wearing yellow and blue hat, pink dress w/flowered under dress, c1880, ... **150.00**

8" h, seated terrier dog, white carved hair, brown streaks, pr, ... **2,650.00**

11" h, shepherd and shepherdess music lesson, man wearing blue coat, brown trousers, reclining lady wearing red laced blue bodice, lilac skirt, drum at side, basket of flowers on base, repairs, c1875, ... **1,820.00**

Fruit Basket, 9" H-H, black headed eagle in multicolored crest on side, reticulated border w/sm multicolored flowerheads at junctures, molded curlicues, ... **400.00**

Lavabo and Pitcher, pitcher, 12 1/2" h, shell molded basin, 14" l z 10" w, Chinese Export designs of armorial

crests of gold, mauve, pink, and green, grey-ivory ground, mauve draped borders, ... **1,250.00**

Plate, 9 1/8" d, 12 sides, Chinese style armorial in center, multicolored floral border, pr, ... **295.00**

Plaque, 8 5/8" d, puce, red, and blue birds, gold rim, "gold anchor" mark, A-$175.00

Pot de Creme, Cov, 2 3/4" h, Sevres style painted red-pink flowers, cobalt, green, and gold trim, gold outlined intertwined handle and knob, celadon green molded saucer, "blue interlaced Ls" mk, set of 6, ... **300.00**

Salt, 3" h x 4 3/4" w, figural clam shell, 3 red, blue, or purple Whelk shell feet, int painted w/exotic bird, insects in landscape, mauve streaked ext border, green rock base, ... **65.00**

Tankard, 6" h, painted scene of classical ruins in mauve leaf cartouche, yellow body, ... **600.00**

Tea Caddy, 6 1/2" h, multicolored Chinese armorial w/raised enamel dots and molded scrolling, gold rims w/hanging fleur-de-lys, ... **75.00**

Tulipiere Pot, 11 1/4" h, urn form body molded w/2 masks, domed reticulated cov, trumpet base, polychromed Chinese Export style crest and florals, (A), ... **235.00**

Urn, Cov, 17" h, oct shape w/circ base, oriental style decorations of panels filled w/yellow, cobalt, iron-red, and gilt florals, dk red Moorish style swirled borders and panels of geometrics, flame knob, ... **1,450.00**

Vase

4 1/2" h

Amphora shape, 6 panels of Kakiemon style gilded branches, green enameled

leaves, red and gold flowers, ... **60.00**

Urn, 13" h, Chinese Export design, red crest, mask handles w/green accents, gilt trim, white ground, pseudo Chinese mks, pr, $6,000.00

Multicolored armorial on front, molded swirls and flowerheads in molded cartouches, gold hanging fleur-de-lys on neck and base, ... **75.00**

7" h, Chelsea style, applied mask and polychrome flowerheads, green, yellow, and pink relief molded curled leaves on base, flared reticulated neck w/blue-green flowerheads at intercises, "gold anchor" mk, ... **150.00**

7 1/2" h

Ball shape w/short neck, lg purple and yellow orchids, aqua glazed ground, Meissen-type mk, ... **650.00**

Dbl gourd shape, spirally molded, Kakiemon palette of exotic birds among prunus from rockwork, flying phoenix on neck w/flower sprays, band of stiff leaves on rim, red sq seal mk, c1900, (A), ... **435.00**

Vase, Cov, 11 3/4" h, hex form, Worcester style painted exotic birds, moths, and insects in scrolling gilt cartouches on blue scale ground, late 19th C, (A), ... **100.00**

c1770

SARREGUEMINES

Lorraine, France
c1770 to Present

History: The Sarreguemines faience factory, one of the most important manufacturers of French faience, was established in Lorraine about 1770 by M. Fabray and Paul Utzscheider.

During the 19th century, pottery and stoneware in the English style were manufactured. Transfer decorations were used frequently. Imitations of Wedgwood's cream-colored earthenware, black basalt, cane, cameos, wall tiles, agate, and marbled wares were made in addition to biscuit figures and groups. Mocha ware and majolica also were manufactured.

Modern production includes faience and porcelain wares.

Museums: Musee Regional de Sarreguemines, Lorraine, France; Sevres Museum, Sevres, France.

Artichoke Plate, 10" d, burgundy edge raised pink swirls, side well, .. **20.00**

Asparagus Dish, 10 1/2" d, relief of red and green tipped white asparagus stalks, rose shell shaped sauce well, ... **85.00**

Asparagus Server, 15" l x 6" h, dbl side by side molded brown basketweave dishes w/relief of blue and white asparagus stalks, center handle, ... **895.00**

Bourdalou, 9 7/8" l, white glazed earthenware, "black Opague de Sarreguemines" mk, c1900, ... **225.00**

Bowl
5" d, fluted body, ftd, lavender stencil design of flowerhead, leaves, w/half circle border, ... **10.00**
10 1/8" d, multicolored decal of Eiffel Tower and grounds in center, blue leaf stick spatter band on border, red inner and outer bands, ... **90.00**

Bowl, Cov, 6" d, 12 paneled white base, molded red plums, purple berries, yellow grapes, green leaves on cov, ... **25.00**

Box, Cov, 9" d x 2 7/8" h, molded brown basketweave, white ball knob, ... **200.00**

Charger
12" d, molded red cherries and strawberries, purple grapes and plums, shaded red apples, shaded green leaves, indented rim, ... **120.00**
12 1/2" d, multicolored named transfer print of "Monument de Sovie Sigismond Va Sovie," hand accented polychromes, dk blue border w/gold bands, ... **75.00**

Cup and Saucer, sm red flowers in blue-green and yellow cartouches, brown ground w/scattered flowerheads, inner rim of hanging swags, flowerhead on int of cup, ... **30.00**

Dish, 14 1/4" l, figural fern leaf, overall green glaze, ... **65.00**

Dish, Cov, 6 1/2" H-H x 4 1/2" h, molded red, green, or purple grapes, green leaves on cov, olive green glazed basket base, "Sarreguemines France" mk, (A), ... **200.00**

Jug, Character, 7" h,
Scotsman, green and red plaid cap, dk brown sideburns, red cheeks, lg white teeth, "imp Viva Les English" on reverse, ... **190.00**
"Upward Eyes," tan face, red cheeks, brown hair, turquoise int, dtd 1902, ... **125.00**

Milk Pitcher, 6" h, relief of hanging red cherries from brown branches, green leaves, brown handle, ... **120.00**

Mustard Pot, Cov, 3 1/2" h, tin glazed, blue, dk red, green, and yellow stylized florals, "Moutarde Bocquet Yvetot-1735" on side, ... **25.00**

*Pitcher, 8 1/2" , 5 3/8" h, rose red cheeks, blue head band, black hair and eyebrows, aqua ints, "imp SARREGUEMINES" mks, **$339.00, $280.00***

Pitcher
4 1/4" h, flowing blue center band of leaves and stems, blue leaf trimmed spout and handle, blue lined rim, "Opaque de Sarreguemines" mk, ... **75.00**

*Pitcher, 8 1/4" h, brown, tan, and rose, turquoise int, mkd, A-**$90.00***

5 3/8" h, blue faux marble top, wide red Greek key band on base flanked by checkerboard bands, "U. & C." mk, c1880, ... **85.00**
12" h, "Louis XV" pattern, scattered yellow and pink roses, blue flowers, off-white ground, woven gilt band on neck and base, fluted ft, gilt braided rope handle, "U & C" mk, chips, ... **225.00**

Plate
7" d, "Fables de la Fontaine," brown transfer, molded basketweave border, brown lined rim, ... **15.00**
7 5/8" d
Military scene in center, border w/"PATRIE," "HONNEUR," and "GLOIRE," black transfer, set of 6 different scenes, ... **275.00**
Relief molded grapes in center, tendrils, and overlapped leaves on border, overall green glaze, ... **90.00**

*Plate, 7 1/2" d, black center transfer, green border transfer, "Digion Sarreguemines" mk, **$45.00***

8" d, multicolored decal

Period couple examining blue hanging cloth, seated woodworking angel, mkd, ... **15.00**

Three bunches of flowers, leaves, and berries on border, blue transfer, "RUBIA U et Cie SARREGUEMINES" mk, ... **20.00**

Two children fishing in countryside, one holding pole, one holding net, "3 Bouge Pas Ca Mord!!!" on rim, mkd, ... **20.00**

8 1/2" d

Green fern fronds in center on lt pink basketweave ground, pink cut out border designs, ... **110.00**

Multicolored transfer of maiden blowing bubbles seated in gazebo, 2 little girls catching bubbles in dresses, gold accented fluting on border, ... **70.00**

8 3/4" d, multicolored transfer of man kneeling w/shoe before maiden and "A La Pantoufle De Cendrillon," "U & C Sarreguemines" mk, c1900, ... **65.00**

Plate, 9" d, dk pink floral, purple, blue, and green leaves, "Floret Vosges Sarreguemines" mark, $35.00

9 1/2" d

"Cluny" pattern, Rouen style geometric flowerhead in center, hanging border swags and lambrequins, blue transfer w/yellow accents, "CLUNY-U & C Sarreguemines" mk, ... **40.00**

"Flore" pattern, flowing black transfer of floral design, dentil

design on rim, "U & C FLORE" mk, ... **20.00**

Lg stylized red rooster on green grass spikes in center, red single stroke designs on border, ... **15.00**

9 3/4" d, majolica style red cherries and strawberries, raised ochre-green leaves, yellow ground, ... **75.00**

Sauceboat, 7 7/8" l, "Evelyne" pattern, scattered red flowers, red streaked rim, ... **20.00**

Soup Plate

9 1/2" d, multicolored transfer of oriental garden flowers, shaped rim, mkd, ... **35.00**

10" d, printed "Ageste" pattern, wheat, cornflowers, and wildflowers, dk red shaped rim, ... **12.00**

Tray, 12 1/2" l x 9 1/2" w, relief molding of 2 red and green apples in center, relief molded yellow-brown and green overlapping leaf ground, "imp SARREGUEMINES" mk, ... **75.00**

Trivet, 7 3/4" sq, multicolored winter scene in center, ribbons and roses at corners, "Obernai U & Cie Sarreguemines" mk, ... **25.00**

Tureen, Cov, 11 1/2" h, "Syra" pattern, blue printed bands of flowerheads and meandering stems, border bands of blue chevrons on dk blue ground, bands of drops, curled handles, loop knob, "U. & Cie Sarreguemines" mk, c1890, ... **395.00**

Urn, 19" h, triangular top and base, dk blue luster ground, brass lion's head and ring handles and ftd base, ... **900.00**

c1890

SCHAFER AND VATER

Thuringia, Germany
1890-1962

History: The Schafer and Vater Porcelain Factory was established in 1890 at

Rudolstadt, Thuringia. The factory produced many decorative pieces, figures, dolls, and novelty ware in hard-paste porcelain. They also were decorators of white ware blanks.

Records of the company ceased in 1962.

Basket, 4" h x 5 1/2" l, green molded overlapping leaf body, applied pink and yellow roses, brown stem overhead handle, imp mk, ... **135.00**

Bottle, 6 3/4" h, white cameos, sage green bkd, med green jasper body, $150.00

Bottle

5 1/2" h

Comical bust of woman w/head tilted upwards, flesh tones, blue eyes, circ orange base, elongated mouth spout holding cork, ... **360.00**

Figural rooster, orange coat, yellow tie, green feathers, white body, "Mr. Cocktail" on green base, ... **150.00**

6 1/4" h, figural man holding glass, "Prosit" on cov, blue and white, ... **165.00**

Candlestick, 2 3/8" h x 5 7/8" l x 3 3/4" w, jasper, white cameo bust on green insert, pink ground, grey handle, imp mk, ... **225.00**

Creamer

4" h, figural

Chinese man, orange and yellow robe, black pony tail handle, figural white goose spout, ... **135.00**

Pig dressed on monk's garb, holding keys, blue, imp mk, ... **185.00**

Candlestick, 3 1/2" h, 5" l, green skirt w/yellow and orange trim, blue base, "imp crown and star" mark, $235.00

4 1/4" h, kneeling woman holding fan, blue wash, imp mk, ... **185.00**

5 1/2" h, figural black and white goat spout, orange coat, ... **300.00**

Cruet, 4 3/4" h, figural smiling face, red cheeks, red fruit and leaf design, green stoppered neck, branch handle, imp mk and "Made in Germany" mk, ... **245.00**

Dish, 5 1/4" d, jasper, green and pink relief of frontal bust of Art Nouveau woman, pink jasper ground, green and pink flowing border, gold accents, imp mk, ... **95.00**

Hatpin Holder, 6" h, pink jasper ground, gold and green accents, "imp crown and star" mark, $395.00

Figure

2 7/8" h, 2 small children hugging, seated in lg rose-pink overstuffed chair, "Everybody's doing it" on base, ... **135.00**

3 1/2" h, brown and white dog w/bee on tail, blue ribbon on neck, "Now Shall I W--Wag It About or Keep It S--Still-" on white base, ... **145.00**

5" h, Googley Eyed Boy, black hair, checkered shirt, lg lt brown shoes, ... **345.00**

Flower Pot, 2 3/4" h x 3" d, w/saucer, jasper, white cameos of winged fairy smelling flower, cherub watering rose tree, dk green jasper ground, ... **70.00**

Inkwell, 4 1/2" h, figural black crow, yellow beak, red legs holding bone, seated on backplate, green to tan shaded base, imp mk, ... **325.00**

Match Holder, 5" h, figural pink w/open red mouth, ... **185.00**

Mug, 3 1/4" h, relief of bellowing elk on sides, orange wash, matte brown ground, zigzag design on rim, ... **85.00**

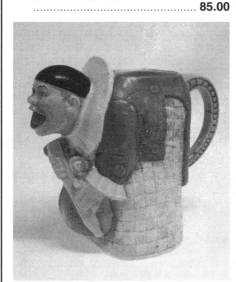

Pitcher, 5 1/2" h, orange jacket, black hat, lt green ground, tan handle, "imp crown and star" mark, $250.00

Plaque, 4" h x 5" l, bisque, mock lt blue basket w/2 white roses, pierced for hanging, unmkd, ... **25.00**

Shaker, 2 1/2" h, jasper, white cameos of gentleman in top hat or lady on sage green ground in white ribbon cartouches, pink jasper ground, ... **70.00**

Sugar Bowl, 2 3/4" h, white bark ground w/relief of orange fruit, green stems, green branch handle w/figural perched on one, imp mk, ... **75.00**

Sugar Shaker, 6 1/8" h, bisque, grey Grecian ladies, coral urns, green foliage, white ground, ... **135.00**

Vase

6" h, white cameo of woman blowing 2 horns on grey ground, hammered bronze body w/red, green, and dk blue enamel jewels, 2 fancy handles, ... **195.00**

6 1/2" h, white jasper ground, blue-green oval w/bust of woman, figural rams head terminals and gold accented green drape handles, pink rim, gold trim, hex base, imp mk, ... **45.00**

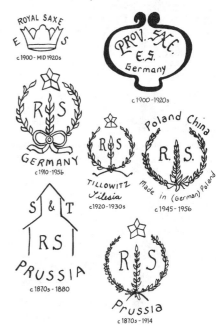

SCHLEGELMILCH PORCELAINS

History: The manufacturing of R.S. Prussia hard paste porcelains began when Erdmann Schleglemilch founded his porcelain factory at Suhl, Thuringia, in 1861. Reinhold Schlegelmilch, Erdmann's brother, established his porcelain factory at Tillowitz, Upper Silesia, in 1869. These two factories marked the beginning of private ownership of porcelain factories in that region.

The founding of these factories coincided with the time when porcelain items were experiencing a big demand, especially in the United States and Canada. The peak exporting years were from the mid-1870s until the early 1900s. The brothers were able to supply large quantities of porcelains by utilizing new industrial production methodology and the availability of cheap labor.

E. S. GERMANY

Suhl, Thuringia
c1900 to c1925

Erdmann's factory at Suhl was associated with the E.S. marks. Some of the marks incorporated "Prov. Saxe," "1861," or "Suhl" in the mark.

The style and decoration of the porcelains were different in shape and decor from the "RSP" examples. Changes reflected fashions of the times. The porcelains had the elegant, flowing lines of the Art Nouveau period rather than the convoluted rococo shape between 1895 and 1905. A great number of "ES" pieces were totally hand painted. After 1905 the porcelain decoration returned to more classical, mythological themes, and to simpler forms. Many of the transfers were in the style of Angelica Kauffmann.

R. S. GERMANY

Tillowitz, Upper Silesia

The forms and decorations of "R.S. Germany" were molded more simply, had more subtle decorations, and reflected the Art Deco period.

Reinhold concentrated on tablewares. Many examples were hand painted. Reinhold used a mark similar to the "RSP" mark at his Upper Silesia factory, except that "Germany" was included instead of "Prussia." The mark was usually under the glaze as opposed to the overglaze "RSP" mark. A number of large American department stores had special patterns created just for their use. Many of the porcelain blanks used for home decorating contain the "RSG" mark. Some exported blanks were decorated professionally by Pickard, a china decorating studio in Illinois.

R. S. PRUSSIA

Erdmann Schlegelmilch

Suhl, Thuringia
1861 -1920

Reinhold Schlegelmilch

Tillowitz, Upper Silesia
1869-1956

Both Erdmann and Reinhold used the "RSP" mark. The famous "Red Mark" first appeared in the late 1870s and was used until the beginning of World War I. Decorative objects and tablewares were back stamped with the trademark featuring the initials "R.S." inside a wreath, a star above, and the word "Prussia" below.

There was a tremendous quantity of items produced with the "RSP" trademark. In addition to art objects, the company also manufactured dresser sets; cake, chocolate, tea and coffee sets; and a large variety of tablewares (including complete dinner sets).

An endless number of "RSP" molds was made. Identical shapes were decorated differently; the same shape was made in a variety of sizes. Many molds produced pieces in the rococo style, including ornately fashioned scrollwork and flowers as part of the design of the blank. Some blanks were exported to the United States for the home decorating market.

Most "RSP" marked porcelains were decorated by transfer or a combination of transfer and enameling or hand applied gilt. Decorations were applied over the glaze. A few pieces were hand painted.

Decoration themes on "RSP" porcelains included animals, birds, figures, florals, portraits, and scenes. Many pieces incorporated more than one theme. Floral themes were the most common; animal and fruit themes were the scarcest.

Background colors were part of the decorating scheme and not the finish or the glaze. These colors were applied over the glaze by the transfer method to highlight the central theme.

A variety of finishes such as glossy, iridescent, luster, matte, pearl, satin, etc. was used to complete an "RSP" piece. Gilt trim often was utilized on borders, bases, handles, feet, or on the outline of a particular design.

The Suhl factory stopped producing R.S. Prussia-marked porcelains in 1920, unable to recover from the effects of World War I. The Tillowitz factory was located in a region where political boundaries kept changing. It finally came under the Polish socialist government control in 1956.

R. S. POLAND

Poland
1945-1956

R.S. Poland pieces have predominately classical decorations or simple designs rather than the ornate or rococo decorations and designs of "RSP" porcelains. Art objects, such as vases and jardinieres, dominated production over common tablewares. After World War II, little export business was done. R.S. Poland examples are quite rare. Reinhold Schlegelmilch's factory came under control of the socialist government in Poland in 1956.

References: Mary Frank Gaston, *The Collector's Encyclopedia of R.S. Prussia & Other R. S. & E.S. Porcelains, 3rd Series*, Collector Books, 1994, *4th Series*, 1995, values updated 2001; Leland & Carol Marple, *R.S. Prussia The Early Years*, Schiffer Publishing, Ltd. 1997; George W. Terrell, Jr., *Collecting R. S. Prussia, Identification and Values*, Books America, 1982; Clifford S. Schlegelmilch, *Handbook of Erdmann and Reinhold Schlegelmilch, Prussia-Germany & Oscar Schlegelmilch, Germany, 3rd Edition*, privately printed, 1973; Mary Frank Gaston, *R.S. Prussia Popular Wares, ID and Value Guide*, Collector Books, 1999; Leland & Carol Marple, *R.S. Prussia, The Wreath & Star*, Schiffer Publications, 2000; Leland & Carol Marple, *R.S. Prussia, The Art Nouveau Years*, Schiffer Publications, 1998; Leland & Carol Marple, *R.S. Prussia, The Formative Years*, Schiffer Publications, 2002.

Collectors' Club: International Association of R.S. Prussia Collectors, Inc., Theresa Newcomer, 357 Kelly Ave, Mount Joy, PA 17552, Membership: $20.00, Quarterly newsletter.

Reproduction Alert: Since the 1960s, R.S. Prussia collecting has grown rapidly. "RSP" pieces are being reproduced. There is a fake RSP red mark in the form of a decal that can be applied, glazed, and fired onto a piece of porcelain. This mark has an overall new appearance when compared to the old mark. There are many reproductions, so marks should be checked carefully.

Japanese porcelain imports try and imitate "RSP" porcelains in type, decor, and mold. There are marked and unmarked examples. Most pieces initially have a paper "Made in Japan" label, but it is removed easily. The Lefton China Company manufactures reproductions.

There are many ways to spot the reproductions. The reproductions and Japanese imports are fairly thick. The scallops, scrolls, and lattice are clumsy rather than delicate. Often the decoration is too bright. The background colors are not subtle, and the transfers are applied poorly. The gold trim lacks patina. These porcelains are sold in gift shops and flea markets.

Collecting Hints: Not all "RSP" is marked. Examples usually can be identified by studying the mold and the decor of an unmarked piece to see if it matches a known mold or design.

E. S. GERMANY

Berry Set, master bowl, 9 1/2" d, 4 bowls, 5 1/8" d, decals of lg red roses and buds, foliage and stems, lt yellow ground, HP gold rims, ... **175.00**

Bowl

8 1/2" d, 5 lobes, gold feathered cartouche w/portrait of black haired Victorian woman wearing blue gown, flowers in hair, burgundy "Tiffany" border w/gold flowers and 5 fleur-de-lys w/reticulated centers, "green E.S. Germany Prov. Saxe" mk, ... **750.00**

10" d, pink shaded magnolias, gold veined green foliage, pink to red shaded ground, cream to red border w/4 cut outs, ... **125.00**

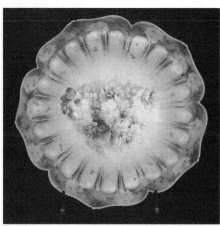

*Bowl, 10 1/2" d, lt red and pink roses in center, shaded green ground, gold trim, satin finish, "Puff" mold, red mk, R.S. Prussia, **$450.00***

Cake Plate, 10" H-H, white or red roses, border of white roses, pale shaded cream ground, gold trim, molded open handles, "E.S. Germany Prov. Saxe" mk, ... **125.00**

Cookie Dish, 8 3/4" d, multicolored fruit in center, bright red inner border, flowers and foliage on border, red rim, red curled handle on end, "green E.S. Germany Prov. Saxe" mk, ... **40.00**

Cup and Saucer, multicolored mythological scene in raised gold cartouche, red and cream panels w/gold swirls and geometrics, ... **65.00**

*Candy Dish, 7 1/2" H-H, white flowers, shaded lt to dk green ground, R.S. Germany, **$125.00***

Dish, 6" w, HP scene of trees, mountains in bkd, end handle, steeple mk, ... **40.00**

Dresser Tray, 10 1/2" l x 7 1/2" w, profile of woman holding 2 roses in center, gold tracery and dots, irid finish, "E.S. Germany Prov. Saxe" mk, ... **700.00**

Ewer
10 3/4" h, red ground w/washed white flowers, overall gold stenciling, fancy gold handle, "green E.S. Germany Prov. Saxe" mk, repair, ... **125.00**
12" h, cascading purple and tan grapes on side, sm bunch of purple grapes, green foliage on reverse, dk peach to cream to green shaded ground, ... **450.00**

*Plate, 6" d, multicolored center, dk red border w/gold overlay, "E.S. Germany Prov. Saxe and shield" mark, **$125.00***

Lemon Server, 6 1/2" d, HP red roofed white cottage, birch tree w/green leaves, loop handle on end, "E.S. Germany Prov. Saxe" mk, ... **10.00**

Plate
8 1/2" d, portrait of "Left Hand Bear" in center frame, orange-red border w/gilt Indian ornaments, "E.S. Germany Prov. Saxe" mk, ... **225.00**
10" d, white center, dk orange and green flower forms and gold accented molded swirls on lt orange to yellow border, shaped rim, "E.S. Germany Prov. Saxe" mk, ... **20.00**

Serving Plate
8 3/4" d, HP fruit cluster in center, wide orange-red inner band, border of flowers and foliage, orange-red rim, orange-red end handle, "E.S. Germany Prov. Saxe" mk, ... **40.00**
9 1/2" d, transfers of Napoleon and Josephine, hanging gold swags, border cartouches of busts of French nobles, center handle, ... **145.00**

Tray, 10 1/2" d, multicolored court scene, green inner border w/gold stenciling, Tiffany finish outer border w/white enamel beading, sculpted rim, "green E.S. Germany Prov. Saxe" mk, ... **575.00**

*Vase, 7" h, brown bird, brown pine ones, tan ground, gold handles, "green E.S. Germany Prov. Saxe" mark, **$200.00***

Vase
8 1/4" h, ovoid, HP dk magenta roses, mint green ground, ornate gold cartouche and netting, orange shaded base, 3 arched gold trimmed handles, gold fancy neck, "green E.S. Germany Prov. Saxe" mk, ... **115.00**
9 3/4" h, tapered form, green and red palm tree, brown trunk on green land, blue mountains in bkd, orange-tan shaded ground, wavy rim, "E.S. Germany Prov. Saxe" mk, ... **175.00**
11 1/2" h, bottle shape, short, flared neck, blue irises, tan ground, ... **1,650.00**

R. S. GERMANY

Basket, 6 3/4" l x 5" w, center overhead handle, Art Nouveau style, pink and white flowers, lt green shaded ground, gold leaf design on border, ... **85.00**

Berry Set, master bowl, 10 1/2" d, 6 bowls, 5 1/2" d, lg pink and red roses in center, gold trimmed meandering borders, red mk, ... **725.00**

Biscuit Barrel, 8" h, white and pink roses, HP accents, green shaded ground, gold outlined molded swirl base, ... **265.00**

Bowl

7 1/4" H-H, Art Nouveau style, white lilies w/yellow centers, green to lt yellow shaded ground, gold accents and molded open handles, ... **60.00**

10 1/4" d, bouquet of red and pink roses in center, MOP finish, raised molded floral relief on border, mkd, ... **50.00**

Cake Plate, 10" H-H, transfer and HP design of red tinged and fuchsia peonies, green stems and leaves, cream to tan and green shaded ground, gold trim, ... **75.00**

Cake Set, master plate, 10" H-H, 6 plates, 6 1/2" d, HP lg white magnolias, green stems, shaded lt brown to cream ground, gold trim, ... **50.00**

Celery Dish, 7 1/2" H-H, bunch of pink dogwood, yellow-green leaves, sprig on inner border, gold curled handles and rim, ... **25.00**

Chocolate Cup and Saucer, pink, tan, and white hanging flowers, shaded tan to white ground, gold rims w/blue enameled dots, "green R.S. Germany wreath" mk, ... **28.00**

Chocolate Pot, 10" h, white azalea pattern, brown shaded ground, "blue R.S. Germany wreath" mk, ... **295.00**

Coffeepot, 9 5/8" h, raised gold edged white irises and leaves, gold stenciled flowers, shaded cobalt ground, ... **1,300.00**

Cracker Box, 8 3/4" H-H, sm red berries, green shaded ground, unmkd, R.S. Prussia, $495.00

Cracker Jar

4 3/4" h x 9" w, pastel pink or yellow rose, lt green foliage, green mk, ... **195.00**

6" h, lg pink or white poppies, brown shaded ground w/yellow and blue accents, wishbone handles, ... **200.00**

Cup and Saucer, lg red tinged white roses, green leaves, shaded tan to cream ground, gold rims, ... **35.00**

Dish, 6 1/4" w, leaf shape w/end handle, 3 groups of yellow flowers at corners, gold rim, ... **100.00**

Hatpin Holder, 4 1/4" h, hex shape, pink rose on pearl luster ground, 6 sm feet, ... **150.00**

Dresser Set, pin tray, 5 1/2" l, hair receiver, 4 1/2" d, hatpin holder, 4 1/2" h, powder box, 4 1/2" d, tray, 11 1/2" H-H, white magnolia blossoms, beige to cream shaded ground, ... **125.00**

Luncheon Service, teapot, 5 1/2" h, 6 cups and plates, 7 1/2" l x 6 3/4" w, creamer, cov sugar bowl, overall blue luster, ... **300.00**

Milk Pitcher, 6" h, red centered lg white roses, brown to cream shaded ground, gold rim and handle outline, blue mk, ... **75.00**

Pitcher, 9 3/4" h, yellow and pink roses and buds, green leaves on sides, lustered mauve rim, "green R.S. Germany" mk, ... **70.00**

Plate

8 1/4" d

HP white tulips, green foliage, green to pink tinted cream shaded ground, gold rim, ... **45.00**

White center, peach border w/pink and peach roses on indentations, gold drop overlay rim, ... **20.00**

8 1/2" d, center pink roses, lt blue to cream ground, gilt accents, mold #90, c1900, ... **135.00**

Plate, 11" H-H, grey boat, red keel, gold trim, blue water, multicolored flags, unmkd, $325.00

8 3/4" d, 2 HP peach lilies, cream to lt green shaded ground, gold rim, "green R.S. Germany wreath" mk, ... **20.00**

Teapot, 5" h, white dogwood blossoms, yellow to brown shaded ground, blue mk, ... **110.00**

Relish Tray, 8" H-H, white and pink flowers, green shaded ground, gold lined rim, blue mark, R.S. Germany, $25.00

Tea Service, pot, 5 1/2" h, creamer, cov sugar bowl, 6 luncheon plates, 6 3/4" l w/6 cups, blue luster ext, white int, ... **300.00**

Tea Set, pot, 4 1/4" h x 8" w, creamer, 2 7/8" h, cov sugar bowl, 4 3/4" h, dogwood pattern, red mks, ... **475.00**

Toothpick Holder, 2 1/2" h, red roses, green foliage, wishbone handles, 4 sm feet, "green R.S. GERMANY wreath" mk, ... **20.00**

Tray, 12" H-H, 3 orange breasted bluebirds, green pine needles on brown branches, ... **195.00**

R. S. POLAND

Creamer, 2" h, Sugar Bowl, 4 1/4" d, white and gold flowers w/green accents, tan and gold ground, gold rims, unmkd, ... **125.00**

Dish, 5 1/4" w, figural leaf shape, leaf stem handle, white glaze, ... **65.00**

Plate, 8 3/4" d, 10 sides, pink or white roses, bluish leaves, shaded ground, wavy border, gold indented rim w/hanging gold chain of crosses, repaired chip, ... **20.00**

Sandwich Tray, 14" H-H, lg lustered red and white poppy blossoms, green stems and leaves, red border w/molded handles, ... **55.00**

Vase, 11" h, yellow, white, and pink roses, yellow to white ground, cobalt base with gilt, matte handles, "green and red R.S. Poland China, Made in (Germany) Poland" marks, $350.00

R. S. PRUSSIA

Bowl

9 1/4" d, "Mill Scene," mold #90, ... **750.00**

9 1/2" d, bouquet of flowers in center, cobalt border, "Tiffany" finish, "Iris" mold, ... **325.00**

10 1/4" d

"Portrait of Summer-Grist Mill" pattern, "Carnation" mold, red mk, ... **1,400.00**

"Seasonal Portrait," red and gold trim, "Fleur-De-Lis" mold, (A), ... **2,800.00**

Bowl, 10 1/2" d, multicolored, red mark, R.S. Prussia, $1,195.00

10 1/2" d

"Diana the Huntress" in center, "Medallion" mold w/"Lubrin, Poteka, and Recaimer," in medallions, hairline, (A), ... **3,200.00**

HP lavender flowers in center, "Icicle" mold, ... **160.00**

Lg spray of pink and white roses in center, green accented molded border flowers, "Carnation" mold, red mk, ... **425.00**

"Madame Recaimer" pattern, Tiffany finish and gold leaves, "Oak Leaf" mold, (A), ... **5,000.00**

Reflecting water lilies pattern, "Icicle" mold, ... **245.00**

Yellow roses and foliage, pale blue to yellow shaded ground, "Hidden Image" mold, unmkd, ... **250.00**

10 3/4" d

Pink rose bouquets and chains on int, "jeweling," mold #130, ... **525.00**

Poppy spray on int center, pearl luster finish, "Fleur-De-Lys" mold, ... **425.00**

Box, 9" w, bone shape

"Midst Snow and Ice" pattern, (A), ... **9,300.00**

Pink roses design, (A), ... **375.00**

Bun Tray, 12" l x 8" w, white lilies and green foliage, cobalt shaded ground, gold lobed rim, red mk, ... **600.00**

Cake Plate

9 1/2" H-H, pink roses, blue-green to yellow shaded ground, "Carnation" mold w/blue-green flowers on border, red mk, ... **325.00**

10" H-H, "Man in Mountain" pattern, "Medallion" mold, red mk, ... **2,500.00**

10 1/4" H-H, "Reflecting Water Lilies" pattern, "Icicle" mold, ... **245.00**

10 1/2" H-H, "Winter Scene," black w/Tiffany finish, "Iris" mold, (A), ... **5,500.00**

11" H-H

Lg bouquet of pink and red roses and foliage, pale blue ground, gold accented border, "Iris" mold, red mk, ... **395.00**

"Peacock and Chickens" pattern, worn gold, mold #304, ... **1,100.00**

11 1/2" H-H, "Surreal Dogwood" pattern, ... **135.00**

11 3/4" H-H, Yellow and red roses, aqua shaded ground, "Dbl Hidden Image" mold, open handles, unmkd, ... **675.00**

Celery Tray, 13" l, yellow, pink, and lavender flowers in center, scattered bunches on lt green shaded border, "Fleur-De-Lys" mold, unmkd, ... **175.00**

Chocolate Pot, 11 3/4" h, hex shape, lg dk red roses, green shadow leaf ground, gold accents, mold #642, ... **675.00**

Chocolate Set, pot, 9" h, 6 cups, dk pink roses, white dogwood, green foliage, pearl luster finish, mold #451, ... **995.00**

Creamer

3 1/2" h, sm lavender flowers, gold stenciled leaves, gold crimped rim, lt blue handle and 4 sm feet, mold #707, red mk, ... **145.00**

4 3/4" h, lilac and magenta flowers, lt green emb drape border, red mk, ... **95.00**

Creamer

3 1/2" h, cov sugar bowl, 5" h, yellow or red roses, shaded green ground, Mold #525, ... **210.00**

7" h, cov sugar bowl, 5 1/4" h, "Melon Eaters" pattern, "Jeweled" mold #643, ... **1,500.00**

Cup and Saucer, stylized white flowers, gold accented leaves, lt green to tan ground lustered ground, mold #451, unmkd, ... **55.00**

Dish, Cov, 3" h x 6 1/4" d, pale red or white roses, green foliage, gold rims and knob, 3 gold outlined scroll feet, red mk, ... **100.00**

Dresser Tray

11 3/4" l x 7 1/2" w, pink roses on shaded cream to green ground, Lily mold, ... **190.00**

13" l x 9" w, swimming swans and gazebo, satin finish, red mk, ... **775.00**

Ferner, 13 1/4" l, w/liner, "Dogwood and Pine" pattern, ... **525.00**

Hair Receiver, 5" d, red or white roses, shaded blue-green ground, gold accented swirls, ... **275.00**

Hatpin Holder, 7 1/2" h, pink roses, satin finish, mold #728, unmkd, ... **595.00**

Mustard Jar, 3 1/4" h, gold encrusted white blossoms, lt green to cream shaded ground, mold #451, ... **450.00**

Pin Box, 4 1/2" d x 2" h, "Ribbon and Jewel" pattern, Mold #8, Red mk, ... **260.00**

Plate, 11" d, white urn w/pink roses, purple and white ground, rope border, red mk, ... **275.00**

Relish Dish, 9 1/2" l x 5" w, "Melon Eaters," gold stippled and jeweled border, red mk, ... **2,250.00**

Sugar Bowl, Cov, 4 3/4" h, "Swallows and Waterlilies" pattern, mold #631, ... **100.00**

Syrup Pitcher, Cov, 4" h, white dogwood blossoms, green shaded ground, ... **125.00**

Talc Holder, 4 1/2" h, lily of the valley, lt green leaves, red mk, ... **575.00**

Tankard

13" h, "Summer Season" pattern w/mill scene, "Stipple Floral" mold, (A), ... **3,500.00**

14" h, domestic animal motif, "Icicle" mold, (A), ... **3,100.00**

15" h, "Dice Throwers" on one side, single "Melon Eater" on reverse, gold accents, "Point and Clover" mold, (A), ... **7,000.00**

Teapot, 6 1/2" h, shaded pink roses, green leaves, gold branches, sm bouquet of pink roses on bk, shaded green to white ground, gold trim, ... **235.00**

Tea Set, pot, 4 1/4" h, creamer, 3 7/8" h, cov sugar bowl, 4 3/4" h, "Dogwood" pattern, ... **475.00**

Tray, 11 1/2" l x 7" w, HP roses and daisies, gold stenciled green shaded border, crimped and stippled border, ... **250.00**

Vase, 14" h, tapered form, 2 sm handles, lion and mate design w/jungle fronds in bkd, (A), ... **13,500.00**

SEVRES AND VINCENNES

Sevres

Paris, France
1738 to Present

History: The Dubois brothers started a small soft paste porcelain factory for the production of decorative flowers at Vincennes in 1738. Encouraged by Madame Pompadour, the factory found favor with Louis XV, who became the chief shareholder in 1753. Louis XV controlled most of the products manufactured at Vincennes as well as throughout the rest of France. Gilding and the use of colored grounds were reserved for his pet projects. The familiar interlaced "L" mark was used during his reign to signify his participation.

In 1756 the factory was moved to Sevres, coming under the watchful eye of its chief benefactor Mme. de Pompadour. The first products were soft paste porcelain pieces decorated in the oriental style. The soft paste porcelain lent itself well to the elaborate rococo style favored by the king and his court. In addition to decorated soft paste, exquisite biscuit porcelain figures were produced, much to the delight of Madame Pompadour.

After the late 1760s, hard paste porcelain gradually replaced the soft paste variety. Styles fell loosely into categories that had taken the names of the benefactors. The period 1753 to 1763 was known as "Pompadour," 1763 to 1786 was "Louis XV," and 1786 to 1793 was "Louis XVI." The products of these periods ranged from small scent bottles to enormous dinner services and vases and urns of monumental size and decoration. The neo-classical styles were heavily favored. Jeweled or heavily enameled pieces first appeared about 1780.

Several directors strongly influenced the products from Sevres. During the directorship of Jean Hellot, about 1745 to 1766, several colors were introduced that have become associated with Sevres porcelain. The earliest ground color was gros bleu (1749) followed by bleu celeste (turquoise, 1752), rose pompadour (pink, 1756), and bleu roi (clear blue, 1763). The use of these colors during specific periods helped date Sevres porcelain.

Following the French Revolution, the company fell into disfavor and did not flourish again until the Napoleonic years. Alexandre Brongniart was appointed director by Lucien Bonaparte in 1800. The Empire style and scenics depicting Napoleon's campaigns and victories dominated the designs during the period. After 1804 soft paste was no longer made. Eventually the factory re-established itself as a leading producer of European hard paste porcelain.

A new range of colors was developed. Ground colors included dark blue, a pale blue called agate, and chrome green. These were seen most frequently in the First Empire Period, 1804 to 1815. Gilding was used extensively during this period. Painters were employed by Brongniart to paint miniature portraits on porcelain shapes that were modeled carefully by artists such as Theodore Brongniart and Charles Parcier.

Between 1800 and 1830, Sevres products included plaques, vases, table services, sculptures, and some very large special pieces. Porcelain plaques made between 1818 and 1848 imitated oil paintings or frescoes. Some vases were made in a neo-classical style that imitated cameos. Napoleon revived the tradition of ordering large table services for his own use or for diplomatic gifts. Post-Revolution monarchs had France glorified as the subject matter for services. Coffee, tea, or breakfast services also were made between 1800 and 1830.

The reign of Louis-Phillipe, 1830 to 1848, saw few changes at Sevres. Brongniart continued with the styles he was using from the early 1800s. White backgrounds were used more frequently for everyday table services. Decorations lessened. Decorations were printed, especially when gilding was used.

Brongniart died in 1847. Jules Dieterle became artistic director from 1852 to 1855; Joseph Nicolle took over from 1856 to 1871. Most of the output of the Sevres factory from 1852 onwards was for imperial residences and diplomatic gifts.

The most important decorative technique of this period was the pate-sur-pate process. This type of decoration was very popular in France and in England. The pate-sur-pate process ended at Sevres in 1897. (See Pate-sur-Pate.)

The Second Empire style at Sevres provided a complete break with the preceding period. This period, 1850-1870, was eclectic. It used the Pompeian style to imitate decoration on classical vases with classical subjects. A return to the rococo forms and decorations of the Louis XV times also occurred during this period.

The Third Republic period, 1870 to 1940, began with difficult conditions at the factory. The factory moved to its present location by the Park of Saint-Cloud. In 1876 the sculptor A. Carrier-Belleuse became artistic director. He remained until his death in 1886.

Many experiments were carried out with different porcelain bodies. Flambe glazes were developed and became popular. During the Carrier-Belleuse period, many different decorating techniques such as painted decoration, pate-sur-pate decoration, and copper glazing were used.

When Alexandre Sandier became director from 1896 to 1916, the factory was reorganized completely. He initiated new shapes and decoration techniques. Sinuous shapes were developed. The human figure was replaced as a decorative motif by painted vegetables, florals, and insects in the new Art Nouveau style. Winding tendrils appeared on vases and plates. Stoneware bodies often were used for the Art Nouveau decorated pieces. Sculpture regained prominence in biscuit porcelain as many busts were modeled.

Marks: For most of the 18th century, painted marks on Sevres porcelain consisted of the royal cypher (interlacing Ls), the date mark, and the identifying insignia of painters and gilders. Marks usually were blue, but could be brown or purple. Initials below the mark indicated the artist. Artists signed their own works as a means of quality control. The Sevres crown was never seen on soft paste examples.

From 1753 to 1793, date letters appeared within the crossed Ls. For example, A = 1753. R = the first letter date used on hard paste. Any letter before R cannot be hard paste Sevres porcelain. From 1793 to 1800, the monogram of the Republic of France (RF) was used with Sevres and a painter's mark to replace the royal cypher. No letter dates were used. The marks were continually changing after that.

References: Carl Christian Dauterman, *Sevres*, Walker & Co. 1969; Carl Christian

Dauterman, *Sevres Porcelain, Makers and Marks of the Eighteenth Century*, The Metropolitan Museum of Art, 1986; W.B. Honey, *French Porcelain of the 18th Century*, Faber & Faber, 1950; Linda Humphries, *Sevres Porcelain from the Sevres Museum 1740 to the Present*, Hund Humpries, 1997; George Savage, *Seventeenth & Eighteenth Century French Porcelain*, Hamlyn Publishing Co. Ltd. 1969.

Museums: Art Institute of Chicago, Chicago, IL; British Museum, London, England; Frick Collection, New York, NY.; Gardiner Museum of Ceramic Art, Toronto, Canada; J. Paul Getty Museum, Los Angeles, CA; Metropolitan Museum of Art, New York, NY; Musee des Arts Decoratifs, Paris, France; Musee du Louvre, Paris, France; Musee Nationale de Ceramique, Sevres, France; Victoria & Albert Museum, London, England; Wadsworth Atheneum, Hartford, CT; Wallace Collection, Hertford House, London, England; Walters Art Gallery, Baltimore, MD; Hillwood Museum & Gardens, Washington, D.C.

Reproduction Alert: A high percentage of pieces with the Sevres marks are fake or questionable. There are some clues to look for to help establish an authentic piece from a fake or reproduction. Nineteenth century Sevres examples had more decoration and more gold than 18th century pieces. Sevres examples were never marked on the lids. A marked lid indicates a fake. Many fakes had chateau marks. Soft paste was more often faked than hard paste since it is more valuable. Some Sevres white blanks were decorated by factory artists at home or at Paris porcelain dealers such as Peres and Ireland. Some blanks were decorated in England by Baldock and Mortlock.

There should be a hole underneath the rim in plates and saucers, created by the support used in the kiln and there should be a black dot from iron oxide. If so, the piece dates from 1752 to 1803-1804 and was fired in the kiln at Sevres. If there are two marks, the piece was refired. If one sees black paint in a hole or a hole with no purpose, then the example is a fake.

The incised mark on a piece must date the same or earlier than the decorator's mark. If the mark on a blank was cut later, the piece was considered a "second" and never decorated at the Sevres factory. Check the painter's sign or symbol to see if it agrees with the letter date. Many Sevres painters produced fakes at home after stealing colors from the factory for decorating. Restorers in France reduced the value of huge quantities of Sevres and Vincennes pieces by regilding chips.

Many colors, such as purple, used on soft paste produced surface bubbles that look like holes because of the gum content. The turpentine used in making hard paste left carbon dots, and there was no bubbling in the colors. One can see scratches in the glaze if pieces of soft paste were used. If the scratches are

melted out, the piece has been refired and is worthless.

Jewelled specimens with any date before 1780 are fakes. "Jewelled Sevres" has transparent raised enamels laid on gold that appeared like inlaid jewels on the surface of the porcelain.

Many Sevres copies were made by Samson. His mark was made to look like two Ls. His glaze was yellowish, not white like Sevres soft paste.

Vincennes

Chateau of Vincennes, Paris, France
1738-1772

History: Gilles and Robert Dubois brought soft paste porcelain manufacturing to the royal chateau at Vincennes in 1738. They were assisted by Orry de Fulvy, Councillor of State and Minister of Finance. After two years, the Dubois brothers failed.

Francois Gravant took over and appointed Charles Adams the director. The king granted many concessions to Adams. The factory entered a period of prosperity.

Vincennes products made between 1745 and 1756 were prized by collectors. Jean-Jacques Bachelier took charge of painting and modeling in 1747. He introduced the use of biscuit porcelain for figure modeling. A Vincennes factory specialty was artificial flowers, popular in Paris around 1750.

In 1753 the king issued an edict giving the exclusive privilege of porcelain-making in France to Adams. He sanctioned the use of the royal cypher, a pair of interlaced "Ls."

The porcelain works were removed from the Chateau of Vincennes to a new building at Sevres in 1756. The firm became the Royal Porcelain Factory of Sevres.

Pierre Antoine Hannong, a Strasbourg potter, established a factory for hard paste porcelain in the vacated buildings at Chateau Vincennes in 1767. He was granted the right to produce porcelain as long as he did not infringe on the Sevres factory's designs. Only a small quantity of porcelains was made. In 1774 the factory was purchased by Seguin, whose patron was the Duc de Chartes. Seguin used the title "Royal Factory of Vincennes." His products duplicated those of many French factories.

Reference: George Savage, *Seventeenth & Eighteenth Century French Porcelain*, Spring Books, 1969.

Museums: British Museum, London, England; Gardiner Museum of Ceramic Art, Toronto, Canada; J. Paul Getty Museum, Los Angeles, CA; The Frick Collection, New York, NY; Victoria & Albert Museum, London, England; Wadsworth Atheneum, Hartford, CT.

Bowl, 15" l, gilt "N" crown and laurel branches, border of multicolored portrait medallions of Bonaparte family on green ground, gilt rim, gilt bellflower ext, " printed iron-red M. Implede Sevres and portrait names, (A), $1,320.00

Achillea and Stand, 6 5/8" h x 8 7/8" l, painted looses bouquets, blue lines and gilt dental rims, gilt branch knob and handles, "blue interlaced Ls and N" mk, did 1766, (A), ... **1,795.00**

Cache Pot, 10" h x 11" d, HP scene of classic couple in garden setting in gilt leaf tied cartouche, reverse w/HP garden flowers in gilt leaf tied cartouche, bleu celeste ground, dore bronze scrolled base, dore bronze lion head handles w/rings, c1880, ... **7,500.00**

Chamber Pot, 8 1/4" w, HP loose bouquets and scattered sprigs, between blue line and gilt dash borders, gilt top rim, gilt husk and dot trimmed handle, "purple interlaced Ls and Y" mk, dtd 1776, (A), ... **1,345.00**

Charger, 17 5/8" d, HP garden flowers in center, bleu celeste border w/gilt accents, c1830, ... **4,450.00**

Cup and Saucer
HP flower painting in gilt cartouche, bleu celeste ground, "blue interlaced Ls ands A" mk, Vincennes, ... **21,000.00**
Painted en grisaille of putti in clouds, green and red laurel berry band between 2 gilt inner bands, bleu nouveau borders w/band of gilt entwined garlands, "blue interlaced Ls and dot" mk, (A), ... **2,030.00**
Painted landscape scene on cup and saucer, reserved in tooled gilt bands, green ground w/gilt entwined foliate scrolls and flower garlands, gilt dentil rims, "blue interlaced Ls, s" mk, did 1771, (A), ... **5,735.00**
Puce painted Patti in clouds, birds on saucer border, gilt dental

rims, "blue interlaced Ls and E" mks, (A), ... **835.00**

Glass Cooler, 4 1/8" h, painted scattered loose bouquets, blue line and gilt sprig rim, curled handles, "blue interlaced Ls and E" mk, (A), ... **1,195.00**

Goblet and Saucer, vert red berries and green vines alternating w/3 gilt entwined vert red lines, gilt scalloped bleu lapis borders, "interlaced Ls and K" mks, (A), $1,440.00

Hot Milk Jug, 5 1/2" h, baluster form, painted bird in landscape reserved in oval tooled gilt band on each side, bleu nouveau ground w/gilt accents and gilt hanging laurels, branch handle, flower knob, "blue interlaced Ls and T" mk, 1772, (A), ... **15,535.00**

Ice Cup, 2 1/2" h, painted flowers in gilt band lined kidney shaped cartouche w/chased designs, reserved on bleu celeste ground accented w/gilt foliate scrolls suspending laurel garlands, "blue interlaced Ls" mks, dtd 1787, pr, (A), ... **5,378.00**

Jewel Box, 4" h x 6 3/8" l x 4 3/4" w, rect, gilt cartouches w/HP flowers on cov and sides, gilt accents on cobalt ground, dore bronze mts, floral bouquet on int cov, sgd "Berkier," did 1771,........................... **3,450.00**

Plate

7 1/2" d, HP courting couple in center, turquoise border w/crowned interlaced Ls in floral gilt cartouche at top, 2 side floral gilt cartouches of HP flowers, Chateau Des Tuileries, ... **215.00**

9 1/2" d

Hanging floral swags forming pentagon from gilt cartouches on bleu celeste border, ... **325.00**

Period couple seated in garden, green border, lobed rim w/gold tracery, "Chateau Des Tuileries, S.37" mk, ... **200.00**

9 3/4" d

Center painted w/loose bouquet, lobed pink border w/molded gilt palm fronds, 3 shaped oval panels painted w/birds in landscape, "blue interlaced Ls and X" mk, (A), ... **11,353.00**

Painted view of cats educating kittens, "L'EDUCATION FELINE" below in beaded gilt surround and gilt scrolls, bleu agate border w/anthemion, bellflowers, and diapering, (A), ... **4,780.00**

Pomade Jar, Cov, 2 7/8" h, cylinder shape, painted loose bouquets in gilt quatrefoil panels reserved on green ground w/gilt edged blue ground surround panels, "blue interlaced Ls and F" mks, (A), ... **33,460.00**

Salt, 4 7/8" l, dbl, bombe form, painted cornflower vines entwined around pink line, blue center line entwined w/berried myrtle garlands, gilt lined openings and base, "blue interlaced Ls, HH" mks, did 1785, pr, (A), ... **8,365.00**

Soup Plate, 9 1/2" d

"CL" monogram under halo of flowers, border w/3 panels of winged Patti in clouds, berried laurel and flower basket below blue ground band, "pink interlaced Ls" mk, c1774, ... **880.00**

Gilt interlaced "LP" w/crown, laurel wreaths, and cherubs in center, blue border w/gilt swags, gilt oak leaf rim, "Sevres, Chateau Tuileries" mks, set of 6, ... **600.00**

Sugar Bowl

2 1/8" h x 3" d, HP bouquet of garden flowers in gilt emb flower, rush, and fern cartouches, gilt dental rim, "blue interlaced Ls and A" mks, Vincennes, (A), ... **1,195.00**

2 1/4" h, painted vignettes of classical ruins and waterfall, figure crossing bridge in shaped oval panels gilt w/leaves and flowers, blue lapis ground, "blue

interlaced Ls, B" mks, 1754, Vincennes, cov missing, ... **550.00**

Tea Service, teapot, 7" h, cream jug, 2 cov sugar bowls, 10 plates, 12 cups and saucers, multicolored portraits of French sovereigns, cobalt and gilt ground, A-$5,720.00

Teapot

5 3/4" h, oviform body, gilt edged bleu celeste foliage scroll borders suspending floral swags and garlands, gilt line and dental rims, ear shaped handle, "blue interlaced Ls and cc" mks, painters mk, did 1780, (A), ... **1,165.00**

6 1/4" h, hard paste, urn shaped, gilt outlined white vert ribs between bands of gilt foliate and dot designs, flat cov w/band of stiff leaves, gilt cone shaped knob, gilt scroll molded handle, gilt lion head spout, "grey fleur-de-lys, Sevres 30" mk, (A), ... **1,795.00**

Tray

9 7/8" l, oblong and lobed, painted floral sprigs in center, bleu celeste border w/gilt accents, did 1755, Vincennes, ... **10,800.00**

16 1/4" l, quatrefoil shape, painted and gilt sm cornflowers and roses in center in gilt beaded band, taupe border w/interlocking scrolls of painted cornflowers, overlapping scroll rim, gilt ribbon and bow handles, "blue interlaced Ls, date" mk, (A), ... **5,975.00**

17 3/4" H-H x 13" w, lobed, HP scene of Chateau de Fontainebleau, cobalt border w/gilt foliage, gilt accented open handles, c1880, ... **9,880.00**

Urn, Cov, 40" h, baluster shape, HP continuous scene of Napoleon in battle, cobalt neck w/gilt eagles, cobalt circ socle w/"N," sq base, cobalt cov w/gilt leaves and flame knob, c1860, pr, ... **89,000.00**

Vase

9" h, tapered baluster shape, blue mottled ground, ormolu mts on foot and rim, ormolu berry clusters and leaves on rim, c1920, Paul Millet, ... **2,200.00**

10 1/2" h, shield shape w/wide shoulder, everted rim, matte purple glaze w/suspended particles, mkd, (A), ... **920.00**

12" h, waisted form, long, slender neck, yellow and ivory crystalline glaze, (A), ... **1,095.00**

13 1/8" h, baluster shape, Japanese cloisonne style gilt edged dk blue peonies and gilt edged brown leaves, white blossoms on neck, blue ground, dtd 1875-80, pr, (A), ... **4,780.00**

14 1/8" h, krater form, upright gilt lion head handles, white ground, gilt lined rim and base, pr, (A), ... **3,346.00**

Wine Cooler, 4 3/8" h, 6" H-H, gilt framed multicolored panel of "Perseus Paying Homage To Gods Of Victory" on front, "Love Laying In Arbor With Nymphs" on reverse, dbl gilt banded rim, scrolled handles, dk blue ground, "interlaced L's and K" mark, A-$1,500.00

Wine Cooler, 7 5/8" h, painted pink chinoiserie designs, gilt accented curl handles, dtd 1753, pr, ... **112,500.00**

c1908

SHAVING MUGS

Austria, England, France, and Germany
c1850-1920

History: Many shaving or barber's mugs were manufactured of pottery or porcelain. Most mugs were shaped like coffee mugs; others had soap drainers and other features incorporated in the designs. Scuttles had double spouts. One spout was used for the razor, and the other for the shaving brush.

Many barber supply companies in the United States imported blank shaving mugs from Limoges and Sevres in France, from Victoria Carlsbad and Imperial Crown China in Austria, from C.T. Germany and Felda China Company in Germany, from A.J. Wilkinson and Goddard in England, and other scattered sources.

The imported, plain white unadorned pottery or porcelain mugs were decorated in the suppliers' workshops. Shaving mugs were not meant to be ornamental. They were designed for the owner's personal use at his favorite barber shop where he went for a daily or weekly shave. Some people considered their private mug a status symbol; others felt it was more hygienic for each man to have his own mug reserved for his personal use.

FRATERNAL

Fraternal shaving mugs bear symbols of the various fraternal orders such as Masons, Elks, Moose, etc. In addition, the Industrial Revolution furnished an incentive for American laborers to unite in national organizations, e.g. the Noble Order of the Knights of Labor and the Grand International Brotherhood of Locomotive Engineers. Symbols of these labor organizations found their way onto shaving mugs just as did the symbols of fraternal groups.

GENERAL

Shaving mugs appeared in quantity after the Civil War and flourished during the Victorian Age. One style of mug featured a photograph of the owner or his family or a favorite painting. It was made by adding a photographic emulsion to the ceramic body and then burning in the resulting image in a kiln.

Simple mugs with the owner's name added to a stock floral design were produced by all the decorating workshops. Scenes of the popular sports of the day also found their way onto shaving mugs.

Mugs with simply a number in gilt were used in hotel barber shops. The numbers corresponded to the hotel room numbers. Decal decorated mugs from Germany contained reproductions of either important people, such as Napoleon or Sitting Bull, well known works of art, or animals, e.g. horses, dogs, etc.

Character shaving mugs, introduced into the United States in about 1900, were manufactured in Austria and Bavaria until the start of World War I. Animal and fish heads were among the popular forms. Some mugs also advertised shaving products like Wildroot.

Barber shop shaving declined after World War I. Safety razors had been invented and perfected and returning soldiers had learned to shave themselves. In addition, Blue Laws forced barber shops to close on Sunday, a popular pre-war shaving day. By 1930 shaving at the barber shop was nearly at an end.

OCCUPATIONAL MUGS

Occupational mugs, indicating the owner's type of work, existed for almost every business, profession, and trade. The mug had a picture featuring the owner's occupation and his name in gold, either above or below the illustration. Lettering was usually in the old English style. Both indoor and outdoor trades were depicted. Some mugs had a scene portraying the owner working at his trade; others illustrated the working tools or emblem of the tradesman.

References: Keith E. Estep, *The Shaving Mug & Barber Bottle Book*, Schiffer Publishing, Ltd. 1995; Robert Blake Powell, *Antique Shaving Mugs of The United States*, published privately, 1978; W. Porter Ware, *Price List of Occupational & Society Emblems Shaving Mugs*, Lightner Publishing Corporation, 1949; Keith Estep, *The Best of Shaving Mugs*, Schiffer Publications, 2001.

Collectors' Club: National Shaving Mug Collectors' Association, Anise Alkin, 544 Line Road, Hazlet, NJ, 07730, Membership: $25.00, Quarterly newsletter.

Museums: Atwater Kent Museum, Philadelphia, PA.; Fort Worth Museum of Science & History, Fort Worth, TX; The Institute of Texas Cultures Museum, San Antonio, TX; Lightner Museum, St. Augustine, FL; The New York Historical Society, New York, NY.

Reproduction Alert: New shaving mugs are manufactured frequently as "replicas" of the past, but these should be recognized easily. Since they were used frequently, old shaving mugs should show definite signs of wear along the handle and the top and bottom rims.

Currently, Japanese companies are making reproduction "occupational" mugs in heavy porcelains similar to the earlier examples. Reproduction mugs from France and Germany appear to be hand painted but are printed by the silk screen process. An experienced collector can spot the difference.

Names on old mugs were larger, and the decoration left ample room for the name. On new mugs the picture is larger and the name looks crowded. Most old mugs were blanks from Germany or France. Old mugs never included the name of the occupation spelled out, only the person's name. Original occupational and fraternal mugs were hand painted and rarely showed wear on the scene. The gold trim does show wear. Perfect gold trim and lettering are rarely found on genuine old shaving mugs.

Collecting Hints: Many collections have been assembled that contain mugs representing over six hundred occupations. Uncommon jobs, such as deep sea diver, are difficult to locate. Mugs picturing obsolete occupations are prized highly by collectors. An occupational mug depicting a profession such as doctor or lawyer are harder to find because professionals were less likely to advertise themselves than were tradesman or neighborhood merchants. Most popular occupational mugs feature men at work.

Violet upper gills, yellow body accents, splashed red base, unmkd, $60.00

FRATERNAL

Brotherhood of Railroad Trainmen, gold emblem w/red and green flags, flanked by gold geometrics, gold name, "T. & V. Limoges France" mk, (A), ... **85.00**

Fraternal Order of Elks, multicolored decal of elk and "B.P.O.E." and gold "Lodge #54," gold name, ... **325.00**

Independent Order of Foresters, brown stag had w/gold I.O.F., flanked by gold sprigs, gold name, ... **60.00**

Independent Order of Longfellows, gold chair w/F.L.T. and multicolored eye, gold name, ... **225.00**

Masonic, gold square and divider w/blue "G" in center, blueberries and gilt leaves at side, gold "Pete Bekin Sr.," worn gold rim, ... **175.00**
Worn gold name, ... **80.00**

Modern Woodsmen of America, blue, red, and gold emblem, gold flanked by gold long stemmed flowers, gold name, (A), ... **50.00**

Odd Fellows,
3 gold links w/"F L T"
HP red clover and green shamrocks, gold name, ... **185.00**
Pink drape w/black and gold geometric designs, gold name, rim, and base bands, c1900, ... **250.00**

3 green links w/"FLT and ODD FELLOWS," in wreath, green print, Austria, ... **70.00**

General, pink, blue, and brown, K.P.M., $550.00

GENERAL

Black horse and white horse in forest setting, gold name, worn gold bands, (A), ... **90.00**

Black scrolling "Ely B. Kirbey," gold banding top and base, Germany, ... **35.00**

Black silhouette of couple seated on bench, yellow bkd, worn gold name, Germany, ... **200.00**

Blue sponging, blue banded handle, (A), ... **248.00**

Blue transfer of 3 bar designs on swirls, emb feather and flower design on border and drain, France, ... **75.00**

Blue Willow pattern, 19th C, ... **125.00**

Brown hanging basket of red and green foliage under red drape border, gold name, worn gold base band, "V & D Austria" mk, ... **150.00**

Brown transfer of intertwined ribbons between beading, "Edge Malkin" mk, ... **125.00**

Decal
Elk standing on grassy ridge, shaded pink base, unmkd, ... **39.00**
Lg red tinged white hibiscus, grey shadow border, Germany, ... **10.00**

Dk red drape over flower sprig, gold name, ... **150.00**

Flow Blue, "Watteau" pattern, Doulton, ... **250.00**

Gold name and leaves in gold bowtie frame, red wrap, worn gold bands top and base, ... **100.00**

Gold name w/red and green border of flowers, full med blue wrap, ... **25.00**

Gold outlined raised white flowerhead on border, blue-green shading at top to cream base, multicolored decals of castles on sides, wavy foot, gold rim, ... **40.00**

High wheeled bicycle, flanked by gold vert leaves, part gold wrap, gold name, (A), ... **1,300.00**

HP
Bluebells, green stems, pink luster base, unmkd, ... **70.00**
Blue robin, yellow breast w/gold "To My Father" in tablet on breast, forest setting, unmkd, ... **50.00**
Lg blue flowerheads, green grasses, diagonal gold name in banner, gold band on base and rim, Limoges, ... **110.00**
Pink wild roses, green foliage, black and gold crisscross base, Limoges, c1890, ... **95.00**
Purple flowers, green foliage, arched gold name, worn gold base bands, "P. Germany" mk, ... **35.00**
Sailor in green slicker, smoking pipe, band of gold hanging keys in bkd, gold rim and outlined handle, ... **155.00**

General, multicolored transfer of horse scene, med blue ground mottled ground, gold rim, $80.00

Multicolored Scene
Gypsy men and women w/ox cart, shaded pink base, Germany, ... **38.00**
Little girl riding on little boy's back, dog at side, tan ring handle, hairline, ... **75.00**

Painted orange-red dragon arched over ewer, sm blue or white periwinkles, green foliage, worn gold name, ... **80.00**

Patriotic, brown and white American eagle holding shield, flanked by American flags, gold name, rim, and base, ... **165.00**

Photographic bust of well dressed young man in gold frame, gold name on foot, "Germany" mk, ... **550.00**

Pink wrap, gold name and sm multicolored flowers in gold cartouche, "T & V. Limoges France" mk, ... **120.00**

Raised gold trimmed "PRESENT" on front, gold band on base, ... **35.00**

General, red roses, green leaves and shadow leaves, "Germany" mark, $40.00

Red, blue, and yellow exotic bird perched on pink flowering branch, copper luster streaks, cobalt border splotches, Germany, ... **40.00**

Red transfer of bluebell flowers, leaves, and branches, ... **30.00**

Relief of bellowing elk on sides, band of drape on rim, matte brown ground w/orange-brown wash, Schafer and Vater, ... **85.00**

Scroll w/gold "EZRA FERRY," purple violets, unmkd, ... **76.00**

Scuttle, purple violets, green leaves, gold trim, $38.00

Sportsman, multicolored scene of hunter shooting rifle, dog at feet in forest, gold name, worn gold stripes, "GDA France" mk, (A), ... **160.00**

Three gold outlined vert panels, 2 w/multicolored scenes of period children courting, third panel of flowers on yellow ground, gold squiggles between panels, unmkd, ... **20.00**

White ironstone
Paneled body, "Maddock & Sons" mk, ... **20.00**
Smooth body, unmkd, ... **50.00**

OCCUPATIONAL

Baker, multicolored scene of 3 men w/table of steaming bread and brick ovens, worn gold name and border bands, (A), ... **300.00**

Occupational, Baker, multicolored scene, gold name, gold trimmed handle, $950.00

Bartender, multicolored scene of bar keep standing behind red bar w/2 patrons in front, worn gold name, "T & V. Limoges France" mk, (A), ... **170.00**

Beer Truck Driver, multicolored scene of man driving beer truck, gold name, (A), ... **1,600.00**

Bicycle Racer, multicolored scene of man riding bicycle on track, gold name, (A), ... **1,200.00**

Book Keep, multicolored scene of man standing in front of slant front desk, stool and waste basket on floor in sq frame, flanked by pink and green flowers, worn gold name, "Limoges France, The World Durfield Koken, St. Louis" mk, (A), ... **900.00**

Brick Maker, multicolored scene of man forming bricks in mold under canopy, gold name, gold base stripe, "D & Co." mk, (A),
.... **1,600.00**

Carpenter, multicolored scene of man planing board at workbench before window, gold name, worn gold bands, "W.G. & Co. Limoges France" mk, (A), ... **500.00**

Carriage Driver, man seated atop horse drawn fancy black carriage, half sea green wrap w/hanging gold half circles and dots, gold name w/gold leaves, (A), ... **200.00**

Cattle Dealer, multicolored scene of steer in field, gold name, (A),
.... **690.00**

Dentist, multicolored scene of dentist pulling tooth from woman in dental chair, worn gold name, worn gold drape and border bands, (A),
.... **1,400.00**

Dry Goods Salesman, multicolored scene of woman at counter w/salesman in dry goods store in rect frame, flanked by gold leaf designs, gold name, "PHL Limoges France" mk, (A), ... **400.00**

Express Wagon Driver, multicolored scene of man driving horse drawn wagon w/"EXP" on side, full black wrap, gold name at top, gold base, crows foot crack, (A), ... **600.00**

Farmer
Multicolored scene of man plowing field behind pair of horses, gold name, (A), ... **690.00**
Two gold crossed ears of corn, worn gold name and base bands, (A),
.... **70.00**

Fireman, multicolored scene of fireman atop horse drawn fire engine, flanked by gold geometrics, worn gold name and bands, "T & V Limoges France" mk, (A),
.... **1,000.00**

Iceman, multicolored scene of man loading ice on red boxcar, gold name, gold rim, (A), ... **450.00**

Laundry Driver, multicolored scene of man driving horse drawn wagon w/"MILTON WET WASH LAUNDRY" on side of wagon, gold name, gold wrap, "T. & V. Limoges France" mk, (A), ... **1,700.00**

Lunch Wagon Owner, multicolored scene of man in wagon w/curtains, gold name and base, (A),
.... **42,550.00**

Milk Wagon Driver, multicolored scene of man driving horse-drawn milk wagon, gold name, (A), ... **800.00**

Musician, multicolored scene of violin and bow, gold cleft above, worn gold name, maroon body, "D. & C." mk, ... **450.00**

Painter, gold paint brushes, worn gold name, unmkd, ... **285.00**

Pharmacist, gold eagle over gold mortar and pestle, worn gold name, ... **550.00**

Photographer, multicolored scene of man photographing seated woman, gold name, gold bands top and base, "MR France, Elite Limoges France" mks, (A), ... **1,300.00**

Plumber, multicolored scene of 2 men working under vanity, purple wrap on upper section, worn gold name, "K.P.M. Germany" mk, (A), ... **700.00**

Policeman, multicolored scene of 2 policemen, robber, and call box, gold name, cracked, (A), .. **6,325.00**

Printing Press Operator, multicolored scene of printing press, gold name, (A), ... **720.00**

Produce Wagon Driver, multicolored worn scene of man w/whip seated in horse drawn wagon, worn gold name, (A), ... **2,760.00**

Railroad Engineer, multicolored scene of locomotive, gold name, (A), ... **460.00**

Sheet Metal Worker, black oven and soldering iron, gold edged black name, Limoges, ... **500.00**

Shoe Clerk, multicolored scene of man waiting on woman, flanked by gold foliage, gold name and line on base, "Limoges France" mk, (A), ... **3,500.00**

Soldier, standing Union soldier in blue uniform, red cape, holding rifle, gold name and "Company H" worn gold bands, (A), ... **1,900.00**

Sulky Driver, multicolored scene of man in racing sulky, trapezoidal gold frame, flanked by gold squiggles, gold name, worn gold band on base, (A), ... **475.00**

Telegrapher, gold telegraph key, gold outlined blue name, ... **345.00**

Watchmaker, gold and colored open pocket watch, flanked by gold geometrics, worn gold striped base and rim, gold name, "PHL Limoges France" mk, (A), ... **250.00**

Water Wagon Driver, multicolored scene of man seated in horse-drawn wagon, gold name, (A), ... **2,760.00**

SCUTTLE

Band of sm pink roses in green wreaths, gold trim, R.S. Prussia red mk, ... **450.00**

Black scene of Blackpool in gold frame, pink luster ground w/molded swirls, ... **20.00**

Blossoming lotus shape, gold outlined MOP petals, green base, gold accented dbl loop handle, Germany, ... **50.00**

Blue and white Dutch scene w/windmill, unmkd, ... **250.00**

Decal of sailing ships on side white ground, Wade, ... **20.00**

Dk orange drip over green body, grey rim, Shelley Harmony series, ... **475.00**

Figural
Black man's head, orange bow tie, ... **250.00**
Pig head, pink snout and ears, ... **265.00**

Flying swallows and blue flowers on body, "gold Souvenir From Brighton" on rim, ... **75.00**

Gilt outlined fluting, unmkd, hairline, ... **15.00**

HP dk pink roses on green ground, gold ovals on olive green neck, lobed rim, brown handle, ... **135.00**

Ironstone, multicolored scattered garden flowers, ... **10.00**

Lg red roses, beaded border, shaded lustered pink rims, ... **90.00**

Lt green shaded rim and base w/molded designs, decal of red flower and green foliage on sides, unmkd, ... **20.00**

Multicolored decal, "JR. G.U.A.M. American Mechanics" worn gold name, **$300.00**

Multicolored decal
American Indian holding flag on front, violets on reverse, gold spattered border, ... **28.00**
Arabs on horseback, Royal Bayreuth, blue mk, ... **215.00**
Steam tractor and "HER MAJESTY BY BURRELL 1897," Wade, ... **10.00**

Overall raised hobnail design, pale green, Germany, ... **40.00**

Shaded yellow to blue borders, gold arched designs, gold dotted handle, ... **65.00**

1925-1945

1890-1910

SHELLEY

Longton, England
Mid-18th Century to Present

History: Members of the Shelley family manufactured pottery at Lane End beginning in the middle of the 18th century. In 1872 Joseph Shelley formed a partnership with James Wileman of Wileman & Co., operator of the Foley China Works. For the next fifty years, the firm used the name Wileman & Co. Percy, Joseph Shelley's son, joined the firm in 1881. Percy became an excellent potter. During his fifty years as head of the firm, he developed the lasting reputation of Shelley china.

During the 1880s, only average quality china was made. Pieces featured one color and poor quality transfers. Percy hired artists to produce dinner services with more elaborate decorations that were intended for the export market. During the 1890s, the wares were more varied, featuring finer patterns and better colorations.

When Joseph died in 1896, Percy assumed complete control and improved all aspects of production and decoration. The artist Rowland Morris modeled "Dainty White," the company's most successfully produced shape until 1966. The shape also was used for many pieces of commemorative ware.

Frederick Rhead, who trained under Solon at Minton and worked at Wedgwood, was employed as artistic director in 1896. Rhead introduced Intarsio, Spano-Lustra, Urbato, Primitf, and Pastello wares, a series of effects used on earthenwares. Intarsio was the most popular. A large number of patterns and styles was made.

Although the firm was still called Wileman & Co. in 1910, the mark utilized the Shelley family name enclosed in an outline shield shape. The art director now was Walter Slater, who had been an apprentice at Minton and spent twenty years working at Doulton.

A new series of Intarsio ware that reflected Art Nouveau motifs was introduced in 1911. Flamboyant ware with flambe glazes and Cloisello ware followed. Under Slater's direction, bone china was developed. Before World War I, Shelley's china dinner services were very popular in the American market.

After the war, Percy's three sons were involved in the firm. By 1922 miniature objects, heraldic and coat of arms, souvenir china and earthenware with engraved views of places of interest, and parian busts of military figures were produced in quantity. During the 1920s, many styles of teawares were made. "Eggshell china" referred to the thinness of the porcelain. Many styles of cups and saucers were made, some having from six to sixteen flutes.

In 1925 the firm's name was changed to Shelley's. Nursery wares decorated by Hilda Cowham and Mabel Lucie Atwell came to the forefront along with "semi-porcelain" domestic china.

The delicate teawares of the 1920s and 1930s established Shelley's reputation. The Queen Anne octagonal shape was one of the best known forms first made in 1926. More than 170 patterns based on about 80 distinct designs were applied to the Queen Anne shape.

More modern shapes such as Vogue and Mode were introduced during the Art Deco period. These shapes were a departure from previous teawares produced by Shelley. The Vogue shape had the wider and shallower teacup and a more definite foot, while the Mode teacup was more upright with a smaller foot. Both were introduced in 1930.

The Eve shape of 1932 had an open triangular handle. Fifty-eight patterns were applied to this shape until 1938. The Regent shape from 1932 had a flared trumpet shape cup. This shape continued unto the 1940s and 50s. Percy retired in 1932.

After World War II, earthenwares were discontinued. China dinnerwares remained in production. Lithographic techniques replaced the "print and enamel" decorations.

In 1965 the firm was renamed Shelley China Ltd. It was acquired by Allied English Potteries in 1966. The family connection with the firm finally ended. Allied merged with the Doulton Group in 1971.

References: Susan Hill, *The Shelley Style*, Jazz Publications, Ltd. 1990; Chris Watkins, William Harvey, and Robert Senft, *Shelley Potteries*, Barrie & Jenkins, 1980; Muriel Miller, *Collecting Shelley Pottery*, Wallace-Homestead, 1997. Jones and Nicholas, *More Shelley China*, Schiffer Publications, 2003. Sherly Burdess, *Shelley Tea Ware Patterns*, Schiffer Publications, 2003; Tina Skinner & Jeffrey Snyder, *Shelley China*, Schiffer Publications, 2001; Robert Prescott-Walker, *Collecting Shelley China*, Francis Jones, 1999.

Collectors' Clubs: National Shelley China Club, P.O. Box 580, Chokoloskee, FL 34138, Membership: $25.00, Quarterly newsletter; www.sweetpea.net/shelleyclub, The Shelley Group, 12 Lilleshall Road, Clayton, Newcastle-Under-Lyme, Staffordshire ST5 3BX, UK, Newsletter.

Biscuit Barrel, 6" h, Art Deco style, mottled med blue glaze, chrome overhead handle, ... **135.00**

Cake Plate, 9 1/2" H-H x 8 1/4" w
"Blue Iris" pattern, Queen Anne shape, ... **45.00**
"Trees at Sunrise" pattern, ... **125.00**

Cake Set, master plate, 9 1/2" l x 8" w, 6 plates, 6 1/4" sq, "Tall Trees" pattern, Queen Anne shape, c1930s, ... **220.00**

Chamberstick, 2" h x 5" d, "Harmony" yellow drip over green ground, yellow ring handle, ... **10.00**

Coffeepot
7" h, "Wild Flowers" pattern, ... **70.00**
8" h, "Red Daisy" pattern, Queen Anne shape, ... **375.00**
9" h, "Regency" pattern, Dainty shape, ... **175.00**

Condiment Dish, 4 3/4" d, "Rose Bud" pattern, 10 flutes, ... **20.00**

Creamer, 2 3/4" h, Sugar Bowl, 2" h x 3 3/8" w, "Primrose" pattern, 6 flutes, ... **110.00**

Cup and Saucer
"Anemone" pattern, Oleander shape, ... **35.00**
"Begonia" pattern, Dainty shape, ... **40.00**
"Blue Daisy" pattern, ... **75.00**
"Buttercup" pattern, Corset shape, ... **30.00**
"Daffodil Time" pattern, Dainty shape, ... **30.00**
"Dog Rose" pattern, Mayfair shape, ... **145.00**
"Honeysuckle" pattern, Regent shape, ... **80.00**
"Golden Harvest" pattern, Henley shape, ... **20.00**
"Maytime" pattern, Henley shape, ... **88.00**
"Primrose" pattern, Dainty shape, ... **35.00**
"Rosebud" pattern, Perth shape, ... **85.00**
"Rose, Pansy, Forget-Me-Not" pattern, Dainty shape, ... **40.00**
"Sheraton" pattern, Gainsborough shape, ... **95.00**
"Sunrise and Tall Trees" pattern, Queen Anne shape, ... **185.00**
"Swirl" pattern, Regent shape, ... **35.00**
"Thistle" pattern, Dainty shape, pink handle, ... **50.00**

Cup and Saucer, Miniature
"Blue Rock" pattern, Dainty shape, ... **75.00**

"Dainty Blue" pattern, ... **395.00**
"Green Charm" pattern, Canterbury shape, ... **235.00**
"Harmony" pattern, Westminster shape, ... **295.00**
"Rose, Pansy, Forget-Me-Not" pattern, Canterbury shape, ... **245.00**

Dish, 4 1/2" d
"Maytime" pattern, ... **20.00**
"Summer Glory" pattern, ... **20.00**

Egg Cup, 2 1/2" h, "Bridal Rose" pattern, Dainty shape, ... **75.00**

Figure, 3 1/8" h, "Boo Boo," green outfit, sgd "Mabel Lucie Atwell," **1,095.00**

Jam Jar, Cov, 2 1/4" h, "Lily-of-the-Valley" pattern, ... **125.00**

Juicer, 3 1/2" h x 3 1/2" d, "Harmony," green and brown mottling, ... **450.00**

Milk Jug, 3 3/4" h, "Archway of Roses" pattern, Cambridge shape, c1942, ... **60.00**

Plate
6" d
"Blue Rock" pattern, Dainty shape, ... **20.00**
"Golden Harvest" pattern, Henly shape, ... **10.00**
7" d, "Begonia" pattern, Dainty shape, ... **15.00**
8" d, "Regency" pattern, Dainty shape, ... **25.00**
10" d, "Regency" pattern, Dainty shape, ... **40.00**

Platter, 12 1/2" l x 10 1/4" w, "Tall Trees and Sunrise" pattern, Queen Anne shape, ... **325.00**

Pudding Mold, 2 1/4" h x 5 3/4" l x 5" w, fluted oval shape, white glaze, "Ritz #2," **88.00**

Sandwich Set, 8" d plate w/well and cup, "Regency" pattern, Dainty shape, ... **55.00**

Sandwich Tray
13" H-H x 4 3/4" w, multicolored scene of fence and garden at ends, lime green trim, ... **25.00**
14" l x 5 1/4" w, "Stocks" pattern, Dainty shape, ... **200.00**

Teapot
5" h
9" l, "Regency" pattern, Dainty shape, ... **215.00**
Figural of Joseph Chamberlain in black and white waistcoat, wearing monocle, hand on hip forms handle, ... **1,050.00**

Teapot, 5 1/4" h, "Rosebud" pattern, $395.00

Orange "Harmony" pattern, green accents, Eve shape, ... **895.00**

4 3/4" h, blue drip over grey-green base, Harmony shape, ... **75.00**

6 1/2" h, "Regency" design, white w/gilt, ... **365.00**

Tea Service, pot, 5 7/8" h, cream jug, 3 1/8" h, cov sugar bowl, 2 3/4" h, cake plate, 6 6/8" d, 4 cups and saucers, "Phlox" pattern, Regent shape, ... **1,500.00**

Tete-A-Tete, teapot, 6 3/4" h, creamer, 3 1/4" h, sugar bowl, 2 7/8" h, cup and saucer, plate, 6" d, "Wild Anemone" pattern, Windsor shape, ... **475.00**

Toast Rack, 5 3/4" l, 3 bar, green dashes and sm florals, gilt accents, ... **55.00**

Trio, "Roses, Pansies, Forget-Me-Nots," $170.00

Trio

"Archway of Roses" pattern, Queen Anne shape, ... **320.00**

"Ashbourne" pattern, Gainesborough shape, ... **235.00**

"Autumn Leaves" pattern, Queen Anne shape, ... **260.00**

"Bellflower" pattern, Eve shape, ... **195.00**

"Black Leafy Tree" pattern, Queen Anne shape, ... **210.00**

"Blue Iris" pattern, Queen Anne shape, ... **225.00**

"Blue Rock" pattern, Dainty shape, ... **90.00**

"Chippendale" pattern, #13216, ... **30.00**

"Cottage #1" pattern, Queen Anne shape, ... **675.00**

"Ivy Print-Autumn Tints" pattern, Fairy shape, ... **65.00**

"Laburnum" pattern, Eve shape, ... **195.00**

"Peaches and Grapes" pattern, Queen Anne shape, ... **210.00**

"Primrose" pattern, Dainty shape, ... **85.00**

"Scarlet Spunge" pattern, Oxford shape, ... **110.00**

"Sunset and Flowers" pattern, Queen Anne shape, ... **185.00**

"Violets" pattern, Dainty shape, ... **150.00**

Tureen, Cov, 11" H-H, "Bouquet" pattern, Dainty shape, ... **90.00**

Vase

5" h

Classic form, 2 loop handles, multicolored oriental scene of bridge, boat, chrysanthemums, and blossoms on med blue ground, yellow int, #8682H, ... **45.00**

Tapered form, flared rim, "Harmony," yellow, grey, green, and orange horiz banding, ... **150.00**

5 7/8" h, figural elf saluting, green uniform, brown basket on bk, Mabel Lucy Atwell, ... **135.00**

7" h, paneled, "Surrey Scenery" pattern, blue shades, orange luster finish, ... **30.00**

7 1/2" h, swollen shape, horiz shaded yellow to brown center band, orange base band, orange band on collar w/wave design, brown rim, ... **110.00**

c1902 *c1887*

SITZENDORF

Thuringia, Germany
1845 to Present

History: A small porcelain factory was founded in 1845 in Thuringia. The Voight brothers managed the factory from 1850 until about 1900. They produced decorative figures and porcelains in the Meissen style.

At the turn of the century, the factory was called Alfred Voight AG. Within a few years, the name was changed to Sitzendorf Porcelain Manufactory, its earlier designation. In 1923 earthenware was added.

The company was semi-nationalized in 1957 and completely nationalized in 1972. The current name is VEB Sitzendorf Porcelain Manufactory.

Bowl, 11" H-H, 6 1/2" h, int w/yellow and mauve flowers in gold circle and scattered flowers, applied pink, purple, and cream flowerheads, green leaves, gold scrolled feet, purple or red sashes on blond putti, Voight Brothers, A-$150.00

Candelabrum, 20 1/2" h, 3 arms w/applied flowerheads and flowerform nozzle and center nozzle, figural period woman in lt blue bodice, black hat, flowered skirt, holding lg open basket, flower encrusted dome base, c1880, ... **700.00**

Centerpiece, 14" h, multicolored bouquet on int, pierced border, ext w/molded and applied flowerheads and polychromed molded swirls, stem w/applied florals, scroll molded base w/cherubs and applied flowerheads, ... **950.00**

Dish, 5 1/4" l, figural brown monkey lying on back, hands on knees, "crowned S slashed Sitzendorf" mk, ... **110.00**

Figure

4 1/8" h, blue bodiced young woman wearing lace skirt w/applied flowers, purple hat and shoes, brown curly hair, circ base, "blue X'd lines" mk, ... **100.00**

4 3/8" h, polychrome seated period boy or girl gathering flowers, boy

w/long box in lap, ftd base, pr, ... **450.00**

Figure, 9 3/4" h, male w/brown hair, med blue coat, salmon and green vest w/gold trim, brown trousers, black shoes, female w/brown hair, dk red vest w/purple ribbon, aqua gown w/purple ribbon, red shoes, gold rococo bases, "blue crowned dble slashed lines" mks, pr, (A), $50.00

4 1/2" h, young girl, pink hat w/blue bow, yellow bodice tied w/red lacing, lt green overdress over pink inner gown, holding pink rose, basket of flowers on arm, chips, "blue crown over lined S" mk, ... **100.00**

5" h, monkey playing gold trumpet, yellow lined puce great coat, flowered vest, blue trousers, gilt scroll molded base, "crowned S" mk, ... **150.00**

5 3/4" h, standing brown haired German country girl, HP red collared black bodice w/green laces, lt brown basket w/red and green flowers on gold lined oct base w/brown fencing in bkd, ... **85.00**

6" h

   9" w

   Period man in blue coat, green and black striped trousers, woman wearing maroon vest, wide flowered skirt, both seated on gold accented sofa, "blue crowned S" mk, ... **520.00**

   Female dancer holding tambourine, pink lace skirt, gold roses, ... **180.00**

7" h x 6" w, seated period lady, blue jacket, flowered white dress, pink

overdress, holding flowerhead in palm, kneeling suitor, dk red coat, lt blue trousers, holding woman's hand, gilt scroll molded base, ... **475.00**

9" h, young boy, brown hair, black hat, red jacket, holding basket of flowers, bird on hand, white rococo base w/gilt accents, "Crown S" mk, ... **175.00**

9 1/4" h, 9 1/2" h, elderly man in blue ribboned white cap, blue flowered waistcoat and trousers, lilac robe, elderly woman blue peaked cap, blue bodice, blue flowered white gown, holding tray of dishes, pr, ... **1,000.00**

Figure, 13 1/4" h, male wearing magenta jacket, green pants, floral vest, female wearing blue vest, maroon and floral skirt, gold scrolled bases, pr, A-$345.00

9 3/8" h, country lady playing tambourine, cobalt jacket, yellow flowered sash, red flowered skirt, lamb on scroll molded base w/applied flowers, "blue crowned slashed lines" mk, ... **340.00**

10 1/2" h, brown haired period woman wearing layers of white lace w/applied flowerheads on hem, white lace bodice, holding 2 lg gold baskets w/applied multicolored flowerheads, gold shoes, scroll molded base w/applied flowerheads, "blue crowned slashed S" mk,

.... **695.00**

12" h, "The Three Graces," 3 entwined female figures, oval base, white glaze, "blue crowned S slash" mk, ... **600.00**

13" h, period man w/curved hat, holding waistcoat w/left hand, scroll molded base, overall white

glaze, "blue crown over lined S" mk, ... **125.00**

Vase

3 3/4" h, 3 seashells standing on end, applied green vines, multicolored roses, ... **300.00**

4 3/4" h, figural open egg shell w/applied multicolored flowerheads, sq base, ... **400.00**

11 1/4" h, cornucopia shape, applied yellow or mauve roses, green foliage, birds and reclining cherub, scroll base, blue slashed lines mk, ... **800.00**

SLIPWARE

Staffordshire, England

Continental

17th C to Present

History: Slip was powdered clay that was mixed with water until a cream-like consistency was achieved. The slip then could be used to decorate pottery in a variety of ways such as trailing, marbling, combing, feathering, and sgraffito.

Trailing was decorating by means of extruding slip or glaze through a nozzle onto the surface of the piece.

Marbling was achieved by trailing different colored slips onto a form that was then either shaken or twisted to produce a pattern.

Combing was done by applying slip and then wiping over the piece with a toothed or pronged instrument or by using the fingers.

Feathering was performed by trailing a line of slip onto a wet ground of a contrasting color. The tip of a feather or another flexible, thin point was then drawn back and forth across the trailed line.

Sgraffito was achieved by cutting, incising, or scratching away a slip coating to reveal the contrasting slip or body underneath.

Colored slips were made by adding a small amount of various oxides to the slip. Slip was an early method to embellish ordinary clay-colored pottery. After the slip decorations were done, the vessel was covered with a lead glaze to make it non-porous and to produce a shiny surface. Slip decoration has been used from the 17th century to the present.

Slipware was made mainly at Wrotham in Kent in Staffordshire. Other manufacturing centers included Essex, Sussex, Somerset, and Devonshire. The earliest piece from Wrotham was dated 1612.

Between 1670 and 1710, the most spectacular pieces of slipware made in Staffordshire were large chargers made by the Tofts, John and William Wright, George Taylor, William Taylor, and Ralph Simpson. Favorite subjects included royal scenes, portraits of popular figures, and cavaliers. Coats of arms, mermaids, Adam & Eve, and the Pelican in her piety were used.

Borders usually had a trellis pattern. Human figures had minimal anatomical details and were painted in a naive fashion. Forms that were slip decorated included tygs, teapots, cradles, baking dishes, puzzle jugs, posset pots, whistles, etc.

Potteries in Devon made large harvest jugs using the sgraffito technique. Decorations included coats of arms, lions, unicorns, ships, mariners' compasses, and floral designs.

Wrotham slip-decorated wares continued to be made until the end of the 18th century. Fleur-de-lys, roses, crosses, stars, and masks were frequent motifs. Tygs, posset pots, two-handled mugs, and candlesticks were made. A distinctive feature of Wrotham ware was handles made by weaving different colored clays together.

Reference: R.G. Cooper, *English Slipware Dishes 1650-1850*, Tiranti, 1968.

Museums: Colonial Williamsburg Foundation, Williamsburg, VA; County Museum, Truro, England; Gardiner Museum of Ceramic Art, Toronto, Canada; Kansas City Art Museum, Kansas City, MO; Plymouth City Museum, Plymouth, England; Royal Albert Museum, Exeter, England; Sheffield City Museum, Sheffield, England.

Bird Feeder, 7 1/8" d, domed drum shape, pierced w/round and sq holes, cream slip fleur-de-lys on dk brown ground, ... **9,000.00**

Bowl, 11 3/4" d, lg brown and green flowerhead in center, green and brown crisscross border, cream ground, ... **25.00**

Cider Jug, 6 1/2" h, blue, brown, and green slip splashes, lt tan ground, orange-brown rim and overhead handle, Jaspe, ... **270.00**

Cup and Saucer, black, brown, tan, and cream slip, brown ground, **$425.00**

Charger, 13 5/8" d, cream and black, orange ground, France, c1870, **$650.00**

Dish, 11 3/4" d, med brown ground, press-molded form, central face, lobed border and scalloped rim, dk brown slip lines separating lobes w/cream dots, pierced for hanging, c1700, (A), ... **2,850.00**

Jug, 9 1/2" h, ovoid, vert green slip stripes, redware body, ... **385.00**

Loaf Pan, 17" l x 14 1/4" w, redware, lt and dk brown comb pattern, white ground, ... **750.00**

Milk Jug, 6" h, wavy red horiz slip, dk blue vert drip, cream ground, Jaspe, ... **120.00**

Milk Mug, 7 1/2" h, applied yellow splotched slip on brown ground, England, ... **50.00**

Milk Pan, 11 1/2" d, green, yellow, and brown slip design on redware body, (A), ... **275.00**

Pitcher
    5" h, trailed white slip zigzags, dots, and "Vs," dk brown ground, white int, ... **35.00**
    8 1/4" h, strap handle, orange, green, and brown slip on white ground, Jaspe, ... **100.00**

Plate, 6" d, cream slip crown over interlaced "CA" and "1898," orange-red ground, Germany, ... **25.00**

Pot, 5 1/4" d, ftd, single handle, wavy cream slip design on redware body, yellow int, Dutch, ... **100.00**

Storage Jar
    5 3/4" h, green, brown, and orange slip on yellow ground, chips, Jaspe, ... **75.00**
    10 1/2" h, 2 ear handles, stoneware, moss green vert slip lines, green-brown ground, mid-19th C, ... **385.00**

Sugar Bowl, Cov, 4 1/2" h, 2 sm handles, brown and green slip, white ground, Jaspe, (A), ... **55.00**

Tray, 11 1/2" l x 6" w, cream swirl slip on redware body, rolled rim, Jaspe, rim chips, ... **245.00**

Tyge, 7 1/2" h, lt tan geometric slip designs on dk brown lower half, brown slip curls on tan border, 3 handles, orange-brown glazed int, England, c1880, ... **1,435.00**

Urn, 8 1/4" h, dbl handles, long neck, redware w/running yellow slip, (A), ... **30.00**

Vase, Cov, 14 1/2" h, brown and cream agate slip over stoneware body, cream satyr mask handles w/horns to rim, ball knob, sq basalt base, "imp Wedgwood" mk, c1773, (A), ... **4,780.00**

SOFT PASTE

English/Continental
17th to 19th Centuries

History: Soft paste, or artificial porcelain, was made during the 17th and 18th centuries in Europe by using glass or a glass substitute that was ground up and mixed with clay. Over the years, the ingredients of soft paste varied.

The glaze was added in the second firing. This glaze was soft. It scratched and chipped easily. If the potter was careless, the glaze could wilt in the kiln and become uneven. The soft paste process was abandoned gradually during the early 19th century when the formula for hard paste porcelain became better understood.

Soft paste porcelain had the translucency of hard paste. It simply was softer and more porous. Since the melting temperatures of soft paste glazes and the colored enamels were similar, the overglaze enamel sank into the glaze and softened the outline of painted decoration. Essentially pigment and surface were melded together.

Soft paste was made in France at Rouen, St. Cloud, Chantilly, Mennecy, Vincennes, and Sevres. English factories making soft paste included Chelsea, Bow, Derby, Worcester, and Liverpool. Most European countries produced soft paste porcelain before switching to hard paste porcelain production.

Bowl
    4 3/4" d, 2 lg yellow centered blue petaled flowerheads, red florals and green foliage, dk red rim and int design, ...**48.00**
    6" d, ftd, 3 polychrome panels of chinoiserie scenes on ext, red,

orange, and purple int rim lines and sm blue dots, (A), ... **300.00**

13 1/2" d, gaudy cobalt to med blue leaves w/swags along border, vining on ext, chips and hairline, (A), ... **285.00**

Coffee Can and Saucer, red transfer of walking oriental man and flowers, chrysanthemums on border, green, blue, and mauve overpaint, ... **25.00**

Coffeepot, 10 1/2" h, center band of brick red and green flowers and foliage, sm blue flowers and green leaves, pink luster accents, (A), ... **780.00**

Creamer, 4" h

5 1/2" w, multicolored enameled basket of flowers on sides, red meandering line above, red chain on rim, ... **25.00**

5 7/8" l, HP pink roses, dk umber leaves, repairs, c1815, ... **65.00**

Cup and Saucer

Enameled green, yellow, red, and lt blue sprigs and cockle shells, puce trim, reeded molding, unmkd, ... **120.00**

HP lt and dk pink, green, and yellow flower sprays, pink luster trim, dbl pink luster lines on rims, Staffordshire, mid-19th C, ... **50.00**

Purple transfers, child watering flowers in center of saucer, HP multicolored floral bands, purple chains on rims, unmkd, ... **32.00**

Sprigs of dk pink flowers on grey-green leaves, unmkd, ... **25.00**

Scattered small blue and red floral sprigs w/green leaves, brown stems, blue lined rims, c1810, ... **185.00**

Cup and Saucer, Handleless

Gaudy blue foliage and border bands, (A), ... **138.00**

Green, blue, pink, and brown flowers, hairline, ... **110.00**

Half pink and half red stylized flowerheads, yellow centered sm blue stylized flowerheads, green foliage, unmkd, ... **30.00**

Pink flowers w/blue and orange buds, (A), ... **50.00**

Scattered sm purple and yellow flowers on branch w/green foliage, c1830, ... **30.00**

Jug, 10" h, relief of florals on sides, red and green flower sprigs, green bands on throat and handle, ... **185.00**

Mug, 8" h, underglazed blue "The Long Eliza" pattern, oriental woman in fenced garden w/parasol, (A), ... **545.00**

Pepper Pot, 4 1/2" h, cobalt scalloped line around shoulder, cobalt feathered top, (A), ... **358.00**

Plate

6 1/2" d, Leeds type painted green and yellow pineapple in center, border band of blue and gold leaves, hairline, (A), ... **550.00**

8 7/8" d, dk red rose, purple columbine, yellow and blue flowers in center, dk purple, green, yellow, and red vine border, (A), ... **110.00**

10" d, small orange and blue sprig w/green leaves in center, border band of blue, orange, and green florals between blue lines, ... **35.00**

Platter, 16" l, oval, HP and printed multicolored oriental flowers in vases, sm trees in boxes, scattered sprigs, rim chip, ... **225.00**

Soup Plate, 9" d, 3 masted sailing ship w/"EAST INDIAMAN SAILING FROM THE DOWNS," black transfer, black lined rim, ... **120.00**

Sugar Bowl, 8" H-H, 7" h, yellow centered mauve flowers, green leaves, purple stems, scattered small blue flowers, $75.00

Sugar Bowl, 5" h x 4 3/4" w, painted sprigs of sm red berries, green leaves, brown stems, black striped knob, ... **175.00**

Teabowl and Saucer, borders of blue printed flowers and cell designs, ... **225.00**

*Teapot, 5 1/4" h x 10" l, sea green leaves and gold leaves and stems, sm pink flowers, c1830-40, **$395.00***

Teapot

7 1/8" h, gaudy blue floral designs, emb leaf handle, beehive knob, hairline, (A), ... **358.00**

9" h, painted gold flower and leaves on sides, twig handle, flower bud knob, ... **45.00**

Fab° de Aranda A — EARLY 19TH CENTURY — 1760-1804

SPAIN-GENERAL

Alcora, Province of Valencia
1726-1858

Count Aranda, assisted by Joseph Olerys of Moustiers and other French workers, established a faience factory in 1726. The original success of this factory was due to the skill of the French painters and the use of French models. The tin-glazed pottery that it produced was quite popular throughout Spain.

By 1737 all the workers were Spanish. Biblical or mythological scenes on large dishes or plaques were among its best pieces. The Count died in 1749. His son took over. A succession of Dukes of Hija owned the factory. When the factory was acquired by private owners in 1858, Francois Martin started to produce hard paste porcelain in imitation of Wedgwood's creamware.

Buen Retiro, near Madrid
1760-1812

King Charles III of Spain established Buen Retiro, near Madrid, using workers from Capodimonte in 1760. Soft paste porcelains were manufactured into services, tea sets, vases, bowls, and figures similar to Capodimonte wares. The factory also specialized in the porcelain tiles that were used to decorate palaces.

By the end of the 18th century, biscuit groups in the Sevres styles, and medallions and plaques in the Wedgwood style, were made. From 1765 until 1790, Giuseppe Gricci was the chief modeler. After his death, Spanish artists influenced the decorations.

Only hard paste wares were made at Buen Retiro after 1800. In 1808 the factory was transformed into a fortress that was destroyed by Wellington in 1812. In 1817 the factory was rebuilt at Moncloa in Madrid and remained in operation until 1850.

Hispano-Moresque, Valencia & Malaga
End of 13th Century to Present

Hispano-Moresque was white enamel, tin-glazed earthenware that was usually decorated with copper or silver metallic lusters. Moorish potters came to Spain, settled in Valencia, Manises, and Paterna, and made their lustered pottery.

Early luster colors were pale and filmy. Later pieces utilized a golden luster and deeper blue tones. As time progressed, the luster became more brassy and metallic in appearance.

Hispano-Moresque flourished for about three hundred years. By the end of the 16th century there was a steady decline, but the technique still continues today in Valencia.

All sorts of vases, drug pots, pitchers, covered bowls, large dishes, and wall tiles are made.

Talavera
15th Century to Present

Talavera pottery was decorated in a peasant-like style with birds, animals, or busts in a blue and dusty-orange motif outlined in purplish-black. Talavera wares were popular with all levels of Spanish society into the 17th century. Monastic coats of arms and the cardinal's hat were decorated in yellow, orange, and green. Shapes included large bowls and two-handled jugs featuring sporting scenes, bullfights, buildings, trees, figures, and animals.

During the mid-18th century, Talavera adopted the styles used at Alcora, which had copied the French style of Moustiers. Today, only ordinary earthenwares are made.

Reference: Alice Wilson Frothingham, *Tile Panels of Spain: 1500-1650*, Hispanic Society of America, 1969.

Museums: Cleveland Museum of Art, Cleveland, OH; Hispanic Society of America, New York, NY; Musee Nationale de Ceramique, Sevres, France; Museo Arquelogical Nacional, Madrid, Spain; Seattle Art Museum, Seattle, WA; Victoria & Albert Museum, London, England.

Albarello, 9 1/2" h, tin glazed, tan kneeling cherub holding bow, basket on back w/blue flowers, 19th C, ... **650.00**

Basket, 8" d x 6 1/4" h, coiled open interwoven rope, med blue, ... **15.00**

Bough Pot, 4" h x 7 1/2" w, faience, 6 pointed star shape, painted blue and iron-red hunter and flying game birds, iron-red sawtooth border w/blue interspersed dots, green and iron-red dashes on sides, ... **475.00**

Bowl

7 1/2" d, Hispano-Moresque, dk red stylized flowers, half loop and band border, copper luster trim, ... **485.00**

Tin Glazed

8" d, blue bud, leaves and stem in center, blue waves on rim, ... **75.00**

8 1/4" d, lg blue painted stylized flowerhead w/dash foliage, border of swags and dash triangles, late 18th C, ... **200.00**

15 1/4" d, polychrome middle eastern temple oriental flowers, int band of blue crosshatching alternating w/flowers, ... **975.00**

Charger, 13 1/8" d, Hispano-Moresque, copper luster, yellow ground, 16th C, **$2,400.00**

Charger

12 1/2" d, Hispano-Moresque, bullseye center, leaf and pod border, raised dot ground, dk red luster, ... **2,250.00**

13" d, Tin Glazed

Blue stylized sm floral sprig in center, half zigzags on border w/leaves and stylized flowerheads, ... **200.00**

Border of stylized manganese flowerheads and meandering vine, stylized orange, blue, yellow, and green flowerheads and foliage,

"blue A.S." mk, early 19th C, ... **210.00**

16" d, blue, yellow, green, orange, maroon, and gold central floral motif circled by blue chain, floral border, ... **135.00**

Dish, 8" d, tin glazed, grey-blue crest of Dominican Order in center, simple florals and foliage on border, rim chips, c1700, ... **565.00**

Drug Jar, 7 1/2" h, oviform w/short, cylindrical neck, faience, blue painted diagonal label w/"So. Edeser" or "Ol. Aparivi," naively painted rabbit, bird, tulip, and wing head of cherub, scrolling foliage on neck, white ground, early 18th C, chips, pr, (A), ... **2,150.00**

Oil Jar, 25" h, amphora shape, stone body w/Delft style polychrome stained glass window design on upper section, fluted neck, c1860, ... **1,250.00**

Pitcher, 6" h, red and green florals, med brown bands, "imp Made in Spain" mark, **$15.00**

Pitcher

5" h, tin glazed, painted brown horse, yellow spotted green saddle, yellow and green foliage, cream ground, c1760, ... **5,500.00**

7" h, ball shape, white, "Waechterbach Spain" mk, ... **10.00**

8 1/4" h, tin glazed, HP multicolored gazelles in trees and hills, brown lined base, blue-black rim, Talavera, late 19th C, ... **295.00**

Plate, 9 1/4" d, relief of brown and tan molded swimming carp, green seaweed streaks, indented border, ... **10.00**

Porringer, 4 3/8" H-H, copper red geometrics and interlaced circles designs, lobed handles, 19th C, ... **25.00**

Urn, 13 3/4" h, tin glazed, molded baluster form w/narrow neck, domed ft, blue painted landscape scene w/bird and scroll, lion's head handles, late 19th C, (A), ... **430.00**

SPATTERWARE

Staffordshire, England
c1800-1850s

Design

History: In design spatter, there were small, shaped areas of spots or dots instead of large continuous overall spattered areas. Some design spatter was done with a stencil or template. Design spatter also was referred to as "structural spatter."

Colors used for design spatter were red, blue, green, and purple. Spatter techniques were combined with hand painted decoration motifs. Decorative center motifs included Adams Rose, Columbine, Dogwood, and Pansy.

Known makers of design spatter were T.W. Barlow, Elsmore and Forster, and Harvey.

General

History: Spatterware was a decoration that appeared on a variety of body compositions including soft paste, creamware, pearlware, and ironstone. It appealed to "popular" tastes because of its inexpensive price and its cheery, colorful, and bright appearance. It was made primarily for export.

Spatter was a stippling or all-over design of color. One or more colors could be used. The color was applied in parallel stripes or concentric bands, leaving a center of white for decoration. With spatter as a border, the center design could be either hand painted or transfer printed.

There were eight basic colors used for spatter: black, blue (the most common), brown, green, pink, purple, red, and yellow (the rarest). Most popular patterns were: Cannon, Castle, Peafowl, Pomegrante, Schoolhouse, and Thistle.

Few pieces of true spatter bore identifying manufacturer's marks. Among the known makers of spatter were Adams, Cotton and Barlow, Harvey, and J. & G. Meakin.

References: Kevin McConnell, *Spongeware and Spatterware*, Schiffer Publishing Co. 1990; Carl F. & Ada F. Robacker, *Spatterware and Sponge*, A.S. Barnes & Co. 1978.

Museum: Henry Ford Museum, Dearborn, MI.

Reproduction Alert: "Cybis" spatter is an increasingly collectible ware made by Boleslow Cybis of Poland. The design utilized the Adams-type peafowl and was made in the 1940s. Some pieces were marked "Cybis" in an impressed mark; some examples were unmarked. The principal shape was cup plates. The body of the ware was harder than true spatter, and the glaze appeared glassy rather than soft.

Many contemporary craftsmen also are reproducing spatterware examples.

Bowl, 8 1/2" d, design dk red inner flowerheads, green, and blue leaves, dk red leaves on border, green lined rim, $130.00

Design

Bowl

8" d, HP red stylized half flowerheads and green foliage on ext, scattered blue stick spatter flowerheads, Belgium, ... **25.00**

11" d, lg painted red, blue, and green stylized flowerhead and leaves in center, stick spatter bands of diamonds on border, "Petrus Regout Maastricht lion" mk, ... **90.00**

Charger

12 1/4" d, inner and border band of stick spatter red and green sprigs and flowers, lg blue foliage between, (A), ... **165.00**

16 1/2" d, lg gaudy fuchsia blossoms in center, lg simple stroke fuchsia or dl blue flowers, green leaves, stick spatter purple starflowers, (A), ... **450.00**

Coffeepot, 8 3/4" h, ironstone, purple and red pansy and green leaves, blue 8 pointed star design spatter on borders, chip under lid, (A), ... **2,200.00**

Creamer

3 1/4" h, black circ stick spatter, (A), ... **55.00**

4" h, center band of stick spatter red flowerheads, blue and green leaves, band of purple stick spatter circ flowerheads on rim and foot, (A), ... **165.00**

Cup and Saucer, Handleless, green and red rainbow spatter, $1,650.00

Cup and Saucer, Handleless

Band of blue or red stick spatter stars, (A), ... **65.00**

Groupings of 3 red flowers, 2 green leaves, green bands encircle int and ext rims, (A), ... **880.00**

Cup and Saucer, Handleless, ironstone, blue and red flowerheads, green leaves, "W.E. Oulsnau & Sons, Burslem" mark, A-$25.00

Miniature, stick spatter brown and purple flowers and green leaves, (A), ... **165.00**

Red and green stick spatter star design, hairline, (A), ... **440.00**

Mustard Jar, Cov, 3" h, blue spatter, c1840, **$395.00**

Mug, 5 3/4" h, center band of stick spatter mauve and goldenrod yellow circles and dots, blue lined rim and base, molded leaf handle terminals, (A), ... **165.00**

Pitcher, 10 1/2" h, band of red star shaped flowerheads, green leaf stick spatter on base and neck, ... **175.00**

Plate, 9 1/2" d, dk blue, dk red flowers and leaves, small green leaves, blue design spatter flowerheads, border of black rabbits on yellow-brown ground, red lined rim, **$495.00**

Plate
8 1/2" d
Border of stick spatter burgundy flower centers, cobalt leaves, single stroke painted green stems and mint green leaves, ... **95.00**
Dk red thistle, blue lily of the valley, green foliage in center, stick spatter red smoke rings on border, (A), ... **468.00**
Painted blue lily of the valley, red rose buds, purple columbine in center, green stick spatter flowerhead border, ... **220.00**

Purple and yellow pansy and green leaves in center, stick spatter band of red 8 pointed stars flanked by blue stripes, (A), ... **275.00**
Violet or dk red painted single stroke stylized flowers on border, green leaves, bunches of sm blue stick spatter flowerheads, dk red rim, ... **70.00**
8 5/8" d, maroon dogwood, green leaves in center stick spatter purple bow design on border between red lines, (A), ... **415.00**
8 3/4" d
Black stick spatter flowerheads, yellow design spatter foliage, (A), ... **70.00**
Border of dk green grapes, stick spatter red and green grape leaves between blue lines, ... **38.00**
Design of red dots in center, green loops on int border, purple loops on ext border, "Cotton & Barlow" mk, (A), ... **138.00**
HP dk red and orange stylized flower, green leaves in center, paneled border w/stick spatter band of blue flowerheads, red rim, ... **175.00**
9" d
Gaudy blue flowers in center, border band of blue stick spatter sm flowerheads, (A), ... **120.00**
Stick spatter yellow centered 5 petal red flowers, curling black stems, green leaves, dk red inner band, stick spatter black dbl diamond border band on ochre ground, dk red rim, ... **100.00**
9 1/8" d, stick spatter red fruit and green leaves, blue rim w/red stripes, (A), ... **193.00**
9 3/8" d, ironstone
Blue and green stick spatter flowers in center w/red and blue foliage, black transfer of running rabbits on border w/green and yellow accents, hairline, (A), ... **413.00**
Red, blue, and green stick spatter flowers in center, black transfer of rabbits,

frogs, and trees on border w/yellow and green accents, (A), ... **468.00**
9 1/2" d, HP naively painted dk blue rooster, red tail and comb, green and red flowers, lt brown ground, border band of blue stick spatter roses, red rim, Swansea, ... **1,080.00**
9 3/4" d
Maroon dogwood, green leaves in center, stick spatter blue rosette border between red lines, (A), ... **360.00**
Stick spatter blue-green clover in center, painted green leaves, 5 pointed star of dk blue stick spatter flowerheads, painted red single stroke half flowerheads on border, blue lined rim, Staffordshire, ... **50.00**
10" d, red border and leaves, flow blue stripes and flowers, (A), ... **275.00**
10 1/2" d, lg red painted stylized trumpet flowers, blue bases, green foliage, scattered stick spatter purple rosettes, (A), ... **130.00**
10 3/4" d, purple stick spatter flowers w/lg blue, red, and green flowers, (A), ... **150.00**

Platter
12" l, oval, band of red roses, sm blue flowers, and green leaves on inner border, border of band of blue stick spatter flowerheads and leaves, red lined rim, Maastricht, ... **135.00**
13 1/2" l x 10 1/4" w, oct, blue printed "Peruvian Horse Hunt," border band of purple stick spatter flowerheads, dbl black lined rim, (A), ... **200.00**
14 1/2" l x 10 1/4" w, oval, ironstone, brown transfer of rabbits and green frog in fenced yellow field, red, green, and blue stick spatter flowers on border, (A), ... **1,100.00**

Soup Plate
8 1/4" d, red plums, purple grapes in center, stick spatter border band of purple cog wheels between red lines, ... **135.00**
8 3/4" d, border band of stick spatter blue flowers, open red roses, green foliage, "Edge Malkin" mk, (A), ... **60.00**

9 1/4" d, stick spatter blue centered purple rayed rosettes in center and border band, (A), ... **248.00**

Sugar Bowl, Cov, 5" h, vert blue, green, and red stick spatter single and dbl circlets, blue striped base, (A), ... **190.00**

Teapot, 8" h, ironstone, purple and yellow pansy and green leaves, blue 8 pointed star stick spatter on borders, chip on spout and lid, (A), ... **1,210.00**

Toddy Plate

6 1/2" d, painted maroon dogwood, green leaves, stick spatter purple roseate border flanked by blue stripes, (A), ... **275.00**

6 5/8" d, purple and yellow pansy, green leaves in center, stick spatter border band of green eight pointed stars between blue stripes, rim chip, (A), ... **330.00**

Waste Bowl, 5 3/4" d, blue and red flowerheads, green leaves, "BB anchor, Royal Arms" mark, **$50.00**

General
Bowl

4 3/4" d, ftd, red and green tulip, yellow spatter body, hairlines, (A), ... **2,310.00**

6 3/4" d, vert red, blue, and green rainbow spatter, blue int rim, hairlines, (A), ... **825.00**

Creamer

3 1/2" h

Paneled, blue spatter on upper half, (A), ... **85.00**

Pink pineapple w/black accents, green foliage, blue spatter rim and base, hairline, (A), ... **3,850.00**

3 3/4" h

Rainbow spatter, red, blue, and green horiz stripes, (A), ... **880.00**

Red and green Adam's Rose design, purple and blue spatter, (A), ... **220.00**

4" h, peafowl w/green, blue, and red rainbow spatter, (A), ... **3,450.00**

4 1/4" h, bulbous

Red flower and bud w/green foliage, blue spatter ground, (A), ... **963.00**

Two brown acorns, teal caps, green leaves, red spatter, (A), ... **880.00**

4 1/2" h

Bulbous, green, blue, and red horiz rainbow spatter, (A), ... **2,860.00**

Red and green tulip variant, blue spatter ground, repairs and stains, (A), ... **578.00**

4 3/4" h, helmet shape, red, green, and blue horiz spatter bands, hairlines, (A), ... **275.00**

5" h, paneled, red and green cockscomb design, blue spatter ground, stains, (A), ... **853.00**

5 5/8" h, paneled, red, green, and peafowl, squiggly branches, blue spatter ground, (A), ... **770.00**

Cup and Saucer, Handleless

Adam's Rose design, red flower, green foliage, red spatter borders, ... **300.00**

Blue and red forget-me-nots, green leaves, blue star shaped outline, hairline on cup, (A), ... **3,630.00**

Blue and red fort, red spatter borders, (A), ... **3,738.00**

Blueberries, green foliage, red spatter borders, (A), ... **4,035.00**

Blue, green, and yellow peafowl, red spatter borders, c1870, ... **1,325.00**

Blue roofed red shed, red spatter borders, ... **2,600.00**

Drape pattern, red, yellow, and green rainbow spatter, rim chip repair, (A), ... **3,080.00**

Green and red parrot on branch, red spatter borders, repaired chip, (A), ... **743.00**

Lg green and red flowerhead, green and red banded spatter borders, c1840, (A), ... **495.00**

Red holly berry and green vine, blue spatter borders, hairline, (A), ... **248.00**

Red schoolhouse, pink roof, brown ground, green trees and grass, red spatter borders, hairlines, (A), ... **825.00**

Red stenciled hex sign in center, red spatter borders, (A), ... **165.00**

Red thistle, green leaves, green and black rainbow spatter borders, (A), ... **23,000.00**

Yellow and blue Dove on green branch, purple spatter borders, (A), ... **2,750.00**

Yellow, blue, red, and green swirl rainbow pattern, (A), ... **23,000.00**

Yellow bullseye, red spatter borders, (A), ... **880.00**

Miniature

Blue, red, green, and yellow rainbow drape spatter, (A), ... **16,100.00**

Green and red tulip, yellow spatter ground, hairlines, (A), ... **1,760.00**

Red and yellow Christmas balls, green drape spatter, (A), ... **7,475.00**

Red, yellow, and green peafowl, blue spatter body, ... **250.00**

Panels of yellow-centered blue and red flowers, green foliage, red and blue rainbow spatter between, (A), ... **6,354.00**

Purple and blue rainbow stripes, (A), ... **385.00**

Red and green berries, purple spatter borders, hairline on saucer, (A), ... **303.00**

Red, green, and dk yellow 6 pointed star, blue spatter borders, (A), ... **1,210.00**

Cup Plate

3 3/8" d, red, green, blue peafowl, red spatter border, (A), ... **44.00**

4 1/2" d, pink and blue rainbow spatter, ... **275.00**

6" d, purple, yellow, and green rainbow drape, (A), ... **1,093.00**

Mug, 2 1/2" h, blue, green, and red peafowl, blue spatter ground, hairline, (A), ... **715.00**

Pitcher

6 3/4" h

Blue spatter drape bands on shoulder, rim, and handle, hairlines, (A), ... **440.00**

Paneled, yellow, green, and red rainbow spatter, repairs, (A), ... **1,840.00**

7 3/8" h, paneled, blue and red-purple rainbow spatter, spout repair, (A), ... **1,705.00**

Sugar Bowl, Cov

4 1/4" h, red, blue, and green horiz rainbow spatter, hairline, (A), ... **220.00**

4 1/2" h, blue cornflower, green leaves, red and yellow drape spatter, repaired knob and rim, (A), ... **2,640.00**

5" h, Rainbow spatter, red, green, and blue vert stripes, bull's eye cov, (A), ... **2,200.00**

Teapot

4 1/4" h, miniature, blue, red, and yellow peafowl on side, tree on reverse, green spatter body, 4 sm feet, molded handle, ... **605.00**

5" h

Red tulip, green leaves, yellow spatter ground, repaired, (A), ... **4,400.00**

Green and yellow rainbow spatter w/purple loops and black spots, restorations, (A), ... **5,060.00**

6 1/2" h, red, yellow, and blue peafowl on branch, green thumbprint spatter, (A), ... **1,870.00**

7 1/4" h, Paneled

Green, red, and blue peafowl, lt red spatter, repairs, (A), ... **495.00**

Red and green thistle, yellow spatter ground, repairs, (A), ... **10,450.00**

10 1/8" h, red transfer of lg flowerheads and delphinium, blue accents, flowerhead knob, red spatter cov, handle, spout, and ft, (A), ... **660.00**

Tea Set, pot, 10 1/2" h, creamer, 6" h, cov sugar bowl, 9" h, paneled, red roses and green foliage on sides, blue spatter ground, ear shaped handles, repairs, (A), ... **1,760.00**

Washbowl

12 1/8" d, blue and purple bullseye in center, blue and purple rainbow spatter border, chip, (A), ... **1,430.00**

14" d, paneled, blue and yellow tulip in center, blue spatter border, (A), ... **1,210.00**

Stone-China
1805-30

SPODE

Shelton, Staffordshire, England
c1797-1833

History: Spode was best known for two important contributions to the ceramic repertoire: the perfection of under-the-glaze transfer printing on earthenware and the introduction of the bone china formula. Josiah Spode I benefited from a five year apprenticeship with Thomas Whieldon. By 1770 he was an established master potter at Stoke-on-Trent at the factory where his successors continue today. Josiah Spode II, 1755 to 1827, opened a showroom and warehouse in London in 1778.

The perfection of transfer printing in blue under-the-glaze on earthenware enabled Spode to copy, at reasonable prices, Chinese blue-painted porcelain. These new examples provided replacements and additions for services that had become increasingly difficult to obtain from Chinese sources.

Earlier English porcelain manufacturers had failed to make large dinner plates and platters with straight enough edges to be commercially saleable. By July 1796, Spode was selling dinnerware that he called "English China" at prices well below those of his established competitors. By 1800 a bone china porcelain containing up to forty percent calcined ox bone had emerged. The credit for perfecting this formula was shared jointly by the two Spodes. Josiah I developed the initial formula, and Josiah II refined it. Josiah Spode II marketed products made with the new formula with such success that within ten years bone china became standard English china.

Josiah II's successful promotion of bone china was achieved in part through the on-glaze decorating of Henry Daniel. The engraving techniques improved greatly. The zenith was reached in 1816 when, two years after the "Tower" pattern appeared, the pattern "Blue Italian" was introduced. Both patterns remain popular to the present day.

In 1813 Spode, responding to the demand for replacement pieces for polychrome Chinese porcelain services, adopted a stone china formula that was patented by J.&W. Turner in 1800. Turner's formula provided a superior body on which to decorate the more costly painted and gilded patterns. The body also matched the delicate grey color of the original Chinese porcelain. Over the years, the formula was improved further and appears in today's market as Spode's Fine Stone China.

When Josiah II moved to Stoke in 1797 after his father's death, he left the management of the London business in the hands of William Copeland, who began his employment with Spode in 1784. Copeland worked with Spode as an equal part-ner. When Spode retired in 1812, Copeland assumed sole charge of the London house. His business acumen, augmented with the help of W.T. Copeland, his son, in 1824, contributed immensely to the success of the Spode enterprise. (See: Copeland-Spode for a continuation of the company's history.

References: Robert Copeland, *Spode & Copeland Marks*, Cassell Academic, 1993; Robert Copeland, *Spode's Willow Pattern & Other Designs After the Chinese*, Blanford Press, 1990; D. Drakard & P. Holdway, *Spode Printed Wares*, Longmans, 1983; Arthur Hayden, *Spode & His Successors*, Cassell, 1925; Leonard Whiter, *Spode: A History of the Family, Factory & Wares, 1733-1833*, Random Century, 1989; Sydney B. Williams, *Antique Blue & White Spode*, David & Charles, 1988; Gillian Neale, *Miller's Blue & White Pottery*, Antique Collectors Club, 2000, Vega Wilkinson, *Spode-Copeland, The Works and Its People 1770-1990*, Antique Collectors' Club, 2002, David Drakard & Paul Holdway, *Spode Transfer Printed Ware, 1784-1833*, Antique Collectors' Club, 1988.

Museums: Cincinnati Art Museum, Cincinnati, OH; City of Stoke-on-Trent Museum, Hanley, England; Jones Museum of Glass & Ceramics, Sebago, ME; Spode Museum, Stoke-on-Trent, UK; Victoria & Albert Museum, London, England.

Collectors' Note: Although there is no collectors' club, inquiries about Spode factory wares may be sent to Historical Consultant, Spode, Stoke-on-Trent, ST4 IBX, England. All inquiries should contain good, clear photographs and full details on the marks.

Bowl, 6 3/8" d x 3 1/8" h, black transfers, pink luster rim, c1820, **$125.00**

Coffee Can and Saucer, Imari pattern, gilt outlined lg cobalt and iron-red leaves, iron-red buds and flowerheads, border of alternating panels of gilt scrolling on cobalt between iron-red buds on white, "Spode Stone China 2061" mk, ... **65.00**

Cup and Saucer, wide med blue band w/gilt sawtooth borders, molded rims, "red SPODE 4041" mk, c1820, ... **65.00**

Dessert Service, Part, 2 biscuit bowls, 10 3/4" l, reticulated fruit basket, 6 plates, 8" d, reticulated cake plate, iron-red and blue exotic bird, red and mauve flowers, olive green ground, gilt trim, "imp Spode" marks, c1810, $1,900.00

Dish, 8" d

Lobed, "Tumbledown Dick" pattern, bird perched on brown prunus, green leaves, pink, blue, and yellow blossoms, c1820s, "imp SPODE" mk, ... **425.00**

Pearlware, "Grape" pattern #3214, blue-purple grapes, green leaves, brown stems and tendrils, c1820, ... **400.00**

Figure, 6 1/4" h, lg purple tinged yellow tulip, sm bud and green leaves on shaped brown base w/grass and sm flower, repair, c1825-30, repair, ... **10,500.00**

Garniture, vase, 8 1/2" h, 2 vases, 5 1/4" h, trumpet shape, painted flowerheads and gilt leaves on mazarine ground, 3 gilt paw feet, gilt rim w/simulated pearls and on base, repaired hairline, chip, pattern #2575, c1810, ... **15,000.00**

Jug, 5 3/4" h, enameled red tinged white morning glories, blue and red buds, green leaves, unglazed redware body, hydra handle, "imp SPODE" mk, ... **330.00**

Meat Platter

19" l x 14 1/2" w, well and tree, "Gothic Castle" pattern, blue transfer, ... **900.00**

21" l x 16 1/2" w, "Jasmine" pattern, blue transfer, ... **1,850.00**

Mug, 3 1/2" h, "New Bridge" pattern, med blue transfer, ... **200.00**

Pitcher, 6 1/2" h, white horse and rider on side, band of white flowerheads on border, lt green ground, "Spode Fortuna England" mk, ... **75.00**

Plate

7 1/2" d, cobalt, iron-red, salmon pink, and gilt tobacco leaf design, border band of cobalt w/gilt curls alternating w/iron-red leaves on white, "imp SPODE NEW STONE" mk, ... **70.00**

8 1/2" d

"Bird and Grasshopper" pattern, med blue transfer, ... **33.00**

Blue "Italian" pattern, "imp SPODE" mk, c1790-1802, set of 6, (A), ... **165.00**

Pearlware, center bouquet of garden flowers, cell pattern band on inner border, scattered looses flowers on border, cell pattern on rim, blue and white, c1805, ... **65.00**

9" d, "Sunflower" pattern, overall blue transfer, ... **20.00**

9 1/2" d

"Peacock and Chrysanthemum" pattern #2023, multicolored, ... **95.00**

Red, mauve, blue, and green oriental style hollow rock and floral ring shrub designs, floral spray border, "Stone China" mk, c1820, ... **95.00**

Soft paste, bold blue and mustard yellow floral and foliate design, "imp SPODE" mk, (A), ... **440.00**

9 3/4" d, "Bird and Grasshopper" pattern, med blue transfer, ... **90.00**

9 7/8" d, "Tiber" pattern, med blue transfer, ... **175.00**

10" d

Blue "Italian" pattern, "imp SPODE" mk, c1790-1802, set of 4, (A), ... **220.00**

"Caramanian Series-Sarcopagi and Sepulchres at the Head of the Harbour at Cacamo," med blue transfer, "imp SPODE 2" mk, ... **175.00**

"Indian Sporting Series-Death of the Bear," med blue transfer, c1810, ... **425.00**

"Jasmine" pattern, blue and white w/mustard accents, gadrooned rim, "imp SPODE" mk, ... **70.00**

Sailing clipper ship in center in sq, seashell border, blue transfer, c1820, ... **850.00**

"Tiber" pattern, med blue transfer, "imp SPODE" mk, ... **195.00**

"Tobacco Leaf" pattern, iron-red, cobalt, green, and salmon, c1840, ... **150.00**

10 1/2" d, "Portland Vase" pattern, red transfer, ... **40.00**

Platter

7 1/2" l x 5 1/2" w, oct w/clipped corners, Kakiemon colors, oriental style prunus tree and chrysanthemums in center, scattered florals on border, "SPODE STONE CHINA" mk, ... **135.00**

11 1/4" l x 8 1/4" w, oct, blue "Italian" pattern, unmkd, (A), ... **220.00**

12 1/2" l

9" w, Oct

HP pink and red roses on border, center armorial of 2 rampant lions, cobalt log, on gilt shield, "imp Spode's New Stone" mk, (A), ... **88.00**

Oriental style lg dk red peonies, brown crooked branch w/green foliage and red flowers, blue stylized clouds, dk red hanging arrowhead inner border, oriental flowers on border, "SPODE STONE CHINA" mk, ... **100.00**

10" w, "Tower" pattern, blue transfer, ... **185.00**

16 3/4" l x 13" w, oct, blue "Italian" pattern, "SPODE" mk, c1790-1802, (A), ... **440.00**

21" l x 16" w, oval, "Grasshopper" pattern, blue transfer, ... **350.00**

Sauceboat, 4 1/4" h x 5 5/8" w, HP center band of green leaves on gilt scrolling stems between gilt bands, band of gilt leaves around neck, gilt lined rim, base, and handle, c1820, "red SPODE" mk, ... **100.00**

Sauce Tureen, 6 1/2" h x 5" H-H, w/underplate, wide cobalt bands, narrow white bands, gilt trim, bands of white enamel dots, gilt dentil band on cov, gilt outlined knob, "Spode Felspar" mk, ... **295.00**

Scent Bottle, 5 3/8" h, green ground w/applied flowerheads, stems, and foliage, gilt accents, c1830, ... **1,750.00**

Soup Plate

9 1/2" d

"Amherst Japan" pattern, iron-red, cobalt, and green flowers in vases in center, c1820, ... **280.00**

Black printed floral sprigs w/rose, rust, yellow, and blue enamel accents, "imp Spode's Stone China" mk, ... **75.00**

"Indian Sporting Series-Chasing After A Wolf" pattern, med blue transfer, "imp SPODE" mk, c1810, ... **450.00**

9 3/4" d, "Rome" pattern, med blue transfer, ... **156.00**

10" d, pearlware, "City of Corinth-Caramanian Series," animal border, blue transfer, "imp SPODE 27" mk, ... **125.00**

Spill Vase

4 1/2" h, Imari palette of peonies, bamboo and oriental flowers in fenced garden, beaded bands on rim, base, and foot, #967 pattern, (A), ... **165.00**

6" h, flared, en grisaille, period hunter and dog or walking man w/fishing pole, gilt flowerhead and foliage on reverse, white ground, gilt horiz banding, raised band of white beading on base and rim, c1810, pr,

.... **3,200.00**

Tray, 9 3/4" l, cobalt, iron red, green, and gold, "imp Spode" mark, **$175.00**

Sugar Box, 6" l, painted polychrome enameled sm flowers and reverse relief of flowers, lt blue ground, gilt rims, gilt molded fruit branch handles, ... **630.00**

Tureen, Cov

7 1/4" H-H x 4 1/4" h, w/undertray, purple, red, yellow, and blue sprigs and band of flowers and green foliage, gold floral knob, figural head handles w/blue and red scale and green facial features, "Stone China" mk,

.... **395.00**

14 3/4" H-H x 11 1/2" h, w/undertray, 17 1/4" l x 12 1/4" w, blue "Italian" pattern, "imp SPODE" mk, c1790-1802, (A), ... **1,430.00**

Vegetable Bowl

9 1/2" l x 7 1/2" w, rect, "Fitzhugh" pattern, blue transfer, ... **65.00**

10 1/2" l, 7" w, oval, iron-red, pink, green, yellow, and gilt flower bouquet in center, cobalt border w/gilt oriental scrolls and black accents, c1817, ... **145.00**

SPONGEWARE

Staffordshire, England

Continental
c1840 to c1900

History: Spongeware, a cut-sponge stamped pattern decoration used on earthenwares and everyday tablewares, was achieved by dipping a sponge in color and applying it to the ware to produce a stamp of the pattern. A single dip of color produced about a dozen impressions. This accounted for the variation in shades.

The stamping technique was invented in Scotland and brought to England about 1845. It was a time-saving device used in decorating inexpensive china that was made mostly for export.

Cut-sponge border patterns included a variety of florals, leaves, scrolls, stars, triangles, hearts, and chains. Some borders supplemented the cut-sponge decoration with hand painting. The center motif also included combinations of cut-sponge and painted decorations.

William Adams and Son of Tunstall was one of the largest English producers of cut-sponge decorated pieces. W. Baker and Company of Fenton; Edge, Malkin and Company of Burslem; and Britannia Pottery of Glasglow were other leading manufacturers of spongeware.

Petrus Regout and Company in Holland, and Villeroy and Boch, in Germany were among the principal Continental manufacturers.

References: Kevin McConnell, *Spongeware and Spatterware, Revised Edition*, Schiffer Publishing Co. 2001; Earl F. & Ada F. Robacker, *Spatterware and Sponge*, A.S. Barnes & Co. 1978; Henry E. Kelly & Arnold A. & Dorothy E. Kowalsky, *Spongeware, 1835-1935; Makers & Patterns*, Schiffer Publications, 2001.

Collecting Hints: Cut-sponge work could be identified by the uneven strength of the color in repeated motifs. Remember, the color supply lessened in the sponge as the pattern was repeated. An uneven interval or space between decorative motifs also indicated spongeware. Border motifs may be overlapped. A smudged effect often occurred because of too much pigment or a worn stamp. If a stamp had a defect in its design, it would be repeated throughout the pattern.

Bowl

5" d, brown and blue sponging, gilt accents, lt green tinged ground, molding on sides, ... **25.00**

8 1/2" d, green sponging, white ground, "Made in England" mk,

.... **60.00**

10 1/4" d

Blue sponging, collar, ... **175.00**

Brown sponging, ... **115.00**

11" d, sparse blue sponging, white ground, dk blue rim, ... **50.00**

11 1/2" d, green and brown sponging, (A), ... **330.00**

12" d, manganese and copper colored sponged freeform stripes, ... **110.00**

12 1/4" d, blue sponging, white ground, (A), ... **100.00**

Bowl, Cov, 2" h x 3 1/4" d, blue sponging, white ground, button knob, (A), ... **248.00**

Butter Crock, Cov, 4" h x 5 5/8" d, blue sponging, white ground, wire bail handle, (A), ... **40.00**

Butter Pat, 3" d, blue sponged border,

.... **45.00**

Cream Pitcher, 5 3/4" h, paneled, blue and white, shaped handle, (A),

.... **120.00**

*Cup and Saucer, child's size, blue sponging, A-***$25.00**

Cup and Saucer, blue sponged borders, white center, Staffordshire, c1850, ... **115.00**

Cup and Saucer, Handleless

Blue and green sponging, (A),

.... **120.00**

Blue and red sponging, ... **80.00**

Blue and tan sponging, (A),

.... **302.00**

Red and green cluster of buds in center, blue and green sponged borders, (A), ... **275.00**

Red tulip, green foliage, red
sponged borders, (A), ... **385.00**

Custard Cup

2 1/4" h x 3 7/8" d, swirled "Turk's
Head" design, blue and brown
sponging, ... **95.00**

2 1/2" h, brown sponging, set of 8,
.... **120.00**

Dessert Plate, 6 7/8" d, blue sponging,
white ground, emb edge scrolling,
(A), ... **90.00**

Egg Cup, 2" h, red sponging, black
lined rim, England, c1850, chips,
.... **48.00**

Flowerpot, 3" h, blue sponging, scribed
horiz bands, ruffled rim, ... **125.00**

Fruit Bowl, 10" d, blue sponging, yellow
ware body, scalloped rim,
.... **80.00**

Jardiniere, 8 1/2" h x 10 3/4" d, blue
sponged body, brown sponged
base and collar, ... **195.00**

Milk Pitcher, 3 1/2" h, yellowware, brown
sponging, Germany, ... **60.00**

Mustard Pot, Cov, 3" h, blue sponged
cov, handle, and body, white ground,
.... **180.00**

Pitcher

6 5/8" h, blue sponging, white
ground, hairline, ... **66.00**

7 1/4" h, lt blue sponging, unmkd,
.... **30.00**

7 1/2" h, vert ribs, bridged spout,
black sponging, ... **250.00**

8 1/2" h, blue sponging, (A),
.... **385.00**

8 3/4" h, tapered shape, overall blue
sponged circles, white ground,
(A), ... **688.00**

8 7/8" h, cylinder shape, blue
sponging, ... **170.00**

11 3/4" h, paneled, grey, red and
black fort, green trees design on
sides, blue sponged borders and
handle, (A), ... **2,090.00**

Plate

8" d

Cream glaze w/brown sponging,
molded rim, (A), ... **85.00**

"The First Nibble," 3 children
fishing, blue transfer, emb
berry and vine red and blue
sponged border, (A),
.... **358.00**

8 1/2" d, red tulip, green leaves, red
and green sponged border, (A),
.... **220.00**

9 1/4" d, fluted and scrolling emb
border, overall blue sponging,
white ground, ... **145.00**

10" d, dk red tulip, green foliage in
center, green sponged border,
(A), ... **630.00**

10 1/4" d, blue sponging, white
ground, ... **225.00**

Platter

9 1/2" l, oval, blue sponging, c1890,
.... **225.00**

12 3/4" l x 8 1/2" w, oval, blue
sponging, ... **120.00**

13" l x 9" w, oval, dk blue sponging,
(A), ... **150.00**

13 3/4" l x 10 1/4" w, rect, curved
sides, blue sponging, white
ground, (A), ... **220.00**

17" l x 13" w, oct, pearlware,
alternating blue and green
sponged border segments,
.... **325.00**

Salt Cellar, 2 1/4" h x 3" d, blue sponged
body and pedestal ft, blue lined rim,
England, ... **85.00**

Serving Bowl, 10 1/4" H-H, blue
sponging, white ground, unmkd,
.... **30.00**

Serving Dish, 9 1/2" l x 8" w, rect, blue
sponging, white ground, (A),
.... **95.00**

*Shaving Mug Insert, 2 3/4" h x 4" d, blue
sponging, white ground, England, c1840,
$165.00*

Soap Dish, 6" l x 4" w, blue sponging,
white ground, ... **125.00**

Soup Plate, 9 1/4" d

Blue "cloud" sponging, white
ground, (A), ... **55.00**

Dk blue sponging, white ground,
scroll molded scalloped rim, (A),
.... **55.00**

Spittoon, 7 1/2" d, blue sponging, white
ground, ... **135.00**

Sugar Bowl, 7 1/2" h, paneled, red tulip,
green foliage, red sponged ground,
lid repair, (A), ... **358.00**

Toddy Plate, 6 1/2" d, red tulip, green
foliage in center, blue and green
sponged border, (A), ... **200.00**

Tray

9 3/4" l x 6 1/2" w, oval, dk blue
sponging, white ground, (A),
.... **120.00**

10" d, blue sponging, white ground,
2 molded wreath handles,
scalloped rim and molded ruffles
on border, (A), ... **55.00**

Vegetable Bowl, 9" l x 7" w, scalloped
rim, blue sponging, white ground,
(A), ... **150.00**

STAFFORDSHIRE-BLUE AND WHITE

England
End of 18th C-1880s

History: Blue and white transfer printed
earthenwares came to the Staffordshire
district of England by the end of the 18th
century. The transfer printing process was
first used by Thomas Turner at Caughley in
Shropshire.

At first, patterns reflected Chinese porcelain designs, and the willow pattern was
featured prominently in many examples.
As the technique improved, scenics featuring abbeys, houses, castles, rivers, and
exotic travel destinations were printed on
wares. A tremendous export market developed because Americans were eager for
scenes of American towns, sites, and historical events of interest.

Florals, birds, and animals also found
their way to earthenwares, as did literary
illustrations from prominent authors such
as Sir Walter Scott and Charles Dickens.

Another area where blue printed wares
were utilized was in children's feeding bottles, pap boats, and feeding cups for use
with invalids.

All blue printed wares were underglaze. Many makers used the same
designs since there were no copyright
laws to protect designs. Wares that were
not marked were very difficult to attribute
to a particular maker.

With the Copyright Act of 1842, copying of designs became much more difficult. Original designs were now registered
to protect from copying for three years and
then there was a renewal option. Makers
could no longer copy engraving from literary works or other books. Since new
sources were needed, designers turned to
romantic scenes, which were then quite
popular.

By the 1880s, there were relatively few
new patterns in use. White dinner services
with printed borders became popular.
Brightly colored dinnerwares also came
into vogue.

References: Arthur Coysh, *Blue-and-
White Transfer Ware 1780-1840*, David
and Charles, 1970; A.W. Coysh and R.K.

Henrywood, *The Dictionary of Blue and White Printed Pottery 1780-1880, Vol II*, Antique Collectors' Club, 1989.

Collectors' Club: Friends of Blue, Mr. R. Govier, 10 Seaview Road, Herne Bay, Kent CT6 6JQ England. Membership: £12, Quarterly bulletins.

Museum: Wellcome Museum, London, England.

Bowl, 10" d, seashells in center, beaded rim, dk blue transfer, Stubbs, ... **895.00**

Butter Dish, Cov, 6 1/4" l x 4 1/4" w x 3" h, "Arden" pattern, vining flowers design, med blue transfer, Burleigh, ... **28.00**

Butter Pat, 2 7/8" d, "Blaize Castle" in center, leaf and flowerhead border, med blue transfer, ... **50.00**

Coffeepot
11" h, high dome shape, English country scene of shepherd boy and flock, country estate in bkd, dk blue transfers, ... **1,795.00**
11 3/4" h, circle of florals and leaves enclosing landscape scene of fox at tree base w/2 hens sitting on branch, cottage and picket fence in bkd on sides, floral and leaf encircling rims, leaf design on handle, med blue transfers, unmkd, (A), ... **605.00**

Creamer, 4 1/4" h, landscape scene of house and beehive, bkd of house and trees, border of floral and berries, med blue transfer, (A), ... **110.00**

Cup and Saucer
"Old English Scenery" pattern, med blue transfers, Heathcote, ... **20.00**
"Rosa" pattern, branches of blossoms, fruit, leaves, and ferns, scrolling border, med blue transfers, "W.& E. Corn" mk, ... **25.00**

Cup and Saucer, Handleless
Overall floral and leaf design, med blue transfers, ... **250.00**
Two cherubic children playing in garden, dk blue transfers (A), ... **125.00**
Urn of flowers w/sparrows, med blue transfers, unmkd, (A), ... **125.00**

Cup Plate, 4 1/4" d, grapes and vines in center, leaf and floral border, dk blue transfer, Stubbs, hairline, ... **120.00**

Dish, 9 1/2" sq, men seining in river, exotic buildings, dk blue transfer, ... **495.00**

Footbath, 19" w, blue printed, int w/lg flowers from urn, ext w/lg bouquets on speckled ground, c1825, (A), ... **2,475.00**

Game Dish, 10 1/2" l, well and tree, "Native Scenery," selling of fish at side of creek, flowerhead border, dk blue transfer, "F. & R. Pratt" mk, ... **100.00**

Gravy Boat, 8" l, "Ancient Rome" pattern, med blue transfer, ... **275.00**

Jug, 4 1/2" h, Dutch shape, "Arden" pattern, vining flowers, med blue transfer, Burleigh, ... **25.00**

Ladle
7 1/8" l, "Fisherman's Hut" pattern, dk blue transfer, unmkd, (A), ... **275.00**
11" l, flowers in urn w/bird, mountain and building in bkd, flowered handle, med blue transfer, ... **325.00**
12 1/4" l, "Sundial" pattern, med blue transfer, unmkd, (A), ... **247.00**

Meat Platter
17 3/4" l x 14" w, "Botanical Beauties" pattern, med blue transfer, Elkin and Newborn, ... **400.00**
18" l, rect, "Durham Ox" pattern, farm cart, 4 cows, and quarry, flowerhead and leaf border, med blue transfer, 19th C, (A), ... **1,125.00**
20 1/2" l, well and tree, "Italian Ruins" pattern, med blue transfer, chip, ... **1,100.00**

Pepper Pot, 5" h, transfer of camels and palm trees, med blue transfer, ... **475.00**

Pitcher
5" h, paneled, mask spout, "Grecian Scroll" pattern, med blue transfer, "T.J. & J. Mayer Longport" mk, ... **100.00**
5 1/2" h, girl picking flowers, boy taking eggs from bird's nest, floral border, dk blue transfer, (A), ... **495.00**
12" h, fruit and leaves pattern, crisscross pattern w/fruit on collar, lt blue transfer, "J.M. & S." mk, ... **275.00**

Plate
6 1/2" d, "Rogers Views," 2 figures on river bank, 2 rowing boats on river, med blue transfer, John Rogers, ... **72.00**
7 1/4" d, pearlware, groups of flowerheads, string rim, med blue transfer, c1830, ... **165.00**

7 1/2" d
Fruit pattern, dk blue transfer, Stubbs, ... **250.00**
Sheltered peasants design, med blue transfer, "R. Hall" mk, ... **380.00**
"The Cowman" pattern, cow in foreground, cowman in bkd, thatched cottage at side, flowerhead border, med blue transfers, c1820, ... **195.00**
7 3/4" d, "Girl Musician" pattern, country house, river, and waterfall, herdsman and girl w/pipe, med blue transfer, Riley, c1820, ... **325.00**
8 1/4" d, "River Fishing" pattern, flower border, med blue transfer, John Meir, ... **155.00**

Plate, 8 3/4" d, med blue transfer, unmkd, **$125.00**

8 7/8" d, fruit in center, floral border, dk blue transfer, "Hill & Henderson New Orleans, Importers" mk, (A), ... **190.00**
9" d
"Classical Antiquities-Ulysses Weeps at the Song of Demodocus," med blue transfer, Clementson, ... **210.00**
"Fisherman's Hut" pattern, med blue transfer, unmkd, c1850, (A), ... **110.00**
"Old Chelsea" pattern, 2 exotic birds in chinoiserie garden, border of floral filled ovals on crisscross ground, med blue transfer, Furnivals, ... **15.00**
Swans on lake in front of country house, floral border, dk blue transfer, unmkd, ... **75.00**
9 1/2" d, pearlware, Indian castle, elephant, mountains and trees in

center, flowerhead border, med blue transfer, unmkd, ... **110.00**

9 7/8" d

"Domestic Cattle," pattern, floral border, med blue transfer, ... **60.00**

Fishermen drying nets in front of classical ruins, floral border, scalloped rim, med blue transfer, (A), ... **55.00**

*Plate 10 1/2" d, "Dr. Syntax Drawing After Nature," med blue transfer, unmkd, **$495.00***

10" d

Boy fishing by trees, scrolling flower border, med blue transfer, ... **25.00**

British manor house, lake, and castle ruins in center, leaf border w/sm flowerheads, med blue transfer, ... **175.00**

Castle and waterfall in center, groups of people on border, med blue transfer, unmkd, ... **50.00**

"Durham Ox" pattern, med blue transfer, c1820, ... **870.00**

Fruit center, flower border, dk blue transfer, "imp Stubbs & Kent, Longport" mk, (A), ... **100.00**

Hunting scene of dog in marsh chasing flying ducks, flower and scroll border, beaded rim, med blue transfer, unmkd, hairline, ... **55.00**

Lg group of fruit in center, floral border, dk blue transfer, unmkd, c1810, ... **450.00**

"Monopteris" pattern, central scene of columned building and travelers, dk blue transfer, John Rogers & Son, ... **175.00**

Oriental scene of bridge, boat, canal, and pagoda in center, oriental flowers and ovals on border, dk blue transfer, ... **30.00**

Seated shepherd w/flute and sheep in center, floral border, med blue transfer, ... **325.00**

10 1/8" d, rabbit hunt w/riders on horseback and dogs, med blue transfer, (A), ... **95.00**

10 1/4" d

"Asiatic Palaces" pattern, med blue transfer, "blue RIDGWAYS ASIATIC PALACES" mk, (A), ... **110.00**

Travelers before classic buildings, dk blue transfer, scalloped rim, "imp Rogers" mk, (A), ... **138.00**

"Wild Rose" pattern, canal scene and English village in center, wild rose border, med blue transfer, c1835-50, ... **40.00**

10 1/2" d

Walking oriental man w/sack over shoulder, village w/temple in bkd, dk blue transfer, (A), ... **90.00**

"Wild Rose" pattern, med blue transfer, George Jones, ... **250.00**

Platter

8 1/2" l x 6 1/4" w, rect, "Boy Piping" pattern, med blue transfer, unmkd, (A), ... **275.00**

11 3/4" l, oval, "Abbey" pattern, med blue transfer, George Jones, c1910, ... **195.00**

13 3/4" l x 11" w, "British Scenery" pattern, med blue transfer, Booth, ... **100.00**

14" l x 10" w, ironstone, "Spring Time" pattern, med blue transfer, "J.F. Wileman & Co." mk, ... **35.00**

16 1/2" l 13" w, "Panoramic Series," lg castle in bkd, group of figures in foreground, band of ovals on border, molded white rim, Ralph Stevenson, ... **895.00**

17" l x 13" w, "Spotted Deer" pattern, diaper border, med blue transfer, unmkd, ... **795.00**

19" l

15" w, "The Villager" pattern, med blue transfer, floral border, rope rim, Turner, c1820, ... **500.00**

"Banana Tree" pattern, lt blue transfer, ... **895.00**

19 1/8" l x 14 3/4" l, Asian river scene w/temple, boat, and fisherman, floral border, dk blue transfer, ... **1,550.00**

20" l x 16" w, ftd, "Royal Cottage" pattern, med blue transfer, "Wm. Barker & Son" mk, ... **850.00**

21" l, "Monopteris" pattern, med blue transfer, Rogers, c1820, ... **1,450.00**

21 1/2" l x 16" w, "Beemaster" pattern, "A Swarm of Bees," med blue transfer, c1820, ... **4,000.00**

21 3/4" l x 16 3/4" w, "Piping Shepherds" pattern, flowerhead and leaf border, med blue transfer, unmkd, ... **1,650.00**

Posset Pot, Cov, 4" h x 5" H-H, chinoiserie floral basket design, scattered vines and buds, ... **375.00**

Potato Bowl, 11 1/2" d, "Italian Buildings" pattern, med blue transfer, beaded rim, "blue ITALIAN BUILDINGS R. HALL" and "imp HALL" mks, c1822-41, (A), .. **247.00**

Sauceboat, 7 1/2" l, "Fisherman's Hut" pattern, woman and child in foreground, fisherman and hut, dk blue transfer, ... **325.00**

Sauce Tureen, 6" h x 8" l, w/undertray, "Rural Scenery" design, med blue transfers, Bathwell & Goodfellow, ... **1,250.00**

Serving Dish, 16 1/2" l, rect, "Elephant" pattern, elephant in oriental garden, flowerhead border, med blue transfer, "imp Rogers" mk, early 19th C, ... **285.00**

Soup Bowl, 9 3/4" d, "Italian Buildings" pattern, med blue transfer, "blue ITALIAN BUILDINGS R. HALL" mk, c1822-41, (A), ... **192.00**

Soup Plate

9 1/2" d, pearlware, "Elephant" pattern, flowerhead border, med blue transfer, "imp Rogers" mk, c1820, ... **100.00**

9 3/4" d

"Cowman" pattern, flowerhead border, dk blue transfer, unmkd, c1825, ... **135.00**

Fruit center, floral border, med blue transfer, (A), ... **195.00**

"Richmond" pattern, dk blue transfer, Adderley, set of 4, ... **65.00**

Soup Tureen, 13" w, "Gothic Ruins" pattern, 2 men on horseback, fisherman, waterfalls, wagon on bridge, med blue transfers, ... **1,250.00**

Sugar Box, Cov

5 1/2" h x 6 1/2" H-H, landscape scene of house and beehive, bkd of house and trees, floral and berry border on cov, med blue transfer, (A), ... **165.00**

5 3/4" h

7" H-H, landscape scene of lg house w/smoke, 3 figures to front, trees and bushes to perimeter on sides, sm flowerheads encircling top rim and cov rim, dk blue transfers, unmkd, rim chips, (A), ... **330.00**

7 1/2" H-H, lg botanical fruit and net ground on body, scrolled gallery on rim, med blue transfer, chip, ... **550.00**

Tankard

4" h, "Gleaners II" pattern, med blue transfer, ... **495.00**

5 3/4" h, "Dragon" pattern, med blue transfer, Booth, ... **120.00**

Tazza, 12 1/2" l x 4" h, "Neptune" pattern, horse drawn chariot and mermaid on dolphin, border of medallions of naval heroes, med blue transfer, ... **875.00**

Tea Service, Part, pot, 6 3/4" h, 11" l, small pot, cov sugar bowl, waste bowl, 10 handleless cups, 11 saucers, "Vase and Flowers" pattern, A-$1,955.00

Teapot

6 1/2" h x 10" w, Venetian boat scene, shell border, dk blue transfer, repaired spout, c1800, ... **850.00**

7" h x 12" l, blue and white overall flowerheads and stems, wishbone handle, dk blue transfer, ... **1,150.00**

8 1/8" h, paneled, blue transfers of classic country scenes w/English countryside and manor house, floral knob, bird spout, unmkd, ... **160.00**

8 1/2" h x 12" w, "Basket of Flowers" pattern, dk blue transfers, ... **675.00**

Tea Strainer, 4" d, oriental village scene in center, floral border, med blue transfer, perforated center, ... **225.00**

Vegetable Bowl, 10 3/4" H-H x 9 1/4" w, "Millford Green" pattern, herder w/goats and village, fruit and flower border, shell molded handles, dk blue transfer, hairline, (A), ... **185.00**

Vegetable Bowl, Cov

6 1/2" h x 11" H-H, hex shape, scroll handles, "Asiatic Palaces" pattern, med blue transfers, "blue RIDGWAYS ASIATIC PALACES" mk, hairline, (A), ... **220.00**

8 3/4" sq x 6" h, "The Boy Piping" pattern, med blue transfers, lion knob, ... **450.00**

9 1/2" d, "Siam" pattern, med blue transfer, "Brown-Westhead, Moore & Co." mk, ... **295.00**

Waste Bowl

5 1/4" d, English country scene of top-hatted fly fisherman, castle in bkd, dk blue transfer, ... **175.00**

6 1/4" d, low ft, pheasants in tree, mountains in bkd, sm birds, med blue transfer, (A), ... **45.00**

1818-35

STAFFORDSHIRE FIGURES

Staffordshire, England
c1740-1900

History: During the 18th century, Staffordshire figures in salt glazed stoneware and Whieldon-type earthenwares with translucent colored glazes were made by the family of Ralph Wood. (See Ralph Wood.)

Obadiah Sherratt's figures from the late 1820s displayed the rustic realism of true peasant art with humor, pathos, and brutality. The modeling was bold and crude; enamel colors were bright. Many figures were quite large. Usually Sherratt's figures were mounted on a table base. The name for the piece often was written on the front. Among his most famous pieces were "The Bull Baiting Group" and "Remus and Romulus." Sherratt also did classical and religious figures.

With the accession of Queen Victoria in 1837, simplicity of design appeared, as well as restraint in the coloring of figures. Nineteenth century earthenware Staffordshire figures were made in a simple, uncomplicated manner, often mass produced at low cost for the cottage rather than for the stately home. They were sold in stalls at county fairs, outside theaters, and by craftsmen who carried trays of figures door-to-door.

The figures featured a flat back, were compact in design, and were mounted on an oval base that was part of the figure. Figures were displayed on mantles, window ledges, bookcases, or Welsh dressers. Only the fronts were visible, so decorations were restricted to the front of the figure. In about 1840, potters made great quantities of mantelpiece ornaments in under-the-glaze colors. Cottage ornaments depicted the homey scenes characteristic of the people that bought them.

The most distinctive color used was the rich, dark, glossy cobalt blue. Additional colors included pink, green, orange, black, and some gold. After 1860 more colors were utilized, including a pale flesh-pink shade. The pottery was harder and whiter than in earlier pieces.

Both human and animal figures were molded. Just about every Victorian kitchen featured a pair of spaniels on either side of the kitchen clock. Greyhounds, poodles, Dalmatians, cats, and even zebras were memorialized in Staffordshire figures. Topical events, heroes and heroines of the times, members of the royal family, and theatrical characters appeared. Churches, cottages, and castles were popular. A unique form was the Victorian watch stand. Few figures were marked with a maker's mark.

Sampson Smith was the most prolific maker of the flat backed figures and Staffordshire dogs. He worked from about 1847 to 1878. Others continued to use his molds to make figures long after his death. In addition to his famous dogs, Sampson Smith is known for figures of castles, churches, cottages, jockeys, Dick Turpin, Toby jugs, politicians, and royalty, including Queen Victoria.

References: T. Balston, *Staffordshire Portrait Figures of the Victorian Age*, Faber & Faber, 1958; Reginald S. Haggar, *Staffordshire Chimney Ornaments*, Phoenix House Ltd. 1955; Pat Halfpenny, *English Earthenware Figures: 1740-1840*, Antique Collectors' Club, Ltd. 1992; J. Hall, *Staffordshire Portrait Figures*, Charles Letts & Co. Ltd. 1972; Adele Kenny, *Staffordshire Spaniels*, Schiffer Publishing, Ltd. 1997; B. Latham, *Victorian Staffordshire Portrait Figures for the Small Collector*, Tiranti, 1953; A. Oliver, *The Victorian Staffordshire Figures: A Guide for Collectors*, Heinemann, 1971; Clive Mason Pope, *A-Z of Staffordshire Dogs*, Antique Collectors' Club, Ltd. 1996; P.D.G. Pugh,

Staffordshire Portrait Figures & Allied Subjects of the Victorian Era, Rev. Ed. Antique Collectors' Club, Ltd. 1987; H.A.B. Turner, *A Collector's Guide to Staffordshire Pottery Figures*, Emerson Books, Inc. 1971. A. & N. Harding, *Victorian Staffordshire Figures, 1875-1962*, Schiffer Publications, 2003; A. & N. Harding, *Miller's Staffordshire Figures of the 19th and 20th Centuries: A Collectors Guide*, 2000; A. & N. Harding, *Staffordshire Figures 1835-75 (Victorian), Portraits, Naval & Military, Theatrical/Literary, Book #1*, Schiffer Publications, 1998, A. & N. Harding, *Staffordshire Figures 1835-75, (Victorian), Religious, Hunters, Pastoral, Occupations, Book #2*, Schiffer Publications, 1998, A. & N. Harding, *Staffordshire Figures, 1835-75 (Victorian), Portraits, Military, Theatrical, Religious, Book #3*, Schiffer Publications, 2000; Adele Kenny, *Staffordshire Animals, History, Styles, & Values*, Schiffer Publications, 1998; Dennis Rice, *Cats in English Porcelain in the 19th Century*, Antique Collectors Club, 2000.

Museums: American Antiquarian Society, Worcester, MA; Brighton Museum, Brighton, England; British Museum, London, England; City Museum and Art Gallery, Stoke-on-Trent, England; The Detroit Institute of Arts, Detroit, MI; Fitzwilliam Museum, Cambridge, England, Victoria & Albert Museum, London, England.

Reproduction Alert: Lancaster and Sandlands are reproducing some of the old Staffordshire models, especially the animal and cottage figures. The colors match the old Staffordshire cobalt blue quite well.

Sampson Smith's figures were reproduced from his original molds from 1948 to 1962, but the colors are less vibrant than the originals.

While old figures were made in press molds, new figures are made in slip molds using a technique called slip casting. A large hole is a sign of slip casting. Many of the new figures are new slip casts with large holes to pour slip into the mold. Old figures had some fine strokes of a paint brush, while modern ones are often colored by swabs or sponges. Old figures had some paint on the back, while new ones have no paint on back. Old figures had more details in overall molding. The gold trim on the old figures was worn with a dull luster. New figures show no wear on the gold and it remains shiny. Reproductions are usually exactly matched pairs, while old figures were seldom exactly the same. The underside of old figures had an even glaze while new glaze is intentionally "aged" or "stressed."

Many reproductions are being made in China. Over eighty different figures and animals are now being made that are direct copies of old pieces found in standard reference books. Even the faults in the figures are being copied. These reproductions are heavier weight and are closer to the originals. They also have smaller firing holes.

Chinese reproductions have dark black crazing to make them look old. They are sprayed with dark colored transparent glaze. They have a rough surface overall, and have streaking in undecorated areas.

Arbor Group, 14 1/2" h, seated Scotsman w/orange striped trousers, red and green plaid sash, seated female in green gown, red headpiece, basket of fruit between and base, red and green fruit on white overhead arbor, ... **250.00**

Bank, 4 5/8" h, salmon pink and white sides, black and white windows, green grass base, gold trim, chip, A-$125.00

Bank
4 1/4" h, head of spaniel, white w/copper luster spots, collar, and lock, slot in head, ... **425.00**
5 3/4" h, cottage, orange, green, and yellow coleslaw trim, (A), ... **110.00**
Bear Baiting, 14" h, rearing black bear, yellow collar and muzzle, leaping black dog, fallen man w/green striped vest, black jacket, yellow trousers, green stepped oblong base, c1830, (A), ... **22,705.00**
Billy Waters and Black Sal, 4 1/2" h, yellow trousers or apron, pink kerchief, gold accents, circ bases w/gold stripe, pr, ... **2,595.00**
Boxers, 9 1/4" h, "HEENAN-SAVERS" on base, yellow pants w/blue belt or pink pants w/orange belt, (A), ... **440.00**

Boxers, 9 1/4" h, "HEENAN" and "SAVERS," yellow and blue or pink and orange, black hair, green-brown base, A-$440.00

Boy on Goat, 12" h, brown coated goat, boy w/red and white cap, ... **365.00**
Boy Holding Bucket, 9" h, standing boy holding 2 buckets, black curly hair, lt blue long coat, orange collar, green bow, brown boots, circ base, ... **270.00**
Camel, 3" h, recumbent, lt olive green shaded body, oval base w/red stripe, (A), ... **385.00**

Cat, 12 1/4" h, grey to black body, green eyes, gold ribbon, pr, $1,500.00

Cat, 3 1/2" h, seated, tan on black patches on white body, green eyes, green base, ... **125.00**
Circus Figures, 8 1/2" h, Louisa Woolford in cobalt jacket, red and green plaid skirt, Andrew Cobbler and Wife, 6 1/2" h, 6" h, seated, man in red vest, black apron and hat, seated woman in red coat, pink apron, pouring liquid from pitcher, animal head under each chair, (A), ... **220.00**
Cow, 2 3/4" h x 3" l, reclining brown sponged white cow, green oval base, c1860, chips, ... **150.00**

Lion, 3 1/4" h x 2 3/4" l, orange-brown mane, lt brown body, oval base, ... **250.00**

Louis Napoleon, 12" h, black hair, cobalt jacket w/gold medals, white sash, red belt, holding feathered black hat, sword at side, leaning on grey stone wall, "LOUIS NAPOLEON" on base, ... **620.00**

Man and Dog, 8 1/4" h, standing man wearing black hat, brown coat, red vest, yellow trousers, black and white dog on green grass base, sq plinth base, c1810, ... **1,250.00**

Mr. Barton as Giaffier, 8" h, blue coat, white and orange turban, chips, ... **200.00**

Money Box, 4 3/4" h, figural cottage, 2 chimneys, white cottage, roof outlined w/green encrusting, red door, green foliage base, slot between chimneys, ... **495.00**

Monkey, 5 1/2" h, manganese monkey clinging to cream tree trunk w/dk brown spots, green shading, rect base w/dk brown stripes, ... **265.00**

Napier, 16" h, standing figure in white military uniform w/gold trim, turquoise base w/raised name, ... **1,125.00**

Old Shakespeare, 7" h, leaning on lectern, holding script, tan coat, cobalt vest, lt blue trousers, ... **495.00**

Orange Sellers, 13 1/2" h, man wearing cocked hat, lt blue scarf, red accented vest, lt blue stockings, yellow box of oranges under arm, woman w/dk red lined shawl, flowered dress, holding box of oranges, flat bk, ... **425.00**

Parrot, 6 1/4" h, press molded, yellow body, green wings w/feather outlines, olive green eyes and beak, head turned, perched on green flared leaf molded base, c1780-90, (A), ... **2,470.00**

Pastille Burner

3" h, hex shape, turreted cottage w/6 lt blue pillars, gold outlined windows, 3 lt blue hex roofs w/gold balls, applied red and green flowerheads and crusted foliage on roof and base, ... **230.00**

3 3/4" h, paneled "toll house," white roof w/applied flowers crusts, orange house w/red door, circ base w/applied flower crusts, c1875, ... **235.00**

5 3/4" h x 4 1/4" w, white cottage, gold outlined windows, door, and chimney, blue encrusted roof and cottage edges, green and brown base, (A), ... **137.00**

7" h, 2 story cottage, brown thatched roof, red outlined chimneys and door, encrusted trim around chimneys, roofs, and green lawn on base, ... **525.00**

7 3/4" h, figural lighthouse, lt orange w/applied foliage, red beacon, gold lined rock base, c1830, ... **1,900.00**

Peter Raising the Lame Man, 10 1/2" h, Peter wearing dk red robe, steel blue sash w/blue-green lining, seated man wearing black jacket, yellow trousers, sq green base w/black molded feet, "Peter Raising The Lame Man Acts CH3" on plaque, c1820, ... **3,300.00**

Plato, 14 1/2" h, bust, dk brown hair and beard, burgundy cloak, marbled socle foot and sq base, late 19th C, (A), ... **420.00**

Polito's Menagerie, 14" w, pearlware, multicolored performers w/instruments, monkey on organ before entrance, lg overhead marquee w/black elephant, lion, tiger, etc, brown rect base w/florals and ribbon-tied swags on 4 bracket feet, Staffordshire, c1820, (A), ... **26,290.00**

Poodle, 4 5/8" h, seated, white w/sanded coats, black muzzles, yellow eyes, gilt collars and locks, opposing pr, (A), ... **413.00**

Praying Mother and Child, 8" h, woman wearing green blouse, orchid sash, flowered print skirt, child in flowered gown kneeling on orange-red cushion, gilt accents, oct base, c1850, ... **650.00**

Prince Albert, 5 3/4" h, cobalt jacket, pink sash, white trousers, seated on orange seat, ... **375.00**

Prussian General, 11" h, flat back, seated on orange-brown horse, green and brown oval base, ... **250.00**

Punch, 11 1/2" h, seated, yellow-gold trimmed sloping hat, red suit w/yellow-gold accents, holding white feather, black spotted white dog on green base w/yellow and black stripes, ... **3,200.00**

Queen Victoria, 10 1/2" h, cobalt cape, green and orange sash, flowered lower gown, c1880, ... **575.00**

Sailor, 10 1/2" h, lt brown hat, black hair, blue shirt, black tie, green grass base, repaired chip, ... **145.00**

Saluki, 3 5/8" h, seated on haunches, white/black splotches, rocky base w/gold lined rim, hairline, ... **750.00**

School House Cottage, cobalt peaked roofs, 3 red doors, green foliage on base, ... **525.00**

Scottish Couple, 7 1/4" h, white w/man in blue stockings, red and green plaid cape, woman in matching skirt, feathered caps, (A), ... **135.00**

Sheep, 5 1/4" h x 4" w, standing ram, white textured body, green bocage w/red and blue flowerheads, brown and green oval base, pr, ... **950.00**

Spaniels, 10" h, white w/black nose, yellow eyes, luster collar and chain, pr, ... **395.00**

Spill Vase, 10 3/4" h, orange w/green and gold accents, (A), $210.00

Spill Vase

5 5/8" h, pearlware, standing tan streaked camel before brown tree trunk spill, green mound base, (A), ... **4,183.00**

6 1/4" h, orange-brown spotted white sheep, multicolored florals on green grass base, dk brown tree trunk spill, ... **850.00**

7 1/2" h, prancing black and white zebra, olive snake wrapped around zebra and tree trunk spill, red lined spill, ... **300.00**

8 1/2" h x 9 1/2" w, standing brown and white standing cow, red-lined green tree trunk spill holder, seated milkmaid wearing green and yellow accented clothing, bocage base, ... **450.00**

10" h x 8" w, figural brown and white cow w/nursing calf, green grass base, green leaf molded spill, c1840, pr, ... **525.00**

Spill Vase, 10 1/4" h, brown, black, blue, and yellow, pr, $1,750.00

11 1/2" h, leaping brown and white stag, green base and tree trunk spill holder, hound on base, c1890, pr, ... **625.00**

12" h, "Fortune Teller," woman in orange cape, blue scarf, lilac gown, reading palm of girl in flowered dress, green and brown spill, Thomas Parr, ... **250.00**

12 1/2" h, "The Rival," couple courting under lg tree spill, man w/dagger watching from behind tree trunk, polychrome and gilt accents, flat bk, ... **625.00**

15" h, "Robin Hood," 2 men and seated dog, white w/red and blue feathers, gold accents, spill vase in bkd, (A), ... **385.00**

16" h, standing huntsman in green jacket, orange belt, black spotted dog at side, orange-lined white tree trunk spill, ... **250.00**

Suckling Calf, 5" h x 6" l, brown spotted calf suckling from black spotted cow, green and brown oval base, ... **225.00**

Temperance, 8 1/2" h, dbl sided figure, man in green jacket, black topper, red bow tie scarf, "Water" on base, reverse w/drunken figure, red scarf undone, lt orange pants, holding bottle, "Gin" on base, ... **250.00**

Tom King, 10 1/2" h, cobalt coat, red tie, flowered vest, black boots, astride tan horse w/black mane and tail, green and brown oval rock base,

"raised TOM KING" on base, c1860, ... **225.00**

Turks, 3 3/4" h, male and female figures in yellow robes, mang spots flanking green bocage, green hollow stand, c1785-1800, pr, ... **7,500.00**

Uncle Tom and Eve, 10 1/2" h, Tom seated on bale of cotton, red and white striped trousers, holding book, offering red flower to standing brown haired Eve, red and yellow hat on base, ... **995.00**

Watch Holder, 8" h, orange castle, central watch well, bocage, gilt accents, gilt lined oval base, flat bk, c1850, ... **150.00**

Whistle, 4" h, black shoeshine, white uniform, red scarf, holding brown shoe, green base, chip, ... **175.00**

Whippets, 7 1/4" h, 7 1/4" l, orange-brown body, black collar and muzzles, black and orange game on base, pr, A-$400.00

Woman and Rabbit, 9 1/2" h, standing woman, mauve trimmed cap, cobalt jacket, green shawl, red and green plaid skirt, holding dead grey rabbit in arm, black spotted dog on black textured white oval base, chip, c1860, ... **335.00**

STAFFORDSHIRE-GENERAL

1700s to Present

History: In the Staffordshire district of England, numerous pottery factories were established that produced a wide variety of wares including figures, flow blue, transfer printed wares, historic blue, and ornamental pieces.

Samuel Alcock and Company established a pottery in Burslem about 1828 that was known for its parian figures, jugs, and decorative wares in the classical style. The pottery also made a wide range of blue-printed earthenwares and bone china. Sir James Duke and nephews took over the firm in 1860.

John and Edward Baddeley produced earthenwares at Shelton between 1786 and 1806. The company manufactured a wide range of tablewares, often enameled in red and black on a cream-ware ground.

Charles Bourne of Foley Pottery made bone china tablewares between 1807 and 1830. His factory equaled those of Spode, Coalport, and Davenport. Pieces could be identified by the pattern numbers and the initials "CB."

The Lane End factory of **Hilditch and Son** made teawares in under-the-glaze blue from 1822 until 1830.

Elijah Mayer established a pottery at Cobden Works, Hanley, about 1705. In 1805 the name changed to Elijah Mayer and Son. Production continued until 1834. The Mayers manufactured black basalt wares, tablewares in cream-colored earthenware, cane wares, and drab stone-wares.

Humphrey Palmer was located at Church Works, Hanley, in 1760. He produced wares popularized by Wedgwood such as black basalts, cream-colored and agate ware vases, and seals and cameos that frequently were modeled by J. Voyez. Most of Palmer's wares were decorative. The pottery went out of business in 1778.

A.J. Wilkinson Ltd. was a Staffordshire pottery firm that operated several factories in the Burslem area beginning in the late 19th century. In 1885 Wilkinson took over the Central Pottery. The plant made white granite ware for the American market. Wilkinson introduced the use of gold luster work on granite ware.

Wilkinson operated the Churchyard Works from 1887 until the early 20th century and the Royal Staffordshire Pottery from c1896 until the present. In 1900 Wilkinson gained control of Mersey Pottery, a subsidiary of Newport Pottery. The factory remained in production until the 1930s. Highly glazed stonewares were made, some of which were designed by Clarice Cliff.

References: P.D. Gordon Pugh, *Staffordshire Portrait Figures & Allied Subjects of the Victorian Era, Rev. Ed.* Antique Collectors' Club, Ltd. 1987; Bernard Rackham, *Early Staffordshire Pottery*, Faber & Faber, 1951; Louis T. Stanley, *Collecting Staffordshire Pottery*, Doubleday, 1963; John Thomas, *The Rise of the Staffordshire Potteries*, Adams & Dart, 1971; Dick Henrywood, *Staffordshire*

Potters 1781-1900: Comprehensive List, Antiques Collector Club.

Museums: City Museum & Art Gallery, Stoke-on-Trent, England; Everson Museum of Art, Syracuse, NY; The Henry Francis DuPont Winterthur Museum, Winterthur, DE; William Rockhill Nelson Gallery of Art, Kansas City, MO.

Biscuit Jar, 6 1/2" h, porcelain, multicolored golfer on side, golf bag on reverse, matte finish, SP rim, cov, and handle, Macintyre, ... **1,100.00**

Bowl, 8 1/2" l x 8 5/8" w, "Yosemite" pattern, brown transfer w/pink, teal, gold accents, "T. & R. Boote" mk, ... **35.00**

Bread Tray, 12" H-H, multicolored center transfer of birds, flowers, and insect, gold trimmed tab handles, "emb GIVE US THIS DAY OUR DAILY BREAD" on sides, ... **135.00**

Cheese Dish, Cov, 7" l x 4 3/8" h, 3 floral sections of pink rose, blue and red florals, green leaves, gilt edge and trim, "Arthur Wood Made in England" mk, $32.00

Cheese Dish, Cov, 6 1/2" d, brown transfer w/colors of English manor home, fruit and florals, relief band of fruit on border, spiral knob, Edge Malkin, ... **125.00**

Chocolate Pot, 8" h, enameled red and white chrysanthemums, green foliage, sprigs, matte dk brown-black ground, pewter lid, c1870, ... **125.00**

Coffeepot
6 5/8" h, baluster form, redware, applied florets, fencing, and vine leaves, acanthus leaf handle terminals, crack, ... **375.00**
10" h, "Homeland" pattern, rural scene w/manor house, border of flowers and geometrics, red transfers, "W.H. Grindley & Co. Ltd. Staffordshire, England" mk, ... **35.00**

Cream and Sugar Set, creamer, 3" h, sugar bowl, 2" h, tray, 6 1/2" l x 4 1/2" w, "Minuet" pattern, garden flowers in gold cartouches, floral borders,

gold accents, Paragon China, ... **75.00**

Creamer
3 1/8" h, baluster form, lion mask feet from shell knees, sprigged cream trailing vines, grapes, and leaves, c1730, (A), ... **1,100.00**
4 1/2" h, black transfer of classic woman draping flowers over funeral urn on each side, purple luster lines, rim, and handle, ... **65.00**
5" h, band of pink stylized flowers, green leaves, blue accents and rim, (A), ... **83.00**

Cup and Saucer, Handleless
Band of blue flowers, green and red leaves, (A), ... **50.00**
"Wreath and Flower" pattern, charcoal grey transfers, c1860, ... **125.00**

Dessert Plate, 11" l x 9" w, "Shrewsbury" shape, multicolored center scene of landscape of viaduct, sm island, and bent trees, pink border, gilt rococo rim, Daniel. **115.00**

Dish, 8 1/2" l, figural green leaf w/sm bunches of fruit, stem handle, c1770, ... **1,485.00**

Gravy Boat, 7 1/2" l x 3 1/4" h, "Old England Gardens" pattern, yellow cottage w/black walk, yellow, orange, pink, and blue florals, blue and green bushes, mustard yellow rim, matte gold handle, "Old England Gardens Swinnertons Staffordshire England" mk, $45.00

Gravy Boat, 7" l, "Calico" pattern, blue sheet transfer, "Crownford China Co. Staffordshire England CALICO" mk, ... **35.00**

Gravy Boat, 8 1/2" l, "Seville" pattern, steel blue transfers, "John Maddock & Sons England Royal Vitreous Seville" mk, $30.00

Grill Plate, 10 3/4" d, pastoral scene in center, grape and vine border, red transfer, Booth, ... **40.00**

Hen On Nest, 8" h x 9" l, w/chicks under wings, tan, grey, and black feathers seated on green grass, tan basket base w/blue accents, ... **150.00**

Honey Pot, 5" h, yellowware body, dk brown glaze on upper half, ear handle, everted rim, ... **150.00**

Hot Milk Jug, Cov, 6 3/4" h, drabware, baluster form, crabstock handle, 3 claw feet and shell knees, sparrow beak spout, sprigged vines w/painted cobalt leaves, c1740, (A), ... **1,900.00**

Inkwell
3 1/8" l x 2 1/2" h, figural reclining white sheep w/applied clay chips, royal blue base w/gold line, ... **50.00**
6" l x 4 1/2" h, inkstand, reclining mottled orange-brown whippet, gold collar, cobalt cushion base w/hole for pen, ... **100.00**

Jug, 6" h, "Ancient Imperial Order of Druids," black transfer, repairs, $150.00

Jug
4 1/2" h, relief molded "Idle Apprentices" design, cobalt coats, orange-brown trousers, green cap, green accented relief molded scrolling, molded mask spout, fancy handle, c1850, ... **115.00**
5 1/4" h, "Quail" pattern, brown transfer, Furnivals, ... **30.00**
6 1/4" h, paneled, "Hydra," blue, brown, green, pink, and iron-red cabbage rose on side, reverse w/tulip, brown rim, snake handle, ... **110.00**
6 1/2" h, alternating diag bands of yellow-centered pink or green daisies, blue lined rim, hairline, ... **55.00**

6 3/4" h, figural bust of "Punch," red sponged cheeks and ears, red streaked eyebrows, cream ground, "Shorter & Son Ltd Stoke-on-Trent Made in England" mk, ... **310.00**

8" h, emb hunting scene w/oak leaves and acorns, molded face on spout, branch handle, cream, "Arthur Wood" mk, ... **55.00**

Junket Bowl, 10" d, ftd, printed blue, red, and green oriental scholars and exotic birds on int, borders and ext, printed wavy rims, ... **260.00**

Mug

4" h, white sprigging of Britannia in chariot, med blue center band ground, fancy handle, ... **195.00**

4 1/2" h, dbl handles, black printed scenes of hunter, dogs, and foxes, floral int border, ... **45.00**

Pepper Pot, 4 1/2" h, gaudy blue and gold drapery w/floral drops, (A), ... **853.00**

Pitcher, 8 3/4" h, pig stealers on one side, farmer's arms on reverse, black transfers, sheet transfer of yellow centered blue flowers and green stems, "From The Experience Of Others Do Thou Learn Wisdom And From Their Failings Correct Thine Own Faults" on base, "gilt 1850 and initials" in black cartouche on front, **$1,700.00**

Pitcher

6 1/4" h, "Calico" pattern, brown sheet transfer of sm flowerheads, leaves, and stems, ... **25.00**

6 3/4" h, sprigged design of sated man drinking and another smoking on white center band, brown base and collar, "imp Turner" mk, ... **400.00**

7 1/2" h, "Dissolution of Parliament," purple transfers, fancy molded handle, chip, ... **375.00**

8" h, oct base, "Chasing the Ostrich" pattern, brown transfer, ... **495.00**

9" h, "Lahore" pattern, purple transfer, "Barker & Till Burslem" mk, hairline, ... **360.00**

Plaque, 9 3/4" l x 8 1/4" w, oval, relief molded brown vulture pecking bound supine figure of Prometheus, red drape, brown rocks, green grass, brown and ochre molded lined border, ... **620.00**

Plate

7 1/8" d, "Thames Tunnel in London 1843," red transfer, molded floral border, lobed rim, unmkd, ... **229.00**

7 1/2" d, "Bombay" pattern, red transfer, John Maddock, ... **12.00**

7 3/4" d, paneled, lg stylized yellow centered red petaled sunflower, green leaves, border band of sm red flowerheads, blue rim, (A), ... **110.00**

11" d, oct, "Centenary of John Wesley and portrait" in center, border of scenes of life, blue-green transfer, "C. Challinor & Co." mk, ... **100.00**

Pitcher, 10" h, black transfers of "El Goucho," "Sweepstakes" on base, clock and "Time Rapid Flys" under spout, **$795.00**

Platter

12" l, oval, "Osborne" pattern, brown transfer of kingfishers in cattails, fish and reed border, "T. Elsmore & Son," **225.00**

13 1/2" l x 10 7/8" w, HP dk red and green sprig in center, similar sprigs on border, (A), ... **143.00**

17 1/2" l x 13 3/4" w, oct, HP gaudy blue feather-like leaf in center, border of stylized tulip heads and feather-like leaves, (A), ... **935.00**

19" l x 14 1/2" w, oval, bunches of chrysanthemums on border, brown transfer w/burgundy, pink, lt yellow, mauve, turquoise, and green highlights, gold accents, lobed rim, c1893, ... **75.00**

Sauceboat, 5 1/8" w, shell molding, blue splash accents, salt glaze, rim chip, c1760, ... **1,325.00**

Soup Plate, 10 1/4" d, gold center design, red, blue, and gold border, gadrooned rim, c1820, **$135.00**

Soup Plate, 8 1/2" d, "Sitka" pattern, brown transfer, "Thomas Hughes & Son" mk, ... **25.00**

Sugar Bowl, 3" w, figural Toby, cobalt jacket, gold trim, red breeches, blue and gold rim, "ALLERTONS EST 1831 MADE IN ENGLAND" mk, (A), ... **88.00**

Sugar Bowl, Cov

5 1/4" h, bulbous, green band w/red flowers and blue drape, black highlights, (A), ... **138.00**

6 1/2" h x 7 1/2" H-H, overall stylized purple tulips and foliage, wavy rim, lyre handles, ... **350.00**

8 1/2" h, paneled, blue floral sprigs on white ironstone body, curled handles, ... **95.00**

Teapot

4" h, globular form, iron-red and cream solid agate, mid-18th C, (A), ... **2,000.00**

5" h

Art Deco style HP yellow, purple, or red poppies, pink ground, figural flower on handle, ... **75.00**

Baluster shape, fluted body, pierced rims, vert green stripes, c1780, (A), ... **350.00**

5 1/2" h x 6 7/8" w, lobed and leaf molded shape, painted flower spray on sides, gilt rims, flower knob, Samuel Alcock, ... **210.00**

7" h, canted corners w/shell motif, black transfers of child in yard w/chalet and mountains, ... **315.00**

7 1/2" h, figural Toby, brown hair, gold trimmed blue jacket, red breeches, branch handle and spout, "ALLERTONS EST 1831. MADE IN ENGLAND" mk, (A), ... **275.00**

Tea Set, pot, 6" h, milk jug, 4" h, sugar bowl, 3" h, HP yellow cattail plant w/brown stems, "Burgess & Leigh Burleigh Ware" mk, ... **90.00**

Tureen, Cov, 5 1/2" h x 7 1/4" H-H, w/ladle, black transfers of shepherd and woman above lake w/castle in bkd, molded leaf handles and knob, (A), ... **385.00**

Vase, 6 1/4" h, swollen shape, yellow or black vert squiggles, red ground, white drip rim, black int, "Poole Pottery England" mk, ... **25.00**

Vegetable Bowl, 9 1/4" l, oct, center rural scene w/castle in bkd, stylized flowerheads on honeycomb ground, dentil rim, red transfer, "Stone China J. Demuth" mk, ... **110.00**

Wall Pocket, 9" w x 8" h, "Camilla" pattern, gilt accents, fluted border, Leigh, ... **10.00**

Water Pitcher, 5 1/2" h, relief of green, yellow, rose and black fish, reptiles, birds, and insects, Greek temple and florals on reverse, green outlined spout, ... **2,550.00**

c1818-1834   c1816-1830   c1828-1830

F.M&CO   J&R.Riley
c1845-1858   1802-1828

ENOCH WOOD & SONS BURSLEM STAFFORDSHIRE
1818-1846

FENTON T.G
1847-1859

ENOCH WOOD & SONS BURSLEM
1818-1846

STAFFORDSHIRE-HISTORIC

English And American Views
1818-1860

History: By 1786 there were eighty different potteries established in the Staffordshire district of England, the center of the English pottery industry. By 1800 the number had grown to almost two hundred. The pottery district included the towns of Burslem, Cobridge, Etruria, Fenton, Foley, Hanley, Lane Delph, Lane End, Longport, Shelton, Stoke, and Tunstall.

After the War of 1812, transfer printed Staffordshire pottery that depicted American historical events, views of cities and towns, tombs of famous individuals, portraits of heroes and other famous people, buildings of important institutions, patriotic emblems, and American landscapes were made for the American market. These historic view pieces allowed the British potters to recapture their dominance of the American market almost immediately upon the end of hostilities. Views were adopted from engravings, paintings, and prints by well-known artists of the period.

Dark blue pieces were favored between 1820 and 1840. This color was inexpensive, easy to secure, covered flaws in the wares, withstood the high temperatures of the kiln, and retained its deep coloration. During the 1830s and 1840s, lighter colors of pink and blue along with black, sepia, and green became popular. Wares made included tea services, dinner services, sets of plates, jugs, etc. Canadian views also were manufactured.

Numerous potteries made the historic blue wares. Each firm had its own distinctive border design and characteristics. The border design was the chief means of identifying a specific maker of an unmarked piece.

English views also were popular. Transfers featuring old and famous castles, abbeys, manor houses, cathedrals, seats of the nobility, famous beauty spots, coastal subjects, English colleges, and London were used on the wares.

William Adams and Enoch Wood were the first manufacturers to produce the English views. Enoch Wood took the lead with the American views. Factories that were established after 1820 concentrated on American views.

William Adams
Stoke, 1827-1831
Tunstall, c1834 to Present

William Adams of Stoke was one of four potters with the name William Adams in the Staffordshire district. In 1819 a William Adams became a partner with William Adams, his father. Later his three brothers joined him. When the father died in 1829, William became the factory's manager.

The firm operated as William Adams and Sons and controlled four potteries at Stoke and one at Tunstall.

Initially, English views, with a foliage border and the name of the scene on the back, were made. Two blue views were manufactured at Stoke. Views done at Tunstall had a border of baskets with roses. The Tunstall plant produced American views in black, light blue, sepia, pink, and green between 1830 and 1840.

William Adams died in 1865. All production was moved to Tunstall. The firm still operates today under the name William Adams & Sons, Ltd.

Carey And Sons
Lane End, 1818-1847

Thomas and John Carey operated the Anchor Works at Lane End between 1818 and 1842. The firm changed names several times during its history. The factory produced English views, some of which were based on Sir Walter Scott's poem "Lady of the Lake."

James And Ralph Clews
Cobridge, 1819-1836

James Clews took over the works of Andrew Stevenson in 1819. Ralph, his brother, joined the firm later. In 1836 James traveled to the United States to establish a pottery in Troy, Indiana, but the venture was a failure. Clews returned to England but never re-established himself as a potter.

Clews made both English and American views. The company made a variety of borders, the most popular having festoons that contained the names of the fifteen existing states.

Thomas Godwin
Burslem Wharf, 1829-1843

Thomas Godwin produced both American and Canadian views in a variety of colors. His borders included nasturtium and morning glories.

Thomas Green
Fenton, 1847-1859

Thomas Green operated the Minerva Works in Fenton from 1847 until his death in 1859. His American view pieces contained variations of William Penn's 1683 Treaty with the Indians. The border was a simple, stenciled design. His printed wares were in green, pink, brown, black, and blue. After his death, his wife and sons managed the firm using the name M. Green & Co. It later became the Crown Staffordshire Porcelain Company.

Ralph Hall
Tunstall, 1822-1849

At the conclusion of a partnership with John Hall, Ralph Hall operated the Swan Bank Works in Tunstall. The firm exported many blue printed wares to America.

Joseph Heath
Tunstall, 1829-1843

Joseph Heath and Company operated a factory at New Field in Tunstall from 1829 to 1843. The company's border design was composed of large roses and scrolls with a beaded band and white edge.

Henshall And Company
Longport, 1790-1828

The firm consisted of a series of different partnerships, with the only recorded mark being that of Henshall and Company. Both English and American views were made. The border motif was comprised of fruit and flowers.

J. And J. Jackson
Burslem, 1831-1843

Job and John Jackson operated the Churchyard Works at Burslem between 1831 and 1843. Many of their American views were not copied by other manufacturers. Their border designs included sprays of roses, a wreath of fine flowers, a beaded band, and a white margin. Their transfer colors were black, light blue, pink, sepia, green, maroon, and mulberry.

Thomas Mayer
Stoke, 1829-1838

In 1829 the Mayer brothers, Thomas, John, and Joshua purchased the Dale Hall Works from Stubbs when he retired. Thomas produced the "Arms of the States" series at Dale Hall Works while the other brothers worked at Cliff Bank. Each factory produced fine ceramics.

Morley And Company
Hanley, 1845-1858

Until 1845 Morley was the sole owner of a pottery firm in Hanley. After that date, the firm experienced a succession of owners. Between 1847 and 1858 it was called Francis Morley and Company. Both American and Canadian views were manufactured.

J. And W. Ridgway And William Ridgway And Company
Hanley, 1814-1830

John and William Ridgway, sons of Job Ridgway, took charge of the Bell Bank Works in 1814 when George Ridgway retired. The brothers produced the "Beauties of America" series in dark blue with the rose leaf border. Their English views featured a border with flowers and medallions of children.

In 1830 the partnership was dissolved. John continued to operate Cauldon Place, Job's old manufactory, and William took charge of Bell Bank. John Ridgway contin-

ued the Cauldon Place Works from 1830 until 1858. In 1855 T.C. Brown-Westhead, Moore & Co. purchased the works.

William Ridgway and Company managed the Bell Bank Works from 1830 until 1859. Edward John, his son, joined the firm. By 1843 he was operating six potteries, mostly in Hanley. "American Scenery" and "Catskill Moss" were two series that were based on Bartlett's etchings. These series were issued in colors of light blue, pink, brown, black, and green.

John And Richard Riley
Burslem, 1802-1828

John and Richard Riley operated at Nile Street between 1802 and 1814 and at the Hill Works in Staffordshire between 1814 and 1828. Mostly they made English views and blue printed dinner services with a border of large leaf-like scrolls and flowers.

John Rogers
Longport, 1815-1842

John and George Rogers operated two factories in Longport in 1802. When George died in 1815, John took Spencer, his son, into the firm. The name changed to "John Rogers and Son," a designation used even after the father died. Rogers produced four American views, three of which featured the Boston State House with a floral border. English views also were made.

Anthony Shaw
Burslem, 1850-1878

Anthony Shaw founded Mersey Pottery at Burslem in 1850. He specialized in views of the Mexican War period.

Andrew Stevenson
Cobridge, 1808-1829

One of the pioneers among English potters to make blue historical, transfer printed ware with American scenes was Andrew Stevenson. W.G. Wall, an Irish artist, went to the United States and supplied the drawings for Stevenson. Stevenson's pieces had a flower-and-scroll border. English views were made with roses and other flowers on the border.

Ralph Stevenson
Cobridge, 1815-1840

Ralph Stevenson used a vine and leaf border on his dark blue historical views and a lace border on his transfers in lighter colors. British and foreign views were made.

Pieces from the works of Ralph Stevenson and Williams (R.S.W.) featured the acorn and oak-leaf border design or the vases of flowers and scrollwork design. Williams was the New York agent for Stevenson.

Joseph Stubbs
Burslem, 1790-1829

Joseph Stubbs established the Dale Hall Works in Burslem in 1790. When he retired in 1829, he sold his pottery to the Mayer brothers. His American views used a border design of eagles with widespread wings among scrolls and flowers. Views included scenes in New Jersey, Boston, New York, and Philadelphia. Stubbs also made English views with a border of foliage and pointed scrolls.

Enoch Wood And Sons
Burslem, 1819-1846

Enoch Wood, sometimes called the "Father of English Pottery," made more marked historical American views than any other Staffordshire manufacturer. In 1819 his firm operated as Enoch Wood and Sons. Enoch died in 1840. Enoch, Joseph, and Edward, his sons, continued the firm with their father's name. The sons sold the firm to Pinder, Bourne, and Hope in 1846.

The company's mark had several variations, but each included the name "Wood." The shell border with the circle around the view was used most frequently, though Wood designed several other unique borders. Many of the views attributed to unknown makers probably were made at the Wood factory.

Enoch Wood and Sons also made British views, including the "English Cities" series, the "London Views" series, the shell border series, and the grapevine border series. In addition, they produced French views such as ceramic portrayals of Lafayette and his home in France, the "Italian Scenery" series, and views of Africa and India. Many of the foreign scenes were copied from engravings after water colors by traveling artists such as William Henry Bartlett.

In addition to views of places, Enoch Wood made other designs including a Scriptural Series of Biblical scenes, a Sporting series of hunting scenes, and a Cupid series showing a variety of cherubs.

William Adams did an animal series. Scriptural subjects were done by Adams, Mason, Jackson, Ridgway, and others.

References: David and Linda Arman, *Historical Staffordshire: An Illustrated Check List*, privately printed, 1974, out of print; David and Linda Arman, *Historical Staffordshire: An Illustrated Check List, First Supplement*, privately printed, 1977, out of print; Ada Walker Camehl, *The Blue China Book*, Tudor Publishing Co. 1946; Elizabeth Collard, *The Potters' View of Canada*, McGill Queen's University Press, 1983; A.W. Coysh and R.K. Henrywood, *The Dictionary of Blue & White Printed Pottery, 1780-1880*, Antique Collectors' Club, 1982; *Volume II*, 1989; Ellouise Baker Larsen, *American Historical Views on Staffordshire China, Third Ed.*, Dover Publications, Inc. 1975; N. Hudson Moore,

The Old China Book, Charles E. Tuttle Co. 1974; Jeffrey B. Snyder, *Historical Staffordshire American Patriots and Views w/Prices*, Schiffer Publishing Ltd. 2000.

Museums: American Antiquarian Society, Worcester, MA; City Museum & Art Gallery, Stoke-on-Trent, England; Henry Ford Museum, Dearborn, MI; The National Museum of History & Technology, Washington, DC; Wellcome Institute of the History of Medicine, London, England; Worcester Art Museum, Worcester, MA; Yale University Gallery of Fine Arts, New Haven, CT.

Bowl, 7 3/4" d, "Hall's Select Views-Warleigh House, Sommersetshire," dk blue transfer, **$325.00**

American Views
ADAMS
Cup Plate, 4 5/8" d, "Fort Edwards, Hudson River," brown transfer, ... **185.00**

Nappy, 8" d, "Schenectady on the Mohawk River, US" red transfer, ... **435.00**

Plate
6 1/4" d, "Monte Video, CT US," red transfer, ... **195.00**
9 1/4" d, "American Views-View Near Conway," flower border, red transfer, ... **240.00**
10" d, "Mitchell and Freeman China and Glass Warehouse," dk blue transfer, ... **1,295.00**
10 1/4" d, "Mt. Vernon," med blue transfer, ... **395.00**

Soup Plate, 10 1/2" d, "Catskill Mountain House US," red transfer, ... **275.00**

Tile, 6 1/4" sq, "The King's Chapel Boston Massachusetts," black transfer, hairlines, ... **75.00**

CLEWS
Cup and Saucer, Handleless, American eagle on urn pattern, dk blue transfers, chip, (A), ... **195.00**

*Coffeepot, 11 1/2" h, "Lafayette at Franklin's Tomb," dk blue transfer, A-***$430.00**

Cup Plate
3 1/2" d
"America and Independence," 3-story mansion in center, partial states border, dk blue transfer, "imp Clews" mk, (A), ... **550.00**
"Landing of Gen. LaFayette" in central oval, floral border, med blue transfer, "imp Clews" mk, (A), ... **1,430.00**
4 1/8" d, "Fort Edwards, Hudson River," mulberry transfer, scalloped and beaded rim, (A), ... **413.00**
4 1/2" d, "Peace and Plenty," full floral border, dk blue transfer, "imp Clews" mk, (A), ... **1,650.00**
4 5/8" d, "Pittsfield Elm," floral border w/vignettes, dk blue transfer, "imp Clews" mk, (A), ... **495.00**
4 3/4" d, medallion portrait bust of Lafayette, "Welcome Lafayette the Nation's Guest," med blue transfer, white leaf molded border, reeded rim, "imp Clews" mk, (A), ... **1,980.00**

*Pitcher, 9" h, "State House on Canal," med blue transfer, olive brown outlined rim and handle, unmkd, A-***$145.00**

Pitcher
4 1/2" h, "Landing of General Lafayette," dk blue transfer, ... **3,200.00**
5 3/4" h, "Welcome Lafayette The Nation's Guest And Our Country's Glory," med blue transfer, star crack, (A), ... **1,440.00**
6 1/2" h, "Landing of General Lafayette," floral border, dk blue transfer, ... **2,200.00**

Plate
6 1/2" d, "States" pattern, dk blue transfer, c1824, ... **575.00**
7 3/4" d
"Landing of General Lafayette at Castle Gardens," med blue transfer, ... **595.00**
"Winter View of Pittsfield, Mass." flower and medallion border, med blue transfer, ... **475.00**
8" d
"Peace and Plenty," fruit and flower border, dk blue transfer, "imp CLEWS ENGLAND" mk, ... **550.00**
"West Point, Hudson River," sepia transfer, ... **225.00**
8 3/4" d
"Picturesque Views-Fort Miller on the Hudson," brown transfer, ... **275.00**
"States" pattern, med blue transfer, "imp CLEWS" mk, ... **365.00**
9" d
"Landing of General Lafayette at Castle Gardens," dk blue transfer, "imp CLEWS WARRANTED STAFFORDSHIRE" mk, (A), ... **413.00**
"Picturesque Views-Baker's Falls, Hudson River," floral border, black transfer, ... **195.00**
10" d, "Lafayette at Castle Gardens," dk blue transfer, "imp Clews" mk, ... **475.00**
10 1/4" d
"Picturesque Views-Near Fishkill Hudson River," black transfer, imp mk, ... **115.00**
"Winter View, Pittsfield Massachusetts," dk blue transfer, ... **470.00**
10 3/4" d, "American Independence Series-Fifteen States," scalloped rim, dk blue transfer, "imp CLEWS WARRANTED

STAFFORDSHIRE" mk, crazing, (A), ... **385.00**

Platter, 18 1/4" l x 13 3/4" w, "English Views-Bristol Hot Springs," med blue transfer, maker unknown, **$1,700.00**

Platter
17" l, "Peace And Plenty," dk blue transfer, (A), ... **1,800.00**
17 1/4" l x 13" w, "Landing of Lafayette," med blue transfer, "imp CLEWS" mk, ... **4,000.00**
17 1/2" l x 14 3/4" w, "Little Falls at Luzerne, Hudson River-Picturesque Views Series," brown transfer, ... **775.00**
18 1/2" l x 15 1/2" w, "New York Customs House-American & Independence" series, States border, dk blue transfer, hairline, ... **3,800.0**
18 3/4" l x 16" w, "Winter View of Pittsfield Dam," dk blue transfer, ... **2,200.00**
19" l x 14 1/2" w, "Peace and Plenty," fruit and flower border, dk blue transfer, ... **2,200.00**
Soup Plate, 9 7/8" d, "Peace and Plenty," dk blue transfer, ... **495.00**

ELSMORE AND FORSTER
Pitcher, 12" h, black transfers of bust of George Washington in wreath on sides, white ironstone, mkd, ... **1,850.00**

GOODWIN
Plate, 9 1/4" d, "Schuylkill Waterworks," pink transfer, ... **275.00**
Platter, 13 1/2" l, "Boston and Bunker Hill," med blue transfer, ... **385.00**
Soup Plate, 10 3/8" d, "The Narrows from Fort Hamilton," lt blue transfer, ... **195.00**

HEATH
Plate, 8" d, "The Residence of the Late Richard Jordan, New Jersey," floral border, med blue transfer, scalloped rim, ... **275.00**

HENSHALL, WILLIAMSON & CO.
Cup Plate, 3 1/2" d, "Holiday Street

Theatre, Baltimore," dk blue transfer, hairline, ... **595.00**
Plate, 9 3/4" d, "Baltimore Exchange-Fruit and Flower Series," med blue transfer, ... **750.00**

J. J. JACKSON
Plate
6 1/4" d, "Gerard's Bank, Philadelphia," purple transfer, ... **235.00**
9" d
"The Race Bridge, Philadelphia-American Scenery" series, purple transfer, ... **195.00**
"The Waterworks, Philadelphia," black transfer, ... **450.00**
10 1/4" d
"City Hall, NY," brown transfer, ... **195.00**
"Hartford Connecticut-American Scenery" series, purple transfer, ... **295.00**

MAKER UNKNOWN
Creamer, 5 3/4" h, black transfer portraits of "General Jackson, The Hero of New Orleans" on med blue center band, copper luster body w/beaded rim, (A), ... **2,200.00**
Cup Plate, 3 3/4" d, "Arms of the United States," partial floral border, med blue transfer, (A), ... **2,860.00**
Bowl, 7 3/4" d, "Near Fishkill," floral border, dk blue transfer, ... **395.00**
Coffeepot, 12 3/4" h, "Lafayette at Franklin's Tomb," dk blue transfers, scrolled ear handle, domed cov, repairs, (A), ... **2,200.00**
Jug, 6 1/8" h, named 13 colonies, view of Mount Vernon, image of George Washington, dk blue transfer, rim chips, (A), ... **1,380.00**
Mug, 2 1/4" h, "Lafayette Crowned at Yorktown," black transfer, pink luster border band, (A), ... **495.00**
Pepper Pot, 4 3/4" h, "Hoboken, New Jersey," med blue transfer, ... **1,255.00**
Pitcher, 11" h, ewer shape, "American Naval Heroes," med blue transfer, ... **1,400.00**
Plate, 10 1/4" d, "Erie Canal Eulogy To DeWitt Clinton," canal boat border, med blue transfer, c1830, ... **350.00**
Soup Plate, 10 1/2" d, "View From Ruggles House Hudson River," med blue transfer, ... **125.00**

MAYER, T.
Cup Plate, 4 1/4" d, "Arms of South Carolina," med blue transfer, unmkd, (A), ... **1,155.00**

RIDGWAY, J. & W.
Basket and Stand, 11" w, pierced basket, "Esplanade and Castle Garden New York" on int, "Deaf and Dumb Asylum, Hartford, Con." and "Almshouse, New York" on ext, "Battle of Bunker Hill" on stand, "Vine" border, dk blue transfers, (A), ... **7,200.00**
Cup Plate, 3 1/2" d, "Customs House, Philadelphia-Beauties of America Series," floral border, unmkd, (A), ... **2,090.00**
Meat Platter, Well and Tree
18 1/2" l, "Pennsylvania Hospital, Philadelphia-Beauties of America" series, dk blue transfer, (A), ... **1,800.00**
20 1/2" l, "Capital, Washington-Beauties of America" series, dk blue transfer, (A), ... **3,300.00**
Plate
7" d
"Insane Hospital, Boston," "Beauties of America" series, med blue transfer, ... **450.00**
"The Valley of Shenandoah from Jefferson's Rock," black transfer, ... **165.00**
8" d, "Library Philadelphia," "Beauties of America" series, med blue transfer, ... **625.00**
9 3/4" d, "City Hall, New York," flower and medallion border, "Beauties of America" series, med blue transfer, ... **495.00**
10 1/4" d, "View from Ruggles House Newburgh," lt blue transfer, ... **165.00**
Platter
9 3/4" l, "Peekskill Landing, Hudson River," lt blue transfer, ... **450.00**
12 5/8" l, "Hospital, Boston-Beauties of America" series, dk blue transfer, (A), ... **1,560.00**
16 3/4" l, "Almshouse, New York-Beauties of America" series, dk blue transfer, (A), ... **1,440.00**
17" l, "The Narrows From Fort Hamilton," med blue transfer, ... **550.00**
Relish Dish, 8 1/4" w, shell shape, "Valley of Shenandoah From Jeffersons Rock," lt blue transfer, ... **275.00**
Sauceboat, 8 1/2" l, "The Narrows From Fort Hamilton, New York," lt blue transfer, ... **275.00**
Undertray, 8 1/4" l x 6" w, oval, "Exchange Charleston-Beauties of

America Series," flowerhead and cartouche border, med blue transfer, ... **895.00**

ROGERS
Cup Plate, 4" d, "Boston Harbor," dk blue transfer, (A), ... **1,210.00**
Plate, 10" d, "Boston State House," med blue transfer, ... **270.00**
Platter, 18 7/8" l, "Boston State House," med blue transfer, ... **1,950.00**

R. STEVENSON AND WILLIAMS
Cup Plate
4 1/8" d, "Octagon Church, Boston," acorn and oak leaf border, dk blue transfer, "imp STEVENSON" mk, (A), ... **1,980.00**
4 1/4" d
"Boston State House," acorn and oak leaf border, med blue transfer, "RS.W." mk, (A), ... **990.00**
"Scudder's American Museum," acorn and oak leaf border, med blue transfer, (A), ... **1,430.00**

Plate
6 1/4" d, "Catholic Cathedral, NY," dk blue transfer, repaired hairline, ... **795.00**
8" d, "New York Battery," white emb border, dk blue transfer, repaired rim chip, ... **395.00**
8 1/2" d
"City Hall, New York," Acorn border, dk blue, ... **750.00**
"Nahant Hotel Near Boston," Acorn and Leaf Series, med blue transfer, ... **795.00**
9" d, "Hospital, Boston," white emb border, dk blue transfer, ... **425.00**
10" d
"Harvard College," Acorn and Oak leaf border, dk blue transfer, ... **475.00**
"New York From Brooklyn Heights," Stevenson, dk blue transfer, ... **1,400.00**
"Park Theatre, New York," acorn and leaf border, dk blue transfer, Ralph Stevenson, ... **550.00**
"Washington Capital," dk blue transfer, R. Stevenson, chip, ... **395.00**

Platter
16 1/2" l, "New York From Heights Near Brooklyn," "Floral and Scroll" border, dk blue transfer, (A), ... **5,400.00**

21" l, "Esplanade and Castle Garden," Vine border, dk blue transfer, (A), ... **4,200.00**
Soup Plate, 10" d, "Harvard College," med blue transfer, "R. & W. Stevenson" mk, ... **450.00**
Toddy Plate, 5" d, "Scudder's American Museum," med blue transfer, crack, ... **795.00**
Vegetable Bowl, 10" l, "Brooklyn Ferry," "Vine" border, dk blue transfer, (A), ... **3,000.00**

STUBBS
Bowl, 10 1/4" d, "Fair Mount Near Philadelphia," "Spread Eagle" border series, dk blue transfer, (A), ... **2,400.00**

Cup Plate
3 1/8" d, "Woodlands Near Philadelphia," med blue transfer, (A), ... **330.00**
3 1/2" d, "Holliday Street Theatre, Baltimore," fruit and flower border, med blue transfer, unmkd, (A), ... **880.00**

Plate
6 1/2" d, "City Hall, New York," eagle and swag border, dk blue transfer, ... **450.00**
7 3/4" d, "Hoboken in New Jersey," "Spread Eagle" border series, dk blue transfer, ... **895.00**
8 3/4" d, "River Schuylkill-Upper Ferry Bridge," med blue transfer, ... **525.00**
10" d, "Bank of the United States, Philadelphia," flowers, and scrolls on border, med blue transfer, ... **750.00**
10 1/4" d, "Fair Mount Near Philadelphia," spread eagle and flower border, med blue transfer, ... **650.00**

Platter
10 3/4" l x 8 3/4" w, "Woodlands, Near Philadelphia," "Spread Eagle" border series, dk blue transfer, ... **1,850.00**
12 3/4" x 10 1/4" w, "Hoboken in New Jersey," spread eagle border, med blue transfer, ... **1,975.00**
17" l, "Mendenhall Ferry," "Spread Eagle" border series, med blue transfer, ... **2,395.00**
18 1/2" l, "Upper Ferry Bridge Across The Schuylkill River in Pennsylvania," med blue transfer, ... **2,100.00**
20 3/4" l x 17" w, "Fair Mount Near Philadelphia," dk blue transfer chip, ... **2,800.00**

Sauce Tureen, Cov and Stand, 9" w, w/ladle, "Upper Ferry Bridge Over River Schuylkill," "Spread Eagle" border series, eagle's head on ladle handle, (A), ... **1,560.00**

Plate, 6 5/8" d, "Hagley, Worchestershire," med blue transfer, "imp Enoch Wood and eagle" mark, A-$60.00

WOOD & SONS
Creamer, 5 1/4" h, "Lafayette at Franklin's Tomb," dk blue transfer, ... **825.00**
Cup and Saucer, Handleless, "Mt Vernon, the Seat of the Late Genl Washington," dk blue transfer, ... **475.00**
Cup Plate
3 5/8" d
"Castle Garden-Battery," Shell border, dk blue transfer, ... **300.00**
"Lafayette and Washington," dk blue transfer, ... **675.00**
4 5/8" d, "Landing of the Pilgrims," bird and scroll border, med blue transfer, "imp Enoch Wood & Sons" mk, (A), ... **440.00**
4 3/4" d, "Boston State House," floral border, lt blue transfer, hairline, (A), ... **770.00**
Pitcher, 7 1/2" h, "Lafayette at the Tomb of Franklin," dk blue transfer, star crack, ... **1,450.00**
Plate
7 1/2" d, "View of Trenton Falls," Shell border, dk blue transfer, ... **395.00**
8 1/2" d, "Marine Hospital, Lexington, Kentucky," shell border, dk blue transfer, ... **350.00**
9" d, "Fall of Montmorenci Near Quebec," dk blue transfer, "imp E. Wood & Sons" mk, ... **595.00**
9 1/8" d, "Baltimore & Ohio Railway-Inclined Plane," dk blue border, ... **1,195.00**

9 1/4" d, "Baltimore & Ohio Railway-Level," dk blue transfer, ... **1,000.00**

9 3/4" d, "Boston State House," dk blue transfer, ... **245.00**

10" d
"Table Rock, Niagara," Shell border, dk blue transfer, ... **550.00**
"Union Line," Shell border, dk blue transfer, ... **895.00**

Platter
14 3/4" l, "Niagara From The American Side," Shell border, dk blue transfer, (A), ... **3,000.00**
17 3/8" l, "State House, New Haven and Yale College-Four Medallion Series," brown transfer, ... **1,795.00**
18 1/2" l, "Castle Garden, Battery, New York," Shell border, dk blue transfer, (A), ... **3,300.00**

Saucer Dish, 5 3/4" d, "Lafayette at Franklin's Tomb," dk blue transfer, "Wood & Sons Burslem" mk, (A), ... **248.00**

Soup Plate, 10" d, "Table Rock, Niagara," dk blue transfer, ... **400.00**

Sugar Bowl, Cov, 5" h x 8" w, "Wadsworth Tower, Avon Connecticut," dk blue transfers, restored lid, ... **625.00**

Teapot
7 1/4" h, "Lafayette at Franklin's Tomb," dk blue transfer, ... **1,200.00**
7 1/2" h x 11 1/2" w, "Wadsworth Tower," Shell border, dk blue transfer, rim chips, (A), ... **935.00**
8 1/4" h, "Commodore MacDonnough's Victory on Lake Champlain," Shell border, dk blue transfers, ... **3,250.00**

English Views
ADAMS
Plate
6" d, "Beckenham Place, Kent," med blue transfer, ... **265.00**
7" d, "Yorkgate, Regent's Park, London," med blue transfer, ... **280.00**
7 7/8" d, "Sunning Hill Park, Berkshire," flower border, dk blue transfer, hairlines, ... **80.00**
8 3/4" d, "The Rookery, Surrey," med blue transfer, "imp WARRANTED STAFFORDSHIRE ADAMS" mk, (A), ... **185.00**

10" d
"Bamborough Castle, Northumberland" med blue transfer, ... **400.00**
"Villa in Regents Park, London," med blue transfer, ... **325.00**

Platter
13 1/2" l x 10 1/2" w, "Bywell Castle, Northumberland," med blue transfer, "imp Adam's Warranted Staffordshire" mk, (A), ... **385.00**
19" l x 15" w, "Windsor Castle," flower and leaf border, beaded rim, dk blue transfer, ... **2,200.00**

Serving Dish, 10 1/2" w, "Highbury College, London-Regent Park Series," dk blue transfer, hairline, ... **495.00**

Tureen, 15" H-H, 9 1/2" h, "Caius College Cambridge," cabbage knob, med blue transfers, "J.W. Ridgway" mark, chip on knob, A-$1,955.00

ASWORTH BROTHERS
Plate, 9" d, "Rideau Canal, Bytown," brown transfer, ... **100.00**

CLEWS
Fruit Basket, 13" l x 8 1/2" w, w/undertray, 10 1/2" l x 8 1/2" w, reticulated, "Select Series- Aysgill Force in Wensleydale," med blue transfer, ... **2,250.00**

Plate
7 5/8" d, "Gunton Hall, Norfolk," dk blue transfer, "imp Clews" mk, ... **225.00**
9" d, "View of Greenwich," foliage and grapevine border, dk blue transfer, imp mk, ... **180.00**
10" d
"Canterbury Cathedral," dk blue transfer, ... **285.00**
"Melrose Abbey," med blue transfer, ... **400.00**
"Wells Cathedral," med blue transfer, ... **375.00**

Soup Plate, 10" d, "Dilston Tower, Northumberland," dk blue transfer,

"imp WARRANTED STAFFORDSHIRE CLEWS" mk, (A), ... **165.00**

HALL R.
Bowl, 12" H-H x 8 1/2" w, w/underplate, reticulated, "R. Hall's Select Views-Luscombe, Devonshire," dk blue transfers, ... **400.00**

Cup Plate, 4" d, "Hampshire Scenery Series-Broadlands," flower border, med blue transfer, ... **45.00**

Plate, 5 1/2" d, "Panshanger, Hertfordshire," med blue transfer, ... **325.00**

Plate
6 1/4" d, "R. Hall's Select Views-Dragorn House, Scotland," dk blue transfer, ... **195.00**
7 3/8" d, "R. Hall's Select Views" "Chashiobury, Herfordshire," dk blue transfer, ... **165.00**
"Eashick Hall, Surrey," flowerhead border, dk blue transfer, ... **175.00**
8 1/2" d, "R. Hall's Select Views-Warleigh House, Somersetshire," dk blue transfer, ... **225.00**
10" d, "R. Hall's Select Views-Pain's Hill, Surrey," dk blue transfer, ... **275.00**

Platter, 15" l x 11 3/4" w, "R. Hall's Select Views-Conway Castle," fruit and flower border, acanthus leaf rim, dk blue transfer, (A), ... **440.00**

HENSHALL & CO.
Plate, 7" d, "Halstead, Essex," fruit and flower border, med blue transfer, c1800, (A), ... **330.00**

Platter, 18 3/4" l x 14 5/8" w, "Compton Verney," fruit and flower border, med blue transfer, ... **2,950.00**

MAKER UNKNOWN
Meat Platter, 14 3/4" l x 11 3/4" w, rect, "Harewood Hall, Yorkshire," med blue transfer, passion flower border, ... **975.00**

Plate
8 3/4" d, "Wistow Hall, Leicestershire," dk blue transfer, (A), ... **385.00**
9" d, "Alnick Castle," passion flower border, med blue transfer, c1830, ... **130.00**
9 3/4" d
"Belvoir Castle," passion flower border, med blue transfer, ... **140.00**
"Wiseton Hall, Nottinghamshire," flowerhead border, dk blue transfer, ... **425.00**

10" d, "Falls of Killarney," dk blue transfer, unmkd, ... **275.00**

10 1/4" d, "Knaresborough Castle, Yorkshire," dk blue transfer, unmkd, ... **215.00**

Platter

12" l x 10" w, oct, "Wakefield Lodge," oak leaf and acorn border, med blue transfer, ... **725.00**

15 1/4" l x 11 3/4" w, "Royal Exchange in London," dk blue transfer, ... **425.00**

Serving Bowl, 9 1/2" l x 9" w, "Dorney Court," oak leaf border, med blue transfer, unmkd, ... **400.00**

Soup Plate, 10" d, "Kirstall Abbey-Antique Scenery Series," med blue transfer, ... **90.00**

Spice Set, tray, 10" H-H x 8 1/2" w, diamond shape, 4 cov jars, 2 1/2" h, scroll handles, "Guy's Cliff, Warwickshire," med blue transfers, ... **975.00**

MORLEY

Butter Keep, Cov, 6 1/4" w, w/underplate, "Georgeville, Provence of Quebec-Lake Series," brown transfers, ... **550.00**

RIDGWAY, J. & W.

Plate, 10" d, "Christ Church, Oxford," morning glory border, med blue transfer, (A), ... **175.00**

Platter, 19 1/2" l x 15 1/2" w, w/drainer, 15" l x 10 3/4" w, "Osterley Park," med blue transfers, c1814-30, unmkd, (A), ... **1,760.00**

Soup Plate, 9 3/4" d, "Pembroke Hall, Cambridge," morning glory border w/medallions of goats and children, med blue transfer, "J. & W. Ridgway" mk, (A), ... **135.00**

RILEY

Gravy Bowl, 7 3/4" l, "Kelmarsh Hall, Northhamptonshire," med blue transfer, ... **275.00**

Plate

6 3/4" d, "King's Cottage, Windsor Park," Large Scroll border, med blue transfer, ... **145.00**

9" d, "Cannon Hall, Yorkshire," scrolling border, med blue transfer, ... **165.00**

10" d

"Gopggerddan Cardiganshire," lg scroll border, med blue transfer, c1825, ... **180.00**

"Hollywell College, Cavan," lg scroll border, dk blue transfer, "J. & R. Riley" mk, ... **235.00**

"Laymouth Castle," med blue transfer, ... **375.00**

Soup Plate, 9" d, "Hollywell Cottage, Cavan," acanthus leaf border, dk blue transfer, (A), ... **125.00**

Tureen, Cov, 13" H-H, "Ballock Castle, Dumbartonshire," lion head handles, med blue transfers, ... **1,200.00**

STEVENSON

Plate

9" d, "Faulkbourn Hall, Cobridge," rose border, med blue transfer, ... **325.00**

10 1/4" d

"Culford Hall, Suffolk," med blue transfer, "A. STEVENSON WARRANTED STAFFORDSHIRE" mk, c1816-30, (A), ... **275.00**

"Faulkbourn Hall Cobridge," med blue transfer, "A. STEVENSON WARRANTED STAFFORDSHIRE" mk, c1816-30, ... **350.00**

WOOD & SONS

Cup Plate, 3 5/8"d, "Shirley House, Surrey," rope twist border, "Imp Enoch Wood & Sons Burslem," med blue transfer, hairline, (A), ... **66.00**

Plate

6 1/4" d, "The Coliseum, Regents Park-London Views," dk blue transfer, "imp WOOD" mk, (A), ... **88.00**

7 1/2" d, "Fontill Abbey, Wiltshire-Far View," Grapevine border, med blue transfer, ... **165.00**

8 3/4" d

"Compton Verney," med blue transfer, "imp Wood" mk, ... **400.00**

"Hawthornden, Edinburghshire," flower border, beaded rim, med blue transfer, ... **75.00**

9 1/4" d

"Hanover Lodge, Regents Park-London Views," dk blue transfer, "imp WOOD" mk, (A), ... **192.00**

"Liverpool-English Cities Series," lt blue transfer, ... **185.00**

10" d

"Guy's Cliff, Warwickshire," Grapevine border, med blue transfer, ... **250.00**

"Wardour Castle, Wiltshire," Grapevine border, med blue transfer, ... **275.00**

10 1/4" d

"Dalguise, Perthshire," Grapevine border, med blue

transfer, "blue DALGUISE PERTHSHIRE" and "imp WOOD & SONS" mk, (A), ... **275.00**

"St. Phillip's Chapel Regent Street-London Views," Grapevine border, dk blue transfer, unmkd, (A), ... **150.00**

"Worcester-English Cities Series," lt blue transfer, ... **95.00**

Sauceboat, 7" l, "Sproughton Chantry," Grapevine border, med blue transfer, hairline, chips, ... **275.00**

Soup Plate

9 1/4" d, "Vue de Chateau Ermenonville," Grapevine border, dk blue transfer, unmkd, (A), ... **190.00**

10" d

"Guy's Cliff, Warwickshire," Grapevine border, med blue transfer, "imp WOOD & SONS BURSLEM" mk, ... **200.00**

"The Holme, Regent's Park-London Views Series," vine, leaf, and grape border, dk blue transfer, ... **295.00**

"Thornton Castle, Staffordshire," dk blue transfer, scalloped rim, (A), ... **95.00**

"Thrybergh, Yorkshire," med blue transfer, ... **275.00**

Soup Tureen, 12 1/4" l, Hollywell Cottage, Caven," Grapevine border, med blue transfer, ... **1,975.00**

Other Views

ADAMS

Cup and Saucer, Handleless, "Ancient Tomb of Bogliopore-Oriental Scenery Series," dk blue transfers, ... **250.00**

Plate, 9 1/8" d, "Moulin sur la Marne a Charenton," dk blue transfer, ... **400.00**

HALL

Cup Plate, 4 1/4" d, "Fakeer's Rock," grape and foliage border, med blue transfer, ... **325.00**

Platter, 19" l x 14 5/8" w, "Palace of St. Germain, France" design, floral border, med blue transfer, "R. Halls Picturesque Scenery" mk, restorations on reverse, (A), ... **440.00**

Undertray, 14" l x 10" w, "Hindu Temple-Hall's Oriental Scenery" pattern, med blue transfer, ... **450.00**

Vegetable Bowl, 12" l x 9" w, "Oriental Scenery-Pagoda Below Patna on the

Ganges," floral border, med blue transfer, "I Hall & Sons" mk, (A), ... **300.00**

MAKER UNKNOWN

Bread Plate, 7 1/4" d, "Batalha, Portugal," med blue transfer, set of 5, (A), ... **413.00**

Drainer, 14 1/2" l, "Pashkov House, Moscow," med blue transfer, (A), ... **660.00**

Pepper Pot, 5" h, "Batalha, Portugal," med blue transfer, ... **515.00**

Pitcher, 9" h, "Bridge of Lucano," leaf border, med blue transfer, ... **985.00**

Plate

8 3/4" d, "Ciala Kavak-Ottoman Empire Series," med blue transfer, ... **250.00**

9 1/2" d, pearlware, "Pashkow House, Moscow," med blue transfer, c1820, repaired chip, ... **75.00**

9 3/4" d, "Batalha, Portugal," med blue transfer, unmkd, ... **295.00**

10" d

"Ponte Rotto," med blue transfer, unmkd, ... **250.00**

"Tchiurluk-Ottoman Empire Series," flower border, med blue transfer, ... **350.00**

10 1/8" d, "Ponte Molle," med blue transfer, ... **195.00**

Platter

13" l x 10" w, oct, "Ponte Rotto," floral border, med blue transfer, ... **875.00**

16 1/2" l x 13" w, "Italian Scenery Series-Ponte Del Palazzo," med blue transfer, ... **895.00**

19" l

14" l, "Bridge at Lucano," med blue transfer, restored hairline, ... **950.00**

14 5/8" w, pearlware, "Oriental Scenery-Tomb of Emperor Auber at Secundra," floral border, med blue transfer, ... **775.00**

WOOD & SONS

Plate

9 1/4" d, "French View Series" "East View of LaGrange, Residence of the Marquis LaFayette," med blue transfer, ... **225.00**

"Moulin Sur La Marne a Charenton," grapes, leaves, and flower border, med blue transfer, ... **525.00**

9 1/2" d, "Vue de la Porte Romaine a Andernach," dk blue transfer, ... **225.00**

10 1/4" d

"French View Series-Vue du Chateau Ermonville," dk blue transfer, "imp SEMI CHINA, eagle, E. WOOD & SONS BUSLEM WARRANTED" mk, chips, (A), ... **165.00**

"Italian Scenery Series-St. Peter's Rome," landscape border, rope rim, dk blue transfer, (A), ... **100.00**

Platter

12 3/4" l x 10" w, "Italian Scenery-Genoa," tree lined border, dk blue transfer, "imp Wood & Sons Burslem" mk, (A), ... **285.00**

16 1/2" l x 13" w, "Vue du Temple de la Philosophie Ermonville," floral and grapevine border, dk blue transfer, "imp WOOD" mk, hairline, (A), ... **400.00**

18 1/2" l, "Christianburg, Danish Settlement On The Gold Coast, Africa," Shell border, dk blue transfer, (A), ... **3,600.00**

Sauce Tureen, 7 1/2" h x 8 1/8" w, w/undertray, "Italian Scenery Series-Terni," flowerhead knob, dk blue transfers, hairline, ... **695.00**

STAFFORDSHIRE-ROMANTIC

England

1830-1860

History: Between 1830 and 1860, the Staffordshire District potters produced a tremendous number of useful dinnerwares intended for everyday dining that featured romantic transfer printed designs.

Romantic wares were printed in blue, red, green, black, brown, purple, and yellow. Some patterns were issued in only one color, while some were produced in a variety of colors. Within each color group, there was a great deal of color variation. Blues ranged from the darkest navy to a pale powder blue to shades of turquoise.

Designs used for romantic wares reflected the tastes of the Victorian age. Scenes with castles, alpine mountain peaks, and rivers evoked a fascination with European travel. Oriental scenery expressed the infatuation of the common man with dreams of faraway places. English scenes were used, but they depicted homes of the nobility, castles, and other important locations.

Floral designs featured realistic flowers, leaves, fruits, and birds that reflected the English love of gardens. Some scenes added insects or butterflies in imitation of the Chinese patterns.

The Victorians loved the architectural and decorative styles of the past. Gothic elements, French designs from the Louis XV and XVI periods, and even Grecian and Roman designs became part of romantic transfer patterns. Classical designs often showed urns or vases in a garden setting. Some pieces contained allegorical stories.

Oriental designs utilized Chinese and Japanese flowers, baskets, exotic birds, flowering trees, pagodas, and urns. East Indian motifs depicted mosques, minarets, desert scenes, and men and women in Arabian or Turkish clothes. Elements of fantasy in these patterns reflected the love of far-off, romantic places, unseen by the common English resident.

Scenic designs were popular. Pastoral scenes showing the typical English countryside featured rolling fields, domestic farm animals, groves of trees, brooks, and ponds. Figures placed in these scenes usually wore Medieval, Elizabethan, or Empire clothing. Greyhounds were a common decorative element.

Although the names of rivers, countries, cities, or towns often were used as titles for these romantic views, the scenes themselves were imaginary. Most of the scenes appeared rather dreamlike in conception. Tall trees, rivers, castles, arched bridges, gazebos, ruins, or fountains were included in the scenes. Borders were either floral, geometric, or featured reserves with landscape scenes.

Some scenes showed local people in their roles as farmers, fishermen, warriors, dancers, etc. In these cases, the scenic background was less prominent. The figures were most important. Other romantic subjects included zoological, religious, moralistic, botanical, marine, or geometric transfers.

In many instances, the designers of the transfers were not known. Many pottery firms purchased their transfers from engraving companies such as Sargeant and Pepper of Hanley. The firm designed the printed patterns and also engraved the copper plates necessary for printing the wares. Popular designs were used by more than one pottery manufacturer.

Romantic transfers were made by many factories. The best known were Adams, Clews, Davenport, Dillon, Dimmock, Hall, Hicks and Meigh, Meigh, Ridgway, Rogers, Spode, Wedgwood, and Wood.

Commonly found patterns included Athena, Andalusia, Asiatic Society, Asiatic

Views, Caledonia, Cyrene, Ivanhoe, Messina, Palestine, Tyrol, Valencia, and Villa.

Hard to find patterns were Belzoni, Carolina, Columbia, Corell, Chinese Marine, Eastern Street Scene, Indian Chief, Italy, Ontario Lake Scenery, Oriental Birds, Temperance Society, and Texian Campaign.

Backstamps were used that reflected the romantic expressions of these Victorian potters. The backstamp was part of the sheet that contained the transfer pattern. When placed on the back of a piece, it indicated the pattern used.

References: Jeffrey B. Snyder, *Romantic Staffordshire Ceramics*, Schiffer Publishing, Ltd. 1997; Petra Williams, *Staffordshire Romantic Transfer Patterns*, Fountain House East, 1978; Petra Williams & Marguerite R. Weber, *Staffordshire II*, Fountain House East, 1986; Petra Williams & Marguerite R. Weber, *Staffordshire III*, Fountain House East, 1998.

Collectors' Clubs: The Transfer Collectors Club, c/o Judi Siddall, 734 Torrega Court, Palo Alto, CA 94303, www.transcollectorsclub.org.

Museums: City Museum & Art Gallery, Stoke-on-Trent, England; Henry Ford Museum, Dearborn, MI.

Basket, 10 3/4" H-H x 3" h, w/undertray, 8 3/4" l, reticulated basket and undertray, "Palmyra" pattern, dk grey transfer, "grey PALMYRA W & B" mk, (A), ... **300.00**

Bowl

7 1/2" d, "Giraffe" pattern, blue transfer, "blue PUBLISHED AUG 30th 1836 AGREEABLY TO THE ACT, STONE CHINA, GIRAFFE" mks, (A), ... **300.00**

8 1/2" d

"Alhambra" pattern, med blue transfer, ... **35.00**

"Pomona" pattern, brown transfer, "J. & Co." mk, ... **90.00**

9 1/4" d, "Roselle" pattern, blue transfer, "Wm Adams & Co." mk, ... **50.00**

9 1/2" d, "Park Scenery" pattern, brown transfer, "Carr & Sons" mk, ... **50.00**

10" d, "Priory" pattern, med blue transfer, "E. Challinor & Co." mk, ... **30.00**

Cake Stand, 11 3/8" d x 2" h, scalloped rim, "Rhine" pattern, lt blue transfer, (A), ... **145.00**

Chestnut Basket, 2 5/8" h x 11 1/2" l x 8 1/2" w, w/undertray, 10 5/8" l x 8 5/8" w, "Marmora" pattern, brown

transfers, reticulated borders on basket and tray, "Brown W.R. & Co. MARMORA, urn and anchor" mk, chip on rim, stapled rim crack, c1834-54, (A), ... **385.00**

Coffeepot, 13 1/2" h, high dome, "Columbus" pattern, purple transfer, Adams, ... **1,150.00**

Compote

10 1/4" d x 4 1/4" h, ftd, "Turkish Landscape" pattern, brown transfer, scalloped rim, (A), ... **300.00**

11 1/4" H-H x 5 3/4" h, 4 spread feet, "Albion" pattern, lt blue transfers, ... **425.00**

Creamer, 5" h, "Boston Mails-Gentlemen's Cabin" pattern, brown transfer, stains, (A), ... **550.00**

Cup and Saucer

"American Marine" pattern, brown transfers, "GLA & Bros." mk, ... **100.00**

"Grecian" pattern, green transfers, Ridgway, ... **12.00**

"Jeddo" pattern, black transfers, Adams, ... **125.00**

Cup and Saucer, Handleless

"Canella" pattern, brown transfer w/yellow, blue, green, and red accents, "E. Challinor" mk, ... **45.00**

Ironstone, "Roselle" pattern, purple transfer, John Meir, ... **45.00**

"Nanking" pattern, med blue transfer, Challinor, ... **45.00**

"Ontario Lake Scenery" pattern, med blue transfers, ... **215.00**

"Palestine" pattern, red transfers, Adams, ... **55.00**

Paneled cup, "Corella" pattern, lavender transfers, ... **210.00**

"Priory" pattern, pink transfer, "E. Challinor" mk, ... **85.00**

"Sydenham" pattern, brown transfer, Clementson, ... **55.00**

"Temple" pattern, purple transfer, "P.W. & Co." mk, ... **40.00**

"Tivoli" pattern, red transfer, "red TIVOLI, MEIGH" mk, (A), ... **55.00**

"Venus" pattern, blue transfer, "P.W. & Co." mk, ... **40.00**

Cup Plate

3 1/2" "Windsor Castle" pattern, red transfer, unmkd, (A), ... **66.00**

4" d

"Chinese Fountains" pattern, brown transfer, ... **85.00**

"Landscape" pattern, med blue transfer, unmkd, (A), ... **66.00**

"Pomerania" pattern, purple transfer, Ridgway, ... **95.00**

"University" pattern, med blue transfer, J. Ridgway, ... **85.00**

4 1/2" d, "Quadrupeds" pattern, hyena, dk blue transfer, chip, ... **150.00**

Drainer

10 3/4" l x 7 1/2" w, "Wild Rose" pattern, med blue transfer, unmkd, ... **495.00**

11 1/4" l x 9" w, "Giraffe" pattern, blue transfer, J. Ridgway, c1836, (A), ... **1,320.00**

Jug, 4" h, "Tyrolean" pattern, green transfer, ... **225.00**

Ladle, 11" l, "Wild Rose" pattern, brown transfer, unmkd, c1820, (A), ... **165.00**

Meat Platter

17 1/2" l x 14" w, "Palmyra" pattern, lt blue transfer, ... **40.00**

19" l x 15 1/2" w, well and tree, "Chinese Pastime" pattern, purple transfer, ... **995.00**

20" l x 16" w, "Abbey" pattern, blue transfer, c1860, ... **375.00**

21 1/2" l x 17 3/4" w, tree and well, "Canova" pattern, brown transfer, George Phillips, (A), ... **1,100.00**

Milk Pitcher, 5 1/8" h, paneled, "Columbian Star" pattern, blue transfer, "John Ridgway" mk, ... **950.00**

Mug

3 1/4" h, "Genevese" pattern, red transfer, "green globe, crown, MINTONS, ENGLAND" mk, c1891, (A), ... **110.00**

3 3/8" h, "Venus" pattern, med blue transfer, "Podmore Walker & Co." mk, ... **185.00**

Pitcher

7 1/2" h, paneled, "Columbia" pattern, med blue transfer, Adams, ... **165.00**

8 1/2" h, "Abbey Ruins" pattern, lt blue transfer, "T. Mayer, Longport" mk, (A), ... **275.00**

9 3/4" h, paneled, "Union" pattern, med blue transfer, "E. Challinor" mk, ... **450.00**

10 1/8" h, "Sardinia" pattern, red transfer, "R. Hall & Co." mk, ... **495.00**

11" h, "Bologna" pattern, purple transfer, Adams, ... **550.00**

11 1/2" h, "Genevese" pattern, brown transfer, unmkd, c1822-36, (A), ... **412.00**

12 1/2" h, "Roselle" pattern, lt blue transfer, repair to spout, ... **495.00**

12 3/4" h, paneled, "Friburg" pattern, med blue transfer, Wm. Davenport, ... **395.00**

Plate

5" d, ironstone, "Cyprus" pattern, black transfer, Davenport, ... **40.00**

5 3/4" d

"Oriental" pattern, med blue transfer, Ridgway, set of 4, ... **25.00**

"Tuscan Rose" pattern, purple transfer, J. & W. Ridgway, ... **95.00**

6" d, Ironstone, "Lozere" pattern, red transfer, "E. Challinor" mk, ... **45.00**

6 1/8" d, "Spanish Convent" pattern, red transfer, ... **85.00**

6 1/2" d

"Geneva" pattern, lt blue transfer, ... **35.00**

"Priory" pattern, med blue transfer, "E. Challinor & Co. Priory" mk, ... **30.00**

7" d, "Asiatic Pheasants" pattern, lt blue transfer, Burgess & Leigh, ... **10.00**

7 3/8" d, "Lucerne" pattern, brown transfer, ... **60.00**

7 1/2" d

"Florentine" pattern, lt blue transfer, Mayer, c1840, ... **60.00**

"Geneva" pattern, lt blue transfer, ... **65.00**

"Millenium" pattern, black transfer, Stevenson, ... **195.00**

"Palestine" pattern, pink transfer, Adams, ... **85.00**

"Persian" pattern, floral border, lavender transfer, ... **65.00**

7 3/4" d, "Cyprus" pattern, brown transfer, "Emery Burslem England" mk, ... **30.00**

7 7/8" d, 12 sides, "Ontario Lake Scenery," med blue transfer, J. Heath, ... **40.00**

8" d

"Carolina" pattern, purple transfer, Hall, ... **110.00**

"Chinese Fountains" pattern, red transfer, ... **85.00**

"Indian" pattern, pink transfer, Adams, ... **150.00**

Plate, 8 1/4" d, "Palestine" pattern, red transfer, "imp Adams" mark, **$85.00**

8 1/4" d

"Ailanthus" pattern, purple transfer w/red, green, yellow, and blue accents, ... **85.00**

"Andalusia" pattern, green transfer, Adams, ... **265.00**

"Aurora" pattern, red transfer, ... **60.00**

"Grecian Scenery" pattern, lavender, "E.W. & S." mk, ... **125.00**

"Indian" pattern, 10 sides, green transfer w/yellow and red accents, "Livesley Powell & Co." mk, c1850, ... **75.00**

"Millenium" pattern, purple transfer, Ralph Stevenson, ... **195.00**

"Palmyra" pattern, med blue transfer, ... **30.00**

Oct, "Manilla" pattern, red transfer, S. Alcock, ... **85.00**

8 1/2" d

"Canova" pattern, red transfer, green border transfer, T. Mayer, ... **145.00**

"Dacca" pattern, black transfer, "DACCA J.C. CO." mk, ... **60.00**

"Morea" pattern, dk blue transfer, J. Goodwin, ... **110.00**

"Park Scenery" pattern, brown transfer, ... **65.00**

"The Sea" pattern, pink transfer, Adams, ... **185.00**

8 5/8" d, "Columbia" pattern, med blue, Adams and Son, ... **35.00**

8 3/4" d

"Asiatic Pheasants" pattern, lt blue transfer, Keeling, ... **55.00**

"Corinthia" pattern, pink transfer, "E. Challinor" mk, ... **75.00**

Ironstone, "Union" pattern, purple transfer, (A), ... **38.00**

"Medici" pattern, 10 sides, purple transfer w/red accents, ... **85.00**

"Pekin" pattern, blue transfer, "J. Clementson" mk, ... **45.00**

"Quadrupeds" pattern, otter, blue transfer, "Hall Quadruped" mk, ... **250.00**

"Swiss Scenery" pattern, brown transfer, ... **60.00**

"Venus" pattern, mulberry transfer, "P.W. & Co." mk, ... **35.00**

8 7/8" d, "Chinese Marine" pattern, blue transfer, Minton, ... **50.00**

Plate, 9" d, "Sicilian" pattern, med blue transfer, **$135.00**

9" d

"Blantyre" pattern, purple transfer, ... **50.00**

"Bosphorus" pattern, brown transfer, "T. & J. Mayer Longport" mk, ... **69.00**

"Davenport" pattern, blue transfer, "imp Davenport and anchor" mk, ... **45.00**

"Hannibal Passing the Alps" pattern, red transfer, (A), ... **137.00**

"Indian Temples" pattern, red transfer, ... **125.00**

"Peruvian Horse Hunt" pattern, med blue transfer, ... **145.00**

"Tyrolean" pattern, green transfer, Hall, ... **225.00**

"Union" pattern, lt purple transfer, Challinor, ... **40.00**

Plate, 10" d, "Quadrapeds" pattern, blue transfer, "R. Hall" mark, $250

10 1/2" d
"Canova" pattern
Blue transfer, "Canova-T. Mayer Longport" mk, ... **48.00**
Green center transfer, red border transfer, Mayer, ... **185.00**
"Fountain Scenery" pattern, purple center, black border, Adams, ... **395.00**
"Indian" pattern, pink transfer, Adams, ... **195.00**
Ironstone
"Boston Mails-Ladies Cabin" pattern, ship and floral border, black transfer, "imp REAL IRONSTONE and printed BOSTON MAIL" mks, hairline, (A), ... **110.00**
"Genoa" pattern, vining border, lt blue transfer, "W. Adams & Sons" mk, ... **85.00**
"Isola Bella" pattern, lt blue transfer, "Wm. Adams & Sons Stone China" mk, ... **50.00**
"Rural Scenery" pattern, dk pink transfer, Heath, ... **165.00**
10 5/8" d, "Canova" pattern, red transfer, ... **175.00**
10 3/4" d
"Marseilles" pattern, med blue transfer, ... **85.00**
"Mogal Scenery" pattern, red transfer, "red MOGAL SCENERY, T MAYER STOKE UPON TRENT," "imp T. MAYER STOKE" mks, (A), ... **135.00**
11" d
"Cologne" pattern, med blue transfer, "Cologne R.S. & S." mk, ... **100.00**
"Genoa" pattern, blue transfer, Davenport, ... **30.00**

Platter
8" l x 6 1/2" w, "Fountain" pattern, red transfer, "E. Wood & Son" mk, ... **295.00**
9 3/4" l x 8" w, "American Marine" pattern, brown transfer, Ashworth, c1862, ... **200.00**
10 3/4" l, "Indian Pagoda" pattern, brown, J. & J. Jackson, ... **425.00**
11" l x 8" w, oct, "Doria" pattern, purple transfer, ... **225.00**
12 1/4" l x 9 1/2" w, "Oriental" pattern, brown transfer, Challinor, ... **295.00**
12 3/4" l x 11" w, "Pagoda" pattern, med blue transfer, "E. Wood & Son" mk, ... **295.00**
13" l, "Canova" pattern, purple transfer, Mayer, ... **450.00**
13 1/2" l x 10 1/2" w, rect, "Columbia" pattern, med blue transfer, ... **225.00**
13 5/8" l x 10 1/4" w, oct, "Ontario Lake Scenery" pattern, lt blue transfer, Heath, ... **200.00**
14" l x 10 5/8" w, rec w/cut corners, "Boston Mails-Gentlemen's Cabin" pattern, black transfer, c1839-41, (A), ... **330.00**
Ironstone, "Ivanhoe" pattern, lt blue transfer, "PW & CO." mk, (A), ... **125.00**
14 1/4" l x 12 1/4" w, "Corinthia" pattern, brown transfer, ... **375.00**
14 1/2" l
12" w, "Asiatic Pheasant" pattern, lt blue transfer, ... **125.00**
12 1/2" w, "Tuscan Rose" pattern, med blue transfer, ... **240.00**
14 7/8" l x 11 7/8" w, "Millenium" pattern, purple transfer, ... **1,050.00**

Platter, 15" l x 11 3/4" w, "Patras" pattern, med blue transfer, "W. & G. H. Ironstone" mk, $275.00

15" l
11 3/4" w, oct, ironstone, "Siam" pattern, lt blue transfer, "J. Clementson" mk, ... **325.00**

12" w, "Dresden Roses" pattern, brown transfer, c1850, (A), ... **165.00**
12 3/4" w, "Napier" pattern, brown transfer, Alcock, crazing, ... **80.00**
15 1/2" l
12 1/2" w
"Cologne" pattern, lt red transfer, Stevenson, ... **495.00**
Oct, "Damascus" pattern, med blue transfer, Enoch Wood, ... **300.00**
"Canova" pattern, red transfer, scalloped rim, "Canova T. Mayer Stoke Upon Trent" mk, (A), ... **330.00**
"Tyrolean" pattern, blue transfer, Ridgway, ... **100.00**
16" l x 12 1/2" w, rect w/cut corners, ironstone, "Friburg" pattern, lt blue transfer, Davenport, ... **130.00**
16 1/2" l
12 1/2" w, oct, "Wild Rose" pattern, med blue transfer, unmkd, c1835, (A), ... **550.00**
14" w, "Wreath & Flowers" pattern, purple transfer, "WREATH & FLOWERS, E.W. & S" mk, ... **335.00**
17" l
13" w, oct, "Non Pariel" pattern, med blue transfer, "T.J. Mayer" mk, ... **875.00**
14" w, "British Palaces" pattern, leaf border, brown transfer, "F. Morley Co." mk, ... **300.00**
15 1/2" w, "Damascus" pattern, brown transfer, Methven & Sons, ... **250.00**
Rect, "Ornithological-Eagle," med blue transfer, ... **475.00**
"Scroll" pattern, brown transfer, canton/comb back, unmkd, c1830, (A), ... **440.00**
17 1/2" l, oct
Ironstone, "Palmyra" pattern, med blue transfer, ... **395.00**
"Non Pariel" pattern, med blue transfer, "T. & J. Mayer Longport" mk, ... **875.00**
17 3/4" l
13 3/4" w, oct, ironstone, "Ardenne" pattern, floral

sprigs on border, med blue transfer, Challinor, (A), ... **247.00**

14" w, "Pompeii" pattern, brown transfer, "brown POMPEII J & G ALCOCK" mk, (A), ... **275.00**

18 1/4" l x 14 1/4" w, "Wild Rose" pattern, brown transfer, unmkd, c1835, (A), ... **358.00**

19" l x 16" w, "Oriental" pattern, lt blue transfer, Ridgway, ... **1,400.00**

19 1/4" l x 15 1/2" w, semi-rect, "Japan Flowers" pattern, lt blue transfer, "Ridgway, Morley, Wear, & Co." mk, ... **900.00**

20" l x 16" w, oct, "Ontario Lake Scenery" pattern, lt blue transfer, ... **350.00**

Potato Bowl, 11 1/2" d, "Italian Buildings" pattern, "blue ITALIAN BUILDINGS R.HALL" mk, (A), ... **220.00**

Punch Bowl, 11" d, "Milan" pattern, brown transfers, South Wales pottery, ... **425.00**

Sauce Dish, 5 1/2" d, "Friburg" pattern, lt blue transfer, Davenport, ... **35.00**

Sauce Tureen, Cov

4 1/4" h x 5 1/2" H-H, "Asiatic Pheasants" pattern, lt blue transfer, Adams, ... **235.00**

6 1/8" h x 8" H-H, w/ladle, "Oriental Scenery" pattern, brown transfer, Thomas Mayer, (A), ... **330.00**

6 3/4" h x 7 1/2" H-H, w/undertray, 8 1/2" l x 7" w, and ladle, "Italian Flower Garden" pattern, brown transfers, John & William Ridgway, c1814-30, (A), ... **357.00**

Soup Bowl, 10" d, "Quadrupeds-Antelope" pattern, dk blue transfer, Hall, ... **330.00**

Soup Plate

9" d

"Alhambra" pattern, dk blue transfer, ... **8.00**

"Grecian" pattern, green transfer, gold rim, Ridgway, ... **14.00**

"Italian Lakes" pattern, black transfer, ... **98.00**

9 1/8" d, "Wild Rose" pattern, brown transfer, c1835, ... **75.00**

9 1/4" d, "Arcadia" pattern, med blue transfer, "M.P. Bell & Co." mk, ... **125.00**

9 1/2" d, "Ontario Lake Scenery" pattern, med blue transfer, "J.

Heath" mk, ... **70.00**

9 3/4" d, "Monopteris" pattern, blue transfer, Bevington & Co., ... **225.00**

10" d, "Venus" pattern, med blue transfer, "P.W. & Co." mk, ... **58.00**

10 1/8" d, "Italian Buildings" pattern, med blue transfer, (A), ... **88.00**

10 1/4" d

"India Temple" pattern, med blue transfer, Ridgway, ... **145.00**

"Peruvian Horse Hunt" pattern, med blue transfer, Goodwin, ... **175.00**

10 1/2" d

"Pantheon" pattern, lt blue transfer, "Ridgway & Morley" mk, ... **95.00**

"William Penn's Treaty" pattern, brown transfer, Thomas Goodwin, c1834-54, (A), ... **220.00**

10 3/4" d, "Rosetta" pattern, purple transfer w/red, green, and blue accents, Challinor, ... **145.00**

11" d, "Geneva" pattern, med blue transfer, Wedgwood, ... **38.00**

Sugar Bowl, Cov

7 1/4" h, gothic shape, "Cologne" pattern, med blue transfers, Alcock, ... **100.00**

8" h x 8" H-H, "Peruvian Hunters" pattern, flower and berry borders, med blue transfers, Goodwin & Ellis, repaired chip, ... **300.00**

Teapot

7" h x 10 1/2" w, "Pearl" pattern, red transfers, Alcock, ... **495.00**

9" h, "Boston Mails-Gentleman's Cabin" pattern, brown transfer, James and Thomas Edwards, "PORCELAIN OPAQUE" mk, spout chip repair, (A), ... **423.00**

Toddy Plate

4 1/2" d, 12 sides, ironstone, "Lozere" pattern, med blue transfer, "E. Challinor" mk, ... **38.00**

5 7/8" d, "Palestine" pattern, black transfer in center, red transfer border, Adams, ... **225.00**

6 3/4" d, "Quadrupeds" pattern, dog, sheep, horses, and squirrel, dk blue transfer, "I. Hall Quadrupeds" mk, (A), ... **206.00**

Tureen, Cov

10" h, w/undertray, 13" l x 11 1/2" w, "India Temple" pattern, med blue

transfers, repairs,.......... **1,295.00**

10 1/4" w x 9" h, "Corinth" pattern, brown transfer, James Edwards, ... **425.00**

11 1/4" h x 15" w, w/undertray, "Boston Mails" pattern, "Gentlemen's Cabin" on cov, "Ladie's Cabin" on undertray, black transfers, "imp PORCELAIN LA PERLE J.E." mk, (A), ... **2,420.00**

13" H-H x 8 1/4" h, "Wild Rose" pattern, brown transfers, unmkd, c1820, (A), ... **385.00**

Tray, 8 3/4" H-H, "Oriental" pattern, med blue transfer, Ridgway, ... **56.00**

Undertray, 8" l x 6" w, oct, "Parisian" pattern, med blue transfer, "Geo. Phillips" mk, ... **175.00**

Vegetable Bowl

10" l x 7" w, "Parthenon" pattern, green transfer, Marley, ... **140.00**

11" l x 8" w, "Parthenon" pattern, green transfer, Marley, ... **160.00**

11 3/4" l x 9 3/4" w, rect, scalloped rim, "Tuscan Rose" pattern, brown transfer, John and William Ridgway, (A), ... **137.00**

Vegetable Bowl, Cov

11" l x 5" h, "India Temple" pattern, med blue transfer, "J.W.R." mk, c1830, ... **475.00**

11 1/2" l x 8 3/4" w x 5" h, "American Marine" pattern, brown transfer, Ashworth, ... **325.00**

Waste Bowl

4 1/2" d, "Tuscan Rose" pattern, black transfer, ... **100.00**

5 1/2" d, stepped, "Venetian Temple" pattern, red transfer, ... **55.00**

STEINS

Germany
1840s to Present

History: A stein is a drinking vessel with a handle and an attached lid that is made to hold beer and ale. The use of a lid differentiates a stein from a mug. Steins range in size from the smallest at 3/10 liters or l/4 liters to the larger at 1, 1 1/2, 2, 3, 4, and 5 liters, and even 8 liters in rare cases. A liter is 1.05 liquid quarts.

General

The finest steins had proportional figures with intricate details that made them appear real. The decorations were made in a separate mold and applied to the body of the stein, giving the piece a raised effect. Etched steins, with the design incised or engraved into the body of the stein, were the most desirable and expensive steins. Artisans used black paint to fill in the lines and then other colors to complete the motif.

The simplest steins to produce were the print under glaze (PUG). A decal or transfer printed scene was applied by the transfer method, the body was covered with an additional coat of transparent glaze, and the piece was refired.

Character or figural steins depicted life-like creations of Indians heads, skulls, animals, Satans, vegetables, buildings, and people. Ernst Bohne's firm produced fine quality figural steins with realistic expressions.

Occupational steins were steins with a decoration or shape that depicted the owner's occupation. A slogan or the owner's name also may have appeared on the stein.

Thumblifts also came in a variety of designs on steins. Steins designed specifically for export to the United States had a United States shield as the thumblift. Other designs included a monkey, owl, jester, lyre, bust of a figure, twin towers, eagle, Munich maid, lion and shield, dwarf, or huntsman.

Mettlach Steins

The most prolific period in the history of stein production occurred in the second half of the 19th century, coinciding with the peak of Mettlach stein manufacture.

Chromoliths made by Mettlach were molded. The designs appeared to be etched by hand. Although the designs seemed three-dimensional, they were smooth to the touch.

Mettlach's cameos or phanoliths had portraits or small scenes in a translucent white clay set against a green or blue background. Even though these were three dimensional, the relief portions were blended into the background without showing seams.

In 1921 when fire destroyed the abbey where Mettlach steins were produced, the company gave up production of chromoliths and cameos. Mettlach's stein competitors included Merkelbach and Wick, Albert Jacob Thewalt, Simon Peter Gerz, and the Girmscheid factory.

Regimental Steins

During the reign of Kaiser Wilhelm II, (1888 to 1918), German reservists frequently purchased souvenir steins that had information such as the owner's name, unit, garrison town, service dates, and rosters of comrades inscribed on them.

Munich was the regimental stein capital. Most of the regimental steins date from the early 1890s.

Other European armies also issued regimental steins after the 1890s. A great variety of transfer scenes, finials, stein bodies, and lids was used for regimental steins. Lid varieties that included the finial type, screw off, fuse, flat, prism, steeple or spindle, helmet, or crown have been identified. The thumblift on the stein usually represented the unit's state of origin or branch of service. Stein body size was usually the standard 1/2 liter. Pottery steins typically had maker's marks, but porcelain steins rarely did.

Mettlach military steins were only made in pottery. They were marked on the bottom with an incised stock or mold number and usually were dated.

References: J.L. Harrell, *Regimental Steins*, The Old Soldier Press, 1979; Gary Kirsner, *German Military Steins 1914-1945, 2nd Ed.* self published, 1996; Gary Kirsner, *The Mettlach Book*, Seven Hills Books, 1983; Gary Kirsner & Jim Gruhl, *The Stein Book, A 400 Year History*, Glentiques, 1999; Dr. Eugene Manusov, *Encyclopedia of Character Steins*, Wallace Homestead, 1976; Dr. Eugene Manusov & Mike Wald, *Character Steins: A Collectors Guide*, Cornwall Books, 1987; R.H. Mohr, *Mettlach Steins & Their Prices, Rev. 4th Ed.* Rockford, 1972; R.H. Mohr, *Mettlach Steins, 9th Ed.* privately printed, 1982; James R. Stevenson, *Antique Steins, A Collectors' Guide*, Cornwall books, 1982; Mike Wald, *HR Steins*, SCI Publications, 1980; J.A. Schmoll & Therese Thomas, *Heinrich Schlitt 1849-1923*.

Collectors' Club: Stein Collectors International, Inc. Marianne Gruskin, P.O. Box 371, Greenlawn, NY 17740-0371, www.mgruskin@aol.com, Membership: $25.00, Magazine *Prosit*.

Museum: Milwaukee Art Center, Milwaukee, WI.

Reproduction Alert: For more than twenty years, several German firms have reproduced regimental-type steins. The reproductions, usually made only in porcelain, have different physical characteristics and historical inaccuracies. The firms have used only the finial type of lid and tapered bodies, as opposed to the straight bodies on original regimentals. Smooth transfers appear on the reproductions. Lids on the reproductions are stamped from a single piece mold and have no seam line.

Collecting Hints: Collectors favor regimental steins with inlaid lids. The inlay is a decorated stoneware disk that is set in a pewter rim. The design in the lid is an extension of the colors and designs on the main body of the stein. A few steins did come without lids or with an all-pewter lid in a variety of designs. Steins with missing lids are generally reduced fifty percent in value.

After the destruction caused by World War II, locating regimental steins became difficult. Occasionally some are found in German attics or barns.

Journals: *The Beer Stein Journal*, P.O. Box 8807, Coral Springs, FL 33075. $20 per year. Quarterly, Publisher: Gary Kirsner; *Regimental Quarterly*, John Harrell, P.O. Box 793, Frederick, MD 21705.

*1 L, tin glazed, blue and white, pewter base and lid, dtd "1744," Germany, **$2,250.00***

Design

.5L

Porcelain, multicolored floral print and ribbon w/German saying, pewter lid and thumbrest, lithophane of couple at table in house, ... **200.00**

Stoneware

Art Nouveau blue salt glazed engraved repeating swirl and shell designs, pewter lid, ... **100.00**

Arts and Crafts, enameled red heart in white circle on green geometric, German saying on front, brown ground, pewter lid and thumblift, ... **285.00**

Chip carved white and turquoise half fans, brown ground, pewter ring base, pewter ring top and lid, Muskau, (A), ... **2,770.00**

Engraved starburst on front w/strapping, grey body, pewter lid, c1800, (A), ... **483.00**

Glazed circle design, dk brown glazed body, pewter base ring and lid, c1920, (A), ... **200.00**

Grey w/engraved cobalt accented birds and floral designs, Westerwald, pewter lid, Westerwald, c1820, (A), ... **780.00**

Incised circle and wave design, blue salt glaze, pewter lid, (A), ... **425.00**

1L, stoneware, etched blue outlined design of bird over German verse, pewter lid, (A), ... **378.00**

1.5L, stoneware, brown w/band of Art Nouveau floral engraving on neck, pewter lid, Merkelbach, (A), ... **242.00**

.25 L, "Munich Child, " black robe, gold vest, dbl tower pewter thumb rest, lithophane of Munich, "Jos. Mayer" on base, c1900, $575.00

Figural

.25L. Friar Tuck, brown robe, "V-sm bee, T7411" mk, Goebel, ... **375.00**

.3L

Smoking Pig, inlaid lid, Schierholz, (A), ... **575.00**

Snake on apple, replaced inlaid lid, E. Bohne & Sohne, (A), .. **392.00**

.5L

Porcelain

Alligator, inlaid lid, E. Bohne & Sohne, (A), ... **695.00**

Bismark, porcelain lid, Schierholz, (A), ... **425.00**

Bismark Radish, inlaid lid, Schierholz, (A), ... **242.00**

Black Student, porcelain inlaid lid, (A), ... **518.00**

Frog, porcelain lid, Schierholz, repaired chip, (A), ... **725.00**

Men standing under umbrella, pewter lid, lithophane, repaired chip, (A), ... **805.00**

Munich Child, black robe, porcelain lid, "Jos. M. Mayer Munchen" mk, (A), ... **362.00**

Munich Child on barrel, porcelain lid, repaired pewter, (A), ... **605.00**

Pig w/cards on chest, inlaid lid, pewter repair, (A), ... **333.00**

Rich man holding bag of money, inlaid lid, Hutschenreuther, hairlines, (A), ... **512.00**

Singing Pig, crossed hoofs, inlaid lid, Schierholz, (A), ... **253.00**

Skull on Book, inlaid lid, E. Bohne & Sohne, (A), ... **518.00**

Pottery

Basket, tan, brown, and green woven design, inlaid rim, (A), ... **310.00**

Clown, red and yellow stripes, inlaid lid, (A), ... **725.00**

Dice, inlaid lid, thumblift repair, (A), ... **830.00**

Fish, inlaid lid, (A), ... **363.00**

Stoneware, owl, purple salt glaze, inlaid lid, "Hauber & Reuther #64" mk, (A), ... **277.00**

1L, porcelain, Munich Child, black robe, turquoise trim, porcelain lid, "Martin Pauson Munchen" mk, (A), ... **775.00**

2L, porcelain, Munich Child, black robe, gold cowl, porcelain lid, repaired damage, "Jos. M. Mayer Munchen" mk, (A), ... **1,210.00**

1 L, etched design, inlaid lid, #2780, Mettlach, $850.00

Mettlach

#715, .5L, PUG, drunken revelers, named cities on base, pewter lid and thumblift, artist sgd, ... **250.00**

#1028, .5L, cameo, brown tree trunk w/white cameos of grapes and wheat ears, panels of man and woman on sides, German saying, ... **100.00**

#1395, .5L, etched scene of French card players, fruit inlaid lid, (A), ... **300.00**

#1467, .5L, relief design of 4 seasons, tan, grey, and brown, inlaid lid, ... **135.00**

#1471, .5L, etched, musicians, inlaid lid, hairlines, (A), ... **145.00**

#1477, .5L, etched design of dwarfs carrying grapes, inlaid lid, (A), ... **465.00**

#1526

601, .5L, PUG, dwarfs in wine cellar, pewter lid, (A), ... **190.00**

1108, .5L, PUG, festive scene, pewter lid, Schlitt, (A), ... **290.00**

#1856, 1L, etched and glazed, post eagle, pewter lid, (A), ... **1,175.00**

#1896, .25L, grey relief design of woman sewing on front, cherub on side, tan clusters of vines, inlaid lid, ... **345.00**

#1909-727, .3L, PUG, dwarfs bowling, "Schlitt," (A), ... **195.00**

#1914, .5L, etched, man holding flag, shield w/German saying, inlaid cov, (A), ... **600.00**

#1915, .5L, etched and PUG of Trier Dom, inlaid lid, ... **850.00**

#1940, 3L, etched, keeper of the cellar, inlaid lid, sgd "Wrath," **1,600.00**

#2001C, .5L, etched and relief scholars, inlaid lid, (A), ... **760.00**

#2007, .5L, etched design of black cat, inlaid lid, (A), ... **695.00**

#2008, .5L, etched design of Trumpeter of Sackingen, inlaid lid, Stuck, (A), ... **725.00**

#2179, .25L, PUG, gnome drinking beer, sgd "Schlitt," **200.00**

#2180, (955), 3.3L, PUG, tavern scene, pewter lid, sgd "Schlitt," **750.00**

#2182, .5L, cameo of drinking and bowling, dk blue ground, inlaid lid, ... **795.00**

#2261-1012, 2.25L, PUG, Germans and Romans drinking, pewter lid, (A), ... **715.00**

#2262-1211, 4.2L, PUG, wedding design, replaced pewter lid, Schlitt, (A), ... **1,690.00**

#2277, .3L, etched design of Heidelberg Castle, inlaid lid w/German sayings, ... **315.00**

#2382, .5L, etched, "The Thirsty Knight," peaked ceramic lid, sgd "H. Schlitt," (A), ... **765.00**

#2482, 1.4L, etched scene of man shooting rifle at target, "jeweled" base, inlaid lid, sgd "Quidenus," **1,650.00**

#2652, .5L, cameo, three scenes of drunken men, castle tower shape, inlaid lid, (A), ... **690.00**

#2716, 1L, etched scene of barmaid serving 2 men, inlaid lid, sgd "Quidenus," **1,100.00**

#2755, .5L, etched knight on white horse, castle lid, pewter knight's head thumblift, (A), ... **1,430.00**

2.2 liter, 15 1/4" h, boy with flute, brown glazes, pewter lid, #2786, Mettlach, A-$575.00

#2782, 4.3L, PUG, Rookwood type cavalier, brown shades, pewter lid, ... **640.00**

#2796, 3L, etched, Heidelberg Castle, inlaid lid, (A), ... **1,095.00**

#2833, .5L, etched design of fraternity students drinking, inlaid lid, (A), ... **485.00**

#2889, .5L, etched design of horseman taking stein from maiden w/German sayings, inlaid lid, ... **390.00**

#2917, 1L, etched and glazed, skyline of Munich, figural inlaid lid of lion w/Bavarian shield, (A), ... **4,225.00**

#2959, .5L, etched design of bowling, inlaid lid, F. Quidenus, chips, (A), ... **200.00**

#2962-15, 3 panels of inlaid WWI scenes on cobalt ground, pewter lid, (A), ... **275.00**

#3091, .5L, etched design of knight drinking, inlaid lid, Schlitt, (A), ... **775.00**

#3193, .5L, etched and glazed man in wreath, inlaid lid, F. Ringer, pewter strap repair, (A), ... **785.00**

Regimental

.5L

Porcelain

1. Komp. II. Bad. Grenard. Regt. K.W.I. No. 110, Mannheim 1911-13, named Grenad. Ohnsmann, 4 side scenes, roster, griffin thumblift, pewter repair, (A), ... **485.00**

2. Bayr. Jager Batl. 4 Comp. Aschaffenburg 1908-10, named Gef. Storath, 2 side scenes, roster, St. Hubertus thumblift, pewter repair, (A), ... **965.00**

3. Esc. 2. Leib-Husar. No. 2 Danzig 1903, named Res. Klemm, 2 side scenes, eagle thumblift, skull and crossbones on front, replaced finial, (A), ... **1,690.00**

3. Pionier Batl. 2. Co. Munchen 1901-03, named Franz Cangauer, 4 side scenes, occupational scene under handle-carpenter, lion thumblift, glass prism inlaid lid w/scene, lines in lithophane, (A), ... **370.00**

4. Batt. 2. Ead. Feld. Art. Regt. Nr. 30. Rastatt 1912-14. named Res. Gef. Eickmeier, 4 side scenes and roster, griffin thumblift, screw lid w/porcelain inlay, Stanhope, pewter strap repair, (A), ... **720.00**

4. Chev. Rgt. 1. Eskadr. Augsburg 1902-05. named Chevauleger Freiberger, 4 side scenes and roster, lion thumblift, lithophane, repaired pewter, (A), ... **290.00**

4. Esk. 3. Bayr. Chevaulgr. Regmt. Dieuze, 1906-09, named Chevauleger Schussele, 4 side scenes, roster, lion thumblift w/stanhope, (A), ... **690.00**

5. Esk. Kgl. Sachs. Karabiner Rgt. Borno, 1910-13, named Karabinier Venus, 4 side scenes, roster, Sachsen thumblift, screw top, green glass jewel, repaired pewter, (A), ... **1,510.00**

8 Comp. Inf. Rgt. No. 120 Ulm-Weingarten 1897-99, named Musk. Schlagenhauf, 4 side scenes, bird thumblift, (A), ... **400.00**

11 Comp. Inftr. Regiment 8. No. 70 Saarbrucken 1903-05, named Res. Kamphausen, 2 side scenes, eagle thumblift, kneeling soldier finial, (A), ... **425.00**

Feldart. Rgt. General-Feldzeugmeister 1. Brandenb. 3. Brandenburg 1904-06, named Res. Paul, 2 side scenes, roster, St. Barbara thumblift, hairlines, (A), ... **518.00**

Hus. Rgt. No.13 Mainz 1900-03, named Res. Zschemisch, 2 side scenes, roster, eagle thumblift w/stanhope scene, repoured pewter strap, (A), ... **435.00**

Kgl. Bay. 3. Inft. Regt. 11. Comp. Augsburg 1907-09, named Josef Bayer, 4 side scenes, roster, lion thumblift, pewter strap repoured, hairline in lithophane, (A), ... **240.00**

1 liter, 13 1/2" h, stoneware, blue and tan accents, grey ground, pewter lid, Simon Peter Gerz, c1900, $420.00

1L

Porcelain, Freiw Sanitatskolone, Trstberg 1908, named Josef

Schmid, pewter lid w/inscription, (A), ... **2,415.00**
Pottery, 3 lg scenes, eagle thumblift, unnamed, (A), ... **605.00**

Scenic

.25L, porcelain, painted panel of mythological man and woman painting on canvas, cherub in foreground, gilt herringbone frame, inlaid lid w/painted scene of sleeping woman and man applying wrap, int lid painted w/couple, crown knob, "blue beehive" mk,
.... **4,500.00**

.5L

Bust of peasant woman on red ground in oval, pewter lid, Germany, ... **145.00**
Faience, ochre, green, and manganese German steepled house and weathervane, blue water in front, manganese and green trees, pewter lid and foot, Germany, ... **4,000.00**
Occupational
Baker, center scene and 2 side scenes, named "Peter Ungeheuer," lithophane, pewter lid, (A), ... **195.00**
Barrel maker, 5 men in workroom, multicolored transfer and enameled, pewter lid, (A), ... **375.00**
Beer brewer, multicolored transfer and enamels, pewter lid, (A), ... **330.00**
Stoneware, multicolored scene of courting couple in green lined reserve on front, German sayings and hanging mug on side in green lined reserve, pewter lid, ... **125.00**

1L, stoneware, occupational, Jockey, multicolored transfer and enamels, named Sebastian Beilmeier, relief pewter lid of man and woman, horse head thumblift, staining, (A), ... **345.00**

3L, stoneware, grey relief of standing king holding foaming stein on blue ground in raised grey cartouche on front, grey relief of cherubs, grapes, sheaves, and leaves on blue ground in cartouches on sides, brown ground between designs, relief mask spout, pewter lid, unmkd, ... **100.00**

5L, center transfer w/enamel accents of classic figures in clouds between gilt tracery accented burgundy bands,

gold handle, Royal Vienna, (A),
.... **965.00**

STIRRUP CUPS

Staffordshire, England
c1770-1890

History: Whieldon made the first earthenware stirrup cups. They dated about 1770 and were in the shape of fox masks. Later animal shapes included deer, stag, hare, and bear heads.

The Staffordshire potters made a wide variety of stirrup cups, and they were rarely marked. Until 1825 the earthenware stirrup cups were well modeled and colored in naturalistic tones. After that date, quality decreased.

During the last quarter of the 19th century, stirrup cups were made in soft paste porcelain by Derby, Rockingham, and Coalport. In addition to wild animal heads, bull dog, bull terrier, setter and Dalmatian heads were manufactured.

Fox Head, 4 5/8" l, pearlware, white glaze, $595.00

Fox Head

3 1/2" l, rust ground, black nose and rim, ... **90.00**
4 1/2" l, HP red w/yellow eyes and rim, (A), ... **465.00**
5" l
Orange-brown head, white face, black muzzle and eyes, c1920s, ... **135.00**
Orange head, black nose and trim, lt green leaf trim and raised berries, ... **225.00**
Porcelain, white w/gilt ears, facial accents, and "Tally Ho," (A),
.... **1,045.00**
Tan body, grey nose, black sponged ears and trim, early 19th C, ... **950.00**
5 1/4" l, HP red w/incised whiskers, black muzzles, gilt trim, repairs, (A), ... **495.00**

5 1/2" l, overall white glaze, hairline,
.... **925.00**
7 1/4" l, brown face, white eyes, vert boot back, black bootstraps, stripes, and handle, ... **4,200.00**
Foxhound, 5" l, dk tan ground, sponged black ears, ... **950.00**
Greyhound Head, 6 1/8" l, lavender glaze, ... **850.00**
Hare, 3 1/4" h, iron-red streaked head, black tipped ears and eyes, curved handle to gold accented cup on top, c1820, ... **4,200.00**

*Hound, 4 1/2" l, brown splashes and ears, black nose, **$1,650.00***

Hound

4 1/2" l, pearlware, brown ears, black nose and eyes, brown rim,
.... **1,650.00**
5" l, tan head w/black and yellow eyes, grey muzzle and nose, black outlined mouth, c1880,
.... **695.00**
5 1/4" l, pearlware, black and white, blue collar, c1815, (A),
.... **1,675.00**
Pug Dog, 3 3/4" l, white glaze,
.... **295.00**
Ram's Head
4 1/2" h, Pratt style, yellow horns, white face, ochre coat, cobalt and ochre trim on collar, (A),
.... **1,045.00**
6 1/2" l, HP brown shades, gilt rim, "blue X'd swords" mk, (A),
.... **495.00**
Viking, 5" h, figural head, red, yellow, and blue lined peaked helmet, brown streaked base, smile face when reversed, "A Cup of Drink Taken By a Fider Aboiut Cup," chips and repairs, ... **1,375.00**

STONEWARE

London and Staffordshire, England
c1670 to Present

History: Stoneware, made from clay to which some sand had been added, was

fired at a higher temperature than ordinary earthenwares and became partly vitrified and impervious to liquids. Often it was glazed by throwing salt into the kiln at full heat. (See: Salt Glaze.)

Stoneware was first made in England in 1672 when John Dwight founded Fulham Pottery and received a patent. He started by making copies of German wine jugs called "graybeards" and also modeled portrait busts, jugs, mugs, and red clay teapots. Dwight died in 1703. Fulham Pottery was carried on by his family. Dwight's examples were unmarked.

In Staffordshire, John and Philip Elers made red stonewares and also introduced salt glazing and other improvements. Stoneware was made by firms throughout the Staffordshire Potteries district. Most stoneware was utilitarian in nature, but some of the useful wares were given a decorative treatment.

The Morleys made brown salt glazed stonewares in Nottingham between 1700 and 1799. Doulton & Watts were the best known and largest manufacture of commercial stonewares. English stoneware is still made, especially by present day studio potters like Bernard Leach, Charles Vyse, and Michael Cardew.

References: J.F. Blacker, *The A.B.C. of English Salt Glaze Stoneware from Dwight to Doulton*, Stanley Paul & Co. 1922; Jonathan Horne, *English Brown Stoneware*, Antique Collectors' Club, Ltd. 1985; Adrean Oswald, R.J.C. Hildyard, & R.G. Hughes, *English Brown Stoneware 1670-1900*, Faber & Faber, 1982; Edwards, *English Dry-Bodied Stoneware, Wedgwood, & Contemporary Manufacturers, 1774-1830*, 1998.

Museums: British Museum, London, England; Cincinnati Art Museum, Cincinnati, OH; County Museum, Truro, England; Victoria & Albert Museum, London, England.

Apothecary Jar, 7" h, straight sides, Switzerland, (A), ... **35.00**
Beaker, 4 3/8" h, flared, loop handle, cobalt cross, brown salt glazed, hairlines, Germany, ... **95.00**
Bottle, 13 1/8" h, bulbous body, ftd, coil handle, cobalt floral design on front, 2 cobalt rings on neck, Westerwald, ... **85.00**
Butter Churn, 16" h, cobalt stylized 3 petal flower in half circle, hanging chain of cobalt circles, band of half circles and dots on cov, wooden paddle, Westerwald, ... **195.00**
Crock
    7 1/2" h, dk blue stylized flower, horiz grooves top and base, blue outlined loop handles, salt glaze, Betschdorf, France, ... **20.00**

9 1/4" h, cobalt stylized flower, cobalt bands under rim, dashes on handles, Westerwald, c1900, ... **125.00**
10 3/8" h, cobalt swept floral design, blue stripes on handles, Westerwald, ... **70.00**
Cup, 3 1/4" h, hand thrown brown stoneware, lt green slip int, salt glaze finish, England, ... **110.00**
Ewer, 10 1/2" h, cobalt relief of bust of woman's head in medallion on front, relief molded cobalt arabesques and meandering vines, mask spout, grey body, Rhineland, 19th C, ... **85.00**
Game Pot, 9 1/4" l x 13 1/2" l, oval, relief of farmers plowing and sowing seeds, brown glaze, applied ram heads on ends, lion knob w/acanthus leaves, hairline, (A), ... **440.00**

Jug, 20 1/2" h, dk blue center band, handle, and rim, tan ground, Germany, $1,250.00

Jug
    6 1/2" h, dry body, blue ground w/white sprigged designs of classical figures, trees, foliage band around collar, (A), ... **50.00**
7 1/8" d, Bellarmine, oval bearded bust on neck, medallion of soldier in wavy oval on body, flat, strap handle, mottled brown ground, ... **1,500.00**
9 1/4" h, bearded mask on neck, rosette on base, dk brown salt glazed, restored handle, ... **325.00**
13 1/2" h, ovoid w/incised rings around spout and shoulder, incised cobalt walking rooster, incised cobalt leaf design, molded strap handle, Germany, (A), ... **193.00**

Mug, 6 3/4" h, "G R" in center molded cartouche w/cobalt flower petals, cobalt circles, manganese incised lines on neck, c1770, Westerwald, ... **895.00**
Oil Jar, 11 7/8" h, 3 strap handles, sm spout, green drip over textured brown body, France, 19th C, chips, ... **175.00**

Pitcher, 8 3/4" h, brown ext, white int, "imp GERMANY" mark, $40.00

Pitcher
    8 1/4" h, olive green, brown, lt blue, white, and tan marbleized body, circ white medallion of emb scene of hunter and dog on front, pewter lid, Staffordshire, (A), ... **605.00**
9" h, raised cobalt outlined alpine flower on sides, cobalt accented rope bands on neck and foot, cobalt German saying on front, grey pebble textured ground, applied handle, chip, ... **350.00**
Pot, 4 1/2" h, "black Rich Preserved Cream-Wigtownshire Creamery Co," tan glazed ground, ... **30.00**
Tankard
    8" h, "G R" in center medallion, center band of cobalt diamonds, incised and cobalt horiz lines, Westerwald, ... **2,400.00**
12" h, horiz ribbing, dbl loop handle, brown glaze, England, ... **25.00**
Teapot
    3 1/4" h, squat shape, brown fluted body, floral knob, "imp S & H BRIDDON" mk, (A), ... **120.00**
4 1/2" h, red stoneware, cylinder shape, relief molded oriental trailing flowering plant on sides,

molded shell, snail, and flower on cov, silver gilt mtd loop handle and lady bust knob, c1720, chips, (A), ... **6,950.00**

Tureen, Cov, 13" h x 11" H-H, molded textured tan ground w/relief molded green grape leaves and stems, brown figural pig handles, pig head and snout knob, Germany, .. **875.00**

Vase

9 1/4" h, jar shape, horiz ribbing, brown curved streaks from collar, blue-grey ground, "Nowotny" mk, ... **650.00**

11 1/4" h, bulbous middle, spread base, flared neck, 2 pierced handles from shoulder to rim, blue and purple threaded and relief starbursts and geometrics, Germany, (A), ... **95.00**

14" h, flared, brown high relief of grape clusters, leaves, and vines, France, c1860, pr, ... **1,500.00**

Water Jug, 14" h, tan glaze on top, buff below, "SOUTHSEA IDEAL MINERAL WATERS LIMITED GREEN ROAD SOUTHSEA" on front, ... **150.00**

Wine Jar

7 1/4" h, incised and painted cobalt bird under spout, flower under handle, grey salt glazed ground, Westerwald, ... **360.00**

12" h, blue-black splashes on grey ground, Westerwald, ... **90.00**

Wine Jar, Cov, 11 3/8" h, sprigged hunting scenes and windmill on brown shaded ground, SP rim and cov, "imp John Cliff & Co. Lambeth" mk, ... **390.00**

Wine Pitcher, 10 3/4" h, incised cobalt checkerboard design, grey body, blue lined rim, ... **195.00**

STRAWBERRY CHINA

Staffordshire, England
1820-1860

History: Strawberry china ware, a soft earthenware produced by a variety of English potteries, was made in three design motifs: strawberry and strawberry leaves (often called strawberry luster); green feather-like leaves with pink flowers (often called cut-strawberry, primrose or old strawberry); and with the decoration in relief. The first two types were characterized by rust-red moldings. Most examples had a creamware ground and were unmarked.

Coffee Can and Saucer, red strawberries, purple luster leaves, tendrils, and rim, age crack, .. **30.00**

Cream Jug, 3 3/4" h, red and green strawberries, (A), ... **95.00**

Cup and Saucer, red berries, green leaves

Pink luster tendrils and trim, ... **50.00**

Red swirled tendrils, lines, ovals, and rims, ... **175.00**

Cup and Saucer, Handleless

Band of red berries w/green foliage, squiggled tendrils, (A), ... **50.00**

Miniature, yellow, green, and brown flowers and fruit, Leeds, repairs, (A), ... **220.00**

Dessert Service, master plate, 11" w x 12 1/2" H-H, 8 plates, 7 1/4" d, group of red strawberries and leaves on borders, gilt outlined lobed rims, "Hackefors Porslin Sweden" mks, ... **175.00**

Mug, 2 7/8" h, lt pink strawberries, lt blue crisscross spatter, (A), ... **412.00**

Plate, 6 3/4" h, black transfer in center, red and green strawberries, relief molded border, **$155.00**

Plate

6 1/4" d, "Strawberry Festival" pattern, Myott, set of 6, ... **10.00**

7 5/8" d, creamware, painted red strawberries w/green stems, pink leaves, pink luster rim, ... **45.00**

7 3/4" d, 12 sides, gaudy ironstone, red, cobalt, green, and copper luster design, ... **100.00**

8 1/2" d, HP red strawberries, white flowers, green leaves, Bavaria, ... **10.00**

8 3/4" d, red berries, purple sprigs, green foliage, scalloped rim, (A), ... **132.00**

9" d, relief molded underglazed cobalt leaves, red strawberries, gilt accents, Staffordshire, c1830, ... **250.00**

9 7/8" d, creamware, 2 lg red strawberries, green foliage in center, sprigs on inner border, pink border w/diamond overlay design, Leeds, ... **425.00**

10 1/4" d, ironstone, 12 sides, red strawberries, pink flowers, flow blue leaves, (A), ... **248.00**

Serving Bowl, 10 1/2" w, quatrefoil shape, red strawberries, red and yellow blossoms, brown stems and green leaves, spiral molded border, gold rim, "James Kent Old Foley" mk, ... **45.00`**

Soup Plate

8 1/4" d, soft paste, red and yellow berries, green leaves, yellow centered blue flowers in pink basket, border of red and yellow strawberries, green leaves, red single stroke flowers and yellow centered red petaled half flowers, (A), ... **880.00**

9 1/2" d, 12 sides, ironstone, gaudy red berries, cobalt stems and tendrils, and green leaves, copper luster trim, rim chip, (A), ... **358.00**

Teapot, 10" l x 6 1/2" h, red strawberries, green foliage, brown lined rims, **$1,250.00**

Teapot, Soft Paste

5" h, sm size w/tall, flaring rim, HP red and green strawberries on lid and shoulder, hairlines, (A), ... **300.00**

6 1/4" h, molded swirl rib bands on center body and collar w/raised strawberries, red, yellow, and lt green enamel accents, repaired lid, (A), ... **330.00**

7" h x 9 1/2" l, pearlware, vert ribbed body, HP mustard yellow strawberries, green leaves and tendrils, blue banded collar and spout rim, ribbed cov w/green leaves and tendrils, and blue band, repairs, (A), ... **100.00**

A
SUSIE COOPER
PRODUCTION
CROWN WORKS,
BURSLEM
ENGLAND
c1932

SUSIE COOPER

Burslem, Staffordshire, England
1932 to Present

History: Susie Cooper studied at the Burslem Art School in Staffordshire in 1922. She made jugs, bowls, and vases in stoneware with Art Nouveau-style incised designs. When Cooper finished her studies, she became a designer for A.E. Grey & Co. Ltd. at Hanley, Staffordshire in 1925.

She founded Susie Cooper Pottery, Burslem in 1932. Cooper designed and manufactured functional-shape earthenware tablewares with bright floral and abstract designs. Cooper introduced the "can" shape for the coffeepot, the straight-sided shape that has become a universal design. Art Deco designs of bright oranges, greens, and browns were found on her later wares.

One of Cooper's most well-known bird shapes was the Kestrel range of tablewares introduced in 1932. Coffee, tea, and dinnerware were all produced in the Kestrel shape, which was so popular it remained in production until the late 1950s. Other bird shapes included Curlew in 1932, Wren in 1934, and Falcon in 1937.

Susie Cooper experimented with many decorating techniques for her wares. She developed the "Crayon Loop" pattern utilizing a crayoning technique, in which color was made into sticks to draw on the wares. She used an aerographing technique for sgraffito patterns as in "Scroll" and "Astral." Cooper also utilized tubelining and "in-glaze" decorations.

For thirty years, Susie Cooper pottery was located at the Crown Works, Burslem. Patterns designed during the 1930s included "Bronze Chrysanthemums," "Scarlet Runner Beans," "A Country Brunch," "Orchids," "Shepherd's Purse," "Dresden Spray," "Nosegay," "Printemps," "Grey Leaf," "Cactus," and "Woodlands."

In addition to tablewares, Susie Cooper made vases, jugs, figures, wall masks, lamp bases, centerpieces, water and lemonade sets, cruet sets, cheese stands, candlesticks, ashtrays, hors d'oeuvres sets, and nursery wares during the 1930s.

She introduced lithography in 1935 to ensure both speed and accuracy. "No. 1017" was a best seller for about twenty years, and Cooper followed with other lithographed patterns. Pattern numbers on pieces indicated whether they were before or after "Dresden Spray," which was helpful in dating.

Wartime, as well as fires in 1942 and 1957, slowed production. Bone china was introduced in the 1950s when Susie Cooper acquired Jason China Company, Ltd. Some of the same patterns were used for both earthenware and bone china. The last earthenware patterns were made in 1964. Bone china patterns in the 1960s included "Persia," "Venetia," "Assyrian Motif," and "Corinthian."

Susie Cooper died in 1994 at age 92. Her pottery eventually became part of the Wedgwood Group and patterns now decorate fine bone china tableware with the Wedgwood-Susie Cooper Design backstamp. The "can" coffeepot shape is still used.

References: Andrew Casey, *Susie Cooper Ceramics, A Collectors Guide*, Jazz Publications, Ltd. 1992; Ann Eatwell, *Susie Cooper Productions*, Victoria & Albert Museum, Faber & Faber, 1987; Reginald G. Haggar, *Century of Art Education in the Potteries*, 1953; Francis Salmon, *Collecting Susie Cooper, 1st Ed.*, Francis Joseph Publications, Ltd. 1995; Judy Spours, *Art Deco Tableware*, Rizzoli, 1988; Adrian Woodhouse, *Susie Cooper*, Tribly Books, l992; Bryn Youds, *Susie Cooper: An Elegant Affair*, Thames & Hudson, Inc. 1996; Bryn Youds, *The Ceramic Art of Susie Cooper*, Thames & Hudson, 1996; General Editors: Andrew Casey & Ann Eatwell, *Susie Cooper, A Pioneer of Modern Design*, Antique Collectors Club, 2002.

Collectors' Club: Susie Cooper Collectors Group, Bryn Youds/Allison Dobbs, P.O. Box 7436, London N12 7QF, UK. Membership: $15.00, Quarterly newsletter.

Museum: Victoria & Albert Museum, London, England.

Berry Set, master bowl, 9 1/4" d, 6 bowls, 5 1/2" d, "Nosegay" pattern, ... **500.00**

Bouillon Cup and Saucer, 4 1/2" H-H, "Dresden Spray" pattern, blue-green border, ... **25.00**

Bowl
  7 5/8" d, "Feathers" pattern, brown shaded border, ... **15.00**
  8 3/4" w x 5" h, w/underplate, modeled lotus blossom, matte white glaze, ... **120.00**
  10" d, "Blue Rings" pattern, ... **45.00**

Cake Plate, 9 1/2" sq, "Nasturtium" pattern, ... **15.00**

Candleholder, 3 3/4" d, "Cornpoppy" pattern, pr, ... **89.00**

Cereal Bowl
  6" d, int w/painted sailboat, yellow sails, red hull, blue and green stylized waves, orange and blue lined rim, "A Susie Cooper Production" mk, ... **150.00**
  6 1/2" d, "Green Spiral" pattern, "A Susie Cooper Production" mk, ... **10.00**

Coffee Cup and Saucer, black conc rings on cup, cream ground, orange int, saucer w/black conc bands and thin orange band, ... **45.00**

Coffeepot, 7 1/4" h, Kestral shape, coffee can and saucer, cream sgraffito crescents, orange ground, "Susie Cooper Crown Works England" marks, coffeepot, $795., coffee can and saucer, $225.00

Coffeepot
  6 1/2" h, grey and red "Tulip" pattern, Rex shape, ... **100.00**
  7 1/2" h, "Patricia Rose" pattern, ... **550.00**

Coffee Service, pot, 7 1/2" h, cream jug, 4 1/4" h, sugar bowl, 4" d, 6 cups and saucers, "Nosegay" pattern, Kestrel shape, ... **600.00**

Cream Jug
  2 3/4" h, "Pink Printemps" pattern, mkd, ... **65.00**
  3 3/8" h, "Dresden Spray" pattern, green int, "A Susie Cooper Production Crown Works Burslem England" mk, ... **55.00**
  3 1/2" h, "Ferndown" pattern, ... **10.00**

Cup and Saucer
  "Astral" shape, lt olive green polka dots, ... **15.00**
  "Can" shape, "Persia" pattern, ... **10.00**
  "Musicians" pattern, ... **10.00**
  "Patricia Rose" pattern, pink rose, cream ground, blue trim, ... **100.00**

Cup and Saucer, Demitasse
"Azalea" pattern, ... **40.00**
"Dresden Spray" pattern, green
        shaded ground, ... **25.00**
"Pineapple" pattern, mauve ground,
        .... **25.00**
Dish, 11" d, 5 blue edged sections
        w/center sauce well, each w/painted
        vegetable in center, blue lined rim,
        mkd, ... **145.00**
Egg Cup, 1 3/4" h, bone china, "Lily"
        pattern, white closed tulip w/green
        foliage, gold rim, ... **55.00**
Gravy Boat, 7 3/4" l, w/undertray, 8 5/8"
        l, dk blue ground w/sgraffito "Scroll"
        design, dk brown rim, "Falcon"
        shape, ... **95.00**

*Jug, 4 3/4" h, "Tiger Lily" pattern, Kestrel shape,
red-brown border and handle, **$50.00***

Jug
3 1/2" h, "Swansea Sprays" pattern,
        pink colorway, ... **69.00**
4 1/2" h, "Dresden Spray" pattern,
        .... **95.00**
4 3/4" h, "Cubist," red, yellow, black,
        blue, and green color blocks,
        steps, and swirls, red handle,
        .... **150.00**
5 1/2" h, carved leaves and stems,
        dashes on rim, overall honey
        brown glaze, "Susie Cooper
        England" mk, ... **100.00**
6 1/4" h, carved oak leaves and
        acorns, grey ground, c1930s,
        .... **95.00**

Meat Platter, 16" l, oval, "Gardinia"
        pattern, ... **30.00**

Milk Jug
3" h, "Swansea Spray" pattern,
        Kestrel shape, ... **80.00**
4" h, "Susan's Red" pattern, ... **80.00**

Pitcher, 8 1/4" h, imp ram motif, overall
        tan glaze, ... **550.00**

Plate
6" d
        Kestrel shape, black, rust-red,
        green, blue, and yellow "Tulip

in Pompadour" pattern, set of
        6, ... **85.00**
"Romance Pink" pattern,
        .... **10.00**
6 1/2" d, "Clematis" pattern, blue
        washed border, "Susie Cooper
        Bone China England Clematis"
        mk, ... **15.00**
7" d, "Cubist" design, multicolored,
        .... **225.00**
8" d
        "Dresden Spray" pattern, pink
        border, ... **5.00**
        "Freesia" pattern, ... **115.00**
        Stylized cowboy w/orange
        checked shirt, black hat,
        holding rope, grey horse,
        orange and red striped rim,
        "Susie Cooper Productions"
        mk, ... **110.00**
        8 5/8" d, green "Assyrian Motif," gilt
        trim, ... **10.00**

*Plate, 9" d, "Dresden Spray" pattern, green
colorway, **$18.00***

9" d
        "Pink Campion" pattern, blue-
        green border, ... **15.00**
        White sgrafitto design of grapes
        and leaves, peach ground,
        swirl rim, ... **18.00**
9 7/8" d, "Dresden Spray" pattern,
        pink border, ... **6.00**
10" d
        "Endon" pattern, brown, green,
        and pink floral border, cream
        ground, "Susie Cooper
        England/1417" mk,
        .... **5.00**
        Matte blue leaf band on inner
        border, ... **40.00**
        "Pink Campion" pattern, blue rim,
        .... **10.00**
        "Priscilla Rose" pattern, wide
        green border, ... **10.00**

"Tiger Lily" pattern, "A Susie
        Cooper Production Crown
        Works Burslem England" mk,
        set of 6, ... **42.00**

Platter
10 1/2" l x 8 3/4" w, "Longleaf"
        pattern, ... **60.00**
14" l x 11" w, oval, "Dresden Spray"
        pattern, shaded green border,
        .... **56.00**
16 1/4" l, "Endon" pattern, brown,
        green, and pink floral border,
        cream ground, "Susie Cooper
        England" mk, ... **40.00**

Preserve Jar, 4" h, red "Polka Dot"
        pattern, ... **20.00**
Serving Plate, 10 1/2" H-H, lily of the
        valley in center, yellow tipped
        handles, ... **40.00**
Soup Plate, 8" d, "Fragrance" pattern,
        .... **15.00**
Sugar Bowl, 3 1/2" h, "Blue Gentian"
        pattern, ... **35.00**

Teapot
5" h, mint green "Polka Dot" pattern,
        .... **45.00**
5 1/2" h, "Whispering Grass" pattern,
        Quail shape, ... **85.00**
6" h x 8 1/2" w, Kestrel shape
        Grey leaf design, ... **168.00**
        Maroon to grey horiz banding,
        .... **250.00**
7 3/4" h, Kestrel shape, green wash
        banding w/green and grey
        dentils, "A SUSIE COOPER
        PRODUCTION CROWN WORKS
        BURSLEM ENGLAND" mk,
        .... **70.00**

Tea Set, pot, 5" h, cream jug, 2 1/2" h,
        sugar bowl, 3 1/2" d x 1 1/2" h,
        "Nosegay" pattern, Kestrel shape,
        .... **700.00**
Trio, cup, saucer, plate, 6 1/2" d, brown
        "Keystone" pattern, ... **20.00**

Vase
5" h, "Glen Mist" pattern, ... **46.00**
11 5/8" h, incised design of squirrel
        seated on haunches eating nut,
        incised curled hills in bkd, cream
        glaze, (A), ... **355.00**

Vegetable Bowl
10" l x 7" w, oval, pink "Patricia Rose"
        pattern, ... **45.00**
10 1/2" H-H, 5 1/2" h, "Tiger Lily"
        pattern, dk pink and green tiger
        lily and foliage on cov, green line
        on int cov rim, arched stem
        handle on cov, ... **145.00**

CAMBRIAN POTTERY
c 1783 - 1810

DILLWYN & CO.
SWANSEA
c 1811 - 1817

BEVINGTON & CO.
c 1817 - 1824

SWANSEA

Wales
c1814 to Early 1820s

History: Swansea potters produced a large variety of earthenwares during the 18th and 19th centuries. Their porcelains, like those of Nantgarw, were very translucent, had fine glazes, and featured excellent floral painting.

After experiencing a lack of funds in 1814, Billingsley and Walker came from Nantgarw to work with Lewis Dillwyn at Swansea. Billingsley and Walker made fine porcelains between 1814 and 1817 at Swansea and then returned to start again at Nantgarw. Production continued at Swansea until the early 1820s. Many Swansea wares were artist decorated.

Swansea Welsh porcelain blanks were quite popular with London decorators.

References: W.D. John, *Swansea Porcelain*, Ceramic Book Co. 1958; Kildare S. Meager, *Swansea & Nantgarw Potteries*, Swansea, 1949; E. Morton Nance, *The Pottery & Porcelain of Swansea & Nantgarw*, Batsford, 1942.

Museums: Art Institute of Chicago, Chicago, IL; Glynn Vivian Art Gallery, Swansea, Wales.

Reproduction Alert: Swansea porcelain has been copied for many decades in Europe and England. Marks should be studied carefully.

Bowl, 7 1/2" d, ftd, pearlware, "Precarious Chinaman" pattern, blue transfer, chip on foot, ... **70.00**

Coffeepot, 10 1/4" h, creamware, red printed "Tea Party No. 1" on side, "The Shepherd" on reverse, dbl strap handle w/flower and leaf terminals, flowerhead knob, c1790, ... **3,750.00**

Cup and Saucer, dry blue rose bunches, gilt dentil rims, "red Swansea" mk, ... **525.00**

Jug

6" h, HP dk red flowerhead, yellow, blue, and yellow centered sm blue flowers, flowing green foliage, band of dk red, blue, and green stylized buds, "SARA MORGANS 1816" under spout, ... **825.00**

6 1/4" h
Oct, multicolored daisies and foliage, dk yellow rim, cream ground, green branch handle, "imp Dillwyn & co. Swansea" mk, ... **350.00**
Pearlware, oriental man in pavilion, 2 courtesans and boy, dog in garden setting w/trees and shrubs, underglaze blue transfer w/orange, yellow, pink, and green enamels, foliate and scroll border, ... **220.00**

Meat Platter, 18 3/4" l, rect, blue printed "Ladies of Llangollen" pattern, flowerhead border, (A), ... **975.00**

Plate

6" d
"St. Michael's Mount Cornwall," black transfer, indented rim w/molded beading, "imp DILLWYN" mk, c1850, ... **185.00**
"Willow" pattern, blue transfer, "imp DILLWYN CO SWANSEA" mk, ... **45.00**

8" d
"Cornflower Sprigs" pattern, emb wicker border, gilt dentil rim, c1816, ... **225.00**
Pink luster heron catching insect in center, arcaded border of green basketweave and pierced rim w/pink luster lined scalloping, c1820, ... **1,890.00**

8 1/4" d, painted spray of dog roses and buds, inner band of gilded foliage and green florets, border molded w/scrollwork, flowers, and ribbons painted w/primrose, forget-me-nots, and strawberry plant, gilded lobed rim, c1815-17, firing crack, (A), ... **740.00**

8 1/2" d
Blue printed chinoiserie scene of stone building and bridge, floral and geometric border,

"imp Dillwyn & Co." mk, ... **80.00**
Overall green molded cos leaf, c1800, ... **125.00**
Pearlware, lg HP multicolored bouquet in center, band of pink luster stylized single stroke florals on border, pink luster rim, c1820, pr, ... **1,050.00**

8 3/4" d
Lt blue printed scattered floral sprays, lace border, shaped rim, "imp DILLWYN SWANSEA" mk, c1830, ... **125.00**
"Verandah" pattern, oriental fencing, florals and flying bird, blue transfer, ... **100.00**

9" d, pearlware, black transfer of 2 masted sailing ship, cannon, anchor, and bucket in foreground, black lined rim, "imp Dillwyn Swansea" mk, ... **245.00**

9 1/4" d, "Cows Crossing Stream" pattern, rural bkd of bridge, mill, and forest, flowerhead border, indented rim, med blue transfer, "imp Dillwyn & Co. Swansea" mk, ... **240.00**

10" d
Blue printed "Elephant" pattern, elephants, fencing, willow trees, ochre rim, c1800, ... **335.00**
"Don Quixote," raised leaf border, blue transfer, "Brameld & Co." mk, hairline, ... **165.00**
Oct, lobed, pearlware, blue printed 2 masted sailing ship and naval implements in center, chinoiserie border of half moons and foliage, ... **1,400.00**
"Women With Baskets" pattern, black transfer, c1829-31, ... **665.00**

Platter

9 5/8" H-H x 5 3/4" w, rect, "Willow" pattern, blue transfer, stilt mks, ... **130.00**
16" l, "Gazebo" pattern, blue, iron-red, and green Imari designs w/gazebo in center, ... **690.00**

Platter, 17 5/8" l, 13 1/8" w, "Long Bridge" pattern, blue transfer, "imp Dillwyn & Co." mark, $995.00

22" l, brown printed shell and flower pattern, repeat on border, band of circles on rim, c1831-50, ... **490.00**

Punch Bowl, 11" d, blue printed "Long Eliza" pattern on ext, "Drink About" on int, ... **1,800.00**

Sugar Box, Cov, 5" h x 6 1/2" w, w/underplate, "Cornflower Sprigs" pattern, emb wicker border, gilt dentil rims, c1816, ... **935.00**

Tray, 11" w, sm iron-red, puce, yellow flowerheads, brown cell design ground, Dillwyn & Co., c1820, $285.00

Teapot

6 1/2" h x 8" w, grapes, leaves, and tendrils, purple transfer, c1817, chip on spout, ... **825.00**

7 1/2" h x 11" l, blue printed "Haymaker" pattern, floral decorated rim, ... **1,235.00**

Vase, 5 7/8" h, urn shape w/everted rim, pedestal ft, gilt ram head handles, painted loose bouquets on each side, gilt neo-classical borders, some restoration, c1817, (A), ... **1,765.00**

c1760-1766

SWEDEN-GENERAL

Marieberg, near Stockholm, Sweden
1758-1788

History: In 1758 Johann Ehrenreich established a factory at Marieberg, near Stockholm, with the intention of making porcelain, but produced faience instead. Pierre Berthevin, a porcelain expert, came to the factory and became director in 1766. Berthevin was the first in Sweden to make porcelain of the soft paste type. Pieces were decorated in the classical designs. Forms included cream jars, pitchers, small vases, and figures. Faience continued to be made and was decorated utilizing the transfer printing technique.

Henrik Sten took over in 1768. Hard paste porcelain was introduced during this period. Only small forms were made; no dinner services were produced. Custard cups, cream pots, and teapots were the most popular shapes. The decoration included both classical and rococo styles. Some figures in Swedish rococo-style costumes were made. Faience manufacturing continued. Strasburg faience was imitated in a table service for Baron Liljencrantz, the factory's owner. Around 1770 attempts were made to duplicate Wedgwood's creamware.

Marieberg was sold to Rorstrand in 1782. Sten resigned. Schumer took over until the works closed in 1788. Marieberg's faience and porcelain pieces were marked.

Gustavsberg Island of Farsta, Sweden
1827 to Present

The Gustavsberg factory was established on the island of Farsta in 1827. The factory first produced faience and later made transfer printed creamware in the English style.

Samuel Gidenius enlarged and modernized the factory during the 1850s. Wilhelm Odelberg took control in 1869. During the 1860s, decorative majolica and bone porcelain were introduced. Parian was made from the 1860s until the late 19th century. After William Odelberg died in 1914, his two sons took over.

Between 1897 and 1914, G. Wennerberg was the artistic director. He made pottery decorated with simple floral designs in the sgraffito technique. In 1937 the firm was called AB Gustavsberg Fabriker.

The dinnerwares featured simple designs. "Blue Flower" has been made since 1870. "Allmoge" was introduced in 1905 and continues to the present day. "Elite" was very popular. "Amulet" in red, blue, or grey was designed by Stig Lindberg, the company's leading artist. Wilhelm Koge, another designer, modeled "Argenta" with silver and green backgrounds inspired by Persian wares. He also created "Pyro," "Praktika II," and "Carrara." Other sets included "Grey Bands" and "Marguente" in the Art Nouveau style.

References: Robin Hecht, *Scandinavian Art Pottery, Denmark & Sweden*, Schiffer Publications, 2000; George Fischler, *Scandinavian Ceramics & Glass: 1940s to 1980s*, Schiffer Publications, 2000.

Museums: American Swedish Institute, Minneapolis, MN; Gustavsberg Ceramics Center, Island of Varmdo, Sweden.

Bowl, 5" d, silver fish blowing bubbles, mottled dk red ground, Gustavsberg Argenta, ... **195.00**

Box, 5 3/4" l x 4" w, silver griffin on cov, mottled green ground, Gustavsberg, ... **150.00**

Bud Vase, 5 7/8" h, silver flower, bud, and foliage, mottled green ground, Gustavsberg, ... **35.00**

Figure, 4" h, 5 1/8" h, tan ground, black incised designs, "Gustavsberg Sweden" paper labels, A-$50.-left, A-$75.00

Figure

3 1/2" l, standing bear w/head turned, vert brown striping, Lisa Larson, Gustavsberg, ... **50.00**

4" h x 4 1/4" l, art pottery, standing cat, incised black eyes and stripes, Lisa Larson, Gustavsberg, ... **75.00**

Plate

8 1/2" d, flowing blue morning glories and vines, bead and bluebell border, "imp GUSTAVSBERG SWEDEN, anchor" mk, ... **48.00**

9 1/2" d, 3 vert stems w/green stylized leaves, white ground, Bersa Lindberg, Gustavsberg, ... **10.00**

10" d, "Krasse" pattern, flowing blue transfer, Gustavsberg, ... **20.00**

Platter, 13 1/4" l x 10 7/8" w, flowing blue floral bouquet in center, oriental style scroll, diaper, and floral border, scalloped rim, "imp anchor, GUSTAVSBERG" mk, ... **235.00**

Soup Plate, 9" d, flowing blue morning glory design, swirl fluted border, gilt rim, "Gustavsberg" mk, ... **50.00**

Toothpick Holder, 2 1/2" h, fluted, sm silver flowers, mottled green ground, silver inner rim, Gustavsberg, Argenta, ... **75.00**

Tray, 6" l x 5" w, rect, silver inlay of steamship, mottled green ground, "Gustavsberg, Argenta Sweden" mk, ... **175.00**

Vase, 10" h, cobalt "Hare's Fur" glaze, Gustavsberg, (A), $1,540.00

Vase

3 3/4" h, stepped gourd shape, irid rose and blue ground, gold trim, c1925, ... **150.00**

5 1/2" h, straight sides, rolled shoulder and base, short neck, silver flowers on mottled green ground, Gustavsberg Argenta, ... **125.00**

6" h, ball shape, med blue stylized flowerheads and leaves on powder blue sponged ground, med blue short collar, Gustavsberg, ... **375.00**

6 1/2" h, bottle shape, mottled Robin's egg and periwinkle blue ground, ... **495.00**

Vase, 8 1/4" h, brown outlined circles, white ground, brown rim, brown clay body, "Gefle Porzlin Fabrikse AB" mark, $1,575.00

7" h, rect shape, silver sailing ship on 4 waves, "WASA 1628" on reverse, blue-green mottled ground, Gustavsberg, ... **45.00**

10" h x 8" d, bulbous shape, short, everted rim, blue "Hare's Fur" glaze, Gustavsberg, ... **2,800.00**

16" h, tapered body, slightly flared neck, lt blue glaze, Gustavsberg, ... **2,200.00**

Vase, 24" l, stoneware, "Dragon Fish," blue and mustard yellow glaze, Gustavsberg, (A), $1,980.00

TEA LEAF IRONSTONE

Staffordshire, England
c1856 to Present

History: The tea leaf pattern started about 1856 when Anthony Shaw of Burslem began decorating his white ironstone with three copper luster leaves. At first it was called "Lustre Band and Sprig." Later names were "Edge Line and Sprig" and "Lustre Spray." The sprig eventually was viewed as a tea leaf, thus giving the pattern its name.

Tons of English tea leaf pattern ironstone china was sent to the United States, where it greatly appealed to American housewives. It was durable, white, and had a simple elegance.

Over thirty English potteries in Staffordshire manufactured wares decorated with the tea leaf pattern. The most prolific were Alfred Meakin Potteries and Anthony Shaw. The tea leaf pattern also was utilized at W.H. Gridley, Alcock Potteries, William Adams, Mellor, Taylor & Co., Wedgwood, and many others. Each company used a slight variation of the tea leaf copper luster pattern. Since all decoration was applied by hand, no two designs were exactly alike, adding to the charm of the ware. Powell & Bishop and Bishop & Stonier also did the design in gold luster.

Tea leaf collectors generally collect pieces made by a specific pottery or with a specific body shape. Teaberry, cinque foil, pinwheel, morning glory, and thistle are also patterns of interest to these collectors.

References: Annise Doring Heaivilin, *Grandma's Tea Leaf Ironstone*, Wallace-Homestead, 1981; Jean Wetherbee, *A Look at White Ironstone*, Wallace-Homestead, 1980.

Museums: Lincoln Home, Springfield, IL; Sherwood Davidson House, Newark, OH; Ox Barn Museum, Aurora, OR.

Collectors' Club: Tea Leaf Club International, Maxine Johnson, P.O. Box 377, Beltron, MO, 64012. Membership: $20.00, *Tea Leaf Readings*, 5 times a year, www.tealeafclub.com

Reproduction Alert: Some recent reproductions are noted for their poor coloration, uneven copper luster decoration, and lower weight. Original ironstone examples are much heavier than newer ceramic pieces.

Baker

6 3/4" sq, rippled rim, Burgess, ... **25.00**

7 3/4" sq, fluted, Alfred Meakin, ... **30.00**

9 3/4" l x 7" w, oval, "H. Burgess" mk, ... **35.00**

Bone Dish, 6" l x 3" w, unmkd, set of 6, ... **275.00**

Bowl

6" d x 3 1/4" h, ftd, "Mellor, Taylor, & Co." mk, ... **45.00**

9" sq, "J. Edwards" mk, ... **65.00**

Butter Pat

2 3/4" sq, Alfred Meakin, ... **8.00**

2 7/7" sq, Funival, ... **10.00**

3" d, Alfred Meakin, ... **22.00**

Casserole, Cov, 6 1/4" h x 10 3/4" l, "Lily of the Valley" pattern, "Anthony Shaw" mk, ... **125.00**

Coffeepot

8 1/2" h, flat sides, Alfred Meakin, ... **210.00**

9 1/2" h, "Empress" pattern, "W. Adams & Sons" mk, (A), ... **270.00**

Coffeepot, 9 1/2" h, Alfred Meakin, $125.00

10" h, "Anthony Shaw" mk,
.... **225.00**
Cup and Saucer, "J. & E. Mayer" mk,
.... **35.00**
Cup and Saucer, Oversize,
"Wedgwood & Co." mk, ... **30.00**
Dish, Rect
5 1/2" l x 4" w, Alfred Meakin,
.... **23.00**
7" l x 5" w, Alfred Meakin, ... **35.00**
Gravy Boat
8" l, "Alfred Meakin" mk, ... **65.00**
8 1/4" l, Wilkinson, ... **95.00**
Nappy, 4 1/4" sq, Bishop & Powell,
.... **15.00**

*Plate, 7 3/4" d, "imp Anthony Shaw" mark,
$37.00*

Plate
7 3/4" d, "Lily of the Valley" pattern,
Anthony Shaw, ... **45.00**
8 1/2" d, 10 sides, Tea Berry design,
unmkd, ... **45.00**
8 5/8" d, "Wedgwood & Co." mk,
.... **12.00**
9" d, Alfred Meakin, ... **10.00**
9 1/2" d, Morning Glory, "Elsmore
Forster" mk, ... **34.00**
9 3/4" d, "Portland" shape, green
and copper luster reverse
teaberry motif, "Elsmore &
Forster" mk, ... **50.00**

9 7/8" d, "Anthony Shaw" mk,
.... **10.00**
10" d, luster rim, Adams, ... **12.00**
Platter
9 1/2" l x 7" w, rect, Alfred Meakin,
.... **10.00**
10 3/4" l, rect, Alfred Meakin,
.... **65.00**
11 3/4" l, rect, Alfred Meakin,
.... **75.00**
12" H-H, x 9" w, oval, molded copper
luster outlined leaf handles,
"Mellor, Taylor & Co." mk,
.... **145.00**
12" l x 9" w, rect, John Edwards,
.... **25.00**
12 1/2" l x 9 7/8" w, oval, "A.J.
Wilkinson," **25.00**
14" l
10" w, "Alfred Meakin" mk,
.... **69.00**
10 1/4" w, straight sides, curved
ends, fluted border, "Royal
Ironstone China, W.H.
Grindley & Sons England"
mk, ... **45.00**
16" l x 13" w, ... **75.00**
Relish Tray, 8" H-H, "Wedgwood & Co."
mk, ... **22.00**
Soap Dish, Cov, 7" H-H, w/drain,
Meakin, ... **145.00**
Soup Plate, 9" d, "Johnson Brothers"
mk, ... **10.00**
Sugar Bowl, Cov
6" h x 6" H-H, ... **25.00**
6 1/2" d, circ, bamboo knob, A.
Shaw, crazing, ... **45.00**
7" h x 6" H-H, Bishop & Powell,
.... **30.00**
7 3/4" h, "Morning Glory" design,
"Portland" shape, Elsmore &
Forster, ... **200.00**
Teapot
8" h, sq shape, Wedgwood & Co.,
chips, ... **200.00**
9" h, bamboo handle, spout, and
knob, "Alfred Meakin" mk,
.... **175.00**
Tray, 7 3/4" H-H x 4 7/8" w, rect, lustered
outlined molded handles, Burgess,
.... **28.00**

*Vegetable Bowl, Cov, 12" H-H, Alfred Meakin,
$165.00*

Vegetable Bowl
8" sq, fluted body, "Wedgwood &
Co." mk, ... **10.00**
8 1/2" l x 8 1/4" w, "Alfred Meakin"
mk, ... **40.00**
8 1/2" sq, J. Edwards, ... **75.00**
Vegetable Bowl, Cov
8 1/4" l x 5 1/2" w, 5" h, "Alfred
Meakin" mk, ... **145.00**
11" l x 6 1/2" w x 5" h, rect, "Alfred
Meakin" mk, ... **195.00**

TEPLITZ

Bohemia, Germany, now Czech Republic
1892-1945

History: Teplitz was a town in Bohemia. Several companies in the Turn-Teplitz area manufactured art pottery in the late 19th and early 20th centuries. Amphora was one of the companies.

Ernst Wahliss of the Alexandria Works in Teplitz manufactured and decorated pieces in the Art Nouveau style. In 1902 the factory bought six hundred molds from the Imperial and Royal Porcelain Manufactory in Vienna and made copies from them of earlier Vienna decorative porcelains and figures. After 1910 the firm manufactured faience wares. In 1925 the firm was called Ernst Wahliss AG. The plant ceased operation in 1934.

Additional Listing: Amphora.

Basket, 6 3/4" h, enameled portrait of seated Arab woman, red and white striped headpiece, green sash, white robe, tray of red pomegranates at side, hammered bronze finish, overhead handle, "Stellmacher Teplitz Austria" mk, ... **395.00**
Bowl
4" h x 7" d, applied purple grapes, red-brown leaves, cream stems and tendrils, cream-grey textured ground, Stellmacher, c1910, chips, ... **395.00**
4 1/2" h x 8 1/2" w, organic, mottled green and grey ground w/gold outlined black triangles, 4 black legs on diamond shaped base, turquoise int, "Stellmacher Teplitz" mk, ... **285.00**

Ewer

9" h, HP pink or white rose sprays, gold trimmed, raised gold dots and ribbing, yellow-green shaded neck w/molded grape clusters, ... **30.00**

14 1/4" h, 2 lg painted purple irises, green and brown foliage on cream ground, irid jade green top and base, gilt accents, reticulated bronze painted serpentine handle w/eared serpent terminals, 4 sm spread feet, "Groschel & Spethmann Company Turn-Teplitz Austria" mk, ... **275.00**

Figures, 12 1/4" h, bisque, tan hair, lt turquoise suit and blouse, lt sea green, brown, and gold bases, "Stellmacher Teplitz" mks, pr, $1,700.00

Figure

7" h, young girl wearing bonnet next to tree stump open vase, beige, ecru, green-gold, and gilt, Ernst Wahliss, c1900, ... **860.00**

17" h, bust of young girl in bonnet, pale green lapels on jacket, molded florals and lace front, scattered gold beads, pale green bonnet w/gold accented applied flowers, ribbons, feathers, and band of fleur-de-lys, "Stellmacher" mk, ... **2,500.00**

19" h, standing period woman wearing gilt floral and feathered pink bonnet, cream gown, long pink gloves w/gilt accents, moss and root base, matte finish, ... **875.00**

21" h x 20" h, nude female w/brown jug on head astride brown bull, child in lap, tan rect base, Stellmacher, ... **7,500.00**

Pitcher

4 1/2" h, lg HP red poppy, green leaves on side, green sprig on

reverse, lt brown shaded ground, ... **30.00**

6 3/8" h, gold molded leaves, flowers, and insects on dk blue-green irid ground, branch handle, ... **425.00**

Planter, 4 7/8" h, red lobster, mottled gunmetal grey ground, Stellmacher, $175.00

Plate, 8 3/4" d, HP green apples, brown stems from wide burnished gold rim, lavender to ivory shade luster ground, "E.W. Turn" mk, ... **68.00**

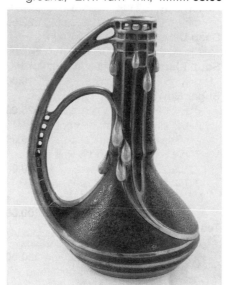

Vase, 9 1/2" h, irid blue applied teardrops, red and green body, "stamped Turn-Teplitz" mark, A-$385.00

Vase

5 1/2" h, corset shape, wide base, everted gold rim, gold outlined red-centered yellow daisies, pink foliage, blue shaded to cream ground, "R.S.K. Teplitz" mk, ... **190.00**

5 7/8" h x 12" d, squat shape, blue-green top, textured cranberry body w/HP enameled Arts and Crafts style white and gold roses,

green leaves, 4 strap handles w/4 smaller handles, gold rim, gold candleholders on top of handles, Paul Daschel, ... **375.00**

6" h, squat body, flared neck, rolled rim, applied red cherries, gold leaves, brown trim, satin green ground, Stellmacher, c1920, ... **165.00**

6 1/2" h

Black bird landing on water, green ground w/black accents, applied loop handles on waist, ... **95.00**

Classic form w/2 gilt reticulated handles from shoulder to rim, gold outlined Moonstone flowers and leaves on yellow ground on upper section, irid blue-purple lower section, "R St K Turn Teplitz" mk, ... **275.00**

Organic molded overlapped leaf form w/handle, orange and yellow w/gilt veining, hairline, (A), ... **432.00**

Tapered shape w/wide shoulder, 2 twisted handles, organic form of molded vine and leaf design, blue and green matte glaze, enamel jewels, Paul Deshcal, (A), ... **1,035.00**

7" h

Heart shape, narrow neck, gold ruffled rim, gold sq ft, gold pierced handles, gold outlined painted violets, green leaves, white ground, "Turn Teplitz Bohemia R St. K" mk, ... **195.00**

Pedestal shape, applied lg red apples, gold leaves, tan molded woven ground, burnished gold rims and triangular handles, "Royal Teplitz Aurora" mk, ... **50.00**

Squat shape, Art Nouveau style, raised blue-green lily pads, raised stems form handles on cream, blue, and green reticulated collar, blue to green shaded ground, "Turn Teplitz Bohemia R St. K" mk, ... **300.00**

7 1/4" h, organic form w/bulbous base, carved and molded stylized trees under speckled gold, brown, and ivory matte glaze, (A), ... **375.00**

8" h

Bulbous shape, 2 sm handles on shoulder, painted red uniformed cavalier holding rifle and sword on grey horse, gilt accents, brown mottled ground, "Teplitz Stellmacher Austria" mk, ... **200.00**

Cylinder shape w/protruding rim, molded stylized tree designs under matte green glaze, (A), ... **1,610.00**

8 1/4" h, wide base tapered to narrow rim, 2 loop handles, HP enameled lavender and white irises, dk brown to lt brown mottled ground, Stellmacher, ... **135.00**

10" h, organic form w/4 small handles on shoulder, matte green, gold, and brown molded lily pads, matte ivory ground w/gold and brown accents, (A), ... **978.00**

12" h, tapered cylinder shape, molded water lilies, fish, and waves on body, figural mermaid wrapped around rim onto body, tan glaze, "Crownoakware Teplitz Austria" mk., ... **995.00**

12 3/8" h, bag base, trumpet neck, wing rim, Art Nouveau terra cotta relief bust of lady wrapped in drape, blue-grey to sage green shading, applied stylized flowerheads and stems, "Grumbach Teplitz Austria" mks, pr, ... **1,450.00**

13 1/4" h, bulbous body, long gilt textured neck, 2 gilt twisted foliate handles, pastel floral bouquet, gilt accents, beige ground, "Turn Teplitz Bohemia R St. K" mk, ... **175.00**

15 1/4" h, tapered shape, straight neck, painted cream and pink mushrooms on base, black vert trees w/gilt accents, pea green ground, Paul Daschel, (A), ... **2,415.00**

c1875

c1880

c1872-1951

TILES

Bristol, Liverpool, and London, England
Denmark, France, Germany, Holland, Italy, Spain, Portugal
1600s to Present

History: Tiles have been used for centuries on floors, walls, fireplaces, chimneys, and facades of houses, palaces, and castles. They even have been installed in furniture such as washstands, hall stands, and folding screens. Tiles cleaned easily and were quite decorative. Numerous public buildings and subways used tiles to enhance their appearances.

The earliest of the **Dutch** tin-glazed tiles featured polychrome figures, landscapes, flowers, and animals. Many used the fleur-de-lys motif in the corners. Additional subjects such as ships, sea monsters, mythical figures, fisherman, farmers, and Biblical subjects appeared in the late 17th century. Tile pictures that were adapted from paintings and engravings of Dutch interiors or landscapes also were made.

Before 1629 at least twenty-five factories in Holland were making tiles, with the Delft potteries the most prolific. After 1650 the Delft potteries became less important. However, all Dutch-made tiles were generically called "Delft" tiles.

Even though the number of factories making tiles diminished during the 18th century, production increased throughout Europe. **Denmark, Germany, Portugal, and Spain** imitated Dutch tiles in their factories. The **Portuguese** tiles featured motifs in two tones of cobalt blue or polychromes. Flemish workers came to **Spain** and introduced the majolica technique. They used a tin-oxide glaze for their decorated tiles.

French tiles were influenced by both Italian and Dutch styles of decoration. In **Italy**, majolica tiles were made in centers such as Florence, Siena, and Venice.

Tiles made in **England** from the 16th through the first half of the 18th century generally followed the Dutch tiles in method of manufacture and design. Polychrome painting—blue and white motifs inspired by Chinese porcelains, birds, landscapes, and flowers—all reflected the strong Dutch influence. Factories that produced tiles were centered in Bristol, Liverpool, and London.

In 1756 John Sadler from Liverpool produced the first transfer printed tiles and revolutionized the tile industry. The use of the transfer printing process on tiles allowed a far greater variety of designs and liberated the tile industry from the old Delft motifs. Transfer printing on tiles was responsible for the growth of the Victorian tile industry.

Herbert Minton was in charge of the production of tiles at Minton. In 1828 he produced encaustic tiles with inlaid decorations, reviving a technique used in medieval Europe. Minton bought Samuel Wright's patent for encaustic tiles in 1830. Minton specialized in tiles for wall decorations in public buildings. Minton began transfer printing tiles in 1850. Minton's Kensington Studio, which was opened in 1871, employed such designers as Moyr Smith, Henry Stacy Marks, and William Wise, who made painted or printed pictorial tiles. Many of Smith's tiles were based on famous literary series.

During the 1870s, decorative wall tiles were in use everywhere. By the 1880s, over one hundred companies in England were producing tiles.

Decorative tiles were a major industry in the Ironbridge Gorge in the late 19th century. Tiles were produced by Maw and Craven Dunnill for church floors, shop counters, public buildings, facades, porches, and many other uses. Maw's factory at Jackfield was the largest decorative tile factory in the world in the 1880s.

The Craven Dunnill firm was formed in 1871 and built its new Jackfield works in 1875. Many encaustic tiles were made for use in new and restored churches. With the revival of the Gothic style, their reproductions of medieval tiles were in great demand.

George Maw and Arthur, his brother, bought the encaustic tile business of the Worcester Porcelain Company in 1850. In addition to floor tiles, they manufactured glazed tiles for walls, porch ways, fireplaces, and washstands. Tiles were either hand painted, transfer printed, or stenciled. They also made ceramic mosaic tiles. The Benthall Works was added to the company in 1883.

In 1892 the Pilkington brothers established a pottery to manufacture tiles and other products at Clifton Junction, Manchester. Many experiments were done. The "Royal" prefix was granted to the company by King George V in 1913, and the company became known as "Royal Lancastrian."

Many designs used on tiles were copied from other fields of art. The Art Nouveau and Art Deco motifs were popular for tile designs.

References: Julian Barnard, *Victorian Ceramic Tiles*, NY Graphic Society Ltd. 1972; Anne Berendsen, *Tiles, A General History*, Viking Press, 1967; C.H. de Jonge, *Dutch Tiles*, Praeger, 1971; Jonathan Horne, *English Tinglazed Tiles*, Jonathan Horne, 1989; Terence A. Lockett, *Collecting Victorian Tiles*, Antique Collectors' Club, Ltd. 2000; Richard & Hilary Myers, *William Morris Tiles: Tile Designs of Morris and His Fellow Workers*, Antique Collectors' Club, Ltd. 1996; Anthony Ray, *English Delftware Tiles*, Faber & Faber, 1973; Anthony Ray, *Liverpool Printed Tiles*, Antique

Collectors' Club, Ltd. 1994; Noel Riley, *Tile Art*, Chartwell Books, Inc. 1987; Hans van Lemmen, *Decorative Tiles Throughout the Ages*, Moyer Bell, 1997; Hans van Lemmen, *Delftware Tiles*, Overlook Press, 1997; Hans van Lemmen, Ed. *Fired Earth: 1000 Years of Tiles in Europe*, Antique Collectors' Club, Ltd. 1991; Hans van Lemmen, *Tiles: A Collectors' Guide, Rev. Ed.*, Intl. Spec. Bk. 1990; H. Wakefield, *Victorian Pottery*, Universe Books, 1965; Wendy Harvey & Sandie Fowler, *Art Nouveau Tiles*, c1890-1914, Schiffer Publications, 2002.

Collectors' Club: Tiles & Architectural Ceramics Society, Kathryn M. Huggins, Reabrook Lodge, 8 Sutton Road, Shrewsbury, Shropshire SY2 6DD UK. Membership: £24, *Glazed Expressions*, Twice yearly magazine, Quarterly newsletter and Journal.

Museums: Boymans-van Beuningen Museum, Rotterdam, Holland; City Museum, Stoke-on-Trent, Hanley, England; Ironbridge Gorge Museum, Teford, England; Lambert van Meerten Museum, Delft, Holland; Victoria & Albert Museum, London, England.

Reproduction Alert: English firms are making copies of 6 x 6" Victorian-era ceramic tiles. Some even have the original artist's signature and 19th century dates. Old tiles are generally thicker, 3/4" or 1/2", while reproductions are 1/4" thick. Old backs have ridges or grooves, while new backs are smooth. New tiles are also transfer printed.

Over sixteen DeMorgan original designs are being reproduced. Some designs are also copies from 18th century tiles as well as the Victorian tiles. Fireplace sets in five-tile sets are also being reproduced.

Collecting Hints: Tiles are becoming increasingly more popular. They are difficult to identify as to manufacturer because they were mass produced and many were unmarked. Some firms only decorated tiles they received from another factory. The method of manufacture may provide clues to the maker. Information on the back of a tile sometimes will indicate the manufacturer or the date that the tile was made.

Condition is an important factor in determining price. Bad cracks, chips, and scratches definitely lower a tile's value. Crazing in the glaze is not uncommon in a tile and usually does not affect the price if it does not detract from the tile's appearance.

3" w x 6" h, tube decorated Art Nouveau style blue tulip, green leaves, white ground, "T. & R. Boote," c1905, ... **35.00**

3 1/4" h x 4 3/4" l, calendar, "Coolidge Homestead," sepia transfer, "Wedgwood Etruria England" mk, ... **95.00**

3 3/4" sq, tin glazed, HP naive peasant holding viola and bow, blue jacket, yellow pantaloons, blue clouds, brown rocks, green bushes, ... **30.00**

4 1/8" sq, carved and raised yellow daisy, brown knobby ground, Minton, ... **95.00**

4 1/2" sq, tube lined black crows, white snow, brown trees and self frame, Porceleyne Fles, ... **80.00**

4 3/4" l x 3 1/4" h, sepia printed calendar, large tree and "Under This Tree Washington First Took Command of the American Army July 3, 1775, Cambridge, Mass." Wedgwood, ... **110.00**

4 7/8" sq, Delft, blue painted w/3 tulips from single foliage base in blue frame, blue dot rim, white ground, Holland, ... **110.00**

5" sq, dk blue design, white ground, Dutch Delft, c1640-60, **$850.00**

5" sq, Tin Glazed

Majolica, white rabbits in center, brown fence, molded green foliage border, Villeroy & Boch, ... **58.00**

Manganese painted floral bouquet, white ground, c1800, rim chips, ... **150.00**

Manganese painted tower, house, and sailboats w/arched trees, stylized flowerheads in corners, white ground, Rotterdam, c1825, ... **150.00**

5 1/8" sq, blue biblical scene of 3 men and snake, stylized ox heads in corners, Delft, 18th C, ... **150.00**

5 7/8" sq, blue printed bust of steer, white ground, Wedgwood, ... **175.00**

6" h x 3" w, tube lined red sailboat on blue water, green and tan bkd, white

clouds and blue sky, Germany, c1900, ... **235.00**

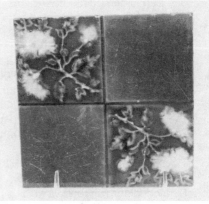

6" sq, 2 dk green sqs, 2 sqs w/yellow flowers, brown streaks and ground, England, **$35.00**

6" sq

"Aesop's Fables-The Hare and the Tortoise," blue and white, Minton & Hollins, c1870, ... **90.00**

Art Nouveau

Celtic knot design, dk blue, ... **30.00**

Olive centered blue petaled flowers, twisted buds, black sinuous stems and shoots, Pilkington, ... **125.00**

Three purple flowerheads, green stems, mauve ribbon, red accents, Gibbons Hinton, c1910, ... **70.00**

Tube lined blue, red, and green stylized peacock feather, grey ground, Germany, ... **265.00**

Yellow stylized iris w/green leaves and stem, red-brown ground, England, ... **45.00**

Arts and Crafts, brown printed scene from Romeo and Juliet, "raised MINTON'S CHINA WORKS STOKE ON TRENT" mk, ... **40.00**

Brown printed w/green accents titled Gareth" from "Idles of the King," two travelers in jerkins w/sacks on sticks over shoulders, maiden seated on columned porch, John Moyr-Smith, Minton, ... **95.00**

Farm Animal Series, cattle, donkey, goat and sheep in mountain setting, blue transfer, Minton and Hollins, ... **200.00**

Green sailing galleon w/side oars, rim chips, William De Morgan, ... **275.00**

Half portrait of cavalier, blue shades, unmkd, ... **20.00**

HP white water lilies, green pads, blue streaked water, France, c1900, ... **125.00**

Incised med blue, tan dk brown foliate design on yellow-brown streaked ground, Martin Brothers, (A), ... **265.00**

"Jack and Jill" design, brown transfer, Minton and Hollins, c1880, ... **115.00**

"K.L. Rose" pattern, dk red old English roses, swirling green foliage, William De Morgan, ... **450.00**

"MacMillan" coat of arms, 2 black rearing lions, red and white scrolling, arm w/sword, yellow shield w/black lion and blue stars, white ground, Pilkington, ... **10.00**

Majolica, 2 HP Dutch women, grey windmill, blue river in bkd, ... **25.00**

Orange and yellow flowers, buds, and stems on white ground, orange vert stripes on sides, England, ... **35.00**

Press molded white flowerheads, green spear leaves, grey ground, Meakin, ... **115.00**

Profile of Queen Victoria, red-brown glaze, "C. Edwards" mk, ... **80.00**

Rabbit in center, panels of stylized florals and leaves separated by bamboo, brown transfer, Minton, ... **58.00**

Raised yellow centered blue flowerhead in center, green 3 petal leaf designs in arms of 4 lobed diamond shape, red outlined fleur-de-lys, green beaded rim, Minton, ... **50.00**

Secessionist lt brown and grey-blue flower and leaves, dk green gloss ground, ... **35.00**

Sepia printed farm yard w/cow and calf, "MINTONS CHINA WORKS STOKE ON TRENT" mk, ... **135.00**

"Village Life" series, dk blue print of peasant woman walking down road w/jug on shoulder, Minton, ... **170.00**

6 1/4" sq
Lg red flowerhead in center, blue and green vert foliage, "Wm De Morgan/Sands End Pottery Fulham" mk, ... **350.00**

Red dot centered turquoise daisies, green stems and foliage, "Wm De Morgan/Sands End Pottery" mk, ... **335.00**

7 7/8" sq, 3 multicolored scenes of kittens playing, border wreath of green leaves, "MONTEREAU" mk, ... **125.00**

8" sq
Art Nouveau Style
Relief molded stylized 8 petaled brown or steel-blue flowers in quatrefoil, club shaped florals on brown corders, Zsolnay, ... **1,000.00**

Three blue morning glories on swirling stems, white curved leaves, olive geometric bkd on cream base, Germany, ... **125.00**

Blue and white printed "November" w/barefoot sailor walking on beach, white border w/blue bellflowers, Wedgwood, ... **325.00**

HP multicolored scene of brown cattle in forest setting, "MONTEREAU L.M. & Cie CREIL" mk, ... **195.00**

Irid pink-purple, and blue-green stylized flowers, "Clement Massier Golfe Juan AM" mk, ... **300.00**

Terra cotta base w/relief of scorpion, blue washed ground, imp "GERMANY" mk, ... **95.00**

8 1/4" l x 4 1/4" h, rect, cuenca leaping brown and tan rabbit, red fruiting green leaf trees, green and lt brown grass, De Porceleyne Fles, (A), ... **1,100.00**

9" sq, blue printed cherub holding cage, Minton, ... **35.00**

11" l x 5 1/2" w, multicolored semi-gloss cuenca scene of Don Quixote chasing sheep, Sancho Panza on hill, black self frame, Spain, c1920, ... **125.00**

12" l x 6" w
HP underglazed multicolored Asian sunset scene of landscape w/mountain, lake, and boat, England, ... **325.00**
Multicolored cuenca design of English landscape w/windmill, lake, trees, mountains in bkd, ... **245.00**

13 1/2" h x 5 1/4" w, rect, white and beige cuenca pelican feeding young, green twisted nest, dk indigo

ground, amber tile borders, mtd on board, De Porceleyne Fles, (A), ... **1,725.00**

14 1/4" h x 6" w, standing grey and white stork, tall green grasses, pyramids in bkd, Holland, ... **375.00**

16 1/2" l x 4 1/4" h, rect, cuenca flotilla of dk brown sailing ships, amber cloud bkd, blue-green sea w/white waves, crystalline green sky, De Porceleyne Fles, (A), ... **460.00**

20" l x 12 1/2" w, rect, tin glazed blue and white Dutch harbor scene of woman on dock holding net, boats in water, c1890, ... **650.00**

Tile Picture

6" h x 12" l, 2 tiles, 6" sq, 2 red eyed green carp swimming by red centered white water lily, green waves, raised "V & B" mks, ... **488.00**

11" sq, 4 tiles, tin glazed, blue stylized flowerhead in center, blue curlicues on border, netted corners, Portugal, ... **100.00**

12" h x 6" w, 2 6" sq tiles, Japanese flowers issuing from grey vase flanked by brown griffons, self framed w/grey border and tan and grey arch overhead, ... **188.00**

16 1/2" h x 11" w, 6 tiles, 5 1/2" sq, painted brown or grey intertwined prancing horses on tan stylized ground, Spain, ... **125.00**

18" l x 6" h, 3 tiles, 6" sq, majolica cuenca scene of green fir trees, brown trunks, green fields w/blue ripple stream, cream, blue, and green mountains in bkd, white clouds, Germany, (A), ... **285.00**

19 1/2" l x 14 1/2" w, 12 5" sq tiles, blue and white Dutch scene of church and public buildings, Dutch, ... **875.00**

24" h x 12" w, 8 tiles, 6" sq, relief of green and brown peacocks facing each other, center grey pedestal, ... **890.00**

25 1/4" l x 10" w, 3 5 1/2" sq tiles, 12 border tiles, 3 aubergine scenes of racing yachts off shore, border of twists w/compass roses at corners, Dutch, ... **950.00**

30" h x 12" w, 10 ties, 6" sq, Art Nouveau style emb white flowers on long stems, pale blue ground, mtd in wood frame, Villeroy and Boch, ... **950.00**

40" sq, 25 tiles, 8" sq, painted goldfish, ocean plants, dk blue water bkd, Longwy, ... **1,100.00**

34" h, 22 1/2" w, blue design, yellow faux marble ground, Portugal, A-**$522.00**

72" h x 47" w, 88 tiles, HP multicolored "The Goose Girl," Royal Doulton, (A), ... **11,000.00**

TOBY JUGS

Staffordshire, England
1775 to Present

History: Toby jugs, first made by English potters from Staffordshire in the 18th century, were drinking vessels. Although they were at the height of their popularity from 1775 to 1825, Toby jugs are still being produced today. After they became outmoded as drinking mugs, they survived as ornamental pieces.

Some of the earliest Toby jugs were made by Ralph Wood and Whieldon at their Burslem potteries in Staffordshire. Some claim the name "Toby" originated with the Uncle Toby character in Laurence Sterne's *Tristram Shandy*. This is subject to debate.

The typical Toby jug featured a seated toper clasping a jug with both hands or holding a glass in one hand and a jug on a knee in the other. The seated figure was usually a male wearing a three cornered hat, each corner of which formed a spout. Figures were dressed in costumes of the period and usually had genial facial expressions. Toby jugs were designed for use in cottages and inns. Variations included standing figures and occasional female figures. Most were usually ten inches tall, while miniatures, which were rarer, measured about three to six-and-one-half inches tall.

Some early Whieldon Toby jugs had the mottled and tortoiseshell underglazed effect. The Ralph Wood jugs had a somewhat whiter body and softer, translucent glazes. After 1780 some overglaze enamels were used. Wedgwood, Pratt, and Davenport, along with other English potters, made Toby jugs.

References: Desmond Eyles, *'Good Sir Toby,'* Doulton & Co. Ltd. 1955; Bernard Rackham, *Early Staffordshire Pottery*, Faber & Faber, 1951; Vic Schuler, *British Toby Jugs, 1st Edition*, Kevin Francis Publishing Ltd. 1986; Vic Schuler, *Collecting British Toby Jugs, 2nd Edition*, Kevin Francis Publishing Ltd. 1987; C.P. Woodhouse, *Old English Toby Jugs*, Mountrose Press, 1949; David C. Fastenau & Stephen M. Mullins, *Toby & Character Jugs of the 20th Century and Their Makers*, Kevin James Publishing, 1999; David C. Fastenau & Stephan M. Mullin, *Companion Price Guide*, Kevin James Publishing, 2000.

Museums: American Toby Jug Museum, Evanston, IL; City Museum & Art Gallery, Stoke-on-Trent, England; Victoria & Albert Museum, London, England.

4 1/2" h, "Beefeater," red and yellow gold uniform, black hat, boots, and handle, white beard, "imp BEEFEATER S/S SHORTER ENGLAND" mk, ... **35.00**

5 1/2" h, Henry VIII, red robe, black hat w/white trim, gold chain around neck w/green and red stones, Wood & Sons, ... **50.00**

6 1/2" h, standing monk, hands on belly, med blue robe, black tricorn, "Creil & Montereau" mk, c1890, ... **165.00**

7" h, brown trimmed black tricorn w/cov, cobalt jacket, pink vest, grey hair, mustard trousers, crossed ankles, holding dotted jug, brown handle, rim chips, ... **440.00**

7 1/2" h, standing "Snuff Taker," black tricorn, dk blue coat, olive green vest, blue stockings, salt glazed stoneware, (A), ... **150.00**

8 1/8" h, standing snuff taker, black tricorn, blue coat, yellow vest, salmon trousers, green and brown rock base, c1860, ... **100.00**

8 3/4" h, Lord Howe, seated, holding jug, overall ochre glaze, c1820, ... **475.00**

9" h

  Seated

    Black tricorn, red warts on face, green greatcoat, yellow breeches, lt blue vest, holding foaming red striped jug, ... **950.00**

    Country Squire-Roger Giles, blue coat, brown vest, yellow breeches, c1890, ... **180.00**

    Holding foaming jug, overall brown treacle glaze, ... **300.00**

Legs crossed, grey tricorn hat, blue coat, turquoise scarf, puce vest, tan trousers, holding white jug w/red stylized flowers, ... **125.00**

Lidded black tricorn, cobalt jacket, green scarf, pink vest, tan trousers, blue trimmed white stockings, X'd ankles, both hands holding flowered jug, c1850, ... **165.00**

Standing "Snuff Taker," black striped white tricorn w/cov, orange coat, grey hair, flowered vest, c1870, hairlines, ... **500.00**

9 1/8" h, pearlware, Ralph Wood type, black tricorn, tan jacket, seated on tan barrel, dk red breeches, green handle, holding brown foaming jug, pipe and sleeping dog on white oct base, Staffordshire, late 18th C, (A), ... **4,950.00**

9 1/4" h

  Black tricorn, cobalt jacket, pot belly, red breeches, seated on green, brown, and yellow sponged base, ... **395.00**

  Cobalt jacket, yellow trousers, holding brown jug, c1870, ... **225.00**

9 3/8" h

  Blue trimmed yellow tricorn hat, puce coat, brown trousers, lt blue stockings, holding brown jug, oct base, repaired chip, ... **110.00**

  Brown tricorn and jacket, yellow vest, lt blue breeches, hands folded on stomach, ... **110.00**

9 1/2" h

  Black tricorn, blue coat, mustard yellow vest, white Ascot, brown breeches, holding flowered jug, oct green base, c1800, Pratt, chip, ... **950.00**

  Brown sponged tricorn, dk red jacket, tan breeches, brown sponged base, lt green seat, holding blue flower decorated pitcher and cup, Yorkshire, c1820, ... **450.00**

  Enamel washes of brown coat, yellow breeches, blue vest, blue sponged stockings, black tricorn, holding pitcher, green base, (A), ... **220.00**

  Pearlware

    Blue-black tricorn, blue sponged coat, yellow tassels on knees, brown splashes on face, holding brown foaming jug, barrel and pipe on white sq base w/canted corners, late 18th C, (A), ... **975.00**

Pratt-type, brown tricorn w/ochre badge, cobalt coat w/ochre dashes, ochre breeches, brown sq base w/canted corners, holding foaming jug, (A), ... **675.00**

W/cov, black tricorn, purple coat, green striped waistcoat, yellow breeches w/red tassels, warty face, holding red flowered jug and pipe, red striped sq base w/canted corners, (A), ... **375.00**

9 3/8" h, black jacket, pink vest, yellow breeches, yellow outlined black hat, brown and green base, c1840, **$895.00**

9 3/4" h

Black tricorn

Grey hair, brown face, dk brown coat, lt tan breeches, holding brown jug, drinking from beaker, ... **1,960.00**

Orange-brown warts on face, dk brown coat, mustard yellow vest, tan breeches, holding foaming jug, ... **695.00**

Wood type, brown transparent glazed coat, green wash vest, tan breeches, brown foaming jug, green chair and handle, ... **1,975.00**

Yellow lined cobalt coat, white vest, dk red trousers, blue hose, green and yellow spatter base, ... **395.00**

Pearlware, blue waistcoat, orange dot white vest, black tricorn hat w/orange dot, mustard trousers, holding dk red jug, c1830, ... **675.00**

Standing fat man w/hands in pockets, cobalt coat, white hat, face, body, blue and brown sponged base, ... **275.00**

10" h

Brown spatter tricorn, transparent green vest and breeches, manganese jacket w/white buttons, holding jug and cup, chip on base, ... **2,250.00**

Creamware, seated figure, tricorn hat, holding foaming jug, brown and green translucent glazes, c1800, repaired hat, (A), ... **530.00**

12 1/4" h, "American Sailor," cobalt jacket, yellow vest, dk red tie, black hat, white trousers w/black stripes, mid-19th C, **$475.00**

Dutch Delft, seated, blue sponged hat, jug, handle, and rock base, blue flowered coat, blue dimples, ... **3,750.00**

Pratt colors, ochre tricorn w/black slashes, open mouth w/teeth, brown coat, green trousers, holding flowered foaming jug, chip on hat, ... **530.00**

10 1/4" h, seated w/goat at feet, holding foaming ale jug, buff glaze, black

tricorn and shoes, Staffordshire, early 19th C, (A), ... **3,750.00**

10 1/2" h

Removable brown and yellow tricorn, rust coat, yellow vest, gold breeches, holding brown jug, ... **395.00**

Seated holding blue striped jug, white w/blue facial accents, blue tricorn, trousers, and coat, blue lined oct base w/blue floral sprig on handle, ... **775.00**

11 1/2" h, Winston Churchill, red hunt coat, black hat, blue bow tie, brown trousers, black boots, grey bulldog at feet, green sq base w/British flag and raised "BULLDOG" on front, Burleigh, ... **195.00**

11 1/2" h, blue coat, yellow vest, iron-red breeches, black shoes and hat, **$895.00**

13 1/4" h, seated Punch, yellow hat w/red peak, red jacket w/yellow flowered collar, yellow trousers, flowered black shoes, late 19th C, "imp Sarreguemines" mk, ... **525.00**

TORQUAY

Torquay District, South Devon, England
1870s-1962

History: G.J. Allen discovered red terra cotta clay on the Watcombe House grounds, just north of Torquay in 1869. The pottery industry in Torquay owed its existence to this discovery.

Allen established the Watcombe Pottery. Charles Brock was appointed manager, and skilled workers were employed from Staffordshire. Watcombe Pottery was established during the peak of the art pottery movement, 1870 to 1900, and found a ready market for its products.

The appeal of the terra cotta wares was the natural color of the clay and the innovative shapes. A small amount of enamel decoration or gilt borders was added. At first, the style was classical, comprised of vases, figures, and busts imitating Greek and Roman originals. Later busts of contemporary and historical celebrities, vases, jars, architectural wares, garden ornaments, and tea services were made.

Watcombe Pottery also was known for its terra cotta plaques. Statues were made for advertising purposes. Enamel decoration of flowers, birds, and fish on ornamental wares was accomplished in a natural style on unglazed terra cotta.

In 1875 Dr. Gillow established the Torquay Terra-Cotta Company Ltd. at Hele Cross, just north of Torquay. Smaller decorative wares, such as statuettes, plaques, vases, figures, and busts were made. Some utilitarian examples also were produced. Products were similar to those made at the Watcombe Pottery.

Torquay Terra-Cotta Company declined. It closed in 1905 as a result of the decline in the Arts and Crafts movement and the shift to more modern styles. Enoch Staddon reopened the Torquay Pottery in 1908 to make pottery rather than terra cotta ware. The factory closed during World War II.

The Aller Vale Pottery, under the direction of John Phillips, started making terra cotta and other art wares in new forms and styles near Torquay in 1881. By 1890 the pottery was catering to holiday visitors who wanted something to take home as a souvenir. Designs were painted in thick colored slip on items prepared with a dip coat of slip of a uniform color. They were finished with a clear glaze. Usually rhymes or proverbs were scratched through the ground so the lettering showed up in the dark red color of the body. This "motto ware" gained tremendous popularity during the early 20th century, not only in resorts, but all over the country.

Watcombe Pottery combined with Aller Vale in 1901 to form the Royal Aller Vale and Watcombe Art Potteries. Watcombe started to manufacture the Aller-type wares. One style of decoration showing the thatched cottage between trees was called "Devon Motto Ware" or "Cottage Ware." In addition to the motto, sometimes the place name was inscribed. Commemorative wares were made. The combined potteries eventually closed in 1962.

During the early part of the 20th century, several smaller potteries such as Longpark Pottery, Burton, and Daison were established in or near Torquay. Most were founded by men who had worked at one of the major potteries in the district. The designs tended to copy the styles used by Aller Vale and Watcombe. When Longpark closed in 1957 and Watcombe in 1962, the red clay pottery industry in Torquay ended.

References: Virginia Brisco, Editor, *Torquay Mottowares*, Torquay Pottery Collectors Society, 1990; D.& E. Lloyd Thomas, *The Old Torquay Potters*, Arthur H. Stockwell Ltd. 1978, Virginia Brisco, *Dartmouth Pottery*, Torquay Pottery Collectors Society, 1993, *Art of the Torquay and South Devon Potters*, Torquay Pottery Collectors Society, 1998.

Collectors' Clubs: North American Torquay Society, Marlene Graham, 214 N. Ronda Road, McHenry, IL 60050, Membership: $20.00, Quarterly magazine *The Torquay Collector*; The Torquay Pottery Collectors Society, 5 Claverdon Drive, Sutton Coldfield, W. Mids B74 3AH, UK. Membership: £12, Quarterly magazine.

Museums: Devonshire Museum, Devonshire, England; Exeter Museums, Exeter, England; Torquay Museum, South Devon, England.

Ashtray

5" w, triangle shape, Cottage design, "A Gentle Reminder" and "Snowden," **25.00**

5 1/4" l x 3 1/4" w, rect, Cottage design, "Better to smoke Here than Hereafter" and "Paignton," **45.00**

Bowl

2" h, green shamrocks, "From Kerry the chosen leaf of bard & chief" on side, Longport, ... **25.00**

4" d, Cottage design, "Actions speak louder than words," Watcombe, ... **10.00**

4 1/2" d, blue, yellow, and rose crocus, green leaves, blue sponged rim and base, "Longpark Torquay England" mk, ... **20.00**

6 1/2" d, dk blue int, cream inner border w/blue, red, green, and yellow lobed designs, "Duee help yourself," **25.00**

9" d, flying seagull design, blue ocean and ground, 3 tabs on rim, Lemon & Crute, ... **55.00**

Candlestick, 3 1/2" h, Scandy design, "Hear all See all Speak nothing" and "last in bed put out the light," "Longpark Torquay" mks, pr, .. **40.00**

Chamberstick

3 1/4" h, Scandy design, "Many are called but few get up" on base, ... **65.00**

5 1/4" h, Scandy design, "Dinna licht yer can'le at bouth ends," **85.00**

Comport, 8" d x 3" h, HP sailing ship at sunset in center, cobalt border, ... **150.00**

Creamer, Cottage Design

3" h,
"Soft words win hard hearts," Watcombe, ... **25.00**
"Take A Little Milk," "Mevrigissey" on front, ... **55.00**

3 3/4" h, "Isle of Wight" and "Help Yourself To Milk," **75.00**

Cup and Saucer

Cottage design
"Everything Has A Bright Side," **20.00**
"Say Little But Think Much," Watcombe, ... **20.00**
"They That Drink Longest Live Longest," **45.00**

Rooster design, "it's unco refreshin while I live I'll crow," Allervale, ... **23.00**

Seagull pattern, white on blue ground, Watcombe, ... **68.00**

Egg Cup

2 1/2" h, ftd, Black Cockeral design, "Fresh laid," **40.00**

3" h, Cottage, "Speak little, Speak well," Watcombe, ... **40.00**

Dish, 4 1/2" d, heart shape, ring handle on end, Cottage design, "Speak little speak well," "Watcombe Devon Motto Ware England" mk, ... **20.00**

Hatpin Holder

4 1/2" h, Cottage design, "A place for everything and everything in its place," Watcombe, ... **75.00**

4 3/4" h, Scandy, "A Place For Hat Pins," **120.00**

Inkwell, Scandy

2" h, "Blot out my past but not my memory," **75.00**

3" h, "Send us a Scrape of your Pen," **35.00**

Jam Dish, 3 1/2" d, Cottage design, "Be aizy wi the Jam" and "Goodringby," **55.00**

Jam Pot

2 1/8" h, white, grey, and black seagull on rocks, med blue ground, Babbacombe, ... **20.00**

4" h, Cottage design, "Help yourself and don'y be shy," **65.00**

Jardiniere, 9 1/2" h x 11 1/2" d, blue water, brown tree trunks, green foliage, green earth mounds, dk brown int, "Torquay Pottery" mk, $495.00

Jardiniere, 8" d x 6 1/4" h, "Piccadilly" pattern, molded stiff leaves on base, ring handles, piecrust rim, turquoise to brown shaded ground top to base, Watcombe, ... **75.00**

Jug

2 1/2" h, Cottage design, "Go aisy wi it now," Dartmouth, ... **26.00**

3 3/4" h, Thistle design, "For Auld Lang Syne," **50.00**

6" h, multicolored pixies and toadstool, blue ground, "Daison Art Pottery Torquay" mk,
.... **75.00**

9 1/2" h, multicolored Stork design, med blue ground, ... **65.00**

Mug

2 3/4" h, Cottage design and "PORTLAND BILL," "Take a little drink," **40.00**

3 1/2" h, Cottage design, "Caernarvon" and "Eichyd Da,"
.... **20.00**

Mustard Jar

2 1/2" h, white, grey, and black seagull on rocks, med blue ground, Babbacombe, ... **38.00**

2 3/4" h, Cottage design, "I improve everything," **55.00**

Nappy, 4 1/4" w, Seagull design, med blue ground, dk brown ext and handle, Watcombe Torquay,
.... **15.00**

Pin Tray

3 1/4" l x 3" w, Cottage design, "A Gentle Reminder," "Watcombe Torquay England" mk, ... **18.00**

3 1/2" l x 2 1/2" w, Seagull design, "Babbacombe Pottery Torquay" mk, ... **15.00**

Pitcher, 5 1/4" h, Cottage design, "Help yourself, don't be shy," "Stratford on Avon" on front, ... **95.00**

Plate, 7" d, "Cottage," brown and cream, "After dinner sit awhile After Supper walk a mile" on border, $55.00

Plate

6 1/4" d, Kerswell Daisy, "Daun tee try tu rin vor you kin walk," Aller Vale, ... **105.00**

6 1/2" d, Cottage design, "To thine own self be true," **45.00**

Puzzle Jug, 4 1/4" h, Scandy design, "The Puzzle," unmkd, ... **475.00**

Sugar Bowl

3" h, ftd, Cottage design, "Take a little sugar," **55.00**

3 1/4" d, "Sweeten to your liking," "Watcombe Torquay Made in England" mk, ... **15.00**

3 3/4" d, Black Cockeral design, "Elp yerzel tu sugar," **75.00**

Tankard, 8" h, red, blue, and yellow leaf and curlicue designs, tan body, blue handle, "Aller Vale HH & Co." mk,
.... **50.00**

Teapot

4" h, center tan band w/"Rax furrit yer haun an help yersel," dk brown top and base, ... **50.00**

6" h, Cottage design, "Take A Cup of Kindness For Auld Lang Syne," "Watcombe Torquay England" mk, ... **60.00**

Tea Stand, 5 1/2" d, Cottage design, "He also serves who only stands and waits" and "Lymouth," "LONGPORT TORQUAY ENGLAND" mk,
.... **50.00**

Tobacco Jar, 6" h, Scandy design, "Lets Have a Smoke and Crack a Joke," "Aller Vale, England" mk, ... **95.00**

Tray, 5 1/4" l x 3 1/4" w, rect, Cottage, "Do not stain to-days blue sky with to-morrows clouds," **72.00**

Tumbler, 4 1/4" h, Cottage design, "There's A Time For All Things,"
.... **18.00**

Vase

3 1/2" h, white dog rose, green leaves on black trellis, green shaded flared neck, 2 brown handles on shoulder, Watcombe,
.... **45.00**

5" h, fan shape, Black Cockerel design, beaded rim, ... **15.00**

8" h, tapered shape, flying white seagulls, brown rocks, blue ground, brown int, Barton Pottery, ... **65.00**

12 1/2" h, moon flask shape, trumpet neck, white enameled swallows on matte terra cotta sides, glazed terra cotta body w/molded lion's head handles, vert turquoise beading on base, Watcombe, ... **750.00**

c 1760-1770

DU PAQUIER 1720-30

VIENNA

Vienna, Austria
1718-1864

Du Paquier
1718-1744

State Factory
1744-1864

History: The Vienna Porcelain Factory, founded in 1718 by Claudius Du Paquier, was the second European factory to produce hard paste porcelain. Meissen was the first. Du Paquier developed high quality white porcelain. The privilege to make porcelain was granted to Du Paquier by the Emperor Charles VI. The decorations of the Du Paquier period fall into three categories: 1) 1725 in which the polychrome Oriental theme was emphasized; 2) 1730-1740, in which polychromed scrolls, landscapes, and figurals in cartouches were dominant, and black and gilt were used to highlight the themes; and 3) the final period, which featured German florals or "Deutch Blumchen" designs similar to the Meissen treatment. The adoption of Meissen styles contributed to the rise of Vienna as one of Meissen's chief rivals. However, unlike Meissen, the Du Paquier factory did not produce a large number of figures.

Du Paquier sold his factory to the Austrian state in 1744. It became the Imperial Porcelain Manufactory and fell under the influence of Empress Maria Theresa. The quality of the porcelain reached its peak during this period, known as the State Period (1744-1864). The Austrian coat of arms was used as the factory mark. Following the Seven Years' War, 1756-1763, which greatly altered the production at Meissen, Vienna porcelain assumed the undisputed leadership in European porcelain.

Between 1747 and 1784, Johann Niedermeyer, the chief modeler, contributed much to the success of the factory by creating rococo-influenced figurals decorated in soft pastel colors. After 1765 the styles from Sevres greatly influenced the decorative styles at Vienna. Anton Grassi came to work at Vienna in 1778. He moved the factory's production away from rococo styles into the neo-classical influences.

Joseph Leithner concentrated on developing new background colors, especially a fine cobalt blue that was a match for Sevres' bleu roi. He introduced a special gold color and enhanced all the colors used at Vienna.

Under the management of Konrad Sorgenthal between 1784 and 1805, the factory produced richly ornamented dinner and tea services, vases, urns, and plates in the neo-classical and Empire styles. Emphasis was placed on the reproduction of paintings by famous artists such as Angelica Kauffmann and Rubens onto porcelain vases, plates, and plaques that were surrounded by gilt frames that often included the painter's name.

Flowers were the principal decorative element used on Viennese porcelains. Seventeenth century Dutch flower paintings were adapted or copied on plates, cups, vases, or plate sets. Many pieces had black backgrounds to make the flowers stand out.

When the Congress of Vienna was held, numerous participants placed orders for services. After this period, the factory experienced a period of stagnation. Competition from the Bohemian factories started to take its toll.

After reaching the very pinnacle of success in the highly competitive porcelain field, the state porcelain factory was forced to close in 1864 due to financial difficulties.

The beehive mark was adopted in 1749. The year was stamped on pieces beginning in 1784.

References: W.B. Honey, *German Porcelain*, Faber & Faber, 1947; George W. Ware, *German & Austrian Porcelain*, Crown Publishers, Inc. 1963.

Museums: Art Institute of Chicago, Chicago, IL; British Museum, London, England; Gardiner Museum of Ceramic Art, Toronto, Canada; Metropolitan Museum of Art, New York, NY; Osterreiches Museum fur Angewandte, Kunst, Vienna, Austria; Smithsonian Institution, Division of Ceramics and Glass, National Museum of American History, Washington DC; Woodmere Art Museum, Philadelphia, PA.

Basket, 11 3/8" H-H, oval, pierced walls, painted fruit and loose sprigs on int, ext w/florets at intercises, green crabstock handles, brown lined rim, "blue shield" mk, c1780, repairs, pr, (A), ... **950.00**

Box, 1 1/2" w, hex shape, HP romantic scene of lady and leaping dog, raised gilding on lid, gilt metal mts, "blue shield" mk, c1820, ... **265.00**

Chocolate Pot, 10 1/2" h, HP garden flowers on sides, gilt rims, gilt accented figural snake handle, gilt accented spout and 3 paw feet, purple flower knob, ... **1,250.00**

Cream Pot, 5 3/4" h, puce painted exotic birds and flower sprays, 3 bird feet, scroll handle, Du Parquier, c1725, (A), ... **2,870.00**

Cup and Saucer, painted red English roses, flower sprigs, blue beehive mk, c1765, firing crack, ... **295.00**

Mug, 2 3/8" h, gilt oval medallion w/gilt intertwined initials in center on white ground, yellow body w/gilt border band and gilt lined base, gilt handle w/foliate terminals, blue beehive mk, ... **60.00**

Plate, 10" d, blue enamel forget-me-nots, blue lined rim, "blue shield" mark, pr, $550.00

Plate, 11 3/4" d, black painted seated putto in classic garden, restraining goose, clouds overhead, foliate scroll, shell and diaper border, gilt accents, c1740, ... **3,500.00**

Perfume Flask, 4 3/4" l, figural infant cap, orange bonnet, w/3 feathers, tied w/puce ribbon, black wrap, swaddled in flowered white blanket, tied w/yellow bow, silver gilt mts, imp shield mk, (A), ... **4,570.00**

Snuff Box, 3 1/2" w, rect, HP Italianate scenes of ruins, cov scene in brown and yellow reeded cartouche w/canted scroll corners, busts and hanging husks, turquoise ground w/border of yellow and brown ovals, same scenes on sides, int cov w/scene of statues and ruins w/o borders, contemporary gilt mts, c1785, (A), ... **19,720.00**

Tureen, 18" h, urn shape, 2 wishbone handles, circ base w/sm feet, band of green ivy on branches, gilt accents, gilt flame knob, ... **5,500.00**

VILLEROY AND BOCH

Mettlach, Germany
1836 to Present

History: Johann Franz Boch founded a dinnerware factory in 1809 in an old Benedictine abbey in Mettlach. This factory merged with the Nicholas Villeroy plant in Wallerfongen, Saar, in 1836 to form the Villeroy and Boch company. The Luxembourg factory founded in 1767 by the Boch brothers also was included in this merger. Eventually there were eight Villeroy and Boch factories in other cities in addition to the main factory at Mettlach. August von Cohausen was the director who instituted the use of the old abbey tower as the factory's trademark.

Stonewares, original in both design and production techniques, were produced starting in the 1840s and were the most famous of the Villeroy and Boch wares. Steins, punch bowls, beakers, wall plaques, beverage sets, drinking cups, hanging baskets, and vases were made.

Chromolith—colored stonewares—used two colors of clay worked side by side but separated by a black intaglio line. Raised decoration was done by applying the design and fusing it to the body of the stoneware pieces. This process was known as etched, engraved, or mosaic inlay.

Motifs included Germanic scenes depicting peasant and student life, and religious and mythological themes. Punch bowls featured garlands of fruit, while steins were adorned with drinking scenes, military events, folk tales, and student life scenes. About 1900, Art Nouveau decorations appeared on plaques, punch bowls, vases, steins, and umbrella and flower stands.

Planolith stoneware plaques were given an initial coating of a delicate green matte color, glazed, and then fired. Figures to decorate the plaques were formed separately, applied to the pre-fired background, and then fired again. These applied decorations were ivory colored and stood out in relief against the green ground. Motifs on plaques included scenes from Greek mythology and Germanic legends.

Cameo stonewares had raised ivory-colored decorations set on light blue or light green backgrounds. There was a less fluid quality to these applied decorations. The stoneware was more dense.

The pinnacle of stoneware production took place between 1880 and 1910. Prominent artists at Mettlach were Christian Warth, Heinrich Schlitt, Fritz Quidenus, Mittein, and Johann Baptist Stahl.

Terra cotta for architectural use was made from 1850; mosaic tiles were made from 1852. Cream-colored earthenwares for domestic use were produced at factories in Dresden from 1853 and in Schramberg from 1883. Around 1890, Mettlach artists manufactured plates and vases decorated in the Delft style and the faience of Rouen.

Around World War I, business had lessened due to unfavorable economic conditions and the lack of unskilled labor. In 1921 a major fire destroyed all molds, formulas, and records of the factory.

Although the factory continued to produce tiles, dinnerwares, and plumbing fixtures, almost fifty years lapsed before the factory revived the production of steins and plaques.

Reference: Gary Kirsner, *The Mettlach Book*, Seven Hills Books, 1983; Therese Thomas, *Villeroy & Boch, 1748-1930*, Self Published.

Museums: Keramik Museum, Mettlach, Germany; Musee de l'Etat, Luxembourg; Munchner-Stadtmuseum, Munich, Germany; Rijksmuseum, Amsterdam, Holland; Sevres Museum, Sevres, France; Villeroy & Boch Archives & Museum, Mettlach, Germany.

Beaker, 5 3/4" h, .25 L, multicolored decal of gnome holding wine bottle, #2842, Mercury mk, ... **168.00**

Biscuit Barrel, 4" h, incised red, blue, white, and dk brown leaves and flowers on brown ground bordered by bands of circles and brown stiff leaves, SP collar, cov, and handle, c1880, castle mk, ... **695.00**

Bowl, 6 1/4" d, floral spray in center, reticulated side panels w/floral sprays and molded gilt swirls, c1900, ... **30.00**

Bread Box, 18" l x 10 1/2" w x 8" h, wood frame w/blue and white Delft style tile inserts, curved ends, early 20th C, (A), ... **2,415.00**

Clock, 15 1/2", chalet shape, etched, black and tan zodiac designs on red-brown circle around clock face, tan and black angel in doorway flanked by chicken and owl, Viking ship on peak, Mettlach, castle mk, (A), ... **4,400.00**

Coffeepot, 9" h, "Burgenland" pattern, blue transfers, ... **75.00**

Cream Pitcher, 4 1/2" h, paneled, Art Nouveau style tan and blue tree design, ... **75.00**

Garniture, 8 1/2", 6 1/2" h, wheat colored ground, silver trim, "V & B Luxemburg" marks, $17,200.00

Jardiniere, 12 1/2" h x 13" d, multicolored scene of Dutch women and children, boats and windmill, reverse w/brown leafless trees, pale blue sky, gold rim, ... **895.00**

Pitcher, 10 5/8" h, relief of man and child playing cards, leaves under rim, mask spout, fancy handle, white glaze, "Villeroy & Boch Dresden" mk, dtd 1888, ... **795.00**

Plaque, 14 1/2" d, etched designs, multicolored, #1385/1384, castle mks, pr, $1,550.00

Plaque, 14" d, PUG, "Stadthaus in Berncastle," "Mettlach mercury, Made in Germany" mark, A- $85.00

Plaque

7 3/4" d, etched drinking cavalier, holding glass aloft, tan rim, Mettlach, #2622, ... **235.00**

9" d, etched bust of Black Forest maiden w/German saying, #2713, Mettlach, (A), ... **360.00**

12 1/4" d, multicolored "Geisenheim on the Rhine" castle, print under glaze, Mercury mk, ... **150.00**

14 1/2" d, etched design of warrior and castle, brown shades, blue bkd, sgd "Schultz," Mettlach, #1385, dtd 1910, ... **775.00**

15" d, etched design of man and woman horseback riding, sgd "Stocke," Mettlach #2041, 2042, pr, ... **3,000.00**

16" d, etched design of elf sitting in flowering tree drinking beer, flying insects, gold rococo border, Mettlach #2133, ... **1,300.00**

17" d, etched design of summer harvest scene, #2899, Mettlach, (A), ... **2,535.00**

18" d, white cameo of Trojan Warriors on boat, green jasper ground, sgd "Stahl," pierced for hanging, Mettlach, ... **850.00**

22 1/2" d, blue and white portrait of Senator Holzschuer, after Durer, #5219, ... **750.00**

Plate

8 3/4" d, lg red cosmos flowerhead in center, border band of pink, red, or blue flowers and green foliage, ... **30.00**

9 1/2" d, relief of gnome standing on another's back watering flower, piecrust inner border, green majolica-type glaze, wide border

of relief of florals and foliage, white glaze, "V.&B. S." mk, ... **45.00**

Platter

12" d, "Burgenland" pattern, red transfer, ... **40.00**

16 1/4" d, relief molded tan scrolls w/incised German sayings on border, dk red accents, Mettlach, ... **425.00**

Punch Bowl, 10" h x 15 1/2" d, w/underplate, white cameos of classic figures, med blue jasper ground, ... **1,280.00**

Serving Dish, 12 3/4" l x 9" w, oval, gaudy lt brown flowers, teal, red, and green foliage sprig in center, same border band w/cobalt cut sponge detail, (A), ... **40.00**

Sugar Bowl, Cov, 4" h x 6" H-H, "Burgenland" pattern, red transfer of country scene, running creek, farmhouse and fencing on sides, red printed Mercury mk, ... **40.00**

Vase

4 1/4" h, ball shape, everted rim, green and silver stylized houses design, c1910, ... **90.00**

5" h, squat ball shape, short neck, "Phoenix" pattern, HP multicolored bird in branches, ... **175.00**

6" h, swollen shape, rolled rim, applied enameled lt blue, yellow and red stylized flowerheads, matte blue ground w/incised meandering gold vines, Mettlach, castle mk, (A), ... **220.00**

9 1/4" h, 5 sides, blue printed oriental floral scene w/lg twisted tree, ... **85.00**

10 1/2" h, 4 sides tapering to top, incised and painted orange and green geometric design on ivory ground, matte finish, Mettlach, (A), ... **978.00**

13" h, tapered shape, short, straight collar, incised and painted orange, green, white, and grey irises and foliage, green ground, swirls on collar, Mettlach, (A), ... **1,495.00**

17" h, amphora shape, 2 rect handles w/rope twist centers, etched design of white and gilt edged yellow-gold swirling leaves, lt blue accents, cobalt ground, Mettlach, castle mk, #2414, ... **750.00**

MODERN MARK   1895

c1900

VOLKSTEDT

Thuringia, Germany
1760 to Present

History: The Volkstedt Porcelain Factory was started about 1760 under the patronage of Johann Friedrich von Schwartzburg-Rudolstadt. The peak of its fame occurred between 1767 and 1797 when the factory was leased to Christian Fonne. A succession of owners followed.

Until 1800 the factory produced mostly ordinary tablewares. These were usually massive in design and decorated in the rococo style. Some fine vases decorated in rococo or formal styles were made. Decorative motifs included small portraits, landscapes, and ornamental maps.

Between 1898 and 1972 Karl Ens occupied one portion of the Volkstedt factory. The firm made decorative porcelains, figures, and gift articles. The company was nationalized in 1972 and named VEB Underglaze Porcelain Factory

During the 20th century, Volkstedt manufactured tablewares, vases, and figures in the Meissen style.

Museum: Victoria & Albert Museum, London, England.

Biscuit Jar, 5 1/2" h, HP garden flowers, gold rims, handles, and knob, Beyer and Boch, ... **295.00**

Bowl, 9 3/4" d, HP white and purple water lily and buds, blue-green water, gold overlay border, artist sgd, "shield, B" mk, $90.00

Bowl, 7 1/4" d x 2 1/4" h, border bands of violets, center bunch, 3 gold feet,

"crowned B in shield" mk, Beyer and Boch, ... **165.00**

Candleholder, 7 1/4" h x 9 1/2" w, 2 arm, 2 pink figural roses applied to center, curved leaves, pr, ... **120.00**

Egg Set, stand, 7 1/4" h x 9 1/8" w, 6 egg cups w/attached bases, 2 1/2" h, HP pink, orange, yellow, and blue florals, gilt trim, repeated on top of server, base w/raised floral designs and gold accents, Beyer and Boch, ... **155.00**

Figure

5 1/2" h, standing harlequin, metallic blue ruffled collar, purple lined suit, holding guitar on base, Karl Ens, ... **135.00**

6" h, young girl w/fluttering goose at feet and flowerheads, beige skin, pink cheeks, blue eyes, blond hair, white wrap, Karl Ens, ... **135.00**

6 1/2" h, ballerina standing on green toe shoes, brown hair, pink lace ruffled sleeves, white lace gown w/pink lace trim and applied flowers, gold accent ed circ base, ... **400.00**

7" h

Art Deco kneeling brown haired nude girl holding flower in each hand, green garden base w/flowers, c1920, ... **545.00**

Figure, 9 1/4" h, brown, tan, cream, and gilt, pr, $650.00

Young couple standing under floppy umbrella, girl wearing flowered dress, basket on arm, boy wearing blue striped pants, molded base, Triebner, Ens, & Eckert, ... **300.00**

8" h x 9" w, white glazed blond haired nude ballerina stretching, arm arched overhead, arm on leg, blue drape and freeform base w/indented ovals, ... **520.00**

9 3/4" h, seated Pan w/brown hair, grey legs, black hooves, playing blue striped pipes to red and rose bird, ... **475.00**

11 1/2" h, dancing ballerina, pink edged white lace gown w/applied flowerheads, brown hair w/blue ribbon, ... **3,000.00**

13" l, nude woman reclining on oval textured base, matte white finish, rim chips, ... **675.00**

Figure, 20" h, white glaze, sgd "Guitav Oppei," A-**$460.00**

Flower Frog, 8 1/2" h, figural seated Pan playing flute, seated on brown rocks and green moss, gold accents, "Muller & Co. Volkstedt" mk, ... **950.00**

Plate, 10" d, HP multicolored scene of 3 children looking at bucket in center, blue luster border w/heavy gold paste geometrics and diapering, c1894, ... **875.00**

WADEHEATH

ENGLAND

c. 1934 +

WADE

Burslem, Stoke-On-Trent

1867-Present

Wade pottery is actually a group of potteries run by members of the Wade family. The most recognizable was the pottery founded as Wade and Myatt by Joseph Wade in 1867. The pottery was known as The Manchester Pottery because it provided ceramic goods to the textile industry in Manchester. In 1882, the name was changed to Wade & Son. In 1889 the company was taken over by George Wade, and under his stewardship, the company flourished. In 1905, Wade bought out the Hallen Pottery, a chief competitor. Son George Albert returned to the firm and the company produced a wide range industrial ceramics. In 1819, it was incorporated as George Wade & Son Ltd.

During the 1920s, the company introduced a line of decorative pottery including figures and gift ware.

In 1891, John and William Wade started J. & W. Wade & Company at the Flaxman Tile Works. Nephew A.J. Wade became a partner. The death of William resulted in John Wade adding Henry Heath as a partner. A.J. Wade Ltd. concentrated on tiles, while Wade Heath & Co stressed earthenware table wares and figures—most notably, the Walt Disney figures. In 1927, A.J. incorporated the two potteries into A.J. Wade, Ltd. and Wade Heath & Co. In 1935, George Albert Wade combined the companies into Wade Pottery, Ltd.

George Wade & Son, Ltd., of Manchester Pottery fame, continued as a separate entity.

The Manchester Pottery opened an art department, hiring Jessica Van Hallen as chief designer. Figures with an Art Deco flavor were given a cellulose finish, which failed over time when exposed to the sun.

Wade Ulster Ltd. was incorporated for the production of insulators in 1950. It was changed to Wade Ireland, Ltd. in 1966. A.J. Wade, Ltd., Wade Heath & Co. Ltd., George Wade & Sons Ltd., and Wade Ireland were combined to form The Wade Group of Potteries, each complementing the other.

By the 1970s, giftware was a large part of the group's products. In addition to producing the usual giftware, Wade Heath specialized in contract work, with distilleries and tobacco companies as major clients.

Wade PDM Ltd. was formed in 1969 for sales, design, and marketing. Wade Ceramics Ltd. is present day representative of the original 1867 firm.

References: Ian Warner and Mike Posgay, *The World of Wade, Book #1*, The Glass Press, Inc., 1997; Ian Warner & Mike Posgay, *The World of Wade, Book #2*; Ian Warner and Mike Posgay, *The World of Figures and Miniatures*, Schiffer Publications, 2003; Pat Murray, *The Charlton Standard Catalog; Wade Whimsical Collectibles*, The Charlton Press; Pat Murray, *The Charlton Standard Catalog of Wade; General Issues*, The Charlton Press; Pat Murray, *The Charlton Standard Catalog of Wade; Decorative Ware*, The Charlton Press; Pat Murray, *The Charlton Standard Catalog of Wade; Tableware, Vol. 3*, The Charlton Press, 1998; Pat Murray, *The Charlton Standard Catalog of Wade; Liquor Containers*, The Charlton Press, 1999; Ian Warner, *Wade Price Trends*; Ian Warner & Mike Posegay, *The World of Wade: Figures & Miniatures*, 2002.

Collectors' Club: Official International Wade Collectors Club, Wade Ceramics Ltd., Royal Works, Westport Road, Burslem, Stoke-on-Trent, St6 4AP England, www.wade.co.uk.

Newsletter: *Wade Watch*, quarterly newsletter, $8.00/year, 8199 Pierson Court, Arvada, CO 80005.

Ashtray

4" sq, center w/multicolored horse and coach scene, green border w/shamrocks, ... **6.00**

4 1/2" w, brown log dish w/figural beige and orange fawn seated on end, "Wade Porcelain Made in England" mk, ... **25.00**

6" d, stylized grey castle, "raised KRONENBOURG," white and red shield, ... **7.00**

Basket, 4 7/8" h x 5 1/2" l x 3 1/8" w, blue molded basketweave design w/yellow and green accents, "Wade England FLAXMAN" mk, ... **15.00**

Bowl, 8" l, figural barge, green glaze, ... **35.00**

Box, Cov, 4" l x 2 1/2" w x 1 1/2" h, figural turtle, brown shades, "WADE-PORCELAIN-MADE IN ENGLAND" mk, ... **15.00**

Cheese Dome, 4 1/2" h x 6" l x 5" w, Heath Cottageware, tan basketweave w/raised red and yellow flowerheads, green leaves, brown knob, "Wade Heath England" mk, ... **20.00**

Creamer, 3 1/4" h, Sugar Bowl, 2" h, Heath, pink and purple flowers, green leaves, gold trim, ... **30.00**

Dish, 3" l x 2 1/2" w, figural leaf shape, brown accents, "Wade Irish Porcelain, Made in Ireland" mk, ... **8.00**

Dispenser, 5 5/8" h, black "GIN" in blue-grey label, blue stripes, metal spigot, ... **15.00**

Egg Cup, 4" h, figural "Harrod's Doorman," green coat, ... **35.00**

Figure

2 1/4" h, "Old King Cole," blue robe, gold crown, ... **5.00**

3 1/2" h, "Wynken," little boy wearing red collared blue gown, holding flowers, flowered green base, ... **100.00**

3 3/4" h, Paddy Reilly, green-brown coat, tan pants, blue vest, ... **80.00**

6" h, Widda Cafferty, brown scarf, blue edged white dress, ... **350.00**

Jam Pot, Cov, 5 1/2" h, w/knife, raised red, purple, and yellow flowerheads, lt yellow basketweave ground, green stem knob, "Wade Heath England" mk, ... **45.00**

Jug

3" h, black printed Tower Bridge, brown ground, silver rims, ... **10.00**

4 1/2" h, "Shooting Star" pattern, black int, ... **30.00**

7 1/2" h, Wadeheath, relief of green and orange budgies on sides, yellow ground, brown handle, c1934-35, ... **200.00**

8" h, paneled, Art Deco "Armari" design, cobalt, iron-red, and gilt Wade Heath, ... **55.00**

9" h, "Flaxmanware," Art Deco emb tulips, leaves, and dots, ivory glaze, Wade Heath, ... **20.00**

10" h, grey figural stone body, green stone base and rim, brown branch handle w/green and yellow figural budgie, "WADE ENGLAND" mk, ... **70.00**

Hot Water Pot, Cov, 8" h, "Heath-Snow White," Dopey, deer, and rabbit, in forest, "WADEHEATH BY PERMISSION WALT DISNEY ENGLAND" mk, ... **975.00**

Money Box, 7" h, figural "Lady Hillary," blue jacket, black dress, holding grey purse, ... **45.00**

Mug

4" h, figural squatting rabbit, tan, ... **6.00**

6 1/4" h, multicolored decal of hunters, amber glaze, incised vert bands on neck, raised bands of squares on base, ... **10.00**

Pipe Rest, 3 1/4" l, standing brown German Shepherd dog on edge of gunmetal grey base, ... **15.00**

Pitcher

5 1/2" h, tan ground, molded gold and tan horiz bands, diag molded swirl bands on front, molded waffle design on base, "WADE ENGLAND" mk, ... **40.00**

Pitcher, 4 3/4" h, "Bramble" pattern, $48.00

6" h

"Beefeater Gin" design, multicolored, white ground, ... **10.00**

Black tribal dancers, black and white circles, white ground, ... **65.00**

6 1/8" h, "Paradise" pattern, lg blue bird, oranges w/green leaves and black stripes, horiz grooved base, 3 loop handle, ... **20.00**

6 1/2" h, "Bramble" pattern, relief molded red and purple berries, green leaves, brown branch handle, grey pebble ground, ... **25.00**

7 3/4" h, Heath, relief of rabbit, bird and chicks, tan tree trunk body w/brown branch handle, mkd, ... **70.00**

9" h, "Empress" pattern, blue and gold vert striping, gold fancy handle, "Wade Empress England" mk, ... **35.00**

Plate

9 1/2" d, "Capri" pattern, maroon and yellow tulips, blue buttercups, curved green leaves, ... **10.00**

10" d, lg painted stylized yellow or red tulip, bluebell flowers, red and green dash leaves and stems, green interrupted lined rim, "WADE ENGLAND" mk, ... **18.00**

10 1/2" d, multicolored transfer of English cottage and garden in center, burgundy piecrust border w/gold tracery, ... **58.00**

10 3/4" d, "Meadow" pattern, ... **20.00**

Posy Bowl

4 1/2" h, figural Pegasus, white w/lt blue tail, hooves, eyes, and mane, ... **60.00**

6 1/2" l, relief of horses, curled handles, beige ground, "WADE ENGLAND" mk, ... **12.00**

Shakers, 4 1/2" h, "Bisto Twins," boy in grey jacket, blue trousers, blond girl, brown hat, yellow shirt, red streaked brown trousers, pr, ... **250.00**

Spill Vase, 4 1/4" h, sm figural blue bird on branch from brown tree trunk spill, "WADE PORCELAIN MADE IN ENGLAND" mk, ... **20.00**

Teapot

5 1/2" h, "Wadeheath Imari" pattern, gilt, iron red, and cobalt designs, c1930, ... **110.00**

6 1/4" h, HP figural Donald Duck, ... **1,050.00**

6 1/2" h, red poppies on sides, ... **15.00**

6 3/4" h, "Beatrice The Ballerina," multicolored decal, ... **33.00**

7" h x 9" l, "Dressage" design, rider in black habit riding white horse sidesaddle, ... **70.00**

7 3/4" w, squat, Flaxman, mottled cream/ivory ground, ... **70.00**

Tea Premiums

1 1/8" h, Wild Boar, tan, ... **3.00**

1 1/8" w, Frog, yellow-green, ... **3.00**

1 1/4" h, Sea Otter, brown, ... **3.00**

1 3/8" h

Camel, tan, ... **5.00**

Fox, red-brown, ... **4.00**

Pine Marten, tan, ... **4.00**

1 1/2" h

Female Monkey, tan, ... **4.00**

Humpty Dumpty, tan, ... **4.00**

Old King Cole, tan and blue, ... **5.00**

Seated Eskimo, brown, ... **6.00**

1 1/2" l

Camel, tan, ... **7.00**

Panther, brown spotting, ... **7.00**

1 5/8" h

Gingerbread Man, dk brown and green, ... **5.00**

Male Monkey, dk brown, ... **5.00**

1 3/4" h

Little Bo Peep, tan and blue, ... **5.00**

Little Red Riding Hood, tan, ... **5.00**

Pied Piper, tan, ... **5.00**

Rabbit, crouching, brown, ... **8.00**

1 3/4" w, butterfly, #196, ... **8.00**

Fawn, brown, ... **3.00**

Seahorse, brown, ... **10.00**

Seated Poodle, ... **5.00**

Tea Set, pot, 6" h, creamer, 4" h, sugar
bowl, 3" h, "Paisley" pattern, "Wades
England" mks, ... **200.00**
Vase
3 1/4" h, squat shape, short, flared
neck, underglazed lg red
flowerhead and leaf, dk brown
ground, ... **35.00**
4 1/2" h x 10" l, gondola shape on
tapered stand, white flowers on
gloss black ground, gold trim,
"red WADE ENGLAND" mk,
.... **25.00**
6 1/2" h, "Gothic" pattern, brown and
green leaf designs, brown
outlined purple and yellow tulips,
"Gothic Wade Heath England"
mk, ... **45.00**
7" h, barrel shape, "Orcadia" pattern,
HP bands of green, orange,
yellow, and green and orange
drip on base, Wadeheath,
.... **35.00**
9" h, tapered cylinder shape, spread
ft, everted rim, "Orcadia" pattern,
matte orange, green, and brown
streaked design, ... **28.00**
Whimsie
1 1/8" h x 1 1/4" l, Pump Cottage,
.... **5.00**
1 1/4" h, Ram, white, green base,
.... **4.00**
1 3/8" h, Koala bear, black, tree
trunk, ... **4.00**
1 1/2" h x 1 1/2" l, Service Station,
.... **10.00**
1 3/4" h x 1 1/2" l, Why Knott Inn,
.... **5.00**
1 7/8" h x 2 1/2" l, The Manor,
.... **6.00**

WEDGWOOD
c1759-1769

***
WEDGWOOD
c1900

WEDGWOOD

Burslem, near
Stoke-on-Trent, England
1759-1769

Etruria factory, England
1769-1940

Barlaston, near
Stoke-on-Trent, England
1940 to Present

History: By 1759 Josiah Wedgwood was
working in Burslem, Staffordshire,
manufacturing earthenware. A partnership
with Bentley was formed shortly after he
moved to his new factory in Etruria in 1769.
The partnership lasted until 1780.
Wedgwood worked in conjunction with
Thomas Whieldon to develop new glazes,
especially green glazes. A tortoiseshell
glaze was also a product of their
partnership.

BLACK BASALT

Black Basalt was fine grained, unglazed
black stoneware made between 1767 and
1796. This term was coined by Josiah
Wedgwood to describe a refined version of
"Egyptian black." In his 1787 catalog,
Wedgwood described his ware as "a black
porcelain biscuit (unglazed body) of nearly
the same properties with the natural stone,
striking fire from steel, receiving a high
polish, serving as a touchstone for metals,
resisting all acids, and bearing without
injury a strong fire—stronger indeed than
the basalts itself." "Egyptian Black" was
used for utilitarian wares and for large relief
plaques, vases, busts, medallions, seals,
and small intaglios. It was a black clay body
that resembled bronze when unpolished.
Both historical and mythological figures and
faces were produced.

BONE CHINA

When Josiah II took over, he introduced
the manufacture of bone china in 1812.
Production continued until 1828. Josiah II
was not satisfied with the product, so it
was discontinued. Bone china was not
manufactured again until 1878.

The forty year period from 1840 to 1880
was one of modernization. Solid jasper
was reintroduced. Parian ware, a fine white
body resembling marble, was produced.
When Wedgwood introduced majolica in
1860, the company was the first to use a
white body and semi-transparent colored
glazes.

When Wedgwood began to manufacture porcelain again in 1878, the products
were of very high quality in texture, color,
glaze, and decoration. The printed mark
with the Portland vase was used on this
porcelain.

Fourth and fifth generations of Wedg-
woods continued to operate the firm into
the 20th century. An interest in late 18th
century design was revived. Commemorative wares were made for the American
market.

CREAMWARE

Wedgwood's creamware utilized a
Cornwall clay that created a lighter,
stronger body of a more uniform texture. It
became designated "Queensware" after
Wedgwood supplied a breakfast set for
Queen Charlotte in 1762.

JASPER

Jasper, probably Josiah Wedgwood's best
known product, was started in 1774.

Known as a "dry body" because it was
non-porous and unglazed, this vitreous
fine stoneware was made in several
shades of blue, green, lilac, yellow,
maroon, black, and white. Sometimes
more than one color was combined.
"Solid" jasper had the body colored
throughout, while white jasper "dip" was a
white jasper body with the color laid on the
surface. Raised figures and ornaments in
white adorned the tremendous variety of
jasper shapes. Classical motifs were most
prominent. Wedgwood's replica of the
Barberini or Portland vase was considered
a high point in production.

PEARLWARE

Pearlware, introduced by Wedgwood in
1779, was whiter than Queensware. Cobalt
oxide was added to the glaze, reacting like
a laundry bluing that whitened clothing.

After Bentley's death in 1780, Wedgwood worked alone until 1790 when his
sons and Thomas Byerley became his
partners. From 1769 until 1780, the firm
was called "Wedgwood and Bentley." It
was simply "Wedgwood" in the decade
from 1780 to 1790. The name became
"Wedgwood Sons and Byerley" between
1790 and 1793, and "Wedgwood & Sons &
Byerley" between 1793 and 1795. Josiah
Wedgwood died in 1795.

REDWARES

Other "dry bodies" or redwares made that
were manufactured between 1776 and
1870 included a) cane ware (pale buff
colored stoneware); b) rosso antico (dark
red to chocolate-colored unglazed
stoneware); c) terra cotta (light red
stoneware); d) drabware (olive-grey
stoneware); and e) white stoneware (pure
white biscuit). Both utilitarian and
decorative wares were made.

WEDGWOOD LUSTERS

Wedgwood lusters were formed by
applying iridescent or metallic films on the
surface of the ceramic wares. The effect
was obtained by using metallic oxides of
gold, silver, copper, etc. Lusters were
applied as embellishments to an
enameled object or as a complete or near-
complete covering to duplicate the effect
of a silver or copper metallic object. The
lusters were decorated by the resist
method.

From 1915 to 1931, Wedgwood produced fairyland lusters from the designs of
Daisy Makeig-Jones. Fairyland lusters
were made in Queensware plaques and
bone china plates and ornamental pieces,
such as vases and bowls. The designs
combined the use of bright underglaze
colors, commercial lusters, and gold printing, often with fantastic and grotesque figures, scenes, and landscapes.

Pattern numbers were painted on the
base of fairyland luster pieces, along with
the Wedgwood marks, by the artist who
decorated them.

A new factory was built at Barlaston, six miles from Etruria. Firing was done at Barlaston in six electric ovens. Production started at the new factory in 1940. Etruria eventually was closed in June 1950.

On May 1, 1959, the company commemorated its bicentenary. During the 1960s, Wedgwood acquired many English firms such as Coalport, William Adams & Sons, Royal Tuscan, Susie Cooper, and Johnson Brothers. Further expansion in the 1970s brought J. & G. Meakin, Midwinter Companies, Crown Staffordshire, Mason's Ironstone, and Precision Studios into the fold. Each company retained its own identity. The Wedgwood Group is one of the largest fine china and earthenware manufacturers in the world.

References: M. Batkin, *Wedgwood Ceramics 1846-1959*, Antique Collectors' Club, 1982; David Buten, *18th Century Wedgwood*, Methuen, Inc. 1980; Una des Fontines, *Wedgwood Fairyland Lustre*, Borne-Hawes, 1975; Alison Kelly, *The Story of Wedgwood*, The Viking Press, 1975; Wolf Mankowitz, *Wedgwood*, Spring Books, 1966; Robin Reilly, *Josiah Wedgwood, 1730-1795*, Pan Books, 1992; Robin Reilly, *The New Illustrated Dictionary of Wedgwood*, Antique Collectors' Club, Ltd. 1995; Robin Reilly, *Wedgwood Jasper*, Thomas Hudson, 1994; Robin Reilly & George Savage, *The Dictionary of Wedgwood*, Antique Collectors' Club, Ltd. 1980; Geoffrey Wills, *Wedgwood*, Chartwell Books, Inc. 1989; Gillian Neale, *Miller's Blue & White Pottery*, Antique Collectors Club, 2000; Michael Herman, *Wedgwood Jasper Ware: A Shape Book & Collectors Guide*, Schiffer Publications, 2003.

Collectors' Clubs: The Wedgwood Society, The Roman Villa, Rockbourne, Fordingbridge, Hants. SP6 3PG, UK. Membership: £7.5, Wedgwood Data Chart, Semi-annual newsletter; The Wedgwood Society of New York, 5 Dogwood Court, Glen Head, NY 11545, Membership: $22.50, *Ars Ceramic Magazine*, Bi-monthly newsletter; The Wedgwood Society of Boston, Adele I. Rogers, 28 Birchwood Drive, Hampstead, NH 03841, Annual Dues: $25.00; Wedgwood International Seminar, 22 DeSavry Crescent, Toronto, Ontario M4S 212 Canada.

Museums: Birmingham Museum of Art, Birmingham, AL; The Brooklyn Museum, Brooklyn, NY; City Museum & Art Gallery, Stoke-on-Trent, England; Henry E. Huntington Library & Art Gallery, San Marino, CA; Jones Museum of Glass & Ceramics, East Baldwin, ME; Nassau County Museum, Sands Point Preserve, NY; R.W. Norton Art Gallery, Shreveport, LA; Victoria & Albert Museum, London, England; Wedgwood Museum, Barlaston, Stoke-on-Trent, England.

Reproduction Alert: Two marks are currently in use on Wedgwood pieces. If neither of these marks appear on a piece, it is probably not Wedgwood.

Basalt, candlesticks, 8 1/2", 9" h, Cupid and Psyche, c1880, pr, $1,750.00

Basalt
Bowl
6 1/4" d, relief molded band of Bacchanalian scenes, c1780, ... **2,250.00**

7 1/4" d, bands of engine turnings, "imp WEDGWOOD" mk, c1880, ... **175.00**

Coffeepot, 8" h, molded classical figures and engine turning, sibyl knob, c1840, ... **1,050.00**

Creamer, 3 1/2" h, "Bacchanalian Boys" design, engine turned vert fluting on base, ... **215.00**

Crocus Pot, 11" l, w/underplate, figural hedgehog w/multiple holes, "imp WEDGWOOD" mk, chip, (A), ... **675.00**

Figure
4 " h, standing poodle, c1930, ... **600.00**

5 3/8" h, pr of Vultures, "imp WEDGWOOD" mk, c1915, ... **1,175.00**

8" h, bust of Robert Burns on circ base, "WEDGWOOD BURNS" on back, ... **200.00**

9 7/8" h, "Autumn," standing partially draped female holding wheat over shoulder, imp title, (A), ... **880.00**

18" h, bust of Mercury, winged helmet, titled socle base, 19th C, (A), ... **1,125.00**

Flower Holder, 12 1/4" h, bowl, 10 1/2" d, center figure of Aphrodite on crested wave, pierced freeform rock, bowl w/inverted rim, early 19th C, (A), ... **765.00**

Inkstand, 3 1/8" h, 2 handled oval tray w/central urn shaped bottle, engine-turned circ inkwell and sand pot, late 18th C, (A), ... **765.00**

Mug, 4 1/8" h, applied oak branches and acorns, handle sprigged w/overlapping oak leaves, "imp WEDGWOOD" mk, c1790, ... **1,050.00**

Oil Lamp, 9 1/2" h x 8 1/2" l, "Vestal," figural female seated on end of Aladdin type lamp pouring oil from pitcher into cov receptacle, flared stem on sq base w/cut corners, "imp Wedgwood" mk, c1800, pr, ... **12,500.00**

Tea Kettle, 6 1/4" h, molded bamboo designs on body and cov, bail handle, (A), ... **1,530.00**

Jasper, urn, 19 1/4" h, white cameos, med blue jasper ground, c1800, $7,250.00

Urn, Cov, 7" h, modeled hanging rope swags, circ socle, sq base, Wedgwood and Bentley, c1770, ... **4,850.00**

Vase
9 1/2" h, trumpet shape, lobed base, molded foliate designs, medallions on border and ft, "imp WEDGWOOD MADE IN ENGLAND" mk, pr, ... **285.00**

9 3/4" h, amphora shape w/leaf molded handles, applied trophies on neck over anthemion band, body w/classical reliefs, 19th C, (A), ... **1,115.00**

Vase, Cov, 12 5/8" h, relief molded Bacchus w/putti and satyrs, classical mask handles, paneled foot and neck molded w/oak leaf wreaths, "imp WEDGWOOD" mk, 19th C, (A), ... **1,200.00**

General

Basket, 6 5/8" d, creamware, open work, dbl woven strand around middle, woven single strand on rim, imp mk, c1800, ... **285.00**

Bowl, 7 7/8" d, "Rosso Antico," applied black meandering border, angular relief on base, "imp WEDGWOOD" mk, ... **2,250.00**

Bowl, Cov, 6 1/8" H-H, w/undertray, Queen's Ware, iron-red and black foliate designs on borders, late 18th C, pr, (A), ... **575.00**

Cereal Bowl, 6 3/8" d, Peter Rabbit-"But around the end of the cucumber frame...," **10.00**

Chocolate Pot, 10 1/4" h, "Ferrara" pattern, purple transfer, "purple FERRARA ETRURIA ENGLAND WEDGWOOD" and imp "MADE IN ENGLAND WEDGWOOD" mk, (A), ... **247.00**

Cream Jug, 2" h, "Encaustic," polychrome enamel bands of arabesque flowers and running laurel, early 19th C, (A), ... **1,525.00**

Dessert Plate, 8 1/4" d, pearlware, iron-red, cobalt, green, and gilt "Chrysanthemum" pattern, c1810, ... **420.00**

Ewer, 7" h, "Etruscan," red classic scenes of wedding on black basalt ground, c1810, ... **4,850.00**

Food Warmer, 10 1/2" h, "Queen's Ware," 2 handled base w/pierced flower design, food pot w/dbl entwined strap handles, acorn knob, early 19th C, (A), ... **825.00**

Game Tureen, Cov, 10 1/2" l x 8" w, bisque, relief molded grapes, vines, and stems on sides, figural rabbit knob, glazed int, pr, ... **1,350.00**

Garniture, 8 1/2" h, 2 vases, 6 1/4" h, Queen's Ware, yellow ground w/relief bands of acanthus, bellflowers, and fruiting vines, late 19th C, (A), ... **1,115.00**

Gravy Boat, 4" h x 8 1/2" l, w/underplate, "Garden" pattern, yellow and black intersecting swirls, Eric Ravilious, 1939, ... **95.00**

Jug, 7 3/4" h, painted white daffodils, green leaves, gold handle, "brown Wedgwood" mk, c1815, ... **2,750.00**

Meat Platter, 15 1/2" l, well and tree, multicolored "Bullfinch" pattern, ... **425.00**

Pepper Pot, 3 1/8" h, queensware, baluster shape, "imp WEDGWOOD" mk, c1785, ... **350.00**

Pitcher, 6 1/4" h, Rosso Antico, glazed int, "imp WEDGWOOD" mk, c1850, ... **110.00**

Plate

9" d, creamware, sm green sprig in center, green outlined reticulated border loops, "imp WEDGWOOD" mk, ... **375.00**

9 1/8" d, creamware, scene of young man selling buns to lady and child, "Buns, Buns, Buns" on reverse, sgd "Lessore," dtd 1863, ... **345.00**

9 1/2" d, creamware, "Liverpool" birds design, black transfers, indented rim, set of 8, ... **3,100.00**

10" d

"Bullfinch" pattern, multicolored, "imp WEDGWOOD ENGLAND" mk, ... **55.00**

"Edinburgh" pattern, aesthetic design of cottage at lake in rect frame, lg jardiniere of flowers w/perched birds in foreground, border of zigzags and flowerheads, blue-green ground, "imp WEDGWOOD" mk, ... **35.00**

Platter, 14 1/2" l x 10 7/8" w, creamware, 2 red-orange stripes on rim, "imp WEDGWOOD" mk, ... **85.00**

Potpourri, Cov, 3 3/4" h, drabware, horiz loop handles, "imp WEDGWOOD" mk, c1820, ... **275.00**

*Soup Plate, 8 3/8" d, red and blue morning glory design in center, blue lined rim, "Morning Glory Wedgwood Patrician" mark, set of 6, **$275.00***

Soup Plate

9 1/8" d, aesthetic, prunus, birds, and pot of peonies in center, multiple rings on border, slate blue transfer, dtd 1883, ... **48.00**

9 1/4" d, "Ivanhoe-Rebecca Repelling the Templar," med blue transfer, ... **85.00**

9 1/2" d, creamware, red enamel crest in center, wavy red lined rim, c1780, ... **595.00**

Sugar Bowl, Cov, 4 1/4" h, "Ferrara" pattern, purple transfer, "purple FERRARA ETRURIA ENGLAND WEDGWOOD" and "imp MADE IN ENGLAND WEDGWOOD" mks, c1891-1900, (A), ... **137.00**

Tea Caddy, 5" h, pearlware, flattened oval shape w/fluted corners and serpentine shoulder, green streaked shoulder border, green accented flower knob, "imp WEDGWOOD" mk, c1785, ... **1,115.00**

*Teapot, 7" l, drabware, "bamboo" pattern, "imp WEDGWOOD" mk, (A), **$100.00***

Teapot, 5 1/2" h, globular, pearlware, underglazed blue printed floral sprays, leaf molded handle and spout, rim chips, 18th C, (A), ... **353.00**

*Teapot, 4 1/2" h, black outlined enameled flowers, terra cotta ground, A-**$70.00***

Tureen, Cov, 9" h x 14" H-H, creamware, pedestal base, ear handles w/molded flowerhead terminals, flowerhead knob w/leaf terminal, c1790, ... **1,250.00**

Jasper

Biscuit Barrel

6 1/4" h, tricolor, white classic figures on dk blue jasper body, lt blue jasper collar w/white stiff leaves, SP rim, cov, and handle, c1880, ... **995.00**

6 1/2" h, white classic cameos amongst trees, lilac jasper

ground, SP rim, cov, and handle, "imp WEDGWOOD" mk, ... **295.00**

Bough Pot, 11 1/8" l, oval, applied white cameos of classic winged cherubs and band of hanging bearded masks and foliage, med blue jasper ground, hairline, late 18th C, (A), ... **1,840.00**

Jasper, box, 7" l x 2 3/4" w, white cameos, dk blue jasper ground, "imp WEDGWOOD MADE IN ENGLAND" mk, $105.00

Box, Cov, 3" w, white cameos of Cupid and lady on cov w/band of roses, Cupids around base, dk blue ground, "WEDGWOOD" mk, ... **165.00**

Basalt, candlesticks, 5 1/4" h x 6" l, "imp WEDGWOOD" mks, c1790, pr, $6,000.00

Candlestick, 6 1/2" h, white cameos of "Poetic Muses" and trees, med blue jasper ground, c1880, pr, ... **1,250.00**

Jasper, candlesticks, 8" h, white cameos, blue jasper ground, "imp WEDGWOOD MADE IN ENGLAND" marks, pr, A-$259.00

Centerpiece, 8" h, "Diceware," green jasper dip on white ground w/applied lilac quatrefoils and white running laurel borders, classical male knob, (A), ... **1,060.00**

Cheese Dish, Cov, 4 1/2" h x 9 1/4" d, white cameos of classic ladies, Cupid on stand, band of leaves on base and cov, leaf terminals on knob, med blue jasper dip ground, "imp WEDGWOOD" mk, ... **455.00**

Claret Jug, 10" h, white cameos of classic figures of woman carrying basket on head and other figures, geometric band on shoulder, med blue jasper dip ground, SP fancy classical handle, collar, cov and spout, "imp WEDGWOOD" mk, ... **1,100.00**

Coffee Cup and Saucer

Three color, white ground w/applied green leaves, lilac berries and florets, lilac drop medallions centering white classical decorations on cup, mid-19th C, (A), ... **1,525.00**

White cameos of "Dancing Hours," band of entwined ribbon on rim, stiff leaves on saucer, sage green ground, "Wedgwood" mk, ... **950.00**

Hot Water Pitcher, 6 1/2" h, white cameos of Grecian ladies and Cupid, raised grape and leaves around neck, hinged SP lid, "WEDGWOOD ENGLAND" mk, ... **175.00**

Jam Jar, 4" h, white cameos of Grecian women and trees, dk blue ground, SP cov, "WEDGWOOD" mk, ... **125.00**

Jug, 5 1/4" h, "Etruscan," applied white cameos of classic figures and statues between floral banded borders on crimson jasper ground, c1920, (A), ... **2,000.00**

Muffineer, 7 1/2" h, white cameos of classic horsemen and women, med blue jasper ground, pierced metal top, "imp WEDGWOOD" mk, ... **250.00**

Mug, 5 1/4" h, cylinder shape, white classic cameos and trees, dk olive green ground, "imp WEDGWOOD ENGLAND" mk, ... **125.00**

Pitcher

4" h, white cameos of 4 classical women and cherub, grape vine around top, crimson ground, "imp WEDGWOOD ENGLAND" mk, ... **500.00**

6 1/2" h, white cameos of Grecian figures, white grapes and leaves around top, metal lid, "WEDGWOOD ENGLAND" mk, ... **175.00**

Plaque

4" h, white cameo bust of "John Peel," med blue jasper ground, "imp WEDGWOOD" mk, c1856, ... **345.00**

13 3/4" l x 6" h, rect, white cameos of Dancing Hours on black ground, white framing of laurel leaves bordered by yellow jasper ground, early 20th C, (A), ... **2,350.00**

14 1/2" l x 6" w, rect, white cameos of groups of boys, black jasper ground, 19th C, pr, (A), ... **3,450.00**

18 1/4" l x 7" h, white cameos of applied scrolling acanthus leaves, banded key border, green jasper dip ground, gilt and ebonized frame, (A), ... **25,850.00**

Portland Vase, 8 1/8" h, white cameos, black jasper ground, mid-19th C, ... **1,850.00**

Potpourri Vase, 18" h, white cameos of the "Bacchanalian Triumph," stiff leaves on base and cov, blue jasper ground, flame knob, horiz handles, c1850, ... **9,500.00**

Ring Tree, 2 3/4" h, blue jasper dip ground w/white cameos of classic figures on base, band of white garlands on rim, c1890s, ... **145.00**

Rose Bowl, 5" d, white cameos of classic figures separated by trees, center starburst and sm 4 petal flowers on cov, 2 white handles, med blue jasper dip ground, c1900, ... **190.00**

Salad Bowl, 7 7/8" d, applied black classic figures between floral festoons ending in ram's heads, yellow jasper dip ground, SP rim, c1930, (A), ... **1,035.00**

Scent Bottle, 4 3/4" l, rect w/cut corners, white cameo of nymph in billowing gown front and reverse, white oval medallion over garland on neck, border chain of sm flowerheads, med blue jasper ground, silver top, ... **1,500.00**

Sugar Bowl, Cov, 4 3/4" h, w/underplate, white cameos of angels and children at play on base, white stiff leaves and radiating green jasper lines on cov and underplate, lt green jasper dip ground, c1780, ... **2,850.00**

Tea Set, pot, 4 1/2" h, creamer, 2 1/2" h, cov sugar bowl, alternating green and lilac vert foliate designs, solid white jasper ground, late 19th C, (A), ... **2,185.00**

Tray, 10" l x 7 1/2" w, oval, white cameo of winged nymph under tree w/cherub and Cupid, white cameo band of grapevines, med blue jasper ground, "imp WEDGWOOD MADE IN ENGLAND" mk, c1900, ... **125.00**

Urn, 8 1/4" h, white cameos of classic figures and floral swags, lt blue jasper dip ground, "imp WEDGWOOD" mk, pr, ... **560.00**

Urn, Cov, 20 1/4" h, white cameos of "Apotheosis of Virgil," figural dolphin handles, Pegasus knob, sq base w/anthemion , med blue jasper ground, dtd 1910, ... **16,500.00**

Vases, 11 1/2" h, white cameos, lt blue jasper ground, c1825, pr, $7,000.00

Vase, Cov, 8 1/4" h, swollen shape, circ socle, sq base, center band of white cameo arabesque floral designs, ribbon border, stiff leaf cov and base, white Cupid knob, lt blue solid jasper, 19th C, pr, (A), ... **2,530.00**

Jasper, vase, Cov, 11" h, white cameos, med blue jasper ground, c1800, $4,200.00

Luster

Bowl

2 3/4" d, oct, "Dragon" luster, lt aqua int w/gold, red, and blue dragon, dk blue luster ext w/purple and gold dragons, "WEDGWOOD MADE IN ENGLAND Z4829" mk, ... **325.00**

3" h x 4 3/4" d, ftd, "Butterfly" luster, MOP int w/multicolored butterfly and blue crosshatched inner border, ruby luster ext w/gold oriental motifs, set of 8, ... **3,500.00**

4 1/4" d, gilt grasshoppers on powder blue luster ground, polychromed floral design on int, (A), ... **295.00**

4 1/2" d, "Butterfly" luster, mottled orange and green ext w/gilt ornaments, MOP int w/multicolored butterfly, Z4830, (A), ... **410.00**

5 3/8" h, stemmed w/flared body, "Dragon" luster, mottled green, brown, blue, and red ext, orange luster int, Z4823, (A), ... **165.00**

8 1/2" h, baluster shape, "Fairyland Luster-Willow" pattern, Z5360, pr, ... **18,850.00**

9" d, "Fairyland Luster-Poplar Trees" pattern on ext, "Elves and Bell Branch" pattern on int, Z4968, (A), ... **2,100.00**

9 1/8" d, "Dragon" luster, blue ext w/dragon, MOP int w/Chinese landscape cartouches, dragons, and cell border, Z4879, (A), ... **645.00**

Dish, 6 1/4" d, 3 sm feet, "Fairyland Luster-Nizami" pattern, Z5494, (A), ... **4,245.00**

Drain, 15" l x 11" w, "Moonlight" luster, pierced, ... **495.00**

Potpourri Urn, 12 3/4" h, mottled purple Moonlight luster w/orange enamel glaze, inner disk lid, c1810, cov missing, (A), ... **382.00**

Tyge, 2" h, 3 handles, "Dragon" luster, gold outlined blue and red dragon on int, aqua luster ground, mottled blue ext w/snake, serpent, or dragon between handles, gold accents, "gold WEDGWOOD MADE IN ENGLAND Porland vase and Z4829" mk, ... **425.00**

Vase, 9" h, "Dragon" luster, gold dragons, mottled blue ext, sea green int, "gold Portland vase, #Z4829," $975.00

Vase

5 1/4" h, "Hummingbird Luster," bottle shape, blue luster ground, ... **370.00**

Vase, 7 3/4" h, Butterfly luster, gold butterflies, green/blue pearl luster ground, orange luster int, $750.00

7 1/2" h, "Fairyland Luster-Candlemas," black ground panel, blue luster frames, (A), ... **9,400.00**

Vase, 9 1/2" h, "Butterfly" luster, gold outlined butterflies, blue-green ext, orange and gold int, c1925, $900.00

Vase, 8 7/8" h, Dragon luster, gold dragons, mottled blue ground, cream int with green line, "WEDGWOOD ENGLAND" mark, pr, $1,000.00

8 7/8" h, bulbous shoulder, tapered base, flared ft, "Argus Pheasant" pattern, (A), ... **2,475.00**

Trumpet Shape

7 3/4" h, "Fairyland Luster-Butterfly Woman" pattern, ... **6,850.00**

9" h, "Fairyland Luster-Candlemas" pattern, ... **10,500.00**

10 1/2" H, "Hummingbird" luster, wide shoulder, narrow base, spread ft, green luster ground, ... **3,500.00**

11" h, cylinder shape, "Dragon" luster, gilt dragon on powder blue luster ground, gilt Greek key and foliate scrolling borders, (A), ... **382.00**

WHIELDON WARE

Fenton Vivien, Stoke-on-Trent, England
1740-1780

History: Thomas Whieldon founded his earthenware factory at Little Fenton in 1740. He began potting small items such as boxes, cutlery handles, chimney pieces, and teapots. Whieldon introduced various metallics into the clay to alter the color of the earthenware body.

Whieldon experimented with colored glazes, attempting to imitate tortoiseshell. Most Whieldon ware is either mottled brownish or greenish in tone.

Several noted potters apprenticed with Whieldon. Josiah Spode is probably the most famous. In 1754 Whieldon took Josiah Wedgwood as a partner. While working for Whieldon, Wedgwood invented a green glaze that was used to decorate fanciful wares in the shapes of pineapples and cauliflowers. Together, Whieldon and Wedgwood continued to make marbled, agate, and tortoiseshell pieces. Wedgwood left in 1759. Whieldon continued producing the variegated wares until the demand for these pieces diminished. He retired in 1780.

No Whieldon pieces were marked. Many earthenware potteries copied Whieldon's tortoiseshell wares between 1740 and 1780. Because no pieces were marked, it is impossible to attribute a piece to a specific factory. The term "Whieldon ware" is now generic.

Reference: F. Falkner, *The Wood Family of Burslem*, Chapman & Hall, 1912.

Museums: City Museum, Stoke-on-Trent, Hanley, England; Fitzwilliam Museum, Cambridge, England; Museum of Art, Rhode Island School of Design, Providence, RI; Sussex Museum & Art Gallery, Brighton, England; Victoria & Albert Museum, London, England; William Rockhill Nelson Gallery of Art, Kansas City, MO.

Bowl, 5 3/8" d, creamware, underglazed translucent brown, blue, yellow, green, and grey, c1760, (A), ... **1,410.00**

Dish, 9 1/2" d, well w/molded leaf veins ground overlaid w/brown branch, 5 blue-grey leaves, raised lip and wide band of crisscrossed lines w/part flower petal, lg green and yellow molded leaves on border, lobed rim, ... **7,500.00**

Figure, 3 1/4" l, reclining lion, brown and cream, green base, c1780, ... **3,500.00**

Fruit Dish, 11" l, oval, pierced border relief molded w/basketweave and fruits, scrolling rim, yellow, green, and brown splashed enamels, c1760, (A), ... **2,470.00**

Milk Jug, 5" h, brown tortoiseshell finish, applied rose and vines, 3 paw feet, c1770, ... **3,000.00**

Plate

8 1/2" w, oct, brown and tan splash, rope rim, c1760, ... **200.00**

9 1/8" d, silver shape, press-molded border of baroque panels w/diamonds and dots separated by chevrons, dk manganese base w/copper green, ochre, and blue-grey splashes, ... **560.00**

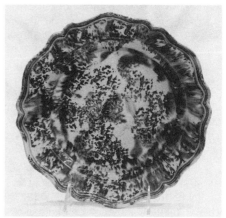

Plate, 9 1/4" d, brown, green, and yellow splashes, cream ground, c1750, hairline, $255.00

9 1/4" d

Mottled, brown, green, and yellow, molded border w/feather medallions and diamond grids, scalloped rim, (A), ... **523.00**

Silver shape, brown tortoiseshell ground w/yellow and green splashes, c1765, ... **310.00**

9 3/8" d, tortoise shell w/brown sponging and blue and green spots, bands on rim, (A), ... **495.00**

9 1/2" d

Brown ground w/green and ochre patches, wavy border w/beaded rim, ... **750.00**

Silver shape, molded diaper and flowerhead panels on border, rope rim, ochre, blue, and copper green splashes on manganese ground, ... **495.00**

10" d, yellow and cream splashes on manganese tortoiseshell ground, c1765, ... **985.00**

Platter

13 3/4" l, rect w/canted corners, brown tortoiseshell finish, milled rim, ... **2,000.00**

15" l, oval, creamware, molded feather edge, scalloped rim, splashed grey and green glazes on sponged brown ground, late 18th C, (A), ... **1,090.00**

16 3/8" l x 12 1/4" w, oct, oval well, raised rim, brown tortoise shell glaze, restored, (A), ... **275.00**

Porringer, 4 3/4" d, applied handle, sponged manganese ground w/ochre and green spotting, star crack, c1770, ... **1,250.00**

Serving Dish, 13 3/4" l, rect w/canted corners, brown tortoiseshell finish milled rim, c1770, ... **2,000.00**

Soup Plate, 9 3/8" d, creamware, molded lattice and basketweave border, scalloped rim, underglaze blue, yellow, and green splashes on grey ground, c1760, (A), ... **350.00**

Teabowl and Saucer, creamware, tortoiseshell underglaze brown enamel, applied relief of gilt flowers and vines, c1760, (A), ... **585.00**

Teapot
4 1/2" h, globular, brown tortoiseshell finish, applied meandering vines and leaves on side, figural bird knob, paw feet, c1770, repairs, ... **3,000.00**

Teapot, 5" h x 7 1/2" w, brown, green, and blue tortoiseshell, "Thomas Whieldon," c1765, $1,785.00

5 1/2" h, relief of scrolling foliage and vines, green and brown tortoiseshell glaze, Staffordshire, c1770, (A), ... **700.00**

WILLOW WARE

English/Continental
1780s to Present

History: Blue willow china was the English interpretation of hand painted blue and white Chinese porcelain exported to England from China in the 16th century. The transfer method of decoration and the under-the-glaze decorating techniques introduced after 1760 provided the methodology to produce willow ware in large quantity.

The first English willow pattern was attributed to Thomas Minton at his Caughley Pottery in Staffordshire in the 1780s. The pattern was called Willow-Nankin.

Josiah Spode developed the first "true" willow pattern in the 1790s. Spode made three different willow patterns. The standard pattern developed in 1810 by Spode was the one that was considered the "true" willow pattern. It differed from the first two patterns in border design and the method by which the transfer pattern was engraved.

Spode's willow pattern had a willow tree in the center leaning over a bridge. A tea house with three pillars forming the portico and located near a large orange tree was behind the center willow tree. Three figures were crossing the bridge towards an island. A man in a boat was on the lake. Two birds were flying towards each other at the top center. Finally, a fence crossed the foreground. The outer border featured several scroll and geometric designs. The inner border consisted of geometric designs that framed the center pattern.

Many manufacturers used transfers that were variations of the Spode willow pattern. Some produced their own original blue willow versions. By 1830 there were more than two hundred makers of willow pattern china in England. English firms still producing blue willow pattern china are Booth's by Royal Doulton, Burleigh, Coalport, Johnson Brothers, Meakin, and Wedgwood.

During the 20th century other countries making willow ware included Belgium, France, Germany, Holland, Ireland, Mexico, Poland, Portugal, and Spain. Potteries in the United States and Japan also make pieces decorated with the blue willow pattern.

A tremendous variety of shapes was made in the blue willow pattern. Many pieces were not marked by the manufacturers, especially during the early period.

The color of the transfer varied with manufacturer. During the 1820s, a pale blue was fashionable. A whole spectrum of blues was used during the Victorian era. Although the most common color was blue, pieces can be found in black, brown, green, pink, yellow, red, and polychrome.

References: Leslie Bockol, *Willow Ware: Ceramics in the Chinese Tradition*, Schiffer Publishing, Ltd. 1995; Robert Copeland, *Spode's Willow Pattern and other designs after the Chinese*, Rizzoli International Publications, Inc. 1980; Mary Frank Gaston, *Blue Willow: An Identification and Value Guide, Revised 2nd Ed.* Collector Books, 2000; Veryl Marie Worth, *Willow Pattern China, Rev. 2nd Ed.* privately printed, 1981; M.A. Harman, *Collecting Blue Willow: Identification & Value Guide*, Collector Books, 2001; Jennifer Lindbeck, *A Collectors Guide To Willow Ware*, Schiffer Publications, 2000; Connie Rogers, *An Encyclopedia of English Willow Pottery*, Schiffer Publications, 2003.

Collectors' Club: International Willow Collectors, P.O. Box 54681, Cincinnati, OH 45254. Membership: $20.00, Newsletters; The Willow Society, 359 Davenport Road, Suite 6, Toronto, M5R 1K5 Canada. Membership: $15.00. *The Willow Transfer Quarterly*, *The Willow Exchange*, and *The Mandarin's Purse* (price guide); *The Willow Word*, Subscription: $25.00, Bimonthly newspaper, Mary Lina Berndt, Publisher, P.O. Box 13382, Arlington, TX 76094; *American Willow Report*, Bimonthly newspaper, Lisa Henze, Publisher.

Reproduction Alert: Teapots, sugar and creamers are being reproduced.

Bourdalou, 4" h x 8 1/2" l, blue, Staffordshire, ... **360.00**

Bowl
4 3/8" d, blue, unmkd, ... **10.00**
9" d, red, "NIMY Fabrication Belge Made in Belgium" mks, ... **10.00**

Butter Pat
2 3/4" d, blue, unmkd, ... **25.00**
3" d, blue, Wedgwood, ... **38.00**
3 3/4" d, blue, "John Maddock & Sons" mk, ... **10.00**

Cake Stand, 9 3/8" d x 5 1/2" h, red, Staffordshire, ... **28.00**

Candy Box, Cov, 7" h, 6 1/2" H-H, bone china, pedestal base, blue, gilt scroll handles, rims, and knob, Coalport, ... **60.00**

Celery Dish, 8 5/8" l, multicolored transfer and accents, "Ashworth Bros. Hanley, England" mark, $185.00

Cereal Bowl
6 1/2" d, blue, Burleigh, ... **7.00**
7 1/4" d, blue, W. Ridgway, ... **9.00**

Charger
11 1/4" d, blue, Petrus Regout, ... **20.00**
12" d, blue, unmkd, ... **20.00**

Cheese Stand, 11 3/4" l, blue, Meir, ... **285.00**

Cream and Sugar Set, creamer, 3 7/8" h, cov sugar bowl, 4 5/8" h x 5 3/8" H-H, blue w/gold trim, "Royal Doulton, Booth's Real Old Willow" mk, ... **35.00**

Creamer, 4" h, oct, blue, Challinor, ... **10.00**

Cup and Saucer
Blue
Fluted, wide gilt rims and handle, Charles Ford, ... **35.00**
"Made in England" mk, ... **5.00**
Gold on black ground, "Booth's Real Old Willow" mk, set of 6, ... **235.00**
Red, Gustavsberg, ... **20.00**

Cup and Saucer, Demitasse, blue, "Booth's Real Old Willow" mk, ... **20.00**

Dish, 9" d, blue, lobed border w/gilt accented lines and curls, Coalport, ... **35.00**

Dish, Cov, 7 3/8" w, blue, scroll knob, England, ... **50.00**

Drain

10 3/4" l x 8" w, blue, Wileman, ... **30.00**

12 3/4" l x 8 3/4" w, blue, Riley, ... **125.00**

Egg Cup

2 1/2" h, blue, "Booth's Real Old Willow" mk, ... **42.00**

4" h, red, unmkd, ... **25.00**

Grill Plate

10" d

Blue, Staffordshire, ... **45.00**

Red, Petrus Regout, ... **140.00**

11" d

Blue, Villeroy & Boch, Made in Saar-Basin, ... **15.00**

Red, "Johnson Brothers" mk, ... **25.00**

Gravy Boat, 7 1/2" l x 4" h, blue, "Ashworth" mk, ... **35.00**

Hot Water Plate, 10 1/4" d, blue, base rim chip, ... **185.00**

Jug

4" h, blue, Allerton, ... **20.00**

5" h, paneled, blue, Sampson Hancock, ... **225.00**

5 1/4" h, blue, unmkd, ... **155.00**

7" h, wavy rim, blue, ... **50.00**

Meat Drain, 14 1/2" l x 11" w, blue, ... **315.00**

Meat Platter

14" l x 11" w, blue, "Booth's Real Old Willow" mk, ... **120.00**

14 1/2" l x 11 3/4" w, blue, George Jones, ... **65.00**

Milk Pitcher, 6" h, rust brown, brown handle w/gold trim, Royal Worcester, ... **120.00**

Mustard Pot, 3" h, metal top and spoon, blue, Copeland, ... **100.00**

Pepper Pot, 3" h, blue, Copeland, ... **40.00**

Pie Dish, 11 1/2" l x 9 1/2" w, blue, Staffordshire, late 19th C, ... **100.00**

Pitcher

6" h, brown, yellow ground, "Royal Worcester, Ovington" mks, ... **115.00**

7" h, blue, gold trim, "Booth's Real Old Willow" mk, ... **35.00**

Plate

4 1/4" d, "YORKSHIRE RELISH" advertising on border, blue, ... **25.00**

*Pitcher, 5 3/8" h, blue, Allerton, **$125.00***

5 1/2" d, blue, Coalport, c1875, ... **25.00**

6" d, blue, "Crown Clarence" mk, ... **5.00**

6" w, oct, blue, "Thos. Hughes & Son, Longport, England" mk, ... **7.00**

6 1/4" d, red, Johnson Brothers, ... **8.00**

6 1/2" d, blue, Foley, ... **4.00**

7" d

Blue, gold trim, "Booth's Real Old Willow" mk, ... **10.00**

Red, "Societe Ceramique Made in Holland Willow" mk, ... **10.00**

7 1/2" sq, red, Johnson Brothers, ... **25.00**

7 5/8" d, oct, blue, "Johnson Brothers" mk, ... **5.00**

8" d, blue, Royal Doulton, ... **8.00**

9 1/2" d, blue, gold trim, "Booth's Real Old Willow" mk, ... **13.00**

10" d

Blue, "Johnson Brothers" mk, ... **5.00**

Pink, "Johnson Brothers" mk, ... **8.00**

Platter

9 1/2" l, blue, Allerton, ... **70.00**

11 1/4" l x 9" w, blue, Allerton, ... **90.00**

11 3/4" l, red, "W.R. Midwinter" mk, ... **26.00**

12 1/2" l x 10" w, oval, red, England, ... **40.00**

13" l x 10" w, rect, blue, unmkd, ... **33.00**

13 1/2" l x 11" w, blue, Burgess & Leigh, ... **85.00**

15 5/8" l, rect, blue, England, ... **500.00**

16" l x 12 1/2" w, w/drain, 10 1/2" l x 7 1/2" w, blue, **895.00**

17 1/2" l x 13 1/2" w, blue, ... **150.00**

17 3/4" l x 14 1/8" w, blue, "RICHD RILEY BURSLEM" mk, (A), ... **385.00**

Punch Bowl, 13 1/8" d, flange ft, blue, unmkd, (A), ... **1,100.00**

Salad Bowl, 6 1/2" d, blue, Staffordshire, ... **8.00**

Sandwich Tray, 11" l x 5 1/4" w, blue, Burleigh Ware, ... **30.00**

Sauceboat, 6" l, blue, Copeland, ... **25.00**

Sauce Dish, 5 1/4" w, blue, "Booth's Old Willow" mk, ... **23.00**

Sauce Ladle, 6" l, blue, c1850, ... **100.00**

Serving Bowl, 8 1/2" d, blue, Ridgway, ... **28.00**

Serving Dish, Divided, 4 1/2" w, blue, Booth, ... **65.00**

Soup Bowl, 8 1/2" d, blue, Grimwades, ... **5.00**

Soup Plate

7 7/8" d, red, "Alfred Meakin" mk, ... **22.00**

9" d

Blue, Ridgway, ... **20.00**

Red, Belgium, ... **30.00**

9 1/4" d, blue, Burgess & Leigh, ... **20.00**

10 1/4" d, blue, Burgess & Leigh, ... **28.00**

10 1/2" d, blue, "blue Mason's crown, PATENT IRONSTONE CHINA drapery" mk, (A), ... **138.00**

Stacked Teapot, 5 3/4" h, blue, ... **495.00**

Sugar Bowl, Cov, 4 1/4" H-H, oct, blue, Challinor, ... **15.00**

Teapot

4 1/4" h, blue, "Booth Real Old Willow" mk, ... **70.00**

5" h, 2 cup, blue, Sadler, ... **40.00**

5 1/8" h, bulbous, domed cov, applied handle w/molded leaf ends, blue, (A), ... **410.00**

6" h, blue, Burleigh Ware, ... **95.00**

Tureen, Cov, 16" H-H x 10 1/2" h, blue, Staffordshire, ... **1,650.00**

Vegetable Bowl

8 1/4" l x 6 1/2" w, oval, blue, Ridgway, ... **25.00**

8 1/4" sq, gold on black, "Booth's Real Old Willow" mk, ... **200.00**

9 1/4" l x 7" w, rect, red, Allerton, ... **15.00**

9 1/2" d, blue, "Johnson Brothers" mk, ... **65.00**

9 3/4" l x 7 1/8" w, blue, Globe Pottery, ... **18.00**

10" H-H x 9" w, blue, hairlines, ... **10.00**

Vegetable Bowl, 8 1/2" d, blue, "W. Ridgway" mk, c1927, **$110.00**

10 1/2" H-H, blue, Ridgway, ... **20.00**
Vegetable Bowl, Cov
  8" sq x 6" h, blue, "Hampson
    Longton" mk, ... **58.00**
  9 1/2" H-H, hooked knob, blue,
    "Newport Pottery Co. Ltd
    Burslem England" mk, ... **75.00**
  10 1/2" l x 6" h, blue, Allerton,
    .... **55.00**
  11" l x 9" w, blue, Allerton, ... **265.00**
  12" l x 9" w, blue, England,
    .... **275.00**
Warming Dish, Cov, 9" d, hot water hole
  at side, blue, "Booth's Made in
  England" mk, ... **450.00**

ENOCH WOOD
& SONS
BURSLEM
STAFFORDSHIRE
1818-1846

ENOCH WOOD & SONS
BURSLEM
1818-1846

WOOD, ENOCH

Fountain Place Pottery,
Burslem,
Staffordshire, England
c1784-1840

History: Enoch Wood came from an
important pottery family that included
Aaron Wood, his father; Ralph Wood, his
cousin; and William Wood, his brother.
After he completed his apprenticeship,
Enoch entered a partnership with Ralph in
1784. They made enamel-colored figures
and Toby jugs using the new over-the-
glaze decoration technique.

In 1790 Enoch Wood entered into a
partnership with Caldwell. The company's
mark was Wood & Caldwell. Enoch bought
out Caldwell in 1819 and formed a new
partnership with Enoch, Joseph, and
Edward Wood, his sons. The firm became
known as Enoch Wood & Sons.

The company made under-the-glaze
blue transfer printed dinnerware, much of
which was exported to America. In addition to the blue historic wares, many
romantic wares were printed in pink, purple, black, sepia, green, or mulberry.
Views used included British, French, Italian, and American scenes. Although views
were the most popular designs, Biblical
scenes, hunting scenes, and cherub
motifs also were made. Many of the
printed designs have the title marked on
the back.

Marked pieces are impressed
"WOOD."

References: A.W. Coysh & R.K.
Henrywood, *The Dictionary of Blue &
White Printed Pottery 1780-1880*,
Antique Collectors' Club, 1982; *Vol. 2*,
1989.

Museums: Cincinnati Art Museum,
Cincinnati, OH; Fitzwilliam Museum,
Cambridge, England; Potsdam Public
Museum, Potsdam, NY.

Chamber Pot, 6" h x 11" w, burnt orange
  and cobalt Amber pattern of lg
  oriental peonies and leaves, green
  serpent handle w/orange head,
  .... **185.00**
Cup Plate, 3 3/4" d, "Cottage in the
  Woods" pattern, dk blue transfer,
  "imp ENOCH WOOD & SONS
  BURSLEM" mk, (A), ... **192.00**

Figure, 7" h x 8" l, tan coat, brown horns, green base, **$4,790.00**

Figure
  7" h, recumbent stag, red-brown, dk
    brown antlers, green oval base,
    restored antlers, ... **725.00**
  7 1/2" h, earthenware, standing
    youth, black hat, underglazed
    brown jacket, green trousers, tan
    bagpipe, standing on green and
    brown rock base, repaired chip,
    .... **750.00**
  7 3/4" h, old woman wearing purple
    cape, blue checked apron,

yellow underdress, holding
  basket and cane, man on crutch
  and cane, purple coat, black
  trousers, black striped vest, sq
  bases w/"OLD AGE" on front,
  c1825, pr, ... **285.00**
18 1/2" h, pearlware, "Eloquence,"
  orator in orchid shirt, ermine-
  lined gold edged purple robe,
  lecturing from tan podium
  holding quill and scrolled paper
  and imp w/mythological figure,
  rect marbleized rect base,
  c1786, (A), ... **1,550.00**
Pitcher, 4" h, applied pink cherubs and
  green and lt brown ground, applied
  band of green flowerheads on collar,
  molded feather design under spout,
  brown luster ground, mkd,
  .... **565.00**
Plate
  5 1/2" d, pearlware, "Spring Vale"
    pattern, flowerhead and grape
    border, rope rim, med blue
    transfer, "Enoch Wood eagle"
    mk, c1818, ... **175.00**
  6 1/2" d, rural scene in center, floral
    border, dk blue transfer,
    .... **275.00**
  7 1/2" d, border band of cobalt
    scrolls and molded fish scales,
    "imp Enoch Wood & Sons
    Burslem" mk, ... **40.00**
  9 1/4" d
    Center design of Valkyries,
      foliage border, dk blue
      transfer, "imp E. Wood &
      Sons Burslem" mk, (A),
      .... **275.00**
    "Cupid Imprisoned" pattern, dk
      blue transfer, "Enoch Wood &
      Sons" mk, ... **350.00**
  10" d, pearlware, family feeding
    swans, flowerhead border, dk
    blue transfer, ... **575.00**
  10 1/4" d, pearlware, spaniel chasing
    birds in center, border of flowers
    in feathered reserves, med blue
    transfer, ... **550.00**
  10 3/8" d, "Fisherman" pattern,
    brown center transfer, blue
    border transfer, scalloped rim,
    (A), ... **248.00**
  10 1/2" d, "Wreath and Flowers"
    pattern, green transfer w/dk
    yellow accents, ... **200.00**
Platter
  12 1/4" l x 9 3/4" w, oval, "English
    Scenery" pattern, blue transfer,
    "Wood & Sons" mk, ... **75.00**

Platter, 13 3/4" l, "Hyde" pattern, green, red, yellow, magenta, and brown, **$65.00**

14 1/2" l x 11 1/2" w, white soft paste, relief molded designs on border, cobalt lined rim, "imp eagle, E. Wood & Sons Burslem" mk, ... **100.00**

17" l x 14" w, "Wreath & Flowers" pattern, Gothic church ruins, river, and mountains, wreath border, brown transfer w/pink enamel accents, ... **550.00**

Quill Holder, 5" l, figural reclining brown shaded lion on dk brown rect base, Wood and Caldwell, ... **1,275.00**

Soup Plate, 10" d, pearlware, beehive in rural England in center, flowerhead border, beaded rim, med blue transfer, ... **450.00**

Vegetable Bowl, Cov, 12" l, rect, "Etruscan" pattern, blue transfers, molded shell handles, lg flower knob, "Enoch Wood & Sons" mk, c1820-40, ... **395.00**

Ra WOOD
BURSLEM
c.1770 - 1801

WOOD, RALPH

near Stoke-on-Trent, England

Ralph Wood the Elder
1754-1772

Ralph Wood the Younger
1760-1795

History: Ralph Wood and Ralph, his son, were the most important makers of earthenware figures and Toby jugs during the second half of the 18th century.

After his apprenticeship, Ralph Wood initially worked for Thomas Whieldon, making salt glazed earthenware and tor-

toiseshell glazed ware. Eventually, he founded his own firm. During the 1750s, Ralph Wood started making figures in cream-colored earthenware with metallic-oxide stained glazes. He kept the colors separate by painting them on with a brush. The modeling of his figures was quite lively. Ralph's figures gained a reputation for portraying the mood and attitude of the character exactly.

Ralph the Younger was a skilled figure maker and joined his father during the 1760s. Ralph the Younger continued the tradition established by his father and eventually produced even more figures than Ralph Wood the Elder. Since Ralph the Younger used many of his father's molds, it is impossible to assign a particular figure to the father or the son with certainty. Later in his career, Ralph the Younger switched to using enamel colors on figures.

Subjects included equestrian figures, contemporary portrait figures, some satyrical groups, classical figures, allegorical figures, and many different animals. All the molded human figures had large hands and well defined, bulging eyes. Ralph Wood also is credited with introducing the Toby jug form. These were very successful and copied by dozens of potters. (See: Toby Jugs.)

In addition to figures and Toby jugs, Ralph Wood's factory also made plaques. John Voyez, a modeler, produced the plaques. Characteristic of Voyez's work were figures with bulging eyes, thick fleshy lips, slightly flattened noses, and a sentimental inclination of the head.

The Woods were the first figure makers to mark their wares with an impressed company mark and sometimes mold numbers. However, some were not marked. "R. Wood" was the mark of Ralph the Elder. "Ra Wood" was the younger's mark.

References: Capt. R.K. Price, *Astbury, Whieldon & Ralph Wood Figures and Toby Jugs*, John Lane, 1922; H A.B. Turner, *A Collector's Guide to Staffordshire Pottery Figures*, Emerson Books, Inc. 1971.

Museums: British Museum, London, England; Cincinnati Art Museum, Cincinnati, OH; City Museum, Stoke-on-Trent, Hanley, England; Fitzwilliam Museum, Cambridge, England.

Figure
6 1/2" h, pearlware, translucent glazes, little girl holding up hem of cream gown, cream cap w/green bow on front, green and brown base, ... **2,800.00**
7" h, pearlware, "Faith," draped standing female holding open book and cross, white glaze, "Ra. Wood Burslem" mk, c1789, missing cross top, ... **770.00**
7" l, reclining ram, lt brown textured body, red splash on back, dk

brown horns and hooves, green leaf base, c1785, ... **4,450.00**

Figure, 7" h, brown shaded deer, green base, unmkd, **$2,750.00**

8" h, standing camel, brown glaze, center support, rect base w/rope border, (A), ... **50,170.00**
8 1/2" h, pearlware, female flower seller, holding basket of flowers, freeform circ base, translucent polychrome glazes, repairs, (A), ... **200.00**
13" h, pearlware, recumbent stag, brown and green glaze, repairs to horns and ears, seated on cushion, rect base, (A), ... **20,440.00**

Milk Jug, 5" h, figural mang covered satyr face, green scaled dolphin on head forming spout and handle, green spread foot, ... **2,500.00**

Sauceboat, 7" w, pearlware, figural brown fox head, green curled base, figural white swan handle, blue streaks, swan form coiled base, white w/blue slashes, c1780-1800, (A), ... **2,870.00**

Spill Vase, 8 1/2" h, "Grieving Widow," seated by green tree trunk spill, blue flowered white dress, ochre edged flowered coat, orange vest, holding rose urn, dog on brown rock base, ... **320.00**

Toby Jug, 9" h, pearlware, blue-black tricorn, brown hair, brown and blue sponged coat, blue and brown striped shirt, yellow breeches, brown outlined chair back, warts on face, c1790, ... **850.00**

Toby Jug, 10" h, black tricorn hat, mustard yellow coat, lt blue vest and stockings, tan keg and dog, **$4,980.00**

WORCESTER

Worcester, England
1751-1892

History: The Worcester pottery was established in 1751. The pieces from the initial years of operation have decorations characterized by a strong dependence on Oriental themes in under-the-glaze blue and on-the-glaze enamel. Production concentrated primarily on making excellent utilitarian wares, mostly tea and dessert sets. Very few purely ornamental pieces were made. The china was symmetrical and featured a smooth glaze. This initial period, 1751 to 1776, was known as the "Dr. Wall" period, named

after one of the original stockholders.

After 1755, transfer printing was used extensively. By 1760 most of the best pieces had the typical Worcester deep blue cobalt under-the-glaze background, done either in a solid or scale motif. Panels were painted with beautiful birds, flowers, and insects.

The factory was managed by William Davis, one of the original partners from the Dr. Wall period. Davis died in 1783; Thomas Flight then purchased the factory. The middle period, also known as the Davis-Flight period, lasted from 1776 to 1793. Neo-classical designs were emphasized. Many of the whiteware blanks used for decoration were purchased from France. There was a limited quantity of fine clay for porcelain production in the area of the Worcester plant. The company received a royal warrant from George III in 1789.

Martin Barr joined the works in 1793. The period from 1793 to 1807 was designated the Flight & Barr period. Patterns continued to be rather plain. Barr's son joined the firm in 1807, resulting in the Barr Flight & Barr period between 1807 and 1813. Decorative motifs from this era were quite colorful and elaborate.

Martin Barr Sr. died in 1813. The time from 1813 to 1840 was called the Flight Barr & Barr period. Patterns continued to be quite colorful, finely painted, and gilded. The quality of porcelains made during the early 19th century was very high. Pieces were richly painted, often featuring gilt trim on a well-potted body with a perfect, craze-free glaze.

In 1840 Flight Barr & Barr merged with the Chamberlain factory and took the name of Chamberlain and Company. The plant moved to Diglis. Quality of production declined during this time.

Kerr and Binns bought the firm in 1852. During the Kerr & Binns period, 1852 to 1862, the factory enjoyed a great artistic recovery. In 1862 R.W. Binns formed the Worcester Royal Porcelain Company Ltd., a company whose products then carried the "Royal Worcester" designation.

References: Franklin A. Barret, *Worcester Porcelain & Lund's Bristol, Rev. Ed.*, Faber & Faber, 1966; Lawrence Branyon, Neal French, John Sandon, *Worcester Blue & White Porcelain, 1751-1790*, Barrie & Jenkins, 1981; Anthony Cast & John Edwards, *Royal Worcester Figurines, First Edition*, Charlton Press, 1997; Geoffrey A. Godden, *Chamberlain-Worcester Porcelain 1788-1852*, Magna Books, 1992; F. Severne Mackenna, *Worcester Porcelain: The Wall Period & Its Antecedents*, F. Lewis Ltd. 1950; H. Rissik Marshall, *Colored Worcester Porcelain of the First Period*, Ceramic Book, 1954; Dinah Reynolds, *Worcester Porcelain 1751-1783: An Ashmolean-Christie's Handbook*, Phaidon-Christie's, 1989; Henry Sandon, Flight & Barr: *Worcester Porcelain 1783-1840*, Antique Collectors' Club, 1978; Henry Sandon, *The Illustrated Guide to Worcester Porcelain*, Herbert Jenkins, 1969; John Sandon, *The Dictionary of Worcester Porcelain, Vol. 1 1751-1851*, Antique Collectors' Club, Ltd. 1996; *1852 to the Present Day, Vol. II*, Antique Collectors' Club, 1997; John Sandon & Simon Spero, *Worcester Porcelain: The Zorensky Collection*, Antique Collectors' Club, Ltd. 1996.

Museums: Art Institute of Chicago, Chicago, IL; British Museum, London, England; City Museum, Weston Park, Sheffield, England; Colonial Williamsburg Foundation, Williamsburg, VA; Dyson Perrins Museum, Worcester, England; Fine Arts Museum of San Francisco, CA; Gardiner Museum of Ceramic Art, Toronto, Canada; Henry Ford Museum, Dearborn, MI; Seattle Art Museum, Seattle, WA; Sheffield City Museum, Sheffield, England; Victoria & Albert Museum, London, England; Brooklyn Museum of Art, Brooklyn, NY; Museum of Fine Arts, Rienzi Decorative Arts Wing, Houston, TX (major collection).

Reproduction Alert: At the end of the 19th century, Samson and other Continental artists copied 18th century Worcester examples. Booths of Turnstall reproduced many Worcester designs utilizing the transfer method. These reproduction pieces also contained copies of the Royal Worcester mark. Even though an earthenware body instead of porcelain was used on the Booth examples, many collectors have been misled by the reproductions.

Basket
    5 1/8" d, lg bouquet of HP flowers in center, loop lattice border w/painted sprigs at intercises, c1765, ... **1,900.00**
    9 5/8" H-H x 7" w, int painted w/polychrome enameled exotic birds on grass, trees in bkd, sm flying birds and insects, open lattice border w/green centered puce flowerheads at intersections on ext, green twisted handles w/flowerhead terminals, c1770, ... **3,300.00**
Beaker, 4 1/2" h, HP multicolored named scene of "CROOME" on front, gilt cartouche w/gilt initials in maroon ground on reverse, gilt rim w/4 petal white flowerheads, Grainger, ... **885.00**
Bowl
    7 1/2" d, black printed profile of "King of Prussia," inscribed battle flags and trophies, sgd "RH Worcester," **1,610.00**

Dessert Dish

10" sq, "Queen Charlotte" pattern, cobalt, iron-red, and gilt swirls, c1775, ... **3,300.00**

11" l x 8" w, melon shape, blue "Gilli Flower" pattern, basketweave border, ... **315.00**

Dessert Service, 6 plates, 9 1/4" d, 2 short compotes, 9 3/8" d, tazza, 6 1/4" h, center painted w/wildflowers in gilt band w/white jewels, turquoise rim w/blue husks and gilt details, late 19th C, (A), ... **1,115.00**

Dish

6 1/2" d, circ and fan shaped vignettes of blue chinoiserie florals or fishing scenes, powder blue ground, scalloped rim, ... **1,400.00**

10" d, "Tobacco Leaf" pattern, cobalt, iron-red, green, and gilt, Flight, Barr, and Barr, ... **1,620.00**

11" l x 7 3/4" w, oval, "Fence" pattern, openwork gilt fence, pagoda, trees w/exotic birds, and plants, band of gilt and orange border panels, scalloped rim, Barr, Flight, Barr, c1805, ... **2,000.00**

12 5/8" w, molded leaf shape, blue printed floral sprays and butterflies, late 18th C, (A), ... **230.00**

Inkwell, 6" h, drum shape w/3 painted named cartouches of Robert Burns homes, white beading on rim, 3 gilt quill holders on cov w/gilt seaweed, triangular marbleized base w/3 gilt sphinx supports, Barr, Flight, and Barr, c1810, ... **11,400.00**

Jug

8" h, molded cabbage leaf body, underglaze blue cornflowers, mask head spout, "C" scroll handle, ... **820.00**

13" h, gilt scrolled panels of multicolored exotic birds on body, insects on neck, blue and gilt scale ground gilt birds, mask spout, "blue chop" mk, ... **650.00**

Milk Jug, 5 1/8" h, cobalt, iron-red, and gilt "Queen Charlotte" pattern, Flight, Barr, and Barr, ... **1,200.00**

Mug, 3 1/4" h, blue printed "Plantation" pattern, c1760-70, ... **630.00**

Pickle Dish, 3 1/2" w, leaf shape, blue "Gilli Flower" pattern, blue streaked rim, c1760, ... **395.00**

Plate

5 7/8" d, blue printed "Pine Cone" pattern, scalloped rim, blue open crescent mk, (A), ... **150.00**

7 1/2" d
Blue "Royal Lily" pattern, scalloped rim, Barr & Flight, ... **95.00**
HP polychrome scattered bouquets and sprigs, fluted border, iron red rim, ... **80.00**

7 5/8" d, "Quail" pattern, Kakiemon colors, Flight and Barr, ... **145.00**

7 3/4" d, "Blind Earl" pattern, molded green and red leaves and stems, buds, and insects, golded lobed rim, c1840, ... **4,000.00**

8 1/4" d, HP seashells and seaweed in center, blue marbleized border, gilt rim on white Greek key design, John Barker, Barr, Flight, and Barr, c1807, repaired crack, ... **5,000.00**

8 3/4" d, iron-red, blue, brown, and yellow oriental flowerheads and ribbons in center and border, Chamberlain, c1815, ... **275.00**

9" d, painted landscape in center, blue "leaf ground" border, gilt outlined indented rim, "G. & Co. W." mk, Grainger, ... **140.00**

9 1/2" d
Center scene of vase w/garden flowers in colors, cobalt and gilt "griffin" type border swirls and sm flowers, shaped rim, Chamberlain, ... **200.00**
Multicolored "Dragon in Compartments" pattern, Chamberlain, c1800, ... **1,100.00**

Platter

11" l x 8" w, cartouches of multicolored flowers, blue scale ground, Dr. Wall, ... **4,390.00**

20 1/4" l x 17" w, shaded blue, red, and green jardiniere in center w/red, blue, and yellow flowers, pale yellow or cobalt border panels w/gilt leaf designs, gilt lined rim, Chamberlain, ... **1,500.00**

Punch Bowl, 5 1/4" h x 12" d, "Queen Charlotte" pattern, red, blue, and gilt, unmkd, ... **7,800.00**

Punch Pot, 8 1/2" h, globular, "Plantation Print," chinoiserie landscape, blue transfer, silver chain on handle to cov, ... **3,750.00**

Salt, 4 1/2" h, figural dolphin supporting shell, circ base, cream glaze, Grainger, ... **400.00**

Sauce Tureen, 7 1/2" h, purple stylized leaves w/gold berries, gold outlined knob, rims, and ring handles, "imp crowned FBB" mk, $1,150.00

Sauceboat

4 3/4" l, blue painted "The Two Porter Landscape" pattern, blue crescent mk, c1770, (A), ... **600.00**

6 1/8" l, HP blue "Strap Flute Sauceboat Floral" pattern, c1770, open crescent mk, ... **625.00**

8" l, figural cos lettuce leaf shape, white molded veined ground w/lt green, yellow, and pink accents, Meissen style polychrome enamel flowers and insects, c1758-62, pr, ... **5,500.00**

Serving Dish, Cov, 10" H-H, w/divided liner, gold lined center yellow band w/painted stylized floral sprays, gilt pineapple knob on 4 gilt lined curved leaves, gilt accented faux branch handles, gadrooned rim on liner, Flight, Barr, and Barr, c1815, ... **12,500.00**

Spoon Tray, 5 3/4" w, hex form, black printed half portrait of King of Prussia, dtd 1757, black enameled lined rim, (A), ... **1,325.00**

Sugar Box, Cov, 4 3/4" h, vert fluted body and cov, HP flowers and sprays, figural leaf and flowerhead knob, gilt lined base and rim, c1770, ... **850.00**

Tankard

4 5/8" h, blue printed chrysanthemums and floral sprigs, blue open crescent mk, c1760-80, ... **545.00**

6" h, blue printed "Parrot Pecking Fruit" pattern, "script W" mk, ... **910.00**

Tazza, 13 1/2" l x 10" w, lobed, oval shape, Japan pattern colors of flowers, gilt fencing, and pagoda, flowering plants, birds in flight and perched on tree branches, border of gilt and orange lozenge shaped panels w/flowerheads and feather designs, "red Barr Flight & Barr Worcester Flight & Barr Coventry Street London Manufacturers To Their Majesties & Royal Family" mk, ... **4,500.00**

Tea and Coffee Service, Part, fluted, "Sevres" style turquoise ground, gilt flower knobs, entwined branch handles, gilt lined rims, teapot and stand, 6 1/8" h, cov cream jug, 5 1/4" h, cov sugar bowl, 4 1/2" h, waste bowl, 6 1/2" d, spoon tray, 5 7/8" l, 2 dishes, 9 3/4" d, 12 teacups, 12 coffee cups, 18 saucers, pseudo Chinese fret mks, c1775, (A), ... **9,560.00**

Teabowl and Saucer
Blue Printed
Blue printed "Fruit Sprigs" pattern, hatched blue crescent mks, c1775, ... **300.00**
"Fence" pattern, blue crescent mks, c1775, ... **480.00**
"Three Flowers" pattern, blue crescent mks, c1775, ... **245.00**
Fluted, "Chequered Tent" pattern in colors, gilt rims, blue fret mk, ... **1,275.00**
HP blue "Mansfield" pattern, open crescent mk, c1770, ... **150.00**
Spiral fluted, HP blue garlands of flowers, int band of sprigs, gilt rims, c1785, ... **90.00**

Tea Canister, 4 3/4" h, fluted, dry blue florals, gilt dentil rims, c1770, ... **265.00**

Teapot
3 1/2" h, "Warbler" pattern, blue underglaze transfer, (A), ... **125.00**
4" h x 9 3/4" l, boat shape, HP band of lg red poppies, gilt leaves on lt green ground between gilt bands, band of gilt foliage on rim, repeat on cov, gilt flame knob, handle, and spout, "imp FBF" mk, c1810, ... **1,600.00**
5 3/4" h, polychrome enamel and gilt panels w/oriental figures, floret knob, (A), ... **330.00**
7 1/2" h, "Queen Charlotte" pattern, Flight and Barr, ... **3,500.00**

Tureen, Cov, 10" H-H, w/undertray, 10 1/4" w, multicolored flowers sprays in gilt lined mirror-shaped cartouches on wet blue ground, green stem handles w/molded flower terminals, green stem knob, gilt edged shaped rims, c1770, ... **15,000.00**

Vase, Cov
8 3/4" h, waisted form, socle ft, gilt and white sq base, painted panel of fruit and butterfly w/landscape bkd in rect frame between white beaded borders, apple green ground, gilt caryatid mask handles, gilt flame formed knob, repairs, Flight, Barr, and Barr, c1820, ... **7,500.00**
15" h, hex panels, multicolored "Dragon in Compartments" pattern, c1770, ... **25,000.00**

Waste Bowl
5 7/8" d x 2 5/8" h, HP blue "Cannonball" pattern, c1770, ... **650.00**
6 1/4" d
3" h, painted blue, turquoise, yellow, green, puce, iron-red, and gilt oriental scenes of boy at table w/yellow fruit, woman holding fan, woman seated on rock at tree, c1768-75, ... **895.00**
Blue "Birds in Branches" pattern, blue crescent mk, ... **450.00**

YELLOW-GLAZED EARTHENWARE

Staffordshire, Yorkshire, Liverpool, England/Wales
c1785 -1835

History: English yellow-glazed earthenware was creamware or pearlware featuring an overall yellow glaze. The principal period of production was between 1785 and 1835. The color varied from a pale to a deep yellow. Yellow glazed earthenware also was known as "canary" or "canary luster" ware.

Most of the yellow-glazed wares were either luster painted, enamel painted, or transfer printed. Sometimes two or three techniques were used on the same pieces. Silver luster was combined the most often with the yellow ground.

Enamel painting on yellow-glazed wares exhibited a wide range in subject matter and technique. The most popular enamel decorative motif was floral. Most flowers were stylized rather than naturalistic. Much of the decoration had a "primitive" or naive feel to the depictions. Iron-red and green were two of the most popular colors. Pastoral landscapes and geometric patterns also were used for enameled decorations.

Transfer printed yellow-glazed wares had the printing done over the glaze. Most patterns were in black, but brown and red were used occasionally. Landscape scenes were the most popular motifs, followed by scenes with birds and animals. Other themes included politics, historical events, sporting scenes, and some mythological figures. Sometimes the transfer prints were over painted in enamel colors.

Yellow-glazed earthenwares were made in nearly all shapes and forms except for complete dinner services. Jugs and pitchers were the most popular forms made.

Yellow-glazed earthenware figures of animals and birds enjoyed great popularity. Some utilitarian pieces such as children's mugs were made in quantity.

Most yellow-glazed earthenware does not contain a maker's mark. Among the identified Staffordshire manufacturers that made the ware were Josiah Wedgwood, Josiah Spode, Davenport, Enoch Wood & Sons, and Samuel Alcock & Co. Rockingham Pottery in Yorkshire made yellow wares; Leeds followed in the north. The Sunderland Pottery made yellow-glazed wares in addition to its more famous pink luster wares. Several potteries in New Castle and Liverpool contributed examples.

Cambrian and Glamorgan, two Swansea potteries, made a considerable number of yellow-glazed pieces. Another Welsh pottery, South Wales in Llanelly, also made yellow wares.

Reference: J. Jefferson Miller II, *English Yellow-Glazed Earthenware*, Smithsonian Institution Press, 1974.

Museums: Art Institute of Chicago, Chicago, IL; City Museum & Art Gallery, Stoke-on-Trent, England; National Museum of American History, Smithsonian Institution, Washington, DC; Nelson-Atkins Museum of Art, Kansas City, MO; Rose Museum, Brandeis University, Waltham, MA.

Bowl, 5 1/4" d, black printed design of woman and child w/bundles of sticks on head, cows grazing before church and house, flowerhead border, yellow glazed ground, c1850s, ... **175.00**

Creamer, 2 3/4" h, miniature, lg red and green flowers, pink luster accents and rim, yellow glazed ground, (A), ... **880.00**

Cup and Saucer, black transfers of mother and child on cup, mother playing piano w/2 children on saucer, yellow glazed ground, unmkd, ... **125.00**

Cup and Saucer, Handleless, black transfer of 2 men fishing in front of castle ruins, yellow glazed ground, hairline on saucer, ... **130.00**

Jug

4" h

Free form w/red satyr face, green, red, and blue dots, black specks, yellow glazed ground, c1820,....... **1,250.00**

Quilted form

Dk brown floral and foliate design, spout repair, (A), ... **165.00**

Green circles, red 4 petal flowers, sm black 4 petal flowers, black rim and lined handle, yellow glazed ground, restored chip, ... **950.00**

5" h, multicolored flowers on sides, yellow glazed ground, c1820, ... **535.00**

5 5/8" h, helmet shape, black printed "Tea Party" pattern, yellow glazed ground, ... **950.00**

5 3/4" h, black transfers of Chatsworth, Derbyshire on sides in silver luster circles, silver luster band on rim, spout, and collar, yellow glazed body, ... **2,500.00**

7" h, lg red cabbage rose, brown and red buds and stems, yellow glazed ground, ... **375.00**

Mug

1 7/8" h, miniature, "BIRDS NEST" on front, 2 young boys w/hoop and stick and nest, maroon transfer, yellow glazed earthenware, chips and hairline, ... **295.00**

2" h

Black transfer of couple walking in woods, church in bkd, yellow glazed body, ... **295.00**

Brown "FOR MY DEAR GIRL," man holding flower, yellow glazed ground, c1820, ... **775.00**

2 1/4" h, silver resist stylized bird on branch, yellow glazed ground, hairline, ... **475.00**

4 3/4" h

Brown outlined cottage w/brown thatched roof, orange splashed ground, green molded horiz ribbing on base, yellow glazed ground, c1830, repaired chips, ... **1,275.00**

Sheep and ram under tree, farmhouse in bkd, black transfer, ear handle, black beaded rim, yellow glazed ground, ... **295.00**

Plate

6" d, enameled red stylized flowerhead in center w/green foliage, dk red rim, yellow glazed ground, c1835, hairline, set of 3, ... **785.00**

8" d

Black transfer of "Vue due Village de Mamren, en Turgove, sur le lae Inferier de Constance," foliage border band, yellow glazed ground, "imp P & H Choisy" mk, ... **185.00**

HP burnt orange carnation, green foliage, burnt orange bellflowers in center, brown lined rim, yellow glazed ground, c1820, ... **195.00**

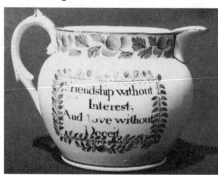

Pitcher, 3 3/4" h, black transfer of "Friendship without Interest, And Love Without Deceit," reverse w/hunting scene of man in rust suit, dog, black birds, rust and green leaves on collar, (A), $155.00

Tankard, 4 1/2" h, young couple holding hands and printed sentiment, green transfer, yellow glazed ground, c1820, ... **1,650.00**

Saucer Dish, 5 1/4" d, Adam Buck design, yellow ground, black transfer, $150.00

Tea Set, pot and stand, 5 3/4" h, 10 3/4" l, creamer, sugar basin, black trim, yellow ground, England, c1810, $1,575.00

Waste Bowl, 6" d, black transfer of mill scene in forest, black lined rim, yellow glazed ground, c1825, ... **750.00**

c 1828 - 1900

ZSOLNAY

Pecs, Funfkirchen

1862 to Present

History: Ignac Zsolnay established a factory in 1853 for the production of utilitarian wares for local markets. Vilmos Zsolnay joined the pottery at Pecs, Funfkirchen, in 1862. Ornamental wares decorated in Persian motifs were added to the line. The factory also produced reticulated and pierced highly decorative ornamental vases similar to those by Fischer. Enamel was used to paint designs onto porcelains, and they were fired at high temperatures. Decorative porcelain-faience was introduced in the 1870s and iridescent glazes in 1890. Zsolnay became the largest ceramics factory in Austria-Hungary.

At the turn of the century, vases and bowls with Art Nouveau decorations and boldly colored glazes were made. Many of the patterns were designed by J. Rippl-Ronai about 1900. An experimental workshop under the direction of V. Wartha produced some luster decorated pieces between 1893 and 1910. Vases in billowing, folded shapes decorated in shades of green, yellow, and blue lusters or in motifs of plants and cloud-like designs were manufactured. A material called "Pyrogranite," which was weather resistant for outdoor ornamentation was perfected. Zsolnay porcelains in fountains, sculptures, and tiles were used to decorate public buildings all over the old Austro-Hungarian empire utilizing special glazes.

Porcelain figurines were added to the line about 1900. These are in great demand today. After World War I, Zsolnay concentrated on industrial porcelain and objects of art.

The factory is called the Alfoldi Porcelain Works today and produces Herend and Zsolnay porcelains.

The Zsolnay factory is still in business. It produces figures with an iridescent glaze called "eosin."

The company's mark is a stylized design representing the five churches of Zsolnay. Sometimes the word "Pecs" also appears.

References: Federico Santi & John Gacher, *Zsolnay Ceramics: Collecting & Culture*, Schiffer, 1998.

Museum: Zsolnay Museum, Pecs, Hungary.

Bowl

4 1/2" h x 6" l, figural Art Nouveau woman at side holding wavy bowl, green-gold eosin glaze, ... **1,465.00**

5 1/4" h x 5 1/2" l, figural duck w/head rotated, red eosin glaze, ... **95.00**

Cache Pot

3" h, melon ribbed, enameled lg yellow and red flowerheads, buds, and foliage, diamond pierced collar, gold accents, ... **45.00**

6 1/2" h, HP lg red or yellow chrysanthemums, brown stems, green leaves, cream ground, reticulated neck, ... **215.00**

Candle Holder, 4 1/4" h, loop handle, blue-green eosin glaze, ... **130.00**

Charger, 15 1/2" d, painted blue, yellow, and mauve flowers, green foliage in center, pink and white floral reticulated border, tower mk, ... **900.00**

Chocolate Pot, 14" h, middle eastern style, pink body, green stem handle, spout, and base w/applied pink flowerheads and spout, ... **600.00**

Figure

3 1/4" h x 3 1/2" w, vulture on branch w/spread wing, irid brown, red, and blue-green glazes, (A), ... **520.00**

3 1/2" l, recumbent fawn, blue-green eosin glaze, sgd "Sirako," **50.00**

6 1/8" h x 7 3/4" l, charging bull, white glaze, grey accents, rect base, artist sgd, ... **950.00**

Figure, 7 1/2" h, green-gold irid glaze, pesces and castle mark, **$325.00**

9" h

Seated Hungarian musician in traditional garb, ovoid base, green-gold eosin glaze, (A), ... **500.00**

Standing man w/hat, smoking pipe, basket on arm, sq base, green-gold eosin glaze, ... **695.00**

9 1/2" h, kneeling nude woman w/raised arms, stepped base, green eosin glaze, ... **895.00**

10 1/2" h, male flutist, orange vest, white bloused shirt, tan britches, black boots, seated on brown rock w/green plant, ... **320.00**

12" h, Art Deco, female nude kneeling on lt blue stone base, brown hair, ... **265.00**

14 3/4" h, seated man w/dying woman across lap, rock base, green-gold eosin glaze, ... **3,875.00**

Jardiniere

5" h x 7" d, gold outlined beige reticulated grill pattern, sm blue center ivory flowers and lg ivory centered blue flowerheads around middle, "Zsolnay Pecs" mk, ... **125.00**

6" h x 9" l x 7" w, panels of painted oriental flowers, red pierced and lobed panels, red lattice rim, ... **2,000.00**

Jug

5" h, red Moorish style curling foliage, gold reticulated handle and base, pinched spout, steeple mk, ... **40.00**

8 1/2" h, front oval w/relief of cherubs drinking and bottle, leaf relief on handle, overall pink glaze, "imp Zsolnay Pecs" mk, ... **975.00**

Match Holder, 2 3/4" h, center barrel w/horiz grooved sides for striking, base w/relief molded red stylized red flowerheads, purple grapes, lime green swirls between, purple luster rim, mkd, ... **885.00**

Pitcher, 9" h, gold, red, and green irid glazes, **$6,000.00**

Pitcher

5 1/2" h, irid red-orange alligator crackle glaze, ... **350.00**

8 1/2" h, Turkish style, brown speckling on yellow ground, "imp Zsolnay Pecs" mk, ... **200.00**

16" h, "secessionist," blue stylized irises w/meandering stems and spear leaves, off-white ground, "5 steeple" mk, ... **315.00**

Plate

8 1/2" d

Painted red or blue flowerheads, swirling leaves in center, gilt outlined reticulated border w/ovals of flowers, brown shaped rim, ... **125.00**

Pink, tan, and cream flowers in center, dbl pierced honeycomb border w/reserves of flowers, "Zsolnay Pecs Hungary" mk, ... **130.00**

8 3/4" d, painted flowers in center on fluted ground w/6 oval cartouches of flowers, gilt pierced swirl border w/gilt flowerheads, imp and printed mkd, ... **135.00**

9 3/4" d, HP orange-red dancing peasant man, zigzag and lined border, wide orange-red banded rim, ... **42.00**

APPENDIX

BRITISH REGISTRATION MARKS
1843 - 1883

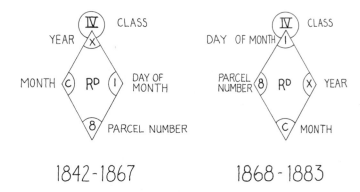

1842 - 1867   1868 - 1883

THE BRITISH REGISTRY MARK

The British Registry mark, or diamond, is found on ceramics manufactured in Great Britain or handled by British agents for foreign manufacturers. The mark was first used in 1842 and continued in use in this form until 1883. The mark is usually found impressed or raised on the ceramic body and indicates that the shape or material was registered or printed when the decoration or pattern was registered.

Through registration of the shape or pattern, the manufacturer was protected from infringement for three years before renewal was necessary. By examining and deciphering this device, the collector can determine the earliest date that a piece was registered, then place it in its proper time frame.

Deciphering the mark is not difficult. All ceramics are classified number IV, as seen at the top of the diamond. Both examples bear this identification.

The 1842 to 1867 diamond is deciphered in the following manner: the top semicircle designates the year, the left one indicates the month, the right one indicates the day of the month, and the bottom one indicates the parcel number that identifies the manufacturer. Below is a table that corresponds to the semicircles in the 1842 to 1867 diamond.

Year	Month for Both Devices	Year
1842-X	January-C or O	1855-E
1843-H	February-G	1856-L
1844-C	March-W	1857-K
1845-A	April-H	1858-B
1846-I	May-E	1859-M
1847-F	June-M	1860-Z
1848-U	July-I	1861-R
1849-S	August-R and September 1-19th, 1857	1862-O
1850-V	September-D	1863-G
1851-P	October-B	1864-N
1852-D	November-K	1865-W
1853-Y	December-A	1866-Q
1854-J		1867-T

From the table on the bottom of page 346, it can be determined that in the sample diamond on the left that the shape or decoration was registered on January 1, 1842.

In 1868, the British Registry mark was altered slightly. The table below corresponds to the diamond used from 1868 to 1883.

Year

1868-X
1869-H
1870-C
1871-A
1872-I
1873-F
1874-U
1875-S

Year

1876-V
1877-P
1878-W from March 1-6
1878-D
1879-Y
1880-J
1881-E
1882-L
1883-K

ADDITIONAL NOTES ON MARKS

Bisque: see Heubach and Sevres for marks.

Creamware: see Leeds and Wedgwood for marks.

Delft: see Bristol and Liverpool for additional marks.

Flow Blue: see Staffordshire General for additional marks.

Majolica: see Keller and Guerin, Minton, and Sarreguemines for additional marks.

Minton: year ciphers were incorporated in some marks.

Mulberry China: see Flow Blue and Staffordshire General for marks.

Parian: see Copeland-Spode and Minton for marks.

Pate-sur-Pate: see Minton and Sevres for marks.

Pearlware: see Clews, Davenport, Ridgway, Staffordshire General, Wedgwood, and Enoch and Ralph Wood for marks.

Piano Babies: see Heubach for marks.

Pitcher and Bowl Sets: see Staffordshire General for additional marks.

Royal Worcester: year ciphers were incorporated in some marks.

Samson: no identifiable marks recorded. Used marks imitating those of Chelsea, Meissen, and Sevres.

Sevres: year ciphers were incorporated in some marks.

Staffordshire Blue and White: see Staffordshire General and Staffordshire Historic marks.

Tea Leaf Ironstone: see ironstone marks.

Tiles: see Minton and Wedgwood for additional marks.

Toby Jugs: see Pratt and Enoch and Ralph Wood for marks.

Wedgwood: year ciphers were included in some marks.

Willow Ware: see Staffordshire General for marks.

GLOSSARY

Applied. Parts or ornaments attached to the body by means of liquid clay (slip). Also called sprigging.

Anthemion. A formal type of decoration in the shape of stylized honeysuckle flowers and leaves.

Bail Handle. An arched fixed or movable overhead handle.

Bargeware. Earthenware of narrow proportions for use on canal boats and barges. These pieces were decorated with florals and luster. Larger pieces featured modeled teapots on the covers or handles.

Bat Printing. The transfer of a design by means of glue-like slabs. Most often used on glazed surfaces.

Bellarmine. Stoneware jug or bottle featuring bearded mask and coat of arms under neck.

Bell-Toy Pattern. Oriental pattern featuring child holding toy composed of stick with bells. Popular pattern at Worcester.

Bianco Sopra Bianco. Decoration on tin-glazed earthenware in opaque white on a slightly bluish or greyish ground. It was employed on Italian maiolica from the early years of the 16th century, and on English delftware in the 18th century.

Bird or Sparrow Spout. Modeled spout in form of open bird beak. These were closely associated with examples fabricated in silver.

Blanc de Chine. French term referring to a translucent white or ivory porcelain covered in thick glaze. Produced by several English and French companies after Chinese originals.

Bleu Lapis. Streaked or veined bright blue ground color often found in combination with gold accents. Used at Vincennes.

Bleu Persan. Dark blue ground color used on Nevers faience, often in conjunction with white or yellow ornamentation.

Blind Earl Pattern. Low relief design of rosebuds, leaves, and insects that covers entire surface. Designed for the blind Earl of Coventry in 1755. The pattern was used at Worcester and Chelsea.

Bocage. Modeled foliage, branches, and flowers that form arbor or canopy background for figures. A method of covering unfinished backs of figures.

Bonbonniere. French term for small covered sweetmeat container.

Cachepot. Ornamental container designed to hold utilitarian flowerpot.

Cartouche. A method of framing or outlining a design, usually with elaborate borders. (See Laub-und-Bandelwerk)

China. Term frequently used to refer collectively to pottery and porcelain, but correctly applies only to porcelain.

Chinoiserie. European decoration utilizing pseudo-Chinese figures, pagodas, and landscapes. Used extensively in early 18th century England and the Continent.

Cloisonne. A French term describing the technique in which copper wire was secured to a body and the ensuing cells filled with enamel, then fired to produce the requested design. This was simulated on ceramic pieces using raised gold lines that substituted for the copper wire. Enamel was then filled into the cells and the entire piece fired.

Cuenca. A technique whereby a pattern is impressed to form ridges, forming cells that hold colors in place prior to firing.

Colors are kept from running together.

Crabstock. Modeled in form of branch or crabapple tree. Found on handles, spouts, and feet.

Dentil. Border treatment of small rectangular blocks giving appearance of teeth. Usually in gilt.

Diapering. Diamond or lozenge-type pattern that is usually repetitive and connected.

Ecuelle. French term for small, covered shallow bowl with double parallel handles. Used for serving soup.

Engine-Turned. Machine-applied design that cuts into the surface of the clay.

Etched. Method of decoration using an acid-resistant covering in which the design is cut, exposed to hydrofluoric acid, and pigment is added to the etched recesses.

Faience. French term for a tin glazing often applied to earthenware bodies. A method of sealing the porous underbody. The term is common to France, Germany, and Scandinavia and is interchangeable with majolica and Delft.

Famille Rose. Chinese-style design that incorporates opaque pink or rose-colored enamels.

Flambe. French term for red-shaded glazes derived from reduced copper.

Fuddling Cup. Group of cups joined together internally and externally, usually with multiple handles.

Gadrooned. Continuous pattern of reeding or fluting used mainly as a border treatment. Inspired from silver examples.

Grisaille. French term for printing in grey shades on porcelain to give the effect of relief.

Hausmalerei. German term for ceramic decorators who worked at home. They purchased whiteware from factories such as Meissen and Vienna, or finished partially decorated pieces.

Imari. Japanese style using designs based on native Japanese textiles. Colors of red and dark underglaze blue predominate.

Istoriato. Italian term for mythical, Biblical, or genre historical scenes that were painted in polychromes on earthenwares. These paints often cover the entire surface of the object.

Kakiemon Style. Based on the Japanese decorations of the Kakiemon family. The main features include asymmetrical patterns of florals, birds, and Orientals in iron-red, yellow, and shades of blue utilizing large masses of white ground in the color scheme. Popular on 18th century Meissen, Chantilly, Chelsea, Bow, and Worcester.

Lambrequin. French term for a scrolled border pattern that consists of hanging drapery, lace and scrollwork, and leaves. This pattern reached its zenith at Rouen.

Laub-und-Bandelwerk. German term meaning leaf and strapwork. This elaborate type of design was used extensively in the cartouche borders at Meissen and Vienna.

Majolica. Introduced in Italy, this tin-glazed surface is the same as faience and Delft, but was initially restricted to the Italian peninsula. This dense glazing was popularized by Minton in the 1850s using the bright colors of lead glazes. See the Majolica category for additional information.

Mon. Japanese inspired form representing circular stylized florals. Frequently incorporated in European interpretations of Oriental designs.

Ozier. German term that describes a molded or painted woven basket-type treatment. Many variations exist, including continuous and interrupted patterns.

Parian. Unglazed biscuit porcelain similar to marble. Introduced and perfected by Copeland, many other English and American manufacturers produced high quality examples.

Posset Pot. Multi-handled pot with center spout designed to hold a mixture of wine or ale and milk.

Potpourri Vase. Designed to hold liquid, flower petals, and herbs. Pierced shoulder or cover allows for the escape of the aromatic scents.

Prunus. Plum blossom-type decoration based on the Chinese symbol for spring.

Putto. Italian term referring to nude or semi-nude young boy. Frequently used as accessory decoration.

Quatrefoil. Shape or design divided in four equal lobes or sections.

Reserve. An area of a design without ground color designated to receive a decorative panel.

Sang de Boeuf. Ox-blood red colored, glazed with islands representing clots, using copper oxide.

Sheet Design. Repetitive design from border to border.

Silver Shape. Copies in porcelain and pottery of existing silver pieces. These usually were reserved for borders, spouts, and handles.

Slip. Clay in a liquid form.

Soft Paste. A form of porcelain fired at lower temperature (about 1200 degrees) than hard paste porcelain, which is fired at 1450 degrees, producing a harder and denser product.

Spill-Vase. A cylindrical vase with flaring mouth, used for holding spills (wood splinters or paper tapers for obtaining a light from the fire).

Transfer Printing. The transfer of a design from prepared copper plates by means of tissue paper. The design, once cut into the copper plates, was prepared with color. A thin sheet of tissue transferred the design to the dry ground of the piece prior to glazing.

Treacle Glaze. A thickly applied pottery glaze that often runs down the side of the ware in much the same way treacle, or molasses would.

Trembleuse. French term used to describe a well or vertical projections found on saucers that were devised to keep accompanying cups from shifting on the saucers. They were designed specifically for those with unsteady hands.

Tube Lining. A method of pottery decoration in which a bag containing liquid clay (slip) is squeezed out of a narrow glass tube onto the surface of fired but undecorated wares, making a thin raised linear design, as though icing a cake.

Additional glossary terms can be found in the following books: Louise Ade Boger, *The Dictionary of World Pottery & Porcelain,* Scribners, 1971; George Savage & Harold Newman, *An Illustrated Dictionary of Ceramics*, Thames and Hudson, Ltd. 1985.

BIBLIOGRAPHY

The following is a listing of general reference books on English and Continental pottery and porcelain that the reader may find useful. A list of marks books is also included.

Continental References
Afterbury, Paul, ed. *The History of Porcelain.* Orbis Publishing, 1982.

Cushion, John. *Continental China Collecting for Amateurs.* Frederick Muller, 1970.

Haggar, Reginard. *The Concise Encyclopedia of Continental Pottery and Porcelain.* Hawthorn Books, Inc., 1960.

Morley-Fletcher, Hugo, and Roger McIllroy. *Christie's Pictorial History of European Pottery.* Prentice-Hall, Inc., 1984.

English References
Bartlett, John A. *British Ceramic Art: 1870-1940.* Schiffer Publishing, Ltd., 1993.

Bergesen, Victoria. *Bergesen's British Ceramics Price Guide.* Barrie & Jenkins, 1992.

Godden, G. A. *British Porcelain.* Clarkson N. Potter, 1974.
— *British Pottery.* Clarkson N. Potter, Inc., 1975.

Hughes, Bernard G. *Victorian Pottery & Porcelain.* Spring Books, 1967.

Lewis, Griselda. *A Collector's History of English Pottery, 4th Ed.* Antique Collectors' Club, Ltd., 1987.

Willis, G. *English Pottery & Porcelain.* Guinness Signatures, 1968.

General References
Cooper, Emmanuel. *A History of Pottery.* St. Martin's Press, 1972.

Cushion, John P. *Pottery and Porcelain Tablewares.* William Morrow & Co., Inc., 1976.

Fay-Halle, Antoinette, and Barbara Mundt, *Porcelain of the Nineteenth Century.* Rizzoli, 1983.

Gleeson, Janet, ed. *Miller's Collecting Pottery and Porcelain.* Reed International Books, Ltd., 1997.

Marks References
Chaffers, W. *Marks & Monograms on European & Oriental Pottery & Porcelain.* William Reeves, 1965.

Cushion, J. P. *Pocket Book of British Ceramic Marks.* Faber & Faber, 1984.

Cushion, J. P., and W. B. Honey, *Handbook of Pottery & Porcelain Marks, 4th Edition.* Faber & Faber, 1981.

Danckert, Ludwig. *Directory of European Porcelain Marks, Makers & Factories, 4th Edition.* N.A.G. Press, 1981.

Godden, G. A., *Encyclopedia of British Pottery & Porcelain Marks.* Barrie & Jenkins, 1996.

Haslam, M. *Marks and Monograms of the Modern Movement.* Lutterworth Press, 1977.

Rontgen, Robert E. *Marks on German, Bohemian & Austrian Porcelain, 1710 to the Present.* Schiffer Publishing, Ltd.

INDEX

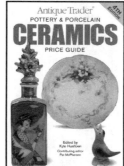